THE MINOR PROPHETS

A COMMENTARY

EXPLANATORY AND PRACTICAL

BY

E. B. PUSEY, D.D.

VOLUME II

MICAH, NAHUM, HABAKKUK, ZEPHANIAH,
HAGGAI, ZECHARIAH AND MALACHI

BAKER BOOK HOUSE
Grand Rapids, Michigan

Library of Congress Catalog Card Number: 55-11418

ISBN: 0-8010-0563-9

First Printing, October 1950
Second Printing, December 1953
Third Printing, June 1957
Fourth Printing, January 1958
Fifth Printing, October 1960
Sixth Printing, March 1962
Seventh Printing, February 1963
Eighth Printing, January 1966
Ninth Printing, November 1968
Tenth Printing, June 1970
Eleventh Printing, November 1971
Twelfth Printing, August 1973

PHOTOLITHOPRINTED BY CUSHING - MALLOY, INC.
ANN ARBOR, MICHIGAN, UNITED STATES OF AMERICA
1973

V. HAGGAI.

INTRODUCTION.

VI. ZECHARIAH.

INTRODUCTION.

VII. MALACHI.

INTRODUCTION.

CONTENTS.

INTRODUCTION

TO

THE PROPHET

MICAH.

MICAH, or Micaiah, this Morasthite, was so called, probably, in order to distinguish him from his great predecessor, Micaiah, son of Imlah, in the reign of Ahab. His name was spoken in its fuller form, by the elders of the land whose words Jeremiah has preserved. And in that fuller form his name is known, where the Greek and Latin translations of the Scriptures are used[a]. By the Syrians, and by the Jews[b] he is still called, as by us, Micah. The fullest and original form is Micaiahu, "who is like the Lord?" In this fullest form, it is the name of one of the Levites sent by Jehoshaphat to teach the people[c], as also of the mother of king Asa[d], (the same name serving sometimes both for men and women). Then according to the habit of abridging names, in all countries, and especially those of which the proper name of the Lord is a part, it is diversely abridged into Micaihu, Micahu[e], whence Micah is readily formed, on the same rule as Micaiah itself from Micaiahu. The forms are all found indifferently. The idolatrous Levite in the time of the Judges[f], and the son of Imlah[g], are both called in the same chapter *Micaihu* and *Micah;* the father of one of Josiah's officers is called *Micaiah* in the book of Kings[h], *Micah* in the Chronicles[i].

The Prophet's name, like those of Joshua, Elijah, Elisha, Hosea, Joel, Obadiah, was significant. Joshua's, we know, was changed of set purpose[k]. The rest seem to have been given in God's Providence, or taken by the Prophets, in order to enunciate truths concerning God, opposed to the idolatries or self-dependence of the people. But the name of Micah or Micaiah, (as *the elders of the land*[l] called him on a solemn occasion, some 120 years afterward) contained more than teaching. It was cast into the form of a challenge. *Who is like the Lord?* The form of words had been impressed on Israel by the song of Moses after the deliverance at the Red sea[m]. In the days of Elijah and that first Micaiah, the strife between God and man, the true Prophet and the false, had been ended at the battle of Ramoth-Gilead; it ceased for a time, in the reigns of Jehu and his successors, because in consequence of his partial obedience, God, by Elisha and Jonah, promised them good: it was again resumed, as the promise to Jehu was expiring, and God's prophets had anew to proclaim a message of woe. *Hast thou found me, O mine enemy*[n]? and, *I hate him, for he doth not prophesy good concerning me, but evil,* Ahab's words as to Elijah and Micaiah, were the types of the subsequent contradiction of the false prophets to Hosea and Amos, which closed only with the destruction of Samaria. Now, in the time of the later Micaiah, were the first dawnings of the same strife in Judah, which

[a] Μιχαίας is used by the LXX. in Jer. xxvi. 18 and Micah i. 1, as also in the other places where the name occurs, except Neh. xi. 17, 22, where for מיכא they have Μιχά. Josephus calls both prophets Μιχαίας, Micah son of Imlah, Ant. 8. 14. 5. and our prophet, Ant. 10. 6. 2. The Vulgate uses for both, Michæas.

[b] They substituted מיכה in the Kri in Jeremiah.

[c] 2 Chr. xvii. 7. [d] Ib. xiii. 2.
[e] Ib. xviii. 8. Keth.
[f] מיכיהו Jud. xvii. 1, 4; מיכה 5, 8, 9, 10.
[g] מיכיהו 1 Kings xxii. 9, 2 Chr. xviii. 7; מיכה 2 Chr. xviii. 14.
[h] 2 Kings xxii. 12. [i] 2 Chr. xxxiv. 20.
[k] Num. xiii. 16. [l] Jer. xxvi. 17, 18.
[m] Ex. xv. 11. [n] 1 Kings xxi. 20. [o] Ib. xxii. 8, 18.

5

hastened and brought about the destruction of Jerusalem under Zedekiah, which re-appeared after the Captivity[p], and was the immediate cause of the second destruction under the Romans[q]. Micah, as he dwells on the meaning of names generally, so, doubtless, it is in allusion to his own, that, at the close of his prophecy, he ushers in his announcement of God's incomparable mercy with the words[r], *Who is a God like unto Thee?* Before him, whatever disobedience there was to God's law in Judah, there was no systematic, organized, opposition to His prophets. There is no token of it in Joel. From the times of Micah it is never missing. We find it in each prophet (however brief the remains of some are), who prophesied directly to Judah, not in Isaiah only, but in Habakkuk[s] and Zephaniah[t]. It deepened, as it hastened toward its decision. The nearer God's judgments were at hand, the more obstinately the false prophets denied that they would come. The system of false prophecy, which rose to its height in the time of Jeremiah, which met and thwarted him at every step[u], and deceived those who wished to be deceived, was dawning in the time of Micah. False prophecy arose in Judah from the self-same cause whence it had arisen in Israel, because Judah's deepening corruption drew down the prophecies of God's displeasure, which it was popular to disbelieve. False prophecy was a gainful occupation. The false prophets had men's wishes on their side. They had the people with them. *My people love to have it so*[x], said God. They forbade Micah to prophesy[y]; prophesied peace[z], when God foretold evil; prophesied for gain[a], and proclaimed war in the Name of God[b] against those who fed them not.

At such a time was Micah called. His name which he himself explains, was no chance name. To the Hebrews, to whom names were so much more significant, parts of the living language, it recalled the name of his great predecessor, his standing alone against all the prophets of Ahab, his prophecy, his suffering, his evidenced truth. The truth of prophecy was set upon the issue of the battle before Ramoth-Gilead. In the presence of Jehoshaphat, king of Judah, as well as of Ahab, the 400 prophets of Ashtaroth had promised to Ahab the prize he longed for. One solitary, discriminating voice was heard amid that clamorous multitude, forewarning Ahab that he would perish, his people would be scattered. On the one side, was that loud triumphant chorus of[c] *all the prophets, Go up to Ramoth-Gilead, and*

prosper; for the Lord shall deliver it into the king's hand. On the other, one solemn voice, exhibiting before them that sad spectacle which the morrow's sun should witness[d], *I saw all Israel scattered upon the hills, as sheep that have not a shepherd, and the Lord said, these have no master, let them return every man to his house in peace.* Micaiah was smitten, imprisoned, and, apparently, ended his ministry, appealing from that small audience of the armies of Israel and Judah to the whole world, which has ever since looked back on that strife with interest and awe; [e] *Hear ye peoples, each one of them.* God, who guided the archer shooting *at a venture*[f], fulfilled the words which He had put into the Prophet's mouth. God's words had found Ahab, although *disguised;* Jehoshaphat, the imperilled[g], returned home, to relate the issue. The conflict between God's truth and idol falsehood was doubtless long remembered in Judah. And now when the strife had penetrated into Judah, to be ended some 170[h] years afterward in the destruction of Jerusalem, another Micaiah arose, his name the old watchword, *Who is like the Lord?* He prefixed to his prophecy that same summons[i] to the whole world to behold the issue of the conflict, which God had once accredited and, in that issue, had given an earnest of the victory of His truth, there thenceforth and for ever.

The prophet was born a villager, in Moresheth Gath, "a village[j]", S. Jerome says; ("a little village[k]", in S. Jerome's own days), "East of Eleutheropolis," where what was "[l]formerly his grave," was "now a church." Since it was his birthplace and his burial-place, it was probably his home also. In the beginning of the reign of Jehoiakim, *the elders of the land*[m] speak of him with this same title, *the Morasthite.* He lingers, in his prophecy, among the towns of the maritime plain (the Shephēlah) where his birthplace lay. Among the ten places in that neighborhood[n], which he selects for warning and for example of the universal captivity, is his native village, "the home he loved." But the chief scene of his ministry was Jerusalem. He names it in the beginning of his prophecy, as the place where the idolatries, and, with the idolatries, all the other sins of Judah were concentrated. The two capitals, Samaria and Jerusalem, were the chief objects of the word of God to him, because the corruption of each kingdom streamed forth from them. The sins which he rebukes are chiefly those of the capital. Extreme oppression[o], violence

p Neh. vi. 14.   q See vol. i. pp. 334–336.
r vii. 18.   s i. 5, ii. 1.   t i. 12.
u See Jer. v. 13, 31, vi. 13–17, viii. 10–12, xiv. 13–16, xx. 1–6, xxiii. 9-end, xxvi. 7, 8, 11, xxvii. 14–18, xxviii., xxix. 8, 9, 21–32.
x Jer. v. 31.   y ii. 6.   z iii. 5.   a iii. 11.

b iii. 5. see note.   c 1 Kings xxii. 12.
d Ib. 17.   e Ib. 28.   f 34.   g 30–3.
h from the beginning of Jotham's reign.
i Hengst. Christ. i. 475.   j Onom.   k Præf. to Mic.
l Ep. 86. ad Eustoch. Epitaph. Paulæ § 14. i. 698.
m Jer. xxvi. 17, 18.   n i. 11–15.   o iii. 2, 3, ii. 2.

among the rich[p], bribing among judges, priests, prophets[q]; building up the capital even by cost of life, or actual bloodshed[r]; spoilation[s]; expulsion of the powerless, women and children from their homes[t]; covetousness[u]; cheating in dealings[x]; pride[y]. These, of course, may be manifoldly repeated in lesser places of resort and of judgment. But it is *Zion and Jerusalem* which are so *built up with blood*[r]; *Zion and Jerusalem*, which are, on that ground, to be *plowed· as a field*[z]; it is *the city* to which *the Lord's voice crieth*[a]; whose *rich men are full of violence*[p]; it is the *daughter of Zion*[b], which is to *go forth out of the city and go to Babylon.* Especially, they are the heads and princes of the people[c], whom he upbraids for perversion of justice and for oppression. Even the good kings of Judah seem to have been powerless to restrain the general corruption.

Micah, according to the title which he prefixed to his prophecy, was called to the prophetic office somewhat later than Isaiah. His ministry began later, and ended earlier. For Uzziah, in whose reign Isaiah began to prophesy, was dead before Micah was called to his office; and Micah probably was called away early in the reign of Hezekiah, whereas some of the chief public acts of Isaiah's ministry fell in the 17th and 18th years of the reign of Hezekiah. Joel, Amos, Obadiah, Jonah, had doubtless been withdrawn to their rest. Hosea alone, in "grey-haired might," was still protesting in vain against the deepening corruptions of Israel.

The contents of Micah's prophecy and his relation to Isaiah agree with the inscription. His prophecy has indications of the times of Jotham, perhaps also of those of Ahaz; one signal prophecy, we know historically, was uttered in the reign of Hezekiah.

It is now owned, well nigh on all hands, that the great prophecy, three verses of which Isaiah prefixed to his 2d chapter, was originally delivered by Micah. But it appears from the context in Isaiah, that he delivered the prophecy in that 2d chapter, in the reign of Jotham. Other language of Micah also belongs to that same reign. No one now thinks that Micah adopted that great prophecy from Isaiah. The prophecy, as it stands in Micah, is in close connection with what precedes it. He had said[d], *the mountain of the house shall be as the high places of the forest;* he subjoins instantly God's reversal of that sentence, *in the latter days.* [e]*And in the last days it shall be that the mountain of the house of the Lord shall be established on the top of the mountains, and peoples shall*

flow unto it. He had said, *Zion shall be plowed as a field, and Jerusalem shall become heaps;* he adds forthwith, in reversal of this[f], *the law shall go forth from Zion, and the word of the Lord from Jerusalem.* The two sentences are joined as closely as they can be; *Zion shall be plowed as a field, and Jerusalem shall become heaps, and the mountain of the house shall become high places of a forest; and it shall be, in the last days, the mountain of the house of the Lord shall be* (abidingly)[g] *established on the top of the mountains.* Every reader would understand, that the elevation intended, was spiritual, not physical. They could not fail to understand the metaphor; or imagine that the Mount Zion, on part of which, (Mount Moriah,) the *house of the Lord* stood, should be physically placed on other hills. But the contrast is marked. The promise is the sequel of the woe; the abiding condition is the reversal of the sentence of its desolation. Even the words allude, the one to the other[h].

In Isaiah, there is no such connection. After the first chapter and its summary of rebuke, warning, threatening, and final weal or woe resting on each class, Isaiah, in his second chapter, begins his prophecy anew with a fresh title[i]; *The word that Isaiah the son of Amos saw concerning Judah and Jerusalem;* and to this he prefixes three verses from Micah's prophecy. He separates it in a marked way from the preceding summary, and yet connects it with some other prophecy by the word, *And*[j]. He himself marks that it is not in its original place here. So then, in the prophet Micah, the close connection with the foregoing marks that it *is* in its original place; Isaiah marked purposely that in his prophecy it is not.

But Isaiah's prophecy belongs to a time of prosperity; such as Judah had not, after the reign of Jotham. It was a time of great warlike strength, diffused through the whole land. The land was full[k], without end, of gold, silver, chariots, horses, of lofty looks and haughtiness. The images which follow[l] are shadows of the Day of Judgment, and extend beyond Judah; but the sins rebuked are the sins of strength and might, self-confidence, oppression, manifold female luxury and bravery[m]. Isaiah prophesies that God would take away their strength[n]. Then they still had it. Judah trusted not at that time in God nor in foreign alliances, but in self. Yet, from the time of Ahaz, trust in foreign help infected them to the end. Even Hezekiah, when he received the messengers of Merodach-baladan[o], fell into the snare; and Josiah probably lost his life, as a vassal

[p] vi. 12.   [q] iii. 11; judges and priests, vii. 3.
[r] iii. 10; bloodshed also, vii. 2.   [s] ii. 8.   [t] ii. 9.
[u] ii. 2.   [x] vi. 10, 11.   [y] ii. 3.   [z] iii. 12. *
[a] vi. 9.   [b] iv. 10.   [c] iii. 1, 9, 11, vi. 12, vii. 3.
[d] iii. 12.   [e] iv. 1.   [f] iv. 2.

[g] It is not ‏יָכוּן‎ but ‏יִהְיֶה־נָכוֹן‎.
[h] The ‏הַר בֵּית יְהוָה‎ iv. 1. to the ‏הַר הַבַּית‎ iii. 12; the ‏יִהְיֶה‎. ‏תִּהְיֶה‎. Hengst.
[i] ii. 1.   [j] ii. 2.   [k] Is. ii. 7, 11.   [l] 12–21.
[m] iii. 16, 23.   [n] iii. 1–3.   [o] Is. xxxix.

of Assyria [p]. This union of inherent strength
and unconcernedness about foreign aid is an
adequate test of days anterior to Ahaz.

But since Isaiah prefixed to a prophecy in
the days of Jotham this great prophecy of
Micah, then Micah's prophecy must have
been already current. To those same days
of strength it belongs, that Micah could
prophesy as a gift, the cutting off [q] of *horses
and chariots*, the destruction *of cities* and *strong
towers*, all, in which Judah trusted instead of
God. The prophecy is a counterpart of
Isaiah's. Isaiah prophesied a day of Judgment, in which all these things should be removed; Micah foretold that their removal
should be a mercy to those who trust in
Christ.

On the other hand, the utter dislocation
of society, the bursting of all the most sacred
bands which bind man to man together, described in his last chapter [r], perhaps belong
most to the miserable decay in the reign of
Ahaz. The idolatry spoken of also belongs
probably to the time of Ahaz. In Jotham's
time [s], *the people sacrificed and burned incense
still in the high places;* yet, under a king so
highly praised [t], these are not likely to have
been in Jerusalem. But Micah, in the very
head of his prophecy, speaks of Jerusalem [u]
as the centre of the idolatries of Judah. The
allusion also to child-sacrifices belongs to the
time of Ahaz, who sacrificed sons of his own [x],
and whose sacrifice others probably imitated.
The mention of the special idolatry of the
time, [y] *the statutes of Omri are kept, and all the
works of the house of Ahab*, belong to the same
reign, it being recorded of Ahaz especially [z],
*he walked in the ways of the kings of Israel and
made also molten images for Baalim;* the
special sin of the house of Ahab. That character too which he describes, that, amid all
that idolatry, practical irreligion, and wickedness, they *leant upon the Lord, and said, Is
not the Lord among us? none evil can come upon
us* [a]; was just the character of Ahaz. Not
until the end of his reign was he so embit-
tered by God's chastisements, that he closed
His temple [b]. Up to that time, even after
he had copied the brazen altar at Damascus,
he still kept up a divided allegiance to God.
Urijah, the high Priest, at the king's command, offered the sacrifices for the king and
the people, while Ahaz used *the brazen altar,
to enquire by* [c]. This was just the half-service
which God by Micah rejects. It is the old
history of man's half-service, faith without
love, which provides, that what it believes
but loves not, should be done for it, and itself
enacts what it prefers. Urijah was to offer
the lawful sacrifices for the king and the
people; Ahaz was to obtain knowledge of the

future, such as he wished in his own way, a
lying future, by lying acts.

Micah renewed under Hezekiah the prophecy of the utter destruction of Jerusalem,
which he had pronounced under Jotham.
The prophets did not heed repeating themselves. Eloquent as they were, they are the
more eloquent because eloquence was not
their object. Even our Lord, with Divine
wisdom, and the more, probably, because He
had Divine wisdom, repeated in His teaching
the same words. Those words sank the deeper,
because often repeated. So Micah repeated
doubtless oftentimes those words, which he
first uttered in the days of Jotham; *Zion shall
be plowed like a field and Jerusalem shall become heaps, and the mountain of the house as the
high places of the forest*. Often, during those
perhaps thirty years, he repeated them in
vain. At the last, they wrought a great repentance, and delayed, it may be for 136
years, the destruction which he was constrained to foretell. Early in the days of Jehoiakim, about 120 years afterward, in the
public assembly when Jeremiah was on trial
for his life, *the elders of the land* said explic-
itly, that the great conversion at the beginning of the reign of Hezekiah, nay, of that
king himself, was wrought by the teaching of
Micah. [d] *Then rose up*, says Jeremiah, *certain
of the elders of the land, and spake to all the assembly of the people, saying, Micah the Morasthite prophesied in the days of Hezekiah king of
Judah, saying, Thus saith the Lord of hosts,
Zion shall be ploughed like a field, and Jerusalem
shall become heaps, and the mountain of the
house, as the high places of the forest. Did Hezekiah king of Judah, and all Judah, put him at
all to death? Did he not fear the Lord, and besought the Lord, and the Lord repented Him of
the evil which He had pronounced against them?*

It may have been that single prophecy
which Micah so delivered; some have
thought that it was his whole book. Jeremiah, at God's command, at one time uttered
single prophecies; at another, the summary
of all his prophecies. This only is. certain,
that the prophecy, whether these words
alone or the book containing them, was delivered to all Judah, and that God moved
the people through them to repentance.

The words, as they occur in Jeremiah, are
the same, and in the same order, as they
stand in Micah. Only in Jeremiah the common plural termination is substituted for the
rarer and poetic form used by Micah [e]. The
elders, then, who quoted them, probably
knew them, not from tradition, but from the
written book of the Prophet. But those
elders speak of Micah, as exercising his prophetic office in the days of Hezekiah. They

---

[p] 2 Kings xxiii. 29, 2 Chr. xxxv. 20–22.
[q] Mic. v. 10, 11, 14.   [r] vii. 5, 6.
[s] 2 Kings xv. 35.
[t] 2 Kings xv. 34, 2 Chr. xxvii. 2, 6.   [u] i. 5.

[x] 2 Kings xvi. 3, 2 Chr. xxviii. 3.   [y] vi. 16.
[z] 2 Chr. xxviii. 2.   [a] iii. 11, vi. 6.
[b] 2 Chr. xxviii. 22–24.   [c] 2 Kings xvi. 15.
[d] Jer. xxvi. 17–19.   [e] םִיָּע for יָּע.

do not say, *he prophesied*, which might have been a single act; but *he was prophesying, hayah nibbah*, a form of speaking which is only used of an abiding, habitual, action. They say also, " he was habitually prophesying, and he said," i. e. as we should say, " in the course of his prophesying in the days of Hezekiah, he said." Still it was to *all the people of Judah* that he said it. The elders say so, and lay stress upon it by repeating it. *Did Hezekiah king of Judah and all Judah put him at all to death?* It must have been then on some of the great festivals, when *all Judah* was gathered together, that Micah so spake to them.

Probably, shortly afterward, in those first years of Hezekiah, Micah's office on earth closed. For, at the outset and in the summary of his prophecy, not incidentally, he speaks of the destruction of Samaria, which took place in the 4th year of Hezekiah, as still to come; and however practical or partial idolatry continued, such idolatry as he throughout describes, did not exist after the reformation by Hezekiah. This conversion, then, of the king and of some considerable part of Judah was probably the closing harvest of his life, after a long seed-time of tears. So God allowed His servant to *depart in peace*. The reformation itself, at least in its fullness, took place after the kingdom of Samaria had come to an end, since Hezekiah's messengers could, unhindered, invite all Israel to join in his great Passover. Probably, then, Micah lived to see the first dawnings only of the first reformation which God wrought by his words.

At the commencement, then, of Hezekiah's reign he collected the substance of what God had taught by him, re-casting it, so to speak, and retaining of his spoken prophecy so much as God willed to remain for us. As it stands, it belongs to that early time of Hezekiah's reign, in which the sins of Ahaz still lived on. Corruption of manners had been hereditary. In Jotham's reign too, it is said expressly, in contrast with himself[f], *the people were still doing corruptly*. Idolatry had, under Ahaz, received a fanatic impulse from the king, who, at last, set himself to close the worship of God[g]. The strength of Jotham's reign was gone; the longing for its restoration led to the wrong and destructive policy, against which Isaiah had to contend. Of this Micah says, such should not be the strength of the future kingdom of God. Idolatry and oppression lived on; against these, the inheritance of those former reigns, the sole residuum of Jotham's might or Ahaz' policy, the breach of the law of love of God and man, Micah concentrated his written prophecy.

This book also has remarkable symmetry. Each of its three divisions is a whole, beginning with upbraiding for sin, threatening God's judgments, and ending with promises of future mercy in Christ. The two later divisions begin again with that same characteristic, *Hear ye*[h], with which Micah had opened the whole. The three divisions are also connected, as well by lesser references to the later to the former, as also by the advance of the prophecy. Judah could not be trusted now with any simple declaration of God's future mercy. They supposed themselves, impenitent as they were and with no purpose of repentance, to be the objects of God's care, and secure from evil. Unmixed promise of good would but foment this irreligious apathy. Hence on the promises at the end of the first portion[i], *and their king shall pass before them and the Lord at the head of them*, he turns abruptly[k], *And I said, Hear, I pray you, Is it not for you to know judgment?* The promise had been to *Jacob* and *the remnant of Israel*[l]. He renews his summons to the[k] *heads of Jacob* and the *princes of the house of Israel*. In like way, the last section, opening with that wonderful pleading of God with His people, follows upon that unbroken declaration of God's mercies, which itself issues out of the promised Birth at Bethlehem.

There is also a sort of progress in the promises of the three parts[l]. In the first, it is of deliverance generally, in language taken from that first deliverance from Egypt. The 2d is objective, the Birth of the Redeemer, the conversion of the Gentiles, the restoration of the Jews, the establishment and nature of His kingdom. The third is mainly subjective, man's repentance, waiting upon God, and God's forgiveness of his sins.

Throughout, the metropolis is chiefly addressed, as the main seat of present evil[m] and as the centre of the future blessings; where the reign of the long-promised Ruler should be[n]; whence the revelation of God should go forth to the heathen[o]; whither the scattered and dispersed people should be gathered[p].

Throughout the prophecy also, Micah upbraids the same class of sins, wrong dealing of man to man, oppression of the poor by the rich[m]. Throughout, their future captivity and dispersion are either predicted[q], or assumed as the basis of the prediction of good[r]. Throughout, we see the contemporary of the prophet Isaiah. Beside that great prediction, which Isaiah inserted verbally from Micah, we see them, as it were, side by side, in that city of God's visitation and of His mercy, prophesying the same respite, the same place of captivity and deliverance from

f 2 Chr. xxvii. 2.   g Ib. xxviii. 22-25, xxix. 7.
h ch. iii.-v. and vi. vii.   i ii. 12.   k iii. 1.
l Hengst. Christ. i. 477, 8.   m See ab. p. 289.
n iv. 2, 7, 8.   o iv. 1, 2.

p iv. 6, 7, vii. 11, 12.
q i. 11, 14-16, ii. 4, 5, 10, (utter abiding destruction of Jerusalem) iii. 12, iv. 10, v. 3.
r ii. 12, 13, iv. 6, 7, 10, vii. 11, 12, 15.

it, the same ulterior mercies in Christ. "[s]The more to establish the faith, God willed that Isaiah and Micah should speak together, as with one mouth, and use such agreement as might the more convict all rebels." Assyria was then the monarchy of the world; yet both prophets promise deliverance from it[t]; both foretell the captivity in the then subordinate Babylon[u]; both, the deliverance from it[x]. Both speak in the like way of the gathering together of God's people from lands[y], to some of which they were not yet dispersed. Isaiah prophesied the Virgin-Birth of Immanuel[z]; Micah, the Birth at Bethlehem of Him *Whose goings forth have been of old, from everlasting*[a]. Both speak in the like way of the reverence for the Gentiles thereafter for her[b], by reason of the presence of their God. Even, in outward manner, Micah, representing himself, as one who *went mourning* and *wailing, stripped and naked*[c], is a sort of forerunner of the symbolic acts of Isaiah[d]. Micah had this also common with Isaiah, that he has a predominance of comfort. He is brief in upbraiding[e], indignant in casting back the pleas of the false prophets[f], concise in his threatenings of woe[g], save where he lingers mournfully over the desolation[h], large and flowing in his descriptions of mercy to come[i]. He sees and pronounces the coming punishment, as absolutely certain; he does not call to repentance to avert it; he knows that ultimately it will not be averted; he sees it irrespectively of time, and says that it will be. Time is an accident to the link of cause and effect. Sin consummated would be the cause; punishment, the effect. He spoke to those who knew that God pardoned on repentance, who had lately had before them that marvelous instance in Nineveh. He dashes to the ground their false security, by reason of their descent from Jacob[k], of God's Presence among them in the Temple[l]; the multitude of their offerings amid the multitude of their sins[m]. He rejects in God's name their false, outward, impenitent, penitence; and thereby the more implies that He would accept a true repentance. They knew this, and were, for a time, scared into penitence. But in his book, as God willed it to remain, he is rather the prophet of God's dealings, than the direct preacher of repentance to individuals. Yet he is the more an evangelic preacher, in that he speaks of repentance, only as the gift of God. He

does not ignore that man must accept the grace of God; but, as Isaiah foretells of the days of the Gospel, *the idols He shall utterly abolish*[n], so Micah first foretells that God would abolish all wherein man relied out of God, all wherein he prided himself[o], every form of idolatry[p], and subsequently describes the future evangelic repentance, submission to, and waiting upon God and His righteousness[q]; and God's free plenary forgiveness[r].

Micah's rapid unprepared transitions from each of his main themes to another, from upbraiding to threatening, from threatening to mercy and then back again to upbraiding, is probably a part of that same vivid perception of the connection of sin, chastisement, forgiveness, in the will and mind of God. He sees them and speaks of them in the natural sequence in which they were exhibited to him. He connects most commonly the sin with the punishment by the one word, *therefore*[s], because it was an object with him to shew the connection. The mercies to come he subjoins either suddenly without any conjunction[t], or with the simple *and*. An English reader loses some of the force of this simplicity by the paraphrase, which, for the simple copula, substitutes the inference or contrast, *therefore, then, but, notwithstanding*[u], which lie in the subjects themselves. An English reader might have been puzzled, at first sight, by the monotonous simplicity of the, *and, and*, joining together the mention of events, which stand, either as the contrast or the consequence of those which precede them. The English version accordingly has consulted for the reader or hearer, by drawing out for him the contrast or consequence which lay beneath the surface. But this gain of clearness involved giving up so far the majestic simplicity of the Prophet, who at times speaks of things as they lay in the Divine Mind, and as, one by one, they would be unfolded to man, without explaining the relation in which they stood to one another. Micah knew that sufferings were, in God's purpose, travail-pains. And so, immediately after the denunciation of punishment, he adds so calmly, "[x]*And* in the last days it shall be;" "*And* thou, Bethlehem Ephratah." Or in the midst of his descriptions of mercies, he speaks of the intervening troubles, as the way to them. *Now*[y] *why dost thou cry aloud?*—*pangs have taken thee, as a woman in travail—be in pain—thou shalt go even unto Babylon; there shalt thou be delivered:* or, [z] *Therefore will He*

[s]Carpz. Introd. p. 365. in Häv. ii. 364.
[t]Is. x. 24-34, xiv. 25, xxx. 31, xxxi. 8, 9, xxxvii. 6, 7, 21-35, Mic. v 5, 6.
[u]Is. xxxix. 6, Mic. iv. 10.
[x]Is. xlviii. 20, Mic. ib.
[y]Is. xi. 11 sqq. Mic. vii. 12.   [z]vii. 14.
[a]v. 2 Eng. (1 Heb.)
[b]Is. xlix. 23, Mic. vii. 17. Häv. ib.
[c]i. 8. see note.   [d]Is. xx. 2, 3.
[e]i. 5, ii. 1, 2, 9-11.   [f]ii. 7, 11, iii. 5-7.

[g]ii. 3, 10, iii. 4, 12, vi. 13-16, vii. 4, 13.
[h]i. 10-16, ii. 4, 5.   [i]iv., v., vii. 7-20.   [k]ii. 7.
[l]iii. 11.   [m]vi. 6, 7.   [n]Is. ii. 18.   [o]v. 9, 10.
[p]v. 11-13.   [q]vii. 8, 9.   [r]Ib. 18, 19.
[s]Not i. 6, vi. 13. but i. 14, ii. 3, 5, iii. 6, 12.
[t]ii. 12, iv. 13.
[u]*Therefore*, i. 6, vi. 13, vii. 7; *then*, iii. 7, vii. 10; *but*, iii. 8, iv. 1, 4, 12, v. 2, vi. 16; *for*, iv. 5; *notwithstanding*, vii. 13.   [x]iv. 1, v. 2 (1 Heb.), add vii. 7.
[y]iv. 9.   [z]v. 3. [2 Heb.]

give thee up until the time, &c. i.e. because He has these good things in store for thee, *He will give thee up, until the time* comes.

With this great simplicity Micah unites great vividness and energy. Thus in predicting punishment, he uses the form of command, bidding them, as it were, execute it on themselves[a]; *Arise, depart:* as, in the Great Day, our Lord shall say, *Depart, ye cursed.* And since God does in us or by us what He commands to be done, he uses the imperative to Zion, alike as to her victories over God's enemies[b], or her state of anxious fear[c].

To that same vividness belong his rapid changes of person or gender; his sudden questions[d]; his unmarked dialogues. The changes of person and gender occur in all Hebrew poetry; all have their emphasis. He addresses the people or place as a whole (*fem.*), then all the individuals in her[e]; or turns away and speaks of it[f]; or contrariwise, having spoken of the whole in the third person, he turns round and drives the warning home to individuals[g]. The variations in the last verse of ch. vi. are unexampled for rapidity even in Hebrew.

And yet the flow of his words is smooth and measured. Without departing from the conciseness of Hebrew poetry, his cadence, for the most part, is of the more prolonged sort, as far as any can be called prolonged, when all is so concise. In some 8 verses, out of 104, he is markedly brief, where conciseness corresponds with his subject, as in an abrupt appeal as to their sins[h], or an energetic announcement of judgment[i] or of mercy[k], or in that remarkable prophecy of both[l], how God would, in mercy, cut off all grounds of human trust. Else, whereas in Nahum and Habakkuk, not quite ⅓, and in the eleven last Chapters of Hosea much less than ⅕, of

the verses contain more than 13 words[m], in Micah above ⅔ (as, in Joel, nearly ⅔) exceed that number[n]. The verses are also distributed in that ever-varying cadence, whereby, in Hebrew poetry, portions of their short sentences being grouped together, the harmony of the whole is produced by the varied dispositions of these lesser groups of 2, 3, 4, and but rarely 5 words; scarcely any two verses exactly corresponding, but all being united by the blending of similar cadences. In Micah, as in all Hebrew poetry, the combination of 3 words is the most frequent, and this, sometimes by itself, sometimes in union with the number 4, making the sacred number 7; or, with 2, making a number which we find in the tabernacle, but which dwells more in the hearts of the disciples of the Crucified. The same exact rhythm seldom recurs, and that, naturally, chiefly in the shorter verses, the longer admitting or requiring more combinations. Wherever also there is more than one pause in the verse, a further and very considerable variety of rhythm may be produced, even when the several clauses of two verses contain the same number of words in the same order. The difference of cadence is far more influenced by the place, where the verse is divided, than by the exact number of words contained in it. The rhetorical force of the distribution of the words into the several clauses depends mainly upon the place of the Athnach or semicolon[o]. The same exact rhythm, (in which both the same number of words occur in the verse, and the verse is divided in the same place) recurs only seven times in Micah, in verses capable of a variation. The other four cases of repetition occur in short verses which have one division only[p] according to the place where the main division of the verse falls.

[a] ii. 10, add i. 11, 13, iv. 10. [b] iv. 13.

[c] v. 1. (iv. 14 Heb.)

[d] i. 5, ii. 7, iii. 1, iv. 9, vi. 3, 6, 10, 11, vii. 18.

[e] i. 11. twice.

[f] i. 2. twice; in i. 13. he returns to the 2d pers.

[g] ii. 3. [h] iii. 10 (5 words), vi. 11 (6 words).

[i] v. 8, and vii. 13, (7 words).

[k] vii. 11 (7 words), vii. 15 (5 words).

[l] v. 13 Heb. (5 words), v. 10 (6 words), v. 11 (7 words).

[m] Out of the 157 verses in Hosea's 11 last chapters, 111 contain fewer than 14 words each, 46 only 14 words or upwards; out of 46, of which the book of Nahum consists (excluding the title) 14 only have more than 13 words; out of 55 of Habakkuk, 17 only have more than 13.

[n] In Micah, 48 out of 104; in Joel, 30 out of 72; in Obadiah, 10 out of 21.

[o] There is less difference between a verse of 14 words, distributed 43, 43 and one of 11, distributed 32, 42, than in a verse whose 10 words were distributed 32,32 or 323,2.

[p] The following summary of these lesser divisions, which are mostly marked by the Hebrew accents, may perhaps give some little idea of the rhythm. Only the degree of subdivision must often be a matter of opinion or taste or ear. Thus, of 5 words which grammatically belong together, one might think that the cadence separated them into 3 and 2; another might take them altogether. But this is a matter of detail only; the principle is unmis-

takable. Again, words which have been artificially joined together in Hebrew by the Makkeph, I have considered as 2 words, if each had a distinct idea. Thus אֶת, when the mere sign of the object, I have not counted; when it is the preposition, "with," I have counted it. In the following list, the verses are ranged according to the number of the words contained in each verse, beginning with the highest. The numbers on the right hand indicate the lesser divisions into which each verse may be distributed. The comma in each set of numbers marks the place of the Athnach or semicolon. The Roman numerals indicate how often any cadence is repeated.

NUMBER OF WORDS IN EACH LESSER DIVISION.

Words.	
24	333422,43 432,3264
22	46,534 14333,44
21	221,423232 4433,34
20	23333,33 333,3134 3333,44 4333,322
19	344,44 34,2253 32,4424
18	43,3233 342,423 3232,44
17	444,32 3433,22 3,4343 2223,332
16	222,433 3433,3 33,4222 44,44
15	32,325 33333,3 432,33 43,233 43,323 (ii) 134,133 43,332 3223,32
14	33,53 (ii) 34,34 23122,22 43,43 432,32 333,23 33,323 43,52 332,33 13,334 43,34 22,3313 2222,33 2222,51

His description of the destruction of the cities or villages of Judah corresponds in vividness to Isaiah's ideal march of Sennacherib q. The flame of war spreads from place to place; but Micah relieves the sameness of the description of misery by every variety which language allows. He speaks of them in his own person r, or to them; he describes the calamity in past s or in future t, or by use of the imperative u. The verbal allusions are crowded together in a way unexampled elsewhere. Moderns have spoken of them, as not after their taste, or have apologized for them. The mighty Prophet, who wrought a repentance greater than his great contemporary Isaiah, knew well what would impress the people to whom he spoke. The Hebrew names had definite meanings.

13	43,33 3,442 332,32 1322,5 222,322 432,4 43,33 322,42
12	32,322 422,22 143,22 224,4 23,34 53,22 24,24 43,23
11	32,33 42,32 (ii) 33,32 23,33 (ii) 24,32 33,23 (ii) 4322 22,43 32,42
10	5,5 33,4 32,32 (ii) 323,2 32,23 (ii) 22,33 2222,2 43,3
9	43,2 4,32 3,33 42,3 22,32 33,3
8	132,2 33,2
7	4,3 (ii) 3, 4 (ii) 3,22
6	3,3 (ii) 22,2
5	3,2 (ii)

To facilitate comparison, I subjoin a like analysis of the other prophets mentioned.

HOSEA.
Eleven last chapters.

22	422253,4 3244,54
21	4433,34 5,242224
20	32,33324 3333,44
19	4343,32 3423,34
18	4,4334 332,2332 2232,423 44,3223
17	43,3322 3332,33 23,4323 3223,223 333,323 3223,43 3442,4
16	2323,24 32,3422 233,323 21214,24 3223,33 3232,33 33,253 42,433
15	344,4 2323,23 3332,4 (ii) 223,242 333,33
14	43,43 44,33 5,432 44,42 43,232 324,32 422,42 33,2222 33,44 3224,3 33,53 4,442 32,333 14,-333
13	33,43 (iii) 34,42 43,33 (ii) 4,333 4,54 34,33 323,32 223,33 22,234 33,34
12	4,44 432,21 33,33 (ii) 222,222 32,34 42,42 222,33 223,32 43,122 43,23 43,32 32,43
11	24,32 323,3 32,33 233,12 33,23 42,23 132,14 32,-42 32,33 33,32 4,43 23,222
10	43,3 (iii) 33,4 (ii) 3,34 3232 (ii) 44,2 24,4 222,22 4,33 33,22 322,3
9	5,13 25,2 3,33 (iii) 33,3 (iii) 232,2 2,322 32,22 (ii) 32,4 22,23 22,32 (ii) 4,32 13,32 2,34 5,4 24,3
8	32,3 (ii) 23,3 (iv) 2222 224 (ii)
7	13,3 (iii) 4,3 (iii) 3,4 (ii) 2,23 22,3 2,32 23,2 31,3 33,1 14,2
6	4,2 (ii) 3,3 (iii) 13,2 (ii)
5	3,2 (vii) 2111 113

JOEL.

25	334,3534
24	322,144332
23	3544,223
22	423,4423
21	5422,422 3335,43
20	16,42313 34,3433
19	224,443
18	22,4433 33,435
17	3332,42 245,33 353,33 1422,35
16	334,42 2242,6 44,44
15	22233,3 2432,22 22222,32 344,4 23,2323 333, 33 34,35

We can well imagine how, as name after name passed from the Prophet's mouth, connected with some note of woe, all around awaited anxiously, to know upon what place the fire of the Prophet's word would next fall; and as at last it had fallen upon little and mighty round about Jerusalem, the names of the places would ring in their ears as heralds of the coming woe; they would be like so many monuments, inscribed beforehand with the titles of departed greatness, reminding Jerusalem of its portion of the prophecy, that x *evil* should *come from the Lord unto the gate of Jerusalem.*

Wonderful must have been his lightning-flash of indignation, as, when the false prophet or the people had forbidden God's word to be spoken, he burst upon them, y *Thou,*

14	53,33 334,4 36,23 1432,4 3332,3
13	34,33 3,55 33,34
12	44,4 34,23 2222,4 5,34 24,33 43,32 32,223
11	22,322 (ii) 223,22 2222,3 (ii) 32,33 3,224 32,42 222,5 4,331 44,3 223,22 2222,3
10	32,32 222,22 22,42 231,4
9	32,22 (iii) 2,43 5,22
8	3,23 22,22 4,22
7	133 3,4 (ii) 3,22 22,3
6	3,3 (iv)

OBADIAH.

21	4333,323
19	4323,43
18	3332,133 34,344 4252,32
17	4242,32
16	5434 32422,3
15	334,23
14	43,43
13	332,23 42,34 4232,2
12	35,22
11	32,33 42,32
10	43,3
9	3,33
7	4,3 32,2
5	32

NAHUM.

21	32232,72
19	2333,55 3233,44
18	32,337
16	34,2322 23,42131
15	323,43 33,522 22222,32 14123,4
14	44,33 (ii) 32221,13 3,2234 234,32
13	42,223 3332,2 323,32
12	33,33 32,34 322,32 (ii) 414,3 42,222 222,222
11	43,4 32,222 22,313 42,32 23,24 322,22
10	42,13 12,223 3,223 32,32
9	32,22 (ii) 23,22
8	23,3 (ii) 24,2 22,22
7	22,21
6	13,2 31,2
5	3,2

HABAKKUK.

24	44,4444
20	4334,33
19	333,1423
18	43,254 3332,43
17	45,35 422,2232 54,44 333,53
15	34,44 332,322 33,234 34,233 43,44 13143,3 3333,3 333,42
14	43,322 332,33 33,44
13	32,422 33,43 23,44
12	323,22 (ii) 33,33 (ii)
11	222,32 32,42 32,33 322,4 42,14
10	322,3 3,34 4,33
9	33,3 (ii) 4,5 24,3 42,3 23,4
8	311,3 22,4 3,32
7	3,4 (ii) 4,3 (ii)
6	3,3 [iv]

q Is. x. 28–32.   r i. 8, 10. see note.
s 9, 10, 11, 12.   t 8.   u 11, 13, 16.
x i. 12.   y ii. 7.

called house of Jacob, shortened is God's Spirit? Or these His doings? And then follow the plaintive descriptions of the wrongs done to the poor, the peaceful [z], the mothers of his people and their little ones. And then again the instantaneous dismissal [a], *Arise and depart.* But, therewith, wonderful also is his tenderness. Burning as are his denunciations against the oppressions of the rich [b], (words less vehement will not pierce hearts of stone) there is an under-current of tenderness. His rebukes evince not indignation only against sin, but a tender sympathy with the sufferers. [c] He is afflicted in the afflictions which he has to denounce. He yearns for his people [d]; nay, until our Lord's Coming, there is scarcely an expression of such yearning longing: he hungers and thirsts for their good [e].

God's individual care of His people, and of each soul in it, had, since David's time [f] and even since Jacob [g], been likened to the care of the shepherd for each single sheep. The Psalm of Asaph [h] must have familiarized the people to the image, as relating to themselves as a whole, and David's deep Psalm had united it with God's tender care of His own in, and over, death. Yet the predominance of this image in Micah is a part of the tenderness of the Prophet. He adopts it, as expressing, more than any other natural image, the helplessness of the creature, the tender individual care of the Creator. He forestalls our Lord's words, *I am the good shepherd*, in his description of the Messiah, gathering *the remnant of Israel together, as the sheep of Bozrah* [i]; His people are as a flock, *lame and despised* [k], whom God would assemble; His royal seat, *the tower of the flock* [l]; the Ruler of Israel should *stand* unresting, *and feed them* [m]; those whom He should employ against the enemies of His people, are *shepherds* [n], under Him, the true shepherd. He sums up his prayer for his people to God as their Shepherd [o]; *Feed Thy people with Thy rod, the flock of Thine heritage.*

Directly, he was a Prophet for Judah only. At the beginning of his book, he condemns the idolatries of both capitals, as the central sin of the two kingdoms. The destruction of Samaria he pronounces at once, as future, absolutely certain, abiding [p]. There he leaves her, declares her *wound incurable*, and passes forthwith to Judah, to whom, he says, that wound should pass, whom that same enemy should reach [q]. Thereafter, he mentions incidentally the infection of Israel's sin

spreading to Judah [r]. Else, after that first sentence on Samaria, the names of Jacob (which he had given to the ten tribes [s]) and Israel are appropriated to the kingdom of Judah [t]: Judah is mentioned no more, only her capital [u]; even her kings are called *the kings of Israel* [x]. The ten tribes are only included in the general restoration of the whole [y]. The future remnant of the two tribes, to be restored after the captivity of Babylon, are called by themselves *the remnant of Jacob* [z]: the Messiah to be born at Bethlehem is foretold as *the ruler in Israel* [a]: the ten tribes are called *the remnant of His brethren*, who were to *return to the children of Israel* [b], i. e. Judah.

This the more illustrates the genuineness of the inscription. A later hand would have been unlikely to have mentioned either Samaria or those earlier kings of Judah. Each part of the title corresponds to something in the prophecy; the name *Micah* is alluded to at its close; his birthplace, the *Morasthite*, at its beginning; the indications of those earlier reigns lie there, although not on its surface [c]. The mention of the two capitals, followed by the immediate sentence on Samaria, and then by the fuller expansion of the sins and punishment of Jerusalem, culminating in its sentence [d], in Micah, corresponds to the brief mention of the punishment of Judah in Amos the Prophet of Israel, and then the fuller expansion of the sins and punishments of Israel. Further, the capitals, as the fountains of idolatry, are the primary object of God's displeasure. They are both specially denounced in the course of the prophecy; their special overthrow is foretold [e]. The title corresponds with the contents of the prophecy, yet the objections of modern critics shew that the correspondence does not lie on the surface.

The taunt of the false priest Amaziah [f] to Amos may in itself suggest that prophets at Jerusalem did prophesy against Samaria. Amaziah, anyhow, thought it natural that they should. Both Isaiah and Micah, while exercising their office at Jerusalem, had regard also to Samaria. Divided as Israel and Judah were, Israel was not yet cut off. Israel and Judah were still, together, the one people of God. The prophets in each had a care for the other.

Micah joins himself on to the men of God before him, as Isaiah at the time, and Jeremiah, Habakkuk, Zephaniah, Ezekiel, subsequently, employed words or thoughts of

[z] 8, 9.   [a] 10.
[b] ii. 1, 2, iii. 1–3, 9–11, vi. 10–12, vii. 2, 3.
[c] i. 8, 9, ii. 1, 2, vii. 5, 6.   [d] i. 8–10, 16, iv. 9, 10.
[e] vii. 1.   [f] Ps. xxiii.   [g] Gen. xlix. 24.
[h] Ps. lxxiv. 1, lxxviii. 52, lxxix. 13, lxxx. 1.
[i] ii. 12.   [k] iv. 6.   [l] Ib. 8.   [m] v. 4. [Eng. 3 Heb.]
[n] Ib. 5. [4 Heb.]   [o] vii. 14.
[p] i. 6, 7.   [q] i. 9.   [r] i. 13.   [s] i. 5.

[t] *Jacob*, ii. 7, iii. 1, 8, 9; *Israel*, i. 14, 15, iii. 1, 8, 9, v. 1, 3, vi. 2.
[u] See ab. p. 6.   [x] i. 14.
[y] *Jacob, all of thee*, ii. 12; *the remnant of Israel*, ib.
[z] v. 7, 8, [8, 9 Heb.]   [a] v. 2. (1 Heb.)
[b] Ib. 3. (2 Heb.)   [c] See ab. p. 8.
[d] iii. 12.
[e] i. 6, 9, 12, iii. 10–12, iv. 10.   [f] See vol. i. p. 321.

Micah[g]. Micah alludes to the history, the laws, the promises, the threatenings of the Pentateuch ; and that in such wise, that it is plain that he had, not traditional laws or traditional history, but the Pentateuch itself before him[h]. Nor were those books before himself only. His book implies not an acquaintance only, but a familiar acquaintance with it on the part of the people. The title, *the land of Nimrod*[i], *the house of bondage*[k], for Egypt, the allusions to the miraculous deliverance from Egypt[l], the history of Balaam ; the whole summary of the mercies of God from the Exodus to Gilgal[m], the faithfulness pledged to Abraham and Jacob[n], would be unintelligible without the knowledge of the Pentateuch. Even single expressions are taken from the Pentateuch[o]. Especially, the whole sixth chapter is grounded upon it. Thence is the appeal to inanimate nature to hear the controversy ; thence the mercies alleged on God's part ; the offerings on man's part to atone to God (except the one dreadful superstition of Ahaz) are from the law; the answer on God's part is almost verbally from the law; the sins upbraided are sins forbidden in the law ; the penalties pronounced are also those of the law. There are two allusions also to the history of Joshua[p], to David's elegy over Saul and Jonathan[q], and, as before said, to the history of Micaiah son of Imlah in the book of Kings. Single expressions are also taken from the Psalms[r] and the Proverbs[s]. In the descriptions of the peace of the kingdom of Christ[t], he appears purposely to have reversed God's description of the animosity of the nations against God's people[u]. He has also two characteristic expressions of Amos. Perhaps, in the image of the darkness which should come on the false prophets[x], he applied anew the image of Amos, adding the ideas of spiritual darkness and perplexity to that of calamity.

The light and shadows of the prophetic life fell deeply on the soul of Micah. The captivity of Judah too had been foretold before him. Moses had foretold the end from the beginning, had set before them the captivity and the dispersion, as a punishment which the sins of the people would certainly bring upon them. Hosea presupposed it[y]; Amos foretold that Jerusalem, like the cities of its heathen enemies, should be burned with fire[z]. Micah had to declare its lasting desolation[a]. Even when God wrought repentance through him, he knew that it was but for a time ; for he foresaw and foretold that the deliverance would be, not in Jerusalem, but at Babylon[b], in captivity. His prophecy sank so deep, that, above a century afterward, just when it was about to have its fulfillment, it was *the* prophecy which was remembered. But the sufferings of time disappeared in the light of eternal truth. Above seven centuries rolled by, and Micah re-appears as the herald, not now of sorrow but of salvation. Wise men from afar, in the nobility of their simple belief, asked, *Where is he that is born King of the Jews?* A king, jealous for his temporal empire, gathered all those learned in Holy Scripture, and echoed the question. The answer was given, unhesitatingly, as a well-known truth of God, in the words of Micah. *For thus it is written in the Prophet.* Glorious peerage of the two contemporary prophets of Judah. Ere Jesus was born, the Angel announced the birth of the Virgin's Son, *God with us*, in the words of Isaiah. When He was born, He was pointed out as the Object of worship to the first converts from the heathen, on the authority of God, through Micah.

[g] See Caspari Micha, 449–455.
[h] See at length, in Caspari, pp. 420–7, and below on the places.   [i] v. 6, (5 Heb.) from Gen. x. 8–12.
[k] vi. 4, comp. Deut. vii. 8, xiii. 5, Ex. xiii. 3, 14, xx. 2. Else only in Josh. xxiv. 17, and Judg. vi. 8, also from the Pent. Casp.
[l] See on ii. 13, vi. 4, vii. 15.   [m] See on vi. 4, 5.
[n] See on vii. 30.
[o] As עלה ii. 13, העלה vi. 4, שלח לפני Ib. שכני vii. 14, זחלי ארץ vii. 17 Casp. לבדד

[p] See on ii. 4, vi. 5.   [q] i. 10.
[r] Casp. 428–30; see on ii. 1, iii. 2, 3, vii. 2, 7, 8, 10.
[s] Casp. 430–2; see on vii. 9, 11.
[t] iv. 3, Joel iii. 10.
[u] כי עת רעה היא ii. 2, Am. v. 13, and הטיף ii. 6, 11, Am. vii. 16. Casp. 443.
[x] Mic. iii. 6, Am. viii. 9.
[y] See on Hos. vi. 11. vol. i. pp. 69, 70.   [z] ii. 5.
[a] iii. 12.   [b] iv. 10.

MICAH.

CHAPTER I.

1 *Micah sheweth the wrath of God against Jacob for idolatry.* 10 *He exhorteth to mourning.*

THE word of the LORD that came to [a] Micah the Morasthite in the days of Jotham, Ahaz, *and*

[a] Jer. 26. 18.

Hezekiah, kings of Judah, [b] which he saw concerning Samaria and Jerusalem.

2 † Hear, all ye people; [c] hearken, O earth, and † all that therein is; and let the Lord GOD [d] be witness against you, the Lord from [e] his holy temple.

[b] Amos 1. 1.
† Heb. *Hear, ye people, all of them.*
[c] Deut. 32. 1.
Is. 1. 2.
† Heb. *the fulness thereof.*
[d] Ps. 50. 7.
Mal. 3. 5.
[e] Ps. 11. 4.
Jonah 2. 7.
Hab. 2. 20.

CHAP. I. VER. 1. *The word of the Lord that came to Micah—which he saw.* No two of the prophets authenticate their prophecy in exactly the same way. They, one and all, have the same simple statement to make, that this which they say is *from* God, and *through* them. A later hand, had it added the titles, would have formed all upon one model. The title was an essential part of the prophetic book, as indicating to the people afterward, that it was not written after the event. It was a witness, not to the prophet whose name it bears, but to God. The prophet bare witness to God, that what he delivered came from Him. The event bare witness to the prophet, that he said this truly, in that he knew what God alone could know,—futurity. Micah blends in one the facts, that he related in words given him by God, what he had seen spread before him in prophetic vision. His prophecy was, in one, *the word of the Lord which came to him,* and a sight *which* he *saw.*

Micah omits all mention of his father. His great predecessor was known as Micaiah *son of Imlah.* Micah, a villager, would be known only by the name of his native village. So Nahum names himself *the Elkoshite;* Jonah is related to be a native *of Gath-hepher;* Elijah, the Tishbite, a sojourner in the despised Gilead [1]; Elisha, of Abelmeholah; Jeremiah, of Anathoth; forerunners of *Him,* and taught by *His* Spirit Who willed to be born at Bethlehem, and, since this, although *too little to be* counted *among the thousands of Judah,* was yet a royal city and was to be the birthplace of the Christ, was known only as *Jesus of Nazareth, the Nazarene.* No prophet speaks of himself, or is spoken of, as born at Jerusalem, *the holy city.* They speak of themselves with titles of lowliness, not of greatness.

Micah dates his prophetic office from kings of Judah only, as the only kings of the line appointed by God. Kings of Israel are mentioned in addition, only by prophets of Israel. He names Samaria first, because, its iniquity being most nearly full, its punishment was the nearest.

2. *Hear, all ye people,* lit. *hear, ye peoples, all of them* Some 140, or 150 years had flowed by, since Micaiah, son of Imlah, had closed his prophecy in these words. And now they burst out anew. From age to age the word of God holds its course, ever receiving new fulfillments, never dying out, until the end shall come. The signal fulfillment of the prophecy, to which the former Micaiah had called attention in these words, was an earnest of the fulfillment of this present message of God.

Hearken, O earth, and all that therein is. The *peoples* or *nations* are never Judah and Israel only: *the earth and the fullness thereof* is the well-known title of the whole earth [2] and all its inhabitants. Moses [3], Asaph [4], Isaiah [5], call heaven and earth as witnesses against God's people. Jeremiah [6], as Micah here, summons *the nations* and the *earth.* The contest between good and evil, sin and holiness, the kingdom of God and the kingdom of Satan, everwhere, but most chiefly where God's Presence is nearest, is *a spectacle to the world, to angels and to men* [7]. The nations are witnesses of God against His own people, so that these should not say, that it was for want of faithfulness or justice or power [8], but in His righteous judgment, that He cast off whom He had chosen. So shall the Day of Judgment *reveal His righteousness* [9]. *Hearken, O earth.* The lifeless earth [10] *trembles at the Presence of God,* and so reproaches the dullness of man. By it he summons man to listen with great reverence to the Voice of God.

[1] 1 Kgs xvii. 1.

[2] In the two passages quoted for the contrary, Jer. viii. 16, Ezek. xii. 19, the context shews that אֶרֶץ is and can only be, *land,* not, *earth,* Jer. *The snorting of his horses is heard from Dan, and they came and devoured the land and the fullness thereof;* where the *land* to which they *came* could plainly be Judea only. In Ezekiel it is not even *the land,* but *her land.* *Say unto the people of the land ; Thus saith the Lord God of the land of Israel,—that her land may be desolate from all the fullness thereof.*
[3] Deut. xxxii. 1.   [4] Ps. l. 7.   [5] i. 2.   [6] vi. 19.
[7] 1 Cor. iv. 9.
[8] Ex. xxxii. 12, Num. xiv. 16, Josh. vii. 8, 9.
[9] Rom. ii. 5.   [10] Ps. cxiv. 7, xcvii. 5.

15

Before CHRIST cir. 758–726.	3 For, behold, 'the LORD cometh forth out of his ᵍ place, and will come	down, and tread upon the ʰ high places of the earth.	Before CHRIST cir. 758–726.
f Is. 26. 21. g Ps. 115. 3.			h Deut 32. 13. & 33. 29. Amos 4. 13.

And let the Lord God be witness against you. Not in words, but in deeds ye shall know, that I speak not of myself but God in me, when, what I declare, He shall by His Presence fulfill. But the nations are appealed to, not merely because the judgments of God on Israel should be made known *to* them by the Prophets. He had not yet spoken of Israel or Judah, whereas he *had* spoken to the nations; *hear, ye peoples.* It seems then most likely that here too he is speaking to them. Every judgment is an earnest, a forerunner, a part, of the final judgment and an ensample of its principles. It is but "the last great link in the chain," which unites God's dealings in time with eternity. God's judgments on one imply a judgment on all. His judgments in time imply a Judgment beyond time. Each sinner feels in his own heart a response to God's visible judgments on another. Each sinful nation may read its own doom in the sentence on each other nation. God judges each according to his own measure of light and grace, accepted or refused. The Heathen shall be judged by *the law written in their heart*[1]; the Jew, by the law of Moses and the light of the prophets; Christians, by the law of Christ. *The word,* Christ saith[2], *that I have spoken, the same shall judge him at the last Day.* God Himself foretold, that the heathen should know the ground of His judgments against His people[3]. *All nations shall say, wherefore hath the Lord done thus unto this land? What meaneth the heat of this great anger? Then men shall say, Because they have forsaken the covenant of the Lord God of their fathers which He made with them, when He brought them forth out of the land of Egypt, &c.* But in that the heathen knew why God so punished His people, they came so far to know the mind of God; and God, Who at no time[4] *left Himself without witness,* bore fresh *witness* to them, and, so far as they neglected it, *against* them. A Jew, wherever he is seen throughout the world, is a witness to the world of God's judgments against sin.

"[5] Christ, *the faithful Witness,* shall *witness against* those who·do ill, *for* those who do well."

The Lord from His holy temple. Either that at Jerusalem, where God shewed and revealed Himself, or Heaven of which it was the image. As David says[6], *The Lord* is *in His holy temple; the Lord's throne* is *in heaven;* and

contrasts His dwelling in heaven and His coming down upon earth. [7] *He bowed the heavens also and came down;* and Isaiah, in like words[8], *Behold, the Lord cometh out of His place to punish the inhabitants of the earth for their iniquity.*

3. *For, behold, the Lord cometh forth,* i. e. (as we now say,) *is coming forth.* Each day of judgment, and the last also, are ever drawing nigh, noiselessly as the nightfall, but unceasingly. *Out of His Place.* "[9] God is hidden from us, except when He sheweth Himself by His Wisdom or Power of Justice or Grace, as Isaiah saith[10], *Verily, Thou art a God Who hidest Thyself.*" He seemeth to be absent, when He doth not visibly work either in the heart within, or in judgments without; to the ungodly and unbelieving He is absent[11], *far above out of their sight,* when He does not avenge their scoffs, their sins, their irreverence. Again He seemeth to go forth, when His Power is felt. "[9] Whence it is said[12], *Bow Thy heavens, O Lord, and come down;* and the Lord saith of Sodom[13], *I will go down now and see, whether they have done altogether according to the cry of it, which is come unto Me.* Or, *the Place* of the Infinite God is God Himself. For the Infinite sustaineth Itself, nor doth anything out of Itself contain It. God *dwelleth* also *in light unapproachable*[14]. When then Almighty God doth not manifest Himself, He abideth, as it were, in *His own Place.* When He manifests His Power or Wisdom or Justice by their effects, He is said to *go forth out of His Place,* i. e. out of His hiddenness. Again, since the Nature of God is Goodness, it is proper and co-natural to Him, to be propitious, have mercy and spare. In this way, *the Place* of God is His mercy. When then He passeth from the sweetness of pity to the rigor of equity, and, on account of our sins, sheweth Himself severe (which is, as it were, alien from Him) He *goeth forth out of His Place.*" "[15] For He Who is gentle and gracious, and Whose Nature it is to have mercy, is constrained, on your account, to take the seeming of hardness, which is not His."

He comes invisibly now, in that it is He Who punisheth, through whatever power or will of man He useth; He shews forth His Holiness through the punishment of unholiness. But the words, which are image-language now, shall be most exactly fulfilled in the end, when, in the Person of our Lord, He

---

[1] Rom. ii. 12–15. [2] S. John xii. 48.
[3] Deut. xxix. 24, 5. [4] Acts xiv. 17. [5] Dion.
[6] Ps. xi. 4. [7] Ps. xviii. 9.

[8] xxvi. 21. [9] Dion. [10] xlv. 15.
[11] Ps. x. 5. [12] Ps. cxliv. 5, Is. lxiv. 1.
[13] Gen. xviii. 21. [14] 1 Tim. vi. 16. [15] S. Jer.

Before
CHRIST
cir. 758-726.

i Judg. 5. 5.
Ps. 97. 5.
Is. 64. 1, 2, 3. Amos 9. 5. Hab. 3. 6, 10.

4 And [i] the mountains shall be molten under him, and the valleys shall be

cleft, as wax before the fire, and as the waters *that are* poured down † a steep place. † Heb. *a descent.*

Before
CHRIST
cir. 758-726.

---

shall *come* visibly to judge the world. " [1] In the Day of Judgment, Christ *shall come down,* according to that Nature which He took, *from His Place,* the highest heavens, and shall cast down the proud things of this world."

And will come down ; not by change of place, or in Himself, but as felt in the punishment of sin; *and tread upon the high places of the earth ;* to bring down the pride of those [2] who " [3] being lifted up in their own conceit and lofty, sinning through pride and proud through sin, were yet created out of earth. For [4] *why is earth and ashes proud ?* " What seems mightiest and most firm, is unto God less than is to man the dust under his feet. The high places were also the special scenes of an unceasing idolatry. " God treadeth *in* the good and humble, in that He dwelleth, walketh, feasteth in their hearts [5]. But He *treadeth upon* the proud and the evil, in that He casteth them down, despiseth, condemneth them."

4. *And the mountains shall be molten under Him.* It has been thought that this is imagery, taken from volcanic eruptions [6]; but, although there is a very remarkable volcanic district just outside of Gilead [7], it is not thought to have been active at times so late as these; nor were the people to whom the words were said, familiar with it. Fire, the real agent at the end of the world, is, meanwhile, the symbol of God's anger, as being the most terrible of His instruments of destruction : whence God revealed Himself as *a consuming fire* [8], and, at this same time said by Isaiah [9]; *For behold, the Lord will come with fire—to render His anger with fury, and His rebuke with flames of fire.*

And the valleys shall be cleft as wax before the fire. It seems natural that the mountains should be cleft; but the valleys [10], so low

already ! This speaks of a yet deeper dissolution ; of lower depths beyond our sight or knowledge, into the very heart of the earth. " [11] This should they fear, who will to be so low ; who, so far from lifting themselves to heavenly things, pour out their affections on things of earth, meditate on and love earthly things, and forgetful of the heavenly, choose to fix their eyes on earth. These the wide gaping of the earth which they loved, shall swallow : to them the *cleft valleys* shall open an everlasting sepulchre, and, having received them, shall never part with them."

Highest and lowest, first and last, shall perish before Him. The pride of the highest, kings and princes, priests and judges, shall sink and melt away *beneath* the weight and Majesty of His glory ; the hardness of the lowest, which would not open itself to Him, shall be cleft in twain before Him.

As wax before the fire [12], melting away before Him by Whom they were not softened, vanishing into nothingness. Metals melt, changing their form only ; wax, so as to cease to be [13].

As the waters poured down (as a stream or cataract, so the word means [14]) *a steep place.* Down to the very edge, it is borne along, one strong, smooth, unbroken current ; then, at once, it seems to gather its strength, for one great effort. But to what end ? To fall, with the greater force, headlong, scattered in spray, foam and froth ; dissipated, at times, into vapor, or reeling in giddy eddies, never to return. In Judæa, where the autumn rains set in with great vehemence [15], the waters must have been often seen pouring in their little tumultuous brooklets down the mountain side [16], hastening to disappear, and disappearing the faster, the more vehemently they rolled along [17]. Both images exhibit

---

[1] S. Jer. Theoph.   [2] See Am. iv. 13, Job ix. 8.
[3] Rup.   [4] Ecclus. x. 9.
[5] 2 Cor. vi. 16, Rev. iii. 20.   [6] Henderson here.
[7] See vol. i. p. 425.   [8] Deut. iv. 24.
[9] lxvi. 15.
[10] Hence some MSS. mentioned in De Rossi's cod. 319, have (as a conjecture) וְהַנְּבָעֹות "the hills."
[11] Sanch.   [12] See Ps. xcvii. 5.
[13] See S. Hil. in Ps. lvii. ℥ 4. מָסַם is used, as to natural objects, only of such melting whereby the substance is wasted, as of manna (Ex. xvi. 21), wax (Ps. lxviii. 3, &c.), or the body through disease (1 Sam. xxv. 37) : then, morally, chiefly of fear.
[14] See Ges. Thes. sub v. from the Punic, Monum. Phœn. p. 418. "There are many waterfalls in Lebanon, one very near and to the N. of the Damascus road. I have also seen one in Anti-libanus on the river Barada, a little above Abil. The stream, named Sheba, which springs from the perpetual snows of Mount Hermon is extremely rapid and has a very steep fall to the Hasbeia which it joins

in Merj-el-Huleh. The Jordan is a continual cataract between el-Huleh and the Lake of Gennesareth ;" (Rev. G. Williams, MS. letter) "a fall of 600 feet in about 10 miles. On the Western bank, high above the rocky bed of the torrent, the water was running rapidly down the steep incline toward the river, which could hardly be less than 150 feet below us." (Id. Col. Church Chron. 1860. Jan. p. 30.). Porter describes the fall of the river Adonis (Five years, ii. 295.) From the height at which the streams rise in the Lebanon chain, there must be many greater or lesser falls.
[15] Hence the Hebrew name גֶּשֶׁם, "heavy rain," for which we have no one word, is used of the autumn and winter rain, Cant. ii. 11.
[16] I have seen this effect for above half an hour (15 miles) on the mountain country near the lakes in a thunderstorm.
[17] "The decrease of the waters (swollen by the rains in the mountains) is usually as rapid as their rise." Burckhardt, Syria, p. 161.

2

5 For the transgression of Jacob *is* all this, and for the sins of the house of Israel. What *is* the transgression of Jacob? *is it*

not Samaria? and what *are* the high places of Judah? *are they* not Jerusalem?

6 Therefore I will make

the inward emptiness of sinners, man's utter helplessness before God. They need no outward impulse to their destruction. "[1] Wax endureth not the nearness of the fire, and the waters are carried headlong. So all of the ungodly, when the Lord cometh, shall be dissolved and disappear." At the end of the world, they shall be gathered into bundles, and cast away.

5. *For the transgression of Jacob is all this.* Not for any change of purpose in God; nor, again, as the effect of man's lust of conquest. None could have any power against God's people, unless it had been given him by God. Those mighty Monarchies of old existed but as God's instruments, especially toward His own people. God said at this time of Assyria, [2] *Asshur, rod of Mine anger, and the staff in his hand is Mine indignation;* and [3], *Now have I brought it to pass, that thou shouldest be to lay waste defenced cities* into *ruinous heaps.* Each scourge of God chastised just those nations, which God willed him to chasten; but the especial object for which each was raised up was his mission against that people, in whom God most shewed His mercies and His judgments. [4] *I will send him against an ungodly nation and against the people of My wrath will I give him a charge.* Jacob and Israel, in this place, comprise alike the ten tribes and the two. They still bare the name of their father, who, wrestling with the Angel, became *a prince with God,* Whom they forgat. The name of Jacob then, as of Christian now, stamped as deserters, those who did not the deeds of their father. *What,* [rather *Who* [5]] *is the transgression of Jacob? Who* is its cause? In whom does it lie? *Is* it *not Samaria?* The metropolis must, in its own nature, be the source of good or evil to the land. It is the heart whose pulses beat throughout the whole system. As the seat of power, the residence of justice or injustice, the place of counsel, the concentration of wealth, which all the most influential of the land visit for their several occasions, its manners penetrate in a degree the utmost corners of the land. Corrupted, it becomes a focus of corruption. The blood passes through it, not to be purified, but to be diseased. Samaria, being founded on apostasy, owing its being to rebellion against God, the home of that policy

which set up a rival system of worship to *His,* forbidden by Him, became a fountain of evil, whence the stream of ungodliness overflowed the land. It became the impersonation of the people's sin, "the heart and the head of the body of sin."

And what [lit. *Who* [5]] are *the high places of Judah?* are they *not Jerusalem?* Jerusalem God had formed to be a centre of unity in holiness; *thither the tribes of the Lord* were to *go up to the testimony of Israel;* there was the unceasing worship of God, the morning and evening sacrifice; the Feasts, the memorials of past miraculous mercies, the foreshadowings of redemption. But there too Satan placed his throne. Ahaz brought thither that most hateful idolatry, the burning children to Moloch *in the valley of the son of Hinnom* [6]. There, [7] *he made him altars in every corner of Jerusalem.* Thence, he extended the idolatry to all Judah. [8] *And in every several city of Judah he made high places to burn incense unto other gods, and provoked to anger the Lord God of his fathers.* Hezekiah, in his reformation, with *all Israel,* [9] *went out to the cities of Judah, and brake the images in pieces and hewed down the statues of Asherah, and threw down the high places and the altars out of all Judah and Benjamin,* as much as out of *Ephraim and Manasseh.* Nay, by a perverse interchange, Ahaz took the *brazen altar,* consecrated to God, for his own divinations, and assigned to the worship of God the altar copied from the idol-altar at Damascus, whose fashion pleased his taste [10]. Since *God and mammon cannot be served* together, Jerusalem was become one great idol-temple, in which Judah brought its sin into the very face of God and of His Worship. The *Holy City* had itself become sin, and the fountain of unholiness. The one temple of God was the single protest against the idolatries which encompassed and besieged it; the incense went up to God, morning and evening, from it; from every head of every street of the city [11], and (since Ahaz had brought in the worship of Baalim [12], and the rites of idolatry continued the same,) from *the roofs* of all their *houses* [13], went up *the incense to Baal;* a worship which, denying the Unity, denied the Being of God.

6. *Therefore* [lit. *And*] *I will make Samaria*

[1] S. Jer.   [2] Is. x. 5.   [3] Ib. xxxvii. 26.   [4] Ib. x. 6.
[5] מי always relates to a personal object, and apparent exceptions may be reduced to this. So AE. Kim. Tanch. Poc.

[6] 2 Chr. xxviii. 3.   [7] Ib. 24.   [8] Ib. 25.
[9] Ib. xxxi. 1.   [10] 2 Kings xvi. 10-16.
[11] Ezek. xvi. 31, 2 Chr. xxviii. 24.   [12] Ib. 2.
[13] Jer. xxxii. 29.

| Before CHRIST cir. 758-726. | Samaria [k] as an heap of the field, *and* as plantings of a vineyard: and I will pour down the stones thereof into the valley, and I will [l] discover the foundations thereof. | 7 And all the graven images thereof shall be beaten to pieces, and all the [m] hires thereof shall be burned with the fire, and all the idols thereof will I lay desolate: for she | Before CHRIST cir. 758-726. |

[k] 2 Kings 19. 25. ch. 3. 12.

[l] Ezek. 13. 14.

[m] Hos. 2. 5, 12.

as an heap of the field, and as plantings of a vineyard. "[1] The order of the sin was the order of the punishment." Samaria's sins were the earliest, the most obstinate, the most unbroken, bound up with its being as a state. On it then God's judgments should first fall. It was a *crown of pride*[2], *resting on the head of the rich valleys*, out of which it rose. Its soil is still rich[3]. "The whole is now cultivated in terraces[4]," "to the summits[5]." Probably, since the sides of hills, open to the sun, were chosen for vineyards, it had been a vineyard, before Shemer sold it to Omri[6]. What it had been, that it was again to be. Its inhabitants cast forth, its houses and gorgeous palaces were to become heaps of stones, *gathered out*[7] to make way for cultivation, or to become the fences of the vegetation, which should succeed to man. There is scarce a sadder natural sight than the fragments of human habitation, tokens of man's labor or his luxury, amid the rich beauty of nature when man himself is gone. For they are tracks of sin and punishment, man's rebellion and God's judgment, man's unworthiness of the good natural gifts of God. A century or two ago, travelers "[8]speak of the ground [the site of Samaria] as strewed with masses of ruins." Now these too are gone. "[3]The stones of the temples and palaces of Samaria have been carefully removed from the rich soil, thrown together in heaps, built up in the rude walls of terraces, and rolled down into the valley below." "[9]About midway of the ascent, the hill is surrounded by a narrow terrace of woodland like a belt. Higher up too are the marks of slighter terraces, once occupied perhaps by the streets of the ancient city." Terrace-cultivation has succeeded to the terraced streets once thronged by the busy, luxurious, sinful, population.

And I will pour down the stones thereof into the valley, of which it was the crest, and which it now proudly surveyed. God Himself would cause it to be poured down (he uses the word which he had just used of the vehemence of the cataract[10]). "[11] The whole face of this part of the hill suggests the idea that the buildings of the ancient city had been thrown down from the brow of the hill. Ascending to the top, we went round the whole summit, and found marks of the same process everywhere."

And I will discover the foundations thereof. The desolation is entire; *not one stone left upon another.* Yet the very words of threatening contain hope. It was to be not a *heap* only, but *the plantings of a vineyard.* The *heaps* betoken ruin; the *vineyard*, fruitfulness cared for by God. Destroyed, as what it was, and turned upside down, as a vineyard by the share, it should become again what God made it and willed it to be. It should again become a *rich valley*, but in outward desolation. Its splendid palaces, its idol temples, its *houses of joy*, should be but heaps and ruins, which are cleared away out of a vineyard, as only choking it. It was built in rebellion and schism, loose and not held together, like a *heap* of stones, having no cement of love, rent and torn in itself, having been torn both from God and His worship. It could be remade only by being wholly unmade. Then should they who believed be branches grafted in Him Who said, [12]*I am the Vine, ye are the branches.*

7. *And all the graven images thereof shall be beaten to pieces.* Its idols in whom she trusts, so far from protecting her, shall themselves go into captivity, broken up for the gold and silver whereof they were made. The wars of the Assyrians being religious wars[13], the idolatry of Assyria destroyed the idolatry and idols of Israel.

And all the hires thereof shall be burned with fire. All forsaking of God being spiritual fornication from Him Who made His creatures for Himself, the *hires* are all which man would gain by that desertion of his God, employed in man's intercourse with his idols, whether as bribing his idols to give him what are the gifts of God, or as himself bribed by them. For there is no pure service, save that of the love of God. God alone can be loved purely, for Himself; offerings to Him Alone are the creature's pure

[1] S. Jer.
[2] Is. xxviii. 1.
[3] Porter, Hdbook, p. 345.
[4] Ib. 344.
[5] Rob. ii. 304. 307.
[6] 1 Kings xvi. 24.
[7] Is. v. 2.
[8] "Cotovicus in the 16th, and Von Troilo in the 17th century." Rob. ii. 307. note 1.

[9] Rob. ii. 304.
[10] ver. 4.
[11] Narrative of Scottish Mission, pp. 293, 4. in Henderson.
[12] S. John xv. 5.
[13] See below Introd. to Nahum.

Before CHRIST cir. 758–726. gathered *it* of the hire of an harlot and they shall return to the hire of an harlot.

8 Therefore [n] I will wail and howl, [o] I will go stripped and naked: [p] I will make a wailing like the

Before CHRIST cir. 758–726.
[n] Is. 21. 3. & 22. 4. Jer. 4. 19.
[o] Is. 20. 2, 3, 4.
[p] Job 30. 29. Ps. 102. 6.

homage to the Creator, going out of itself, not looking back to itself, not seeking itself, but stretching forth to Him and seeking Him for Himself. Whatever man gives to or hopes from his idols, man himself is alike his object in both. The *hire* then is, alike what he gives to his idols, *the gold whereof he makes* his *Baal* [1], the offerings which the heathen used to lay up in their temples, and what, as he thought, he himself received back. For he gave only earthly things, in order to receive back things of earth. He hired their service to him, and his earthly gains were his hire. It is a strong mockery in the mouth of God, that they had these things from their idols. He speaks to them after their thoughts. Yet it is true that, although God overrules all, man does receive from Satan [2], *the god of this world* [3], all which he gains amiss. It is the price for which he sells his soul and profanes himself. Yet herein were the heathen more religious than the Christian worldling. The heathen did offer an ignorant service to they knew not what. Our idolatry of mammon, as being less abstract, is more evident self-worship, a more visible ignoring and so a more open dethroning of God, a worship of a material prosperity, of which we seem ourselves to be the authors, and to which we habitually immolate the souls of men, so habitually that we have ceased to be conscious of it.

And all the idols thereof will I lay desolate, lit. *make a desolation.* They, now thronged by their worshipers, should be deserted; their place and temple, a waste. He thrice repeats *all; all her graven images, all her hires, all her idols; all* should be destroyed. He subjoins a threefold destruction which should overtake them; so that, while the Assyrian broke and carried off the more precious, or burned what could be burned, and, what could not be burned, nor was worth transporting, should be left desolate, all should come to an end. He sets the whole the more vividly before the mind, exhibiting to us so many separate pictures of the mode of destruction.

For from the hire of a harlot she gathered them, *and to the hire of a harlot they shall return.* "[4] The wealth and manifold provision which (as she thought) were gained by fornication

with her idols, shall go to another harlot, Nineveh; so that, as they went a whoring in their own land, they should go to another land of idols and fornication, the Assyrians." They [5] *turned their glory into shame, changing the glory of the incorruptible God into an image made like unto corruptible man;* and so it should turn to them into shame. It sprung out of their shame, and should turn to it again. "Ill got, ill spent." Evil gain, cursed in its origin, has the curse of God upon it, and makes its gainer a curse, and ends accursedly. "Make not ill gains," says even a Heathen [6], "ill gains are equal to losses;" and another [7], "Unlawful sweetness a most bitter end awaiteth."

Probably, the most literal sense is not to be excluded. The degrading idolatrous custom, related of Babylon and Cyprus [8], still continued among the Babylonians at the date of the book of Baruch [9], and to the Christian era [10]. S. Augustine speaks of it as having existed [11] among the Phœnicians, and Theodoret [12] says that it was still practiced by some in Syria. The existence of the idolatrous custom is presupposed by the prohibition by Moses [13]; and, in the time of Hosea self-desecration was an idolatrous rite in Israel [14]. In the day of Judgment, when the foundation of those who build their house upon the sand, shall be laid bare, the riches which they gained unlawfully shall be burned up; all the idols, which they set up instead of God, "[15] the vain thoughts, and useless fancies, and hurtful forms and images which they picture in their mind, defiling it, and hindering it from the steadfast contemplation of divine things, will be punished. They were the hire of the soul which went astray from God, and they who conceived them will, with them, become the prey again of that infernal host which is unceasingly turned from God."

8. *Therefore I will [would* [16]*] wail [*properly *beat* [17], i. e. on the breast], *and howl.* "Let me alone," he would say, "that I may vent my sorrow in all ways of expressing sorrow, beating on the breast and wailing, using all acts and sounds of grief." It is as we would say, "Let me mourn *on*," a mourning inexhaustible, because the woe too and the cause of

---

[1] See Hos. ii. 8. vol. i. p. 32. [2] S. Matt. iv. 9.
[3] 2 Cor. iv. 4. [4] S. Jer. [5] Rom. i. 23.
[6] Hesiod. Ἔ. κ. ʽ Η. 354. L.
[7] Pindar Isthm. vii. 67, 8. L. [8] Herod. i. 199.
[9] vi. 43. [10] Strabo, xvi. 1. 20.

[11] dabant. de Civ. Dei iii. 10. [12] on this place.
[13] Deut. xxiii. 18. [14] See on Hos. iv. 14, p. 31.
[15] Dion.
[16] He thrice repeats the optative אֶסְפְּדָה וְאֵילִילָה אֵילְכָה. [17] סָפַד.

Before
CHRIST
cir. 758–726. dragons, and mourning as
the † owls.

† Heb. *daughters
of the owl.*
‖ Or, she is
grievously sick
of her wounds.

9 For ‖ her wound *is*
incurable; for ᑫ it is
ᑫ 2 Kings 18. 13. Is. 1. 6, 7, 8.

come unto Judah; he is Before
CHRIST
cir. 758–726.
come unto the gate of
my people, *even* to Jerusalem.

---

grief was unceasing. The Prophet becomes
in words, probably in acts too, an image of
his people, doing as they should do hereafter.
He mourns, because and as they would have
to mourn, bearing chastisement, bereft of all
outward comeliness, an example also of repentance, since what he did were the chief
outward tokens of mourning.

I will [*would*] *go stripped* [*despoiled*[1]] *and
naked.* He explains the acts, that they
represented no mere voluntary mourning.
Not only would he, representing them, go
bared of all garments of beauty, as we say
"half-naked[2]" but *despoiled* also, the proper
term of those plundered and stripped by an
enemy. He speaks of his doing, what we
know that Isaiah did, by God's command,
representing in act what his people should
thereafter do. "[3] Wouldest thou that I should
weep, thou must thyself grieve the first."
Micah doubtless went about, not speaking
only of grief, but grieving, in the habit of
one mourning and bereft of all. He pro-
longs in these words the voice of wailing,
choosing unwonted forms of words, to carry
on the sound of grief[4].

I will make a wailing like the dragons [*jackals*[5]] *and mourning as the owls* [*ostriches*[6]].
The cry of both, as heard at night, is very
piteous. Both are *doleful creatures,* dwelling
in desert and lonely places. "The[7] jackals
make a lamentable howling noise, so that
travelers unacquainted with them would
think that a company of people, women or
children, were howling, one to another."

"Its howl," says an Arabic natural historian[8], "is like the crying of an infant." "We
heard them," says another[9], "through the
night, wandering around the villages, with a
continual, prolonged, mournful cry." The
ostrich, forsaking its young[10], is an image of
bereavement. "[11] As the ostrich forgets her
eggs and *leaves them as though they* were *not
her's,* to be trampled by the feet of wild
beasts, so too shall I go childless, spoiled and
naked." Its screech is spoken of by travelers as "[12] fearful, affrighting." "[13] During the lonesome part of the night they
often make a doleful and piteous noise. I
have often heard them groan, as if they were
in the greatest agonies."

"[14] I will grieve from the heart over those
who perish, mourning for the hardness of the
ungodly, as the Apostle had [15] *great heaviness
and continual sorrow in* his *heart* for his brethren, the impenitent and unbelieving Jews.
Again he saith [16], *who is weak and I am not
weak? Who is offended, and I burn not?* For
by how much the soul is nobler than the
body, and by how much eternal damnation is
heavier than any temporal punishment, so
much more vehemently should we grieve
and weep for the peril and perpetual damnation of souls, than for bodily sickness or any
temporal evil."

9. *For her* [Samaria's] *wound*[17], [lit. *her
wounds, or strokes,* (the word is used especially
of those inflicted by God[18],) each, one by
one,] *is incurable.* The idiom is used of
inflictions on the body politic[19] or the

---

[1] *Barefoot* is expressed in Hebrew by יָחֵף. Since
then Micah does not use the received term for *barefoot,* and does use the word expressing "stripped,"
"despoiled," the E. V. is doubtless right, agreeing
with the Latin against the LXX. and Syr.

[2] See on Amos ii. 16. p. 178. n. 6. Seneca says:
"Some things, though not [exactly] true, are comprised under the same word, for their likeness. So
we call illiterate, one not altogether uninstructed,
but who has not been advanced to higher knowledge.
So he who has seen one illhabited and in rags, says
that he had seen one 'naked.'" de benef. v. 13.
Sanch.

[3] Hor. A. P. 102, 3.

[4] שִׁילְלָה and אֵילְכָה carry on the sound of
שִׁילֵל, the textual reading, is doubtless
right, although without example; אֵילְכָה has analogy with other words but, common as the word is,
stands alone in the word itself. Each bears out
the other.

[5] The תֵן, which occurs only in the plural תַנִים,
is distinct from the תַנִין, plur. תַנִינִים, although
they touch on each other, in that תַנִין sing. is
written תַנִים, Ezek. xxix. 3, and the poetic plur. of

תֵן, תַנִין occurs in the text, Lam. iv. 3. The Syr.
(and Chaldee, properly) and Tanchum oftentimes
render it "jackal." Pococke first, of moderns,
brought out this meaning. See his note here.

[6] The בַת יַעֲנָה "female ostrich" (the תַחְמָס
probably being the male ostrich) may be so called
from יָעֵן, (Syr. *glutton,* like its Arabic name na'am)
or from its shrill cry, יָעֲנָה.

[7] Pococke, who had heard them in Syria, &c.

[8] Demiri, in Bochart, iii. 12. T. iii. p. 181. ed. Leipz.
"It howls by night only." Id.

[9] Olearius, Itin. Mosc. et Pers. iv. 17. Boch. Ib.
p. 183.

[10] Job xxxix. 16.   [11] S. Jer.

[12] Sandys' Travels, L. ii. fin.

[13] Shaw, Travels, T. ii. p. 349.   [14] Dion.

[15] Rom. ix. 1.   [16] 2 Cor. xi. 29.

[17] The construction of the E. V. is beyond question preferable to that of the E. M. It is the common
emphatic idiom, in which the plural subject and
singular predicate are joined to express, that the
thing asserted is true not only of all generally but
of each individually.

[18] Lev. xxvi. 21, Nu. xi. 33, Deut. xxviii. 59, 61, &c.

[19] Nah. iii. ult. Jer. xxx. 12, 15.

Before
CHRIST
cir. 758-726.
r 2 Sam. 1. 20.

10 ¶ r Declare ye *it* not at Gath, weep ye not at all :

in the house of || Aphrah s roll thyself in the dust.

|| That is, *dust.*

Before
CHRIST
cir. 758-726.
s Jer. 6. 26.

mind [1], for which there is no remedy. The *wounds* were very *sick*, or incurable, not in themselves or on God's part, but on Israel's. The day of grace passes away at last, when man has so steeled himself against grace, as to be morally dead, having deadened himself to all capacity of repentance.

For it is come unto [*quite up to* [2]] *Judah ; he,* [the enemy,] *is come* [lit. hath *reached,* touched,] *to* [*quite up to* [2]] *the gate of my people, even to* [*quite up to* [2]] *Jerusalem.* "[3] The same sin, yea, the same punishment for sin, which overthrew Samaria, shall even come unto, *quite up to Judah.* Then the Prophet suddenly changes the gender, and, as Scripture so often does, speaks of the one agent, the centre and impersonation of the coming evil, as sweeping on over Judah, *quite up to the gate* of his *people, quite up to Jerusalem.* He does not say here, whether Jerusalem would be taken [4]; and so, it seems likely that he speaks of a calamity short of excision. Of Israel's wounds only he here says, that they are *incurable ;* he describes the wasting of even lesser places near or beyond Jerusalem, the flight of their inhabitants. Of the capital itself he is silent, except that the enemy *reached, touched, struck* against it, *quite up to it.* Probably, then, he is here describing the first visitation of God, when [5] *Sennacherib came up against all the fenced cities of Judah and took them,* but Jerusalem was spared. God's judgments come step by step, leaving time for repentance. The same enemy, although not the same king, came against Jerusalem who had wasted Samaria. Samaria was probably as strong as Jerusalem. Hezekiah prayed ; God heard, the Assyrian army perished by miracle ; Jerusalem was respited for 124 years.

10. *Tell it not in Gath.* Gath had probably now ceased to be ; at least, to be of any account [6]. It shows how David's elegy lived

in the hearts of Judah, that his words were used as a proverb, (just as we do now, in whose ears it is yearly read), when, as with us, its original application was probably lost. True, Gath, reduced itself, might rejoice the more maliciously over the sufferings of Judah. But David mentions it as a chief seat of Philistine strength [7]; now its strength was gone.

The blaspheming of the enemies of God is the sorest part of His chastisements. Whence David prays [8], *let not mine enemies exult over me ;* and the sons of Korah, [9] *With a sword in my bones, mine enemies reproach me, while they say daily unto me, where* is *thy God ?* and Ethan [10]; *Thou hast made all his enemies to rejoice. Remember, Lord, the reproach of Thy servant—wherewith Thine enemies have reproached, O Lord, wherewith they have reproached the footsteps of Thine anointed.* It is hard to part with home, with country, to see all desolate, which one ever loved. But far, far above all, is it, if, in the disgrace and desolation, God's honor seems to be injured. The Jewish people was then God's only home on earth. If *it* could be extinguished, who remained to honor Him ? Victories over them seemed to their heathen neighbors to be victories over Him. He seemed to be dishonored without, because they had first dishonored Him within. Sore is it to the Christian, to see God's cause hindered, His kingdom narrowed, the Empire of Infidelity advanced. Sorer in one way, because he knows the price of souls, for whom Jesus died. But the world is now the Church's home. "The holy Church throughout all the world doth acknowledge Thee !" Then, it was girt in within a few miles of territory, and sad indeed it must have been to the Prophet, to see this too hemmed in. *Tell it not in Gath,* to the sons of those who, of old, defied God.

Weep not at all [lit. *weeping* [11], *weep not*].

---

[1] Jer. x. 19, xv. 18. נחלה in Nahum and Jer. xxx. 15. is exactly equivalent to the אנוש in Micah. In Jer. xxx. 12, אנוש לשברך stands parallel with it. Isaiah (xvii. 11) has כאב.

[2] עד in each of the three places. [3] S. Jer.

[4] עד includes the whole country, *quite up to.* It does not necessarily include the place, *quite up to* which it reaches. It does not, probably, 2 Kings xviii. 8. See on Am. i. vol. i. p. 245.

[5] 2 Kings xviii. 13.

[6] See on Am. vi. 2. vol. i. p. 305.

[7] Parallel with Ashkelon.

[8] Ps. xxv. 2. [9] Ps. xlii. 10. [10] Ps. lxxxix. 42, 50.

[11] The conjecture of Reland (Pal. p. 534) "in Acco weep not," as if בכו were for בעכו, is against the Hebrew idiom, and one of the many abuses of Hebrew parallelism, as if Hebrew writers were tied down to exactness of parallelism, and because the Prophet mentions the name of a city in two clauses, he must in the third. The Prophet never would have used one of the commonest idioms in Hebrew, the emphatic use of the Inf. Abs. with the finite verb, unless he had meant it to be understood, as any one must understand the three Hebrew words, בכו אל תבכו. The sacred writers wrote to be understood. It is contrary to all principles of language, not to take a plain idiom in its plain sense. The Verss. Vulg. Aq. Symm. so render it. The LXX. (from a reading in which, οἱ Ἐνακείμ or οἱ ἐν Ἀχείμ, Reland made his οἱ ἐν Ἀχώ) is full of blunders. They render also תבכו as if it were תבנו, ἀνοικοδομεῖτε; בבית, ἐξ οἴκου; לעפרה κατὰ γέλωτα. The ע is but seldom omitted in Hebrew. (Of the instances given by Gesenius, p. 976, בל for בעל is the Chaldee name of the idol; בי for בעי, uncertain, at most; למו for לעכו (Ps. xxvii. 8) wrong. There remains then in, Hebrew, only the single

Before CHRIST cir. 758-726. 11 Pass ye away, || thou †inhabitant of Saphir, having thy [t] shame naked: the inhabitant of || Zaanan

|| Or, *thou that dwellest fairly.*
† Heb. *inhabitress.*
[t] Is. 20. 4. & 47. 2, 3. Jer. 13. 22. Nah. 3. 5.
|| Or, *the country of flocks.*

came not f o r t h in the mourning of || Beth-ezel; he shall receive of you his standing. Before CHRIST cir. 758-726.

|| Or, *a place near.*

Weeping is the stillest expression of grief. We speak of "weeping in silence." Yet this also was too visible a token of grief. Their weeping would be the joy and laughter of God's enemies.

In the house of Aphrah, [probably, *In Beth-leaphrah*] *roll thyself in the dust* [better, as the text, *I roll myself in dust* [1]]. The Prophet chose unusual names, such as would associate themselves with the meanings which he wished to convey, so that thenceforth the name itself might recall the prophecy. As if we were to say, "In Ashe I roll myself in ashes."—There was an Aphrah near Jerusalem [2]. It is more likely that Micah should refer to this, than to the Ophrah in Benjamin [3]. He shewed them, in his own person, how they should mourn, retired out of sight and hidden, as it were, in the dust. " [4] Whatever grief your heart may have, let your face have no tears; go not forth, but, *in the house of dust,* sprinkle thyself with the ashes of its ruins."

All the places thenceforth spoken of were in Judah, whose sorrow and desolation are repeated in all. It is one varied history of sorrow. The names of her cities, whether in themselves called from some gifts of God, as Shaphir, (*beautiful;* we have *Fair*ford, *Fair*field, *Fair*burn, *Fair*light,) or contrariwise from some defect, Maroth, *Bitterness* (probably from brackish water) Achzib, *lying,* (doubtless from a winter-torrent which in summer failed) suggest, either in contrast or by them-

selves, some note of evil and woe. It is Judah's history in all, given in different traits; her "beauty" turned into shame; herself free neither to go forth nor to "abide;" looking for good and finding evil; the strong (Lachish) strong only to flee; like a brook that fails and deceives; her *inheritance* (Mareshah) inherited; herself, taking refuge in dens and caves of the earth, yet even there found, and bereft of her glory. Whence, in the end, without naming Judah, the Prophet sums up her sorrows with one call to mourning.

11. *Pass ye away* [lit. *Pass thou* (fem.) *away to* or *for yourselves* [5], disregarded by God and despised by man] *pass* the bounds of your land into captivity, *thou inhabitant of Shaphir, having thy shame naked,* [better, *in naked-ness,* and *shame* [6]]. *Shaphir* [*fair*] was a village in Judah, between Eleutheropolis and Ashkelon [7]. There are still, in the Shephelah, two villages called Sawafir [8]. It, once *fair,* should now go forth in the disgrace and dishonor with which captives were led away.

The inhabitants of Zaanan came not forth. *Zaanan* (abounding in *flocks*) was probably the same as Zenan of Judah, which lay in the Shephelah [9]. It, which formerly *went forth* [10] in pastoral gladness with the multitude of its flocks, shall now shrink into itself for fear.

The mourning of Beth-Ezel [lit. *house of root,* firmly rooted] *shall take from you its standing* [11]. It too cannot help itself, much less be a stay to others. They who have

---

pronunciation of Amos נשקה for נשקעה viii. 8.

See ab. p. 216. Robinson observes, "The Semitic letter ע in particular, so unpronounceable by other nations, has a remarkable tenacity. Of the very many Hebrew names, containing this letter, which still survive in Arabic, our lists exhibit only two or three in which it has been dropped; and perhaps none in which it has been exchanged for another letter." (i. 255. n. 2.) His only instances are Jib for Gibeon (where the whole syllable has been dropped) i. 456; Jelbon for Gilboa (ii. 316); Yafa for Yaphia Josh. xix. 12, (doubtful) ii. 342; and Endor (which I doubt) ii. 360. Anyhow they are but three names, in which, in the transfer into another language, ע has been dropped at the end, and one at the beginning of a word, none in the middle. In fact also Acco (Acre) was probably never in the possession of Israel. It is only mentioned in the Old Testament, to say that *Asher did not drive out* its *inhabitants* (Judg. i. 31). This interpretation which has become popular, 1) violates the Hebrew idiom; 2) implies a very improbable omission of a "tenacious letter;" 3) is historically unnatural, in that the Prophet would thus forbid Judah to weep in a city where there were none even of Israel. Yet of late, it has been

followed by Hitz. Maur. Umbreit, Ewald, thought probable by Gesenius and Winer, and adopted even by Dr. Henderson.
[1] The Kethib התפלשתי is, as usual, to be preferred to the correction, the Kri, התפלשי.
[2] R. Tanchum of Jerusalem, here.
[3] Josh. xviii. 23, 1 Sam. xiii 17.
[4] S. Jer. Rup. [5] עברי לכם.
[6] The construction, עריה בשת is like עינוה בשת meekness, righteousness, Ps. xlv. 5. בשת is the quality, *shame.* [7] Onom.
[8] Scholz, Reisen, p. 255. Robinson, ii. 34, says, "There are three villages of this name near each other." "There is yet a village Snaphir, two hours S. E. of Ashdod." Schwartz (of Jerusalem) Das Heil. Land, p. 87. "a Sapheria one hour N. W. of Lod." [Lydda] (Ib. p. 105.)
[9] Josh. xv. 27, coll. 33. "There is a village Zanabra, 1. hour S. E. of Moresha." Schwartz, 74.
[10] יאן, whence זאנן, is itself probably connected with אצי.
[11] I have preferred the division of the Syr. and Vulg. because, if joined as in the E. V. the last clause has no definite subject, and there is no allusion to the meaning of Beth haezel.

Before
CHRIST
cir. 750.
12 For the inhabitant of Maroth ‖ waited carefully

‖ Or, *was grieved.*
u Amos 3. 6.

for good: but [u] evil came down from the LORD unto the gate of Jerusalem.
13 O thou inhabitant of

Before
CHRIST
cir. 750.
[x] Lachish, bind the chariot to the swift beast: she *is* the beginning of the sin to the daughter of Zion: for the transgressions of Israel were found in thee.

x 2 Kings 18. 14, 17.

---

been wont to go forth in fullness, shall not go forth then, and they who abide, strong though they be, shall not furnish an abiding place. Neither in going out nor in remaining, shall anything be secure then.

12. *For the inhabitant of Maroth [bitterness] waited carefully for good.* She *waited carefully*[1] for the good which God gives, not for the Good which God *is.* She looked, longed for, good, as men do; but therewith her longing ended. She longed for it, amid her own evil, which brought God's judgments upon her. *Maroth* is mentioned here only in Holy Scripture, and has not been identified. It too was probably selected for its meaning. *The inhabitant of bitternesses, she,* who was in *bitternesses,* or, it may be, *rebellions*[2], were as the home in which she dwelt, which ever encircled her, in which she reposed, wherein she spent her life, *waited for good!* Strange contradiction! yet a contradiction, which the whole un-Christian world is continually enacting; nay, from which Christians have often to be awakened, to look for good to themselves, nay, to pray for temporal good, while living in bitternesses, bitter ways, displeasing to God. The words are calculated to be a religious proverb. "Living in sin," as we say, *dwelling in bitternesses, she looked for good!* *Bitternesses!* for it is [3] *an evil* thing *and bitter, that thou hast forsaken the Lord thy God, and that My fear is not in thee.*

But [For] evil came down from the Lord unto the gate of Jerusalem. It came, like the brimstone and fire which God rained upon Sodom and Gomorrah, but as yet *to the gate of Jerusalem,* not upon itself. "[4] Evil came down upon them from the Lord, i. e. *I* was grieved, *I* chastened, *I* brought the Assyrian upon them, and from *My* anger came this affliction

upon them. But it was removed, *My* Hand prevailing and marvelously rescuing those who worshiped My Majesty. For the trouble shall *come to the gate.* But we know that Rabshakeh, with many horsemen, came to Jerusalem and all-but touched the gates. But he took it not. For in one night the Assyrian was consumed." The two *for's* are seemingly co-ordinate, and assign the reasons of the foreannounced evils[5], on man's part and on God's. On man's, in that he looked for what could not so come, good: on God's, in that evil, which alone could be looked for, which, amid man's evil, could alone be good for man, came from Him. Losing the true Good, man lost all other good, and dwelling in the bitterness of sin and provocation, he dwelt indeed in bitterness of trouble.

O thou inhabitant of Lachish, bind the chariot to the swift beast [steed.] Lachish was always a strong city, as its name probably denoted, (probably "compact[6].") It was one of the royal cities of the Amorites, and its king one of the five, who went out to battle with Joshua[7]. It lay in the low country, Shephēlah, of Judah[8], between Adoraim and Azekah[9], 7 Roman miles S. of Eleutheropolis[10], and so, probably, close to the hill-country, although on the plain; partaking perhaps of the advantages of both. Rehoboam fortified it. Amaziah fled to it from the conspiracy at Jerusalem[11], as a place of strength. It, with Azekah, alone remained, when Nebuchadnezzar had taken the rest, just before the capture of Jerusalem[12]. When Sennacherib took *all the defenced cities of Judah,* it seems to have been his last and proudest conquest, for from it he sent his contemptuous message to Hezekiah[13]. The whole power of the great king seems to have

---

[1] חוּל is used in the sense of יָחַל, Gen. viii. 10, and in Hif. Jud. iii. 25, in Pil. Job xxvi. 15, and in Hithpal. Ps. xxxvii. 7. Here too it has the construction of יָחַל with לְ, as it has in Job xxvi, and as it has not in the sense of the E. M. "was grieved."
Such an idiom as חוּל לְטוֹב, "to be in pain for (lost) good," does not occur in Hebrew, and would be equivocal, since the idiom *is* used for "longed for (expected) good." חוּל also, "grieved," occurs only Jer. v. 3. Used of the "writhing" of the birth-pangs, it is joined with no preposition; in the sense "feared," it is joined only with the מִלִּפְנֵי, כִּפְנֵי, מִן of the object of fear.
[2] מְרָתִים from מָרָה occurs Jer. 1. 21.
[3] Jer. ii. 19.   [4] S. Cyr.   [5] 3–11.
[6] from the Arab. The bilitteral root לְךְ seems to

have been an onomato-poet. In Arabic the sense of "striking" occurs in لكز لكع لكم, لكد, لكت, لكا لكخ. Thence the idea of parts "impinging on one another," "cleaving close to," in لكا [لكي; "griping," لكد, لكت, لكي; "cleaving close together," "compact," in لكع لكد, لكد. These senses account for all the Arabic words, beginning with لك. The only Hebrew roots, so beginning, are לכד, took, and לכש.

[7] Josh. x. 3.   [8] Ib. xv. 33. 39.   [9] 2 Chr. xi. 9.
[10] Onom.   [11] 2 Kgs xiv. 19.
[12] Jer. xxxiv. 7.   [13] Is. xxxvi. 1, 2.

Before
C H R I S T
cir. 750.

ʸ 2 Sam. 8. 2.
2 Kings 18.
14, 15, 16.
‖ Or, *for.*

14 Therefore shalt thou ʸgive presents ‖ to Moresheth-gath: the houses

of ‖ ᶻAchzib *shall be* a lie to the kings of Israel.

Before
C H R I S T
cir. 750.

‖ That is, *a lie.*
ᶻ Josh. 15. 44.

been called forth to take this stronghold. The Assyrian bas-reliefs, the record of the conquests of Sennacherib, if (as the accompanying inscription is deciphered), they represent the taking of Lachish, exhibit it as "[1]a city of great extent and importance, defended by double walls with battlements and towers, and by fortified out-works. In no other sculptures were so many armed warriors drawn up in array against a besieged city. Against the fortifications had been thrown up as many as ten banks or mounts compactly built,—and seven battering-rams had already been rolled up against the walls." Its situation, on the extremity probably of the plain, fitted it for a dépôt of cavalry. *The swift steeds* [2], to which it was bidden to bind the chariot, are mentioned as part of the magnificence of Solomon, as distinct from his ordinary horses [3]. They were used by the posts of the king of Persia [4]. They were doubtless part of the strength of the kings of Judah, the cavalry in which their statesmen trusted, instead of God. Now, its swift horses in which it prided itself should avail but to flee. Probably, it is an ideal picture. Lachish is bidden to bind its chariots to horses of the utmost speed, which should carry them far away, if their strength were equal to their swiftness. It had great need; for it was subjected under Sennacherib to the consequences of Assyrian conquest. If the Assyrian accounts relate to its capture, impalement and flaying alive [5] were among the tortures of the captive-people; and awfully did Sennacherib, in his pride, avenge the sins against God Whom he disbelieved.

She is the beginning of the sin to the daughter of Zion. "[6]She was at the gate through which the *transgressions of Israel* flooded Judah." How she came first to apostatise and to be the infectress of Judah, Scripture does not tell us [7]. She scarcely bordered on Philistia; Jerusalem lay between her and Israel. But the course of sin follows no geographical lines. It was the greater sin to Lachish that she, locally so far removed

from Israel's sin, was the first to import into Judah the idolatries of Israel. Scripture does not say, what seduced Lachish herself, whether the pride of military strength, or her importance, or commercial intercourse, for her *swift steeds,* with Egypt, the common parent of Israel's and her sin. Scripture does not give the genealogy of her sin, but stamps her as the heresiarch of Judah. We know the fact from this place only, that she, apparently so removed from the occasion of sin, became, like the propagators of heresy, the authoress of evil, the cause of countless loss of souls. *Beginning of sin to*—, what a world of evil lies in the three [8] words!

14. *Therefore shalt thou give* [bridal] *presents to Moresheth Gath. Therefore!* since Judah had so become a partaker of Israel's sins, she had broken the covenant, whereby God had given her the land of the Heathen, and she should part with it to aliens. The *bridal presents,* lit. *the dismissals,* were the dowry [9] with which the father *sent away* [10] his daughter, to belong to another, her *lord* [11] or husband, never more to return. *Moresheth,* [lit. *inheritance,*] *the inheritance* which God gave her, was to be parted with; she was to be laden [12] with gifts the enemy. Judah should part with her, and her own treasure also.

The houses of Achzib shall be a lie. Achzib, so called probably from *a winter brook* (achzab) was to become what its name imported, a resource which should fail just in the time of need, as the winter brooks in the drought of summer. [13] *Wilt Thou be unto me as a failing brook, waters which are not sure?* This Achzib, which is recounted between Keilah and Mareshah [14], was probably one of the oldest towns of Palestine, being mentioned in the history of the Patriarch Judah [15]. After having survived about 1000 years, it should, in time of need, fail. *The kings of Israel* are here the kings of Judah. When this prophecy was to be accomplished, the ten tribes would have ceased to have any political existence, the remnant in their own land would have no head to look to, except the line of David,

part of the chain of fortified cities furthest removed from Israel on the S. W.

[1] Layard, Nin. and Bab. p. 149.
[2] The רֶכֶשׁ was undoubtedly a swift horse, probably from its rapid striking of the earth. (Arab.) The word is used of riding horses in Syr. Chald. Talm. Nasor. see Ges. "horses of good breed and young," R. Jonah in Kim. Ib.
[3] 1 Kgs iv. 28. Eng. (v. 8. Heb.)
[4] Esther viii. 10, 14.
[5] Layard, Ib. and 150.
[6] S. Jer.
[7] Rosenm. and others from him, by mistake, attribute it to a supposed situation of Lachish, "lying on the frontier of" Israel; whereas it was

[8] רֵאשִׁית חַטַּאת ל.
[9] 1 Kgs ix. 16. [10] Jud. xii. 9. [11] בַּעַל.
[12] שִׁלּוּחִים עַל מוֹרֶשֶׁת נַת lit. "bridal presents on Moresheth Gath." Hitzig thinks that in מוֹרֶשֶׁת there is an allusion to מְאֹרָשֶׂת, "espoused;" but this would be a contradictory image, since the bridal-presents were given in espousing, not to one already espoused, and they were to be given not to Gath but to the invader.
[13] Jer. xv. 18. [14] Josh. xv. 44.
[15] in the unlengthened form כְזִיב Gen. xxxviii. 5.

Before
CHRIST
cir. 750.

ᵃ Josh. 15. 44.
‖ Or, *the glory of
Israel shall
come, &c.*

15 Yet will I bring
an heir unto thee, O
inhabitant of ᵃMare-
shah : ‖ he shall come

unto ᵇAdullam the glory
of Israel.

16 Make thee ᶜbald,
and poll thee for thy ᵈdeli-

Before
CHRIST
cir. 750.

ᵇ 2 Chr. 11. 7.
ᶜ Job 1. 20.
　　Isai. 15. 2.
　　& 22. 12.
ᵈ Lam. 4. 5.　　Jer. 7. 29. & 16. 6. & 47. 5. & 48. 37.

---

whose good kings had a care for them.
Micah then, having prophesied the utter destruction of Samaria, speaks in accordance
with the state of things which he foresaw and
foretold [1].

15. *Yet will I bring an heir* [*the heir* [2], him
whom God had appointed to be *the heir*, Sen-
nacherib] *unto thee, O inhabitant of Mareshah.
Mareshah*, (as the original form of its name
denotes [3],) lay on the summit of a hill. "Its
ruins only were still seen," in the time of
Eusebius and S. Jerome, "in the second mile
from Eleutheropolis [4]." "[5] Foundations still
remain on the south-eastern part of the remarkable Tell, south of Beth-Jibrin." Rehoboam fortified it also [6]. Zerah the Æthiopian
had *come to* [7] it, probably to besiege it, when
Asa met him, and *God smote the Æthiopians
before* him, *in the valley of Zephathah* thereat.
In the wars of the Maccabees, it was in the
hands of the Edomites [8]. Its capture and
that of Adora are mentioned [9] as the last act
of the war, before the Edomites submitted to
John Hyrcanus, and were incorporated in
Israel. It was a powerful city [10], when the
Parthians took it. As Micah writes the name,
it looked nearer to the word "inheritance [11]."
Mareshah (*inheritance*) shall yet have *the heir*
of God's appointment, the enemy. It shall
not inherit the land, as promised to the faithful, but shall itself be inherited, its people
dispossessed. While it, (and so also the soul
now) held fast to God, they were the heritage
of the Lord, by His gifts and grace; when, of
their own free-will, those, once God's heritage, become slaves of sin, they passed and
still pass, against their will, into the possession of another master, the Assyrian or Satan.
He [i. e. the heir, the enemy] *shall come
unto Adullam, the glory of Israel* [12]; i. e. he who
shall dispossess Mareshah, *shall come quite unto
Adullam*, where, as in a place of safety, *the
glory of Israel*, all in which she gloried, should
be laid up. Adullam was a very ancient
city, being mentioned in the history of the
patriarch Judah [13], a royal city [14]. It too
lay in the Shephelah [15]; it was said to be
10 [16] or 12 [17] miles East of Eleutheropolis;

but for this, there seems to be scarcely place
in the Shephelah. It was one of the 15
cities fortified by Rehoboam [18]; one of the 16
towns, in which (with their dependent villages) Judah settled after the captivity [19]. It
contained the whole army of Judas Maccabæus [20]. Like Lachish, it had probably the
double advantages of the neighborhood of
the hills and of the plain, seated perhaps at
the roots of the hills, since near it doubtless
was the large *cave of Adullam* named from it.
The line of caves, fit for human habitation,
which extended from Eleutheropolis to
Petra [21], began Westward of it. "[22] The
valley which runs up from Eleutheropolis
Eastward, is full of large caves; some would
hold thousands of men. They are very extensive, and some of them had evidently been
inhabited." "[22] The outer chamber of one
cavern was 270 feet long by 126 wide; and
behind this were recesses and galleries,
probably leading to other chambers which
we could not explore. The massive roof was
supported by misshaped pieces of the native
limestone left for that purpose, and at some
places was domed quite through to the surface, admitting both light and air by the
roof." The name of *Adullam* suggested the
memory of that cave, the refuge of the Patriarch David, the first of their line of kings, in
extreme isolation and peril of his life.
Thither, the refuge now of the remaining
glory of Israel, its wealth, its trust, its boast,—
the foe should come. And so there only remained one common dirge for all.

16. *Make thee bald, poll* [lit. *shear* [23]] *thee
for thy delicate children.* Some special ways
of cutting the hair were forbidden to the
Israelites, as being idolatrous customs, such
as the rounding the hair in front, cutting it
away from the temples [24], or between the
eyes [25]. All shearing of the hair was not forbidden [26]; indeed to the Nazarite it was commanded, at the close of his vow. The removal of that chief ornament of the countenance was a natural expression of grief, which
revolts at all personal appearance. It belonged, not to idolatry, but to nature [27]. *Thy*

---

[1] See ab. Introd. p. 5.　　　[2] הַיּׂרֵשׁ.
[3] מֹרֵאשָׁה (from רֹאשׁ) Jos. xv. 44.　　[4] Onom.
[5] Rob. ii. 67, 8.　　[6] 2 Chr. xi. 8.　　[7] Ib. xiv. 9. sqq.
[8] Jos. Ant. xii. 8. 6.　[9] Ib. xiii. 9. 1.　[10] Ib. xiv. 13. 9.
[11] מֹרַשָׁה like מוֹרָשָׁה. In the Chron. it is spelled
as in Micah.
[12] The Eng. Marg. has, in the same general sense,
unto Adullam shall come the glory of Israel.
[13] Gen. xxxviii. 1. 12. 20.　　　[14] Jos. xii. 15.
[15] Ib. xv. 35.　[16] Eus.　[17] S. Jer.　[18] 2 Chr. xi. 7.

[19] Neh. xi. 30.　　　　　[20] Macc. xii. 38.
[21] see S. Jer. ab. p. 235.
[22] Rev. G. Williams, MS. letter.
[23] see on Am. viii. 10. vol. i. p. 327.
[24] Lev. xix. 27. against Arab idolatry. See Herod.
iii. 8.　　[25] Deut. xiv. 1.　　[26] as Hitzig says.
[27] See Job i. 20, early Greece, (Il. 23, 46, 135 sqq.
Alcestis 429. non-Egyptian nations, (Herod. ii. 36.)
Persians, (Ib. ix. 24.) Scythians, (Ib. iv. 71.) Thessa-
lians, Macedonians (Plut. Pelop. 34.)

cate children ; enlarge thy baldness as the eagle ; for

they are gone into captivity from thee.

delicate children. The change was the more bitter for those tended and brought up delicately. Moses from the first spake of special miseries which should fall on *the tender and very delicate. Enlarge thy baldness ;* outdo in grief what others do ; for the cause of thy grief is more than that of others. The point of comparison in *the Eagle* might either be the actual baldness of the head, or its moulting. If it were the baldness of the head, the word translated *eagle* [1], although mostly used of the Eagle itself, might here comprehend the Vulture [2]. For entire baldness is so marked a feature in the vulture, whereas the "bald-headed Eagle" was probably not a bird of Palestine [3]. On the other hand, David, who lived so long among the rocks of Palestine, and Isaiah seem to have known of effects

of moulting upon the *Eagle* in producing, (although in a less degree than in other birds,) a temporary diminution of strength, which have not in modern times been commonly observed. For David says [4], *Thou shalt renew, like the eagle, thy youth,* which speaks of fresh strength after temporary weakness; and Isaiah [5], *They that trust in the Lord shall put forth* [6] *fresh strength ; they shall put forth pinion-feathers* [7] *like eagles,* comparing the fresh strength which should succeed to that which was gone, to the eagle's recovering its strong pinion-feathers. Bochart however says unhesitatingly, " [8] At the beginning of spring, the rapacious birds are subject to shedding of their feathers which we call moulting." If this be so, the comparison is yet more vivid, For the baldness of the vulture belongs to

[1] The etymology, (Arab. nasara "tore with the beak,") belongs rather to the eagle with its sharp, than to the vulture with its long, piercing beak. (The Kamoos, Freytag's authority for rendering *nasr vulture,* only says "a bird," adding that it is the name of "the constellation," i. e. Aquila. In Ulug Begh Tab. Stell. 49, 50. the okab and the *nasr* both occur as names of the constellation. Kazwini in Ideler [Sternkunde p. 385] says that the 'okab is three stars of the form of the flying nasr.) Leo Afr. [Descr. Afr. ix. 56.] says that "the largest species of eagle is called Nesir." 2) Unless *nesher* be the golden Eagle, there is no Hebrew name for it, whereas it is still a bird of Palestine, and smaller eagles are mentioned in the same verse, Lev. xi. 13; viz. *the ossifrage,* פֶּרֶס, and *the black eagle,* עָזְנִיָּה, so called from its strength, like the valeria, of which Pliny says, "the melanætos or valeria, least in size, remarkable for strength, blackish in color." x. 3. The same list of unclean birds contains also the *vulture,* דַּיָּה, Deut. xiv. 13, (as it must be, being a gregarious bird, Is. xxxiv. 15.) in its different species; (Deut. ib.) *the gier-eagle,* (i. e. Geyer) [vulture] eagle, gypaetos, or vultur percnopterus, (Hasselquist, Forskal, Shaw, Bruce in Savigny p. 77.) partaking of the character of both, (רָחָם) Lev. xi. 18. Deut. xiv. 17.) together with the *falcon* (דָּאָה Lev. xi. 14.) and *hawk,* with its subordinate species, (נֵץ לְמִינֵהוּ) Lev. xi. 18. Deut. xiv. 15.

[2] In this case, *nesher,* being a name taken from a quality common to birds of prey, might at once be a generic term, corresponding to the modern term, (aves) *rapaces,* and might also designate what all account the king of birds. Its Greek name ἀετός is doubtless the Hebrew, עַיִט, (Bochart ii. 2. p. 170.) a generic name for birds of prey. The Gypaetos forms a link between the vulture and the eagle. Seeing the prey afar, lofty flight out of human sight, strength of pinion, building nests in the rocks, attributed in H. Scr. to the *nesher,* belong also to the vulture. The feeding on dead bodies belongs especially to the vulture, although affirmed of eagles also if the body be not decayed. The Arabic *nasr* seems to comprise the vulture also. See in Boch. ii. 27. T. iii. p. 79 sqq. Savigny says, "Nisr is a generic name which has always been translated Aquila, but now the people and Arabic naturalists use it to designate the great vulture." (Descr. de l'Eg. i. 73.) and of 'Okab, "'Okab is a generic name, but it becomes specific for the small black eagle which, properly speaking, is the 'Okâb." (Ib. 85.)

[3] "The only 'bald-headed Eagle' is an American

rather than an European species. Though it is not exclusively of the new world, it is yet rarely seen in the old, and then chiefly in the Northern latitudes." Dr. Rolleston, MS. letter, who kindly guided me to the modern authorities quoted above.   [4] Ps. ciii. 5.   [5] xl. 31.

[6] חָלַף *to succeed to* (as in Arab. whence Chaliph) is used of the fresh shoots of grass, (Ps. xc. 5, 6.) of the stump of a felled tree, putting forth fresh suckers, Job xiv. 7. then, causatively, of the *putting forth fresh strength,* in contrast with the exhaustion and utter stumbling of the young and strong. In Arab. conj. iv. one of its many special meanings is "put forth fresh feathers" after moulting.

[7] Bochart ii. 1. T. ii. p. 745. So the LXX πτεροφυήσουσιν. S. Jer. assument pennas. So also Syr. Saad. חֶגְלָה is used of bringing flesh on the bones, (Ez. xxxvii. 6.) putting on the figures of Cherubim on the veil, (2 Chr. iii. 14.) gold on a shield, (1 Kgs x. 17.) dress, 2 Sam. i. 24. Am. viii. 10. The E. V. (lit. "they shall ascend a pinion [i. e. with a pinion] like eagles,") would not be too bold, but for the correspondence of Ps. ciii. 5. The word אֵבֶר, rendered *wings* E. V., is, in Ezek. xvii. 3, distinguished from the *wing* itself and the *plumage ;* as is אֶבְרָה Job xxxix. 13. In Ps. lxviii. 14. אֶבְרוֹת must be the pinion-feathers, not the pinions; and so אֶבְרָה in Ps. xci. 4. In Job xxxix. 26, the denom. יַאֲבֵר might mean the same, (Boch. Ib.) the first hemistich describing the acquiring the new feathers, the 2d the emigration of the hawks. The radical meaning of אֵבֶר is strength.

[8] Bochart, Hieroz. ii. 1. p. 744, 5. The Kamoos quotes, among the 10 characteristics of the *Anook,* (the Rachma, Heb. רָחָם), "It flies in the time of shedding its feathers and is not imperilled in its young plumage, &c." Boch. ii. 26. T. iii. p. 57. Demetrius Const. in his Ἱερακοσοφ. gives remedies for making fresh feathers put forth fast, (c. 17.) and grow quick, (c. 18.) and against diseases in moulting, (c. 32.) showing that birds of prey are liable to the same law as other birds. (See Buffon, Hist. Nat. i. 44, 5. 69, 70.) Cuvier says, "In certain states of moulting, you see in the plumage [of the royal eagle] the white at the base of the feathers. It is then called Falco Canadensis." (Règne Animal.) To this Grey adds, that the names Melanaetos and Mogilnik (in Gmelin) only describe it when moulting. (Cuvier Anim. Kingd. vi. 33.) So then the change at moulting is so great, that the royal eagle, when moulting, has been thought to be four different species.

CHAPTER II.

1 *Against oppression.* 4 *A lamentation.* 7 *A reproof of injustice and idolatry.* 12 *A
promise of restoring Jacob.*

WOE to them ᵃ that de-
vise i n i q u i t y, and
ᵇ work e v i l u p o n their
beds! when the morning is
light, they practise it, be-

ᵃ Hos. 7. 6.
ᵇ Ps. 36. 4.

its matured strength, and could only be an external likeness. The moulting of the eagle involves some degree of weakness, with which he compares Judah's mournful and weak condition amid the loss of their children, gone into captivity[1].

Thus closes the first general portion of the prophecy. The people had cast aside its own Glory, God; now its sons, its pride and its trust, shall go away from it.

" [2] The eagle, laying aside its old feathers and taking new, is a symbol of penitence and of the penitents who lay aside their former evil habits, and become other and new men. True, but rare form of penitence! " S. Gregory the Great thus applies this to the siege of Rome by the Lombards. " [3] That happened to her which we know to have been foretold of Judea by the Prophet, *en-
large thy baldness like the eagle.* For baldness befalls man in the head only, but the eagle in its whole body; for, when it is very old, its feathers and pinions fall from all its body. She lost her feathers, who lost her people. Her pinions too fell out, with which she was wont to fly to the prey; for all her mighty men, through whom she plundered others, perished. But this which we speak of, the breaking to pieces of the city of Rome, we know has been done in all the cities of the world. Some were desolated by pestilence, others devoured by the sword, others racked by famine, others swallowed by earthquakes. Despise we them with our whole heart, at least, when brought to nought; at least with the end of the world, let us end our eagerness after the world. Follow we, wherein we can, the deeds of the good." One whose commentaries S. Jerome had read, thus applies this verse to the whole human race. " O soul of man! O city, once the mother of saints, which wast formerly in Paradise, and didst enjoy the delights of different trees, and wast adorned most beautifully, now being cast down from thy place aloft, and brought down unto Babylon, and come into a place of captivity, and having lost thy glory, make thee bald and take the habit of a penitent; and thou who didst fly aloft like an eagle, mourn thy sons, thy offspring, which from thee is led captive."

CHAP. II. The Prophet had declared that evil should come down on Samaria and Jerusalem for their sins. He had pronounced them sinners against God; he now speaks of their hard unlovingness toward man, as our Blessed Lord in the Gospel speaks of sins against Himself in His members, as the ground of the condemnation of the wicked. The time of warning is past. He speaks as in the person of the Judge, declaring the righteous judgments of God, pronouncing sentence on the hardened, but blessing on those who follow Christ. The sins thus visited were done with a high hand; first, with forethought:

1. *Woe,* all woe, woe from God; " [4] the woe of temporal captivity; and, unless ye repent, the woe of eternal damnation, hangeth *over* you." *Woe to them that devise iniquity.* They *devise* it, " [5] they are not led into it by others, but invent it out of their own hearts." They plot and forecast and fulfill it even in thought, before it comes to act. *And work evil upon their beds.* Thoughts and imaginations of evil are works of the soul[6]. *Upon their beds*[7], which ought to be the place of holy thought, and of communing with their own hearts and with God[8]. Stillness must be filled with thought, good or bad; if not with good, then with bad. The chamber, if not the sanctuary of holy thoughts, is filled with unholy purposes and imaginations. Man's last and first thoughts, if not of good, are especially of vanity and evil. The Psalmist says[9], *Lord, have I not remembered Thee in my bed, and thought upon Thee when I was waking?* These men thought of sin on their bed, and did it on waking. *When the morning is light,* lit. *in the light of the morning,* i. e. instantly, shamelessly, not shrinking from the light of day, not ignorantly, but knowingly, deliberately, in full light. Nor again through infirmity, but in the wantonness of might, *because it is in the power of their hand*[10], as, of old, God said[11], *This they begin to do, and now nothing will be restrained from them which they have imagined to do.* " [12] Impiously mighty, and mighty in impiety."

[13] See the need of the daily prayer, " Vouchsafe, O Lord, to keep us this day without sin;" and " Almighty God, Who hast brought

---

[1] In Greek also the loss of wealth by pillage is compared to moulting, not in Aristoph. Av. 284–6. only, but in Philostratus, "he moults as to the wealth," p. 273.
[2] Lap.   [3] in Ezek. Hom. 18, fin. L.
[4] Dion.   [5] Rup. Rib.

[6] Ps. lviii. 2.   [7] See Ps. xxxvi. 4.
[8] Ib. iv. 4.   [9] lxiii. 6.
[10] This phrase can have no other meaning, Gen. xxxi. 29. Prov. iii. 27; nor the corresponding phrase with the negative, Deut. xxviii. 32. Neh. v. 5.
[11] Gen. xi. 6.   [12] Rup.   [13] from lap.

Before
CHRIST
cir. 730.

c Gen. 31. 29.
d Isai. 5. 8.

‖ Or, *defraud.*

cause ^c it is in the power of their hand.

2 And they covet ^d fields, and take *them* by violence; and houses, and take *them* away : so they ‖ oppress a

man and his house, even a man and his heritage.

3 Therefore thus saith the Lord ; Behold, against ^e this family do I devise an evil, from which ye shall

Before
CHRIST
cir. 730.

e Jer. 8. 3.

---

us to the beginning of this day, defend us in the same by Thy mighty power, that we may fall into no sin, &c." The illusions of the night, if such be permitted, have no power against the prayer of the morning.

2. *And they covet fields and take* them *by violence,* [*rend* them *away*] *and houses, and take* them *away.* Still, first they sin in heart, then in act. And yet, with them, to covet and to rob, to desire and to take, are the same. They were prompt, instantaneous, without a scruple, in violence. So soon as they coveted, they took [1]. Desired, acquired ! Coveted, robbed ! "They saw, they coveted, they took," had been their past history. They did violence, not to one only, but, touched with no mercy, to whole families, their little ones also ; *they oppressed a man and his house.* They spoiled not goods only, but life, *a man and his inheritance ;* destroying him by false accusations or violence and so seizing upon his inheritance [2]. Thus Ahab first coveted Naboth's vineyard, then, through Jezebel, slew him ; and " [3] they *who devoured widow's houses,* did at the last plot by night against Him of Whom they said, *Come, let us kill Him, and the inheritance shall be our's ; and in the morning, they practiced it,* leading Him away to Pilate." ^d [4] Who of us desires not the villas of this world, forgetful of the possessions of Paradise ? You see men join field to field, and fence to fence. Whole places suffice not to the tiny frame of one man." " [5] Such is the fire of concupiscence, raging within, that, as those seized by burning fevers cannot rest, no bed suffices them, so no houses or fields content these. Yet no more than seven feet of earth will suffice them soon. [6] Death only owns, how small the frame of man."

3. Such had been their habitual doings. They had done all this, he says, as one continuous act, up to that time. They were habitually *devisers of iniquity, doers of evil* [7]. It was ever-renewed. By night they sinned in heart and thought ; by day, in act. And so he speaks of it in the present. *They do it* [8]. But, although renewed in fresh acts, it was one unbroken course of acting. And so

he also uses the form, in which the Hebrews spoke of uninterrupted habits, *They have coveted, they have robbed, they have taken* [9]. Now came God's part.

Therefore, thus saith the Lord, since they oppress whole families, *behold* I will set Myself *against this* whole *family* [10]; since they *devise iniquity, behold I* too, Myself, by Myself, in My own Person, *am devising.* Very awful is it, that Almighty God sets His own Infinite Wisdom against the devices of man and employs it fittingly to punish. "I am devising no common punishment, but one to bow them down without escape ; *an evil from which* —He turns suddenly to them, *ye shall not remove your necks, neither shall ye go haughtily.*" " [5] Pride then was the source of that boundless covetousness," since it was pride which was to be bowed down in punishment. The punishment is proportioned to the sin. They had done all this in pride ; they should have the liberty and self-will wherein they had wantoned, tamed or taken from them. Like animals with a heavy yoke upon them, they should live in disgraced slavery. The ten tribes were never able to *withdraw their necks* from the yoke. From the two tribes God removed it after the 70 years. But the same sins against the love of God and man brought on the same punishment. Our Lord again spake the woe against their covetousness [11]. It still shut them out from the service of God, or from receiving Him, their Redeemer. They still *spoiled the goods* [12] of their brethren. In the last dreadful siege, " [13] there were insatiable longings for plunder, searching-out of the houses of the rich ; murder of men and insults of women were enacted as sports ; they drank down what they had spoiled, with blood." And so the prophecy was for the third time fulfilled. They who withdraw from Christ's easy yoke of obedience shall not remove from the yoke of punishment ; they who, through pride, will not bow down their necks, but *make* them *stiff,* shall be bent low, that they *go not* upright or *haughtily* any more. [14] *The Lord alone shall be exalted in that Day. For it is an evil time.* Perhaps he gives a more special meaning to

---

[1] The force of חמדו ונזלו.

[2] Comp. the woes, Is. v. 7. on oppression; 8 covetousness.

[3] Theoph.   [4] S. Jer.   [5] Rib.

[6] Juv. Sat. x. 172, 3.   [7] פעלי רע, חשבי און.

[8] יעשוה.   [9] חמדו גזלו נשאו.

[10] as in Am. iii. 1. vol. i. p. 270.
[11] S. Luke xvi. 13, 14. xi. 39. S. Matt. xxiii. 14, 23, 25. S. Mark xii. 40.
[12] Heb. x. 34.
[13] Jos. B. J. iv. 9. 10. add v. 1.   [14] Is. ii. 11.

f Amos 5. 13.
Eph. 5. 16.

g Hab. 2. 6.
h 2 Sam. 1. 17.
† Heb. *with a
lamentation of
lamentations.*

not remove your necks;
neither shall ye go haughtily: f for this time *is* evil.

4 ¶ In that day shall
one g take up a parable
against you, and h lament
† with a doleful lamenta-

tion, *and* say, We be utterly spoiled: i he hath
changed the portion of my
people: how hath he re-
moved *it* from me! ‖ turning away he hath divided
our fields.

i ch. 1. 15.

‖ Or, *instead of
restoring.*

---

the words of Amos [1], that *a time of* moral *evil*
will be, or will end in, *a time*, full of *evil*, i. e.
of sorest calamity.

4. *In that day shall one take up a parable
against you.* The *mashal* or *likeness* may, in
itself, be any speech in which one thing is
likened to another; 1) "figured speech," 2)
"proverb," and, since such proverbs were
often sharp sayings against others, 3) "taunting figurative speech." But of the person
himself it is always said, he *is made, becomes a
proverb* [2]. To *take up* or *utter* such a speech
against one, is, elsewhere, followed by the
speech itself; [3] *Thou shalt take up this parable
against the king of Babylon, and say, &c.* [4] *Shall
not all these take up a parable against him, and
say, &c.* Although then the name of the
Jews has passed into *a proverb of reproach* [5],
this is not contained here. The parable here
must be the same as the *doleful lamentation*, or
dirge, which follows. No mockery is more
cutting or fiendish, than to repeat in jest
words by which one bemoans himself. The
dirge which Israel should use of themselves
in sorrow, the enemy shall take up in derision, as Satan does doubtless the self-con-
demnation of the damned. "[6] Men do any
evil, undergo any peril, to avoid shame.
God brings before us that deepest and eternal
shame," *the shame and everlasting contempt*, in
presence of Himself and angels and devils
and the good [7], that we may avoid shame by
avoiding evil.

And lament with a doleful lamentation. The
words in Hebrew are varied inflections of a
word imitating the sounds of woe. It is the
voice of woe in all languages, because the
voice of nature. *Shall wail a wail of woe* [8], It
is the funeral dirge over the dead [9], or of the
living doomed to die [10]; it is sometimes the

measured mourning of those employed to call
forth sorrow [11], or mourning generally [12].
Among such elegies, are still Zion-songs [13],
(elegies over the ruin of Zion,) and mourn-
ings for the dead [14]. The word *woe* is thrice [15]
repeated in Hebrew, in different forms, according to that solemn way, in which the
extremest good or evil is spoken of; the
threefold blessing, morning and evening,
with the thrice-repeated name of God [16],
impressing upon them the mystery which
developed itself, as the Divinity of the
Messiah and the personal agency of the Holy
Spirit were unfolded to them. The dirge
which follows is purposely in abrupt brief
words, as those in trouble speak, with scarce
breath for utterance. First, in two words,
with perhaps a softened inflection [17], they
express the utterness of their desolation.
Then, in a threefold sentence, each clause
consisting of three short words, they say what
God had done, but name Him not, because
they are angry with Him. God's chastisements irritate those whom they do not
subdue [18].

The portion of my people He changeth;
How removeth He (it) as to *me!*
To a rebel [19] our fields He divideth.

They act the patriot. They, the rich, mourn
over "the portion of *my* people" (they say)
which they had themselves despoiled: they
speak, (as men do,) as if things were what
they ought to be: they hold to the theory
and ignore the facts. As if, because God had
divided it to His people, therefore it so remained! as if, because the poor were in
theory and by God's law provided for, they
were so in fact! Then they are enraged at
God's dealings. *He removeth the portion as
to me;* and to whom giveth He our fields?

---

[1] v. 13.
[2] Deut. xxviii. 37. 1 Kings ix. 7. 2 Chr. vii. 20. Ps.
xliv. 15. lxix. 12. Jer. xxiv. 9. Ezek. xiv. 8.
[3] Is. xiv. 4.   [4] Hab. ii. 6.   [5] Jer. l. c.
[6] Rib.   [7] Ps. lii. 6, 7, Is. lxvi. 24.
[8] נָהָה נְהִי נִהְיָה from the sounds, הוֹי passim,
הוֹ Am. v. 16. הָהּ Ezek. ii. 10. הָהּ, i. q. אֲהָהּ Ezek.
xxx. 2.
[9] Jer. xxxi. 15.   [10] Ez. xxxii. 18.
[11] Am. v. 16. Jer. ix. 17, 19.
[12] 1 Sam. vii. 2. Jer. ix. 18.
[3] צִינִית Fürst s. v.   [14] הַזְכָרָה Id.
[15] There is no plea for separating נִהְיָה in the
sense, "it has been," like "fuit Ilium." By itself
נִהְיָה would rather be, "it came to pass." אָכִי
also, which follows, explains what the proverb and

dirge is, as in Isaiah and Habakkuk. The single
word הָיָה, actum est, is no dirge. The feminine
and masculine together make up a whole as in Is.
iii. 1; or it might stand as a superlative, as in the
Eng. Marg.
[16] Num. vi. 24–26.
[17] שָׂדוּר נְשַׁדָּנוּ The ָ for the ֹ repeating the
sound oo.
[18] See ab. on Am. vi. 10. p. 207.
[19] שׁוֹבֵב, "backsliding," occurs Jer. xxxi. 22. and,
of Ammon, xlix. 4. This rendering is favored by
the contrast between the לִי and the לְשׁוֹבֵב, and
gives an adequate meaning to the לְ in the לִשׁוֹבֵב;
whereas, as part of the infinitive, it is superfluous,
and unusual as superfluous.

5 Therefore thou shalt have none that shall [k] cast a cord by lot in the congregation of the LORD.

To a rebel! the Assyrian, or the Chaldee. They had deprived the poor of their portion of *the Lord's land* [1]. And now they marvel that God resumes the possession of His own, and requires from them, not the fourfold [2] only of their spoil, but His whole heritage. Well might Assyrian or Chaldee, as they did, jeer at the word, *renegade. They* had not forsaken their gods;—but Israel, what was its whole history but a turning back ? [3] *Hath a nation changed their gods, which yet are no gods? But My people have changed their glory for that which doth not profit.*

Such was the meaning in their lips. The word *divideth* had the more bitterness, because it was the reversal of that first *division* at the entrance into Canaan. Then, with the use of this same word [4], the division of the land of the heathen was appointed to them. Ezekiel, in his great symbolic vision, afterward prophesied the restoration of Israel, with the use of this same term [5]. Joel spoke of the parting of their land, under this same term, as a sin of the heathen [6]. Now, they say, God *divideth our fields,* not to us, but to the Heathen, whose lands He gave us. It *was* a change of act : in impenitence, they think it a change of purpose or will. But what lies in that, *we be utterly despoiled ?* Despoiled of everything; of what they felt, temporal things; and of what they did not feel, spiritual things. Despoiled of the land of promise, the *good things* of this life, but also of the Presence of God in His Temple, the grace of the Lord, the image of God and everlasting glory. *Their portion* was *changed,* as to themselves and with others. As to themselves, riches, honor, pleasure, their own land, were changed into want, disgrace, suffering, captivity; and yet more bitter was it to see others gain what they by their own fault had forfeited. As time went on, and their transgression deepened, the exchange of the portion of that former people of God became more complete. The casting-off of the Jews was the grafting-in of the Gentiles. [7] *Seeing ye judge yourselves unworthy of everlasting life, lo ! we turn to the Gentiles.* And so they who were [8] *no people,* became *the people of God,* and they who were His people, became, for the time, [9] *not My people :* and [10] *the adoption of sons, and the glory, and the covenants, and the lawgiving, and the service* of God, *and the promises,* came to us Gentiles, since to us Christ Himself our *God blessed for ever* came, and made us His.

How hath He removed. The words do not say what *He* removed. They thought of His gifts, the words include Himself [11]. They say How! in amazement. The change is so great and bitter, it cannot be said. Time, yea eternity cannot utter it. *He hath divided our fields.* The land was but the outward symbol of the inward heritage. Unjust gain, kept back, is restored with usury ; [12] *it taketh away the life of the owners thereof.* The vineyard whereof the Jews said, *the inheritance shall be ours,* was taken from them and given to others, even to Christians. So now is that awful change begun, when Christians, leaving God, their only unchanging Good, turn to earthly vanities, and, for the grace of God which He withdraws, have these only for their fleeting portion, until it shall be finally exchanged in the Day of Judgment. [13] *Son, remember that thou in thy lifetime receivedst thy good things, and likewise Lazarus evil things ; but now he is comforted and thou art tormented.*

Israel defended himself in impenitence and self-righteousness. He was already the Pharisee. The doom of such was hopeless. The prophet breaks in with a renewed, *Therefore.* He had already prophesied that they should lose the lands which they had unjustly gotten, the land which they had profaned. He had described it in their own impenitent words. Now on the impenitence he pronounces the judgment which impenitence entails, that *they* should not be restored

5. *Therefore thou shalt have none that shall cast a cord by lot in the congregation of the Lord. Thou,* in the first instance, is the impenitent Jew of that day. God had promised by Hosea [14] to restore Judah ; shortly after, the Prophet himself foretells it [15]. Now he forewarns these and such as these, that they would have no portion in it. They had [16] *neither part nor lot in this matter.* They, the not-Israel then, were the images and ensamples of the not-Israel afterward, those who seem to be God's people and are not ; members of the body, not of the soul of the Church ; who have a sort of faith, but have not love. Such was afterward the *Israel after the flesh,* which was *broken off,* while the true Israel was restored, passing out of themselves into Christ. Such, at the end, shall be

[1] See on Hos. ix. 3. vol. i. p. 88.
[2] Ex. xxii. 1. 2 Sam. xii. 6. S. Luke xix. 8.
[3] Jer. ii. 11.
[4] Num. xxvi. 53, 55, 6. Josh. xiii. 7. xiv. 5. xviii. 2, 5, 10. xix. 51.   [5] xlvii. 21.   [6] iv. 2. [ili. 3. Eng.]
[7] Acts xiii. 46.   [8] Rom. x. 19.   [9] Hos. i. 9.

[10] Rom. ix. 4, 5.
[11] קִסְמָ is mostly transitive: it was intransitive ii. 3, and is so (if not Kal) Prov. xvii. 13.
[12] Prov. i. 19.   [13] S. Luke xvi. 25.
[14] See on Hos. v. 11. vol. i. p. 60.
[15] ii. 12.   [16] Acts viii. 21.

Before CHRIST cir. 730.

6 || † [1] Prophesy ye not, *say they to them that* prophesy : they shall not prophesy to them, *that* they shall not take shame.

7 ¶ O *t h o u   t h a t   a r t*

|| Or, *Prophesy not as they prophesy.*
† Heb. *Drop, &c.*
Ezek. 21. 2.
[1] Isai. 30. 10.
Amos 2. 12.
& 7. 16.

named the house of Jacob, is the spirit of the LORD || straitened ? *are* these his doings ? do not my words do good to him that walketh † uprightly ?

Before CHRIST cir. 730.
|| Or, *shortened ?*
† Heb. *upright ?*

those, who, being admitted by Christ into *their portion,* renounce the world in word not in deed. Such shall have "[1] no portion for ever *in the congregation of the Lord.* For [2] *nothing defiled shall enter there, nor whatsoever worketh abomination or a lie, but they which are written in the Lamb's book of life."*

The ground of their condemnation is their resistance to light and known truth. These not only [3] *entered not in,* themselves, but, being hinderers of God's word, *them that were entering in,* they *hindered.*

6. *Prophesy ye not,* say they to them that *prophesy ; they shall not prophesy to them, that they shall not take shame.* The words are very emphatic in Hebrew, from their briefness, *Prophesy not ; they shall indeed prophesy ; they shall not prophesy to these ; shame shall not depart* [4]. The people, the false prophets, the politicians, forbade God and Micah to prophesy ; *Prophesy not.* God, by Micah, recites their prohibition to themselves, and forewarns them of the consequences.

Prophesy ye not, lit. *drop not.* Amaziah and the God-opposing party had already given an ungodly meaning to the word [5]. " Drop not," " distill not," thus unceasingly, these same words, ever warning, ever telling of [6] *lamentation and mourning and woe ; prophesying not good concerning us, but evil* [7]. So their descendants *commanded* the Apostles [8] *not to speak at all or to teach in the Name of Jesus.* [9] *Did we not straitly command you, that ye should not teach in this Name ?* [10] *This man ceaseth not to speak blasphemous words against this holy place and the law.* God answers ; *They shall certainly prophesy.* The Hebrew word is emphatic [11]. The Prophets had their commission from God, and Him they must obey, whether Israel [12] *would hear or whether they would forbear.* So must Micah and Isaiah [13] now, or Jeremiah [14], Ezekiel, and the rest afterward. *They shall not prophesy to these.* He does not say only, *They shall not prophesy to them,* but, *to these ;* i. e. they shall prophesy to others who would receive their words : God's word would not be stayed ; they who would hearken shall never be de-

prived of their portion ; but *to these* who despise, *they shall not prophesy.* It shall be all one, as though they did not prophesy ; the soft rain shall not bedew *them.* The barnfloor shall be dry, while the fleece is moist [15]. So God says by Isaiah [16]; *I will also command the clouds that they rain no rain upon it.* The dew of God's word shall be transferred to others. But so *shame* [lit. *shames* [17], manifold shame,] *shall not depart,* but shall rest upon them for ever. God would have turned away the shame from them ; but they, despising His warnings, drew it to themselves. It was the natural fruit of their doings ; it was in its natural home with them. God spake to them, that they might be freed from it. They silenced His Prophets ; deafened themselves to His words ; so it *departed not.* So our Lord says [18], *Now ye say, we see ; therefore your sin remaineth ;* and S. John Baptist [19], *The wrath of God abideth on him.* It hath not now first to come. It is not some new thing to be avoided, turned aside. The sinner has but to remain as he is ; the shame encompasseth him already ; and only *departeth* not. The *wrath of God* is already upon him, and *abideth on him.*

7. *O thou that art named the house of Jacob ;* as Isaiah says [20], *Hear ye this, O house of Jacob, which are called by the name of Israel—which make mention of the God of Israel, not in truth, nor in righteousness. For they call themselves of the holy city, and stay themselves upon the God of Israel.* They boasted of what convicted them of faithlessness. They relied on being what in spirit they had ceased to be, what in deeds they denied, children of a believing forefather. It is the same temper which we see more at large in their descendants ; [21] *We be Abraham's seed and were never in bondage to any man ; how sayest Thou, ye shall be made free ?* [22] *Abraham is our Father.* It is the same which S. John Baptist and our Lord and S. Paul reproved. [23] *Think not to say within yourselves, we have Abraham to our father.* [24] *If ye were Abraham's children, ye would do the works of Abraham. Now ye seek to kill Me, a Man that hath told you the truth—This did not*

[1] Rib.   [2] Rev. xxi. 27.   [3] S. Luke xi. 52.
[4] Poc. gives this distribution of the words from Abulwalid v. נטף.
[5] See on Am. vii. 16. vol. i. p. 322.
[6] Ezek. ii. 10.   [7] 1 Kings xxii. 18.
[8] Acts iv. 18. v. 40.   [9] Ib. v. 28.   [10] Ib. vi. 13.
[11] יטיפון.   [12] Ezek. ii. 5. 7.   [13] xxviii. 9-14. 22.
[14] i. 7. 17. xxvi. 10-15.   [15] Judg. vi. 37.
[16] Is. v. 6.
[17] כלמות as שועות, omnigenæ salutes, manifold salvation.
[18] S. John ix. 41.   [19] Ib. iii. 36.   [20] xlviii. 1.
[21] S. John viii. 33.   [22] Ib. 39.
[23] S. Matt. iii. 9.   [24] S. John viii. 39, 40.

8 Even † of late my peo-
ple is risen up as an enemy:
† Heb. *yesterday.*
† Heb. *over* ye pull off the robe † with
against a garment.

the garment f r o m them
that pass by securely as
men averse from war.

Abraham. [1] *He is not a Jew which is one outwardly, neither is that circumcision which is outward in the flesh.—Behold thou art called a Jew,
and restest in the law and makest thy boast of
God, and knowest His Will and approvest the
things that are more excellent—&c.* The Prophet answers the unexpressed objections of
those who forbade to prophesy evil. "Such
could not be of God," these said; "for God
was pledged by His promises to *the house of
Jacob.* It would imply change in God, if He
were to cast off those whom He had chosen."
Micah answers; "not God is changed, but
you." God's promise was to Jacob, not to
those who were but *named* Jacob, who called
themselves after the name of their father,
but did not his deeds. *The Spirit of the Lord
was not straitened* [2], so that He was less long-
suffering than heretofore. *These,* which He
threatened and of which they complained,
were *not His doings,* not what He of His own
Nature did, not what He loved to do, not
His, as the Author or Cause of them, but
theirs. God is Good, but to those who can
receive good, *the upright in heart* [3]. *God is
only Loving unto Israel.* He is all Love;
nothing but [4] Love: all His ways are Love;
but it follows, unto *what* Israel, the true
Israel, *the pure of heart.* [5] *All the paths of the
Lord are mercy and truth ;* but to whom ? *unto
such as keep His covenant and His testimonies.*
[6] *The mercy of the Lord is from everlasting to
everlasting ;* but *unto them that fear Him.* But,
they becoming evil, His good became to them
evil. Light, wholesome and gladdening to the
healthful, hurts weak eyes. That which is
straight cannot suit or fit with the crooked.
Amend your crookedness, and God's ways
will be straight to you. *Do not My words do
good ?* He doth speak [7] *good words and comfortable words.* They are not only *good,* but *do
good.* [8] *His word is with power.* Still it is

with those who *walk uprightly ;* whether
those who forsake not, or those who return
to, the way of righteousness. God flattereth
not, deceiveth not, promiseth not what He
will not do. He cannot [9] *speak peace where
there is no peace.* As He saith, [10] *Behold the
goodness and severity of God; on them which
fell, severity, but toward thee, goodness, if thou
continue in His goodness.* God Himself could
not make a heaven for the proud or envious.
Heaven would be to them a hell.

8. *Even of late* [lit. *yesterday* [11].] " [12] He
imputeth not past sins, but those recent and,
as it were, of yesterday." *My people is risen
up vehemently* [13]. God upbraideth them tenderly by the title, *Mine own people,* as S. John
complaineth [14], *He came unto His own, and His
own received Him not.* God became not *their*
enemy, but they arose as one man,—*is risen
up,* the whole of it, as *His.* In Him they
might have had peace and joy and assured
gladness, but they arose in rebellion against
Him, requiting Him evil for good, (as bad
Christians do to Christ,) and brought war
upon their own heads. This they did by
their sins against their brethren. Casting off
the love of man, they alienated themselves
from the love of God.

Ye pull off [*strip off violently* [15]] *the robe with
the garment,* lit. *over against the cloak.* The
salmah [16] is the large enveloping cloak, which
was worn loosely over the other dress, and
served by night for a covering [17]. *Eder* [18],
translated *robe,* is probably not any one garment, but the remaining dress, the comely,
becoming [19], array of the person. These they
stripped violently off from persons, peaceable,
unoffending, off their guard, *passing by securely, men averse from war* [20] and strife. These
they stripped of their raiment by day, leaving them half-naked, and of their covering
for the night. So making war against God's

---

[1] Rom. ii. 17–28.
[2] קצר רוח, (as in part Zech. xi. 8,) as opposed to
ארך אפים (Ex. xxxiv. 6. &c. longanimis, longsuffering,) and i. q. קצר אפים Prov. xx. 17, coll. 29.

[3] Ps. lxxiii. 1.   [4] The force of אך.

[5] Ps. xxv. 10.   [6] Ps. ciii. 17. S. Luke i. 50.
[7] Zech. i. 13.   [8] S. Luke iv. 32.   [9] Jer. vi. 14.
[10] Rom. xi. 22.

[11] אתמגל is i. q. אתמול, in Is. xxx. 33.
[12] S. Jer.

[13] יקומם, in Isaiah (xliv. 26. lviii. 12. lxi. 4.) transitive, but only of the raising up, rebuilding of ruins.
The use of קומם actively in that one sense is no
ground for taking it so, where the idea is different.
To *raise up* an adversary is expressed by הקים

Mic. v. 4. Am. vi. 14. 1 Kings xi. 14. and so raising
up evil also.
[14] i. 11.
[15] חפשטון. This is intensive, as in Arabic.
[16] שלמה here and Ex. xxii. 8. i. q. שמלה, elsewhere.
[17] Deut. xxii. 17.
[18] אדר occurs here only. There is no ground to
identify it with the well-known אדרת. It is not
likely that the common garment should have been
called, this once, by a different name; nor that the
אדרת, a wide enfolding garment, (see on Jonah iii.
6. vol. i. p. 416,) should have been worn together
with the שלמה.
[19] This meaning seems to lie in the root; comp.
στολή, array, apparel, dress.
[20] שוב is doubtless an adjective form, distinct
from the participle שב, (Is. lix. 20.) like מודי Jer.
ii. 21.

3

Before
C H R I S T
cir. 730.
9 The || women of my
people have ye cast out
from their pleasant houses ;
from their children have

|| Or, *wives.*

ye taken away my glory Before
C H R I S T
cir. 730.
for ever.

10 Arise ye, and depart;
for this *is* not *your* [m] rest :   [m] Deut. 12. 9.

---

peaceful people, they, as it were, made war
against God.

9. *The women of my people have ye cast out
from their pleasant houses*, [lit. *from her pleasant
house,*] each from her home. These were
probably the widows of those whom they had
stripped. Since the houses were their's,
they were widows ; and so their spoilers were
at war with those whom God had committed
to their special love, whom He had declared
the objects of His own tender care, *the widows
and the fatherless.* The widows they *drove
vehemently forth* [1], as having no portion in the
inheritance which God had given them, as
God had driven out their enemies before
them, each *from her pleasant house,* the home
where she had lived with her husband and
children in delight and joy.

From [*off*] *their* [*young* [2]] *children have ye
taken away My glory.* Primarily, the glory,
comeliness, was the fitting apparel which God
had given them [3], and laid upon them [4], and
which these oppressors stripped *off* from them.
But it includes all the gifts of God, wherewith God would array them. Instead of the
holy home of parental care, the children
grew up in want and neglect, away from all
the ordinances of God, it may be, in a strange
land. *For ever.* They never repented, never
made restitution ; but so they incurred the
special woe of those who ill-used the unprotected, the widow, and the fatherless. The
words *for ever* anticipate the punishment.
The punishment is according to the sin.
They never ceased their oppression. They,
with the generation who should come after
them, should be deprived of God's *glory,* and
cast out of His land forever.

10. *Arise ye and depart.* Go your way, as
being cast out of God's care and land. It
matters not whither they went. *For this is
not your rest.* As ye have done, so shall it be
done unto you. As ye cast out the widow
and the fatherless, so shall ye be cast out ; as

ye gave no rest to those *averse from war,* so
shall ye have none.   [5] *He that leadeth into
captivity shall go into captivity ; he that killeth
with the sword must be killed with the sword.*
The land was given to them as a temporary
rest, a symbol and earnest of the everlasting
rest to the obedient. So Moses spake [6], *ye
are not as yet come to the rest* [7] *and the inheritance which the Lord your God giveth you. But
when ye go over Jordan, and dwell in the land
which the Lord your God giveth you to inherit,
and when He giveth you rest* [8] *from your enemies
round about, so that ye dwell in safety, &c.* And
Joshua [9], *Remember the word which Moses commanded you, saying, The Lord your God giveth
you rest* [10]. But the Psalmist had warned
them, that, if they hardened their hearts like
their forefathers, they too would *not enter into
His rest* [11].

Because it is polluted [lit. *because of* its *pollution* [12]] by idolatry, by violence, by uncleanness. So Moses (using the same word) says,
the land is defiled [13] by the abominations of the
heathen ; and warns them, *that the land spue
you not out, when you defile it, as it spued out the
nations which were before you.* Ezekiel speaks
of that *defilement* [14], as the ground why God
expelled Israel [15].   *It shall destroy you, even
with a sore* [lit. *sharp*] *destruction* [16]. It is a
sore thing to abuse the creatures of God to
sin, and it is unfit that we should use what
we have abused. Hence Holy Scripture
speaks, as though even the inanimate creation took part with God, *made subject to vanity, not willingly,* and could not endure those
who employed it against His Will.

The words, *Arise, depart ye, for this is not
your rest,* became a sort of sacred proverb,
spoken anew to the soul, whenever it would
find rest out of God.   "[17] We are bidden to
think of no rest for ourselves in any things
of the world ; but, as it were, *arising* from the
dead, to stretch upwards, and walk after the
Lord our God, and say, *My soul cleaveth hard*

---

[1] תגרשון is doubly intensive, as the intensive
form with the emphatic ן. It is the word used of
God's driving out the nations before Israel, (Ex.
Jud. &c.) or of man being driven out of Paradise,
(Gen. iii. 24,) Hagar being cast out. (Gen. xxi. 10.)
The word itself, by its rough sound, expresses the
more of harshness ; and that as opposed to softness, תענוג'ה. This is the same word as that rendered *delicate,* i. 16.

[2] מעל עולליה.

[3] as Hos. ii. 11. דני I. H. Mich.
[4] Ez. xvi. 14. Id.
[6] Deut. xii. 9. 10. add 1 Kings viii. 56.

[7] אל המנוחה, the same word.

[5] Rev. xiii. 10.

[8] הניח.

[9] i. 13.   [10] מניח.
[11] Ps. xcv. 11. comp. למנוחתך Ps. cxxxii. 8.
מנוחתי 14.
[12] as pointed in most accurate copies, without
Metheg.   [13] תטמא Lev. xviii. 27. בטמאכם 28.
[14] Ezek. xxxvi. 17.
[15] Ezek. xxxvi. 18. add Jer. ii. 7.
[16] This is the common rendering of חבל. Others,
with Sal. B. Mel. have understood it of travail-pains,
(Cant. viii. 5. Ps. vii. 15.) but this would have the
opposite sense of bringing forth, re-birth, not of
ejection. (See Is. lxvi. 8.) The sharp bitter pang
would express the pains of travail, not its fruitlessness or that they were cast out any whither. Fruitlessness of travail-pangs is expressed, if intended,
(as in Is. xxvi. 18.)   [17] S. Jer.

Before
CHRIST
cir. 730.
because it is ⁿpolluted, it shall destroy *you*, even with a sore destruction.

ⁿ Lev. 18. 25, 28. Jer. 3. 2.
‖ Or, *walk with the wind, and lie falsely.*
º Ezek. 13. 3.

11 If a man ‖ º walking in the spirit and falsehood do lie, *saying*, I will proph-

esy unto thee of wine and of strong drink ; he shall even be the prophet of this people.

12 ¶ ᵖ I will surely assemble, O Jacob, all of

Before
CHRIST
cir. 730.

ᵖ ch. 4. 6, 7.

---

after Thee. This if we neglect, and will not hear Him Who saith, *Awake thou that sleepest, and arise from the dead, and Christ shall give thee light*, we shall indeed slumber, but shall be deceived and shall not find rest ; for where Christ enlighteneth not the risen soul, what seemeth to be rest, is trouble." All rest is wearisome which is not in Thee, O our God.

11. *If a man walking in the spirit and falsehood*, lit. *in spirit* [not *My* Spirit] *and falsehood*, i. e. in a lying spirit ; such as they, whose woe Ezekiel pronounces ¹, *Woe unto the foolish prophets who walk after their own spirit and what they have not seen* ² ; *prophets out of their own hearts*, who ³ *prophesied a vision of falsehood, and a destruction and nothingness* ⁴ ; *prophesied falsehood ; yea, prophets of the deceit of their hearts*. These, like the true prophets, *walked in spirit* ; as Isaiah speaks of *walking in righteousness* ⁵, and Solomon of one *walking in the frowardness of the mouth* ⁶. Their habitual converse was in a spirit, but of falsehood. If such an one *do lie*, saying, *I will prophesy unto thee of wine and strong drink*. Man's conscience must needs have some plea in speaking falsely of God. The false prophets had to please the rich men, to embolden them in their self-indulgence, to tell them that God would not punish. They doubtless spoke of God's temporal promises to His people, the land *flowing with milk and honey*. His promises of abundant harvest and vintage, and assured them, that God would not withdraw these, that He was not so precise about His law. Micah tells them in plain words, what it all came to; it was a prophesying of *wine and strong drink*.

He shall even be the prophet of this people, lit. *and shall be bedewing this people*. He uses the same words, which scorners of Israel and Judah employed in forbidding to prophesy. They said, *drop not ;* forbidding God's word as a wearisome dropping. It wore away their patience, not their hearts of stone. He tells them, *who* might speak to them without wearying, of *whose* words they would never tire, *who* might do habitually ⁷ what they

forbade to God,—one who, in the Name of God, set them at ease in their sensual indulgences. This is the secret of the success of everything opposed to God and Christ. Man wants a God. God has made it a necessity of our nature to crave after Him. Spiritual, like natural, hunger, debarred from or loathing wholesome food, must be stilled, stifled, with what will appease its gnawings. Our natural intellect longs for Him ; for it cannot understand itself without Him. Our restlessness longs for Him ; to rest upon. Our helplessness longs for Him, to escape from the unbearable pressure of our unknown futurity. Our imagination craves for Him ; for, being made for the Infinite, it cannot be content with the finite. Aching affections long for Him ; for no creature can soothe them. Our dissatisfied conscience longs for Him, to teach it and make it one with itself. But man does not want to be responsible, nor to owe duty ; still less to be liable to penalties for disobeying. The Christian, not the natural man, longs that his whole being should tend to God. The natural man wishes to be well-rid of what sets him ill at ease, not to belong to God. And the horrible subtlety of false teaching, in each age or country, is to meet its own favorite requirements, without calling for self-sacrifice or self-oblation, to give it a god, such as it would have, such as might content it. "⁸ The people willeth to be deceived, be it deceived," is a true proverb. *Men turn away their ears from the truth* ⁹ which they dislike ; and so *are turned unto fables* which they like. They who *receive not the love of the truth,—believe a lie* ¹⁰. If men *will not retain God in their knowledge, God giveth them over to an undistinguishing mind* ¹¹. They who would not receive our Lord, coming in His Father's Name, have ever since, as He said, *received them who came in their own* ¹². Men teach their teachers how they wish to be mistaught, and receive the echo of their wishes as the Voice of God.

12. *I will surely assemble, O Jacob, all of thee ; I will surely gather the remnant of Israel*. God's

---

¹ Ezek. xiii. 3.   ² Ib. 2. 17.
³ Jer. xiv. 14, הזון שקר, as here רוח ושקר.
⁴ Ib. xxiii. 26. add נבא׳ם שקר xxvii. 10, 14,
16. or בשקר Jer. xxix. 9. נבא׳ חלמות שקר Ib.
xxiii. 32.
⁵ xxxiii. 15. הלי צדרות.

⁶ הולך עקשות פה Pr. vi. 12. elsewhere with ב.
⁷ The force of היה מטיף.
⁸ Populus vult decipi, decipiatur.
⁹ 2 Tim. iv. 4.
¹⁰ 2 Thess. ii. 11. 12.
¹¹ Rom. i. 28.   ¹² S. John v. 43.

Before CHRIST cir. 730.

thee; I will surely gather the remnant of Israel; I will put them together [q] as the sheep of Bozrah, as the flock in the midst of their fold: [r] they shall make great noise by reason of *the multitude of* men.

[q] Jer. 31. 10.

[r] Ezek. 36. 37.

mercy on the penitent and believing being the end of all His threatenings, the mention of it often bursts in abruptly. Christ is ever the Hope as the End of prophecy, ever before the Prophets' mind. The earthquake and fire precede the still small voice of peace in Him. What seems then sudden to us, is connected in truth. The Prophet had said [1], where was not their rest and how they should be cast forth; he saith at once how they should be gathered to their everlasting rest. He had said, what promises of the false prophets would *not* be fulfilled [2]. But, despair being the most deadly enemy of the soul, he does not take away their false hopes, without shewing them the true mercies in store for them. "[3] Think not," he would say, "that I am only a prophet of ill. The captivity foretold will indeed now come, and God's mercies will also come, although not in the way, which these speak of." The false prophets spoke of worldly abundance ministering to sensuality, and of unbroken security. He tells of God's mercies, but after chastisement, to *the remnant of Israel*. But the restoration is complete, far beyond their then condition. He had foretold the desolation of Samaria [4], the captivity of Judah [5]; he foretells the restoration of *all Jacob*, as one. The images are partly taken (as is the Prophet's wont,) from that first deliverance from Egypt [6]. *Then*, as the image of the future growth under persecution, God multiplied His people exceedingly [7]; then [8] *the Lord went before them by day in a pillar of a cloud to lead them the way;* then God *brought them up* [9] *out of the house of bondage* [10]. But their future prison-house was to be no land of Goshen. It was to be a captivity and a dispersion at once, as Hosea had already foretold [11]. So he speaks of them emphatically [12], as a great throng, *assembling I will assemble, O Jacob, all of thee; gathering I will gather the remnant of Israel.* The word, which is used of the gathering of a flock or its lambs [13], became, from Moses' prophecy [14], a received word of the gathering of Israel from the dispersion of the captivity [15]. The return of the Jews from Babylon was but a faint shadow of the fulfillment. For, ample as were the terms of the decrees of Cyrus [16] and Artaxerxes [17], and widely as that of Cyrus was diffused [18], the restoration was essentially that of Judah, i. e. Judah, Benjamin and Levi [19]: the towns, whose inhabitants returned, were those of Judah and Benjamin [20]; the towns, to which they returned, were of the two tribes. It was not a gathering of *all Jacob;* and of the three tribes who returned, there were but few gathered, and they had not even an earthly king, nor any visible Presence of God. The words began to be fulfilled in the *many* [21] *tens of thousands* who believed at our Lord's first Coming; and *all Jacob*, that is, all who were Israelites indeed, *the remnant according to the election of grace* [22], were gathered within the one fold of the Church, under One Shepherd. It shall be fully fulfilled, when, in the end, *the fullness of the Gentiles shall come in, and all Israel shall be saved* [23]. *All Jacob* is the same as *the remnant of Israel*, the true Israel which remains when the false severed itself off; all the seed-corn, when the chaff was winnowed away. So then, whereas they were now scattered, *then*, God saith, *I will put them together* [in one fold] *as the sheep of Bozrah*, which abounded in sheep [24], and was also a strong city of Edom [25]; denoting how believers should be fenced within the Church, as by a strong wall, against which the powers of darkness should not prevail, and the wolf should howl around the fold, yet be unable to enter it, and Edom and the heathen should become part of the inheritance of Christ [26]. *As a flock in the midst of their fold*, at rest, "[27] like sheep, still and subject to their shepherd's voice. So shall these, having one faith and One Spirit, in meekness and simplicity, obey the one rule of truth. Nor shall it be a small number;" for the place where they

1 ver. 10. 2 ver. 11. 3 S. Jer.
4 i. 6. 5 i. 16. ii. 4. 6 Hengst. Christ. i. 499.
7 Ex. i. 12. 8 Ib. xiii. 21.
9 Ex. iii. 8, 17. Lev. xi. 45. The people *went up*. Ex. xiii. 18. add. xii. 38. i. 10.
10 See below, vi. 4.
11 See on Hos. vi. 11. vol. i. p. 70. ix. 17. p. 97.
12 אסף אאסף, קבץ אקבץ. 13 Is xl. 11. xiii. 14.
14 Deut. xxx. 3, 4. see Neh. i. 9.
15 See below, iv. 6. Ps. cvi. 47. cvii. 3. Is. xi. 12. xliii. 5. liv. 7. lvi. 8. Zeph. iii. 19, 20. Jer. xxiii. 3. xxix. 14. xxxi. 8, 10. xxxii. 37. Ezek xi. 17. xx. 34, 41. xxviii. 25. xxxiv. 13. xxxvii. 21. xxxviii. 8. xxxix. 27. Zech. x. 10.
16 Ezr. i. 2–4. 17 vii. 13. 18 Ib. i. 1.
19 Ib. i. 5. ii. 1. iv. 1. x. 7, 9. Josephus, who alone mentions that Ezra sent a copy of Artaxerxes' letter to him, "to all those of his nation who were in Media," and that "many of them, taking their property, came to Babylon, longing for the return to Jerusalem," adds, "but the whole people of Israelites [i. e. the great mass] remained where they were." Ant. xi 5. 2.
20 Ezr. ii. Neh. vii. 21 *μυριάδες* Acts xxi. 20.
22 Rom. xi. 5. 23 Ib. xi. 25, 6.
24 Is. xxxiv. 6.
25 See on Am. i. 12. vol. i. p. 252.
26 See on Am. ix. 12. vol. i. p. 337. 27 Rup.

13 The breaker is come up before them : they have

broken up, and have passed through the gate, and are

shall be gathered shall be too narrow to contain them, as is said in Isaiah ; *Give place to me, that I may dwell*[1].

They shall make great noise (it is the same word as our *hum*, "the hum of men,") *by reason of the multitude of men.* He explains his image, as does Ezekiel[2], *And ye are My flock, the flock of My pasture ; men are ye ; I, your God, saith the Lord God :* and, [3] *As a flock of holy things, as the flock of Jerusalem in her solemn feasts ; so shall the waste cities be full of a flock of men, and they shall know that I am the Lord.* So many shall they be, that "throughout the whole world they shall make a great and public sound in praising God, filling Heaven and the green pastures of Paradise with a mighty hum of praise ; " as St. John saw[4] *a great multitude which no man could number,* "[5] with one united voice praising the Good Shepherd, Who smoothed for them all rugged places, and evened them by His Own Steps, Himself the Guide of their way and the *Gate* of Paradise, as He saith, *I am the Door ;* through Whom, *bursting through* and *going before,* being also the Door of the way, the flock of believers shall break through *It.* But this Shepherd is their *Lord* and *King.*" Not their King only, but the Lord God ; so that this, too, bears witness that Christ is God.

13. *The Breaker is come up (gone up) before them ; they have broken up, (broken through*[6]) *and have passed the gate, and have gone forth.* The image is not of conquest, but of deliverance. They *break through,* not to enter in but to *pass through the gate* and *go forth.* The wall of the city is ordinarily *broken through,* in order to make an entrance[7], or to secure to a conqueror the power of entering in[8] at any time, or by age and decay[9]. But here the object is expressed, to *go forth.* Plainly then they were confined before, as in a prison ; and the gate of the prison was burst open, to set them free. It is then the same image as when God says by Isaiah[10] ; *I will say to the North, give up ; and to the South, Hold not back,* or[11], *Go ye forth of Babylon, Say ye, the Lord hath redeemed His servant Jacob ;* or, with the same reminiscence of God's visible leading of His people out of Egypt, [12] *Depart ye, depart ye ; for ye shall not go out with haste, nor yet by flight, for the Lord God shall go before you, and the God of Israel* will be *your reward ;* or as Hosea describes their restoration[13] ; *Then shall the children of Judah and the children of Israel be gathered together and appoint themselves one Head, and they shall go up out of the land*[14]. Elsewhere, in Isaiah, the spiritual meaning of the deliverance from the prison is more distinctly brought out, as the work of our Redeemer[15]. *I will give Thee for a covenant of the people, for a light of the Gentiles, to open the blind eyes, to bring out the prisoners from the prison, them that sit in darkness out of the prison-house ;* and[16], *the Spirit of the Lord God is upon Me, because the Lord hath anointed Me to proclaim liberty to the captives, and the opening of the prison to them that are bound.*

From this passage, the "Breaker-through" was one of the titles of the Christ, known to the Jews[17], as One Who should be "[18] from below and from above" also ; and from it they believed that "[19] captives should come up from Gehenna, and the Shechinah," or the Presence of God, "at their head."[20] He then, Who shall break the way, the King and Lord Who shall *go up before them,* shall be the Good Shepherd, Who puts them together in the fold. And this He doth when, as He saith, [21] *He putteth forth His own sheep, and He goeth before them, and the sheep follow Him, for they know His Voice.* How doth He go before them but by suffering for them, leaving them an example of suffering, and opening the entrance of Paradise ? The Good Shepherd *goeth up* to the Cross, [22] *and is lifted up from the earth, laying down His Life for His sheep, to draw all men unto* Him. He *goeth up,* trampling on death by His resurrection ; He *goeth up* above the heaven of heavens, and sitteth on the Right Hand of the Father, opening the way before them, so that the flock, in their lowliness, may arrive where the Shepherd went before in His Majesty.

---

[1] xlix. 20.   [2] xxxiv. 31.   [3] Ib. xxxvi. 38.
[4] Rev. vii. 9.   [5] Rup.
[6] פָּרַץ is to *break through,* as, enemies surrounding one, 2 Sam. v. 20. 1 Chr. xiv. 11. *break in pieces* so as to scatter, Ps. lx. 3. *break through or down* a wall, (see references in 30, 31, 33,) and with בְּ, "burst upon," of God's inflictions, Ex. xix. 22, 24. 2 Sam. vi. 8. Ps. cvi. 29. 1 Chr. xiii. 11. xv. 13.
[7] Ps. lxxx. 13. lxxxix. 41. Is. v. 5. Neh. ii. 13.
[8] Prov. xxv. 28. 2 Kgs xiv. 13. 2 Chr. xxv. 23. xxvi. 6.
[9] 2 Chr. xxxii. 5.   [10] xliii. 6.   [11] Ib. xlviii. 20.
[12] lii. 11, 12. תֵּצֵאוּ, as here וְיֵצְאוּ ; and הֹלֵךְ לִפְנֵיכֶם corresponding to עָלָה לִפְנֵיכֶם.

[13] i. 11. (ii. 2. Heb.)
[14] עָלוּ מִן הָאָרֶץ in reference to Egypt, (see on Hos. i. 11. vol. i. p. 26) as here עָלָה.
[15] Is. xlii. 6, 7.
[16] Is. lxi. 1.   [17] Huls. Theol. Jud. pp. 143, 144.
[18] R. Mos. Haddars. in Mart. Pug. Fid. p. 432. It is interpreted of the Messiah in the Bereshith Rabba, § 48. f. 47. 2. (Schöttg. de Mess. p. 61.) the Echa Rabbathi, f. 60. 2, (Ib. p. 69.) the Pesikta Rabbathi, f. 60. 1, (Ib. p. 135.) and the Midrash Mishle, ad c. vi. 1. (Ib. ad loc. p. 212.) So also Jonathan, Rashi, Tanchum, Abarbanel in Poc.
[19] Quoted by Pearson on the Creed, art. 6, note y.
[20] Rup.   [21] S. John x. 4.   [22] Ib. 15. xii. 32.

Before
CHRIST
cir. 730.
ˢ Hos. 3. 5. gone out by it : and ˢ their king shall pass before them,

ᵗ and the LORD on the head of them.

Before
CHRIST
cir. 730.
ᵗ Is. 52. 12.

And when He thus breaketh through and openeth the road, they also *break through and pass through the gate and go out by it*, by that Gate, namely, whereof the Psalmist saith [1], *This is the Gate of the Lord ; the righteous shall enter into It*. What other is this *Gate* than that same Passion of Christ, beside which there is no gate, no way whereby any can enter into life ? Through that open portal, which the lance of the soldier made in His Side when crucified, and *there came thereout Blood and Water, they shall pass and go through*, even as the children of Israel passed through the Red Sea, which divided before them, when Pharaoh, his chariots and horsemen, were drowned." " [2] He will be in their hearts, and will teach and *lead* them ; He will shew them the way of Salvation, [3] *guiding their feet into the way of peace*, and they shall pass through the strait and narrow gate which leadeth unto life ; of which it is written [4], *Enter ye in at the strait gate ; because strait is the gate and narrow is the way which leadeth unto life, and few there be that find it. And their King shall pass before them*, as He did, of old, in the figure of the cloud, of which Moses said [5], *If Thy Presence go not, carry us not up hence ; and wherein shall it be known that I have found grace in Thy sight, I and Thy people, is it not in that Thou goest up with us ?* and as He then did when He passed out of this world to the Father. *And the Lord on* (that is, *at*) *the head of them*, as of His army. " [6] For *the Lord is His Name*, and He is the Head, they the members ; He the King, they the people ; He the Shepherd, they the sheep of His pasture. And of this *passing through* He spake [7], *By Me if any man enter in, he shall be saved, and shall go in and out and find pasture*. For a man *entereth in*, when, receiving the faith, he becomes a sheep of this Shepherd, and *goeth out*, when he closeth this present life, and then findeth the pastures of unfading, everlasting life ; " " [2] passing from this pilgrimage to his home, from faith to sight, from labor to reward." Again, as describing the Christian's life here, it speaks of progress. " [8] Whoso shall have entered in, must not remain in the state wherein he entered, but must *go forth* into the pasture ; so that, in entering in should be the beginning, in *going forth and finding pasture*, the perfecting of graces. He who entereth in, is contained within the bounds of the world ; he who goeth forth, goes, as it were, beyond all

created things, and, counting as nothing all things seen, shall *find pasture* above the Heavens, and shall feed upon the Word of God, and say [9], *The Lord is my Shepherd*, (and feedeth me,) *I can lack nothing*. But this going forth can only be through Christ ; as it followeth, *and the Lord at the head of them*." Nor, again, is this in itself easy, or done for us without any effort of our own. All is of Christ. The words express the closeness of the relation between the Head and the members ; and what He, our King and Lord, doth, they do, because He Who did it for them, doth it in them. The same words are used of both, shewing that what they do, they do by virtue of His Might, treading in His steps, walking where He has made the way plain, and by His Spirit. What they do, they do, as belonging to Him. He *breaketh through*, or, rather, in all is *the Breaker-through*. They, having broken through, *pass* on, because He *passeth before them*. He will [10] *break in pieces the gates of brass, and cut in sunder the bars of iron*. He breaketh through whatever would hold us back or oppose us, all might of sin and death and Satan, as Moses opened the Red Sea, for [11] *a way for the ransomed to pass over ;* and so He saith, [12] *I will go before thee, I will break in pieces the gates of brass, and cut in sunder the bars of iron, and I will give thee the treasures of darkness, and hidden riches of secret places*. So then Christians, following Him, the *Captain of their salvation*, strengthened by His grace, must burst the bars of the flesh and of the world, the chains and bonds of evil passions and habits, force themselves through the narrow way and narrow gate, do violence to themselves, [13] *endure hardness, as good soldiers of Jesus Christ*. The title of our Lord, the *Breaker-through* [14], and the saying, *they break through*, together express the same as the New Testament doth in regard to our being partakers of the sufferings of Christ. [15] *Joint heirs with Christ, if so be that we suffer with Him, that we may be also glorified together.* [16] *If we be dead with Him, we shall also live with Him ; if we suffer, we shall also reign with Him.* [17] *Forasmuch then as Christ hath suffered for us in the flesh—arm yourselves likewise with the same mind.*

The words may include also the removal of the souls of the just, who had believed in Christ before His Coming, into Heaven after His Resurrection, and will be fully completed when, in the end, He shall cause His faithful

[1] Ps. cxviii. 20.   [2] Dion.   [3] S. Luke i. 79.
[4] S. Matt. vii. 13, 14.   [5] Ex. xxxiii. 15, 16.
[6] Rup.   [7] S. John x. 9.
[8] S. Jer.   [9] Ps. xxiii. 1.   [10] Is. xlv. 2.
[11] Ib. li. 10.   [12] Ib. xlv. 2, 3.   [13] 2 Tim. ii. 3.

[14] פָרֵיץ. It is from the same word as Pharez, Judah's son, whose birth was typical. Gen. xxxviii. 29.   [15] Rom. viii. 17.
[16] 2 Tim. ii. 11, 12.   [17] 1 Pet. iv. 1.

CHAPTER III.

1 *The cruelty of the princes.* 5
The falsehood of the prophets.
8 *The security of them both.*

ᵃ Jer. 5. 4, 5.

AND I said, Hear, I pray
you, O heads of Jacob,
and ye princes of the house
of Israel; ᵃ *Is* it not for
you to know judgment?

2 Who hate the good,
and love the evil; who

pluck off their skin from
off them, and their flesh
from off their bones;

3 Who a l s o ᵇ eat the
flesh of my people, and
flay their skin from off
them; and t h e y break
their bones, and chop them
in pieces, as for the pot,
and ᶜ as flesh within the
caldron.

ᵇ Ps. 14. 4.

ᶜ Ezek. 11. 3, 7.

---

servants, in body and soul, to *enter into the
joy of their Lord.*
CHAP. III. ver. 1. *And I said.* God's love
for us is the great incitement, constrainer,
vivifier of His creature's love. Micah had
just spoken of God's love of Israel; how He
would gather them into one fold under One
Shepherd, guard them, lead them, remove
all difficulties before them, be Himself their
Head and enable them to follow Him. He
turns then to them. These are God's doings;
this, God has in store for you hereafter.
Even when mercy itself shall require chastisement, He doth not cast off forever. The
desolation is but the forerunner of future
mercy. What then do ye? The Prophet
appeals to them, class by class. There was
one general corruption of every order of men,
through whom Judah could be preserved,
princes[1], prophets[2], priests[3]. *The salt had
lost its savor; wherewith could it be seasoned?*
whereby could the decaying mass of the
people be kept from entire corruption?
*Hear, I pray you, O heads of Jacob, and ye
princes of the house of Israel.* He arraigns
them by the same name, under which He
had first promised mercy. He had first
promised mercy to *all Jacob* and *the remnant
of Israel.* So now he upraids the *heads of
Jacob,* and *the princes of the house of Israel,* lest
they should deceive themselves. At the
same time he recalls them to the deeds of
their father. Judah had succeeded to the
birthright, forfeited by Reuben, Simeon and
Levi; and in Judah all the promises of the
Messiah were laid up. But he was not like
the three great Patriarchs, *the father of the
faithful,* or the meek Isaac, or the much-
tried Jacob. The name then had not the
reminiscences, or force of appeal, contained
in the titles, *seed of Abraham,* or Isaac, or
Israel.
Is it not for you to know judgment? It is a

great increase of guilt, when persons neglect
or pervert what it is their special duty and
office to guard; as when teachers corrupt
doctrine, or preachers give in to a low standard of morals, or judges pervert judgment.
The *princes* here spoken of are so named
from judging, "deciding[4]" causes. They are
the same as the *rulers,* whom Isaiah at the
same time upbraids, as being, from their sins,
rulers of Sodom[5], whose [6] *hands* were *full of
blood.* They who *do* not right, in time cease,
in great measure, to know it. As God withdraws His grace, the mind is darkened and
can no longer see it. So it is said of Eli's
sons, they[7] *were sons of Belial, they knew
not the Lord;* and, [8] *Into a malicious soul Wisdom shall not enter, nor dwell in a body that is
subject unto sin.* Such "[9] attain not to know
the judgments of God which are *a great deep:*
and the depth of His justice the evil mind
findeth not." But if men will not *know judgment* by doing it, they shall by suffering it.
2. *Who hate the good and love the evil;* i. e.
they hate, for its own sake, *that* which is good,
and love *that* which is evil. The Prophet is
not here speaking of their *hating good* men,
or *loving evil* men, but of their hating *goodness*
and loving *wickedness*[10]. "[9] It is sin not to
love good; what guilt to hate it! it is faulty,
not to flee from evil, what ungodliness to love
it!" Man, at first, loves and admires the
good, even while he doth it not; he hates
the evil, even while he does it, or as soon as
he has done it. But man cannot bear to be
at strife with his conscience, and so he ends
it, by excusing himself and telling lies to
himself. And then, he hates the truth or
good with a bitter hatred, because it disturbs
the darkness of the false peace with which
he would envelop himself. At first, men
love only the pleasure connected with the
evil; then they make whom they can, evil,
because goodness is a reproach to them: in

---

¹ 1–4.   ² 5–7   ³ 11.
⁴ קָצִין from קָצָה, "cut, decide," whence Cadhi.
⁵ The word is the same, Is. i. 10.

⁶ Ib. 15.   ⁷ 1 Sam. ii. 12.
⁸ Wisd. i. 4.   ⁹ S. Jer.
¹⁰ This appears from the Kethib רָעָה.

Before
CHRIST
cir. 710.

[d] Ps. 18. 41.
Prov. 1. 28.
Is. 1. 15.
Ezek. 8. 18.
Zech. 7. 13.

4 Then [d] shall they cry unto the LORD, but he will not hear them: he will even hide his face from them at that time, as they

have behaved themselves ill in their doings.

5 ¶ Thus saith the LORD [e] concerning the prophets that make my

Before
CHRIST
cir. 710.

[e] Is. 56. 10, 11.
Ezek. 13. 10.
& 22. 25.

the end, they love evil for its own sake [1]. Heathen morality too distinguished between the incontinent and the unprincipled [2], the man who sinned under force of temptation, and the man who had lost the sense of right and wrong. "[3] *Every one that doeth evil, hateth the light.* Whoso longeth for things unlawful, hateth the righteousness which rebuketh and punisheth [4]."

Who pluck off their skin from off them, and their flesh from off their bones. He had described the Good Shepherd ; now, in contrast, he describes those who ought to be "shepherds of the people," to feed, guard, direct them, but who were their butchers ; who did not shear them, but flayed them ; who fed on them, not fed them. He heaps up their guilt, act by act. First they flay, i. e. take away their outer goods ; then they break their bones in pieces, the most solid parts, on which the whole frame of their body depends, to get at the very marrow of their life, and so feed themselves upon them. And not unlike, though still more fearfully, do they sin, who first remove the skin, as it were, or outward tender fences of God's graces ; (such as is modesty, in regard to inward purity ; outward demeanor, of inward virtue ; outward forms, of inward devotion ;) and so break the strong bones of the sterner virtues, which hold the whole soul together ; and with them the whole flesh, or softer graces, becomes one shapeless mass, shred to pieces and consumed. So Ezekiel says [5]; *Woe to the shepherds of Israel that do feed themselves; should not the shepherds feed the flock ? Ye eat the fat and ye clothe you with the wool, ye kill them that are fed, ye feed not the flock. The diseased have ye not strengthened, &c.*

4. *Then shall they cry unto the Lord. Then.* The Prophet looks on to the Day of the Lord, which is ever before his mind. So the Psalmist, speaking of a time or place not expressed, says, [6] *There were they in great fear.* He sees it, points to it, as seeing what those to whom he spoke, saw not, and the more awfully, because he saw, with super-human and so with certain vision, what was *hid from their eyes.* The *then* was not then, *in the time of grace,* but when the Day of grace should be over, and the Day of Judgment should be

come. So of that day, when judgment should set in, God says in Jeremiah [7], *Behold I will bring evil upon them which they shall not be able to go forth of, and they will cry unto Me, and I will not hearken unto them.* And David [8], *They cried and there was none to save ; unto the Lord, and He answered them not.* And Solomon [9]; *Whoso stoppeth his ears at the cry of the poor, he shall cry himself and shall not be heard.* And St. James [10], *He shall have judgment without mercy, that hath shewed no mercy.* The prayer is never too late, until judgment comes [11]; the day of grace is over, when the time of judgment has arrived. "They shall cry unto the Lord, and shall not be heard, because they too did not hear those who asked them, and the Lord shall turn His Face from them, because they too turned their face from those who prayed them."

He will even hide His Face. He will not look in mercy on those who would not receive His look of grace. *Your sins,* He says by Isaiah, *have hid His face from you, that He heareth not.* O what will that turning away of the Face be, on which hangs eternity !

As. There is a proportion between the sin and the punishment. [12] *As I have done, so God hath requited me. They have behaved themselves ill in their doings.* lit. *have made their deeds evil.* The word rendered *doings* is almost always used in a bad sense, *mighty deeds,* and so deeds with a high hand. Not ignorantly or negligently, nor through human frailty, but with set purpose they applied themselves, not to amend but to *corrupt their doings,* and make them worse. God called to them by all His *prophets, make good your doings*[13] ; and they, reversing it, used diligence to *make their doings evil.* "[14] All this they shall suffer, because they were not rulers, but tyrants ; not Prefects, but lions ; not masters of disciples, but wolves of sheep ; and they sated themselves with flesh and were fattened, and, as sacrifices for the slaughter, were made ready for the punishment of the Lord. Thus far against evil rulers ; then he turns to the false prophets and evil teachers, who by flatteries subvert the people of God, promising them the knowledge of His word."

5. *The prophets that make My people err,* flattering them in their sins and rebellions,

[1] Rom. i. 32.
[2] The ἀκρατής and ἀκόλαστος of Aristotle.
[3] S. John iii. 20.   [4] Dion.   [5] xxxiv. 2–4. add 5–10.
[6] Ps. liii. 5.   [7] xi. 11.   [8] Ps. xviii. 41.   [9] Prov. xxi. 13.
[10] ii. 13.   [11] See on Hos. v. 6. vol. i. p. 58.

[12] Judg. i. 7. "As the Jews speak 'measure for measure'." Poc. from Abarb.
[13] Jer. xxxv. 15. הֵיטִיבוּ מַעַלְלֵיכֶם ; here, הָרֵעוּ מַעַלְלֵיהֶם.
[14] St. Jer.

Before CHRIST cir. 710

people err, that ᶠbite with their teeth, and cry, Peace; and ᵍhe that putteth not into their mouths, they even prepare war against him :

6 ʰTherefore night shall *be* unto you, †that

ᶠch. 2. 11. Matt. 7. 15.
ᵍEzek. 13. 18, 19.

ʰIs. 8. 20, 22. Ezek. 13. 23. Zech. 13. 4. †Heb. *from a vision.*

ye shall not have a vision; and it shall be dark unto you, †that ye shall not divine; ¹and the sun shall go down over the prophets, and the day shall be dark over them.

Before CHRIST cir. 710.

†Heb. *from divining.*
¹Amos 8. 9.

---

promising that they shall go unpunished, that God is not so strict, will not put in force the judgments He threatens. So Isaiah saith ¹ ; *O my people, they which lead thee, mislead thee ;* and ², *the leaders of this people are its misleaders, and* they that are *led of them are destroyed.* And Jeremiah ³, *The prophets have seen for thee vanity and folly ; and they have not discovered thine iniquity to turn away thy captivity, and have seen for thee false burdens and causes of banishment.* No error is hopeless, save what is taught in the Name of God.

That bite with their mouths. The word ⁴ is used of no other biting than the biting of serpents. They were doing real, secret evil *while they cry,* i. e. *proclaim peace ;* they bit, as serpents, treacherously, deadlily. They fed, not so much on the gifts, for which they hired themselves to ⁵ *speak peace when there was no peace,* as on the souls of the givers. So God says by Ezekiel ⁶, *Will ye pollute Me among My people for handfuls of barley and for pieces of bread, to slay the souls that should not die, and to save the souls alive that should not live, by your lying to My people that hear your lies ?* *Because with lies ye have made the heart of the righteous sad, whom I have not made sad ; and strengthened the hands of the wicked, that he should not return from his wicked way, by promising him life—therefore ye shall see no more vanity nor divine divinations.* It was with a show of peace that Joab slew Abner and Amasa, and with a kiss of peace Judas betrayed our Lord.

And he that putteth not into their mouths, they prepare war against him, lit. *and* (i.e. forthwith ; it was all one ; bribes refused, war proclaimed,) *they sanctify war against him.* Like those of whom Joel prophesied ⁷, they proclaim war against him in the Name of God, by the authority of God which they had taken to themselves, speaking in His Name Who had not sent them. So when our Lord fed the multitude, they would *take*

¹ iii. 12.   ² ix. 16. (15, Heb.)   ³ Lam. ii. 14.
⁴ רשׁן Gen. xlix. 17. Num.' xxi. 8, 9. Prov. xiii. 32.

Eccl. x. 8, 11. Am. v. 19. ix. 3. Hence, Kimchi, "While they proclaim peace, and flatter the people, it is as if they bit it with the teeth." So A. E. also and Tanch. in Poc.

Him by force and make Him a king ; when their hopes were gone and they saw that His *Kingdom was not of this world,* they said, *Crucify him, crucify Him.* Much more the Pharisees, who, because He rebuked their covetousness, their devouring widows' houses, their extortion and excess, their making their proselytes more children of hell than themselves, said, *Thou blasphemest.* So, when the masters of the possessed damsel whom St. Paul freed, ⁸ *saw that the hope of their gains was gone,* they accused him, that he *exceedingly troubled their city, teaching customs not lawful to be received.* So Christians were persecuted by the Heathen as "⁹ hating the human race," because they would not partake of their sins ; as "¹⁰ atheists," because they worshiped not their gods; as "¹¹ disloyal" and "public enemies," because they joined not in unholy festivals ; as "unprofitable," because they neglected things not profitable but harmful. So men are now called "illiberal," who will not make free with the truth of God ; "intolerant," who will not allow that all faith is matter of opinion, and that there is no certain truth ; "precise," "censorious," who will not connive at sin, or allow the levity which plays, mothlike, around it and jests at it. The Church and the Gospel are against the world, and so the world which they condemn must be against them ; and such is the force of truth and holiness, that it must carry on the war against them in their own name.

6. *Therefore night shall be unto you, that ye shall not have a vision.* In the presence of God's extreme judgments, even deceivers are at length still ; silenced at last by the common misery, if not by awe. The false prophets had promised peace, light, brightness, prosperity ; the night of trouble, anguish, darkness, fear, shall come upon them. So shall they no more dare to speak in the Name of God, while He was by His judgments speaking the contrary in a way which all must hear. They abused God's gifts and long-suffering

⁵ Ezek. xiii. 10.   ⁶ Ib. 19, 22, 23
⁷ See on Joel iii. vol. i. p. 207.
⁸ Acts xvi. 19–21.
⁹ Tertullian, Apol. c. 10. and note k. Oxf. Tr.
¹⁰ Ib. c. 35. ad Scap. c. 2.
¹¹ Ib. 42, 43.

7 Then shall the seers be ashamed, and the diviners confounded: yea, they

† Heb. *upper lip.*

shall all cover their † lips;

8 ¶ But truly I am full of power by the spirit of

k Ps. 74. 9.
Amos 8. 11.

against Himself: they could misinterpret His long-suffering into favor, and they did it: their visions of the future were but the reflections of the present and its continuance; they thought that because God was enduring, He was indifferent, and they took His government out of His Hands, and said, that what He appeared to be now, He would ever be. They had no other light, no other foresight. When then the darkness of temporal calamity enveloped them, it shrouded in one common darkness of night all present brightness and all sight of the future.

"[1] After Caiaphas had in heart spoken falsehood and a prophecy of blood, although God overruled it to truth which he meant not, all grace of prophecy departed. [2] *The law and the prophets prophesied until John. The Sun of Righteousness went down over them, inwardly and outwardly, withdrawing the brightness of His Providence and the inward light of grace.*" So Christ Himself forewarned; [3] *Walk while ye have the light, lest darkness come upon you.* And so it has remained ever since. [4] *The veil has been on their hearts.* The light is in all the world, but they see it not; it arose to lighten *the Gentiles,* but they *walk on still in darkness.* As opposed to holiness, truth, knowledge, Divine enlightening of the mind, bright gladness, contrariwise darkness is falsehood, sin, error, blindness of soul, ignorance of Divine things, and sorrow. In all these ways, did the Sun go down *over them,* so that the darkness weighed heavily *upon them.* So too the inventors of heresies pretend to see and to enter into the mysteries of Christ, yet find darkness instead of light, lose even what they think they see, fail even of what truth they seem most to hold; and they shall be in night and darkness, being *cast into outer darkness;* [5] *sinning against the brethren, and wounding the weak conscience of those for whom Christ died.*

7. *They shall cover their lips,* lit. *the hair of the upper lip* [6]. This was an action enjoined on lepers [7], and a token of mourning [8]; a token then of sorrow and uncleanness. With their lips they had lied, and now they should cover their lips, as men dumb and ashamed. *For there is no answer of God,* as these deceivers had pretended to have. When all things shall come contrary to what they had

promised, it shall be clear that God did not send them. And having plainly no answer of God, they shall not dare to feign one *then.* "[9] Then not even the devils shall receive power to deceive them by their craft. The oracles shall be dumb; the unclean spirit shall not dare to delude." "[10] All this is spoken against those who, in the Church of Christ, flatter the rich, or speak as menpleasers, out of avarice, ambition, or any like longing for temporal good, to whom that of Isaiah [11] fitteth; *the leaders of this people* [they who profess to *lead* them *aright*] *mislead them, and they that are led of them are destroyed.*"

8. *And truly I,* [lit. *contrariwise I,*] i.e. whereas they shall be void and *no word in them, I am full of* (or *filled with*) power *by the Spirit of the Lord and of judgment and might.* The false prophets [12] *walked after their own spirit.* Their only power or influence was from without, from favoring circumstances, from adapting themselves to the great or to the people, going along with the tide, and impelling persons whither they wished to go. The power of the true prophet was inherent, and that by gift of *the Spirit of the Lord* [13]. And so, while adverse circumstances silenced the false prophets, they called forth the more the energy of the true, whose power was from Him in Whose Hands the world is. The adverse circumstances to the false prophets were God's judgments; to the true, they were man's refractoriness, rebellion, oppressiveness. *Now* was the time of the false prophets; *now,* at a distance, they could foretell hardily, because they could not yet be convicted of untruth. When trouble came, they went *into the inner chamber to hide* [14] themselves. Micah, amid *the wild tumult of the people* [15], was fearless, upborne by Him who controls, *stills,* or looses it, to do His Sovereign Will.

I am filled with power. So our Lord bade His Apostles [16], *Tarry ye, until ye be endued with power from on high* [17] : *ye shall receive power, after that the Holy Ghost is come upon you;* and [18] *they were all filled with the Holy Ghost.* The three gifts, *power, judgment, might,* are the fruits of the One Spirit of God, through Whom the Prophet was filled with them. Of these, *power* is always strength residing in the person, whether it be the *power* [19] or *might of wisdom* [20] of Almighty God Himself,

[1] Rup.
[2] S. Matt. xi. 13.
[3] S. John xii. 35.
[4] 2 Cor. iii. 15.
[5] 1 Cor. viii. 12.
[6] Kim.
[7] Lev. xiii. 45.
[8] Ezek. xxiv. 17, 22.
[9] S. Jer.
[10] Dion.
[11] iii. 12.
[12] Ezek. xiii. 3.
[13] The use of אֶת before רוּחַ יְיָ only, shews plainly

that the objects of the verb are כֹּחַ, מִשְׁפָּט, גְּבוּרָה, and that the אֶת is "with" "through," as in Gen. iv. 1.
[14] 1 Kgs. xxii. 25.
[15] Ps. lxv. 7.
[16] S. Luke xxiv. 49.
[17] Acts i. 8.
[18] Ib. ii. 4.
[19] Ex. xv. 6. xxxii. 11. Num. xiv. 17, &c.
[20] Job xxxvi. 5.

Before
C H R I S T
cir. 710.
the LORD, and of judg-ment, and of might, [1] to declare unto Jacob his transgression, and to Israel his sin.

[1] Is. 58. 1.

9 Hear this, I pray you, ye heads of the house of Ja-cob, and princes of the house of Israel, that abhor judg-ment, and pervert all equity.

Before
C H R I S T
cir. 710.

or *power* which He imparts [1] or implants [2]. But it is always power lodged *in* the person, to be put forth by him. Here, as in St. John Baptist [3] or the Apostles [4], it is Divine power, given through God the Holy Ghost, to accomplish that for which he was sent, as St. Paul was endued with might [5], *casting down imaginations and every high thing that exalteth itself against the knowledge of God, and bringing into captivity every thought to the obedience of Christ.* It is just *that*, which is so wanting to human words, which is so characteristic of the word of God, *power*. Judgment is, from its form [6], not so much discernment in the human being, as "the thing judged," pronounced by God, the righteous judgment of God, and righteous judgment in man conformably therewith [7]. It was what, he goes on to say, the great men of his people *abhorred* [8], equity. With this he was filled. This was the substance of his message, right judgment to be enacted by them, to which he was to exhort them, or which, on their refusal, was to be pronounced upon them to be executed upon them. *Might* is courage or boldness to deliver the message of God, not awed or hindered by any adversaries. It is that holy courage, of which St. Paul speaks [9], *that utterance may be given unto me, that I may open my mouth boldly, to make known the mystery of the gospel, for which I am an ambassador in bonds, that therein I may speak boldly, as I ought to speak.* So too, after the Apostles had been [10] *straitly threatened that they should speak no more in the Name of Jesus, all*, having prayed, *were filled with the Holy Ghost*, and spake *the word of God with boldness.* "[11] Whoso is so strengthened and arrayed, uttereth fiery words, whereby hearers' hearts are moved and changed. But whoso speaketh of his own mind, doth good neither to himself nor others."

So then, of the three gifts, *power* expresses the Divine might lodged in him; *judgment*, the substance of what he had to deliver; *might* or *courage*, the strength to deliver it in face of human power, persecution, ridicule, death.

"[12] These gifts the Prophets know are not their own, but are from the Spirit of God, and are by Him inspired into them. Such was the spirit of Elijah, unconquered, energetic, fiery, of whom it is said, [13] *Then stood up Elias as fire, and his word burned like a lamp.* Such was Isaiah [14], *Cry aloud, spare not, lift up thy voice like a trumpet, and shew My people their transgression and the house of Jacob their sins.* Such was Jeremiah [15]; *Therefore I am full of the fury of the Lord; I am weary of holding in. I have set thee for a trier among My people, a strong fort; and thou shalt know and try their ways.* Such was John Baptist, who said [16], *O generation of vipers, who hath warned you to flee from the wrath to come?* Such was Paul, who, when he [17] *reasoned of temperance, righteousness and judgment to come*, made Felix tremble, though unbelieving and ungodly. Such were the Apostles, who, when they had received the Holy Spirit, [18] *brake*, with a mighty breath, *ships* and *kings of Tarshish.* Such will be Elias and Enoch at the end of the world, striving against Anti-Christ, of whom it is said [19], *If any man will hurt them, fire proceedeth out of their mouth and devoureth their enemies.*"

9. *Hear this, I pray you.* The Prophet discharges upon them that *judgment*, whereof, *by the Spirit of God*, he was *full*, and which they *abhorred; judgment* against their perversion of judgment. He rebukes the same classes as before [20], *the heads* and *judges*, yet still more sternly. They *abhorred judgment*, he says, as a thing loathsome and *abominable* [21], such as men cannot bear even to look upon; they not only dealt wrongly, but they *perverted*, distorted, *all equity:* "[22] that so there should not remain even some slight justice in the city." *All equity;* all of every sort, right, rectitude, uprightness, straight-forwardness [23], whatever was right by natural conscience or by God's law, they distorted, like the sophists making the worse appear the better cause. Naked violence crushes

---

[1] Deut. viii. 18. Judg. xvi. 5. 9, 19.
[2] Deut. viii. 17. and passim.   [3] S. Luke i. 17.
[4] S. Luke xxiv. 49.   [5] 2 Cor. x. 5.   [6] מִשְׁפָּט.
[7] As in Prov. i. 3. Is. i. 21. v. 7.   [8] ver. 9.
[9] Eph. vi. 19, 20.   [10] Acts iv. 18, 31.
[11] Dion.
[12] Lap.   [13] Ecclus. xlviii. 1.   [14] lviii. 1.
[15] vi. 11, 21.   [16] S. Matt. iii. 7.
[17] Acts xxiv. 25.
[18] Ps. xlviii. 8.   [19] Rev. xi. 5.   [20] iii. 1.

[21] מַתְעִיבִים, one of the two strongest Hebrew words to express abomination, comp. תּוֹעֵבָה. [22] S. Jer.
[23] Frequent as the adj. יָשָׁר, "right, upright," is, the abstract יֹשֶׁר occurs here only in the O. T. The original force is "straight," "even," and hence "straight-forwardness, rectitude." The idea of "evenness" (which Ges. denies) belonged to the root in early times, the names of the two "plains," *Sharon*, and *Mishor* in Reuben (Deut. iii. 10. iv. 43.) being formed from it.

Before
CHRIST
cir. 710.

m Jer. 22. 13.
n Ezek. 22. 27.
Hab. 2. 12. Zeph. 3. 3.

10 ^m They build up Zion with ⁿ † blood, and Jerusalem with iniquity.

† Heb. *bloods.*

11 ^o The heads thereof judge for reward, and ^p the priests thereof teach for

Before
CHRIST
cir. 710.

o Is. 1. 23.
Ezek. 22. 12.
p Jer. 6. 13.   Hos. 4. 18. ch. 7. 3.

the individual; perversion of equity destroys the fountain-head of justice. The Prophet turns from them in these words, as one who could not bear to look upon their misdeeds, and who would not speak to them; *they pervert; building; her heads, her priests, her prophets;* as Elisha, but for the presence of Jehoshaphat, would not look on Jehoram, nor see him[1]. He first turns and speaks of them, as one man, as if they were all one in evil;

10. *They build up* [lit. *building, sing.*] *Zion with blood.* This may be taken literally on both sides, that, the rich built their palaces, "with wealth gotten by bloodshed[2]," by rapine of the poor, by slaughter of the saints," as Ezekiel says[3], *her princes in the midst thereof are like wolves, to shed blood, to destroy souls, to get dishonest gain.* Or by *blood* he may mean that they indirectly took away life, in that, through wrong judgments, extortion, usury, fraud, oppression, reducing wages or detaining them, they took away what was necessary to support life. So it is said[4]; *The bread of the needy is their life, he that defraudeth him thereof is a man of blood. He that taketh away his neighbor's living slayeth him, and he that defraudeth the laborer of his hire is a bloodshedder.* Or it may be, that as David prayed to God, [5] *Build Thou the walls of Jerusalem,* asking Him thereby to maintain or increase its well-being, so these men thought to promote the temporal prosperity of Jerusalem by doings which were unjust, oppressive, crushing to their inferiors. So Solomon, in his degenerate days, made the *yoke* upon his people and his *service grievous*[6]. So ambitious monarchs by large standing-armies or filling their exchequers drain the life-blood of their people. The physical condition and stature of the poorer population in much of France was lowered permanently by the conscriptions under the first Emperor. In our wealthy nation, the term poverty describes a condition of other days. We have had to coin a new name to designate the misery, offspring of our material prosperity. From our wealthy towns, (as from those of Flanders,) ascends to heaven against us "[7] the cry of 'pauperism' i.e. the cry of distress, arrived at a condition of system and of power, and, by an unexpected curse, issuing from the very development of wealth.

The political economy of unbelief has been crushed by facts on all the theatres of human activity and industry." Truly we *build up Zion with blood,* when we cheapen luxuries and comforts at the price of souls, use Christian toil like brute strength, tempt men to dishonesty and women to other sin, to eke out the scanty wages which alone our selfish thirst for cheapness allows, heedless of everything save of our individual gratification, or the commercial prosperity, which we have made our god. Most awfully was *Zion built with blood,* when the Jews shed the innocent Blood, that [8] *the Romans* might not *take away* their *place and nation.* But since He has said[9], *Inasmuch as ye did it not unto one of the least of these My brethren, ye did it not unto Me,* and, [10] *Saul, Saul, why persecutest thou Me?* when Saul was persecuting Christ's members, then, in this waste of lives and of souls, we are not only wasting the Price of His Blood in ourselves and others, but are anew slaying Christ, and that, from the self-same motives as those who crucified Him. [11] *When ye sin against the members, ye sin against Christ.* Our commercial greatness is *the price of His Blood*[12]. In the judgments on the Jews, we may read our own national future; in the woe on those through whom *the weak brother perishes for whom Christ died*[13], we, if we partake or connive at it, may read our own.

11. *The heads thereof judge for reward.* Every class was corrupted. One sin, *the root of all evil*[14], covetousness, entered into all they did. It, not God, was their one end, and so their God. *Her heads,* the secular authority, who [15] *sat to judge according to the law, judged,* contrary to the law, *for rewards.* They sat as the representatives of the Majesty of God, in Whose Name they judged, Whose righteous Judgment and correcting Providence law exhibits and executes, and they profaned it. To *judge for rewards* was in itself sin, forbidden by the law[16]. To refuse justice, unless paid for it, was unjust, degrading to justice. The second sin followed hard upon it, to judge unjustly, absolving the guilty, condemning the innocent, justifying the oppressor, legalizing wrong.

And her priests teach for hire. The Lord was *the portion and inheritance*[17] of the priest. He had his sustenance assigned him by God,

[1] 2 Kgs iii. 14.   [2] S. Jer.   [3] xxii. 27.
[4] Ecclus. xxxiv. 21, 22.   [5] Ps. li. 18.
[6] 1 Kgs. xii. 4.
[7] Lacordaire, Conférences, T. ii. p. 300.
[8] S. John xi. 48.   [9] S. Matt. xxv. 45.

[10] Acts ix. 4.   [11] 1 Cor. viii. 12.
[12] S. Matt. xxvii. 6.   [13] 1 Cor. viii. 11.
[14] 1 Tim. vi. 10.   [15] Acts xxiii. 3.
[16] Ex. xxiii. 8. Deut. xvi. 19.
[17] Num. xviii. 20. Deut. xviii. 2.

Before
CHRIST
cir. 710.

q Is. 48. 2.
Jer. 7. 4.
Rom. 2. 17.

hire, and the prophets thereof divine for money: q yet will they lean upon

the LORD, † and say, *Is* not the LORD among us? none evil can come upon us.

and, therewith, the duty to [1] *put difference between holy and unholy, and between clean and unclean, and to teach all the statutes,* which God had commanded. Their *lips* were to *keep knowledge* [2]. This then, which they were bound to *give,* they sold. But " [3] whereas it is said to the holy, [4] *Freely ye have received, freely give,* these, producing the answer of God upon the receipt of money, sold the grace of the Lord for a covetous price." Probably too, their sin co-operated with and strengthened the sin of the judges. Authorized interpreters of the law, they, to please the wealthy, probably misinterpreted the law. For wicked judges would not have given a price for a righteous interpretation of the law. The civil authorities were entrusted by God with power to execute the law; the priests were entrusted by Him with the knowledge to expound it. Both employed in its perversion that which God gave them for its maintenance. The princes obtained by bribery the misjudgment of the priests and enforced it; the priests justified the injustice of the Princes. So Arian Bishops, themselves hirelings [5], by false expositions of Scripture, countenanced Arian Emperors in the oppression of the faithful. " [6] They propped up the heresy by human patronage ; " the Emperors " [7] bestowed on " them their " reign of irreligion." The Arian Emperors tried to efface the Council of Nice by councils of Arian Bishops [8]. Emperors perverted their power, the Bishops their knowledge. Not publicly only but privately doubtless also, these *priests taught* falsely *for hire,* lulling the consciences of those who wished to deceive themselves as to what God forbade, and to obtain from His priests answers in His Name, which might explain away His law in favor of laxity or sin. So people now try to get ill-advised to do against God's will what they are bent on doing ; only they get ill-advised for nothing. One who receives money for giving an irresponsible opinion, places himself in proximate peril of giving the answer which will please those who pay him. " [9] It is Simony to teach and preach the doctrine of Christ and His Gospel, or to give answers to quiet the conscience, for money. For the immediate object of these two acts, is the calling forth of faith, hope, charity, penitence, and

other supernatural acts, and the reception of the consolation of the Holy Spirit; and this is, among Christians, their only value. Whence they are accounted things sacred and supernatural ; for their immediate end is to things supernatural; and they are done by man, as he is an instrument of the Holy Ghost."

" [10] Thou art permitted, O Priest, *to live* [11], not to luxuriate, from the altar. [12] *The mouth of the ox which treadeth out the corn is not muzzled.* Yet the Apostle [13] abused not the liberty, but [14] *having food and raiment,* was *therewith content ;* [15] *laboring night and day, that he might not be chargeable to anybody.* And in his Epistles he calls God to witness that he [16] *lived holily and* without avarice in the Gospel of Christ. He asserts this too, not of himself alone but of his disciples, that he had sent no one who would either ask or receive anything from the Churches [17]. But if in some Epistles he expresses pleasure, and calls the gifts of those who sent, the *grace* [18] *of God,* he gathers not for himself but for the [19] *poor saints at Jerusalem.* But these *poor saints* were they who of the Jews first believed in Christ, and, being cast out by parents, kinsmen, connections, had lost their possessions and all their goods, the priests of the temple and the people destroying them. Let such poor receive. But if on plea of the poor, a few houses are enriched, and we eat in gold, glass and china, let us either with our wealth change our habit, or let not the habit of poverty seek the riches of Senators. What avails the habit ·of poverty, while a whole crowd of poor longs for the contents of our purse ? Wherefore, *for our sake* who are such, *who build up Zion with blood and Jerusalem by iniquity, who judge for gifts, give answers for rewards, divine for money,* and thereon, claiming to ourselves a fictitious sanctity, say, *Evil will not come upon us,* hear we the sentence of the Lord which follows. *Sion and Jerusalem and the mountain of the temple,* i. e. the temple of Christ, *shall,* in the consummation and the end, when [20] *love shall wax cold* and the faith shall be rare [21], *be plowed as a field and become heaps as the high places of a forest ;* so that, where once were ample houses and countless heaps of corn, there should only be a poor cottage, keeping up the show

[1] Lev. x. 10, 11. add Deut. xvii. 10, 11. xxxiii. 10. Hag. ii. 11 sqq.
[2] Mal. ii. 7.   [3] S. Jer.   [4] S. Matt. x. 8.
[5] S. Ath. ag. Arians, i. 8. p. 191. and n. c. Oxf. Tr.
[6] Id. ii. 43. p. 341.
[7] Counc. Arim. § 3. p. 77.
[8] Pusey's Councils of the Church, p. 118–180, &c.

[9] Less de Justit. ii. 35. de Simonia Dub. 13. p. 389. L.
[10] S. Jer.   [11] 1 Cor. ix. 13.   [12] Ib. 9.   [13] Ib. 18.
[14] 1 Tim. vi. 8.   [15] 1 Thess. ii. 6. 2 Thess. iii. 8.
[16] 1 Thess. ii. 10.   [17] 2 Cor. xii. 17, 18.
[18] Ib. viii. 6. 7.   [19] Rom. xv. 26.
[20] S. Matt. xxiv. 12.   [21] S. Luke xviii. 8.

Before
C H R I S T
cir. 710.

ʳ Jer. 26. 18. ch. 1. 6.

12 Therefore shall Zion for your sake be ʳ plowed *as* a field, ˢ and Jerusalem shall become heaps, and ᵗ the

Before
C H R I S T
cir. 710.

ˢ Ps. 79. 1.   ᵗ ch. 4. 2.

of fruit which has no refreshment for the soul."

The three places, Zion, Jerusalem, the Temple, describe the whole city in its political and religious aspects. Locally, Mount Zion, which occupies the South-West, "had upon it the Upper city," and "was by much the loftier, and length-ways the straighter." Jerusalem, as contrasted with Zion, represented the lower city, "¹ supported" on the East by Mount Acra, and including the valley of Tyropœon. South of Mount Acra and lower than it, at the South Eastern corner of the city, lay Mount Moriah or the Mount of the Lord's House, separated at this time from Mount Acra by a deep ravine, which was filled up by the Asmonæan princes, who lowered Mount Acra. It was joined to the N. E. corner of Mount Zion by the causeway of Solomon across the Tyropœon. The whole city then in all its parts was to be desolated.

And her prophets divine for money. The word rendered², *divine*, is always used in a bad sense. These prophets then were false prophets, *her prophets* and not God's, which *divined*, in reality or appearance, giving the answer which their employers, the rich men, wanted, as if it were an answer from God. ³ Yet they also *judge for rewards,* who look rather to the earthly than to the spiritual good ; they *teach for hire,* who seek in the first place the things of this world, instead of teaching for the glory of God and the good of souls, and regarding earthly things in the second place only, as the support of life.

And say, Is not the Lord among us ? And after all this, not understanding their sin, as though by their guilt they purchased the love of God, they said in their impenitence, that they were judges, prophets, priests, of God. *They do all this,* and yet *lean on the Lord ;* they stay and trust, not in themselves, but in God ; good in itself, had not they been evil ! *And say, Is not the Lord among us ? none evil can [shall] come upon us.* So Jeremiah says ⁴, *Trust ye not in lying words saying, The temple of the Lord, the temple of the Lord, The temple of the Lord are these.* " ⁵ He called them *lying words,* as being ofttimes repeated by the false prophets, to entice the credulous people to a false security" against the threatenings of God. As though God could not forsake His own people, nor cast away

Zion which He had *chosen for an habitation for Himself,* nor profane His own holy place ! Yet it was true that God *was among them,* in the midst of them, as our Lord was among the Jews, though they knew Him not. Yet if not in the midst of His people so as to hallow, God is in the midst of them to punish. But what else do we than these Jews did, if we lean on the Apostolic line, the possession of Holy Scripture, Sacraments, pure doctrine, without setting ourselves to gain to God the souls of our Heathen population ? or what else is it for a soul to trust in having been made a member of Christ, or in any gifts of God, unless it be *bringing forth fruit with patience ?* " ⁶ Learn we too hence, that all trust in the Merits of Christ is vain, so long as any wilfully persist in sin." " ⁶ Know we, that God will be in us also, if we have not faith alone, nor on this account rest, as it were, on Him, but if to faith there be added also the excelling in good works. For *faith without works is dead.* But when with the riches of faith works concur, then will God indeed be with us, and will strengthen us mightily, and account us friends, and gladden us as His true sons, and free us from all evil."

12. *Therefore shall Zion for your sake [for your sake shall Zion] be plowed as a field.* They thought to be its builders ; they were its destroyers. They imagined to advance or secure its temporal prosperity *by bloods ;* they (as men ever do first or last,) ruined it. Zion might have stood, but for these its acute, far-sighted politicians, who scorned the warnings of the prophets, as well-meant ignorance of the world or of the necessities of the state. They taught, perhaps they thought, that *for Zion's sake* they, (act as they might,) were secure. Practical Antinomians ! God says, that, *for their sake,* Zion, defiled by their deeds, should be destroyed. The fulfillment of the prophecy was delayed by the repentance under Hezekiah. *Did he not,* the elders ask ⁷, *fear the Lord and besought the Lord, and the Lord repented Him of the evil which He had pronounced against them ?* But the prophecy remained, like that of Jonah against Nineveh, and, when man undid and in act repented of his repentance, it found its fulfillment.

Jerusalem shall become heaps, [lit. *of ruins* ⁸,] and *the mountain of the house,* Mount Moriah, on which the *house of God* stood, *as the high*

¹ Jos. B. J. v. 4. 1.
² In Prov. xvi. 10. (quoted as an exception) it is used of that penetrating acuteness which is like a gift of divination ; as we speak of "divining a person's thoughts, purposes," &c.

³ From Dion.   ⁴ vii. 4.
⁵ Sanch.
⁶ J. H. Mich.
⁷ Jer. xxvi. 19.
⁸ עִיִּין from עָוָה, "distort, pervert, subvert."

mountain of the house as || the high places of the forest.

places of the forest, lit. *as high places of a forest.* It should return wholly to what it had been, before Abraham offered up the typical sacrifice of his son, a wild and desolate place covered with tangled *thickets* [1].

The prophecy had a first fulfillment at its first capture by Nebuchadnezzar. Jeremiah mourns over it; [2] *Because of the mountain of Zion which is desolate, foxes walk* [habitually [3]] upon it. Nehemiah said, [4] *Ye see the distress that we are in, how Jerusalem lieth waste;* and Sanballat mocked at the attempts to rebuild it, as a thing impossible; [5] *Will they revive the stones out of the heaps of dust, and these too, burned?* and the builders complained ; [6] *The strength of the bearers of burdens is decayed* [lit. *sinketh* under them], *and there is much dust, and we are not able to build the wall.* In the desolation under Antiochus again it is related ; [7] *they saw the sanctuary desolate, and the altar profaned, and the gates burned up, and shrubs growing in the courts, as in a forest or in one of the mountains.* When, by the shedding of the Blood of the Lord, they [8] *filled up the measure of their fathers,* and called the curse upon themselves, [9] *His Blood be upon us and upon our children,* destruction came upon them to the uttermost. With the exception of three towers, left to exhibit the greatness of Roman prowess in destroying such and so strong a city, they " [10] so levelled to the ground the whole circuit of the city, that to a stranger it presented no token of ever having been inhabited." He " *effaced* the rest of the city," says the Jewish historian, himself an eyewitness [11]. The elder Pliny soon after, A. D. 77, speaks of it, as a city which *had been* .

and was not. " [12] Where *was* Jerusalem, far the most renowned city, not of Judæa only, but of the East," " [13] a funeral pile." With this corresponds S. Jerome's statement, " [14] relics of the city remained for fifty years until the Emperor Hadrian." Still it was in utter ruins [15]. The toleration of the Jewish school at Jamnia [16] the more illustrates the desolation of Jerusalem where there was none. The Talmud [17] relates how R. Akiba smiled when others wept at seeing a fox coming out of the Holy of holies. This prophecy of Micah being fulfilled, he looked the more for the prophecy of good things to come, connected therewith. Not Jerusalem only, but well-nigh all Judæa was desolated by that war, in which a million and a half perished [18], beside all who were sold as slaves. "Their country to which you would expell them, is destroyed, and there is no place to receive them," was Titus' expostulation [19] to the Antiochenes, who desired to be rid of the Jews their fellow-citizens. A heathen historian relates how, before the destruction by Hadrian, " [20] many wolves and hyænas entered their cities howling." Titus however having left above 6000 [21] Roman soldiers on the spot, a civil population was required to minister to their wants. The Christians who, following our Lord's warning, had fled to Pella [22], returned to Jerusalem [23], and continued there until the second destruction by Hadrian, under fifteen successive Bishops [24]. Some few Jews had been left there [25]; some very probably returned, since we hear of no prohibition from the Romans, until after the fanatic revolt under Barcocheba. But the fact that when toward

[1] Gen. xxii. 13. סֻבך.   [2] Lam. v. 18.   [3] הלכו.
[4] Neh. ii. 17.   [5] Ib. iv. 2. [iii. 34. Heb.]
[6] Ib. 10. [iv. 4. Heb.]   [7] 1 Macc. iv. 38.
[8] S. Matt. xxiii. 32.   [9] Ib. xxvii. 25.
[10] Joseph. B. J. vii. 1. 1.   [11] Ib. vi. 9. 1.
[12] Nat. Hist. v. 14.
[13] Pliny says of Engedi, "Below these was the town Engadda, second only to Jerusalem in fertility and palm-groves, now a second funeral pile." [bustum] N. H. v. 18. See at length in Deyling de Æliæ Capit. Orig. in his Obss. sacr. v. 436–490. and on the whole subject Lightfoot, Chronicon de Excidio urb. Hieros. Opp. ii. 136 sqq. Tillemont, Hist. d. Emp. T. i. Ruine des Juifs ; T. ii. Révoltes des Juifs ; Munter, d. Jud. Krieg unt. Traj. u. Hadr. (translated in Dr. Robinson's Bibl. Sacr. T. iii. 1st series) who, however, gives too much weight to very late authorities. Jost, Gesch. d. Juden, B. xii.
[14] Ep. 129. ad Dard. fin.
[15] Pliny speaks of R. Jose (who lived before Hadrian) "praying in one of the ruins of Jerusalem," but only when on a journey. Berachoth, f. 3. The context implies that they were utter ruins.
[16] Gittin, f. 56. Jost, iii. 184. Anhang, p. 165.
[17] Maccoth, fin.   [18] Josephus' numbers.
[19] Jos. B. J. vii. 5. 2.   [20] Dio lxix. 14.
[21] " The tenth legion and some troops of horse and companies of foot." (Jos. Ib. vii. 1. 2.) The

legion was 6000 men; the troop, 64; the company, 100.
[22] Eus. H. E. iii. 5.
[23] S. Epiph. de Mens. c. 15. p. 171.
[24] Eus. H. E. iv. 5. "from written documents."
[25] Josephus makes Eleazar say in the siege of Masada, "Jerusalem has been plucked up by the roots, and the only memorial of it remaining is the camp of those who took it, still seated on its remains. Hapless elders sit by the dust of the temple, and a few women preserved by the enemy for the foulest insolence." B. J. vii. 8. The statement of S. Epiphanius (de Mens. 15. p. 170.) "in that part of Zion which survived after the desolation, there were both parts of dwellings around Zion itself and seven synagogues which alone stood in Zion as cabins, one of which survived till the time of Bishop Maximus and the Emperor Constantine, as a hut in a vineyard," is remarkably confirmed by the independent Latin statement of the Bourdeaux pilgrim. "Within the wall of Zion appears the place where David had his palace; and of seven synagogues, which were there, one only has remained, the rest are ploughed and sowed." Itin. Hieros. p. 592, ed. Wess. Optatus also mentions the 7 synagogues. (iii. 2. Edd. before Dupin, and all MSS. but one. See p. 53.) Before the destruction there are said to have been 480. Echa Rabbathi, f. 52. col. 2. f. 71. col. 4.

the close. of Trajan's reign they burst out simultaneously, in one wild frenzy[1], upon the surrounding Heathen, all along the coast of Africa, Libya, Cyrene, Egypt, the Thebais, Mesopotamia, Cyprus[2], there was no insurrection in Judæa, implies that there were no great numbers of Jews there. Judæa, aforetime the centre of rebellion, contributed nothing[3] to that wide national insurrection, in which the carnage was so terrible, as though it had been one convulsive effort of the Jews to root out their enemies[4]. Even in the subsequent war under Hadrian, Orosius speaks of them, as "[5] laying waste the province of Palestine, *once their own*," as though they had gained possession of it from without, not by insurrection within it. The Jews assert that in the time of Joshua Ben Chananiah (under Trajan) " the kingdom of wickedness decreed that the temple should be rebuilt[6]." If this was so, the massacres toward the end of Trajan's reign altered the policy of the Empire. Apparently the Emperors attempted to extinguish the Jewish, as, at other times, the Christian faith. A heathen Author mentions the prohibition of circumcision[7]. The Jerusalem Talmud[8] speaks of many who for fear *became uncircumcised*, and renewed the symbol of their faith

"[9] when Bar Cozibah got the better, so as to reign 2½ years among them." The Jews add, that the prohibition extended to the keeping of the sabbath and the reading of the law[10]. Hadrian's city, Ælia, was doubtless intended, not only for a strong position, but also to efface the memory of Jerusalem by the Roman and Heathen city which was to replace it. Christians, when persecuted, suffered ; Jews rebelled. The recognition of Barcocheba, who gave himself out as the Messiah[11], by Akibah[12] and " all the wise [Jews] of his generation[13]," made the war national. Palestine was the chief seat of the war, but not its source. The Jews throughout the Roman world were in arms against their conquerors[14]; and the number of fortresses and villages which they got possession of, and which were destroyed by the Romans[15], shews that their successes were far beyond Judæa. Their measures in Judæa attest the desolate condition of the country. They fortified, not towns, but "[16] the advantageous positions of the country, strengthened them with mines and walls, that, if defeated, they might have places of refuge, and communication among themselves underground unperceived." For two years, (as appears from the coins struck by Barcocheba[17],) they

[1] sub uno tempore, quasi rabie efferati. Oros. L. vii. B. P. vi. 437. " as if rekindled by some dreadful seditious spirit." Eus. H. E. iv. 2.
[2] Oros. Dio mentions Cyrene, Egypt, Cyprus; to these Eusebius adds Mesopotamia; also in S. Jer. Chron. A. D. 117.
[3] Abulfaraj (A. D. 1270.) mentions an *invasion* of Judæa by one whom the Egyptian Jews made their king; and whom " the Roman armies sought and slew with some ten thousands of Jews everywhere." (Hist. Ar. p. 120. Chron. Syr. p. 56.) He is too late to be an authority; but his account equally implies that there was no rebellion in Judæa.
[4] Dio speaks of their destroying 220,000 Romans and Greeks in Cyrene; committing much the same horrors in Egypt; destroying 240,000 in Cyprus. lxviii. 32. The Jews, ascribing this to Barcocheba, say that they destroyed " in Africa a great multitude of Romans and Greeks like the sand on the sea-shore innumerable," and in Egypt more than 200,000 men; and in Cyprus, so as to leave none. Zemach David, f. 27. 1. in Eisenmenger, Entd. Jud. ii. 655. (The coincidence is remarkable, but the statement is too late. to have any independent value.) Orosius says that " Libya was so desolated through the slaughter of its peasants, that, had not Hadrian re-colonized it, it would have remained empty." l. c.
[5] l. c. Sulpicius Severus in like way speaks of the Jews " wishing to rebel, essaying to plunder Syria and Palestine." ii. 4.   [6] Bereshith Rabba, c. 64.
[7] Spartian Hadrian, c. 14. It was repealed by Antonine. See Munter, § 26.
[8] Yebammoth, f. 9. 1. and R. Nissim. (See in Lightfoot, Chron. Opp. ii. 143.) Berachoth f. 16. 2. in Jost B. xii. Anhang n. 21.
[9] R. Nissim in Lightfoot, l. c.
[10] Jost xii. 9. p. 228.
[11] Eus. H. E. iv. 6. Zemach David, f. 27. in Eisenmenger, Entd. Jud. ii. 654. " He was called Bar Cocheba, because he interpreted, as said of himself, *a star shall arise out of Jacob, &c.* (Num. xxiv. 17.) Shalshalet hakkabbala (in De Voisin on Martini, Pug. Fid. p. 265.) Sanhedrin, Chelek. (Mart. p. 320.)
[12] " And R. Akibah himself, when he saw him, said of him, This is the king Messiah, as it is in the

Echa Rabbathi on the verse Lam. ii. 2." (Ib.) " He applied Hagg. ii. 6, 7. to him " (quoting v. 7. " *I will bring the desire of the nations to Jerusalem.*") Sanh. Chelek in Mart. See more of him Wolf, Bibl. Hebr. i. n. 1801. R. Bechai said, God revealed to him things unknown to Moses. (Ib.) See also Midrash Cant. in Mart. p. 320. Bartolocci, Bibl. Rabb. p. 274.
[13] Maimon. Yad Chazaka, Sanhedrin, c. 11. in Mart. p. 873. " R. Akiba and all the wise of his generation thought that he was the Messiah, until he was slain in his iniquities, and it was known that he was not." This was doubtless the ground of their death, mentioned in the Avoda Zara. See p. 128 sqq. F. C. Ewald, trans.
[14] " The Romans made no account of them at first, but when all Judæa was moved and all the Jews throughout the world were set in commotion and conspired and publicly and privately inflicted much evil on the Romans, and many foreigners helped them in hope of gain, and the whole world was shaken, Hadrian sent his best general against them." Dio Cass. lxix. 13.
[15] " 50 fortresses of much account and 985 very well-known villages." Dio C. (almost a contemporary) Ib. 14.   [16] Ib. 12.
[17] De Saulcy, Numismatique Judaique, p. 156–70. The coins bear the inscription " the 1st year of the redemption of Jerusalem," " the first " and " second year of the freedom of Jerusalem." Two of them are cast upon coins of Trajan and Vespasian. Ib. p. 162. The Abbé Barthélémi (App. to Bayer Num. Hebr. Sam. Vind. L. iii. p. ix.–xi.) mentions four of Trajan's, recast by Barcocheba. Bayer mentions coins of the 3d and 4th year, but anonymous. (Num. Hebr. Sam. p. 171.) De Saulcy supposes these to belong to the revolt against Vespasian. (p. 153, 4.) The title and the name "Simon" which probably Barcocheba took, were doubtless intended to recall the memory of the Maccabees. The Jerusalem Talmud speaks of money with the impress of Ben Coziba, (" son of a lie" as the Jews changed his name.) Lightfoot, Opp. ii. 143. Mr. Vaux, keeper of the coins, British Museum, tells me that these coins (of which some are in the British Museum) are certainly genuine. See also Madden, p. 161–182.

had possession of Jerusalem. It was essential to his claim to be a temporal Messiah. They proposed, at least, to "rebuild their temple [1]" and restore their polity." But they could not fortify Jerusalem. Its siege is just named [2]; but the one place which obstinately resisted the Romans was a strong city *near* Jerusalem [3], known before only as a deeply indented mountain tract, Bether [4]. Probably, it was one of the strong positions, fortified in haste, at the beginning of the war [5].

The Jews fulfilled our Lord's words [6], *I am come in My Father's Name and ye receive Me not; if another shall come in his own name, him ye will receive.* Their first destruction was the punishment of their Deicide, the crucifixion of Jesus, the Christ; their second they brought upon themselves by accepting a false Christ, a robber [7] and juggler [8]. "580,000 are said to have perished in battle [9]," besides "an incalculable number by famine and fire, so that all Judæa was made well-nigh a desert." The Jews say that "[10] no olives remained in Palestine." Hadrian "[11] destroyed it," making it "[12] an utter desolation" and "effacing all remains of it." "We read [13]," says St. Jerome [14], "the expedition of Ælius Hadrianus against the Jews, who so destroyed Jerusalem and its walls, as, from the fragments and ashes of the city to build a city, named from himself, Ælia." At this time [15] there appears to have been a formal act, whereby the Romans marked the legal annihilation of cities; an act esteemed, at this time, one of most extreme severity [16]. When a city was to be built, its compass was marked with a plough; the Romans, where they willed to unmake a city, did, on rare occasions, turn up its soil with the plough. Hence the saying, "[17] A city with a plough is built, with a plough overthrown." The city so ploughed forfeited all civil rights [18]; it was counted to have ceased to be. The symbolical act under Hadrian appears to have been directed against both the civil and religious existence of their city, since the revolts of the Jews were mixed up with their religious hopes. The Jews relate that both the city generally, and the Temple, were ploughed. The ploughing of the city was the last of those mournful memories, which made the month Ab a time of sorrow. But the ploughing of the temple is also especially recorded. S. Jerome says, "[19] In this [the 5th Month] was the Temple at Jerusalem burnt and destroyed, both by Nebuchadnezzar, and many years afterward by Titus and Vespasian; the city Bether, whither thousands of Jews had fled, was taken; the Temple was ploughed, as an insult to the conquered race, by Titus Annius Rufus." The Gemara says, "[20] When Turnus, [or it may be "when Tyrant] Rufus ploughed the porch," [of the temple.] Perhaps Hadrian meant thus to declare the desecration of the site of the Temple, and so to make way for the further desecration by his temple of Jupiter. He would declare the worship of God at an end. The horrible desecration of placing the temple of Ashtaroth over the Holy Sepulchre [21] was probably a part of the same policy, to make the Holy City utterly Heathen. The "Capitoline [22]" was part of its new name in honor of the Jupiter of the Roman Capitol. Hadrian intended, not to rebuild Jerusalem, but to build a new city under his own name. "[23] The city being thus bared of the Jewish nation, and its old inhabitants having been utterly destroyed, and

[1] S. Chrys. adv. Jud. v. 10. He does not apparently mean that they actually began it.
[2] Eus. Dem. Ev. ii. 38. vi. 18. The Samaritan Chronicle (c. 47. ed. Juynboll) gives an account of a siege by Adrian in which it mixes up fables and facts belonging to the siege of Titus, (which it omits,) but I do not see any traces of traditional fact.
[3] Eus. H. E. iv. 6.
[4] The Rev. G. Williams, (Holy City, i. 209–13,) has at once identified *Bether* with the name, *the mountains of Bether*, (Cant. ii. 17,) and ruins, "khirbet el yehûd," (ruins of the Jews) near the village still called Bittir near Jerusalem. (See Robinson's or Kiepert's map.) There are traces both of fortifications and excavations, such as Dio speaks of. *Bether* as well as *Bithron* beyond Jordan (2 Sam. ij. 29.) had their name from deep *incisions*. (See the use of בָּתַר, בְּתֵר, בֶּתֶר, Gen. xv. 10.)
[5] Dio Cass. lxix. 12.
[6] S. John v. 43.
[7] "given to murder and robbery." Eus. H. E. iv. 6. See Maimonides above, n. 13.
[8] S. Jer. Apol. 2. c. Ruf. §31. He pretended to breathe fire, a trick ascribed by Florus iii. 19 to Eunus, author of the servile war in Sicily. Vallars.
[9] Dio l. c.
[10] Talm. Jesus. Pea 7 in Lightfoot, l. c.
[11] Appian de reb. Syr. 50. "Jerusalem, which Ptolemy king of Egypt first destroyed: then, when

rebuilt, Vespasian razed to the ground, and again Hadrian, in my time."
[12] S. Chrys. l. c. §11.
[13] S. Jerome then took this statement from written history.   [14] in Joel i. 4.
[15] The Mishnah places it after the capture of Bether. "On the 9th of Ab, it was decreed against our fathers, that they should not enter the land; and the Temple was laid desolate the first and second time; and Bether was taken; and the city was ploughed." Taanith, c. 5. §6. Mishna ii. p. 382. ed. Surenhus. Rashi regards this as a fulfillment of Jer. xxvi. 18. and of this place. Ib. p. 383. col. 2. Buxtorf quotes also Yotseroth, (Jewish hymns,) c. Comm. f. 35. l. for the fact. Lex. Rabb. p. 916.
[16] Seneca de clem. i. 26. Deyl.
[17] Isidor. lxxv. 1. &c.
[18] "If the usufruct [annual produce] be left to a city, and the plough be passed over it, (as befell Carthage,) it ceases to be a city, and so by a sort of death it ceases to have the usufruct." Modestinus in l. Si usus fructus 21. ff quibus modis usus fructus amittatur. L.
[19] On Zech. viii. 16, 17. S. Jerome has the same order as the Talmud.
[20] Taanith, l. c. The Jerusalem Talmud has "the temple" for "the porch."
[21] Eus. Vit. Const. iii. 26. Socr. i. 17. Soz. ii. 1. S. Jer. Ep. 58, ad Paul. §3.
[22] Col. Æl. Capitol. i. 2. Colonia Ælia Capitolina.
[23] Eus. H. E. iv. 6.

an alien race settled there, the Roman city which afterward arose, having changed its name, is called Ælia in honor of the Emperor Ælius Hadrianus." It was a Roman colony [1], with Roman temples, Roman amphitheatres. Idolatry was stamped on its coins [2]. Hadrian excluded from it, on the North, almost the whole of Bezetha or the new city, which Agrippa had enclosed by his wall, and, on the South, more than half of Mount Zion [3], which was left, as Micah foretold, to be *ploughed as a field.* The Jews themselves were prohibited from entering the Holy Land [4], so that the heathen Celsus says, "[5] they have neither a clod nor a hearth left." Ælia, then, being a new city, Jerusalem was spoken of, as having ceased to be. The Roman magistrates, even in Palestine, did not know the name [6]. Christians too used the name Ælia [7], and that, in solemn documents, as the Canon of Nice [8]. In the 4th century the city was still called Ælia by the Christians [9], and, on the first Mohammedan coin [10] in the 7th century, it still bore that name. A series of writers speak of the desolation of Jerusalem. In the next century Origen addresses a Jew, "[11] If going to the earthly city, Jerusalem, thou shalt find it overthrown, reduced to dust and ashes, weep not, as ye now do." "[12] From that [Hadrian's] time until now, the extremest desolation having taken possession of the place, their once renowned hill of Zion— now no wise differing from the rest of the country, is cultivated by Romans, so that we ourselves have with our own eyes observed the place ploughed by oxen and sown all over. And Jerusalem, being inhabited by aliens, has to this day the stones gathered out of it, all the inhabitants, in our own times too, gathering up the stones out of its ruins for their private or public and common buildings. You may observe with your own eyes the mournful sight, how the stones from

the Temple itself and from the Holy of holies have been taken for the idol-temples and to build amphitheatres." "[13] Their once holy place has now come to such a state, as in no way to fall short of the overthrow of Sodom." S. Hilary, who had been banished into the East, says, "[14] The Royal city of David, taken by the Babylonians and overthrown, held not its queenly dignity under the rule of its lords; but, taken afterward and burnt by the Romans, it now is not." S. Cyril of Jerusalem, Bishop of the new town, and delivering his catechetical lectures in the Church of the Holy Sepulchre, pointed out to his hearers the fulfillment of prophecy; "[15] The place [Zion] is now filled with gardens of cucumbers." "If they [the Jews] plead the captivity," says S. Athanasius [16], "and say that on that ground Jerusalem is not." "The whole world, over which they are scattered," says S. Gregory of Nazianzum [17], "is one monument of their calamity, their worship closed, and the soil of Jerusalem itself scarcely known."

It is apparently part of the gradual and increasing fulfillment of God's word, that the ploughing of the city and of the site of the Temple, and the continued cultivation of so large a portion of Zion, are recorded in the last visitation when its iniquity was full. It still remains *ploughed as a field.* "[18] At the time I visited this sacred ground, one part of it supported a crop of barley, another was undergoing the labor of the plough, and the soil, turned up, consisted of stone and lime filled with earth, such as is usually met with in the foundations of ruined cities. It is nearly a mile in circumference." "[19] On the S. E. Zion slopes down, in a series of cultivated terraces, sharply though not abruptly, to the sites of the Kings' gardens.—Here and round to the S. the whole declivities are sprinkled with olive trees, which grow luxuriantly among the narrow slips of corn."

[1] Col. Æl. Capitol. i. e. Colonia Ælia Capitolina.
[2] See Roman coins in De Saulcy, p. 171-187. from Hadrian, A. D. 136, to Hostilian, A. D. 250.
[3] See Pierotti's excellent map of Jerusalem, (also reduced in his "Jerusalem explored." n. 3.)
[4] Eusebius, l. c. affirms this on the authority of Aristo of Pella, a contemporary; Tertullian says, "they are not permitted, even in the right of strangers, to greet their native land so much as with the sole of their foot." (Apol. c. 21. p. 45 Oxf. Tr. and adv. Jud. c. 13.) S. Jerome affirms the same. (on Is. vi. 11-13. and on Dan. ix. end.) Celsus urges the fact of their total expulsion as a proof of God's breach of promise; (in Orig. c. Cels. viii. 69.) and Origen agrees as to the fact. S. Justin speaks of their expulsion (as a nation) after their defeat, (Dial. c. 110.) so that, when he speaks of Jerusalem only, (Apol. i. 47.) it may have been that he spoke of it alone, as sufficing for the prophecy which he was explaining. The prohibition was subsequently limited to Jerusalem, with the well-known concession to behold it without entering, one day in the year, to weep. Itin. Hieros. p. 591. S. Hil. on Ps. 58. § 7. S. Jer. on Zeph. i. 15, 16, &c. Both S. Chrysostom and S. Augustine speak of the Jews, as excluded from Jerusalem. "Dost thou for thy sins, O Jew,

remain so long out of Jerusalem?" S. Chrys. adv. Jud. vi. 2. "They were excluded from the place where they crucified Christ; now that place is full of Christians who praise Him; it hath no Jew." S. Aug. in Ps. lxii. n. 18. "Now thou seekest a Jew in the city of Jerusalem, and findest not." in Ps. cxxiv. n. 3.
[5] L. c.   [6] Eus. de mart. Pal. c. 11.
[7] "In the suburbs of what is now Ælia." Eus. H. E. ii. 12. add. vi. 20. de mart. Pal. c. 11. (Deyl.)
[8] Can. vii.
[9] "From that [Hadrian's] time until now, it is called Ælia from the name of him who conquered and destroyed it." (S. Chrys. adv. Jud. v. 11 T. i. p. 645.) "Which is now Ælia." S. Jer. Ep. 129. ad. Dard. § 5.
[10] De Saulcy, p. 188.
[11] In Jos. Hom. xvii. 1. Opp. ii. 438.
[12] Eus. Dem. Ev. viii. 8. p. 406.
[13] Ib. v. 23. p. 250.   [14] S. Hil. in Ps. 131. § 18.
[15] Lect. xvi. 9. § 18. see Oxf. Tr.
[16] de Incarn. n. 39. T. i. p. 81. Ben.
[17] Orat. 6. § 18. Ben.
[18] Richardson's Travels, p. 359. quoted by Keith on Prophecy, p. 257.
[19] Porter, Hdbook, p. 92.

Before
CHRIST
cir. 710.

CHAPTER IV.

1 *The glory,* 3 *peace,* 8 *kingdom,*
11 *and victory of the church.*

BUT ^ain the last days it shall come to pass, *that* the mountain of the house

^a Is. 2. 2, &c.
Ezek. 17. 22, 23.

Not Christians only, but Jews also have seen herein the fulfillment upon themselves of Micah's words, spoken now "26 centuries ago."

IV. 1. But [*And*] in the last days it shall come to pass. God's promises, goodness, truth, fail not. He withdraweth His Presence from those who receive Him not, only to give Himself to those who will receive Him. Mercy is the sequel and end of chastisement. Micah then joins on this great prophecy of future mercy to the preceding woe, as its issue in the order of God's Will. *And it shall be.* He fixes the mind to some great thing which shall come to pass; *it shall be.* Then follows, in marked reference to the preceding privations, a superabundance of mercy. For *the mountain of the house,* which should be as a *forest* and which was *left unto* them *desolate,* there is *the mountain of the Lord's house established; for the heap of dust and the ploughed field,* there is the flowing-in of the Gentiles; for the *night* and *darkness,* that *there shall be no vision,* there is the fullness of revelation; for corrupt judgment, teaching, divining, a law from God Himself going forth through the world; for the building of Jerusalem with blood, one universal peace.

In the last days, lit. *the end* [1] *of the days,* i. e. of those days which are in the thoughts of the speaker. Politically, there are many beginnings and many endings; as many endings as there are beginnings, since all human polity begins, only to end, and to be displaced in its turn by some new beginning, which too runs its course, only to end. Religiously, there are but two consummations. All time, since man fell, is divided into two halves, the looking forward to Christ to come in humility; the looking forward to His Coming in glory. These are the two events on which man's history turns. To that former people the whole period of Christ's kingdom was one future, the fullness of all* their own shadows, types, sacrifices, services,

prophecies, longings, being. The *end of their days* was the beginning of the new Day of Christ: the coming of His Day was necessarily the close of the former days, the period of the dispensation which prepared for it. The Prophets then by the words, *the end of the days,* always mean the times of the Gospel [2]. *The end of the days* is the close of all which went before, the last dispensation, after which there shall be no other. Yet this too hast *last days* of its own, which shall close God's kingdom of grace and shall issue in the Second Coming of Christ; as the end of those former days, which closed the times of "the law," issued in His First Coming. We are then at once living in the *last times,* and looking on to a *last time* still to come. In the one way St. Peter speaks [3] of *the last times,* or *the end of the times* [4], *in* which *Christ was manifested for* us, in contrast *with the foundations of the world, before* which He *was foreordained.* And St. Paul contrasts God's [5] *speaking to the fathers in the Prophets,* and *at the end of these days* [6] *speaking to us in the Son;* and of our Lord coming [7] *at the end, consummation, of the times* [8]*, to put away sins by the sacrifice of Himself;* and says that the things which befell the Jews [9] *were written for our admonition, unto whom the ends of the times* [10] [i. e. of those of the former people of whom he had been speaking] *are come;* and St. John speaks of this as [11] *the last time.* In the other way, they contrast the *last days,* not with the times before them but with their own, and then plainly they are a last and distant part of this their own *last time.* [12] *The Spirit speaketh expressly, that in the latter times some shall depart from the faith:* [13] *In the last days perilous times shall come:* [14] *There shall come at the end of the days scoffers:* [15] *They told you that there should be mockers in the last time.* The Jews distributed all time between "this world" and "the coming world [16]," including under "the coming world" the time of grace under the Messiah's reign, and the future glory. To us the

---

[1] Gesenius adduces, as the single instance in which אַחֲרִית is to mean "sequel," Is. xlvi. 10, where "the end" answers to "the beginning," רֵאשִׁית אַחֲרִית. It is the *end* of the year, Deut. xi. 12; the *end* of a person, Pr. v. 4, Ps. xxxvii. 37; of a nation, Jer. xxxi. 17: of a thing, i. e. its issue, Pr. xxiii. 32; "the *end* of the sea," Ps. cxxxix. 9. The phrase is rendered rightly by the Ch. יוֹמַיָּא סוֹף. The ἐπ' ἐσχάτου τῶν χρόνων of S. Paul, S. Peter and S. Jude is nearly the translation of בְּאַחֲרִית הַיָּמִים.

[2] Hos. iii. 5. Is. ii. 2. Jer. xxiii. 20. xxx. 24. xlviii. 47. xlix. 39. Ezek. xxxviii. 16. Dan. x. 14. Daniel uses it in Chaldee. (ii. 28.) Nebuchadnezzar's dream which he is interpreting ended in the kingdom of Christ. On the Jewish agreement, see on Hos. iii. 5. p. 25. n. 10.

[3] 1 Ep. i. 20.

[4] According to the reading ἐπ' ἐσχάτου τῶν χρόνων, preferred by Alter and Tischendorf.

[5] Heb. i. 1.

[6] ἐπ' ἐσχάτου τῶν ἡμερῶν τούτων, preferred by Griesbach, Matthiæ, Scholz, Tisch.

[7] Heb. ix. 26.

[8] ἐπὶ συντελείᾳ τῶν αἰώνων, comp. S. Matt. xiii. 40.

[9] 1 Cor. x. 11.

[10] τὰ τέλη τῶν αἰώνων.

[11] 1 Ep. ii. 18.

[12] 1 Tim. iv. 1. ἐν ὑστέροις χρόνοις.

[13] 2 Tim. iii. 1. ἐν ἐσχάταις ἡμέραις.

[14] 2 Pet. iii. 3. ἐπ' ἐσχάτου τῶν ἡμερῶν, preferred by Griesb., Alter, Matthæi, Scholz.

[15] Jude 18. ἐν ἐσχάτῳ χρόνῳ or ἐπ' ἐσχάτου τοῦ χρόνου, preferred by Scholz, Tisch.

[16] עוֹלָם הַזֶּה and עוֹלָם הַבָּא. See Schöttg de Messia i. 2. 4. p. 23–27.

of the LORD shall be es-
tablished in the top of the
mountains, and it shall be

exalted above the hills;
and people shall flow
unto it.

names have shifted, since this present world [1]
is to us the kingdom of Christ, and there remains nothing further on this earth to look
to, beyond what God has already given us.
Our future then, placed as we are between
the two Comings of our Lord, is, of necessity,
beyond this world [2].
The mountain of the house of the Lord shall be
[abidingly] established. He does not say
merely, *it shall be established.* Kingdoms may
be established at one time, and then come to
an end. He says, *it shall be a thing estab-*
lished [3]. His saying is expanded by Daniel;
[4] In the days of these kings shall the God of
heaven set up a kingdom which shall not be de-
stroyed for ever, and it shall abide for ever. The
house of the Lord was the centre of His worship, the token of His Presence, the pledge
of His revelations and of His abiding acceptance, protection, favor. All these were
to be increased and continuous. The image
is one familiar to us in the Hebrew Scriptures. People were said to *go up* [5] to it, as
to a place of dignity. In the Psalm on the
carrying of the Ark thither, *the hill of God* is
compared to the many-topped mountains of
Basan [6], (the Hermon-peaks which bound
Basan,) and so declared to be greater than
they, as being the object of God's choice.
The mountain where God was worshiped
rose above the mountains of idolatry. Ezekiel, varying the image, speaks of the Gospel as an overshadowing cedar [7], *planted by*
God *upon an high mountain and an eminent, in*
the mountain of the height of Israel, under
which *should dwell all fowl of every wing;*
and, in his vision of the Temple, he sees this,
the image of the Christian Church, [8] *upon a*
very high mountain. Our Lord speaks of His
Apostles and the Church in them, as [9] *a city*
set upon a hill which cannot be hid. The seat
of God's worship was to be seen far and wide;
nothing was to obscure it. It, now lower
than the surrounding hills, was then to be as
on the summit of them. Human elevation,
the more exalted it is, the more unstable is
it. Divine greatness alone is at once solid
and exalted. The new kingdom of God was
at once to be *exalted above the hills,* and *estab-*
lished on the top of the mountains; exalted, at
once, above everything human, and yet
established, strong as the mountains on which

it rested, and unassailable, unconquerable,
seated secure aloft, between heaven, whence
it came and to which it tends, and earth, on
which it just rests in the sublime serenity of
its majesty.
    The image sets forth the supereminence of
the Lord's House above all things earthly.
It does not define wherein that greatness
consists. The flowing in of the nations is a
fruit of it [10]. The immediate object of their
coming is explained to be, to learn to know
and to do the will of God [11]. But the new
revelation does not form all its greatness.
That greatness is from the Presence of God,
revealing and evermore teaching His Will,
ruling, judging, rebuking, peacemaking [12].
" [13] The *mountain of the Lord's House* was then
exalted above the hills by the bodily Presence
of Christ, when He, in the Temple built on
that mountain, spake, preached, worked so
many miracles; as, on the same ground,
Haggai saith [14], *the glory of this latter house shall*
be greater than the glory of *the former.*"
" [15] This *mountain,* the Church of Christ,
transcends all laws, schools, doctrines, religions, Synagogues of Jews and Philosophers, which seemed to rise aloft among men,
like mountain-tops, yea, whatever under the
sun is sublime and lofty, it will overpass,
trample on, subdue to itself."
    Even Jews have seen the meaning of this
figure. Their oldest mystical book explains
it [16]. "*And it shall be in the last days,* when
namely the Lord shall visit the daughter of
Jacob, then shall *the mountain of the house of*
the Lord be firmly established, i. e. the Jerusalem which is above, which shall stand firmly
in its place, that it may shine by the light
which is above. (For no light can retain its
existence, except through the light from
above.) For in that time shall the light
from above shine sevenfold more than before; according to that [17], *Moreover the light of*
the moon shall be as the light of the sun; and the
light of the sun shall be sevenfold, as the light of
seven days, in the day that the Lord bindeth up
the breach of His people and healeth the stroke of
their wound." Another, of the dry literal
school, says [18], "It is well known that the
house of the Temple is not high. The meaning then is, that its fame shall go forth far,
and there shall return to it from all quarters

[1] S. Matt. xiii. 40. Eph. i. 21. Tit. ii. 12.
[2] S. Mark x. 30. S. Luke xviii. 30. xx. 35. Eph. l.
c. Heb. vi. 5. Attention to this language of Holy
Scripture and the distant future which it looks on
to, should have saved misbelievers from imagining
that Apostles erroneously expected a near end of
the world.
[3] יהיה נכון, as in 1 Kgs ii. 45, of the throne of

David. "It is an expression denoting continuance
and perpetuity, that it shall continually remain on
its settlement." Poc. from Abarb.
[4] ii. 44.   [5] See on Hos. i. 11. vol. i. p. 26.
[6] Ps. lxviii. 16, 17.   [7] xvii. 22, 23.   [8] xl. 2.
[9] S. Matt. v. 14.   [10] iv. 1, 2.   [11] iv. 2.   [12] iv. 3, 4.
[13] Dion.   [14] ii. 9.   [15] Lap.   [16] Zohar, f. 93.
[17] Is. xxx. 26.   [18] Aben Ezra.

2 And m a n y nations shall come, and say, Come,

and let us go up to the mountain of the LORD,

persons with offerings, so that it shall be, as if it were on the top of all hills, so that all the inhabitants of the earth should see it."

Some [1] interpret *the mountain* to be Christ, Who is called *the Rock* [2], on the confession of Whom, God-Man, *the house of the Lord,* i. e. the Church is built [3], *the precious Corner-stone* [4], which is laid, beside which *no foundation can be laid* [5]; *the great mountain,* of which Daniel [6] prophesied. It is *firmly established,* so that *the gates of Hell shall not prevail against the Church,* being built thereon; *exalted above hills and mountains,* i. e. above all beside, greater or smaller, which has any eminence; for He in truth is [7] *highly exalted and hath a Name above every name,* being [8] *at the Right Hand* of God *in the heavenly places, far above all principality and power and might and dominion, and every name that is named, not only in this world but also in that which is to come ;* and *all things are under His Feet.* And this for us, in that He, the Same, is *the Head over all things to the Church which is His Body, the fullness of Him that filleth all in all.* " [9] He is God and Man, King and Priest, King of kings, and a Priest abiding for ever. Since then His Majesty reacheth to the Right Hand of God, neither mountains nor hills, Angels nor holy men, reach thereto ; for [10] *to which of the Angels said God at any time, Sit thou on My Right Hand ?* "

" [11] Aloft then is the Church of God raised, both in that its Head is in heaven and the Lord of all, and that, on earth, it is not like the Temple, in one small people, but [12] *set on a hill that it cannot be hid,* or remain unseen even to those far from it. Its doctrine too and life are far above the wisdom of this world, shewing in them nothing of earth, but are above; its wisdom is the knowledge and love of God and of His Son Jesus Christ, and its *life is hid with Christ in God,* in those who are justified in Him and hallowed by His Spirit." In Him, it is lifted above all things, and with the eyes of the mind beholdeth (as far as may be) the glory of God, soaring on high toward Him Who is the Author of all being, and, filled with Divine light, it owneth Him the Maker of all.

And people, [peoples, nations,] *shall flow unto* [lit. *upon]* it. A mighty tide should set in

to the Gospel. The word [13] is appropriated to the *streaming in* of multitudes, such as of old poured into Babylon, the merchant-empress of the world [14]. It is used of the distant nations who should throng in one continuous stream into the Gospel, or of Israel streaming together from the four corners of the world [15]. So Isaiah foretells [16], *Thy gates shall be open continually ; they shall not be shut day nor night ; that they may bring unto thee the forces of the Gentiles, and that their kings* may *be brought.* These were to *flow upon it,* perhaps so as to cover it, expressing both the multitude and density of the throng of nations, how full the Church should be, as the swollen river spreads itself over the whole champaign country, and the surging flood-tide climbs up the face of the rock which bounds it. The flood once covered the highest mountains to destroy life ; this flood should pour in for the saving of life. " [17] It is a miracle, if waters ascend from a valley and flow to a mountain. So is it a miracle that earthly nations should ascend to the Church, whose doctrine and life are lofty, arduous, sublime. This grace of Christ effecteth, mighty and lofty, as being sent from heaven. As then waters, conducted from the fountains by pipes into a valley, in that valley bound up and rise nearly to their original height, so these waters of heavenly grace, brought down into valleys, i. e. the hearts of men, make them to bound up with them into heaven and enter upon and embrace a heavenly life."

2. *And many nations shall come.* Isaiah [18] added the world *all* to Micah's prophecy. So our Lord said, [19] *This Gospel of the kingdom shall be preached in all the world for a witness unto all nations ;* and the elect are to be gathered out *of all nations and kindreds and people and tongues* [20]. *All nations shall flow into it.* The *all* might be many or few. Both prophets say that those *all* should be many. Judah probably knew already of many. The history of Genesis gave them a wide-expanding knowledge of the enlargement of mankind after the flood, in Europe, Asia, Africa, as they then existed in their nations. The sons of Japhet had already spread over the whole coast of our Western sea, and far

---

[1] Tert. c. Jud. i. 3. Orig. c. Cels. ii. 33. S. Cypr. Test. ii. 18. Euseb. Ecl. Proph. iv. 1. p. 171. ed. Ox. S. Jerome here, S. Aug. de Civ. D. xviii. 30. Ps. Basil on Is.
[2] 1 Cor. x. 4–6.
[3] S. Matt. xvi. 18. see Note Q. on Tertull. p. 492 sqq. Oxf. Tr.
[4] Is. xxviii. 16. 1 Pet. ii. 6. Eph. ii. 20.
[5] 1 Cor. iii. 11.
[6] Dan. ii. 35.
[7] Phil. ii. 9.   [8] Eph. i. 20–23.

[9] from Rup.   [10] Heb. i. 13.
[11] from S. Cyr.
[12] S. Matt. v. 14.
[13] נָהַר (from נְהִי river, stream) is used only figuratively.
[14] Jer. li. 44.
[15] Ib. xxxi. 12. It is used in these places only, and Is. ii. 2.
[16] Is. lx. 11. add Rev. xxi. 25, 26.
[17] Lap.   [18] Is. ii. 2.
[19] S. Matt. xxiv. 14.   [20] Rev. vii. 9.

and to the house of the
God of Jacob; and he

will teach us of his ways,
and we will walk in his

North; the Cimmerians[1], or Cwmry, Scandinavians[2], Carpathians[3], (probably Celts,) Armenians[4], (including the kindred Phrygians,) Scythians[5], Medes, Ionians[6], Æolians[7], Iberians[8], Cypriotes[9], Dardani[10], Tybarenes[11], Moschi[12], and the Turseni[13], or perhaps the Thracians. On the East, the sons of Shem had spread in Elam, Asshur, Arrapachitis[14]; they occupied the intervening tract of Aram; in the N. W. they reached to Lydia. Southward the sons of Joktan were in Arabia. Micah's hearers knew how, of the sons of Ham, Cush had spread far to the S. E. and S. from Babylonia to Æthiopia; Egypt they remembered too well, and, beyond it, they knew of the far-scattered tribes of the Libyans, who extended along the coast of Africa. Phœnician trade filled up this great outline. They themselves had, in Solomon's time, traded with India[15]; about this time, we know that they were acquainted with the furthest East, China[16]. Such was the sight before the human mind of the Prophet; such the extent of the nations whom his people knew of. Some were the deadly enemies of his people; some were to be its conquerors. He knew that the ten tribes were to be abidingly *wanderers among the nations*[17], despised by them [18]; "a people, the strangers and sojourners of the whole world[19]." He knew many of those nations to be sunk in idolatry, viciousness; proud, contemptuous, lawless; he saw them fixed in their idolatries. *All people will walk every one in the name of his god.* But he saw what eye of man could not see, what the will of man could not accomplish, that He, whom now Judah alone partially worshiped, would turn the hearts of His creatures to Himself, to seek Him, not in their own ways, but as He should reveal Himself at Jerusalem. Micah tells them distinctly, that those who should believe would be a great multitude from *many nations.* In like way Isaiah expresses the great multitude of those for whom Christ should atone. [20] *He bare the sin of many.* [21] *By*

knowledge of Him shall My righteous Servant make many righteous. And our Lord Himself says; [22] *The Son of man came to give His life a ransom for many.* [23] *This is my Blood—which is shed for many for the remission of sins.* In Micah's time not one people, scarcely some poor fragments of the Jewish people, went up to worship God at Zion, to call to remembrance His benefits, to learn of Him. Those who should thereafter worship Him, should be *many nations.*

And say, exhorting one another, in fervor and mutual love, as Andrew exhorted his brother Simon, and Philip Nathanael, and the woman of Samaria those of her city, to come to Christ: and so all since, who have been won by Him, by word or example, by preaching or by deed, in public or in private, bear along with them others to seek Him Whom they themselves have found.

Let us go up, leaving the lowness and earthliness of their former conversation, and mounting upward on high where Christ is, desiring righteousness, and athirst to know His ways.

To the house of the God of Jacob. They shall seek Him as Jacob sought Him, "[24] who left his father's house and removed into another land, was a man of heavy toils and served for hire, but obtained special help from God, and, undistinguished as he was, became most glorious. So too the Church, leaving all Heathen wisdom, and having its conversation in Heaven, and therefore persecuted and enduring many hardships, enjoys now glory with God."

And He, i. e. *the God of Jacob* of Whom he had just spoken, *shall teach us of His ways.* They do not go to God, because they know Him, but *that* they *may* know Him. They are drawn by a mighty impulse toward Him. Howsoever attracted, they come, not making bargains with God, (as some now would,) what they should be taught, that He should reveal to them nothing transcending reason, nothing exceeding or contradicting their

which came with the creatures themselves; a Sanskrit name for elephant, *ibha,* שֶׁנְהַבִּים ivory,

---

[1] Gomer.
[2] Ashkenaz, Scandinavia, Scanzia in Jornandes. Knobel, Völkertafel d. Genesis, p. 35.
[3] Riphath, from whom also the Montes Riphæi are named.
[4] Togarmah.   [5] Magog.   [6] Javan.
[7] Elishah, Αἰολεῖς or Αἰλεῖς, Knobel; *Elis,* Boch. iii. 4.
[8] Tarshish. "Tarseis, whence the Iberians." Eus. (Tuch ad loc.)
[9] Chittim.   [10] Dodanim.   [11] Tubal.   [12] Meshech.
[13] Tiras, Tyrseni, (Tuch,) Thracians, Boch. iii. 2. Knob.
[14] Arphaxad, Gen. x. 22.
[15] As appears from the Tamul name for the peacock קֹף Tam. *tôgai* 1 Kgs x. 22; the Sanskrit or Malabar name for the ape, קוֹף *kapi;* (Ib. see Ges.)

lit. "elephant's tooth;" (Ib.) and a Malabar name for a wood, *al gum, val gu* (ka.) See Max Müller, Science of language, p. 205. ed. 3. Ophir itself, (which is mentioned in connection with these things,) Max Müller identifies, beyond question, with the Abiria of Ptolemy above Pattalene; the people, "called by Hindu Geographers *Abhira* and "the *Ahirs*" in "Macmurdo's account of the province of Cutch." Ib.
[16] Is. xlix. 12. see Gesenius Thes. p. 948–50.
[17] See on Hos. ix. 17. vol. i. p. 97.
[18] See on Hos. viii. 8. vol. i. p. 83.
[19] S. Greg. Naz. Or. 22. n. 2.   [20] Is. liii. 12.
[21] Ib. 11.   [22] S. Matt. xx. 28.
[23] Ib. xxvi. 28. add Rom. v. 15.   [24] Theoph.

paths: for the law shall go forth of Zion, and the word

of the LORD from Jerusalem.

notions of God; they do not come with reserves, that God should not take away *this* or *that* error, or should not disclose anything of His incomprehensibleness. They come in holy simplicity, to learn whatever He will condescend to tell them; in holy confidence, that He, the Infallible Truth, will teach them infallibly. They say, *of His ways.* For all learning is by degrees, and all which all creatures could learn in all eternity falls infinitely short of His truth and Holiness. Nay, in all eternity the highest creature which He has made and which He has admitted most deeply into the secrets of His Wisdom will be as infinitely removed as ever from the full knowledge of His Wisdom and His Love. For what is finite, enlarged, expanded, accumulated to the utmost degree possible, remains finite still. It has no proportion to the Infinite. But even here, all growth in grace implies growth in knowledge. The more we love God, the more we know of Him; and with increased knowledge of Him come higher perceptions of worship, praise, thanksgiving, of the character of faith, hope, charity, of our outward and inward acts and relations to God, the unboundedness of God's love to us and the manifoldness of the ways of pleasing Him, which, in His love, He has given us. Since then the whole Christian life is a growth in grace, and even St. Paul, [1] *forgetting those things which are behind and reaching forth to those which are before, pressed toward the mark for the high calling of God in Christ Jesus,* then St. Paul too was ever learning, in intensity, what he knew certainly by revelation, *of His ways.* Again, as each blade of grass is said to differ from another, so, and much more, each soul of man which God has created for Himself. No one ever saw or could imagine two human beings, in whom the grace of God had unfolded itself in exactly the same way. Each saint will have his distinct beauty around the Throne. But then each will have learnt *of His ways,* in a different proportion or degree. His greatest saints, yea His Apostles, have been pre-eminent, the one in one grace, another in another. St. John Baptist came as a pattern of repentance, and contempt of self; St John the Evangelist, stands out pre-eminent in deep tender burn-

ing personal love; St. Paul in zeal to spread the knowledge of Christ Crucified; St. Mary Magdelene in loving penitence. Even the Blessed Virgin herself, under inspiration, seems, in part, to speak of her *lowly lowness* [2], as that which God specially regarded in her, when He made her the Mother of God. Eternity only will set forth the fullness of the two words [3], *He will teach us of His ways.* For eternity will shew, how in all [4] *worketh that one and the self-same Spirit, dividing to every man severally as He will;* and how the countless multitude of the redeemed have corresponded to His gifts and drawings. " [5] The way of the life to God-ward is one, in that it looketh to one end, to please God; but there are many tracks along it, as there are many modes of life;" and each several grace is a part of the way to God.

And we will walk in His paths, " [6] by believing, hoping, loving, well-doing, and bearing patiently all trouble." " [7] For it sufficeth not to believe, unless we act as He commandeth, and strive to enter on His ways, *the strait and narrow path which leadeth unto life.* He Himself then, when He had said, [8] *Go, teach all nations, baptizing them in the Name of the Father, and of the Son, and of the Holy Ghost,* added, *teaching them to observe all things whatsoever I have commanded you.*" They say too, *we will walk,* i. e. *go on from strength to strength,* not stand still after having labored for a while to do His Will, but hold on to all His ways and to Himself Who is *the Way, until they appear before the Lord in Zion.*

For the law, [lit. *law* [9],] *shall go forth from Zion.* These are the Prophet's words, declaring why the nations should so flock to Zion. For he says, *shall go forth,* but the nations were not gathered to Zion, until the Gospel was already gone forth. He speaks of it as *law* simply, not *the* Jewish *law* as such, but a rule of life [10] from God. Man's better nature is ill at ease, being out of harmony with God. It cannot be otherwise. Having been made in His likeness, it must be distressed by its unlikeness; having been made by Him for Himself, it must be restless without Him. What they indistinctly longed for, what drew them, was the hope to be conformed by Him to Him. The sight of superhuman holiness, life, love, endurance, ever won and

---

[1] Phil. iii. 13, 14.
[2] S. Luke i. 48. ταπείνωσις in Prov. xvi. 19. LXX. is, "lowliness." The whole phrase ἐπέβλεψεν ἐπὶ τὴν ταπείνωσιν τῆς δούλης αὐτοῦ, corresponds more to the use in 1 Kgs (Sam.) i. 11. 2 Kgs xvi. 12. 2 Kgs xiv. 26. Neh. ix. 9. Ps. ix. 13. LXX. where the prominent sense is *low estate.* Perhaps, as in יָנְי, the two meanings are blended.
[3] יורנו מדרכיו. [4] 1 Cor. xii. 11. [5] Theoph.

[6] Dion. [7] Rup. [8] S. Matt. xxviii. end.
[9] תורה, not התורה.
[10] תורה is always *law,* not, as some have said, "religion," or "doctrine" generally. It is used without the article, in this sense, as rule of life, (Prov. vi. 23. xxviii. 4, 7, 9. xxix. 18.) such as the Heathen had not, (Lam. ii. 9.) but which should be revealed to them, (here, Is. ii. 3. li. 4.) The תורה corresponds with the יורנו.

3 ¶ And he shall judge among many people, and rebuke strong nations afar off; and they shall

wins those without to the Gospel or the Church. Our Lord Himself gives it, as the substance of Prophecy [1], *that repentance and remission of sins should be preached in His Name among all nations beginning at Jerusalem.* The image may be that of a stream, issuing forth from Jerusalem [2] and watering the whole world. "[3] The law of the Gospel and the word of the Apostles, beginning from Jerusalem, as from a fountain, ran through the whole world, watering those who approached with faith." But in that it *went forth*, it may be meant, that it left those from among whom it *went forth*, and "[4] Zion was indeed desolate of the law and Jerusalem bared of the Divine word." "[5] The word of God *passed* from Jerusalem to the Gentiles." "[6] For the shadow was done away, and the types ceased, and sacrifices were abolished, and everything of Moses was, in the letter, brought to a close."

He does not say here, through whom God would so teach, but he does speak of a direct teaching of God. He does not say only, "God will give us a law," or "will make a revelation of Himself." He speaks of a Personal, direct, continuous act of teaching by God, carried on upon earth, whether the teacher be our Lord's word spoken once on earth, which does *not pass away* [7], or God the Holy Ghost, as teaching in the Church and in the hearts which receive Him. The words which follow speak of a personal reign, as these speak of personal teaching.

3. *And He shall judge among many people and rebuke strong nations afar off.* Hitherto, they had walked each *in their own ways* [8]; now, they sought to be *taught in the ways of God.* Before, they had been lords of the world; now they should own a Judge higher than themselves. They were no common, but *mighty* [9] nations, such as had heretofore been the oppressors of Israel. They were to be many, and those mighty, nations. He should "[10] not only command, but *rebuke*, not weak or petty nations only, but mighty, and those not only near but afar." Mohammed had moral strength through what he stole from the law and the Gospel, and by his owning Christ as the Word of God. He was a heretic, rather than a heathen. Fearful scourge as he was, and as his successors have been, all is now decayed, and no *mighty nation* is left upon earth, which does not profess the Name of Christ.

He shall rebuke them; for it was an office of the Holy Ghost [11] *to reprove the world as to its sin, the righteousness* of Christ, *the judgment* of *the prince of this world.* The Gospel conquered the world, not by compromises or concordants, but by convicting it. It alone could *rebuke* with power; for it was, like its Author, all-holy. It could rebuke with efficacy; for it was the word of Him Who *knew what is in man.* It could rebuke with awe; for it knew the secrets of eternal Judgment. It could rebuke winningly; for it knew [12] *the love of Christ which passeth knowledge.* Its martyrs suffered and rebuked their judges; and the world was amazed at the impotence of power and the might of suffering. It rebuked the enthroned idolatry of centuries; it set in rebellion by its rebukes every sinful passion of man, and it subdued them. Tyrants, whom no human power could reach, trembled before its censures. Then only is it powerless, if its corrupted or timid or paralyzed ministers forfeit in themselves the power of rebuke.

And they shall beat their spears into ploughshares. "All things are made new in Christ." As the inward disquiet of evil men makes them restless, and vents itself toward others in envy, hatred, maliciousness, wrong, so the inward peace whereof He saith, *My peace I give unto you,* shall, wherever it reacheth, spread out abroad and, by the power of grace, bring to "[13] all nations unity, peace, and concord." All, being brought under the one empire of Christ, shall be in harmony, one with the other. As far as in it lies, the Gospel *is* a Gospel of peace, and makes peace. Christians, as far as they obey Christ, are at peace, both in themselves and with one another. And this is what is here prophesied. The peace follows from His rule. Where He judges and rebukes, there even the mighty *beat their swords into ploughshares.* The universal peace, amid which our Lord was born in the flesh, the first which there had been since the foundation of the Roman empire, was, in God's Providence, a fruit of His kingdom. It was no chance coincidence, since nothing is by chance. God willed that they should be contemporaneous. It was fitting that the world should be still, when its Lord, the Prince of peace, was born in it. That outward cessation of public strife, though but for a brief time, was an image how His peace spread backward as well as

[1] S. Luke xxiv. 47.
[2] See on Joel iii. 18. vol. i. p. 212.
[3] Theod.
[4] S. Cyr.
[5] S. Jer.
[6] Rup.
[7] S. Matt. xxiv. 35.
[8] Is. liii. 6.
[9] עַם, which originally signified bound together, (coll. Arab.) thence used of the closing of the eyes,

(Is. xxix. 10. xxxiii. 15.) included the idea of number. The secondary idea of strength, (as we use "well-knit,") is so prominent, that the idea of number, in the verb, only occurs in Ps. xl. 13. Jer. xv. 8; in the adj. Num. xxxii. 1.
[10] Rib.
[11] S. John xvi. 8-11.
[12] Eph. iii. 19.
[13] Litany.

beat their swords into b plowshares, and their

spears into || pruning-hooks : nation shall not

forward, and of the peace which through Him, our Peace, was dawning on the world. " [1] First, according to the letter, before That Child was born to us, [2] *on* Whose *shoulder the government is,* the whole world was full of blood ; people fought against people, kings against kings, nations against nations. Lastly, the Roman state itself was torn by civil wars, in whose battles all kingdoms shed blood. But after that, at the time of the Empire of Christ, Rome gained an undivided empire, the world was laid open to the journeys of Apostles, and the gates of cities were open to them, and, for the preaching of the One God, one single empire was formed. It may too be understood as an image, that, on receiving the faith of Christ, anger and unrestrained revilings were laid aside, so that each *putteth his hand to the plough and looketh* not *back,* and, breaking in pieces the shafts of contumelies, seeketh to reap spiritual fruit, so that, *others laboring, we enter into their labors ;* and of us it is said, *They shall come with joy, bringing their sheaves* [3]. Now no one fighteth ; for we read, [4] *Blessed are the peacemakers ;* no one learneth to [5] *strive, to the subverting of the hearers. And every one shall rest under his vine,* so as to press out that [6] *Wine which gladdeneth the heart of man,* under that [7] *Vine,* whereof the *Father is the Husbandman ;* and *under his fig tree,* gathering the sweet [8] *fruits of the* Holy *Spirit, love, joy, peace,* and the rest."

The fathers had indeed a joy, which we have not, that wars were not between Christians; for although "just wars are lawful," war cannot be on both sides just; very few wars have not, on both sides, what is against the spirit of the Gospel. For, except where there is exceeding wickedness on one side, or peril of further evil, the words of our Lord would hold good, in public as in private, [9] *I say unto you, that ye resist not evil.*

This prophecy then is fulfilled 1) in the character of the Gospel. " [10] The law of the Gospel worketh and preserveth peace. For it plucketh up altogether the roots of all war, avarice, ambition, injustice, wrath. Then, it teacheth to bear injuries, and, so far from requiting them, willeth that we be prepared to receive fresh wrongs. He saith, [11] *If any one smite thee on the right cheek, turn to him the other also, &c.* [12] *I say unto you, Love your enemies, &c.* For neither did the old law give

these counsels, nor did it explain so clearly the precept implied in them, nor had it that wonderful and most efficacious example of the patience and love of Christ, nor did it supply grace, whereby peace could be preserved ; whereas now the first fruits of the Spirit are *love, joy, peace, long-suffering, gentleness, goodness."* 2) The prophecy has been fulfilled within and without, among individuals or bodies of men, in body or mind, in temper or in deed, as far as the Gospel has prevailed. [13] *The multitude of them that believed were of one heart and of one mind ;* one, through One indwelling Spirit ; one, though a great multitude, through one bond of love. " [14] See how these Christians love one another ; " " see how ready they are to die for one another," was, in the third century, a heathen proverb as to Christian love. " [15] They love one another, almost before they know one another." " [16] Their first lawgiver has persuaded them that they are all brethren." "We (which grieves you,) " the Christian answered [17], "so love one another, because we know not how to hate. We call ourselves 'brethren' which you take ill, as men who have one Father, God, and are sharers in one faith, in one hope, coheirs." For centuries too, there was, for the most part, public peace of Christians among themselves. Christian soldiers fought only, as constrained by the civil law, or against Barbarian invaders, to defend life, wife, children, not for ambition, anger, or pride. Christians could then appeal, in fulfillment of the prophecy, to this outward, the fruit of the inward, peace. "We," says an early martyr [18], "who formerly stained ourselves with mutual slaughter, not only do not wage war with foes, but even, in order not to lie and deceive those who consume us, willingly professing Christ, meet death." " From the coming of the Lord," says another martyr [19], "the New Testament, reconciling unto peace, and a life-giving law, went forth into all lands. If then another law and word, going forth from Jerusalem, produced such peace among the nations which received it, and thereby *reproved much people* of want of wisdom, then it would follow that the prophets spake of some other. But if *the law of liberty,* that is, the law of God preached by the Apostles, which went forth out of Jerusalem to all the world, worked

[1] S. Jer.   [2] Is. i
[3] Ps. cxxvi. 6.   [4] S. Matt. v. 9.   [5] 2 Tim. ii. 14.
[6] Ps. civ. 15.   [7] S. John xv. 1.   [8] Gal. v. 22.
[9] S. Matt. v. 39.   [10] Rib.   [11] S. Matt. v. 39–42.
[12] Ib. 44–48.   [13] Acts iv. 32.
[14] Tertull. Apol. c. 39. "For they themselves hate one another." " For they themselves are more

ready to slay one another," are Tertullian's statements as to the contemporary condition of the Heathen, which their amazement at Christian love rather confirms.   [15] Minut. Felix, p. 81. ed. Ouz.
[16] Lucian. de morte Peregrini, i. 507. ed. Græv.
[17] Min. F. p. 312, 3.
[18] S. Justin M. Apol. i. 39.   [19] S. Iren. iv. 34. 4.

| Before CHRIST cir. 710. | lift up a sword against nation, °neither shall | they learn war any more. | Before CHRIST cir. 710. |

such a transformation, that swords and spears of war He wrought into plough-shares and pruning-hooks, instruments of peace, and now men know not how to fight, but, when smitten, yield the other cheek, then the prophets spake of no other, but of Him who brought it to pass." " Even from this," says Tertullian [1], "you may know that Christ was promised, not as one mighty in war, but as a peace-bringer. Either deny that these things were prophesied, since they are plain to see ; or, since they are written, deny that they are fulfilled. But if thou mayest deny neither, thou must own that they are fulfilled in Him, of Whom they are prophesied." "Of old [2]," says St. Athanasius, " Greeks and Barbarians, being idolaters, warred with one another, and were fierce toward those akin. For through their implacable warfare no one might pass land or sea, unarmed. Their whole life was passed in arms ; the sword was to them for staff and stay. They worshiped idols, sacrificed to demons, and yet from their reverence for idols they could gain no help to correct their minds. But when they passed into the school of Christ, then, of a truth, pricked in mind, they wondrously laid aside their savage slaughters, and now think no more of things of war ; for now all peace and friendship are alone their mind's delight. Who then did this, Who blended in peace those who hated one another, save the Beloved Son of the Father, the common Saviour of all, Christ Jesus, Who, through His love, endured all things for our salvation ? For of old too, the peace which should hold sway from Him was prophesied, *they shall beat their swords into ploughshares.* Nor is this incredible, since now too, the Barbarians with innate savageness, while they yet sacrifice to their idols, are mad with one another, and cannot for one hour part with their swords. But when they have received the teaching of Christ, forthwith for ever they turn to husbandry ; and, in lieu of arming their hands with swords, stretch them out to prayer. And altogether, instead of warring with one another, they arm themselves against the devil and demons, warring against them with modesty and virtue of soul. This is a token of the Godhead of the Saviour. For what men could not learn among idols, this they have learned from Him. Christ's disciples, having no war with one another, array themselves against demons by their life and deeds of virtue, chase

them and mock their captain the devil, chaste in youth, enduring in temptation, strong in toils, tranquil when insulted, unconcerned when despoiled."

And yet later, S. Chrysostom says, " [3] Before the Coming of Christ, all men armed themselves against this service, and cities fought with cities, and everywhere were men trained to war. But now most of the world is in peace ; all engage in mechanical art or agriculture or commerce, and few are employed in military service for all. And of this too the occasion would cease, if we acted as we ought and did not need to be reminded by afflictions." " [4] After the Sun of righteousness dawned, so far are all cities and nations from living in such perils, that they know not even how to take in hand any affairs of war.—Or if there be still any war, it is far off at the extremity of the Roman Empire, not in each city and country, as heretofore. For then, in any one nation, there were countless seditions and multiform wars. But now the whole earth which the sun surveys from the Tigris to the British isles, and therewith Lybia too and Egypt and Palestine, yea, all beneath the Roman rule,—ye know how all enjoy complete security, and learn of war only by hearsay." S. Cyril [5] and Theodoret [5] carry on this account into the fifth century after our Lord's Coming. Christians then during those four centuries could point to a present fulfillment of prophecy, when we, for our sins, can only speak of the past. [6] *The Lord's hand is not shortened, that it cannot save : neither His ear heavy, that it cannot hear ; but our iniquities have separated between us, and our God, and our sins have hid His Face from us, that He will not hear.* Those first Christians could urge against the Jews the fulfillment of their prophecies herein, where the Jews can now urge upon us their seeming non-fulfillment ; " [7] In the time of King Messiah, after the wars of Gog and Magog, there shall be peace and tranquillity in all the world, and the sons of men shall have no need of weapons, but these promises were not fulfilled." The prophecy is fulfilled, in that the Gospel is a Gospel of peace and makes peace. Christians, as far as they obey Christ, are at peace both in themselves and with one another. The promises of God are perfect on His part : He is faithful to them. But He so wills to be freely loved by His intelligent creatures whom He formed for His love,

---

[1] adv. Marc. iii. 21.
[2] de Incarn. Verbi Dei, c. 51, 2.
[3] in Ps. xliv. §3. T. v. p. 186.

[4] in Is. ii. n. 5. T. vi. p. 24, 5.
[5] on Is. ii. and here.   [6] Is. lix. 1, 2.
[7] R. Isaac, Munim. Fid. i. 5. 7. et all.

4 [d] But they shall sit
every man under his vine

and under his fig tree;
and none shall make *them*

afraid: for the mouth of
the L o r d of hosts hath
spoken *it*.

5 For [e] all people will

---

that He does not force our free-agency. We can fall short of His promises, if we will. To those only who will it, the Gospel brings peace, stilling the passions, quelling disputes, banishing contentions, removing errors, calming concupiscence, soothing and repressing anger, in individuals, nations, the Church; giving oneness of belief, harmony of soul, contentment with our own, love of others as ourselves; so that whatever is contrary to this has its origin in something which is not of Christ nor of His Gospel.

4. *But (And) they shall sit every man, under his vine and under his fig-tree.* Palestine was a home of the vine and the fig-tree. Vineyards were a common property, possessed by all but the very poor[1], or even by them[2]. The land was[3] *a land of bread and vineyards.* The vine was the emblem of the people, in Psalmists and Prophets[4]. The bunch of grapes or the vine-leaf appear as characteristic emblems on Jewish coins[5], chiefly in the times of their revolts under Vespasian and Hadrian[6]. The fig is also mentioned as part of the characteristic fruitfulness of Palestine[7]. It too was an universal property[8]. Both formed natural arbors; the fig had its name probably from its length[9], the vine from the arch made by its drooping boughs[10]. Both formed, in those hot countries, a grateful shade. The vine, rising with its single stem, was spread over trellis-work or by props, so as to enclose a considerable space[11]. Even in Italy, a single vine shaded a portico[12]. In Palestine it grew *by the walls of the house*[13]. Rabbins relate how their forefathers sat and studied under the fig-tree[14], as Nathanael was doubtless meditating or praying under one, when Jesus, being God, saw him[15].

[1] This is implied in the laws concerning them, as Ex. xxiii. 11. Lev. xix. 10. xxv. 3, 4. Deut. xx. 6, &c. comp. Num. xvi. 14. Deut. vi. 11. 1 Sam. viii. 14. xxii. 7. 2 Kgs. xviii. 32. Ps. cvii. 37. Prov. xxxi. 16.
[2] Neh. v. 4. Jer. xxxix. 10.   [3] 2 Kgs. xviii. 32.
[4] Ps. lxxx. 8 sqq. Is. iii. 14. v. 1 sqq. xxvii. 2. Jer. ii. 21, xii. 10. Ezek. xv. xvii. 5–10. xix. 10. Hos. x. 1.
[5] The bunch of grapes appears on coins of Herod Archelaus, Madden, Jew, Coinage, p. 94, 5. also of Tiberius, Ib. p. 144. See De Saulcy, p. 134. 140, 1. The golden vine, given by Alexander to the Romans is mentioned by Strabo. (Jos. Ant. 14, 31.) The vine-tree stood at the porch of the Temple for receiving alms. Middoth 3. 8. in Levy Jüd. Münz. p. 134. Madden,.p 210.
[6] Madden, p. 162, 4, 7, 8. 170, 2, 3, 7. 180. 206, 7, 8, 9. See also De Saulcy, p. 160, 1, 2, 4, 5, 6, 7, &c.
[7] Deut. viii. 8.   [8] 2 Kgs xviii. 32.
[9] תְּאֵנָה (its name still in the East) from יָאַן i. q. תָּנַן.   [10] גֶּפֶן i. q. גָּבַן.
[11] "We passed the evening, under a large vine, whose stem was about 1½ foot in diameter. Its height was 30 feet; its branches had to be propped

It exhibits a picture of domestic peace, each family gathered in harmony and rest under the protection of God, each content with what they have, neither coveting another's, nor disturbed in their own. Wine is explained in Holy Scripture to be an emblem of gladness, and the fig of sweetness[16]. "[17] For exceeding sweet is the word of the Saviour, and it knoweth how to gladden man's heart; sweet also and full of joy is the hope of the future, wherewith we are enriched in Christ.

Such had been Israel's lot in the peaceful days of Solomon[18], the peace of whose times had already been made the image of the Gospel[19]; the coming of the Queen *of the South from the uttermost parts of the earth, to hear the wisdom of Solomon*[20], had made her kingdom to be selected as an emblem of those who should *fall down before* Christ and *serve Him*[21]. "[22] Such is that most quiet fearlessness which the law of Christ bringeth, as being the law of charity, peace, and concord."

And none shall make them afraid. "[23] Neither man, nor devil; for the Lord hath given us power to [24] *tread on serpents and scorpions, and over all the power of the enemy,* and said, *nothing shall by any means hurt you,* and bade us, [25] *fear not them which kill the body.*" Witness the might which He gave to His Apostles and Martyrs.

For the mouth of the Lord of Hosts hath spoken it. The Prophets often add this, when what they say, seems, for its greatness, past belief. Yet it will be, because He hath spoken it, *the Lord* Who changeth not, *the Lord of Hosts,* to Whose commands all creatures are subject, Whose word is truth with Whom to speak is to do.

5. *For all people will walk, every one in the*

up; and so it covered an arbor more than 50 feet wide and long. I remembered Micah. I have seen in this land the people living under both the fig and the vine; the fig between Jerusalem and Arimathea; the vine, here [Beitjin.]" Schulz. Leit. v. 285. in Paulus Reisen, vii. 103.
[12] Plin. N. H. xiv. 3.   [13] Ps. cxxviii. 3.
[14] "R. Haia and his disciples—others say, R. Akiba, used to rise very early and sit and study under a fig-tree." Bereshith Rabba in Winer Reallex. [wrong reference.]
[15] S. John i. 48.
[16] Jud. ix. 11. 13. "The דְּבֵלָה is the fig, distinguished for its more perfect sweetness, so that none such can be found, save in the land of Israel." Maimonid. in Demai c. ii. § 1. in Cels. Hierob. ii. 369. "It is appropriated to the food of man." Id. de jure anni 7 et jubil. c. v. § 8. Ib. Our Lord made it, as well as the grape, the figure of good fruit, which an evil nature could not bear. S. Matt. vii. 16. S. Luke vi. 44.
[18] 1 Kings iv. 25.   [19] Ps. lxxii.   [20] S. Matt. xii. 42.
[21] Ps. lxxii. 10, 11.   [22] Lap.   [23] Theoph.
[24] S. Luke x. 19.   [25] S. Matt. x. 28.

walk every one in the name
of his god, and ' we will walk

in the name of the Lord
our God for ever and ever.

*name of his god, and we will walk in the name of
the Lord our God.* Hitherto unsteadfastness
had been the very characteristic sin of Israel.
It was "[1] constant only in its inconstancy,"
ever [2] *falling away like their forefathers, starting
aside like a broken bow.* The heathen persevered in their worship, because it was evil or
had evil in it, not checking but feeding their
passions. Israel did not persevere in his, because it required him to deny himself things
unlawful. [3] *Hath a nation changed their gods
which are yet no gods ? But My people have
changed their glory for that which doth not profit.*
Henceforth, the Prophet professeth for his
people, the true Israel, that he will be as
steadfast in good, as the heathen in evil; so
our Lord sets forth [4] *the children of this world
in their generation,* as an example of wisdom to
the children of light.

"[5] They who are eager to go up into the
mountain of the Lord, and wish to learn thoroughly His ways, promise a ready obedience, and receive in themselves the glories
of the life in Christ, and undertake with their
whole strength to be earnest in all holiness.
'For let every one,' he saith, 'in every
country and city go the way himself chooseth,
and pass his life, as to him seemeth good;
but our care is Christ, and His laws we will
make our straight path ; we will walk along
with Him ; and that not for this life only,
present or past, but yet more for what is beyond.' [6] *It is a faithful saying. For they who
now suffer with Him,* shall walk with Him
forever, and *with Him be glorified, and with
Him reign.* But *they* make Christ their care,
who prefer nothing to His love, who cease
from the vain distractions of the world, and
seek rather righteousness and what is pleasing
unto Him, and to excell in virtue. Such an
one was the divine Paul; for he writeth, [7] *I
am crucified with Christ; and now no longer I
live, but Christ liveth in me;* and again [8], *I determined not to know anything among you, save
Jesus Christ, and Him crucified.*"

To *walk* is so uniformly in Holy Scripture
used of a person's moral or religious "ways[9]"
(as we say), that the Prophet here too is
doubtless speaking of the opposite religious
ways of the Heathen and of the future people
of God. The *name* was often, in Hebrew, expressive of the character; and, in regard to

God Himself, that Name which He vouchsafed to give to Himself[10], expressed His
Self-existence, and, as a result, His Unchangeableness and His Faithfulness. The
names, by which it was foretold that Christ
should be called, express both His Deity and
attributes[11]; the human Name, which He
bare and vouchsafes to bear yet, was significant of His office for us, Saviour[12]. *To praise
the Name of the Lord* then, is to praise Him in
that character or relation which He has revealed to us. "[13] He *walketh in the Name of
the Lord,* who ordereth every act and motion
worthily of the vocation wherewith he is
called, and, [14] *whether he eateth or drinketh, doth
all to the glory of God.*" This promise hath its
own reward ; for it is *for ever and ever.* They
who *walk in the Name of the Lord,* shall *walk* [15]
*before Him in the land of the living, for ever and
ever.* Such walk on, with quickened steps,
lingering not, *in the Name of the Lord our God,*
i. e. doing all things in His Name, as His
great Name requires, conformed to the holiness and all other qualities which His Name
expresseth. *For ever and ever,* lit. *for ever and
yet,* or, more strictly still, *for that which is hidden and yet,* which is the utmost thought of
eternity we can come to. Time indeed has
no relation to eternity ; for time, being God's
creature, is infinite. Still, practically to us,
our nearest conception of eternity, is existence, on and on and on, an endless, unchanging, ever-prolonged future, lost in distance
and *hidden* from us, and then, *and yet,* an
ever-to-come *yet,* which shall' never come to
an end. Well then may we not faint, as
tho' it were long to toil or to do without this
or that, since the part of our way which lies
amid toils and weariness is so short, and will
soon be at an end; what lies beyond, in joy,
is infinite in infinite joy, ever full and still
ever a *yet* to come.

The Prophet says, *we will walk;* "[16] uniting himself in longing, hope, faith, to the sons
of the New Testament, i. e. Christians, as his
brethren, re-born by the grace of the same
Christ ;" "[17] ministers of the Old, heirs of
the New Testament, because they loved
through that same faith whereby we
love ; believing in the Incarnation, Passion,
Resurrection of Christ yet to be, as we believe in it, having been."

[1] Rib.　　　[2] Ps. lxxviii. 57.　　　[3] Jer. iii. 11.
[4] S. Luke xvi. 8.　　　　　　　　　[5] S. Cyr.
[6] 2 Tim. ii, 11, 12. Rom. viii. 17. Rev. iii. 4.
[7] Gal. ii. 20.　　　　　　　　[8] 1 Cor. ii. 2.
[9] As to *walk in God's statutes,* (Ezek. v. 6, 7, &c.
and seven other places) *in His judgments,* (Ps. lxxxix.
31. Ez. xxxvi. 27.) *in His commandments,* (2 Chr. xvii.
4.) *in His law,* (Ps. lxxviii. 10 &c.) *in His fear,* (Neh.
v. 9.) and, in the corresponding place in Isaiah, *in*

the light of the Lord. (Is. ii. 5.) see Ges. Thes. v. הלך.
p. 378. and above on Mic. ii. 11. p. 35.　So again to
walk with God, (Gen. v. 22.) or *before God,* (Ib. xvii.
1.) or *contrary to God.* (Lev. xxvi. 21.)
[10] יהוה See on Hos. xii. 5. vol. i. p. 119.
[11] Is. vii. 14. Immanuel, i. e. God with us; ix. 6.
Wonderful, Counsellor, Mighty God, &c.
[12] S. Matt. i. 21.　　[13] Theoph.　　[14] 1 Cor. x. 31.
[15] Ps. cxvi. 9.　[16] Tir.　[17] S. Aug. c. 2 Epp. Pelag. iii. 4.

Before
C H R I S T
cir. 710.

6 In that day, saith the LORD, ^g will I assemble her that halteth, ^h and I will gather her that is driven out, and her that I have afflicted ;

7 And I will make her

g Ezek. 34. 16.
Zeph. 3. 19.
h Ps. 147. 2.
Ezek. 34. 31.
& 37. 21.

that halted ⁱ a remnant, and her that was cast far off a strong nation : and the LORD ^k shall reign over them in mount Zion from henceforth, even for ever.

8 ¶ And thou, O tower

Before
C H R I S T
cir. 710.

i ch. 2. 12.
& 5. 3, 7, 8.
& 7. 18.
k Is. 9. 6.
& 24. 23.
Dan. 7. 14, 27.
Luke 1. 33.
Rev. 11. 15.

6. *In that day,* i. e. in that day of Christ and of His Gospel, of grace and salvation, *the last days* of which he had been speaking. Hitherto he had prophesied the glory of Zion, chiefly through the coming-in of the Gentiles. Now he adds, how the Jews should, with them, be gathered by grace into the one fold, in that long last day of the Gospel, at the beginning, in the course of it, and completely at the end[1].
Her that halteth. The Prophet resumes the image of the scattered flock, under which he had before[2] foretold their restoration. This was no hope of his own, but *His* word Who cannot fail. The course of events, upon which he is entering, would be, at times, for their greatness and their difficulty, past human belief. So he adds straightway, at the outset, *saith the Lord.* To *halt* is used of bodily lameness[3], and that, of a flock, worn out by its wanderings[4]. It is used also of moral halting[5], such as had been a chief sin of Israel, serving partly God, partly Baal[6]; God, with a service of fear, Baal with a service of that counterfeit of love, sensuality. So it was *sick,* both in body and soul, and *driven out*[7] also, and *afflicted.*
7. *And her that was cast off a strong nation.* The prophecy, that there should be a remnant, was depressing. Yet what a remnant should it be! A remnant, which should multiply like the stars of heaven or the sand on the sea-shore. Israel had never been a *strong nation,* as a kingdom of this world. At its best estate, under David, it had subdued the petty nations around it, who were confederated to destroy it. It had never competed with the powers of this world, East or West, Egypt or Nineveh, although God had at times marvelously saved it from being swallowed up by them. *Now,* the remnant of Judah, which itself was but a remnant of the undivided people, was to become *a strong nation.* So Isaiah prophesied, [8] *A little one shall become a thousand, and a small one a strong nation.* Plainly not in temporal greatness, both because human strength was not, and could not be, its characteristic, and be-

cause the Prophet had been speaking of spiritual restoration.
"[9] *Strong* are they, whom neither torture nor allurements can separate from the love of Christ." "Strong are they, who are strong against themselves." Strong were they who said [10], *We ought to obey God rather than men,* and [11], *Who shall separate us from the love of Christ? shall tribulation, or distress, or persecution, or famine, or nakedness, or peril, or sword?* Nay, in all these things we are more than conquerors through Him that loved us. God does not only restore in the Gospel ; He multiplies exceedingly. " [12] I will so clothe her with the spirit of might, that, as she shall be fruitful in number, so shall she be glorious in victories, so that of her it shall be said [13], *Who is she that looketh forth as the morning, fair as the moon, clear as the sun, terrible as an army with banners?*" For, not to name those, whose whole life is one warfare against invisible enemies and the evil desires of the flesh, who shall count the martyrs of Christ ? We know that that *remnant* and *strong nation* owe wholly to grace all which they are, as they themselves in the Revelations give thanks ; [14] *Thou wast slain and hast redeemed us to God by Thy Blood, out of every kindred and tongue and people and nation, and hast made us unto our God kings and priests, and we shall reign on the earth ;* that same Lord, of Whom it is here said, *The Lord shall reign over them in Zion from henceforth even forever.* The visible kingdom of God in Judah was often obscured, kings, princes, priests, and false prophets combining to encourage one another in rebellion against God. In the captivity it even underwent an almost total eclipse by the over-shadowing of earthly power, save when the Divine light flashed forth for an instant in the deeds or words of power and wisdom, related by Daniel. *Henceforth,* i. e. from the time, when *the law should go forth out of Zion,* God should *indeed* reign, and that kingdom should have no end.
8. *And thou, O tower of the flock.* " ' Tower of Ader,' which is interpreted ' tower of the flock,' about 1000 paces (a mile) from Beth-

1 Rom. xi. 26.   2 ii. 12, 13.   3 Gen xxxii. 32.
4 Zeph. iii. 19.
5 Ps. xxxv. 15. xxxviii. 18.
6 1 Kings xviii. 21. The word is different here.
7 נִדָּחָה is used with the same image of the dis-

persed flock, Zeph. iii. 19. Ez. xxxiv. 4. 16. and
הַדִּיחוֹן Jer. l. 17.
8 Ix. 22.   9 Gloss.   10 Acts v. 29.
11 Rom. viii. 35, 37.   12 Rup.   13 Cant. vi. 10.
14 Rev. v. 9, 10.

of ‖ the flock, the strong
hold of the daughter of
‖ Or, *Edar :* Gen. 35, 21.

Zion, unto thee shall it
come, even the first domin-

lehem," says St. Jerome[1] who lived there,
" and foresignifying [in its very name] by a
sort of prophecy the shepherds at the Birth
of the Lord." There Jacob fed his sheep[2],
and there (since it was hard by Bethlehem)
the shepherds, keeping watch over their flocks
by night, saw and heard the Angels singing,
"Glory to God in the highest, and on earth
peace, good will toward men." The Jews inferred from this place that the Messiah
should be revealed there[3].

Stronghold [Ophel[4]] *of the daughter of Zion.*
Ophel was a strong place in the South of
Jerusalem, the last which the wall, enclosing
Zion, reached, before, or as, it touched on the
Eastern porch of the temple[5], with whose
service it was connected. We know that,
after the captivity, the Nethinim, who did
the laborious service of the temple, dwelt
there[6]. It lay very near to the priests' district[7]. It was probably a lower acclivity,
"swelling out," (as its name seems to mean[8],)
from the mountain of the temple. In the
last war, it was held together with "[9] the
temple, and the adjoining parts to no slight
extent, and the valley of Kedron." It was
burnt[10] before the upper city was taken. It
had been encircled by a wall of old; for
Jotham "[11] built greatly *upon* its wall."
Manasseh "[12] encircled it," (probably with an
outer wall) "and raised it exceedingly," i. e.
apparently raised artificially the whole level.

Yet, as a symbol of all Jerusalem, Ophel
is as remarkable, as the " tower of the flock "
is as to Bethlehem. For Ophel, although
fortified, is no where spoken of, as of any account[13]. It is not even mentioned in the
circuit of the walls, at their dedication under
Nehemiah[14], probably as an outlying spot.
It was probably of moment chiefly, as giving,

an advantage to an enemy who might
occupy it.

Both then are images of lowliness. The
lonely Shepherd tower, for Bethlehem, the
birthplace of David ; Ophel for Jerusalem,
of which it was yet but an outlying part,
and deriving its value probably as an outwork of the temple. Both symbols anticipate
the fuller prophecy of the littleness, which
shall become great in God. Before the mention of the greatness of the *dominion to come,*
is set forth the future poverty to which it
should come. In lowliness Christ came, yet
is indeed a Tower protecting and defending
the sheep of His pasture, founded on earth
in His Human Nature, reaching to Heaven
in His Divine ; [15] *a strong Tower ; the righteous
runneth into it, and is safe.*

Unto thee shall it come ; (lit. *unto thee shall
it come* [16], *and there shall arrive* &c.) He saith
not at first what shall come, and so raises the
soul to think of the greatness of that which
should come. The soul is left to fill up what
is more than thought can utter. *Unto thee,*
(lit. *quite up to thee* [17].) No hindrances should
withhold it from coming. Seemingly it was
a great way off, and they in a very hopeless
state. He suggests the difficulty even by his
strength of assurance. One could not say, *it
shall come quite up to thee,* of that which in the
way of nature would readily come to any one.
But amid all hindrances God's Might makes
its way, and brings His gifts and promises to
their end. *And there shall arrive.* He twice
repeats the assurance, in equivalent words,
for their fuller assurance, "[18] to make the
good tidings the gladder by repeating and
enforcing them."

The first or *former, dominion.* The word
often stands, as our "former[19]," in contrast

[1] de loc. Hebr. Areulf A. D. 670 found "a Church
of the Shepherds," a mile from Bethlehem. Early
trav. in Pal. p. 6. The Migdal Edar is mentioned
also in the Mass. Shekalim c. 7. 4. " Of the herds,
in the space between Jerusalem and 'the tower of
the flock' and on both sides, the males are for
burnt-offerings, the female for peace-offerings. R.
Jehuda says, whatever male animals are found
(there) thirty days before the passover fit for it, are
to be used thereto." in Sepp. Heil. Land. ii. 470.
[2] Gen. xxxv. 21.
[3] Ps. Jon. on Gen. xxxv. 21. " This is the place,
where in the last days Messiah shall be revealed."
[4] Ophel, like many other Hebrew Proper names,
did not lose its original appellative meaning, and
so in the 6 places, where it occurs in the prose
books, keeps the article ; 2 Chron. xxvii. 3. xxxiii.
14. Neh. iii. 26, 7. xi. 21. and 2 Kings v. 24. in which
last place it may very possibly be a place in Samaria, named after that in Jerusalem. It occurs without the art. here and Is. xxxii. 14. and in Josephus,
'Οφλᾶς. The E. V. retains the word as a Proper
name in the historical books, 2 Chron. and Neh.
[5] " The oldest wall was hard to be taken on account of the ravines, and the ridge above them on

which it was built.—On the West—turning to the S.
over the pool of Siloam, and then again bending
Eastward to Solomon's pool, and extending to a
place which they call Ophlas, it was joined on to the
Eastern porch of the temple." Jos. B. J. v. 4. 2.
[6] Neh. iii. 26. xi. 21.   [7] Ib. iii. 28.
[8] Like *tumulus* from *tumeo.* Fürst. It is used of
a local tumor in Arab. and in Deut. xxviii. 27. 1 Sam.
v. 6. 12. vi. 4. 5. and of the swelling of pride. Num.
xiv. 44. Hab. ii. 4.   [9] by John. Jos. B. J. v. 6. 1.
[10] Together with "the archive, Acra, the Council-
hall." Ib. vi. 6. 3. after the destruction of the temple.
Ib. vi. 4. 5–7.   [11] 2 Chron. xxvii. 3.   [12] Ib. xxxiii. 14.
[13] Josephus calls it, "that which was called Ophlas."
B. J. v. 4. 2. vi. 6. 3.
[14] Neh. xii. 31–40.   [15] Prov. xviii. 10.
[16] The Masorethes seem rightly to have marked
this by the accents.   [17] עָדַיִךְ.   [18] Rup.
[19] So, the *former* time, (Is. viii. 23.) *deeds,* (2 Chron.
ix. 29. xvi. 11, xx. 34,) *king,* (Num. xxvi. 26,)
tables, (Ex. xxxiv. 1.) *benefits,* (Ps. lxxxix. 50.) *days,*
(Deut. iv. 32, x. 10.) *kings,* (Jer. xxxiv. 5,) *prophets,*
(Zech. i. 4, vii. 7. 12.) *temple,* (Ezr. iii. 12. Hagg. ii. 3.
9.) See Ges. Thes. p. 1251.

Before CHRIST cir. 710.

ion; the kingdom **shall** come to the daughter of Jerusalem.

9 Now why dost thou cry out aloud? [1] *is there* no king in thee? is thy counsellor perished? for [m] pangs have taken thee as a woman in travail.

[1] Jer. 8. 19.

[m] Is. 13. 8. & 21. 3. Jer. 30. 6. & 50. 43.

10 Be in pain, and labor to bring forth, O daughter of Zion, like a woman in travail: for now shalt thou go forth out of the city, and thou shalt dwell in the field, and thou shalt go *even* to Babylon; there shalt thou be de-

Before CHRIST cir. 710.

---

with the "later." It is not necessarily the *first*, strictly; and so here, not the *dominion* of David and Solomon exclusively. Rather the Prophet is placed in spirit in the later times when the kingdom should be suspended, and foretells that *the former dominion*, i. e. that of the line of David, should come to her, not in its temporal greatness, but the line itself. So the Angel said, [1] *He shall be great and shall be called the Son of the Highest, and the Lord God shall give unto Him the throne of His father David, and He shall reign over the house of Jacob for ever.*

The [A] *kingdom to the daughter of Jerusalem*, i. e. a kingdom, which should not be *of* her, but which should come *to* her; not her's by right, but by *His* right, Who should merit it for her, and, being King of kings, makes His own, [2] *kings and priests unto God and His Father.*

The Jews themselves seem to have taken these words into their own mouths, just before they rejected Him, when they hoped that He would be a king, such as they wished for. [3] *Blessed be the kingdom of our father David that cometh in the Name of the Lord.* And in a distorted form, they held it even afterward [4].

9. *Now.* The prophet places himself in the midst of their deepest sorrows, and out of them he promises comfort. *Why dost thou cry out aloud? is there no King in thee? is thy Counsellor perished*[5]? Is then all lost, because thou hast no visible king, none to counsel thee or consult for thee[5]? Very remarkably he speaks of their *King* and *Counsellor* as one, as if to say, "When all beside is gone, there is One Who abides. Though thou be a captive, God will not forsake thee. When thou hadst no earthly king, [6] *the Lord thy God* was *thy King.* He is the First, and He is the Last. When thou shalt have no other, He, thy King, ceaseth not to be." "[7] Thou

shouldest not fear, so long as He, Who counselleth for thee, liveth; but He liveth for ever." Thy *Counsellor*, He, Who is called [8] *Counsellor*, Who counselleth for thee, Who counselleth thee, will, if thou obey His counsel, make birth-pangs to end in joy.

For pangs have taken thee, as a woman in travail, resistless, remediless, doubling the whole frame, redoubled until the end, for which God sends them, is accomplished, and then ceasing in joy. The truest comfort, amid all sorrow, is in owning that the travail-pains must be, but that the reward shall be afterward. "[7] It is meet to look for deliverance from God's mercy, as certainly as for punishment from our guilt; and that the more, since He who foretold both, willingly saves, punishes unwillingly." So the prophets adds.

10. *Be in pain, and labor to bring forth*, (lit. *Writhe and burst forth*,) as if to say, "thou *must* suffer, but thy suffering and thy joy shall be one. Thou canst not have the joy without the suffering. As surely as thou sufferest, thou shalt have joy. In all sorrow, lose not faith and hope, and [9] *thou shalt be sorrowful, but thy sorrow shall be turned into joy.*" "[10] Good daughter, be very patient in the pangs, bear up against your sorrows," so shall the birth be nigh. Yet for the time she must *go forth out of the city* into captivity. *And thou shalt dwell in the field*, houseless, under tents, as captives were wont to be kept, until all were gathered together to be led away; a sore exchange for her former luxury, and in requital of their oppression[11].

And thou shalt go even to Babylon. Not Babylon, but Assyria was the scourge of God in Micah's time. Babylon was scarcely known, *a far country*[12]. Yet Micah is taught of God to declare that thither shall the two tribes be carried captive, although the ten

[1] S. Luke 1. 32, 3.   [2] Rev. i. 6.
[3] S. Mark xi. 10.
[4] Targ. "And thou, O Messiah of Israel, who art hid on account of the sins of the congregation of Israel, to thee the kingdom will come," giving to עֹפֶל the sense of אֹפֶל. (as in the LXX. Vulg. Aq. Symm. Syr.) and thence obtaining the sense

"hidden," in reference to their fable that He was born before the destruction of the temple and hidden by God.
[5] Comp. Hos. xiii. 10.   [6] 1 Sam. xii. 12.
[7] Mont.   [8] Is. ix. 6.
[9] S. John xvi. 20.
[10] S. Cyr.   [11] Am. vi. Micah ii. 8, 9.
[12] 2 Kings xx. 14.

Before
CHRIST
cir. 710.

livered; there the LORD
shall redeem thee from the
hand of thine enemies.

n Lam. 2. 16.

11 ¶ [n] Now also many
nations are gathered
against thee, that say, Let

her be defiled, and let our
eye [o] look upon Zion.

12 But they know not
[p] the thoughts of the LORD,
neither understand they
his counsel: for he shall

Before
CHRIST
cir. 710.

o Obad. 12.
ch. 7. 10.
p Is. 55. 8.
Rom. 11. 33.

were carried captive by Assyria. *There [1]
shalt thou be delivered, there the Lord shall
redeem thee from the hand [2] of thine enemies.*
God's judgments, or purifying trials, or visitation of His saints, hold their way, until
their end be reached. They who suffer them
cannot turn them aside; they who inflict
them cannot add to them or detain them.
The prisonhouse is the place of deliverance
to Joseph and St. Peter; the Red-sea to
Israel; the judges were raised up, when Israel
was mightily oppressed; Jabesh-Gilead was
delivered when the seventh day was come [3];
the walls of Jerusalem were the end of Sennacherib; Judah should have long been in
the very hand and grasp of Babylon, yet
must its clenched *hand* be opened.

11. *Now also.* [*And now.*] The prophet
had already spoken of the future before them,
with this word *Now.* Then, he distinctly
prophesied the captivity to Babylon. Twice
more he begins anew; as Holy Scripture, so
often, in a mystery, whether speaking of evil
or of good, of deliverance or of punishment,
uses a threefold form. In these two, no mention is made of the enemy, and so there is some
uncertainty. But the course must apparently
be either backward or forward. They must
either be two nearer futures before the Captivity, or two more distant after it. This
second gathering might, in itself, either be
that of the Assyrian hosts under Sennacherib
out of all the nations subject to him; or that
of the many petty nations in the time of the
Maccabees, who took advantage of the
Syrians' oppression, to combine to eradicate
the Jews [4]. If understood of Sennacherib,
the prophet, having foretold the entire captivity of the whole people to Babylon, would
have prophesied the sudden destruction of a
nearer enemy, whose miraculous and instantaneous overthrow should be the earnest of
the destruction of Babylon and of their
deliverance from it. This would suit well
with the description, *He shall gather them as
sheaves to the floor,* and would correspond well
with the descriptions in Isaiah. On the
other hand, whereas *this* description would
suit any other event, in which man gathered
his strength against God and was overthrown,

the following words, *Arise and thresh, O
daughter of Zion,* &c, fit better with the victories of the Maccabees, in which Israel was
active, than with the overthrow of Sennacherib, in which they were wholly passive,
and God did all for them, as Isaiah and
Nahum foretell the same overthrow [5]. Then
also, if the course of the description was
backward, 1) the captivity in Babylon, 2)
the destruction of Sennacherib, there is no
earlier event to correspond with [6] *the smiting
of the judge of Israel on the cheek.* The malice
also of the nations gathered against Zion
suits better with the abiding character of the
petty nations, and of their hereditary envy
against Israel and its high claims. To
Nineveh and Babylon, Israel was but one
little corner of ground, which rounded their
territory and connected them with Egypt.
They disdained them, even while they sought
to subdue them. Micah describes the exultation of petty rivalry.

That say, let her be defiled. The bad have a
keen eye for the haltings and inconsistencies
and falls of God's people, for which they are
ever on the watch. Like Satan, they are
first tempters, then the accusers; first dese-
crators, then sanctimonious justiciaries. God,
in His judgment, leaves what has been inwardly defiled to be outwardly profaned. [7] *If
any man defile the temple of God, him shall God
destroy; for the temple of God is holy, which
temple are ye.* [8] *The faithful city had become a
harlot.* [9] *The land had become polluted by its
inhabitants.* Now it was to be polluted
by the enemy. Its seducers ask for the
judgment of God. "It has become like
us in its deeds; let it no more be distinguished from us by the name of the people
of God."

And let our eye look upon Zion, with pleasure
upon its desolation, and feed itself with its
misery. " [10] Where the eye, there love;
where the hand, there pain." [11] *They opened
their mouth wide against me: they said, Aha,
Aha, our eye hath seen.* The world hates the
Church; Edom, Israel; it cannot be satisfied
with beholding its chastisements [12]. The
sufferings of the Martyrs were the choice
spectacle of the Heathen.

[1] See on Hos. ii. 15.
[2] lit. " the hollow of the hand," and so " the
grasp."
[3] 1 Sam. xi. 3. 10. 11.
[4] 1 Macc. v. 1, 2.

[5] Is. x. 24-34. xiv. 24, 5. xvii. 12-14. xxix. 7, 8. Nah.
i. 10-13.   [6] v. 1-4. Heb.   [7] 1 Cor. iii. 17.   [8] Is. i. 21.
[9] Jer. iii. 9. Ps. cvi. 38. Is. xxiv. 5.
[10] Proverb in Lap.   [11] Ps. xxxv. 21.
[12] Mic. vii. 10. Ob. 12.

Before CHRIST cir. 710.

q Is. 21. 10.
r Is. 41. 15, 16.
Jer. 51. 33.

gather them �q as the sheaves into the floor.

13 ʳ Arise and thresh, O daughter of Zion : for I will make thine horn iron, and I will make thy hoofs brass : and thou shalt ˢbeat in pieces many people : ᵗand I will consecrate their gain unto the LORD, and their substance unto ᵘthe Lord of the whole earth.

Before CHRIST cir. 710.

s Dan. 2. 44.
t Isai. 18. 7.
& 23. 18.
& 60. 6, 9.
u Zech. 4. 14.
& 6. 5.

12. *But they know not the thoughts of the Lord, neither understand they His counsel.* The heathen did, for their own ends, what God willed for His. The first step was the same ; God willed that His people should be punished ; they willed to punish them. But all which lay beyond, they saw not ; that God willed (on their repentance) to pardon His own people, but to punish themselves for their pride[1] and cruelty[2]. "[3] Almighty God corrects the elect through the reprobate, as with a rod ; after which He condemns the reprobate eternally, as when the son has been disciplined, the rod is cast into the fire."

For He shall gather them as the sheaves into the floor. The multitude of the sheaves hinders not the threshing ; the multitude of God's enemies hinders not their destruction. They think that they strengthen themselves, as they gather together ; God sees them but as ripened and fitted for destruction, gathered into one bundle together, to perish together. God gathers them, not by constraint or force, but by giving free scope to their own wayward wills, and overruling these to His ends.

13. *Arise* (it may be,) from the dust in which they were lying, *I will make thine horn iron, and I will make thy hoofs brass.* Threshing in the East is partly with oxen, partly with wheels of iron, or with planks set with sharp flints on an open place made hard to this end. The Prophet joins another image, with this and represents Judah as being by God endued with strength, first as with a *horn of iron*[4] to cast the enemy to the ground, and then with *hoofs of brass,* wherewith to trample them to dust, as the stubble and chaff. *And I will consecrate their gain unto the Lord,* i. e. to Myself ; the Lord gathered them into the floor by His Providence ; the Lord gave His people strength to subdue them ; and now, in His own Person, He says, I will complete My own work.

The very image of the "threshing" implies that this is no mere destruction. While the stubble is *beaten* or bruised to small pieces, and the chaff is far more than the wheat, and is carried out of the floor, there yet remains the seed-corn. So in the great judgments of God, while most is refuse, there yet remains over, what is severed from the lost heap and wholly *consecrated* to Him. Whatever things were the object of the "Cherem[5]" or "thing devoted to the Lord," could not be redeemed, but must remain wholly the Lord's. If it had life, it was to be put to death[6]. And so the use of the word here may the rather shew, how those converted to God, and who became *gain,* hallowed to Him, were to pass through death to life, to die to themselves that they might live to Him : what was evil was to be slain in them, that they themselves might live.

The Israelites and God's dealings with them are [7] *ensamples of us upon whom the ends of the world are come.* And so the whole section fits wonderfully with the condition of the single soul.

She who halteth is "[8] the soul, who would serve God, yet not so as wholly to give up the service of the world, which it had in Baptism renounced, who, after it had gone astray like a lost sheep, and been scattered amid the manifoldness of earthly things, was gathered again into the fold, to love One only, long for One only, give itself to One," its Good Shepherd, and over it the Lord reigneth for ever, if, taught by experience the deceitfulness of Satan's promises, and stung by the sense of its own thanklessness and vileness, and conscious of the peril of self confidence, it abideth more closely than others with God. *He shall gather her that is driven out,* i. e. "[9]He shall restore her, from whom He had, for the time, withdrawn His grace," *and her that was afflicted,* trouble being God's most effectual instrument, in recalling the soul to Himself. "[10]For *the Lord raiseth them that are bowed down. And will make her that halteth, a remnant,* placing her among the elect and holy, *and her that was cast off strong ;* for Christ giveth oft to such souls great richness of Divine graces, so that [11]*where sin abounded, grace* should *much more abound.*" "[8]To it, when enlightened and purified by affliction and by repentance, it is promised, that its Lord, the Great King, shall come to it, and again reign in it, which is the great bliss of souls in grace. For then doth the soul really reign, when it submits wholly to Christ, Whom to serve is to reign, and so, under Him, receives power to command its

---

1 Is. x. 7. 12.   2 Zech. i. 15. 19.   3 Dion.   4 1 Kings xxii. 11.
5 Lev. xxvii. 28.   6 Ib. 29.   7 1 Cor. x. 11.   8 Rib.   9 Dion.   10 Ps. cxlvi. 8.   11 Rom. v. 20.

CHAPTER V.

1 *The birth of Christ.* 4 *His kingdom.* 8 *His conquest.*

NOW gather thyself in troops O daughter of

troops: he hath laid siege against us: they shall [a] smite the judge of Israel with a rod upon the cheek.

[a] Lam. 3. 30.
Matt. 5. 39.
& 27. 30.

wrong desires, and rule itself;" that great and wonderful power which the Evangelist expresses in words so brief, [1] *To them gave He power to become the sons of God.* Thus He maketh it strong, so that [2] *neither death, nor life, nor angels, nor principalities, nor powers, can separate it from the love of God which is in Christ Jesus our Lord.* Then, " he describes the condition of the soul fluctuating between good and evil, called one way by God through inward inspirations, and another way by the enticements and habits of sin. And, wishing to follow God, yet not to be without its sinful pleasures, and knowing this to be impossible, it is in anguish and hesitates. Her the prophet justly rebukes, ' *why thus cry aloud,* as though thou must be led captive by the Devil, not knowing or unable to extricate thyself? *Hast thou no King,* aided by Whose power, thou mayest fight against all enticements, habit, the flesh?' Paul felt this and cried aloud, [3] *I see another law in my members, warring against the law of my mind, and bringing me into captivity to the law of sin which is in my members. O wretched man that I am, who shall deliver me from the body of this death?*" You see his grief. But he despairs not. He knows that he has *a King. I thank God through Jesus Christ our Lord.* Or why grievest thou, as if thou hadst no *counsellor,* by whose counsels to free thee from these snares? *Thy Counsellor* indeed *perished* on the Cross, but for thy sake, that thou mayest live. He died, to destroy him who hath the power of death. But He rose the third day and is still with thee; at the Right Hand of the Father He still reigns Immortal forever. See how many counsels He has left thee in the Gospel, how many admonitions, whereby thou mayest lead a happy and tranquil life. Now *pain seizes thee like a woman in travail.* For such a soul *travails,* having conceived inspirations from God, which it wishes to obey, but that the flesh, overcome by concupiscence, resists, and so it never brings forth, nor experiences that joy, whereof the Lord speaketh, [4] *When she is delivered of the child, she remembereth no more the anguish, for joy that a man is born into the world.* Wherefore he adds; *be in pain,* for thou art indeed in travail; thou wilt not cease to be in pain, until thou bring forth. *Thou wilt go forth, &c.* " [5] God, by a provision of His great mercy, allows lukewarm souls, who will be at no pains to gain grace, to fall into foulest sins, in order

that, owning at last their misery, they may cease to be lukewarm, and with great ardor of soul may embrace virtue. For, warned by the result, they understand that they themselves emboldened the tempter, (for he chiefly attacks the lukewarm and remiss,) and they become ardent in the conflict and in well-doing." Wherefore he says, *thou shalt go forth out of the city,* that City of God, whereof He *is the Builder and Maker* [6], which is gladdened by the river of His spirit; " and it dwells in the open field, unprotected, ready to be a prey, in the broad way of its own concupiscences, out of *the narrow road which leadeth to life, and goeth even to Babylon,* the city of ' confusion,' in tumult and din and unrest, and the distractions of this life." Yet even there shall it be delivered, like the poor Prodigal, who came to himself in a far country, when worn out by its hard service. Even there it must not despair, but remember, with him, its Father's house, its former home, the Heavenly Jerusalem. Its pains within or without, whereby it is brought back, are travail-pains. Though all is dark, it must not say, *I have no Counsellor.* For its Redeemer's Name is [7] *Counsellor,* " [8] one Counsellor of a thousand." " [9] Thine Intercessor never dies." Out of the very depth of misery will the Divine Mercy draw thee. Though thou seem held by the strong hand of the enemy, and he seems to triumph over thee and to jeer thee, [10] *There, there so would we have it, we have devoured him,* and hosts of devils seek thy utter destruction, and thou seem to be [11] *delivered over* to them *to the destruction of the flesh; yet is it only that the spirit may be saved in the Day of the Lord.* Even Satan, when he is tormenting souls, *knows not the thoughts of the Lord, nor understands His counsels,* how, by the very pain which he inflicts, God is bidding them, *Rise* and " [5] look up to heaven and long for heavenly things and trample on all which they had hitherto foully served, honor or vain glory or covetousness or lust;" how He will *exalt their horn in the Lord, make* it strong as iron that they should *do all things through Christ in strengthening them,* and conquer all through the might of Christ; how He should *bruise Satan under their feet shortly,* and they consecrate wholly to God their whole strength, every power of soul and body which hitherto had been the adversary's.

V. 1. *Now gather thyself in troops, O daughter*

[1] S. John i. 12.   [2] Rom. viii. 38, 9.   [3] Rom. vii. 23, 24.
[4] S. John xvi. 21.   [5] Rib.   [6] Heb. xi. 10.   [7] Is. ix. 6.

[8] Ecclus. vi. 6.   [9] Christian Year.
[10] Ps. xxxv. 25.   [11] 1 Cor. v. 5.

2 But thou, [b] Beth-le-

[b] Matt. 2. 6. John 7. 42.

hem Ephratah *though* thou

of troops. The *daughter of troops* is still the same who was before addressed, Judah. The word is almost always [1] used of "bands of men employed in irregular, marauding, inroads." Judah is entitled *daughter of troops*, on account of her violence, the robbery and bloodshed within her [2], as Jeremiah says [3], *Is this house which is called by My Name become a den of robbers in your eyes?* She then who *had spoiled* [4] should now be *spoiled;* she who had formed herself in bands to lay waste, shall now be gathered thick together, in small bands [5], unable to resist in the open field ; yet in vain should she so gather herself; for the enemy was upon her, in her last retreat.

This description has obviously no fulfillment, except in the infliction by the Romans. For there was no event, *before* the invasion by Sennacherib and accordingly in the prophet's own time, in which there is any seeming fulfillment of it. But then, the second deliverance must be that by the Maccabees ; and this siege, which lies, in order of time, beyond it, must be a siege by the Romans. With this it agrees, that whereas, in the two former visitations, God promised, in the first, deliverance, in the second, victory, here the Prophet dwells on the Person of the Redeemer, and foretells that the strength of the Church should not lie in any human means [6]. Here too Israel has no *king*, but a *judge* only. Then the "gathering in robber-bands" strikingly describes their internal state in the siege of Jerusalem ; and although this was subsequent to and consequent upon the rejection of our Lord, yet there is no reason why the end should be separated from the beginning since the capture by Titus was but the sequel of the capture by Pompey, the result of that same temper, in which they crucified Jesus, because He would not be their earthly king. It was the close of the organic existence of the former people ; after which the *remnant* from among them with the Gentiles, not Israel after the flesh, were the true people of God.

He hath laid siege against us. The Prophet, being born of them, and for the great love he bore them, counts himself among them, as St. Paul mourns over his brethren after the flesh. *They shall smite the judge of Israel with a*

rod upon the cheek. So St. Paul said to him who had made himself high priest, [7] *God shall smite thee, thou whited wall; for sittest thou to judge me after the law, and commandest me to be smitten contrary to the law.* It is no longer "the king" (for they had said, [8] *We have no King but Cæsar*) but *the judge of Israel*, they who against Christ and His Apostles gave wrong judgment. As they had smitten contrary to the law, so were the chief men smitten by Titus, when the city was taken. As they had done it, was done unto them. To be smitten on the face, betokens shame ; to smite with the rod, betokens destruction. Now both shall meet in one ; as, in the Great Day, the wicked [9] *shall awake to shame and everlasting contempt*, and shall *perish for ever*.

2. *But [And] thou, Bethlehem Ephratah.* With us, the chequered events of time stand in strong contrast, painful or gladdening. Good seems to efface evil, or evil blots out the memory of the good. God orders all in the continuous course of His Wisdom. All lies in perfect harmony in the Divine Mind. Each event is the sequel of what went before. So here the Prophet joins on, what to us stands in such contrast, with that simple, *And.* Yet he describes the two conditions as bearing on one another. He had just spoken of *the judge of Israel* smitten on the cheek, and, before [10], that Israel had neither *king* nor *counsellor;* he now speaks of *the Ruler in Israel*, the Everlasting. He had said, how Judah was to become mere *bands* of men ; he now says, how the *little Bethlehem* was to be exalted. He had said before, that the *rule of old* was to come to *the tower of the flock, the daughter of Jerusalem;* now, retaining the word [11], he speaks of the Ruler, in Whom it was to be established. Before he had addressed *the tower of the flock;* now, *Bethlehem.* But he has greater things to say now, so he pauses [12], *And thou!* People have admired the brief appeal of the murdered Cæsar, "Thou too, Brutus." The like energetic conciseness lies in the words, *And thou! Bethlehem Ephratah.* The name Ephratah is not seemingly added, in order to distinguish Bethlehem from the Bethlehem of Zabulon, since *that* is but once named [13], and Bethlehem here is marked to be the *Bethlehem Judah* [14], by the addition, *too little to be among the thou-*

troops" is the only known sense of התגודד, Jer. v. 7, except that of "making incisions in one's flesh," which is obviously irrelevant here.

[6] v. 8-15. [7] Acts xxiii. 3. [8] St. John xix. 15.

[9] Dan. xii. 2. [10] iv. 9.

[11] ממשלה iv. 8. כושל v. 1. Heb.
[12] As marked by the accent, "double Garesh." Casp. [13] Jos. xix. 15.
[14] Its name in Jud. xvii. 7-9. xix. 1, 2. 18. Ruth i. 1, 2. 1 Sam. xvii. 12.

[1] i. e. except Job xxv. 3. (where it is used of the armies of God) and Job xxix. 25. In Job xix. 5. it is used metaphorically of the "host" of evils sent against Job. S. Jerome renders "filia latronis," and says that Aq. Symm. Theod. and Ed. V. agree with that rendering.
[2] ii. 8. iii. 2. &c. Hos. v. 10.
[3] Jer. vii. 11. comp. S. Matt. xxi. 13. [4] Is. xxxiii. 1.
[5] תתגודדי and גדוד בת are manifestly to be taken in corresponding senses. That of "gathering in

be little [c]among the [d]thou- || sands of Judah, *yet* out of

[c] 1 Sam. 23. 23.   [d] Ex. 18. 25.

---

sands of Judah. He joins apparently the usual name, *Bethlehem,* with the old Patriarchal, and perhaps poetic[1] name *Ephratah,* either in reference and contrast to that former birth of sorrow near Ephratah[2], or, (as is Micah's wont,) regarding the meaning of both names. Both its names were derived from "fruitfulness;" "House of Bread" and "fruitfulness;" and, despite of centuries of Mohammedan oppression, it is fertile still[3].

It had been rich in the fruitfulness of this world; rich, thrice rich, should it be in spiritual fruitfulness. "[4]Truly is Bethlehem, 'house of bread,' where was born[5] *the Bread of life, which came down from heaven,*" "[6]Who with inward sweetness refreshes the minds of the elect," [7]*Angel's Bread,* and "[4]Ephratah, fruitfulness, whose fruitfulness is God," the Seed-corn, stored wherein, died and *brought forth much fruit,* all which ever was brought forth to God in the whole world.

Though *thou be little among the thousands of Judah,* lit. *small to be,* i. e. *too small to be among* &c. Each tribe was divided into its thousands, probably of fighting men, each thousand having its own separate head[8]. But the thousand continued to be a division of the tribe, after Israel was settled in Canaan[9]. The *thousand* of Gideon was *the meanest in*

Manasseh[10]. Places too small to form a thousand by themselves were united with others, to make up the number[11]. So lowly was Bethlehem that it was not counted among the possessions of Judah. In the division under Joshua, it was wholly omitted[12]. From its situation, Bethlehem can never have been a considerable place. It lay and lies, East of the road from Jerusalem to Hebron, at six miles from the capital[13]. It was "[14]seated on the summit-level of the hill country of Judæa with deep gorges descending East to the Dead Sea and West to the plains of Philistia," "2704 feet above the sea[15]." It lay "[16]on a narrow ridge," whose whole length was not above a mile[16], swelling at each extremity into a somewhat higher eminence, with a slight depression between[17]. "[18]The ridge projects Eastward from the central mountain range, and breaks down in abrupt terraced slopes to deep valleys on the N. E. and S." The West end too "[19]shelves gradually down to the valley." It was then rather calculated to be an outlying fortress, guarding the approach to Jerusalem, than for a considerable city. As a garrison, it was fortified and held by the Philistines[20] in the time of Saul, recovered from them by David, and was one of the 15 cities [21]fortified by Rehoboam. Yet it remained an unimportant

---

[1] Ps. cxxxii. 6.   [2] Gen. xxxv. 19. xlviii. 7.
[3] "The district country around Bethlehem abounds in fields, vineyards, hills, valleys, olive-yards, fig-trees, and is especially supported by wines and corn." Quaresm. Elucid. Terræ S. ii. 620. "Round the hill is fruitful garden and corn land." Russegger iii. 79. "The terraces, admirably kept, and covered with rows of luxuriant olives, intermixed with the fig and vine, sweep in graceful curves round the ridge, regular as stairs." Porter Hdbook, p. 206. "It is still one of the best-cultivated and most fertile parts of Palestine." Rev. G. Williams in Smith's Gr. and R. Geogr. Add. Volney ii. 298.   [4] in vit. S. Jer. Ep. 108. de vit. Paulæ. n. 10.
[5] S. Joh. vi. 48, 51.   [6] S. Greg. Hom. 8. in Ev.
[7] Ps. lxxviii. 25.   [8] Num. i. 16. x. 4.
[9] Jos. xxii. 21. 30. 1 Sam. x. 19. xxiii. 23.
[10] Jud. vi. 15.
[11] As in 1 Chron. xxiii. 11. four brothers, not having many sons, were counted as one "house." Hengst.
[12] Jos. xv.   The LXX interpolate it in Jos. xv. 59.
[13] Eus. S. Jer. de loc. Hebr. "6 miles [in the 6th mile, S. Jer.] from Ælia to the South, near the road which leadeth to Hebron." Itin. Hieros. p. 598. "From Jerusalem, as you go to Bethlehem, on the high road at 4 miles on the right is the monument where Rachel, Jacob's wife, was buried. Thence 2 miles on the left is Bethlehem where our Lord Jesus Christ was born." "Two parasangs," (6 miles) Benj. Tud (i. 40. ii. 90.) "6 miles," Arculf, (Early travels in Pal. p. 6.) Bernard (Ib. 29.) Sæ, wulf, (Ib. 44.) "2 hours." Maundrell, (Ib. 455.) Robinson. (Ib 470.)   [14] Thomson, The land ii. 509.
[15] van de Velde memoir p. 180. "convent at Bethlehem, 2704 Eng. feet." Russ.
[16] Arculf in Early Travels in Palestine p. 6.
[17] Ritter Erdk. xvi. 285. and Russ. in n 15.
[18] Porter's Hdbook i. 207. "It stands upon an eminence surrounded by small valleys or depres-

sions, devoted to the culture of the olive and vine." —"From this height there is a pretty steep slope on both the North and Southern sides, particularly the former, the two Wadis or gorges which form its boundaries. On the flanks of these Wadis are the principal gardens, vineyards, and plantations of olives and figs. They unite a little to the E. of the town, and form what is called the Wadi-et-Taamarah from the village of Beit-Taamr, in the neighborhood." Wilson, Lands i. 394. "A narrow ridge, surrounded on all sides by valleys." Arculf. Ib. "On the N. the other side of the deep, abruptly-sinking, valley, on the top of the hill, lay Bethlehem." V. Schubert ii. 493, coming from the south. "It stands on the slope of a hill, of difficult ascent, at least by night." Lord Lindsay p. 240. "The first sight of Bethlehem has something strangely picturesque. It lies quite on a bare summit in the Jura limestone of Palestine, 2338 Paris feet above the sea. The summit is divided by a shallow saddle-back. On the West side lies Bethlehem, on the East the great monastery and Church, like a fortress over the precipice, which falls into the deep valley." Russegger iii. 79. "The little city of David, seated on a lofty hill, shines, like a brilliant crown, among the mountains of Judah." Mislin. c. 32. iii. 6. From one spot, you can see the Church of Bethlehem, where our Saviour was born; the Church of the Holy Sepulchre where He was buried; the Mount of Olives whence He ascended to heaven." Id. Ib.
[19] Grove in Smith Dict. of Bib. "Toward the W. the hill is higher than the village, and then sinks down very gradually toward Wadi Ahmed." Rob. i. 470.   [20] 2 Sam. xxiii. 14.
[21] 2 Chron. xi. 6. "A low wall without towers surrounds the brow of the hill, and overlooks the valley." Arculf. p. 6. "scarcely a ¼ of an hour." Ritter p. 286.

thee shall he come forth ‖ unto me *that is* to be

place. Its inhabitants are counted with those of the neighboring Netophah, both before[1] and after[2] the captivity, but both together amounted after the captivity to 179[3] or 188[2] only. It still does not appear among the possessions of Judah[4]. It was called a city[5], but the name included even places which had only 100 fighting men[6]. In our Lord's time it is called *a village*[7], a *city*[8], or a strong spot[9]. The royal city would become *a den of thieves.* Christ should be born in a lowly village. "[10] He Who had taken the form of a servant, chose Bethlehem for His Birth, Jerusalem for His Passion."

St. Matthew relates how the Chief Priest and Scribes in their answer to Herod's enquiries, *where Christ should be born*[11], alleged this prophecy. They gave the substance rather than the exact words, and with one remarkable variation, *art not the least among the princes of Judah.* St. Matthew did not correct their paraphrase, because it does not affect the object for which they alleged the prophecy, the birth of the Redeemer in Bethlehem. The sacred writers often do not correct the translations, existing in their time, when the variations do not affect the truth[12]. Both words are true here. Micah speaks of Bethlehem, as it was in the sight of men; the chief priests, whose words St. Matthew approves, speak of it as it was in the sight of God, and as, by the Birth of

Christ, it should become. "[13] Nothing hindered that Bethlehem should be at once a small village and the Mother-city of the whole earth, as being the mother and nurse of Christ Who made the world and conquered it." "[14] That is *not the least,* which is the house of blessing, and the receptacle of Divine grace." "[15] He saith that the spot, although mean and small, shall be glorious. And in truth," adds S. Chrysostom, "the whole world came together to see Bethlehem, where, being born, He was laid, on no other ground than this only." "[16] O Bethlehem, little, but now made great by the Lord, He hath made thee great, Who, being great, was in thee made little. What city, if it heard thereof, would not envy thee that most precious Stable and the glory of that Crib? Thy name is great in all the earth, and *all generations call thee blessed.* [17] *Glorious things are* everywhere *spoken of thee, thou city of God.* Everywhere it is sung, that *this Man is born in her, and the Most High Himself shall stablish her.*

Out of thee shall He come forth to Me that is to be Ruler in Israel [lit. shall (one) come forth to Me *to be Ruler.*] Bethlehem was too small to be any part of the polity of Judah ; out of her was to come forth One, Who, in God's Will, was to be its Ruler. The words *to Me* include both *of Me* and *to Me.* Of Me, i. e. "[18] by My Power and Spirit," as Gabriel said, [19] *The Holy Ghost shall come upon thee, and*

---

[1] 1 Chron. ii. 54.   [2] Neh. vii. 26.
[3] Ezr. ii. 21. 2.   [4] Neh. xi. 25–30.
[5] Ruth i. 19. Ezr. ii. 1. with 21. Neh. vii. 6. with 26.
[6] Am. v. 3.   [7] S. John vii. 42.
[8] S. Luke ii. 4.   [9] Jos. Ant. v. 2. 8. (χώριον)
[10] S. Leo de Epiph. Serm. 1.   [11] S. Matt. ii. 4–6.
[12] See on Am. ix. 12. vol. i. p. 328. Pococke has employed much learning to make this passage verbally accord with the allegation of it by the chief priest recorded by S. Matthew (Notæ miscell. on the Porta Mosis, Works i. 134–9). He follows the eminent authority of Abulwalid (followed by R. Tanchum and a Hebr. Arab. Gloss.) in supposing צָעִיר, "little," to have had the opposite sense of "great," and that it actually had that meaning in Jer. xlviii. 4. Zech. xiii. 7. In neither of those passages, however, have צָעִיר, צָעַר, that meaning, nor do the cases alleged of words containing opposite meanings bear out such an one as this. For the two senses, although differing at last, can be traced up to one common source, which could not be done as to צָעִיר. Thus 1) קָדֹשׁ, "holy," is used of idolatrous consecrations which were in fact horrible desecrations, (see on Hos. iv. 14. vol. i. p. 52.) 2) נֶפֶשׁ, "soul," is used of the "person," as we speak of "1000 souls." Thence the idiom מַת נֶפֶשׁ, lit. "the soul of one dead," Lev. xxi. 11. Num. vi. 6 ; then in one idiom מֵת לְנֶפֶשׁ, "defiled as to the dead," but נֶפֶשׁ does not signify one alive or dead indifferently. 3) בֵּרֵךְ, lit. "bent the knee," prayed, includes prayers for evil as well as for good, cursing as well as blessing. 4) חֶסֶד love, piety, hence

perhaps, what is forbidden by natural piety, (Lev. xx. 17.) and a reproach ; (Prov. xiv. 34. Ib. xxv. 10.) unless different roots have accidentally coalesced, (see Fürst Conc.) as in שָׂכַל, to use "insight," hence wisdom, and סָכַל vacillate, hence folly, meet in one Syriac word; or our *let,* "hinder," is from *lata,* "slow;" *latyan,* "retard;" Goth. our *let,* "allow," from "*letan*" i. q. lassen.) In Arabic this is the more common on account of the severance of the different tribes who spoke it, before Mohammed united them into one, as the same word receives modifications in different languages of Europe. The meaning, "great" also, if it could be obtained for צָעִיר, would still not yield the meaning desired. For לִהְיוֹת implies a comparison. It means *little to be in the thousands of Judah* i. e. too little. If צָעִיר were rendered *great,* it would still be "great to be among the thousands" &c. i. e. too great to be. Chald. Lxx. Syr. and the Latin in S. Aug. de Civ. D. xviii. 30. give another explanation, *it is little that thou shouldest be.* This does not agree better with the words in St. Matthew, and is against the idiom. In this idiom 1) צָעִיר is not used, but mostly מִעֵט, or נָקֵל Is. xlix. 6. or קָטֹן 2 Sam. vii. 19. 2) The person spoken to is always expressed.
[13] S. Greg. Naz. Orat. 18. in patr. § 17.
[14] S. Chrys. Quod Christus sit Deus § 3. i. 561.
[15] S. Ambr. Ep. 70. § 11.
[16] S. Bern. Serm. 1 in Vig. Nativ. § 4. i. 763.
[17] Ps. lxxxvii. 3.   [18] Theoph.   [19] S. Luke i. 35.

Before CHRIST cir. 710.
[e]ruler in Israel; [f]whose goings forth have been

• Gen. 49. 10. Is. 9. 6. f Ps. 90. 2. Pro. 8. 22, 23. John 1. 1.

from of old, from † ever-lasting.

Before CHRIST cir. 710.

† Heb. *the days of eternity.*

the power of the *Highest shall overshadow thee, therefore also that Holy Thing which shall be born of thee, shall be called the Son of God.* To Me, as God said to Samuel[1], *I will send thee to Jesse the Bethlehemite; for I have provided Me a king among his sons.* So now, one shall *go forth* thence *to Me,* to do My Will, to My praise and glory, to reconcile the world unto Me, to rule and be Head over the true Israel, the Church. He was to *go forth out of* Bethlehem, as his native-place[2]; as Jeremiah[3] says, *His noble shall be from him, and his ruler shall go forth out of the midst of him*[4]; and Zechariah[5], *Out of him shall come forth the cornerstone; out of him the nail, out of him the battlebow, out of him every ruler together.* Before, Micah had said to *the tower of Edar, Ophel of the daughter of Zion, the first rule shall come to thee;* now, retaining the word, he says to Bethlehem, *out of thee shall come one to be a ruler*[6]. The judge of Israel had been smitten; now there should *go forth out of* the little Bethlehem, One, not to be a judge only, but a *Ruler.*

Whose goings forth have been *from of old, from everlasting,* lit. *from the days of eternity. Going forth* is opposed to *going forth;* a *going forth out of* Bethlehem, to a *going forth from eternity;* a *going forth,* which then was still to come, (the Prophet says, *shall go forth,*) to a *going forth* which had been long ago, "[7]not from the world but from the beginning, not in the days of time, but *from the days of eternity.* For[8] *in the beginning was the Word, and the Word was with God, and the Word was God. The Same was in the beginning with God. In the end of the days,* He was to go forth from Bethlehem; but, lest he should be thought then to have had His Being, the Prophet adds, His *goings forth are from everlasting.*" Here words, denoting eternity and used of the eternity of God, are united together to impress the belief of the Eternity of God the Son. We have neither thought nor words to conceive eternity; we can only conceive of time lengthened out without end. "[9]True eternity is boundless life, all existing at once," or "[10] duration without beginning and without end and without change."

The Hebrew names, here used, express as much as our thoughts can conceive or our words utter. They mean literally, *from afore,* (i. e. look back as far as we can, that from which we begin is still "before,") "*from the days of that which is hidden.*" True, that in eternity there are no divisions, no succession, but one everlasting "now;" one, as God, in whom it is, is One. But man can only conceive of Infinity of space as space without bounds, although God contains space, and is not contained by it; nor can we conceive of Eternity, save as filled out by time. And so God speaks after the manner of men, and calls Himself [11] *the Ancient of Days,* "[12] being Himself the age and time of all things; before days and age and time," "the Beginning and measure of ages and of time." The word, translated *from of old,* is used. elsewhere[13] of the eternity of God. [14] *The God of before* is a title chosen to express, that He is *before* all things which He made. [15] *Dweller of afore* is a title, formed to shadow out His ever-present existence. Conceive any existence *afore* all which else you can conceive, go back *afore* and *afore* that; stretch out backward yet *before* and *before* all which you have conceived, ages *afore* ages, and yet *afore,* without end,—then and there God was. That *afore* was the property of God. Eternity belongs to God, not God to eternity. Any words must be inadequate to convey the idea of the Infinite to our finite minds. Probably the sight of God, *as He is,* will give us the only possible conception of eternity. Still the idea of time prolonged infinitely, although we cannot follow it to infinity, shadows our eternal being. And as we look along that long vista, our sight is prolonged and stretched out by those millions upon millions of years, along which we can look, although even if each grain of sand or dust on this earth, which are countless, represented countless millions, we should be, at the end, as far from reaching to eternity as at the beginning. *The days of eternity* are only an inadequate expression, because every conception of the human mind must be so. Equally so is every other, [16] *From everlasting to everlasting;* [17]from

[1] 1 Sam. xvi. 1.

[2] When יָצָא is used of actual descent, it is in relation to the actual parent, to "go forth out of the womb," "out of the loins," "out of the bowels," "out of thee," Gen. xlvi. 26. Job i. 21. Jer. i. 5. Gen. xxxv. 11, xv. 4, xvii. 6. 2 Kings xx. 18. יֵרְכוֹ יָצָא

יצא, מבטן, מרחם, מחלצי, ממעי, ממך

[3] xxx. 21.　　[4] משלו מקרבו יצא　　[5] x. 4.

[6] משל (v. 1. Heb.) refers back to הממשלה iv. 8.

[7] Rup.　　[8] S. John i. 1. 2.

[9] S. Anselm Monol. c. 24. L.

[10] Rich. Vict. de Trin. ii. 4. L.　　[11] Dan. vii. 9.

[12] Dionys. de Div. Nom. c. 10. x. 5.　　[13] Hab. i. 12.

[14] אֱלֹהֵי קֶדֶם Deut. xxxiii. 27. So אֵל עוֹלָם Gen. xxi. 33. Is. xl. 28.

[15] יֹשֵׁב קֶדֶם Ps. lv. 20.

[16] מֵעוֹלָם עַד עוֹלָם Ps. xc. 2. ciii. 17.

[17] מֵעוֹלָם Ps. xciii. 2. and of Divine Wisdom, or God the Son, Prov. viii. 23.

everlasting; [1] *to everlasting;* [2] *from the day,* i. e. since the day was. For the word, *from,* to our minds implies time, and time is no measure of eternity. Only it expresses præexistence, an eternal Existence backward as well as forward, the incommunicable attribute of God. But words of Holy Scripture have their full meaning, unless it appear from the passage itself that they have not. In the passages where the words, *for ever, from afore,* do not mean eternity, the subject itself restrains them. Thus *for ever,* looking onward, is used of time, equal in duration with the being of whom it is written, as [3], *he shall be thy servant for ever,* i. e. so long as he lives in the body. So when it is said to the Son [4], *Thy throne, O God, is for ever and ever,* it speaks of a kingdom which shall have no end. In like way, looking backward, [5] *I will remember Thy wonders from old,* must needs relate to time, because they are marvelous dealings of God in time. So again [6], *the heavens of old,* stand simply contrasted with the changes of man. But [7] *God of old* is the Eternal God. [8] *He that abideth of old* is God enthroned from everlasting In like manner the *goings forth* here, opposed to a *going forth* in time, (emphatic words being moreover united together,) are a going forth in eternity.

The word, *from of old,* as used of being, is only used as to the Being of God. Here too then there is no ground to stop short of that meaning; and so it declares the eternal *going-forth,* or Generation of the Son. The plural, *goings forth,* may here be used, either as words of great majesty [9], "God," "Lord," "Wisdom," (i. e. Divine [9]) are plural; or because the Generation of the Son from the Father is an Eternal Generation, before all time, and now, though not in time, yet in eternity still. As then the prophet saith, "*from the days* of eternity," although eternity has no parts, nor beginning, nor "*from,*" so he may say *goings forth,* to convey, as we can receive it, a continual going-forth. We think of Eternity as unending, continual, time; and so he may have set forth to us the Eternal Act of the *Going Forth* of the Son, as continual acts.

The Jews understood, as we do now, that Micah foretold that the Christ was to be born at Bethlehem, until they rejected Him, and were pressed by the argument. Not only did

the chief priests formally give the answer, but, supposing our Lord to be of Nazareth, some who rejected Him, employed the argument against Him. [10] *Some said, Shall Christ come out of Galilee?* *Hath not the Scripture said, that Christ cometh of the seed of David, and out of the town of Bethlehem, where David was?* They knew of two distinct things: that Christ was 1) to be *of the seed of David;* and 2) *out of the town of Bethlehem.* Christians urged them with the fact, that the prophecy could be fulfilled in no other than in Christ. "[11] If He is not yet born, who is to go forth as a Ruler out of the tribe of Judah, from Bethlehem, (for He must needs come forth out of the tribe of Judah, and from Bethlehem, but we see that now no one of the race of Israel has remained in the city of Bethlehem, and thenceforth it has been interdicted [12] that any Jew should remain in the confines of that country)—how then shall a Ruler be born from Judæa, and how shall he *come forth out of Bethlehem,* as the Divine volumes of the Prophets announce, when to this day there is no one whatever left there of Israel, from whose race Christ could be born?" The Jews at first met the argument, by affirming that the Messiah *was* born at Bethlehem on the day of the destruction of the temple [13]; but was hidden for the sins of the people. This being a transparent fable, the Jews had either to receive Christ, or to give up the belief that He was to be born at Bethlehem. So they explained it, "The Messiah shall go forth thence, because he shall be of the seed of David who was out of Bethlehem." But this would have been misleading language. Never did man so speak, that one *should be* born in a place, when only a remote ancestor had been born there. Micah does not say merely, that His family came out of Bethlehem, but that He Himself should thereafter come forth thence. No one could have said of Solomon or of any of the subsequent kings of Judah, that they *should* thereafter come forth from Bethlehem, any more than **they** could now say, 'one shall come forth from Corsica,' of any future sovereign of the line of Napoleon III., because the first Napoleon was a Corsican; or to us, 'one *shall come* out of Hanover,' of a successor to the present dynasty, born in England, because George I. came from Hanover in 1714.

---

[1] לְעֹולָם Ps. ix. 8. xxix. 10.
[2] מִיֹּום Is. xliii. 13.   [3] Ex. xxi. 6.
[4] Ps. xlv. 6.
[5] Ib. lxxvii. 12.   [6] Ib. lxviii. 34.
[7] Deut. xxxiii. 27.
[8] קֶדֶם יֵשֵׁב Ps. lv. 20.
[9] הַכָּמֹות קְדֹשִׁים, אֲדֹנָי אֱלֹהִים Prov. i. 20. ix. 1.
[10] S. John vii. 41, 2.
[11] Tert. c. Jud. c. 13. R. Isaac, Chizzuk Emunah, in Wagenseil tela ignea Sat. p. 278. tries to evade it.

[12] By Hadrian. See ab. on iii. 12. p. 76. Reland p. 647, understands this of a prohibition to approach Bethlehem itself.
[13] See at length Martini Pugio fidei ii. 6. f. 279, from the Jerusalem Talmud Berachoth [f. 5.] and the old mystical books, Bereshith Rabba on Gen. xxx. 41, and the Echa R. on Lam. i. 16. (These last passages have been mutilated.) See also Schoettg. T. ii. p. 196. on Is. lxvi. 7. The fable of His concealment occurs in Jonath. on Micah iv. 8, (see ab. p. 62,) and in Trypho in S. Just. Dial. § 8.

3 Therefore will he give them up, until the time

that [g] she which travaileth hath brought forth: then

[g] ch. 4. 10.

3. *Therefore*, since God has so appointed both to punish and to redeem, *He*, God, or the Ruler "Whose goings forth have been from of old from everlasting," Who is God with God, *shall give them up*, i. e. withdraw His protection and the nearness of His Presence, *giving them up* 1) into the hands of their enemies. And indeed the far greater part never returned from the captivity, but remained, although willingly, in the enemy's land, outwardly shut out from the land of the promise and the hope of their fathers[1]. But also, 2) all were, more than before, [2]*given up*, to follow their own ways. God was less visibly present among them. Prophecy ceased soon after the return from the captivity, and many tokens of the nearness of God and means of His communications with them, the Ark and the Urim and Thummim were gone. It was a time of pause and waiting, wherein the fullness of God's gifts was withdrawn, that they might look on to Him Who was to come. *Until the time that she which travaileth hath brought forth, i. e.* until [3] *the Virgin* who should *conceive and bear a Son and call His Name Emmanuel, God with us*, shall give birth to *Him* Who shall save them. And then shall be Redemption and joy and assured peace. God provides against the fainting of hearts in the long time before our Lord should come.

Then [*And.*] There is no precise mark of time such as our word *then* expresses. He speaks generally of what should be after the Birth of the Redeemer. *The remnant of His brethren shall return unto the children of Israel.* *The children of Israel* are the true Israel, *Israelites indeed*[4]; they who are such, not in name[5] only, but indeed and in truth. *His brethren* are plainly the brethren of the Christ; either because Jesus vouchsafed to

be born [6]*of the seed of David according to the flesh*, and of them [7]*as concerning the flesh Christ came, Who is over all, God blessed for ever ;* or as such as He makes and accounts and [8] *is not ashamed to call, brethren*, being sons of God by grace, as He is the Son of God by nature. As He says, [9]*Whosoever shall do the will of My Father which is in Heaven, the same is My brother and sister and mother ;* and, [10] *My brethren are these who hear the word of God and do it.* The *residue* of these, the Prophet says, shall *return to*, so as to be joined with [11], *the children of Israel ;* as Malachi prophesies, [12] *He shall bring back the heart of the fathers to* [13] *the children, and the heart of the children to* [13] *the fathers.* In the first sense, Micah foretells the continual inflow of the Jews to that true Israel who should first be called. All in each generation, who are the true Israel, shall be converted, made one in Christ, saved. So, whereas, since Solomon, all had been discord, and, at last, the Jews were scattered abroad everywhere, all, in the true Prince of Peace, shall be one[14]. This has been fulfilled in each generation since our Lord came, and shall be yet further in the end, when they shall haste and pour into the Church, and so *all Israel shall be saved*[15].

But "[16] the promise of God was not only to Israel after the flesh, but *to all*" also *that were afar off, even as many as the Lord our God should call*[17]. All these may be called *the remnant of His brethren*, even those that were, before, *aliens from the commonwealth of Israel and afar off*, [18]*but now, in Christ Jesus, made one* with them ; all, brethren among themselves and to Christ their ruler. "[16] Having taken on Him their nature in the flesh, He is not ashamed to call them so, as the Apostle speaketh, confirming it out of the Psalm, where in the Person of Christ he saith [19], *I will*

[1] As in 2 Chron. xxxvi. 17.
[2] Acts vii. 42. Rom. i. 24. 26. 28.
[3] Is. vii.14. The context requires, that the Mother here spoken of should be the Mother of the Messias. For the Birth is spoken of before (v. 2) and *his brethren*, וְאֶחָיו, in this v. can be no other than the brethren of *Him* Who is so born. The evasion, that it is only a figure for the end of the travail, gives an unmeaning sense, for it would signify, "He shall give them up, until He cease to give them up." It is also contrary to the idiom ; since in the O. T. travail pangs are an emblem of suffering, not of the subsequent joy, and Israel is spoken of, both before and after, unfiguratively ; "He shall give *them* up" and as "the children of Israel," so that a figurative mention of them in between would be unsuited to the context.
[4] S. John i. 47.   [5] Rom. ix. 6. &c.   [6] Ib. i. 3.
[7] Ib. ix. 5.   [8] Heb. ii. 11.   [9] S. Matt. xii. 50.
[10] S. Luke viii. 21.
[11] "עַל stands in its first meaning of 'place,' where one thing moves to another, and so abides on it ;" Ewald, in Hengst. who quotes 2 Chr. xxx.

9, "when you return to (עַל) the Lord," and Mal. iii. 24. Heb. as to the religious meaning. So contrariwise, "they returned to (עַל) the iniquities of their forefathers." (Jer. xi. 10.) In all the cases mentioned by Fürst, (Conc. p. 1109–11,) the original idea "over" remains in some force; "the waters returned upon the Eg.," Ex. xiv. 26; "and they returned *unto* Pihahiroth (encamping there), Num. xxxiii. 7; "man would return *to* the dust," (so as to dwell there,) Job xxxiv. 15; "the dog returned *to* his vomit, (taking it up again,) Prov. xxvi. 11, "the wind returneth to its circuits," (so as to rest where it began,) Eccl. i. 6; "My prayer shall return *into* my bosom," (so as to rest there, or, from God in blessing upon himself,) Ps. xxxv. 13. In Neh. iv. 6.
[12] Mal. iii. 24. Heb.   [13] עַל.
[14] See Hosea i. 11. Is. xi. 10. &c.   [15] Rom. i. 26.
[16] Poc.   [17] Acts ii. 39.
[18] Eph. ii. 12–14.   [19] Ps. xxii. 22.
תשׁובוּ עלינוּ, "return so as to be with us," the idiom is the same as in this place.

ʰ the remnant of his brethren shall return unto the
children of Israel.

4 ¶ And he shall stand

and || ¹ feed in the strength
of the LORD, in the majesty of the name of the
LORD his God; and they

Before
CHRIST
cir. 710.

|| Or, *rule.*
¹ Is. 40. 11.
& 49. 10.
Ezek. 34. 23.
ch. 7. 14.

declare Thy name unto My brethren. There is
no reason to take the name, *brethren,* here in
a narrower sense than so to comprehend all
¹ *the remnant whom the Lord shall call,* whether
Jews or Gentiles. The word "brethren" in
its literal sense includes both, and, as to both,
the words were fulfilled.

4. *And He shall stand.* The Prophet continues to speak of personal acts of this Ruler
Who was to be born. He was not to pass
away, not to rule only by others, but by Himself. To *stand* is the attitude of a servant,
as Jesus, although God and Lord of all, said
of Himself, ² *He shall come forth and serve them;*
³ *The Son of Man came not to be ministered unto,
but to minister. He shall stand* as a Shepherd ⁴,
to watch, feed, guard them, day and night;
He shall stand, as St. Stephen saw Christ
⁵ *standing on the Right Hand of God,* "⁶ to succor all those who suffer for Him." "⁷ For
to sit belongs to one judging; to stand, to one
fighting or helping." *He shall stand,* as abiding, not to pass from them, as Himself saith,
⁸ *Lo, I am with you alway, even unto the end of
the world:* and He shall *feed* His flock by His
Spirit, His Word, His Wisdom and doctrine,
His example and life; yea, by His own Body
and Blood ⁹. They whom He feedeth ¹³ *lack
nothing.*

In the strength of the Lord. He, Who feedeth them with Divine tenderness, shall also
have Divine might, His Father's and His
own, to protect them; as He saith, ¹¹ *My
sheep hear My Voice, and I know them and they
follow Me, neither shall any man pluck them out
of My Hand. My Father Which gave them Me
is greater than all, and no man is able to pluck
them out of My Father's Hand. I and My
Father are One.* With authority, it is said ¹²,
*He commandeth even the unclean spirits and they
come out.* His feeding or teaching also was
¹³ *with authority, and not as the scribes.*

*In the Majesty of the Name of the Lord His
God,* as St. John says ¹⁴, *We beheld His Glory, the
Glory as of the Only-Begotten of His Father;*
and He saith, ¹⁵ *All power is given unto Me in*

heaven and in earth; so that the Divine Glory
should shine through the Majesty of His
teaching, the power of His Grace, upholding
His own, and the splendor of the miracles
wrought by Him and in His Name. *Of the Name
of the Lord;* as He saith again, ¹⁶ *Holy Father,
keep through Thine own Name those whom Thou
hast given Me, that they may be one as We are.
While I was with them in the world, I kept them
in Thy Name.* "¹⁷ Whoever then is sent to
feed His flock must *stand,* i. e. be firm and
unshaken; feed, not sell, nor slay; and
feed in might, i. e. in Christ." *His God,* as
our Lord Himself, as Man, saith, ¹⁸ *Unto My
Father, and your Father, and to My God and
your God.* But that Majesty He Himself
wields, as no mere man can; He Himself is
invested with it. "¹⁹ To ordinary kings God
is strength ²⁰, or gives strength ²¹; men have
strength in God; this Ruler is clad in the
strength of the Lord, that same strength,
which the Lord hath, Whose is strength. Of
Him, as Israel's King, the same is said as of
the Lord, as King of the whole earth ²²; only
that the strength of the Messiah is not His
own, but the Lord's. He is invested with
the strength of the Lord, because He is Man;
as Man, He *can* be invested with the *whole*
strength of the Lord, only because He is also
God."

And they shall abide (lit. *sit, dwell*) in rest
and security and unbroken peace under
Christ their Shepherd and their King;
they shall not wander to and fro as heretofore. "²³ He, their Shepherd, shall *stand;
they* shall *sit.*" "The word ²⁴ is the more
emphatic, because it stands so absolutely.
This will be a sitting or dwelling, which will
indeed deserve the name. The original
promise, so often forfeited by their disobedience should be perfectly fulfilled; ²⁵ *and ye shall
dwell in your land safely, and I will give peace
in the land, and ye shall lie down, and none shall
make you afraid.* ²⁶. And this is the result of
the greatness of the promised Ruler, as the

¹ Joel ii. 32.   ² S. Luke xii. 37.
³ S. Matt. xx. 28.   ⁴ See Is. lxi. 5.
⁵ Acts vii. 55.   ⁶ Collect for S. Stephen's Day.
⁷ S. Greg. Hom. 29. in Evang. n. 7.
⁸ S. Matt. xxviii. 20.   ⁹ S. John vi.
¹⁰ S. Matt. xxiii. 1.   ¹¹ S. John x. 27–30.
¹² S. Luke iv. 36.   ¹³ S. Matt. vii. 29.
¹⁴ S. John i. 14.   ¹⁵ S. Matt. xxviii. 18.
¹⁶ S. John xvii. 11, 12.   ¹⁷ Theoph.
¹⁸ S. John xx. 17. Lipmann, in Nizzachon, objects,
that, "as God, He has no God; as Man, He is not
from everlasting to everlasting," not knowing, as a
Jew, the Divine Personality of our Lord, whence,

He being "not two but one Christ," (Ath. Creed),
both the attributes of His Divine and Human Nature can be said of Him. (in Poc.) R. Tanchum
owns, that the Ruler here spoken of can, for His
greatness, be no other than the Messiah. (Ib.)
¹⁹ Casp.   ²⁰ Ps. xxviii. 7. cxl. 7.   ²¹ 1 Sam. ii. 10.
²² Ps. xciii. 1.   ²³ from Casp.   ²⁴ יֵשֵׁב.
²⁵ Lev. xxvi. 5, 6. "comp. Hos. ii. 20. [18 Eng.] Is.
xiv. 30. xxxii. 18. Jer. xxiii. 8. Ezek. xxxiv. 25, 6.
xxxiv. 25, 28. xxxvii. 25. xxxviii. 8. Zech. xiv. 10, 11."
Casp.
²⁶ Am. ix. 14. Mic. iv. 4. Both use the same word
as here.

Before
C H R I S T
cir. 710.

k Ps. 72. 8.
Is. 52. 13.
Zech. 9. 10.
Luke 1. 32.
l Ps. 72. 7. Is. 9. 6. Zech. 9. 10. Luke 2. 14. Eph. 2. 14.

shall abide: for now ᵏshall he be great unto the ends of the earth.

5 And this *man* ˡshall

be the peace, when the As- syrian shall come into our land: and when he shall tread in our palaces, then

Before
C H R I S T
cir. 710.

---

like promise of the Psalm is rested on the immutability of God[1]; *Thou art the Same, and Thy years shall have no end. The children of Thy servants shall dwell[2], and their seed shall be established before Thee.* For it follows,"

For now, (in the time which Micah saw as did Abraham with the eye of faith,) *now,* in contrast to that former time of lowliness. His life shall be divided between a life of obscurity, and a life of never-ending greatness. *Shall He be great unto the [very[3]] ends of the earth,* embracing them in His rule, (as David and Solomon had foretold[4],) and so none shall harm those whom He, the King of all the earth, shall protect. The universality of protection is derived from an universality of power. To David God says, [5]*I have made thee a great name, like the name of the great that are in the earth.* Of Uzziah it is said[6], *His name went forth far; for he was marvelously helped, until he was strong;* but of the Messiah alone it is said, that His power should reach to the ends of the earth ; as God prophesies of Himself, that His [7]*Name should be great among the Heathen.* So Gabriel said to His Mother, [8] *This,* Whom she should bear, *shall be great.*

5. *And this Man shall be the Peace. This,* emphatically, i. e. "This Same," as is said of Noah, [9]*This same shall comfort us,* or, in the song of Moses, of the Lord, [10]*This Same is my God.* Of Him he saith, not only that He brings peace, but that He Himself[11] is that Peace ; as St. Paul saith, [12]*He is our Peace,*

and Isaiah calls Him [13]*the Prince of peace,* and at His Birth the heavenly host pro- claimed [14]*peace on earth;* and He [15]*preached peace to you which were afar off, and to them that were nigh;* and on leaving the world He saith, [16]*Peace I leave with you, My Peace I give unto you. He shall be our Peace,* within by His Grace, without by His Protection. " [17]Wouldest thou have peace with God, thine own soul, thy neighbor ? Go to Christ Who is our Peace," and follow the footsteps of Christ. "Ask peace of Him Who is Peace. Place Christ in thy heart and thou hast placed Peace there."

When the Assyrian shall come into our land, and when he shall tread in our palaces. Assur stands for the most powerful and deadliest foe, "ghostly and bodily," as the Assyrian then was of the people of God. For since this plainly relates to the time after Christ's coming, and, (to say the least,) after the cap- tivity in Babylon and deliverance [18] from it, which itself followed the dissolution of the Assyrian Empire, the Assyrians cannot be the literal people, who had long since ceased to be [19]. In Isaiah too the Assyrian is the type of Anti-Christ and of Satan[20]. As Christ is our Peace, so one enemy is chosen to repre- sent all enemies who [21] *vex the Church,* whether the human agents or Satan who stirs them up and uses them. "By the Assyrian," says St. Cyril, "he here means no longer a man out of Babylon, but rather marks out the in- ventor of sin, Satan. Or rather, to speak fully, the implacable multitude of devils, which

[1] Ps. cii. 27, 28.   [2] יְשִׁכוּנ.   [3] עַד.
[4] Ps. ii. 8. " the ends of the earth for His posses- sion;" Ps. lxxii. 8. " from the river *unto* (עַד) the ends of the earth." In both cases the אַפְסֵי אָרֶץ as here. See " Daniel the Proph." p. 480.
[5] 2 Sam. vii. 9.   [6] 2 Chron. xxvi. 15. add Ib. 8.
[7] Mal. i. 11. 14.
[8] S. Luke i. 32. οὗτος ἔσται μέγας,
[9] Gen. v. 29.   [10] Ex. xv. 2.
[11] The word " this " *might* grammatically be taken as agreeing with " peace." " This [viz. this thing] shall be our peace," as Eccl. vi. 9, נֵם זֶה הֶבֶל, "this too is vanity;" Ex. iii. 15, זֶה זִכְרִי, "this is My memorial," i. e. הֶז is not necessarily personal. But this would not alter the sense. For, " this thing is our peace," must necessarily refer to what had been said, viz. the greatness, majesty, tender care of the Messiah. It is most natural to take הֶז=οὗτος, as a person, since a person was the sub- ject of the verse before.
[12] Eph. ii. 14.   [13] Is. ix. 6.   [14] S. Luke ii. 14.
[15] Eph. i. 17.   [16] S. John xiv. 27.   [17] Lap.
[18] iv. 10.
[19] A disbeliever in prophecy writes, " If he would quote Micah as designating Bethlehem for the birthplace of the Messiah, he cannot shut his eyes

to the fact that the Deliverer to come from thence was to be a *contemporary* shield against the Assy- rian." Dr. Williams in Ess. and Rev. p. 68. Not " contemporary," unless it be certain that Psalm- ists and Prophets cannot identify themselves with the past and future of their people. The course of events interposed shews, that the deliv- erance was *not* to be contemporary. As the Psalm- ist speaking of the passage of the Red Sea, says, *there did we rejoice in Him,* (Ps. lxvi. 6.) making himself one with them ; as Micah himself, speak- ing of times after the desolation of the land, (vii. 13.) says, " He will turn again, He will have com- passion upon *us*;" (Ib. vii. 19.) nay, as our Lord Himself says to the Apostles, " I am with *you* alway, even to the end of the world," (S. Matt. xxviii. 20.) i. e. with them and their successors to the end of time ; so Micah, who had sorrowed with his people in their sorrows, (i. 8. 10.) here rejoices with them in a deliverance far away, after God should for a long time have given them up, v. 3. and which he should not see. " Even L. Bauer translated, ' And if another Assur,' comparing the passage of Virgil which Castalio had already quoted, ' Alter erit tum Tiphys, et altera quæ vehat Argo Delectos heroas.' " Hengst.
[20] Is. x. and including Babylon Ch. xiv.
[21] Acts. xii. 1.

Before
C H R I S T
cir. 710.
shall we raise against him seven shepherds, and eight

† Heb. *princes of* † principal men.
men.
† Heb. *eat up.*

6 And they shall † waste the land of Assyria with the sword and the land of

ᵐ Nimrod ‖ in the entrances thereof: thus shall he ⁿ deliver *us* from the Assyrian, when he cometh into our land, and when he treadeth within our borders.

Before
C H R I S T
cir. 710.

ᵐ Gen. 10. 8, 10,
11.
‖ Or, *with her
own naked
swords.*
ⁿ Luke 1. 71.

spiritually ariseth against all which is holy, and fights against the holy city, the spiritual Zion, whereof the Divine Psalmist saith, *Glorious things are spoken of thee, thou city of God.* For Christ dwelleth in the Church, and maketh it, as it were, His own city, although by His Godhead filling all things. This city of God then is a sort of land and country of the sanctified and of those enriched in spirit, in unity with God. When then the Assyrian shall come against our city, i. e. when barbarous and hostile powers fight against the saints, they shall not find it unguarded." The enemy may tread on the land and on its palaces, i. e. lay low outward glory, vex the body which is of earth and the visible temple of the Holy Ghost, as he did St. Paul by *the thorn in the flesh, the minister of Satan to buffet him,* or Job in mind body or estate, but [1] *after that he has no more than he can do;* he cannot hurt the soul, because nothing can *separate us from the love of Christ,* and [2] Christ Who is our Peace is in us; and of the saint too it may be said, [3] *The enemy cannot hurt him.* [4] Much as the Church has been vexed at all times by persecutions of devils and of tyrants, Christ has ever consoled her and given her peace in the persecutions themselves: [5] *Who comforteth us in all our tribulation, that we may be able to comfort them which are in any trouble, by the comfort wherewith we are comforted of God. For as the sufferings of Christ abound in us,* so our *consolation also aboundeth by Christ.* The Apostles [6] *departed from the presence of the council, rejoicing that they were counted worthy to suffer shame for His Name.* And St. Paul writeth to the Hebrews, [7] *ye had compassion of me in my bonds, and took joyfully the spoiling of your goods, knowing that ye have in heaven a better and more enduring substance.*

Then shall we raise against him seven shepherds and eight principal men (lit. *anointed,* although elsewhere used of heathen princes.)

The *shepherds* are manifestly inferior, spiritual, shepherds, acting under the One Shepherd, by His authority, and He in them. The *princes of men* are most naturally a civil power, according to its usage elsewhere [8]. The *seven* is throughout the Old Testament a symbol of a sacred whole, probably of the union of God with the world [9], reconciled with it; *eight,* when united with it, is something beyond it [10]. Since then *seven* denotes a great, complete, and sacred multitude, by the *eight* he would designate "an incredible and almost countless multitude." "[4] So in defence of the Church, there shall be raised up very many shepherds and teachers (for at no time will it be forsaken by Christ;) yea by more and more, countlessly, so that, however persecutions may increase, there shall never be wanting more to teach, and exhort to, the faith."

6. *And they shall waste,* lit. *feed on,* and so *eat up.* They who were shepherds of their own people, should consume their enemies. Jeremiah uses the same image. [11] *The shepherds with their flocks shall come unto her; they shall pitch tents against her round about; they shall feed, each his space.* So Joshua and Caleb say, [12] *They,* (the inhabitants of Canaan,) *are bread for us.* So it was said to St. Peter, [13] *Arise, Peter, kill and eat;* and what once *was common,* defiled *and unclean,* shall turn to the nourishment and growth of the Church, and be incorporated into Christ, being made part of His Body.

And the land of Nimrod. Babylon, which should displace Assyria, but should carry on its work of chastising God's people, is joined by Micah, as by Isaiah [14], as an object of His judgment. In Isaiah, they are the actual Assyria [15] and Babylon [16] whose destruction is foretold, yet so as to shadow out rebellion against God in its intensest form, making itself independent of, or measuring itself against, God. Hence, probably, here alone in holy Scripture, Babylon is called *the land of Nimrod,* as indeed he founded it [17], but therewith was the author of the tower of Babel also, which was built in *rebellion* against God,

---

[1] S. Luke xii. 4.　　　　[2] Rup.
[3] Ps. lxxxix. 22.　　[4] Rib.　　[5] 2 Cor. i. 4, 5.
[6] Acts. v. 41.　　　　　　[7] x. 34.
[8] Jos. xiii. 21, Ps. lxxxiii. 12, Ezek. xxxii. 30. The word stands rather in contrast with מֹשֵׁל than as equivalent to it, since מָשִׁיחַ is always used of one, anointed by God, נָגִיד, unless it be in this place, never.
[9] See Bähr Symbolik, ii. 107. sqq.

[10] See on Amos i. 3. vol. i. p. 234. This instance in Micah so far differs from the others, that the two numbers are not united with one substantive; and, unless *the shepherds* and *the princes of men* be the same class of persons, (which scarcely seems probable,) they have kindred, yet different, subjects.
[11] vi. 3.　　[12] Num. xiv. 9.　　[13] Acts x. 13.
[14] Is. x. 5-34, xiii-xiv. 27.　　[15] Is. x. 12-15.
[16] xiv. 13-15.　　　　　　　　　[17] Gen. x. 10.

Before CHRIST cir. 710.
o ver. 3.
Deut. 32. 2.
p Ps. 72. 6.
& 110. 3.

7 And °the remnant of Jacob shall be in the midst of many people ᴾas a dew from the LORD, as the

showers upon t h e grass, that tarrieth not for man, nor waiteth for the sons of men.

Before CHRIST cir. 710.

whence his own name was derived[1]. Assyria then, and the world-empire which should succeed it, stand as representing the God-opposed world.

In the entrances thereof, [lit. *in the gates thereof*[2].] The shepherds of Israel shall not act on the defensive only, but shall have victory over the world and Satan, carrying back the battle into his own dominions, and overthrowing him there. Satan's malice, so far from hurting the Church, shall turn to its good. Wherein he hoped to waste it, he shall be wasted; wherein he seemed to triumph, he shall be foiled. So it has been ever seen, how, under every persecution, the Church grew. " [3] The more it was pressed down, the more it rose up and flourished;" "[4] Shivering the assault of the Pagans, and strengthened more and more, not by resisting, but by enduring." Yet all, by whomsoever done, shall be the work of Christ Alone, enduring in martyrs, teaching in pastors, converting through the Apostles of Heathen nations. Wherefore he adds:

Thus, [*And*] *He shall deliver* us *from the Assyrian.* Not *they,* the subordinate shepherds, but He, the Chief Shepherd until *the last enemy shall be destroyed* and *death shall be swallowed up in victory, shall deliver,* whether by *them* or by Himself as He often so doth,— not *us* only (the saying is the larger because unlimited) but—*He shall deliver,* absolutely. Whosoever shall be delivered, He shall be their deliverer; all, whom He Alone knoweth, Who Alone [5] *knoweth them that are His.* [6] *Neither is there salvation in any other.* [7] *Whoso glorieth, let him glory in the Lord.* Every member of Christ has part in this, who, through the grace of God, "has power and strength to have victory and to triumph against the devil, the world, and the flesh " —not he, but the grace of God which is with him; and much more, all, whether Apostles or Apostolic men, or Pastors, or Bishops and Overseers, who, by preaching or teaching or

prayer, bring those to the knowledge of the truth, who [8] *sat in darkness and the shadow of death,* and by whom [9] *God translates us into the kingdom of His dear Son.*

7. *And the remnant of Jacob.* Micah [10], as well as Isaiah [11], had prophesied, that a *remnant* only should *return unto the Mighty God.* These, though very many in themselves, are yet but a *remnant* only of the unconverted mass; yet this, [12] *the remnant, who shall be saved,* who believe in Christ, [13] *the little flock,* of whom were the Apostles and their disciples, *shall be, in the midst of many people,* whom they won to the faith, as John in Asia, Thomas in India, Peter in Babylon and Rome, Paul well-nigh in the whole world, what? something to be readily swallowed up by their multitude? No, but *as a dew from the Lord, as the showers from the grass, which tarrieth not for man, nor waiteth for the sons of men,* quickening to life that, which, like soon-withered [14] grass, no human cultivation, no human help, could reach.

In the Gospel and the grace of Christ there are both, gentleness and might; softness, as *the dew,* might as of *a lion.* For " [15] Wisdom reacheth from one end to another *mightily ;* and *sweetly* doth she order all things." *The dew* is, in Holy Scripture, a symbol of Divine doctrine. [16] *My doctrine shall drop as the rain, my speech shall distill as the dew, as the small rain upon the tender herb, and as the showers upon the grass.* The dew comes down from heaven, is of heavenly not of earthly birth, transparent, glistening with light, reflecting the hues of heaven, gentle, slight, weak in itself, refreshing, cooling the strong heats of the day [17], consumed itself, yet thereby preserving life, falling on the dry and withered grass wherein all nature droops, and recalling it to freshness of life. And still more in those lands, where from the beginning of April to the end of October [18], the close of the latter and the beginning of the early rain, during all the hot months of summer, the life of all herb-

[1] Lit. "We will rebel." There is no other even plausible etymology.
[2] The E. V. has followed the analogy of the " Caspiæ pylæ," &c. and has paraphrased, " openings " or " gates " by " entrances," as if they were " the gates of the country;" which, however, belongs only to narrow entrances, such as Thermopylæ. The rendering in the E. M. " with their own drawn swords," (from Aq. and Ed. v. A. E. and Kim.) is owing to a slavish adherence to parallelism, פְּתִיחוֹת, &c. " drawn swords," (Ps. lv. 22.) is fem. after the analogy of חֶרֶב itself. The uniform meaning of פֶּתַח "opening," "door," " port," "gate," is plainly not to be deserted in a single case, on the ground of parallelism only. The fem.

aff. also belongs naturally to the land, *her's,* not *their's,* i. e. the people's.
[3] S. Anton. in S. Athan. vit. ej. c. 79.
[4] S. Aug. de Ag. Christ. c. 12. and other fathers quoted Tertull. Apol. c. ult. n. a. Oxf. Tr.
[5] 2 Tim. ii. 19.   [6] Acts iv. 12.
[7] 2 Cor. x. 17.   [8] Ps. cvii. 10.   [9] Col. i. 13.
[10] iv. 7.   [11] x. 21.   [12] Rom. ix. 27.
[13] S. Luke xii. 32.
[14] שָׁשַׁב. See Ps. cii. 5, 12, 2 Kings xix. 26, Is. xxxvii. 27.   [15] Wisd. viii. 1.   [16] Deut. xxxii. 2.
[17] Ecclus. xviii. 16, xliii. 22.
[18] Called אֵיתָן, because only " perennial " streams still flowed.

Before
CHRIST
cir. 710.

8 ¶ And the remnant of Jacob shall be among the Gentiles in the midst of many people as a lion among the beasts of the forest, as a young lion among the flocks of ‖sheep: who, if he go through,

‖ Or, *goats.*

both treadeth down, and teareth in pieces, and none can deliver.

9 Thine hand shall be lifted up upon thine adversaries, and all thine enemies shall be cut off.

Before
CHRIST
cir. 710.

age depends upon the dew alone[1]. *Showers*[2] are so called from the "multitude" of drops, slight and of no account in themselves, descending noiselessly yet penetrating the more deeply. So did the Apostles "[3] bedew the souls of believers with the word of godliness and enrich them abundantly with the words of the Gospel," themselves dying, and the Church living the more through their death[4], quenching the fiery heat of passions, and watering the dry and barren soil, that it might bring forth fruits unto Christ. Yet, they say[5], *the excellency of the power was of God and not of us,* and [6] *God gave the increase.* For neither was their doctrine [7] *of man nor by man ;* but it came from heaven, the Holy Spirit teaching them invisibly and making *unlearned and ignorant* men *mighty in word and deed.* " [8] Whence these and these alone the Church of Christ looks up to, as furnishing the rule of truth." " [9] The herb, upon which this dew falleth, groweth to God without any aid of man, and flourisheth, and needeth neither doctrines of philosophers, nor the rewards or praises of men."

8. *And the remnant of Jacob shall be as a young lion.* " [10] What more unlike than the sweetness of the dew and the fierceness of the lion? What so different as the gentle shower distilling on the herb, and the savageness or vehemence of a *lion roaring among the flocks of sheep?* Yet both are ascribed to *the remnant of Jacob.* Why? Because the Apostles of Christ are both tender and severe, tender in teaching and exhorting, severe in rebuking and avenging. How does Paul teach, [11] *God was in Christ reconciling the world unto Himself, and hath committed unto us the word of reconciliation ; now then we are ambassadors for Christ, as though God did beseech you by us: we pray you in Christ's stead, be ye reconciled to God!* What sweeter than the dew of love, the shower of true affection? And so, on to that, "our heart is enlarged." They are such drops of dew as no one could doubt came from [12] *the Lord, the Father of our*

Lord Jesus Christ, the Father of mercies and the God of all comfort. Yet the same Apostle after a little writes, [13] *This is the third time I am coming to you. I told you before and foretell you, and being absent now I write to them which heretofore have sinned and to all others, that if I come again, I will not spare, since ye seek a proof of Christ speaking in me.* See the severity of a master, like the roaring of *a lion among the beasts of the forest.* For such surely are they whom he rebukes for *the* [14] *uncleanness and fornication and lasciviousness which they had committed.* Was he not to such as a lion [15] ? Was not Peter such, when he rebuked Ananias first and then Sapphira his wife, and they fell down and gave up the ghost? They *tread down* or [16] *cast down imaginations and every high thing that exalteth itself against the knowledge of God;* as Christ Himself, Who spake in them, is both a lamb and the [17] *Lion of the tribe of Judah,* and nothing is so terrible as [18] *the wrath of the Lamb.*

And none can deliver. " [19] For as the Apostles past from nation to nation, and trod down Heathenism, subduing it to Christ, and taking within their net the many converted nations, none could withdraw from the Apostles' doctrine those whom they had converted." The Heathen world " [20] cried out that the state is beset, that the Christians are in their fields, their forts, their islands." " [21] We are a people of yesterday, and yet we have filled every place belonging to you, cities, islands, castles, towns, assemblies, your very camp, your tribes, companies, palace, senate, forum ! We leave you your temples only. We can count your armies, our numbers in a single province will be greater."

9. *Their hand shall be lifted up upon their adversaries.* The might of the Church is the Might of Christ in her, and the glory of the Church is His from Whom it comes and to Whom it returns. It is all one, whether this be said to Christ or to the *remnant of Jacob,* i. e. His Church. Her *enemies* are His, and her's only because they are His,

[1] On its importance to vegetable life, see Gen. xxvii. 28, Deut. xxxiii. 13, 28, Hag. i. 10, Zech. viii. 12.
[2] רביבים. It occurs Deut. xxxii. 2. Ps. lxv. 11. (Heb.) lxxii. 6, as especially refreshing.
[3] S. Cyr. [4] 2 Cor. iv. 12. [5] Ib. 7.

[6] 1 Cor. iii. 6, 7. [7] Gal. i. 12. [8] Rup.
[10] Rup. [11] 2 Cor. v. 19—vi. 11. [12] Ib. i. 3.
[13] Ib. xiii. 1-3. [14] Ib. xii. 21.
[15] See again 1 Cor. v. 2–5. [16] 2 Cor. x. 5.
[17] Rev. v. 5. [18] Ib. vi. 16. [19] Dion.
[20] Apol. c. 1. p. 2. Oxf. Tr. [21] Ib. c. 37. p. 78.

Before CHRIST cir. 710.

q Zech. 9. 10.

r Is. 2. 6.

s Zech. 13. 2.

10 [q] And it shall come to pass in that day, saith the LORD, that I will cut off thy horses out of the midst of thee, and I will destroy thy chariots:

11 And I will cut off the cities of thy land, and throw down all thy strong holds:

12 And I will cut off witchcrafts out of thine hand and thou shalt have no *more* [r] soothsayers:

13 [s] Thy graven images also will I cut off, and thy || standing images out of the midst of thee; and thou shalt [t] no more worship the work of thine hands.

14 And I will pluck up thy groves out of the midst of thee: so will I destroy thy || cities.

15 And I will [u] execute vengeance in anger and fury upon the heathen, such as they have not heard.

Before CHRIST cir. 710.

|| Or, *statues.*

t Is. 2. 8.

|| Or, *enemies.*

u Ps. 149. 7. ver. 8. 2 Thess. 1. 8.

---

and hate her as belonging to Him. They *shall be cut off*, either ceasing to be His enemies, or ceasing to be, as Julian or Arius or Anti-Christ, [1] *whom the Lord shall consume with the spirit of His Mouth and shall destroy with the brightness of His Coming.* And in the end, Satan also, over whom Christ gave the Apostles [2] *power to tread on all the power of the Enemy*, shall be *bruised under our feet* [3].

10. *And it shall come to pass in that day*, of grace in the kingdom of Christ and of His Presence in the Apostles and with the Church, *I will cut off thy horses out of the midst of thee.* The greater the glory and purity of the Church, the less it needs or hangs upon human aid. The more it is reft of human aid, the more it hangs upon God. So God promises, as a blessing, that He will remove from her all mere human resources, both what was in itself evil, and what, although good, had been abused. Most of these things, whose removal is here promised, are spoken of at the same time by Isaiah, as sin, or the occasion of sin, and of God's judgments to Judah. [4] *Soothsayers*, (the same word) *horses, chariots, idols the work of their hands; high towers, fenced walls.* "[5] I will take, from thee all arms wherewith, while unconverted, thou opposedst the faith," all which thou settest up as idols in place of God. (Such are witchcrafts, soothsayers, graven images, images of Ashtaroth.) "I will take from thee all outward means and instruments of defence which aforetime were turned into pride and sin;" as horses and chariots. Not such shall be the arms of the Church, not such her strongholds. *A horse is a vain thing to save a man.* Her arms shall be the despised Cross of shame; her warriors, they who bear it; their courage, to endure in holy patience and meekness; their might, the Holy Spirit within them; their victories, through death, not of others, but their Master's and, in His, their own. They shall overcome the world, as He overcame it, and through Him Alone and His Merits Who overcame it by suffering.

11–15. *I will cut off the cities of thy land.* So God promised by Zechariah [6], *Jerusalem shall be inhabited as towns without walls; for I will be unto her a wall of fire round about.* The Church shall not need the temptation of human defence; for God shall fence her in on every side. Great cities too, as the abode of luxury and sin, of power and pride, and, mostly, of cruelty, are chiefly denounced as the objects of God's anger. Babylon stands as the emblem of the whole city of the world or of the devil, as opposed to God. "[7] The first city was built by Cain; Abel and the other saints *had no continuing city* [8]" here. *Cities* then will include "[7] all the tumults and evil passions and ambition and strife and bloodshed, which Cain brought in among men. Cities are collectively called and are Babylon, *with whom*, (as in the Revelations we hear a voice from heaven saying), [9] *the kings of the earth committed fornication and the merchants of the earth are waxed rich through the abundance of her delicacies;* and of which it is written, [10] *And a mighty Angel took up a stone like a great millstone, and cast it into the sea, saying, Thus with violence shall that great city, Babylon, be thrown down, and shall be found no more at all.* "Great rest then is promised to holy Zion i. e. the Church, when the cities or strongholds of the land [strongholds, as they are, of earthliness] shall be destroyed.

[1] 2 Thess. ii. 8. [2] S. Luke x. 19. [3] Rom. xvi. 20. [4] Is. ii. 6–8. 15. [5] Rib. Lap.

[6] ii. 4, 5. [7] Rup. [8] Heb. xiii. 14. [9] Rev. xviii. 3. [10] Ib. 21.

Before
CHRIST
cir. 710.

CHAPTER VI.

1 *God's controversy for unkindness,* 6 *for ignorance,* 10 *for injustice,* 16 *and for idolatry.*

HEAR ye now what the LORD saith; Arise;

contend thou ‖ before the mountains, and let the hills hear thy voice.

2 ^aHear ye, O mountains, ^bthe LORD's controversy, and ye strong foun-

Before
CHRIST
cir. 710.

‖ Or, *with.*
ª Deut. 32. 1.
Ps. 50. 1, 4.
Is. 1. 2.
ᵇ Hos. 12. 2.

For together with them are included all objects of desire in them, with the sight whereof the citizens of the kingdom of God, while pilgrims here, are tempted; whereof the wise man saith, *Vanity of vanities, all is vanity.*" The fulfillment reaches on to the Day of Judgment, when the Church shall finally receive glory from the Lord, and be ¹*without spot and wrinkle.* All looks on to that Day. The very largeness of the promise, which speaks, in its fullest sense, of the destruction of things, without which we can hardly do in this life, (as cities ²,) or things very useful to the needs of man, (as horses,) carries us on yet more to that Day when there will be no more need of any outward things; "³ when the heavy body shall be changed, and shall have the swiftness of angels, and shall be transported whither it willeth, without *chariots* and *horses* ; and all things which tempt the eye shall cease ; and no evil shall enter ; and there shall be no need of *divining,* amid the presence and full knowledge of God, and where the ever-present Face of God, Who is Truth, shall shine on all, and nothing be uncertain or unknown ; nor shall they need to form in their souls images of Him Whom His own *shall see as He Is ;* nor shall they esteem anything of self, or the work of their own hands ; but God shall be All in all." In like way, the woe on those who obey not the truth, also looks on to the end. It too is final. There is nothing to soften it. Punishments in the course of life are medicinal. Here no mention is made of Mercy, but only of *executing vengeance ;* and that, *with wrath and fury ;* and that, *such as they have not heard.* For as *eye hath not seen, nor heart conceived the good things laid up in store for those who love* God, so neither the evil things prepared for those who, in act, shew that they hate Him.

Ch. VI. The foregoing prophecy closed with the final cleansing of the Church and the wrath of God resting on the wicked, when, as St. Paul saith, ⁴ *The Lord Jesus shall be revealed from heaven with His mighty angels, in flaming fire, taking vengeance on them that*

know not God, and that obey not the Gospel of our Lord Jesus Christ: who shall be punished with everlasting destruction from the presence of the Lord, and from the glory of His power ; when He shall come to be glorified in His Saints, and to be admired in all them that believe. The Prophet here begins his third and last summons to judgment, in the Name, as it were, of the All-Holy Trinity, against Whom they had sinned.

1. *Hear ye now what the Lord saith :* If ye will not hear the rebuke of man, hear now at last the word of God. "*Arise* thou, Micah." The prophet was not willing to be the herald of woe to his people ; but had to *arise* at the bidding of God, that he might not ⁵ *be rebellious like that rebellious house. Stand up ;* as one having all authority to rebuke, and daunted by none. He rouses the hearer, as shewing it to be a very grave urgent matter, to be done promptly, urgently, without delay. *Contend thou before* [better, as in E. M. *with* ⁶] *the mountains.* Since man, who had reason, would not use his reason, God calls the mountains and hills, who ⁷ *unwillingly,* as it were, had been the scenes of their idolatry, as if He would say, "ᵇ Insensate though ye be, ye are more sensible than Israel, whom I endowed with sense; for ye feel the voice and command of God your Creator and obey Him ; they do not. I cite you, to represent your guilty inhabitants, that, through you, they may hear My complaint to be just, and own themselves guilty, repent, and ask forgiveness." "The altars and idols, the blood of the sacrifices, the bones and ashes upon them, with unuttered yet clear voice, spoke of the idolatry and guilt of the Jews, and so pronounced God's charge and expostulation to be just. Ezekiel is bidden, in like way, to prophesy against *the mountains of Israel*⁹, *I will bring a sword upon you, and I will destroy your high places, and your altars shall be desolate.* "¹⁰ Lifeless nature without voice tells the glory of God ; without ears it hears what the Lord speaks ¹¹."

2. *Hear, ye strong* [or, it may be, *ye enduring* ¹²,] *foundations of the earth.* Mountains

¹ Eph. v. 27.
² In ver. 14. Jon. has "I will cut off thy *enemies,*" whence E. M. But although זֶר stands for זֵר "enemy" 1 Sam. xxviii. 16, and plur. Ps. cxxxix. 20, (in both places with affix,) here every object mentioned is of things, *belonging* to Judah, its own.
³ Rup.   ⁴ 2 Thess. i. 7–10.   ⁵ Ezck. ii. 8.

⁶ This is the uniform sense of רִיב with אֵת as well as with עִם. See Num. xx. 13, Jud. viii. 1, Prov. xxv. 9, Is. xlv. 9, 1. 8, Jer. ii. 9, Neh. v. 7, xiii. 11, 17. (all, in Fürst Conc.)
⁷ Rom. viii. 20.   ⁸ Lap.   ⁹ Ezek. vi. 2–5.
¹⁰ Poc.   ¹¹ Ps. xix. 3, S. Luke xix. 40.
¹² אֵיתָנִים. See Ges. Lex. p. 644.

Before
CHRIST
cir. 710.

dations of the earth: for ^cthe LORD hath a controversy with his people, and he will plead with Israel.

3 O my people, ^dwhat have I done unto thee?

c Is. 1. 18.
& 5. 3, 4.
& 43. 26.
Hos. 4. 1.

d Jer. 2. 5, 31.

and wherein have I wearied thee? testify against me.

4 ^eFor I brought thee up out of the land of Egypt, and redeemed thee out of the house of servants; and I sent before

Before
CHRIST
cir. 710.

e Ex. 12. 51.
& 14. 30.
& 20. 2.
Deut. 4. 20.
Amos 2. 10.

and rocks carry the soul to times far away, before and after. They change not, like the habitable, cultivated, surface of the earth. There they were, before the existence of our short-lived generations; there they will be, until time shall cease to be. They have witnessed so many vicissitudes of human things, themselves unchanging. The prophet is directed to seize this feeling of simple nature. "They have seen so much before me," Yes! "then they have seen all which befell my forefathers; all God's benefits, all along, to them and to us, all their and our unthankfulness."

He will plead with Israel. God hath a strict severe judgment [1] with His people, and yet vouchsafes to clear Himself before His creatures, to come down from His throne of glory and place Himself on equal terms with them. He does not *plead* only, but mutually (such is the force of the word) *impleads with* [2] His people, hears if they would say aught against Himself, and then gives His own judgment [3]. But this willingness to hear, only makes us condemn ourselves, so that we should be without excuse before Him. We do owe ourselves wholly to Him Who made us and hath given us all things richly to enjoy. If we have withdrawn ourselves from His Service, unless He dealt hardly with us, we dealt rebelliously and ungratefully with Him. God brings all pleas into a narrow space. The fault is with Him or with us. He offers to clear Himself. He sets before us His good deeds, His Loving kindness, Providence, Grace, Long-suffering, Bounty, Truth, and contrasts with them our evil deeds, our unthankfulness, despitefulness, our breach of His laws, and disorderings of His creation. And then, in the face of His Goodness, He asks, "What evil have I done, what good have I left undone?" so that our evil and negligences should be but a requital of His. For if it is evil to return evil for evil, or not to return good for good, what evil is it to return

evil for His exceeding good! As He says by Isaiah, [4] *What could have been done more to My vineyard and I have not done in it. Wherefore, when I looked that it should bring forth grapes, brought it forth wild grapes?* And our Blessed Lord asks; [5] *Many good works have I shewed you from My Father. For which of those works do ye stone Me?* [6] *Which of you convinceth Me of sin? And if I say the truth, why do ye not believe Me?* Away from the light of God, we may plead excuses, and cast the blame of our sins upon our temptations, or passions, or nature, i. e. on Almighty God Himself, Who made us. When His light streams in upon our conscience, we are silent. Blessed if we be silenced and confess to Him then, that we be not first silenced in the Day of Judgment. [7] *Righteous Job* said, [8] *I desire to reason with God;* but when his *eye saw Him,* he said, [9] *wherefore I abhor myself, and repent in dust and ashes.*

3. *O My people.* This one tender word [10], twice repeated [11], contains in one a whole volume of reproof. It sets before the eyes God's choice of them of His free grace, and the whole history of His loving-kindness, if so they could be ashamed of their thanklessness and turn to Him. "Mine," He says, "ye are by creation, by Providence, by great deliverances and by hourly love and guardianship, by gifts of nature, the world, and grace; such things have I done for thee; what against thee? *what evil have I done unto thee?*" [12] *Thy foot did not swell these forty years,* for He upbears in all ways where He leads. *Wherefore have I wearied thee?* for [13] *His commandments are not grievous. Thou hast been weary of Me, O Israel,* God says by Isaiah [14], *I have not wearied thee with incense; thou hast wearied Me with thine iniquities.*

4. *For I brought thee up out of the land of Egypt, and redeemed thee out of the house of servants.* What wert thou? What art thou? Who made thee what thou art? God reminds them. They *were* slaves; they *are* His people in the heritage of the heathen, and that by

[1] רִיב.   [2] יְתוֹכֵחַ.
[3] Comp. Is. xliii. 26, Jer. ii. 5, 6, 9. So יָעֲנָה בִי, "testify against Me," (ver. 3.) is a judicial term, lit. "answer against Me," i.e. "answer judicial interrogatories," then generally "depose," "testify," Num. xxxv. 30, Deut. xix. 18, Job xv. 6, Ruth i. 21, Is. iii. 9, lix. 12, Jer. xiv. 7.

[4] Is. v. 4.
[6] Ib. viii. 46.
[7] Job i. 8. ii. 3, Ezek. xiv. 20.
[9] xlii. 5, 6.
[11] Here and v. 5.
[12] Deut. viii. 4.
[14] Is. xliii. 22–24.

[5] S. John x. 32.

[8] Job xiii. 3.
[10] עַמִּי.

[13] 1 S. John v. 3.

Before CHRIST cir. 710.	thee Moses, Aaron, and Miriam.	what Balaam the son of Beor answered him from	Before CHRIST cir. 710.
f Num. 22. 5. & 23. 7. & 24. 10, 11. Deut. 23. 4, 5. Josh. 24. 9, 10. Rev. 2. 14.	5 O my people, remember now what f Balak king of Moab consulted, and	g Shittim unto Gilgal; that ye may know h the righteousness of the LORD.	g Num. 25. 1. & 33. 49. Josh. 4. 19. & 5. 10. h Judg. 5. 11.

His *outstretched arm*. God mentions some heads of the mercies which He had shewn them, when He had made them His people, His redemption of them from Egypt, His guidance through the wilderness, His leading them over the last difficulty to the promised land. The use of the familiar language of the Pentateuch [1] is like the touching of so many key-notes, recalling the whole harmony of His love. *Moses, Aaron, and Miriam* together, are Lawgiver, to deliver and instruct; Priest, to atone; and Prophetess [2] to praise God; and the name of Miriam at once recalled the mighty works at the Red Sea and how they *then* thanked God.

5. *Remember now*. The word translated *now* is a very tender one, like our "*do* now remember" or "*do* remember," beseeching instead of commanding. "[3] I might command, but I speak tenderly, that I may lead thee to own the truth." *What Balak king of Moab consulted, and what Balaam the son of Beor answered him*. God did not only raise up Moses, Aaron, Miriam, out of their brethren, but He turned the curse of the alien Balaam into a blessing; and that, not for their righteousness, (for even then they were rebellious,) but against their deserts, out of His own truth and righteousness. Not that the curse of Balaam could in itself have hurt them; but, in proportion to his reputation, it would have infused great energy into their enemies, and its reversal must have struck a great panic into them and into others. Human might having failed in Sihon and Og, Balak sought superhuman. God shewed them by their own diviner, that it was against them. Even after they had seduced Israel, through Balaam's devilish counsel, Midian seems to have been stricken by God with panic, and not to have struck a blow [4].

From Shittim unto Gilgal. The words are separated by the Hebrew accent from what went before. It is then probably said in concise energy for, "Remember too from Shittim to Gilgal," i. e. all the great works of God *from Shittim* [5], the last encampment of Israel out of the promised land, where they so sinned in Baal-peor, *unto Gilgal*, the first

in the promised land, which they entered by miracle, where the Ark rested amid the victories given them, where the Covenant was renewed, and [6] *the reproach of Egypt was rolled away*. Remember all, from your own deep sin and rebellion to the deep mercy of God.

That ye may know the righteousness [*righteousnesses*] *of the Lord;* His Faithfulness in performing His promises to Abraham, Isaac, and Jacob. God speaketh of His promises, not as what they were in themselves, mere mercy, but as what they became, through that gracious and free promise, *righteousness*, in that He had bound Himself to fulfill what He had, out of mere grace, promised. So in the New Testament He saith, [7] *God is not unrighteous that He should forget your works and labor which proceedeth of love;* and, [8] *He is faithful and just to forgive us our sins*. Micah speaks, by a rare idiom, of the *righteousnesses* [9] *of the Lord*, each act of mercy being a separate effluence of His Righteousness. The very names of the places suggest the righteous acts of God, the unrighteous of Israel. "[10] But we too, who desire with unveiled face to behold the glory of the Lord, and have Abraham really for our father, let us, when we have sinned, hear God pleading against us, and reproving us for the multitude of His benefits. For we too once served Pharaoh and the people of Egypt, laboring in works of mire and clay; and He redeemed us Who gave Himself a Redemption for all; that we, the redeemed of the Lord [11], *whom He redeemed out of the hand of the enemy and gathered from the lands, might say, His mercy endureth for ever*. He sent also before our face Moses, the spiritual Law, and Aaron the High Priest, not bearing the typical Ephod and Urim, but having in His Forehead the seal of holiness which God the Father sealed; and Miriam, the foreshewing of prophets. Recollect we too what *he* thought against us who willed to devour us, the true Balak, Satan, who laid snares for us through Balaam, *the destroyer of the people*, fearing lest we should cover his land and occupy it, withdrawing the earthly-minded from his empire."

---

[1] העלתיך מארץ מצרים see Gen. l. 24. בית עברים Ex. xiii. 3. 14, xx. 2, Deut. viii. 14, xiii. 10; and united, as here, with פדה, Deut. vii. 8; xiii. 5.
[2] Ex. xv. 20. [3] Dion. [4] Num. xxxi. 49.
[5] See on Hos. ix. 10. vol. i. p. 93. and on Jo. iii. 18. vol. i. p. 212. [6] Jos. v. 9.

[7] Heb. vi. 10. [8] 1 S. John i. 9.
[9] צדקות, only occurs beside Jud. v. 11. (bis) 1 Sam. xii. 7 thence צדקתיך, Dan. ix. 16. Else only Ps. ciii. 6.
[10] From S. Jer. [11] Ps. cvii. 1-3.

Before
CHRIST
cir. 710.

6 ¶ Wherewith shall I come before the Lord, *and* bow myself before the high God? shall I come before him with burnt offerings, †with calves †of a year old?

7 ¹Will the Lord be pleased with thousands of rams, *or* with ten thousands of ᵏrivers of oil? ¹shall I give my firstborn *for* my transgression, the fruit of my †body *for* the sin of my soul?

8 He hath ᵐshewed

†Heb. *sons of a year?*
¹ Ps. 50. 9.
& 51. 16.
Isai. 1. 11.

Before
CHRIST
cir. 710.

ᵏ Job. 29. 6.
¹² Kings 16. 3.
& 21. 6. & 23. 10.
Jer. 7. 31.
& 19. 5.
Ezek. 23. 37.
† Heb. *belly.*
ᵐ Deut. 10. 12.
1 Sam. 15. 22.
Hos. 6. 6.
& 12. 6.

6, 7. *Wherewith shall I come before the Lord?* The people, thus arraigned, bursts in, as men do, with professions that they would be no more ungrateful; that they will do anything, everything—but what they ought. With them it shall be but " Ask and have." They wish only to know, *with what* they shall come? They would *be beforehand* ¹ with Him, anticipating His wishes; they would, with all the submission of a creature, *bow* ², prostrate themselves before God; they acknowledge His High Majesty, who dwelleth on high ³, *the most High God*, and would *abase themselves* ⁴ before His lofty greatness, if they but knew, "how" or "wherewith." They would give of their best ; sacrifices the choicest of their kind, which should be wholly His, whole-burnt-offerings, offered exactly according to the law ⁵, *bullocks of a year old*; then too, the next choice offering, the rams; and these, as they were offered for the whole people on very solemn occasions, in vast multitudes, *thousands* or ten thousands ⁶; the *oil* which accompanied the burnt sacrifice, should flow in rivers ⁷ ; nay, more still ; they would not withhold their sons, their first born sons, from God, part, as they were, of themselves, *or any fruit of their own body*. They enhance the offering by naming the tender relation to themselves ⁸. They would offer everything, (even what God forbade) excepting only what alone He asked for, their heart, its love and its obedience ⁹. The form of their offer contains this; they ask zealously, " with *what* shall I come." It is an outward offering only, a *thing* which they would bring. Hypocritical eagerness! a sin against light. For to enquire further, when God has already revealed anything, is to deny that He has revealed it. It comes from the

wish that He had *not* revealed what He *has* revealed. " ¹⁰ Whoso, after he hath found the truth, discusseth anything further, seeketh a lie." God had told them, long before, from the time that He made them His people, what he desired of them ; So Micah answers,

8. *He hath shewed thee.* Micah does not tell them *now*, as for the first time; which would have excused them. He says, *He hath shewed thee ; He*, about Whose mind and will and pleasure they were pretending to enquire, *the Lord* their God. He *had* shewn it to them. The law was full of it. He shewed it to them, when He said, ¹¹ *And now, Israel, what doth the Lord thy God require of thee, but to fear the Lord thy God, to walk in all His ways, and to love Him and to serve the Lord thy God with all thy heart and with all thy soul, to keep the commandments of the Lord and His statutes which I command thee this day for thy good?* They had asked, " *with what* outward *thing* ¹² shall I come before the Lord;" the prophet tells them, " what *thing* is *good*," the inward man of the heart, righteousness, love, humility.

And what doth the Lord require [*search, seek*] *of thee?* The very word ¹³ implies an earnest search within. He would say, " ¹⁴ Trouble not thyself as to any of these things, burnt-offerings, rams, calves, without thee. For God seeketh not thine, but thee ; not thy substance, but thy spirit; not ram or goat, but thy heart." " ¹⁵ Thou askest, what thou shouldest offer for thee? Offer thyself. For what else doth the Lord seek of thee, but thee? Because, of all earthly creatures, He hath made nothing better than thee, He seeketh thyself from thyself, because thou hadst lost thyself."

To do judgment, are chiefly all acts of

⁴ The word occurs only of one sinking, bowed down, amid persecutions, Ps. lvii. 7; of the "bowed down," whom God raiseth up, Ps. cxlv. 14, cxlvi. 8; and in Is. lviii. 5, of "ostentatious outward humiliation before God." So probably here, where alone the reflective occurs.
⁵ Lev. ix. 2, 3.
⁶ At Solomon's dedication, 22,000 oxen and 120,000 sheep, 1 Kings viii. 63; by Hezekiah, 2000 bullocks and 17,000 sheep, 2 Chron. xxx. 24; by Josiah, 30,000 lambs and kids for the paschal offerings and 3000 bullocks. Ib. xxxv. 7.

⁷ Comp. Job xx. 17, "rivers " (נהרי as here) "of streams of honey and cream." Oil was used in all meal-offerings which accompanied the burnt-offering, Lev. ii. 1, 2. 4–7, vii. 10. 12, and so entered into the daily sacrifice, Ex. xxix. 40, and all sacrifices of consecration, Ex. xxix. 2, 23, Lev. vi. 15, 21, Num. viii. 8.
⁸ See Deut. xxviii. 53.   ⁹ Conc. Chalc. Act. 3.
¹⁰ The enquiry, v. 7, was, *Will the Lord be pleased?* הֲיִרְצֶה יְיָ. The subject of, *He hath shewn thee*, is obviously that same Lord.
¹¹ Deut. x. 12, 13.   ¹² בַּמָּה, 6. מַה טוֹב, 8.
¹³ דרש.   ¹⁴ Rup.   ¹⁵ S. Aug. Serm. 48. ad loc. § 2.

Before CHRIST cir. 710.
ⁿ Gen. 18. 19.
Isai. 1. 17.

thee, O man, what *is* good; and what doth the LORD require of thee, but ⁿ to do

justly, and to love mercy, and to † walk humbly with thy God?

Before CHRIST cir. 710.
† Heb. *humble* thyself *to walk*.

equity; *to love mercy,* all deeds of love. *Judgment,* is what right requires; *mercy,* what love. Yet, secondarily, "to do judgment" is to pass righteous judgments in all cases; and so, as to others, [1] *judge not according to the appearance, but judge righteous judgment;* and as to one's self also. Judge equitably and kindly of others, humbly of thyself. " [2] Judge of thyself in thyself without acceptance of thine own person, so as not to spare thy sins, nor take pleasure in them, becau²e *thou* hast done them. Neither praise thyself in what is good in thee, nor accuse God in what is evil in thee. For this is wrong judgment, and so, not judgment at all. This thou didst, being evil; reverse it, and it will be right. Praise God in what is good in thee; accuse thyself in what is evil. So shalt thou anticipate the judgment of God, as He saith, [3] *If we would judge ourselves, we should not be judged of the Lord."* He addeth, *love mercy;* being merciful, out of love, [4] *not of necessity, for God loveth a cheerful giver.* These acts together contain the whole duty to man, corresponding with and formed upon the mercy and justice of God [5]. All which is due, anyhow or in any way, is of *judgment;* all which is free toward man, although not free toward God, is of *mercy.* There remains, *walk humbly with thy God;* not, *bow thyself* only before Him, as they had offered [6], nor again *walk with Him* only, as did Enoch, Noah, Abraham, Job; but *walk humbly* (lit. *bow down* [7] *the going*) yet still *with thy God;* never lifting up thyself, never sleeping, never standing still, but ever walking on, yet ever *casting thyself down;* and the more thou goest on in grace, the more cast thyself down; as our Lord saith, [8] *When ye have done all these things which are commanded you, say, We are unprofitable servants; we have done that which was our duty to do.*

It is not a "crouching before God" displeased, (such as they had thought of,) but the humble love of the forgiven; *walk humbly,* as the creature with the Creator, but in love, *with thine* own *God. Humble* thyself with God, Who humbled Himself in the flesh; *walk on* with Him, Who is thy Way. Neither humility nor obedience alone would be true graces; but to cleave fast to God, because He is thine *All,* and to *bow thyself down,* because

thou art nothing, and thine All is He and of Him. It is altogether a Gospel-precept; bidding us, [9] *Be ye perfect, as your Father which is in Heaven is perfect;* [10] *Be merciful, as your Father also is merciful;* and yet, in the end, have [11] *that same mind which was also in Christ Jesus, Who made Himself of no reputation.*

The offers of the people, stated in the bare nakedness in which Micah exhibits them, have a character of irony. But it is the irony of the truth and of the fact itself. The creature has nothing of its own to offer; [12] *the blood of bulls and goats cannot take away sin;* and the offerings, as they rise in value, become, not useless only but, sinful. Such offerings would bring down anger, not mercy. Micah's words then are, for their vividness, an almost proverbial expression of the nothingness of all which we sinners could offer to God. " [13] We, who are of the people of God, knowing that [14] *in His sight shall no men living be justified,* and saying, [15] *I am a beast with Thee,* trust in no pleas before His judgment-seat, but pray; yet we put no trust in our very prayers. For there is nothing worthy to be offered to God for sin, and no humility can wash away the stains of offences. In penitence for our sins, we hesitate and say, *Wherewith shall I come before the Lord?* how shall I come, so as to be admitted into familiar intercourse with my God? One and the same spirit revolveth these things in each of us or of those before us, who have been pricked to repentance, 'what worthy offering can I make to the Lord?' This and the like we revolve, as the Apostle saith; [16] *We know not what to pray for as we ought; but the Spirit itself maketh intercession for us with groanings which cannot be uttered.* 'Should I offer myself wholly as a burnt-offering to Him?' If, understanding spiritually all the Levitical sacrifices, I should present them in myself, and offer my first-born, i. e. what is chief in me, my soul, I should find nothing worthy of His greatness. Neither in ourselves, nor in ought earthly, can we find anything worthy to be offered to reconcile us with God. For the sin of the soul, blood alone is worthy to be offered; not the blood of calves, or rams, or goats, but our own; yet our own too is not offered, but given back, being due already [17]. The Blood of Christ Alone suf-

[1] S. John vii. 24.   [2] S. Aug. l. c.   [3] 1 Cor. xi. 31.
[4] 2 Cor. ix. 7.   [5] Ps. ci. 1. lxi. 7.   [6] v. 6.
[7] הַצְנֵעַ לֶכֶת The root only occurs beside in the form צְנוּעִים Prov. xi. 2, where it is opposed to *pride.* In the Targg. Afel is = Heb. הַצְנִיעַ. The noun is also used of humility. The Arabic has no

bearing upon it, all its meanings being derived from the original "formed."
[8] S. Luke xvii. 10.   [9] S. Matt. v. 48.
[10] S. Luke vi. 36.   [11] Phil. ii. 5, 7.   [12] Heb. x. 4.
[13] from S. Jer. S. Cyr. Rup. Dion.
[14] Ps. cxliii. 2.   [15] Ib. lxxiii. 22.
[16] Rom. viii. 26.   [17] Ps. cxvi. 8.

Before
CHRIST
cir. 710.

9 The LORD'S voice crieth unto the city, and ‖ *the man of* wisdom shall

|| Or, *thy name
shall see that
which is.*

see thy name: hear ye the rod, and who hath appointed it.

Before
CHRIST
cir. 710.

ficeth to do away all sin." "[1] The whole is said, in order to instruct us, that, without the shedding of the Blood of Christ and its Virtue and Merits, we cannot please God, though we offered ourselves and all that we have, within and without; and also, that so great are the benefits bestowed upon us by the love of Christ, that we can repay nothing of them."

But then it is clear that there is no teaching in this passage in Micah, which there is not in the law [2]. The developments in the Prophets relate to the Person and character of the Redeemer. The law too contained both elements; 1) the ritual of sacrifice, impressing on the Jew the need of an Atoner; 2) the moral law, and the graces inculcated in it, obedience, love of God and man, justice, mercy, humility, and the rest. There was no hint in the law, that half was acceptable to God instead of the whole; that sacrifice of animals would supersede self-sacrifice or obedience. There was nothing on which the Pharisee could base his heresy. What Micah said, Moses had said. The corrupt of the people offered a half-service, what cost them least, as faith without love always does. Micah, in this, reveals to them nothing new; but tells them that this half-service is contrary to the first principles of their law. *He hath shewed thee, O man, what is good.* Sacrifice, without love of God and man, was not even so much as the body without the soul. It was an abortion, a monster. For one end of sacrifice was to inculcate the insufficiency of all our good, apart from the Blood of Christ; that, do what we would, [3] *all* came *short of the glory of God.* But to substitute sacrifice, which was a confession that at best we were miserable sinners, unable, of ourselves, to please God, for any efforts to please Him or to avoid displeasing Him, would be a direct contradiction of the law, antinomianism under the dispensation of the law itself.

Micah changes the words of Moses, in order to adapt them to the crying sins of Israel at that time. He then upbraids them in detail, and that, with those sins which were patent, which, when brought home to them, they could not deny, the sins against their neighbor.

9. *The voice of the Lord crieth unto the city,* i.e. Jerusalem, as the metropolis of their wealth and their sin, the head and heart of their offending. *Crieth,* aloud, earnestly, intently, so that all might hear. So God says, [4] *Doth not wisdom cry? and understanding put forth her voice? She crieth at the gates,— unto you, O men, I cry, and my voice is to the sons of men;* and Isaiah prophesied of St. John Baptist, as [5] *the voice of one crying in the wilderness;* and our Lord saith, [6] *He that heareth you, heareth Me. And the man of wisdom shall see Thy Name.* The voice of God is in the hearing of all, but *the wise* only *seeth the Name of* God [7]. The word rendered *wisdom* means, *that which is* [8], and so, that which alone *is,* which alone has any real solid being, because it alone abides, *wisdom,* or counsel according to God. Such as are thus wise shall *see the Name of God,* (as Jeremiah says to his *generation* [9], *See ye the word of the Lord.*) They shall see His power and majesty and all which His Name expresses, as they are displayed severally in each work of His: He shall speak to them by all things wherein He is; and so seeing Him now *in a glass darkly,* they shall hereafter see all, His Glory, His Goodness, His Love, Himself, *face to face.*

Hear ye the rod, i.e. the scourge of the wrath of God. The name and the image recall the like propecies of Isaiah, so that Micah in one word epitomises the prophecies of Isaiah, or Isaiah expands the word of Micah. [10] *The rod in thine hand is My indignation;* [11] *As if the rod lifted up Him, Who is not wood;* [12] *He lifteth up his rod against thee;* [13] *Thou hast broken the rod* (which is) *on his*

[1] Dion.
[2] As is so often said, in order to depreciate the law, e. g. in Dr. Stanley's J. Church p. 448.
[3] Rom. iii. 23.
[4] Prov. viii. 1, 3, 4.   [5] Is. xl. 3. S. Matt. iii. 3.
[6] S. Luke x. 16.
[7] This, the simplest, is the most energetic rendering. Other possible renderings of the simple words, וְתוּשִׁיָּה יִרְאֶה שְׁמֶךָ, come to the same. Such are, "And wisdom (i. e. wholly wise) is he who regards Thy Name;" or "Thy Name (i. e. Thou, such as Thy name expresses of Thee) beholdeth wisdom," i. e. the really wise, or religious; or, "And wisdom is it, that one regards Thy Name;" or, with the change of a vowel (יִרְאָה for יִרְאֶה), "and wisdom is it, to fear Thy Name." In regard to the use

of the abstract, *wisdom,* for the concrete, *the wise,* Poc. compares Prov. xiii. 6, "wickedness overthrows sin," i. e. the sinner, and Ib. xx. 1. '*wine*' for *a man of wine.* He quotes also אָמַר קֹהֶלֶת, Eccl. i. 2. in illustration of the anomaly of gender, and vii. 8, מִתְנָה יְאַבֵּד.
[8] There is no other even plausible etymology of תּוּשִׁיָּה, than יֵשׁ, whose 3d radical appears in אִיתַי in Daniel, and in Syriac, and in אִיתִיאֵל, Heb. See "Daniel the Proph." p. 49.
[9] Jer. ii. 31. add "Ex. xx. 18, *and all the people saw* קוֹלֹת *the voices,* or *thunderings,* and, *see the smell of my son,* Gen. xxvii. 27." Poc.
[10] Is. x. 5.   [11] Ib. 15.   [12] Ib. 24.   [13] Ib. ix. 3. Heb.

Before
C H R I S T
cir. 710.

10 ¶ || Are there yet the treasures of wickedness in the house of the wicked, and the † scant measure ° *that is* abominable?

11 || Shall I count *them*

‖ Or, Is there
yet unto every
man an house
of the wicked,
&c.
† Heb. *measure*
of leanness,
Amos 8. 5.
° Deut 25. 13–16. Prov. 11. 1. & 20. 10, 23.
‖ Or, *Shall I be pure with, &c.*

pure with ᴾ the w i c k e d balances, and with the bag of deceitful weights?

12 For the rich m e n thereof are full of violence, and the inhabitants thereof

Before
C H R I S T
cir. 710.

ᴾ Hos. 12. 7.

---

shoulder; [1] *The Lord hath broken the rod of the wicked;* [2] *whereon the grounded* [i. e. fixed by the decree of God] *staff shall pass.*

And Who hath appointed it, i. e. beforehand, fixing the time and place, when and where it should come. So Jeremiah says, [3] *How canst thou* (sword of the Lord) *be quiet, and the Lord hath given it a charge to Ashkelon and to the sea-shore? there hath He appointed it.* He Who has *appointed it,* changeth not His decree, unless man changeth; nor is He lacking in power to fulfil it. He will surely bring it to pass. All which can be thought of, of fear, terror, motives to repentance, awe, hope, trust, is in that word *Who.* It is God; hopes and fears may be infinite.

10. *Are there* [4] *yet,* still after all the warnings and long-suffering of God, *the treasures of wickedness in the house of the wicked? Treasures of wickedness* are treasures gotten by wickedness; yet it means too that the wicked shall have no treasure, no fruit, but his wickedness. He treasureth up treasures, but of wickedness; as St. James saith, [5] *Ye have heaped treasure together for the last days,* i. e. of *the miseries that shall come upon them* [6]. The words stand over against one another; *house of the wicked, treasures of wickedness;* as though the whole *house of the wicked* was but a "treasure-house of wickedness." Therein it began; therein and in its rewards it shall end. *Are there yet?* the Prophet asks. There shall soon cease to be. The treasure shall be spoiled; the iniquity alone shall remain.

And the scant ephah (lit. *"ephah of leanness"* E. M.) *which is abominable?* Scant itself, and, by the just judgment of God, producing scantness, emaciated and emaciating [7]; as He says, [8] *He gave them their desire, and sent leanness withal into their soul;* and St. James [9], *it shall eat your flesh as it were fire.* Even a heathen said, "[10] Gain gotten by wickedness is loss;" and that, as being "*abominable*" or "*accursed*" or, one might say, "be-

wrathed [11]," lying under the wrath and curse of God. "[12] What they minish from the measure, *that* they add to the wrath of God and the vengeance which shall come upon them; what is lacking to the measure shall be supplied out of the wrath of God." The Ephah was a corn-measure [13], containing about six bushels; the rich, in whose house it was, were the sellers; they were the necessaries of life then, which the rich retailers of corn were selling dishonestly, at the price of the lives of the poor [14]. Our subtler ways of sin cheat ourselves, not God. In what ways do not competitive employers use the *scant measure which is accursed?* What else is all our competitive trade, our cheapness, our wealth, but scant measure to the poor, making their wages *lean,* full and overflowing with the wrath of God?

11. *Shall I count them pure?* rather, (as E. M.) *Shall I be pure* [15]? The Prophet takes for the time their person and bids them judge themselves in him. If it would defile me, how are ye, with all your other sins, not defiled? All these things were expressly forbidden in the law. [16] *Ye shall do no unrighteousness in judgment, in mete-yard, in weight or in measure. Just balances, just weights, a just ephah and a just hin, shall ye have;* and, [17] *Thou shalt not have in thy bag divers weights, a great and a small. Thou shalt not have in thine house divers measures, a great and a small. For all that do such things, and all that do unrighteousness are an abomination unto the Lord thy God.* Yet are not these things common even now?

12. *For the rich men thereof,* i. e. *of the city* [18], *are full of violence.* It had been little, had thieves and robbers lived by violence, but now, (as Isaiah at the same time upbraids them,) [19] *her princes* were become *companions of thieves.* Not the poor out of distress, but the rich, out of wantonness and exceeding covetousness and love of luxury, not only did

---

[1] Ib. xiv. 5.　　[2] Ib. xxx. 32.
[3] Jer. xlvii. 7. יָעַד is used in regard to time, 2 Sam. xx. 5. It is used of both time and place in the Arab. Conj. iii. as in מוֹעֵד, and the Syr.
[4] אַשׁ i. q. יֵשׁ, as in 2 Sam. xiv. 19, the א occurring together with the י (here indicated by the vowel) in Arab. Chald. Syr. Sam. Pers. and Heb. אִתַּי See n. 5.
[5] S. Jam. v. 3.　　[6] Ib. 1.　　[7] See v. 14.

[8] Ps. cvi. 15.　　[9] v. 3.
[10] Chilon in Diog. Laert. i. 4.　　[11] זְעוּמַת.
[12] Rib.　　[13] Am. viii. 5.
[14] It seems necessary, I see, in so-called Christian London, to advertise in shops, that bread is of its alleged weight.
[15] זָכַה in Kal is only intransitive.
[16] Lev. xix. 35, 36.
[17] Deut. xxv. 13, 15, 16. add Prov. xi. 1. xvi. 11. xx. 10.　　[18] ver. 9.　　[19] Is. i. 23.

Before
CHRIST
cir. 710.
have spoken lies, and [q] their tongue *is* deceitful in their

[q] Jer. 9. 3, 5, 6, 8.

mouth.

13 Therefore also will I [r] make *thee* sick in smiting thee, in making *thee* desolate because of thy sins.

[r] Lev. 26. 16.
Ps. 107. 17.

14 [s] Thou shalt eat, but

[s] Lev. 26. 26.
Hos. 4. 10.

Before
CHRIST
cir. 710.

not be satisfied; and thy casting down *shall be* in the midst of thee; and thou shalt take hold, but shalt not deliver; and *that* which thou deliverest will I give up to the sword.

---

wrong but were *filled*, not so much with riches, as *with violence.* Violence is the very meat and drink wherewith they are filled, yea, and wherewith they shall be filled, when it is returned upon their heads.

And the inhabitants thereof have spoken lies. Fraud is itself lying, and lying is its inseparable companion. "[1] Lying followeth the gathering together of riches, and the hard wont to lay up riches hath a deceitful tongue." The sin, he saith, is spread throughout all *her inhabitants;* i. e. all of them, as their wont, have spoken lies, and, even when they speak not, the lie is ready; *their tongue is deceitful* (lit. *deceit*) *in their mouth.* It is *deceit*, nothing but deceit, and *that*, deceit which should "[2] overthrow" and ruin others. One intent on gain has the lie ever ready to be uttered, even when he speaks not. It lurks concealed, until it is needed.

13. *Therefore also will I*, [lit. *And I too*,] i. e. this dost thou, and thus will I too do. "[3] As thou madest sick the heart of the poor oppressed, so will I, by My grievous and severe punishments, *make thee sick,*" or *make thy wound incurable*, as in Nahum [4], *thy wound is grievous*, lit. *made sick. In making thee desolate because of thy sins.* The heaping up riches shall itself be the cause of thy being waste, deserted, desolate.

14. *Thou shalt eat, but not be satisfied.* The correspondence of the punishment with the sin shall shew that it is not by chance, but from the just judgment of God. The curse of God shall go with what they eat, and it shall not nourish them. The word, *thou*, is thrice repeated [5]. As God had just said, *I too*, so here, *Thou. Thou,* the same who hast plundered others, *shalt thyself eat, and not be satisfied;* "*thou* shalt sow, and not reap; *thou* shalt tread the olive, and thou shalt not anoint thee with oil." "Upon extreme but ill-gotten abundance, there followeth extreme want. And whoso," adds one [6], "seeth not this in our ways and our times is abso-

lutely blind. For in no period have we ever read that there was so much gold and silver, or so much discomfort and indigence, so that those most true words of Christ Jesus seem to have been especially spoken of us, [7] *Take heed, for a man's life consisteth not in the abundance of the things which he possesseth.*" And is not this true of us now?

Thy casting down shall be in the midst of thee. Where thou hast laid up thy treasures, or rather thy wickedness, there thou shalt *sink down*, or give way, from inward decay, in the very centre of thy wealth and thy sin. They had said, [8] *Is not the Lord in the midst of us? None evil can come upon us.* Micah tells them of a different indweller. God had departed from them, and left them to their inherent nothingness. God had been their stay; without God, human strength collapses. Scarcely any destruction is altogether hopeless save that which cometh from within. Most storms pass over, tear off boughs and leaves, but the stem remains. Inward decay or excision alone are humanly irrecoverable. The political death of the people was, in God's hands, to be the instrument of their regeneration.

Morally too, and at all times, inward emptiness is the fruit of unrighteous fullness. It is disease, not strength; as even Heathen proverbs said; "the love of money is a dropsy; to drink increaseth the thirst," and "amid mighty wealth, poor;" and Holy Scripture, [9] *The rich He sendeth empty away.* And truly they must be empty. For what can fill the soul, save God? "[10] This is true too of such as, like the Bishop of Sardis, [11] *have a name that they live and are dead*," "[12] such as do some things good, feed on the word of God, but attain to no fruit of righteousness;" "who corrupt natural and seeming good by inward decay; who appear righteous before men, are active and zealous for good ends, but spoil all by some secret sin or wrong end, as vain-glory or praise of men, whereby they lose the praise of God. *Their casting down shall be in the midst of* them. The

---

[1] S. Jer.
[2] רְכִיָּה from רכה. It is used of the tongue in Ps. lii. 4, ci. 7, cxx. 2, 3; of a bow, Ps. lxxviii. 57, Hos. vii. 16.
[3] Poc.
[4] iii. 19.
[5] אַתָּה once in v. 14. twice in v. 15.

[6] Arias Montanus, a Spaniard. His Commentary on the Minor Prophets was published at Antwerp, 1571.
[7] S. Luke xii. 15.
[8] iii. 11.
[9] S. Luke i. 53, comp. 1 Sam. ii. 5.
[10] Rib.
[11] Rev. iii. 1.
[12] Dion.

Before
C H R I S T
cir. 710.
ᵗ Deut. 28. 38, 39,
40.
Amos 5. 11.
Zeph. 1. 13.
Hag. 1. 6.

15 Thou shalt ᵗ sow, but thou shalt not reap; thou shalt tread the olives, but thou shalt not anoint thee

with oil; and sweet wine, but shalt not drink wine.

16 ¶ For ‖ the statutes of ᵘ Omri are ˣ kept, and

Before
C H R I S T
cir. 710.
‖ Or, he doth
much keep the
&c.
ᵘ 1 Kings 16. 25,
26.
ˣ Hos. 5. 11.

meaning of the whole is the same, whether the word be rendered *casting down*, i. e. down-fall, (lit. *sinking down* [1],) or *emptiness*, especially of the stomach, perhaps from the feeling of "sinking."

Thou shalt take hold to rescue or *remove* to a safe place from the enemy, those whom he would take from thee, *but shalt not* wholly *deliver; and that which thou deliverest* for a time, *will I give up to the sword*, i. e. the children for whose sake they pleaded that they got together this wealth; as, now too, the idols, for whose sake men toil wrongly all their life, are often suddenly taken away. Their goods too may be said to be *given to the sword*, i. e. to the enemy.

15. *Thou shalt sow, but thou shalt not reap.* Micah renews the threatenings of the law [2], which they had been habitually breaking. Those prophecies had been fulfilled before, throughout their history; they have been fulfilled lately in Israel for the like oppression of the poor [3]. Their frequent fulfillment spoke as much of a law of God's righteousness, punishing sin, as the yearly supply in the ordinary course of nature spoke of His loving Providence. It is the bitterest punishment to the covetous to have the things which they coveted, taken away before their eyes; it was a token of God's Hand, that He took them away, when just within their grasp. The prophet brings it before their eyes, that they might feel beforehand the bitterness of forgetting them. "[4] They should lose, not only what they gained unjustly, but the produce of their labor, care, industry, as, in agriculture, it is said that there is mostly much labor, little fraud, much benefit." Harvest is a proverb for joy; [5] *they joy before Thee according to the joy in harvest;* [6] *wine maketh glad the heart of man, and oil is to make him a cheerful countenance.* But the harvest shall be turned into sorrow, [7] the oil and wine shall be taken away, when all the labor had been employed. Yet, since all these operations in nature are adapted to be, and are used as, symbols of things spiritual, then the words which describe them are adapted to be spiritual proverbs. Spiritually, " [8] *he soweth and reapeth not, who*

[9] *soweth to the flesh, and of the flesh reapeth corruption,* things corruptible, and inward decay and condemnation. He *treadeth the olive,* who, by shameful deeds contrary to the law, [10] *grieveth the Holy Spirit of God,* and therefore obtaineth not gladness of spirit; he maketh *wine, yet drinketh not wine,* who teacheth others, not himself." They too *take hold but do not deliver,* who *for awhile believe and in time of temptation fall away,* who repent for a while and then fall back into old sins, or in other ways *bring no fruit to perfection;* taking up the Cross for awhile and then wearying; using religious practices, as, more frequent prayer or fasting, and then tiring; cultivating some graces and then despairing because they see not the fruits. These tread the olive, but are not anointed with the oil of the Holy Spirit of grace, who " [11] end by doing for the sake of man, what they had thought to do out of the love for God, and abandon, for some fear of man, the good which they had begun."

16. *For the statutes of Omri are kept,* rather, (like E. M. *he doth much keep,*) *And he doth keep diligently for himself.* Both ways express much diligence in evil [12]. To "keep God's commandments" was the familiar phrase, in which Israel was exhorted, by every motive of hope and fear, to obedience to God. [13] *I know him,* God says of Abraham, *that he will command his children and his household after him, and they shall keep the way of the Lord, to do judgment and justice.* This was the fundamental commandment immediately after the deliverance from Egypt upon their first murmuring. [14] *The Lord made there* (at Marah) *for them a statute and ordinance, and said, If thou wilt diligently hearken to the voice of the Lord thy God, and wilt do that which is right in His sight, and wilt give ear to His commandments and keep all His statutes, I will put none of these diseases upon thee which I have brought upon the Egyptians.* In this character He revealed Himself on Mount Sinai, as [15] *shewing mercy unto thousands of them that love Me and keep My commandments.* This was their covenant, [16] *Thou hast avouched the Lord this day to be thy God and to walk in His ways, and to keep His statutes and His commandments and*

---

[1] It is possible, as Gesenius conjectures, that שׁוֹע (a ἅπ. λεγ.) is a transposed form of the Arab. שׁוֹה; more probably it may be from the bi-literal שׁוֹע, which gave rise to the other forms, שׁוֹע, שׁוֹשׁ.
[2] Lev. xxvi. 16, Deut. xxviii. 30. 38–41.
[3] Am. v. 11.   [4] Mont.   [5] Is. ix. 3.
[6] Ps. civ. 15.

[7] Comp. Is. xvi. 9, 10, Jer. v. 17, xlviii. 37.
[8] Theoph.   [9] Gal. vi. 8.   [10] Eph. iv. 30.   [11] Rib.
[12] In the construction of the E. V. (which is possible) the force of the union of the sing. verb with the plural noun would be that "the statutes of Omri, one and all, are kept diligently."
[13] Gen. xviii. 19.   [14] Ex. xv. 25, 26.   [15] Ib. xx. 6.
[16] Deut. xxvi. 17.

all the works of the house of ʸ Ahab, and ye walk in their c o u n s e l s; that I should make thee ᶻ a ‖ de-

ʸ 1 Kings 16. 30, &c.
& 21. 25, 26.
2 Kin. 21. 3.
ᶻ 1 Kings 9. 8. Jer. 19. 8.   ‖ Or, *astonishment*.

solation, and the inhabitants thereof an hissing: therefore ye shall bear the ᵃ reproach of my people.

ᵃ Isai. 25. 8.
Jer. 51. 51.
Lam. 5. 1.

His judgments and to hearken unto His voice. This was so often enforced upon them in the law, as the condition upon which they should hold their land, if they kept *the covenant*[1], *the commandments*[2], *the judgments*[3], *the statutes*[4], *the testimonies*[5], *the charge*[6] of the Lord. Under this term all the curses of the law were threatened, if they [7] *hearkened not unto the voice of the Lord* their *God, to keep His commandments and His statutes which* He commanded them. Under this again the future of good and evil was, in Solomon, set before the house of David; of unbroken succession on his throne, if [8] *thou wilt keep My commandments;* but contrariwise, *if ye or your children will not keep My commandments and My statutes,* banishment, destruction of the temple, and themselves to be [9] *a proverb and a byword among all people.* This was the object of their existence, [10] *that they might keep His statutes and observe His laws.* This was the summary of their disobedience, [11] *they kept not the covenant of God.* And now was come the contrary to all this. They had *not* kept the commandments of *God;* and those commandments of man which were the most contrary to the commandments of God, they *had* kept and did keep diligently. Alas! that the Christian world should be so like them! What iron habit or custom of man, what fashion, is not kept, if it is against the law of God? How few are not more afraid of man than God? Had God's command run, *Speak evil one of another, brethren,* would it not have been the best kept of all His commandments? God says, *speak not evil;* custom, the conversation around, fear of man, say, *speak evil;* man's commandment is kept; God's is not kept. And no one repents or makes restitution; few even cease from the sin.

Scripture does not record, what was the special aggravation of the sin of Omri, since the accursed worship of Baal was brought in by Ahab[12], his son. But, as usual, "like father, like son." The son developed the sins of the father. Some special sinfulness of Omri is implied, in that Athaliah, the murderess of her children, is called after her grandfather, Omri, not after her father, Ahab[13]. Heresiarchs have a deeper guilt than their followers, although the heresy itself is commonly developed later. Omri settled for a while the kingdom of Israel, after the anarchy which followed the murder of Elah, and slew Zimri, his murderer. Yet before God, *he did worse than all before him, and he walked in all the way of Jeroboam*[14]. Yet this too did not suffice Judah; for it follows, *And all the doings of the house of Ahab,* who again [15] *did evil in the sight of the Lord above all that were before him and served Baal;* Ahab, to whom none [16] *was like in sin, who did sell himself to work wickedness in the sight of the Lord.* These were they, whose statutes Judah now kept, as diligently and accurately as if it had been a religious act. They kept, not *the statutes of the Lord,* but *the statutes of Omri;* they kept, as their pattern before their eyes, *all the doings of the house of Ahab,* his luxury, oppression, the bloodshedding of Naboth; and they *walked* onward, not, as God bade them, *humbly with Him,* but *in their counsels.* And what must be the end of all this? *that I should make thee a desolation.* They acted, as though the very end and object of all their acts were *that,* wherein they ended, their own destruction and reproach[17].

Therefore ye shall bear the reproach of My people. The title of *the people of God* must be a glory or a reproach. Judah had gloried in being God's people, outwardly, by His covenant and protection; they were envied for the outward distinction. They refused to be so inwardly, and gave themselves to the hideous, desecrating, worship of Baal. Now then what had been their pride, should be the aggravation of their punishment. *Now* too we hear of people everywhere zealous for a system, which their deeds belie. Faith, without love, (such as their character had been,) feels any insult to the relation to God, which

---

[1] Ex. xix. 5. *the words of this covenant,* Deut. xxix. 9.

[2] המצוה or כל המצוה, or מצות יי Lev. xxii. 31, xxvi. 3, Deut. iv. 2, vi. 17, vii. 11, viii. 6, 11, x. 13, xi. 1, 8, 22, xiii. 5, Heb. 19, xv. 5. xix. 9, xxvii. 1. xxviii. 9, xxx. 10.

[3] משפט Lev. xviii. 5, 26, xx. 22, Deut. vii. 11, viii. 11, xi. 1.

[4] חקות or חקים Lev. xviii. 5, 26, xx. 8, 22. Deut. iv. 40, vi. 17, vii. 11, x. 13, xi. 1, xxx. 10.

[5] עדות Deut. vi. 17.

[6] משמרת Lev. xviii. 30, Deut. xi. 1.
[7] Deut. xxviii. 15.   [8] 1 Kings ix. 4–6.
[9] Ib. 7.   [10] Ps. cv. 45.   [11] Ib. lxxviii. 11.
[12] The worship of Baal was the result of Ahab's marriage with *Jezebel, the daughter* of one, whose name designates his devotedness to that idolatry, *Ethbaal,* (i.e. "with the help of Baal.") And this marriage is spoken of as Ahab's act, not his father's. 1 Kings xvi. 31.
[13] 2 Kings viii. 26. 2 Chron. xxii. 2.
[14] 1 Kings xvi. 25, 26. [15] Ib. 30–33. [16] Ib. xxi. 20.
[17] See on Hos. viii. 4. vol. i. p. 81.

CHAPTER VII.

1 *The church, complaining of
her small number,* 3 *and the
general corruption,* 5 *putteth
her confidence not in man, but
in God.* 8 *She triumpheth
over her enemies.* 14 *God
comforteth her by promises,* 16
by confusion of the enemies, 18
and by his mercies.

WOE is me! for I am as
† when they have
gathered the summer fruits,
as [a] the grapegleanings of
the vintage: *there is* no
cluster to eat: [b] my soul
desired the firstripe fruit.

† Heb. *the
gatherings of
summer.*
[a] Isai. 17. 6.
& 24. 13.

[b] Is. 28. 4.
Hos. 9. 10.

---

by its deeds it disgraces. Though they had
themselves neglected God, yet it was a heavy
burden to them to *bear* the triumph of the
heathen over them, that God was unable to
help them, or had cast them off. [1] *These are
the people of the Lord and are gone forth, out of
His land.* [2] *Wherefore should they say among
the heathen, where is their God?* [3] *We are confounded, because we have heard reproach, shame
hath covered our faces, for strangers are come into
the sanctuaries of the Lord's house.* [4] *We are become a reproach to our neighbors, a scorn and
derision to them that are round about us.* [5] *Thou
makest us a reproach to our neighbors, a scorn and
derision to them that are round about us. Thou
makest us a byword among the heathen, a shaking
of the head among the people. My confusion is
daily before me, and the shame of my face hath
covered me, for the voice of him that slandereth
and blasphemeth, by reason of the enemy and the
avenger.* The words, *the reproach of My people,* may
also include " [6] the reproach wherewith God
in the law [7] threatened His people if they
should forsake Him ", which indeed comes to
the same thing, the one being the prophecy,
the other the fulfillment. The word *hissing*
in itself recalled the threat to David's house
in Solomon; [8] *At this house,* which is high,
*every one that passeth by it shall be astonished and
hiss.* Micah's phrase became a favorite expression of Jeremiah [9]. So only do God's
prophets denounce. It is a marvelous
glimpse into man's religious history, that
faith, although it had been inoperative and
was trampled upon without, should still survive ; nay, that God, Whom in prosperity
they had forsaken and forgotten, should be
remembered, when He seemed to forget and
to forsake them. Had the captive Jews abandoned their faith, the reproach would have
ceased. The words, *ye shall bear the reproach*

of *My people* are, at once, a prediction of their
deserved suffering for the profanation of
God's Name by their misdeeds, and of their
perseverance in that faith which, up to that
time, they had mostly neglected.

CHAP. VII. The Prophet's office of threatening woe is now over. Here, out of love, he
himself crieth woe unto himself. He hath
[10] *continual sorrow in heart* for his people. He
bewails what he cannot amend, and, by bewailing, shews them how much more they
should bewail it, over whose sins he sorrows ;
how certain the destruction is, since there is
none to stand in the gap and turn away the
wrath of God, no "ten righteous," for whose
sake the city may be spared. " [11] These
words flow out of the fount of pity, because
the good zeal, wherewith the Holy seem to
speak severely, is never without pity. They
are wroth with the sins, they sympathize
with the sinner." So Isaiah mourned for the
judgment, which he prophesied against the
world, [12] *Woe is me!* he sorrowed even for
Moab [13] ; and Joel, [14] *Alas for the day!* and
Jeremiah in that exclamation of impas-
sioned sorrow ; [15] *Woe is me, my mother, that
thou hast borne me a man of strife and a man of
contention to the whole world !*

1. *Woe* [16] *is me ! for I am,* as when they have
gathered the summer fruits [17], *as the grape-glean-
ings of the vintage. The vineyard of the Lord of
hosts,* Isaiah said at the same time [18], is *the
house of Israel, and the men of Judah His pleasant plants.* Isaiah said, *it brought forth wild
grapes ;* Micah, that there are but gleanings,
few and poor. It is as though Satan pressed
the vineyard of the Lord, and made the most
his prey, and few were left to those who glean
for Christ ; [19] *the foxes have eaten the grapes.*
Some few remain too high out of their reach,
or hidden behind the leaves, or, it may be,
[20] falling in the time of gathering, fouled,

---

[1] Ezek. xxxvi. 20.
[2] Joel ii. 17. See vol. i. pp. 185, 186.
[3] Jer. li. 51. [4] Ps. lxxix. 4. [5] Ps. xliv. 13-16.
[6] Rib. and others in Poc. [7] Deut. xxviii. 36.
[8] 1 Kgs. ix. 8.
[9] שְׁרֵקָה Jer. li. 37. לִשְׁרֵקָה Jer. xix. 8. xxv. 9, 18.
xxix. 18. Else it is only used by Hezekiah, 2 Chron.
xxix. 8.
[10] Rom. ix. 2. [11] Rup. [12] Is. xxiv. 16.
[13] Ib. xv. 5. xvi. 11. [14] Joel i. 15. [15] Jer. xv. 10.
[16] אַלְלַי. The word occurs beside only in Job

x. 15. but it is the cry of nature. Among the Greeks
it is chiefly of joy or triumph, but of sorrow too; in
Latin chiefly of sorrow, "ululo," our, "howl."
[17] lit. *as the gatherings of the fig-harvest.* It is one
of those concise comparisons, which have to be
filled up. In prose it would be, "I am as one who,
at the gatherings of the fig-harvest, should still look
for fruit on the trees." The meaning, "summer,"
E. M. is doubtless a secondary sense of the word,
resulting from the fact, that the main fig harvest
was about the summer solstice.
[18] Is. v. 7. [19] Cant. ii. 15. [20] Poc. from Tanch.

Before
C H R I S T
cir. 710.
ᶜPs. 12. 1.
& 14. 1, 3.
Is. 57. 1.
‖ Or, *godly*, or,
merciful.
ᵈHab. 1. 15.

2 The ᶜ‖ good *man* is
perished out of the earth :
and *there is* none upright
among men : they all lie in
wait for blood ; ᵈ they hunt

every man his brother with
a net.

3 ¶ That they may do
evil with both hands earnestly, ᵉ the prince asketh,

---

sullied, marred and stained, yet left." So in
the gleaning there may be three sorts of souls ;
[1] *two or three in the top of the uppermost bough,*
which were not touched ; or those unripe,
which are but imperfect and poor ; or those
who had fallen, yet were not wholly carried
away. These too are all sought with difficulty ; they had escaped the gatherer's eye,
they are few and rare ; it might seem at first
sight, as though there were none. *There is
no cluster to eat ;* for the vintage is past, the
best is but as a sour grape which sets the teeth
on edge. *My soul desired the first-ripe fig* [2].
These are they which, having survived the
sharpness of winter, ripen early, about the
end of June ; they are the sweetest [2] ; but
he longed for them in vain. He addressed a
carnal people, who could understand only
carnal things, on the side which they *could*
understand. Our longings, though we pervert them, are God's gift. As they desired
those things which refresh or recruit the
thirsty body, as their whole self was gathered
into the craving for that which was to restore
them, so was it with him. Such is the longing of God for man's conversion and salvation; such is the thirst of His ministers;
such, their pains in seeking, their sorrow in
not finding. "[3] There were none, through
whose goodness the soul of the prophet might
spiritually be refreshed, in joy at his growth
in grace, as St. Paul saith to Philemon, [4] *refresh my bowels in the Lord.* So our Lord saith
in Isaiah, [5] *I said, I have labored in vain, I have
spent my strength for nought and in vain.* [6] *Jesus was grieved at the hardness of their hearts.*
"[7] The first-ripe fig may be the image of
the righteous of old, as the Patriarchs or the
Fathers, such as in the later days we fain
would see."
    2. *The good* [or *godly,* or *merciful,* E. M.]
man. The Hebrew word contains all. It is
"he who loveth tenderly and piously" God,
for His own sake, and man, for the sake of
God. Mercy was probably chiefly intended,
since it was to this that the prophet had exhorted [8], and the sins which he proceeds to

speak of, are against this. But imaginary
love of God without love of man, or love of
man without the love of God, is mere self-
deceit. *Is perished out of the earth,* i. e. by an
untimely death [9]. *The good* had either been
withdrawn by God *from the evil to come* [10], or
had been cut off by those who *laid wait for
blood ;* in which case their death brought a
double evil, through the guilt which such
sin contracted, and then, through the loss of
those who might be an example to others,
and whose prayers God would hear. The
loving and *upright,* all, who were men of
mercy and truth, had ceased. They who
were left, *all lie in wait for blood,* lit. *bloods* [11], i. e.
bloodshedding ; *all,* as far as man can see ; as
Elijah complains that he was left alone.
Amid the vast number of the wicked, the
righteous were as though they were not.
Isaiah, at the same time, complains of the
like sins, and that it was as though there were
none righteous ; [12] *Your hands are defiled with
blood, and your fingers with iniquity ; your lips
have spoken lies, your tongue hath muttered perverseness. None calleth for justice, nor any
pleadeth for truth.* Indirectly, or directly,
they destroyed life [13]. To violence they add
treachery. The good and *loving* had perished,
and all is now violence ; the upright had
ceased, and all now is deceit. *They hunt every
man his brother with a net.* Every man is the
brother of every man, because he is man,
born of the same first parent, children of the
same Father: yet they lay wait for one
another, as hunters for wild beasts [14].
    3. *That they may do evil with both hands ear-
nestly,* [lit. *upon evil both hands to do well,*] i. e.
"both their hands are upon evil to do it
well," or "earnestly [15]," as our translation
gives the meaning ; only the Hebrew expresses more, that evil is their good, and
their good or excellence is in evil. Bad men
gain a dreadful skill and wisdom in evil, as
Satan has ; and cleverness in evil is their delight. "[16] They call the evil of their hands
good." *The prince asketh, and the judge* asketh
(or, it may more readily be supplied, *judgeth,*

[1] Is. xvii. 6.
[2] The *bikkurah, boccore, Albacora.* (Span.) See
Shaw's Travels p. 370. Its goodness was proverbial.
See Hos. ix. 10, Is. xxviii. 4, Jer. xxiv. 2.
[3] Dion.   [4] Philem. 20.   [5] Is. xlix. 4.
[6] S. Mark iii. 5.   [7] From Rib.
[8] חֶסֶד vi. 8. חֶסֶד vii. 2.   [9] נָבַז.
[10] Is. lvii. 1. where אֲבָד is, in like way, used.
[11] See Hos. v. 2, and Mic. iii. 10, *They build up Zion
with bloods :* Isaiah says in like way, *Your hands are
full of bloods.* i. 15.

[12] Is. lix. 2, 3.
[13] See ab. p. 44, on iii. 10.
[14] Comp. Ps. xxxv. 7, lvii. 7, cxl. 6, Jer. v. 26.
[15] הֵיטֵב, like our, "do it well," can signify "do it
thoroughly;" yet not so as to supersede the idea
of its being "done well" in the mind of the actor.
The two cases cited to the contrary, the thorough
destruction of the calf, (Deut. ix. 21,) and of the
house of Baal, (2 Kings xi. 18,) were, of course, good
acts. So to "search well." Deut. xvii. 4, xix. 18.
[16] S. Jer.

[f] and the judge *asketh* for a reward; and the great *man*, he uttereth † his mischievous desire: so they wrap it up.

4 The best of them [g] *is* as a brier: the most upright *is sharper* than a thorn hedge: the day of thy watchmen *and* thy

visitation cometh; now shall be their perplexity.

5 ¶ [h] Trust ye not in a friend, put ye not confidence in a guide: keep the doors of thy mouth from her that lieth in thy bosom.

6 For [i] the son dishonoreth the father, the daughter riseth up against her

doth that which is his office,) against right *for a reward*, (which was strictly forbidden [1],) *and the great man he uttereth his mischievous desire*, (or *the desire of his soul*.) Even the shew of good is laid aside; whatever the heart conceives and covets, it utters;—mischief to others and in the end to itself. The mischief comes forth from the soul, and returns upon it. The *elders and nobles in the city* [2], as well as Ahab, took part, (as one instance,) in the murder of Naboth. The *great* man, however, here, is rather the source of the evil, which he induces others to effect; so that as many as there were great, so many sources were there of oppression. All, prince, judges, the great, unite in the ill, and this not once only, but they are ever doing it [3], and *so they wrap it up*, (lit. twist [4], intertwine it.) Things are twisted, either to strengthen, or to pervert or intricate them. It might mean, they *strengthen* it, that which their soul covets against the poor, or they *pervert* it, the cause of the poor.

4. *The best of them is as a brier;* the gentlest of them is a thorn, [5] strong, hard, piercing, which letteth nothing unresisting pass by but it taketh from it, "robbing the fleece, and wounding the sheep." *The most upright*, those who, in comparison of others still worse, seem so, *is sharper than a thorn hedge*. (lit. *the upright, than a thorn hedge*.) They are not like it only, but worse, and that in all ways; none is specified, and so none excepted; they were more crooked, more tangled, sharper. Both, as hedges, were set for protection; both, turned to injury. "[6] So that, where you would look for help, thence comes suffering." And if such be the best, what the rest?

The day of thy watchmen and thy visitation

cometh. When all, even the good, are thus corrupted, the iniquity is full. Nothing now hinders the *visitation*, which *the watchmen*, or prophets, had so long foreseen and forewarned of. *Now shall be their perplexity* [7]; *now*, without delay; for the day of destruction ever breaketh suddenly upon the sinner. [8] *When they say, peace and safety, then sudden destruction cometh upon them.* [9] *Whose destruction cometh suddenly at an instant.* They had perplexed the cause of the oppressed; they themselves were tangled together, intertwined in mischief, as a thorn-hedge. They should be caught in their own snare; they had perplexed their paths and should find no outlet.

5. 6. *Trust ye not in a friend.* It is part of the perplexity of crooked ways, that all relationships are put out of joint. Selfishness rends each from the other, and disjoints the whole frame of society. Passions and sin break every band of friendship, kindred, gratitude, nature. "Every one *seeketh his own.*" Times of trial and of outward harass increase this; so that God's visitations are seasons of the most frightful recklessness as to everything but self. So had God foretold [10]; so it was in the siege of Samaria [11], and in that of Jerusalem both by the Chaldeans [12] and by the Romans [13]. When the soul has lost the love of God, all other is but seeming love, since *natural affection* is from Him, and it too dies out, as God gives the soul over to itself [14]. The words describe partly the inward corruption, partly the outward causes which shall call it forth. There is no real trust in any, where all are corrupt. The outward straitness and perplexity, in which they shall be, makes *that* to crumble and fall

• [1] Deut. xvi. 19. See ab. iii. 11.
[2] 1 Kings xxi. 8, 11.
[3] The force of the partic. דִּבֶּר שׁוֹאֵל.
[4] עָבַת, the verb, is a ἅπ. λεγ. What remains of the root has the meaning of "twisted," (in עֲבֹת, "a rope") or "entangled," (in עֲבֹת, עֲבֹת "thick boughs.")
[5] The Heb. חֵדֶק seems to have been different from the Arab. which is a "solanum," (Cels. Hierob.

ii. 35.) but Prov. xv. 19, (where it occurs beside), shews that it served as a hedge. [6] S. Jer.
[7] In the Hebrew the two words "mesucah," "thorn hedge," and "mebucah," "perplexity," are alike in sound.
[8] 1 Thess. v. 3.
[9] See Is. xxx. 13. comp. 2 Pet. ii. 1, "swift destruction;" Prov. i. 27, "cometh as a whirlwind," Ps. xxxv. 8, "unawares."
[10] Deut. xxviii. 53. [11] 2 Kings vi. 28.
[12] Lam. iv. 3-16. [13] Jos. B. J. vi. 3. 8.
[14] Rom. i. 28.

Before
C H R I S T
cir. 710.

mother, the daughter in law against her mother in law; a man's enemies *are* the men of his own house.

7 Therefore [k] I will look unto the LORD; I will wait for the God of my salvation: my God will hear me.

Before
C H R I S T
cir. 710.

k Isai. 8. 17.

to pieces, which was inwardly decayed and severed before. The words deepen, as they go on. First, *the friend*, or neighbor, the common band of man and man; then *the guide*, (or, as the word also means, one *familiar*, united by intimacy, to whom, by continual intercourse, the soul was *used ;*) then the wife who lay in the bosom, nearest to the secrets of the heart; then those to whom all reverence is due, *father* and *mother*. Our Lord said that this should be fulfilled in the hatred of His Gospel. He begins His warning as to it, with a caution like that of the prophet ; [1] *Be ye wise as serpents*, and *beware of men*. Then He says, how these words should still be true [2]. There never were wanting pleas of earthly interest against the truth. He Himself was *cut off*, lest [3] *the Romans should take away their place and nation*. The Apostles were accused, that they meant to *bring this Man's Blood upon* the chief priests [4]; or as [5] *ringleaders of the sect of the Nazarenes, pestilent fellows and movers of sedition, turning the world upside down, setters up of another king ; troublers of the city ; commanding things unlawful for Romans to practice ; setters forth of strange gods ; turning away much people ; endangering not men's craft only, but the honor of their gods ; evil doers*. Truth is against the world's ways, so the world is against it. Holy zeal hates sin, so sinners hate it. It troubles them, so they count it, *one which troubleth Israel* [6]. Tertullian, in a public defence of Christians in the second century, writes, " [7] Truth set out with being herself hated ; as soon as she appeared, she is an enemy. As many as are strangers to it, so many are its foes ; and the Jews indeed appropriately from their rivalry, the soldiers from their violence, even they of our own household from nature. Each day are we beset, each day betrayed ; in our very meetings and assemblies are we mostly surprised." There was no lack of pleas. " [8] A Christian thou deemest a man guilty of every crime, an enemy of the gods, of the Emperors, of law, of morals, of all nature ; " "factious," "au-

thors of all public calamities through the anger of the heathen gods," "impious," "atheists," "disloyal," "public enemies." The Jews, in the largest sense of the word *they of their own household*, were ever the deadliest enemies of Christians, the inventors of calumnies, the authors of persecutions. "What other race," says [9] Tertullian, "is the seed-plot of our calumnies ? " Then the Acts of the Martyrs tell, how Christians were betrayed by near kinsfolk for private interest, or for revenge, because they would not join in things unlawful. " [10] So many are the instances in daily life, [of the daughter rising against the mother] that we should rather mourn that they are so many, than seek them out."—" I seek no examples, [of those of a man's own household being his foes] they are too many, that we should have any need of witness." " [11] Yet ought we not, on account of these and like words of Holy Scripture, to be mistrustful or suspicious, or always to presume the worst, but to be cautious and prudent. For Holy Scripture speaketh with reference to times, causes, persons, places." So St. John saith, [12] *Believe not every spirit, but try the spirits, whether they are of God*.

7. *Therefore*, (*And.*) when all these things come to pass and all human help fails, *I*, for my part, *will look unto*, (lit. *on*) *the Lord* God, the Unchangeable. The prophet sets himself, *I*, with emphasis, against the multitude of the ungodly. When all forsake, betray, fail, when [13] *love* is *waxed cold*, and men, in the last days, shall be [14] *lovers of their ownselves*, not *lovers of God*, I,—he does not say, "will trust," but—*will*, " [16] with the eye of the heart contemplating, loving, venerating God most High, and weighing His mercy and justice," *gaze intently* [15] with the devotion of faith toward Him, though I see Him not: yet so too I will rest *in* Him [16] and *on* Him, as the eyes are wont to rest in trust and love and dependence, and as, on the other hand, the Eyes of God [17] *espy into* man and dwell *on* him, never leaving him unbeheld. I will *espy* Him, although from afar, with the eyes

[1] S. Matt. x. 16. 17.   [2] Ib. 21, 35, 36.
[3] S. John xi. 48.   [4] Acts v. 28.
[5] Acts xxiv. 5. xvi. 20, 21. xvii. 6, 7, 18. 1 Pet. ii. 12.
[6] 1 Kings xviii. 17.
[7] Tert. Apol. c. 7. p. 17. Oxf. Tr.
[8] Ib. c. 2. p. 7. O. T. 38. 10. (and note k. Oxf. Tr.)
24, 28, 40, and notes e. f.; ad Scap. c, 2.
[9] Tert. ad Nat. i. 24. "The most atrocious calumnies against the Christians," S. Justin M. says, "were invented and circulated from country to

country by the Jews." Apol. i. 49. See also Dial c. Tryph. § 16. 108. c. Cels. vi. 27.
[10] S. Jer.   [11] Dion.   [12] 1 John iv. 1.
[13] S. Matt. xxiv. 12.   [14] 2 Tim. iii. 2, 4.
[15] אֶשְׁבֶּה, intensive, (as in Ps. v. 4.) "will espy intently," as toward that which can be seen only by intent gazing; and with בּ pers. "so as to dwell upon."
[16] Comp. Ps. xxv. 15. cxxiii. 1. cxli. 8.
[17] Ps. lxvi. 7.

Before
CHRIST
cir. 710.

1 Prov. 24. 17.
Lam. 4. 21.
m Ps. 37. 24. Prov. 24. 16.

8 ¶ [1] Rejoice not against me, O mine enemy: [m] when I fall, I shall arise; when I sit in darkness, [n] the LORD *shall be* a light unto me.

Before
CHRIST
cir. 710.

n Ps. 27. 1.

of the soul, as a watchman, (the word is the same,) looking for His Coming and announcing it to others; and until He comes, *I will wait* [*I would wait*] with trust unbroken by any troubles or delay, as Job saith, [1] *Though He slay me, yet will I put my trust in Him.* The word is almost appropriated to a longing waiting for God [2]. *For the God of my salvation.* This too became a wonted title of God [3], a title, speaking of past deliverances, as well as of confidence and of hope. Deliverance and salvation are bound up with God, and that, in man's personal experience. It is not only, "Saviour God," but "God, *my* Saviour," Thou who hast been, art, and wilt be, my God, my saving God. It is a prelude to the name of Jesus, our Redeeming God. *The Lord will hear me.* His purpose of waiting on God he had expressed wistfully. *I would wait* [4]; for man's longing trust must be upheld by God. Of God's mercy he speaks confidently, *the Lord will hear me,* He, Who is ever "more ready to hear than we to pray." He has no doubts, but, as Abraham said, [5] *the Lord will provide,* so he, *The Lord will hear me.* So, when Jehoshaphat prayed, [6] *We have no might against this great company that cometh against us, neither know we what to do, but our eyes are upon Thee;* God answered by the prophet, *Be not afraid nor dismayed by reason of this great multitude; for the battle is not yours, but God's.* Micah unites with himself all the faithful as one, "in the unity of the spirit," wherein all are one band, looking, waiting, praying for His Coming in His kingdom. "[7] God is our only refuge and asylum in things desperate, and rejoices to help in them, in order to shew His supreme Power and Goodness especially to those who believe, hope, and ask it. Therefore all mistrust and despondency is then to be supremely avoided, and a certain hope and confidence in God is to be elicited. This will call forth the help

of God assuredly, yea though it were by miracle, as to Lot in Sodom, to Moses and the people from Pharaoh, to David from Saul, to Hezekiah from Sennacherib, to the Maccabees from Antiochus. This our proverbs express [8], how God aids, when there is least sign of it."

8. *Rejoice not against me, O mine enemy.* The Prophet still more makes himself one with the people, not only as looking for God, but in penitence, as Daniel bewails [9] *his own sins and the sins of his people.* The *enemy* is Babylon and *Edom* [10]; and then, in all times, (since this was written for all times, and the relations of the people of God and of its enemies are the same,) whosoever, whether devils or evil men, rejoice over the falls of God's people. *Rejoice not;* for thou hast no real cause; *the triumphing of the ungodly,* and the fall of the godly, [11] *is but for a moment. When I fall, I shall arise;* (lit. *when I have fallen, I have arisen;*) expressing both the certainty and speed of the recovery. To fall [12] and to arise is one. "[13] The fall of infirmity is not grave, if free from the desire of the will. Have the will to rise, He is at hand Who will cause thee to rise." "[14] Though I have sinned, Thou forgivest the sin; though I have fallen, thou raisest up; lest they, who rejoice in the sins of others, should have occasion to exult. For we who have sinned more, have gained more; for Thy grace maketh more blessed than our own innocence."

When I sit in darkness, the Lord shall be a light unto me. "[15] He does not say 'lie,' but *sit;* she was not as one dead, without hope of life, but she sat solitary as a widow, helpless, unable to restore herself, yet waiting for God's time. The darkness of the captivity was lightened by the light of the prophetic grace which shone through Daniel and Ezekiel, and by the faithfulness of the three

---

[1] Job xiii. 15.

[2] אוֹחִילָה לְ, as in Ps. xxxviii. 16. xlii. 6, 12, xliii. 5, cxxx. 5, 2 Kings vi. 33, Lam. iii. 24. יָחֵל is almost appropriated to one who so *waiteth* for God. Abs. Hifil, Lam. iii. 21. Pi. Job vi. 11, xiv. 14, Ps. lxxi. 14. יָחִיל, adj. Lam. iii. 26. and Prop. Name "Waiter" on God, as expressed in יַחְלְאֵל. Pi. with לְ, Ps. xxxi. 25, xxxiii. 22, lxix. 4; with אֶל, of God, Ps. cxxx. 7, cxxxi. 3; with לְ, of the *word* of God, Ps. cxix. 74, 81, 114, 147; of His *mercy,* Ps. xxxiii. 18, cxlvii. 11; of His *judgments,* Ps. cxix. 43; of His *Arm,* Is. li. 5; of His *law,* Is. xlii. 4. Transitively, Ps. cxix. 49. So תּוֹחֶלֶת, abs. Pr. x. 28. Lam. iii. 18; with לְ, Ps. xxxix. 8.

[3] "God of *my* salvation," (יִשְׁעִי,) Ps. xviii. 47, (2 Sam. xxii. 47.) xxv. 5, xxvii. 9, Hab. iii. 18. "God, my s." Ps. lxii. 8. "God of our s." Ps. lxv. 6, lxxix. 9, lxxxv. 5. "God of thy s." Is. xvii. 10. "God of his s." Ps. xxiv. 5. "Rock of our s." Ps. xcv. 1.

[4] אוֹחִילָה, optat.   [5] Gen. xxii. 8, 14.
[6] 2 Chron. xx. 12, 15.   [7] Lap.
[8] Deus ex machinâ.   [9] Dan. ix. 10.
[10] Obad. 10. 12. Ps. cxxxvii. 7.   [11] Ps. xxx 5.

[12] נָפַל is used of the fall of a people, Am. v. 2, viii. 14, Is. xxiv. 20; of a king and his people, 2 Kings xiv. 10; of many individuals, Is. viii. 15. In Prov. xxiv. 16. it is used of the fall of the righteous, from which he shall rise, in contrast with the stumbling (יִכָּשְׁלוּ) of the wicked, without recovery.
[13] S. Ambr. in Ps. 37. [38 Eng.] v. 15.
[14] Ib. v. 47.   [15] Mont.

Before
CHRIST
cir. 710.

º Lam. 3. 39.

P Ps. 37. 6.

9 º I will bear the indignation of the LORD, be-
cause I have sinned against
him, until he plead my
cause, and execute judg-
ment for me: P h e w i l l

bring me forth to the light,
and I shall b e h o l d his
righteousness.

10 || Then *she that is* mine
enemy s h a l l see *it*, and
q shame shall cover her

Before
CHRIST
cir. 710.

|| Or, And thou
wilt see her that
is mine enemy,
and cover her
with shame.

q Ps. 35. 26.

children, and the brightness of Divine glory
shed abroad through them, when Nebuchadnezzar proclaimed to all people that their
God was [1] *God of gods and Lord of kings*,
and that none should [2] *speak anything amiss
against Him*. Still more when, at the close
of the captivity, they were delivered from
sorrow, trouble, bondage, death, to joy, rest,
freedom, life. Yet how much more in Christ,
(for Whom this deliverance prepared,) when
[3] *the people that walked in darkness have seen a
great light: they that dwell in the land of
the shadow of death, upon them hath the light
shined*. God is not only our light, as "[4] restoring us" outwardly "to gladness, freedom,
happiness, whereof light is a symbol, as
darkness is of sorrow, captivity, adversity,
death." Scripture speaks of God, in a di-
recter way, as being Himself our light. [5] *The
Lord is my light*. [6] *The Lord shall be unto thee
an everlasting light*. He calls Himself, [7] *The
light of Israel*. He is our light, by infusing
knowledge, joy, heavenly brightness, in any
outward lot. He does not say, "after darkness, comes light," but *when I shall sit in
darkness*, then, *the Lord is light unto me*. The
sitting in darkness is the occasion of the light,
in that the soul or the people in sorrow turns
to Him Who is their light. In their sin,
which was so punished, they were turned
away from the light.

9. *I will bear the indignation of the Lord,
because I have sinned against Him*. This is the
temper of all penitents, when stricken by
God, or under chastisement from Him. [8] *It
is the Lord, let Him do what seemeth Him
good*. [9] *So let him curse, because the Lord hath
said unto him, curse David. Who shall then
say, Wherefore hast thou done so?* [10] *He putteth his mouth in the dust; if so be there may
be hope*. The penitent owns the just sentence
of God, and, knowing that he deserves far
more than God inflicts, is thankful to endure
it, until He remove it, *until He plead my
cause and execute judgment for me*, i. e. until
God Himself think the punishments inflicted, enough, and judge between me and
those through whose hands they come. The
judgments which God righteously sends, and
which man suffers righteously from Him, are

unrighteously inflicted by those whose malice
He overrules, whether it be that of evil men
(as the Assyrian or the Chaldæan or the Edomite) or of Satan. The close of the chastisements of His people is the beginning of the
visible punishment of *their* misdeeds, who
used amiss the power which God gave them
over it. Whence it is said, [11] *Daughter of
Babylon, the wasted! blessed he that rewardeth
thee as thou hast served us*. But all is of the
mercy of God. So He saith, *He shall bring
me forth to the light* of His Countenance and
His favor and His truth. Micah speaks in
the name of those who were penitent, and so
were forgiven, and yet, in that they were
under punishment, seemed to lie under the
wrath of God. For, although God remits
at once the eternal penalty of sin, yet we see
daily, how punishment pursues the forgiven
sinner, even to the end of life. The light of
God's love may not, on grounds which He
knoweth, shine unchequered upon him. We
should not know the blackness of the offence
of sin, and should never know the depth of
God's mercy, but for our punishment. The
indignation of God toward the penitent is an
austere form of His love. So then penitents may well say, in every grief or sickness
or visitation or disappointment, *I will bear
the indignation of the Lord, because I have sinned
against Him*. He says, *I shall behold His
righteousness*, because they had a righteous
cause against man, although not toward God,
and God in His just judgment on their enemies shewed Himself as the righteous Judge
of the world.

10. *Then [And]* she that is *mine enemy shall
see it, and shame shall cover her which said unto
me, Where is He* [12], He of Whom thou boast-
est, *the Lord thy God?* The cause of her
gladness then is, that the blasphemies of the
enemy of God were to cease. This was the
bitterest portion of her cup, that they said
daily, "*Where is now thy God?* let Him come
and save thee;" as though He could not, or
as though He loved her not, and she vainly
presumed on His help. Even when fallen,
it was for *His* sake that she was hated, Who
seemed to be overcome in her: as He was
hated in His Martyrs, and they asked,

[1] Dan. ii. 47.   [2] Ib. iii. 29.
[3] Is. ix. 2.   [4] Lap.
[5] Ps. xxvii. 1.
[6] Is. lx. 19.   [7] Ib. x. 17.   [8] 1 Sam. iii. 18.

[9] 2 Sam. xvi. 10.
[10] Lam. iii. 29.
[11] Ps. cxxxvii. 8.
[12] איו. The pronoun is inserted emphatically.

Before CHRIST cir. 710.
r Ps. 42. 3, 10. & 79. 10. & 115. 2. Joel 2. 17. s ch. 4. 11.

which said unto me, r Where is the LORD thy God? s mine eyes shall be-

Before CHRIST cir. 710.
† Heb. she shall be for a treading down.
t 2 Sam. 22. 43. Zech. 10. 5.

hold her: now † shall she be trodden down t as the mire of the streets.

"[1] Where is the God of the Christians?" Now the taunt was closed, and turned back on those who used it. The wheel, which they had turned against her, rolled round on themselves. They who had said, *Let our eye look on Zion,* now were ashamed that their hope had failed. *They* had longed to feed their sight *on* her miseries; Zion had her reverent gladness in *gazing* on [2] *the righteousness of God.* Babylon was trodden down by the Medes and Persians, and they whom she had let captive beheld it. Daniel was in the palace, when Belshazzar was slain.

The soul of one, who has known the chastening of God, cannot but read its own history here. The sinful soul is at once the object of the love of God and hath that about it which God hates. God hates the evil in us, even while He loves us, being, or having been, evil. He forgives, but chastens. His displeasure is the channel of His goodpleasure. Nathan said to David, [3] *The Lord hath put away thy sin,* but also, *the sword shall never depart from thy house.* It is part of His forgiveness to cleanse the soul with a [4] *spirit of burning.* "It seemeth to me," says St. Jerome, "that *Jerusalem* is every soul, which had been the temple of the Lord, and had had the vision of peace and the knowledge of Scripture, and which afterward, overcome by sins, hath fallen captive by its own consent, parting from that which is right in the sight of God, and allowing itself to sink among the pleasures of the world." So then "[5] captive, and tortured, she saith to Babylon, i. e. the confusion of this world and the power of the enemy which ruleth over the world, and sin who lordeth it over her, *Rejoice not against me, O mine enemy; when I fall, I shall arise;*" "[6] from sin by repentance, and from tribulation by the consolation of the Holy Spirit, Who, after weeping, poureth in joy. *For* [7] *the Lord helpeth them that are fallen,* and saith by the Prophet, [8] *Shall they fall and not arise?* and [9], *I have no pleasure in the death of the wicked; but that the wicked turn from his way and live. If I walk in darkness, the Lord is my light!* For although [10] *the rulers of the darkness of this world* have deceived me, and I [11] *sit in darkness and in the shadow of death,* and [12] *my feet stumble upon the dark mountains,* yet [13] *to them who sit in the region and shadow of death, light is sprung up,*

[1] Ep. of Churches of Vienne and Lyons, in Eus. H. E. v. 1 fin.
[2] אראה בצדקתו ver. 9, corresponding to תראינה בה, v. 10.
[3] 2 Sam. xii. 10, 13.   [4] Is. iv. 4.   [5] S. Cyr.

and [14] *light shineth in darkness,* and [15] *the Lord is my light, and my salvation; whom then shall I fear?* and I will speak to Him and will say, [16] *Thy word is a lamp unto my feet, and a light unto my path.*" "He draweth me from the darkness of ignorance and from the black night of sin, and giveth a clear view of future bliss, and brighteneth the very inmost soul within." "[6] Even if a mist have come upon me and I have been in darkness, I too shall find the light, i. e. Christ; and the Sun of Righteousness arising on my mind shall make it white." *I will bear* patiently, yet gladly, *the indignation of the Lord,* "[6] all adversity, trial, tribulation, persecution, which can happen in this life;" *because I have sinned against Him,* "and such is the enormity of sin, offered to the Majesty and dishonoring the Holiness of God, and such punishment doth it deserve in the world to come, that if we weigh it well, we shall bear with joy whatever adversity can befall us." "[5] For although for a short time I be out of His Presence, and be [17] *given to an undistinguishing mind,* yet, seeing I suffer this rejection justly, I will bear the judgment, for I am not chastened in vain." [18] *All chastening for the present seemeth not to be joyous but grievous, nevertheless afterward it yieldeth the peaceable fruit of righteousness unto them who are exercised thereby.* "[19] The soul, feeling that it hath sinned, and hath the wounds of sins and is living in dead flesh and needs the cautery, says firmly to the Physician, 'Burn my flesh, cut open my wounds, all my imposthumes. It was my fault, that I was wounded; be it my pain, to endure such sufferings and to regain health.' And the true Physician shews to her, when whole, the cause of His treatment, and that He did rightly what He did. Then after these sufferings, the soul, being brought out of outer darkness, saith, *I shall behold His Righteousness,* and say, [20] *Thou, O Lord, art upright; Righteous are Thy judgments, O God.* But if Christ is [21] *made unto us wisdom and righteousness and sanctification and redemption,* he who, after the indignation of God, saith that he shall *see His Righteousness,* promiseth to himself the sight of Christ." "[5] Then, having considered in her mind the grace of the righteousness in Christ and the overthrow of sin, the soul, in full possession of herself,

[6] Dion.   [7] Ps. cxlvi. 8.   [8] Jer. viii. 4.
[9] Ezek. xxxiii. 11.   [10] Eph. vi. 12.
[11] Ps. cvii. 10.   [12] Jer. xiii. 16.   [13] Is. ix. 2.
[14] S. John i. 5.   [15] Ps. xxvii. 1.   [16] Ps. cxix. 105.
[17] Rom. i. 28.   [18] Heb. xii. 11.   [19] S. Jer.
[20] Ps. cxix. 137.   [21] 1 Cor. i. 30.

Before
CHRIST
cir. 710.

u Amos 9. 11, &c.

11 *In* the day that thy
u walls are to be built, *in*
that day shall the decree
be far removed.

Before
CHRIST
cir. 710.

x Is. 11. 16.
& 19. 23. &c.
& 27. 13.
Hos. 11. 11.
|| Or, *even to.*

12 *In* that day *also* x he
shall come even to thee
from Assyria, || and *from*
the fortified cities, and from

---

crieth out, *Mine enemy shall see it, &c.* For,
after that Christ came unto us, justifying
sinners through faith, the mouth of the ungodly One is stopped, and the Author of sin
is put to shame. He hath lost his rule over
us, and sin is trodden down, *like mire in the
streets,* being subjected to the feet of the saints.
But the blotting-out of sin is the Day of
Christ." "[1] And, because the end of all
punishment is the beginning of good," God
saith to the poor, penitent, tossed, soul, "*the
walls* of virtues *shall be built up* in thee, and
thou shalt be guarded on all sides, and the
rule of thine oppressors shall be far removed, and thy King and God shall come
unto thee, and *all the ends of the earth shall
see the salvation of God.*" "[2] All this shall
be most fully seen in the Day of Judgment."

11, 12. On this confession of unworthiness and trust the message of joy bursts in,
with the abruptness [3] and conciseness of
Hosea or Nahum:

A day to build thy fences; [i. e. cometh;]
That day, far shall be the decree;
That day, and he shall come quite to thee [4];
and there follows, in a longer but still remarkably measured and interrupted cadence [5], the
statement of the length and breadth from
which the people shall come to her;

*Up to and from Assyria and the cities of strong-
land* [Egypt;]

Up to and from strong-land and even to river
[Euphrates;]
*And sea from sea, and mountain to moun-
tain.*

It is not human might or strength which
God promises to restore. He had before
predicted, that the kingdom of the Messiah
should stand, not through earthly strength [6].
He promises the restoration, not of city
walls, but of the *fence* of the vineyard [7] of
God, which God foretold by Isaiah that He
would *break down* [8]. It is a peaceful renewal
of her estate under God's protection, like
that, with the promise whereof Amos closed
his prophecy ; [9] *In that day I will raise up the
tabernacle of David that is fallen, and close up
the breaches thereof.* This *decree,* which he
says *shall be far* away, might in itself be the
decree either of God or of the enemy [10]. The
sense is the same, since the enemy was but
the instrument of God. Yet it seems more
in accordance with the language of the prophets, that it should be the decree of man.
For the decree of God for the destruction of
Jerusalem and the captivity of His people
was accomplished, held its course, was fulfilled. The destruction, captivity, restoration, were parts of one and the same decree
of God, of which the restoration was the last
accomplished in time. The restoration was
not the removal, but the complete fulfillment,
of the decree. He means then probably,

---

3 Hence the omission of the preposition עַד before
עָרֵי מָצוֹר and יָם, and of any preposition in the
last clause, וְהַר חָרַר.

4 The three sentences, which begin with יוֹם, are
manifestly each complete in itself.

5 Ver. 12 is divided into four clauses, of which
each consists of four words, and these in pairs;

" Yôm hoo, ve'adeica yabo
leminni asshur, ve'arê mâtsôr,
ooleminni matsôr, ve' ad nahar
veyam miyyam, vehar hahar.

6 v. 9-13.

7 גֶּדֶר is the wall of a vineyard, Num. xxii. 24, Is.
v. 5, Ps. lxxx. 13; a wall pushed down, Ps. lxii. 4;
one in which a serpent might lurk, Eccl. x. 8; a
wall with gaps in it, Ezek. xiii. 5, xxii. 30; the wall
of the court of the temple, Ib. xlii. 7; a fence, Ezr.
ix. 9. It is no where used of "the wall of a city."
גָּדֵר too is the wall of the court of the temple, Ezek.
xliii. 10; the wall of a vineyard, Prov. xxiv. 31.
גְּדֵרָה is "a sheepfold," Num. xxxii. 16, 24, 36, 1
Sam. xxiv. 4, Zeph. ii. 6; fences under which locusts lodge, Nah. iii. 17; in the open field, Jer. xlix.
3, Hos. ii. 8. Heb.; fences, Ps. lxxxix. 41. Heb.
8 Is. v. 5. 9 ix. 11.

10 חֹק is used chiefly of a "statute" of God, either

those positive laws given by Moses, (its common
use) or such laws as God has impressed upon the
physical world, Job xxvi. 10, xxviii. 26, xxxviii. 10,
33, Prov. viii. 29, Jer. v. 22. xxxi. 35, 6; of the time
appointed by God for man's life, Job xiv. 5, 13; a
decree of God, Job xxiii. 14, Ps. ii. 7, Zeph. ii. 2; of a
portion of food appointed by God, Job xxiii. 12,
Prov. xxx. 8, Ezek. xvi. 27; by man, Gen. xlvii. 22,
Prov. xxxi. 15; of a statute made by man, Gen.
xlvii. 26, 1 Sam. xxx. 25; a custom, Jud. xi. 39, (Plur.
Jer. xxxii. 11, Ez. xx. 18.); a task appointed by
man, Ex. v. 14. But in all cases the idea of "appointment," is prominent; so that although חֹק
expresses the law of God determining the bounds
of the sea or the term of man's life, it cannot therefore signify a mere point in space or time. חָרַר
also, with which it is united by alliteration, (probably to fix the words in men's memories,) is not to
"expand," but to "be far off." Then also יָרִים, corresponding to לִבְנוֹת which implies a future, must
itself be a future, not a mere aorist or vivid present.
These three observations together exclude such
renderings as, "the decree for thy restoration shall
be promulged far and wide;" "the decree of God
shall not be confined to Babylon but shall extend to
other countries." "In that day, the interval is distant:" (Ew.) "the bound set to her will be far off,"
i. e. Israel shall be enlarged.

the fortress even to the river, and from sea to sea, and *from* mountain to mountain.

that the *decree* of the enemy, whereby he held her captive, was to remove and *be far* off, not by any agency of her's [1]. The people were to stream to her of themselves. One by one, shall all thy banished, captive, scattered, children be brought *quite* home *unto thee* from all parts of the earth, whither they have been driven, *from Assyria, and from strong-land.* The name *Matsor*, which he gives to Egypt, modifying its ordinary dual name *Mitsraim*, is meant, at once to signify "Egypt [2]" and to mark the strength of the country; as, in fact, "[3] Egypt was on all sides by nature strongly guarded." A country, which was still strong relatively to Judah, would not, of itself, yield up its prey, but held it *straitly;* yet it should have to disgorge it. Isaiah and Hosea prophesied, in like way, the return of Israel and Judah from Assyria and from Egypt [4]. *And from strong-land even to the river* [Euphrates]; the ancient, widest, boundary of the promised land [5]; *and from sea to sea, and from mountain to mountain.* These last are too large to be the real boundaries of the land. If understood geographically, it would by narrowing those which had just been spoken of, from Egypt to the Euphrates. Joel likens the destruction of the Northern army to the perishing of locusts in the two opposite seas, the Dead sea and the Mediterranean [6]; but the Dead sea was not the entire Eastern boundary *of all Israel.* Nor are there any mountains on the South, answering to Mount Libanus on the North. Not the mountains of Edom which lay to the South-East, but *the desert* [7] was the Southern boundary of Judah. In the times too of their greatest prosperity, Edom, Moab, Ammon, Syria, had been subject to them. The rule of the Messiah *from sea to sea* had already been predicted by Solomon [8], enlarging the boundaries of the promised land to the whole compass of the world, *from the sea,* their bound westward, *to* the further encircling *sea* beyond all habitable land, in which, in fact, our continents are large islands [9]. To this, Micah adds a new description, *from mountain to mountain,* including, probably, all subdivisions in our habitable earth, as the words,

sea to sea, had embraced it as a whole. For, physically and to sight, mountains are the great natural divisions of our earth. Rivers are but a means of transit. The Euphrates and the Nile were the centres of the kingdoms which lay upon them. Each range of mountains, as it rises on the horizon, seems to present an insuperable barrier. No barrier should avail to hinder the inflow to the Gospel. As Isaiah foretold that all obstacles should be removed [10], *every valley shall be exalted, and every mountain and hill shall be made low,* so Micah prophesies, *from mountain to mountain they shall come.*

The words are addressed as a promise and consolation to the Jews, and so, doubtless, the restoration of the Jews to their own land after the captivity is foretold here, as Micah had already foretold it [11]. But is the whole limited to this? He says, with remarkable indefiniteness, *there shall come* [12]. He does not say, *who* "shall come." But he twice sets two opposite boundaries, from which men should come; and, since these boundaries, not being coincident, cannot be predicted of one and the same subject, there must be two distinct incomings. The Jews were to come from those two countries, whither its people were then to be carried captive or would flee. From the boundaries of the world, the world was to come.

Thus Micah embraces in one the prophecies, which are distinct in Isaiah, that not only God's former people should *come from Egypt and Assyria,* but that Egypt and Assyria themselves should be counted as one with Israel [13]; and while, in the first place, the restoration of Israel itself is foretold, there follows that conversion of the world, which Micah had before promised [14], and which was the object of the restoration of Israel. This was fulfilled to Jews and heathen together, when the *dispersed* of the Jews were gathered into one in Christ, *the Son of David* according *to the flesh,* and the Gospel, *beginning at Jerusalem,* was spread abroad among all nations. The promise is thrice repeated, *It is the day,* assuring the truth thereof, as it were, in the Name of the All-Holy Trinity.

---

[1] This is conveyed by the simple neuter, יַרְחִק, "shall be far off."

[2] As it certainly does in Isaiah at the same date, Is. xix. 6, xxxvii. 25, (2 Kings xix. 24.).

[3] Diod. Sic. i. 31.

[4] Is. xi. 11. xxvii. 13. Hos. xi. 11.

[5] Gen. xv. 18, Ex. xxiii. 31, Deut. i. 7, xi. 24, Jos. i. 4, 1 Kings iv. 21, 24.

[6] Joel ii. 20.

[7] Ex. xxiii. 31, Num. xxxiv. 3, Deut. xi. 24.

[8] Comp. Ps. lxxii. 8. See "Daniel the Prophet," p. 479 sqq.

[9] See Aristot. de mundo c. 3. in "Daniel the Prophet," p. 625. Strabo speaks as though Homer too knew the fact that the sea encircled the land, "hinting at those in East and West, in that they were washed by the Ocean."

[10] Is. xl. 4.

[11] Mic. iv. 10.

[12] יָבוֹא, not, "they shall come;" nor again is it, "he," Israel, "shall come," since they were to come *to* Israel, "there shall come *to thee;*" nor is it an individual, since one person could not come from all these places.

[13] Is. xix. 23-25.   [14] iv. 1-3.

Before
CHRIST
cir. 710.

‖ Or, *After that
it hath been.*
y Jer. 21. 14.
ch. 3. 12.

13 ‖ Notwithstand-
ing the land shall be desolate because of them that
dwell therein, y for the fruit
of their doings.

14 ¶ ‖ Feed thy people
with thy rod, the flock of
thine heritage, which
dwell solitarily *in* z the
wood, in the midst of Car-

Before
CHRIST
cir. 710.

‖ Or, *Rule.*
Ps. 28. 9.
ch. 5. 4.
z Is. 37. 24.

13. *Notwithstanding* [*And*] *the land* (i. e.
that spoken of, the land of Judah) *shall be
desolate*, not through any arbitrary law or the
might of her enemies, but through the sins
of the people, *because of them that dwell therein,
for the fruit of their doings.* Truly "the fruit
of *their* doings," what they did to please
themselves, of their own minds against God.
As they sow, so shall they reap. This sounds
almost as a riddle and contradiction beforehand; "the walls built up," "the people
gathered in," and "the land desolate." Yet it
was all fulfilled in the letter as well as in spirit.
Jerusalem was restored; the people was
gathered, first from the captivity, then to
Christ; and yet the land was again desolate
through the fruit of their *doings* who rejected
Christ, and is so until this day.
The prophet now closes with one earnest
prayer [1]; to which he receives a brief answer,
that God would shew forth His power anew,
as when He first made them His people[2].
On this, he describes vividly the awed submission of the world to *their* God [3], and closes
with a thanksgiving of marveling amazement at the greatness and completeness of
the forgiving mercy of God [4], ascribing all to
His free goodness [5].
14. *Feed Thy people with Thy rod.* The
day of final deliverance was still a great way
off. There was a weary interval before them
of chastisement, suffering, captivity. So
Micah lays down his pastoral office by committing his people to Him Who was their
true and abiding Shepherd. Who that has
had the pastoral office, has not thought, as
the night drew nigh *in which no man can work,*
"what will be after him?" Micah knew and
foretold the outline. It was for his people a
passing through the valley of the shadow of death.
Micah then commits them to Him, Who had
Himself committed them to him, Who alone
could guide them through it. It is a touching parting with his people; a last guidance
of those whom he had taught, reproved, rebuked, in vain, to Him the Good Shepherd
Who led Israel like a flock. The *rod* is at
times the shepherd's staff [6], although more
frequently the symbol of chastisement. God's
chastisement of His people is an austere form
of His love. So He says, [7] *If his children for-*

sake My law, I will visit their offences with a rod
and their sin with scourges : nevertheless My loving-kindness will I not utterly take from them.
The flock of Thine inheritance. So Moses
had appealed to God, [8] *Destroy not Thy people
and Thine inheritance which Thou hast redeemed
through Thy greatness—They are Thy people and
Thine inheritance ;* and Solomon, in his dedica-
tion-prayer, that, on their repentance in
their captivity, God would forgive His people, [9] *for they be Thy people and Thine inheritance which Thou broughtest forth out of Egypt ;*
and Asaph, [10] *O Lord, the heathen are come into
Thine inheritance ;* and again, [11] *Why doth
Thine anger smoke against the sheep of Thy pasture ? Remember the tribe of Thine inheritance
which Thou hast redeemed ;* and Joel, [12] *Spare
Thy people and give not Thine heritage to reproach ;* and a Psalmist, [13] *They break in
pieces Thy people, O Lord, and afflict Thine
heritage ;* and Isaiah, [14] *Return for thy servants'
sake, the tribes of Thine inheritance.* The appeal excludes all merits. Not for any deserts
of their's, (for these were but evil,) did the
Prophets teach them to pray ; but because
they were God's property. It was His
Name, which would be dishonored in them ;
it was His work, which would seemingly
come to nothing ; it was He, Who would be
thought powerless to save. Again, it is not
God's way, to leave half-done what He has
begun. [15] *Jesus, having loved His own which
were in the world, loved them unto the end.* God's
love in creating us and making us His, is the
earnest, if we will, of His everlasting love.
We have been the objects of His everlasting
thought, of His everlasting love. Though
we have forfeited all claim to His love, He
has not forfeited the work of His Hands ;
Jesus has not forfeited the price of His Blood.
So holy men have prayed ; " [16] I believe that
Thou hast redeemed me by Thy Blood : per-
mit not the price of the Ransom to perish."
" [17] O Jesus Christ, my only Saviour, let not
Thy most bitter Passion and Death be lost or
wasted in me, miserable sinner ! "
Which dwell solitarily, or *alone.* Micah uses
the words of Balaam, when he had been constrained by God to bless Israel. [18] *The people shall dwell alone and shall not be reckoned
among the nations.* Moses had repeated them,

[1] v. 14.   [2] v. 15.   [3] v. 16, 17.   [4] v. 18, 19.   [5] v. 20.
[6] שֵׁבֶט Lev. xxvii. 32, Ps. xxiii. 4.
[7] Ps. lxxxix. 31, 33.   [8] Deut. ix. 26, 29.
[9] 1 Kings viii. 51.   [10] Ps. lxxix. 1.
[11] Ps. lxxiv. 1, 2.   [12] Joel ii. 17.   [13] Ps. xciv. 5.

[14] Is. lxiii. 17.   [15] S. John xiii. 1.
[16] Bp. Andrewes Preces quotid. Græc. p. 150.
Tracts for the Times, No. 88. p. 66.
[17] Paradise for the Christian Soul. On the Passion
c. 5.   [18] Num. xxiii. 9

Before
CHRIST
cir. 710.

mel: let them feed *in* Bashan and Gilead, as in the
days of old.

15 [a] According to the
days of thy coming out of
the land of Egypt will I

Before
CHRIST
cir. 710.

[a] Ps. 68. 22.
& 78. 12.

[1] *Israel shall dwell in safety alone.* This alone-
ness among other nations, then, was a blessing, springing from God's being in the midst
of them [2], the deeds which He did for
them [3], the law which He gave them [4]. So
Moses prayed, [5] *Wherein shall it be known
here, that I and Thy people .have found grace in
Thy sight?* is it *not in that Thou goest with us?
So shall we be separated, I and Thy people, from
all the people that are on the face of the earth.* It
was, then, a separate appeal to God by all His
former loving-kindness, whereby He had
severed and elected His people for Himself.

In the wood, in the midst of Carmel. God
[6] *turneth a fruitful land into barrenness for the
wickedness of them that dwell therein. He turneth the wilderness into a standing water and dry
ground into watersprings.* Isaiah at the same
time used the like image, that [7] *Lebanon shall
be turned into a fruitful field* [Carmel], *and the
fruitful field* [Carmel] *shall be esteemed as a
forest* [8]. The wild forest was to be like the
rich domestic exuberance of Carmel [9]. He
would say, "Feed Thy people in Babylon,
which is to them a wild homeless tract, that
it may be to them as their own peaceful Carmel." Without God, all the world is a wilderness; with God, the wilderness is Paradise.

Let them feed in Bashan and Gilead. The
former words were a prayer for their restoration. Gilead and Bashan were the great
pasture-countries of Palestine [10], "[11] a wide
tableland, with undulating downs clothed
with rich grass throughout," where the cattle
ranged freely. They were the first possessions, which God had bestowed upon Israel;
the first, which they forfeited. Micah prays
that God, Who protected them in their desolation, would restore and protect them in the
green pasture where He placed them. They
are a prayer still to *the Good Shepherd* Who
laid down His life for His sheep [12], our Lord
Jesus Christ, that He would feed His flock
whom He has redeemed, who have been *given*

to Him as *an inheritance* [13], *the little flock* [14], to
which *it is* the *Father's good pleasure to give
the kingdom,* which cleaveth to Him and shall
be heirs with Him [15]. "[16] Christ feedeth His
own with a rod, guiding them gently, and repressing by gentle fears the tendency of believers to listlessness. He *bruiseth* as *with a
rod of Iron,* not them, but the rebellious disobedient and proud, who receive not the
faith; believers He instructs and forms tenderly, [17] *feeds them among the lilies,* and leads
them into good pastures and rich places,
namely the Divinely-inspired Scriptures,
making the hidden things thereof clear
through the Spirit to those of understanding,
that they [18] *may grow up unto Him in all things
which is the Head, even Christ,* with minds
well-fed and nourished and gladdened with
all spiritual delights. But the chosen and
elect *dwell solitarily,* being apart from the rest
who think only of the things of earth, and
give themselves to the pleasures of sense. So
then these, having the mind at rest, freed
from the vain and abominable tumults, are
placed apart as *in a wood* and in a *mountain.*
By the *wood* you may understand, the rich
and varied and solid instruction (as it were
trees and flowers) both in doctrine and life;
by the *mountain,* what is high and lofty. For
none of the wisdom, accounted of in the
Church, is low. They are *fed in Bashan and
Gilead, as in the days of old,* rich pastures;
for the mind of the holy is beautified, de-
lighting itself in the contemplation of the
inspired Scriptures, and filled, as it were,
with a certain richness, and shares without
stint all excellence in thought or in deed;
and that, not for a brief and narrow season,
but for ever. For what gladdeneth the flesh
falleth therewith and fadeth and hasteth
away like a shadow; but the participation of
the good things from above and of the Spirit,
stretcheth out along endless ages."

15. *According to the days of thy coming out*

[1] Deut. xxxiii. 28. In both cases, as in 'Micah,
שכן is used; as also in Jer. xlix. 31, of Hazor
dwelling in security alone. The idiom ישב, בדד
"sit alone," is different. It occurs first of the
separation of the leper, "he shall sit alone, without
the camp shall his dwelling be (מושב)," Lev. xiii.
46; then of an individual in sorrow, Jer. xv. 17,
Lam. iii. 28; and, in one case, of the deserted city
personified, Lam. i. 1.   [2] Ex. xxxiii. 16, Deut. iv. 7.
[3] Ex. xxxiv. 10, Deut. iv. 34.   [4] Deut. iv. 8. 33.
[5] Ex. xxxiii. 16.   [6] Ps. cvii. 34, 5.   [7] Is. xxix/17.
[8] והכרמל ליער יחשב. The phrase recurs Is.
xxxii. 15, except that the Kethib omits the article,
which makes the contrast of יער and כרמל exactly the same as in Micah.
[9] See on Am. i. 2. vol. i. p. 233.
[10] See on Am. i. 3. vol. i. p. 234; iv. 1. p. 280.

[11] Rev. G. H. Palmer in Dr. Stanley Pal. p. 320.
See also Porter's Handbook, p. 307 sq. "One can
scarcely get over the impression that he is roam-
ing through some English park. The graceful
hills, the rich vales, the luxuriant herbage, the
bright wild-flowers, the plantations of evergreen
oak, pine, and arbutus, now a tangled thicket, and
now sparsely scattered over the gentle slope, as if intended to reveal its beauty, the little rivulets fringed
with oleander, &c.—such are the features of the
mountains of Gilead." p. 310. "The country from
Jerash to *Wady Gâbes* [Jabesh Gilead] 8 hours,
resembles in scenery that from es-Salt to Jerash.
We have the thickly wooded hills, the deep and
fertile valleys, and the luxuriant pasturage in every
part of it." p. 316. See also Thomson, The Land and
the Book, i. 304.   [12] S. John x. 11, 15.   [13] Ps. ii. 8.
[14] S. Luke xii. 32.   [15] Rom. viii. 17.   [16] S. Cyr.
[17] Cant. vi. 3.   [18] Eph. iv. 15.

Before
C H R I S T
cir. 710.

b Is. 26. 11.

shew unto him marvelous
things.

16 ¶ The nations b shall
see and be confounded at

all their might : c they shall
lay *their* hand upon *their*
mouth, their ears shall be
deaf.

Before
C H R I S T
cir. 710.

c Job 21. 5.
& 29. 9.

---

of the land of Egypt. God answers the prayer, beginning with its closing words [1]. Micah had prayed, " Turn Thy people *like the days of old* [2] *;*" God answers, "*like the days of thy coming* [2] *out of the land of Egypt.*" Micah had said, 'in the name of his people, [3] *I shall behold His Righteousness ;* God answers, *I will make him to behold marvelous things.* The word *marvelous things* [4] was used of God's great marvels in the physical world [5], or the marvelous mercies of His Providence toward individuals or nations [6], and especially of those great miracles, which were accumulated at the deliverance from Egypt [7], and the entrance of the promised land [8] which was its completion. The reference to the Exodus must have led them to think of actual miracles ; since, in regard to the Exodus, it is used of nothing else. But there were no miracles at the return from the captivity. [9] *When the Lord turned again the captivity of Zion,* said a Psalmist of the returned people, *we were like them that dream. The Lord hath done great things for us ; we are glad.* Great things, but not miraculous. The promise then kept the people looking onward, until He came, [10] *a Prophet mighty in word and deed,* as to Whom St. Peter appealed to the people, that He was [11] *approved of God among you by miracles and wonders and signs, which God did by Him in the midst of you, as ye yourselves also know ;* Who gave also to them who believed on Him power to do [12] *greater works than He did,* through His own power, *because* He went to His *Father ;* and when they believed, He *shewed to him,* viz. to the whole people gathered into the One Church, Jew and Gentile, yet more *marvelous things,* things, every way more marvelous and beyond nature than

those of old, [13] *the unsearchable riches of Christ, the mystery which from the beginning of the world hath been hid in God.*

16. *The nations shall see.* God had answered, what He would give to His own people, to *see.* Micah takes up the word [14], and says, what effect this sight should have upon the enemies of God and of His people. The world should still continue to be divided between the people of God and their adversaries. Those who are converted pass from the one to the other ; but the contrast remains. Assyria, Babylon, Egypt, pass away or become subject to other powers ; but the antagonism continues. *The nations* are they, who, at each time, waste, oppress, are arrayed against, the people of God. When the Gospel came into the world, the whole world was arrayed against it [15]. These then, he says, *shall see,* i. e. *the marvelous works* of God, which God should shew His people, *and be ashamed at,* i. e. *because of all their might,* their own might. They put forth their whole might, and it failed them against the *marvelous* might of God. They should array might against might, and *be ashamed* at the failure of *all their might* [16]. The word *all* is very emphatic ; it implies that they had put forth *all,* and that *all* had failed them, and proved to be weakness. So the Heathen might was often put to shame and gnashed its teeth, when it could avail nothing against the strength to endure which God gave to His martyrs. Its strength to inflict and to crush was baffled before the hidden might of God's Spirit. *They shall lay their hand upon their mouth,* in token that they were reduced to silence, having no more to say [17] ; for He promised, [18] *I will give you a mouth and wis-* and mostly with this aggravation, that they had trusted in it, and it had failed them. See Hos. iv. 19, " *they shall be ashamed because of their sacrifices ;* x. 6, *because of their own counsel*" (see on Hos. x. 6. vol. i. p. 10) ; "They shall be afraid and *ashamed because of Ethiopia, their expectation, and of Egypt, their glory,*" Is. xx. 5 ; "*because of the oaks, which ye have desired,*" Ib. i. 29 ; "*thou shalt be ashamed because of Egypt, as thou wast ashamed because of Assyria,*" Jer. ii. 36 ; " Moab shall be *ashamed because of Chemosh, as the house of Israel was ashamed because of Bethel their confidence,*" Ib. xlviii. 13 ; add xli. 13. The idiom itself, מִגְּבוּרָתָם בּוֹשִׁים, "*ashamed because of their might,*" occurs in Ezek. xxxii. 30, of the nations, which had perished in war. In a few cases, the idiom is used of the source of shame, where the idea of previous trust in them is less prominent, as in Ezek. xxxvi. 32, Zeph. iii. 11. But here, this is involved in the subject itself, and is illustrated by Ezek. xxxii. 30.

[17] See the use of the idiom in Jud. xviii. 19. Job. xxi. 5, xxix. 9, xl. 4, Prov. xxx. 32.

[18] S. Luke xxi. 15. comp. Acts v. 29.

---

[1] Casp.

[2] כִּימֵי עוֹלָם ver. 14. כִּימֵי צֵאתְךָ ver. 16. The word עוֹלָם is necessarily restrained to time, in that it relates to man's past, and *that,* according to the context, a limited past, the time of their coming out of Egypt. This does not interfere with its use as to eternity. See ab. on Mic. v. 2. p. 67.

[3] ver. 9. Casp.   [4] נִפְלָאוֹת.

[5] Job v. 9, xxxvii. 5, 14.

[6] Ps. ix. 2, xxvi. 7, lxxi. 17, lxxii. 18, &c.

[7] Ex. iii. 20, Jud. vi. 13, Neh. ix. 17, Ps. lxxviii. 4, 11, 32, cv. 2, 5, cvi. 7, 22.

[8] Ex. xxxiv. 10. Of the passage of the Jordan, Jos. iii. 5.

[9] Ps. cxxvi. 1, 3.   [10] S. Luke xxiv. 19.

[11] Acts ii. 22. [12] S. John xiv. 12. [13] Eph. iii. 8, 9.

[14] אֶרְאֶנּוּ end of ver. 15 ; יִרְאוּ beg. of ver. 16. Casp.

[15] See ab. p. 92.

[16] This is the force of בּוּשׁ with מִן. מִן designates, as usual, the cause and source of the shame ;

Before CHRIST cir. 710.

17 They shall lick the ^d dust like a serpent, ^e they shall move out of their holes like || worms of the

^d Ps. 72. 9.
Is. 49. 23.
^e Ps. 18. 45.
|| Or, *creeping things.*

earth: ^f they shall be afraid of the LORD our God, and shall fear because of thee.

Before CHRIST cir. 710.

^f Jer. 33. 9.

---

dom, which all your adversaries shall not be able to gainsay nor resist; and they had to own, [1] *indeed a notable miracle hath been done by them, and we cannot deny it. Their ears shall be deaf;* they shall be silent, as though they had heard nothing, as if they were both dumb and deaf [2]. Yet it seems too that they are wilfully deaf, *shutting their ears* out of envy and hatred, that they might not hear what great things God had done for His people, nor hear the voice of truth and be converted and healed. "[3] The nations and the Emperors of the nations saw, Jews and Gentiles saw, and were ashamed at all their might, because their might, great as it was accounted, upheld by laws and arms, could not overcome the mighty works, which the Good Shepherd did among His people or flock by His rod, i.e. by His power, through weak and despised persons, the aged, or oftentimes even by boys and girls. They were then ashamed at all their might which could only touch the [4] *earthen vessels,* but could not take away the *treasure* which was in them. What shall I say of the wisdom of those same nations? Of this too they were ashamed, as he adds, *They shall put their hands upon their mouths.* For, in comparison with the heavenly wisdom, which spake by them and made their tongues eloquent, dumb was all secular eloquence, owning by its silence that it was convicted and confounded."

17. *They shall lick the dust like a [the] serpent.* To *lick the dust,* by itself, pictures the extreme humility of persons who cast themselves down to the very earth [5]. To lick it "like *the* serpent" seems rather to represent the condition of those who share the serpent's doom [6], whose lot, viz. earth and things of earth, they had chosen [3]. *They shall move out of their holes,* or, better, *shall tremble,* (i.e. " *come tremblingly,"*) *out of their close places* [7], whether these be *strong places* or *prisons,* as the word, varied in one vowel [8], means. If it be *strong places,* it means, that "[9] the enemies of God's people should, in confusion and tumultuously with fear, leave their strongholds, wherein they thought to be se-

cure, not able to lift themselves up against God and those by Him sent against them." *Like worms of the earth,* lit. *creeping things,* or, as we say, *reptiles* [10], contemptuously. *They shall be afraid of,* or rather *come trembling to, the Lord our God;* it is not said *their,* but *our* God, Who hath *done so great things for us. And shall fear because of* [lit. *from*] *Thee, O* Lord, of Whom they had before said, *Where is the Lord thy God?*

It is doubtful, whether these last words express a "servile fear," whereby a man turns away and flees *from* [11] the person or thing which he fears, or whether they simply describe fear of God [12], the first step toward repentance. In Hosea's words [13], *they shall fear toward the Lord and His goodness,* the addition, *and His goodness,* determines the character of the fear. In Micah, it is not said that the fear brings them into any relation to God. He is not spoken of, as becoming, any how, *their* God, and Micah closes by a thanksgiving, for God's pardoning mercy, not to them but to His people.

And so the Prophet ends, as he began, with the judgments of God; to those who would repent, chastisement, to the impenitent, punishment: "sentencing Samaria, guilty and not repenting [3]," to perpetual captivity; "to Jerusalem, guilty but repenting, promising restoration. So from the beginning of the world did God; so doth He; so shall He unto the end. So did He shew Himself to Cain and Abel, who both, as we all, sinned in Adam. Cain, being impenitent, He wholly cast away; Abel, being penitent," *and through faith offering a better sacrifice than Cain,* and "*bringing forth fruits worthy of repentance,* He accepted." So He hath foreshewn as to the end [14]. "[3] And that we may know how uniformly our Judge so distinguisheth, at the very moment of His own Death while hanging between the two thieves, the one, impenitent and blaspheming, He left; to the other, penitent and confessing, He opened the gate of paradise; and, soon after, leaving the Jewish people unrepentant, He received the repentance of the

[1] Acts iv. 16.
[2] As in Ps. xxxviii. 14, "I was as a man that heareth not, and in whose mouth are no reproofs."
[3] Rup.   [4] 2 Cor. iv. 7.
[5] As in Ps. lxxii. 9. Is. xlix. 23.
[6] Gen. iii. 14, Is. lxv. 25.
[7] So our Version renders the word in Ps. xviii. 45, 2 Sam. xxii. 46.
[8] מִסְגָּר masc. Is. xxiv. 22, xlii. 7, Ps. cxlii. 8; here and in Ps. xviii. 46, מִסְגֶּרֶת fem.

[9] Poc.
[10] The idiom occurs beside only in Deut. xxxii. 24, with the variation only of עָפָר for אֶרֶץ.
[11] יָרֵא with מִן Ps. iii. 7, xxvii. 1, Job v. 21. See Ges. Thes. p. 804.
[12] יָרֵא with מִן is used of a fear of God, whereby one is kept from evil. Lev. xix. 14. Yet also generally of fear of God, Ps. xxxiii. 8.
[13] Hos. iii. 5.   [14] S. Matt. xxv.

Before
C H R I S T
cir. 710.
g Ex. 15. 11.
h Ex. 34. 6, 7.
Jer. 50. 20.
i ch. 4. 7.
& 5. 3, 7, 8.
k Ps. 103. 9.
Is. 57. 16.
Jer. 3. 5.

18 [g] Who *is* a God like unto thee, that [h] pardoneth iniquity, and passeth by the transgression of [i] the remnant of his heritage? [k] he retaineth not his anger

for ever, because he delighteth *in* mercy.

19 He will turn again, he will have compassion upon us ; he will subdue our iniquities ; and thou

Before
C H R I S T
cir. 710.

Gentiles." Thus the Prophet parts with both out of sight ; the people of God, feeding on the rich bounty and abundance of God, and His *marvelous* gifts of grace above and beyond nature, multiplied to them above all the wonders of old time ; the enemies of God's people looking on, not to admire, but to be ashamed, not to be healthfully ashamed, but to be wilfully deaf to the voice of God. For, however to *lay the hand on the mouth* might be a token of reverent silence, the *deafness of the ears* can hardly be other than the emblem of hardened obstinacy. What follows, then, seems more like the unwilling creeping-forth into the Presence of God, when they cannot keep away, than conversion. It seems to picture the reprobate, who would not[1] *hear the Voice of the Son of God and live*, but who, in the end, shall be forced to hear it out of their *close places* or *prisons*, i. e. the grave, and come forth in fear, when they shall [2] *say to the mountains, Fall on us ; and to the hills, Cover us.* Thus the Prophet brings us to the close of all things, the gladness and joy of God's people, the terror of His enemies, and adds only the song of thanksgiving of all the redeemed.

18. *Who is a God* (and, as the word means, *A Mighty God,*) *like unto Thee ?* He saith not, [3] *Who hast made heaven and earth, the sea and all that therein is ;* nor, [4] *Who telleth the number of the stars ; and calleth them all by their names ;* nor, [5] *Who by His strength setteth fast the mountains and is girded about with power ;* but Who forgivest ! For greater is the work of Redemption than the work of Creation. *That pardoneth,* and *beareth* and *taketh away* also, *and passeth by the transgression of the remnant of His heritage,* i. e. His heritage, which is a remnant still when [6] *the rest are blinded ;* and this, not of its merits but of His mercy ; since it is not His nature to *retain His anger for ever ;* not for anything in them, but *because He delighteth in mercy,* as He saith, [7] *I am merciful, saith the Lord, and I will not keep anger for ever.* [8] *I am He that blotteth out thy transgressions for Mine own sake, and will not remember thy sins.* "[9] For although God for a time is angry with His elect, chastening them mercifully in this life, yet in the end He hath

compassion on them, giving them everlasting consolations."

Moses, after the completion of his people's deliverance at the Red Sea, used the like appeal to God, in unmingled joy. Then the thanksgiving ran, [10] *glorious in holiness, awful in praises, doing wonders.* Now, it ran in a more subdued, yet even deeper, tone, taken from God's revelation of Himself after that great transgression on Mount Sinai, [11] *forgiving iniquity and transgression and sin.* With this, Micah identified his own name[12]. This was the one message which he loved above all to proclaim ; of this, his own name was the herald to his people in his day. *Who is like the Lord,* the Pardoner of sin, the Redeemer from its guilt, the Subduer of its power ? For no false god was ever such a claim made. The heathen gods were symbols of God's workings in nature ; they were, at best, representatives of His Government and of His displeasure at sin. But, being the creatures of man's mind, they could not freely pardon, for man dared not ascribe to them the attribute of a freely-pardoning mercy, for which he dared not hope. *Who is a God like to Thee,* mighty, not only to destroy but to pardon ? is the wondering thanksgiving of time, the yet greater amazement of eternity, as eternity shall unveil the deep blackness of sin over-against the light of God, and we, seeing God, as He Is, shall see what that Holiness is, against which we sinners sinned, The soul, which is truly penitent, never wearies of the wondering love, *Who is a God like unto Thee ?*

19. *He will turn again,* Who seemed to be turned away from us when we were turned away from Him[13]. *He will subdue, or trample under foot,* our worst enemy, *our iniquities,* as He saith, [14] *He shall bruise Satan under your feet shortly.* Hitherto, sinful passions had not rebelled only, but had had the mastery over us. Sin subdued man ; it was his lord, a fierce tyrant over him ; *he* could not subdue *it.* Holy Scripture says emphatically of man under the law, that he was *sold under sin*[15], a slave under a hard master, oppressed, weighed down, and unable to throw off the bondage. [16] *We have before proved both Jews and Gen-*

1 S. John. v. 25.
2 S. Luke xxiii. 30, Rev. vi. 16.   3 2 Ex. xx. 11.
4 Ps. cxlvii. 4.   5 Ps. lxv. 6.   6 Rom. xi. 7.
7 Jer. iii. 12.   8 Is. xliii. 25.   9 Dion.
10 Ex. xv. 11.

11 נָשָׂא עָוֹן וָפֶשַׁע, Ex. xxxiv. 7 ; Micah, dividing the clauses, inserted עֹבֵר עַל before פֶּשַׁע. Casp.
12 See Introd. to Micah, ab. p. 5.   13 See Jo. ii. 14.
14 Rom. xvi. 20.   15 Ib. vii. 14.   16 Ib. iii. 9.

Before CHRIST cir. 710. will cast all their sins into the depths of the sea.

20 [1] Thou wilt perform the truth to Jacob, *and the* Before CHRIST cir. 710.

[1] Luke 1. 72, 73.

tiles, that they are all under sin ; [1] *the Scripture hath concluded all under sin.* Under the Gospel, God, he says, would subdue sin "under *us,*" and make it, as it were, our "footstool[2]." It is a Gospel before the Gospel. God would pardon; and *He,* not *we,* would subdue sin to us. He would bestow, "[3]of sin the double cure, Save us from its guilt and power." [4] *Not I, but the grace of God, which was with me.*

And Thou wilt cast,—not, some ("[5]for it is impious to look for a half-pardon from God") but—*all their sins into the depths[6] of the sea,* so that as in the passage of the Red Sea there was not one Egyptian left of those who pursued His people, so neither shall there be one sin, which, through Baptism and on Repentance, shall not through His free mercy be pardoned. As they, which [7] *sank as lead in the mighty waters,* never again rose, so shall the sins, unless revived by us, not rise against us to condemnation, but shall in the Day of Judgment be sunk in the abyss of hell, as if they had never been.

20. *Thou wilt perform the truth to Jacob* and *the mercy to Abraham.* What was free *mercy to Abraham,* became, when God had once promised it, His *truth. Abraham* also stands for all those, who in him and his Seed should be blessed, those who were [8] *aliens from the commonwealth of Israel, and strangers from the covenants of promise, having no hope, and without God in the world,* in no covenant or relation with God, as well as those who were the children of the faith ; heathen, as well as Jews. *Jacob* represents those who were immediately his children, such of the children of Israel, as were also the true Israel and *children of faithful Abraham.* In both ways the gift to Abraham was *mercy,* to Jacob, *truth.* So also St. Paul saith [9], "Jesus Christ was a Minister of the circumcision for the *truth* of God, to confirm the promises made to the fathers, and that the Gentiles might glorify God for *His mercy.*" Yet *mercy and truth* [10], together, *are all the paths of the Lord ;* they [11] *met together* in Christ; yea Christ Himself is full of Mercy as well as [12] *Truth :* and woe were it to that soul to whom He were Truth without mercy. "[13] For to be saved, we look not so much to the truth of

the Judge as to the mercy of the Redeemer." And *mercy,* in the counsel of God, reacheth wider than *truth ;* for *truth* is given to Jacob, the father of one nation, Israel; but mercy to Abraham, [14] *the father of many nations.* Isaac, it may be, is not here mentioned, because all to whom the blessing should come are already spoken of in Jacob and Abraham ; in Jacob, all to whom the promise was first made; in Abraham, all nations of the world in whom should be blessed in his Seed, through the mercy of God overflowing the bounds of that covenant. Isaac is, in his sacrifice, chiefly a type of our Lord Himself.

Which Thou hast sworn unto our fathers. [15] *That by two immutable things, in which it was impossible for God to lie, we might have a strong consolation.*

From the days of old. [16] From eternity, in the counsel of God ; in promise, from the foundation of the world, as is said in the hymn of Zacharias [17], *As He spake by the mouth of His holy Prophets, which have been since the world began.* [18] The inspired hymns of the Blessed Virgin Mary and of Zachariah take up the words of the prophet, and shew that they are already fulfilled in Christ, although they shall be more and more fulfilled unto the world's end, as Jew and Gentile are brought into His fold ; [19] *He remembering His mercy, as He spake to our fathers, to Abraham and to his seed for ever.* [20] *To perform the mercy promised to our fathers, and to remember His holy covenant, the oath which He sware to our father Abraham that He would grant unto us.* "I too," St. Jerome subjoins, "sealing the labor of my little work by calling upon the Lord, will say at the close of this tract, *O God, who is like unto Thee ?* Take away the iniquity of Thy servant, pass by the sin of my decayed soul, and send not Thine anger upon me, nor rebuke me in Thy indignation ; for Thou art full of pity and great are Thy mercies. Return and have mercy upon me ; drown mine iniquities, and cast them into the depth of the sea, that the bitterness of sin may perish in the bitter waters. Grant the truth which Thou didst promise to Thy servant Jacob, and the mercy which Thou didst pledge to Abraham Thy friend, and free my

[1] Gal. iii. 22.
[2] בֶּבֶשׁ, "footstool," 2 Chr. ix. 18. (as in Syr. Ch.) from the same root.
[3] Hymn, "Rock of ages."
[4] 1 Cor. xv. 10.
[5] S. Amb. ap. Alb.
[6] מְצוֹלוֹת doubtless is meant to refer back to מְצוֹלוֹת, Ex. xv. 5, and so, to suggest the image of

the destruction at the Red Sea, and its completeness.
[7] Ex. xv. 10.
[8] Eph. ii. 12.
[9] Rom. xv. 8, 9.
[10] Ps. xxv. 10.
[11] Ps. lxxxv. 10.
[12] S. John i. 14.
[13] Rup.
[14] Gen. xvii. 5, Rom. iv. 17.
[15] Heb. vi. 18.
[16] Alb.
[17] S. Luke i. 70.
[18] Poc.
[19] S. Luke i. 54, 56.
[20] Ib. 72–74.

Before
C H R I S T
cir. 710.
mercy to Abraham, ^m which
thou hast sworn unto our

^m Ps. 105. 9, 10.

fathers from the days of
old.

Before
C H R I S T
cir. 710.

soul, as Thou didst sware to my fathers in
the days of old; [1] *As I live, saith the Lord
God, I have no pleasure in the death of the
wicked, but that the wicked turn from his way and*

[1] Ezek. xxxiii. 11.

live. Then shall mine enemy see and be
crowned with *confusion,* who now saith unto
me, *where is now thy God?"* Amen, Amen, O
Good Lord Jesu.

INTRODUCTION

TO

THE PROPHET

NAHUM.

THE prophecy of Nahum is both the complement and the counterpart of the book of Jonah. When Moses had asked God to shew him His glory, and God had promised to let him see the outskirts of that glory, and to proclaim the Name of the Lord before him, *the Lord*, we are told, *passed by before him and proclaimed,* [a] *The Lord, the Lord God, merciful and gracious, longsuffering and abundant in goodness and truth, keeping mercy for thousands, forgiving iniquity and transgression and sin, and that will by no means clear the* guilty. God proclaimed at once His mercy and His justice. Those wondrous words echo along the whole of the Old Testament. Moses himself [b], David [c], other Psalmists [d], Jeremiah [e], Daniel [f], Nehemiah [g], plead them to God or rehearse some part of them in thanksgiving. Joel repeated them as a motive to repentance [h]. Upon the repentance of Nineveh, Jonah had recited to God the bright side of that His declaration of Himself, [i] *I knew that Thou art a gracious God and merciful, slow to anger and of great goodness*, repeating to God His words to Moses, and adding, *and repenting of the evil*. Nineveh, as appears from Nahum, had fallen back into the violence of which it had repented. Nahum then, in reference to that declaration of Jonah, begins by setting forth the awful side of the attributes of God. First, in a stately rhythm, which, in the original, reminds us of the gradual Psalms, he enunciates the solemn threefold declaration of the severity of God to those who will be His enemies.

[k] *A jealous God and Avenger is the Lord :*
An Avenger is the Lord, and lord of wrath ;
An Avenger is the Lord to His adversaries :
And a Reserver of wrath *to His enemies.*

Then, he too recites that character of mercy recorded by Moses, [l] *The Lord is slow to anger, and great in power*. But anger, although slow, comes, he adds, not the less certainly on the guilty ; [l] *and will not at all clear the* guilty. The iniquity is full. As a whole, there is no place more for repentance. Nineveh had had its prophet, and had been spared, and had sunk back into its old sins. The office of Nahum is to pronounce its sentence. That sentence is fixed. [m] *There is no healing of thy bruise.* Nothing is said of its ulterior conversion or restoration. On the contrary, Nahum says, [n] *He will make the place thereof an utter desolation.*

The sins of Nineveh spoken of by Nahum are the same as those from which they had turned at the preaching of Jonah. In Jonah, it is, [o] *the violence of their hands.* Nahum describes Nineveh as [p] *a dwelling of lions, filled with prey and with ravin, the feeding-place of young lions, where the lion tore enough for his whelps ;* [q] *a city of bloods, full of lies and robbery,* from which *the prey departeth not.*

But, amid this mass of evil, one was eminent, in direct antagonism to God. The character is very peculiar. It is not simply of rebellion against God, or neglect of Him. It is a direct disputing of His Sovereignty. The prophet twice repeats the characteristic expression, *What will ye devise so vehemently* [r]

---

[a] Ex. xxxiv. 6, 7. [b] Num. xiv. 17, 18.
[c] Ps. lxxxvi. 15, ciii. 8, cxlv. 8.
[d] Ps. cxi. 4, cxii. 4, cxvi. 5. [e] xxxii. 18, 19.
[f] ix. 4. [g] ix. 17. [h] ii. 13. [i] Jon. iv. 2. [k] i. 2.

[l] Ib. 3. [m] iii. 19. [n] i. 8. [o] iii. 8.
[p] Nah. ii. 11, 12. [q] Ib. iii. 1.
[r] Ib. i. 9, מַה תְּחַשְּׁבוּן. The verb is doubly intensive, both as Piel, and as having the intens. ן.

against the Lord? [s] *devising evil against the Lord;* and adds, *counsellor of evil.* This was exactly the character of Sennacherib, whose wars, like those of his forefathers, (as appears from the cuneiform inscriptions [t],) were religious wars, and who blasphemously compared God to the local deities of the countries, which his forefathers or himself had destroyed [u]. Of this enemy Nahum speaks, as *having "*gone forth ;*" out of thee* (Nineveh) *hath gone forth* [x] *one, devising evil against the Lord, a counsellor of Belial.* This was past. Their purpose was inchoate, yet incomplete. God challenges them, [r] *What will ye devise so vehemently against the Lord?* The destruction too is proximate. The prophet answers for God, *"*[y] *He Himself,* by Himself, *is* already *making an utter end.*" To Jerusalem he turns, *"*[z] And *now I will break his yoke from off thee, and will break his bonds asunder.*" Twice the prophet mentions the device against God ; each time he answers it by the prediction of the sudden utter destruction of the enemy, while in the most perfect security. [a] *While they are intertwined as thorns, and swallowed up as their drink, they are devoured as stubble fully dry ;* and, [b] *If they be perfect,* unimpaired in their strength, *and thus many, even thus shall they be mown down.* Their destruction was to be, as their numbers, complete. With no previous loss, secure and at ease, a mighty host, in consequence of their prosperity, all were, at one blow, mown down ; *"and he* (their king, who *counselled against the Lord) shall pass away* and perish. *"* The abundance of the wool in the fleece is no hindrance to the shears," nor of the grass to the scythe, nor of the Assyrian host to the will of the Lord. After *he,* the chief, had thus *passed away,* Nahum foretells that remarkable death, in connection with the house of his gods ; [c] *Out of the house of thy gods I will cut off the graven image and the molten image: I will make thy grave.* There is no natural construction of these words, except, *I will make* it *thy grave*[d]. Judah too was, by the presence of the Assyrian, hindered from going up to worship at Jerusalem. The prophet bids proclaim peace to Jerusalem ; *keep thy feasts—for the wicked shall no more pass through thee.* It was then by the presence of the wicked, that they were now hindered from keeping their feasts, which could be kept only at Jerusalem.

The prophecy of Nahum coincides then with that of Isaiah, when Hezekiah prayed

against Sennacherib. In the history [e], and in the prophecy of Isaiah, the reproach and blasphemy and rage against God are prominent, as an evil design against God is in Nahum. In Isaiah we have the messengers sent to blaspheme [f]; in Nahum, the promise, that *the voice of thy messengers shall no more be heard.* Isaiah prophesies the fruitlessness of his attempt against Jerusalem [g] ; his disgraced return ; his violent death in his own land [h] ; Nahum prophesies the entire destruction of his army, his own passing away, his grave. Isaiah, in Jerusalem, foretells how the spontaneous fruits of the earth shall be restored to them [i], and so, that they shall have possession of the open corn-country ; Nahum, living probably in the country, foretells the free access to Jerusalem, and bids them to [k] *keep their feasts,* and *perform the vows,* which, in their trouble, they had promised to God. He does not only foretell that they may, but he enjoins them to do it. The words, [l] *the emptiers have emptied them out and marred their vine branches,* may relate to the first expedition of Sennacherib, when, Holy Scripture says, he [m] *came up against all the fenced cities of Judah and took them,* and Hezekiah gave him *thirty talents of gold, and 300 talents of silver.* Sennacherib himself says [n], "Hezekiah, king of Judah, who had not submitted to my authority, forty-six of his principal cities, and fortresses and villages depending upon them of which I took no account, I captured, and carried away their spoil. And from these places I captured and carried off as spoil 200,150 people," &c. This must relate to the first expedition, on account of the exact correspondence of the tribute in gold, with a variation in the number of the talents of silver, easily accounted for [o]. In the first invasion Sennacherib relates that he besieged Jerusalem. "[p] Hezekiah himself I shut up in Jerusalem his capital, city, like a bird in a cage, building towers round the city to fence him in, and raising banks of earth against the gates, so as to prevent escape." It is perhaps in reference to this, that, in the second invasion, God promises by Isaiah ; [q] *He shall not come into this city, and shall not shoot an arrow there ; and shall not present shield before it, and shall not cast up bank against it.* Still, in this second invasion also, Holy Scripture relates, that [r] *the king of Assyria sent Rabshakeh from Lachish to Jerusalem unto king Hezekiah with a great army.* Per-

---

[s] i. 11. [t] See on "Daniel the Prophet," pp. 444, 5.
[u] Is. xxxvi. 18-20, xxxvii. 10-13. [x] i. 11. אצי.
[y] i. 9. כָּלָה הוּא עֹשֶׂה. [z] i. 13. וְעַתָּה.
[a] i. 10. [b] i. 12. [c] i. 14.
[d] So Chald. Syr. S. Jer. and moderns, as soon as they have no bias, e. g. Ros. Ew. It is not *asah,* but *sim;* i. e. not ποιεῖν, but θεῖναι; not, in our sense, I will "make a grave," but "I will set" or "make" something else, viz. the house of his gods of which Nahum had just spoken, "to be his grave."

[e] 2 Kings xix. 4, 22-28. [f] Is. xxxvii. 4, 23-29.
[g] Ib. 33, 34. [h] Ib. 7.
[i] 2 Kings xix. 29, Is. xxxvii. 30.
[k] Nah. i. 15, ii. 1. [2 Heb.] [l] Ib. ii. 2. [3. Heb.]
[m] 2 Kings xviii. 13, 14, Is. xxxvi. 1.
[n] Dr. Hincks in Layard Nin. and Bab. pp. 143, 4. Sir H. Rawlinson, quoted ib. and Rawl. Bampt. L. p. 141.
[o] See Layard ib. pp. 144, 5. Rawl. B. L. p. 143.
[p] Sir H. Rawl. transl. in B. L. ib. [q] xxxvii. 33.
[r] Ib. xxxvi. 2. 2 Kings xviii. 17.

haps it is in regard to this second expedition, that God says, [s] *Though I have afflicted thee, I will afflict thee no more;* i. e. this second invasion should not desolate her, like that first. Not that God absolutely would not again afflict her, but not now. The yoke of the Assyrian was then broken, until the fresh sins of Manasseh drew down their own punishment.

Nahum then was a prophet for Judah, or for that remnant of Israel, which, after the ten tribes were carried captive, became one with Judah, not in temporal sovereignty, but in the one worship of God. His mention of Basan, Carmel and Lebanon alone, as places lying under the rebuke of God, perhaps implies a special interest in Northern Palestine. Judah may have already become the name for the whole people of God who were left in their own land, since those of the ten tribes who remained had now no separate religious or political existence. The idol-centre of *their* worship was gone into captivity.

With this agrees the old tradition as to the name of the birth-place of Nahum, *the Elkoshite.* "Some think," says St. Jerome [t], "that Elcesæus was the father of Nahum, and, according to the Hebrew tradition, was also a prophet; whereas Elcesi [u] is even to this day a little village in Galilee, small indeed, and scarcely indicating by its ruins the traces of ancient buildings, yet known to the Jews, and pointed out to me too by my guide." The name is a genuine Hebrew name, the *El,* with which it begins, being the name of God, which appears in the names of other towns also, as, El'ale, Eltolad, Elteke, Eltolem. The author of the shortlived Gnostic heresy of the Elcesaites, called Elkesai, ēlkasai, ēlxai, ēlxaios, Elkasaios [u], probably had his name from that same village. Eusebius mentions Elkese, as the place "whence was Nahum the Elkesæan." S. Cyril'of Alexandria says, that Elkese was a village somewhere in Judæa.

On the other hand *Alcush,* a town in Mosul, is probably a name of Arabic origin, and is not connected with Nahum by any extant or known writer, earlier than Masius toward the end of the 16th century [x], and an Arabic scribe in 1713 [y]. Neither of these mention the tomb. "The tomb," says Layard [z], "is a simple plaster box, covered with green cloth, and standing at the upper end of a large chamber. The house containing the tomb is a modern building. There are no inscriptions, nor fragments of any antiquity near the place." The place is now reverenced by the Jews, but in the 12th century Benjamin of Tudela [a] supposed his tomb to be at Ain Japhata, South of Babylon. Were anything needed to invalidate statements above 2000 years after the time of Nahum, it might suffice that the Jews, who are the authors of this story, maintain that not Jonah only but Obadiah and Jephthah the Gileadite are also buried at Mosul [b]. Nor were the ten tribes placed there, but "[c] in the cities of the Medes." The name Capernaum, "the village of Nahum," is probably an indication of his residence in Galilee. There is nothing in his language peculiar to the Northern tribes. One very poetic word [d], common to him with the song of Deborah, is not therefore a "provincialism," because it only happens to occur in the rich, varied, language of two prophets of North Palestine. Nor does the occurrence of a foreign title [e] interfere with "purity of diction." It rather belongs to the vividness of his description.

The conquest of No-Ammon or Thebes and the captivity of its inhabitants, of which Nahum speaks, must have been by Assyria itself. Certainly it was not from domestic disturbances [f]; for Nahum says, that the people were carried away captive [g]. Nor was it from the Ethiopians [h]; for Nahum speaks of them, as her allies [i]. Nor from the Carthaginians [j]; for the account of Ammianus [k], that "when first Carthage was beginning to expand itself far and wide, the Punic generals, by an unexpected inroad, subdued the hundred-gated Thebes," is merely a mistaken gloss on a statement of Diodorus, that "[l] Hanno took Hekatompylos by siege;" a city, according to Diodorus himself [m], "in the desert of Libya." Nor was it from the Scythians [n]; for Herodotus, who alone speaks of their maraudings and who manifestly exaggerates them, expressly says, that Psammetichus induced the Scythians by presents not to enter Egypt [o]; and a wandering predatory horde does not besiege or take strongly-fortified towns. There remain then only the Assyrians. Four successive Assyrian Monarchs, Sargon, his son, grandson and great grandson, Sennacherib, Esarhaddon, Asshurbani-pal, from B. C. 718 to about B. C. 657,

---

[s] Nah. i. 12.　　　　　　[t] Præf. to Nah.
[u] Ἐλκεσαί, Ἐλκασαί, (Theod. Fab. i. 27.) Ἠλκασαί, (Hippol. Philosoph. ix. 4. &c.) Ἠλξαί, Ἠλξαῖος, Ἐλκεσσαῖος, S. Epiph. Hær, xix. 5, xxx. 3, liii. 1. Ἐλκασαῖος or Ἐλκεσαῖος, Method. Conviv. in Combef. Nov. Coll. p. 234. A.
[x] Assem. Bibl. Or. i. 525.　　[y] Ib. iii. 1. 352.
[z] Nin. i. 233.　　[a] Travels i. 310. ed. Asher.
[b] Niebuhr Voyage en Arabie ii. 289, 90.
[c] 2 Kings xvii. 6.
[d] דרה = רוד of the "circling" of the forefeet of the horse in his speed, Nah. iii. 2, Jud. v. 22.

[e] טפסר, doubtless a Ninevite title, probably signifying "noble prince," from סבכר, as Prof. Lee conjectured. Lee denies that it bears in Persian the meaning ascribed to it by Bohlen. Richardson renders *tâbsâr,* "an elevated window;" Vüllers notes, "in others it occurs not." Gesenius was satisfied with no explanation of those before him.
[f] Ewald's theory.　[g] iii. 10.　[h] Vitringa, Grot.
[i] iii. 9.　[j] Heeren.　[k] xvii. 4.
[l] Excerpt. ex L. xxiv. T. ii. p. 565.
[m] v. 18. T. i. p. 263.
[n] Gesenius Lit. Zeit. 1841. n. 1.　　[o] i. 105.

conquered in Egypt [p]. The hostility was first provoked by the encouragement given by Sabacho the Ethiopian (Sab'e [q], in the cuneiform inscriptions, S b k, in Egyptian), the So of Holy Scripture [r], to Hoshea to rebel against Shalmaneser [s]. Sargon, who, according to his own statement, was the king who actually took Samaria [t], led three expeditions of his own against Egypt. In the first, Sargon defeated the Egyptian king in the battle of Raphia [u]; in the second, in his seventh year, he boasts that Pharaoh became his tributary [x]; in a third, which is placed three years later, Ethiopia submitted to him [y]. A seal of Sabaco has been found at Koyunjik, which, as has been conjectured [z], was probably annexed to a treaty. The capture of Ashdod by the Tartan of Sargon, recorded by Isaiah [a], was probably in the second expedition, when Sargon deposed its king Azuri, substituting his brother Akhinit [b]: the rebellion of Ashdod probably occasioned the third expedition, in which as it seems, Isaiah's prophecy was fulfilled, that Egyptians and Ethiopians, young and old, should be carried captive by the king of Assyria. The king of Ashdod, Yaman, is related to have fled to Egypt, which was subject to Merukha or Meroe; and to have been delivered up by the king of Meroe who himself fled to some unnamed desert afar, a march of (it is conjectured) months [c]. The king of Meroe, first, from times the most distant, became tributary. "[d] His forefathers had not" in all that period "sent to the kings my ancestors to ask for peace and to acknowledge the power of Merodach." The fact, that his magnificent palace, "one of the few remains of external decoration," Layard says [e], "with which we are acquainted in Assyrian architecture," "seems" according to Mr. Fergusson [f], "at first sight almost purely Egyptian," implies some lengthened residence in Egypt or some capture of Egyptian artists.

Of Sennacherib, the son of Sargon, Josephus writes, "[g] Berosus, the historian of the Chaldee affairs, mentions the king Sennacherib, and that he reigned over the Assyrians, and that he warred against all Asia and Egypt, saying as follows." The passage of Berosus itself is wanting, whether Josephus neglected to fill it in, or whether it has been subsequently lost; but neither Chaldee nor

Egyptian writers record expeditions which were reverses; and although Berosus was a Babylonian, not an Assyrian, yet the document, which he used, must have been Assyrian. In the second expedition of Sennacherib, Rabshakeh, in his message to Hezekiah, says, [h] *Behold thou trustest upon the staff of this bruised reed, upon Egypt.* The expression is remarkable. He does not speak of Egypt, as a power, weak, frail, failing, but, passively, as *crushed* [i] by another. It is the same word and image which he uses in his prophecy of our Lord, *a bruised reed (kaneh ratsuts) shall He not break,* i. e. He shall not break that which is already bruised. The word implies, then, that the king of Egypt had already received some decided blow before the second expedition of Sennacherib. The annals of Sennacherib's reign, still preserved in his inscriptions, break off in the eighth of his twenty-two years [k], and do not extend to the time of this second expedition against Hezekiah [l]. Nor does Holy Scripture say, in what year this 2d expedition took place. In this he defeated "[m] the kings of Egypt and the king of Meroe at Altakou [Elteke] and Tamna [Timnatha]."

Sennacherib's son Esarhaddon appears for the time to have subdued Egypt and Ethiopia, and to have held them as kingdoms dependent on himself. "He *acquired* Egypt and the inner parts of Asia," is the brief statement of Abydenus [n]: (i. e. of Berosus.) "He established" (his son relates) "twenty kings, satraps, governors in Egypt [o]," among which can be recognized Necho, (the father of Psammetichus) king of Memphis and Sais; a king of Tanis, or Zoan (now Sân); Natho (or, according to another copy, Sept), Hanes, Sebennytus, Mendes, Bubastis, Siyout or Lycopolis, Chemmis, Tinis, and No. These were all subordinate kings; for so he entitles each separately in the list, although he sums up the whole, "[p] These are the names of the Kings, Pechahs, Satraps who in Egypt obeyed my father who begat me." Tearcho or Taracho himself, "king of Egypt and Ethiopia [q]," was in like way subject to Esarhaddon. The account of the revolt, which his son Asshur-bani-pal quelled, implies also a fixed settlement in Egypt. The 20 kings were involved in the rebellion through fear of Taracho, but there is notice of other servants of Esarhaddon who remained faithful and were

[p] See Rawlinson Five Empires ii. 409–486.
[q] Oppert, les rapports de l' Eg. et de l' Ass. p. 12.
[r] אֹנִיס. In the LXX, in different MSS. Σωά, Σοβά, Σωβά, Σουβά; in the Complut. Σουά Vulg. Sua. Sir G. Wilkinson in Rawl. Herod. [s] 2 Kings xvii. 4.
[t] Layard, Nin. and Bab. p. 618, Rawl. Herod. i. 472, Five Empires ii. 406.
[u] Rawl. Five Emp. ii. 414. [x] Rawl. Ib. pp. 415, 6.
[y] Rawl. Ib. pp. 416, 7.
[z] Rawl. Herod. i. 473, note 1. [a] xx. 1.
[b] Inscription in Oppert, les rapports de l' Eg. &c. p. 18.
[c] Ib. p. 19. [d] Ib. [e] Nin. and Bab. p. 130.

[f] Palaces of Nineveh and Persepolis restored, p. 223, quoted by Layard Ib. Rawl. Her. i. 474.
[g] Ant. x. 1. 4. [h] 2 Kings xviii. 21.
[i] רָצוּץ, "quassatum," Vulg. Gesenius says well, "It differs from שָׁבַר in this, that רָצַץ signifies, 'broke, crushed,' without severance of the parts; שָׁבַר signifies, 'broke asunder.'"
[k] Rawl. Her. i. 478. [l] See Rawl. i. 479, note 1.
[m] Inscr. in Oppert Rapports pp. 26, 27.
[n] In Eus. Chron. Arm. P. i. c. 9.
[o] Inscr. in Opp. Ib. pp. 51, 53. [p] Ib. p. 58.
[q] Ib. pp. 51, 62, 63.

maltreated by Taracho[r]. Asshur-bani-pal says also, that he strengthened his former garrisons[s]. One expedition of Esarhaddon (probably toward the close of his reign, since he does not mention it in his own annals which extend over eight years) is related by his son Asshur-bani-pal. "[t]He defeated Tirhakah in the lower country, after which, proceeding Southward, he took the city, where the Ethiopian held his court," and assumed the title, "[u]king of the kings of Egypt and conqueror of Ethiopia." On another inscription in a palace built for his son, at Tarbisi, now Sherif-khan, he entitles himself "[x]king of the kings of Egypt, Pathros, Ethiopia." We do not, however, find the addition, which appears to recur upon every conquest of a people not before conquered by Assyria, "which the kings, my fathers, had not subdued." This addition is so regular, that the absence of it, in itself, involves a strong probability of a previous conquest of the country.

The subdual apparently was complete. They revolted at the close of the reign of Esarhaddon (as his son Asshur-bani-pal relates) from fear of Taracho[y] rather than from any wish of their own to regain independence. Asshur-bani-pal accordingly, after the defeat of Taracho, forgave and restored them[z]. Even the second treacherous revolt was out of fear, lest Taracho shall return[a], upon the withdrawal of the Assyrian armies. This second revolt and perhaps a subsequent revolt of Urdamanie[b] a stepson of Taracho, who succeeded him, Asshur-bani-pal seems to have subdued by his lieutenants[c], without any necessity of marching in person against them. Thebes was taken and retaken; but does not appear to have offered any resistance. Taracho, upon his defeat at Memphis, fled to it, and again abandoned it as he had Memphis, and the army of Asshur-bani-pal made a massacre in it[d]. Once more it was taken, when it had been recovered by Urdamanie[e], and then, if the inscriptions are rightly deciphered, strange as it is, the carrying off of men and women from it is mentioned in the midst of that of "great horses and apes." "Silver, gold, metals, stones, treasures of his palace, dyed garments, berom and linen, great horses, men, male and female, immense apes —they drew from the midst of the city, and brought as spoils to Nineveh the city of my dominion, and kissed my feet."

All of those kings having been conquerors of Egypt, the captivity of No might equally have taken place under any of them. All of them employed the policy, which Sargon apparently began, of transporting to a distance those whom they had conquered[f]. Yet it is, in itself, more probable, that it was at the earlier than at the later date. It is most in harmony with the relation of Nahum to Isaiah that, in regard to the conquest of Thebes also, Nahum refers to the victory over Egypt and Ethiopia foretold by Isaiah, when Sargon's general, the Tartan, was besieging Ashdod. The object of Isaiah's prophecy was to undeceive Judah in regard to its reliance on Egypt and Ethiopia against Assyria, which was their continual bane, morally, religiously, nationally. But the prophecy goes beyond any mere defeat in battle, or capture of prisoners. It relates to conquest within Egypt itself. For Isaiah says, "[g]the king of Assyria shall lead into captivity Egyptians and Ethiopians, young and old." They are not their choice young men[h], the flower of their army, but those of advanced age and those in their first youth[i], such as are taken captive, only when a population itself is taken captive, either in a marauding expedition, or in the capture of a city. The account of the captivity of No exactly corresponds with this. Nahum says nothing of its permanent subdual, only of the captivity of its inhabitants. But Esarhaddon apparently did not carry the Egyptians captive at all[k]. Every fact given in the Inscriptions looks like a permanent settlement. The establishment of the 20 subordinate kings, in the whole length and breadth of Egypt, implies the continuance of the previous state of things, with the exception of that subordination. No itself appears as one of the cities settled apparently under its native though tributary king[l].

In regard to the fulfillment of prophecy, they who assume as an axiom, or petitio principii, that there can be no prophecy of distant events, have overlooked, that while they think that, by assuming the later date, they bring Nahum's prophecy of the capture of Nineveh nearer to its accomplishment, they remove in the same degree Isaiah's prophecy of the captivity of Egyptians and Ethiopians, young and old, from its accomplishment. "Young and old" are not the prisoners of a field of battle; young and old of the Ethiopians would not be in a city of

[r] Inscr. in Opp. p. 64. [s] Ib. pp. 58, 68.
[t] Rawl. 5 Emp. ii. 474, 5.
[u] Ib. 475. He also entitles himself, "king of Assyria, Babylon, Egypt, Meroe and Ethiopia." Oppert Sargonides, p. 53. Rawl. Ib. 484.
[x] Inscript. Oppert Rapp. p. 41.
[y] Ib. p. 58. [z] Ib. [a] Ib. p. 59. [b] p. 77
[c] Ib. 70. where he speaks of *sapite-ya* (שׁפֶטַי) "my judges" pp. 77, 78. In another inscription, however, Oppert observes that Asshurbanipal speaks, as if he had been there in person. pp. 73-76. It has

been observed, long since, that the Assyrian monarchs speak at times of what was done by their generals as done by themselves. This, however, scarcely appears here, where he says "I returned in safety to Nineveh." p. 76.
[d] Ib. 66, 68.
[e] Ib. p. 79. In p. 75 it is said that Urdamanie abandoned No and fled to Kipkip.
[f] See on Am. i. 5, vol. i. p. 240.
[g] Is. xx. 4. [h] בחורים. [i] נערים וזקנים.
[k] Rawl. Ib. 474, 475. [l] Rawl. Ib. p. 485.

lower Egypt. If Isaiah's prophecy was not fulfilled under Sargon or Sennacherib, it must probably have waited for its fulfillment until this last subdual by Asshurbanipal. For the policy of Esarhaddon and also of Asshurbanipal, until repeated rebellions wore his patience, was of settlement, not of deportation. If too the prophecy of Nahum were brought down to the reign of Asshurbanipal, it would be the more stupendous. For the empire was more consolidated. Nahum tells the conqueror, flushed with his own successes and those of his father, that he had himself no more inherent power than the city whose people he had carried captive. Thebes too, like Nineveh, dwelt securely, conquering all, unreached by any ill, sea-girt, as it were, by the mighty river on which she rested. She too was strengthened with countless hosts of her own and of allied people. Yet she fell. Nineveh, the prophet tells her, was no mightier, in herself. Her river was no stronger defence than that sea of fresh water, the Nile; her tributaries would disperse or become her enemies. The Prophet holds up to her the vicissitudes of No-amon, as a mirror to herself. As each death is a renewed witness to man's mortality, so each marvelous reverse of temporal greatness is a witness to the precariousness of other human might. No then was an ensample to Nineveh, although its capture was by the armies of Nineveh. They had been, for centuries, two rivals for power. But the contrast had far more force, when the victory over Egypt was fresh, than after 61 years of alternate conquest and rebellion.

But, anyhow, the state of Nineveh and its empire, as pictured by Nahum, is inconsistent with any times of supposed weakness in the reign of its last king: the state of Judah, with reference to Assyria, corresponds with that under Sennacherib but with none below. They are these. Assyria was in its full unimpaired strength [m]. She still blended those two characters so rarely combined, but actually united in her and subsequently in Babylon, of a great merchant and military people. She had, at once, the prosperity of peace and of war. Lying on a great line of ancient traffic, which bound together East and West, India with Phœnicia, and with Europe through Phœnicia, both East and West poured their treasures into the great capital, which lay as a centre between them, and stretched out its arms, alike to the Indian sea and the Mediterranean. Nahum can compare its merchants only to that which is countless by man,

the locusts or the stars of heaven [n]. But amid this prosperity of peace, war also was enriching her. Nineveh was still sending out its messengers (such as was Rabshakeh), the leviers of its tribute, the demanders of submission. It was still one vast lion-lair, its lions still gathering in prey from the whole earth [o], still desolating, continually, unceasingly, in all directions [p], and now, specially, devising evil against God and His people [q]. Upon that people its yoke already pressed, for God promises to break it off from them [r]; the people was already afflicted, for God says to it, *Though I have afflicted thee, I will afflict thee no more* [s], viz. by this invader. The solemn feasts of Judah were hindered through the presence of ungodly invaders; Belial, the counsellor of evil spoken of under that name, already passing through her [t]. War was around her, for he promises that one should publish peace upon her mountains [t]. This was the foreground of the picture. This was the exact condition of things at Hezekiah's second invasion, just before the miraculous destruction of his army. Sennacherib's yoke was heavy; for he had exacted from Hezekiah *three hundred talents of silver and thirty talents of gold* [u]; Hezekiah had not [x] *two thousand horsemen; the great host* [y] of the Assyrians encircled Jerusalem. They summoned it to surrender on the terms, that they should pay a new tribute, and that Sennacherib, whenever it pleased him, should remove them to Assyria [z].

At no subsequent period were there any events corresponding to this description. Manasseh was carried captive to Babylon by Esarhaddon; but probably this was no formidable or resisted invasion, since the book of Kings passes it over altogether, the Chronicles mention only that the Assyrian generals took Manasseh prisoner in a thicket [a], accordingly not in Jerusalem, and carried him to Babylon. Probably, this took place, in the expedition of Esarhaddon to the West, when he settled in the cities of Samaria people of different nations, his captives [b]. The capture of Manasseh was then, probably, a mere incident in the history. Since he was taken among the thickets, he had probably fled, as Zedekiah did afterward, and was taken in his place of concealment. This was simply personal. No taking of towns is mentioned, no siege, no terror, no exaction of tribute, no carrying away into captivity, except of the single Manasseh. The grounds of his restoration are not mentioned. The Chronicles mention only the religious aspect

[m] i. 12. ii. 12.   [n] iii. 16.
[o] ii. 12, 13.   [p] iii. 19.   [q] i. 9, 11.   [r] i. 13.
[s] i. 12.   [t] i. 15.   [u] 2 Kings xviii. 14.   [x] Ib. 23.
[y] Ib. 17.   [z] Ib. 31, 32.
[a] 2 Chron. xxxiii. 11. The uniform meaning of לכד is "took, took prisoner;" of חוחים, "thorns;" the singular only, חוח, in one of the two places in

Job, is "a hook," in the other it is a "thorn." לכד, which occurs 120 times in the O. T., never means "dragged captive." The meaning ascribed to the words, "bound him with chains," is wholly conjectural. לכד does not mean "bound," nor חוחים "chains."
[b] Ezr. iv. 2, 9, 10.

of his captivity and his restoration, his sin and his repentance. But it seems probable that he was restored by Esarhaddon, upon the same system of policy, on which he planted subjects of his own in Samaria and the country around Zidon, built a new town to take the place of Zidon, and joined in the throne of Edom one, brought up in his own palace. For, when restored, Manasseh was set at full liberty to fortify Jerusalem[c], as Hezekiah had done, and to put "[c] captains of war in all the cities of Judah." This looks as if he was sent back as a trusted tributary of Esarhaddon, and as a frontier-power against Egypt. At least, sixty years afterward, we find Josiah, in the like relation of trust to Nebuchadnezzar, resisting the passage of Pharaoh-Necho. However, the human cause of his restoration must remain uncertain. Yet clearly, in their whole history, there is nothing to correspond to the state of Judæa, as described by Nahum.

A recent critic writes, "[d] Nahum's prophecy *must* have been occasioned by an expedition of mighty enemies against Nineveh. The whole prophecy is grounded on the certain danger, to which Nineveh was given over; only the way in which this visible danger is conceived of, in connection with the eternal truths, is here the properly prophetic." Ewald does not explain how the danger, to which "Nineveh was given over" was *certain*, when it did not happen. The explanation must come to this. Nahum described a siege of Nineveh and its issue, as certain. The description in itself might be either of an actual siege, before the Prophet's eyes, or of one beheld in the Prophet's mind. But obviously no mere man, endowed with mere human knowledge, would have ventured to predict so certainly the fall of such a city as Nineveh, unless it was "given over to certain danger." But according to the axiom received in Ewald's school, Nahum, equally with all other men, could have had only human prescience. Therefore Nahum, prophesying the issue so confidently, must have prophesied when Nineveh was so "given over." The à priori axiom of the school rules its criticism. Meanwhile the admission is incidentally made, that a prophecy so certain, had it related to distant events, was what no man, with mere human knowledge, would venture on. Ewald accordingly thinks that the prophecy was occasioned by a siege of Phraortes; which siege Nahum expected to be successful; which however failed, so that Nahum was mistaken, although the overthrow which he foretold came to pass afterward! The siege, however, of Nineveh by Phraortes is a mere romance. Herodotus, who alone attributes to Phraortes a war with

Assyria, has no hint, that he even approached to Nineveh. He simply relates that Phraortes "subdued Asia, going from one nation to another, until, leading an army against the Assyrians, he perished himself, in the 22d year of his reign, and the greater part of his army." It is not necessary to consider the non-natural expositions, by which the simple descriptions of Nahum were distorted into conformity with this theory, which has no one fact to support it. Herodotus even dwells on the good condition of the Assyrian affairs, although isolated from their revolted allies, and seemingly represents the victory as an easy one. And, according to Herodotus, whose account is the only one we have, Phraortes (even if he ever fought with the Ninevites, and Herodotus' account is not merely the recasting of the history of another Median Frawartish who, according to the Behistun Inscription, claimed the throne of Media against Darius, and perished in battle with him[e]) had only an unorganized army. Herodotus says of Cyaxares, his son, "[f] He is said to have been more warlike far than his forefathers, and he first distributed Asiatics into distinct bands, and separated the spearmen and archers and horsemen from one another, whereas, before, everything had alike mixed into one confused mass." Such an undisciplined horde could have been no formidable enemy for a nation, whom the monuments and their history exhibit as so warlike and so skilled in war as the Assyrians.

Another critic[g], then, seeing the untenableness of this theory, ventures (as he never hesitated at any paradox) to place the prophet Nahum, as an eye-witness of the first siege of Cyaxares.

Herodotus states that Cyaxares, the son of Phraortes, twice besieged Nineveh. First, immediately after his father's death, to avenge it[f]; the second, after the end of the Scythian troubles, when he took it[h]. The capture of Nineveh was in the first year of Nabopolassor B. C. 625. The accession of Cyaxares, according to Herodotus, was B. C. 633. Eight years then only elapsed between his first siege and its capture, and, if it be true, that the siege lasted two years, there was an interval of six years only. But, at this time, the destruction of Nineveh was no longer a subject of joy to Judah. Since the captivity of Manasseh, Judah had had nothing to fear from Assyria; nor do we know of any oppression from it. Holy Scripture mentions none. The Assyrian monuments speak of expeditions against Egypt; but there was no temptation to harass Judah, which stood in the relation of a faithful tributary and an outwork against Egypt, and which, when Nineveh fell, remained in the same relation to its

c 2 Chron. xxxiii. 14.   d Ewald, Proph. i. 349.
e In Rawl. i. 409.   f i. 103.

g Hitzig, followed by Davidson, iii. 293.
h i. 106.

conquerors, into whose suzerainty it passed, together with the other dependencies of Assyria. The relation of Josiah to Babylon was the continuation of that of Manasseh to Esarhaddon.

The motive of this theory is explained by the words, " With a confidence, which leaves room for no doubt, Nahum expects a siege and an ultimate destruction of Nineveh. The security of his tone, nay that he ventures at all to hope so enormous a revolution of the existing state of things, must find its explanation in the circumstances of the time, out of the then condition of the world ; but not till Cyaxares reigned in Media, did things assume an aspect, corresponding to this confidence." It is well that this writer doffs the courteous language, as to the " hopes," " expectations," " inferences from God's justice," and brings the question to the issue, " there is such absolute certainty of tone," that Nahum must have had either a Divine or a human knowledge. He acknowledges the untenableness of any theory which would account for the prophecy of Nahum on any human knowledge, before Cyaxares was marching against the gates of Nineveh. Would human knowledge have sufficed then ? Certainly, from such accounts as we have, Nineveh might still have stood against Cyaxares and its own rebel and traitorous general, but for an unforeseen event which man could not bring about, the swelling of its river.

But, as usual, unbelief fixes itself upon that which is minutest, ignores what is greatest. There are, in Nahum, three remarkable predictions. 1) The sudden destruction of Sennacherib's army and his own remarkable death in the house of his god. 2) The certain, inevitable, capture of Nineveh, and that, not by capitulation or famine, not even by the siege or assault, which is painted so vividly, but the river, which was its protection, becoming the cause of its destruction. 3) Its utter desolation, when captured. The first, men assume to have been the description of events past ; the second, the siege, they assume to have been present ; and that, when human wisdom could foresee its issue ; the third, they generalize. The first is beyond the reach of proof now. It was a witness of the Providence and just judgment of God, to those days, not to our's. A brief survey of the history of the Assyrian Empire will shew, that the second and third predictions were beyond human knowledge.

The Assyrian Empire dated probably from the ninth century before Christ. Such, it has been pointed out, is the concurrent result of the statements of Berosus and Herodotus.

[i] Gen. x. 10, 11.
[k] וַיֵּצֵא not יָצָא הַהוּא הָאָרֶץ מִן.
[l] אַשּׁוּרָה Gen. xxv. 18.

Moses, according to the simplest meaning of his words, spake of the foundation of Nineveh as contemporary with that of Babylon. [i] *The beginning of the kingdom of Nimrod, he relates, was Babel and Erech, and Accad and Calneh, in the land of Shinar. Out of that land went forth Asshur, and builded Nineveh.* Oppressed probably and driven forth by Nimrod, Asshur and his Semitic descendants went forth from the plain of Shinar, the Babylonia of after-ages. Had Moses intended to express (what some have thought), that *Nimrod* " went forth out of that land to Assyria," he would doubtless have used the ordinary style of connected narrative ; " [k] *And* he went forth thence." He would probably also have avoided ambiguity, by expressing that Nimrod " went forth *to* Asshur [l]," using a form, which he employs a little later. As it is, Moses has used a mode of speech, by which, in Hebrew, a parenthetic statement would be made, and he has not used the form, which occurs in every line of Hebrew narrative to express a continued history. No one indeed would have doubted that such was the meaning, but that they did not see, how the mention of Asshur, a son of Shem, came to be anticipated in this account of the children of Ham. This is no ground for abandoning the simple construction of the Hebrew. It is but the history, so often repeated in the changes of the world, that the kingdom of Nimrod was founded on the expulsion of the former inhabitants. Nimrod began his kingdom ; "Asshur went forth."

It is most probable, from this same brief notice, that Nineveh was, from the first, that aggregate of cities, which it afterward was. Moses says, " [m] And he builded Nineveh and Rehoboth-Ir and Calach and Resen, between Nineveh and Calach ; this is that great city [n]." This cannot be understood as said exclusively of Nineveh ; since Nineveh was mentioned first in the list of cities, and the mention of the three others had intervened ; and, in the second place where it is named, it is only spoken of indirectly and subordinately ; it is hardly likely to be said of Resen, of whose unusual size nothing is elsewhere related. It seems more probable, that it is said of the aggregate of cities, that they formed together one great city, the very characteristic of Nineveh, as spoken of in Jonah.

Nineveh itself lay on the Eastern side of the Tigris, opposite to the present Mosul. In later times, among the Syrian writers, Asshur becomes the name for the country, distinct from Mesopotamia and Babylonia [o], from which it was separated by the Tigris,

[m] Gen. x. 11, 12.
[n] הָעִיר הַגְּדֹלָה.
[o] Bar-Hebr. in Tuch de Nino urbe pp. 9, 10.

and bounded on the North by Mount Niphates.

This distinction, however, does not occur until after the extinction of the Assyrian empire. On the contrary, in Genesis, Asshur, in one place, is spoken of as West [p] of the Hiddekel or Tigris, so that it must at that time have comprised Mesopotamia, if not all on this side of the Tigris, i. e. Babylonia. In another place, it is the great border-state of Arabia on the one side, as was Egypt on the other. *The sons of Ishmael*, Moses relates [q], *dwelt from Havilah unto Shur that is before Egypt, as thou goest to Assyria ;* i. e. they dwelt on the great caravan-route across the Arabian desert from Egypt to Babylonia. Yet Moses mentions, not Babylon, but Asshur. In Balaam's prophecy [r], Asshur stands for the great Empire, whose seat was at one time at Nineveh, at another at Babylon, which should, centuries afterwards, carry Israel captive.

Without entering into the intricacies of Assyrian or Babylonian history further than is necessary for the immediate object, it seems probable, that the one or other of the sovereigns of these nations had an ascendency over the others, according to his personal character and military energy. Thus, in the time of Abraham, Chedorlaomer king of Elam, in his expedition against the kings of Sodom and Gomorrah, took with him, as subordinate allies, the kings of Shinar, (or Babylon) and Ellasar, as well as *Tidal king of nations*, a king probably of Nomadic tribes. The expedition was to avenge the rebellion of the petty kings in the valley of Siddim against Chedorlaomer, after they had been for twelve years tributary. But, although the expedition closed with the attack on the five kings of Sodom and Gomorrah, Admah, Zeboim, and Zoar, its extent on the East side of the Jordan from Ashteroth Karnaim in Basan to Elparan (perhaps Elath on the Red Sea), and the defeat of the giant tribes, the Rephaim, Zuzim, Emim, Horites, the Amalekites and the Amorites in their several abodes, seems to imply one of those larger combinations against the aggressions of the East, which we meet with in later times [s]. It was no insulated conflict which

spread over nearly three degrees of latitude. But it was the king of Elam, not the king of Babylon or of Asshur, who led this expedition; and those other kings, according to the analogy of the expeditions of Eastern monarchs, were probably dependent on him. It has been observed that the inscriptions of a monarch whose name partly coincides with that of Chedorlaomer, viz. Kudurmabuk, or Kudurmapula, shew traces of a Persian influence on the Chaldee characters; but cuneiform decipherers having desponded of identifying those monarchs [t], Chedorlaomer appears as yet only so far connected with Babylon, that its king was a tributary sovereign to him or a vice-king [u] like those of later times, of whom Sennacherib boasts, "Are not my princes altogether kings ?"

Assyria, at this time, is not mentioned, and so, since we know of its existence at an earlier period, it probably was independent. Lying far to the North of any of the nations here mentioned, it, from whatever cause or however it may have been engaged, took no share in the war. Subsequently also, down to a date almost contemporary with the Exodus, it has been observed that the name of Asshur does not appear on the Babylonian inscriptions, nor does it swell the titles of the king of Babylon [x]. A little later than the Exodus, however, in the beginning of the 14th century B. C., Asshur and Egypt were already disputing the country which lay between them. The account is Egyptian, and so, of course, only relates the successes of Egypt. Thothmes III, in his fortieth year, according to Mr. Birch, received tribute from a king of Nineveh [y]. In another monument of the same monarch, where the line, following on the name Nineveh, is lost, Thothmes says that he " [z] erected his tablet in Naharaina (Mesopotamia) for the extension of the frontiers of Kami" [Egypt]. Amenophis III, in the same century, represented Asiatic captives [a], with the names of Patana [Padan-Aram], Asuria, Karukamishi [Carchemish "]. "On another column are Saenkar (Shinar), Naharaina, and the Khita (Hittites)." The mention of these contiguous nations strengthens the impression that the details of the interpretation are accurate. All

---

[p] Gen. ii. 14. There is no reason, with Keil, to disturb the rendering. קֵדְמָה is most naturally rendered *Eastward*, in the other three places; Michmash was E. S. E. of Bethaven (1 Sam. xiii. 5), but was not *over-against* it, being some four miles from it, in a valley. The battle which began at Michmash, *passed over to Bethaven*. (1 Sam. xiv. 23.) The Philistines too were obviously facing Saul who was at Gilgal (1 Sam. xiii. 12). In Ezek. xxxix. 11, the words "*eastward of the sea*," express that the carcases were outside the promised land. In Gen. iv. 16, Cain was not one to linger *over-against* the lost *Eden*. Probably he went *Eastward*, because then too the stream of population went Westward. In Isaiah vii. 20 the king of Assyria is spoken of as *beyond the river*, i. e. the Euphrates.

[q] Gen. xxv. 18.

[r] Num. xxiv. 22.

[s] Sir H. Rawl. in Rawl. Herod. i. 446.

[t] "On the one hand the general resemblance of Kudurmapula's legends to those of the ordinary Chaldæan monarchs is unquestionable; on the other hand, it is remarkable that there are peculiarities in the forms of the letters, and even in the elements composing the names upon his bricks which favor his connection with Elam." Sir H. Rawlinson in Rawl. Herod. i. 436.

[u] Rawl. Five Empires i. 206.

[x] Ib. p. 447.

[y] From statistical Tablet of Karnak, quoted by Layard Nin. and Bab. c. xxvi. p. 631, Birch in Archæologia Vol. xxxv. pp. 116–66.

[z] Ib. p. 630, note 1.

[a] Ib.

these inscriptions imply that Assyria was independent of Babylon. In one, it is a co-ordinate power; in the two others, it is a state which had measured its strength with Egypt, under one of its greatest conquerors, though, according to the Egyptian account, it had been worsted.

Another account, which has been thought to be the first instance of the extension of Babylonian authority so far northward, seems to me rather to imply the ancient self-government of Assyria. "[b] A record of Tiglath-pileser I. declares him to have rebuilt a temple in the city of Asshur, which had been taken down 60 years previously, after it had lasted for 641 years from the date of its first foundation by Shamas-Iva, son of Ismi-Dagon." Sir H. Rawlinson thinks that it is probable (although only probable)[c], that this Ismi-Dagon is a king, whose name occurs in the brick-legends of Lower Babylonia. Yet the Ismi-Dagon of the bricks does not bear the title of king of Babylon, but of king of Niffer only [d]: "his son," it is noticed, "does not take the title of king; but of governor of Hur[e]." The name Shamas-Iva nowhere occurs in connection with Babylonia, but it *does* recur, at a later period, as the name of an Assyrian Monarch [f]. Since the names of the Eastern kings so often continue on in the same kingdom, the recurrence of that name, at a later period, makes it even probable, that Shamas-Iva was a native king. There is absolutely nothing to connect his father Ismi-Dagon with the Ismi-Dagon king of Niffer, beyond the name itself, which, being Semitic, may just as well have belonged to a native king of Nineveh as to a king of Lower Babylonia. Nay, there is nothing to shew that Ismi-Dagon was not an Assyrian Monarch who reigned at Niffer; for the name of his father is still unknown; there is no evidence that his father was ever a king, or, if a king, where he reigned. It seems to me in the last degree precarious to assume, without further evidence, the identity of the two kings. It has, further, yet to be shewn that Lower Babylonia had, at that time, an *empire*, as distinct from its own local sovereignty. We know from Holy Scripture of Nimrod's kingdom in Shinar, a province distinct from Elymais, Mesopotamia, Assyria, and probably Chaldæa. In Abraham's time, 1900 B. C., we find again a king of Shinar. Shinar again, it is supposed, appears in Egyptian inscriptions, in the 14th century, B. C.[g]; and, if so, still distinct from Mesopotamia and Assyria. But all this implies a distinct kingdom, not an empire.

Again, were it ever so true, that Shamas-

Iva was a son of a king in Lower Babylonia, that he built a temple in Kileh-Shergat, as being its king, and that he was king, as placed there by Ismi-Dagon, this would be no proof of the continual dependence of Assyria upon Babylonia. England did not continue a dependency of France, because conquered by William of Normandy. How was Alexander's empire broken at once! Spain under Charles the V. was under one sovereignty with Austria; Spain with France had, even of late, alike Bourbon kings. A name would, at most, shew an accidental, not a permanent, connection.

But there is, at present, no evidence implying a continued dependence of Assyria upon Babylon. Two facts only have been alleged; 1) that the cuneiform writing of inscriptions at Kileh-Shergat, 40 miles South of Nineveh, has a Babylonian character; 2) that, on those bricks, four names have been found of inferior Satraps.

But 1) the Babylonian character of the inscriptions would show a dependence of civilization, not of empire. Arts flourished early at Babylon, and so the graven character of the Inscriptions too may have been carried to the rougher and warlike North. The garment, worked at Babylon, was, in the 15th century B. C., exported as far as Palestine, and was, for its beauty, the object of Achan's covetousness [h].

2) In regard to the satraps whose names are found on the bricks of Kileh-Shergat, it does not *appear*, that they were tributary to *Babylon* at all; they may, as far as it appears, have been simply inferior officers of the Assyrian empire. Anyhow, the utmost which such a relation to Babylon would evince, if ever so well established, would be a temporary dependence of Kileh-Shergat itself, not of Nineveh or the Assyrian kingdom. Further, the evidence of the duration of the dependency would be as limited at its extent. Four satraps would be no evidence as to this period of 700 years, only a century less than has elapsed since the Norman conquest. The early existence of an Assyrian kingdom has been confirmed by recent cuneiform discoveries, which give the names of 8 Assyrian kings, the earliest of whom is supposed to have reigned about 3½ centuries before the commencement of the Assyrian Empire [i].

The "empire," Herodotus says [k], "Assyria held in Upper Asia for 520 years;" Berosus[l], "for 526 years." The Cuneiform Inscriptions give much the same result. Tiglath-pileser [m], who gives five years' annals of his own victories, mentions his grandfather's grandfather,

---

[b] Sir H. Rawlinson from the Shergat Cylinders in Rawl. Herod. Ess. vi. i. 433. note 1.
[c] Ib. p. 456. note 5.   [d] Ib. p. 437.   [e] Ib. § 7.
[f] Sir H. Rawlins., Journ. As. Soc. xvi. P. 1. Ann. Rep. p. xii. sq. Rawl. Herod. i. p. 466.

[g] Mr. Birch in Layard, Nin. and Bab. p. 631.
[h] Josh. vii. 21.
[i] Rawl. 5 Emp. ii. 291; comp. i. 212.
[k] i. 95.   [l] Fragm. 11.
[m] Rawl. Her. i. 457.

the 4th king before him, as the king who " first organized the country of Assyria," who " established the troops of Assyria in authority." The expression, " established in authority," if it may be pressed, relates to foreign conquest. If this Tiglath-pileser be the same whom Sennacherib, in the 10th year of his own reign, mentions as having lost his gods to Merodach-ad-akhi, king of Mesopotamia, 418 years before [n], then, since Sennacherib ascended the throne about 703 B.C.[o], we should have B.C. 1112 for the latter part of the reign of Tiglath-pileser I., and counting this and the six preceding reigns at 20 years each [p], should have about 1252 B.C. for the beginning of the Assyrian empire. It has been calculated that if the 526 years, assigned by Berosus to his 45 Assyrian kings, are (as Polyhistor [q] states Berosus to have meant) to be dated back from the accession of Pul who took tribute from Menahem, and so from between B.C. 770 and B.C. 760, they carry back the beginning of the dynasty to about 1290 B.C. If they be counted, (as is perhaps more probable) from the end of the reign of Pul [r], i. e. probably B.C. 747, " the era of Nabonassar," the Empire would commence about 1273 B.C. Herodotus, it has been shewn [s], had much the same date in his mind, when he assigned 520 years to the Assyrian empire in upper Asia, dating back from the revolt of the Medes. For he supposed this revolt to be 179 years anterior to the death of Cyrus B.C. 529 (and so, B.C. 708)+a period of anarchy before the accession of Deioces. Allowing 30 years for this period of anarchy, we have 738 B.C.+520, i. e. 1258 B.C., for the date of the commencement of Assyrian empire according to Herodotus. Thus, the three testimonies would coincide in placing the beginning of that Empire anyhow between 1258 and 1273 B.C.

But this Empire started up full-grown. It was the concentration of energy and power, which had before existed. Herodotus' expression is " rulers of Upper Asia." Tiglath-pileser attributes to his forefather, that he " organized the country," and " established the armies of Assyria in authority." The 2d king of that list takes the title of " ruler over the people of Bel [t]," i. e. Babylonia. The 4th boasts to have reduced " all the lands of the Magian world." Tiglath-pileser I. claims to have conquered large parts of

Cappadocia, Syria from Tsukha to Carchemish, Media and Muzr. According to the inscription at Bavian [u], he sustained a reverse, and lost his gods to a king of Mesopotamia, which gods were recovered by Sennacherib from Babylon. Yet this exception the more proves that conquest was the rule. For, had there been subsequent successful invasions of Assyria by Babylonia, the spoils of the 5th century backward would not have been alone recovered or recorded. If the deciphering of the Inscriptions is to be trusted, Nineveh was the capital, even in the days of Tiglath-pileser I. For Sennacherib brought the gods *back*, it is said, and put them in their places, i. e. probably where he himself reigned, at Nineveh. Thence then they were taken in the reign of Tiglath-pileser. Nineveh then was *his* capital also.

Of an earlier portion we have as yet but incidental notices; yet the might of Assyria is attested by the presence of Assyrian names in the Egyptian dynastic lists, whether the dynasties were themselves Assyrian, or whether the names came in through matrimonial alliances between two great nations [x].

With few exceptions, as far as appears from their own annals (and these are in the later times confirmed by Holy Scripture), the Assyrian Empire was, almost whenever we hear of it, one long series of victory and rapine. It is an exception, if any monarch is peaceful, and content to " repair the buildings [y] " in his residence, " leaving no evidence of conquest or greatness." Tiglathi-Nin, father of the warlike Asshur-i-danipal or Sardanapalus, is mentioned only in his son's monument, " [z] among his warlike ancestors, who had carried their arms into the Armenian mountains, and there set up stelæ to commemorate their conquests." Civil wars there were, and revolutions. Conquerors and dynasties came to an untimely end; there was parricide, fratricide; but the tide of war and conquest rolled on. The restless warriors gave no rest. Sardanapalus terms himself, " [a] the conqueror from the upper passage of the Tigris to Lebanon and the great sea, who all countries, from the rising of the sun to the going down thereof, has reduced under his authority." His son, Shalmanubar or Shalmaneser, in his thirty-five years of reign led, in person twenty-three military expeditions. 20,000,16,000, are the

[n] Dr. Hincks, from Bavian Inscription in Layard Nin. and Bab. pp. 212,3.

[o] His annals mention that, having expelled Merodach-baladan in the first year of his reign, he set up Belib in Babylon (Hincks in Layard Bab. and Nin. 140, 1); but, in the Canon of Ptolemy, the date of Belib is B. C. 703.

[p] Rawl. gives this as the average of Assyrian reigns (Five Empires ii. 93.). The whole calculation is his. An interregnum of 20 years, carries the whole back to the date of Berosus 1273 B.C.

[q] In Euseb. Chron. Arm. pp. 40, 1.

[r] 2 Kings xv. 19.   [s] Rawl. Herod. i. 407.

[t] Rawl. i. 458.

[u] Layard N. and B. 207–12. 614. Rawl. 459.

[x] Rawlinson's conjecture. Five Emp. ii. 335. The period is one of " obscurity," as Rawl. says, but that very obscurity forbids our deciding, as he does, that it was one of " extraordinary weakness and depression."

[y] Asshur-adan-akhi and three following kings. See Rawl. Her. i. 460. The accession of Asshur-adan-akhi was placed by some, referred to by Rawl. Ib., at B. C. 1050, by himself, at B. C. 950, Five Emp. ii. 291.   [z] Sir H. Rawl. Ib. in Rawl. Her. i. 460, n. 7.

[a] In Layard N. and B. pp. 361, 2 Rawl. p. 461.

numbers of his enemies left dead upon a field of battle with Benhadad and Hazael [b]. Cappadocia, Pontus, Armenia, Media, Babylonia, Syria, Phœnicia [c], 15 degrees of longitude and 10 of latitude, save where the desert or the sea gave him nothing to conquer, were the range of his repeated expeditions. He circled round Judæa. He thrice defeated Benhadad with his allies (on several occasions, twelve kings of the Hittites). His own army exceeded on occasions 100,000 fighting men. Twice he defeated Hazael. Israel under Jehu, Tyre, Sidon, 24 kings in Pontus, kings of the Hittites, of Chaldæa, 27 kings of Persia are among his tributaries [d]; "the shooting of his arrows struck terror," he says, "as far as the sea" [Indian Ocean]; "he put up his arrows in their quiver at the sea of the setting sun." His son Shamasiva apparently subdued Babylonia, and in the West conquered tribes near Mount Taurus, on the North the countries bordering on Armenia to the South and East, the Medes beyond Mount Zagros, and "[e] the Zimri [f] in upper Luristan." His son Ivalush III. or IV. received undisturbed tribute from the kingdoms which his fathers conquered, and ascribes to his god Asshur the grant of "[g] the kingdom of Babylon to his son." Thus "Assyria with one hand grasped Babylonia; with the other Philistia and Edom; she held Media Proper, S. Armenia, possessed all Upper Syria, including Commagene and Amanus, bore sway over all the whole Syrian coast from Issus to Gaza, and from the coast to the desert." Tiglath-pileser II. and Shalmaneser are known to us as conquerors from Holy Scripture [h]. Tiglath-pileser, we are told from the inscriptions, warred and conquered in Upper Mesopotamia, Armenia, Media, Babylonia, drove into exile a Babylonian prince, destroyed Damascus, took tribute from a Hiram king of Tyre, and from a Queen of the Arabs [h]. And so it continued, until nearly the close of the Monarchy.

The new dynasty which began with Sargon were even greater conquerors than their predecessors. Sargon, in a reign of seventeen or nineteen years, defeated the king of Elam, conquered in Iatbour beyond Elam, reigned from Ras, a dependency on Elam, over Poukoud (Pekod), Phœnicia, Syria, &c. to the river of Egypt, in the far Media to the rising sun, in Scythia, Albania, Parthia, Van, Armenia, Colchis, Tubal to the Moschi: he

placed his lieutenants as governors over these countries, and imposed tribute upon them, as upon Assyrians; he, probably, placed Merodach-Baladan on the throne of Babylon, and after 12 years displaced him; he reduced all Chaldæa under his rule; he defeated "Sebech (i. e., probably, So), Sultan of Egypt, so that he was heard of no more;" he received tribute from the Pharaoh of Egypt, from a Queen of Arabia and from Himyar the Sabæan. To him first the king of Meroe paid tribute. He finally captured Samaria: he took Gaza, Kharkar, Arpad and Damascus, Ashdod (which it cost Psammetichus 29 years to reconquer), and Tyre, (which resisted Nebuchadnezzar for 13 years). He added to the Satrapy of Parthia, placed a Satrap or Lieutenant over Commagene and Samaria, Kharkar, Tel-Garimmi, Gamgoum, Ashdod, and a king of his own choice over Albania. He seized 55 walled cities in Armenia, 11, which were held to be "inaccessible fortresses;" and 62 great cities in Commagene; 34 in Media; he laid tribute on the "king of the country of rivers." He removed whole populations at his will; from Samaria, he carried captive its inhabitants, 27,800, and placed them in "cities of the Medes [i];" he removed those of Commagene to Elam; all the great men of the Tibareni, and the inhabitants of unknown cities, to Assyria; Cammanians, whom he had conquered, to Tel-Garimmi, a capital which he rebuilt; others whom he had vanquished in the East he placed in Ashdod: again he placed "Assyrians devoted to his empire" among the Tibareni; inhabitants of cities unknown to us, in Damascus; Chaldæans in Commagene [k]. "[1] The Comukha were removed from the extreme North to Susiana, and Chaldæans were brought from the extreme South to supply their place." "Seven kings of Iatnan, seven days' voyage off in the Western seas, whose names were unknown to the kings" his "fathers, hearing of" his "deeds, came before" him to Babylon with "presents:" as did the king of Asmoun, who dwelt in the midst of the Eastern sea (the Persian gulf). He placed his statue, "writing on it the glory of Asshur his master," in the capital of Van, in Kikisim (Circesium) as also in Cyprus, which he does not name, but where it has been discovered in this century [m]. The Moschian king, with his 3000 towns, who had never submitted to the

[b] Rawl. Ib. 464, 5.
[c] Nimrud Obelisk translated by Dr. Hincks, in Dubl. Univ. Mag. Oct. 1853. pp. 422, 5, 6. Rawl. Her. i. 462.
[d] Dr. Hincks, Athenæum N. 1476. p. 174. Rawl. Ib. Five Emp. ii. 360.
[e] Rawl. Herod. i. 466. Five Emp. ii. 374.
[f] Jer. xxv. 25.
[g] Rawl. Her. i. 467, Five Empires ii. 380.
[h] Rawl. Her. i. 470.　[i] 2 Kings xvii. 6, xviii. 11.
[k] The above account of Sargon is taken from Op-

pert's Inscriptions Assyriennes des Sargonides, p. 19-40, extracted from the Annales de Philosophie Chrétienne T. vi. (5e série). Oppert, p. 8, gives as the meaning of his name, "actual king," "roi de fait." Sargon himself, if Oppert has translated him rightly, gives as its meaning, "righteous prince," (שַׂר־כֵּן) p. 38.
[l] Rawl. 5 Emp. ii. 423. This statement is not in Oppert's Inscriptions.
[m] Now in the Royal Museum at Berlin. Layard, Bab. p. 618.

kings his predecessors, sent his submission and tribute to him.

Sennacherib, the son of Sargon, says of himself, "Assour, the great Lord, has conferred on me sovereignty over the peoples; he has extended my dominion over all those who dwell in the world. From the upper Ocean of the setting sun to the lower Ocean of the rising sun, I reduced under my power all who carried aloft their head." He defeated Merodach Baladan and the king of Elam together[n]; took in one expedition, "[n] 79 great strong cities of the Chaldæans and 820 small towns;" he took prisoners by hundreds of thousands; 200,150 in his first expedition against Hezekiah, from 44 great walled cities which he took and little villages innumerable[o]; 208,000 from the Nabathæans and Hagarenes[p]: he employed on his great buildings 360,000 men, gathered from Chaldæa and Aramæa, from Cilicia and Armenia[q]; he conquered populations in the North, which "had of old not submitted to the kings my brothers[r]," annexed them to the prefecture of Arrapachitis and set up his image[r]; he received tribute from the governor of Khararat[r], wasted the 2 residence-cities, 34 smaller cities of Ispahara king of Albania, joining a part of the territory to Assyria, and calling its city, Ilhinzas, the city of Sennacherib[s]; he reduced countries of "Media, whose names the kings his brothers had not heard[s]; he set a king, Toubaal, over the great and little Sidon, Sarepta, Achzib, Acco, Betzitti, Mahalliba; the kings of Moab, Edom, Bet-Amman, Avvad, Ashdod, submitted to him[t]; he defeated an "innumerable host" of Egyptians at Altakou[u] [Elteke]; sons of the king of Egypt fell into his hands; he captured Ascalon, Bene-Barak, Joppa, Hazor[u]; put back at Amgarron [Migron] the expelled king Padi, who had been surrendered to Hezekiah[x]; gave portions of the territory of Hezekiah to the kings of Ashdod, Migron, Gaza[y]; he drove Merodach-baladan again to Elam, captured his brothers, wasted his cities, and placed his own eldest son, Assurnadin, on the throne of Babylon[z]; took seven impregnable cities of the Toukharri, placed like birds' nests on the mountains of Nipour[z]; conquered the king of Oukkou in Dayi, among mountains which none of his ancestors had penetrated; took Oukkou and 33 other cities[a]; attached Elam, "crossing" the Persian gulf "in Syrian vessels[a];" capturing the men, and destroying the cities[b]; in

another campaign, he garrisoned, with prisoner-warriors of his own, cities in Elam which his father had lost[o]; destroyed 34 large cities and others innumerable of Elam[o]. His account of his reign closes with a great defeat of Elam, whom the escaped Souzoub had hired with the treasures of the temples of Babylon, and of 17 rebel tribes or cities, at Khalouli, and their entire subdual[d]. He repelled some Greeks in Cilicia, set up his image there, with a record of his deeds, and built Tarsus, on the model of Babylon[e]. It has been noticed, what a "keen appreciation of the merits of a locality[f]" his selection of its site evinced. The destruction of his army of 185,000 men, at the word of God, might well deter him from again challenging the Almighty; but we have seen, in the wars of Napoleon I., that such losses do not break the power of an empire. It was no vain boast of Sennacherib, that he had *gathered all the earth, and carried captive the gods of the nations.* The boast was true; the application alone was impious. God owned in him the instrument which He had formed, *the rod of His anger.* He condemned him, only because *the axe boasted itself against Him Who hewed therewith.* Victorious, except when he fought against God, and employed by God to *tread down the people as the mire of the streets[g],* Sennacherib was cut off as God foretold, but left his kingdom to a victorious son.

His son, Esarhaddon, takes titles, yet more lofty than those of Sennacherib. He calls himself, "[h] King of Assyria, Vicar of Babylon, King of the Sumirs and Accads, King of Egypt, Meroe and Cush, who reigned from sunrising to sun-set, unequalled in the imposition of tributes." In Armenia, he killed Adrammelech[i], his half-brother, one of his father's murderers, who fled to Armenia, probably to dispute thence his father's crown. In every direction he carried his conquests further than his powerful father[k]. He speaks of conquests in the far Media, "[l] where none of the kings, our fathers," had conquered, whose kings bore well-known Persian names[m].

They and their subjects were carried off to Assyria. Others, who "[n] had not conspired against the kings my fathers and the land of Assyria, and whose territories my fathers had not conquered," submitted voluntarily in terror, paid tribute and received Assyrian governors. In the West, he pursued by sea a king of Sidon who rebelled, divided the Syrians in strange countries, and placed

[n] Oppert Sarg. p. 41.
[o] Ib. p. 45. [p] Layard Bab. p. 141.
[q] Rawl. Her. i. 476. [r] Opp. pp. 42, 3. [s] Ib. p. 43.
[t] pp. 43, 4. [u] p. 44. [x] pp. 44, 5. [y] p. 45.
[z] p. 46. [a] p. 47. [b] pp. 47, 8. [c] pp. 48.
[d] pp. 49–51.
[e] Polyhist. in Eus. Chr. i. c. 5. Abyden. ib. c. 9.
[f] Rawl. 5 Emp. ii. 456.
[g] Is. x. 5–15, xxxvi. 18–20. [h] Oppert p. 53.

[i] Abyden. in Eus. Chron. Arm. p. 53.
[k] The murder then of Sennacherib was no sign of the decadence of the empire, but one of the common fruits of the polygamy of Eastern monarchs.
[l] Oppert pp. 56, 7. [m] Sitirparna and Iparna.
[n] Ib. Two of the names again, Rawl. observes (5 Emp. ii. 473), are Aryan, Zanasana and Ramatiya; a 3d is Arpis.

mountaineers, whom his bow had subdued in the East, with a governor, in a castle of Esarhaddon which he built in Syria. He warred successfully in Cilicia, Khoubousna, and destroyed 10 large cities of the Tibareni and carried their people captive; trod down the country of Masnaki, transported rebels of Van; he established on the Southern shore that son of Merodach-baladan who submitted to him, removing the brother who trusted in Elam, himself reigned in Babylon[o], whither he carried Manasseh[p]. He reconquered "the city of Adoumou (Edom), (the city of the power of the Arabs,) which Sennacherib had conquered, and carried off its people to Assyria;" he named as Queen of the Arabs, Tabouya, born in his palace; put the son of Hazael on his father's throne. An expedition to "[q] a far country to the bounds of the earth beyond the desert," Bazi (Buz), reached by traversing 140 farsakhs (?) of sandy desert, then 20 farsakhs (?) of fertile land and a stony region, Khazi (Uz), looks like an expedition across Arabia, and, if so, was unparalleled except by Nushirvan. Some of the other names are Arabic. Anyhow, it was a country, whither none of his predecessors had gone; he killed 8 kings, carried off their subjects and spoils. He conquered the Gomboulou in their marshes. Twelve kings on the coast of Syria whom he recounts by name, (Ba'lou king of Tyre, Manasseh king of Judah, and those of Edom, Maan, Gaza, Ascalon, Amgarron, Byblos, Aradus, Ousimouroun, Bet-Ammon, Ashdod) and 10 kings of Yatnan in the sea (Cyprus),—Ægisthus (Ikistousi), King of Idalion (Idial), Pythagoras (Pitagóura) K. of Citium (Kitthim), Ki—, K. of Salamis (Silhimmi), Ittodagon ("Dagon is with him," Itoudagon), K. of Paphos (Pappa), Euryalus (Irieli), K. of Soli (Sillou), Damasou, K. of Curium (Kuri,) Ounagousou, K. of Limenion (Limini), Roumizu, K. of Tamassus (Tamizzi,) Damutsi of Amti-Khadasti, Puhali of Aphrodisium (Oupridissa)[r],—held their rule from him.

The names of the countries, from which he brought those whom he settled in Samaria, attest alike his strength and the then weakness of two of the nations, which afterward concurred to overthrow his empire. The colonists, according to their own letters to Artaxerxes[s], comprehended, among others, *Babylonians; Archevites* i. e. inhabitants of Erech, mentioned in Genesis[t], as, together with Babel, part of the beginning of the kingdom of Nimrod ; *Susanchites,* i. e. inhab-

itants of Susiana or Chusistan ; *Dehavites, Daans* in Herodotus[u], one of the wandering Persian tribes, whose name (Taia) still exists[x] ; *Elamites*[y], or the dwellers on the Persian gulf, bordering on Susiana ; *Apharsites* or the Persians in their original abode in Paraça, Paraiç, now Farsistan. It seems also probable that the *Apharsachites*[z] are those more known to us as Sacæ or Scythians, whom Esarhaddon says that he conquered[a] ; and that the *Apharsachthites* (with the same word *Aphar* prefixed) are the Sittaceni on the Caspian. The *Dinaites* and the *Tarphelites* are as yet unidentified, unless the Tarpetes[b] of the Palus Mæotis near the Sittaceni, or the Tapiri [c] in Media be a corruption of the name. The Samaritan settlers add, *And the rest of the nations, whom the great and noble Asnapper carried captive, and settled in the cities of Samaria and the rest on this side the river.* Under this general term, they include the Mesopotamian settlers brought from Avvah and Sepharvaim, and those from Hamath[d], probably wishing to insist to the Persian Monarch on their Persian, Median, or Babylonian descent. They attest at the same time that their forefathers were not willingly removed but *transported, carried into exile*[e], and accordingly that Esarhaddon, in whose reign they were removed, had power in all these countries. The condensation also of settlers from twelve nations in so small a space as the cities of Samaria (analogous as it is to the dispersion of the Jews over so many provinces of their captors) illustrates the policy of these transportations, and the strength which they gave to the empire. Nations were blended together among those foreign to them, with no common bond except their relation to their conqueror. A check on those around them, and themselves held in check by them, they had no common home to which to return, no interest to serve by rebelling. Esarhaddon built 36 temples in Assyria by the labor of foreign slaves, his captives, who worshiped his gods[f].

This collection of people of twelve nations in the cities of Samaria represents moreover one portion only of the conquests of Esarhaddon, and, for the most part, that furthest from Judæa. For the principle of the policy was to remove them far from their own land. Ethiopian and Egyptian captives would be placed, not here whence they could easily return, but, like Israel in the cities of the Medes, whence they could find no escape. The son of Esarhaddon, Asshurbanipal [g] II., yet further enlarged and consolidated

---

[o] Babyl. tablet in Rawl. Her. i. 482.
[p] 2 Chr. xxxiii. 11.

[q] Oppert p. 56. Rawl. 5 Emp. ii. 470, 1. Oppert does not identify the names of distances.

[r] Rawl. Herod. i. 483, 4. 5 Emp. ii. 483, Oppert p. 58.
[s] Ezr. iv. 9.   [t] Gen. x. 10.   [u] i. 125.
[x] Ritter Erdk. vii. 668.   [y] Is. xxi. 2, xxii. 6.

[s] Ezr. v. 6. Rawl. Journ. of Asiat. Soc. xv. p. 164.
[a] Rawl. Her. i. 481.   [b] Strabo xl. 2. 8. 11.
[c] Id. xl. 8. and 13. 2.   [d] 2 Kgs xvii. 24.

[e] הַגְלִי Ezr. iv. 10.

[f] Assyr. texts p. 16, Oppert p. 57, Rawl. 5 Emp. ii. 482.

[g] Or Asordanes, Layard Nin. and B. p. 452.

the conquests of his conquering father. His expeditions into Egypt have been already dwelt upon; his victories were easy, complete. Tirhaka, himself a great conqueror, fled into unknown deserts beyond reach of pursuits. His step-son Urdaminie attempted to recover his kingdom, was defeated at once, fled and his capital was taken. In Asia, he took away the king of Tyre, who offended him; made conquests beyond Mt. Taurus, where his fathers had never been [h]; received an embassy from Gyges; attached to Assyria a tract of Minni or Persarmenia, took the capital of Minni; took Shushan [i] and Badaca, slew their kings, united Susiana to Babylonia; subdued anew Edom, Moab, Kedar, the Nabathæans; received the submission of the king of Urarda, Ararat [k]. While Assyria was extended wider than before, its old enemies were more incorporated with it, or, at least, more subdued; it was more at one within itself. Egypt, the great rival Empire, had tried to shake off the yoke, but was subdued; no people in Syria or the valley of the Euphrates stirred itself; the whole tract within the Taurus, once so rife with enemies, lay hushed under his rule: hushed were the Hittites, Hamathites, the Syrians of Damascus, the Tibareni who had once held their own against his father; war was only at the very extremities, in Minni or Edom, and that, rather chastisement than war; Babylon was a tranquil portion of his empire, except during the temporary rebellion of the brother, whom he had placed over it, and whom he pardoned. His death, amid the tranquil promotion of literature [l], when he had no more enemies to conquer or rebels to chasten, left his empire at the zenith of its power, some 22 years before its destruction. *Calno* had become, as Sennacherib boasted [m], *like Carchemish; Hamath like Arpad; Samaria as Damascus*. He [n] *had removed the bounds of the people* and *gathered all the earth, as one gathereth eggs, left* by the parent bird, undefended even by its impotent love. There was not a cloud on the horizon, not a token whence the whirlwind would come. The bas-reliefs attest, that neither the energy nor the cruelty of the Assyrians were diminished [o].

Of those twenty-two years, we have nothing reliable except their close. There was probably nothing to relate. There would not be anything, if Asshurbanipal had consolidated his empire, as he seems to have done, and if his son and successor inherited his father's later tastes, and was free from the thirst of boundless conquest, which had

characterized the earlier rulers of Assyria. Anyhow, we know nothing authentic. The invasion of Assyria by Phraortes, which Herodotus relates, is held, on good grounds, to be a later history of a rebellion against Darius Hystaspes, adapted to times before the Medes became one nation [p]. There was no reason why it should not have been recorded, had it taken place, since it is admitted to have been a total defeat, in which Phraortes lost his life [q]. The invasion of the Scythians, which is to have stopped the siege of Nineveh under Cyaxares, was reported in a manifestly exaggerated form to Herodotus. The 28 years, during which Herodotus relates the Scythian rule to have lasted [r], is longer than the whole of the reign of the last king of Assyria; and yet, according to Herodotus, is to have been interposed between the two sieges of Cyaxares. And as its empire gave no sign of decay, so far as we can trace its history within 22 years before its destruction, so, with the like rapidity, did the empire rise, which was to destroy it. The account which Herodotus received, that the Medians had thrown off the yoke of Assyria before Deioces [s], is in direct contradiction to the Assyrian inscriptions. This was, they state, the time, not of the revolt, but of the conquest of Media. They are confirmed by Holy Scripture, which says that the Assyrian king [Sargon] placed *in the cities of the Medes* [t] his Israelitish captives. The utmost, which Herodotus ascribes to Deioces however, is, that he consolidated the six Median tribes and built a capital, Agbatana [u]. It is an union of wild hordes into one people, held together for the time by the will of one man and by their weariness of mutual oppressions. Even according to their accounts, Cyaxares (about B. C. 633, i. e. 8 years before the fall of Nineveh) first organized the Median army; the Greeks, in the time of Æschylus, believed Cyaxares to have been the first of the Median kings [x]; rebels in Media and Sagartia claimed the Median throne against Darius, as descended from Cyaxares, as the founder of the Monarchy [y].

Further, the subsequent history supports the account of Abydenus against Herodotus, that not the Medes, but the rebel general of the last Monarch of Nineveh was, with his Babylonian troops, the chief author of the destruction of Nineveh. The chief share of the spoil, where no motives of refined policy intervene, falls to the strongest, who had chief portion in the victory. "The Medes," says Herodotus, "took Nineveh, and conquered all Assyria, except the Babylonian

[h] Rawl. remarks that the names are new.
[i] The name is spelt as in Daniel.
[k] Rawl. 5 Emp. ii. 484–93.   [l] Ib. 495, 6.
[m] Is. x. 9.
[n] Ib. 13, 14.
[o] See plates in Layard Nin. and B. pp. 457, 8. Rawl.

5 Emp. iii. 504, and Layard Monuments Ser. 2. Pl. 47, 49. quoted Ib.
[p] Rawl. Herod. i. 408, 9.   [q] Herod. i. 402.
[r] Ib. 106.   [s] i. 95, 6.   [t] 2 Kgs xvii. 6.
[u] Her. i. 101.   [x] Persæ 761–4.
[y] Behistun Inscr., quoted by Rawl. Her. i. 409.

portion [z]." But Babylon was no spared province, escaping with its independence as a gain. Babylonia, not Media, succeeded to the Southern and Western dominions of the Assyrian empire, and the place, where Nineveh had stood, Cyaxares retaining the North. This was a friendly arrangement, since subsequently too we find a Babylonian prince in the expedition of Cyaxares against Asia Minor, and Medians assisting Nebuchadnezzar against the king of Egypt [a]. Abydenus represents the Babylonians and Medes, as equal [b], but exhibits the rebel general, as the author of the attack. "[c] After him [Sardanapal], Sarac held the empire of Assyria, who, being informed of a horde of mingled troops which were coming against him from the sea, sent Busalossor [Nebopalassar] general of his army, to Babylon. But he, having determined to revolt, betrothed to his son, Nebuchodrossor, Amuhea, daughter of Asdahag, prince of the Medes, and soon made a rapid attack on Nineveh. King Sarac, when he knew the whole, set the palace Evorita on fire. Then Nebuchodrossor, attaining to the empire, encircled Babylon with strong walls."

The "horde of mingled troops" "from the sea" were probably those same Susians and Elymæans, whom the Assyrians had, in successive reigns, defeated. If the account of Herodotus were true, the father of the Median Monarch had perished in conflict with Assyria. The grandfather of the Assyrian Monarch had himself reigned in Babylon. Assyria ruled Babylon by viceroys to the end. It has been noticed that Nahum mentions no one enemy who should destroy Nineveh. True, for no one enemy did destroy her.

Even now its fall is unexplained. The conquests of its Monarchs had not been the victories of talented individuals. They were a race of world-wide conquerors. In the whole history, of which we have the annals, they are always on the aggressive. They exacted tribute where they willed. The tide of time bore them on in their conquests. Their latest conquests were the most distant. Egypt, her early rival, had been subdued by her. The powers, which did destroy her, had no common bond of interest. They were united, for one reign, not by natural interests, but, as far as we see, by the ambition of two individuals. These crushed, at once and for ever, the empire which for so many centuries had been the ravager of the world. But who could have foreseen such a combination and such results, save God, in Whose hands are human wills and the fate of empires?

The fiery empire of conquerors sank like a tropic sun. Its wrath had burned, unassuaged, "from" (in their own words) "the rising to the setting sun." No gathering cloud had tempered its heat or allayed its violence. Just ere it set, in those last hours of its course, it seemed, as if in its meridian. Its bloodstained disk cast its last glowing rays on that field of carnage in Susiana; then, without a twilight, it sank beneath those stormy waves, so strangely raised, at once and for ever. All, at once, was night. It knew no morrow.

Its fall is inexplicable still. It may have accelerated its own destruction by concentrating the fierce Chaldees at Babylon. It was weakened by the revolt of its own general, and with him the defection of an army. Still, in those days, the city of 1200 towers, each 200 feet high, its ordinary wall 100 feet high and of such breadth, that three chariots could drive on it abreast [d], could not be taken by mounds, except by some most gigantic army with patience inexhaustible. Famine could not reduce a city, which, in its 60 miles in circumference, enclosed, like Babylon, space for [e] much cattle, and which could, within its walls, grow corn enough for its population of 600,000. With its perennial supply of provision, it might have laughed to scorn a more formidable foe than the Medes, Elamites and Babylonians, unaccustomed to sieges, except in as far as any had fought in its armies, while the Ninevites possessed the hereditary skill of centuries. Babylon, smaller than Nineveh [f], was at rest amidst the siege of the more powerful grandson of Cyaxares. Cyrus could only take it by stratagem; Darius Hystaspes, by treachery. Then, every Ninevite was a warrior. Their descendants, the Curds, are still among the fiercest and most warlike people of Asia. The bas-reliefs, which bear internal evidence of truth, exhibit a wonderful blending of indomitable strength of will, recklessness of suffering, inherent physical energy, unimpaired by self-indulgence. A German writer on art says [g], "You recognize a strong thickset race, of very powerful frame, yet inclined to corpulence, a very peculiar blending of energy and luxury.—The general impression of the figures, whether men, women or eunuchs, has uniformly something earnest and imposing." An English writer says still more vividly; "[h] All the figures indicate great physical development, animal propensities very strongly marked, a calm, settled ferocity, a perfect nonchalance amidst the most terrible scenes; no change of feature takes place, whether the individual is inflict-

[z] i. 106. [a] Rawl. Herod. i. 415, 6.
[b] Conf. Tobit xiv. 15. "Before he died, he heard of the destruction of Nineveh, which was taken by Nabuchonosor and Ahasuerus."
[c] Euseb. Chron. P. 1. c. 9.

[d] Diod. Sic. ii. 3. [e] Jon. iv. 11.
[f] Strabo xvi. p. 757.
[g] Kugler Kunst-Geschichte, (2) p. 75, 6. in Strauss Nahum p. li.
[h] Edwards in Kitto Scr. Lands. pp. 50, 1.

ing or experiencing horrid sufferings.—The pictures are very remarkable as indicating the entire absence of higher mental and moral qualities: and the exuberance of brutal parts of man's nature. At the same time there is not wanting a certain consciousness of dignity and of inherent power. There is a tranquil energy and fixed determination, which will not allow the beholder to feel any contempt of those stern warriors."

How then could it fall? The prophecy of Nahum describes, with terrible vividness, a siege; the rousing of its king from a torpor of indolence; [i] *he remembereth his nobles;* the orderly advance, the confused preparations for defence; and then, when expectation is strung, and we see besiegers and besieged prepared for the last decisive strife, there is a sudden pause. No human strength overthrows the city. [k] *The gates of the rivers shall be opened, and the palace shall be dissolved. And it is decreed, she shall be led away captive.* Her captivity follows on the opening of *the gates of the rivers.* The *rivers,* ordinarily her strength, were also her weakness. The annals of Sennacherib relate, how he repaired a palace which had been undermined by the Tigris. "[l] The small palace, which was become very ruinous in every part, because the river Tigris, during 16 years, had undermined and ravaged it, [I repaired.]" Dionysius, the Jacobite Patriarch, relates how in his own time, A. D. 763, "[m] the Tigris, overflowing, laid waste all the towns around it, and especially Mosul" (opposite to Nineveh). Barhebræus, in four different years, mentions the destruction of houses in Bagdad through the overflow of the Tigris [n]. He mentions also a city-wall, overthrown by an inundation, so that 3000 men were drowned in their houses [o]. Ives relates [p]; "The Bishop (of Babylon) remembers that" about 1733 "the Euphrates and Tigris were so overflown, that the whole country between them appeared as one large sea. Over all the plain between Bagdad and Hilla, people could pass only in boats. The water flowed quite up to the glacis, the ditch was full, the city also overflown, and the foundation of most of the buildings hurt; 300 houses were entirely destroyed. To prevent as much as possible" the recurrence of such a calamity, "the Turks now face the foundation-wall of their houses with a composition of charcoal, ashes, and Demar (bitumen)." "The river Khosar," also, which would be swollen by the same causes as the Tigris, "entered the city," says Ainsworth [q], "by an aperture in the walls on the East side, which appears to have

formed part of the original plan and to have been protected by a gateway and walls, vestiges of which still remain." "The Khausser," says Mr. Rich [r], "is generally drawn off for irrigating the cotton-plantations in the alluvial ground of the river; when it is much overflowed, it discharges itself into the Tigris above the bridge." "[s] The Khausser now [Dec. 1. after "very heavy tropical rain,"] discharges itself direct into the Tigris, and brings an immense body of water." "[t] After rain, it becomes an impetuous torrent, overflowing its banks and carrying all before it." "[s] The stone-bridge was carried away one night by the violence of the Khausser, on a sudden inundation." On a lesser swelling of the river,—"[s] the water-wheels were removed" in precaution "and the bridge of boats opened." Cazwini, the Arabic geographer, speaks of "[u] the rivers of Nineveh."

Ctesias, being a writer of suspected authority, cannot safely be alleged in proof of the fulfillment of prophecy. Yet in this case his account, as it is in exact conformity with the obvious meaning of the prophecy of Nahum, so it solves a real difficulty, how Nineveh, so defended, could have fallen. It seems certain that the account of the siege taken from him by Diodorus, is that of the last siege. It has been remarked [x] that the only event of the siege, known from any other source, viz. that the last Assyrian king, when he had learned the combination of the Medes and Babylonians against him, set fire to his palace, is related also by Ctesias. Ctesias has also the same fact, that the Babylonian revolt was recent; the name of the revolted general in Ctesias, Belisis, is the latter half of that given to him by Abydenus [y], Nebopalassar, omitting only the name of the god, Nebo. The rest of the history is in itself probable. The success of the Assyrian monarch at first against the combined armies, and the consequent revelry, are that same blending of fierceness and sensuality which is stamped on all the Assyrian sculptures, continued to the end. The rest of his relation, which, on account of the facts of nature, which we know, but which, since they are gathered from sources so various, Ctesias probably did not know, is, in itself, probable, accounts for what is unaccounted for, and corresponds with the words of Nahum. It is, "[s] Sardanapalus, seeing the whole kingdom in the greatest danger, sent his three sons and two daughters with much wealth to Paphlagonia to Cotta the Governor, being the best-disposed of his subjects. He himself

[i] ii. 5, [6.]   [k] ii. 6, 7. [7, 8.]   [l] Assyr. Texts p. 7.
[m] Ass. B. O. ii. 112.
[n] A. D. 835, 941, 988, 1211. Barh. p. 153, 188, 204. 500.
[o] Ib. p. 153.   [p] Voyage 1773. p. 281.
[q] Travels ii. 142, 3.   [r] Koordistan, ii. 56.
[s] Ib. p. 64.   [t] Layard N. and B. p. 77.

[u] Quoted by Tuch de Nino urbe p. 24.
[x] Rawl. Her. i. 413.
[y] Abydenus in Euseb. Chron. Can. P. i. c. 9.
[s] In Diod. Sic. ii. 27. Diodorus has "Euphrates" in conformity with his own error, that Nineveh was on that river.

sent by messengers to all his subjects for forces, and prepared what was needed for the siege. He had an oracle handed down from his forefathers, that no one should take Nineveh, unless the river first became an enemy to the city. Conceiving that this never would be, he held to his hopes, purposing to abide the siege and awaited the armies to be sent by his subjects." "The rebels, elated by their successes, set themselves to the siege, but on account of the strength of the walls, could in no wise injure those in the city." "But these had great abundance of all necessaries through the foresight of the king. The siege then being prolonged for two years, they pressed upon it; assaulting the walls and cutting off those therein from any exit into the country." "In the 3d year, the river, swollen by continuous and violent rains, inundated a part of the city and overthrew 20 stadia of the wall. Then the king, thinking that the oracle was fulfilled, and that the river was plainly an enemy to the city, despaired of safety. And, not to fall into the enemy's hands, he made an exceeding great pile in the palace, heaped up there all the gold and silver and the royal apparel, and having shut up his concubines and eunuchs in the house formed in the midst of the pile, consumed himself and all the royalties with them all. The rebels, hearing that Sardanapalus had perished, possessed themselves of the city, entering by the broken part of the wall."

Yet Nahum had also prophesied [b]; "the fire shall devour thy bars;" "fortify thy strong holds, there shall the fire devour thee;" "I will burn her chariots in the smoke," and all the ruins of Nineveh still speak from beneath the earth where they lie interred, that, overthrown as they have been by some gigantic power, fire consumed them within. "[c] The palaces of Khorsabad (Dur Sarjina) and Nimrud shew equal traces of fire with those of Koyunjik." "[d] The recent excavations have shown that fire was a great instrument in the destruction of the Nineveh palaces. Calcined alabaster, masses of charred wood and charcoal, colossal statues split through with the heat, are met with in parts of the Ninevite mounds, and attest the veracity of prophecy." "[e] It is evident from the ruins that Khorsabad and Nimroud were sacked, and set on fire."

Yet this does not exhaust the fullness of the prophecy. Nahum not only foretold the destruction of Nineveh, that it should be empty, void, waste, there is no healing of thy

bruise, but in emphatic words, that its site also should be a desolation. With an overrunning flood He shall make the place thereof (mekomah) a desolation [f]. This was then new in the history of the world. Cities have remained, while empires passed away. Rome, Constantinople, Athens, Damascus, Alexandria, Venice, abide, although their political might is extinct. No or Thebes itself survived its capture by Sargon and a yet later loss of its inhabitants nearly two centuries, when the more fatal conquest of Cambyses, and perhaps the rise of Memphis perpetuated its destruction. Nahum foretells emphatically as to Nineveh, "He will make the place thereof an utter consumption." Not only would God destroy the then Nineveh; but the very place or site thereof should be an utter desolation. There was, then, no instance of so great a city passing away. Such had not been Babylonian, Assyrian, Egyptian policy. It had become an established policy in Sennacherib's time to remove populations, not to destroy cities. And these two policies were incompatible. For a conqueror who would remove populations must have, whither to remove them. Nineveh itself had conquered Babylon and Shushan, and the cities of the Medes; but had placed her own lieutenants in them. The mere destruction of such a city as Nineveh was "contrary to experience." Even later than this, Babylon, notwithstanding its rebellions, was spared by its first conqueror, and survived to be the grave of its second, Alexander. Xenophon describes Nineveh under the name of Mespila (of which Mosul has been supposed to be a corruption) "[g] a wall, void, large, lying against the city—the basement was of polished stone, full of shells, its width 50 feet, its height 50 feet. Thereon was built a wall of brick, its breadth 50 feet, the height 100; the circuit was six farsangs," i. e. 22½ miles. The shell remained; the tumult of life was gone. Its protecting bulwarks remained; all, which they protected, had disappeared. They had forgotten already on the spot what it had been or by whom it had perished. "[h] The Medes inhabited it formerly. It was said that Media, a king's wife, had fled thither, when the Medes were losing their power through the Persians. The Persian king, besieging this city, could not take it, either by time or force; but Zeus made the inhabitants senseless, and so it was taken." A little later, Alexander marched over its site to gain the world, not knowing that a world-empire, like that which he gave his life to found, was buried under

[b] iii. 13. 15. ii. 13.
[c] Rawl. Herod. i. 488. quoting "Layard Nin. and its Remains i. 12, 27, 40. &c. Nin. and B. [of Nimrud] p. 351, 357, 359. &c. Vaux Nineveh and Persepolis p. 196–8. Botta Letter ii. p. 26. iii. p. 41. &c." "They [the human-headed bulls] had suffered, like all those previously discovered, from the fire." Lay. N. and B.

p. 71. "It [the wall] contained some fragments of calcined sculptured alabaster, evidently detached from the bas-reliefs on the walls." Ib. Add of Kouyunjik, Athenæum N. 900. Jan. 25. 1845. p. 99.
[d] Rawl. Ib. note 2.
[e] Bonomi p. 461.   [f] i. 8.
[g] Anab. iii. 4. 10.   [h] Ib. 12.

his feet[1]. Gaugamela, near which Darius lost his empire, must have been close to its site. Yet three centuries, and history, not its mere neighbors only, had forgotten when it had perished. Strabo says[k], "It was effaced immediately after the destruction of the Syrians." Nearly two centuries later is Lucian's saying, "[1]Nineveh has perished, and there is no trace left where it once was." Yet before this time, in the reign of Claudius, the Romans had built a new Nineveh which they called by his name "Ninive Claudiopolis." In the 6th century, it is mentioned as a Christian see[m]. Its episcopate was taken away, probably on account of its decline, early in the 9th century; and it was united to Mosul[n]. It was still in being at the beginning of the 14th century[o]. Yet, in the 12th century, as a whole, "[p] it was desolate, but there were there many villages and castles." This was not the Nineveh of prophecy; but it too was swept away, and a few coins alone attest the existence of the Roman city. "The city, and even the ruins of the city," relates Gibbon[q] of the last victory of Heraclius, "had long since disappeared; the vacant space afforded a spacious field for the operation of the two armies." A line of lofty mounds, on the East of Tigris, long drew but a momentary gaze from the passers-by; a few cottages surmounted the heaps, which entombed the palaces of kings, who were the terror of the East; the plough turned up, unheeded, the bricks, which recorded their deeds; the tide of war swept over it anew; the summer's sands again filled up "[r] the stupendous mass of brick-work, occasionally laid bare by the winter rains." The eyes rested on nothing but "[r] the stern shapeless mound, rising like a hill from the scorched plain." "[r] The traveler is at a loss to give any form to the rude heaps, upon which he is gazing. Those of whose works they are the remains, unlike the Roman and the Greek, have left no visible traces of their civilization or of their arts; their influence has long since passed away. The scene around him is worthy of the ruin he is contemplating; desolation meets desolation; a feeling of awe succeeds to wonder, for there is nothing to relieve the mind, to lead to hope, or to tell of what has gone by. Those huge mounds of Assyria made a deeper impression upon me, gave rise to more serious thoughts and more earnest reflection, than the temples of Baalbec and the theatres of Ionia."

In 1827, Buckingham still wrote[s]: "we came in about an hour to the principal mounds which are thought to mark the site of the ancient Nineveh. There are four of these mounds, disposed in the form of a square; and these, as they shew neither bricks, stones, nor other materials of building, but are in many places overgrown with grass, resemble the mounds left by entrenchments and fortifications of ancient Roman camps. The longest of these mounds runs nearly N. and S. and consists of several ridges of unequal height, the whole appearing to extend for four or five miles in length. There are three other distinct mounds, which are all near to the river, and in the direction of E. and W.—There are appearances of mounds and ruins extending for several miles to the southward; and still more distinctly seen to the Northward of this, though both are less marked than the mounds of the centre. The space between these is a level plain, over every part of the face of which, broken pottery, and the other usual debris of ruined cities are seen scattered about." "Mounds and smaller heaps of ruins were scattered widely over the plain, sufficient to prove, that the site of the original city occupied a vast extent." Niebuhr had ridden through Nineveh unknowingly. "[t] I did not learn that I was at so remarkable a spot, till near the river. Then they showed me a village on a great hill, which they call Nunia, and a mosque, in which the prophet Jonah was buried. Another hill in this district is called Kalla Nunia, or the Castle of Nineveh. On that lies a village Koindsjug. At Mosul, where I dwelt close by the Tigris, they showed me in addition the walls of Nineveh, which in my journey through I had not observed, but supposed to be a set of hills." "It is well-known," begins an account of the recent discoveries[u], "that in the neighborhood of Mosul, travelers had observed some remarkable mounds, resembling small hills, and that Mr. Rich had, thirty years ago, called attention to one called *Koyunjik*, in which fragments of sculpture and pottery had been frequently discovered."

And yet, humanly speaking, even if destroyed, it was probable before-hand, that it would not altogether perish. For a town near its site was needed for purposes of commerce. Of the two routes of commerce from the Persian gulf to the North by the Euphrates or by the Tigris, the Tigris-route was free from the perils of the arid wilderness, through

[1] It is noticed, that Arrian alone mentions the name of Nineveh; and he too speaks of it, in relation to the course of the Tigris, not of the battle. "The lake, into which the Tigris discharges itself, which, flowing by the city Ninus formerly a great and wealthy city, forms the country between it [Tigris] and the Euphrates." Ind. p. 197. ed. Vall.
[k] xvii. 1. 3.   [1] Charon c. 23.
[m] See Ass. B. O. iii. 1. p. 104.

[n] By Josua Bar Nun Catholicus A. D. 820–824. Ass. iii. p. 344, coll. p. 165.
[o] Ebedjesu, who died A. D. 1318, (Ass. i. 539.) wrote to the Ninevites on the plague. Ass. iii. 1. 143.
[p] Benjamin Tud. p. ⅃⅃ ed. Asher.   [q] c. 46.
[r] Layard, Nineveh i. pp. 6, 7.
[s] Travels ii. 49–52, 62.
[t] Reisebeschr. ii. 353.
[u] W. S. V. Vaux in Geogr. Dict. ii. 438.

which the line by the Euphrates passed. If, for the downward course, the Euphrates itself was navigable, yet the desert presented a difficulty for caravans returning upward from the Persian gulf. Arrian, who mentions the two lines of travel, says that Alexander, having crossed the Euphrates at Thapsacus, chose the less direct line by the Tigris, as [x] having a better supply of all things, food for his cavalry, and a less scorching heat. The mention of Haran (afterward Carrhœ) Canneh, and Asshur in Ezekiel, (in one verse [y]) seems to indicate the continuation of the same line of commerce with Tyre, which must have existed from præhistoric times (i. e. from times of which we have no definite historic account), since there is no ground to question the statement of the Phœnicians themselves in Herodotus, that they had come from the Erythræan sea [z], i. e. the Persian gulf. The later hindrances to the navigation of the Tigris by the great dams (probably for irrigation), were of Persian date; but they could have had no great effect on the actual commerce; since for the greater part of the upward course on the Tigris line, this also must, on account of the rapidity of the river, have been by caravans. The route was still used in the middle ages [x]. "[b] The ancient road and the modern one on the upper Tigris follow, pretty nearly throughout, the same line, it being determined by the physical necessities of the soil." In the 16th century, "[c] from the head of the Persian gulf two commercial lines existed : by one of them goods were carried some way up the Euphrates, and then by land to Bir, Aleppo, Iskenderun. By the other they followed the Tigris to Baghdad and were carried by Diyar-Bekr and Sivas to Terabuzum." [But Mosul was necessarily on the way from Baghdad to Diyar Bekr]. Mosul still lies on the line of commerce, from the Persian gulf, Basrah, Baghdad, Mosul, Mardin, Diyar-Bekr to Iskenderun, the port of Aleppo [d], or Trebizond [Tarabuzum [e].] It still carries on some commerce with Kurdistan and other provinces [f] [beside Diyar-Bekr and Baghdad]. Col. Chesney, in 1850, advocated the advantages of extending the line of commerce by British stations at Diyar-Bekr and Mardin,

in addition to and connection with those already existing at Baghdad and Mosul [g]. There is, in fact, a consent as to this. Layard writes; "[h] The only impediment between the Syrian coast and the Tigris and Euphrates in any part of their course, arises from the want of proper security. The navigation of the Persian gulf is, at all times, open and safe ; and a glance at the map will shew that a line through the Mediterranean, the port of Suedia, Aleppo, Mosul, Baghdad, Busrah, and the Indian Ocean to Bombay is as direct as can well be desired. With those prospects, and with the incalculable advantages, which a flourishing commerce and a safe and speedy transit through, perhaps, the richest portions of its dominions would confer upon the Turkish empire, it would seem that more than Eastern apathy is shown in not taking some steps, tending to restore security to the country watered by the Tigris and Euphrates." Ainsworth suggests a still wider commerce, of which Mosul might be the centre. "[i] With a tranquil state of the surrounding country, Mosul presents mercantile advantages of no common order.—There are several roads open to Persia, across the mountains ; a transit from five to seven days, and by which, considering the short distance and good roads from Mosul to Iskenderun, British manufactures might be distributed into the heart of Persia, in a time and at an expense, which the line of Trebizond Erzrum and Tabriz, that of Bushire and Baghdad, or the Russian line of Astrakhan Bakhu and Mazenderan can never rival."

But although marked out by these advantages for continuance, even when its power was gone, Nineveh was to perish and it perished. Nor ought it to be alleged, that in other cases too, "if the position of the old capital was deemed, from political or commercial reasons, more advantageous than any other, the population was settled in its neighborhood, as at Delhi, not amidst its ruins." For 1) there was, at the time of Nahum, no experience of the destruction of any such great city as Nineveh ; 2) In the case of conquest, the capital of the conquering empire became, ipso facto, the capital of the whole ; but this did not, in itself, involve

---

[x] Arr. iii. 7. The same route was recommended to Antiochus the great. Polyb. v. 51. Xenophon relates the scarcity in Cyrus' advancing army on the Euphrates route, Anab. i. 5. 4 ; Dio Cassius, the sufferings of the army of Severus L. lxxv. 1.
[y] Ezek. xxvii. 23. "Eden" (Ib.) is mentioned in 2 Kgs xix. 12, as having been subdued by Assyria; "Chalmad" remains unknown; "Sheba" spread too widely to the desert of Syria (Strabo xvi. 4. 21.) for the mention of it to be any indication that those thus grouped together did not live in the same direction.
[z] Herod. i. 1. vii. 89 and Rawlinson ib. and App. to B. vii. Essay 2. T. iv. pp. 241. sqq.
[a] Abulpharaj Hist. Dyn. p. 218 sqq. quoted by Tuch de Nino urbe p. 32. Col. Chesney counts Mosul among the flourishing commercial centres

in the time of Abu'l Abbas A. D. 749. Expedition ii. 581.
[b] Ainsworth Travels ii. 337. Tuch quotes also Campbell's Land journey to India, p. 252, that "the merchants still, from the nature of the country, go from the Persian gulf to Armenia and Syria and thence again to Bagdad by the same route through Mosul and Arbela, by which large bodies of men went formerly."   [c] Chesney's Expedition ii. 589.
[d] Ib ii. 595.   [e] Ib. 596.   [f] Ib. i. 21.
[g] "The Tigris being already provided with stations at Bagdad and Mosul—it only requires another at Diyar Bekr, and the neighboring town of Mardin, since the connection of the former places with the countries about it would speedily cause a revival of its ancient commerce." Chesney Expedition ii. 602.
[h] Nin. and Bab. p. 469.   [i] Travels ii. 127.

the destruction of the former. Babylon, from having been the winter residence of Cyrus, became the chief residence of the Persian Emperor at the time of Alexander, and continued to exist for many centuries, after the foundation of Seleucia, although it ceased to be a great city[k]. And this, notwithstanding its two rebellions under Darius[l], and that under Xerxes[m]. There was no ground of human policy against Nineveh's continuing, such as Mosul became, any more than Mosul itself. It existed for some time, as a Christian See.

The grandeur, energy, power, vividness of Nahum, naturally can be fully felt only in his own language. The force of his brief prophecy is much increased by its unity. Nahum had one sentence to pronounce, the judgments of God upon the power of this world, which had sought to annihilate the kingdom of God. God, in His then kingdom in Judah, and the world, were come face to face. What was to be the issue? The entire final utter overthrow of whatever opposed God. Nahum opens then with the calm majestic declaration of the majesty of God; Who God is, against whom they rebelled; the madness of their rebellion, and the extinction of its chief: (c. 1); then in detail, what was to come long after that first overthrow, the siege and capture of Nineveh itself, (c. 2.); then, in wider compass, the overthrow of the whole power (c. 3.). It was to be the first instance, in the history of mankind, of a power so great, perishing and forever. Nahum's office was not, as Jonah's, to the people itself. There is then no call to repentance, no gleam of God's mercy toward them in this life. Nineveh was to perish wholly, as the habitable world had perished in the time of Noah. The only relief is in the cessation of so much violence. There is no human joy expressed at this destruction of the enemy of God and of His people; no sorrow, save that there can be no sorrow; "[n] who will bemoan her? whence shall I find comforters for her?"

In conformity with this concentration of

Nahum's subject, there is little in outward style or language to connect him with the other Prophets. His opening (as already observed [o]) bears upon God's declarations of mercy and judgment; but, Nineveh having filled up the measure of its iniquites, he had to exhibit the dark side of those declarations; how much lay in those words, "that will by no means clear the guilty." "[p] Jonah and Nahum form connected parts of one moral history, the remission of God's judgment being illustrated in the one, the execution of it in the other: the clemency and the just severity of the Divine government being contained in the mixed delineation of the two books." His evangelic character just gleams through, in the eight tender words, in which he seems to take breath, as it were; "Tôb Yhvh lemaōz beyōmtsarah, veyōdēah chōsē bo," "Good is God (Yhvh), refuge in day of trouble, and knowing trusters in Him[q];" then again, in the few words, which I think Isaiah expanded, "Lo on the mountains the feet of a good-tidings-bearer, peace-proclaimer[r]." Else there is only the mingled tenderness and austereness of truth, which would sympathize with the human being, but that that object had, by putting off all humanity, alienated all which is man. "Who will bemoan her? Whence shall I seek comforters for thee?" Who? and Whence? None had escaped evil from her. "Upon whom hath not thy wickedness passed continually?"

It is difficult for us, who have to gather up our knowledge of the sacred language from the fragments which remain, in which also the number of words forms and idioms, which stand out singly here and there, seem but so many specimens of lost treasure, to judge with any certainty, whether any approximation of idiom, which we may observe, implies any connection between the writers in whom it occurs. Nahum has, especially in his picture of the capture of Nineveh, so many of those ἅπαξ λεγόμενα, consisting often of slight modifications[t], his language is so rich and so original, that one the more doubts whether

[k] See Dict. of Greek and Rom. Geogr. i. 358.
[l] Behistun Inscr. in Rawl. Herod. ii. 595–597. 608.
[m] Ctesias Exc. Pers. 22.   [n] iii. 7.   [o] p. 556.
[p] Davison on Prophecy, p. 369.   [q] N. i. 7.

[r] Nah. ii. 1. הִנֵּה עַל הֶהָרִים רַגְלֵי מְבַשֵּׂר מַשְׁמִיעַ שָׁלוֹם. Is. lii. 7. מַה נָּאווּ עַל הֶהָרִים רַגְלֵי מְבַשֵּׂר מַשְׁמִיעַ שָׁלוֹם. It seems to me impossible that Nahum, had he been adapting the words of Isaiah, would have left out the tender מַה נָּאווּ at the beginning, or the triumphant softly-flowing continuation, מְבַשֵּׂר טוֹב מַשְׁמִיעַ יְשׁוּעָה עֹמֵר אֹמֵר לְצִיּוֹן מָלַךְ אֱלֹהָיִךְ at the end.

[t] The following, at least in form or idiom, stand alone in Nahum; the condensed forms וַיְבַשֵּׁהוּ (though with analogies) i. 4; סְבוּאִים i. 10; נָבוֹךְ i. 12; מֹט, else מוֹטָה as "yoke" i. 13; זְמוֹרִים masc.

ii. 3; מְתֻלָּעִים (denom. from תּוֹלַעַת ii. 4; פְּלָדֹת Ib. בְּרוֹשִׁים like μελία, ἐλάτη, "abies," of the spear, (Ib. הָרְעָלוּ "are quivered;" verb too ἅπ.) Ib. יִשְׁתַּקְשְׁקוּן (form) ii. 5. יְרוֹצֵצוּ (form) Ib. סֹבֶךְ ("covered way") ii. 6. וְהֻצַּב "and it is decreed" ii. 8 (See Ib.) גֻּלְּתָה (form, the meaning is determined by גֻּלָּה See Ib.) Ib. מְזָהֲנוֹת ("moaning") Ib. מְתֹפְפֹות (form and metaphor; Kal once Ps. lxviii. 26) Ib. לְבָבְהֶן masc. plur. Ib. הִיא מֵימֵי ii. 9. מְבוּקָה and בּוּקָה תְּבוּנָה (like "apparatus") ii. 10. מְבֻלָּקָה (a fem. part. "void" and, as to the form, used as an abstract; elsewhere is only the act. part. kal. בּוֹלֵק Is. xxiv. 1) ii. 11. פִּק "shaking" (of

in those idioms, in which he seems to approximate to other prophets, the expressions in common do not belong to the common stock of the language; and that the more, since mostly [u] part of the idiom only coincides. the

knees) Ib מְחֻקַּק, form, ii. 13. (else Nif. 2 Sam. xvii. 23; noun, מְחֻקַּק Job vii. 15) הִבְעַרְתִּי בָעָשָׁן (prægn. idiom) ii. 14. פֶּרֶק (in this sense) iii. 1. דהר (the verb) iii. 2. (noun, דהרה, Jud. v. 22.) מֵעַר (i. q. עֶרְוָה iii. 5. שְׁקָצִים (only instance of etymol. meaning) iii. 6. רֳאִי (as, "spectacle") Ib. רֶתְקֻן (part. pass. fem. as noun Is. xl. 19) iii. 10. הִתְכַּבֵּד (of oppressive number) iii. 15. מִנְעָרִים iii. 17. נָפֻשׁוּ iii. 18. כֵּהָה iii. 19.

[u] The correspondence is complete between Jo. ii. 6. כָּל פָּנִים קִבְּצוּ פָארוּר. and Nah. ii. 11. פְּנֵי כֻלָּם קִבְּצוּ פָארוּר.

[x] Dr Henderson (in addition to Nah. ii. 1, Is. lii. 7, see note r.) (connects a) שֶׁטֶף עֹבֵר כָּלָה יַעֲשֶׂה Nah. i. 8 and כָּלָה הוּא עֹשֶׂה i. 9 with וְעָבַר שֶׁטֶף Is. viii. 8 and כָּלָה וְנֶחֱרָצָה־עֹשֶׂה Is. x. 23; b) בּוּקָה וּמְבוּקָה וּמְבֻלָּקָה N. ii. 11, with בּוֹקֵק הָאָרֶץ and וּבוֹלְקָהּ Is. xxiv. 1. c) יְחַלְחָלָה בְּכָל מָתְנָיִם ii. 11, מָלְאוּ מָתְנַי חַלְחָלָה Is. xxi. 3. But in) a כָּלָה עָשָׂה is an idiom used not in Is. only but in Jeremiah (5 times) in Ezekiel (twice) Zephaniah and Nehemiah. It is then an ordinary Hebrew idiom. The peculiarity of Isaiah, that in both places (Is. x. 23, xxviii.22) he adds וְנֶחֱרָצָה, does not occur in Nahum. Nahum also has not the verb שָׁטַף, which Isaiah uses in 5 places; Isaiah does not use the noun שֶׁטֶף, which Nahum has, and which occurs in a Psalm of David (xxxii. 6). Nahum too speaks of a flood which shall pass over and overwhelm; Isaiah, of a man who should pass over and pass away. In b) there is only in common, that Isaiah joins the two like-sounding words בקק and בלק as active verbs (of which, the word common to the two prophets must be older than the Prophet Nahum (comp. "Balak" in the Pent.). Nahum unites two nouns, one from a different root בוק, the other a pass. intens. part. מְבֻלָּקָה, as an abstract noun. The gradual lengthening of the alliterate form occurs in Nahum only. Two of the three words in Nahum are ἅπ. λεγ. c) The mention of חַלְחָלָה, "great writhing anguish," in connection with the loins, is more remarkable, since חַלְחָלָה occurs in those places only and Ez. xxx. 4, 9 (with the same constr. with בְּ; yet מֻזְעָקָה (although not חַלְחָלָה) occurs with בְּמָתְנִים Ps. lxvi. 11. It may then only be an accidental coincidence of the same term.

O. Strauss thinks that d) Nah. i. 13 is from Is. x. 27; e) i. 5 from Is. xlvii. 2. 3; f) Nah. iii.7 from Is. li. 19. But in d and e there is no characteristic word the same; in Nah. i. 13 there is only the common imagery of breaking the yoke. מוֹט masc. occurs in Nahum only; מוֹסְרוֹת נתק in Ps. ii. 3 (of men rebelling) and Jerem. 3 times. It is then a common idiom. In f. there is the correspondence of the idiom מִי יָנוּד לָךְ in Is. (which also occurs Jer. xv. 5) in N. מִי יָנוּד לָהּ, but with the difference that in Is. God speaks of the heaviness of a sorrow

rest is different [x]. As for the so-called Syriasms or other peculiarities of language which Hitzig would have to be evidences of a later date [y], and from some of which others would infer that Nahum lived at Nineveh itself, which He will comfort; Nahum speaks of desolation which none can comfort. The construction of נוד with לְ occurs Job ii. 11, xlii. 11, Jer. xvi. 5, xxii. 10, xlviii. 17; in Job and Ps. lxix. 21 נוד is united with נחם. The expression seems then to belong to the common stock of the language; the idiom מִי אֲנַחֲמֵךְ "Who (in what character) shall I comfort thee?" is peculiar to Isaiah.

Hitzig further would have it, that, "נִכְבַּדִּים occurs in N. iii. 10 exactly as in Is. xxiii. 9 alone beside;" whereas the only correspondence is, that Isaiah has the idiom, "honored of earth," "all honored of earth," נִכְבַּדֵּי אָרֶץ; Nahum has, with the affix, "her honored," נִכְבַּדֶּיהָ as Ps. cxlix. 8. נִכְבְּדֵיהֶם.

[y] Of the forms or words, which Hitzig would make characteristic of a later time

1) שְׂעֹרָה i. 3 is only orthographically different from the more common, סְעָרָה; yet not only does שְׂעָרָה occur Job ix. 17, and the masc. שַׂעַר, Is. xxviii.2, but the verb is written with שׂ in the same meaning, Ps. l. 3, lviii. 10, Job xxvii. 21.

2) קַנּוֹא occurs in Jos. xxiv. 19, the oldest book next to the Pentateuch, and having much in common with it (see on Dan. p. 312 note 2), and in no later book. קַנָּא occurs 5 times in the Pentateuch; this form קַנָּא (not קַנּוֹא) survived in the Chaldee.

3) נָפֻשׁוּ iii. 18, is simply Nif. from פּוּשׁ, a word as old as the Pentateuch, since the river, Pishon, פִּישׁוֹן, is derived from it. Hitzig obtains his "pronunciation" by making it kal, נָפְשׁוּ, a word not extant in Heb.

4) "The form of the suffix of the 2d person, ii. 14," מַלְאָכֵכֶה, which has been urged by all writers on his side, is the more singular ground of argument, because it turns entirely on the vowels, which only represent a tradition of the expiring language. Gesenius calls it "an especial form, which perhaps ought properly to be pronounced כָה, as masc., out of which the punctuator first made כָּה, in order in some sort of way to indicate the feminine" (Lehrg. p. 216). Written מַלְאֲכֶבָה, it is only the full and original form of the pronominal affix, כָה (from אָנֹכָה for אַתָּה), as it is found in the Pentateuch, אֵיכָה Gen. iii. 9, יָדְכָה Ex. xiii. 16, אֹתָכָה Ex. xxix. 35. Nahum chose it probably as a fuller form. It occurs in a Psalm of David, cxxxix. 5, at the close, כַּפֶּכָה, and in Jer. xxix. 25, בְּשִׁמְכָה: as also with the verb, יֶעֶצְרְכָה 1 Kgs xviii. 44, and, in the pause, תִּנְצְרֶכָּה Prov. ii. 11, יִמְצָאֶכָה, 1 Kings xviii. 10. Mss. have, some מַלְאָכֵכֶה (19 De Rossi, 3 by correction, and 3 early Edd. De R.) "many have מַלְאָכֵכָה;" 3 of De R. and 3 or 4 in the first instance, had the regular מַלְאָכֵכָה. The messengers were the king's messengers (Is. xxxvi. 2. 12. 13, xxxvii.4. 6. 9. 17. 24.) and so the masculine form is in its place. Punctuators probably (as Ges. conjectured) wished to assimilate it to the preceding feminines; Ewald lays down that כָה is a dialectic difference (p. 638 note) and uses it as an argument

"the wish has been father to the thought."
One only solid ground there would be why
Nahum should not have written his pro-

for Nahum's living near Nineveh (Proph. i. 350).
Davidson (iii. 301.) follows Hitzig.

5) "The form of the suffix of the 3d person, i. 13,
ii. 4. comp. Hab. iii. 10." The form הוּ lies nearer
to the original הוא, than the contracted וֹ; it also
occurs in the word לְמִינֵהוּ, 14 times in the Pentateuch (in Gen. 8 times, Levit. 5 times, Deut. once);
it occurs most (Ges. observes, Lehrg. p. 213) in
words ending in ה, as מַרְאֵהוּ 10 times (3 in Levit.)
שָׂדֵהוּ 7 times (5 in Gen. Ex. Lev.) עָלֵהוּ in Ps. i.
Ezek. twice, Jerem. once; מִקְנֵהוּ in Gen. 4 times,
Exod. twice, Job twice: although רָעָה absolutely
occurs 3 times only, רָעָה is the rule: it occurs 114
times, of which 42 are in the Pentateuch. The
form הוּ also occurs in פִּילַגְשֵׁהוּ Jud. xix. 24, וַרֵהוּ
Job xxv. 3. It is united with the plur. noun in
אַשָׁרֵהוּ Prov. xix. 18, and רֵעֵהוּ for רֵעֵיהוּ 1 Sam.
xxx. 26, Job xlii. 10; also יָדֵיהוּ Hab. iii. 10, עֵינֵיהוּ
Job xxiv. 23. It is obviously used by Nahum for its
more stately sound.

6) "The meaning of נָבֵל iii. 6," is one attributed
to it by Hitz. only.

7) "As Pilpel occurs more and more in later
times, so הַלְחָלָה ii. 11, (comp. יִשְׁתַּחְשְׁקוּן ii. 5)
only occurs in Is. xxi. 3, Ez. xxx. 4. 9." Pilpel is
formed on exactly the same principle, as the other
rarer intensive conjugations, the doubling of those
letters of the root, most capable of being doubled.
In כִּלְכֵל, it occurs from Genesis downward. The
use of the word הַלְחָלָה by two contemporaries,
Isaiah and Nahum, was nothing remarkable.

8) "So, plainly שׁוּב ii. 3 could only in later times
be used transitively, otherwise than as united with
שְׁבוּת." Why? If שׁוּב is transitive in the phrase,
שׁוּב שְׁבוּת, "restore the captivity" of Jacob, the
corresponding phrase, שָׁב אֶת גָּאוֹן is but a variation of the phrase, such as would naturally occur in
any original writer. שׁוּב is transitive, also in Ps.
lxxxv. 5, and Ezek. xlvii. 7, (since if intrans., as
Abulwalid pointed out, it would have been בְּשׁוּבִי
not בְּשׁוּבָן) if not in Num. x. 36. Gesenius also
pointed out that the corresponding Arab رَجَعَ is
both transitive, and intransitive, so that the use of
the causative conj. أَرْجَعَ is dialectic, according to
Djauhari, or less pure (See Lane sub v. T. i. p. 1038).
It is consistent in Hengst. to deny the transitive
meaning of שׁוּב altogether, but not to make any
idiomatic difference between שָׁב שְׁבוּת and שָׁב
גָּאוֹן as belonging to different dates.

9) "מְצוּרָה (ii. 2) in the sense of munitio, first occurs in the Chronicles." In the Chronicles, the
phrase is different. The idiom is a slight variation
of the old masc., עִיר מָצוֹר Ps. xxxi., 22. lx., 11
(which the Chronicles too has, 2 C. viii. 5). The
Chronicles, on whatever ground, mostly adopt the
feminine form in speaking historically of the fortified cities built in Judah; once in the sing.
עָרֵי מְצֻלָה 2 C. xiv. 5; else with two plurals עָרֵי
מְצֻרוֹת, 2 C. xi. 10. 23. xii. 4. xiv. 5. xxi. 3. In one
place only, having ended a verse, xi. 10, "and in
Benjamin עָרֵי מְצֻרוֹת," the writer begins the
next, (omitting the עָרֵי) "and he strengthened
אֶת הַמְּצֻרוֹת." Nor is there anything characteristic of a later period in the use of the feminine;

phecy, when, according to all history, it
could alone have any interest for Judah,
long before the event itself, viz. if He to

and, any how, since the Chronicles were compiled
after the captivity, probably by Ezra, the use of the
same form could have proved nothing, as to whether
a book were written 85 years, sooner or later, before
the captivity.

"Also the Hebrew of Nahum is in part impure;
מַפְסֵר iii. 17, is probably not Semitic." It probably
is Semitic (see above p. 108) and Assyrian. The occurrence of what probably is a title of an Assyrian
commander, not only fits the times of Nahum, when
Assyrian invasions had begun, but the occurrence
of an official title, (like that of "Pechah" elsewhere, see Daniel the Prophet pp. 570, 571,) without
any Syriasms, belongs to Nahum's time and life in
Palestine. When three officers of Hezekiah understood Assyrian (Is. xxxvi. 11.), there is nothing surprising in the mention of an Assyrian title. Pechah
is also an Assyrian title, occurring in the Inscriptions in the plural "pahati," Oppert Rapports p. 51.
52. 53. 57. 65. 74. "Tartan," in Isaiah and 2 Kings, is
also probably an Assyrian title, since Rabsaris,
"Chief of the Eunuchs," "Rab-shakeh, Chief-cup-
bearer," (with which Tartan is united in 2 Kings
xviii. 17) are names of officers. Yet no satisfactory
etymology has been found for "Tartan."

10) "סָכַב, stands in Arabic meaning." The
coincidence with *Arabic* would have proved nothing;
but Nahum uses סָכַב in its common meaning. In
Arabic also it signifies "deceived," not (as Hitzig
would have it) "meshed."

11) "נָהַג, ii. 8, in Syriac meaning." נָהַג, not in
Syriac only, but in Arabic, signifies to be "violently
out of breath;" but this, which is its only meaning
which could be brought to bear on this passage, does
not suit it, whereas that suggested by the Hebrew
itself does. In Nahum it is evidently a modification
of the biliteral הַג, in the same sense as הָגָה which
is used of the low moaning of the dove, Is. xxxviii.
14, lix. 11; and the subst. הָגָה "moaning" is united
with קִינִים and הִי (for נְהִי) Ezek. ii. 10. Another
modification of the biliteral is הָגִין Ps. v. 2,
xxxix. 4.

12) "and דֹהַר too, iii. 2 (only beside in the song
of Deborah Jud. v. 22) is probably equally only a
Syriasm;" i. e. supposing its meaning to be derived
from דּוּר "circle," the substitution of ה for ו occurs
oftenest in Aramaic. In the root דּוּר itself however, the nearest correspondence of Hebrew with
any Semitic dialect is not with the Syriac but with
the Arabic; דּוּר "generation" and the Arab. דֹּהֵר
"prolonged time," but also the period of life (see
Lane p. 923); whereas the Syr. דֹּהֵרָא only signifies
"a mill." But Hitzig himself sets aside these last,
with the observation, "these appearances however
are sufficiently explained, if the home of Deborah
was also Nahum's country, a border-country toward
Syria, inhabited in part by non-Israelites."

13) Hitzig makes neither הָעֵץ nor the Queen's name
and so Assyrian, nor פַלְדוֹת, although he has his
own fantastic meaning for each, derived from mis-
application of the Arabic. The alleged Syriasm in
פַלְדוֹת rests on an odd ground-work. The Syriac
word פַלְדָא has not been found in any Syriac
author; in one of three Syro-Arab Lexica (Bar-
Bahlul's) it is explained by the Arabic word, "fûlâdso." This in its turn is interpreted by the Persian, which again has, in Vüllers, no Persian etymology. On the other hand the Arabic "faladsa"
"cut," conj. ii. "cut to pieces," does give a good
etymology for any sharp instrument, as the
"scythe" of a scythed chariot.

Yet this is the evidence on which Davidson tells
the unlearned (Introd. iii. 301), "The language is
pure and classical with a few exceptions, as נָהַג to
mourn, ii. 8, דֹהַר iii. 2, פַלְדוֹת ii. 4. which are Syri-

Whom all, past and future, are present, could not or did not declare beforehand things to come ᶻ. If there be prophecy, the siege of

asms.—These Syriasms cannot well be explained by the native locality of the prophet, which was toward the border-land of Syria and inhabited in part by people who were not Israelites, because other prophets of the Northern kingdom do not use Syriac words or idioms. They imply intimate contact with a people beyond Palestine." Yet נהן does not, in this sense, exist beyond Palestine; דהר was, in the time of the Judges, used within it, and the Arabic does give an etymology for פלדות, natural and adequate, which Syriac does not. The only difficulty is, that the Arabic word for "steel" is not a pure Semitic form, like the Hebrew, but a Persian, "fûlâdso" or "fâlûdso." Yet the Arabic has also the genuine Arabic form "maflûdso" "formed of steel," of a sword. The direct connection of פלדות with "fûlâdso" or "fâlûdso" must be given up, since it seems that the direct connection of the Arabic faladsa and fûlâdso or fûlûdso must be abandoned. For Prof. F. Justi whose judgment Prof. Max Müller kindly obtained for me says; "The Arabic fûlâdso must be borrowed from the Persian pûlâdo, not conversely (as Freytag and Vüllers also assume in their Lexica); for Persian retains the f in Arabic words which it adopts, but Arabic changes a Persian p into f, because it has no p. So Arabic again changes a Persian d, especially between or after vowels, always into ds. The relation of the Arabic fûlâdso, fâlûdso, with the root faladsa is consequently only apparent, whence the derivation of

פלדות from פלד is also shewn to be untenable, especially since this Hebrew root is not evidenced

Nineveh might be as vividly presented to the Prophet's mind, as if he saw it with his bodily eyes ª.

but assumed." Yet as relates to the Hebrew פלד, since the Heb. ד is often interchanged with the Arab. ds ("which in some Arab. dialects is pronounced d" Ges.), the etym. from the Arabic faladsa, "cuts," lies nearer to it than any other, designating a sharp instrument. It is remarkable that the Heb-Arab. Lexicogr., Abraham B. David and Abulwalid, were not aware of any connected Arabic root, both regarding פלד as inverted from לפיד. The Syr. בלצוציתא "spark" or "sparks" (which Ew. compares, Proph. ii. p. 11) is too remote, insulated, uncertain, not being connected with any known root, and being written also בלסוסיתא. See Dr. P. Smith's Lex. Syr. s. v. "The Arab.ברצ" (Ib.) must be a mis-print.

ᶻ "Did Nahum predict the downfall of Nineveh a century before the event? If he was a younger contemporary of Isaiah, he did so. He prophesied, say some, about the 14th year of Hezekiah and graphically painted the overthrow of Assyria's metropolis. The interval consists of about one hundred years. Is not the analogy of Prophecy violated here? If a specific event be foretold long before it happened, what becomes of the canon or principle that prophecy presents nothing more than the prevision of events in the immediate future? [Dr. Ds. italics.] The principle in question is almost axiomatic." [Introd. iii. 298.] It passes for an axiom in the school, whose results Dr. Davidson gives to the English; i. e. it is a petitio principii applied to each prophecy in turn.

ª "Nahum must have seen this peril with his own eyes." Ewald Proph. i. 349.

NAHUM.

CHAPTER I.

1 *The Majesty of God in goodness to his people, and severity
against his enemies.*

THE burden ᵃ of Nine-
veh. The book of the
vision of Nahum the El-
koshite.

1. *The' burden* [1]. " [2] The word 'massa' [burden] is never placed in the title, save when the vision is heavy and full of burden and toil." *Of Nineveh.* The prophecy of Nahum again is very stern and awful. Nineveh, after having "repented at the preaching of Jonah," again fell back into the sins whereof it had repented, and added this, that, being employed by God to chasten Israel, it set itself, not to inflict the measure of God's displeasure, but to uproot the chosen people, in whom was promised the birth of Christ [3]. It was then an Antichrist, and a type of him yet to come. Jonah's mission was a call to repentance, a type and forerunner of all God's messages to the world, while the day of grace and the world's probation lasts. Nahum, "the full of exceeding comfort," as his name means, or "the comforter" is sent to [4] *reprove the world of judgment.* He is sent, prominently, to pronounce on Nineveh its doom when its day of grace should be over, and in it, on the world, when it and [5] *all the works therein shall be burned up.* In few words he directly comforteth the people of God [6]; else the comfort even to her is indirect, in the destruction of her oppressor. Beside this, there is nothing of mercy or call to repent-

ance, or sorrow for their desolation [7]; but rather the pouring out of the vials of the wrath of God on her and on the evil world, which to the end resists all God's calls and persecuteth His people. The book of Jonah proclaimeth God, *a gracious God and merciful, slow to anger and of great kindness, Who repenteth Him of the evil.* Nahum speaketh of the same attributes, yet closes with, *and will not at all acquit the wicked.* " [3] The Merciful Himself, Who is by Nature Merciful, the Holy Spirit, seemeth, speaking in the prophet, to *laugh at their calamity.*" All is desolation, and death. The aggression against God is retorted upon the aggressor; one reeling strife for life or death; then the silence of the graveyard. And so, in its further meaning, " [2] the prophecy belongs to the close of the world and the comfort of the saints therein, so that whatsoever they see in the world, they may hold cheap, as passing away and perishing and prepare themselves for the Day of Judgment, when the Lord shall be the Avenger of the true Assyrian." So our Lord sets forth the end of the world as the comfort of the elect. *When these things begin to come to pass, then look up and lift up your heads, for your redemption draweth come.* In regard to the use of מַשָּׂא (1 C. xv. 22, 27,) where the E. V. has, "for song," if it related to the voice at all, it must (like the "on Alamoth," "on Sheminith" vv. 20, 21, which probably designate two notes of music, "treble" and the "octave," "bass") have signified some character of voice, as "alto," according to the meaning of מַשָּׂא, "lift up." But, considering (as Hengstenberg has noticed, Christol. on Zech. ix. 1.) the use of מַשָּׂא in places where it can only mean "burden" as also throughout Num. iv. (19, 24, 27, 31, 32, 47, 49,) it seems probable, that in 1 C. xv. too, it signifies "bearing" (as in E. M. "carriage"). For the "bearing the ark" is spoken of immediately afterward as a matter of much skill. "When God helped the Levites, the bearers of the ark of the covenant of the Lord," נֹשְׂאֵי אֲרוֹן בְּרִית ‏ (1 C. xv. 26); and the writer speaks of the dress of "all the Levites who bare the ark" "*and* the singers" v. 27, as two classes. Even Bertheau defends this meaning, and solidly. In Lam. ii. 14, מַשְׂאוֹת שָׁוְא is united with מַדּוּחִים "expulsions." The context seems to require more than is in the rendering, "sayings of vanity," which would be less strong than הֲ‏זוּ‏ לְ‏ ו שָׁוְ‏א "have seen for thee vanity." "The burdens of vanity," which the false prophets professed to see, would be heavy prophecies against the enemy, that they should be driven from the land of Israel. Comp. Zedekiah's enquiry, Jer. xxi. 1, 2, and Hananiah's prophecy Jer. xxviii. 2. 11.

---

[1] So, beyond question, מַשָּׂא should be rendered. Since נָשָׂא is no where used of mere speaking, it is beforehand improbable that מַשָּׂא should mean "speech ;" and this, apart from the consideration that "the speech of Babylon, Damascus, Egypt, Moab, Tyre, Dumah," "the valley of vision," "the desert of the sea," "Nineveh," would be an inexpressive expression for a speech concerning them. For, in one place only, (Is. xxi. 13.) is it expressed that the burden is *upon* (בְּ) Arabia. Else prepositions are only used to determine the relation of מַשָּׂא with the object (בְּ, Zech. ix. 1. עַל, Ib. xii. 1. אֶל, Mal i. 1.) when that object is already separated from מַשָּׂא; "the burden of the word of the Lord upon" Ib. נָשָׂא, "lift up" when used alone for נָשָׂא קוֹל "lifted up" [the voice], is always used of "loud speaking," Is. xlii. 2, 11, Job xxi. 12, and so Is. iii. 7, "loudly protest." Eleven times in Isaiah (xiii. 1, xiv. 28, xv. 1, xvii. 1, xix. 1, xxi. 1, 11, 13, xxii. 1, xxiii. 1, xxx. 6.) in Ezek. xii. 10, Hab. i. 1, Mal. i. 1, מַשָּׂא is followed by a heavy prophecy, as it is here. Zech. ix. 1, also is a heavy prophecy, against those whom Alexander would conquer; Zech. xii. 2, begins with a heavy prophecy against Judah and Jerusalem. Prov. xxx. xxxi, are rebukes; in Prov. xxxi., it is expressly added, "wherewith his mother admonished him." The blasphemy also, rebuked by Jeremiah (xxiii. 33, 34, 36), presupposes that the meaning of מַשָּׂא, at which they mocked, was a heavy prophecy. "What fresh burden has God for us?" they asked mockingly, not believing that the evil which Jeremiah prophesied would

[2] S. Jer. [3] Rup.
[4] S. John xvi. 6, 8. [5] 2 Pet. iii. 10. [6] i. 15.
[7] As in Jerem. iii. 12, viii. 18, 21.

9

2 ‖ God *is* [b]jealous, and [c]the Lord revengeth; the

‖ Or, *The Lord is a jealous God, and a revenger,* &c.
[b] Ex. 20. 5. & 34. 14. Deut. 4. 24. Josh. 24. 19.
[c] Deut. 32. 35. Ps. 94. 1. Isa. 59. 18.

LORD revengeth, and † *is* furious; the LORD will

† Heb. *that hath fury.*

nigh [1]." This is the highest fulfillment of the prophecy; for "then will the wrath of God against the wicked be fully seen, Who now patiently waiteth for them for mercy."

The book of the vision of Nahum the Elkoshite. "[2] He first defines the object of the prophecy, whereto it looks; then states who spake it and whence it was;" the human instrument which God employed. The fuller title, "*The book of* the vision of Nahum," (which stands alone) probably expresses that it was not, like most prophecies, first delivered orally, and then collected by the prophet, but was always (as it is so remarkably) one whole. "The weight and pressure of this 'burden' may be felt from the very commencement of the book."

2. *God is jealous and the Lord revengeth.* Rather (as the E. M.) [3] *A God very jealous and avenging is the Lord.* The Name of God, YHVH, "He Who Is," the Unchangeable, is thrice repeated, and thrice it is said of Him that He is an Avenger. It sheweth both the certainty and greatness of the vengeance, and that He Who inflicteth it, is the All-Holy Trinity, Who have a care for the elect. God's jealousy is twofold. It is an intense love, not bearing imperfections or unfaithfulness in that which It loves, and so chastening it; or not bearing the ill-dealings of those who would injure what It loves, and so destroying them. To Israel He had revealed Himself, as a[4] *jealous God, visiting iniquity* but *shewing mercy;* here, as jealous for His people against those who were purely His enemies and the enemies of His people[5], and so His jealousy burneth to their destruction, in that there is in them no good to be refined, but only evil to be consumed.

The titles of God rise in awe; first, *intensely jealous*[6] and *an Avenger;* then, *an Avenger*

[1] S. Luke xxi. 28.

[2] S. Cyr. On the prophet, and his country which S. Cyril says, he had "learned by tradition to be expressed by the addition, the Elkoshite," see the Introduction p. 357.

[3] אֵל קַנּא is used as an attribute of God Ex. xx. 5. xxxiv. 14. Dt. iv. 24. v. 9. vi. 15, as is קַנּוֹא אֵל, the form used here, Jos. xxiv. 19. It is observed that, in prose, אֵל is almost uniformly used with an adj. אֵל עֶלְיוֹן, אֵל חַי, אֵל גָּדוֹל וְנוֹרָא, אֵל רַחוּם וְחַנּוּן, אֵל דֵּעוֹת, אֵל עוֹלָם, or a noun אֵל רֳאִי שַׁדָּי.

[4] Ex. xx. 5, 6.   [5] See Zech. i. 14.

[6] The form קַנּא being intensive.

[7] בַּעַל חֵמָה occurs once only beside, and that, of man, Pr. xxix. 22; but בַּעַל אַף also Pr. xxii. 24.

and *a Lord of wrath;* One Who hath it laid up with Him, at His Command, and the more terrible, because it is so; the Master of it, (not, as man, mastered by it[7]); having it, to withhold or to discharge; yet so discharging it, at last, the more irrevocably on the finally impenitent. And this He says at the last, *an Avenger to* [8] *His adversaries,* (lit. "those who hem and narrow Him in"). The word *avenged*[9] is almost appropriated to God in the Old Testament, as to punishment which He inflicts, or at least causes to be inflicted[10], whether on individuals[11], or upon a people, (His own[12] or their enemies[13], for their misdeeds. In man it is a defect[14]. Personal vengeance is mentioned only in characters, directly or indirectly censured, as Samson[15] or Saul[16]. It is forbidden to man, punished in him, claimed by God as His own inalienable right. [17] *Vengeance is Mine and requital.* [18] *Thou shalt not avenge nor keep up against the children of My people.* Yet it is spoken of, not as a mere act of God, but as the expression of His Being. [19] *Shall not My soul be avenged of such a nation as this?*

And a Reserver of wrath for His enemies, the hardened and unbelieving who hate God, and at last, when they had finally rejected God and were rejected by Him, the object of His aversion. It is spoken after the manner of men, yet therefore is the more terrible. There is *that* in God, to which the passions of man correspond; they are a false imitation of something which in Him is good, a distortion of the true likeness of God, in which God created us and which man by sin defaced. "[20] Pride doth imitate exaltedness: whereas Thou Alone art God exalted above all. Ambition, what seeks it, but honors and glory? whereas Thou Alone art to be honored above

[8] נקם with ל p., only beside Ez. xxv. 12.

[9] נקם.

[10] Nu. xxxi. 2, 3. Ps. cxlix. 9. Hence almost the same as, punished by law, Ex. xxi. 20, 21.
[11] Gen. iv. 15. 24. 1 Sam. xxiv. 12. 2 Sam. iv. 8. 2 Kings ix. 7. Jer. xi. 20. xv. 15. xx. 12.
[12] Lev. xxvi. 25. Ps. xcix. 8. Ez. xxiv. 8.
[13] Deut. xxxii. 41, 43. Ps. xviii. 48. Is. xxxiv. 8. xxxv. 4. xlvii. 3. lix. 17. lxi. 2. lxiii. 4. Mi. v. 14. Jer. xlvi. 10. l. 15. 28. li. 6. 11. 36. Ezek. xxv. 14. 17.
[14] מתנקם, a self-avenger, Ps. viii. 3. xliv. 17. It is punished by God Ezek. xxv. 12, 15, being moreover unjust; Jer. xx. 10. 12. Lam. iii. 60. coll. 64.
[15] Jud. xv. 7. xvi. 20.
[16] 1 Sam. xiv. 24. xviii. 25. Else only historically Pr. vi. 34. Esth. viii. 13. David thanks God for keeping him from it toward Nabal 1 Sam. xxv. 32, 33.
[17] Deut. xxxii. 35, comp. Ps. xciv. 1.
[18] Lev. xix. 18.   [19] Jer. v. 9. 29. ix. 9.
[20] S. Aug. Conf. B. ii. n. 13. 14.

take vengeance on his ad-
versaries, and he reserveth
wrath for his enemies.

3 The LORD *is* ^dslow to
anger, and ^egreat in power,
and will not at all acquit ^d Ex. 34. 6, 7.
Neh. 9. 17.
^e Job 9. 4.   Ps. 103. 8. Jonah 4. 2.

---

all and glorious for evermore. The cruelty of the great would fain be feared; but who is to be feared but God Alone, out of Whose power what can be wrested or withdrawn, when, or where, or whither, or by whom? The tendernesses of the wanton would fain be counted love: yet is nothing more tender than Thy charity; nor is aught loved more healthfully than that Thy truth, bright and beautiful above all. Curiosity makes semblance of a desire of knowledge; whereas Thou supremely knowest all. Yea, ignorance and foolishness itself is cloaked under the name of simplicity and uninjuriousness: because nothing is found more single than Thee; and what less injurious, since they are his own works which injure the sinner? Yea, sloth would fain be at rest; but what stable rest beside the Lord? Luxury affects to be called plenty and abundance; but Thou art the fullness and never-failing plenteousness of incorruptible pleasures. Prodigality presents a shadow of liberality: but Thou art the most overflowing Giver of all good. Covetousness would possess many things; and Thou possessest all things. Envy disputes for excellency: what more excellent than Thou? Anger seeks revenge: who revenges more justly than Thou? Fear startles at things unwonted or sudden, which endanger things beloved, and takes fore-thought for their safety; but to Thee what unwonted or sudden, or who separateth from Thee what Thou lovest? Or where but with Thee is unshaken safety? Grief pines away for things lost, the delight of its desires; because it would have nothing taken from it, as nothing can from Thee. Thus doth the soul seek without Thee what she findeth not pure and untainted, till she returns to Thee. Thus all pervertedly imitate Thee, who remove far from Thee, and lift themselves up against Thee. But even by thus imitating Thee, they imply Thee to be the Creator of all nature; whence there is no place, whither altogether to retire from Thee." And so, in man, the same qualities are good or bad, as they have God or self for their end. "¹The joy of the world is a passion. Joy in the Holy Spirit or to joy in the Lord is a virtue. The sorrow of the world is a passion. The sorrow according to God which worketh salvation is a virtue. The fear of the world

which hath torment, from which a man is called fearful, is a passion. The holy fear of the Lord, which abideth for ever, from which a man is called reverential, is a virtue. The hope of the world, when one's hope is in the world or the princes of the world, is a passion. Hope in God is a virtue, as well as faith and charity. Though these four human passions are not in God, there are four virtues, having the same names, which no one can have, save from God, from the Spirit of God." In man they are "passions," because man is so far "passive" and suffers under them, and, through original sin, cannot hinder having them, though by God's grace he may hold them in. God, without passion and in perfect holiness, hath qualities, which in man were jealousy, wrath, vengeance, unforgivingness, a "rigor of perfect justice toward the impenitent, which punisheth so severely, as though God had fury;" only, in Him it is righteous to punish man's unrighteousness. Elsewhere it is said, ² *God keepeth not for ever,* or it is asked, ³ *will He keep for ever?* and He answers, ⁴ *Return, and I will not cause Mine anger to fall upon you; for I am merciful, saith the Lord, I will not keep for ever.* Man's misdeeds and God's displeasure remain with God, to be effaced on man's repentance, or ⁵ *by his hardness and impenitent heart man treasureth up unto himself wrath in the day of wrath and of the revelation of the righteous judgment of God, Who will reward each according to his works.*

3. *The Lord is slow to anger.* Nahum takes up the words of Jonah ⁶ as he spoke of God's attributes toward Nineveh, but only to shew the opposite side of them. Jonah declares how God is *slow to anger,* giving men time of repentance, and if they do repent, *repenting Him also of the evil;* Nahum, that the long-suffering of God is not *slackness,* that *He is long-suffering to usward, not willing that any should perish, but that all should come to repentance.*

And strong in power⁷. Divine long-suffering goes along with Divine power. God can be long-suffering, because He can, whenever He sees good, punish. His long-suffering is a token, not of weakness, but of power. He can allow persons the whole extent of trial, because, when they are past cure, He can end it at once. ⁸ *God is a righteous judge, strong*

¹ Rup.
² Ps. ciii. 9. The idiom נֹטֵר לְאֹיְבָיו stands alone.
³ Jer. iii. 5.   ⁴ Ib. 12.
⁵ Rom. ii. 5. 6.   ⁶ iv. 2.

⁷ The full form וְגָדוֹל כֹּחַ, Cheth. belongs probably to the stately character of Nahum. The like occurs only in Ps. cxlv. 8. גְּדָל חָסֶד.
⁸ Ps. vii. 11.

| Before CHRIST cir. 713. | *the wicked :* *'the* LORD *hath* his way in the whirl- wind and in the storm, | and the clouds *are* the dust of his feet. | Before CHRIST cir. 713. |
| † Ps. 18. 7, &c. & 97. 2. Hab. 3. 5, 11, 12. | | 4 **g** He rebuketh the sea, | **g** Ps. 106. 9. Isa. 50. 2. Matt. 8. 26. |

and patient, and God wratheth [1] *every day.* The wrath cometh only at the last, but it is ever present with God. He cannot but be dis- pleased with the sin; and so the Psalmist describes in the manner of men the gradual approximation to its discharge. [2] *If he* (the sinner) *will not return* [from evil or to God], *He will whet His sword ; He hath trodden His bow and directed it : He hath prepared for him instruments of death ; He hath made his arrows burning.* We see the arrow with unex- tinguishable fire, ready to be discharged, waiting for the final decision of the wicked, whether he will repent or not, but that still *the Day of the Lord* will *come* [3]. He *will not at all acquit* [4]. The words occur originally in the great declaration of God's attributes of mercy by Moses, as a necessary limitation of them [5]; they are continued to God's people, yet with the side of mercy predominant [6]; they are pleaded to Himself [7]; they are the sanction of the third commandment [8]. He *will not acquit* of His own will, apart from His justice. So He saith [9], *I can of Mine own self do nothing,* i. e. (in part), not as unjust judges, who *call good evil and evil good,* following their own will, not the merits of the case; but, *as I hear, I judge, and My judgment is just.* He can- not even have mercy and spare unjustly, nor without the lowliness of penitence. Even if it be Jerusalem, over which He wept, or His *companion,* His *own familiar friend* [10], He, Who is no *accepter of persons,* cannot of mere favor forgive the impenitent.

The Lord hath His way in the whirlwind and in the storm. The vengeance of God comes at last swiftly, vehemently, fearfully, irresist- ibly. *When they say, Peace and safety, then sudden destruction cometh upon them* [11], and all creation stands at the command of the Cre- ator against His enemies. *He shall take to Him His jealousy for complete armor, and make the creature His weapon, for the revenge of His enemies* [12].

And the clouds are the dust of His feet. Per- haps the imagery is from the light dust raised by an earthly army, of which Nahum's

word is used [13]. The powers of heaven are arrayed against the might of earth. On earth a little dust, soon to subside ; in heaven, the whirlwind and the storm, which sweep away what does not bow before them. The vapors, slight in outward seeming [14], but formed of countless multitudes of mist-drops, are yet dark and lowering, as they burst, and resist- less. " The *Feet* of God are that power where- by He trampleth upon the ungodly." So it is said to the Son, *Sit Thou on My Right Hand until I make Thine enemies Thy footstool.* Tem- pests have also, without figure, been used to overthrow God's enemies [15].

4. *He rebuketh the sea, and maketh it dry* [16], delivering His people, as He did from Pha- raoh [17], the type of all later oppressors, and of Antichrist. *His word is with power ; to de- stroy them at once with one rough word* [18]. The restlessness of the barren and troubled sea is an image of the wicked [19]. *And drieth up all the rivers,* as He did Jordan. His coming shall be far more terrible than when all *the hearts* of the inhabitants of the land *did melt* [20]. *Bashan languisheth and Carmel ; and the flower of Lebanon languisheth.* Bashan was richest in pastures ; Carmel, according to its name, in gardens and vineyards ; Lebanon, in vines also and fragrant flowers [21], but chiefly in the cedar and cypress ; it had its name from the whiteness of the snow, which rests on its summit. These mountains then together are emblems of richness, lasting beauty, fruitful- ness, loftiness ; yet all, even that which by nature is not, in the variety of seasons, wont to fade, dries up and withers before the re- buke of God. But if these thing are *done in a green tree, what shall be done in the dry ?* All freshness, beauty, comeliness, shew of out- ward nature, shall fade as grass ; all ornament of men's outward graces or gifts, all mere shew of goodness, shall fall off like a leaf and perish. If the glory of nature perishes be- fore God, how much more the pride of man ! Bashan also was the dwelling-place of the race of giants, and near Libanus was Damas- cus ; yet their inhabitants *became as dead men*

[1] The word expresses continuously present action, םֵעֹנ. The lxx added *strong and patient* to bring out the meaning.
[2] Ib. 12. 13.   [3] 2 Pet. iii. 9, 10.   [4] וְנַקֵּה לֹא יְנַקֶּה.
[5] Ex. xxxiv. 7. The Samaritan Pentateuch char- acteristically changes the words into וְנַקֵּה לוֹ יְנַקֶּה "the innocent shall be held guiltless by him."
[6] Jer. xxx. 11. xlvi. 28.   [7] Nu. xiv. 18.
[8] Ex. xx. 7. Deut. v. 11.   [9] John v. 30.
[10] Ps. lv. 14.   [11] 1 Thess. v. 3.
[12] Wisdom v. 17.   [13] Ezek. xxvi. 10.

[14] אבק occurs six times in the O. T. It is by itself " light dust " Ex. ix. 9. De. xxviii. 24. Is. v. 24, but has רַק added Is. xxix. 5.
[15] Ex. xiv. 27. Josh. x. 11. Judges v. 20. 1 Sam. ii. 10. and vii. 10. 2 Sam. xxii. 15.
[16] The contracted form, וַיַּבְּשֵׁהוּ is again for emphasis. The like contraction יֵרַד occurs in Lam. iii. 53. יֵרַע Ib. 33. וַיֵּשְׁרַם 2 Chr. xxxii. 30. Kri.
[17] Ps. cvi. 9.   [18] Wisd. xii. 9.   [19] Is. lvii. 20.
[20] Josh. ii. 11.   [21] Hos. xiv. 7, Cant. iv. 11.

and maketh it dry, and drieth up all the rivers:

ʰ Isa. 33. 9.

ʰ Bashan languisheth, and Carmel, and the flower of Lebanon languisheth.

¹ Ps. 68. 8.
ᵏ Judg. 5. 5.
Ps. 97. 5.
Mic. i. 4.
¹ 2 Pet. 3. 10.

5 ¹ The mountains quake at him, and ᵏ the hills melt, and ¹ the earth is burned at his presence, yea, the

world, and all that dwell therein.

6 Who can stand before his indignation? and ᵐ who ᵐ Mal. 3. 2. can † abide in the fierce- † Heb. *stand up.* ness of his anger? ⁿ his ⁿ Rev. 16. 1. fury is poured o u t like fire, and the r o c k s are thrown down by him.

---

and their power shrank to nothing at the word of God.

5. *The mountains quaked at Him, and the hills melted,* as of their own accord. The words are a renewal of those of Amos ¹. Inanimate nature is pictured as endowed with the terror, which guilt feels at the presence of God. All power, whether greater or less, whatsoever lifteth itself up, shall give way in that Day, which shall be ² *upon all the cedars of Lebanon that are high and lifted up, and upon all the oaks of Bashan, and upon all the high mountains, and upon all the hills that are lifted up. And the earth is burned* [rather *lifteth itself up* ³]; as in an earthquake it seems, as it were, to rise and sink down, lifting itself as if to meet its God or to flee. What is strongest, shaketh ; what is hardest, melteth ; yea, the whole world trembleth and is removed. "⁴ If," said even Jews of old, "when God made Himself known in mercy, to give the law to His people, the world was so moved at His Presence, how much more, when He shall reveal Himself in wrath ! " The words are so great that they bear the soul on to the time, when the heaven and earth shall flee away from the Face of Him *Who sitteth on the throne, and the elements shall melt with fervent heat* ⁵. And since all judgments are images of the Last, and the awe at tokens of God's Presence is a shadow of the terror of that coming, he adds,

6. *Who can stand before His indignation?* This question appeals to our own consciences, that we cannot ⁶. It anticipates the self-con-

viction at every day of God's visitation, the forerunners of the last. The word rendered " indignation " is reserved almost exclusively to denote the wrath of God ⁷. "⁸ Who can trust in his own righteousness, and, for the abundance of his works or consciousness of his virtues, not be in need of mercy ? *Enter not into judgment with Thy servant, O Lord, for in Thy sight shall no man living be justified ;* and in Job it is said truly, *Behold He put no trust in His servants, and His Angels He charged with folly. How much less in them that dwell in houses of clay, whose foundation is in the dust, which are crushed before the moth* ⁹ ? It were needless now to prove, that man's own deserts suffice to no one, and that we are not saved but by the grace of God, *for all have sinned and come short of the glory of God* ¹⁰. Wherefore he saith, *before His indignation,* standing face to Face before Him in wrath."

lit. in the Face of : guilt cannot look in the face of man, how much less, of God. The bliss of the righteous is the punishment of the wicked, to behold God face to Face. For "⁸ whoso trusteth in his own works deserveth His indignation, and thinking he standeth, righteously does he fall."

His fury is poured out ¹¹ *like fire,* sweeping away, like a torrent of molten fire, him who presumeth that he can stand before His Face, as He did the cities of the plain ¹², the image of the everlasting fire, which shall burn up His enemies on every side ¹³. *And rocks are thrown down.* The rocks are like so many towers ¹⁴ of nature, broken down and crushed

---

¹ Am. ix. 13. התמונג occurs beside only in Ps. cvii. 26, of the heart of man through terror. Delitzsch (on Hab. p. 156) supposed that the hithpael or hithpalel conveyed "the operation of an outward cause, completing itself within the subject, as it were in continued vibrations," alleging Ew. Lehrb. 124 a, coll. התבקע Mic. i. 4, התנעש Ps. xviii. 8, התרעע התפורר, Is. xxiv. 19, התקלקל Jer. iv. 24, but there is no ground for making the form at once passive and reflective; and it is less vivid.

² Is. ii. 13, 14.

³ נשא intrans. as Ps. lxxxix. 10, בשוא גליו, of the sea. With this agrees the constr. מפני "from His Presence," as the cause of its fear. The E. V. " is burned " is taken from Rashi.

⁴ Jon. ⁵ Rev. xx. 11 ; 2 Pet. iii. 10.

⁶ As in Jo. ii. 11, Mal. iii. 2; renewed Rev. vi. 17.

⁷ The noun זעם (used here) occurs 21 times in the O. T.; of men only once; the verb זעם occurs 13 times, 5 times only of man's anger.

⁸ Rup. ⁹ Job iv. 18, 19. ¹⁰ Rom. iii. 23.

¹¹ נתך is used of the pouring out of God's wrath, Jer. vii. 20, xlii. 18, 2 Chr. xii. 7 (as more commonly שפך); here its native meaning is brought out the more, by adding כאש.

¹² Gen. xix. ¹³ Ps. xcvii. 3. l. 3, lxviii. 3, xviii. 8.

¹⁴ נתץ (not in the dialects) is used 34 times of the " breaking down " of walls, buildings, a statue, altar, shrine; in Ps. lviii. 7. only, of the teeth of lions, and, by metaphor, of men in Ps. lii. 7, Job xix. 10. Three times it is used elliptically.

Before
C H R I S T
cir. 713.

o 1 Chr. 16. 34.
Ps. 100. 5.
Jer 33. 11.
Lam. 3. 25.
|| Or, *strength.*
p Ps. 1. 6.
2 Tim. 2. 19.

7 °The LORD *is* good,
a || strong hold in the day
of trouble; and P he knoweth them that trust in
him.

Before
C H R I S T
cir. 713.

q Dan. 9. 26.
& 11. 10, 22, 40.

8 q But with an over-
running flood he will make
an utter end of the place
thereof, and darkness shall
pursue his enemies.

---

by Him lit. *from Him.* It needeth not any
act of God's. He wills and it is done. Those
who harden themselves, are crushed and
broken to pieces, the whole fabric they had
built for themselves and their defences,
crumbling and shivered. If then they, whose
hearts are hard as rocks, and bold against all
peril, and even Satan himself, whose [1] *heart is
as firm as a stone, yea, as hard as a piece of the
nether millstone,* shall be crushed then, who
shall abide ?

7. *The Lord is good: a stronghold in the day
of trouble.* "Good and doing good," and full
of sweetness; alike good and mighty ; Good
in giving Himself and imparting His goodness to His own; yea [2] *none is good, save
God ;* Himself the stronghold wherein His
own may take refuge; both in the *troubles of*
this life, in which [3] *He will not suffer us to be
tempted above that we are able,* and in that Day,
which shall hem them *in* on every side, and
leave no place of escape except Himself.

And He knoweth them that trust in Him ;
so as to save them ; as Rahab was saved when
Jericho perished, and Lot out of the midst
of the overthrow and Hezekiah from the
host of Sennacherib. He *knoweth* them with
an individual, ever-present, knowledge [4]. He
says not only, " He shall own them," but He
ever *knoweth them.* So it is said ; [5] *The Lord
knoweth the way of the righteous,* [6] *The Lord knoweth the days of the upright;* and our Lord
says, [7] *I know My sheep;* and S. Paul, [8] *The
Lord knoweth them that are His.* God speaks
of this knowledge also in the past, of His
knowledge, when things as yet were not, *I
have known thee by name ;* or of loving kindness in the past, [9] *I knew thee in the wilderness,*
[10] *you alone have I known of all the families of
the earth,* as contrariwise our Lord says, that
He shall say to the wicked in the Great Day,
[11] *I never knew you.* That God, being what He
is, should take knowledge of us, being what we
are, is such wondrous condescension, that it

involves a purpose of love, yea, His love
toward us, as the Psalmist says admiringly,
*Lord, what is man that Thou takest knowledge
of him* [12] ?

Them that trust in Him. It is a *habit,* which
has this reward ; *the trusters in Him* [13], *the
takers of refuge in Him.* It is a continued unvarying trust, to which is shewn this ever-
present love and knowledge.

Yet this gleam of comfort only discloseth
the darkness of the wicked. Since those who
trust God are they whom God knoweth, it
follows that the rest He knoweth not. On
this opening, which sets forth the attributes
of God toward those who defy Him and
those who trust in Him, follows the special
application to Nineveh.

8. *But with an overrunning flood He will make
an utter end of the place thereof* [14], i. e. of Nineveh, although not as yet named, except in
the title of the prophecy, yet present to the
Prophet's mind and his hearers, and that the
more solemnly, as being *the* object of the
wrath of God, so that, although unnamed, it
would be known so to be. Image and reality,
the first destruction and the last which it
pictures, meet in the same words. Nineveh
itself was overthrown through the swelling
of the rivers which flowed round it and
seemed to be its defence [15]. Then also, the
flood is the tide of the armies, gathered from
all quarters, Babylonians [16], Medes, Persians,
Arabians, Bactrians, which like a flood should
sweep over Nineveh and leave nothing standing. It is also the flood of the wrath of God,
in Whose Hands they were, and Who, by
them, should *make a full end of it,* lit. *make the
place thereof a thing consumed,* a thing which
has ceased to be. For a while, some ruins
existed, whose name and history ceased to
be known ; soon after, the ruins themselves
were effaced and buried [17]. Such was the
close of a city, almost coeval with the flood,
which had now stood almost as many years

---

[1] Job xli. 24. [2] S. Luke xviii. 19. [3] 1 Cor. x. 13.
[4] יֹדֵעַ. [5] Ps. i. 6. [6] Ps. xxxvii. 18.
[7] S. John x. 14. 27. [8] 2 Tim. ii. 19. [9] Hos. xiii. 5.
[10] Am. iii. 2. [11] S. Matt. vii. 23. [12] Ps. cxliv. 3.

[14] It is the well known construction חוֹסֵי, in
which, the verb being united with its object by a
preposition, (like our "trust in,") the "in Him"
stands as gen. as marked by the stat. const. חוֹסֵי,
as it were "all trusters of Him," as כָּל חֹסֵי בוֹ Ps.
ii. 12, כָל חֹסֵי בָךְ Ps. v. 12. Elsewhere the art. is

used to express the class, הַחֹסִים בוֹ 2 Sam. xxii.
31 (Ps. xviii. 31.) Ps. xxxiv. 23, לַחוֹסִים בָּךְ, Ps.
xxxi. 20. לַחוֹסִים בוֹ Pr. xxx. 5. הַחוֹסָה בִי Is.
lvii. 13.

[14] So Ezek. xi. 13, xx. 17, כָּלָה being the second
object of the verb, "He made them as a thing consumed," or עֹשֶׂה is used abs. as in v. 9. or with אֶת
Jer. v. 18.
[15] See on ii. 6. [16] Diod. Sic. ii. 25.
[17] See ab. Introd. pp. 122, 123.

Before CHRIST cir. 713.	9 [r] What do ye im-agine against the LORD? [s] he will make an utter	end: affliction shall not rise up the second time.	Before CHRIST cir. 713.

[r] Ps. 2. 1.
[s] 1 Sam. 3. 12.

as have passed since Christ came, but which now defied God. Marvelous image of the evil world itself, which shall flee away from the Face of Him Who sat on the throne[1], *and there was found no place for it.*

And darkness shall pursue His enemies; better, *He shall pursue His enemies* into *darkness*[2]. Darkness is, in the O. T., the condition, or state in which a person is, or lives; it is not an agent, which pursues. Isaiah speaks of the [3] *inhabitants of darkness*[4], *entering into darkness;* [5] *those who are in darkness. The grave is all* [6] *darkness,* [7] *darkness, and the shadow of death.* Hence even Jews rendered, " [8] He shall deliver them to hell." Into this darkness it is said, God shall pursue them, as other prophets speak of being *driven forth into darkness*[9]. The darkness, the motionless drear abode, to which they are driven, anticipates the being cast into *the outer darkness, where shall be weeping and gnashing of teeth.* " [10] The vengeance of God on " those who remain "His enemies " to the last, " ends not with the death of the body; but evil spirits, who are darkness and not light, pursue their souls, and seize them." They would not hear Christ calling to them, [11] *Walk, while ye have the light, lest darkness come upon you.* [12] *They are of those that rebel against the light; they know not the ways thereof, nor abide in the paths thereof.* [13] *They loved darkness rather than light.* And so they were driven into the darkness which they chose and loved.

9. The Prophet had in few words summed up the close of Nineveh; he now upbraids them with the sin, which should bring it upon them, and foretells the destruction of Sennacherib. Nineveh had, before this,

[1] Rev. xx. 11.
[2] So S. Jer. The punctuators marked this by the Makkef, יִרְדֹּף־חֹשֶׁךְ.
[3] Is. xlii. 7.   [4] Ib. xlvii. 5.   [5] Ib. xlix. 9.
[6] Ps. lxxxviii. 12. Job xvii. 13.   [7] Job x. 21.
[8] Jon.
[9] Is. viii. 22. וַאֲפֵלָה מְנֻדָּח Jer. xxiii. 12. בָּאֲפֵלָה יִדַּחוּ וְנָפְלוּ בָהּ " in darkness, into which they shall be driven and fall therein."
[10] Rup.   [11] S. John xii. 35.   [12] Job xxiv. 13.
[13] S. John iii. 19.   [14] 2 Kings xviii. 35.
[15] Ib. xix. 16.   [16] See xix. 15-34.
[17] The Hebrew form is doubly emphatic, תְּחַשְּׁבוּן. The same construction occurs with אֶל, "towards," Hos. vii. 15, וְאֵלַי יַחְשְׁבוּ רָע (in the same general sense as the stronger עַל Nah. i. 11, Dan. xi. 24), in אֶל שַׁדַּי יִתְגַבֵּר Job xv. 25, יָרוּץ אֵלָיו "runneth at" i. e. against Him (God) Ib. 26. חָשַׁב is not simply "think," but "excogitated," "calculated" (Lev. 5 times), "devised" Pr. xvi. 9; with לְ and inf. "to do

been the instrument of chastising Israel and Judah. Now, the capture of Samaria, which had cast off God, deceived and emboldened it. Its king thought that this was the might of his own arm; and likened the Lord of heaven and earth to the idols of the heathen, and said, [14] *Who are they among all the gods of the countries, that have delivered their country out of mine hand, that the Lord should deliver Jerusalem out of mine hand?* He sent [15] *to reproach the living God* and [16] *defied the Holy One of Israel.* His blasphemy was his destruction. It was a war, not simply of ambition, or covetousness, but directly against the power and worship of God.

What will ye so mightily [17] *devise, imagine against the Lord?* He [18] Himself, by Himself, *is* already *making an utter end.* It is in store; the Angel is ready to smite. Idle are man's *devices,* when the Lord *doeth.* [19] *Take counsel together, and it shall come to nought; speak the word, and it shall not stand: for God is with us.* While the rich man was speaking comfort to his soul as to future years, God was making an utter end. *Thou fool, this night shall thy soul be required of thee.* [20] *Affliction shall not rise up the second time:* as he says afterward, *Though I have afflicted thee, I will afflict thee no more* [21]. *God,* He had said, *is good for a refuge in the day of affliction;* now, personifying that affliction, he says, that it should be so utterly broken, that it should rise up no more to vex them, as when a serpent's head is, not wounded only but, crushed and trampled under foot, so that it cannot again lift itself up. The promises of God are conditioned by our not falling back into sin. He saith to Nineveh, " God will

evil to " Pr. xxiv. 8. In kal, also, חָשַׁב מַחֲשָׁבָה is used for "devising against," alike with עַל Jer. xi. 19. xviii. 11. 18. xlix. 30, and with אֶל Jer. xlix. 20. l. 45; and with עַל in a good sense, Jer. xxix. 11. חָשַׁב is used also of "thinking over" the past, Ps. lxxvii. 6. cxix. 59; with לְ and inf. "thinking over," in order to know, Ps. lxxiii. 16; with acc. p. "take account of " Ps. cxliv. 3, 2 Kgs xii. 16; but in none of these cases with אֶל.
[18] The use of the pronoun in Heb. is again emphatic. [19] Is. viii. 10.
[20] Others have understood this, "affliction shall not rise up the second time," but shall destroy at once, utterly and finally (comp. 1 Sam. xxvi. 8. 2 Sam. xx. 10.): but 1) the idiom there, לֹא אֶשְׁנֶה לוֹ, "he did not repeat to him," as we say, "he did not repeat the blow," is quite different: 2) it is said, "affliction shall not rise up," itself, as if it could not. The causative of the idiom occurs in 2 Sam. xii. 11. הִנְנִי מֵקִים עָלֶיךָ רָעָה "lo, I will cause evil to rise up against thee." [21] v. 12.

10 For while *they be* folden together ^t *as* thorns,

^u**and while they are** drunken *as* **drunkards,**

^xthey shall be devoured as stubble fully dry.

11 There is *one* come out of thee, ^ythat imagin-

not deliver Judah to thee, as He delivered the ten tribes and Samaria." Judah repented under Hezekiah, and He not only delivered it from Sennacherib, but never afflicted them again through Assyria. Renewal of sin brings renewal or deepening of punishment. The new and more grievous sins under Manasseh were punished, not through Assyria but through the Chaldeans.

The words have passed into a maxim, "God will not punish the same thing twice," not in this world and the world to come, i. e. not if repented of. For of the impenitent it is said, ¹ *destroy them with a double destruction.* Chastisement here is a token of God's mercy; the absence of it, or prosperous sin, of perdition; but if any refuse to be corrected, the chastisement of this life is but the beginning of unending torments.

10. *For while they be folden together as thorns* ², i. e. as confused, intertwined, sharp, piercing, hard to be touched, rending and tearing whosoever would interfere with its tangled ways, and seemingly compact together and strong ; *and while they are drunken as their drink* ³, not "drinkers ⁴" only but literally "drunken," swallowed up, as it were, by their drink which they had swallowed, mastered, overcome, powerless, *they shall be devoured as stubble fully dry* ⁵, rapidly, in an instant, with an empty crackling sound, unresisting, as having nothing in them which can resist. Historically, the great defeat of the Assyrians, before the capture of Nineveh, took place while its king, flushed with success, was giving himself to listlessness ; and having distributed to his

soldiers victims, and abundance of wine, and other necessaries for banqueting, the whole army ⁶ was negligent and drunken." In like way Babylon was taken amid the feasting of Belshazzar ⁷ ; Benhadad was smitten, while ⁸ *drinking himself drunk in the pavilions, he and the kings, the thirty and two kings that helped him.* And so it may well be meant here too, that Sennacherib's army, secure of their prey, were sunk in revelry, already swallowed up by wine, before they were swallowed up by the pestilence, on the night when the Angel of the Lord went out to smite them, and, from the sleep of revelry, they slept the sleep from which they shall not awake until the Judgment Day. God chooseth the last moment of the triumph of the wicked, when he is flushed by his success, the last of the helplessness of the righteous, when his hope can be in the Lord Alone, to exchange their lots. ⁹ *The righteous is delivered out of trouble, and the wicked cometh in his stead.* Spiritually, " ¹⁰ the false fullness of the rich of this world, is real leanness ; the greenness of such grass (for *all flesh is grass*) is real dryness. Marvelous words, *fully dry.* For what is dryness but emptiness? " They are perfected, but in dryness, and so perfectly prepared to be burned up. " The thorns had, as far as in them lay, choked the good seed, and hated the Seed-corn, and now are found, like stubble, void of all seed, fitted only to be burned with fire. *For those who* feast themselves *without fear is* ¹¹ *reserved the blackness of darkness for ever.*"

11. *There is one come out of thee* i. e. Nineveh, *that imagineth* ¹², deviseth ¹³, *evil* ¹⁴, *against the*

" Out of thee, Judah, is gone away, withdrawn, he who devised evil against the Lord." But a person is said to " go forth " out of that which is his abode, from the city, gate, &c. or, to war. In the exceptions, Is. xlix. 17, " thy destroyers and wasters shall go forth from thee," it is implied that thay had long sojourned there, and were to give place to the children, who should return. In Jer. xliii. 12, where it is said of Nebuchadnezzar, *he shall go forth thence in peace,* it is first said, *he shall set up his throne there and shall array himself with the land of Egypt, as a shepherd putteth on his garment ;* i. e. he shall make it wholly his own.

¹ Jer. xvii. 18.
² עַד סִרִים lit. " quite up to," so as altogether to equal ; as עַד תַּכְלִית, Job. xi. 7, עַד בְּנֵי יְהוּדָה, 1 Chr. iv. 27.   ³ סְבָא, wine, Is. i. 22. Hos. iv. 18.
⁴ As elsewhere סֹבְאִים, Deut. xxi. 20, Pr. xxiii. 20, 21, סוֹבֵא Cheth. Ez. xxiii. 42.
⁵ מָלֵא is best united with יָבֵשׁ. מָלֵאָה is used of ripe corn, Ex. xxii. 28. Dt. xxii. 9 ; but this may be so called, from the ear being full. The idiom, in which מָלֵא is joined with the verb, קָרְאוּ אַתְרִיךְ מָלֵא Jer xii. 6, is different, being derived from a phrase, קָרְאוּ מַלְאוּ " cry aloud, fill," i. e with a full voice, Jer. iv. 5. Schultens compares Arab. נָעַל וַמְלֵא " he did and filled "=did fully. For the imagery of the devouring of the stubble by fire, see Is. v. 24. xlvii. 14. Jo. ii. 5. Ob. 18.   ⁶ Diod. Sic. ii. 26.
⁷ Dan. v. 1-30.   ⁸ 1 Kings xx. 16.
⁹ Pr. xi. 8.   ¹⁰ Rup.   ¹¹ Jude 12, 13.
¹² Those who explain this of the past, render,

¹³ As Ps. xxxv. 4. חָשְׁבֵי רָעָתִי.
¹⁴ בְלִיַּעַל occurs 18 times, combined with עַד, בֵּן, בַּת, בְּנֵי, אִישׁ, אֲנָשִׁים, אָדָם, "a son, daughter, sons, man, men, witness." יוֹעֵץ בְּ is a similar composition. Else it only occurs with דָּבָר Ps. xli. 9, ci. 3, and as an adj. De. xv. 9 ; as personal 2 Sam. xxiii. 6. Nah. ii. 1. also הָאֹמֵר בְּ Job xxxiv. 18. There is then no ground to take it here, or Ps. xviii. 5, and 2 Sam. xxii. 5, with נַחְלֵי, as signifying " destruction."

Before
C H R I S T
cir. 713.
eth evil against the LORD, † a wicked counsellor.

† Heb. *a counsellor of Belial.*

12 Thus saith the LORD;

‖ Or, *If they would have been at peace, so should they have been many, and so should they have been shorn, and he should have passed away.*

‖ Though *they be* q u i e t, and likewise m a n y, yet thus ᶻ shall they be † cut down, when he shall ª pass through. Though I have

ᶻ 2 Kings 19. 35, 37.   † Heb. *shorn.*
ª Isa. 8. 8. Dan. 11. 10.

afflicted thee, I will afflict thee no more.

13 F o r n o w w i l l I ᵇ break his yoke from off thee, and will burst thy bonds in sunder.

14 And the LORD hath given a commandment

Before
C H R I S T
cir. 713.

ᵇ Jer. 2. 20. & 30. 8.

Lord, Sennacherib, [1] *the rod of God's anger,* yet who "*meant* not so," as God meant. "And this was his counsel," as is every counsel of Satan, "that they could not resist him, and so should withdraw themselves from the land of God, [2] *into a land like their own,* but whose joy and sweetness, its vines and its fig-trees, should not be from God, but from the Assyrian, i. e. from Satan."

12. *Though they be quiet and likewise many, yet thus shall they be cut down.* lit. *If they be entire* [3], i. e. sound, unharmed, unimpaired in their numbers, unbroken in their strength, undiminished, perfect in all which belongeth to war ; *and thus many, even thus shall they be mown down* (or *shorn*), *and he passeth away* [4]. With might outwardly unscathed, *without hand* [5], and *thus many* i. e. many, accordingly, as being unweakened ; as many as they shall be, *so shall they be mown down* [6], *and he,* their head and king, *shall pass away* and perish [7]. Their numbers shall be, as their condition before, perfect ; their destruction as their numbers, complete. It is wonderful how much God says in few words ; and how it is here foretold that, with no previous loss, a mighty host secure and at ease, in consequence of their prosperity, all are at one blow *mown down,* like the dry grass before the scythe, are cut off and perish ; and one, their king, *passeth away,* first by flight, and then by destruction. As they had shorn the glory of others [8], so should they be shorn and cut down themselves.

Though I have afflicted thee, I will afflict thee [9] *no more,* unless by new guilt thou compel Me.

God always relieves us from trouble, as it were with the words [10], *sin no more, lest a worse thing come unto thee.* In the end, afflictions shall be turned into joy, and *God shall wipe away all tears from their eyes ; and there shall be no more death, nor sorrow, nor crying, neither shall there be any more pain* [11].

13. *For now will I break his yoke from off thee.* God, lest His own should despair, does not put them off altogether to a distant day, but saith, *now.* Historically, the beginning of the fall is the earnest of the end. By the destruction of Sennacherib, God declared His displeasure against Assyria ; the rest was matter of time only. Thus Haman's wise men say to him, [12] *If Mordecai be of the seed of the Jews, before whom thou hast begun to fall, thou shalt not prevail against him, but shalt surely fall before him ;* as He saith in Isaiah, [13] *I will break the Assyrian in My land, and upon My mountains tread him under foot ; then shall his yoke depart from off them, and his burden depart from off their shoulders.* " [14] In that He saith, not 'I will loose,' 'will undo,' but 'I will break,' 'will burst,' He sheweth that He will in such wise free Jerusalem, as to pour out displeasure on the enemy. The very mode of speaking shews the greatness of His displeasure against those who, when for the secret purpose of His judgments they have power given them against the servants of God, feed themselves on their punishments, and moreover dare to boast against God, as did the Assyrian, [15] *By the strength of my hand I have done it, and by my wisdom.*"

14. *And the Lord hath given a commandment*

---

[1] Is. x. 5-7.   [2] Is. xxxvi. 16, 17.

[3] שָׁלֵם is used of physical entireness, completeness, or mental integrity. In one place only, Gen. xxxiv. 21, שְׁלֵמִים אִתָּנוּ is doubtless rendered rightly "peaceable with us," as שְׁלֹמִי Ps. vii. 5, but not in the frequent idiom לְבָב, לֵב שָׁלֵם, whether with or without עִם, and never by itself.

[4] So it seems better to render it, than, as in the E. V., *and he shall pass through.* The word means alike "pass away" or "pass through," but the act spoken of is later than the *cutting down* of the army, and so probably the *passing away,* or flight of its king, to his destruction or final passing away.
[5] Dan ii. 34.

[6] גֵּז is used of sheep-shearing, cutting off the hair in sorrow ; גֵּז is "mown grass, fleece cut." Here alone, it is a metaphor, like that of יִגָּלֵחַ, Is. vii. 20.   [7] Comp. Ps. xlviii. 4.   [8] Is. vii. 20.
[9] עָנָה "afflicted" relatively to God, is said of His chastisement of His people (Deut. viii. 2. 2 Kgs xvii. 20) or of individuals (Ps. lxxxviii. 8. xc. 15. cii. 24. cxix. 75. Job xxx. 11.) but no where of the enemies of God, whose *destruction* moreover is here spoken of. It cannot then refer to the Assyrian, as some have done. The double omission of the י in עִנִּתִךְ was probably for the rhythm.

[10] S. John v. 14.   [11] Rev. xxi. 4.   [12] Esth. vi. 13.
[13] Is. xiv. 25.   [14] Rup.   [15] Is. x. 13.

Before
C H R I S T
cir. 713.
concerning thee, *that* n o
more of thy name be sown:
out of the house of thy
gods w i l l I cut off the

graven image and the mol-
ten image: [e] I will make thy
grave; for thou art vile.
15 Behold [d] u p o n the

Before
C H R I S T
cir. 713.

e 2 Kin. 19. 37.
d Isa. 52. 7.
Rom. 10. 15.

concerning thee, O Assyrian. In the word "I
have afflicted *thee*," the land of Israel is addressed, as usual in Hebrew, in the feminine;
here, a change of gender in Hebrew shews
the person addressed to be different. "[1] By
His command alone, and the word of His
power, He cut off the race of the Assyrian, as
he says in Wisdom, of Egypt, [2] *Thine Almighty word leaped down from Heaven, out of
Thy royal throne ; as a fierce man of war into the
midst of a land of destruction, and brought Thine
unfeigned commandment as a sharp sword, and
standing up filled all things with death,*" or else
it may be, He gave command to the Angels
His Ministers. God commandeth beforehand, that, when it cometh to pass, it may
be known "[3] that not by chance," nor by the
will of man, "nor without His judgment but
by the sentence of God" the blow came.

No more of thy name be sown, as Isaiah saith,
[4] *the seed of evildoers shall never be renowned.*
He prophesies, not the immediate but the
absolute cessation of the Assyrian line. If
the prophecy was uttered at the time of Sennacherib's invasion, seventeen years before
his death, not Esarhaddon only, but his son
Asshurbanipal also, whose career of personal
conquest, the last glory of the house of the
Sargonides and of the empire, began immediately upon his father's reign of thirteen
years, was probably already born. Asshurbanipal in this case would only have been
thirty-one, at the beginning of his energetic
reign, and would have died in his fifty-second
year. After him followed only an inglorious
twenty-two years. The prophet says, *the
Lord hath commanded.* The decree as to
Ahab's house was fulfilled in the person of
his second son, as to Jeroboam and Baasha
in their sons. It waited its appointed time,
but was fulfilled in the complete excision of
the doomed race.

*Out of the house of thy gods will I cut off
graven image and molten image*[5]; as thou hast
done to others[6], it shall be done to thee.
"[7] And when even the common objects of
worship of the Assyrian and Chaldean were

not spared, what would be the ruin of the
whole city!" So little shall thy gods help
thee, that "[8] there shalt thou be punished,
where thou hopest for aid. *Graven and molten image* shall be thy grave ; amid altar and
oblations, as thou worshipest idols," thanking
them for thy deliverance, "shall thy unholy
blood be shed," as it was by his sons Adrammelech and Sharezer[9]. *I will make* it [10] *thy
grave;* "[7] what God *maketh* remains immovable, cannot be changed. But He "maketh
thy grave" in hell, where not only that rich
man in the Gospel hath his grave; but all
who are or have been like him, and especially
thou, O Asshur, of whom it is written,
[11]*Asshur is there and all her company; his
graves are about him: all of them slain, fallen
by the sword. Whose graves are set in the sides
of the pit and her company is round about her
grave: all of them slain, fallen by the sword,
which caused terror in the land of the living.*
Graven and molten image, the idols which men
adore, the images of their vanity, the created
things which they worship instead of the
true God (as they *whose god is their belly*), in
which they busy themselves in this life, shall
be their destruction in the Day of Judgment.

For thou art vile. Thou honoredst thyself and dishonoredst God, so shalt thou be
dishonored [12], as He saith, [13] *Them that honor
Me I will honor, and they that despise Me shall
be lightly esteemed.* So when he had said to
Edom, [14] *thou art greatly despised,* he adds the
ground of it, [15] *The pride of thine heart hath
deceived thee. For thou art vile.* Great, honored, glorious as Assyria or its ruler were in
the eyes of men, the prophet tells him, what
he was in himself, being such in the eyes of
God, light, empty, as Daniel said to Belshazzar, [16] *Thou art weighed in the balances, and
found wanting,* of no account, vile [17].

15. *Behold upon the mountains, the feet of
him that bringeth good tidings, that publisheth
peace.* From mountain-top to mountain-top
by beacon-fires they spread the glad tidings.
Suddenly the deliverance comes, sudden its
announcement. *Behold!* Judah, before hin-

[1] Alb.   [2] Wisd. xviii. 15. 16.   [3] S. Jer.   [4] xiv. 20.

[5] פֶּסֶל וּמַסֵּכָה are so joined De. xxvii. 15. Jud.
xvii. 3, 4, xviii. 14.

[6] Is. xxxvii. 19.   [7] Rup.   [8] S. Jer.
[9] Is. xxxvii. 38.

[10] He does not use the word עָשָׂה "made," but
שִׂים "appointed" it, set it to be. "There I will
make thy grave." Jon. Even Ew. has "making
them thy grave."

[11] Ez. xxxii. 22, 23.   [12] From Dion.
[13] I Sam. ii. 30.   [14] Ob. 2.   [15] Ib. 3.   [16] Dan. v. 27.
[17] So in Job's confession of himself, xl. 4, which,

as addressed to God, can only be said of his
intrinsic worthlessness. It stands contrasted with
those whom God honors (אָכְבֵּד) 1 Sam. ii. 30; in
Hif. "held cheap" (2 Sam. xix. 44, Ez. xxii. 7.) put
to dishonor, Is. viii. 23. (contrasted with הכביד).
In Gen. xvi. 4. 5, it is added "in the eyes of"
another; it is used of a thing, 1 Sam. xviii. 23. 2
Kgs iii. 18. The physical sense "were lightened"
(of the waters of the deluge, Gen. viii. 11.) does not
authorize the interpretation of some, "art lessened
in number;" nor would this be a ground why God
should make its grave.

Before
C H R I S T
cir. 713.

† Heb. *feast*.

mountains the feet of him
that bringeth good tidings,
that publisheth peace! O
Judah, † keep thy solemn

feasts, perform thy vows:
for † ᵉ the wicked shall no
more pass through thee;
ᶠ he is utterly cut off.

Before
C H R I S T
cir. 713.

† Heb. *Belial*.
ᵉ ver. 11, 12.
ᶠ ver. 14.

dered by armies from going up to Jerusalem, its cities taken [1], may now again *keep the feasts* there, and *pay the vows*, which "in trouble she promised;" *for the wicked* one, the ungodly Sennacherib, *is utterly cut off, he shall no more pass through thee;* "the army and king and empire of the Assyrians have perished." But the words of prophecy cannot be bound down to this. These large promises, which, as to this world, were forfeited in the next reign, when Manasseh was taken captive to Babylon, and still more in the seventy years' captivity, and more yet in that until now, look for a fulfillment, as they stand. They sound so absolute. "I will afflict thee *no more*," "the wicked shall *no more* pass through thee," "he is utterly (lit. *the whole of him*) cut off." Nahum joins on this signal complete deliverance from a temporal enemy, to the final deliverance of the people of God. The invasion of Sennacherib was an avowed conflict with God Himself. It was a defiance of God. He would make God's people, his; he would *cut it off, that it be no more a people, and that the name of Israel may be no more in remembrance* [2]. There was a more "evil counsellor" behind, whose agent was Sennacherib. He, as he is the author of all murders and strife, so has he a special hatred for the Church, whether before or since Christ's Coming. Before, that he might cut off that Line from whom *the Seed of the woman* should be born, which should destroy his empire and crush himself, and that he might devour the Child who was to be born [3]. Since, because her members are his freed captives, and she makes inroads on his kingdom, and he hates them because he hates God and Christ Who dwells in them. As the time of the birth of our Lord neared, his hate became more concentrated. God overruled the hatred of Edom or Moab, or the pride of Assyria, to His own ends, to preserve Israel by chastising it. Their hatred was from the evil one, because it was God's people, the seed of Abraham, the tribe of Judah, the line of David. If they could be cut off, they of whom Christ was to be born according to the flesh, and so, in all seeming, the hope of the world, were gone. Sennacherib then was not a picture only, he was the agent of Satan, who used his hands, feet, tongue, to blaspheme God and war against His people. As then we have respect not to the mere agent, but

to the principal, and should address him through those he employed (as Elisha said of the messenger who came to slay him, [4] *is not the sound of his master's feet behind him?*), so the Prophet's words chiefly and most fully go to the instigator of Sennacherib, whose very name he names, *Belial*. It is the deliverance of the Church and the people of God which he foretells, and thanks God for. To the Church he says in the Name of God, *Though I have afflicted thee, I will afflict thee* no more [5]. The *yoke* which He will burst is the yoke of *the* oppressor, of which Isaiah speaks, and which the Son, to be born of a Virgin, "the Mighty God, the Prince of Peace," was to *break* [6]; the yoke of sin and the bands of fleshly pleasure and evil habits, wherewith we were held captive, so that henceforth we should walk upright, unbowed, look up to heaven our home, and *run the way of Thy commandments when Thou hast set my heart at liberty*. Behold, then, *upon the mountains*, i. e. above all the height of this world, *the feet of him that bringeth good tidings*, i. e. of remission of sins and sanctification by the Spirit and the freedom and adoption as sons, and the casting out of the Prince of this world, *that publisheth peace. O Judah*, thou, the true people of God, *keep thy solemn feasts*, the substance of the figures of the law." "[7] He who is ever engaged on the words, deeds and thoughts of Him, Who is by nature Lord, the Word of God, ever liveth in His days, ever keepeth Lord's days. Yea he who ever prepareth himself for the true life and abstaineth from the sweets of this life which deceive the many, and who cherisheth not the mind of the flesh but chastens the body and enslaves it, is ever keeping the days of preparation. He too who thinketh that Christ our Passover was sacrificed for us, and that we must keep festival, eating the flesh of the Word, hath no time when he keepeth not the Passover, ever passing over in thought and every word and deed from the affairs of this life to God, and hasting to His city. Moreover whoso can say truthfully, *we have risen together with Christ*, yea and also, *He hath together raised us and together seated us in the heavenly places in Christ*, ever liveth in the days of Pentecost; and chiefly, when, going up into the upper room as the Apostles of Jesus, he giveth himself to supplication and prayer, that he may become meet for the rushing mighty wind

[1] 2 Kings xviii. 13.   [2] Ps. lxxxiii. 4.
[3] Rev. xii. 4.

[4] 2 Kings vi. 32.   [5] v. 12.   [6] ix. 4. and 6.
[7] Orig. c. Cels. viii. n. 22.

Before
CHRIST
cir. 713.

CHAPTER II.

1 *The fearful and victorious armies of God against Nineveh.*

H E ‖ ᵃ that dasheth in pieces is come up before thy face: ᵇ keep the

Before
CHRIST
cir. 713.

‖ Or, *The dis-
perser,* or,
hammer.

ᵃ Jer. 50. 23.   ᵇ Jer. 51. 11, 12. ch. 3. 14.

from heaven, which mightily effaceth the evil in men and its fruits, meet too for some portion of the fiery tongue from God." " ¹ Such an one will keep the feast excellently, having the faith in Christ fixed, hallowed by the Spirit, glorious with the grace of adoption. And he will offer to God spiritual sacrifice, consecrating himself for an odor of sweetness, cultivating also every kind of virtue, temperance, continence, fortitude, endurance, charity, hope, love of the poor, goodness, longsuffering : for *with such sacrifices God is well pleased.* Every power of the enemy, which before had dominion over him, *shall pass through no more,* since Christ commanded the unclean spirits to depart into the abyss and giveth to those who love Him power to resist the enemy, and subdue the passions, and destroy sin and *tread on serpents and scorpions and every power of the enemy."* And these feasts were to be kept "² in the spirit not in the letter. For what availeth it to keep any feast without, unless there be the feast of contemplation in the soul ? " Wherefore he adds, *and pay thy vows,* i. e. thyself, whom in Baptism thou hast vowed : *for the Wicked One shall no more pass through thee.* "² For from what time, O Judah, Christ, by dying and rising again, hallowed *thy feasts,* he can *no longer pass through thee.* Thenceforth he perished wholly. Not that he has, in substance, ceased to be, but that the death of the human race, which through his envy came into this world, the two-fold death of body and soul, wholly perisheth. Where and when did this Belial perish ? When died the death which he brought in, whence himself also is called Death ? When Christ died, then died the death of our souls ; and when Christ rose again, then perished the death of our bodies. When then, *O Judah* thou *keepest thy feasts,* remember that thy very feast is He, of Whom thou sayest that by dying He conquered death and by rising He restored life. Hence it is said, *Belial shall no more pass through thee.* For if thou look to that alone, that Sennacherib departed, to return no more, and perished, it would not be true to say, Belial hath wholly perished ! For after him many a Belial, such as he was, passed through thee, and hurt thee far more. Perchance thou sayest, ' so long as Nineveh standest, how sayest thou, that Belial has wholly perished ? So long as the world standeth, how shall I be comforted, that death hath perished ? For lo ! persecutors armed with death have stormed, and besides

them, many sons of Belial, of whom Anti-Christ will be the worst. How then sayest thou, that Belial has wholly perished ?' It follows, *the Scatterer hath gone up before thee.* To Judah in the flesh, Nebuchadnezzar who went up against Nineveh, was worse than Sennacherib. Who then is He Who went up before thee, and dispersed the world, that great Nineveh, that thou shouldest have full consolation ? Christ who descended, Himself ascended ; and as He ascended, so shall He come to *disperse* Nineveh, i. e. to judge the world. What any persecutor doth meanwhile, yea or the Devil himself or Anti-Christ, hath been eading from the truth, that Belial hath *wholly perished. The prince of this world is cast out.* For nothing which they do, or can do, hinders, that both deaths of body and soul are swallowed up in *His* victory, Who hath ascended to heaven ? Belial cannot in the members kill the soul, which hath been made alive by the death of the Head, i. e. Christ; and as to the death of the body, so certain is it that it will perish, that thou mayest say fearlessly that it hath perished, since Christ the Head hath risen." Each fall of an enemy of the Church, each recovery of a sinful soul being a part of this victory, the words may be applied to each. The Church or the soul are bidden to *keep the feast* and *pay their* vows, whatever in their trouble they promised to God. " ³ It is said to souls, which confess the Lord, that the devil who, before, wasted thee and bowed thee with that most heavy yoke hath, in and with the idols which thou madest for thyself, perished; *keep thy feasts* and *pay* to God *thy vows,* singing with the Angels continually, for *no more shall Belial pass through thee,* of whom the Apostle too saith, *What concord hath Christ with Belial ?* The words too, *Behold upon the mountains* the feet of him that bringeth good tidings, that publisheth peace" belong, in a degree, to all preachers of the Gospel. " ⁴ No one can preach peace, who is himself below and cleaveth to earthly things. For wars are for the good things of earth. If thou wouldest preach peace to thyself and thy neighbor, be raised above the earth and its goods, riches and glory. Ascend to the heavenly mountains, whence David also, lifting up his eyes, hoped that his help would come."

C. II. The Prophet, having foretold the destruction of Sennacherib, and in him how the enemy of Judah is wholly cut off, goes on to describe the destruction of Nineveh, and

¹ S. Cyr.   ² Rup.   ³ S. Jer.   ⁴ Theoph.

Before CHRIST cir. 713. munition, watch the way, make *thy* loins strong, fortify *thy* power mightily.

c Isa. 10. 12. Jer. 25. 29.
‖ Or, *the pride of Jacob as the pride of Israel.*

2 c For the LORD hath turned away ‖ the excellency of Jacob, as the excellency of Israel: for d the emptiers have e m p t i e d them out, and marred their vine branches.

Before CHRIST cir. 713.

d Ps. 80. 12. Hos. 10. 1.

---

with it of his whole kingdom, and, under it, of Anti-Christ and Satan.

1. *He that dasheth in pieces*, rather, *the Disperser*[1], the instrument of God, whereby he should *break her in pieces like a potter's vessel*, or *should scatter* her in all lands, *is come up against thy face*, O Nineveh, i. e. either, *over against thee*[2], confronting her as it were, face to face, or directed *against thee*[3]. From the description of the peace of Judah, the Prophet turns suddenly to her oppressor, to whom, not to Judah, the rest of the prophecy is directed. Jacob and Israel are spoken *of*, not *to*[4]. The destroyer of Nineveh *went up against the face of Nineveh*, not in the presence of Judah and Jacob, who were far away and knew nothing of it. *Keep the munition.* While all in Judah is now peace, all in Nineveh is tumult. God Whom they had defied, saying that Hezekiah could not [5] *turn away the face of one captain of the least of* his *servants*, now bids them prepare to meet him whom He would send against them. *Gird up thy loins now, like a man*[6]. Thou who wouldest lay waste others, now, if thou canst, keep thyself. The strength of the words is the measure of the irony. They had challenged God; He in turn challenges them to put forth all their might.

Fence thy defences[7], we might say. Their strong walls, high though they were, unassailable by any then known skill of besiegers, would not be secure.

The prophet uses a kindred and allusive word, that their protection needed to be itself protected ; and this, by one continued watchfulness. *Watch*, he adds, *the way :* espy out [8] (as far as thou canst), the coming of the enemy ; *strengthen the loins*, the seat of strength[9]. Elsewhere they are said to be *girded up* for

any exertion. *Fortify thy strength exceedingly.* The expression is rare[10] : commonly it is said of some part of the human frame, knees, arms, or mind, or of man by God.

The same words are strong mockery to those who resist God, good counsel to those who trust in God. *Keep the munition, for He Who keepeth thee will not sleep* [11] ; *watch the way*, by which the enemy may approach from afar, for Satan approacheth, sometimes suddenly, sometimes very stealthily and subtly, *transforming himself into an angel of light.* "[12] *Watch* also *the way* by which thou art to go, as it is said, [13] *Stand ye in the ways, and see, and ask for the old paths, where is the good way, and walk therein ;* so that, having stood in many ways, we may come to that Way which saith, *I am the Way.*" Then [14], *make thy loins strong*, as the Saviour commandeth His disciples, *Let your loins be girded about*[15], and the Apostle says, [16] *Stand therefore, having your loins girt about with truth ;* for nothing so strengtheneth as the Truth. For Christ being the Truth, whoso with his whole heart hath believed in Christ, is strong against himself, and hath power over the loins, the seat of the passions. Then, since this warfare is hard, he adds, be strong, *fortify thy power mightily ;* resist not listlessly, but vehemently ; and that, in His strength Who hath strengthened our nature, taking it to Himself and uniting it with the Godhead. For without Him, strong though thou be, thou wilt avail nothing.

2. *For the Lord hath turned away* (rather *restoreth*) *the excellency of Jacob*, speaking of what should come, as already come. For Nineveh falls, because God restores His people, whom it had oppressed. The restoration of God's favor to His Church is the sea-

---

1 מֵפִיץ is a partic. used as a proper name. מֵפִיץ is indeed used as a noun=מַפֵּץ as united with the *sword* and arrow, and so an instrument of war, *battle axe* or the like (Prov. xxv. 18.), like מַפֵּץ (Jer. li. 20.), used of Nebuchadnezzar by God. Yet the like phrase עָלָה הַפָּרִץ (Mic. ii. 13.) and the use itself of עָלָה, "went up," make it probable that an agent is meant. הַפִּיץ is always "dispersed ;" the sense, "broke in pieces," occurs only in פּוֹצֵץ Jer. xxiii. 29, פַּצֵּץ Job. xvi. 12, הַתְפּוֹצֵץ Hab. iii. 6, תְּפוֹצוֹתִיכֶם Jer. xxv. 34, and in נֶפֶץ, נָפֵץ.

2 As Gen. xxxii. 22, תַעֲבֹר עַל פָּנָיו ; Job iv. 15, רוּחַ עַל פָּנַי יַחֲלֹף.

3 As Ps. xxi. 13, תְּכוֹנֵן עַל פְּנֵיהֶם which is supported by the use of עָלָה עַל, "went up against," as 2 Kgs xvii. 3, xviii. 25, Jo. i. 6.
4 ver. 2. Jon., Rashi, Kim., Abarb. would have it, that Judah is addressed.
5 Is. xxxvi. 9.
6 Job. xl. 7.
7 נָצוֹר מִצֻּרָה The Imp. נָצוֹר would have expressed a simple command ; the Infin. says, what has to be done.
8 צָפָה.
9 The use of the adj. אַמֵּץ "strong" Dan. vii. 7, shows that the meaning of the root was not lost, though occurring only in the adj. and מָתְנַיִם.
10 It occurs Prov. xxiv. 5, of the man of understanding, and Am. ii. 14, of what man cannot do.
11 Ps. cxxi. 3.   12 S. Jer.   13 Jer. vi. 16.
14 From S. Jer.   15 Luke xii. 35.   16 Eph. vi. 14.

Before
CHRIST
cir. 713.

3 The shield of his mighty men is made ᵉred, the valiant men *are* || in scarlet : the chariots *shall be* with || flaming torches in the day of his prepara-

ᵉ Isa. 63. 2, 3.
|| Or, *dyed scarlet.*

|| Or, *fiery torches.*

tion, and the fir trees shall be terribly shaken.

4 The chariots shall rage in the streets, they shall justle one against another in the broad ways :

Before
CHRIST
cir. 713.

---

son of His punishment of their enemies ; as, again, His displeasure against her enemies is a token of His favor to her. When Herod was smitten by God, [1] *the word of God grew and multiplied.* A long captivity was still before Judah, yet the destruction of the Assyrian was the earnest that every *oppressing city* should *cease* [2].

The excellency of Jacob. The word, *excellency,* is used in a good or bad sense ; bad, if man takes the excellency to himself ; good, as given by God. This is decisive against a modern popular rendering ; "[3] *has returned to* the excellency of Jacob ; " for Scripture knows of no *excellency of Jacob,* except God Himself or grace from God. Jacob, if separated from God or left by Him, has no excellency, to which God could return.

As the excellency of Israel. Both the ten and the two tribes had suffered by the Assyrian. The ten had been carried captive by Shalmanezer, the two had been harassed by Sennacherib. After the captivity of the ten tribes, the name Jacob is used of Judah only. It may be then, that the restoration of God's favor is promised to each separately. Or, [4] there may be an emphasis in the names themselves. Their forefather bore the name of *Jacob* in his troubled days of exile ; that of *Israel* was given him on his return [5]. It would then mean, that the afflicted people (Jacob) shall be restored to its utmost glory as Israel. The sense is the same.

For the emptiers have emptied them out. Their chastisement is the channel of their restoration. Unlike the world, their emptiness is their fullness, as the fullness of the world is its emptiness. The world is cast down, not to arise ; for [6] *woe to him that is alone when he falleth : for he hath not another to help him up.* The Church *falleth,* but *to arise* [7] : the people is restored, because it had borne chastening [8] ; *for the Lord hath restored the excellency of Jacob ;*

for the emptiers have emptied them out and marred their vinebranches [9], i. e. its fruit-bearing branches, that, as far as in them lay, it should not bear fruit unto God ; but to cut the vine is, by God's grace, to make it shoot forth and bear fruit more abundantly.

3, 4. Army is arrayed against army ; the armies, thus far, of God against the army of His enemy ; all without is order ; all within, confusion. The assailing army, from its compactness and unity, is spoken of, both as many and one. The might is of many ; the order and singleness of purpose is as of one. *The shield,* collectively, not *shields. His mighty men ;* He, who was last spoken of, was Almighty God, as He says in Isaiah ; [10] *I have commanded My consecrated ones ; I have also called My mighty ones, them that rejoice in My highness.*

Is reddened, either with blood of the Assyrians, shed in some previous battle, before the siege began, or (which is the meaning of the word elsewhere [11]), an artificial color, the color of blood being chosen, as expressive of fiery fierceness. *The valiant men are in scarlet ;* for beauty and terror, as, again being the color of blood [12]. It was especially the color of the dress of their nobles [13], one chief color of the Median dress, from whom the Persians adopted their's [14]. *The chariots shall be with flaming torches,* literally *with the fire of steels* [15], or of sharp incisive instruments. Either way the words seem to indicate that the chariots were in some way armed with steel. For steel was not an ornament, nor do the chariots appear to have been ornamented with metal. Iron would have hindered the primary object of lightness and speed. Steel, as distinct from iron, is made only for incisiveness. In either way, it is probable, that scythed chariots were already in use. Against such generals, as the younger Cyrus [16] and Alexander [17], they were of no avail ; but they

---

1 Acts xii. 24.　　　　　2 Is. xxxiii. 1.
3 See ab. Intr. p. 127. n. 8.
4 Sanct.　　　　　　　5 Gen. xxxii. 28.
6 Eccles. iv. 10.　　　　7 Micah vii. 8.
8 Ez. xxxvi. 3, 6, 7.　　9 See Ps. lxxx. 12, 13.
10 Is. xiii. 3.
11 The form מָאְדָּם is used five times in Exodus of the artificial color of the dyed ramskins. But there is no proof of any such custom as to the shields. If reddened by actual blood, it must have been in a previous battle, since Nahum is thus far describing the preparations, בְּיוֹם הֲכִינוֹ. The gleaming of the brass of the shields in the sun

(1 Macc. vi. 39) could hardly be called *their* being reddened.
12 Ælian V. H. vi. 6. Val. Max. ii. 6. 2.
13 Xenophon (Cyrop. viii. 3. 3) implies that they were costly treasures which Cyrus distributed.
14 Strabo xi. 13. 9.
15 On פְּלָדוֹת see Introd. pp. 127–129.
16 At Cunaxa, Xen. Anab. i. 8.
17 At Arbela, Arr. iii. 13, Q. Curt. iv. 51, and, upon experience, by Eumenes, "haud ignarus pugnæ," Liv. xxxvii. 41, Appian Syr. 33. Diodorus (xvii. 58.) describes their terrible vehemence, when not evaded. Uneven ground naturally disordered them. Tac. Agr. c. 36. Vegetius iii. 24.

Before
C H R I S T
cir. 713.

† Heb. *their
show.*

‖ Or, *gallants.*

†they s h a l l seem like torches, they shall run like the lightnings.

5 He shall recount his ‖ w o r t h i e s: they shall

stumble in t h e i r walk; they shall make haste to the wall thereof, and the †defence s h a l l be pre-pared.

Before
C H R I S T
cir. 713.

† Heb. *covering,
or, coverer.*

must have been terrific instruments against undisciplined armies. The rush and noise of the British chariots disturbed for a time even Cæsar's Roman troops[1]. They were probably in use long before.[2] Their use among the ancient Britons[3], Gauls[4] and Belgians[5], as also probably among the Canaanites[6], evinces that they existed among very rude people. The objection that the Assyrian chariots are not represented in the monuments as armed with scythes is an oversight, since those spoken of by Nahum may have been Median, certainly were not Assyrian. *In the day of His preparation*[7], when He mustereth the hosts for the battle; *and the fir-trees shall be terribly shaken ;* i. e. fir-spears[8] (the weapon being often named from the wood of which it is made) shall be made to quiver through the force wherewith they shall be hurled.

The chariots shall rage (or *madden*[9], as the driving of Jehu is said to be *furiously,* lit. *in madness*) *in the streets.* The city is not yet taken; so, since this takes place *in the streets* and *broad ways,* they are the confused preparations of the besieged. *They shall justle one against another,* shall run rapidly to and fro, restlessly ; *their show* (*E. M.*) is *like torches,* leaving streaks of fire, as they pass rapidly along. *They shall run* vehemently[10], *like the lightnings,* swift but vanishing.

5. *He shall recount his worthies.* The Assyrian king wakes as out of a sleep, lit. " he *remembers* his mighty men[11] ; " *they stumble in their*

walk, lit. *paths*[12], not through haste only and eager fear, but from want of inward might and the aid of God. Those whom God leadeth stumble not[13]. "[14] Perplexed every way and not knowing what they ought to do, their mind wholly darkened and almost drunken with ills, they reel to and fro, turn from one thing to another, and in all " labor in vain.

They shall make haste to the walls thereof, and the defence (lit. *the covering*) *shall be prepared.* The Assyrian monuments leave no doubt that a Jewish writer[15] is right in the main, in describing this as a covered shelter, under which an enemy approached the city; "a covering of planks with skins upon them ; under it those who fight against the city come to the wall and mine the wall underneath, and it is a shield over them from the stones, which are cast from off the wall."

The monuments, however, exhibit this shelter, as connected not with mining but with a battering ram, mostly with a sharp point, by which they loosened the walls[16]. Another covert was employed to protect single miners who picked out single stones with a pick-axe[17]. The Assyrians sculptures shew, in the means employed against or in defence of their engines, how central a part of the siege they formed[18]. Seven of them are represented in one siege[19]. The " ram[20] " is mentioned in Ezekiel as the well-known and ordinary instrument of a siege.

[1] De bell. Gall. iv. 33, 34.
[2] Ctesias, who speaks of them as long prior (quoted by Diod. Sic. ii. 5.) is, on Persian matters, much better authority than Xenophon who (Cyrop. vi. 1. as explained by Arrian, Tactic. c. 3.) attributes their invention to Cyrus. For Xenophon, who was a good witness as to what he saw, shews himself ignorant of the previous history (See ab. p. 123). He himself quotes Ctesias as an authority (Anab. i. 8.). The exaggerations of Ctesias are probably those of his Persian informants.
[3] Sil. Ital. viii. 417, 418. Tac. Agric. 35, 36. Mela iii. 6. Jornandes de reb. Goth. c. 2.
[4] Mela iii. 6.
[5] Lucan i. 426. S. Jerome in Is. ult.
[6] The use of a little iron, more or less, in strengthening the wheels &c., could hardly entitle them to be called "chariots of iron." Jos. xvii. 16, 18. Jud. i. 19, iv. 3, 13.
[7] רכב as in Jer. xlvi. 14, Ez. vii. 14, xxxviii. 7.
[8] See on Hos. xiv. 8. vol. i. p. 140.
[9] The words are adopted by Jeremiah xlvi. 9.
[10] רצץ Intensive from רוץ.
[11] As iii. 18. Jud. v. 13. Neh. iii. 5.
[12] So the Heb. text. Their many ways may be opposed to the oneness of the army of God (See v. 3).
[13] Is. lxiii. 13.   [14] S. Cyr.   [15] Kimchi.

[16] See in Rawlinson's 5 Empires ii. 78. "All of them [the battering-rams] were covered with a frame-work of ozier, wood, felt, or skins, for the better protection of those who worked the implement;—some appear to have been stationary, others in early times had six wheels, in the later times four only. Sometimes with the ram and its framework was a moveable tower, containing soldiers, who, at once, fought the enemy on a level and protected the engine."
[17] See picture in Rawl. 5 Emp. ii. 82.
[18] " Fire was the weapon usually turned against the ram, torches, burning tow or other inflammable substances being cast from the walls upon its framework." To prevent this [its being set on fire], the workers of the ram were sometimes provided with a supply of water; sometimes they suspended from a pole in front of their engine, a curtain of leather, or some other non-inflammable substance. In a bas-relief (Layard's *Monuments,* Series ii. Pl. 21.) where an enormous number of torches are seen in the air, every battering-ram is so protected. Or the besieged sought to catch the point of the ram by a chain, drawing it upwards; the besieger with metal hooks to keep it down." from Rawl. Ib. pp. 79, 80, referring further to Layard's *Monuments,* Series i. Pl. 17, 19.
[19] Ib. p. 79.   [20] Ezek. iv. 2.

6 The gates of the rivers shall be opened, and the palace shall be ‖ dissolved.

7 And ‖ Huzzab shall be ‖ led away captive, she shall be brought up, and

Before
C H R I S T
cir. 713.

‖ Or, that which was established,
‖ Or, discovered. or, there was a stand made.

Thus v. 3. describes the attack ; v. 4, the defence ; the two first clauses of v. 5, the defence ; the two last, the attack. This quick interchange only makes the whole more vivid.

" [1] But what availeth it to build the house, unless the Lord build it? What helpeth it to shut the gates, which the Lord unbarreth?" On both sides is put forth the full strength of man; there seems a stand-still to see, what will be, and God brings to pass His own work in His own way.

6. *The gates of the rivers shall be opened, and the palace shall be dissolved.* All gives way in an instant at the will of God; the strife is hushed; no more is said of war and death; there is no more resistance or bloodshed; no sound except the wailing of the captives, the flight of those who can escape, while the conquerors empty it of the spoil, and then she is left a waste. The swelling of the river and the opening made by it may have given rise to the traditional account of Ctesias, although obviously exaggerated as to the destruction of the wall. The exaggerated character of that tradition is not inconsistent with, it rather implies, a basis of truth. It is inconceivable that it should have been thought, that walls, of the thickness which Ctesias had described, were overthrown by the swelling of any river, unless some such event as Ctesias relates, that the siege was ended by an entrance afforded to the enemy through some bursting-in of the river, had been true. Nahum speaks nothing of the wall, but simply of the opening of *the gates of the rivers*, obviously the gates, by which the inhabitants could have access to the rivers [2], which otherwise would be useless to them except as a wall. These *rivers* correspond to the *rivers*, the artificial divisions of the Nile, by which No or Thebes was defended, or [3] *the rivers of Babylon* which yet was washed by the one stream, the Euphrates. But Nineveh was surrounded and

guarded by actual rivers, the Tigris and the Khausser, and, (assuming those larger dimensions of Nineveh, which are supported by evidences so various [4]) the greater Zab, which was "called [5] the frantic Zab' on account of the violence of its current." "The Zab contained (says Ainsworth [6]), when we saw it, a larger body of water than the Tigris, whose tributaries are not supplied by so many snow-mountains as those of the Zab." Of these, if the Tigris be now on a level lower than the ruins of Nineveh, it may not have been so formerly. The Khausser, in its natural direction, ran through Nineveh where, now as of old, it turns a mill, and must, of necessity, have been fenced by *gates*; else any invader might enter at will; as, in modern times, Mosul has its "gate of the bridge." A break in these would obviously let in an enemy, and might the more paralyze the inhabitants, if they had any tradition, that the river alone could or would be their enemy, as Nahum himself prophesied. Subsequently inaccuracy or exaggeration might easily represent this to be an overthrow of the walls themselves. It was all one, in which way the breach was made.

The palace shall be dissolved. The prophet unites the beginning and the end. The river-gates were opened ; what had been the fence against the enemy became an entrance for them : with the river, there poured in also the tide of the people of the enemy. *The palace*, then, the imperial abode, the centre of the empire, embellished with the history of its triumphs, sank, was *dissolved* [7], and ceased to be. It is not a physical loosening of the sun-dried bricks by the stream which would usually flow harmless by ; but the dissolution of the empire itself. " [1] The temple i. e. his kingdom was destroyed." The palaces both of Khorsabad and Kouyunjik lay near the Khausser [8] and both bear the marks of fire [9].

7. The first word should be rendered, *And*

---

[1] S. Jer.
[2] Such explanations as "gates whereby the enemy poured in as rivers" (Ros.), or "gates of Nineveh which was guarded by rivers" (Ew.) or "of the streets, where the inhabitants surged like rivers" (Hitz.) are plainly not literal.
[3] Ps. cxxxvii. 1.
[4] See Introd. to Jonah, vol. i.
[5] Kaswini, quoted by Tuch p. 35.
[6] Ainsw. Tr. ii. 327.
[7] The word, which occurs 18 times, is used of the melting of the earth at the voice or presence or touch of God, Ps. xlvi. 7, Nah. i. 5, Am. ix. 5; of the "melting away" of a multitude, 1 Sam. xiv. 16; of all Philistia, Is. xiv. 31; (act.) of God working the dissolution of one being, Job xxx. 22, or of many,

Is. lxiv. 6; of the hearts of people, melting for fear, Ex. xv. 15, Jos. ii. 9, 24, Ps. lxxv. 4, cvii. 26. Jer. xlix. 23, Ez. xxi. 20 : once only it is used physically of water, of the clods softened by showers, Ps. lxv. 11; and in the ideal image "the hills shall melt," being dissolved, as it were, in the rich stream of the abundant vintage. Am. ix. 13.
[8] See Introduction to Jonah, vol. i. Asshurbanipal, the last great monarch of Assyria, built his palace on the mound of Kouyunjik. (Rawl. 5 Emp. ii. 496). "The Khosr-su, which runs on this side of the Khorsabad ruins, often overflows its banks, and pours its waters against the palace-mound. The gaps, N. and S. of the mound, may have been caused by its violence." Ib. i. 358.
[9] See ab. p. 122 n. c.

Before
C H R I S T
cir. 713.

f Isa. 38. 14.
& 59. 11.
‖ Or, *from the
days* that she
hath been.

‖ Or, *cause* them
to turn.

her maids shall lead *her* as
with the voice of ᶠ doves,
tabering upon their breasts.

8 But Nineveh *is* ‖ of
old like a pool of water:
yet they shall flee away.
Stand, stand, *shall they cry;*
but none shall ‖ look back.

9 Take ye the spoil of

silver, take the spoil of
gold: ‖ for *there is* none
end of the store *and* glory
out of all the † pleasant
furniture.

10 She is empty, and
void, and waste: and the
ᵍ heart melteth, and ʰ the
knees smite together, ⁱ and

Before
C H R I S T
cir. 713.

‖ Or, *and* their
infinite store,
&c.
† Heb. *vessels of*
desire.

ᵍ Isa. 13. 7.
ʰ Dan. 5. 6.
ⁱ Jer. 30. 6.

---

it is decreed ; She shall be laid bare. It is de-
creed[1]. All this took place, otherwise than
man would have thought, because it was the
will of God. *She* (the people of the city,
under the figure of a captive woman) *shall be*
laid bare[2], in shame, to her reproach; *she*
shall be brought up[3], to judgment, or from
Nineveh as being now sunk low and depressed; *and her maids,* the lesser cities, as
female attendants on the royal city, and their
inhabitants represented as women, both as
put to shame and for weakness. The whole
empire of Nineveh was overthrown by Nebopalassar. Yet neither was the special
shame wanting, that the noble matrons and
virgins were so led captives in shame and
sorrow. They *shall lead her, as with the voice*
of doves, moaning, yet, for fear, with a subdued voice.

8. *But Nineveh is of old like a pool of water*
i. e. of many peoples[4], gathered from all quarters and settled there, her multitudes being
like the countless drops, full, untroubled,
with no ebb or flow, fenced in, *from the days*
that she hath been, yet even therefore stagnant
and corrupted[5], not "a fountain of living
waters," during 600 years of unbroken empire; even lately it had been assailed in
vain[6]; now its hour was come, the sluices
were broken; the waters poured out. It was
full not of citizens only, but of other nations
poured into it. An old historian says[7],
"The chief and most powerful of those whom
Ninus settled there, were the Assyrians, but
also, of other nations, whoever willed." Thus
the pool was filled; but at the rebuke of the
Lord they flee. *Stand, stand,* the Prophet
speaks in the name of the widowed city;
"shut the gates, go up on the walls, resist the
enemy, gather yourselves together, form a

band to withstand," *but none shall look back* to
the mother-city which calls them; all is forgotten, except their fear; parents, wives,
children, the wealth which is plundered,
home, worldly repute. So will men leave all
things, for the life of this world. [8] *All that a*
man hath, will he give for his life. Why not for
the life to come?

9. *Take ye the spoil of silver, take the spoil of*
gold. Nineveh had not hearkened of old to
the voice of the Prophet, but had turned
back to sin; it cannot hearken now, for fear.
He turns to the spoiler to whom God's judgments assigned her, and who is too ready to
hear. The gold and silver, which the last
Assyrian King had gathered into the palace
which he fired, was mostly removed (the
story says, treacherously) to Babylon. Ar-
baces is said to have borne this and to have
removed the residue, to the amount of many
talents, to Agbatana, the Median capital[9].
For there is none end of the store. Nineveh
had stored up from her foundation until then,
but at last for the spoiler. [10] *When thou shalt*
cease to spoil, thou shalt be spoiled. Many [11]
perish and leave their wealth to others. [12] *The*
wealth of the sinner is laid up for the just. And
glory out of all the pleasant furniture, [lit. as in
the Margin, "glory out of all vessels of desire"] i. e. however large the spoil, it would
be but a portion only; yet all their wealth,
though a more than enough for the enemy and
for them, could not save them. Her "glory,"
was but a "weight" to weigh her down, that
she should not rise again[13]. Their wealth
brought on the day of calamity, availed not
therein, although it could not be drawn dry
even by the spoiler. "[14] They could not spoil
so much as she supplied to be spoiled."

10. *She is empty and void and waste.* The

---

¹ This is the simple rendering of הֻצַּב, Hof. of
נָצַב. In Ch. יַצִּיב, "firm," Dan. vi. 13; "reliable,"
Dan. ii. 45, vii. 16; יַצִּיבָא "certainly," Dan. iii. 24,
מִן־יַצִּיב "of a certainty," Dan. ii. 8. Also in Phœn.;
Ges. Thes. p. 66. The retention of Huzzab as a
proper name for the queen, is derived from R.
Samuel Hannagid in Ibn Ezra. The ground for
this, alleged in Rashi, viz. the use of נָצְבָה Ps. xlv.
10, betrays its origin. Kimchi, with the same
etymology, explains it of the palace.

² The meaning of גֻּלְּתָה (*ăπ.*) is determined by
that of the active גָּלָה, which is always "laid bare,"
not "carried captive."
³ As in c. iii. 5. Is. xlvii. 2, 3.
⁴ Rev. xvii. 1.   ⁵ See Jer. xlviii. 11.
⁶ By Cyaxares Her. i. 106.
⁷ Ctesias ap. Diod. ii. 3.   ⁸ Job ii. 4.
⁹ Diod. Sic. ii. 28.   ¹⁰ Is. xxxiii. 1.
¹¹ Ps. xlix. 10.   ¹² Pr. xiii. 22.
¹³ Zech. v. 8. Ex. xv. 10.   ¹⁴ S. Jer.

much pain *is* in all loins,
and [k] the faces of them all
gather blackness.

[k] Joel 2. 6.

11 Where *is* the dwell-
ing of [l] the lions, and the
feedingplace of the young
lions, where the lion *even*
the old lion, walked, *and*
the lion's whelp, and none
made *them* afraid?

[l] Job 4. 10, 11.
Ezek. 19. 2–7.

12 The lion did tear in
pieces e n o u g h f o r his
whelps, and strangled for
his lionesses, and filled his
holes with prey, and his
dens with ravin.

13 [m] B e h o l d, I *a m*
a g a i n s t thee, saith the
LORD of hosts, and I will
burn her chariots in the

[m] Ezek. 29. 3.
& 38. 3. & 39.
1 ch. 3. 5.

---

completeness of her judgment is declared first
under that solemn number, Three, and the
three words in Hebrew are nearly the same [1],
with the same meaning, only each word
fuller than the former, as picturing a growing
desolation; and then under four heads (in all
seven) also a growing fear. First *the heart*,
the seat of courage and resolve and high purpose, *melteth;* then *the knees smite together*,
tremble, shake, under the frame; then, *much
pain is in all loins*, lit. "strong pains as of a
woman in travail," writhing and doubling the
whole body, and making it wholly powerless
and unable to stand upright, shall bow the
very loins, the seat of strength [2], *and*, lastly,
the faces of them all gather blackness [3], the fruit
of extreme pain, and the token of approaching dissolution.

11. *Where is the dwelling of the lions, and the
feeding place of the young lions?* Great indeed
must be the desolation, which should call
forth the wonder of the prophet of God. He
asks "where is it?" For so utterly was Nineveh to be effaced, that its place should scarcely
be known, and now is known by the ruins
which have been buried, and are dug up. The
messengers of her king had asked, [4] *Where
are the gods of Hamath and of Arpad? of Sepharvaim, Hena, and Ivah?* And now of her it
is asked, "Where is Nineveh?" It had *destroyed utterly all lands*, and now itself is utterly
destroyed. The lion dwelt, fed, walked there,
up and down, at will; all was spacious and
secure; he terrified all, and none terrified
him; he tore, strangled, laid up, as he willed,
booty in store; but when he had filled it to
the full, he filled up also the measure of his
iniquities, and his sentence came from God.
Nineveh had set at nought all human power,
and destroyed it; now, therefore, God appeareth in His own Person.

13. *Behold I*, Myself, *am against thee* [lit.

toward thee]. God, in His long-suffering, had,
as it were, looked away from him; now He
looked toward [5] him, and in His sight what
wicked one should stand? *Saith the Lord of
hosts*, Whose power is infinite and He changeth not, and all the armies of heaven, the
holy angels and evil spirits and men are in
His Hand, whereto He directs or overrules
them. *And I will burn her chariots in the
smoke.* The Assyrian sculptures attest how
greatly their pride and strength lay in their
chariots. They exhibit the minute embel-
lishment of the chariots and horses [6]. Almost inconceivably light for speed, they are
pictured as whirled onward by the two [7] or,
more often, three [8] powerful steeds with eye
of fire [9], the bodies of the slain [10] (or, in peace,
the lion [11]) under their feet, the mailed warriors, with bows stretched to the utmost,
shooting at the more distant foe. Sennacherib gives a terrific picture of the fierceness
of their onslaught. "The armor, the arms,
taken in my attacks, swam in the blood of
my enemies as in a river; the war-chariots,
which destroy man and beast, had, in their
course, crushed the bloody bodies and limbs [12]."
All this their warlike pride should be but
fuel for fire, and vanish in smoke, an emblem
of pride, swelling, mounting like a column
toward heaven, disappearing. Not a brand
shall then be saved out of the burning; nothing half-consumed; but the fire shall burn,
until there be nothing left to consume, as, in
Sodom and Gomorrah [13], *the smoke of the country
went up as the smoke of a furnace.* And the
sword of the vengeance of God *shall devour the
young lions*, his hope for the time to come, the
flower of his youth; *and I will cut off thy prey*,
what thou hast robbed, and so that thou
shouldest rob no more, but that thy spoil
should utterly cease *from the earth, and the
voice of thy messengers shall be no more heard,*

---

[1] See ab. p. 125–6. *bookah, oomebookah, oomebullakah.*
[2] Prov. xxxi. 17.   [3] See on Joel ii. 6.
[4] 2 Kings xviii. 34.   [5] As in Ps. xxxvii. 20.
[6] See Rawl. 5 Empires ii. 4–21.
[7] Rawl. Ib. 10. 11. 13.
[8] Layard Monuments, Series i. Plate 18, 21, 23,
27, 28.

[9] See a striking illustration in Rawl. ii. 15. (from
Boutcher.)
[10] Layard Ser. i. 27. 28. ii. 45. 46.
[11] Rawl. Ib. 13. Layard Ninev. ii. 77.
[12] In Oppert Sargonides p. 51. The general accuracy of the deciphering is alone presupposed.
[13] Gen. xix. 28.

Before
CHRIST
cir. 713. smoke, and the sword shall devour thy young lions: and I will cut off thy prey

from the earth, and the voice of [n] thy messengers shall no more be heard. Before
CHRIST
cir. 713.
[n] 2 Kin. 18. 17,
19. & 19. 9, 23.

such as Rabshakeh, whereby they insulted and terrified the nations and blasphemed God.

In the spiritual sense, Nineveh being an image of the world, the prophecy speaks of the inroad made upon it through the Gospel, its resistance, capture, desolation, destruction. First, He that *ruleth with a rod of iron*, came and denounced *woe to it because of offenses;* then His *mighty* ones [1] in His Name. Their shield is red, *the shield of faith*, kindled and glowing with love. Their raiment too is red, because they wash it in the Blood of the Lamb, and conquer through the Blood of the Lamb, and many shed their own blood *for a witness to them. The day of His preparation* is the whole period, until the end of the world, in which the Gospel is preached, of which the prophets and apostles speak, as *the* day of salvation [2]; to the believing world a day of salvation; to the unbelieving, of preparation for judgment. All which is done, judgments, mercy, preaching, miracles, patience of the saints, martyrdom, all which is spoken, done, suffered, is part of the one preparation for the final judgment. The chariots, flashing with light as they pass, are [3] *the chariots of salvation*, bearing the brightness of the doctrine of Christ and the glory of His truth throughout the world, enlightening while they wound; the "spears" are the word of God, slaying to make alive.

On the other hand, in resisting, the world clashes with itself. It would oppose the Gospel, yet knows not how; is "maddened with rage, and gnashes its teeth, that it can prevail nothing [4]." On the *broad ways* which lead to death, where *Wisdom uttereth her voice* and is not heard, it is hemmed in, and cannot find a straight path; its chariots dash one against another, and yet they breathe their ancient fury, and run to and fro like lightning, as the Lord saith, *I beheld Satan, as lightning, fall from Heaven* [5]. Then shall they *remember their mighty* ones, all the might of this world which they ascribed to their gods, their manifold triumphs, whereby in Heathen times their empire was established; they shall gather strength against strength, but it shall be powerless and real weakness. While they prepare for a long siege, *without hand* their gates give way; the kingdom falls, the world is taken captive by a blessed captivity, suddenly, unawares, as one says in the second century; "[6] Men cry out that the state is beset, that the Christians are in their fields, in

their forts, in their islands!" These mourn over their past sins, and beat their breasts, in token of their sorrow; yet sweeter shall be the plaint of their sorrow, than any past joy. So they shall mourn as doves, and their mourning is as melody and the voice of praise in the ear of the Most High. One part of the inhabitants of the world being thus blessedly taken, the rest are fled. So in all nearness of God's judgments, those who are not brought nearer, flee further. "*They flee, and look not back,* and none heareth the Lord speaking, *Return, ye backsliding children, and I will heal your backslidings* [7]. So then, hearing not His Voice, *stand, stand*, they flee away from His presence in Mercy, into darkness for ever. Such is the lot of the inhabitants of this world; and what is the world itself? The prophet answers what it has been. *A pool of water*, into which all things, the riches and glory, and wisdom, and pleasures of this world, have flowed in on all sides, and which gave back nothing. All ended in itself. The water came from above, and became stagnant in the lowest part of the earth. "[5] For all the wisdom of this world, apart from the sealed fountain of the Church, and of which it cannot be said, *the streams thereof make glad the city of God* nor are of those waters which, above the heavens, praise the Name of the Lord, however large they may seem, yet are little, and are enclosed in a narrow bound." These either are hallowed to God, like the spoils of Egypt, as when the eloquence of S. Cyprian was won through the fishermen [8], or the gold and silver are offered to Him, or they are left to be wasted and burned up. *All which is in the world, the lust of the flesh, and the lust of the eyes, and the pride of life, all under the sun,* remain here. "[9] If they are thine, take them with thee. *When he dieth, he shall carry nothing away, his glory shall not descend after him* [10]. True riches are, not wealth, but virtues, which the conscience carries with it, that it may be rich for ever." The seven-fold terrors [11], singly, may have a good sense [4], that the stony *heart* shall be melted, and the stiff *knees,* which before were not bent to God, be bowed in the Name of Jesus. Yet more fully are they the deepening horrors of the wicked in the Day of Judgment, when *men's hearts shall fail them for fear and for looking after those things which are coming on the earth* [12], closing with the everlasting confusion of face, *the shame and everlasting contempt,* to which the wicked

---

[1] From Dion. [2] Is. xlix. 8. 2 Cor. vi. 2.
[3] Habak. iii. 8. [4] S. Jer. [5] S. Luke x. 18.
[6] Tert. Apol. c. 1. and p. 3. not. 9. Oxf. Tr.

[7] Jer. iii. 22. [8] The Apostles. S. Aug.
[9] S. Bern. in Adv. Serm. 4. [10] Ps. xlix. 17.
[11] v. 10. [12] S. Luke xxi. 26.

Before
CHRIST
cir. 713.

† Heb. city of
bloods.
▲ Ezek. 22. 2, 3.
& 24. 6. 9.
Hab. 2. 12.

CHAPTER III.

1 *The miserable ruin of Nineveh.*

WOE to the †ᵃ bloody city! it is all full of

lies *and* robbery; the prey departeth not;

2 The noise of a whip, and ᵇ the n o i s e of the

shall rise. As the vessel over the fire is not cleansed, but blackened, so through the judgments of God, whereby the righteous are cleansed, the wicked gather but fresh defilement and hate. Lastly, the Prophet asks, *Where is the dwelling of those who had made the world a den of ravin, where the lion,* even *the devil* who is *a roaring lion,* and all Anti-Christs[1], destroyed at will; where Satan made his dwelling in the hearts of the worldly, and *tore in pieces for his whelps,* i. e. slew souls of men and gave them over to inferior evil spirits to be tormented, and *filled his holes with prey,* the pit of hell with the souls which he deceived[2]? The question implies that they shall not be. [3] *They which have seen him shall say, Where is he?* God Himself answers, that He Himself will come against it to judgment, and destroy all might arrayed against God; and Christ [4] shall *smite the Wicked one with the rod of His Mouth,* and the [5] *sharp two-edged sword out of His mouth shall smite all nations,* and *the smoke of their torment ascendeth up for ever and ever* [6]; and it should no more oppress, nor " any messenger of Satan " go forth to harass the saints of God.

C. III. The prophecy of the destruction in Nineveh is resumed in a dirge over her; yet still as future. It pronounces a woe, yet to come [7].

1. *Woe to the bloody city,* lit. *city of bloods* [8], i. e. of manifold bloodshedding, built and founded in blood [9], as the prosperity of the world ever is. Murder, oppression, wresting of judgment, war out of covetousness, grinding or neglect of the poor, make it a *city of bloods.* Nineveh, or the world, is a city of the devil, as opposed to the " city of God." " [10] Two sorts of love have made two sorts of cities; the earthly, love of self even to contempt of God; the Heavenly, love of God even to contempt of self. The one glorieth in itself, the other in the Lord." " [11] Amid the manifold differences of the hu-

man race, in languages, habits, rites, arms, dress, there are but two kinds of human society, which, according to our Scriptures, we may call two cities. One is of such as wish to live according to the flesh; the other of such as will according to the Spirit." " Of these, one is predestined to live for ever with God; the other, to undergo everlasting torment with the devil." Of this city, or evil world, Nineveh, *the city of bloods,* is the type.

It is all full of lies and robbery, better, *it is all lie; it is full of robbery* [*rapine*]. *Lie* includes all falsehood, in word or act, denial of God, hypocrisy; toward man, it speaks of treachery, treacherous dealing, in contrast with open violence or rapine [12]. The whole being of the wicked is one lie, toward God and man; deceiving and deceived; leaving no place for God Who is the Truth; seeking through falsehood things which fail. Man [13] *loveth vanity and seeketh after leasing.* All were gone out of the way. " [14] There were none in so great a multitude, for whose sake the mercy of God might spare so great a city." *It is full,* not so much of booty as *of rapine* and violence. The sin remains, when the profit is gone. Yet it ceaseth not, but persevereth to the end; *the prey departeth* [15] *not;* they will neither leave the sin, nor the sin them; they neither repent, nor are weary of sinning. Avarice especially gains vigor in old age, and grows by being fed. *The prey departeth not,* but continues as a witness against it, as a lion's lair is defiled by the fragments of his prey.

2. *The noise* [lit. *voice*] *of the whip.* There is cry against cry; the voice of the enemy, brought upon them through the voice of the oppressed. Blood hath a voice which *crieth* [16] to heaven; its echo or counterpart, as it were, is the cry of the destroyer. All is urged on with terrific speed. The chariot-wheels quiver [17] in the rapid onset; the chariots bound, like living things [18]; the earth echoes

---

[1] 1 John ii. 18.　　[2] Dion.　　[3] Job xx. 7.
[4] Is. xi. 4.　[5] Rev. i. 16, xix. 15. 21.　[6] Rev. xiv. 11.
ᵗ הוֹי, when signifying " woe," is always of future woe, as lies in the word itself. It is used of classes of persons 25 times; against people, Samaria, Jerusalem or foreign nations, 13 times; of the past only as to the wailings at funerals. 1 Kgs xiii. 30, Jer. xxii. 18, xxxiv. 5.
[8] As in E. M. The phrase occurs Ezek. xxii. 2, xxiv. 6. 9. So אִישׁ, אַנְשֵׁי, בֵּית, " a man " (2 Sam. xvi. 7, 8. Ps. v. 7) " men " (Ps. xxvi. 9, lv. 24, lix. 3, cxxxix. 19, Pr. xxix. 10) " a house " (2 Sam. xxi. 1) " of bloods," guilty of manifold bloodshed.
[9] Hab. ii. 12, Jer. xxii. 13.

[10] S. Aug. de Civ. D. xiv. 28.　　[11] Ib. c. l.
[12] פֶּרֶק *ăm.* The verb is used of the merciless " tearing " of the lion, " rending and there is no deliverer." Ps. vii. 3.　　[13] Ps. iv. 2.　　[14] Alb.
[15] יָמִישׁ is intrans. except in Mic. ii. 3, 4.
[16] Gen. iv. 10.
[17] רַעַשׁ of the chariots, Jer. xlvii. 3, of the war-horse, Job. xxxix. 24, of the loud tumult of battle, Is. ix. 4, Jer. x. 22.
[18] רָקַד is used of the dancing of children, Job xxi. 11, of David before the ark, 1 Chr. xv. 29, of the satyrs, Is. xiii. 21. Even when used of the tremb-

Before
CHRIST
cir. 713.

rattling of the wheels, and
of the pransing horses, and
of the jumping chariots.

3 The horseman lifteth

† Heb. *the flame of the sword, and the light-ning of the spear.*

up both † the bright sword
and the glittering spear:
and *there is* a multitude of
slain, and a great number
of carcases; and *there is*
none end of *their* corpses;

they stumble upon their
corpses:

4 Because of the multi-
tude of the whoredoms of
the wellfavored harlot, ᶜ the
mistress of witchcrafts,
that selleth nations through
her whoredoms, and fami-
lies through her witch-
crafts.

Before
CHRIST
cir. 713.

ᶜ Isa. 47. 9. 12.
Rev. 18. 2, 3.

---

with the whirling swiftness[1] of the speed of
the cavalry. The Prophet within, with the
inward ear and eye which heareth the *mysteries of the Kingdom of God*[2] and seeth
things to come, as they shall come upon the
wicked, sees and hears the scourge coming,
with[3] a great noise, impetuously; and so describes it as present. Wars and rumors of
wars are among the signs of the Day of Judgment. The *scourge,* though literally relating
to the vehement onset of the enemy, suggests
to the thoughts, the scourges of Almighty
God, wherewith He chastens the penitent,
punishes the impenitent; the *wheel,* the swift
changes of man's condition in the rolling-on
of time. [4] *O God, make them like a rolling thing.*

3. *The horseman lifteth up,* rather, *leading
up*[5]: *the flash of the sword, and the lightning
of the spear.* Thus there are, in all, seven inroads, seven signs, before the complete destruction of Nineveh or the world; as, in
the Revelations, all the forerunners of the
Judgment of the Great Day are summed up
under the voice of seven trumpets[6] and
seven vials. "[7] God shall not use horses and
chariots and other instruments of war, such
as are here spoken of, to judge the world,
yet, as is just, His terrors are foretold under
the name of those things, wherewith this
proud and bloody world hath sinned. For
so *all they that take the sword shall perish with
the sword*[8]." They who, abusing their power,
have used all these weapons of war, especially

against the servants of God, shall themselves
perish by them, and there shall be *none end
of their corpses,* for they shall be corpses for
ever: for, dying by an everlasting death,
they shall, without end, be without the true
life, which is God." *And there is a multitude
of slain.* Death follows on death. The Prophet views the vast field of carnage, and
everywhere there meets him only some new
form of death, *slain, carcases, corpses,* and
these in *multitudes,* an *oppressive heavy number,*
without end, so that the yet living *stumble* and
fall *upon the carcases* of the slain. So great
the multitude of those who perish, and such
their foulness; but what foulness is like sin?

4. *Because of the multitude of the whoredoms
of the well-favored harlot.* There are *multitudes of slain,* because of the *multitude of whoredoms* and love of the creature instead of the
Creator. So to Babylon Isaiah saith, "[9] they
[loss of children and widowhood] shall come
upon thee in their perfection *for* the multitude of thy sorceries, for the great abundance
of thine enchantments." The actual use of
enchantments[10], for which Babylon was so infamous, is not elsewhere attributed to the
Assyrians. But neither is the word elsewhere
used figuratively; nor is Assyria, in its
intimate relation to Babylon, likely to have
been free from the longing, universal in
Heathendom, to obtain knowledge as to the
issue of events which would affect her. She
is, by a rare idiom, entitled "*mistress*[11] of

---

ling of the mountains before God, they are compared to living things, a calf, Ps. xxix. 6, rams, Ps.
cxiv. 4. 6. It is used also of the locusts, Jo. ii. 5.
[all]. Mostly, as here, it is intensive. In Syr. Pa.
is "danced;" in Arabic the insulated רָקְדָאן is
used of "bounding as a kid." See Lane s. v.
[1] The root only occurs beside Jud. v. 22. "Then
smote [the earth] the horse-hoofs from the whirlings, the whirlings [probably "whirling speed"
דַּהֲרֹת i. q. דְּרוֹר] of his mighty ones" [i. e. steeds. Jer.
viii. 16. xlvii. 3. l. 11.].   [2] S. Matt. xiii. 11. 16.
[3] 2 Pet. iii. 10. The words in Hebrew are purposely chosen with rough sounds, (r) "*ra'ash,*
doher, merakkedah."   [4] Ps. lxxxiii. 14.
[5] This division is the more likely, because the
words stand very broken, mostly in pairs, describing, as it were, by the very order of the words, the
successive onsets, wherewith the destruction from
God should break in upon them.

[6] Rev. vi. viii. The foreboding cry "woe! woe!"
before the destruction of Jerusalem, an image also
of the Day of Judgment, was also seven-fold. See
above on c. ii. 10.
[7] Rup.   [8] S. Matt. xxvi. 52.   [9] Is. xlvii. 9.
[10] כְּשָׁפִים (always plural) are spoken of as to Jezebel, 2 Kgs ix. 22; Babylon, Is. l. c. and as to be
abolished by God in Judah; Micah v. 11. Those
who used them, מְכַשְּׁפִים, were employed by Pharaoh, Ex. vii. 11, and Nebuchadnezzar, Dan. ii. 2;
were strictly forbidden to Israel (Ex. xxii. 17. De.
xviii. 10.); their employment was one chief offence
of Manasseh. (2 Chr. xxxiii. 6.)
[11] בַּעֲלַת (fem.) only occurs beside in 1 Kgs xvii.
17, of the widow of Zarephath, who, as being a
widow, was the mistress of the house, and of the
witch of Endor, as בַּעֲלַת אוֹב, 1 Sam. xxviii. 7.

Before CHRIST cir. 713.
d ch. 2. 13.
e Isa. 47. 2, 3.
Jer. 13. 22, 26.
Ezek. 16. 36.
Mic. 1. 11.

5 ^d Behold, I *am* against thee, saith the LORD of hosts; and ^e I will discover thy skirts upon thy face,

^f and I will shew the nations thy nakedness, and the kingdoms thy shame.

Before CHRIST cir. 713.

f Hab. 2. 16.

enchantments," having them at her command, as instruments of power. Mostly, idolatries and estrangement from God are spoken of as *whoredoms,* only in respect of those who, having been taken by God as His own, forsook Him for false gods. But Jezebel too, of whose offences Jehu speaks under the same two titles [1], was a heathen. And such sins were but part of that larger all-comprehending sin, that man, being made by God for Himself, when he loveth the creature instead of the Creator, divorceth himself from God. Of this sin world-empires, such as Nineveh, were the concentration. Their being was one vast idolatry of self and of *the god of this world.* All, art, fraud, deceit, protection of the weak against the strong [2], promises of good [3], were employed, together with open violence, to absorb all nations into it. The one end of all was to form one great idol-temple, of which the centre and end was man, a rival worship to God, which should enslave all to itself and the things of this world. Nineveh and all conquering nations used fraud as well as force, enticed and entangled others, and so sold and deprived them of freedom [4]. Nor are people less sold and enslaved, because they have no visible master. False freedom is the deepest and most abject slavery. All sinful nations or persons extend to others the infection of their own sins. But, chiefly, the "wicked world," manifoldly arrayed with fair forms, and "beautiful in the eyes of those who will not think or weigh how much more beautiful the Lord and Creator of all," spreads her enticements on all sides, *the lust of the flesh, and the lust of the eye, and the pride of life,* "her pomps and vanities," worldly happiness and glory and majesty, and ease and abundance, deceives and sells mankind into the power of Satan. It is called *well-favored* [lit. *good of grace*], because the world has a real beauty, nor, "[5] unless there were a grace and beauty in the things we love, could they draw us to them." They have their beauty, because from God; then are they deformed, when

"[6] things hold us back from God, which, unless they were in God, were not at all." We deform them, if we love them for our own sakes, not in Him; or for the intimations they give of Him. "[7] Praise as to things foul has an intensity of blame. As if one would speak of a skilled thief, or a courageous robber, or a clever cheat. So though he calls Nineveh *a well-favored harlot,* this will not be for her praise, (far from it !) but conveys the heavier condemnation. As *they,* when they would attract, use dainty babblings, so was Nineveh a skilled artificer of ill-doing, well provided with means to capture cities and lands and to persuade them what pleased herself." She selleth not *nations* only but *families,* drawing mankind both as a mass, and one by one after her, so that scarce any escape.

The adultery of the soul from God is the more grievous, the nearer God has brought any to Himself, in priests worse than in the people, in Christians than in Jews, in Jews than in Heathen; yet God espoused mankind to Him when He made him. His dowry were gifts of nature. If this be adultery, how much sorer, when betrothed by the Blood of Christ, and endowed with the gift of the Spirit !

5. *Behold I am against thee, saith the Lord of Hosts.* "[8] I will not send an Angel, nor give thy destruction to others; I Myself will come to destroy thee." "[7] She has not to do with man, or war with man: He Who is angered with her is *the Lord of hosts.* But who would meet God Almighty, Who hath power over all, if He would war against him ?" In the Medes and Persians it was God who was against them. *Behold I am against thee,* lit. *toward thee.* It is a new thing which God was about to do. *Behold !* God in His long-suffering had seemed to overlook her. Now, He says, *I am toward thee,* looking at her with His all-searching eye, as her Judge. Violence is punished by suffering; deeds of shame by shame. All sin is a whited sepulchre, fair without, foul

[1] 2 Kgs ix. 22.
[2] 2 Kgs xvi. 7-9, 2 Chr. xxviii. 20, 21.
[3] Is. xxxvi. 16, 17.
[4] See Joel iii. 3. The word מָכַר, as the act of selling, implies elsewhere, "to part with into the hands of another." This is implied, even where (as in De. xxxii. 30, Ps. xliv. 13) it is not expressed to whom they were sold. But here the nations were not, as nations, sold by Assyria into the hands of others, but retained in its own power. Yet since מָכַר occurs 80 times throughout the O. T. in the one

sense "sell," and its derivatives מִמְכָּר, מִמְכֶּרֶת, מֶכֶר, 14 times, it is against all idiom to assume that, in this one case, it meant "deceived" (as the Arab. כַבַר, with acc. p. and בְ of thg.); nor were the enchantments an instrument of deceit; the word then must here too retain its sense of depriving of liberty, "selling" to slavery or death.
[5] S. Aug. Conf. iv. 13.
[6] Ib. x. 27 and iv. 12 and note m.
[7] S. Cyr.   [8] S. Jer.

<table>
<tr><td>

Before
C H R I S T
cir. 713.

g Mal. 2. 9.

h Heb. 10. 33.

6 And I will cast abominable filth upon thee, and
^g make thee vile, and will set thee as ^h a gazingstock.

7 And it shall come to pass *that* all they that look

</td><td>

upon thee ⁱ shall flee from thee, and say, Nineveh is laid waste: ^k who will bemoan her? whence shall I seek comforters for thee?

8 ^l Art thou better than

Before
C H R I S T
cir. 713.

i Rev. 18. 10.
k Jer. 15. 5.

l Amos 6. 2.

</td></tr>
</table>

within. God will strip off the outward fairness, and lay bare the inward foulness. The deepest shame is to lay bare, what the sinner or the world veiled within. *I will discover thy skirts*[1], i. e. the long flowing robes which were part of her pomp and dignity, but which were only the veil of her misdeeds. *Through the greatness of thine iniquity have thy skirts been discovered*, says Jeremiah in answer to the heart's question, *why have these things come upon me? Upon thy face*, where shame is felt. The conscience of thy foulness shall be laid bare before thy face, thy eyes, thy memory continually, so that thou shalt be forced to read therein, whatsoever thou hast done, said, thought. *I will shew the nations thy nakedness*, that all may despise, avoid, take example by thee, and praise God for His righteous judgments upon thee. The Evangelist heard *much people in heaven saying Alleluia* to God that *He hath judged the whore which did corrupt the earth with her fornication*[2]. And Isaiah saith, *They shall go forth and look upon the carcases of the men that have transgressed against Me*[3].

6. *And I will cast abominable filth upon thee*, "[4] like a weight, that what thou wouldest not take heed to as sin, thou mayest feel in punishment." *Abominable things had God seen*[5] in her doings; with abominable things would he punish her. Man would fain sin, and forget it as a thing past. God *maketh* him to *possess the iniquities of his youth*[6], and bindeth them around him, so that they *make* him to appear what they are, *vile*[7]. [8] *These things hast thou done and I kept silence;—I will reprove thee and set them in order before thine eyes. And will set thee as a gazing-stock*, that all, while they gaze at thee, take warning from thee[9]. [10] *I will cast thee to the ground ; before kings will I give thee, for them to gaze*

upon thee. "[11] Whoso amendeth not on occasion of others, others shall be amended on occasion of him."

7. *All they that look upon thee shall flee from thee* through terror, lest they should share her plagues, as Israel did, when the earth swallowed up Corah, Dathan and Abiram ; and they who [12] *had been made rich by Babylon, stand afar off, for the fear of her torment. All they who look on thee.* She was set as a thing to be *gazed at*[13]. He tells the effect on the gazers. *Each one who so gazed*[14] at her should *flee;* one by one, they should *gaze*, be scared, flee[15]. Not one should remain. *Who will bemoan her?* Not one should pay her the passing tribute of sympathy at human calamity, the shaking of the head at her woe[16]. Who had no compassion, shall find none.

8. *Art thou better*[17], more populous or more powerful, *than the populous No?* rather *than No-Ammon*, so called from the idol Ammon, worshiped there. No-Ammon, (or, as it is deciphered in the Cuneiform Inscriptions, *Nia*), meaning probably "the portion of Ammon[18]," was the sacred name of the capital of Upper Egypt, which, under its common name, Thebes, was far-famed, even in the time of Homer, for its continually accruing wealth, its military power, its 20,000 chariots, its vast dimensions attested by its 100 gates[19]. Existing earlier, as the capital of Upper Egypt, its grandeur began in the 18th dynasty, after the expulsion of the Hyksos, or Semitic conquerors of Egypt. Its Pharaohs were conquerors, during the 18th–20th dynasties, B. C. 1706–1110, about six centuries. It was then the centre of a world-empire. Under a disguised name[20], its rulers were celebrated in Greek story also, for their world-wide conquests. The Greek statements have in some main points been verified by the

[1] שׁוּלַיִךְ always plural, for their profuseness, as we speak of "robes." It is the word used in the same image, Jer. xiii. 22. 26; Isaiah has the like, שֹׁבֶל. Is. xlvii. 2.

[2] Rev. xix. 1. 2.   [3] lxvi. 24.   [4] Alb.
[5] Jer. xiii. 27.   [6] Job. xiii. 26.
[7] Comp. Wisdom iv. 18.   [8] Ps. l. 21.
[9] Comp. 2 Chron. vii. 20.   [10] Ezek. xxviii. 17.
[11] Ptol. Prov. ap. Alb.   [12] Rev. xviii. 15.

[13] רְאִי.   [14] כָּל־רֹאַיִךְ.
[15] Comp. Ps. xxxi. 11. lxiv. 8.   [16] Comp. Job xvi. 4, 5.
[17] תֵּיטְבִי, for תִּיטְבִי, as יִיקַר Ps. lxxii. 14, אֵלְכָה Mic. i. 8.

[18] As the LXX. (from their acquaintance with Egypt) render, μερίς Ἀμμών. The Coptic MSS. Martyrologies mention "the place of Ammon," (Jablonski Opp. i. 163) and the Hieroglyphics. Lepsius, Chronol. d. Æg. i. 272. The common name Ap-t or T-ap was the original of the name Thebes, by which it became known to the West through the Greeks.

[19] Il. ix. 381–4, [all the wealth] "as much as comes to the Egyptian Thebes, where most possessions are laid up in the houses, which hath a hundred gates, and from each, 200 men go forth with horses and chariots."

[20] Sesostris. Herod. ii. 102–110, and notes in Rawl. Her.; Diod. i. 53–59, Strabo xv. 1. 6. xvi. 4. and 7. xvii. 1. 5.

Before
CHRIST
cir. 713.
‖ † populous ᵐ No, that was
situate among the rivers,
† that had the waters round

| Or, nourishing.
† Heb.
No Amon.   ᵐ Jer. 46. 25, 26. Ezek. 30. 14–16.

about it, whose ramparts
was the sea, *and* her wall
was from the sea?
Before
CHRIST
cir. 713.

decipherment of the hieroglyphics. The monuments relate their victories in far Asia, and mention Nineveh itself among the people who paid tribute to them. They warred and conquered from the Soudan to Mesopotamia. A monument of Tothmosis I. (1066 B. C.) still exists at Kerman, between the 20th and 19th degrees latitude, boasting, in language like that of the Assyrian conquerors; "All lands are subdued, and bring their tributes for the first time to the gracious god[1]." "The frontier of Egypt," they say[2], "extends Southward to the mountain of Aptâ (in Abyssinia) and Northward to the furthest dwellings of the Asiatics." The hyperbolic statements are too undefined for history[3], but widely-conquering monarchs could alone have used them. "[4]At all periods of history, the possession of the country which we call Soudan (the Black country) comprising Nubia, and which the ancients called by the collective name of Kous [Cush] or Æthiopia, has been an exhaustless source of wealth to Egypt. Whether by way of war or of commerce, barks laden with flocks, corn, hides, ivory, precious woods, stones and metals, and many other products of those regions, descended the Nile into Egypt, to fill the treasures of the temples and of the court of the Pharaohs: and of metals, especially gold, mines whereof were worked by captives and slaves, whose Egyptian name *noub* seems to have been the origin of the name Nubia, the first province S. of Egypt." "The conquered country of Soudan, called Kous in the hieroglyphic inscriptions, was governed by Egyptian princes of the royal family, who bore the name of 'prince royal of Kous.'"

But the prophet's appeal to Nineveh is the more striking, because No, in its situation, its commerce, the sources of its wealth, its relation to the country which lay between them, had been another and earlier Nineveh. Only, as No had formerly conquered and exacted tribute from all those nations, even to Nineveh itself, so now, under Sargon and Sennacherib, Nineveh had reversed all those successes, and displaced the Empire of Egypt by its own, and taken No itself. No had, under its Tothmoses, Amenophes, Sethos, the

Ousertesens, sent its *messengers*[5], the leviers of its tribute, had brought off from Asia that countless mass of human strength, the captives, who (as Israel, before its deliverance, accomplished its hard labors) completed those gigantic works, which, even after 2000 years of decay, are still the marvel of the civilized world. Tothmosis I., after subduing the Sasou, brought back countless captives from Naharina[6] (Mesopotamia); Tothmosis III., in 19 years of conquests, (1603–1585 B. C.) "[7] raised the Egyptian empire to the height of its greatness. Tothmosis repeatedly attacked the most powerful people of Asia, as the Routen (Assyrians?) with a number of subordinate kingdoms, such as Asshur, Babel, Nineveh, Singar; such as the Remenen or Armenians, the Zahi or Phœnicians, the Cheta or Hittites, and many more. We learn, by the description of the objects of the booty, sent to Egypt by land and sea, counted by number and weight, many curious details as to the industry of the conquered peoples of central Asia, which do honor to the civilization of that time, and verify the tradition that the Egyptian kings set up stelæ in conquered countries, in memory of their victories. Tothmosis III. set up his stele in Mesopotamia, 'for having enlarged the frontiers of Egypt.'" Amenophis too is related to have "[8]taken the fortress of Nenii (Nineveh)." "[8]He returned from the country of the higher Routen, where he had beaten all his enemies to enlarge the frontiers of the land of Egypt:" "[8]he took possession of the people of the South, and chastised the people of the North:" "at Abd-el-Kournah" he was represented as "[9]having for his footstool the heads and backs of five peoples of the S. and four peoples of the N. or Asiatics." "[9]Among the names of the peoples, who submitted to Egypt, are the Nubians, the Asiatic shepherds, the inhabitants of Cyprus and Mesopotamia." "[10]The world in its length and its breadth" is promised by the sphinx to Tothmosis IV. He is represented as "[11]subduer of the negroes." Under Amenophis III., the Memnon of the Greeks, "[12]the Egyptian empire extended Northward to Mesopotamia, Southward to the land of Karou." He enlarged and beautified No,

[1] Brugsch Hist. d'Eg. p. 88.
[2] Ib. and (Tothmosis iii.) p. 109.
[3] "Notwithstanding the length of the like texts, recording the victories gained by the Pharaohs, the historical subject is treated as accessory, as an occasion of repeating, for the thousandth time, the same formulas, the same hyperbolic words, the same ideas." Brugsch pp. 89.

[4] Brugsch ib. p. 89–107.   [5] Nah. ii. 13.
[6] Brugsch p. 90.
[7] Ib. p. 104, the summary of pp. 95–103.
[8] Ib. p. 111.
[9] Ib. 112.
[10] On the sphinx of Gizeh Ib. p. 113.
[11] In the Isle of Konosso near Philæ Ib. p. 114.
[12] Ib. pp. 114, 115.

which had from him the temple of Louksor, and his vocal statue, "¹ all people bringing their tributes, their children, their horses, a mass of silver, of iron and ivory from countries, the roads whereto we know not." The king Horus is saluted as "² the sun of the nine people; great is thy name to the country of Ethiopia;" "² the gracious god returns, having subdued the great of all people." Setj I. (or Sethos) is exhibited³, as reverenced by the Armenians, conquering the Sasou, the "Hittites, Naharina (Mesopotamia), the Routen (Assyrians?) the Pount, or Arabs in the S. of Arabia, the Amari or Amorites, and Kedes, perhaps Edessa." Rameses II., or the great ⁴ (identified with the Pharaoh of the Exodus⁵), conquered the Hittites in the N.; in the S. it is recorded, "⁶ the gracious god, who defeated the nine people, who massacred myriads in a moment, annihilated the people overthrown in their blood, yet was there no other with him." The 20th Dynasty (B. C. 1288–1110) began again with conquests. "⁷ Rameses III. triumphed over great confederations of Libyans and Syrians and the Isles of the Mediterranean. He is the only king who, as the monuments shew, carried on war at once by land and sea." Beside many names unknown to us, the Hittites, Amorites, Circesium, Aratus, Philistines, Phœnicia, Sasou, Pount, are again recognized. North, South East and West are declared to be tributary to him, and of the North it is said, "⁸ The people, who knew not Egypt, come to thee, bringing gold and silver, lapis-lazuli, all precious stones." He adorned Thebes with the great temple of Medinet-Abou⁹ and the Ramesseum¹⁰. The brief notices of following Rameses' speak of internal prosperity and wealth : a fuller account of Rameses XII. speaks of his "¹¹ being in Mesopotamia to exact the annual tribute," how "the kings of all countries prostrated themselves before him, and the king of the country of Bouchten [it has been conjectured, Bagistan, or Ecbatana] presented to him tribute and his daughter." "¹² He is the last Pharaoh who goes to Mesopotamia, to collect the annual tributes of the petty kingdoms of that country." On this side of the Euphrates, Egypt still retained some possessions to the time of Necho; for it is said, "¹³ the king of Babylon had taken from the river of Egypt unto the river Euphrates all that pertained to the

king of Egypt." Thebes continued to be embellished alike by "the high-priests of Ammon," who displaced the ancient line¹⁴, and kings of the Bubastite Dynasty, Sesonchis I. or Sisak ¹⁵, Takelothis II.¹⁶, and Sesonchis III¹⁷. The Ethiopian dynasty of Sabakos and Tearko or Tirhaka in another way illustrates the importance of No. The Ethiopian conquerors chose it as their royal city. Thither, in the time of Sabakos, Syria brought it tribute ¹⁸; there Tirhaka set up the records of his victories ¹⁸; and great must have been the conqueror, whom Strabo put on a line with Sesostris ¹⁹. Its site marked it out for a great capital; and as such the Ethiopian conqueror seized it. The hills on either side retired, encircling the plain, through the centre of which the Nile brought down its wealth, connecting it with the untold riches of the south. "²⁰ They formed a vast circus, where the ancient metropolis expanded itself. On the West, the Lybian chain presents abrupt declivities which command this side of the plain, and which bend away above Bab-el-molouk, to end near Kournah at the very bank of the river. On the East, heights, softer and nearer, descend in long declivities toward Louksor and Karnak, and their crests do not approach the Nile until after Medamout, an hour or more below Karnak." The breadth of the valley, being about 10 miles ²¹, the city (of which, Strabo says, "²² traces are now seen of its magnitude, 80 stadia in length") must have occupied the whole. "²³ The Ζam city embraced the great space, which is now commonly called the plain of Thebes and which is divided by the Nile into two halves, an Eastern and a Western, the first bounded by the edge of the Arabian wilderness, the latter by the hills of the dead of the steep Libyan chain." The capital of Egypt, which was identified of old with Egypt itself ²⁴, thus lay under the natural guardianship of the encircling hills which expanded to receive it, divided into two by the river which was a wall to both. The chains of hills, on either side were themselves fenced in on East and West by the great sand-deserts unapproachable by an army. The long valley of the Nile was the only access to an enemy. It occupied apparently the victorious army of Asshur-banipal ²⁵ "a month and ten days" to march from Memphis to Thebes. "²⁶ At Thebes itself there are still remains of walls

1 In Brugsch p. 116.
2 Ib. pp. 124, 125.   3 Ib. pp. 128–132.
4 ib. pp. 137 sqq.   5 Ib. p. 156.   6 Ib. p. 158.
7 Ib. p. 183.   8 Ib. p. 190.   9 Ib. p. 191.
10 Ib. pp. 197, 198.   11 Ib. p. 207.   12 Ib. p. 210.
13 2 Kgs xxiv. 7.   14 Brugsch p. 212.
15 Ib. pp. 224–227.   16 Ib. p. 223.   17 Ib. p. 235.
18 Ib. p. 244.
19 xv. 1. 6. He mentions him again for his extensive removals of people, which implies extensive conquests. i. 3. 21.   20 Joanne et Isambert, Itinéraire de l' Orient. p. 1039.

21 Smith Bibl. Dict. v. Thebes.   22 xvii. 1. 46.
23 Brugsch Geogr. d. Alt. Æg. p. 176.
24 "In old times Thebes [the Thebais] was called Egypt." Herod. ii. 15. "Formerly Egypt was called Thebes." Aristot. Meteor. i. 14.
25 Inscr. in Oppert, Rapports. pp. 74, 78, 85.
26 Miss Harris, the learned daughter of a learned Egyptologist; "In several hieroglyphical inscriptions and notably in a papyrus in Miss Harris' possession, partly deciphered by her father and herself, there are minute accounts of fortresses existing at that date, about the time of the Exodus,

and fortifications, strong, skillfully constructed, and in good preservation, as there are also in other Egyptian towns above and below it. The crescent-shaped ridge of hills approaches so close to the river at each end as to admit of troops defiling past, but not spreading out or manœuvering. At each of these ends is a small old fort of the purely Egyptian, i. e. the Ante-Hellenic period. Both above and below there are several similar crescent sweeps in the same chain of hills, and at each angle a similar fort."

All successive monarchs, during more centuries than have passed since our Lord came, successively beautified it. Everything is gigantic, bearing witness to the enormous mass of human strength, which its victorious kings had gathered from all nations to toil for its and their glorification. Wonderful is it now in its decay, desolation, death ; one great idol-temple of its gods and an apotheosis of its kings, as sons of its gods. "[1] What spires are to a modern city, what the towers of a cathedral are to the nave and choir, *that* the statues of the Pharaohs were to the streets and temples of Thebes. The ground is strewed with their fragments ; the avenues of them towered high above plain and houses. Three of gigantic size still remain. One was the granite statue of Rameses himself, who sat on the right side of the entrance to his palace.—The only part of the temple or palace, at all in proportion to him, must have been the gateway, which rose in pyramidal towers, now broken down and rolling in a wild ruin down to the plain." It was that self-deifying, against which Ezekiel is commanded to prophesy ; [2] *Speak and say ; thus saith the Lord God ; Behold, I am against thee, Pharaoh king of Egypt, the great dragon that lieth in the midst of his rivers, which hath said, My river is mine own, and I have made it for myself.* "[3] Everywhere the same colossal proportions are preserved. Everywhere the king is conquering, ruling, worshiping, worshiped. The palace is the temple. The king is priest. He and his horses are ten times the size of the rest of the army. Alike in battle and in worship, he is of the same stature as the gods themselves. Most striking is the familiar gentleness, with which,

one on each side, they take him by each hand, as one of their own order, and then, in the next compartment, introduce him to Ammon, and the lion-headed goddess. Every distinction, except of degree, between divinity and royalty is entirely levelled." Gigantic dimensions picture to the eye the ideal greatness, which is the key to the architecture of No. "[3] Two other statues alone remain of an avenue of eighteen similar or nearly similar statues, some of whose remnants lie in the field behind them, which led to the palace of Amenophis III., every one of the statues being Amenophis himself, thus giving in multiplication what Rameses gained in solitary elevation." "[4] Their statues were all of one piece." Science still cannot explain, how a mass of nearly 890 tons[5] of granite was excavated at Syene, transported [6] and set up at Thebes, or how destroyed[7].

"[8] The temper of the tools, which cut adamantine stone as sharply and closely as an ordinary scoop cuts an ordinary cheese, is still a mystery." Everything is in proportion. The two sitting colossi, whose "breadth across the shoulders is eighteen feet, their height forty-seven feet, fifty-three above the plain, or, with the half-buried pedestal, sixty feet, were once connected by an avenue of sphinxes of eleven hundred feet with what is now 'Kom-el-Hettán,' or 'the mound of sand-stone,' which marks the site of another palace and temple of Amenophis III. ; and, to judge from the little that remains, it must have held a conspicuous rank among the finest monuments of Thebes. All that now exists of the interior are the bases of its columns, some broken statues, and Syenite sphinxes of the king, with several lion-headed figures of black granite[9]." The four villages, where are the chief remaining temples, Karnak, Luksor, Medinet-Abou, Kournah, form a great quadrilateral[10], each of whose sides is about one and a half mile, and the whole compass accordingly six miles. The avenue of six hundred sphinxes, which joined the temple of Luksor with Karnak must have been one and a half mile long[11] : *one* of its obelisks is a remarkable ornament of Paris. Mostly massiveness is the characteristic, since strength and might were their

she supposes, and of their armaments and garrisons." Thebes then was fortified, as well as Nineveh, and Homer is confirmed by the Hieroglyphical inscriptions.
[1] Stanley Sin. and Pal. Introd. p. xxxviii..
[2] Ezek. xxix. 3.   [3] Stanl. Ib. p. xxxix.
[4] Wilkinson Anc. Eg. iii. 266.
[5] "about 887 tons, 5½ hundred weight." Wilkinson Mod. Eg. ii. 145.
[6] "The obelisks, transported from the quarries of Syene at the first cataract, in latitude 24° 5′ 23″ to Thebes and Heliopolis, vary in size from 70 to 93 feet in length. They are of one single stone, and the largest in Egypt (that of the great temple at Karnak) I calculate to weigh 297 tons. This was brought about 138 miles from the quarry to where it now stands ; those taken to Heliopolis, more than

800 miles. The power, however, to move the mass was the same, whatever might be the distance, and the mechanical skill which transported it five or even one, would suffice for any number of miles. The two colossi of Amenophis iii., of a single block each, 47 feet in height, which contain about 11,500 cubic feet, are made of a stone not known within several days journey of the place ; and at the Memnonium is another of Rameses which, when entire, weighed upwards of 887 tons, and was brought from E'Sooan to Thebes, 138 miles." Wilk. Anc. Eg. iii. 329, 330.   [7] See Wilk. Mod. Eg. ii. 144.
[8] Nozrani in Eg. and Syr. p. 278.
[9] Wilkinson Mod. Eg. ii. 157, 158. 160. 162.
[10] Joanne et Isambert, Itiner. de l' Orient pp. 1039, 1040.
[11] Two kilometres, Joan. et Isamb. p. 1060.

ideal. Yet the massive columns still preserved, as in the temple of Rameses II.[1], are even of piercing beauty[1]. And for the temple of Karnak ! Its enclosure, which was some two miles in circumference[2], bears the names of Monarchs removed from one another, according to the Chronology, by above two thousand years[3]. "[4] A stupendous colonnade, of which one pillar only remains erect, once extended across its great court, connecting the W. gate of entrance with that at its extremity. The towers of the Eastern gate are mere heaps of stones, poured down into the court on one side and the great hall on the other ; giant columns have been swept away like reeds before the mighty avalanche, and one hardly misses them. And in that hall, of 170 feet by 329 feet, 134 columns of colossal proportions supported its roof; twelve of them, 62 feet high and about 35 in circumference, and on each side a forest of 66 columns, 42 feet 5 in. in height. Beyond the centre-avenue are seen obelisks, gateways and masses of masonry ; every portion of these gigantic ruins is covered with sculpture most admirably executed, and every column has been richly painted."

"[5] Imagine a long vista of courts and doorways and colonnades and halls ; here and there an obelisk shooting up out of the ruins, and interrupting the opening view of the forest of columns.—This mass of ruins, some rolled down in avalanches of stone, others perfect and painted, as when they were first built, is approached on every side by avenues of gateways. E. and W., N. and S., these vast approaches are found. Some are shattered, but in every approach some remain ; and in some can be traced, beside, the further avenues, still in parts remaining by hundreds together, avenues of ram-headed sphinxes. Every Egyptian temple has, or ought to have, one of those grand gateways, formed of two sloping towers, with the high perpendicular front between." Then, over and above, is "their multiplied concentration.—Close before almost every gateway in

this vast array were the colossal figures, usually in granite, of the great Rameses, sometimes in white and red marble, of Amenophis and of Thothmes. Close by them, were pairs of towering obelisks, which can generally be traced by pedestals on either side.—You have only to set up again the fallen obelisks which lie at your feet ; to conceive the columns, as they are still seen in parts, overspreading the whole ; to reproduce all the statues, like those which still remain in their august niches, to gaze on the painted walls and pillars of the immense hall, which even now can never be seen without a thrill of awe, and you have ancient Thebes before you." And most of those paintings were records of their past might. "[6] There remained on the massive buildings Egyptian letters, recording their former wealthiness ; and one of the elder priests, bidden to interpret his native language, related that of old 700,000 of military age dwelt there ; and with that army king Rhamses gained possession of Libya, Ethiopia, the Medes and Persians, the Bactrian and Scythian ; and held in his empire the countries which the Syrians and Armenians and neighboring Cappadocians inhabit, the Bithynian also and Lycian to the sea. There were read too the tributes imposed on the natives, the weight of silver and gold ; the number of arms and horses, and the gifts to the temples, ivory and frankincense, and what supplies of corn and utensils each nation should pay, not less magnificent than are now enjoined by Parthian violence or by Roman power."

That was situate lit. *the dweller, she that dwelleth.* Perhaps the Prophet wished to express the security and ease[7], in which she dwelt *among the rivers*. They encircled, folded round her, as it were, so that she was a little world in herself, secluded from all who would approach to hurt her. The Prophet's word, *rivers*[8], is especially used of the branches or canals of the Nile, which is also called *the sea*[9]. The Nile passed through No, and doubtless its canals encircled it.

---

[1] Memnonium. See Hoskins, Winter in upper and lower Eg. Frontispiece.
[2] 13 Stadia. (Diod. S. i. 46.) "It will be found to surpass the measurement of the historian by at least two or three stadia." Wilkins. ii. 249.
[3] Osirtasen i, placed at 2803. B. C. to Tirhaka, 693. B. C., Wilkinson Mod. Eg. ii. 250. 252.
[4] Lord Lindsay Letters on Egypt, &c., pp. 98, 99.
[5] Stanley, Sinai and Pal. p. xli.   [6] Tac. Ann. ii. 60.
[7] In Zech. i. 11, this is brought out by the addition of the word וְשֹׁקֶטֶת "and at rest ;" in Zech. vii. 7,
by וּשְׁלֵוָה, "and tranquil." In Rev. xviii. 7, "I sit a queen," the addition, "as a queen" points to the other meaning, of יָשַׁב, "sat enthroned."
[8] Yeorim.
[9] Is. xviii. 2, xix. 5. In Arabic, the Nile is called "the sweet sea" in contrast with "the salt sea," or "the encircling sea;" a title given by Egyptian writers to the Mediterranean, as being connected with the Ocean. Egyptian writers mostly add an

epithet to אֶלְבַּחְר, to designate the sea, because אֶלְבַּחְר, simply, is the Nile; as in India it is the Ganges; in Mesopotamia, the Euphrates. De Sacy Chrest. Arab. ii. 14, 15. ed. 2. The "white Nile" is called "Bahr-el-Abiad," the "blue Nile" Bahr-el-Azrek, and the great Ethiopian tributary to the Nile, the Albara, "Bahr-el-Aswad," "the black sea." Baker, Nile tributaries, p. 91. אֶלְבַּחְר is also used of the Tigris. Lane sub v. At Thebes, the Nile is usually about half a mile in width, but, at the inundation, overflowing the plain, especially upon the western bank, for a breadth of two or more miles. Smith Bib. Dict. v. Thebes. "When the Nile overflows the country, the cities alone appear, surmounting it, like the islands in the Ægean ; the rest of Egypt becomes a sea." Herod. ii. 97. "The water of the Nile is like a sea." Plin. H. N. xxxv. 11. "Homer gives to the river, the name 'Ocean,' because the Egyptians in their own language call the Nile, Ocean." Diod. S. i. 96.

Before
C H R I S T
cir. 713.

9 Ethiopia and Egypt
were her s t r e n g t h, and
it was infinite; Put and
Lubim were † thy helpers.
10 Yet *was* she carried

† Heb. *in thy help.*

away, she went into cap-
tivity: [n] her young children also were dashed in
pieces [o] at the top of all
the streets: and they [p] cast

Before
C H R I S T
cir. 713.

[n] Ps. 137. 9.
Isa. 13. 16.
Hos. 13. 16.
[o] Lam. 2. 19.
[p] Joel 3. 3.
Obad. 11.

Egypt is said by a Heathen to be " [1] walled
by the Nile as an everlasting wall." *Whose
rampart* was [*rampart* is] *the sea. Wall* and
rampart [2] are, properly, the outer and inner
wall of a city, the wall and forewall, so to
speak. For all walls and all defences, her
enfolding walls of sea would suffice. Strong
she was in herself; strong also in her helpers.
9. *Ethiopia and Egypt were her strength ;* lit.
Egypt was *strength* [3], *and Ethiopia, and boundless*. He sets forth first the imperial might
of No; then her strength from foreign, subdued power. The capital is a sort of impersonation of the might of the state; No, of
Egypt, as Nineveh, of Assyria. When the
head was cut off or the heart ceased to beat,
all was lost. The might of Egypt and
Ethiopia was the might of No, concentrated
in her. They were *strength*, and that strength
unmeasured by any human standard. *Boundless* was the *strength*, which Nineveh had
subdued: *boundless*, the *store* [4] which she
had accumulated for the spoiler; *boundless* [5]
the carcases of her slain. *And it was infinite.*
" The people that came up with the king out
of Egypt, were without number [6]." The
Egyptians connected with Thebes are counted
by a heathen author [7] at seven millions.
Put or *Phut* [8] is mentioned third among the
sons of Ham, after Cush and Mizraim [9].
They are mentioned with the Ethiopians in
Pharaoh's army at the Euphrates [10], as joined
with them in the visitation of Egypt [11]; with
Cush in the army of Gog [12]; with Lud in
that of Tyre [13]; a country and river of that
name were, Josephus tells us [14], " frequently
mentioned by Greek historians." They
dwelt in the Libya, conterminous to the
Canopic mouth of the Nile [15].

And Lubim. These came up against
Judah in the army of Shishak [6] against
Rehoboam, and with the Ethiopians, " a huge
host" under Zerah the Ethiopian against
Asa [16]. The Ribou or Libou appear on the
monuments as a people conquered by Me-
nephthes [17] and Rameses III. [18] They were
still to be united with Egypt and the Ethiopians in the times of Antiochus Epiphanes [19];
so their connection with Egypt was not
broken by its fall. Those unwearied enemies
had become incorporated with her; and
were now her help. These were (E. M.) *in
thy help ;* set upon it, given up to it [20]. The
prophet appeals to No herself, as it were,
" Thou *hadst* strength." Then he turns away,
to speak of her, unwilling to look on the
miseries which he has to portray to Nineveh, as the preludes of her own. Without
God, vain is the help of man.

10. *Yet* was *she* [*also* [21]] *carried away,* lit.
She also became *an exile* [22] band, her people
were carried away, with all the barbarities of
Heathen war. All, through whom she
might recover, were destroyed or scattered
abroad ; *the young,* the hope of another age,
cruelly destroyed [23]; *her honorable men* enslaved [24], *all her great men* prisoners. God's
judgments are executed step by step. Assyria herself was the author of this captivity,
which Isaiah prophesied in the first years of
Hezekiah when Judah was leaning upon
Egypt [25]. It was repeated by all of the
house of Sargon [26]. Jeremiah and Ezekiel
foretold fresh desolation by Nebuchadnezzar [27]. God foretold to His people [28], *I gave
Egypt for thy ransom, Ethiopia and Seba for
thee ;* and the Persian monarchs, who fulfilled prophecy in the restoration of Judah,

[1] Isocr. Busir. ap. Boch. Phal. i. 1. p. 7.

[2] חֵיל and חוֹמָה, joined Lam. ii. 8, חֵל וחומה.
It included the space between the two walls (pomœrium) 2 Sam. xx. 15, 1 Kgs xxi. 23. It is the whole
circuit of the wall as contrasted with the palaces
of Zion, in Ps. xlviii. 14, cxxii. 7. As is common in
Hebrew poetry, " wall and forewall," which together
make one subject, are placed in the parallel
columns. " Murus et antemurale" S. Jer. on Is.
xxvii. " the lesser wall, which is before the
greater," Rabb. ap. Kim. " the wall and the son
of the wall." R. Chanina. Ib.
[3] Not lit. " *her* strength." It is עָצְמָה, not עָצְמָה;
the abstract for the concrete, as אֵימָה Job xli. 6,
גֵּאוּת Ib. 7.   [4] ii. 10.
[5] iii. 3. קְצֶה וְאֵין in each.

[6] 2 Chron. xii. 3.
[7] Cato in Steph. Byz. ap. Boch. iv. 27.

[8] Translated Lybians Jer. xlvi. 9, Ez. xxx. 5,
xxxviii. 5.   [9] Gen. x. 6.   [10] Jer. l. c.
[11] Ez. xxx. 5.   [12] Ib. xxxviii. 15.
[13] Ib. xxix. 10.   [14] Jos. Ant. i. 6. 2.
[15] See Ges. Thes. s. v.
[16] 2 Chron. xvi. 8. coll. Ib. xiv. 9.
[17] B. C. 1341–1321 (Brugsch p. 172).
[18] 1288 B. C. Ib. 186, 190, 191.   [19] Dan. xi. 43.
[20] בְּעֶזְרִי Ps. xxxv. 2; בְּעֶזְרִי Ex. xviii. 4.
קוּמָה בְעֶזְרָתִי
[21] The word is emphatic; " *She also,*" her young
children *also*. The same word *also* is repeated.
[22] חַגּוֹלָה might be either " captivity" or " the
captives." But בַּגּוֹלָה הָלַךְ occurs 5 times, בָּא
בַגּוֹלָה, 3 times; but לַגּוֹלָה with neither.
[23] See Hos. xiv. Is. xiii. 16. 2 Kgs viii. 12.
[24] See Joel iii. 3.   [25] See Is. xx.
[26] See ab. pp. 117, 118.
[27] Jer. xlvi. 25, 26. and Ezekiel xxx. 14–16.
[28] Is. xliii. 3.

Before
C H R I S T
cir. 713.

lots for her honorable men, and all her great men were bound in chains.

11 Thou also shalt be [q]drunken: thou shalt be hid, thou also shalt seek strength because of t h e enemy.

[q]Jer. 25. 17, 27.
ch. 1. 10.

12 All thy strongholds *shall be like* [r]fig trees with the firstripe figs: if they be shaken, they shall even fall into the mouth of the eater.

13 Behold, [s]thy people in the midst of thee *are*

Before
C H R I S T
cir. 713.

[r]Rev. 6. 13.

[s]Jer. 50. 37.
& 51. 30.

---

fulfilled it also in the conquest of Egypt and Ethiopia. Both perhaps out of human policy in part. But Cambyses' wild hatred of Egyptian idolatry fulfilled God's word. Ptolemy Lathyrus carried on the work of Cambyses; the Romans, Ptolemy's. Cambyses burnt its *temples*[1]; Lathyrus its four-or five-storied private houses[2]; the Roman Gallus levelled it to the ground[3]. A little after it was said of her, "[4]she is inhabited as so many scattered villages." A little after our Lord's Coming, Germanicus went to visit, not it, but "[5]the vast traces of it." "[6]It lay overwhelmed with its hundred gates" and utterly impoverished. No was powerful as Nineveh, and less an enemy of the people of God. For though these often suffered from Egypt, yet in those times they even trusted too much to its help[7]. If then the judgments of God came upon No, how much more upon Nineveh! In type, Nineveh is the image of the world as oppressing God's Church; No, rather of those who live for this life, abounding in wealth, ease, power, and forgetful of God. If, then, *they* were punished, who took no active part against God, fought not against God's truth, yet still were sunk in *the cares and riches and pleasures of this life*, what shall be the end of those who openly resist God?

11. *Thou also.* As thou hast done, so shall it be done unto thee. The cruelties on No, in the cycle of God's judgments, draw on the like upon Nineveh who inflicted them. *Thou also*[8] *shalt be drunken* with the same cup of God's anger, entering within thee as wine doth, bereaving thee of reason and of counsel through the greatness of thy anguish, and bringing shame on thee[9], and a stupefaction like death. *Thou shalt be hid, a thing hidden*[10]

from the eyes of men, *as though thou hadst never been.* Nahum had foretold her complete desolation: he had asked, where is she? Here he describes an abiding condition; strangely fulfilled, as perhaps never to that extent besides; her palaces, her monuments, her records of her glorious triumphs existed still in their place, but hidden out of sight, as in a tomb, under the hill-like mounds along the Tigris. *Thou also shalt seek strength,* or a *strong-hold from the enemy*[11], out of thyself, since thine own shall be weakness. Yet in vain, since God, is not such to thee[12]. "They *shall seek,* but not find." "For then shall it be too late to cry for mercy, when it is the time of justice." *He shall have judgment without mercy, that hath shewed no mercy*[13]

12. *All thy strong-holds shall be like figtrees, with the first ripe figs,* hanging from them[14]; eagerly sought after[15], to be consumed. Being ripe, they are ready to fall at once; *if they be shaken;* it needeth but the tremulous motion, as when trees wave in the wind[16], *they shall even fall into the mouth of the eater,* not costing even the slight pains of picking them from the ground[17]. So easy is their destruction on the part of God, though it cost more pains to the Babylonians. At the end of the world it shall be yet more fulfilled[18], for then God will use no human instrument, but put forth only His own Almightiness; and all strong-holds of man's pride, moral or spiritual, shall, of themselves, melt away.

13. *Behold, thy people in the midst of thee are women.* Fierce, fearless, hard, iron men, such as their warriors still are portrayed by themselves on their monuments, they whom no toil wearied, no peril daunted, shall be, one and all, their whole *people, women.* So

---

[1] Diod. Sic. i. 46. Strabo xvii. 1. 45.
[2] They had been destroyed shortly before Diodorus Sic. Ib. 45, 46.
[3] "She was destroyed to the ground." S. Jer. Chron. Eus. A. 1989.
[4] Strabo l. c.   [5] Tac. Ann. ii. 62.
[6] Juv. Sat. xv. 6.   [7] See Is. xxx. &c.
[8] אַתְּ־נַם takes up הִיא־נַם v. 10.
[9] The two images are united in Ob. 16.
[10] The force of the substantive verb with the pass. part. נַעֲלָמָה תְּהִי as in Zech. iii. 3; as, with the act. part., it expresses continued action; Gen. i. 6, xxxvii. 2, De. ix. 7, 22, 24, xxviii. 29, 2 Sam. iii. 6,

Job i. 14, Ps. x. 14, cxxii. 2, Is. xxx. 20. See Ew. Lebrb. n. 168[c].
[11] מִגְּרָם מַחֲסֶה, as Is. xxv. 4, מֵעֹז מֵאוֹיֵב, "a refuge from the storm."
[12] i. 7.   [13] S. Jas. ii. 13.
[14] הָאֵנִים עִם בְּכוּרִים, as Cant. iv. 13, רִמּוֹנִים עִם מְגָדִים פְּרִי
[15] See ab. p. 66 on Mic. v. 1. It is not here the specific word, בִּכּוּרָה, but בִּכּוּרִים, "the first-fruits," in the same sense, as in Nu. xiii. 20, בִּכּוּרֵי עֲנָבִים "the first ripe grapes."
[16] נוּעַ is used of this, Is. vii. 2; here, as in Am. ix. 9. Nif.   [17] S. Jer.   [18] Rev. vi. 13.

women: the gates of thy land shall be set wide open

unto thine enemies: the
fire shall devour thy ᵗbars.
Before
C H R I S T
cir. 713.

ᵗ Ps. 147. 13. Jer. 51. 30.

Jeremiah to Babylon, "¹ they shall become, became, women." He sets it before the eyes. *Behold, thy people* are *women ;* against nature they are such, not in tenderness but in weakness and fear. Among the signs of the Day of Judgment, it stands, *men's hearts failing them for fear*². Where sin reigns, there is no strength left, no manliness or nobleness of soul, no power to resist. *In the midst of thee,* where thou seemest most secure, and, if any where, there were hope of safety. The very inmost self of the sinner gives way.

To thine enemies (this is, for emphasis, prefixed) not for any good to thee, but *to thine enemies shall be set wide open the gates of thy land,* not, *thy gates,* i. e. the gates of their cities, (which is a distinct idiom), but *the gates of the land* itself, every avenue, which might have been closed against the invader, but which was *laid open.* The Easterns³, as well as the Greeks and Latins⁴, used the word "gate" or "doors" of the mountain-passes, which gave an access to a land, but which might be held against an enemy. In the pass called "the Caucasian gates," there were, over and above, doors fastened with iron bars⁵. At Thermopylæ or, as the inhabitants called them, Pylæ⁶, "gates," the narrow pass was further guarded by a wall⁷. Its name recalls the brilliant history, how such approaches might be held by a devoted handful of men against almost countless multitudes. Of Assyria, Pliny says, "⁸ The Tigris and pathless mountains encircle Adiabene." When those *gates of the land* gave way, the whole land was laid open to its enemies.

The fire shall devour thy bars. Probably, as elsewhere, the *bars* of the gates, which were mostly of wood, since it is added expressly of

some, that they were of the iron ⁹ or brass ¹⁰. "¹¹ Occasionally the efforts of the besiegers were directed against the gate, which they endeavored to break open with axes, or to set on fire by application of a torch.—In the hot climate of S. Asia wood becomes so dry by exposure to the sun, that the most solid doors may readily be ignited and consumed." It is even remarked in one instance that the Assyrians "¹² have not set fire to the gates of this city, as appeared to be their usual practice in attacking a fortified place."

So were her palaces buried as they stood, that the traces of prolonged fire are still visible, calcining the one part and leaving others which were not exposed to it, uncalcined. "¹³ It is incontestable that, during the excavations, a considerable quantity of charcoal, and even pieces of wood, either half-burnt or in a perfect state of preservation, were found in many places. The lining of the chambers also bears certain marks of the action of fire. All these things can be explained only by supposing the fall of a burning roof, which calcined the slabs of gypsum and converted them into dust. It would be absurd to imagine that the burning of a small quantity of furniture could have left on the walls marks like these which are to be seen through all the chambers, with the exception of one, which was only an open passage. It must have been a violent and prolonged fire, to be able to calcine not only a few places, but every part of these slabs, which were ten feet high and several inches thick. So complete a decomposition can be attributed but to intense heat, such as would be occasioned by the fall of a burning roof.

"Botta found on the engraved flag-stones scoria and half-melted nails, so that there is no an enemy," and in the idiom שַׁד אלתער, "stopped the gap," like עמד בפרץ Ez. xxii. 30. The phrase, שער האריץ, recurs Jer. xv. 7.

---

¹ Jer. l. 37, li. 30. ² S. Luke xxi. 26.

³ Freytag (sub. v. בָּאב) says that the Pyrenees are called in Arab. גבל אלאבואב "the mountain of gates," and' that the Portæ Caspiæ are called בָּאב אלאבואב. "Bab Bmaria" is the name of a pass in Libanon to the Litany, Ritter Erdk. xvii. 93. 94. 138. 218; "Bab-el-Howa" "gate of the winds" is said to be a mountain gorge (Ritter xviii. 849. Buckingham gives the name to a gate of Bosra. Travels among Arabs ii. 200). Bab-el-Mardin is the name of a mountain-pass in the Masius chain (Ritter xi. 263. 393. 464), "a remaakable gap or notch in the chain of Mt. Masius, behind which is situated the city of Mardin." Forbes on the Sinjar Hills, Mem. R. Geogr. Soc. 1839 p. 421. The name "Bab-el-mandeb" shews that the name "door" is given to narrow straits also, as is that of πύλαι (See Lidd. and Scott Lex. v. πύλη). The Arab. תָעַר only incidentally illustrates the idiom, being, not a "gate" (as Röd. in Ges. Thes.) but "a gap, interstice, hence a mountain-pass, an access to a country," and specifically "a border-country toward

⁴ The Κάσπιαι πύλαι (Strabo xi. 12. 13), the Αὐδίαι Ib. xiii. 65). See further Lidd. and Sc. l. c.) the πύλαι τῆς Κιλικίας καὶ τῆς Συρίας, Xen. Anab. i. 4. 14, the "Amanicæ Pylæ" (Q. Curt. iii. 20). Pliny speaks of the "portæ Caucasiæ" (H. N. vi. 11) or "Iberiæ" (Albaniæ Ptol. v. 12.) Ib. 15.

⁵ "After these are the Caucasian gates (by many very erroneously called the Caspian gates), a vast work of nature, the mountains being suddenly interrupted, where are doors, &c." Plin. H. N. vi. 11.

⁶ Herod. vii. 201.   ⁷ Ib. 176. 208.

⁸ Plin. H. N. vi. 9. quoted by Tuch ii. 1.

⁹ Ps. cvii. 16, Is. xlv. 2.   ¹⁰ 1 Kgs iv. 13.

¹¹ Rawl. 5 Emp. ii. 83. who relates how "the city of Candahar was ignited from the outside by the Affghanees, and was entirely consumed in less than an hour." Note.

¹² Bonomi Nin. p. 205. ed. 2. on Botta plate 93. See also Ib. p. 221, 222. 225.

¹³ Ib. Sect. iv. c. 1, pp. 245-247.

14 Draw thee waters for the siege, ᵘ fortify thy strong holds: go into clay, and tread the mortar, make strong the brickkiln.

15 There shall the fire devour thee; the sword shall cut thee off, it shall eat thee up like ˣ the cankerworm: make thyself

doubt that these appearances had been produced by the action of intense and long-sustained heat. He remembers, beside, at Khorsabad, that when he detached some bas-reliefs from the earthy substance which covered them, in order to copy the inscriptions that were behind, he found there coals and cinders, which could have entered only by the top, between the wall and the back of the bas-relief. This can be easily understood to have been caused by the burning of the roof, but is inexplicable in any other manner. What tends most positively to prove that the traces of fire must be attributed to the burning of a wooden roof is, that these traces are perceptible only in the interior of the building. The gypsum also that covers the wall inside is completely calcined, while the outside of the building is nearly everywhere untouched. But wherever the fronting appears to have at all suffered from fire, it is at the bottom; thus giving reason to suppose that the damage has been done by some burning matter falling outside. In fact, not a single bas-relief in a state to be removed was found in any of the chambers, they were all pulverized."

The soul which does not rightly close its senses against the enticements of the world, does, in fact, open them, and *death is come up into our windows*[1], and then "[2] whatever natural good there yet be, which, as *bars*, would hinder the enemy from bursting in, is consumed by the fire," once kindled, of its evil passions.

14. *Draw thee waters for the siege ; fortify thy strongholds.* This is not mere mockery at man's weakness, when he would resist God. It foretells that they shall toil, and that, heavily. Toil is added upon toil. Nineveh did undergo a two years' siege. *Water* stands for all provisions within. He bids them, as before[3], strengthen what was already strong; *strongholds*, which seemed to "cut off" all approach. These he bids them strengthen, not repairing decays only but making them *exceeding strong*[4]. *Go into clay.* We seem to see all the inhabitants,

[1] Jer. ix. 21. [2] S. Jer. [3] ii. 1.
[4] 2 Chr. xi. 12.
[5] Is. xliv. 12, sqq.
[6] חמר and טיט are united as synonymes Is. xli. 25, where the טיט is that which the potter treadeth, יוצר ירמס טיט.
[7] Rawl. 5 Emp. i. 476.
[8] Wilk. Anc. Eg. ii. 99. [9] Anab. iii. 4, 4.
[10] See Is. xxvii. 10, 11. [11] Ps. xlix. 11.
[12] S. Luke xii. 19, 20.
[13] התכבד expresses more than mere number.

like ants on their nest, all poured out, every one busy, every one making preparation for the defence. Why had there been no need of it ? What needed she of towers and fortifications, whose armies were carrying war into distant lands, before whom all which was near was hushed ? Now, all had to be renewed. As Isaiah in his mockery of the idol-makers begins with the forging of the axe, the planting and rearing of the trees, which were at length to become the idol[5], Nahum goes back to the beginning. The neglected *brick-kiln*, useless in their prosperity, was to be *repaired ;* the clay[6], which abounded in the valley of the Tigris[7], was to be collected, mixed and kneaded by treading, as still represented in the Egyptian monuments. The conquering nation was to do the work of slaves, as Asiatic captives are represented, under their taskmasters[8], on the monuments of Egypt, a prelude of their future. Xenophon still saw the massive brick wall, on the stone foundation[9].

Yet, though stored within and fenced without, it shall not stand[10].

15. *There,* where thou didst fence thyself, and madest such manifold and toilsome preparation, *shall the fire devour thee.* All is toil within. The fire of God's wrath falls and consumes at once. Mankind still, with mire and clay, build themselves Babels. *They go into clay,* and become themselves earthly like the mire they steep themselves in. They make themselves strong, as though they thought *that their houses shall continue forever*[11], *and say,* [12] *Soul, take thine ease, eat, drink and be merry.* God's wrath descends. *Thou fool, this night thy soul shall be required of thee. It shall eat thee up like the canker-worm.* What in thee is strongest, shall be devoured with as much ease as the locust devours the tender grass. The judgments of God, not only overwhelm as a whole, but find out each tender part, as the locust devours each single blade. *Make thyself many as the cankerworm,* as though thou wouldest equal thyself in oppressive number[13] to those instruments of God.

כבד retains always the idea of weight, gravity or oppressiveness. *We* say "heavy hail" Ex. ix. 18, 24. It is used of the plague of flies, Ib. viii. 20, and, as here, of the locusts, Ib. x. 14; of the host, with which Esau opposed Israel, Nu. xx. 20, (adding וּבְיָד חֲזָקָה); of that sent with Rabshakeh to Jerusalem, Is. xxxvi. 2. and of the great train of the Queen of Sheba, camels laden with very much gold and precious stones, 1 Kgs x. 2. כבד occurs above

many as the cankerworm, make thyself many as the locusts.

16 Thou hast multiplied

thy merchants above the
stars of heaven: the cankerworm ‖ spoileth, and fleeth away. ‖ Or, *spreadeth himself.*

---

vengeance of God, gathering from all quarters armies to help thee; yea, though thou make thy whole self[1] one oppressive multitude, yet it shall not avail thee. Nay, He saith, thou hast essayed to do it.

16. *Thou hast multiplied thy merchants above the stars of Heaven;* not numerous only but glorious in the eyes of the world, and, as thou deemest, safe and inaccessible; yet in an instant all is gone.

The commerce of Nineveh was carried back to præhistoric times, since its rivers bound together the mountains of Armenia with the Persian gulf, and marked out the line, by which the distant members of the human family should supply each others' needs. "Semiramis," they say[2], "built other cities on the Euphrates and the Tigris, where she placed emporia for those who convey their goods from Media and Parætacene. Being mighty rivers and passing through a populous country, they yield many advantages to those employed in commerce; so that the places by the river are full of wealthy emporia." The Phœnicians traced back their Assyrian commerce (and as it seems, truly) to those same præhistoric times, in which they alleged, that they themselves migrated from the Persian gulf. They commenced at once, they said[3], the long voyages, in which they transported the wares of Egypt and Assyria. The building of "Tadmor in the wilderness[4]" on the way to Tiphsach (Thapsacus) the utmost bound of Solomon's dominions[5], connected Palestine with that commerce. The great route for couriers and for traffic, extending for fifteen hundred or sixteen hundred miles in later times, must have lain through Nineveh, since, although no mention is made of the city which had perished, the route lay across the two rivers[6], the greater and lesser Zab, of which the greater formed the Southern limit of Nineveh. Those two rivers led up to two mountain-passes which opened a way to Media and Agbatana; and pillars at the summit of the N. pass attest the use of this route over the Zagros chain about

700 B. C.[7] Yet a third and easier pass was used by Nineveh, as is evidenced by another monument, of a date as yet undetermined[8]. Two other lines connected Nineveh with Syria and the West. Northern lines led doubtless to Lake Wan and the Black Sea[9]. The lists of plunder or of tribute, carried off during the world-empire of Egypt, before it was displaced by Assyria, attest the extensive imports or manufactures of Nineveh[10]; the titles of "Assyrian nard, Assyrian amomum, Assyrian odors, myrrh, frankincense[11], involve its trade with the spice countries: domestic manufactures of hers apparently were purple or dark-blue cloaks[12], embroidery, brocades[13], and these conveyed in chests of cedar; her metallurgy was on principles recognized now; in one practical point of combining beauty with strength, she has even been copied[14].

A line of commerce, so marked out by nature in the history of nations, is not changed, unless some preferable line be discovered. Empires passed away, but at the end of the 13th century trade and manufacture continued their wonted course and habitation. The faith in Jesus had converted the ancient heathenism; the heresy of Mohåmmedanism disputed with the faith for the souls of men; but the old material prosperity of the world held its way. Mankind still wanted the productions of each others' lands. The merchants of Nineveh were to be dispersed and were gone: itself and its remembrance were to be effaced from the earth, and it was so; in vain was a new Nineveh built by the Romans; that also disappeared; but so essential was its possession for the necessities of commerce, that Mosul, a large and populous town, arose over against its mounds, a city of the living over-against its buried glories; and, as *our* goods are known in China by the name of our great manufacturing capital, so a delicate manufacture imposed on the languages of Europe (Italian, Spanish, French, English, German) the name of Mosul[15].

---

iii. 3. of the heavy mass of corpses. In Ex. ix. 3, it is used of a grievous pestilence (Gesenius' instances Thes. s. v.).
[1] The two genders, התכבדי, התכבד, are probably joined together, the more strongly to express universality, as מִשֶּׁעַן וּמִשְׁעֵנָה, Is. iii. 1; and Nahum himself unites טֶרֶף and טַרְפָה in two parallel clauses, ii. 13. [2] Diod. ii. 11.
[3] Herod. i. 1. [4] 1 Kgs ix. 18. [5] Ib v. 4. (iv. 24.)
[6] Herod. ii. 52. [7] See Rawl. 5 Emp. ii. 180, 181.
[8] Ib. 181, 182. [9] Ib. 182, 183.

[10] "Dishes of silver with their covers; a harp of brass inlaid with gold; 823 pounds of perfumes" (Brugsch Hist. d' Eg. p. 100); "10 pounds of true lapis lazuli, 24 pounds of artificial lapis lazuli; vessels laden with ebony and ivory, precious stones, vases, (Ib. p. 203); beside· many other articles, which cannot yet be made out.
[11] See Rawl. 5 Emp. ii. 191, 192.
[12] נְלוֹמֵי תְכֵלֶת, Ez. xxvii. 24. [13] ברומים
[14] Layard Nin. and Bab. p. 191.
[15] "All those cloths of gold and of silk which we call

Before
CHRIST
cir. 713.

⁷ Rev. 9. 7.

17 ⁷ Thy crowned *are* as the locusts, and thy captains as the great grass-

hoppers, which camp in the hedges in the cold day, *but* when the sun ariseth

Before
CHRIST
cir. 713.

Even early in this century, under a mild governor, an important commerce passed through Mosul, from India, Persia, Kurdistan, Syria, Natolia, Europe[1]. And when European traffic took the line of the Isthmus of Suez, the communication with Kurdistan still secured to it an important and exclusive commerce. The merchants of Nineveh were dispersed and gone. The commerce continued over-against its grave.

The cankerworm spoileth and fleeth away; better, *the locust hath spread itself abroad* (*marauded*) *and is flown.* The prophet gives, in three words[2], the whole history of Nineveh, its beginning and its end. He had before foretold its destruction, though it should be oppressive as the locust; he had spoken of its commercial wealth; he adds to this, that other source of its wealth, its despoiling warfares and their issue. The heathen conqueror rehearsed his victory, " I came, saw, conquered." The prophet goes farther, as the issue of all human conquest, "I disappeared." *The locust* [Nineveh] *spread itself abroad* (the word is always used of an inroad for plunder[3]), destroying and wasting, everywhere: it left the world a desert, and was gone[4]. Ill-gotten wealth makes poor, not rich. Truly they who traffic in this world, are more in number than they who, seeking treasure in Heaven, shall *shine as the stars* for ever and ever. For *many are called,*

but few are chosen. And when *all the stars of light* " shall abide and *praise God*[5], these men, though multiplied like the locust, shall, like the locust, pass away, destroying and destroyed. They abide for a while in the chillness of this world; when the Sun of righteousness ariseth, they vanish. This is the very order of God's Providence. As truly as locusts, which in the cold and dew are chilled and stiffened, and cannot spread their wings, *fly away* when the sun is hot and are found no longer, so shalt thou be dispersed and thy place not any more be known[6]. It was an earnest of this, when the Assyrians, like locusts, had spread themselves around Jerusalem in a dark *day of trouble and of rebuke and of blasphemy*[7], God was entreated and they were not. Midian *came up like the grasshopper for multitude*[8]. In the morning they had fled[9]. What is the height of the sons of men? or how do they spread themselves abroad?" At the longest, after a few years it is but as the locust *spreadeth himself and fleeth away,* no more to return.

17. *Thy crowned* are *as the locust, and thy captains as the great locusts.* What he had said summarily under metaphor, the prophet expands in a likeness. *The crowned*[10] are probably the subordinate princes, of whom Sennacherib said[11], *Are not my princes altogether kings?* It has been observed that the head-dress of the Assyrian Vizier has the orna-

---

'muslins' (Mossulini) are of manufacture of Mosul." Marco Polo, Travels c. 6. p. 37. ed. 1854. " The manufactures from fine transparent white cotton, like the stuffs now made in India under that name and like the bombazines manufactured at Arzingan, received in the following centuries the name 'muslins;' but not the silk brocades interwoven with gold, which had their name Baldachini from Baldak i. e. Bagdad, and perhaps were manufactured at that time at Mosul, unless indeed this name 'muslin' was then given to gold-brocades as wares of Mosul." Ritter Erdk. x. 274, 275. " There is a very large deposition of merchandise [at Mosul] because of the river, wherefore several goods and fruits are brought thither from the adjacent countries, both by land and water, to ship them for Bagdad." Rauwolf's Travels P. 2, c. 9. p. 205. A. 1573. Niebuhr still witnessed "the great traffic carried on there, as also linen manufactures, dyeing and printing [of stuffs]."

[1] Olivier Voyage (1808) ii. 359. In 1766, one caravan, in which Niebuhr travelled, had 1300 camelloads of gall-apples from Kurdistan. It supplied yearly 2000 centners of them. Nieb. ii. 274.

[2] ‏ילק פשט ויעף‎.

[3] Jud. ix. 44 bis, 1 Sam. xxiii. 27, xxvii. 8, 10, xxx. 1, 1 Chr. xiv, 9, 13, 2 Chr. xxv. 13, xxviii. 18. The object, against which the attack is directed, is joined on with ‏אל‎ Jud. xx. 37, 1 Sam. xxvii. 8, 10, xxx. 1, or ‏על‎, Jud. ix. 33, 44, 1 Sam. xxiii. 27, xxvii. 10; even as to the object of plunder, "camels" Job i.

17. The place (Hos. vi. 1) or country (1 Chr. xiv. 9, 13, 2 Chr. xxv. 13, xxviii. 18) is joined with ‏ב‎, and once (1 Sam. xxx. 14) stands in the accus. The idiom ‏פשט בגדיו‎, " put off his clothes," is distinct. The object of the verb is always added Lev. vi. 4, xvi. 23, 1 Sam. xix. 24, Cant. v. 3, Ez. xxvi. 16, xliv. 19, Neh. iv. 17; except that, in Is. xxxii. 11, it is implied by the context, "strip ye, make ye bare." Credner's theory then (followed by Ewald Proph. iii. 14. ed. 2.) that ‏ילק‎ signifies the locust in its last moulting, which strips off the involucra of its wings, is contrary to the use of ‏פשט‎, as well as to that of ‏ילק‎. See on Joel vol. i. p. 149. Gesenius, under ‏פשט‎, contradicts the explanation which he had given under ‏ילק‎ from Credner.

[4] ‏עוף‎ is used of shortness of human life; "like a dream he flieth away," (‏יעוף‎) Job xx. 8; "and we fly away" ‏ונעפה‎, Ps. xc. 10. "Ephraim, like a bird, their glory flieth away," ‏יתעופף‎, Hos. ix. 11, add Pr. xxiii. 5, of unjust wealth.
[5] Ps. cxlviii. 3.   [6] See c. i. 8.   [7] Is. xxxvii. 3.
[8] Judg. vi. 4, 5, vii. 12.   [9] Judg. vii. 21.
[10] The punctuation of ‏מנזריך‎ is compared by Jewish grammarians too to ‏מקדש‎ Ex. xv. 17; ‏ממגרח‎ Jo. i. 17.   [11] Is. x. 8.

11

Before
C H R I S T
cir. 713.

‖ Ex. 15. 16.
Ps. 76. 6.
ª Jer. 50. 18.
Ezek. 31. 3, &c.

they flee away, and their
place is not known where
they *are.*

18 ᶻ Thy shepherds
slumber, O ª king of As-

syria: thy ‖ nobles shall
dwell *in the dust:* thy people is ᵇ scattered upon the
mountains, and no man
gathereth *them.*

Before
C H R I S T
cir. 713.

‖ Or, *valiant
ones.*
ᵇ 1 Kin. 22. 17.

---

ment which "¹ throughout the whole series
of sculptures is the distinctive mark of royal
or quasi-royal authority." "² All high officers of state, *the crowned captains,* were adorned
with diadems, closely resembling the lower
band of the royal mitre, separated from the
cap itself. Such was that of the vizier,
which was broader in front than behind, was
adorned with rosettes and compartments, and
terminated in two ribbons with embroidered
and fringed ends, which hung down his
back." *Captain* is apparently the title of
some military office of princely rank. One
such Jeremiah ³, in a prophecy in which he
probably alludes to this, bids place over the
armies of Ararat, Minni, and Ashchenaz, to
marshall them against Babylon, against
which he summons the cavalry *like the rough
locust.* The *captains* are likened to the *great
caterpillars* ⁴, either as chief in devastation,
or as including under them the armies under
their command, who moved at their will.
These and their armies now subsided into
stillness for a time under the chill of calamity, like the locust "⁵ whose nature it is, that,
torpid in the cold, they fly in the heat." The
stiffness of the locusts through the cold,
when they lie motionless, heaps upon heaps,
hidden out of sight, is a striking image of
the helplessness of Nineveh's mightiest in
the day of her calamity; then, by a different
part of their history, he pictures their entire disappearance. "⁶ The locusts, are commonly taken in the morning when they are
agglomerated one on another, in the places
where they passed the night. As soon as the
sun warms them, they fly away." *When the
sun ariseth, they flee away* ⁷, lit. *it is chased
away* ⁸. One and all; all as one. As at
God's command the plague of locusts, which

He had sent on Egypt, was removed ⁹; *there
remained not one locust in all the coasts of Egypt;*
so the mighty of Nineveh were driven forth,
with no trace where they had been, where
they were. *The wind carried them away* ¹⁰;
*the wind passeth over him and he is not, and his
place knoweth him no more* ¹¹. *The triumphing
of the wicked is short, and the joy of the ungodly
for a moment: though his excellency mount up
to the heavens, and his head reach unto the clouds,
yet he shall perish for ever; they which have seen
him shall say, where is he? He shall fly away, as
a dream, and shall not be found; neither shall
his place any more behold him* ¹².

Where they are. So Zechariah asks, *Your
fathers, where are they* ¹³? History, experience,
human knowledge can answer nothing. They
can only say, where they are *not.* God
Alone can answer that much-containing word,
Where-they ¹⁴. They had disappeared from
human sight, from their greatness, their visible being, their place on earth.

18. *Thy shepherds,* i. e. they who should
counsel for the people's good and feed it, and
keep watch over their flocks by night, but are now
like their master, the *King of Assyria,* are his
shepherds not the shepherds of the people
whom they care not for; these *slumber,* at
once through listlessness and excess, and now
have fallen asleep in death, as the Psalmist
says ¹⁵, *They have slept their sleep.* The prophet speaks of the future, as already past in
effect, as it was in the will of God. All "the
shepherds of the people ¹⁶," all who could
shepherd them, or hold them together, themselves sleep *the sleep of death;* their *mighty
men dwelt* ¹⁷ in that abiding-place, where they
shall not move or rise ¹⁸, the grave; and so
as Micaiah, in the vision predictive of
Ahab's death ¹⁹, saw *all Israel scattered on the*

---

¹ Rawl. 5. Empires i. 115.
² Gosse, Assyria p. 463, who remarks that " the
Ten Thousand in Xerxes' army," crossed the Hel-
lespont " crowned with garlands." Herod. vii. 55.
³ Jer. li. 27. On the word, סבכר, see ab. p. 107.
n. e.
⁴ גוב גבי, doubtless the common superlative,
like עבד עבדים Gen. ix. 25.
⁵ S. Jer. copied by S. Cyr. and Theod.
⁶ Casalis, on the proverb of the Bassouto, " locusts are taken in the heap." Etudes sur la langue
Sechuana ɼ. 87. Paris 1842, referred to by Ewald ad
loc. who also refers to Ibn Babuta (in the Journ.
As. 1843, March, p. 240.) " The chase of locusts is
made before sunrise; for then they are benumbed
by the cold and cannot fly."
⁷ יום קרה, "the cold day," (also Prov. xxv. 20),
of course does not mean "night," (as Hitzig &c.)

nor (as Ew. &c.) does זרח השמש mean anything
but " sunrise," of which it is used 8 times beside,
Gen. xxxii. 32, Ex. xxii. 2, Jud. ix. 33, 2 Sam. xxiii.
4, 2 Kgs iii. 22, Ps. civ. 22, Eccl. i. 5, Jon. iv. 8; but
the locusts, having been benumbed by a cold day,
plainly would not be warmed till the sunrise of the
following day.
⁸ נודד, passive.   ⁹ Ex. x. 19.   ¹⁰ Is. xli. 16.
¹¹ Ps. ciii. 16.   ¹² Job xx. 5-9.   ¹³ Zech. i.
¹⁴ אים, contracted for איה הם.
¹⁵ Ps. lxxvi. 6, נמו שנתם.
¹⁶ Homer, passim. ¹⁷ Comp. משכן Is. xxii. 16.
¹⁸ " They cannot rise " Rashi. " It means the rest
of death, and so שכנה דומה נפשי Ps. xciv. 6,
כבודי לעפר ישכן Ps. vii. 6." Sal. Ben Mel. "are
still and move not." A. E.   ¹⁹ 1 Kgs xxii. 17.

Before
C H R I S T
cir. 713. 19 *There is* no †healing
of thy bruise; °thy wound

† Heb. *wrinkling.* ° Mic. 1. 9.

is grievous: ᵈall that hear
the bruit of thee shall clap

Before
C H R I S T
cir. 713.

ᵈ Lam. 2. 15. Zeph. ii. 15. See Isa. 14. 8, &c.

---

hills, as sheep that have not a shepherd, so the people of the Assyrian monarch shall be *scattered on the mountains,* shepherdless, and that irretrievably ; *no man gathereth* them.

19. *There is no healing* [lit. *dulling*] *of thy bruise;* it cannot be softened or mitigated ; and so *thy wound is grievous* [lit. *sick*], incurable, for when the wound ever anew inflames, it cannot be healed. The word, *bruise,* is the more expressive, because it denotes alike the abiding wound in the body [1], and the shattering of a state, which God can heal [2], or which may be great, incurable [3]. When the passions are ever anew aroused, they are at last without remedy ; when the soul is ever swollen with pride, it cannot be healed ; since only by submitting itself to Christ, " broken and contrite " by humility, can it be healed. Nineveh sank, and never rose ; nothing soothed its fall. In the end there shall be nothing to mitigate the destruction of the world, or to soften the sufferings of the damned. The *rich man, being in torments,* asked in vain that Lazarus might *dip the tip of his finger in water and cool my tongue.* *All that hear the bruit of thee shall clap the hands over thee,* for none can grieve at thy fall.

Nineveh sinks out of sight amid one universal, exulting, exceeding joy [4] of all who heard the report of her. *For upon whom hath not thy wickedness passed continually ?* " In that he asketh, *upon whom hath not thy wickedness passed continually?* he affirmeth most strongly that his evil did pass upon all continually." His *wickedness,* like one *continual* flood, which knew no ebb or bound, had *passed* upon the whole world and each one in it ; now at length it had passed away, and *the whole earth is at rest, is quiet ; they break forth into singing* [5].

It is not without meaning, that having throughout the prophecy addressed Nineveh (in the feminine), now, in the close [6], the prophet turns to him in whom all its wickedness is, as it were, gathered into one, the soul of all its evil, and the director of it, its king. As Nineveh is the image of the world, its pomps, wealth, luxury, vanity, wickedness, oppression, destruction, so its king is the image of a worse king, the Prince of this world. " [7] And this is the song of triumph of those, over whom *his wickedness has passed,* not rested, but they have escaped out of his hands. Nahum, ' the comforter,' had *rebuked*

the world of sin ; now he pronounces that *the prince of this world is judged. His shepherds* are they who serve him, who *feed the flock of the slaughter,* who guide them to evil, not to good. These, when they *sleep,* as all mankind, *dwell* there; it is *their abiding-place ;* their sheep are *scattered on the mountains,* in the heights of their pride, because they are not of the sheep of Christ; and since they would not be gathered of Him, they *are scattered,* where *none gathereth.*" " The king of Assyria (Satan) knoweth that he cannot deceive the sheep, unless he have first laid the shepherds asleep. It is ever the aim of the devil to lay asleep souls that watch. In the Passion of the Lord, he weighed down the eyes of the Apostles with heavy sleep, whom Christ arouseth [8], *Watch and pray, lest ye enter into temptation ;* and again, *What I say unto you, I say unto all, watch ! And no man gathereth them,* for their shepherds themselves cannot protect themselves. In the Day of God's anger, *the kings of the earth and the great men, and the rich men and the chief captains, and the mighty men, and every bondman, and every free man, hid themselves in the dens and in the rocks of the mountains* [9]. Such are his shepherds, and his sheep ; but what of himself ? Truly his *bruise* or *breaking* can *not be healed ;* his *wound* or smiting is *incurable ;* that namely whereby, when *he came* to Him *in* Whom he *found nothing* [10], yet *bruised His heel,* and exacted of Him a sinner's death, *his own head was bruised.*" And hence *all who have ears to hear,* who hear not with the outward only, but with the inner ears of the heart, *clap the hands over thee,* i. e. give to God all their souls' thanks and praise, raise up their eyes and hands to God in heaven, praising Him Who had *bruised Satan under their feet.* Ever since, through the serpent, the evil and malicious One lied, saying, *ye shall not surely die,* eat and *ye shall be as gods,* hath *his evil, continually* and unceasingly, from one and through one, *passed upon all* men. As the Apostle saith, *As by one man, sin entered into the world, and death by sin, and so death passed upon all men, for that all have sinned* [11]. *Upon whom* then hath not *his sin passed ?* Who hath not been *shapen in iniquity ?* and whom did not *his mother conceive in sin ?* Yet, it *passeth* only, for *the world itself also passeth away,* and we pass away from it, and all the evil it can do us, unless we share in its evil, is not abiding, but passing. This then is the cause, and a

---

[1] Lev. xxi. 19. [2] Ps. lx. 4, Is. xxx. 26.
[3] Jer. xxx. 12.
[4] תִּקְעוּ כַף, only here and Ps. xlvii. 2, expressing joy.

[5] Is. xiv. 7. [6] v. 18, 19.
[7] S. Jer. Rup.
[8] S. Mat. xxvi. 41. [9] Rev. vi. 15.
[10] S. John xiv. 30. [11] Rom. v. 12.

Before
C H R I S T
cir. 713.
the hands over thee: for
upon whom hath not thy

wickedness passed contin-
ually?
Before
C H R I S T
cir. 713.

great cause, why *all that hear the bruit of thee* should *clap the hands over thee ;* because thee, whose *wickedness passed* through one *upon all,* One Man, Who Alone was without sin, contemned and bruised, while He freed and justified from wickedness them who *hearing* rejoiced, and rejoicing and believing, *clapped*

the hands over thee. Yet they only shall be glad, upon whom his *wickedness,* although it *passed,* yet abode not, but in prayer and good deeds, by the grace of God, they lifted up their hands to Him Who overcame, and Who, in His own, overcometh still, to Whom be praise and thanksgiving for ever and ever. Amen.

INTRODUCTION

TO

THE PROPHET

HABAKKUK.

HABAKKUK is eminently the prophet of reverential, awe-filled faith. This is the soul and centre of his prophecy. One word alone he addresses directly to his people. It is of marvel at their want of faith. [a] *Behold among the heathen and gaze attentively, and marvel, marvel; for I am working a work in your days; ye will not believe, when it is declared unto you.* He bids them *behold,* and *gaze,* for God is about to work in their own days; he bids them prepare themselves to *marvel,* and *marvel on;* for it was a matter, at which political wisdom would stagger; and they, since they had not faith, would not believe it. The counterpart to this, is that great blessing of faith, which is the key-stone of his whole book, [b] *the just shall live by his faith.*

Isaiah had foretold to Hezekiah that his treasures should be carried to Babylon, his sons be eunuchs in the palace of its king [c]. He had foretold the destruction of Babylon and the restoration of the Jews [d]. Prophecy in Habakkuk, full as it is, is almost subordinate. His main subject is, that which occupied Asaph in the 73d Psalm, the afflictions of the righteous amid the prosperity of the wicked. The answer is the same; the result of all will be one great reversal, the evil drawing upon themselves evil, God crowning the patient waiting of the righteous in still submission to His holy Will. *The just shall live by his faith,* occupies the same place in Habakkuk, as *I know that my Redeemer liveth,* does in Job [e], or *Thou shalt guide me with Thy counsel, and after that receive me into glory,* in Asaph [f].

His first subject [g] is, faith struggling under

the oppressive sight of the sufferings of the good from the bad within God's people; the second [h], the sufferings at the hands of those who are God's instruments to avenge that wickedness. The third [i], that of his great hymn, is faith, not jubilant until the end, yet victorious, praying, believing, seeing in vision what it prays for, and triumphing in that, of which it sees no tokens, whose only earnest is God's old loving-kindnesses to His people, and His Name, under which He had revealed Himself, "He Who Is," the Unchangeable.

The whole prophecy is, so to speak, a colloquy between the prophet and God. He opens it with a reverential, earnest, appeal to God, like that of the saints under the heavenly Altar in the Revelations [k], *How long?* The prophet had prayed to God to end or mitigate the violence, oppressions, strife, contention, despoiling, powerlessness of the law, crookedness of justice, entrapping of the righteous by the wicked [l]. God answers [m], that a terrible day of retribution was coming, that He Himself would raise up the Chaldees, as the instruments of His chastisements, terrible, self-dependent, owning no law or authority but their own will, deifying their own power, sweeping the whole breadth of the land, possessing themselves of it, taking every fenced city, and gathering captives as the sand. This answers the one half of Habakkuk's question, as to the prosperity of the wicked among his people. It leaves the other half, as to the condition of the righteous, unanswered. For such scourges of God swept

---

[a] i. 5.　　　[b] ii. 4.　　　[c] Is. xxxix. 6, 7.
[d] Is. xii. xiii. xlvii.　　　[e] Job xix. 25.

[f] Ps. lxxiii. 24.　　[g] c. i.　　[h] c. ii.　　[i] c. iii.
[k] Rev. vi. 10.　　[l] i. 2-4.　　[m] Ib. 6-11.

165

away the righteous with the wicked. Habakkuk then renews the question as to *them*.
But, as Asaph began by declaring his faith,
[n]*All-good is God to Israel*, the true Israel, *the
pure of heart*, so Habakkuk, " Israel would
not die, because He, their God, is Unchangeable." [o]*Art not Thou of old, O Lord, my God,
my holy One? we shall not die; Thou, O Lord,
hast set him* [the Chaldee] *for judgment, and
Thou, O Rock, hast founded him to chasten.*
Then he appeals to God, " Why then is
this? *Thou art of purer eyes than to behold
evil—wherefore keepest Thou silence, when the
wicked devoureth him who is more righteous than
he?*" This closes the first chapter and the first
vision, in which he describes, with the vividness of one who saw it before him, the irresistible invasion of the Chaldæans. Israel was
meshed as in a net; should that net be
emptied [p]?

The second chapter exhibits the prophet
waiting in silent expectation for the answer.
This answer too dwells chiefly on those retri-
butions in this life, which are the earnest
of future judgments, the witness of the
sovereignty of God. But although in few
words, it does answer the question as to the
righteous, that he has abiding life, that he
lives and shall live. God impresses the importance of the answer in the words [q], *Write
the vision* i. e. the prophecy, *and make it plain
on the tables*, whereon the prophet was wont
to write [r], *that he may run who reads it.* He
says also, that it is for a time fixed in the
mind of God, and that however, in man's
sight, it might seem to *linger*, it would not be
aught behind the time [s]. Then he gives the
answer itself in the words, [t] *Behold his soul
which is puffed up is not upright in him; and
the just shall live by his faith.* The swelling
pride and self-dependence of the Chaldee
stands in contrast with the trustful submission of faith. Of the one God says, it has no
ground of uprightness, and consequently will
not stand before God ; of faith, he says, *the
righteous shall live by it.* But the life plainly
is not the life of the body. For Habakkuk's
ground of complaint was the world-wasting
cruelty of the Chaldees. The woe on the
Chaldee which follows is even chiefly for
bloodshed, in which the righteous and the
wicked are massacred alike. The simple
word, *shall live*, is an entire denial of death, a
denial even of any interruption of life. It
stands in the same fullness as those words of
our Lord, [u] *because I live, ye shall live also.*
The other side of the picture, the fall of the

Chaldees, is given in greater fullness, because
the fulfillment of God's word in things seen
was the pledge of the fulfillment of those
beyond the veil of sense and time. In a
measured dirge he pronounces a five-fold woe
on the five great sins of the Chaldees, their
ambition [v], covetousness [x], violence [y], insolence [z], idolatry [a]. It closes with the powerlessness of the Chaldee idols against God,
and bids the whole world be hushed before
the presence of the One God, its Maker,
awaiting His sentence.

Then follows the prayer [b], that God would
revive His work for Israel, which now seemed
dead. He describes the revival as coming,
under the images of God's miraculous deliverances of old. The division of the Red Sea
and the Jordan, the standing-still of the sun
and moon under Joshua, are images of future
deliverances ; all nature shakes and quivers
at the presence of its Maker. Yet not it,
but the wicked were the object of His displeasure. The prophet sees his people
delivered as at the Red Sea, just when the
enemy seemed ready to sweep them away,
as with a whirlwind. And, in sight of the
unseen, he closes with that wondrous declaration of faith, that all nature should be desolate, all subsistence gone, everything, contrary to God's promises of old to His people,
should be around him, *and I will rejoice in
the Lord, I will exult for joy in the God of my
salvation.*

This prophecy is not less distinct, because
figurative. Rather it is the declaration of
God's deliverance of His people, not from
the Chaldees only, but at all times. The
evil is concentrated in one Evil one, who
stands over against the One anointed. *Thou
art gone forth for the salvation of Thy people ;
for salvation with Thine anointed One. Thou
crushedst the head out of the house of the wicked
One, laying bare the foundation unto the neck*,
i. e. smiting the house, at once, above and
below ; with an utter destruction. It belongs
then the more to all times, until the closing
strife between evil and good, Christ and
Antichrist, the ἄνομος and the Lord. It includes the Chaldee, and each great Empire
which opposes itself to the kingdom of God,
and declares that, as God delivered His
people of old, so He would unto the end.

It may be that Habakkuk chose this name
to express the strong faith, whereby he embraced the promises of God. At least, it
means one who " strongly enfolds [c]."

Perhaps too it is on account of the form in

---

[n] Ps. lxxiii. 1.   [o] Hab. i. 12.

[p] Ib. 17.   [q] ii. 2.   [r] עַל הַלֻּחוֹת.

[s] ii. 3.   [t] ii. 4.   [u] S. John xiv. 19.
[v] ii. 5. 8.   [x] ii. 9–11.   [y] ii. 12–14.
[z] ii. 15–17.   [a] ii. 18–20.   [b] c. iii.
[c] There is no other form exactly like חֲבַקּוּק.

Yet it is manifestly intensive. It most resembles

the form אָהַבְהַב "loved intensely." This form,
in חֲצַרְצַר, הַטַרְטַר, is changed into הֶטּוֹצַר חַטוֹטֵר.
Equally חֲבַקּבּוּק might be pronounced Habakkuk,

the second בּ being, as Delitzsch suggested, merged
in the קּ, for greater facility of pronunciation. The
וּ is a form like נַעֲצוּץ שַׁעֲרוּרָה, שְׁקַעֲרוּרוֹת,

which his prophecy is cast, as being spoken (with the exception of that one verse) to God or to the Chaldæan, not to his own people, that he added the title of Prophet to his name. *The burden which Habakkuk the prophet did see* [d]. For, however the name "prophet" includes all to whom revelations from God came, it is nowhere, in the Old Testament, added as the name of an office to any one, who did not exercise the practical office of the Prophet. Our Lord quotes David as *the Prophet* [e], and God says to Abimelech of Abraham [f], *He is a Prophet*, and, in reference to this, the Psalmist speaks of the Patriarchs, as Prophets [g]. *He reproved kings for their sakes, saying, Touch not Mine anointed and do My prophets no harm*, and Hosea speaks of Moses as a prophet [h], and St. Peter says of David [i], *He being a prophet*. But the title is nowhere in the Old Testament added to the name as it is here, *Habakkuk the prophet*, and as it is elsewhere Samuel the prophet [k], the prophet Gad [l], Nathan the prophet [m], Ahijah the prophet [n], the prophet Jehu [o], Elijah the prophet [p], Elisha the prophet [q], Shemaiah the prophet [r], the prophet Iddo [s], the prophet Obed [t], Isaiah the prophet [u], Jeremiah the prophet [v], Haggai the prophet [x], unless any have exercised the prophetic office. The title of *the Prophet* is not, in the Old Testament, added to the names of Jacob or even of Moses or David or Solomon or Daniel, although they all prophesied of Christ.

Since Holy Scripture often conveys so much incidentally, it may be that a large range of ministerial office is hinted in the words "write on *the* tables;" for "*the* tables" must have been well-known tables, tables upon which prophets (as Isaiah) and probably Habakkuk himself was accustomed to write. The writing of a few emphatic unexplained words in a public place, which should arouse curiosity, or startle passers-by, would be in harmony with the symbolical actions, enjoined on the prophets and used by them. The *Mene, Mene, Tekel, Upharsin*, had, from their mysteriousness, an impressiveness of their own, apart from the miracle of the writing.

The words appended to the prophecy, *to the chief singer*, (as we should say, "the leader of the band") *with* or *on my stringed instruments*, imply, not only that the hymn became part of the devotions of the temple, but that Habakkuk too had a part in the sacred music

which accompanied it. The word so rendered, *neginothai*, could only mean *my stringed instruments*, or "my song accompanied with music," as Hezekiah says [y], *we will sing my songs on the stringed instruments, neginggen neginothai*. But in Habakkuk's subscription, "To the chief musician *binginothai*," *neginoth* can have no other meaning than in the almost identical inscription of Psalms, "[z] To the chief musician *binginoth*," nor this any other than *with stringed instruments*, "instruments struck with the hand [a]." The addition, "with *my* stringed instruments," shews that Habakkuk himself was to accompany his hymn with instrumental music, and since the mention of *the chief musician* marks out that it was to form part of the temple-service, Habakkuk must have been entitled to take part in the temple-music, and so must have been a Levite. The Levitical order then had its prophet, as the sacerdotal in Jeremiah and Ezekiel. The tradition in the title to Bel and the Dragon, whatever its value, agrees with this; "[b]from the prophecy of Ambakum, son of Jesus, of the tribe of Levi."

This, however, does not give us any hint as to the time when Habakkuk prophesied. For, bad as were the times of Manasseh and Amon, their idolatry consisted in associating idols with God, setting them up in His courts, bringing one even into His temple [c], not in doing away His service. They set the two services, and the two *opinions* [d], side by side, adding the false, but not abolishing the true, "consenting to differ," leaving to the worshipers of God their religion, while forcing them to endure, side by side, what seemed an addition, but what was, in fact, a denial. Habakkuk then might have been allowed to present his hymn for the temple-service, while the king placed in the same temple the statue of Astarte, and required its devil's worship to be carried on there. The temple was allowed to go into some degree of decay, for Josiah had it repaired; but we read only of his removing idols [e], not of his having to restore the disused service of God. Of Ahaz it is recorded, that [f] *he shut up the doors of the house of the Lord*, which Hezekiah had to open [g]. Nothing of this sort is told of Manasseh and Amon.

Habakkuk, however, has two hints, which determine his age within a few years. He says that the invasion of the Chaldæans was to be in the days of those to whom he speaks;

; yet it is impossible that the reduplication should be meaningless. (as Ew. 157. a. p. 405. ed. 7.)

[d] i. 1. add iii. 1.　　　　[e] S. Matt. xiii. 35.
[f] Gen. xx. 7.　　[g] Ps. cv. 14–15.　　[h] Hos. xii. 13.
[i] Acts ii. 30.　　　　　　[k] 2 Chr. xxxv. 18.
[l] 1 Sam. xxii. 5.　[m] 1 Kgs i. 32.　[n] 1 Kgs xi. 29.
[o] Ib. xvi. 7, 12.　[p] Ib. xviii. 36.　[q] 2 Kgs vi. 12.
[r] 2 Chr. xii. 5.　　[s] Ib. xiii. 22.　[t] Ib. xv. 8.
[u] 2 Kgs xix. 2, xx. 1.

[v] Jer. xxviii. 6, xxxvi. 26, 2 Chr. xxxvi. 12.
[x] Ezr. v. 1, vi. 14.　　　　[y] Is. xxxviii. 20.
[z] Ps. iv. vi. liv. lv. lxi. lxvii. lxxvi.
[a] Coll. 1 Sam. xvii. 16, 23, xviii. 10, xix. 9, 2 Kgs iii. 15.
[b] Cod. Chis. of LXX from Origen's Tetraplar and the Syro-Hexaplar.
[c] 2 Kgs xxi. 7.　　　　[d] 1 Kgs xviii. 21.
[e] 2 Kgs xxiii. 6.　　　　[f] 2 Chr. xxxviii. 24.
[g] Ib. xxix. 3.

in your days [h]. Accordingly he must have spoken to adults, many of whom would survive that invasion of Nebuchadnezzar, in the 4th year of Jehoiakim B. C. 605. He can hardly have prophesied before B. C. 645, about the close of Manasseh's reign; for at this date, those who were 20 at the time of the prophecy, would have been 60, at the time of its commenced fulfillment at the battle of Carchemish. On the other hand, in that he speaks of that invasion as a thing incredible to those to whom he was speaking, he must have prophesied before Babylon became independent by the overthrow of Nineveh, B. C. 625. For when Babylon had displaced Nineveh, and divided the Empire of the East with Media and Egypt, it was not a thing incredible, that it would invade Judah in their own days, although it was beyond human knowledge to declare that it certainly would. The Babylonian Empire itself lasted only eighty-nine years; and, to human sight, Judah had as much or more to fear from Egypt as from Babylon. The Median Empire also might as well have swallowed up Judah for the time, as the Babylonian.

The relation of Zephaniah to Habakkuk coincides with this. Zephaniah certainly adopted the remarkable words [i], lit. [k] *Hush at the presence of the Lord God*, from Habakkuk's fuller form [l], *the Lord is in His holy temple; hush at His presence all the earth.*

But Zephaniah prophesied under Josiah, before the destruction of Nineveh B. C. 625, which he foretold [m]. Habakkuk was also, at latest, an earlier contemporary of Jeremiah who, in one place, at least, in his earlier prophecies, used his language [n], as he does so often, of set purpose, that of the prophets before him, in order to shew that the fullness of their prophecies was not yet exhausted. But Jeremiah began to prophesy in the thirteenth year of Josiah B. C. 629 [o]. Habakkuk, on the other hand, joins himself on with the old prophets and Psalms by the employment of language of Isaiah [p] and perhaps of Micah [q], by the use of language of Deuteronomy [r], and by the expansion of a Psalm of Asaph in his own Psalm [s], but does not systematically renew their prophecies like Jeremiah [t] or Zephaniah [u].

The ministry then of Habakkuk falls in the latter half of the reign of Manasseh or the earlier half of that of Josiah, (for the reign of Amon, being of two years only, is too short to come into account), and there is no decisive evidence for either against the other. In the reign of Manasseh, we are expressly told, that there were prophets, sent to foretell a destruction of Jerusalem as complete as that of Samaria, on account of the exceeding wickedness, into which Manasseh seduced his people. *The Lord spake by His servants, the prophets, saying, Because Manasseh king of Judah hath done these abominations, and hath made Judah also to sin with his idols, Therefore thus saith the Lord God of Israel, Behold, I am bringing such evil upon Jerusalem and Judah, that whosoever heareth of it, both his ears shall tingle. And I will stretch over Jerusalem the*

---

[i] Dr. Davidson says, " Delitzsch [with many others] maintains from a comparison of Hab. ii. 20, with Zeph. i. 7, that the former preceded the latter.—The premises are by no means safe or valid " [and, following Umbreit,] " ' Be silent before the Lord God' (Zeph. i. 7.) sounds like a proverb: part of it having been already used by Amos (vi. 10)," iii. 304. 305. Amos has only the single word הַס " hush !" which is, of course no fragment of a proverb. Nor was there any lack of expressions to bid men be still before their Maker. Delitzsch (ad. loc. p. 102.) puts together the following; Ps. xcvi. 9. חִילוּ סִפָּנָיו 1 Chr. xiv. 7. מִלִּפְנֵי אֲדוֹן חוּלִי אֶרֶץ; כָּל־הָאָרֶץ xvi. 30, חִילוּ מִלְּפָנָיו כָּל־הָאָרֶץ; Ps. xxxiii. 8, וַיִּירְאוּ מִיָּי" כָּל הָאָרֶץ, and the Psalm of Asaph," מִשְׁמִים הִשְׁמַעַתָּ דִּין אֶרֶץ יָרְאָה וְשָׁקְטָה; not to speak of other possible combinations, with חָשָׁה דָּמַם, הֶחֱרִישׁ, (which is thought to be only a stronger pronunciation of it. Kim. also explains הַס by שָׁתַק.) When then a writer, who uses much the language of those before him, has an idiom which occurs once beside in Holy Scripture, there being many other expressions, which might equally have been used, any one unbiassed would think that he adopted the language of the other. Stähelin admits the connection, but inverts the argument, contrary to the character of both prophets.

[k] Zeph. i. 7. [l] Hab. ii. 20. [m] Zeph. ii. 13, sqq.
[n] Hab. i. 8, קַלּוּ מִנְּמֵרִים סוּסָיו וְחַדּוּ מִזְּאֵבֵי עָרֶב

---

seems to have suggested the like description of the Chaldee cavalry, Jer. iv. 13, קַלּוּ מִנְּשָׁרִים סוּסָיו, although, with the slight variation, which he commonly used, Jeremiah has כְּשָׁרִים, after David probably on Saul and Jonathan, קַלּוּ מִנְּשָׁרִים 2 Sam. i. 23, the remaining instance of this likeness. זְאֵבֵי עֶרֶב recurs in Zeph. iii. 3, and in Jer. v. 6, only. Jer. xxii. 13, in the reign of Jehoiakim, is also a reminiscence of Habakkuk ii. 12; and Jer. li. 58, in the 4th year of Zedekiah, of Hab. ii. 13.

[o] Jer. i. 2, xxv. 3.
[p] Hab. ii. 14, is from Is. xi. 9; the form of Hab. i. 5, seems suggested by Is. xxix. 9; the standing on the watch-tower Hab. ii. 1, occurs in Is. xxi. 8; the writing on tables occurs in Is. viii. 1, xxx. 8, and Hab. ii. 2; the imagery, " he hath enlarged his desire as hell," (הִרְחוּב כִּשְׁאוֹל נַפְשׁוֹ) Hab. ii. 5, was probably suggested by Is. v. 14. שְׁאוֹל הִרְחִיבָה; נַפְשָׁהּ the introduction of a מָשָׁל, Hab. ii. 6, as Is. xiv. 4, both over Babylon ; the union of הֶלֶק and עָבַר Is. viii. 8, and Hab. i. 11; from Küper Jerem. p. 153. Havernick Symb. ad defend. authentiam vat. Ies. c. xiii.—xiv. 23. p. 37 sqq. in Delitzsch Hab. p. viii.
[q] Hab. ii. 12. and Mic. iii. 10.
[r] From Deut. xxxii. xxxiii. See below.
[s] Ps. lxxvii. 17-21, in Hab. iii. 10-15.
[t] On the relation of Jeremiah to Obadiah and Isaiah, see Introd. to Obad. vol. i. pp. 344-348.
[u] See Introd. to Zephaniah, below.

line of Samaria and the plummet of the house of Ahab; and I will wipe Jerusalem as a man wipeth a dish, wiping it and turning it upside down; and I will forsake the remnant of their inheritance, and deliver them into the hand of their enemies, and they shall become a prey and spoil to all their enemies [x].

The sinful great men of Manasseh's and Amon's court and judicature are but too likely to have maintained their power in the early years of the reign of Josiah. For a boy of eight years old (at which age Josiah succeeded his father [y]) could, amid whatsoever sense of right and piety, do little to stem the established wrong and ungodliness of the evil counsellors and judges of his father and grandfather. The sins, which Jeremiah denounces, as the cause of the future captivity of Jerusalem, are the very same, of which Habakkuk complains, " oppression, violence, spoil [z]." Jeremiah speaks, in the concrete, of total absence of right judgment [a], as Habakkuk, in the abstract, of the powerlessness of the law [b]. Zephaniah gives the like picture of those earlier years under Josiah [c]. But Habakkuk's description would not suit the later years of Josiah, when judgment and justice *were* done. *Did not thy father,* Jeremiah appeals to Jehoiakim [d], *eat and drink, and do judgment and justice, and then it was well with him; he judged the cause of the poor and needy, then it was well with him; was not this to know Me? saith the Lord* [e]. But while there is nothing to preclude his having prophesied in either reign, the earliest tradition places him in the close of the reign of Manasseh [f].

Modern critics have assigned an earlier or

later date to Habakkuk, accordingly as they believed that God did, or did not, reveal the future to man, that there was or was not, superhuman prophecy. Those who denied that God did endow His prophets with knowledge above nature, fell into two classes; 1) Such as followed Eichhorn's unnatural hypothesis, that prophecies were only histories of the past, spoken of, as if it were still future, to which these critics gave the shameless title of " vaticinia post eventum [g]." These plainly involved the prophets in fraud. 2) Those who laid down that each prophet lived at a time, when he could, with human foresight, tell what would happen. Would that those who count certainty, as to even a near future, to be so easy a thing, would try their hands at predicting the events of the next few years or months, or even days [h], and, if they fail, acknowledge God's Truth ! This prejudice, that there *could* be no real prophecy, ruled, for a time, all German criticism. It cannot be denied, that " the unbelief was the parent of the criticism, not the criticism of the unbelief." It is simple matter of history, that the unbelief came first; and, if men, à priori, disbelieved that there *could* be prophecy, it must needs be a postulate of their criticism, that what seemed to be prophecy *could* not have belonged to a date, when human foresight did not suffice for positive prediction. I will use the words of Delitzsch rather than my own ;

" [i] The investigation into the age of Habakkuk could be easily and briefly settled, if we would start from the prejudice, which is the soul of modern criticism, that a prediction of the future, which rested, not on human in-

---

[x] 2 Kgs xxi. 11-14. [y] Ib. xxii. 1, 2 Chr. xxxiv. 1.

[z] חָמָס וָשֹׁד Jer. vi. 7, as Hab. i. 3, שֹׁד וחמס; Zeph. speaks of חמס ומרמה, i. 9.

[a] Jer. vi. 19. " My law they have despised it ; " v. 28. " they have not judged the cause, the cause of the fatherless, and they prosper ; and the judgment of the poor have they not judged."

[b] Hab. i. 4, "the law is chilled, and judgment will never go forth ; for the wicked encompasseth the just ; therefore judgment goeth forth perverted."

[c] Zeph. i. 9. where he too foretells the punishment of those, " which fill their masters' houses with violence and deceit, חָמָס וּמִרְמָה " and iii. 1-4.

[d] Jer. xxii. 15, 16.

[e] Dr. Davidson rightly says, "the spoiling and violence, there (i. 2, 3.) depicted, refer to the internal condition of the theocracy, not to external injuries " (p. 305) ; but then he contradicts himself and Jeremiah, when he says, (p. 305) following Ewald (Proph. ii. 30.), " The safest conclusion respecting the time of the prophet, is that he lived in the time of Jehoiakim (606-604. B. C.), *when the kingdom of Judah was in a good moral condition, justice and righteousness having entered into the life of the people after Josiah's reforms,* and idolatry having almost disappeared."

[f] "Seder Olam, from which Abarbanel, R. Dav. Ganz in Zemach David, p. 21, and Rabbins drew their opinion." Carpzoff Introd. P. iii. p. 410.

[g] Eichhorn (Einl.) Bertholdt (Einl.) Justi Habakkuk neu übersetzt 1841. Wolf, der Proph. Hab. &c. 1822.

[h] At every early stage of the great conflict (August 1870) it was remarkable how day after day journalists professed themselves to be at fault, as to the most immediate future. On one point only they were agreed that the war would be " long and severe." Then it was thought that one month would see its beginning and its end. " The course of the present war," says a journal not wanting in self-reliance, " has gone far to verify the paradox, that nothing is certain but the unexpected. At any rate, *nothing has happened but the unforeseen.* Neither king nor Emperor, neither French nor German government or people had formed any anticipation of the events of the month now ending. The French expected to invade Germany, and they have been invaded themselves. The Germans, though confident of ultimate success, expected a long and toilsome conflict, whereas a month has brought them almost to the gates of Paris. The calculation of all parties as to the political effects of the war have been equally mistaken." *The Times,* Aug. 31st. And yet men, who, with our full information, would not risk a prediction as to the issue of things immediately before their eyes, think it so easy for Jewish prophets, living in their own small insulated country, to foretell certainly that Babylon would prevail over Egypt, when they knew either country only as their own superior, and political sagacity and feeling was on the side of Egypt.

[i] Der Proph. Habakkuk Einleit. pp. iv-vi.

ferences or on a natural gift of divination, but on supernatural illumination, is *impossible*. For since Habakkuk foretold the invasion of the Chaldees, he must, in such case, have come forward at a time, at which natural acuteness could, with certainty, determine beforehand that sad event ; accordingly in or after the time of the battle of Carchemish in the 4th year of Jehoiakim [j] 606 B. C. In this decisive battle Nebuchadnezzar defeated Pharaoh Necho, and it was more than probable that the king of Babylon would now turn against Judæa, since Jehoiakim, the son of Josiah, had been set on the throne by Pharaoh Necho [k], and so held with Egypt. And this is in reality the inference of modern critics. They bring the Chaldæans so close under the eyes of the prophet, that he could, by way of nature, foresee their invasion ; and so much the closer under his eyes, the more deeply the prejudice, that there is no prophecy in the Biblical sense of the word, has taken root in them, and the more consistently they follow it out. 'Habakkuk prophesied under Jehoiakim, for,' so Jäger expresses himself, ' since Jehoiakim was on the side of the Egyptians, *it was easy to foresee, that* [l] ; &c.' Just so Ewald ; '[m] One night readily be tempted to think, that Habakkuk wrote, while the pious king Josiah was still living ; but since the first certain invasion of the Chaldæans, of which our account speaks [n], falls within the reign of king Jehoiakim, somewhat between 608–604 B. C. we must abide by this date.' Hitzig defines the dates still more sharply, according to that principle of principles, to which history with its facts must adapt itself unconditionally. ' The prophet announces the arrival of the Chaldæans in Judæa, as something marvelous.' Well then, one would imagine, that it would follow from this, that at that time they had not yet come. But no! 'Habakkuk,' says Hitzig, ' introduces the Chaldæans as a new phænomenon, as yet entirely unknown ; he *prophesied accordingly* at their *first* arrival into Palestine. But this beyond question falls in the reign of Jehoiakim [o]. In Jehoiakim's fourth year, i. e. 606, they had fought the battle at Carchemish ; in 605 *the Chaldæan army seems to have been on its march ;* the writing of Habakkuk is placed most correctly in the beginning of the year 604,' accordingly, at the time, when the Chaldæans were already marching with all speed straight on Jerusalem, and (as Hitzig infers from Hab. i. 9.) after they had come down from the North along the coast, were now advancing from the West, when they, as Ewald too remarks (resting, like Maurer on i. 2–4), '[p] already

stood in the holy land, trampling everything under foot with irresistible might, and allowing their own right alone to count as right.' Holding fast to that naturalist *à priori*, we go yet further. In ii. 17, the judgment of God is threatened to the Chaldæan, on account of the violence practiced on Lebanon, and the destruction of its animals. Lebanon is, it is said, the holy land ; the animals, its inhabitants : in iii. 14, 17, the prophet sees the hostile hordes storming in : the devastation wrought through the war stands clearly before his eyes. This is not *possible*, unless the Chaldæan were at that time already established in Judæa. However, then, c. i. was written *before* their invasion, yet c. ii., iii. must have been written after it. ' Wherefore,' says Maurer, ' since it is evident from Jer. xlvi. 2, and xxxvi. 9, that the Chaldæans came in the year B. C. 605, in the 9th month of the 5th year of the reign of Jehoiakim, it follows that c. i. was written at that very time, but c. ii. at the beginning of B. C. 604, the 6th of Jehoiakim.'

"Turn we away from this cheap pseudo-criticism, with its ready-made results, which sacrifices all sense for historical truth to a prejudice, which it seems to have vowed not to allow to be shaken by anything. It seeks at any cost to disburden itself of any prophecy in Scripture, which can only be explained through supernatural agency ; and yet it attains its end, neither elsewhere nor in our prophet. Chapter ii. contains a prediction of the overthrow of the Chaldæan empire and of the sins whereby that overthrow was effected, which has been so remarkably confirmed by history even in details, that that criticism, if it would be true to its principles, must assume that it was written while Cyrus, advancing against Babylon was employed in punishing the river Gyndes by dividing it off into 360 channels." This major premiss, " there *can* be no superhuman prediction of the future," (in other words, " Almighty God, if He knows the future, cannot disclose it ! ") still lurks under the assumptions of that modern school of so-called criticism. It seems to be held no more necessary, formally to declare it, than to enounce at full length any axiom of Euclid. Yet it may, on that very ground, escape notice, while it is the unseen mainspring of the theories, put forth in the name of criticism. "That Habakkuk falls at a later time," says Stähelin, " is clear out of his prophecy itself ; *for he speaks of the Chaldæans*, and the controversy is only, whether he announces their invasion, as Knobel, Umbreit, Delitzsch, Keil [q] hold, or presupposes it, as Ewald, Hit-

[j] Jer. xlvi. 2.   [k] 2 Kgs xxiii. 34, 35.
[l] "Facile erat prævidere fore ut &c." Jäger de ord. proph. minor: chronol. ii. 18. sqq.
[m] Proph. iii. 30. ed. 2.

[n] 2 Kgs xxiv. 1.   [o] Ib. 2.
[p] Proph. iii. 29. ed. 2.
[q] Stähelin mixed up Delitzsch and Keil, who believed in superhuman prediction, and Knobel &c.

zig, E. Meier maintain. To me the first opinion appears the right, since not only do i. 5. sqq. plainly relate to the future, but the detailed description of the Chaldæans points at something which has not yet taken place, at something hitherto unknown, and the terror of the prophet in announcing their coming, i. 12. sqq., recurs also iii. 1, 16, 17; and so, I think, that the time of Habakkuk's activity may be placed very soon after the battle of Carchemish, in the first half of the reign of Jehoiakim, and so his prophecy as contemporary with Jeremiah xxv." "Habakkuk," says De Wette, "lived and prophesied in the Chaldee period. It is, however, matter of dispute at what point of time in this period he lived. i. 5. sqq. clearly points to its beginning, the reign of Jehoiakim. Even ch. iii. seems to require no later point of time, since here the destruction of Judah is not yet anticipated. He was then Jeremiah's younger contemporary. Rightly do Perschke, Ranitz, Stickel, Knobel, Hitzig, Ewald, let the prophet prophesy a little before the invasion of the Chaldæans in Judah, which the analogy of prophecy favors;" for prophecy may still be human at this date, since so far it foretells only, what any one could foresee. A prophet of God foretells, these critics admit, an invasion which all could foresee, and does not foretell, what could not humanly be foreseen, the destruction of Jerusalem. The theory then is saved, and within these limits Almighty God is permitted to send His prophet. Condescending criticism!

Mostly criticism kept itself within these limits, and used nothing more than its axiom, "there was no prophecy." The freshness and power of prophetic diction in Habakkuk

who denied it, joining himself on to the class in general and ignoring the radical difference. Dr. Davidson assumes the same principle. "As he mentions the Chaldæans by name, and his oracle refers to them, he lived in the Chaldæan period.— The safest conclusion respecting the time of the prophet is that he lived in the time of Jehoiakim 606–604. B. C." "To put the prophet in Manasseh's reign is incorrect *because* the Chaldæans were not a people formidable to the Jews at that time." (Introd. iii. pp. 304, 305.) And so Habakkuk, without superhuman knowledge, could not foretell it!

r "Thus the verb קָלַם occurs, only beside in the books of Kings and in Ezekiel." Stähelin. "The diction is pure and classical. Yet he has some late words, as קָלֶם i. 10, which appears only in Kings and Ezekiel." Dr. Davidson. The primitive form קָלָם, which is alleged, does not occur at all; only קָלֶם Ez. xvi. 31. and הִתְקַלֶּם with בְ, "mock at," 2 Kgs ii. 23, Hab. i. 10, Ez. xxii. 5, as denominatives from קֶלֶס Ps. xliv. 14. lxxix. 4, and Jer. xx. 8. There is nothing to show that it is a late word, though occurring for the first time in the history of Elisha. In Aramaic, (not in Onk. or Jon. it has the opposite meaning, "praised." In the excep-

deterred most from that other expedient of picking out some two or three words as indicative of a later style. Stähelin however says; "His language too, although *on the whole* pure and without Aramaisms," (truly so! since there is not even an alleged or imagined Aramaism in his prophecy,) "still betrays, in single cases, the later period." And then he alleges that 1) one *verb* r "only occurs beside in the books of Kings and in Ezekiel;" 2) another word, " s *with the exception of Nahum*, only in Jeremiah and Malachi ;" 3) "the image of the cup of destiny only occurs in prophecies subsequent to Jeremiah." Marvelous precision of criticism, which can infer the date of a book from the facts, 1) that a *verb*, formed from a *noun*, occurs four times only in Holy Scripture, in 2 Kings, Habakkuk, and Ezekiel, whereas the *noun* from which it is derived occurs in a Psalm, which fits no later time than David's t; 2) that a word, slightly varied in pronunciation from a common Hebrew word u, occurs only in Nahum, Habakkuk, Jeremiah, and Malachi, once in each, when that word is the basis of the name of the river *Pishon*, mentioned in Genesis, and Stähelin himself places Nahum in the reign of Hezekiah ; or that 3) no *prophet* before Jeremiah speaks of the image of the "cup of destiny v," whereas the portion given by God for good w or for ill x, occurs under that same image in Psalms of David and Asaph; and if the question is to be begged as to the date of Isaiah li. 17, 22, the corresponding image of "drinking wine, of reeling," occurs in a Psalm of David y, and being "drunk, but not with wine" is imagery of an earlier chapter in Isaiah z; the image occurs fully in Obadiah a.

Such criticism is altogether childish. No

tions in Chaldee, Ges. seems rightly to conjecture, that it signifies ironical praise, as in Shem. rabba s.

27. In Ps. xliv. 14. קְלָסָא is retained for the Heb. קֶלֶס.

s "פּוּשׁ i. 8. with the exception of Nah. iii. 18. only besides in Jeremiah and Malachi." Stähelin, "פּוּשׁ i. 8. in Jeremiah and Malachi besides;" Dr. Davidson; who avoids the absurdity of arguing relative lateness of diction from a word, occurring in Nahum, by omitting this fourth instance, but therewith falsifying the facts before him.
t Ps. xliv. 14.
u פּוּשׁ (whence פִּישׁוֹן Gen. ii. 11.) an early variation of פּוּץ, שׁ for צ, as Rashi observes on Nah. iii. 18.
v "The image of 'the cup of destiny' ii. 16, first occurs in the prophets after Jeremiah; and Hab. ii. 16. itself seems to refer to Jerem. xlix. 12." Stähelin pp. 288, 289. "The cup of judgment (ii. 16.) does not occur in the prophets before Jeremiah; whether Habakkuk refers in ii. 16. to Jer. xlix. 12. is doubtful, though Stähelin ventures to assert it;" Dr. Davidson (iii. 303) acknowledging, as usual, the source of his statements, where he dissents in one of them.
w David, Ps. xi. 6. Asaph, lxxv. 8.
x David. Ps. xvi. 5. xxiii. 5. y Ps. lx. 5. [3 Eng.]
z Is. xxix. 9. a ver. 16.

one would tolerate it, except that it is adduced to support a popular and foregone conclusion. It would be laughed to scorn, were it used by believers in revelation. In the small remains of the Hebrew Scriptures and language, an induction, if it is to be of any value, must be very distinct. The largeness of Greek literature enables critics to single out Homeric, Herodotean, Æschylean, Pindaric words. In Hebrew we meet with ἅπαξ λεγόμενα in perhaps every prophet, in many Psalms; but it requires far more than the occurrence of the word in one single place, to furnish any even probable inference, that it was framed by the Prophet or Psalmist himself. Still less can it be inferred safely that because, in the scanty remains of Hebrew, a word does not occur before e. g. a certain historical book, it did not exist before the date of that book. Rather the occurrence of any word in language so simple as that of the historical books, is an evidence that it did exist and was in common use at the time. Poets and orators coin words, in order to give full expression for their thoughts. The characteristic of the sacred historians, both of the Old and New Testament, is to relate the facts in most absolute simplicity. It would be a singular "history of the Hebrew language," which should lay down as a principle, that all those are later words, which do not happen to occur before the books of Kings, Habakkuk, or any other prophet, whom this criticism is pleased to rank among the later books. What are we to do with Habakkuk's own ἅπαξ λεγόμενα? Granted, that he framed some of them, yet it is impossible that he framed them all. As specimens of the results of such a critical principle, that words, occurring for the first time in any book, are characteristic of the date of that word, let us only take roots beginning with s. Had then the Hebrew no name for nails (as distinct

from hooks, pegs [b],) before those whom these critics would make late writers [c], as Ecclesiastes and Isaiah xli ? Or had they none for ceiling a building before the book of Kings [d]; although the ark had a third story [e], and Lot speaks of "the shadow of my roof [f]? " Or had they none for a " decked vessel" before Jonah [g], although the Indian names of Solomon's imports show that Ophir, whither his navy sailed, was in India, Ophir itself being Abhira in the province of Cutch [h] ? Or had they no name for "divided opinions" before Elijah [i]? Seed shed, which sprang up in the second year, was known in the Pentateuch [k]; but that of the third year would, on that hypothesis, remain unknown till Hezekiah [l]; nor did the Hebrews express to "drag along the ground," till Hushai [m], and, after him, Jeremiah. They had no name for winter, as distinct from autumn, until the Canticles [n], and, but for the act of the Philistines in stopping up [o] Abraham's wells, it might have been said that Hebrew had no word for this act, till the time of Jehoshaphat [p].

Or as to the criticism itself, קֶלֶס is to be a later word, because, except in that Psalm of the sons of Corah, it occurs first in the history of Elisha [q]. Perhaps it is so rare (and this may illustrate the history of Elisha) because, as used, it seems to have been one of the strongest words in the language for " derision ; " at least the verb is used in an intensive form only, and always of strong derision [r]. But then, did the old Hebrews never use derision ? Happy exception for one nation, if they never used it wrongly or had no occasion to use it rightly ! Yet even though (by a rare exception) Ewald allows the second Psalm to be David's, (Job however being placed about the 7th century B. C.) the evidence for לָעַג, as strong a word, would be of the time of David [s]. "Scorning" "scoffing,"

[b] וָו, יָתֵד.

[c] מַסְמְרִים Is. xli. 7, מַסְמְרִים 1 Chr. xxii. 3, מַסְמְרוֹת Jer. x. 4, מסמרות 2 Chr. iii. 9. מַשְׂמְרוֹת Eccl. xii. 11.

[d] סִפֻּן 1 Kgs vi. 9, סָפוּן 1 Kgs vii. 3, 7, Jer. xxii. 14, Hagg. i. 4, (סְפוּן) Dt. xxxiii. 21. שָׂפוּן Ib. 19, is i. q. (צָפוּן). אָחוּז, "hold together," occurs 1 Kgs vi. 6, 10, Ezek. xli. 6; טָלַל lit. " overshadowed " Neh. iii. 15; צֻצּוּעַ occurs also 1 Kgs vi. 5, 6, 10.

[e] שָׁלִישִׁים, Gen. vi. 16, as in 1 Kgs vi. 8. Ez. xlii. 3.

[f] קֹרָה Gen. xix 8. as being " beamed." Conf. קֹרָה " laid beams," (met.) Ps. civ. 3. else 2 Chr. xxxiv. 11, Neh. ii. 8, iii. 3, 6 ; קוֹרָה beam 2 Kgs vi. 2, 5, 2 Chr. iii. 7. Cant. i. 17. מְקָרֶה Eccl. x. 18.

[g] סְפִינָה ἅπ. Jon. i. 5. See vol. i. p. 375.

[h] See ab. on Micah iv. p. 62.

[i] 1 Kgs xviii. 21. As " branches," סְעִפִּים first occurs in Isaiah, (xvii. 6. xxvii. 10, and the denom.

סְעֵף, Ib. x. 33. and סַרְעַפּוֹת, סְעַפּוֹת, סַרְעַפּוֹת in Ezek. xxxi. 5. 6. 8.

[k] סָפִיחַ Lev. xxv. 5. 11. Else only with שַׁחַ or שָׂחִים. סָחִישׁ 2 Kgs xix. 29, שָׂחִים. Ib. xxxvii. 30.

[m] סָחַב 2 Sam. xvii. 13. Jer. xv. 3, xxii, 19, xlix. 20. So סָחָה " swept" occurs only Ezek. xxvi. 4. סָחוּ Lam. iii. 45. but סָחוּף is used by Solomon Prov. xxviii. 3.

[n] סְתָו Cant. ii. 11.

[o] סָתַם Gen. xxvi. 15. 18.

[p] סָתַם 2 Kgs iii. 19. 25. 2 Chr. xxxii. 3. 4. Nif. of closing breaches in a wall, Neh. iv. 1.

[q] 2 Kgs ii. 23.

[r] Pih. Ez. xvi. 31. Hithp. 2 Kgs l. c., Hab. ι. c., Ez. xxii. 5, who has also קַלָּסָה.

[s] לָעַג. The verb occurs Ps. ii. 4, xxii. 8, lix. 9, lxxx. 7, Prov. i. 26, xvii. 5, xxx. 17. Job ix. 23, xi. 3, xxi. 3, xxi. 19, Is. xxxiii. 19. xxxvii. 22, Jer. xx. 7,

(unless Psalm i. be allowed to be David's) did not begin till Solomon's time[t]. "Mocking" was yet later[u]. As belongs to a rude people, insult was only shewn in acts, of which התעלל is used[v]; and from those simple times of the Patriarchs, they had no stronger word than "to laugh at[w]." For this is the only word used in the Pentateuch[x]. But to what end all this? To prove that Habakkuk had no superhuman knowledge of what he foretold? Prophecy occupies, as I said, a subordinate place in Habakkuk. He renews the "burden" of former prophets, both upon his own people and upon the Chaldæans; but he does not speak even so definitely as they. His office is rather to enforce the connection of sin and punishment: he presupposes the details, which they had declared. Apart from those chapters, which pseudo-criticism denies to Isaiah[y], on account of the distinctness of the temporal prophecies, Isaiah had, in plainest words, declared to Hezekiah the carrying away of all the royal treasures to Babylon, and that his offspring should be eunuchs there[z]; Micah had declared not only the complete desolation of Jerusalem[a], but that the people should be "[b]carried to Babylon, and there delivered, there redeemed from the hands of the enemy." In the 13th year of Josiah, B. C. 628, and so, three years before the fall of Nineveh, while Babylon was still dependent on Nineveh and governed by a vice-roy, and while Nabopolassar was still in the service of the king of Nineveh, Jeremiah foretold, that *[c] evil should break forth from the North upon all the inhabitants of the land, and all the families of the kingdoms of the North shall come and set every one his throne at the entering of the gates of Jerusalem and against all the walls thereof round about and against all the cities of Judah*, to execute the *judgments* of God *against them for their wickedness*. This was his dirge over his country for twenty-three years[d], ere yet there was a token of its fulfillment. Babylon had succeeded to Nineveh in the West and South-

West, and Judah had fallen to the share of Babylon; but the relation of Josiah to Nabopolassar was of a tributary sovereign, which rebellion only could disturb. The greater part of Nabopolassar's 21 year's reign are almost a blank[e]. Chastisement had come, but from the South, not from the North. Eighteen years had passed away, and Josiah had fallen, in resisting Pharaoh-Necho in discharge of his fealty to the king of Babylon. Pharaoh-Necho had taken away one king of Judah, Jehoahaz, the people's choice, whose continued fealty to Babylon represents their minds, and had set up another, Jehoiakim. For three years Judah's new allegiance was allowed to continue. Who, but God, could tell the issue of the conflict of those two great armies at Carchemish? Egypt with her allies, the Ethiopians, Phut and Lud, were come, *rising up like a flood[f], covering the earth* with her armies, as her rivers, when swollen, made her own land one sea. Necho had apparently in his alliance all the kings of the countries West of the Euphrates: for to them all, in connection with Egypt and subordinate to her, does Jeremiah at that moment give to drink the cup of the wrath of God; to [g] *Pharaoh king of Egypt, and his servants and his princes and all his people, and all the mingled people* [his auxiliaries] *and all the kings of the land of* Uz, and *all the kings of the land of the Philistines and Ashkelon and Azzah and Ekron and the remnant of Ashdod; Edom and Moab and the children of Ammon; and all the kings of Tyrus, and all the kings of Zidon and the kings of the isle beyond the sea* [probably Caphtor[h], or Crete, or Cyprus] *Dedan and Tema and Buz, and those whose hair is shorn* [Arabians[i]] *and all the kings of Arabia and all the kings of the mingled people that dwell in the desert, and all the kings of Zimri* [[k] descendants of Abraham and Keturah.] It was a mighty gathering. *All the kings of Elam, and all the kings of the Medes, all the kings of the North far and near*, all was hostile to Babylon; for all were to drink of the cup beforehand, at the hands of the king of Babylon, *and then the king of Sheshach* [Babylon]

2 Chr. xxx. 10, Neh. ii. 19, iii. 33. לַעַג Job. xxxiv. 7, Ps. cxxiii. 4, Hos. vii. 16, Ez. xxiii. 32, xxxvi. 4. with

קֶלֶס Ps. xliv. 19. lxxix. 4.

[t] לִיץ part. occurs 14 times in Prov. Ps. i. 1. and Is. xxix. 20. לִיץ *l* (the verb), Pr. ix. 12. לוֹצְצִים Hos. vi. 5. הִתְלוֹצֵץ Is. xxviii. 22. הַלִּיץ Ps. cxix. 51 Pr. iii. 34, xiv. 9, xix. 28.

[u] הִתֵּל Job xvii. 2, 1 Kgs xviii. 27.

[v] הִתְעַלֵּל with בְּ of the pers. Num. xxii. 29, of Balaam's ass; 1 Sam. xxxi. 4, Jer. xxxviii. 19, 1 Chr. x. 4, of apprehended insult from an enemy.

[w] צָחַק Gen. xix. 14, xxi. 9. insult in act, Ib. xxxix. 14, 17, revived from Genesis, Ez. xxiii. 32, elsewhere שָׂחַק.

[x] The exact meaning of שִׂמְצָה (Ex. xxxii. 25) is uncertain. The E. V. "shame" follows most of the Heb. Intt., yet with an improbable etymol. "Whisper" seems the most probable meaning of Job iv. 12. xxvi. 14, from which that of "ill-report" is possible. The Arabic gives nothing nearer than "hurried in speech."

[y] Is. xiii. xiv. 1-23, xl. sqq.

[z] Is. xxxix. 6, 7.   [a] Mic. iii. 12.
[b] Ib. iv. 10.   [c] Jer. i. 14-16.
[d] Ib. xxv. 3. see also v. 15-17, vi. 1. 22-25, x. 22. Also in the collection of all his prophecies from the time of Josiah, which God bade him make in the 4th year of Jehoiakim, Jer. xxxvi. 2. 29, he provides them also with a saying against idolatry (in Chaldee) for their use in their captivity in Chaldæa. x. 11.   [e] Rawl. 5 Emp. iii. 484.
[f] Jer. xlvi. 8. 9.   [g] Ib. xxv. 19-24.
[h] Jer. xlvii. 4.   [i] Herod. iii. 8.
[k] Gen. xxv. 2. 1 Chr. i. 32. (זִמְרִי for זִמְרָן.)

was *to drink after them.* Necho was one of the most enterprising monarchs[1]. Nabopolassar had shewn no signs of enterprise. Nebuchadnezzar, the first and last conqueror of the Babylonian empire, though the alliance with Media and his father's empire had been cemented by his marriage, had, as far as we know, remained inactive during 20 years of his father's life[m]. He was as yet untried. So little did he himself feel secure as to his inheritance of the throne, even after his success at the head of his father's army, that his rapid march across the desert, with light troops, to secure it, and its preservation for him by the chief priest, are recorded in a very concise history[n]. Neither Egypt nor Jehoiakim foresaw the issue. Defeat taught neither. Two voices only gave, in God's name, one unheeded warning. Pharaoh Hophra, the Apries of Herodotus, succeeded Pharaoh Necho in his self-confidence, his aggressions, his defeat. " I am against thee," God says[o], " Pharaoh, king of Egypt, the great dragon that lieth in the midst of his rivers, *which hath said, My river* is *mine own and I have made* it *for myself.*" " It is said," relates Herodotus[p], " that Apries believed that there was not a god which could cast him down from his eminence, so firmly did he think that he had established himself in his kingdom."

For a time, Nebuchadnezzar must have been hindered by Eastern wars, since, on Jehoiakim's rebellion and perjury, he sent only *bands of the Chaldees,* with *bands* of tributary nations, the Syrians, Moabites, Ammonites, against him[q]. But not in his time only, even after the captivity under his son Jehoiachin and his men of might[r], the conviction that Nebuchadnezzar could be resisted, still remained in the time of Zedekiah both in Egypt and Judah. Judah would have continued to hold under Babylonia that same position toward Egypt which it did under Persia, only with subordinate kings instead of governors. Apart from God's general promise of averting evil on repentance, Jeremiah, too, expressly tells Israel, " [s] If thou wilt put away thine abominations out of My sight, *thou shalt not remove ;* " " [t] Then will I cause you to dwell in this place, in the land that I gave to your fathers, for ever and ever." And " in the beginning of the reign of Jehoiakim[u]," " [v] The Lord sent me to prophesy against this house and against this city all the words which ye have heard. Therefore

now amend your ways and your doings and obey the voice of the Lord your God, *and the Lord will repent Him of the evil that He hath pronounced against you.*" Still later, to Zedekiah, " [w] The nations that bring their neck under the yoke of the king of Babylon and serve him, *them will I let remain still in their own land, saith the Lord ; and they shall till it and dwell therein.*" " [x] I have sent unto you all My servants the prophets, rising up early and sending them, saying, Return ye now every man from his evil way and amend your doings, and go not after other gods to serve them, and *ye shall dwell in the land which I have given to you and to your fathers.*" Even on the very verge of the capture of Jerusalem, Jeremiah promised to Zedekiah[y] ; " If thou wilt go forth to the king of Babylon's princes ;—*this city shall not be burned with fire.*" Pharaoh Hophra was still strong enough to raise the siege of Jerusalem, when invested by the Chaldæan army[z]. Jeremiah had the king, his princes, his prophets, all the people of the land against him, because he prophesied that Jerusalem should be burned with fire, that those already taken captives should not return, until the whole had been carried away, and the seventy years of captivity were accomplished[a]. The warning and the promise of Jeremiah's inaugural vision had its accomplishment. " [b] I have made thee a defenced city, and an iron pillar, and brazen walls, *against the king of Judah, against the princes thereof and against the people of the land ;* and they shall fight against thee, but they shall not prevail against thee ; for I am with thee, saith the Lord, to deliver thee." Had it been matter of human foresight, how was it, that all nations, all their politicians, all their wise men, all their prophets, all Judah, kings, priests, princes, people, were blinded, (as in Him of Whom Jeremiah was a shadow,) and Jeremiah alone saw? " Vaticinia post eventum " are, in one sense, easy ; viz. to imagine, after an event has taken place, that one could have foreseen it. And yet who, after the retreat to Corunna, could have foreseen the victories of the Peninsular war ? Or, when that tide of 647,000 men[c] was rolling on toward Russia, who could imagine that only a small fraction of those hosts should return, that they should capture Moscow, but find it a tomb ; and hunger and cold, reaching at last to 36 degrees below Zero, should destroy more than the sword ? " [d] What was the principal adversary of this tremendous power ? By whom was it checked

---

[1] As shewn in his attempt to make a canal across the isthmus of Suez (Herod. ii. 158.) and in the circumnavigation of Africa. Ib. iv. 42.
[m] The battle of Carchemish was in the 4th of Jehoiakim. Jer. xlvi. 1. 2.
[n] Berosus in Joseph. c. Ap. i. 19. Opp. ii. 450.
[o] Ezek. xxix. 3.   [p] Herod. ii. 16.
[q] 2 Kgs xxiv. 2.   [r] Ib. 14–16.   [s] Jer. iv. 1.

[t] Ib. vii. 7, add xvii. 25, 26. xxii. 2–5.
[u] Ib. xxvi. 1.   [v] xxvi. 12. add ib. 2, 3.
[w] xxvii. 11.   [x] xxxv. 15.   [y] xxxviii. 17.
[z] Jer. xxxvii. 5.   [a] xxv. 11, 12. xxix. 10.
[b] Jer. i. 18, 19, renewed xv. 20.
[c] " Imperial muster rolls in Chambray Vol. i. App. No. 2." Alison Hist. of Europe x. 629.
[d] Dr. Arnold lect. on· Hist. ii. 139.

and resisted and put down? By none and by nothing but the direct and manifest interposition of God."

The distinctness and perseverance of the prophecy are the more remarkable, because the whole of the greatness of the Chaldæan empire was that of one man. Assyria, in this one case, overreached itself in its policy of transporting conquered populations. It had, probably to check the rebellions of Babylon, settled there a wild horde, which it hoped would neither assimilate with its people, nor itself rebel. Isaiah relates the fact in simple words: *Behold the land of the Chaldæans; this people was not; the Assyrian founded* [f] *it for them that dwelt in the wilderness.* This does not seem to me necessarily to imply, that the wild people, for whom Assyria founded it, were Chaldæans [g] or Curds, whom the king of Assyria had brought from their Northern dwellings in the Curduchæan mountains [h] near Armenia, where Sennacherib conquered. Isaiah simply uses the name, *the land of the Chaldæans*, as does Jeremiah [i] after him, as the name of Babylonia; the word *Babylonia*, had it existed, might have been substituted for it. Of this, he says, that *it was not*, i. e. was of no account [k], but that *Assur founded it for wild tribes*, whom he placed there. Whence then he brought those tribes, Isaiah does not say. Æschylus (although indeed in later times) as well as Isaiah and Jeremiah, speak of the population of Babylon, as mingled of various nations; and the language is too large to be confined simply to its merchant-settlers. In Æschylus [l], "the all-mingled crowd," which "it sends out in long array," are its military contingents. It is its whole population, of which Isaiah and Jeremiah say, it will flee, each to his own land. [m] *It* [Babylon] *shall be as a chased roe, and as a sheep which no man gathereth; they shall, every man, turn to his own people, and flee every man to his own land. For fear of the oppressing sword they shall turn every one to his people:* [n] *And they shall flee, every one to his own land.*

Thus Babylonia received that solid accession of strength which ultimately made it a

powerful people, sixty years before the beginning of the reign of Josiah; its ancient and new elements would take some time to blend: they did not assume importance until the capture of Nineveh; nor had Judah any reason to dread anything from them, until itself rebelled, early in the reign of Jehoiakim. But 18 years before the death of Josiah, while Judah was a trusted and faithful tributary kingdom, Jeremiah foretold that evil should come upon them from the North, i. e. as he himself explains it, from the Chaldees [o]. Even then if Habakkuk were brought down to be a contemporary of Jeremiah, still in the 13th year of Josiah, there was nothing to fear. Judah was not in the condition of an outlying country, which Babylonian ambition might desire to reduce into dependence on itself. It was already part of the Babylonian empire, having passed into it, in the partition with Assyria, and had no more to fear from it, than any of the conquered nations of Europe have now from those who have annexed them, unless they rebel. God alone knew the new ambition of the kings of the smitten and subdued Egypt, their momentary success, Josiah's death, Judah's relapse into the old temptation of trusting in Egypt—all, conditions of the fulfilment of Habakkuk's and Jeremiah's prophecies. Edom, Moab, Ammon, Tyre, Zidon, sent embassadors to Zedekiah, to concert measures of resistance against Nebuchadnezzar [p]; they were encouraged by their [q] *diviners, dreamers, enchanters, sorcerers, which spake* to them, *ye shall not serve the king of Babylon.* One alone told them that resistance would but bring upon them destruction, that submission was their only safety; there was prophecy against prophecy [r], among these nations, in Jerusalem, in Babylon [s]; the recent knowledge of the political aspect of Babylon deterred not the false prophets there; all, with one voice, declared the breaking the yoke of the king of Babylon: Jeremiah only saw, that they were framing for themselves [t] *yokes of iron.* Had Jehoiakim or Zedekiah, their nobles, and their people possessed that human fore-

---

[e] Is. xxiii. 13.

[f] Jon. unites Asshur with the preceding זֶה הָעָם לֹא הָיָה אַשּׁוּר and so Syr. and Oxf. Arab. S. Jer. divides as the E. V., though with an opposite sense. "Talis populus non fuit." The E. V. is from Kim. The rendering, "This people was not Asshur," i. e. no longer Asshur, or not like Asshur, is very obscure; and יְסָד is everywhere "grounded it, that it might be," (Comp. Ps. civ. 8, Hab. i. 12. and the common use of יְסֹד "founded a city, building, temple,") not that it should cease to be.

[g] With this the only objection to the simple rendering falls away, that Jeremiah speaks of the Chaldees, as an *ancient nation.* Jer. v. 15.

[h] Xen. Cyrop. iii. 2. 7 and 12. Anab. iv. 3, 4. v. 5. 9. vii. 8. 14.

[i] Jer. xxiv. 5, l. 8. 25, li. 4; and, united with the name Babylon, xxv. 12, l. 1. 45, Ezek. xii. 13, as Isaiah does *Chasdim* alone, xlviii. 14, 20.

[k] Coll. לֹא עָם Deut. xxxii. 21, לֹא אִישׁ Ps. xxii. 7. See the like in the Classics in Perizon. Orig. Bab. c. vi. p. 70. sqq. and from him in Vitr.

[l] Æsch. Pers. 52, 53, 54. [m] Is. xiii. 14.

[n] Jer. l. 16.

[o] There ought to be no question as to the identity of the invasion from the north, Jer. i. 15, vi. 22, x. 22, and Jeremiah's own summary of his prophecies from the 13th of Josiah, xxv. 3-9 when he names Nebuchadnezzar; only then there would be definite prediction. Hence the mare's nest as to the dread of the Scythians, who marched down the sea coast and returned, being bought off by Psammetichus, doing no harm to Judah by this passing expedition.

[p] Jer. xxvii. 3. [q] Ib. 9.

[r] Jer. v. 12–14. xiv. 14–16. xxiii. 16, 17, 21, 25–27, 30 sqq. xxvii. 14, 15–18, xxviii.

[s] Jer. xxix. 8, 9, 15, 21, 24, sqq.

[t] xxviii. 13, 14.

sight which that pseudo-critical school holds to be so easy, Judah had never gone into captivity to Babylon. But He Who *fashioneth the heart of man* knoweth alone the issue of the working of those hearts, which He over-rules.

From the necessity of its case, the pseudo-critical school lowers down the words, in which Habakkuk declares the marvelousness of the event which he foretells, and the unbelief of his people. " Look well," he bids them, " marvel ye, marvel on; for I will work a work in your days which ye will not believe, when it shall be told you." It is " something which had not hitherto been, something hitherto unknown," says Stahelin [u]. Yet things hitherto unknown, are not therefore incredible. " It is clear from the contents," says Bleek [v], " that the Chaldees had at that time already extended to the West their expeditions of conquest and destruction, and on the other side, that this had only lately begun and that they were not yet come to Judah and Jerusalem, so that here they were hitherto little known." " The appearance of the Chaldees as world-conquerors was, in Judah, then a quite new phenomenon," says Ewald [w]. " The description of the Chaldees altogether is of such sort, that they appear as a people still little known to the Jews," says Knobel [x]. " That which is incredible for the people consists therein, that God employs just the Chaldees, such as they are described in what follows, for the unexpected chastisement of Israel," says even Umbreit [y].

What was there incredible, that, when the king of Jerusalem had revolted from Babylon, and had sided with Egypt, its chief enemy, the Chaldæans, should come against it? As soon might it be said to be incredible that France should invade Prussia, when its hundred thousands were on their march toward the Rhine. During the reign of Manasseh it was incredible enough, that any peril should impend from Babylon; for Babylon was still subordinate to Assyria: in the early years of Josiah it was still incredible, for his thirty-one years were years of peace, until Pharaoh Necho disputed the cis-Euphratensian countries with Babylon. When the then East and West came to Carchemish, to decide whether the empire should be with the East or with the West, nothing was beyond human foresight but the result. Expectation lately hung suspended, perplexed between the forces of Europe. None, the most sagacious, could predict for a single day. Men might sur-

mise; God only could predict. For three and twenty years Jeremiah foretold, that the evil would come from the North, not from the South. The powers were well-balanced. Take Habakkuk's prophecy as a whole— not that the Chaldæans should invade Judæa, (which in Jehoiakim's time was already certain) but that Egypt should be a vain help, and that the Chaldæans should mesh its people like *the fishes of the sea*, yet they should still have to disgorge them, because God's judgment would come upon them also. This too were incredible. Incredible it was to the kings, the wise, the politicians, the political prophets of Judæa, that Jerusalem itself should be taken. Incredible it was, and there was much human reason for the incredulity. Egypt and Assyria had been matched during centuries. Until the Sargonides, Egypt had, during centuries, the unbroken advantage. But the Sargonides had passed away. Yet Chaldæa had not, alone, prevailed against Assyria. Why should the yet untried Babylonian be so certain of success, when the whole West of the Euphrates was banded together against him, and fought within their own ground? *The kings of Elam and the kings of the Medes* [z] were now, as under Cyrus, enemies of Babylon. Babylon had enemies before and behind. But God had raised up Nebuchadnezzar to be *the hammer of the whole earth* [a], and had given those cis-Euphratensian lands which leagued against him *into the hands of Nebuchadnezzar the king of Babylon, My servant,* God says [b], *and all nations shall serve him and his son and his son's son, until the very time of his land come; and then many nations and great kings shall serve themselves of him.* Whence this combination of almost superhuman but short-lived might, this certainty of wide sway down to the third generation, this certainty of its cessation afterward? There was no time for decay. Alexander's empire was yet more short-lived, but it was divided among his successors. Alexander had, by his genius, founded his own empire, which the able generals, whom he had trained, divided among themselves. In the Chaldæan empire, we have an enterprising conspirator, who seizes an occasion, but does little beside which is recorded, nothing alone, nothing, beside that first grasp at power, for himself. He appears only as the ally of Media [c]: then a son, a world-wide conqueror, with a genius for consolidating the empire which he inherited, forming an impregnable city, which should also be a province, filling his empire with fortresses [d], but leaving none after him

[u] Einl. p. 218.   [v] Einl. ins. A. T. pp. 545, 546.
[w] Die Proph. ii. 29. see also Delitzsch's quotation from him ab. p. 170.
[x] Die Proph. u. Hebr. ii. 292. Dr. Davidson's sentences are chiefly gleaned from him.

[y] Kl. Proph. p. 286.
[z] Jer. xxv. 25.   [a] Ib. l. 23.
[b] Ib. xxvii. 6. 7.   [c] Herod. i. 74.
[d] See Daniel the Prophet pp. 118. 122, Rawl. 5 Empires iii. 496 sqq.

to maintain what he had so consolidated. By whom could this be foreknown save by Him, with Whom alone it is, *to root out and to pull down and to destroy and to throw down, to build and to plant* [e] ?

It has been common to praise the outside of Habakkuk's prophecy, the purity of his language, the sublimity of his imagery. Certainly it is, humanly speaking, magnificent: his measured cadence is impressive in its simplicity. He too has words and forms, which are peculiar to him among the remains of Hebrew [f]. But his eminence is rather the condensed thought, expressed often in the simplest words; as when, having carried on the tide of victory of the Chaldæan to its height, everything human subdued before him, all resistance derided, he gathers up his fall and its cause in those eight words, " [g] Then sweeps-he-by, wind, and-passes, and-is-guilty; this his-strength (is) his-god." Yet more striking is the religious greatness, in which he sums up the meaning of all this oppressiveness of man. " [h] *Thou*, Lord, has placed him for judgment,

and, O Rock, has founded him to correct." Or, take the picture, prolonged relatively to his conciseness, of the utter helplessness of God's people, meshed, hooked, dragged in their net; their captors worshiping the instrument of their success, revelling in their triumph, and then the sudden question, " [i] *Shall they therefore empty their net?* " He waits to hear the answer from God. Or, again, the antiphonal dirge of the materials of the blood-built city over him [k]. Or the cutting off of every stay, sustenance, hope, promise of God, and, amid this universal crash, what does he ? It is not as the heathen, " [l] fearless will the ruins strike him : " but, " [m] And I," as if it were the continuance and consequence of the failure of all human things ; " I would exult in the Lord, I would bound for joy in the God of my salvation." His faith triumphs most, when all, in human sight, is lost.

> " Ill which Thou blessest is most good,
> And unblest good is ill ;
> And all is right which seems most wrong,
> So it be Thy sweet Will."

[e] Jer. i. 10.
[f] The most remarkable, have, of course, been singled out of old ; as, מִנְכָּה, i. 9, יָעֲבֹט טּ, ii. 6, קִיקָלוֹן ii. 16. Others are partly emphatic forms, as מִזָּעֵעַ, ii. 7, or are in some way, even though slight, peculiar to him. מְיֻקָּל, i. 4 (not in the verb), הִתְמַהְמְהוּ i. 5. יְהִיתַן ii. 17 (the form), מַסֵּכָה ii. 18. הֶעָרֵל ii. 16. מוֹדַד, הַתְּפוֹצֵץ, iii. 6. תָּעוּר iii.

9. עֲלִיצֻת iii. 14. קְצֹת ii. 10. עֻפְלָה i. 4. נֹוהַ ii. 5. חֶבְיוֹן iii, 4. רֹגֶז iii, 2. תָּפוּשׂ ii. 19, מְעוּרִים ii. 15. חֹדֶר i. 8, כְּפִישׁ ii. 11. מִשְׁסוֹת ii, 7. רַחֵם iii. 2, צָלַל quiver (of the lips) iii. 16, חֹמֶר (of sea) iii. 15. They will recur for notice in the Comm.

[g] Hab. i. 11.   [h] Ib. 12.   [i] Ib. 17.   [k] ii. 11.
[l] Hor. Od. iii. 3. 8.   [m] iii. 10.

12

HABAKKUK.

CHAPTER I.

1 *Unto Habakkuk, complaining of the iniquity of the land,* 5 *is shewed the fearful vengeance by the Chaldeans.* 12 *He complaineth that vengeance should be executed by them who are far worse.*

THE burden which Habakkuk the prophet did see.

2 O LORD, how long shall I cry, ᵃ and thou wilt not hear! *even cry out un-*

ᵃ Lam. 3. 8.

CHAP. I., Ver. 1. *The burden*[1] *which Habakkuk the prophet did see.* The prophet's name signifies "strong embrace." The word in its intensive form is used both of God's enfolding the soul in His tender supporting love[2], and of man clinging and holding fast to Divine wisdom[3]. It fits in with the subject of his prophecy, faith, cleaving fast to God amid the perplexities of things seen. "[4] He who is spiritually Habakkuk, cleaving fast to God with the arms of love, or enfolding Him after the manner of one holily wrestling, until he be blessed, enlightened, and heard by Him, is the seer here." "Let him who would in such wise fervidly embrace God and plead with Him as a friend, praying earnestly for the deliverance and consolation of himself and others, but who sees not as yet, that his prayer is heard, make the same holy plaint, and appeal to the clemency of the Creator." "[5] He is called 'embrace' either because of his love to the Lord; or because he engages in a contest and strife and (so to speak) wrestling with God." For no one with words so bold ventured to challenge God to a discussion of His justice and to say to Him, "Why, in human affairs and the government of this world is there so great injustice?"

The prophet. The title, *the prophet,* is added only to the names of Habakkuk, Haggai, Zechariah. Habakkuk may the rather have added it to his name, because prominently he expostulates with God, like the Psalmists, and does not speak in the name of God to the people. The title asserts that he exercised the pastoral office of the prophets, although not directly in this prophecy[6].

Did see. "[7] God *multiplied visions,* as is written[8], and Himself spake to the prophets, disclosing to them beforehand what should

be, and all but exhibiting them to sight, as if already present. But that they determined not to speak from their own, but rather transmit to us the words from God, he persuades us at the outset, naming himself a Prophet, and shewing himself full of the grace belonging thereto."

2. *O Lord, how long shall I cry,* lit. *how long have I cried so intensely* to Thee[9]? For it is ever the cry of the creature to Him Who alone can hear or help, its God[1]. Of this cry the Prophet expresses that it had already lasted long. In that long past had he cried to God and no change had come. There is an undefined past, and this still continues[10]. *How long,* as Asaph cries, *how long hast Thou been,* and, it is implied, wilt Thou be *wroth against the prayer of Thy people?* as we should say, *how long shall Thy wrath continue?* The words which the Prophet uses relate to domestic strife and wrong between man and man; violence[11], iniquity, strife, contention[12], nor are any of them used only of the oppression of a foreign enemy. He complains too of injustice too strong for the law, and the perversion of justice[13]. And on this the sentence is pronounced. The enemy is to be sent for *judgment* and *correction*[14]. They are then the sins of Judah which the Prophet rehearses before God, in fellow-suffering with the oppressed. God answers that they shall be removed, but by the punishment of the sinners.

Punishment does not come without sin, nor does sin endure without punishment. It is one object of the Old Testament to exhibit the connection between sin and punishment. Other prophets, as commissioned by God, first denounced the sins and then foretold the punishment of the impenitent. Habakkuk appeals to God's justice, as requiring

---

[1] On the word *burden* see on Nah. i. 1. p. 129. n. 1.
[2] תָּבֵק Cant. ii. 6. viii. 3.　[3] Prov. iv. 8.　[4] Dion.
[5] S. Jer. Abarbanel has the like, "He strengthens himself in pleading his cause with God as to the prosperity of Nebuchadnezzar as if he was joined with God for the cause of his people." Pref. to Ezek. pp. 123, 4, 124. 1.
[6] See ab. p. 20.　[7] S. Cyr.　[8] Hos. xii. 10.
[9] שֻׁוֵּעַ only occurs in the intensive form, and always of the cry to God, expressed by אֶל. or implied, except perhaps Job xxxv. 9.
[10] עַד־מָתַי עִוַּעְתִּי, as Ps. lxxx. 6. עַד־מָתַי עָשַׁנְתָּ.

and Exod. xvi. 28. עַד־אָנָה מֵאַנְתֶּם and Ex. x. 3, עַד־מָתַי מֵאַנְתָּ [all.]
[11] חָמָס וְשֹׁד are united of individual internal violence, Jer. vi. 7. xx. 8. Ez. xlv. 9. Am. iii. 10: even שֹׁד וָשֶׁבֶר Is. lix. 7. and שֹׁד alone Ps. xii. 6. Job xxiv. 9. Pr. xxi. 7. xxiv. 2. Hab. ii. 17. כֹּזָב וָשֹׁד Hos. xii. 2. אוֹן וְעָמָל occur Ps. lv. 11, in Habakkuk's order; inverted in Ps. x. 7. אוֹן, עָמָל שׁוֹא occur in three clauses in Is. lix. 4. עָמָל, אוֹן, with מִרְמָה Job xv. 35.
[12] i. 3.　[13] i. 4.　[14] i. 12.

to thee *of* violence, and thou wilt not save!

3 Why dost thou shew

me iniquity, and cause *me* to behold grievance? for spoiling and violence *are*

---

its infliction. On this ground too this opening of the prophecy cannot be a complaint against the Chaldees, because *their* wrong would be no ground of the punishment which the prophet denounced, but the punishment itself, requiting wrong to man through human wrong.

"[1] The prophet considers the person of the oppressed, enduring the intolerable insolence and contumely of those wonted to do wrong, and very skilfully doth he attest the unutterable loving kindness of God. For he exhibits Him as very forbearing, though wont to hate wickedness. But that He doth not forthwith bring judgment on the offenders, he showed clearly, saying that so great is His silence and long-suffering, that there needeth a strong cry, in that some practise intolerable covetousness against others, and use an unbridled insolence against the weak. For his very complaints of God's endurance of evil attest the immeasurable loving kindness of God."

"[1] You may judge hence of the hatred of evil in the Saints. For they speak of the woes of others as their own. So saith the most wise Paul, [2] *who is weak and I am not weak? who is offended, and I burn not?* and bade us [3] *weep with those who weep,* shewing that sympathy and mutual love are especially becoming to the saints."

The Prophet, through sympathy or fellow-suffering with the sufferers, is as one of them. He *cries* for help, as himself needing it, and being in the misery, in behalf of which he prays. He says, *How long shall I cry?* standing, as it were, in the place of all, and gathering all their cries into one, and presenting them before God. It is the cry, in one, of all which is wronged to the God of Justice, of all suffering to the God of love. "When shall this scene of sin, and confusion, and wrong be at an end, and the harmony of God's creation be restored? How long shall evil not exist only, but prevail?" It is the cry of the souls under the altar [4], *How long, O Lord, Holy and True, dost Thou not judge and avenge our blood on them that dwell on the earth?* It is the voice of the oppressed against the oppressor; of the Church against the world; weary of hearing the Lord's Name

blasphemed, of seeing wrong set up on high, holiness trampled under foot. It is in its highest sense His Voice, Who, to sanctify our longings for deliverance, said in the days of His Flesh, [5] *I cry in the daytime, but Thou hearest not.*

Even cry out aloud (it is the cry of anguish). "[6] We cry the louder, the more we cry from the heart, even without words; for not the moving of the lips, but the love of the heart sounds in the ears of God." *Even cry out unto Thee.* Whether as an exclamation or a continuance of the question, *How long?* the prophet gathered in one the prolonged cry of past and future. He *had* cried; he should cry on, *Violence* [7]. He speaks as if the one word, jerked out, as it were, wrung forth from his inmost soul, was, *Violence,* as if he said this one word to the God of Justice and love.

3. *Why dost Thou shew me iniquity, and cause me to behold,* or rather, *Why beholdest Thou* [8] *grievance?* God seemed to reverse what He had said by Balaam, [9] *He hath not beheld iniquity in Jacob, and hath not seen grievousness in Israel;* and "[10] Thou hast seen, for *Thou* [emph.] beholdest grievousness *and wrong, to put it in Thy hand,*" i. e. Thou layest it up in Thy hand, to cast it back on the head of the evil-doer. Now He seemed to behold it and leave it unpunished, which yet Habakkuk says to God below, He could not do; [11] *Thou canst not look upon iniquity.* What then did this mean? What was the solution?

All forms and shapes of sin are multiplied; oppressive *violence* [12], such as *covered the earth* before the flood, and brought it down; which Nineveh had to put away [13], and it was spared; *iniquity,* i. e. what is unequal and contrary to truth, falsehood; *grievance* lit. burdensome wearisome *toil; spoiling,* or open robbery; *strife and contention,* both through perversion of the law and, without it, through endless jarrings of man with man. Sin recoils on the sinner. So what he beholds is not *iniquity* only, but (in the same word) *vanity; grievance;* which is a burden both to him who suffers, and yet more to him who inflicts. For nothing is so burdensome as sin, nothing so empty as wickedness.

---

[1] S. Cyr.   [2] 2 Cor. xi. 29.
[3] Rom. xii. 15.   [4] Rev. vi. 10.
[5] Ps. xxii. 2.   [6] Dion.

[7] הן חמם ושר אקרא as אזעק חמם Jer. xx. 8. אצעק חמם Job. xix. 7. [all of this construction.]

[8] Since הביט, occurring 67 times, is certainly no where else used causatively of its common meaning, *behold, look,* and Habakkuk himself uses it four

times beside in that meaning הביט, "look," i. 5. with אל, i. 13. with על ii. 13. with acc. pers. i. 13. it is wholly improbable that it should be used here of "causing to look;" the more, since he has not marked the supposed exceptional use by adding the affix, תביטני. There is no ground to assume a causative of a causative.
[9] Nu. xxiii. 21.   [10] Ps. x. 14.   [11] i. 13.
[12] חמם Gen. vi. 11, 13.   [13] Jonah iii. 8.

before me: and there are *that* raise up strife and contention.

4 Therefore the law is s l a c k e d, and judgment

doth never go forth: for the ᵇ wicked doth compass about the righteous; therefore || wrong judgment proceedeth.

ᵇ Job. 21. 7.
Ps. 94. 3, &c.
Jer. 12. 1.

|| Or, *wrested.*

And while to him who suffers, the suffering is temporal, to him who inflicts it, it is eternal. And yet the prophet and whoso prays against ungodliness, "[1] must commiserate him who doth wrong yet more, since they hurt what is most precious, their own soul, and that eternally." All then is full of evil. Whithersoever the Prophet looks, some fresh *violence is before* him; it confronts him on every side; *strife hath arisen*[2], come up, exists where it was not before; *contention lifteth itself*[3] on high, bowing down all beside.

4. *Therefore,* i. e. Because God seemed not to awake to avenge His own cause, men promised themselves that they might sin on with impunity. Sin produces sin, and wrong, wrong; it spreads like an infectious disease, propagating itself, and each, to whom it reaches, adds to its poison. At last, it reached those also, who should be in God's stead to restrain it. The Divine law itself is silenced, by the power of the wicked, by the sin of the judge, the hopelessness of all. When all around is evil, even those not yet lost are tempted to think; "Why should I be other than they? what evil befalls them? Why stand alone?" Even a Psalmist[4] speaks as if tempted to *speak even as they. These are the ungodly who prosper in the world; they increase in riches; verily I have cleansed my heart in vain, and washed my hands in innocency;* and Solomon[5], *Because sentence against an evil work is not executed speedily, therefore the heart of the sons of men is fully set in them to do evil.*

The law is slacked, lit. *is chilled*[6] (as we say, "is paralyzed,") through lack of the fire of love. This is what our Lord says, [7] *Because iniquity shall abound, the love of many shall wax cold.* The Divine law, the source of all right, being chilled in men's hearts, *judgment,* i. e. the sentence of human justice, as conformed

to Divine, *doth never go forth*[8]. Human sense of right is powerless, when there is not the love of God's law. It seems ever ready to act, but ever falls short, like an arrow from an unstrung bow. The man seems ever *about* to do right; he judges, sees, aright; all but does it; yet at last always fails. It *goes not forth. The children are come to the birth, and there is not strength to bring forth*[9].

For the wicked doth compass about[10] the righteous, laying snares for him, as the Jews for our Lord; evil is too strong for a weak will to do right, and overbears it. Pilate sought in many ways, how he might deliver Jesus, yet at last did deliver Him into their hands.

Therefore wrong judgment proceedeth, lit. *judgment proceedeth wrested*[11]. He had said, "*it never goes forth;*" never, that is, in its true character; for, when it does *go forth,* it is distorted. "[12] For gifts or favor or fear or hate the guiltless are condemned and the guilty acquitted, as saith the Psalmist, [13] *How long will ye judge unjustly and accept the persons of the ungodly ?*" "[14] *Judgment goes forth* perverted in the seat of man's judgment (the soul), when, bribed by the pleasures of sense, it leans to the side of things seen, and the Ungodly one, the rebel angel, besets and overpowers him who has the sense of right; for it is right that things seen should give way to things unseen; [15] *for the things which are seen are temporal, but the things which are not seen are eternal.*" Why then all this? and how long? Why does God bring it before him and He Who is *of purer eyes than to behold iniquity, behold grievance,* which His Holy Eyes could not endure? Neither the Unseen Presence of God nor the mission of the Prophet checks. If he rebuke, no one hearkened; if he intercedes for sinners, or against sin, God made as though He would

---

[1] Theoph.
[2] The Lxx. Syr. S. Jer. so divide; γέγονε κρίσις καὶ ὁ κριτὴς λαμβάνει, "et factum est judicium et contradictio potentior." So Tanchum. The E. V. has followed Jon. Kim. Aben Ezra.
[3] נָשָׂא intrans., as in Ps. lxxxix. 10; Nah. i. 5.
[4] Ps. lxxiii. 15, 12, 13.   [5] Eccl. viii. 11.
[6] It is used of Jacob's heart, who could not believe the good tidings, Gen. xlv. 26; the numbing of the comfortless heart of the penitent through grief (Nif.) Ps. xxxviii. 9. The Psalmist, holding on in prayer, denies it of himself. Ps. xxvii. 3. They quote "friget lex."   [7] S. Matt. xxiv. 12.

[8] According to the uniform use of לָנֶצַח, 31 times and נֶצַח 6 times. This uniform usage cannot be overborne by the analogy of Is. xlii. 3. לֶאֱמֶת

יוֹצִיא מִשְׁפָּט, "He shall bring forth judgment to truth," as Syr. here, "with sincerity," Rashi, "according to truth."
[9] Is. xxxvii. 3.

[10] הַכְתִּיר, "encompass for hostile end," ᶦas כָּתַר Jud. xv. 43. Ps. xx. 13. "The wicked," רָשָׁע is collective, as implied by the word "encompass." "The righteous" is, in contrast, determined, אֵת הַצַּדִּיק.

[11] מְעֻקָּל. The root occurs only in intensive forms; in the verb here only; crooked ways are עֲקַלְקַלּוֹת Jud. v. 6. Ps. cxxv. 5. the Serpent is called עֲקַלָּתוֹן,

Isa. xxvii. 1.   [12] Dion.   [13] Ps. lxxxii. 2.
[14] Theoph.   [15] 2 Cor. iv. 18.

Before
C H R I S T
cir. 626.

e Is. 29.14.
Acts 13. 41.

5 ¶ e Behold ye among the heathen, and regard, and wonder marvellously; for *I* will work a work in

your days, *which* ye will not believe, though it be told *you.*

6 For, lo, d || I raise up

Before
C H R I S T
cir. 626.

d Deut. 28. 49. 50.
Jer. 5. 15.
|| fulfilled.
2 Chr. 36. 6.

not hear. God answers that, though to man's impatience the time seems long, judgment shall come, and that, suddenly and speedily. While the righteous is enquiring, *how long?* and the wicked is saying [1], *My Lord delayeth His coming,* He is come, and seen in the midst of them. The whole tone of the words suddenly changes. The Jews flattered themselves that, being the people of God, He would not fulfill His threats upon them. They had become like the heathen in wickedness; God bids them look out among them for the instrument of His displeasure. It was an aggravation of their punishment, that God, Who had once chosen *them,* would now choose these whom He had not chosen, to chasten them. So Moses had foretold; [2] *They have moved Me to jealousy by that which is not God; they have provoked Me to anger with their vanities; and I will move them to jealousy with not-a-people, I will provoke them to anger with a foolish nation.* There were no tokens of the storm which should sweep them away, yet on the horizon. No forerunners yet. And so He bids them gaze on among the nations, to see whence it should come. They might have expected it from Egypt. It should come whence they did not expect, with a fierceness and terribleness which they imagined not. *Regard,* look narrowly, weigh well what it portends; *and wonder marvelously;* lit. *be amazed, amazed.* The word is doubled [3], to express how amazement should follow upon amazement; when the first was passing away, new source of amazement should come; for [4] *I will work a work in your days, which ye will not believe, though it be told you.* So incredible it will be, and so against their wills! He does not say, "ye would not believe if it were told you;" much less, "if it were told you *of others;*" in which case the chief thought would be left unexpressed. No condition is expressed. It is simply foretold, what was verified by the whole history of their resistance to the Chaldees until the capture of the city; "Ye will not believe, when it shall be told you." So

it ever is. Man never believes, that God is in earnest, until His judgments come. So it was before the flood, and to Sodom, and Lot's sons-in-law; so it was to Ahab and Jezebel; so as to this destruction of Jerusalem by the Chaldæans, and that which is shadowed forth, by the Romans. So Jeremiah complained, [5] *They have belied the• Lord, and said, it is not He; neither shall evil come upon us; neither shall we see sword nor famine,* and, [6] *I am in derision daily; every one mocketh me.   For since I spake, I cried out, I cried violence and spoil; because the word of the Lord was made a reproach unto me, and a derision daily;* and Isaiah, [7] *Who hath believed our report?* and St. John Baptist speaks as though it were desperate; [8] *O generation of vipers, who hath warned you to flee from the wrath to come?* and our Lord tells them, [9] *Your house is left unto you desolate.* And yet they believed not, but delivered Him up to be put to death, *lest* that should be, which did come, *because* they put Him to death. [10] *If we let Him thus alone, all men will believe on Him; and the Romans shall come, and take away both our place and nation.* St. Paul [11], then, applies these words to the Jews in his day, because the destruction of the first temple by Nebuchadnezzar was an image of the destruction of the second (which by Divine appointment, contrary to man's intention, took place on the same day [12]), and the Chaldæans were images of the Romans, that second Babylon, heathen Rome; and both foreshowed the worse destruction by a fiercer enemy, the enemy of souls, the spiritual wasting and desolation which came on the Jew first, and which shall come on all who disobey the Gospel. So it shall be to the end. Even now the Jews believe not, Whose work their own dispersion is; His, Who by them was crucified, but Who hath [13] *all power in heaven and in earth.* The Day of Judgment will come like a thief in the night to those who believe not or obey not our Lord's words.

6. *For lo.* So God announces a future, in which His Hand shall be greatly visible,

[1] S. Matt. xxiv. 48.   [2] Deut. xxxii. 21.
[3] As in Ps. cxviii. 11, סַבּוּנִי גַם סְבָבוּנִי, Hos. iv. 18,
אָהֵכוּ הֵבוּ, Zeph. ii. 1. הִתְקוֹשְׁשׁוּ וְקוֹשּׁוּ. If suggested by Is. xxix. 9, הִתְמַהְמְהוּ וּתְמָהוּ "be perplexed and marvel," Habakkuk changed the phrase, preserving the alliteration.
[4] The "I" is omitted in the Hebrew, probably for conciseness, as if it were the finite verb. Del. quotes as omissions of the 3d person, Ps. xxii. 29. lv. 20; of the second 1 Sam. ii. 24. vi. 3. Ps. vii. 10.

Hab. ii. 10. Ewald adds "after הִנֵּה Gen. xli. 1. Ex. vii. 15. viii. 16, and without it, Ps. xxii. 29, xxxiii. 5. 7. lxvi. 7. xcvi. 13. Lehrb. p. 516. ed. 7.
[5] Jer. v. 12.   [6] Ib. xx. 7, 8.
[7] Is. liii. 1.   [8] S. Matt. iii. 7.
[9] Ib. xxiii. 38. S. Luke xiii. 35.   [10] S. John xi. 48.
[11] Some of the words as there quoted (from the then received translation, the LXX.) differ; the sense is the same.
[12] Jos. de B. J. vii. 14.   [13] S. Matt. xxviii. 18.

the Chaldeans, *that* bitter and hasty nation, which shall march through the † breadth of the land, to possess the dwellingplaces *that are* not their's.

7 They *are* terrible and dreadful: ||their judgment and their dignity

shall proceed of themselves.

8 Their horses also are swifter than the leopards, and are more † fierce than the *e* evening wolves : and their horsemen shall spread themselves, and their horsemen shall come from

Before CHRIST cir. 626.

† Heb. *breadths.*

‖ Or, *from them shall proceed the judgment of these, and the captivity of these.*

Before CHRIST cir. 626.

† Heb. *sharp.*

e Jer. 5. 6. Zeph. 3. 3.

---

whether more or less distant. In His sight it is present. *I raise up.* God uses the free-will and evil passions of men or devils to His own ends ; and so He is said to *raise up*[1] those whom He allows to be stirred up against His people, since the events which His Providence permits, favor their designs, and it rests with Him to withhold them. They lift themselves up for some end of covetousness or pride. But there is a higher order of things, in which God orders their actions to fulfill by their iniquities His righteousness. *The Chaldæans, that bitter*[2] *and hasty*[3] *nation.* "[4] To its might and warlike boldness almost all the Greeks who have written histories of the barbarians, witness." *Which shall march through the breadth of the land,* rather, *the earth,* lit. " to the breadths of the earth," reaching to its whole length and breadth, all its dimensions[5], as in the description of Gog and Magog, [6] *the number of whom is as the sand of the sea ; and they went up on the breadth of the earth ;* unhindered, not pent up, but spreading abroad, where they will, over the whole earth. All before it, is one wide even plain which it overspreads and covers, like a flood, and yet is not spent nor exhausted. *To possess the dwelling-places that are not theirs.* As God's people had done, so should it be done to them. Spoiling and violence within [7] attract oppression from without. The overcharged atmosphere casts down the lightning upon them. They had expelled the weak from their dwelling[8] ; others shall possess theirs. Yet this scourge too shall pass by, since, although the Chaldæan did God's

Will, he willed it not, but his own[9]. The words, *not theirs,* lit. *not to him* [*lo-lo*[10]] stand with a mysterious fullness of meaning. The dwelling places *not being his* by right, shall not remain *his,* although given to him, while God wills.

7. *They are terrible*[11] *and dreadful.* He describes them, first in themselves, then in act. They are terrible, and strike fear through their very being, their known character, before they put it forth in act. *Their judgment and their dignity shall proceed of themselves. Judgment* had *gone forth* in God's people *wrested*[12] ; now shall it go forth against them at the mere will of their master, who shall own no other rule or Lord or source of his power. His own will shall be his only law for himself and others. His elevation[13] too is, in his own thought, from himself. He is self-sufficing ; he holds from no other, neither from God nor man. His *dignity* is self-sustained ; his *judgment* irresponsible, as if there were none[14] *higher than he.* He has, like all great world-powers, a real dignity and majesty. He infuses awe. The dignity is real but faulty, as being held independently of God. This is a character of Antichrist[15], a lawless insolence, a lifting up of himself.

8. *Their horses are swifter* [lit. *lighter,* as we say, " light of foot"] *than leopards.* The wild beast intended is the panther, the lightest, swiftest, fiercest, most blood-thirsty of beasts of prey. "[16] It runs most swiftly and rushes brave and straight. You would say, when you saw it, that it is borne through the air." "[17] It bounds exceedingly and is very exceed-

---

[1] הקים is so used, 1 Kings xi. 14, 23. Am. vi. 14, and of evil (in the abstract) 2 Sam. xii. 11. Zech. xi. 16, as also העיר Ezek. xxiii. 22. 2 Chr. xxi. 16. and against Babylon, Is. xiii. 17. xli. 2, 25. Jer. l. 9. li. 1. 11.

[2] מר. In Jud. xviii. 25. 2 Sam. xvii. 8, the less concise מר נפש is used.

[3] נמהר as Is. xxxii. 4. [4] S. Jer.

[5] מרחבי (plur.) occurs here only. Isaiah has " the fullness of the breadth of Thy land, O Immanuel " viii. 8, and in the same sense v. 9. כל מרחקי ארץ " all the far places of the earth." (also ἁπ.)

[6] Rev. xx. 8. 9. [7] i. 2–4. [8] Mic. ii. 9.

[9] See Isa. x. 6, 7. [10] לא לו.

[11] אים occurs here only and Cant. vi. 4. 10. compared with the "bannered host," but the root is common in אימה. [12] i. 4.

[13] שאת is not in itself, "*self*-elevation" (as Kim. "that he will exalt himself above the nations") but simply "elevation;" from God, Gen. iv. 7, or His Providence, Ib. xlix. 3, Ps. lxii. 5. It is used of the majesty of God, Job xiii. 23.

[14] Eccl. v. 8. [15] Dan. xi. 36. 2 Thess. ii. 4.

[16] Oppian Cyneg. iii. 75. sq.

[17] S. Cyr. See more fully in Daniel the Prophet p. 77. n. 3.

far; [f]they shall fly as the eagle *that* hasteth to eat.

[f]Jer. 4. 13.
‖ Or, *the supping up of their faces, &c.* or, *their faces shall look toward the east.*
† Heb. *the opposition of their faces toward the east.*

9 They shall come all for violence: ‖ †their faces shall sup up *as* the east wind, and they shall gath-

er the captivity as the sand.

10 And they shall scoff at the kings, and the princes shall be a scorn unto them : they shall de-

---

ingly light to spring down on whatever it pursues." *More fierce* [1] *than the evening wolves* [2], i. e. than they are when fiercest, going forth to prey when urged to rabidness by hunger the whole day through. Such had their own judges been [3], and by such should they be punished. The horse partakes of the fierceness of his rider in trampling down the foe [4]. *Their horsemen shall spread themselves* [lit. *widespread are their horsemen*], *and their horsemen from far shall come.* Neither distance of march shall weary them, nor diffusion weaken them. So should Moses' prophecy be again fulfilled. [5] *The Lord shall raise against thee a nation from far, from the ends of the earth, as the eagle flieth ; a nation whose tongue thou shalt not understand ; a nation of fierce countenance, which shall not regard the person of the old, nor show favor to the young.* *They shall fly as the eagle that hasteth* [lit. *hasting* [6]] *to eat,* " [7] not to fight, for none shall withstand ; but with a course like the eagle's, to whom all fowl are subdued, *hasting* but to *eat.*" *Behold,* Jeremiah says of Nebuchadnezzar [8], *he shall fly as an eagle and spread his wings over Moab ;* and, he repeats the words, [9] *over Bozrah.* Our *pursuers,* Jeremiah says [10], *are swifter than the eagles of the heavens.* Ezekiel likens him to [11] *a great eagle with*

great wings full of feathers ; in Daniel's vision he is [12] *a lion with eagle's wings.*

9. *They shall come all for violence.* Violence had been the sin of Judah [13], and now shall be her punishment. It had been *ever before* the prophet ; all were full of it. Now should *violence* be the very end, one by one, of all the savage horde poured out upon them ; *they all,* *each one of them* [14], *come for violence. Their faces shall sup up* [15] *as the east wind* [16]. " As at the breath of the burning wind all green things dry up, so at sight of these all shall be wasted." They shall sweep over everything impetuously, like the east wind, scorching, blackening, blasting, swallowing up all, as they pass over, as the East wind, especially in the Holy Land, sucks up all moisture and freshness. *And they shall gather the captivity* [i. e. *the captives*] *as the sand,* countless, as the particles which the East wind raises, sweeping over the sand-wastes, where it buries whole caravans in one death.

10. *And they* [lit. *he,* the word stands emphatically, *he,* alone against all *the kings* of the earth] *shall scoff at the kings* and all their might, taking them away or setting them up at his pleasure and caprice, subduing them as though in sport [17] ; *and princes,* (lit. *grave and majestic) shall be a scorn unto them* [*him*] [18].

---

[1] lit. *sharp* "acer." חדד (except of the scales of the crocodile Job xii. 22) is used elsewhere only of the sharpening of iron against iron (Hif.) Pr. xxvii. 17 ; (Hof.), of the sword Ezek. xxi. 14, 15, 26. חדד as an epithet of the sword (iv. times). In Arabic חַד, conj. i. ii. iv. x. is to "sharpen ;" הוֹדָאר,חֹרָאר "sharp," of a knife, sword ; חָרִיד met., "sharp of intellect," &c. also of sword.
[2] Comp. Jer. v. 6. [3] Zeph. iii. 3.
[4] The horse and his rider are regarded as one. Nahum had spoken of the cavalry in the armies against Nineveh (Nah. iii. 2); in Judith they are numbered in the proportion of one-tenth to the footmen of Holofernes (Judith ii. 5, 15.). They were the more formidable to Judah which had footmen only. Under Persian rule Babylonia was a great breeding place for horses. Rawl. 5 Empires iii. 317.
[5] Deut. xxviii. 49, 50. מרחוק occurs in both.
[6] חָשׁ as partic. In the finite verb, it had been חוּשׁ like יָכֹסוּ ii. 14, יַהֲלֹכוּ iii. 11, יֹטְשׁ Job ix. 26. Del. [7] S. Jer. [8] Jer. xlviii. 40. [9] Ib. xlix. 22.
[10] Lam. iv. 19. [11] Ezek. xvii. 3. [12] Dan. vii. 4.
[13] v. 3. 4.
[14] As כֻּלֹּה Ps. xxix. 9, Is. i. 23, ix. 16, Jer. vi. 13, viii. 6. 10, xv. 10. כֻּלֹּה Jer. xx. 7.
[15] מְגַמַּה, *απ. λεγ.* The sense "swallowing" is given by Jos. Kimchi, A. E., Rashi, Ob. Sip., Menahem B. Saruk, taking גֹּמֶם as i. q. נָגְמָא, quoting

Job xxxix. 24 or Gen. xxiv. 17. Thence A. E. obtains the meaning " before, straight on," quoting Targ. Abulwalid, followed by Tanchum, compares the Arab. הַם, "purposed," and thence derives the meaning " direction." The Arab. מַ, (appetivit, Fr.) signifies "approached" not "desired." Gesenius " the *collection* of their faces," i. e. all of them, involves the use of a *απ. λεγ.* to express, without emphasis, what is expressed everywhere by the common word, כֹּל. Symm. has προσοψις, and so Syr.
[16] קָדִימָה occurs else only in Ezek. xi. 1, and 16 times in c. xl.-xlviii. of the ideal city and temple as " Eastwards." But except in the far-fetched explanation of Abarb. (mentioned also by Tanchum) that they ravaged, not to settle, but to return home with their booty, " Eastwards " would have no meaning. Yet " forwards " is just as insulated a rendering as that adopted by J. and D. Kim., A. E., Rashi, Ob. Sip., Sal. B. Mel. Arab Tr. (following Jon.) " the East-wind ;" קָדִימָה standing as a met. instead of a simile the ה being regarded as paragogic, as in לֵילָה. So also Symm. *ανεμος καυσων.* S. Jer., "ventus urens."
[17] Comp. Benhadad's drunken commands, 1 Kings xx. 18.
[18] Comp. Job xli. 29.

ride every strong hold;
for they shall heap dust,
and take it.

11 Then shall *his* mind

change, and he shall pass
over, and offend, ᵍ *imputing*
this his power unto his
god.

ᵍ Dan. 5. 4.

So Nebuchadnezzar *bound* Jehoiakim¹ *in fetters to carry him to Babylon;* then, on his submission made him for three years a tributary king², then on his rebellion sent bands of Chaldees and other tributaries against him³; and then, or when Nebuchadnezzar took Jehoiachin, Jeremiah's prophecy was fulfilled, that he should *be buried with the burial of an ass, dragged and cast forth beyond the gates of Jerusalem⁴, his dead body cast out in the day to the heat and in the night to the frost⁵,* then Nebuchadnezzar took away Jehoiachin; then Zedekiah. He had also many kings captive with him in Babylon. For on his decease Evil-Merodach brought Jehoiachin out of his prison after 27 years of imprisonment, *and set his throne above the throne of the kings that were with him in Babylon⁶.* Daniel says also to Nebuchadnezzar⁷, *Thou, O king, art a king of kings: for the God of heaven hath given thee a kingdom, power and strength and glory. And wheresoever the children of men dwell, the beasts of the field and the fowls of heaven hath He given into thine hand and hath made thee ruler over all.*

They [*he*] *shall deride every strong hold,* as, aforetime, when God helped her, Jerusalem laughed the Assyrian to scorn⁸; *for they* [*he*] *shall heap dust, and take it,* as Nebuchadnezzar did Tyre, whose very name (*Rock*) betokened its strength. "⁹ He shall come to Tyre, and, casting a mound in the sea, shall make an island a peninsula, and, amid the waves of the sea, land shall give an entrance to the city."

The *mount,* or heaped-up earth, by which the besiegers fought on a level with the besieged, or planted their engines at advantage, was an old and simple form of siege, especially adapted to the great masses of the

Eastern armies. It was used in David's time¹⁰; and by the Assyrians¹¹, Egyptians¹², Babylonians¹³, and afterward the Persians¹⁴. Here he describes the rapidity of the siege. To heap up dust and to capture were one.

It needed no great means; things slight as the dust sufficed in the hands of those employed by God. Portion by portion, ¹⁵ *the King of Babylon took all that pertained to the king of Egypt, from the river of Egypt unto the river Euphrates.*

11. *Then shall his mind change,* or, better, *Then he sweeps by* ¹⁶, *a wind* ¹⁷, *and passes* ¹⁸, *and is guilty; this his strength is his god.* The victory was completed, all resistance ended. He sweeps by, as his own Euphrates, when over-filled by the swelling ¹⁹ of all its tributary streams, riseth up over all its banks, and overwhelms all where it passes; as a wind which sweepeth ²⁰ over the desert : *and passes over* all bounds and laws, human and Divine, *and is guilty* and stands guilty before God, making himself as God, *This his power is his god.* God had said to Israel, ²¹ *I will be to thee God.* The Chaldæan virtually said, *this my strength is to me my god.* This Nebuchadnezzar's own words speak; ²² *Is not this great Babylon, that I have built for the house of the kingdom by the might of my power, and for the honor of my majesty?* And the statue which was to be worshiped, was, very probably, of himself²³, as the intoxication of pride has made other heathen kings or conquerors, Alexander or Darius²⁴. Belshazzar said, ²⁵ *I will be like the Most High,* and the prince of Tyre said, ²⁶ *I am a god,* and Anti-Christ shall ²⁷ *exalt himself above all that is called god,* and, *as God, sit in the temple of God, shewing himself that he is god.* Such is all pride. It sets itself in the place of God,

¹ 2 Chr. xxxvi. 6. Dan. i. 2.
² 2 Kings xxiv. 1.   ³ Ib. 2.   ⁴ Jer. xxii. 19.
⁵ Ib. xxxvi. 30. On the one hand, the expression "slept with his fathers" does not necessarily imply that Jehoiakim died a peaceful death, since it is used of Ahab (1 Kings xxii. 40) and Amaziah (2 Kings xiv. 20, 22.) On the other, Jeremiah's prophecy was equally fulfilled, if the insult to his corpse took place when Nebuchadnezzar took away Jehoiachin three months after his father's death. See Daniel the Prophet, pp. 399, 402, 403. Josephus attributes both the death and disgrace to Nebuchadnezzar. Ant. x. 6. 3.
⁶ 2 Kgs xxv. 27, 28.
⁷ Dan. ii. 37. 38. and iv. 22.   ⁸ Is. xxxviii. 22.
⁹ S. Jer.   ¹⁰ 2 Sam. xx. 15.   ¹¹ 2 Kgs xix. 32.
¹² Ez. xvii. 17.
¹³ Jer. vi. 6. xxii. 24, xxxiii. 4, Ezek. iv. 2, xxi. 22 [27 Heb.], xxvi. 8.
¹⁴ Herod. i. 162.   ¹⁵ 2 Kings xxiv. 7.
¹⁶ חלף is used of the overflowing of a river, Is.

viii. 8. of a wind chasing, Ib. xxi. 1, of the invisible presence of God passing by, Job ix. 11. or a spirit, Ib. iv. 15. of the swift passing of our days, like ship or eagle, Ib. ix. 26. of idols utterly passing away, Is. ii. 18, of rain past and gone, Cant. ii. 11. It is, together with רבע, used of transgressing God's law, Is. xxiv. 5. It is always intrans., except as piercing the temples of man Jud. v. 26, or himself Job xx. 24.
¹⁷ רוה, i. q. כרוה, metaphor for simile, as Ps. xi. 1. xxii. 14. (13 Eng.) xc. 4. Job xxiv. 5. Is. li. 12. &c. רוה can hardly be i. q. יהור.
¹⁸ רבע "pass over" (with חלף, as here,) Is. viii. 8. Nah. i. 8. Hab. iii. 10; "transgress," passim; "pass away," Ps. xxxvii. 6, Job xxxiv. 20, Nah. i. 12.
¹⁹ Is. viii. 8.   ²⁰ Ib. xxi. 1.
²¹ Ex. vi. 7.   ²² Dan. iv. 30.
²³ See Daniel the Prophet, p. 443.
²⁴ See ib. p. 446.   ²⁵ Is. xiv. 14.
²⁶ Ezek. xxviii. 2.   ²⁷ 2 Thess. ii. 4.

Before
CHRIST
cir. 626.

h Ps. 90. 2.
& 93. 2.
Lam. 5. 19.

12 ¶ ʰ *A r t* thou not
from everlasting, O LORD
my God, mine Holy One?

we shall not die. O LORD,
ⁱ thou hast ordained them
for judgment;   and, O

Before
CHRIST
cir. 626.

¹² Kin. 19. 25.
Ps. 17. 13.
Is. 10. 5, 6, 7.   Ezek. 30. 25.

it ceases to think itself His instrument, and
so is a god to itself, as though its eminence
and strength were its own, and its wisdom
the source of its power [1], and its will the
measure of its greatness. The words, with
a 'Divine fullness, express severally, that the
king shall *sweep* along, shall *pass* over all
bounds and all hindrances, and shall *pass
away*, shall *be guilty* and shall *bear his guilt* [2]:
and so they comprise in one his sin and his
punishment, his greatness and his fall. And
so forty years afterward Nebuchadnezzar,
[3] *whom he would, he slew ; and whom he would,
he kept alive; and whom he would, he set up;
and whom he would, he put down; but when his
heart was lifted up, and his mind hardened in
pride, he was deposed from his kingly throne, and
they took his glory from him;* [4] *there fell a voice
from heaven, The kingdom is departed from thee;*
and Belshazzar, [5] *in the same night that he
lifted up himself against the Lord of heaven, was
slain.*
12. The prophet, having summed up the
deeds of the enemy of God in this his end,
sets forth his questions anew. He had appealed against the evil of the wicked of his
people; he had been told of the vengeance
by the Chaldæans. [6] But the vengeance is
executed by them who are far worse. How
then ? The answer is, "Wait to the end, and
thou shalt see." What remains are the
triumphs of faith ; the second chapter closes
with the entire prostration of the whole
world before God, and the whole prophecy
with joyous trust in God amid the entire
failure of all outward signs of hope. Here,
like the Psalmists [7] and Jeremiah [8], he sets
down at the very beginning his entire trust in
God, and so, in the name of all who at any
time shall be perplexed about the order of
God's judgments, asks how it shall be, teaching us that the only safe way of enquiring
into God's ways is by setting out with a living conviction that they [9] *are mercy and truth.*
And so the address to God is full of awe and
confidence and inward love. For " [10] God
placeth the oil of mercy in the vessel of
trustfulness."

Art not Thou (the word has always an emphasis) *Thou*, and not whatsoever or whosoever it be that is opposed to Thee, (be it
Nebuchadnezzar or Satan) *from everlasting*
lit. *from before* [11] ? Go back as far as man can
in thought, God was still *before;* and so,
much more *before* any of His creatures, such
as those who rebel against Him. *O Lord*, it
is the Proper Name of God, [12] *Which is and
Which was and Which is to come,* I AM, the
Unchangeable ; *my God,* i. e., whereas his
own might is (he had just said) the heathen's
god, the Lord is his; *mine Holy One:*—one
word, denoting that God is his God, sufficeth
him not, but he adds (what does not elsewhere
occur) *mine Holy One,* in every way, as hallowing him and hallowed by him : " [13] Who
hallowest my soul, Holy in Thine Essence,
and Whom as incomparably Holy I worship
in holiness." All-Holy in Himself, He becometh the Holy One of him to whom He
imparteth Himself, and so, by His own gift,
belongeth, as it were, to him. The one word
in Hebrew wonderfully fits in with the truth,
that God becomes one with man by taking
him to Himself. It is full of inward trust
too, that he saith, " *my God, mine Holy One,*"
as S. Paul saith, [14] *Who loved me, and gave
Himself for me,* i. e., as S. Augustine explains
it, " [15] O Thou God Omnipotent, Who so carest
for every one of us, as if Thou caredst for
him only ; and so for all, as if they were but
one." The title, *my Holy One,* includes his
people with himself; for God was *his* God,
primarily because he was one of the people
of God ; and his office was for and in behalf
of his people. It involves then that other
title which had been the great support of
Isaiah [16], by which he at once comforted his
people, and impressed upon them the holiness of their God, the holiness which their
relation to their God required, *the Holy One
of Israel.* Thence, since Habakkuk lived, for
his people with himself, on this relation to
God, as *my God, my Holy One,* and that God,
the Unchangeable; it follows, " *We shall not
die* [17]." There is no need of any mark of inference, " *therefore* we shall not die." It *is* an

[1] See Ezek. xxviii. 2–5.
[2] םשא includes both.   [3] Dan. v 19. 20.
[4] Ib. iv. 31.   [5] Ib. v. 23, 30.
[6] Heading of Chap. i.
[7] Asaph, Ps. lxxiii. Ethan Ps. lxxvi.
[8] Jer. xii. 1.   [9] Ps. xxv. 10.
[10] S. Bern. de Annunt. Serm. 3. n. 3.
[11] See on Micah v. 2.   [12] Rev. i. 8.   [13] Dion.
[14] Gal. ii. 9.   [15] Conf. iii. 11.
[16] Isaiah uses it in his prophetic answer to Hezekiah (2 Kgs xix. 22. Is. xxxvii. 23,) also in the
earlier chapters 12 times and "his holy One" (of

Israel) x. 17; in the chapters xl–lxvi, 14 times, and
"his holy One" "your holy One" of or to Israel
xlix. 7. xliii. 35. Else it occurs only in Ps. lxxviii.
41 (Asaph's), lxxxix. 19 (Ethan's), lxxi. 22 [Anon.,
but in Book ii.] and Jer. l. 29, li. 5.
[17] The "tikkune sopherim" or so-called "corrections of the scribes" I think, appear to almost any
one who examines them, not to imply any correction of the text of Holy Scripture, but as meant to
suggest what would have come naturally into the
mind of the writer, unless for some reason he had
chosen what stands written. Thus here, the obvi-

Before
CHRIST
cir. 626.
† mighty God, thou hast
† established them for correction.

13 [k] *Thou art* of purer
eyes than to behold evil,
and canst not look on ‖ in-

† Heb. *rock.*
Deut. 32. 4.
† Heb. *founded.*
[k] Ps. 5. 5.
‖ Or, *grievance.*

iquity : [1] wherefore lookest
thou upon them that deal
treacherously, *and* holdest
thy tongue when the wicked
devoureth *the man that is*
more righteous than he ?

Before
CHRIST
cir. 626.

[1] Jer. 12. 1.

---

inference, but it so lay in those titles of God, *He Is, My God, My Holy One,* that it was a more loving confidence to say directly, *we shall not die.* The one thought involved the other. God, the Unchangeable, had made Himself their God. It was impossible, then, that He should cast them off or that they should perish. *We shall not die,* is the lightning thought of faith, which flashes on the soul like all inspirations of God, founded on His truth and word, but borne in, as it were, instinctively without inference on the soul, with the same confidence as the Psalmist says [1], *The Lord hath chastened me sore ; but He hath not given me over unto death ;* and Malachi, [2] *I am the Lord, I change not ; therefore ye sons of Jacob are not consumed.* "[3] Thou createdst us from the beginning ; by Thy mercy we are in being hitherto." Thy *gifts and calling are without repentance* [4]. "Did we look to his might ; none of us could withstand him. Look we to Thy mercy, Thine alone is it that we live, are not slain by him, nor led to deeds of death." *O Lord*, again he repeats the Name of God, whereby He had revealed Himself as their God, the Unchangeable ; *Thou,* whose *mercies fail not, hast ordained them for judgment,* not for vengeance or to make a full end, or for his own ends and pleasure, but to *correct* Thine own [5] *in measure,* which he, exceeding, sinned.[6]

And O mighty God [lit. *Rock*]. It is a bold title. *My rock* is a title much used by David [7], perhaps suggested by the fastnesses amid which he passed his hunted life, to ex-

press, that not in them but in His God was his safety. Habakkuk purposely widens it. He appeals to God, not only as Israel's might and upholder, but as the sole Source of all strength, the Supporter of all which is upheld [8], and so, for the time, of the Chaldæan too. Hence he continues the simple image : *Thou hast founded him.* "[9] Thou hast made him to stand firm as the foundation of a building ; " *to reprove* or *set before* those who have sinned against Thee, what they had done. Since then God was the Rock, Who had *founded them,* from Him Alone had they strength ; when He should withdraw it, they must fall. How then did they yet abide, who abused the power given them and counted it their own ? And this the more, since

13. *Thou art of purer eyes than to behold evil.* The prophet repeats his complaint, (as troubling thoughts are wont to come back, after they have been repelled,) in order to answer it more strongly. All sin is hateful in God's sight, and in His Holy Wisdom He cannot endure to *look toward iniquity.* As man turns away from sickening sights, so God's abhorrence of wrong is pictured by His not being able to *look toward* it. If He looked toward them, they must perish [10]. Light cannot co-exist with darkness, fire with water, heat with cold, deformity with beauty, foulness with sweetness, nor is sin compatible with the Presence of God, except as its Judge and punisher. Thou *canst not look.* There is an entire contradiction between God and unholi-

---

ous contrast to "Thou art of old ; " might be, (they would say) "Thou wilt continue to be ; " " *Thou* wilt not die," וְלֹא תָמוּת ; but since it were unbefitting to speak of death in regard to God, even in denying it, the prophet said לֹא נָמוּת, "we shall not die." But no thoughtful Jewish critic could ever have believed that Habakkuk could have said to God, *Thou wilt not die.* It would also, while irreverent to God, have omitted the whole consolation to his people. Of Jewish Commentators, Kim., A. E., Abarb. Tanch., do not think it worth while to allude to the correction ; Sal. B. Melech mentions it, to reject it ; Rashi quotes it as the writing of the prophet. Several of the 18 Tikkune Sopherim are childish ; no one of value. The Chaldee follows the suggestion, paraphrasing, " Thy word abideth for ever ; " the LXX, not. Ewald corrects as the Chaldee. The Tikk. Soph. are given in Buxtorf Lex. Chald. pp. 2631, sqq. A glance will shew that they are no real corrections.
[1] Ps. cxviii. 18. [2] Mal. iii. 6.
[3] S. Jer. [4] Rom. xi. 29.
[5] Jer. x. 24. xxx. 11.

[6] See Isa. x. 5. xlvii. 6. Zech. i. 15.
[7] Ps. xviii. 2. 46. xix. 15. xxviii. 1. lxii. 6. 7. cxliv. 1. else only in Deut. xxxii. 1. Ps. xcii. 15. anon. Else Moses speaks in his Song of "the Rock," "our Rock," "their Rock," "Rock of his salvation," "the Rock who begat thee," [Deut. xxxii. 4, 31, 30. 15, 18.] and in reference to Deut. lxxviii. 35, and Hannah, "there is no rock like our God," 1 Sam. ii. 2, and David asks, "Who is a rock beside Thee ? " 2 Sam. xxii. 31, and calls Him "the Rock of Israel," 2 Sam. xxiii. 3, "the Rock of my strength " Ps. lxii. 8, and Ethan says that God entitled David to call Him "Rock of my salvation," Ps. lxxxix. 26. and Asaph calls Him, " the Rock of my heart." Ps. lxxiii. 26. Isaiah in his song entitles God "the Rock of ages," Isa. xxvi. 4. also "the Rock of Israel," xxx. 29, "the rock of thy [Israel's] strength," xvii. 10. Let it occurs only in two anonymous Psalms, "the rock of my refuge," Ps. xciv. 22, "of our salvation," xcv. 1.
[8] "Thou Who art the Rock of all ages hast founded him to reprove by him all the nations of the earth." Kim.
[9] Kim. [10] Ps. civ. 32.

Before
CHRIST
cir. 626.

‖ Or, *moving.*

ᵐ Jer. 16. 16.
Amos 4. 2.

14 And makest men as the fishes of the sea, as the ‖ creeping things, *that have* no ruler over them?

15 They ᵐ take up all of them with the angle,

they catch them in their net, and gather them in their ‖ drag: therefore they rejoice and are glad.

16 Therefore ⁿ they sacrifice unto their net,

Before
CHRIST
cir. 626.

‖ Or, *flue net.*

ⁿ Deut. 8. 17.
* Isai. 10. 13.
& 37. 24, 25.

---

ness. And yet, *wherefore lookest thou upon,* viewest, as in Thy full sight [1], yea, as it would seem, with favor [2], bestowing on them the goods of this life, honor, glory, children, riches, as the Psalmist saith; [3] *Behold these* are *the ungodly, who prosper in the world, they increase in riches?* Why lookest thou upon *them that deal treacherously, holdest Thy tongue,* puttest restraint [4], as it were, upon Thyself and Thine own attribute of Justice, *when the wicked devoureth the man that is more righteous than he?* [5] *In God's sight no man living can be justified;* and in one sense Sodom and Gomorrah were less unrighteous than Jerusalem, and [6] *it shall be more tolerable for* them *in the day of Judgment,* because they sinned against less light; yet the actual sins of the Chaldee were greater than those of Jerusalem, and Satan's evil is greater than that of those who are his prey. To say that Judah was more righteous than the Chaldæan does not imply any righteousness of the Chaldæan, as the saying that [7] *God ransomed Jacob from the hand of* one *stronger than he,* does not imply any strength remaining to Israel. Then, also, in all the general judgments of God, the righteous too suffer in this world, whence Abraham intercedes for Sodom, if there were but ten righteous in it; lest [8] *the righteous be destroyed with the wicked.* Hence God also spared Nineveh in part as having [9] *more than sixscore thousand persons that cannot discern between their right hand and their left hand,* i. e. good from evil. No times were fuller of sin than those before the destruction of Jerusalem, yet the fury of the Assassins fell upon the innocent. And so the words, like the voice of the souls under the Altar [10], become the cry of the Church at all times against the oppressing world, and of the blood of the Martyrs from Abel to the end, *Lord, how long?* And in that the word Righteous [11] signifies both " one righteous man," and the whole class or generation of the righteous, it speaks both of Christ the Head and of all His members in whom (as

by Saul) He was persecuted. The *wicked* also includes all persecutors, both those who slew the Lord Christ, and those who brought His servants before judgment-seats, and blasphemed His Name [12], and caused many to blaspheme, and slew whom they could not compel. And God, all the while, seemeth to look away and to regard not.

14. *And makest men as the fishes of the sea,* dumb, helpless, in a stormy, restless element, no cry heard, but themselves swept away in shoals, with no power to resist, *as the creeping things,* whether of the land (as it is mostly used), or the sea [13]. Either way it is a contemptuous name for the lowest of either. *That have no ruler over them;* none to guide, order, protect them, and so a picture of man deprived of the care and providence of God.

15. *They take up all of them* [lit. *he taketh up all of it*] the whole race as though it were one, *with an angle; they catch them,* [lit. *he sweepeth it away*] *in their* [*his*] *net.* One fisherman is singled out who partly by wiles [as by the bait of *an angle*], partly by violence, [the net or drag] sweeps away [14] and gathers as his own the whole kind. Nebuchadnezzar and the Chaldæans are herein a faint image of Satan, who casts out his baits and his nets in the stormy sea of this life, taking some by individual craft, sweeping others in whole masses, to do evil; and whoso hath no ruler, and will not have Christ to reign over him [15], he allures, hurries, drags away as his prey. " [16] Adam clave to his hook, and he drew him forth out of Paradise with his net; and covered him with his drags, his varied and manifold deceits and guiles. And *by one many became sinners,* and in Adam we *all died,* and all saints afterward were with him alike cast out of Paradise. And because he deceived the first man, he ceaseth not daily to slay the whole human race."

16. *Therefore they sacrifice unto their net, and burn incense unto their drag.* [lit. *he* sacrifices unto *his* &c.] Whatever a man trusts in, is

[1] The preposition אֶל is left out in this place, as if to make the contrast stronger. God cannot endure to *look toward* (אֶל) iniquity, and yet He does not only this, but beholdeth it, contemplateth it, and still is silent.
[2] So the word means mostly; " regard favorably;" except Ps. x. 14. where it is said that God beheld ungodliness to avenge it. [3] Ps. lxxiii. 12.
[4] הַחֲרֵשׁ translated " keep silent " Ps. xxxv. 22. l. 21. implies an acting on a person's self.
[5] Ps. cxliii. 2.

[6] S. Matt. x. 15. xi. 24. S. Mark vi. 11. S. Luke x. 12.
[7] Jer. xxxi. 11. Del.　[8] Gen. xviii. 23.
[9] Jon. iv. 11.　[10] Rev. vi. 10.
[11] Singular in Hebrew, yet so that it may be said of many.　[12] S. Jas. ii. 6, 7.　[13] Ps. civ. 25.
[14] The word גָּרַר, *garar,* expresses by its sound the grating noise of the pebbles on the sea-shore. The word is singular, although it *might* be a collective.
[15] S. Luke xix. 4.　[16] S. Jer.

and burn incense unto their drag; because by them their portion *is* fat, and their meat || † plenteous.

17 Shall they therefore empty their net, and not spare continually to slay the nations?

CHAPTER II.

1 *Unto Habakkuk, waiting for an answer, is shewed that he must wait by faith.* 5 *The judgment upon the Chaldean for unsatiableness,* 9 *for covetousness,* 12 *for cruelty,* 15 *for drunkenness,* 18 *and for idolatry.*

I WILL ª stand upon my watch, and set me upon

his god. If a man relies to compass his end by his strength, or his wisdom, or his forethought, or his wealth, his armies or navies, these his forces are his God. So the Assyrian said, [1] *By the strength of my hand I did it; and by my wisdom, for I am prudent;* and God answered, *Shall the axe boast itself against him that heweth therewith?* The coarse forms of idolatry only embody outwardly the deep inward idolatry of the corrupt human mind. The idol is [2] *set up in the heart* first. There have not indeed been wanting savage nations, who in very deed worshiped their arms [3]; those of old worshiped spears as immortal gods [4]; Even now we are told of some North American Indians " [5] who designate their bow and arrow as the only beneficent deities whom they know." Among the civilized Romans, the worship of the eagles, their standards [6], to whom they did sacrifice [7], was no other nor better. The inward idolatry is only a more subtle form of the same sin, the evil spirit which shapes itself in the outward shew. Here the idolatry of self is meant, which did not join creatures with God as objects of worship; but, denying Him in practice or misbelief, became a God to itself [8]. So Habakkuk had said, *this his strength is his God.* His idol was himself.

Because by them their portion is fat, and their meat plenteous (lit. as in E. M., *well-fed*). All the choicest things of the world stood at his command, as Nebuchadnezzar boasted [9], and all the kingdoms of the world and their glory, all the knowledge and wisdom and learning of the world, and the whole world itself, were Satan's lawful prey [10]. " [11] Nebu-

chadnezzar, as by a hook and meshes and line, swept into his own land both Israel himself and other nations, encompassing them. Satan, as it were, by one line and net, that of sin, enclosed all, and Israel especially, on account of his impiety to Christ. *His food was choice.* For Israel was chosen above the rest, as from a holy root, that of *the fathers,* and having the *law* as a *schoolmaster,* and being called to the knowledge of the one true God. Yet he, having this glory and grace, was taken with the rest. *They* became his prey by error; but Israel, knowing Him Who is by nature God, slaying ungodlily Him Who was by nature His Begotten Son and Who came as Man, were taken in his nets."

17. *Shall they therefore empty their net, and not spare continually to slay the nations?* The prophet, like Isaiah [12], stands at the very last point, before the fury and desire of the enemy was fulfilled. Men, like fish, were gathered together for a prey; he who had taken them was rejoicing and exulting beforehand in his booty; his portion and meat were the choice of the earth; the prophet looks on, as it were, and beholds the net full; there is but one step more; "Shall he empty it? Shall he then devour those whom he has caught? and so cast his emptied net again unceasingly, pitilessly, to slay the nations?" This question he answers in the next chapter; A Deliverer will come.

II. 1. *I will stand [I would stand now],* as a servant awaiting his master, *upon my watch* [or *keep* [13]], *and set me* [plant myself firmly] *upon the tower* [lit. *fenced place,* but also one

[1] Is. x. 13. 15.   [2] Ezek. xiv. 4.
[3] The Scythians. Herod. iv. 62. Lucian Jov. Tragœd. 42. p. 275, Arnob. vi. § 11, Mela. ii. 1. Clem. Al. Protr. iv. p. 40, ed. Pott., Amm. Marc. xxvi. 2. The Quadi did the same. Id. xvii. 12. fin. The chance discovery of one of these sacred swords of the Scythian kings made Attila think himself "made prince of the whole world." Jordanes de Get. orig. c. 35, from Priscus, a contemporary.
[4] Justin L. 43. c. 3.
[5] Waitz die Indianer Nord-Americas 1867 p. 127. quoted by Ewald.
[6] See Tertull. Apol. c. 16 and note e. f. g. p. 38. Oxf. Tr.

[7] Joseph. de Bell. Jud. vi. 32.
[8] A heathen poet, wishing to express this irreverence, puts into a warrior's mouth this prayer: "Now may my right hand, to me god, and the weapon which I brandish, be my helper!" Virg. Æn. vii. 648. add Stat. x. 545. iii. 645, sq. So the *Times* said at the beginning of the late war, "The French almost worshiped the mitrailleuse as a goddess." They idolized, it would say, their invention, as if it could do what God alone could.
[9] Dan. iv. 30. comp. 22.
[10] S. Luke iv. 6. S. John xii. 31. Isa. xlix. 24.
[11] S. Cyr.   [12] Isa. xviii. 4, 5.
[13] Ib. xxi. 8. מִשְׁמָר in the same sense Jer. li. 12.

Before CHRIST cir. 626.
† Heb. *fenced place.*
b Ps. 85. 8.
|| Or, *in me.*
|| Or, *when I am argued with.*
† Heb. *upon my reproof,* or, *arguing.*

the † t o w e r, b and will watch to see what he will say || unto me, and what I shall answer || † when I am reproved.

2 And the LORD an-

swered me, and said, c Write the v i s i o n, and make *it* plain upon tables, that he may run that readeth it.

3 For d the vision *is* yet

Before CHRIST cir. 626.
c Isai. 8. 1. & 30. 8.
d Dan. 10. 14. & 11. 27, 35.

straitened and narrowly hemmed in], *and will watch* (it is a title of the prophets [1], as espying, by God's enabling, things beyond human ken); I will *espy out,* to see a long way off, *to see* with the inward eye, *what He will say unto me* [lit. [2] *in me*]; first revealing Himself in the prophets " within to the inner man ; " then, through them. *And what I shall answer when I am reproved* [3], or, *upon my complaint,* lit. *upon my reproof or arguing ;* which might mean, either that others argued against him, or that he had argued, pleaded in the name of others, and now listened to hear what God would answer *in* him [4], and so he, as taught by God, should answer to his own plea. But he had so pleaded with God, repeatedly, *Why is this?* He has given no hint, that any complained of or reproved him.

" [5] By an image from those who, in war and siege, have the ward of the wall distributed to them, he says, *I will stand upon my watch.*" " [6] It was the wont of the Saints, when they wished to learn the things of God, and to receive the knowledge of things to come through His voice in their mind and heart, to raise it on high above distractions and anxieties and all worldly care, holding and keeping it unoccupied and peaceful, rising as to an eminence to look around and contemplate what the God of all knowledge should make clear to them. For He hateth the earth-bound and abject mind, and seeks hearts which can soar aloft, raised above earthly things and temporal desires." The prophet takes his stand, apart from men and the thoughts and cares of this world, on his

lonely watch, as Moses on the rock, keeping himself and kept by God, and planted firm, so that nothing should move him, fenced around though straitened in [7], as in a besieged camp committed to his ward, looking out from his lofty place what answer God would give as to times long distant, and what answer he should give first to himself, and to those to whom his office lay, God's people.

2. The answer is, that it is indeed for a long time yet. *Write the vision,* that it may remain for those who come after and not be forgotten, *and make it plain* [8] *upon the tables,* whereon he was wont to write [9]; that it, in large lasting characters, *that he may run that readeth it,* that it may be plain to any, however occupied or in haste. So Isaiah too was bidden to write the four words, *haste-prey-speed-spoil.*

3. *For the vision is yet for an [the] appointed time.* [10] Not for the present, but to develop itself in the course of time, down to a season which God only knows ; as it is subsequently repeated, [11] *for the end is yet for the appointed time ;* [12] *for it is for the appointed time of the end ;* and is explained, [13] *for the vision is yet for the days ;* [14] *for it is for many days ;* [15] the house of Israel say, *The vision that he seeth,* is *for many days* and he *prophesieth of the times far off;* yet it should haste toward the end, toward its fulfillment, so that, if it is not at once fulfilled, it should be surely waited for. " [16] It shall certainly be; not in vain hath it been shewn, but as certainly to be. For whatever hath been shewn to come and to be, will come and be."

But at the end it shall speak [17] [or *it breatheth,*

---

[1] Hence צוֹפֶה "watchman," the "prophet" Isa. lii. 8. Jer. vi. 17. Ezek. iii. 17. xxxiii. 7. Kal; of the prophets, Pih. Mic. vii. 4; of looking up to God, Ps. v. 4; with בְּ Mic. vii. 7.
[2] S. Jer.
[3] The Rabb. Kim. A. E. Rashi, Tanch. Sal. B. Mel., Abarb. take it as the E. V., probably thinking the other to be too bold as expression toward God.
[4] See Num. xii. 6. and on Zech. i. 19.
[5] Theodᵃ.   [6] S. Cyr.
[7] Symm. Theod. Aq. agree in this sense of narrowness.
[8] Etymologically, בָּאַר means "engrave," lit. *dig:* like so many other words, which come to mean "write," as כָּתַב with חָצַב,חָטַב Ges.; סָפַר γράφειν, eingraben, graben, engrave, [Id.] but it only occurs as "make clear, explain," De. xxvii. 8. So Kim. &c.
[9] לוּחַ is a table or tablet, on which Isaiah too was bidden to write what was to last, though in parallelism with a "book." Isa. xxx. 8. "the tablets which

boys write on." A. E. comp. Ezek. xvii. 14. Jer. xxx. 2.
[10] Ewald ad loc.; but therewith the theory of a mere human foresight is abandoned.
[11] Dan. xi. 27. *for it is for the appointed time,* ib. 35.
[12] Ib viii. 19.   [13] Ib. x. 1, 14.
[14] Ib. viii. 26.   [15] Ezek. xii. 27.   [16] Theodᵉ.
[17] The E. V. follows the Rabbins [Kim. Comm., A. E., Tanch., Rashi, Abarb.] so far in rendering יָפֵחַ "speak." Yet in all the cases of both roots, פוּחַ, נָפַח, except Prov. xii. 17, יָפִיחַ אֱמוּנָה, the root is used not of mere "speaking " but of "breathing out" like ἐμπνέων ἀπειλῆς (Acts xi. 1.) "breathing out threatening." In five cases it occurs in the one idiom, "breatheth out lies," יָפִיחַ כְּזָבִים, Pr. vi. 19, xiv. 5, 25, xix. 5, 9. In other idioms יָפִיחַ בָּהֶם "speak." יָפִיחַ לוֹ, Ps. x. 5, xii. 6, it is still used of puffing at "contemptuously." Else the Kal is used of the cool air of the evening Cant. ii. 17. iv. 6, and Hifil

for an appointed time, but at the end it shall speak, and not lie: though it tar-|| ry, wait for it; because it will [e]surely come, it will not tarry.

[e] Heb. 10. 37.

---

hasteth to the end], not simply "to its own fulfillment," but to that *time of the end* which should close the period assigned to it, during which it should continually be putting itself forth, it should come true in part or in shadow, gleams of it should here and there part the clouds, which, until the end, should surround and envelop it. Being God's truth, he speaks of it as an animate living thing, not a dead letter, but running, hasting on its course, and accomplishing on its way that for which it was sent. The will and purpose of God hasteth on, though to man it seemeth to tarry; it can neither be hurried on, nor doth it linger; before *the appointed time* it cometh not; yet it hasteth toward it, and *will not be behindhand* when the time comes. It does *not lie*, either by failing to come, or failing, when come, of any jot or tittle. *Though it tarry* or *linger* [1], continually appearing, giving signs of itself, yet continually delaying its coming, *wait for it; because it will surely come, it will not be behindhand* [2], when the time comes. [3] *He cometh quickly* also, as He saith; because "[4]though the delay of His Coming and of the fulfillment of the vision seem long, yet, in comparison with eternity, it is very short. In His First Coming, He taught why God permitteth these things; in the Second, He shall teach by experience, how good it it is for the good to bear the persecution of the evil; whence S. Peter also has to say,[5] *The Lord is not slack concerning His promise, as some men count slackness.*" The words seem to belong, in the first instance, to the vision itself; but the vision had no other existence or fulfillment than in Him Who was the Object of it, and Who, in it, was foreshadowed to the mind. The coming of the vision was no other than His Coming. The *waiting*, to which he exhorts, expresses the religious act, so often spoken of,[6] of waiting for God, or His counsel, or His promised time. The sense then is wholly the same,

when S. Paul uses the words of the Coming of our Lord Himself,[7] *Yet a little while, and He that shall come, will come and will not tarry.* S. Paul, as well as Habakkuk, is speaking of our Lord's Second Coming; S. Paul, of His Coming in Person, Habakkuk, of the effects of that Coming[8]; but both alike of the redressing of all the evil and wrong in the world's history, and the reward of the faithful oppressed. At His First Coming He said, [9] *Now is the judgment of this world; now shall the prince of this world be cast out.* He came to [10]*put down the mighty from their seat, and to exalt the humble and meek;* but much more in the Second, when [11] *He shall come to judge the world with righteousness and the people with His truth,* and to [12]*reward every man according to his works.* At all times He seemeth continually to linger, to give signs of His Coming, yet He cometh not; when the appointed season shall come, He shall be found not to be "later" than His word. Yea, all time shall shrink up into a little moment in the presence of a never-ending ever-present eternity.

"[13]Having named no one expressly, he says, *wait for him,* wait for him although delaying, and halt not in thy hope, but let it be rooted and firm, even if the interval be extended. For the God of all seemeth to suggest to the mind of the Prophet, that He who was foretold would surely come, yet to enjoin on him to wait for Him on account of the interval. He who believeth My word shall possess life, for this is the reward of those who honor God, and a good reward of His benevolence. He who admitteth faith and love to dwell in his heart hath as a requital, un-aging life and forgiveness of sins and sanctification by the Spirit." "[14] He shall live; for [15] *God is not the God of the dead but of the living,*" [16] *Whoso liveth and believeth in Me, shall never die.*"

It will not lie. God vouchsafes to speak of

---

of "causing to blow," Ib. iv. 16. Else it is only used (metaph.) of blowing up, kindling, (as we say) stirring up a city to strife Pr. xxix. 8, and blowing up the fire of the wrath of God, Ez. xxi. 36. הָתֵּיפַחַ is used of the deep sigh of agony Jer. iv. 31. and יָפֵחַ דָּמָס Ps. xxvii. 12. "breathing forth violence" stands united with "false witness" as in the Prov. If understood then of speaking, it would be "breathing of the end" (לֹ relating to the subject of the speech, as so often) which would be much the same as, breatheth panting toward the end, (like שָׁאַף לְ, Eccl. i. 5.)

[1] הַתְמַהְמַהּ (no kal.) seems to be compound of מָה, מַה, why, why? the answer of one procrastinating. It occurs thrice in the Pent., twice in Judges, else only in 2 Sam. xv. 19, in the prophets

Is. xxix. 9, and in Ps. cxix. 60. of religious procrastinating. In Arab. are the like forms מַהְמָה and נִהְנָה.
[2] לֹא תְאַחֵר.
[3] Rev. xxii. 7.   [4] from Dion.
[5] 2 S. Pet. iii. 9.
[6] Ps. xxxiii. 20. Isai. viii. 17. xxx. 18. lxiv. 3. Zeph. iii. 8. Dan. xii. 12. Ps. cvi. 13.
[7] Heb. x. 37.
[8] The vivid words, in themselves, rather express a personal agent; what would be figure as to the vision are simple words as to Him Who was foreshown. Whence the Lxx change the gender and interpret the clause of a person, "He who shall come."   [9] S. John xii. 31.
[10] S. Luke i. 52.   [11] Ps. xlvi. 13.
[12] S. Matt. xvi. 27.   [13] S. Cyr.   [14] Alb.
[15] S. Matt. xxii. 32.   [16] S. John xi. 26.

4 Behold, his soul *which*
is lifted up is not upright

in him: but the *'*just shall
live by his faith.

f John 3. 36. Rom. 1. 17. Gal. 3. 11. Heb. 10. 38.

Himself, as we should be ashamed to speak of one whom we love, teaching us that all doubts question His truth. [1] *God is not a man, that He should lie: hath He said and shall He not do it?* [2] *The strength of Israel shall neither lie nor repent.* [3] *God that cannot lie, promised before the world began.* Therefore it follows, *wait for Him*, as Jacob says, [4] *I have waited for Thy salvation, O Lord.*

4. *Behold, his soul which is lifted up* [lit. *swollen* [5]] *is not upright in him.* The construction is probably that of a condition expressed absolutely. *Lo, swollen is it, not upright is his soul in him.* We should say, "His soul, if it be swollen [6], puffed up, is not upright in him." The source of all sin was and is pride. It is especially the sin of all oppressors, of the Chaldee, of Anti-Christs, and shall be of the Anti-Christ. It is the parent of all heresy, and of all corruption and rejection of the Gospel. It stands therefore as the type of all opposed to it. Of it he says, it is in its very inmost core [*in him*] lacking in uprightness. It can have no good in it, because it denies God, and God denies it His grace. And having nothing upright in it, being corrupt in its very inmost being, it cannot stand or abide. God gives it no power to stand. The words stand in contrast with the following, the one speaking of the cause of death, the other of life. The soul, being swollen with pride, shuts out faith, and with it the Presence of God. It is all crooked in its very inner self or being. S. Paul gives the result, [7] *if any man draw back, my soul hath no pleasure in him.* The prophet's words describe the proud man who stands aloof from God, in himself; S. Paul, as he is in the Eyes of God. As that which is swollen in nature cannot be straight, it is clean contrary that the soul should be swollen with pride and yet upright. Its moral life being destroyed in its very inmost heart, it must perish.

" [8] Plato saith, that properly is straight, which being applied to what is straight, touches and is touched everywhere. But God is upright, Whom the upright soul touches and is touched everywhere; but what is not upright is bent away from God. [9] *God is good unto Israel, the upright in heart.* [10] *The upright love thee.* [11] *The way of the just is*

uprightness, *Thou, most Upright, doth weigh the path of the just.*" But the *just shall live by his faith.* The accents emphasize the words [12], *The just, by his faith he shall live.* They do not point to an union of the words, *the just by his faith.* Isaiah says that Christ should *justify many by the knowledge of Himself* [13], but the expression, *just by his faith*, does not occur either in the O. or N. T. In fact, to speak of one really righteous [14] as being " righteous by his faith " would imply that men could be righteous in some other way. *Without faith*, S. Paul says at the commencement of his Old Testament pictures of giant faith, [15] *it is impossible to please God.* Faith, in the creature which does not yet see God, has one and the same principle, a trustful relying belief in its Creator. This was the characteristic of Abraham their father, unshaken, unswerving, belief in God Who called him, whether in leaving his own land and going whither he knew not, for an end which he was never to see; or in believing the promise of the son through whom that Seed was to be, in Whom all the nations of the world should be blessed; or in the crowning act of offering that son to God, knowing that he should receive him back, even from the dead. In all, it was one and the same principle. [16] *His belief was counted to him for righteousness*, though the immediate instance of that faith was not directly spiritual. In this was the good and bad of Israel. [17] *The people believed.* [18] *They believed the Lord and His servant Moses.* [19] *Then believed they His word, they sang His praise.* This contrariwise was their blame. [20] *In this ye did not believe the Lord.* [21] *Ye rebelled against the commandment of the Lord your God, and believed Him not, nor hearkened to His voice.* [22] *They forgat God their Saviour; they despised the pleasant land, they believed not His word.* And God asks, [23] *How long will it be, ere this people believe Me, for all the signs which I have shown among them?* [24] *Anger came upon Israel, because they believed not in God, and in His salvation trusted not.* [25] *For all this they sinned still, and believed not His wondrous works.* Even of Moses and Aaron God assigns this as the ground, why they should not bring His people into the land which He gave them, [26] *Because ye believed Me not, to sanctify Me in*

[1] Nu. xxiii. 19.   [2] 1 Sam. xv. 29.
[3] Tit. i. 2.   [4] Gen. xlix. 18.
[5] עֻפְּלָה See on Micah iv. 8. p. 62, note 8.
[6] In the Lxx ἐὰν ὑποστείληται. הִנֵּה is used thus absolutely, the condition being implied, Deut. xiii. 15, 16. In Ex. viii. 22. the future is used absolutely with הֵן.

[7] Heb. x. 39.   [8] Alb.   [9] Ps. lxxiii. 1.
[10] Cant. i. 4.   [11] Is. xxvi. 7.   [12] See Delitzsch.
[13] בְּרַעְתּוֹ יַצְדִּיק Is. liii. 11.   [14] As צַדִּיק always is.
[15] Heb. xi. 6.   [16] Gen. xv. 6.   [17] Ex. iv. 31.
[18] Ib. xiv. 31.   [19] Ps. cvi. 12.   [20] Deut. i. 32.
[21] Ib. ix. 23.   [22] Ps. cvi. 21, 24. [23] Num. xiv. 11.
[24] Ps. lxxviii. 21, 22. [25] Ib. 32.   [26] Num. xx. 20.

the eyes of the children of Israel (at Meribah). This was the watchword of Jehoshaphat's victory, [1] *Believe in the Lord your God and ye shall be established; believe His prophets, so shall ye prosper.* This continued to be one central saying of Isaiah. It was his own commission to his people; [2] *Go and say to this people; hear ye on, and understand not; see ye on and perceive not.* In sight of the rejection of faith, he spake prominently of the loss upon unbelief; [3] *If ye will not believe, surely ye shall not be established;* and, [4] *Who hath believed our report?* he premises as the attitude of his people toward Him, the Centre of all faith, Jesus. Yet still, as to the blessings of faith, having spoken of Him, [5] *Thus saith the Lord God, Behold, I lay in Zion for a foundation, a stone, a tried stone, a precious cornerstone,* he subjoins, *he that believeth in Him shall not make haste.*

So it had been the key-note of Habakkuk to his people, *Ye will not believe when it is declared unto you.* Here he is bid to declare contrariwise the blessing on belief. *The just shall live by his faith.* The faith, then, of which Habakkuk speaks, is faith, in itself, but a real, true confiding faith. It is the one relation of the creature to the Creator, unshaken trust. The faith may vary in character, according as God reveals more or less of Himself, but itself is one, a loving trust in Him, just as He reveals Himself. " [6] By this faith in God, each righteous person begins to live piously, righteously, holily, peacefully and divinely, and advanceth therein, since in every tribulation and misery, by this faith and hope in God he sustains, strengthens, and increases this life of the soul. He says then, *the just lives by faith,* i. e., the unbelieving and unrighteous displeases God, and consequently will not live by the true, right, peaceful and happy life of grace, present righteousness, and future glory, because God is displeased with him, and *he* places his hopes and fears, not in God, but in men and man's help and in created things. But the righteous who believeth in God shall live a right, sweet, quiet, happy, holy, untroubled life, because, fixed by faith and hope in God Who is the true Life, and in God's promises, he is dear to God, and the object of His care.

" This sentence, *the just shall live by faith,* is universal, belonging at once to Jews and Christians, to sinners who are *first* being justified, as also to those who are already justified. For the spiritual life of each of these begins, is maintained and grows through faith. When then it is said, *the just shall live by his faith,* this word, *his,* marks the cause, which both begins and preserves life. The just, believing and hoping in God, begins to

live spiritually, to have a soul right within him, whereby he pleases God; and again, advancing and making progress in this his faith and hope in God, therewith advances and makes progress in the spiritual life, in rightness and righteousness of soul, in the grace and friendship of God, so as more and more to please God."

Most even of the Jewish interpreters have seen this to be the literal meaning of the words. It stands in contrast with, illustrates and is illustrated by the first words, *his soul is swollen, is not upright in him.* Pride and independence of God are the centre of the want of rightness; a steadfast cleaving to God, whereby *the heart,* as Abraham's, *was stayed on God,* is the centre and cause of the life of the righteous. But since this stayedness of faith is in everything the source of the life of the righteous, then the pride, which issues in want of rightness of the inmost soul, must be a state of death. Pride estranges the soul from God, makes it self-sufficing, that it should not need God, so that he who is proud cannot come to God, to be by Him made righteous. So contrariwise, since by his faith doth the righteous live, this must be equally true whether he be just made righteous from unrighteous, or whether that righteousness is growing, maturing, being perfected in him.

This life begins in grace, lives on in glory. It is begun, in that God freely justifies the ungodly, accounting and making him righteous for and through the Blood of Christ; it is continued in faith which worketh by love; it is perfected, when faith and hope are swallowed up in love, beholding God. In the Epistles to the Romans [7] and the Galatians [8] St. Paul applies these words to the first beginning of life, when they who had before been dead in sin, began to live by faith in Christ Jesus Who gave them life and made them righteous. And in this sense he is called "just," although before he comes to the Faith he is unjust and unrighteous, being unjustified. For St. Paul uses the word not of what he was before the faith, but what he is, when he lives by faith. Before, not having faith, he had neither righteousness nor life; having faith, he at once has both; he is at once *just* and *lives by his faith.* These are inseparable. The faith by which he lives, is a living faith, [9] *faith which worketh by love.* In the Epistle to the Hebrews [10], St. Paul is speaking of *their* endurance in the faith, once received, whose faith is not shaken by the trial of their patience. They who look on beyond things present, and fix their minds steadfastly on the Coming of Christ, will not suffer shipwreck of their faith, through any troubles of this time. Faith is the founda-

[1] 2 Chron. xx. 20. [2] Is. vi. 9. [3] Ib. vii. 9.
[4] Ib. liii. 1. [5] Ib. xxviii. 16.

[6] Lap. in Rom. i. 17. [7] Rom. i. 17.
[8] Gal. iii. 11. [9] Ib. v. 6. [10] Heb. x. 38.

13

Before
CHRIST
cir. 626.

|| Or, *How much more.*

ᵍ Prov. 27. 20.
& 30. 16.

5 ¶ || Yea also, because he transgresseth by wine, *he is* a proud man, neither keepeth at home, who enlargeth his desire ᵍ as hell,

and *is* as death, and cannot be satisfied, but gathereth unto him all nations, and heapeth unto him all people:

tion of all good, the beginning of the spiritual building, whereby it rests on The Foundation, Christ. *Without faith it is impossible to please God,* and so the *proud* cannot please Him. Through it, is union with Christ and thereby a divine life in the soul, even a life[1] *through faith in the Son of God,* holy, peaceful, self-possessed[2], enduring to the end, being [3] *kept by the power of God through faith unto salvation ready to be revealed in the last time.*

5. This general rule the Prophet goes on to apply in words which belong in part to all oppressors and in the first instance to the Chaldæan, in part yet more fully to the end and to Anti-Christ. *Yea also, because he transgresseth by wine* [or better, *Yea, how much more, since wine is a deceiver*[4]], as Solomon says[5], *Wine is a mocker, strong drink is raging, and whosoever erreth thereby shall not be wise,* and, [6] *In the end it biteth like a serpent and pierceth like an adder;* and Hosea, [7] *Whoredom and wine and new wine take away the heart.* As wine at first gladdens, then deprives of all reason, and lays a man open to any deceit, so also pride. And whereas all pride deceives, how much more[8], when men are either heated and excited by the abuse of God's natural gifts, or drunken with prosperity and hurried away, as conquerors are, to all excess of cruelty or lust to fulfill their own will, and neglect the laws of God and man. Literal drunkenness was a sin of the Babylonians under the Persian rule, so that even a heathen says of Babylon, "[9] Nothing can be more corrupt than the manners of that city, and more provided with all to rouse and en-

tice immoderate pleasures;" and "the Babylonians give themselves wholly to wine, and the things which follow upon drunkenness." It was when flushed [10] with wine, that Belshazzar, *with his princes his wives and his concubines,* desecrated the sacred vessels, insulted God in honor of his idols, and in the night of his excess "was slain." Pride blinded, deceived, destroyed him. It was the general drunkenness of the inhabitants, at that same feast, which enabled Cyrus, with a handful of men, to penetrate, by means of its river, the city which, with its provisions for many years [11] and its impregnable walls, mocked at his siege. He calculated beforehand on its feast [12] and the consequent dissolution of its inhabitants; but for this, in the language of the heathen historian, he would have been caught "[13] as in a trap," his soldiery drowned.

He is a proud man[14], *neither keepeth at home.* It is difficult to limit the force of the rare Hebrew word rendered, [15] *keep at home;* for one may cease to dwell or abide at home either with his will or without it; and, as in the case of invaders, the one may be the result of the other. He who would take away the home of others becomes, by God's Providence, himself homeless. The context implies that the primary meaning is the restlessness of ambition; which abides not at home, for his whole pleasure is to go forth to destroy. Yet there sounds, as it were, an undertone, "he would not abide in his home, and he shall not." We could scarcely avoid the further thought, could we translate by a

---

[1] Gal. ii. 20.   [2] S. Luke xxi. 19.   [3] 1 S. Pet. i. 5.
[4] Jon. agrees "as one erring through wine." Kim. A. E. Rashi, Abarb. Tanch. (in one explanation) take it personally; Kim. supplying שתה "drinker of wine;" A. E. and Tanch. regarding יין as יין איש, quoting מרי Ez. ii. 8. and תפלה Ps. cix. 4. which they explain in the same way.
[5] Prov. xx. 1.   [6] Ib. xxiii. 32.   [7] Hosea iv. 11.
[8] אף כי as in 1 Sam. xxiii. 3. Ezek. xxiii. 40. It adds to the previous sentence; whether we should express it by *how much more,* if an affirmative had preceded; or *how much less,* if a negative. The *more* or *less* lies in the relation of the sentences, not in the כי אף.
[9] Q. Curt. v. 1.   [10] See Daniel the Prophet, p. 450.
[11] Xen. Cyrop. vii. 4, 5, 6.
[12] "When then he [Cyrus] heard that there was a feast in Babylon, in which all the Babylonians drink and revel all the night, on this, &c." Ib. 11, on the drunkenness see Ib. 9. 10.
[13] Herod. i. 19.
[14] יהיר, in the only other place, Pr. xxi. 24, stands

in connection with זד and לץ; in Chald. it is "arrogant," (see instances in Levy Chald. Wört.) as in Nasor. (ap. Ges.). The Arab. only supplies יהר "perseverance in litigation:" the meaning "prominence, swelling" is assumed only. The Arab. תיהור (in Ges. Hitz.) is from האר (med. ו) and signifies "a sand-heap," not as heaped up, but as sinking asunder, "corruens," (the central meaning of האר.)
[15] נוה, נאה, seems to be of the same root as ναίω, whence נות בית "dweller in the house," Ps. lxviii. 13; נוה, נוה, abode: נויה Pr. N. probably the same, and נאות also. The derived sense "becoming" (lit. "sit well on" "bene sedet alicui," Ges.) exists in נאוה Ps. xciii. 5; "beautiful," Cant. i. 10. Is. lii. 7; and in נוה Jer. vi. 2. It is the basis of Hif. אנוהו "will praise Him." Either gives a good sense. The Vulg. takes the derived sense "decorabitur."

Before CHRIST cir. 626.	6 Shall not all these [h] take up a parable against him, and a taunting pro-	verb against him, and say, ‖ Woe to him that increas- eth *that which is* not his!	Before CHRIST cir. 626.
[h] Mic. 2. 4.			‖ Or, *Ho, he.*

word which does not determine the sense, "he will not home," "he will not continue at home." The words have seemed to different minds to mean either; as they may [1]. Such fullness of meaning is the contrary of the am- biguity of Heathen oracles; they are not alternative meanings, which might be justi- fied in either case, but cumulative, the one on the other. The ambitious part with present rest for future loss. Nebuchadnezzar lost his kingdom and his reason through pride, received them back when he humbled himself; Belshazzar, being proud and im- penitent, lost both his kingdom and life.

Who enlargeth his desire, lit. *his soul.* The soul becomes like what it loves. The ambi- tious man is, as we say, "all ambition;" the greedy man, "all appetite;" the cruel man, "all savagery;" the vain-glorious, "all vain- glory." The ruling passion absorbs the whole being. It is his end, the one object of his thoughts, hopes, fears. So, as we speak of "largeness of heart," which can embrace in its affections all varieties of human inter- ests, whatever affects man, and "largeness of mind" uncramped by narrowing prejudices, the Prophet speaks of this "ambitious man widening his soul," or, as we should speak, "appetite," so that the whole world is not too large for him to long to grasp or to devour. So the Psalmist prays not to be delivered into the murderous *desire* of his enemies [2], (lit. *their soul,*) and Isaiah, with a metaphor almost too bold for our language, [3] *Hell hath enlarged her soul, and opened her mouth beyond measure.* It devours, as it were, first in its cravings, then in act.

As hell, which is insatiable [4]. He saith, *enlargeth;* for as hell and the grave are year by year fuller, yet there is no end, the desire *enlargeth* and becometh wider, the more is given to it to satisfy it. *And* [*he* [5]] *is* [*him- self*] *as death,* sparing none. Our poetry would speak of a destroyer as being "like the angel of death;" his presence, as the presence of death itself. Where he is, there is death. He is as terrible and as destroying as the death which follows him. *And can- not be satisfied.* Even human proverbs say, "[6] The love of money groweth as much as the money itself groweth." "The avaricious is

ever needy." [7] *He that loveth silver shall not be satisfied with silver.* For these fleeting things cannot satisfy the undying soul. It must hunger still; for it has not found what will allay its cravings [8].

But gathereth, lit. *And hath gathered*—He describes it, for the rapidity with which he completes what he longs for, as. though it were already done, —*unto him all nations, and heapeth unto him all people.* One is still the subject of the prophecy, rising up at succes- sive times, fulfilling it and passing away, Nebuchadnezzar, Alexander, Attila, Timur, Genghizchan, Hunneric, scourges of God, all deceived by pride, all sweeping the earth, all in their ambition and wickedness the unknowing agents and images of the evil One, who seeks to bring the whole world under his rule. But shall it prosper?

6. *Shall not all these* [9] *take up a parable against him, and a taunting proverb against him?* Nebuchadnezzar gathered [10] *all people, nations, and languages, to worship the golden image which he had set up.* The second Babylon, heathen Rome, sought to blot out the very Christian Name; but mightier were the three children than the King of Babylon; mightier, virgins, martyrs, and children than Nero or Decius. These shall rejoice over Babylon, that [11] *God hath avenged them on her.*

Woe to him that increaseth that which is not his! Truly wealth ill-gotten by fraud or oppression, *is not his,* who winneth it, before he had it, nor when he hath it, but a *woe.* It is *not his;* the *woe* is his. *Woe unto him.* He shall have no joy in what he gaineth, and what he hath he shall lose. *How long?* What is the measure of thine impiety and greediness and cruelty? Yet if these are like hell, without measure, there remains another *How long?* How long will the for- bearance of God endure thee, which thou art daily exhausting?

This is then the end of all. The conqueror sweeps to him *all nations* and gathereth to him *all peoples.* To what end? As one vast choir in one terrible varied chant of all those thousand thousand voices, to sing a dirge over him of the judgments of God which his ill-doings to them should bring upon him, a

---

[1] A. E. Abarb. Tanch. Rashi, following Jon. take it of his privation of home. Kim. either of the shortness of Nebuchadnezzar's empire, or his own being driven forth with the wild animals, Dan. iv. 31–33. Del. illustrates the sense of forced "non- abiding" by בְּלִי יָלִין Ps. xlix. 13, "abideth not;" לֹא שָׁכֵן אֶרֶץ Pr. x. 30, "shall not inhabit the earth;" שָׁכֵן נוֹתָר ‖ Pr. ii. 21.

[2] Ps. xxvii. 12. Comp. Ps. xli. 3 [2 Eng.] Ezek. xxvi. 27. [3] Is. v. 14. [4] Prov. xxx. 15.
[5] וְהוּא. It is not an unmeaning change as though it belonged only to the simplicity of Hebrew con- struction; but emphatic, "and *he.*"
[6] Juv. Sat. xiv. 139. [7] Eccl. v. 10.
[8] S. Aug. Conf. and n. a. iv. 8.
[9] אֵלֶּה כֻלָּם v. 6, referring to the כָּל הָעַמִּים, בְּל, הַגּוֹיִם v. 5. [10] Dan. iii. 4, 5. [11] Rev. xviii. 20.

how long? and to him that
ladeth himself with thick
clay!

7 Shall they not rise up

suddenly that shall bite
thee, and awake that shall
vex thee, and thou shalt
be for booties unto them?

fivefold Woe, woe, woe, woe, woe! Woe for
its rapacity! Woe for its covetousness!
Woe for its oppression! Woe for its insolence to the conquered! Woe to it in its
rebellion against God! It is a more
measured rhythm than any besides in Holy
Scripture; each of the fivefold woes comprised in three verses, four of them closing
with the ground, *because, for.* The opening
words carry the mind back to the fuller picture of Isaiah. But Isaiah sees Babylon as
already overthrown; Habakkuk pronounces
the words upon it, not by name, but as certainly to come, upon it and every like enemy
of God's kingdom. With each such fall,
unto the end of all things, the glory of God
is increased and made known. Having, for
their own ends, been unconscious and even
unwilling promoters of God's end, they, when
they had accomplished it, are themselves
flung away. The pride of human ambition,
when successful, boasts "woe to the conquered." Since *whom the Lord loveth He
chasteneth,* the ungodly saying of the heathen
is reversed, and it stands, "Man sympathizes
with the conquering side, God with the conquered." It is a terrible thought that men
should have been the instruments of God,
that they should, through ambition or other
ends short of God, have promoted His ends
which they thought not of, and then should
be *weighed in the balance and found wanting,*
and themselves be flung away.

"[1] Gentiles also departed from their wor-
ship under Satan, and having deserted him
who aforetime called them, ran unto Christ.
For Satan gathered what was *not his;* but
Christ received what was His. For, as God,
He is Lord of all."

*And to him that ladeth himself with thick
clay*[2]. It is the character of these proverbs
to say much in few words, sometimes in one,

[1] S. Cyr.
[2] The word עַבְטִיט naturally suggests the divis-
ion into עָב and טִיט which has been adopted by
Syr. "cloud of mud," and S. Jer. doubtless from his
Hebrew Instructor "densum lutum," as A. E., J.
and D. Kimchi, Rashi, Abarb., R. Tanchum; Poc.
Arab. Vers. which is not Saadiah's (Hunt. 206.) R.
Samuel Hannagid, Joshua, Japhet, (quoted by A.
E.) Sal. B. Mel., explaining it "abundance of clay."
Kimchi (Shorashim) admits the possibility of its
being derived from עָבַט sub v., but himself says
it is a compound word. Saadiah Ben Denan Lex.
Heb.–Arab. [Bodl. Or. 612.] alone positively derives
it from עָבַט. The objection that there are no compound appellatives in Hebrew is contrary to the
evidence of such words, as צַלְמָוֶת, בְּלִיָּה, בְּלִיַּעַל,
and amid the predominance of compound words,

and more than appears. So the word translated *thick-clay,* as if it were two words, in
another way means in an intensive sense, "a
strong deep pledge." At best gold and silver
are, as they have been called, red and white
earth. "[3] What are gold and silver but
red and white earth, which the error of
man alone maketh, or accounteth precious?
What are gems, but stones of the earth?
What silk, but webs of worms?" These he
"maketh heavy upon" or "against himself"
[so the words strictly mean]. "For *he*
weigheth himself down with thick clay, who,
by avarice multiplying earthly things, hems
himself in by the oppressiveness of his own
sin, imprisons and, as it were, buries the
soul, and heaps up sin as he heaps up
wealth." With toil they gather what is not
worthless only, but is a burden upon the
soul, weighing it down that it should not
rise Heavenwards, but should be bowed
down to Hell. And so in that other sense
while, as a hard usurer, he heaps up the
pledges of those whom he oppresses and im-
poverishes, and seems to increase his wealth,
he does in truth *increase against himself a
strong pledge,* whereby not others are debtors
to him, but he is a debtor to Almighty God
Who careth for the oppressed. [4]*He that
gathereth riches and not by right, shall leave
them in the midst of his days and at his end
shall be a fool.*

7. *Shall not they rise up suddenly that shall bite
thee, and awake that shall vex thee?* The destruction of the wicked is ever sudden at
last. Such was the flood[5], the destruction of
Sodom, of Pharaoh, of the enemies of God's
people through the Judges, of Sennacherib,
Nineveh, Babylon by the Medes and Persians. Such shall the end be[6]. As he by
his oppressions had *pierced* others (it is the
word used of the oppression of usury[7]), so

as Proper Names, it would be monstrous to assume
that a Prophet could not have compounded a word.
On the other hand, the forms כְּמִירִיר, סַנְרִיר,
חַכְלִיל, שַׁפְדִיר, are remarkable analogies in favor
of its being a single word. It was probably formed
to suggest both thoughts, as it has.
[3] S. Bern. Serm. 4. in Adv.   [4] Jer. xvii. 11.
[5] S. Luke xvii. 26. 27.
[6] S. Matt. xxiv. 43. 44. xxv. 13. S. Luke xvii. 26–
30. xxi. 34. 35. 1 Thess. v. 3. 2 Pet. iii. 10. Rev.
xvi. 15.
[7] כָּל דְּבַר אֲשֶׁר יִשֵּׁךְ lit. "everything which shall
bite," De. xxiii. 20. הִשֵּׁךְ (De. xxiii. 20. 21 bis) is
properly a denom. from נָשֵׁךְ, explained to be "what
bites the giver and takes something of his from
him." Mezia 60. b. in Del. The הַכְּרֻבָה, v. 6. suggested תַּרְבִּית, and this, favored by the conception

Before
CHRIST
cir. 626.

i Isai. 33. 1.

k ver. 17.

8 [1] Because thou hast spoiled many nations, all the remnant of the people shall spoil thee; [k] because

of men's † blood, and *for* the violence of the land, of the city, and of all that dwell therein.

Before
CHRIST
cir. 626.

† Heb. *bloods.*

---

should it be done to him. "[1] The Medes and Persians who were before subject to the Babylonian empire, and whose kings were subject to Nebuchadnezzar and his successors, rose up in and awaked, i. e., stirred themselves up in the days of Belshazzar to rebel against the successors of Nebuchadnezzar which sat on his throne, like a man who awaketh from sleep." The words *awake, arise,* are used also of the resurrection, when the worm of the wicked gnaweth and dieth not [2].

And thou shalt be for booties unto them? The common phrase is modified to explain the manifoldness of the plunder [3] which he should yield. So Jeremiah, [4] *Chaldæa shall be a spoil ; all that spoil her shall be satisfied, saith the Lord.* "[5] We may hear Him Who saith, [6] *How can one enter into a strong man's house, and spoil his goods, except he first bind the strong man ? and then he will spoil his house.* For, as soon as He was born of the holy Virgin, He began to spoil his goods. For the Magi came from the East—and worshiped Him and honored Him with gifts and became a first-fruits of the Church of the Gentiles. And being vessels of Satan, and the most honored of all his members, they hastened to Christ."

8. *Because,* [or *For*]. The Prophet assigns the reason of the *woes* he had just pronounced. *Thou* [7] [emph.], *thou hast spoiled many nations, all the remnant of the people shall spoil thee.* So Isaiah, [8] *When thou shalt cease to spoil, thou shalt be spoiled ; when thou shalt make an end to deal treacherously, they shall deal treacherously with thee.* Boundless as his conquests were, each remaining people, tribe, or family shall be his foe. "[9] Having subdued very many, thou shalt be destroyed by few, and they who long endured thy tyranny, arising as from sleep, shall compass thy destruction ; and thou shalt pay the penalty of thy countless slaughters and thy great ungodliness and thy lawless violence to cities

which thou madest desolate of inhabitants." Nothing was too great or too little to escape this violence.

All the remnant. "[9] As thou, invading, didst take away the things of others, in like way shall what appertaineth to thee be taken away by those who are left for vengeance." Jeremiah foretold of Elam *in the beginning of the reign of Zedekiah* [10], (in expansion of the prophecy in the reign of Jehoiakim [11]) ; *Thus saith the Lord of hosts, Behold, I will break the bow of Elam, the chief of their might. And upon Elam I will bring the four winds from the four quarters of the heavens, and will scatter them toward all these winds, and there shall be no nation whither the outcasts of Elam shall not come. For I will cause Elam to be dismayed before her enemies ; but it shall come to pass in the latter days, that I will bring again the captivity of Elam, saith the Lord.* Elam is also counted by Ezekiel [12] among those who, together with Pharaoh, should be brought down to the grave, with *Asshur, Meshech, Tubal, Edom and all the Zidonians,* by the king of Babylon. They were then all which remained [13] of the nations which he had conquered, who should be gathered against his house. *Because of men's blood and of the violence of* i. e. *to the land, as the violence of,* i. e. *to* [14], *Lebanon,* and *men's blood* is their blood which was shed. *To land, city, and all dwellers therein. Land* or *earth, city,* are left purposely undefined, so that while that in which the offence culminated should be, by the singular, specially suggested, *the violence* *to* Judah and Jerusalem, the cruelty condemned should not be limited to these. *The violence* was dealt out to the whole *land* or *earth,* and in it, to cities, and in each, one by one, to all its inhabitants. Babylon is called, [15] *the hammer of the whole earth ;* [16] *a golden cup in the Lord's hand, that made all the earth drunken ;* [17] *a destroying mountain, which destroyeth the whole earth ; the whole earth is at*

---

of the Chaldæans as a pitiless creditor, concentrated in עֹבְטִיט, suggested נֶשֶׁךְ, (which is often united with תַּרְבִּית) ; and this suggested the remarkable designation of those who were to execute the Divine retribution on the Chaldæans by the word, נֹשְׁכֶ.   [1] Abarb. quoted by Del.
[2] See Isaiah xiv. 11. lxvi. 24.
[3] הָיָה לִמְשׁוֹסוֹת. Elsewhere sing. לִמְשֻׁסָּה.
[4] Jer. l. 10.   [5] See S. Cyr.   [6] S. Matt. xii. 29.
[7] כִּי אַתָּה.   [8] Isaiah xxxiii. 1.
[9] Theod.   [10] Jer. xlix. 34–39.
[11] The prophecies against the heathen nations Jer. xlvi.-li. were in the same order in the main as in Jer. xxv. 19-26, beginning with Egypt and end-

ing in Babylon, and containing between these, the Philistines (with Tyre and Zidon incidentally), Moab, Ammon, Edom, Kedar, Hazor, Elam ; Elam being in both cases the last before Babylon itself.
[12] Ezek. xxxii. 17-32.
[13] As יֶתֶר הַגּוֹיִם הָאֵלֶּה Josh. xxiii. 12, יֶתֶר אֶת יֶתֶר הָעָם ,אֶת יֶתֶר הֶהָמוֹן Ex. x. 5; הַפְּלֵטָה 2 Kings xxv. 11; אֶת יֶתֶר הָעָם הַנִּשְׁאָרִים Jer. xxxix. 9.
[14] Hab. ii. 17, חָמָס is united with the gen. of the object, Gen. xvi. 5. Jud. ix. 24. Jo. iv. 19. Ob. 10. Jer. li. 35 ; with that of the subject, Ps. vii. 17, lviii. 3, Ezek. xii. 19. [all.]
[15] Jer. l. 23.   [16] Ib. li. 7.   [17] Ib. 25.

Before
CHRIST
cir. 626.

9 ¶ Woe to him that
[1] ‖ coveteth an evil covetousness to his house, that
he may [m] set his nest on
high, that he may be de-

livered from the †power
of evil!

10 Thou hast consulted
shame to thy house by cutting off many people, and

Before
CHRIST
cir. 626.

† Heb. *palm of
the hand.*

[1] Jer. 22. 13.
‖ Or, *gaineth an
evil gain.*
[m] Jer. 49. 16.
Obad. 4.

rest and is quiet [1], after Babylon, *which made it
to tremble* [2], is overthrown.

So Satan had by violence and deceit subdued the whole earth, yet Christ made him a
spoil to those whom he had spoiled, and the
strong man was bound and his goods spoiled
and himself trampled underfoot. Yet here
as throughout the prophets, it is a "remnant" only which is saved. " [3] Satan too
was spoiled by the remnant of the people,
i. e. by those justified by Christ and sanctified in the Spirit. For the remnant of
Israel was saved."

9. *Woe to him that coveteth an evil covetousness
to his house* [or, with accents, *that coveteth
covetousness or unjust gain, an evil to his house.*]
What man coveteth seems gain, but is *evil to
his house* after him, destroying both himself
and his whole family or race with him [4].
That he may set his nest on high, as an eagle, to
which he had likened the Chaldee [5]. A
heathen called "strongholds, the nests of
tyrants." The nest was placed "on high"
which means also "heaven," as it is said,
[6] *though thou set thy nest among the stars;* and
the tower of Babel was to [7] *reach unto heaven;*
and the Anti-Christ, whose symbol the King
of Babylon is, says, [8] *I will exalt my throne
above the stars of God.* Babylon lying in a
large plain, on the sides of the Euphrates, the
image of its eagle's-nest on high must be
taken, not from any natural eminence, but
wholly from the works of man. Its walls,
and its hanging gardens were among "the
seven wonders of the world." Eye witnesses
speak of its walls, encompassing at the least
100 square miles [9], " [10] and as large as the
land-graviat of Hesse Homberg;" those
walls, 335, or 330 feet high, and 85 feet
broad [11]; a fortified palace, near 7 miles in
circumference; gardens, 400 Greek feet
square, supporting at an artificial height
arch upon arch, of "at least 75 feet," forest
trees; a temple to its god, said to have been

at least 600 feet high. Had we, creatures of
a day, no one above us, Nebuchadnezzar's
boast had been true [12], *Is not this great Babylon
that I have builded for the house of the Kingdom
by the might of my power and for the honor of my
majesty?* He had built an *eagle's nest,* which
no human arm could reach, encircled by
walls which laughed its invaders to scorn,
which no then skill could scale or shatter or
mine. Even as one sees in a picture the vast
mounds which yet remain [13], one can hardly
imagine that they were, brick upon brick,
wholly the work of man.

To be delivered from the hand [*grasp*] *of
evil;* that it should not be able to reach him.
Evil is spoken of as a living power [14], which
would seize him, whose grasp he would defy.
It was indeed a living power, since it was
the Will of Almighty God, Whose servant
and instrument Cyrus was, to chasten Babylon, when its sins were full. Such was the
counsel, what the result? The *evil* covetousness which he wrought, brought on him the
evil, from which, in that nest built by the
hard toil of his captives, he thought to deliver himself.

10. *Thou hast consulted shame to thy house,
the cutting off many people, and sinning against
thy soul.* The wicked, whether out of passion
or with his whole mind and deliberate choice
and will, takes that *counsel,* which certainly
brings *shame* to himself and his *house,* according to the law of God, whereby He [15] *visits
the iniquities of the fathers upon the children unto
the third and fourth generation of them that hate
Him,* i. e. until by righteousness and restitution the curse is cut off. [16] *He that is greedy
of gain troubleth his own house.* So Jeremiah
says, [17] *Thus saith the Lord, Is it Me they are
vexing?* is it *not themselves, for* [18] *the confusion
of their faces?* i. e. with that end and object.
Holy Scripture overlooks the means, and
places us at the end of all. Whatever the
wicked had in view, to satisfy ambition,

[1] Is. xiv. 7.   [2] Ib. 16.   [3] S. Cyr.
[4] בָּצַע עֶצַע elsewhere stand, without an epithet,
it being itself evil, Prov. i. 19. xv. 27. Jer. vi. 13. viii.
10. and Ezek. xxii. 27. [all]
[5] i. 8. Comp. Jer. xx. 16.   [6] Obad 4.
[7] Gen. xi. 4.   [8] Is. xiv. 13.
[9] Herodotus, giving probably the extent of the
outer wall, makes it a square 120 stades each way,
and so 56 miles in circuit [i. 178]. Ctesias, giving
probably the dimensions of the inner-wall, makes
the circumference 360 stades, 41–42 miles, and so
enclosing 100 square miles [Diod. Sic. ii. 7. sqq.].
[10] Rawl. 5 Empires iii. 340.
[11] It is remarkable that the larger dimensions are

the oldest, given by eye-witnesses. Rawlinson has
pointed out one case in which the later reduced the
dimensions artificially, "softening down the cubits
of Herodotus into feet." 5 Empires iii. 348 note.
See the whole vivid description, Ib. pp. 338–361.
[12] Dan. iv. 30.
[13] See in Smith's Bible Dict. i. 152. Rawl. 5 Empires iii. 353.
[14] מִכַּף occurs in 19 other places with verbs signifying deliverance, [see Fürst Conc. p. 568.] and in
all of living agents.   [15] Ex. xx. 5.
[16] Prov. xv. 27.   [17] Jer. vii. 19.
[18] לְמַעַן בֹּשֶׁת.

hast sinned *against* thy soul.

11 For the stone shall cry out of the wall, and

the || beam out of the tim-ber shall || answer it.

12 ¶ Woe to him that buildeth a town with

avarice, passion, love of pleasure, or the rest of man's immediate ends, all he was doing was leading on to a further end, shame and death. He was bringing about, not only these short-lived, but the lasting ends beyond, and these far more than the others, since that is the real end of a thing which abides, in which it at last ends. He consulted to cut off many people and was thereby (though he knew it not) by one and the same act, *guilty of* and *forfeiting his own soul*[1].

11. *For the stone shall cry out of the wall, and the beam out of the timber shall answer it.* All things have a voice, in that they are[2]. God's works speak that, for which He made them. [3] *The heavens declare the glory of God.* [4] *The valleys are clad with corn, they laugh, yea, they sing;* their very look speaks gladness. " [5]For the creation itself proclaims the glory of the Maker, in that it is admired as well made. Wherefore there are voices in things, although there are not words." Man's works speak of that in *him,* out of which and for which *he* made them. Works of mercy go up for a memorial before God, and plead there; .great works, wrought amid wrong and cruelty and for man's ambition and pride, have a voice too, and *cry out* to God, calling down His vengeance on the oppressor. Here *the stones of the wall,* whereby the building is raised, and *the beam,* the tye-beam, *out of the timber-*work[6] wherewith it is finished, and which, as it were, crowns the work, join, as in a chorus, *answering* one another, and in a deep solemn wailing, before God and the whole world, together chant "Woe, Woe." Did not the blood and groans of men cry out to God, speechless things have a voice to appeal to Him[7]. Against Belshazzar the wall had, to the letter, words to speak.

Each three verses forming one stanza, as it were, of the dirge, the following words are probably not directly connected with the former, as if the woe, which follows, were, so to speak, the chant of these inanimate witnesses against the Chaldæans; yet they stand connected with it. The dirge began with woe on the wrongful accumulation of wealth from the conquered and oppressed people: it continues with the selfish use of the wealth so won.

12. *Woe to him that buildeth a town with blood, and establisheth a city by iniquity!* Nebuchadnezzar " [8]encircled the inner city with three walls and the outer city also with three, all of burnt brick. And having fortified the city with wondrous works, and adorned the gates like temples, he built another palace near the palace of his fathers, surpassing it in height and its great magnificence." He seemed to strengthen the city, and to stablish it by outward defences. But it was built through cruelty to conquered nations, and especially God's people, and by oppression, against His holy Will. So there was an inward rottenness and decay in what seemed strong and majestic, and which imposed on the outward eye; it would not stand, but fell. Babylon, which had stood since the flood, being enlarged contrary to the eternal laws of God, fell in the reign of his son. Such is all empire and greatness, raised on the neglect of God's laws, by unlawful conquests, and by the toil and sweat and hard service of the poor. Its aggrandizement and seeming strength is its fall. Daniel's exhortation to Nebuchadnezzar, [9]*Redeem thy sins by righteousness, and thine iniquities by shewing mercy on the poor,* implies that oppressiveness had been one of his chief sins.

1 נפשׁ תּשׂא Prov. xx. 2. comp. נפשׁו חמס Ib. viii. 36. The contemporaneousness of the act is expressed by the participle; the pronoun is omitted as in i. 5.

2 The Arabs have an expression for it, לסאן אלחאל, lit. "The tongue of the situation."
3 Ps. xix. 1.   4 Ib. lxv. 13.   5 S. Cyr.
6 So the word is best understood, since the "beam" bears the same relation to the "wood-work" as the "stone" to the "wall," i. e. is a part of it, כפה in Ch. signifying "to bind," like כפה Dan. iii. 20, 21, 23, 24. So Kim. The other sense given, that it is a half-brick, such as is worked into the mode of building, called by us "bricknogging," which R. Tanchum of Jerusalem also knew in the East, seems unsuited here; 1) because it is speaking of magnificent building; the interlacing of brick with wood is for economy, since the wood, interlacing the bricks, holds them together, though

the wall be thin; 2) the half-bricks naturally enter into this mode of building, but are neither the chief nor a prominent part of it. 3) Neither is the woodwork apparently in such way one, that it can stand as a whole. Tanchum and Parchon adopt this rendering, and Rashi on Taanit 11 a (ap. Del.) not in his Comm.; Symm. Theod. Syr. έ have σύνδεσμος, S. Jer. in the same sense, ἱμάντωσις, and LXX. κάνθαρος. The other sense given does not account for the wood "out of the timber," since it would rather be "out of the stone-work." S. Cyril says, "the other versions have ἔνδεσμος ξύλου, so that they named the crown of the house and the complexity of the wood, i. e., the band, κάνθαρος, because they as with many feet supported the roof which lay upon it.
7 See S. Luke xix. 40.
8 Berosus Hist. Chald. L. iii. ap. Joseph. Antiq. x. 11. and ç. Ap. i. 20.
9 Dan. iv. 27.

Before
C H R I S T
cir. 626.

ⁿ † blood, and stablisheth a
city by iniquity!

13 Behold, *is it* not of
the LORD of hosts °that
the people shall labor in
the very fire, and the people shall weary themselves
|| for very vanity?

ⁿ Jer. 22. 13.
Ezek. 24. 9.
Mic. 3. 10.
Nah. 3 1.
† Heb. *bloods.*
° Jer. 51. 58.

|| Or, *in vain ?*

14 For the earth shall
be filled || with the ᴾ knowl-
edge of the glory of the
LORD, as the waters cover
the sea.

15 ¶ W o e unto h i m
that giveth his neighbor
drink, that p u t t e s t thy

Before
C H R I S T
cir. 626.

|| Or, *by knowing
the glory of the
Lord.*
ᴾ Isai. 11. 9.

---

13. *Behold, is it not of the Lord of hosts that
[the] people [nations] shall labor* ¹ *in [for] the
very fire* [lit. *to suffice the fire*]? By God's
appointment, the end of all their labor is for
the fire, what may *suffice* it to consume. This
is the whole result of their labor ; and so it
is as if they had toiled for this ; they built
ceiled palaces and gorgeous buildings, only
for the fire to consume them.
*And peoples shall weary themselves for very
vanity.* They *wearied themselves,* and what
was their reward ? What ha l they to suffice
and fill them ? *Emptiness.* This is *from the
Lord of hosts,* Whom all the armies of heaven
obey and all creatures stand at His command
against the ungodly, and in Whose Hand are
all the hosts of earth, and so the oppressor's
also, to turn as He wills.
Near upon the first stage of the fulfillment,
Jeremiah reinforces the words with the name
of Babylon ; ² *Thus saith the Lord of hosts!* *The
broad walls of Babylon shall be utterly destroyed,
and her high gates shall be burned with fire ; and
the people shall labor in vain [for vanity], and the
folk in [for] the fire, and they shall be weary.*
14. *For the earth shall be filled with the
knowledge of the glory of the Lord.* Habakkuk
modifies in a degree the words of Isaiah
which he embodies, marking that the destruction of Babylon was a stage only toward
the coming of those good things which God
taught His people to long for, not their very
coming. All the world should be then full
of the knowledge of the glory of the Lord,
not, as yet, wholly of Himself. " ³ When
Babylon shall be overthrown, then shall the
power of the might of the Lord be known
unto all. So shall the whole earth be filled
with the glory of the Lord, as the waters
cover the bottom of the sea. This as to the
letter. But it is plain, that the Devil also
and Anti-Christ, and the perverse teaching
of heretics, built a city in blood; i. e., their
own Church, with the destruction of those

whom they deceive. . . . . . But when they
fail in the fire, (either this fire which is felt,
or consumed in the fire of the devil their
prince, or burned up with the fire whereof
the Lord says, *I came to send a fire upon the
earth,* and so brought back from their former
course, and doing penitence), the whole earth
shall be filled with the glory of the Lord,
when, at the preaching of the Apostles, their
sound shall go out into all the world, as waters
covering the sea, i. e., all the saltness and
bitterness of the world which Satan had
rained down and the earth had drunk, the
waters of the Lord shall cover, and cause the
place of their ancient bitterness not to appear." " ⁴ *For the Spirit of the Lord filled the
earth,* and when He filled it, *the earth was
filled with the knowledge of the glory of the Lord,*
so that unlearned and ignorant men became
wise and eloquent, and earthly became
heavenly, yea, they who were earth became
heaven, knowing the Glory of the Lord, declaring the Glory of God, not any how, but
as waters cover the sea. Great as must be
waters, which would cover the sea, or compared to which the sea were nothing, far
greater is the miracle, when the abundance
of heavenly wisdom, given to the simple,
surpassed the sea, i. e., the wisdom of all
mankind." This verse being already a received image of the spread of the Gospel ⁵, it
would of itself be understood to include this
also; but more generally, it declares how
upon all the judgments of God, a larger
knowledge of Him would follow. " ⁶ All
things are full of Christ, Who is the Glory
of the Father; wherefore also He said, ⁷ *I
have glorified Thee on earth, I have finished the
work which Thou gavest me to do.*"
15. From cruelty the Prophet goes on to
denounce the woe on insolence. *Woe unto
him that giveth his neighbor* (to whom he owes
love) *drink* [lit. *that maketh him drink*] ; *that
puttest* ⁸ *thy bottle* ⁹ *to him, and makest him*

---

¹ יָגַע with בְ "labor upon " Josh. xxiv. 13. Isa.
lxii. 8. and boldly, of God, Ib. xliii. 22. and Hif.
" cause to labor with " Isa. xliii. 23.
² Jer. li. 58.   ³ S. Jer.   ⁴ Rup.
⁵ Isaiah xi. 9.   ⁶ S. Cyr.   ⁷ S. John xvii. 4.
⁸ סָפַח is rendered " approaching " to "joining "
by Tanch., A. E., Rashi Kim. Sal. B. Mel. Abarb. ;

" pouring " Ch. Symm. Both senses exist in the
verb; and the efforts of Ges. and Papenheim (ap. Del.)
to reduce all the usages under either, force some.
⁹ The E. V. has taken חֲמָתְךָ as irregular from
חֵמָה "flask," with Kim., A. E., Sal. ben Mel.;
" poison," Ch. Abulw.· " wrath," Rashi, Abarb.;
" flask " or " wrath," Tanch.

Before
C H R I S T
cir. 626.

q Hos. 7. 5.
r Gen. 9. 22.
‖ Or, *more with
shame than
with glory.*
s Jer. 25. 26, 27.
& 51. 57.

q bottle to *him*, and makest *him* d r u n k e n also, that thou mayest r look on their nakedness!

16 Thou art filled ‖ with shame for glory : s drink thou also, and let thy foreskin be u n c o v e r e d : the cup of the LORD's right hand shall be turned unto

thee, and shameful spewing *shall be* on thy glory.

17 For the violence of Lebanon shall cover thee, and the spoil of beasts, *which* made them afraid, t because of men's blood, and for the violence of the land, of the city, and of all that dwell therein.

---

drunken also, [1] *that thou mayest look* [*gaze with devilish pleasure*] *on their nakedness.* This may either be of actual insults (as in the history of Noah), in keeping certainly with the character of the later Babylonians, the last wantonness of unbridled power, making vile sport of those like himself (*his neighbor*), or it may be drunkenness through misery [2] wherein they are bared of all their glory and brought to the lowest shame. The *woe* falls too on all, who in any way intoxicate others with flattering words or feigned affection, mixing *poison* under things pleasant, to bring them to shame.

16. *Thou art filled with shame for glory.* Oppressors think to make themselves great by bringing others down, to *fill* themselves with riches, by spoiling others. They loved shame [3], because they loved that, which brought shame ; they were filled with shame, in that they sated themselves with shamefulness, which was their shame within, before, in the just judgment of God, shame came on them from without. [4] *Their glory was in their shame.* They shall be filled, yea, he says, *they are* already filled [5] ; they would satisfy, gorge themselves, with all their hearts' desires ; they are *filled to the full*, but *with shame* instead of *glory* which they sought, or which they already had. *From* and *for* [6] a state of *glory*, they were filled with contempt.

Drink thou also, and let thy foreskin be uncovered : thy shame like those whom thou puttest to shame, only the greater in being uncircumcised. *The cup of the Lord's*

Right Hand shall be turned [*round*] *unto thee* [or *against thee*]. It had gone round the circuit of the nations whom God had employed him to chasten, and now, the circle completed, it should be brought round to himself, [7] *With what measure ye mete, it shall be measured unto you again.* So Jeremiah says, [8] *And the king of Sheshach shall drink after them ;* and of Edom, [9] *To thee also shall the cup be brought round.* Thou, a man, madest man to drink of the cup of *thine* anger : the cup shall be brought round to thee, but not by man ; to thee it shall be given by *the Right Hand of the Lord,* which thou canst not escape ; it shall be [10] *the cup of the wine of the fierceness of the wrath of Almighty God ;* as Asaph had said, [11] *There is a cup in the Lord's hand ; it is full of mixture, and He poureth out therefrom ; but the dregs thereof all the ungodly of the earth shall suck them out, shall drink them.*

And shameful spewing [12] *shall be on thy glory.* "[13] With the shame of thy spewing shalt thou bring up all thou hast swallowed down, and from the height of glory shalt thou be brought to the utmost ills." The shame of the ungodly cometh forth from himself ; the shame he put others to is doubled upon himself ; and the very means which he had used to fill himself with glory and greatness, cover the glory which by nature he had, with the deeper disgrace, so that he should be a loathsome and revolting sight to all. Man veils foul deeds under fair words ; God, in His word, unveils the foulness.

17. *For the violence of Lebanon* i. e., done to

---

[1] וְאַף שָׁכֵר The inf. abs. continuing the previous action of the finite verb, as in Gen. xli. 43. Is. ix. 20. Jer. xiv. 5, or after the inf. constr. 1 Sam. xxii. 13. xxv. 26. 33. Jer. vii. 18. &c. See in Ewald Lehrb. p. 839. ed. 7.   [2] Isaiah xxix. 9.
[3] Hos. iv. 8.   [4] Phil. iii. 19.
[5] שָׂבַע has nowhere the reflective meaning, "satiated himself with " (as Del.) ; it simply expresses a state.
[6] מִן includes both.   [7] S. Matt. vii. 2.
[8] Jer. xxv. 26.   [9] Lam. iv. 21.   [10] Rev. xvi. 19.
[11] Ps. lxxvi. 8.
[12] קִיקָלוֹן *might* be simply an intensive, modified

from קָלְקלוֹן, as כּוֹכָב from כָּכָב, תַּצוֹצָרוֹת for חַצְרְרוֹת, &c. Ew. Lehrb. p. 408. It was regarded as a compound word by S. Jerome's Hebrew instructor, " vomitus ignominiæ," the Midrash Ester Rabb. 121. c. (in Del.) Kim. Sal. B. Mel. as suggested by the mention of the drinking, (as in Jer. xxv. 27.). Ibn Ezra, Tanchum, Abarb. give both. In any case, as in יַבְטִיט, the word was probably framed to suggest the two words, into which it is naturally resolved, קִיא קָלוֹן, like קִיא צֹאָה Is. xxviii. 8. and the image Is. xix. 14. The form is enlarged by Hab. from the previous קָלוֹן, but the doubling occurs in קִלְקֵל Nu. xxi. 5.   [13] S. Jer.

Before
CHRIST
cir. 626.

u Is. 44. 9, 10.
& 46. 2.

18 ¶ ᵘ What profiteth the graven image that the maker thereof hath graven it ; the molten image, and

a ˣ teacher of lies, that † the maker of his work trusteth therein, to make ʸ dumb idols ?

Before
CHRIST
cir. 626.

ˣ Jer. 10. 8, 14.
Zech. 10. 2.
† Heb. *the fash-
ioner of his
fashion.*

ʸ Ps. 115. 5. 1 Cor. 12. 2.

Lebanon, whether the land of Israel of which it was the entrance and the beauty [1], or the temple [2], both of which Nebuchadnezzar laid waste ; or, more widely, it may be a symbol of all the majesty of the world and its empires, which he subdues, as Isaiah uses it, when speaking of the judgment on the world [3]. *It shall cover thee, and the spoil* [i. e., *spoiling, destruction*] *of beasts* [the inhabitants of Lebanon] *which made them afraid,* or more simply, *the wasting of wild beasts* [4] *shall crush* [5] *them*[selves]," i. e., as it is in irrational nature, that " the frequency of the incursions of very mischievous animals becomes the cause that men assemble against them and kill them, so their [the Chaldæans'] frequent injustice is the cause that they haste to be avenged on thee [6]." Having become beasts, they shared their history. They spoiled, scared, laid waste, were destroyed. " Whoso seeketh to hurt another, hurteth himself." The Chaldæans laid waste Judæa, scared and wasted its inhabitants ; the end of its plunder should be, not to adorn, but to *cover* them, overwhelm them as in ruins, so that they should not lift up their heads again. Violence returns on the head of him who did it ; they seem to raise a lofty fabric, but are buried under it. He sums up their past experience, what God had warned them beforehand, what they had found.

18. *What profiteth* [*hath profited* [7]] *the graven image, that the maker therefore hath graven it ?* What did Baal and Ashtaroth profit you ? What availed it ever but to draw down the wrath of God ? Even so neither shall it profit

the Chaldæan. As their idols availed them not, so neither need they fear them. Sennacherib and Nebuchadnezzar were propagandists of their own belief and would destroy, if they could, all other worship, false or true [8] : Nebuchadnezzar is thought to have set up his own image [9]. Anti-Christ will set himself up as God [10]. We may take warning at least by our own sins. If we had no profit at all from them, neither will the like profit others. This the Jews did, in the main, learn in their captivity.

The molten image and teacher of lies. It is all one whether by *teacher of lies* we understand the idol [11], or its priest [12]. For its priest gave it its voice, as its maker created its form. It could only seem to teach through the idol-priest. Isaiah used the title *teacher of lies,* of the false prophet [13]. It is all one. Zechariah combines them ; [14] *The teraphim have spoken vanity, and the diviners have seen a lie, and have had false dreams.*

That the maker of his work trusteth therein. This was the special folly of idolatry. The thing made must needs be inferior to its maker. It was one of the corruptions of idolatry that the maker of his own work should trust in what was wholly *his* own *creation,* what, not God, but himself created, what had nothing but what it had from himself [15]. He uses the very words which express the relation of man to God, " the Framer " and " the thing framed." [16] *O your perverseness ! Shall the framer be accounted as clay, that the thing made should say of its Maker, He made me not, and the thing framed say of its Framer, He*

---

[1] See Is. xxxvii. 24. and, as a symbol, Jer. xxii. 6, 23. Ez. xvii. 3 ; but it is used as a symbol of Sennacherib's army, Is. x. 34, and the king of Asshur is not indeed spoken of under the name as a symbol (in Ezek. xxi. 3.) but is compared to it.

[2] See on Zech. xii. 1.　　　　[3] Is. ii. 13.

[4] בְּהֵמוֹת is used of beasts of prey, Deut. xxvii. 24.

[5] As in Is. vii. 8. and מְחִתָּה Ps. lxxxix. 40, Pr. x. 14, xiii. 3, xiv. 14, xviii. 7.

[6] R. Tanchum. He had after Abulwalid, which Kimchi quotes and approves, explained the first part of the verse ; " This is a likeness framed as to him, that he was like a beast of prey which attacketh the animals in their lairs ; and Lebanon is mentioned on account of the multitude of animals in it. He says then, thy wrong to the inhabitants of Lebanon shall overwhelm thee." He gives also the rendering, followed in the E. V., but prefers his own. He gives the two ways of deriving יְחִיתָן from חתת and חִית [6]. Rashi follows the same construction. " The wasting of thy beasts and forces, because they have wasted My people Israel, it shall crush them [selves]."

[7] מָה הוֹעִיל. Samuel warned them, " Serve the

Lord with all your heart, and turn ye not aside ; for [it would be] after vanities, which will not profit, nor deliver, for they are vain : " and Jeremiah tells their past ; " their prophets prophesied by Baal ; and after things יוֹעִילוּ לֹא which profit not, have they gone." Elsewhere the idol is spoken of as a thing, " which *will* not profit " (fut.) " My people hath changed its glory יוֹעִיל בְּלֹא for that which profiteth not," Jer. ii. 8. 11. So Isaiah, " Who hath formed a god, לְבִלְתִּי הוֹעִיל, not to profit." Is. xliv. 9. 10. " The makers of a graven image are all of them vanity, and their desirable things יוֹעִילוּ בַל will not profit."

[8] 2 Kgs xviii. 32–35, xix. 12–18, xxv. 9, Is. x. 10, 11. See also Lectures on Daniel pp. 447–449 ed. 2.
[9] Dan. iii. See Lectures on Dan. pp. 442.
[10] 2 Thess. ii. 4. Rev. xiii. 15–17. [11] Abarb. Kim.
[12] AE. Tanch. [13] Is. ix. 14. [14] Zech. x. 2.
[15] In Hebrew this is made stronger by the sameness of the words, יֹצֵר יָצַר *yotser yitsro* E. M. " fashioner of his fashion." Again " dumb idols " are *elilim illemim,* the second word only slightly varying from the first. [16] Is. **xxix. 16.**

Before
CHRIST
cir. 626.

19 Woe unto him that saith to the wood, Awake; to the dumb stone, Arise, it shall teach! Behold, it *is* laid over with gold and silver, [z] and *there is* no

ᵃ Ps. 135. 17.

breath at all in the midst of it.

20 But ᵃ the LORD *is* in his holy temple: † ᵇ let all the earth keep silence before him.

Before
CHRIST
cir. 626.

ᵃ Ps. 11. 4.
† Heb. *he silent
all the earth
before him.*
ᵇ Zeph. 1. 7.
Zech. 2. 13.

---

hath no hands? The idol-maker is "the creator of his creature," of his god whom he worships. Again the idol-maker makes *dumb idols* [lit. *dumb nothings*] in themselves nothings, and having no power out of themselves; and what is uttered in their name, are but *lies.* And what else are man's idols of wealth, honor, fame, which he makes to himself, the creatures of his own hands or mind, their greatness existing chiefly in his own imagination, before which *he* bows down himself, who is the image of God?

19. But then the greater is the *Woe* to him who deceiveth by them. The prophet passes away from the the idols as "nothings" and pronounces "woe" on those who deceive by them. He [1] first expostulates with them on their folly, and would awaken them. *What hath it profited* [2]? Then on the obstinate he denounces "woe." *Woe unto him that saith to the wood, Awake; to the dumb stone, Arise.* Self-made blindness alone could, in the light of truth, so speak; but yet more lies in the emphatic word, *It.* The personal pronoun stands emphatically in Hebrew; *He* shall teach, lo, *He* (this same of whom he speaks) this is *It* which *shall teach:* It, and not the living God. And yet this same *It* (the word is again emphatic) he points, as with the finger, to it, *behold, It is laid over with, held fast by* [3], *gold and silver,* so that no voice could escape, if it had any. *And there is no breath at all in the midst of it* [4], lit. *All breath, all which is breath, there is none within it;* he first suggests the thought, breath of every sort, and then energetically denies it all [5]; no life of any sort, of man, or bird, or beast, or creeping thing; [6] none, good or bad; from God or from Satan; none whereby it can do good or do evil; for which it should be loved or feared. Evil spirits may have made use of idols: they could not give them life, nor dwell in them.

The words addressed to it are the language of the soul in the seeming absence or silence of God [7], but mockery as spoken to the senseless stone, as Elijah had mocked the Baal-

priests [8], *peradventure he sleepeth and must be awaked.*

20. And now having declared the nothingness of all which is not God, the power of man or his gods, he answers again his own question, by summoning all before the Presence of the Majesty of God.

And the Lord. He had, in condemning them, pictured the tumult of the world, the oppressions, the violence, bloodsheddings, covetousness, insolence, self-aggrandizement of the then world-empire, and had denounced woe upon it; we see man framing his idols, praying to the lifeless stones; and God, of Whom none thought, where was He? These were men's ways. "*And* the Lord," he joins it on, as the complement and corrective of all this confusion, *The Lord is in His holy temple,* awaiting, in His long-suffering, to judge. *The temple of God* is where God enshrines Himself, or allows Himself to be seen and adored. "God is wholly everywhere, the whole of Him no where." There is no contrast between His temple on earth, and His temple in heaven. He is not more locally present in heaven than in earth. It were as anthropomorphic but less pious to think of God, as confined, localized, in heaven as on earth; because it would be simply removing God away from man. Solomon knew, when he built the temple, that *the heaven and heaven of heavens could not contain* [9] God. The *holy temple,* which could be destroyed [10], toward which men were to pray [11], was the visible temple [12], where were the symbols of God's Presence, and of the atoning Sacrifice; but lest His presence should be localized, Solomon's repeated prayer is, [13] *hear Thou in heaven Thy dwelling place;* [14] *hear Thou in heaven.* There is then no difference, as though in earlier books the " holy temple " meant that at Jerusalem, in the later, " the heavens." In the confession at the offering of the *third year's tithes,* the prayer is, [15] *look down from Thy holy habitation, from heaven;* and David says, [16] *the Lord is in His holy temple, the Lord's throne is in heaven;*

---

[1] Rup.
[2] As in Ps. cxv. 5. 1 Cor. xii. 2.
[3] The meaning of תָּפַשׂ elsewhere. " Here it means ' surrounds,' for that which encircles a thing, is as if it held it on every side." Tanch.
[4] Comp. Jer. x. 14 repeated li. 17.
[5] As in the Hebraism of the N. T. οὐ δικαιωθήσεται πᾶσα σάρξ Rom. iii. 20.

[6] Is. xli. 23. Jer. x. 5.
[7] Ps. vii. 7, xxxv. 23, xliv. 24. lix. 6, Is. li. 9. Del.
[8] 1 Kgs xviii. 26, 27.　　[9] 1 Kgs viii. 27.
[10] Ps. lxxix. 1.
[11] Ps. v. 7. cxxxviii. 2. Jon. ii. 4.
[12] 1 Kgs viii. 29, 30, 35, 38, 42, 44, 48.
[13] Ib. 30, 39, 43, 49.　　[14] Ib. 32, 34, 36, 45.
[15] De. xxvii. 15.　　[16] Ps. xi. 4.

CHAPTER III.

1 *Habakkuk in his prayer trem-*
bleth at God's majesty. 17
The confidence of his faith.

A PRAYER of Habak-
kuk the prophet [a] || up-
on Shigionoth.

[a] Ps. 7, title.
|| Or, *according*
to variable songs, or, *tunes, called in Hebrew, Shigionoth.*

and, [1] *He heard my voice out of His temple—*
He bowed the heavens also and came down ; and,
[2] *In His temple doth every one say, Glory.* The
simple words are identical though not in the
same order as those, in which David, in the
same contrast with the oppression of man,
ushers in the judgment and final retribution
to good and bad, by declaring the unseen
presence of God on His Throne in heaven,
beholding and trying the sons of men.
In His Presence, all the mysteries of our
being are solved. *The Lord is in His holy
Temple,* not, as the idols in temples made with
hands, but revealing Himself in the visible
temple, " [3] dwelling in the Son, by Nature
and Union, as He saith, [4] *The Father Who
dwelleth in Me doeth the works ;* in each one
of the bodies and souls of the Saints by His
Spirit [5], in the Blessed, in glory ; in the
Heavens, by the more evident appearance of
His Majesty and the workings of His Power ;
" [6] everywhere by Essence, Presence, and
Power, *for in Him we live, and move, and have
our being ;* nowhere as confined or inclosed."
Since then God is in Heaven, beholding the
deeds of men, Himself Unchangeable, Almighty, All-holy, *let all the earth keep silence
before Him,* lit. *hush before Him all the earth,*
waiting from Him in hushed stillness the
issue of this tangled state of being. And to
the hushed soul, hushed to itself and its own
thoughts, hushed in awe of His Majesty and
His Presence, before His face, God speaks [7].
III. 1. *A prayer* [8] *of Habakkuk.* The *prayer*
of the prophet, in the strictest sense of the
word, is contained in the words of verse 2.
The rest is, in its form, praise and thanksgiving, chiefly for God's past mercies in the
deliverance from Egypt and the entering
into the promised land. But thanksgiving
is an essential part of prayer, and Hannah
is said to have *prayed,* whereas the hymn
which followed is throughout one thanksgiving [9]. In that also these former deliverances were images of things to come, of every
deliverance afterward, and, especially, of that

complete Divine deliverance which our Lord
Jesus Christ wrought for us from the power
of Satan [10], the whole is one prayer. "Do, O
Lord, as Thou hast done of old ; forsake not
Thine own works. Such were Thy deeds
once ; fulfill them now, all which they
shadowed forth." It is then a prayer for the
manifestation of God's power, and therewith
the destruction of His enemies, thenceforth
to the Day of Judgment. "[11] Having completed the discourse about Babylon, and having fore-announced most clearly, that those
who destroyed the holy city and carried
Israel captive shall be severely punished, he
passes suitably to the mystery of Christ, and
from the redemption which took place partially in one nation, he carries on the discourse to that universal redemption, whereby
the remnant of Israel, and no less the whole
world has been saved."
Upon Shigionoth. The title, *Shiggaion,*
occurs but once besides [12]. *Upon,* in the titles
of the Psalms, is used with the instrument [13],
the melody [14], or the first words of the hymn,
whose melody has been adopted [15]. The two
first are mentioned by a Jewish Commentator [16] with others, " in his delight," or " his
errors," in the sense, that God will forgive
them. This, which the versions and Jewish
commentators mostly adopt, would be a good
sense, but is hardly consistent with the
Hebrew usage. *Shiggaion of David,* as a title
of a Psalm, must necessarily describe the
Psalm itself, as *Midsmor of David, Michtam of
David, Tephillah of David, Maschil of David.*
But *Shiggaion,* as a " great error," is not a
title : nor does it suit the character of the
Psalm, which relates to calumny not to error.
It probably, then, means a psalm with music
expressive of strong emotion, " erratic " or
" dithyrambic." Habakkuk's title, *on Shigionoth* [plur.] then would mean *upon,* or (as we
should say,) " set to " music of psalms of this
sort [17]. The number " three " remarkably
predominates in this psalm [18], yet so that
long measures are succeeded by very short.

[1] Ps. xviii. 6. 9.
[2] Ib. xxix. 9.
[3] S. Jer.
[4] S. John xiv. 10.
[5] 1 Cor. vi. 19.
[6] Dion.
[7] See S. Augustine's words to his mother before
her death, Conf. ix. 10.
[8] Tephilloth is a title of the collection of David's
Psalms ending with Ps. lxxii. (Ib. ver. 20.) Three of
David's Psalms are entitled Tephillah, Ps. xvii.
lxxxvi. cxlii. Moses' Psalm xc., and anonymous cii.
◦ ותתפלל 1 Sam. ii. 1.
[10] 1 Cor. x. 11.
[11] S. Cyr.
[12] Ps. vii.
[13] on Neginoth, Ps. iv. vi. lv. Nehiloth, Ps. v.
Gittith, Ps. viii. Shoshannim, Ps. xlv. Mahalath,
Ps. liii.

[14] on Sheminith, Ps. vi. Alamoth Ps. xlvi.
[15] Perhaps " upon Muthlabben," Ps. ix. " on
Aiieleth Shahar," Ps. xxii. " on Yonath-elem-
rekokim," Ps. lvi.
[16] R. Tanchum.
[17] Since שגה " erred " is common to Hebrew and
Aramaic, it is improbable that שגיון should be i. q.
Syr. סוגיתא a " hymn of praise," from סג, beside
that the Heb. שׂ does not interchange with Syr. ס.
[18] Ver. 6 has 15 words, in five combinations, of
three words ; vv. 3 and 10 have 12 words, in four 3s :
vv. 4, 9, 19. have 9 words in three 3s : vv. 5, 12, 15
and 18 have 6 words in two 3s : ver. 17 is divided into
433433 ; ver. 8 is 33332 ; ver. 11 is 433 ; ver. 16 is

2 O LORD, I have heard
† thy s p e e c h, *and* was
† Heb. *thy report,* or, *thy hearing.*

afraid : O LORD, || ᵇ revive
thy work in the midst
|| Or, *preserve alive.*
ᵇ Ps. 85. 6.

2. *O Lord, I have heard* i. e. with the inward ear of the heart, *Thy speech,* (rather as E. M. *Thy report,* i. e. the report of Thee [1]) i. e. what may he heard and known of God, or, what he had himself heard [2]. The word contains in one both that which God had lately declared to the Prophet, the judgments of God upon the wicked of the people, and upon those who, with their own injustice, wrought on them the righteous judgments of God, and that the work of the Lord would be wrought in His time for those who in patience wait for it ; and also still more largely, what might be heard of God, although, as it were, but a little whisper of His greatness and of the Majesty of His workings.

And was afraid, not " fearful " but *afraid* in awe, as a creature, and amazed at the surpassing wonderfulness of the work of God. Well may man stand in awe " [3] at the Incarnation of the Only Begotten Son, how earth should contain Him uncontained by space, how a Body was prepared for Him of the Virgin by the Holy Ghost, and all the works whereby He shall work the salvation of mankind, the Cross, the Death, Resurrection and Ascension, uniting things opposite, a Body with One incorporeal, Death with Life, Resurrection with Death, a Body in Heaven. All is full of wonder and awe." " [4] This is not a servile fear, but a holy fear which endureth forever, not one which *love casteth out,* but which it bringeth in, wherein angels praise, dominions adore, powers stand in awe at the Majesty of the Eternal God."

O Lord, revive Thy work. God's Word seems, often, as it were, dead and *come utterly to an end for evermore* [5], while it is holding on its own course, as all nature seems dead for a while, but all is laid up in store, and ready to shoot forth, as by a sort of resurrection. " [4] The Prophet prophesying prayeth, that it should come quickly, and praying prophesieth that it shall so come." All God's dealings with His people, His Church, each single soul, are part of one great work, perfect in itself [6] ; glory and majesty [7] ; all

which the godly meditateth on [8] ; which those busied with their own plans, do not look to [9] ; it is manifested in great doings for them or with them, as in the Exodus the Psalmist says, [10] *We have heard with our ears, yea, our fathers have told us what work Thou didst in their days, in the times of old ;* [11] *They proved Me and saw My work ;* with it He makes His own glad [12] ; after it has been withdrawn for a while, *He sheweth it to His servants* [13] ; it issues in judgments on the ungodly, which men consider and declare [14].

The great work of God on earth, which includes all His works and is the end of all, is the salvation of man through Jesus Christ. This great work seemed, as it were, asleep, or dead, as trees in winter, all through those 4000 years, which gave no token of His Coming. Included in this great work is the special work of the Hand of God, of which alone it is said, *God said, Let Us make man in Our Image after Our Likeness* [15] ; and, *we are the clay and Thou our Potter, and we are all the work of Thy Hands* [16] ; and *Thy Hands have made me and fashioned me together round about* [17], —man ; whom, being dead as to the life of the soul through the malice of Satan, Christ revived by dying and rising again. He was *dead in trespasses and sins,* and like a carcase putrefying in them, and this whole world one great charnel-house, through man's manifold corruptions, when Christ came to awaken the dead, and they who heard lived [18].

Again, the Centre of this work, the special Work of God, that wherein He made all things new, is the Human Body of our Lord, the Temple which was destroyed by Death, and within three days raised up.

The answer to Habakkuk's enquiry, *How long ?* had two sides. It had given assurance as to the end. The trial-time would not be prolonged for one moment longer than the counsel of God had foredetermined. The relief would *come, come ; it would not be behindhand.* But meantime? There was no comfort to be given. For God knew that deepening sin was drawing on deepening chastise-

---

3332223. This forces itself on every reader. Del. quotes the Meor. Enaim, i. 60, " The prayer of Habakkuk goeth on threes."

[1] Except in the one phrase אֹ֫זֶן שְׁמַע " hearing of ear " (Job xlii. 5. Ps. xviii. 45.) the personal gen. after שְׁמַע is that of the object, " the report of Jacob," Gen. xxix. 13. " of Solomon," 1 Kgs x. 1. 2 Chron. ix. 1. " of Tyre," Is. xxiii. 5 with the affix שִׁמְעֵךְ *the report of thee,* Nu. xiv. 15, De. ii. 25. Nah. iii. 19. שִׁמְעָהּ *the report of her* [wisdom] Job xxviii.

22. שָׁמְעִי *the report of Me* [God], Is. lxvi. 19. שִׁמְעָם *the report of them,* Jer. xxxvii. 5. l. 43.

[2] as שְׁמוּעָה Ob. 1, and thence Jer. xlix. 14. See on Hosea vii. 12.   [3] Theoph. from S. Cyr.
[4] Rup.   [5] Ps. lxxvii. 8.
[6] De xxxii. 4.   [7] Ps. cxl. 3.
[8] Ib. lxxvii. 3. cxliii. 35.   [9] Is. v. 12.
[10] Ps. xliv. 2. פֹּעַל פֵּעֲלָת.   [11] Ps. xcv. 9.
[12] Ib. xcii. 3.   [13] Ib. xc. 6.
[14] Ib. lxiv. 10. In all these cases sing. פָּעַל.
[15] Gen. i. 26.   [16] Is. lxiv. 8.
[17] Job x. 8.   [18] S. John v. 25.

of the years, in the midst of the years make

known; in wrath remember mercy.

ment. But in that He was silent as to the intervening time and pointed to patient expectation of a lingering future, as their only comfort, He implies that the immediate future was heavy. Habakkuk then renews his prayer for the years which had to intervene and · to pass away. *In the midst of the years,* before that *time appointed*[1], when His promise should have its full fulfillment, before those years should come to their close, he prays; *revive Thy work.* The years include all the long period of waiting for our Lord's first Coming before He came in the Flesh; and now for His second Coming and the *restitution of all things.* In this long period, at times God seems to be absent, as when our Lord was asleep in the boat, while the tempest was raging; at times He bids *the storm to cease and there is a great calm.* This, in those long intervals, when God seems to be absent, and to leave all things to time and chance, and love waxes cold, and graces seem rare, is the prayer of Habakkuk, of Prophets and Psalmists, of the Church, [2] *Return, we beseech Thee, O God of hosts, look down from heaven, behold and visit this vine.* [3] *O God, why hast Thou cast us off for ever? Why withdrawest Thou Thy hand, Thy right hand? For God is my king of old, working salvation in the midst of the earth.* [4] *Awake, awake, put on strength, Thou Arm of the Lord; awake, as in the ancient days, in the generations of old. Art thou not It which did smite Rahab, didst wound the dragon? Art thou not It which didst dry the sea, the waters of the great deep, which didst make the depths of the sea a way for the ransomed to pass over ?* [5] *Stir up Thy might and come, save us.* [6] *Renew our days, as of old.* So our Lord taught His Church to pray continually, whenever she prayed, *Thy kingdom come,* longing not for His final Coming only, but for the increase of His glory, and the greater dominion of His grace, and His enthronement in the hearts of men, even before its complete and final Coming. *In the midst of the years revive Thy work,* is the Church's continual cry.

In the midst of the years make known, lit. *Thou wilt make known: in wrath Thou wilt remember mercy;* and so (as we use the word *wilt*) the Prophet, at once, foretelleth, expresseth his faith, prayeth. God had made known His work and His power in the days of old. In times of trouble He seems *like a God who hideth Himself.* Now, he prays Him to *shine* forth and help; *make known* Thy work, before Thou fulfill it, to revive the

drooping hopes of man, and that all may see that *Thy word is truth.* *Make* Thyself *known* in Thy work, that, when the time cometh to [7] *make an end of sin* by the Death of Thy Son, Thy Awful Holiness, and the love wherewith Thou hast [8] *so loved the world,* may be the more known and adored.

In wrath Thou wilt remember mercy. So David prayed, [9] *Remember Thy tender-mercies and Thy loving-kindnesses; for they are from old.* *Thou wilt remember* that counsel for man's redemption which has been from the foundation of the world: for we seem in our own minds to be forgotten of God, when He delayeth to help us. God remembereth mercy [10] in anger, in that in this life He never chastens without purposes of mercy, and His Mercy ever softeneth His judgments. His Promise of mercy, that the Seed of the woman shall bruise the serpent's head, went before the sentence of displeasure, [11] *Dust thou art, and unto dust shalt thou return.* " [12] He reveals His wrath that He may scare us from sin and so may not inflict it;" and when at last He inflicteth it, He hath mercy on the remnant who flee to His Mercy, that we be not like Sodom and Gomorrah. [13] *While we were yet sinners,* and God was wroth, *Christ died for us,* and [14] *He saved us, not for works which we had done, but out of His great Mercy,* and took away sin, and restored us to life and incorruption.

God had already promised by Micah, [15] *According to the days of thy coming out of the land of Egypt, I will show him marvelous things.* Isaiah had often used the great events of that deliverance as the symbols of the future. So now Habakkuk, in one vast panorama, as it were, without distinction of time or series of events, exhibits the future in pictures of the past. In the description itself which follows, he now speaks in the past, now in the future; of which times the future might be a vivid present; and the past a prophetic past. As a key to the whole, he says, *God shall come,* indicating that all which follows, however spoken, was a part of that future. In no other way was it an answer to that prayer, *Revive Thy work.* To foretell future deliverances in plain words, had been a comfort; it would have promised a continuance of that work. The unity and revival of the work is expressed, in that the past is made, as it was, the image of the future. That future was to be wondrous, superhuman; else the past miracles had been no image of it. It was

---

[1] מוֹעֵד.
[3] Ib. lxxiv. 1, 11, 12.
[4] Is. li. 9, 10.
[6] Lam. v. 21.
[2] Ps. lxxx. 14.
[5] Ps. lxxx. 3.
[7] Dan. ix. 24.

[8] S. John iii. 16.
[10] S. Luke i. 54, 72.
[12] S. Jer.
[14] Tit. iii. 5.
[9] Ps. xxv. 6.
[11] Gen. iii. 19.
[13] Rom. v. 8.
[15] Mic. vii. 15.

3 God came from ‖ Te-
man, ^c and the Holy One

^c Deut. 33. 2. Judg. 5. 4. Ps. 68. 7.

from mount **Paran.** Selah.
His glory c o v e r e d the

---

to be no mere repetition of the future; and to mark this, the images are exhibited out of their historical order.

3. *God came* (lit. *shall come*) *from Teman. God shall come*, as He came of old, clothed with majesty and power; but it was not mere power. The centre of the whole picture is, as Micah and Isaiah had prophesied that it was to be, a new revelation; [1] *The law shall go forth from Zion, and the word of the Lord from Jerusalem.* [2] *I will give Thee for a covenant to the people* [Israel], *for a light of the Gentiles.* So now, speaking of the new work in store, Habakkuk renews the imagery in the Song of Moses[3], in Deborah's Song[4], and in David[5]; but there the manifestation of His glory is spoken of wholly in time past, and Mount Sinai is named. Habakkuk speaks of that coming as yet to be, and omits the express mention of Mount Sinai, which was the emblem of the law[6]. And so he directs us to another Lawgiver, Whom God should *raise up like unto Moses,* yet with a law

[1] Is. ii. 3. Mic. iv. 2.
[2] Is. xliv. 5.
[3] Deut. xxxiii. 2.
[4] Jud. v. 5.
[5] Ps. lxviii. 7.
[6] S. Cyr.
[7] Deut. xxxiii. 2.
[8] זָרַח is used in prose too, of the rising sun (with שֶׁמֶשׁ) Gen. xxxii. 32, Ex. xxii. 3, Jud. ix. 33, 2 Sam. xxiii. 4, 2 Kgs iii. 22, Jon. iv. 8.
[9] הוֹפִיעַ is used of the light of the sun Job iii. 4, x. 22; of the manifestation of God apart from any physical emblem Ps. l. 2, lxxx. 2, xciv. 1; and of God, favoring *the counsel of the wicked.* Job x. 3.
[10] *Mount* Paran is only mentioned in Deuteronomy and Habakkuk, and was probably taken by Habakkuk from Moses, who himself knew it. *The wilderness of Paran* must have lain W. or S. of the *wilderness of Zin,* which formed the Southern border of Judah (Nu. xiii. 21. Josh. xv. 1.). The history of Ishmael implies that part of it lay toward Egypt (Gen. xii. 21.); that of *Hadad the Edomite,* shews that it lay between Midian and Egypt (1 Kgs xi. 18); but there being, (as far as it is ascertained), no natural boundary between it and the wilderness of Zin, the name Paran is apparently used in a wider sense as comprehending the desert of Zin, whence Kadesh is placed both in Paran (Nu. xiii. 26.) and more commonly in Zin (Nu. xx. 1, xxvii. 14, xxxiii. 36, 37, xxxiv. 4, Josh. xv. 3.), and the wilderness near it is also called *the wilderness of Kadesh* (Ps. xxix. 8.). The name of *the wilderness of Zin* does not occur after Joshua; and that of Paran may have extended over the whole desert cretaceous plateau up to the borders of Edom, now called Badiet-et-Tih, the "wilderness of the wanderings," whose Western extremity lies North of the crescent-shaped Jebel-et-Tih, which separates it from the lower part of the peninsula. (See Map in Sinaitic survey.) Hence Nabal is related to have fed his flocks in Paran (1 Sam. xxv. 5.) and Eilparan "the terebinth of Paran," (Gen. xiv. 6.) *by the wilderness,* the bound of the inroad of Chedorlaomer, may have had its name from the wilderness. *Mount* Paran might be anywhere connected with this wilderness on the West. "Mount Serbal is perhaps the most striking mountain in the peninsula; it rises abruptly to a height of more than 4000 feet above the valleys at its base, and its summit, a sharp ridge about three miles

of life, and tells how He Who spake the law, God, shall come in likeness of our flesh.
And the Holy One from Mount Paran. In the earliest passage three places are mentioned, in which or from which the glory of God was manifested; with this difference however, that it is said, [7] *The Lord came from Sinai,* but His glory *arose,* as we should say *dawned* [8] *unto them from Seir,* and *flashed forth* [9] from Mount Paran [10]. Seir and Mount Paran are joined together by the symbol of the light which *dawned* or *shone forth* from them. In the second passage, the Song of Deborah, *Seir* and *the field of Edom* are the place whence God came forth; *Sinai melted* [11] at His presence. In the 68th Psalm the mention of Edom is dropped; and the march through the wilderness under the leading of God, is alone mentioned, together with the shaking of Sinai. In Habakkuk, the contrast is the same as in Moses; only *Teman* stands in place of *Seir* [12]. *Teman* and *Mount Paran* are named probably, as the two opposed

long, is broken into a series of peaks varying little in altitude, but rivaling each other in the beauty and grandeur of their outline. It is three miles from Wady Feiran;" "in one or two points from which its highest peak is visible." Ordnance Survey of Peninsula of Sinai pp. 143, 144. "When seen from a distance Serbal presents a boldness of outline and an appearance of massive isolation which entitled it to rank as one of the grandest and most distinctive features of the peninsula." (Palmer's desert of the Exodus p. 169.) What is now called Jebel Feiran is too low to be taken into account. It is but an eminence, rising on one side 810 feet above the Wady Feiran; on the other side, 795 feet, and above the sea 2800; so that in the same neighborhood Mount Serbal is above twice its height, 6443 feet above the sea at its highest peak. (Sinaitic Survey, Mount Serbal, sections.) This mountain has this advantage, that it is connected with Wady Feiran or Paran, through which Moses led Israel to Mount Sinai. The name is remarkable, as having been given by Israel, since it has a Hebrew etymology, "the beautiful " or "the leafy," and all travelers praise the richness of the valley, even amid the decay of fertility consequent on neglect. It has no Arabic etymology. (See Palmer, l. c. p. 20.) S. Jerome says, from his Hebrew teacher apparently, "Pharan is a place near to Mount Sinai." ad loc.
The striking mountain of Edom had its own name Hor, which in the eleven places in which it is named in the Pentateuch is always called הֹר הָהָר "Hor, the mountain." Nu. xx. 22, 23, 25, 27. xxi. 4. xxxiii. 37, 38, 41. xxxiv. 7, 8. De. xxxii. 19. Prof. Palmer having shewn Ain Gadis to be Kadesh (l. c. c. iv. p. 373. sqq.) says, "To one encamped in the wilderness of Kadesh, i. e. in the open plain into which Wady Gadis debouches, Jebel Magrah would be always the most conspicuous object in the scene." (Ib. p. 510.) This is a plateau, 70 miles long and 40–50 miles broad, "projecting into the Tih, much as the Tih projects into Sinai." Ib. p. 288, 9.
[11] Jud. v. 4, 5.
[12] As it stands connected with Edom, Ob. 9. Jer. lix. 7, 20, 21. with Dedan also, Jer. xlix. 8, Ezek. xxv. 13.

heavens, and the earth || was full of his praise.

boundaries of the journeyings of Israel through the desert. They came to Mount Sinai through the valley, now called Wady Feiran [1] or Paran; Edom was the bound of their wanderings to their promised land [2]. God Who guided, fed, protected them from the beginning, led them to the end. Between *Paran* also and Edom or *Teman* was the gift of the Spirit to the seventy, which was the shadow of the day of Pentecost; there, was the brazen serpent lifted up, the picture of the healing of the Cross [3]. *If* Mount Paran *be* near Kadesh, then Moses in the opening of his song describes the glory of God as manifested from that first revelation of His law on Mount Sinai; then in that long period of Israel's waiting there to its final departure for the promised land, when Mount Hor was consecrated and God's awful Holiness declared in the death of Aaron.

He Who *shall come*, is God [4], the *Holy One* (a proper Name of God [5]). Perfect in Holiness, as God, the Son of God, and as Man also all-holy, with a human will, always exactly accompanying the Divine Will, which was

"the passion of His Heart"
Those Three-and-thirty years."

On this there follows a pause denoted by Selah [6], (which occurs thrice according to the mystery of that number,) that the soul may dwell on the greatness of the majesty and mercy of God.

Selah. There is no doubt as to the general purport of the word, that it is a musical direction, that there should be a pause, the music probably continuing alone, while the mind rested on the thought, which had just

been presented to it; our "interlude [7]." It is always placed at some pause of thought, even when not at the end of a strophe, or, as twice in this hymn [8], at the end of the verse. S. Gregory of Nyssa modifies this thought, supposing "Selah" to express a pause made by the writer, that "[9] while the psalmody, with which David's prophesying was accompanied, went on in its course, another illumining of the Holy Spirit, and an addition to the gift according to knowledge, came for the benefit of those who received the prophecy, he, holding in his verse, gave time for his mind to receive the knowledge of the thought, which took place in him from the Divine illumining. He defines it to be "a sudden silence in the midst of the Psalmody for the reception of the illumining."

His Glory covered the heavens, and the earth was full of His praise. This is plainly no created glory, but anticipates the Angelic Hymn, [10] *Glory to God in the highest, and on earth peace, good-will toward men,* or, as the Seraphim sing first, glory to God in Heaven, [11] *Holy Holy Holy is the Lord God of Sabaoth,* and then, *the whole earth is full of His glory;* and Uncreated Wisdom saith, [12] *I alone compassed the circuit of Heaven, and walked in the bottom of the deep.* Nor are they our material heavens, much less this lowest heaven over our earth, nor is *His glory* any lightning at Mount Sinai, but the boundless Majesty [13] of God, which rules, encompasses, fills, penetrates the orbs of heaven and all its inhabitants, and yet is not enclosed nor bounded thereby. Those who are made as the heavens by the indwelling of God He spiritually *covers*, filling [14] them with the light of glory and splendor of grace and brightness of

---

[1] Sinaitic Survey c. 5. 149–155.
[2] Nu. xx. 14–20. Deut. ii.   [3] Rib.
[4] The sing. אֱלוֹהַּ occurs 41 times in the book of Job; else only 16 times in all the O. T., and 8 times only of the true God, (twice in Moses' song Deut. xxxii. 15, 17; in a Psalm of David, Ps. cxxxix. 19, of Asaph, l. 22, Anon. Ps. cxiv. 7; in Proverbs xxx. 5, here, and in Nehemiah's prayer, (in which there are so many reminiscences from the Pentateuch. See in "Daniel the Prophet" pp. 356, 357.) Else it is used of the Godhead (*Who is God except, &c.* in David Ps. xviii. 32, *is there any God besides Me?* Is. xliv. 8); "any God" including the true God Dan. xi. 3. And five times it is used of a false god; in Hab. i. 11; three times in Dan. xi. 38, 39; and by Sennacherib 2 Chr. xxxii. 15. There is then no basis of induction as to its occurring in later Hebrew and poetic books; since its use is mostly a peculiarity of the book of Job, the other 16 cases are sporadic and in no one sense.
[5] Whence in the Hebrew, though the subject, it has no article, as in Is. xl. 25, and Job vi. 11.
[6] It occurs here only besides the Psalms. It occurs thrice in Ps. iii. xxxii. lxvi. lxviii.
[7] διάψαλμα in Lxx. Theod. Symm. Syr.
[8] In Ps. lv. 20. lvii. 4. Hab. iii. 3, 9, alone, it is not

at the end of the verse. Eight Psalms only, out of 39 Psalms which have it, have not the title "For the chief musician," Ps. 32, 48, 56, 82, 83, 87, 89, 143.

5 of these are מִזְמוֹר; 2, מַשְׂכִּיל (32 and 89), one without any inscription (48). The most probable etymology seems to be סֶלַה,=סָלַל and so our "alto;" whether the ה be added to סַל or it be an imperative with paragogic ה like אֲשִׁיעָה Ps. cxix. 117, נִשְׁתַּעֲיָה Is. xli. 23, although there is no extant instance of this imperative. There is equally no instance of the form from סָלַל (as Ewald Ps. i. 179, Lehrb. § 216. c. p. 544) since נָתָן 1 Kgs ii. 40, is only a Var. Read. for the received נָתַה which is borne out by נָתַן Jos. xix. 13.

[9] Tract 2 in Ps. Inscr. &c. T. i. p. 329.
[10] S. Luke ii. 14.   [11] Is. vi. 3.   [12] Ecclus. xxiv. 5.
[13] דֹּד is used of the Divine Majesty Job xxxvii. 22. Ps. viii. 2. xx. 30. with הָדָר Ps. xcvi. 6, (1 Chr. xvi. 27,) civ. 1, cxi. 3, cxlv. 5, cxlviii. 11; ironically to man, as impossible for him, Job xl. 10. It is used as imparted to the Messiah Ps. xxi. 6, or being in Him, Ps. xlv. 4.   [14] Dion.

Before
C H R I S T
cir. 626.

4 And *his* brightness || was as the light; he had

Before
C H R I S T
cir. 626.

wisdom, as it saith, *Is there any number of His armies, and upon whom doth not His light arise* [1] *? and so the earth was full of His praise,* i. e. the Church militant spread throughout the world, as in the Psalm, [2] *The Lord's name is praised from the rising up of the sun unto the going down of the same,* and, [3] *O Lord, our Lord, how excellent is Thy name in all the earth. Who hast set Thy glory above the heavens.*

4. *And His Brightness,* that wherein God dwelleth, [4] *the brightness of the Lord's glory,* before which darkness fleeth [5], *was as the light,* or as the sun. Out of the midst of the darkness, wherewith God, as it were, [6] hid Himself, the Brightness of the *inapproachable Light* wherein He *dwelleth,* gleams forth [7], bright as the brightest *light* gathered into one, which man knows of and whereon he cannot gaze. So amid the darkness of the humiliation of His Presence in the flesh, [8] *we beheld His Glory, the Glory as of the Only-Begotten of the Father;* and [9] *the people that walked in darkness see a great light,* "not dim [10] nor weak, nor shadowed, like that of Moses, but pure unimaginable light of the knowledge of God." The Brightness too of His Flesh was like the light of the Godhead on Mount Tabor ; for the Godhead flashed through. " [11] As often as He did His marvelous works, He put forth His *Brightness* (tempered for His creatures, since they could not approach the depth of His light, yet) *as light* to enlighten men to know Him. Yet the Brightness issues from the Light, co-existing with it, and in it, while issuing from it. And so the words aptly express, how He Who is the

[12] *Brightness of the Father's Glory and the express Image of His Person,* the [13] *Brightness of the Eternal Light, the unspotted mirror of the Power of God, and the Image of His Goodness,* is as the Light from Whom He is, " [14] Light of Light," Equal to the Father by Whom He was Begotten; as S. John says, [15] *That was the true Light, which lighteneth every man that cometh into the world.* As He prayeth, [16] *Glorify Thou Me with Thine Own Self with the Glory Which I had with Thee before the world was.*

He had horns coming out of His Hand. " [17] Horns are everywhere in Holy Scripture the emblem of strength." It may be, that here "rays" are likened to horns, as the face of Moses is said, with the same image, to have "sent forth rays [18] " after he had long been in the presence of God. So it may be a mingled image of the Glory and might ; Light, which was also might. But "horns," though they may be a symbol of "light," are not of "lightning ;" and the Hand of God is used as an emblem of His Power, His protection, His bounty, His constraining force on His prophets. It is nowhere used of the side or sides [19]. We have two images combined here ; "horns" which in every other place in which they are used as a metaphor, is an emblem of power ; and "from the hand of" which, wherever it is used of a person, means that the thing spoken of had been in his hand or power really or virtually [20]. Both then combine in the meaning that the might came forth from the directing agency of God Who wielded it.

[1] Job xxv. 3. [2] Ps. cxii. 3. [3] Ib. viii. 1.
[4] Ezek. x. 4. [5] Ps. xviii. 12.
[6] Ex. xix. 9, 16. xx. 21. [7] Ib. xxiv. 10.
[8] S. John i. 14. [9] Is. ix. 2. [10] Theoph.
[11] Rup. [12] Heb. i. 3. [13] Wisd. vii. 25.
[14] Nicene Creed. [15] S. John i. 9.
[16] Ib. xvii. 5. [17] S. Jer. Dion.
[18] קֶרֶן Ex. xxxiv. 29. 30. 35. which is compared by

Kim. Rashi, A. E. Abulw. Abarb. Tanch. Abendana. This is illustrated further by the use of " horns " as a hieroglyphic for the sun, Champollion Grammar p. 359. in Ges. and קַרְנְתָא "horns" of the sun, Buxt. (not in Levy). The title of Ps. xxii. עַל אַיֶּלֶת הַשַּׁחַר "according to the hind of the morning," may bear upon it, since אַיַלְתָא דְשַׁחרא in the Jerus. Talm. (originally quoted by Lightfoot, Horæ Hebr. on S. Mark xvi. 2) is used of the first rays of light, which usher in the dawn, the rays appearing solid like horns. In Arab. too عَزَالَة is a name of the sun, though Arab. authorities differ about its use, and عَزَالَة الصَّحَا is the "sun at the time called صَحَا," some part of the clear day. And Hariri uses "the horn of the gazelle" قَرْنُ الْعَزَالَة (as explained by De Sacy) of those

same first rays. But Kim. gives as the meanings of אֵשׁ הֹשׁ hind (literally) or day-star, or sunrise.
[19] As even Del. and Keil. יָד is used of the side of the river Ex. ii. 5, and with the prepositions אֶל, עַד, בְּעַד (See Ges.) but with מִן, once only *from the side of the country* Nu. xxiv. 4; on which, see note 20. end.
[20] מִיַד occurs in the O. T. with the gen. of the noun or pronoun, 197 times; in the plural 5 times. Of these, the greatest number are with verbs of *delivering,* הִצִּיל, 71; הֹשִׁיעַ, 18; *redeem,* פָּדָה, 3, גָּאל, 3; *brought forth,* הֹוצִיא, 1; *rescued,* פָּרַק, 1; *guard,* שָׁמַר, 2; *escape,* מִלַּט, 9, פָּלַט, 1; *flee,* בָּרַח, 1; לָקַח, *took by force,* 11; *took, received,* 22; *took unawares from,* גָּנַל, 2; *receive and offer,* הִקְרִיב, 1; *consecrate from,* הִקְדִּישׁ, 1; *sprinkled* (blood), זָרָה 2; *bought,* קָנָה, 7; *accept,* רָצָה, 2; *give,* נָתַן, 1; *collect,* אָסַף, 1; *eat from,* אָכַל 1; בָּרָה, 2; *drank,* שָׁתָה 1; *seek,* בָּקַשׁ, 7; *require of,* דָּרַשׁ, 5; *judged and avenged,* שָׁפַט, 3; *avenged,* נָקַם, 1; *rend,* קָרַע, 3; *cause to fall from,* הִפִּיל, 2; *strike from,* הִכָּה, 2; *cut off from,*

14

‖ horns *coming* out of his hand: and there

‖ Or, *bright beams out of his side.*

was the hiding of his power.

When then did light or might, which lay, as it were, before in the Hand of God, go forth from it? For *the Hand of God* is always symbolic of His might, whether put forth, or for the time laid up in it. The form of the words remarkably corresponds to those of Moses, in the preface to the blessing on the tribes, which Habakkuk had in mind, [1] *From His right hand was a fiery law for them,* and S. Paul says that the glory of Moses' face which he received from the Presence of God, was a symbol of the glory of the law. [2] *The ministration of death written and engraven on stone was glorious, so that the children of Israel could not steadfastly behold the face of Moses for the glory of his countenance.* The law, being given by God, had a majesty of its own. The Psalms bear witness to its power in converting, enwisening, rejoicing, enlightening the soul [3]. They in whose heart it was, none of their steps slided [4]. The whole 119th Psalm is one varied testimony of its greatness and its power. It was a guide on the way; it was a schoolmaster unto Christ [5], by Whom it was fulfilled. But itself bare witness of the greater glory which should come forth from the Hand of God. [6] *If that which is done away were glorious, much more that which remaineth is glorious.* " [7] The horn signifieth power, when it is spoken of God the Father exhibiting to us God the Son : [8] *He hath raised up a horn of salvation for us,* and again, [9] *His horn shall be exalted in honor.* For all things which were marvelously done were glorious. The Only-Begotten came then in our form, and, in regard to the Flesh and the Manhood, enduring the appearance of our weakness, but, as God, invisible in might and easily subduing whom He willed."

And what has been the weapon of His warfare, whereby He has subdued the might of Satan and the hearts of men, but *the horns* of His Cross, whereto His Sacred Hands were once fastened by the sharp nails, where was the *hiding of His Power,* when His Almightiness lay hid in His Passion [10], and He was [11] *a worm and no man; a reproach of men and the despised of the people?* Now it is the

Sceptre laid upon His Shoulder [12], the ensign and trophy of His rule, the Rod of His Strength [13], terrible to devils, salvation to man. In it lay His might, although concealed, as He said, [14] *I, if I be lifted up from the earth, will draw all men unto Me.* His Might was lodged there, although hidden. It was *the hiding-place of His power.* The Cross was [15] *to the Jews a stumbling-block, and unto the Greeks foolishness; but unto them which are called, both Jews and Greeks, Christ Crucified was the Power of God and the Wisdom of God.* Through the Cross was [16] *all power given to Him both in Heaven and earth.* [17] *There was given Him dominion and glory and a kingdom, that all people, nations, and languages should serve Him.* From Him shall go forth all power in earth; by His Hands shall be given the vacant thrones in Heaven, as He saith, [18] *To him that overcometh will I grant to sit with Me in My Throne, even as I also overcame and am set down with My Father in His Throne. There* too *was the hiding of His Power,* in that there, in His Cross, is our shelter [19], and in His pierced Side our hiding-place, where we may take refuge from Satan and our sins ; for therein is Power. [20] *Neither shall any pluck them out of My Hand.* Light and darkness ever meet in God. His inapproachable light is darkness to eyes which would gaze on it. [21] *He covereth Himself with Light as with a garment.* His light is the very veil which hideth Him. His Light is darkness to those who pry into Him and His Nature; His darkness is light to those who by faith behold Him. He *emptied Himself* [22] and hid Himself ; He hid the power of His Godhead in the weakness of the Manhood, and so [23] *He Who commanded the light to shine out of darkness, hath shined in our hearts, to give the light of the knowledge of the glory of God, in the Face of Jesus Christ.* " [24] In the Cross was for a while His might hidden, when He said to His Father, [25] *My soul is exceeding sorrowful even unto death, and, Father, if it be possible, let this cup pass from Me,* and on the Cross itself, [26] *Father, into Thy Hands I commend My Spirit.*"

shew the insignia of His kingdom, by which horns, pushing and thrusting the invisible and opposing powers, He drove them away." Euseb. Dem. Evang. vi. 15. Add S. Cyprian Test. ad Quirin. ii. 21. p. 57. Oxf. Tr. "The horns in His Hands, what are they, but the trophy of the Cross?" S. Aug. de Civ. Dei xviii. 32.　[15] 1 Cor. i. 23, 24.　[16] S. Matt. xxviii. 18.
[17] Dan. vii. 14.　　　　　　　[18] Rev. iii. 21.
[19] As in the proper names, Ezr. ii. 61. *Habaiah* "whom God hideth i. e., protecteth ;" *Yehubbah* "hidden, protected." 1 Chron. vii. 34. Comp. Is. xxvi. 20.　[20] S. John x. 28.　[21] Ps. civ. 3.
[22] Phil. ii. 8.　　[23] 2 Cor. iv. 6.　　[24] S. Jer.
[25] S. Matt. xxvi. 38, 39.　[26] S. Luke xxiii. 13.

הַכְרִית, 1; נָגוֹר, 1; cast, שָׁלַךְ; *reproach from,* חֵרְפָּתִי; *by writing from,* בִּכְחֹב, 1; *letters from,* אַגֶּרֶת, 1; *officers appointed by* פְּקִידִים, 1. *strengthened*

from the hands of God, 1. The verb *was,* הָיָה, is expressed once; it lies in the sentence thrice ; once only it means *from the side of a country,* Nu. xxiv. 4. in which there can be no ambiguity.
[1] Deut. xxxiii. 2.　[2] 2 Cor. iii. 7.　[3] Ps. xix. 8.
[4] Ib. xxxvii. 31.　[5] Gal. iii. 24.　[6] 2 Cor. iii. 11.
[7] S. Cyr.　　[8] S. Luke ii. 69.　[9] Ps. cxi. 9.
[10] Is. liii. 3.　　[11] Ps. xxii. 6.　[12] Is. ix. 6.
[13] S. John xii. 32.
[14] Ps. cx. 2. "The words, Horns are in His Hands,

Before
C H R I S T
cir. 626.

d Nah. 1. 3.
|| Or, *burning
diseases,*
Deut. 32. 24.
o Ps. 18. 8.

5 ^d Before him went the pestilence, and || ^e burning coals went forth at his feet.

6 He stood and measured the earth: he beheld, and drove asunder the nations; ^f and the ^g everlast-

Before
C H R I S T
cir. 626.

f Nah. 1. 5.
g Gen. 49. 26.

---

5. *Before Him went* [*goeth*] *the pestilence;* then to consume His enemies. ¹ *I will send My fear before thee, and will destroy all the people, to whom thou shalt come,* and the lightnings are a token that ² *they which hate Him, flee before Him, and the wicked perish at the Presence of God.* So, on His Ascension, Herod and Pilate were smitten by Him, and Elymas and Simon Magus before His Apostles, and whatsoever hath lifted itself up against Him hath perished, and Antichrist shall perish ³ *at the breath of His mouth,* and all the ungodly in the Day of Judgment.

And burning coals (rather, as E. M., *burning fever* ⁴) *went forth at His Feet,* i. e., followed Him. Messengers of death went as it were before Him, as the front of His army, and the rear thereof was other forms of death ⁵. Death and destruction of all sorts are a great army at His command, going before Him as heralds of His Coming, (such as are judgments in this world) or attendants upon Him, at the Judgment when He appeareth ⁶ in His Kingdom, when ⁷ *they shall gather out of His Kingdom all things that offend, and them which do iniquity, and shall cast them into a furnace of fire.*

6. *He stood* ⁸, *and measured* ⁹ *the earth.* Joshua, after he had conquered the land, meted it out and divided it among the people. He Who should come, should measure out the earth in its length and breadth, that *earth* which His glory *filleth. He stood,* as S. Stephen saw Him, ¹⁰ *standing at the Right Hand of God;* and Isaiah saith, ¹¹ *The Lord standeth up to plead, and standeth to judge the people.* He had not need to go forth, but, in the abode of His glory, *He stood and* beheld and with His Eye *measured the earth,* as His own, whereas, before the Cross, it lay under ¹² *the Prince of this world,* and he had said, ¹³ *it is delivered unto me, and unto whomsoever I will, I give it. He measureth* it, and gave it to His Apostles, ¹⁴ *All power is given unto Me in heaven*

and in earth. Go ye into all the world, and preach the Gospel to every creature, and, ¹⁵ *their sound is gone out into all lands, and their words into the ends of the world.* He measureth it also, surveying and weighing all who dwell therein, their persons, qualities, deeds, good or bad, to requite them, as *Judge of quick and dead;* as David cast down Moab and measured them with a line, ¹⁶ *to put to death and to keep alive.*

He beheld, and drove asunder the nations, or, *made the nations to tremble* ¹⁷. When Israel came out of Egypt and God divided the Red sea before them, they sang, ¹⁸ *The people shall hear and be afraid; terror shall take hold of the inhabitants of Palestina; the mighty men of Moab, trembling shall take hold of them; all the inhabitants of Canaan shall melt away; fear and dread shall fall on them; by the greatness of Thy power they shall be still as a stone.* Fear and awe were to be renewed. All nearness of God brings terror to sinful man. When the news came through the wise men, that they had ¹⁹ *seen in the East the star of Him* Who was *born, King of the Jews,* not *Herod the King* only *was troubled,* but *all Jerusalem with him.* Pilate ²⁰ *was afraid* when he condemned Him: the High Priests wondered *whereunto this should grow,* and expostulated, ²¹ *ye have filled Jerusalem with your doctrine, and intend to bring this Man's blood upon us.* Heathendom was as a beleaguered city, mastered by an ubiquitous Presence, which they knew not how to meet. "²² The state is beset: the Christians are in their fields, in their forts, in their islands. Every sex, age, condition, and now even rank is going over to this sect." The fierceness of the persecutions was the measure of their fear. They put forth all human might to stamp out the spark, lest their gods, and the greatness of the empire which they ascribed to their gods, should fall before this unknown power.

And the everlasting mountains were scattered ;

out by Hithpo. "extended himself," 1 Kgs xvii. 21. By an interchange of dentals מוֹד might be = מוֹט, and so Ch. LXX. but in no other case do the two forms coexist in Hebrew.
¹¹ Is. iii. 13.   ¹² 1 Cor. ii. 5.   ¹³ S. Luke iv. 6.
¹⁴ S. Matt. xxviii. 18. S. Mark xvi. 15.
¹⁵ Ps. xix. 4.   ¹⁶ 2 Sam. viii. 2.
¹⁷ נָתַר being used of outward leaping of the locust, Lev. xi. 12, נָתַר, of the inward leaping of the heart, Job xxxvii. 1. either seems admissible. The inward terror was the forerunner and often the instrument of the outward-dispersion.
¹⁸ Ex. xv. 15, 16.   ¹⁹ S. Matt. ii. 1-3.
²⁰ S. John xix. 8.   ²¹ Acts v. 24, 28.
²² Tertull. Apol. init. p. 2. Oxf. Tr.

¹ Ex. xxiii. 27.   ² Ps. lxviii. 1. 2.   ³ Ib. xi. 4.
⁴ De. xxxii. 2. (where also it is sing., as only beside in בְּנֵי רֶשֶׁף Job v. 7.) So A. E. "Burning coals" is from Kim. Tanch. gives as different opinions "sparks" or "arrows" or "pestilence;" but the meanings "sparks, arrows," are ascribed only to the plur. Ps. lxxvi. 4. lxxxviii. 48. Cant. viii. 6. The central meaning is probably "burning heat."
⁵ "Before Him is sent the angel of death and His word goeth forth, a flame of fire." Jon.
⁶ 2 Tim. vi. 1.   ⁷ S. Matt. xiii. 51, 42.
⁸ It is "a metaphor of his giving victory to Israel." Tanch.
⁹ So Kim. A. E. Rashi. Tanch. Vulg. It is borne

ing mountains were scattered, the perpetual hills did bow: his ways *are* everlasting.

7 I saw the tents of || Cushan || i n affliction : *and* the curtains of the land of Midian did tremble.

|| Or, *Ethiopia.*
|| Or, *under afflic-tion,* or, *vanity.*

the perpetual hills did bow; all power, great or small, gave way before Him. All which withstood was scattered asunder, all which in pride lifted itself up was brought low, although before the coming of the Saviour it had ever gone with neck erect, and none could humble its pride. There is something so marvelous about those ancient mountains. There they stood before man was on the earth; they are so solid, man so slight; they have survived so many generations of man; they will long survive us; they seem as if they would stand forever; the apter symbol how nothing should stand before the might of God. To the greater pride the heavier lot is assigned; the mountains lifted on high above the earth and, as it were, looking down upon it, are scattered or dispersed, as when a stone flieth in pieces under the stroke of the hammer. The "hills" are bowed down only; and this may be the pride of man humbled under the yoke of Christ.

His Ways are Everlasting. "Everlasting" is set over against "everlasting." The "everlasting" of the creature, that which had been as long as creation had been, co-existing with its whole duration, its most enduring parts, are as things past and gone; *the everlasting mountains, the hills of eternity,* have been scattered in pieces and bowed, and are no more. Over against these stands the ever-present eternity of God. *His ways are everlasting,* ordered everlastingly, existing everlastingly in the Divine Mind, and, when in act among us, without change in Him. The prophet blends in these great words, things seemingly contrary, *ways* which imply progress, *eternity* which is unchangeable. "[1] God ever worketh, and ever resteth; unchangeable, yet changing all; He changeth His works, His purpose unchanged." "[2] For Thou art Most High, and art not changed, neither in Thee doth to-day come to a close; yet in Thee it doth come to a close; because all such things also are in Thee. For they had no way to pass away, unless Thou heldest them together. And since *Thy years fail not,* Thy years are one To-day. How many of our's and our fathers' years have flowed away through Thy to-day; and from it received the measure and the mould of such being as they had; and still others shall flow away, and so receive the mould of their degree of

being. But Thou art still the Same; and all things of to-morrow, and all beyond, and all of yesterday, and all behind it, Thou wilt do in this to-day, Thou hast done in this to-day."

To these His goings, a highway is made by the breaking down of all which exalted itself, as Isaiah had said,[3] *The loftiness of man shall be bowed down, and the haughtiness of men shall be made low, and the Lord Alone shall be exalted in that day;* and,[4] *The voice of him that crieth in the wilderness, Prepare ye the way of the Lord, make straight in the desert a highway for our God. Every valley shall be exalted, and every mountain and hill shall be made low.*

"[5] The Everlasting ways of the Everlasting God are Mercy and Truth,—by these Ways are the hills of the world and the proud demons, the princes of the darkness of this world, bowed down, who knew not the way of mercy and truth nor remembered Its paths. What hath he to do with truth, who is a liar and the father of it, and of whom it is written, *he abode not in the Truth?* But how far he is from Mercy, our misery witnesseth, inflicted on us by him. When was he ever merciful, who was *a murderer from the beginning?*—So then those swelling hills were bowed down from the Everlasting Ways, when through their own crookedness they sunk away from the straight ways of the Lord, and became not so much ways as precipices. How much more prudently and wisely are other hills bowed down and humbled by these ways to salvation! For they were not bowed from them, as parting from their straightness, but the Everlasting Ways themselves bowed down. May we not now see the hills of the world bowed down, when those who are high and mighty with devoted submission bow themselves before the Lord, and worship at His Feet? Are they not bowed down, when from their own destructive loftiness of vanity and cruelty, they are turned to the humble way of mercy and truth?"

7. *I saw* (in prophetic vision [6]), *the tents of Cushan in* (lit. *under*) *affliction.* On the Coming of the Lord there follows the visitation of those alien from Him [7]. Cushan-Rishathaim was the first, whose ambition God overruled to chasten His people [8]. It has been remarked [9], that as *king of Aram-Naha-*

[1] S. Aug. Conf. i. 4 p. 3. Oxf. Tr.
[2] Ib. 10. p. 6.   [3] Is. ii. 17.   [4] Ib. xl. 3.
[5] S. Bern. in Ps. Qui habitat. Serm. xi. 8.
[6] 1 Kgs xxii. 17.

[7] As in Joel ii. iii. Mic. iv. 1-10 and iv. 11. v. 1. v. 2. &c. v. 15.   [8] Jud. iii. 8-10.
[9] R. S. Poole in Smith's Bible Dict., Art. Cushan. Often as Cush or Ethiopia is mentioned in the Old

8 Was the LORD displeased against the rivers? *was* thine anger against the rivers? *was* thy wrath

against the sea, ʰ that thou didst ride upon thine horses *and* ‖ thy chariots of salvation?

Before
CHRIST
cir. 626.

ʰ Deut. 33. 26, 27.
Ps. 68. 4.
& 104. 3.
ver. 15.

‖ Or, *thy chariots* were *salvation?*

---

raim or North Mesopotamia, he was probably sovereign of the Aram, from which Balak king of Moab, allied with Midian, sent for Balaam to curse Israel. *Midian* was the last enemy who, at the very entrance of the promised land, seduced God's people into idolatry and foul sin and lusts. Midian became then the object of the wrath of God [1]. They were also among the early oppressors of Israel, leaving [2] *no sustenance for Israel, neither sheep nor ox nor ass,* driving them for refuge to dwell in *the dens and the mountains, caves and fastnesses,* consuming the produce of their land *like locusts,* so that he whom God raised up as their subduer, was *threshing* even *in a wine-press to hide it from* them. Both the kingdom of Aram-Naharaim and Midian disappear from history after those great defeats. Midian, beside its princes, [3] lost, by mutual slaughter, *one hundred and twenty thousand men who drew sword.* It left its name as a proverb for the utter destruction of those who sought to exterminate the people of God. [4] *Do unto them as unto the Midianites; —make them and their princes like Oreb and Zeeb; all their princes as Zebah and as Zalmunnah, who said, let us take to ourselves the houses of God in possession.* It was an exterminating warfare, which rolled back on those who waged it. So Isaiah sums up an utter breaking-off of the yoke and the rod of the oppressor, as being [5] *as in the day of Midian.* The same word, *aven,* is nothingness, iniquity, and the fruit of iniquity, *trouble* [6], (since iniquity is emptiness and opposed to that which *is,* God and His Goodness, and ends in sorrow) ; so then Cushan is seen as lying as all sinners do, *weighed down* by and *under* what is very "emptiness." *Tents* and *curtains* are emblems of what shall pass away, under which the wicked shelter themselves from the troubles of this present life, as from heat and rain, "but which [7] in themselves decay, and are consumed by fire." *The curtains of*

Testament, and in twelve of the sacred writers, Historians, Psalmists, Prophets; from Genesis to Esther (Moses, Job, Chronicles, Esther, David) (Ps. lxviii.), sons of Corah (Ps. lxxxvii.), Amos, Nahum, Zephaniah, Jeremiah, Ezekiel, and Ethiopians by Daniel, it is uniformly used not Cushan. Cush also is retained in Ch. and Syr. and was the name in use in the time of Josephus (Ant. i. 62.) One cannot then doubt, that Jon. and the Talmud (Sanh. 105 in Delitzsch) were right in regarding Cushan as designating him who is so called in the Holy Scriptures, not Ethiopia, which is never so called. Kim., Rashi, A. E., Abarb. follow the Targum. Only Tanchum, identifying the two clauses, says "Cushan is one of the names of Midian or one of its tribes, and it is also called Cush," Zipporah being identified

Midian tremble. The prophet uses the present to shew that he was not speaking of any mere past terror, but of that terror, which should still seize those opposed to God. The word "wrath" "*rogez*" echoes through the hymn [8] ; here the wicked tremble, "*yirgezu,*" under it, to perish; afterward the Prophet [9], to live.

8. *Was the Lord displeased against the rivers?* The Prophet asks the question thrice, as to the two miracles of the dividing of the Red Sea and the river Jordan, thereby the more earnestly declaring, that God meant somewhat by these acts and beyond them. He asks, as Daniel [10] and Zechariah [11] asked, what was the truth of the things which they saw. God's dealings with His former people were as much ensamples of what should be with us [12], as the visions shewn to the prophets. Hereafter too, there shall be [13] *signs in the sun, and in the moon, and in the stars ; and upon the earth distress of nations, with perplexity, the sea and the waves roaring ;* there shall be deepening plagues upon the sea and the rivers and fountains of waters ; and *every living soul in the sea shall die* [14]. But God's purpose therein aforetime was not as to the sea or the rivers, but for the salvation of His elect ; so shall it be to the end. Mighty as may be the *mighty waves of the sea* which lift themselves up against the Lord, *mightier on high is the Lord* [15]. " [16] As Thou didst dry up the Jordan and the Red sea, fighting for us ; for Thou wert not wroth with the rivers or the sea, nor could things without sense offend Thee; so now mounting Thy chariots, and taking Thy bow, Thou wilt give salvation to Thy people ; and the oaths which Thou swarest to our fathers and the tribes, Thou wilt fulfil for ever."

Thou didst ride upon Thy horses, as though God set His army, [17] *the Hosts which do His pleasure,* against the armies of earth, as the Prophet's servant had his eyes opened to see,

with Moses' Cushite wife. Nu. xii. 1. Even Ewald says, "The people, כושי, which can neither according to language nor context stand for כוש :" though he guesses it to be a little people near Midian. ad loc.
[1] Nu. xxv. 17.   [2] Jud. vi. 4. 11.
[3] Ib. viii. 10.   [4] Ps. lxxxiii. 9, 11, 12.
[5] Is. ix. 4.
[6] Job v. 6. xxvi. 14; Jer. iv. 15. Hos. ix. 4. not in Ps. lv. 4. nor (as Ges.) in Job iv. 8. Ps. xxii. 8. Is. lix. 4.
[7] S. Greg. Mor. viii. 9.   [8] ver. 2.   [9] v. 16.
[10] vii. 16.   [11] c. 1.   [12] 1 Cor. x. 11.
[13] S. Luke xxi. 25. Rev. viii. 6.   [14] Rev. xvi. 3.
[15] Ps. xciii. 4.   [16] S. Jer.   [17] Ps. ciii. 12.

9 Thy bow was made quite naked, *according to* the oaths of the tribes,

[1] *the mountain was full of horses and chariots of fire round about Elisha.* " [2] Yet amidst so many thousands of horses and chariots, there was no rider; He was the Rider and Ruler of those horses, of Whom the Psalmist says, [3] *Thou that sittest above the Cherubim, shew Thyself.* With such horses and such chariots was Elijah also *taken up into Heaven.*"
And *Thy chariots of salvation,* lit. *Thy chariots are salvation.* Not, as in human armies, except as far as they are the armies of God, to destruction. The end of God's armies, His visitations and judgments, is the salvation of His elect, even while they who are inwardly dead, perish outwardly also. Nor, again, do they *prepare* for the deliverance for which He intends them. With God, to will is to do. His chariots *are* salvation. His help is *present help.* His *chariots* are the tokens and channels of His Presence to aid. And so, they who bore His *Name before the Gentiles, and kings, and the children of Israel, chosen vessels* to bear it, are, in a yet fuller sense, His *chariots,* which are *salvation.* They " [2] are holy souls, upon which the word of God cometh, to save them and others by them. [4] *I have compared thee,* saith the Spouse, *to a company of horses in Pharaoh's chariots.* However holy the soul, yet compared to God, it is like the chariot of Pharaoh; and a beast, yet still *a beast, before Thee* [5] ." Yet such an one, as endowed with might and ready obedience, and swiftness and nobleness to bear the word of God, and through His might Whom they bore, not their own, nor making it their own, bearing down everything which opposed itself. " [6] The object of the Prophet, is to shew that the second dispensation is better and more glorious, and of incomparably better things than the old. For of old He led Israel forth, through the bodily service of Moses, changing into blood the rivers of Egypt, and doing signs and wonders; then dividing the Red Sea, and carrying over the redeemed, and choking in the waters the most warlike of the Egyptians. But when the Only-Begotten Word of God became Man, He withdrew the whole human race under heaven from the tyranny of Satan, not changing rivers into blood, nor pouring forth His anger upon waters, nor dividing waves of the sea, nor bringing destruction upon men, but rather destroying the murderous Serpent himself, and taking away the sin

even thy word. Selah.

|| [1] Thou didst cleave the earth with rivers.
[1] Ps. 78. 15, 16. & 105. 41.

|| Or, *Thou didst cleave the rivers of the earth.*

which had been invented by him and for him, and loosing the unconquered might of death, and calling all to the knowledge of God, through the holy Apostles, who, running forth their course under the whole Heaven and bearing about the Name of Christ, were rarely rightly had in admiration. He saith then, O Lord, most worthy to be heard are those things, of which Thou hast Thyself been the Doer, and what Thou hast anew wrought is far better than what Thou didst through Moses. For Thou wilt not inflict wrath on rivers, nor shew Thy might on the sea; not in these things will Thy Divine and marvelous power gleam forth, but *Thou wilt ride upon Thy horses,* and *Thy chariots are Salvation.* What may these horses be? The Blessed Disciples, Apostles and Evangelists, they who took on them wholly the yoke of all His Divine will, they, the noble, the obedient, ready for all things, whatsoever should please Him; who had Christ to sit upon them, whereof one is the Blessed Paul, of whom Himself saith, [7] *He is a chosen vessel unto Me, to bear My Name before the Gentiles.* Of fiery speed were these Horses, encompassing the whole earth; so then the chariots of God are said to be *ten thousand times ten thousand* [8]. For countless, each in their times, and after them, became leaders of the people, and subjected the neck of the understanding to the yoke of the Saviour, and bare about His Glory throughout the whole earth, and rightly divided the word of truth, and subdued the whole earth, as with the speed of horsemen."

His chariots are salvation; " [6] for they ran not in vain, but to save cities and countries and nations together, Christ overthrowing the empires of devils, who, so to speak, divided among themselves the whole earth, subduing its dwellers to their own will."

9. *Thy bow was made quite naked.* The word is repeated for emphasis. Lit. (In) *nakedness* [9] *it was laid naked;* the sheath being laid aside and cast away, as Isaiah says, [10] *Kir laid bare the shield.* The [11] *bow* represents the threat of the vengeance of Almighty God, from which it is at length discharged, if not turned aside; the longer the string is drawn, the sharper issueth the arrow. So then the more the coming of the day of judgment is delayed, the stricter is the severity of the judgment then issuing. So long as judg-

[1] 2 Kgs vi. 15.   [2] S. Jer.
[3] Ps. lxxx. 1.
[4] Cant. i. 9.   [5] Ps. lxxiii. 23.
[6] S. Cyr.   [7] Acts ix. 15.   [8] Ps. lxviii. 17.

[9] עֶרְיָה, acc. abs. as עֶרְיָה בֹשֶׁת Mic. i. 11., for the inf. abs.   [10] Is. xxii. 6.
[11] S. Greg. Mor. xix. 9. n. 54, Comp. S. Aug. in Ps. lix. n. 6.

Before
CHRIST
cir. 626.

k Ex. 19. 16, 18.
Judg. 5. 4, 5.
Ps. 68. 8. & 77. 18. & 114. 4.

10 ^k The mountains saw thee, *and* they trembled: the overflowing of the wa-

ter passed by : the deep uttered his voice, *and* ^l lifted up his hands on high.

ment is delayed, the bow seems laid up in its sheath. God's judgments mostly strike suddenly ¹ *as with a swift arrow*, because men regard them not, coming from a bow at a distance which they see not. His more signal judgments He makes bare in sight of all. *According to the oath of* [*to*] *the tribes ;* ² *the oath which He sware unto our father Abraham,* which oath He often renewed to Abraham, Isaac and Jacob, and again to David ³. This oath, the *word* and promise of God, was the pledge of the deliverance of His people, that they *should be saved from their enemies, and from the hand of all that hate them.* It lay, as it were, covered and hid, so long as God completed it not. *Selah.* A pause followeth, wherein to meditate on all which is contained in the *word* or promise of God, which is all time and eternity.

Thou didst cleave the earth with [i. e., *into*] *rivers.* Sea and river had become dry land for the passing through of God's people; again, the rock, struck by Moses' rod, was split, so that *rivers ran in the dry places.* Until that Rock, Which was Christ, was stricken, and ⁴ *out of His Side came Blood and water,* the whole world was desert and barren ; then it was turned into streams of water, and " ⁵ now not four but twelve streams went forth from the Paradise of Scriptures." For from the One Fountain which is Christ, there issue many streams, even as many as convey the waters of His teaching, to *water the earth.*

10. *The mountains saw Thee, and they trembled,* lit. *they tremble.* While man is insen-

sate, inanimate nature feels and attests the presence of its Maker. *It saw, it trembles.* To see, feel, tremble, were one. The Prophet does not follow a bare order of events, or bind himself to miracles which actually took place. The mountains tremble with earthquakes, or seem to be shaken by the thunders which they re-echo. And so they are signs, how what is firmest and closes up the way to man, trembles at the Presence of God. Whatever is lifted up shall be bowed down before Him ⁶. But the word *trembled,* is that used especially of travail pangs ⁷, and so it may spiritually denote that " ⁸ they who conceive the fear of God shall bring forth unto salvation." *The overflowing* i. e., the impetuous, sweeping, flow, *of the water* ⁹ (or *of waters*), such as in themselves would bear all before them, *pass by* harmless. The more they swell, the more they expend themselves, and pass away. "The whole force of persecution, wherewith they vexed Thy people, at sight of Thee passed away," like a torrent which rages and disappears, and, by raging, the sooner wastes itself.

The deep uttered his voice, and lifted up his hands ¹⁰ *on high.* The noise of the waves, when God brought the strong East wind over it and ¹¹ *rebuked* it, was as a cry to God ; the waves, as they swelled, were like hands lifted up to Him, and stricken one against the other. There is no distinct ground against a slightly different rendering, ¹² *the deep uttered his voice, the height lifted up his hands* i. e., to One yet higher, Whom height and depth owned as their Lord and worshiped.

¹ Ps. lxiv. 7.
² S. Luke i. 73. The E. V. takes the common words שְׁבֻעוֹת and מַטּוֹת in their common senses, and אֹמֶר (which is a poetic word) agreeably to them. שְׁבוּעָה, "oath" occurs 27 times: the plur. שְׁבֻעוֹת here and Ezek. xxi. 28. The other meaning, *weeks,* which occurs 9 times (chiefly of the "feast of weeks," four times in De. xvi.), is plainly irrelevant here. מַטּוֹת occurs 24 times beside of the tribes of Israel; twice only of the "rods" set against that of Aaron (Ex. vii. 12, Nu. xvii. 21.). אֹמֶר "speech" is used of the "promise of God," certainly Ps. lxxvii. 9. The construction is likewise easy, מַטּוֹת is the gen. of the obj. after שְׁבֻעוֹת, and both in apposition with the preceding clause, and אֹמֶר with them. This construction and meaning of שְׁבֻעוֹת מַטּוֹת, and meaning of אֹמֶר, and the construction with .שׂ מִ. is that of Jon. followed by Kim. Rashi Abarb. Tanch. So also S. Jer. Only A. E. taking מַטּוֹת as spears, explains, that "His spears were sworn to establish the word of God."
³ See Mic. end (ab. p. 104.) Ps. lxxxix. 3. cxxxii. 11.

⁴ S. John xix. 24. ⁵ S. Jer.
⁶ See Zech. iv. 7.
⁷ The LXX. so translate, "shall be in birth-pangs."
⁸ Theoph.
⁹ זֶרֶם is used apparently both of the "flow of waters and their strong current," as Tanch. explains it here; or of a violent storm breaking upon a thing. Its union with rain, Is. iv. 6, hail, Is. xxviii. 2. xxx. 30, the mountains, Job xxiv. 8, fits in with or requires the meaning "storm ;" its union with mighty overflowing (שֶׁטֶף מַיִם) waters Is. xxviii. implies "a current;" "a storm against a wall" קִיר זֶרֶם, Is. xxv. 4, might suit either; the verb זְרַמְתָּם, "hast swept them away," Ps. xc. 5, implies "a flood;" the mention of the clouds Ps. lxxvii. 18, "a storm." Kim. Rashi, Abarb. explain it here of water on the earth; A. E. of waters descending.
¹⁰ מֵרוֹם = רוּם which stands as the acc. of direction with *lifted up the eyes* Is. xxxvii. 23. xl. 26.
¹¹ Ps. cvi. 9.
¹² So S. Jer., Rashi, A. E.; רוּם being a ἅπ. λεγ., one cannot say that it *might* not mean this. The metaphor would be dropped.

Before CHRIST cir. 626.	11 ^m The sun *and* moon stood still in their habita-

^m Josh. 10. 12, 13.
‖ Or, *thine arrows walked in the light, &c.*
ⁿ Josh. 10. 11.
Ps. 18. 14.
& 77. 17, 18.

11 ^m The sun *and* moon stood still in their habitation: ‖ at the l i g h t of thine ⁿ arrows they went, *and* at the shining of thy glittering spear.

	Before CHRIST cir. 626.

12 Thou didst march through the land in indignation, ^o thou didst thresh the heathen in anger.   ^o Jer. 51. 33. Amos. 1. 3. Mic. 4. 13.

13 Thou wentest forth for the salvation of thy

---

11. *Sun* and *moon stood still in* [as one act[1], retiring *into*] *their habitation.* They withdrew, as it were, in the midst of the great tempest, wherein [2] *God cast down great stones from heaven upon His enemies and they died ; and the sun stood still, and the moon stayed.* The sun too withdrew itself in the great darkness at the Crucifixion, as not bearing to look upon the Death of its Maker, when the majesty of the Sun of Righteousness was darkened o'er; and signs in the sun and in the moon there shall be to the end.

At the light of Thine arrows they went. " [3] There was no need of the sun by day, nor of the moon by night; for by the light of Thine arrows can the sons of men hold their way."

" [4] This is a mystical interpretation, as you see; this is like the promise of the Most High; [5] *the sun shall be no more for thy light by day, neither for brightness shall the moon give light unto thee, and the Lord shall be to thee an everlasting light.*" The judgments of God are a light to His people, while they are the destruction of His enemies; in them they [6] *learn righteousness.* The arrows are God's judgments, as they threaten and wound from afar; *the shining of Thy glittering* [lit. *of the lightning of Thy*] *spear*, when close at hand. When all other light is withdrawn, and the *Sun*, our Lord, is hardly beheld in the darkness of the last days, and the *moon*, the Church, shall not give her light, Christ not shining upon her as before, because *iniquity shall abound, and the love of many shall wax cold*, and *stars*, many who seem to shine with the light of grace, *shall fall from heaven*, His own shall walk on and advance in holiness, " [7] from strength to strength [8], from good to better, from the way to their home," by the bright light of the lightning of God's Judgments, wherein His glory [9] shall be manifested. *Arrows and spears* are part of the spiritual armory of God, wherewith *the people are subdued unto Him ;* " [10] armory, not wherewith He is girt but which He giveth to those who are meet; bright and as it were full of

lightning. For most transparent is virtue." They went then at the light of Thine arrows; " [10] because to those who love sin virtue has no beauty, nor, as yet, any brightness. But to those who know her she is nothing less than lightning, bright and transparent, so that whoso hath her is easily known to all around. The disciples then, first having the lightning of Thine arms, shall lead others also to its Light. Admiring and conceiving in themselves those virtues which are the arms of Christ, they shine forth to others, a gleam, as it were, of the bright flash of light inherent in those graces." " [11] They were enlightened and began, by preaching, to send forth shining words of truth. But those words are Thine arrows, shining arrows, shewing by their light the way of life, and by their sharp point pricking the hearts of people unto repentance."

12. *Thou didst tread the earth in indignation.* The word *tread* [12] is used of very solemn manifestations of God [13], of His going to give to His own victory over their enemies [14]. Not *the land* only, as of old, but *the earth* is the scene of His judgments; the *earth* which was *full of His praise*, which He *meted out* [15], which contained the nations whom He chastened, the whole earth. *Thou dost thresh the heathen in anger.* Not then only, but at all times unto the end, *distress of nations and perplexity* are among the shoots of the fig-tree, which betoken that the everlasting [16] *summer is nigh at hand.* Jerusalem, when it had slain the Prince of Life, was given over to desolation and counted like the heathen. It became the synagogue, not the Church ; and so in the destruction of Jerusalem (as it is an image of the destruction of the world) was that again fulfilled, *Thou dost march through the earth in indignation, Thou dost thresh the heathen in anger.*

13. *Thou wentest forth.* Even a Jew says of this place, " [17] The past is here used for the future; and this is frequent in the

---

[1] עָמַד sing. with the asyndeton שֶׁמֶשׁ יָרֵחַ;
" Every word which needs לְ (to) at the beginning has הַ at the end, i. e. the הַ replaces it." Rashi. Tanchum says the הַ is for grandeur; Kim. Sal. b. Mel. say it is like הַ in לַיְלָה. The " habitation " they explain to be heaven, like מָעוֹן.

[2] Jos. x. 11–13.   [3] A. E.   [4] Tanch.   [5] Is. lx. 19.
[6] Ib. xxvi. 9.   [7] Dion.   [8] Ps. lxxxiv. 7.

[9] The word "shining" is the same as "brightness," v. 4.
[10] S. Cyr.   [11] Rup.   [12] צָעַד.
[13] Jud. v. 4. Ps. lxviii. 8 ; of the procession of the ark 2 Sam. vi. 13. It is denied as to the idols, Jer. x. 5.
[14] " The voice of a treading " קוֹל צַעֲדָה 2 Sam. v. 24. 1 Chr. xiv. 15.
[15] iii. 3, 6.   [16] S. Luke xxi. 25–31.   [17] Kimchi.

Before
C H R I S T
cir. 626.
ᵖ Josh. 10. 24.
& 11. 8, 12.
Ps. 68. 21.

people, *even* for salvation with thine anointed; ᵖthou woundest the head out of

the house of the wicked, † by discovering the foundation unto the neck. Selah.

Before
C H R I S T
cir. 626.
† Heb. *making
naked.*

language of prophecy; for prophecy, although it be future, yet since it is, as it were, firmly fixed, they use the past concerning it." The Prophet speaks again in the past, perhaps to fix the mind on that signal going-forth, when God destroyed Pharaoh, the first enemy who essayed to destroy the chosen line. This stands at the head of all those dispensations, in which God put or shall put forth His might to save His people or destroy their enemies. All is with Him one everlasting purpose; the last were, as it were, embodied in the first: were it not for the last, the first would not have been. Prophecy, in speaking of the first, has in mind all the rest, and chiefly the chiefest and the end of all, the full salvation of His people through Jesus Christ our Lord. *Thou wentest forth*[1], i. e., "[2] Thou, the Unseen God, gavest signs which may be seen of Thy Presence or coming to men." *Thou wentest forth,* not by change of place, for Thou art not bounded; Thou art without change; but by shewing Thy power, and doing something anew openly *for the salvation of Thy people, even for salvation with*[3] *Thine Anointed,* God, from the first, helped His people through single persons, Moses, Joshua, each of the Judges, accustoming them to receive deliverance by one, and to gather together all their hopes in One. To Moses He said, [4] *I will be with thee,* and to Joshua, [5] *As I was with Moses, so I will be with thee,* and to Cyrus, [6] *I will go before thee,* preparing His people to receive that nearer Presence with His Christ, of which our Lord says: [7] *Believest thou not, that I am in the Father, and the Father in Me? The Father that Dwelleth in Me, He doeth the works.* "[8] The Son of God, God Invisible, became Man, visible; and with Him, so going forth, the Holy Spirit went forth *to the salvation of His people,* so as to give a visible sign of His Coming. For upon His Christ Him-

self, Him Who was anointed with the Holy Ghost[9], He *descended in a bodily Shape, as a Dove.* So He *went forth to the Salvation of His people,* i. e., to save His people with His Christ, our Saviour;" and again, on the Day of Pentecost, when that other Comforter came, *Whom,* He said, *I will send unto you from the Father,* and in Whose Presence His own promise was fulfilled, *Lo, I am with you always, even unto the end of the world.* His Presence was manifested both in the remission of sins, and the parting of graces among all, and in the [10] *signs and wonders, and divers miracles, and gifts of the Holy Ghost,* wherewith *God bare witness to the Apostles,* when [11] *they went forth, the Lord working with them, and confirming the word with signs following.* A going forth to judgment, at the end of the world, is foretold in the like image of warfare [12].

Thou woundedst [crushedst] the head out of the house of the wicked. One wicked stands over against One anointed, as in Isaiah, [13] *He shall smite the earth with the rod of His mouth, and with the breath of His lips shall He slay the wicked;* and David speaks of one, [14] *He shall smite the head over a great land;* and S. Paul speaks of [15] *that Wicked, whom the Lord shall consume with the spirit of His mouth, and shall destroy with the brightness of His Coming.* Him He shall destroy at once from above and below; overthrowing his kingdom from the foundation. From above, his head was crushed in pieces; from below, the house was razed from its very foundations. So Amos said, [16] *The Lord said, Smite the capital, and the lintel [threshold[17]] strike, and wound them in the head, all of them;* and with a different image, [18] *I destroyed his fruit from above, and his roots from beneath.* First, the head is struck off, crushed; then the house from the foundations to its neck; then as it were the headless walls. The image of *the neck* may

[1] Comp. בצאתך, בצעדך Jud. v. 4. Ps. lxviii. 8 of the great manifestation of God at Sinai; so of the judgment of the world, יצא מִמְקוֹמוֹ Is. xxvi. 21.   [2] Rup.
[3] The E. V. is doubtless right. So Aquila, although a Jew, rendered, and the 5th Version. The 6th, a Christian, translated, "Thou wentest forth to save Thy people through Jesus, Thy Christ." So also the Vulgate and other old Jewish authorities. Rachmon (in Martini Pug. Fid. f. 534.) notes "that the word *eth* means *with,* as in Gen. xxxvii. 2. xxxix. 2." For although it might be used to mark the object only after a verbal noun, it is not likely that the construction would have been changed, unless the meaning were different. Had *eth* been only the sign of the object, there was no occasion for inserting it at all, and it would probably have been avoided, as only making the sentence ambiguous,

in that it may more obviously be taken in the sense adopted by Aq. and the Vulgate and the E. V. The LXX and two early heretics who disbelieved the Divinity of our Lord (Theodot. and Symm.) render "to save Thy Christs." The LXX is wrong moreover, in that *the Anointed* is never used of the people, but of single persons only, who were shadows of the Christ. "Thine anointed" is understood of one individual, "the king of Judah," by A. E. "Saul and David," by Rashi; "Moses" by Abarb.; "Hezekiah" by Tanch.; but "Messiah Ben David" by Kim. Sal. b. Mel.

[4] Ex. iii. 12.   [5] Josh. i. 5.   [6] Is. xlv. 2.
[7] S. John xiv. 10.   [8] Rup.   [9] Acts x. 38.
[10] Heb. ii. 4.   [11] S. Mark xvi. 20.
[12] Rev. xvii. 14. xix. 11. sqq.   [13] Is. xi. 4.
[14] Ps. cx. 6.   [15] 1 Thess. iv. 8.   [16] Am. ix. 1.
[17] The same word is used Zeph. ii. 14. Ps. cxxxvii. 7.   [18] Am. ii. 9.

Before
CHRIST
cir. 626.

14 Thou didst strike
through with his staves
the head of his villages:
they † came out as a

† Heb. *were*
tempestuous.

whirlwind to scatter me:
their rejoicing *was* as
to devour the poor se-
cretly.

Before
CHRIST
cir. 626.

be the rather used to recall, that as the house
of God is built of living stones, so the kingdom of the evil one is made of living dead,
who shall never cease to exist in an undying
death. The bruising of Satan, the head or
prince of this evil world, is the deliverance
of the world. His head was bruised, when,
by the Death of our Lord, *the Prince of this
world* was *cast out; he is crushed out of the
house of the wicked,* whenever he, the *strong
man,* is bound and cast out, and "the soul of
the sinner which had been his abode, becomes the house of God, and righteousness
dwelleth there and walketh in her."

"¹ Thou didst not leave any error or vice
in the world unshaken, either what was concealed, like the foundation of a house; or
that which was open, as the neck of the body
is open;" *to the neck,* where the destruction
from above ceased, so that nothing remained
unsmitten. "¹ For they being, by the fiery
tongues which Thou shewedst without, made
fervent and strong, wise and eloquent, ceased
not, until they made known to all, what folly
was this world's wisdom, what sacrilege its
sacred worship." "² His secret counsels He
laid bare, as the Apostle says, ³ *We are not
ignorant of his devices;* and, *to another is given
the discerning of spirits.*"

14. *Thou didst strike through with his staves
the head of his villages*⁴. The destruction
comes not upon himself only, but upon the
whole multitude of his subjects; and this not
by any mere act of Divine might, but *with
his own staves,* turning upon him the destruction which he prepared for others. So it
often was of old. When the Midianites and
Amalekites and the children of the east⁵
wasted Israel in the days of Gideon, ⁶ *the
Lord set every man's sword against his fellow,*

even throughout all the host; and when God delivered the Philistines into the hand of Jona-
than⁷; so was it with *Ammon Moab and the
inhabitants of Mount Seir,* at the prayer of
Jehoshaphat and his army⁸. And so it shall
be, God says, at the end, of the army of God;
every man's sword shall be against his brother⁹,
and Isaiah says, ¹⁰ *every man shall eat the flesh
of his own arm,* and Zechariah, ¹¹ *a great tumult
from the Lord shall be among them; and they
shall lay every man hold on the hand of his
neighbor, and his hand shall rise up against the
hand of his neighbor.* So Pharaoh drove Israel to the shore of the sea, in which he himself perished; Daniel's accusers perished in
the den of lions, from which Daniel was delivered unharmed¹²; and so. Haman was
hanged on the gallows which he prepared
for Mordecai¹³. So it became a saying of
Psalmists, ¹⁴ *He made a pit and digged it, and
is fallen into the ditch which he made; his mischief shall return upon his own head, and his
violent dealing shall come down upon his own
pate:* and this from above, sent down by God.
The heathen too observed that there was
"no juster law than that artificers of death
by their own art should perish." This too
befell him, when he seemed to have all but
gained his end. *They came* [*out*] *as a whirlwind to scatter me,* with whirlwind force, to
drive them asunder to all the quarters of the
heavens, as the wind scatters the particles of
¹⁵ cloud, or ¹⁶ *as the stubble which passeth away by
the wind of the wilderness.* Pharaoh at the
Red Sea or Sennacherib, sweep all before
them. Pharaoh said, ¹⁷ *I will pursue, I will
overtake, I will divide the spoil; my lust shall be
satisfied upon them; I will draw my sword, my
hand shall destroy them.*

Their rejoicing. It is no longer one enemy.

zite," very possibly, was originally "paganus "
"one who dwelt in villages." This rendering is
adopted by chief Jewish interpreters; Kim. "cities
of the plain, which have no fort nor wall." So
Abulw. Tanch. "land;" Rashi, Abarb. "his cities
and villages;" A. E. keeps the word, but implies
the meaning, on Zech. ii. 8. Kim. Sal. b. Mel.
obtained the sense of "forces" herein, that they
"shall come in great numbers, and so dwell in
Jerusalem, as פְּרָזִים, who dwell in פְּרָזוֹת, who
spread in the whole place, who have no wall to
enclose them." This explains Jon. "the forces of
Pharaoh," as hordes too large to be enclosed in
walls, and perhaps the LXX. δυνάσται.

¹ Rup.   ² Dion.   ³ 2 Cor. ii. 11. 1 Cor. xii. 10.
⁴ The meaning "leaders, prefects of soldiers"
has been obtained for פְרָז by Ges. &c. by a misap-
plication of the Arab. פָּרַז "distinguished " which
in conj. ii. signifies "defined for a person," but only
in the idiom פְרָז עֲלֵי בְרֹאשִׁי "defined for me by
his own counsel," which gains its meaning only
from the עַל. That of the E. V. is furnished, in
most places, by the passages themselves. As in
Ezek. xxxviii. 11, where "a land of פְּרָזוֹת " is
expanded into "where they all dwell without wall;
and bar and double gates they have not;" and
Deut. iii. 5, "all these were fenced cities, with high
wall, double gates and bar, beside cities of הַפְּרָזִי,"
and 1 Sam. vi. 18, "from the fenced city to the
village of הַפְּרָזִי " and Zech. ii. 8. "Jerusalem
shall dwell as פְּרָזוֹת for the multitude of men and
cattle therein; and I, saith the Lord, will be a wall
of fire around." In Esther ix. 19, cities הַפְּרָזוֹת
are contrasted with Shushan v. 18, and "the Periz-

⁵ Jud. vi. 3, 4.   ⁶ Ib. vii. 22.
⁷ 1 Sam. xiv. 12, 16, 20.   ⁸ 2 Chron. xx. 22, 23.
⁹ Ezek. xxxviii. 21.   ¹⁰ Is. ix. 20.
¹¹ Zech. xiv. 13.   ¹² Dan. vi. 24.   ¹³ Esth. vii. 10.
¹⁴ Ps. vii. 5. add ix. 15, x. 2, xxxv. 8, lvii. 6, xciv.
23. cxli. 10. Prov. v. 22. xxvi. 27. Eccl. x. 8.
¹⁵ Job xxxvii. 11.   ¹⁶ Jer. xiii. 24. add xviii. 17.
Is. xli. 16. Del.   ¹⁷ Ex. xv. 9.

Before CHRIST cir. 626.

q Ps. 77. 19. ver. 8.
|| Or, *mud.*

15 q Thou didst walk through the sea with thine horses, *through* the || heap of great waters.

16 When I heard, r my belly trembled; my lips quivered at the voice: rottenness entered into my

Before CHRIST cir. 626.

r Ps. 119. 120. Jer. 23. 9.

The malice of the members was concentrated in the head; the hatred concentrated in him was diffused in them. The readiness of instruments of evil to fulfill evil is an incentive to those who conceive it; those who seem to ride the wave are but carried on upon the crest of the surge which they first roused. They cannot check themselves or it. So the ambitious conceiver of mischief has his own guilt; the willing instruments of evil have theirs. Neither could be fully evil without the other. Sennacherib had been nothing without those fierce warriors who are pictured on the monuments, with individual fierceness fulfilling his will, nor the Huns without Attila, or Attila without his hordes whose tempers he embodied. Satan would be powerless but for the willing instruments whom he uses. So then Holy Scripture sometimes passes from the mention of the evil multitude to that of the one head, on earth or in hell, who impels them; or from the one evil head who has his own special responsibility in originating it, to the evil multitude, whose responsibility and guilt lies in fomenting the evil which they execute.

Their rejoicing. He does not say simply "they rejoice to," but herein is their exceeding, exulting joy. The wise of this earth glories in his wisdom, the mighty man in his might, the rich in his riches: the truly wise, that he understandeth and knoweth God. But as for these, their exultation is concentrated in this,—savagery; in this is their jubilation; this is their passion. Psalmists and pious men use the word to express their exulting joy in God: men must have an object for their empassioned souls; and these, in cruelty.

As it were to devour the poor secretly. From the general he descends again to the individual, but so as now to set forth the guilt of each individual in that stormy multitude which is, as it were, one in its evil unity, when each merges his responsibility, as it were, in that of the body, the horde or the mob, in which he acts. *Their exultation,* he says, is that of the individual robber and murderer, who lies wait secretly in his ambush, to spring on the defenceless wanderer, to slay him and devour his substance.

Premeditation, passion, lust of cruelty, cowardice, murderousness, habitual individual savagery and treachery, and that to the innocent and defenceless, are all concentrated in the words, *their exultation is, as it were, to devour the poor secretly,* i. e. *in their secret haunt.*

Pharaoh had triumphed over Israel. [1] *They are entangled in the land, the wilderness hath shut them in.* He rejoiceth in having them wholly in his power, as a lion has his prey in his lair, *in secret,* unknown to the Eyes of God Whom he regarded not, with none to behold, none to deliver. "[2] They gloried in oppressing the people of Israel, even as the cruel man glories in secretly rending and afflicting the needy, when without fear they do this cruelty, nor heed God beholding all as Judge." The invisible enemies too rejoice very greatly in the ruin of our souls. [3] *Lest mine enemy say, I have prevailed against him: for if I be cast down, they that trouble me will rejoice at it.* [4] *O Lord and governor of all my life, leave me not to their counsels and let me not fall by them.* Yet God left them not in his hands; but even *brake the head of Leviathan in pieces.*

15. *Thou didst walk through the sea with Thine horses.* God Himself is pictured as leading them on the way, Himself at the head of their multitude, having, as Asaph said of old, [5] *His path in the sea.* So Isaiah, [6] *Who leddest them in the depths;* and Zechariah, [7] *And he shall pass through the sea.* God was literally there; for [8] *in Him we live and move and have our being.* He Who "is wholly everywhere but the whole of Him nowhere" manifested His Presence there. Such anthropomorphisms have a truth, which men's favorite abstractions have not.

Through the heap [9] *of great waters,* as of old, [10] *the waters stood as a heap,* and *He made the waters to stand as a heap.* The very hindrances to deliverance are in God's Hands a way for His ends. The waves of the Red sea rose in heaps, yet this was but a readier way for the salvation of His people and the destruction of their enemies. "[2] God prepareth ever a way for His elect in this present evil world, and leadeth them along the narrow way which leadeth unto life."

16. *When I heard,* better, *I heard and* &c.

opinion of others that it is "mud" but choosing the other.) A. E. chooses the sense, "mud." Rashi paraphrases, "as the sand of the sea." For that of Ges., "the boiling of the waters," there is absolutely no authority.

[1] Ib. xiv. 3.   [2] Dion.   [3] Ps. xiii. 4.
[4] Ecclus. xxiii. 1.
[5] דרכם בים as Ps. lxxvii. 20, בים דרכך.
[6] Is. lxiii. 13.   [7] Zech. x. 11.   [8] Acts xvii. 28.
[9] So Jon. Kim. (comparing Ex. xv. 8 and חמרים Ex. viii. 10.) Sal. b. Mel. Tanch. (mentioning the   [10] Ex. xv. 8. Ps. lxxviii. 13.

bones, and I trembled in myself, that I might rest in the d a y o f trouble:

when he cometh up unto the people, he will ‖ invade them with his troops.

‖ Or, *cut them in pieces.*

The prophet sums up, resuming that same declaration with which he had begun, *I heard, I was afraid.* Only now he expresses far more strongly both his awe at God's judgments and his hopes. He had just beheld the image of the destruction of Pharaoh, the end of the brief triumphing of the wicked and of the trials of God's people. But awful as are all the judgments of God upon the enemies of His people, it was not this alone which was the object of his terror. *This* was deliverance. It was the whole course of God's dispensations, which he had heard; God's punishment of His people for their sins, and the excision of their oppressors, who, in His Providence, fulfilling their own evil end, executed His chastisements upon them. The deliverances, which shadowed out the future, had their dark side, in that they *were* deliverances. The whole course of this world is one series of man's unfaithfulnesses or sins, God's chastisements of them through their fellow-sinners, and His ultimate overthrow of the aggressors. Those first three centuries of glorious martyrdoms were, on the one side, the malice and hatred of Satan and the world against the truth; on the other side, the prophets of those days told their people that they were the chastisements of their sins. Future deliverance implies previous chastisement of those delivered. The prophet then, at the close, in view of all, for himself and all whose perplexities he represented and pleaded before God, chooses his and their portion. "Suffer here and rest forever!" "Endure here any terror, any failure of hopes, yet trust wholly in God, have rest in the day of trouble and sing the endless song!" Again

he casts himself back amid all the troubles of this life.

I heard [i. e. that speech of God uttering judgments to come] *and my belly* [1], the whole inward self, bodily and mental, all his hidden powers, *trembled* [2], "vibrated" as it were, " [3] in every fibre of his frame," at the wrath of God; *my lips quivered* [4] *at the voice* of God, so that they almost refused their office and could hardly fulfill the prophetic duty and utter the terrors which he had heard; his very strongest parts, the *bones,* which keep the whole frame of man together, that he be not a shapeless mass, and which remain unconsumed long after the rest has wasted away in the grave, *rottenness entered into them,* corruption and mouldering eating into them [5]; *and I trembled in myself* [lit. *under me* [6]] so that he was a burden to himself and sank unable to support himself, *that I might rest in the day of trouble.* All up to this time was weariness and terror, and now at once all is repose; the prophet is carried, as it were, over the troubles of this life and the decay of the grave to the sweetness of everlasting rest [7]. I, the same, suffer these things, terror, quivering, rottenness in the very bones themselves. *I* [lit.] *who shall rest* [8] *in the day of trouble.* *I* who had not rest until then, shall enter into rest then in the very day of trouble to all who found their rest in the world not in God, the day of judgment. [9] *Blessed is the man whom Thou chastenest, O Lord, and teachest him in Thy law, that Thou mayest give him patience in time of adversity, until the pit be digged up for the ungodly.*

" [10] O my soul; had we daily to bear tortures, had we for a long time to endure hell

[1] בטן is used of the inward part of man, which "prepareth mischief," Job xv. 35; the spirit whereof constrains one, Ib. xxxii. 18; the chambers of which are searched out by the spirit of man, as the lamp of God, Prov. xx. 27; as cleansed by stripes Ib. 30; where the words of the wise are guarded, Ib. xxii. 18; which should not be filled with the East wind, Job xv. 2. In the like way in the N. T. "from his belly, κοιλία, shall flow living waters," S. John vii. 38. In Arab. בטן is the "inner meaning;" בטן "he knew the inner, the intrinsic, state of the case;" with ב p., "became intimate with;" conj. x. with acc., "penetrated a thing." So also באטן אל "that which is within," of facts, thoughts, mind. See Lane. All are derivative senses. בטן has nothing in common with Ar. בטל, as Ges.

[2] "ragaz," twice repeated in this verse, takes up, as it were, "rogez" wrath v. 2. [3] Del.

[4] צלל occurs of the tingling of the ear, 1 Sam. iii. 11. 2 Kgs xxi. 12. Jer. xix. 3. "From the fear at the meaning of this sound which he has heard his lips trembled in speaking, and he uttered their words with a trembling sound." Tanch.

[5] רקב (the root) is used of the decay of wood and of the bones, and Pr. x. 7, of "the name of the wicked."

[6] As 2 Sam. ii. 23. "he died" as we say, "on the spot," sinking down dead.

[7] The very softness of the original word אנוח stands in contrast with the rigidness in the words tirgaz, rakab, regaz, tsarah.

[8] נוח is uniformly "rest." It is used of rest from labor, from calamities, [Is. xxiv. 7 Job iii. 26.] rest *in* a place, with ב, or *on* (על) it; of the Holy Spirit resting on a person (with על). But its meaning is uniformly of rest, not of silence as to a thing [as Ges.] nor does שׁ החריש furnish any analogy, since this in itself signifies "*kept* silence." Nor can it mean "wait patiently for," for נ חם "rest" is the very opposite of "waiting for," חכה, which necessarily involves a degree, even if of subdued unrest. Then, too יחל, קוה, חכה, are used of waiting, looking for good, not for evil.

[9] Ps. xciv. 12, 13.

[10] Man. ap. App. S Aug. T. vi. c. 21.

Before
CHRIST
cir. 626.

17 ¶ Although the fig tree shall not blossom, neither *shall* fruit *be* in the vines; t h e labor of the olive shall † fail, and the

† Heb. *lie.*

fields shall yield no meat; the flock shall be cut off from the fold, and *there shall be* no herd in the stalls :

Before
CHRIST
cir. 626.

itself, that we might see Christ in His glory and be the companion of His Saints, were it not worth enduring all sorrow, that we might be partakers of so exceeding a good, such exceeding glory?"

When he cometh up unto the people, he shall invade them with his troops, or, which is probably meant, *when he cometh up who shall invade them* [1]. It is a filling out of *the day of trouble* [2]. However near the trouble came, he, under the protection of God and in firm trust in Him, would be at rest in Him. The troubles of God's prophets are not the outward troubles, but the sins of their people which bring those troubles, the offence against the majesty of God, the loss of souls. Jeremiah was more at rest in the court of the prison, than when all the people did curse him [3] for telling them God's Truth. He who fears God and His judgments betimes, shall rest in perfect tranquillity when those judgments come. The immediate trouble was the fierce assault of the Chaldees whose terror he had described ; and this, picturing, as through the prophecy, all other judgments of God even to the last, when devils shall contend about the souls of men, as Satan did about the body of Moses.

[1] This is the simplest construction, and is that adopted by Kim. Abarb. In the rendering "in the coming up of a people," the ל would, as Tanchum observes, be superfluous, and יגודנו would be more natural than יגודנו. But the prophet would not needlessly make his language ambiguous. Had he meant, "in the coming up of *a* or *the* people," he would have used the common עם לעלות or לעלות לעלות העם. The construction of עלה with ל instead of על, "to" for "against," is exceptional. But עלה occurs with the equivalent אל of the person, and in one case with ל (as we say "go up to") Gen. xliv. 24, 34. xlv. 9. Ex. xix. 3, 24. xxiii. 1, 12. xxxii. 30. Deut. x. 1. Josh. x. 4, 6. Jud. iv. 5. xii. 3. xvi. 5. (לה) 18. 1 Sam. vi. 20. x. 3, xiv. 9, 12. xxiii. 19. 2 Kgs i. 11. xii. 4, and this, in a hostile sense Jud. xx. 23, 2 Sam. v. 19, Jer. xlix. 28, 31. עם also, is used without the art. (as a sort of proper name) of the Jewish people, Is. xxvi. 11. xliv. 6. גוד occurs Gen. xlix. 19. there also with acc.; יתנודד, our, "troop" (verb) Jer. x. 7. See also Mic. v. 14, p. 79.
[2] יום צרה is a general term which occurs also Is. xxxvii. 3, more commonly with ב, ביום צרה, Ps. xx. 2, l. 15, Pr. xxiv. 10, xxv. 19, Jer. xvi. 19, Ob. 12, 14, Nah. i. 7. Zeph. i. 15. as עת צרה occurs Jer. xxx. 7. Dan. xii. 1. בעת צרה, Is. xxxiii. 2. Jer. xiv. 8. xv. 11; ביום צרתי Gen. xxxv. 3, Ps. lxxvii. 3, lxxxvi. 7; בעת צרתם Jud. x. 14. צרתכם Neh. ix. 27. There is no ground then to limit it to the Chaldæan or Assyrian period.
[3] Jer. xv. 10.

17. *Although* [lit. *For* [4]] *the figtree shall not blossom.* The Prophet repeats his confidence in God, premising his knowledge that all human hopes should fail. I know, he says, all stay and support shall fail; he numbers from the least to the greatest, the fruits of trees, the fig, vine and olive, for sweetness, gladness, cheerfulness [5], whereof the well-being of the vine and figtree furnishes the proverbial picture of peace and rest. These shall either not *shoot forth,* or shall at time of fruit-gathering have no *produce* [6], or having, as it were, labored to bring forth fruit shall *lie* [7], and fail: yet further "the staff of life" itself shall fail; *the fields shall yield no meat;* all the fields, as though they were but one [8], shall have one common lot, barrenness. Yet more; the flocks shall be cut off [9] from the fold ; not those only, feeding abroad in fields and open plains, shall be driven away, but they shall be carried away by the enemy from the folds, where they seemed penned securely ; and not these only, but *there shall be no herd in the stalls* [10], even the stronger animals shall utterly fail ; every help for labor, or for clothing, or for food shall cease ; he speaks not of privation, partial failure, but of the entire loss of all things,

[4] The adversative or exceptional force attributed to כי, always lies in the relation of the two sentences, not in the כי itself, which is always causative, "for" or "because." [5] Ps. civ. 15.
[6] יבול occurs here only of the produce of trees; 10 times of the earth itself directly; in Ps. lxxvii. 1, its produce, as the result of human culture, is מעשה. יבול ביתו; and Job xx. 28 יבים, יבולם; occurs here only of the fruit, being an application of the common idiom עשה פרי.
[7] כחש as Hos. ix. 2.
[8] שדמות, (an old word Deut. xxxii. 32) with no known etymology, is used, in three out of the four places in which it certainly occurs, in relation to place : "fields of Gomorrah" Deut. l. c. "f. of Kidron 2 Kgs xxiii. 4." "f. of Heshbon" Is. xvi. 8. It occurs in a fifth, (if, as is probable, the Kri is right,) "all the fields unto the brook Kidron" i. e. reaching to it, Jer. xxxi. 40. As a collective, it is joined with a sing. verb here, and Is. xvi. 8.
[9] גזר occurs intrans. here only. In Arab. also it is commonly used, but intrans. of "water which sunk " or retired. See Lane.
[10] רפתים, here only, but clear from the context. In Buxtorf's instance, מצאה ברפת "found it in a stall," the word is very probably used in the sense ascribed to it here by tradition as "well known in the language of the ancient (doctors) who say in the sing. רפת בקר." Tanch. "House of oxen." Kim. "See Mishnah Bava Bathra ii. 3. vi. 4." Munk on Tanch. The Arab. רפת "chopped straw" could hardly furnish a name for a stall.

Before CHRIST cir. 626.	18 ⁸Yet I will ᵗrejoice in the LORD, I will joy in the God of my salvation.	19 The LORD God *is* ᵘmy strength, and he will make my feet like ˣhinds *feet*, and he will make me	Before CHRIST cir. 626.
⁸ Job. 13. 15. ᵗ Isai. 41. 16. & 61. 10.			ᵘ Ps. 27. 1. ˣ 2 Sam. 22. 34. Ps. 18. 33.

no meat from the fields, no herd in the stalls; and what then? And I will rejoice in the Lord, I will joy in the God of my salvation. The words are very impressive, as they stand in the Hebrew. " For," he says, " the fig-tree shall not blossom, *and* there is no fruit in the vines, the labor of the olive *hath* failed ; " (the Prophet does not look on, only to these things, but in his mind stands in the midst of them [1], they are done, and he amid them, feeling their effects) " and the field *hath* yielded no food ; the flock hath been cut off from the fold, *and* there is no herd in the stall ; *and I*"—He relates it as the result of all which had gone before ; such and such was the state of fruit-trees, vintage, harvest, flocks and herds ; such was the aspect of all nature, living or inanimate ; all was barren, disappointing ; all had failed and was gone ; and then at last he comes to himself, *and I ;* what is he doing, when all nature and every seeming hope is dead ? thus and thus it is with them ; *and I—will rejoice.* He almost uses the expression as to the exultation of the enemy, adopting the same word only in a softer form. " *Their exulting* joy was " concentrated in this, " as to devour the poor secretly ; " *he* too had " exulting joy." There is a joy against joy : a joy of theirs in the possession of all which their rapacity covets, in the possession of all things : a joy of his amid the privation of all things. He contrasts the two joys, as David had of old ; [2] *the men of the world, whose portion is in this life, whose belly Thou fillest with Thy hid treasure ; they are sated of children and leave their substance to their babes : I,* he adds, *I shall behold Thy Presence in righteousness, I shall be sated, in the awakening, with Thine image.* So Habakkuk, *I will* not rejoice only, but *shout for joy* [3] ; and not so only, but *I will bound for joy ;* and this not for a time only ; both words express a drawing, yearning [4] of the soul, and this yet more and more, *I will shout for joy and would shout on ; I will bound for joy and would bound on.* But whence the source of this measureless unutterable joy ? *In the Lord,* the Unchangeable God, *Who is and was and is to*

come, I AM, (it is the incommunicable Name) ; in the God of my salvation : it is almost the Name of Jesus [5] ; for JESUS is salvation, and the Name means " the Lord is Salvation ; " whence the words are here rendered even by a Jew [6], " in God the Author of my redemption," and yet more sweetly by a father [7], " in God my Jesus." In Him his joy begins, to Him and in Him it flows back and on ; before he ventures, amid all the desolation, to speak of joy, he names the Name of God, and, as it were, stays himself in God, is enveloped and wrapped round in God ; *and I* (the words stand in this order) *and I in the Lord would shout for joy.* He comes, as it were, and places himself quite close to God, so that nothing, not even his joy should be between himself and God ; " *and I in the Lord.*" All creation, as it had failed, ceases to be ; all out of God : he speaks of nothing but himself and God, or rather himself *in God ;* and as He, God, comes before his joy, as its source, so in Him does he lose himself, with joy which cannot be contained, nor expressed, nor rest, but utters itself in the glad motions of untiring love. *I would bound for joy in my Saving God.* Truly all our joy is, to be in Him in Whom is all Good, Who is all Goodness and all Love.

19. *The LORD God is my strength.* The prophet does not inwardly only exult and triumph in God, but he confesses also in words of praise, that in Him he hath all things, that He is All things in him. And as he had confessed the Father, under the Name whereby He revealed Himself to Moses, and the Son, " the Lord God of my salvation," so he confesses [8] God the Holy Ghost, Who, in us, is our strength. *He* is our strength, so that through Him, we *can do all things ; He* is *our strength,* so that without Him, we can do nothing ; *He* is *our strength,* so that when we put forth strength, we put forth nothing of our own, we add nothing of our own, we use not our own strength, of which we have none, but we *do* use His ; and we have It ever ready to use, as if it were our own. For it is *not* our own and it *is* our

---

[1] The first future לֹא תִפְרַח, " *shall* not *flourish* " determines that all which follows is future in act, though present to the prophet's mind.

[2] Ps. xvii. 13, 15.

[3] עָלַז, like ἀλαλάζω. It is used of exultation in the holiness of God, Ps. lx. 8. cviii. 8. before God, Ps. lxviii. 5, God being the implied Object, Zeph. iii. 14. Ps. xxviii. 7. xcvi. 12. cxlix. 5. of the evil in evil Jer. xi. 15. l. 11, li. 39. Ps. xciv. 3.

[4] This is the force of the optative אָגִילָה. אֶעֱלוֹזָה. אֶגִילָה, recurs in Ps. lx. 8. cviii. 8.

[5] Jesus in Heb. יְשׁוּעַ, here יֵשַׁע.

[6] Chald. The Syr. "God my Redeemer." LXX. "God my Saviour."

[7] S. Aug. de Civ. D. xviii. 32. " To me what some MSS. have ; ' I will rejoice in God my Jesus,' seems better than what they have, who have not set the Name itself, (but saving) which to us it is more loving and sweeter to name." [8] Rup.

Before
CHRIST
cir. 626.

y Deut. 32. 13. & 33. 29.

to ʸ walk upon mine high places. To the chief

singer on my † stringed instruments.

Before
CHRIST
cir. 626.

† Heb. *Neginoth*, Ps. 4, title.

own; not our own, i. e., not from or of ourselves; but our own, since It is in us, yea He the Lord *our God* is *our strength*, not without us, for He is *our* strength, but in us. And so he says further, how we can use it as our own. *He will make my feet like hinds*, which bound upward through His imparted strength, and, when scared by alarms here below, flee fearless to their native rocks, spring from height to height, and at last shew themselves on some high peak, and standing on the Rock, look down on the whole world below their feet and upward on high. Even so, ¹ when at the end of the world all shall fail, and *the love of many shall wax cold*, and the Church, which is likened to the fig tree the vine and the ² olive, shall yield no fruits, and sweetness shall be corrupted by vanities, and the oil of mercy shall be dried up, and lamps go out, and its promises shall fail and it shall *lie*, having *a show of goodness, but denying the power of it; in words confessing God, and in works denying Him;* and through their own negligences, or the carelessness of pastors, the sheep of Christ shall perish from His very fold, and they who should be strong to labor ³ shall cease, God's elect shall joy in Him, "beholding His goodness, and loving Him in all things, and He will give them free affections, and fervid longings of holy love, whereby they shall not walk only, but *run the way of* His *commandments* and prevail over the enemies of their salvation."

¹ Chiefly from Dion. Comp. S. Jer.
² S. Luke xiii. 6. Is. v. 1. xxi. 33. &c. Rom. xi. 17.
³ 1 Cor. ix. 9, 10.

Yet though this strength is inward, and used by man, still God Who gives it, Himself guides it. Not man shall *direct his own ways*, but *He will make me to walk* (as on a plain *way*) *upon my high places*. Steep and slippery places and crags of the rocks are but *ways* to the safe height above, to those whom God *makes to walk* on them; and since he has passed all things earthly, what are *his high places*, but the heavenly places, even his home, even while a pilgrim here, but now at the end, much more his home, when not *in hope* only, but in truth, he is *raised up together*, and *made to sit together in heavenly places in Christ Jesus* ⁴?

And now what remains then, but that this song of praise should be for ever? And so it is not without meaning, nor was of old thought to be so ⁵, that there stand here, at the end, words which elsewhere in the Psalms always stand at the beginning. Nor is it anywhere else, "upon *my* stringed instruments." *To the chief singer on my stringed instruments.* To Him to Whom all praise is due, through Whom we praise Himself, His Spirit pleading in us, for us, *upon my stringed instruments*. He Himself, providing, as it were, and teaching the prelude of the endless song, and by His spirit, breathing upon the instrument which He has attuned, and it giving back faithfully, in union with the heavenly Choir with whom it is now blended, the Angelic Hymn, "Glory to God in the Highest."

⁴ Eph. ii. 6.
⁵ It is commented upon as part of the text by S. Cyril and S. Jerome.

INTRODUCTION

TO

THE PROPHET

ZEPHANIAH.

ZEPHANIAH was called to his office, at all events not long after Habakkuk. As his time was near to that of Habakkuk, so his subject also was kindred. Both lived when, for the sins of the reign of Manasseh, God had pronounced upon Jerusalem an irreversible sentence of destruction. The mission of both was not to the whole people whose sentence was fixed, but to the individuals who would *flee from the wrath to come.* The form of Habakkuk's prophecy was (as we might say) more subjective; that of Zephaniah, more objective. Habakkuk exhibits the victory of faith in the oppressed faithful; how it would hold to God amid the domestic oppressions, amid the oppressions of the Chaldees by whom those oppressions were to be punished, and, when all shall seem to fail, should, in the certainty of its unseen life, joy in its God. The characteristic of Zephaniah is the declaration of the tenderness of the love of God for that remnant of Israel, [a] *the afflicted and poor people,* whom God would *leave in the midst of* them.

Zephaniah has, like Habakkuk, to declare the judgment on the world. He renews the language of Joel as to "the day of the Lord," and points it to nations and individuals. He opens with the prophecy of one wide destruction of the land and all the sinners in it, its idolaters and its oppressors, its princes, its royal family, its merchants, its petty plunderers, who used rapine under color of their masters' name, and brought guilt on themselves and them. Nothing is either too high or too low to escape the judgments of God.

But the visitation on Judah was part only of a more comprehensive judgment. Zephaniah foretells the wider destruction of enemies of God's people on all sides; of Philistia, Moab, Ammon, on each side of them, and the distant nations on either side, Ethiopia (which then included Egypt) and Assyria. All these particular judgments contain principles of God's judgments at all times. But in Zephaniah they seem all to converge in the love of God for the remnant of His people. The nation he calls [b] *a nation not desired.* Individuals he calls to God; [c] *it may be, ye shall be hid in the Day of the Lord's anger.* He foretells a sifting time, wherein God would *take away the proud among her* [d]; yet there follows a largeness of Gospel promise and of love [e], the grounds of which are explained in the Gospel, but whose tenderness of language is hardly surpassed even by the overwhelming tenderness of [f] *the love of Christ which passeth knowledge.*

The prophet's own name "the Lord hath hid" corresponds with this. The Psalmist had said, using this same word, "[g] He shall *hide* me in His tabernacle in the day of evil: in the secret of His tabernacle He shall hide me;" and, "O how great is Thy goodness, which Thou hast *laid up* [h] for them that fear Thee. Thou shalt hide them in the secret of Thy presence from the pride of man. Thou shalt *keep them secretly* [i] in a pavilion from the strife of tongues." "[k] They take counsel against Thy *hidden* ones."

The date which Zephaniah prefixed to his prophecy, has not been disputed; for no one

---

a Zeph. iii. 12.   b ii. 1.   c ii. 3.
d iii. 11, 12.   e iii. 12–17.   f Eph. iii. 19.
g Ps. xxvii. 5. ‏יִצְפְּנֵנִי‎.

h ‏צָפַנְתָּ‎.
i Ps. xxxi. 19. 20. ‏תִּצְפּוּם‎.
k Ps. lxxxiii. 4. ‏צְפוּנֶיךָ‎.

15

225

felt any interest in denying it. Those who disbelieve definite prophecy invented for themselves a solution, whereby they thought that Zephaniah's prophecy need not be definite, even though uttered in the time of Josiah; so the fact remained unquestioned.

The unwonted fullness with which his descent is given implies so much of that personal knowledge which soon fades away, that those who speak of other titles, as having been prefixed to the books, or portions of books of the prophets, by later hands, have not questioned this. The only question is, whether he lived before or in the middle of the reformation by Josiah. Josiah, who came to the throne when eight years old B. C. 641, began the reformation in the twelfth year of his reign [1], when almost twenty ; B. C. 630. The extirpation of idolatry could not, it appears, be accomplished at once. The finding of the ancient copy of the law, during the repairs of the temple in the eighteenth year of his reign [m], B. C. 624, gave a fresh impulse to the king's efforts. He then united the people with himself, bound all the people present to the covenant [n] to keep the law, and made a further destruction of idols [o] before the solemn passover in that year. Even after that passover some abominations had to be removed [p]. It has been thought that the words, [q] *I will cut off the remnant of Baal from this place*, imply that the worship of Baal had already in some degree been removed, and that God said, that He would complete what had been begun. But the emphasis seems to be rather on the completeness of the destruction, as we should say, that He would efface every remnant of Baal, than to refer to any effort which had been made by human authority to destroy it.

The prophet joins together, *I will cut off the remnant of Baal, the name of the Chemarim.* The cutting off *the name of the Chemarim*, or idolatrous priests, is like that of Hosea [r], *I will take away the names of Baalim out of her mouth, and they shall no more be remembered by their name.* As the cutting off of *the name of the Chemarim* means their being utterly obliterated, so, probably, does *the cutting off the remnant of Baal.* The worship of Baal was cut off, not through Josiah, but (as Zephaniah prophesied) through the captivity. Jeremiah asserts its continuance during his long prophetic office [s].

In the absence of any direct authority to the contrary, the description of idolatry by Zephaniah would seem to belong to the period, before the measures to abolish it were begun. He speaks as if everything were full of idolatry [t], the worship of Baal, the worship of the host of heaven upon the housetops, swearing by Malcham, and probably the clothing with strange apparel.

The state also was as corrupt [u] as the worship. Princes and judges, priests and prophets were all alike in sin ; the judges distorted the law between man and man, as the priests profaned all which related to God. The princes were roaring lions ; the judges, evening wolves, ever famished, hungering for new prey. This too would scarcely have been, when Josiah was old enough to govern in his own person. Both idolatry and perversion of justice were continued on from the reign of his father Amon. Both, when old enough, he removed. God Himself gives him the praise, that he [v] *did judgment and justice, then* it was *well with him ; he judged the cause of the poor and needy, then* it was *well with him ; was not this to know Me ? saith the Lord.* His conversion was in the eighth year of his reign. Then, *while he was yet young,* he began to *seek after the God of David his father.*

The mention of the *king's children* [w], whom, God says, He would punish in the great day of His visitation, does not involve any later date. They might, anyhow have been brothers or uncles of the king Josiah. But, more probably, God declares that no rank should be exempt from the judgments of that day. He knew too that the sons of Josiah would, for their great sins, be then punished. The sun of the temporal rule of the house of David set in unmitigated wickedness and sorrow. Of all its kings after Josiah, it is said, they *did evil in the sight of the Lord ;* some were distinguished by guilt ; all had miserable ends; some of them aggravated misery.

Zephaniah then probably finished his course before that 12th year of Josiah, (for this prophecy is one whole) and so just before Jeremiah was, in Josiah's 13th year, called to his office, which he fulfilled for half a century, perhaps for the whole age of man.

The foreground of the prophecy of Zephaniah remarkably coincides with that of Habakkuk. Zephaniah presupposes that prophecy and fills it up. Habakkuk had prophesied the great wasting and destruction through the Chaldæans, and then their destruction. That invasion was to extend beyond Judah (for it was said *he shall scoff at kings* [x]), but was to include it. The instrument of God having been named by Habakkuk, Zephaniah does not even allude to him. Rather he brings before Judah the other side, the agency of God Himself. God

---

[1] 2 Chr. xxxiv. 3–7.
[m] 2 Kgs xxii. 2 Chr. xxxiv. 8–28.
[n] 2 Kgs xxiii. 3. 2 Chr. xxxv. 31.
[o] 2 Kgs xxiii. 4–20. 2 Chr. xxxiv. 33.
[p] 2 Kgs xxiii. 24.

[q] Zeph. i. 4.   [r] Hos. ii. 17.
[s] Jer. ii. 8. vii. 9. xi. 13. xix. 5. xxxii. 29.
[t] i. 4. 5.   [u] iii. 3, 4.
[v] Jer. xxii. 15, 16.   [w] See bel. on Zeph. i. 8.
                          [x] Hab. i. 10.

would not have them forget Himself in His instruments. Hence all is attributed to God. [y] *I will utterly consume all things from off the land, saith the Lord. I will consume man and beast ; I will consume the fowls of the heaven, and the fishes of the sea, and the stumblingblocks with the wicked, and I will cut off man from the land, saith the Lord. I will also stretch out Mine hand upon Judah; and I will cut off the remnant of Baal. In the day of the Lord's sacrifice, I will punish the princes, &c. In the same day also I will punish all those &c. I will search Jerusalem with candles. The great day of the Lord is near, and I will bring distress upon, &c. O Canaan, land of the Philistines, I will even destroy thee. The Lord will be terrible upon them. Ye Ethiopians also, ye shall be slain by My sword. And He will destroy Nineveh.* The wicked of the people had [z] *said in their heart, The Lord will not do good, neither will He do evil.* Zephaniah inculcates, throughout his brief prophecy, that there is nothing, good or evil, of which He is not the Doer or Overruler.

But the extent of that visitation is co-extensive with that prophesied by Habakkuk. Zephaniah indeed speaks rather of the effects, the desolation. But the countries, whose desolation or defeat he foretells, are the lands of those, whom the Chaldæans invaded, worsted, in part desolated. Beside Judah, Zephaniah's subjects are Philistia, Moab, Ammon, Ethiopia (which included Egypt), Nineveh. And here he makes a remarkable distinction corresponding with the events. Of the Ethiopians or Egyptians, he says only, [a] *ye shall be slain by My sword.* Of Assyria he foretells [b] the entire and lasting desolation ; the capitals of her palaces in the dust; her cedar-work bare ; flocks, wild-beasts, pelican and hedgehog. taking up their abode in her. Moab and Ammon and Philistia have at first sight the two-fold, apparently contradictory, lot ; *the remnant of My people,* God says, [c] *shall possess them ; the coast shall be for the remnant of the house of Judah;* and, that they should be a perpetual desolation. This also was to take place, after God had brought back His people out of captivity. Now all these countries were conquered by the Chaldæans, of which at the time there was no human likelihood. But they were not swept away by one torrent of conquest. Moab and Ammon were, at first, allies of Nebuchadnezzar, and rejoiced at the miseries

of the people, whose prophets had foretold their destruction. But, beyond this, Nineveh was at that time more powerful than Egypt. Human knowledge could not have discerned, that Egypt should suffer defeat only, Nineveh should be utterly destroyed. It was the wont of the great conquerors of the East, not to destroy capitals, but to re-people them with subjects obedient to themselves. Nineveh had held Babylon by viceroys ; in part she had held it under her own immediate rule. Why should not Babylon, if she conquered Nineveh, use the same policy? Humanly speaking, it was a mistake that she did not. It would have been a strong place against the inroads of the Medo-Persian empire. The Persians saw its value so far for military purposes, as to build some fort there [d]; and the Emperor Claudius, when he made it a colony, felt the importance of the well-chosen situation [e]. It is replaced by Mosul, a city of some " [f] 20000 to 40000 " inhabitants. Even after its destruction, it was easier to rebuild it than to build a city on the opposite bank of the Tigris. God declared that it should be desolate. The prediction implied destruction the most absolute. It and its palaces were to be the abode of animals which flee the presence of man ; and it perished [g].

Again, what less likely than that Philistia, which had had the rule over Israel, strong in its almost impregnable towns, three of whose five cities were named for their strength, Gaza, *strong*; Ashdod, *mighty* ; Ekron, *deep-rooting*; one of which, Ashdod, about this very time, resisted for 29 years the whole power of Egypt, and endured the longest siege of any city of ancient or modern times —what, to human foresight, less likely, than that Philistia should come under the power of the *remnant of the house of Judah*, when returned from their captivity? Yet it is absolutely foretold [h]. *The sea-coast shall be for the remnant of the house of Judah; they shall feed thereupon : in the houses of Ashkelon they shall lie down in the evening. For the Lord their God shall visit them, and restore their captivity.* As unlikely was it, that Moab and Ammon, who now had entered upon the territory of the two and a half tribes beyond Jordan, should themselves become the possession of the remnant of Judah. Yet so it was.

It is then lost labor, even for their own ends, when moderns, who believe not definite prophecy, would find out some enemy [i] whom

[y] Zeph. i. 2, 4, 8, 9, 13, 14, 17. ii. 5, 11, 12, 13.
[z] i. 12.   [a] ii. 12.   [b] ii. 13-15.
[c] ii. 9.
[d] Amm. Marcell. xxiii. 22. The Ninos taken by Meherdates A.D. 59. was on the site of the old Ninos, on the other side of the Tigris. Tac. Ann. xii. 13.
[e] The existence of the Nineve Claudiopolis is attested by coins. See Vaux in Smith's Dict. of Greek and Roman Geogr. v. Ninus.

[f] See Keith Johnstone. Dict. of Geography [ed. 1864, and ed. 1867.
[g] See on Nahum, ab. pp. 122-125.   [h] ii. 7.
[i] The Père Paul Pezron (Essai d'un Comm. lit. et. hist. sur les prophétes 1697) assumed three irruptions of the Scythians : the first prophesied by Amos and Joel; the second, in the reign of Josiah about 631. B. C.; the third, prophesied (he thinks) by Ezek. xxxviii. xxxix. Baseless as all this is, the characteristic of the late writers is not the

Zephaniah may have had in mind in fore-telling this wide destruction. It still remains that all that Zephaniah says beforehand was fulfilled. It is allowed that he could not foretell this through any human foresight. The avowed object in looking out for some power, formidable in Zephaniah's time, is, that he could not, by any human knowledge, be speaking of the Chaldæans. But the words stand there. They were written by Zephaniah, at a time when confessedly no human knowledge could have enabled man to predict this of the Chaldæans; nay, no human knowledge would have enabled any-one to predict so absolutely a desolation so wide and so circumstantially delineated.

That school however has not been willing to acquiesce in this, that Zephaniah does *not* speak of the instrument, through whom this desolation was effected. They will have it, that they know, that Zephaniah had in his mind one, who was *not* the enemy of the Jews or of Nineveh or of Moab and Ammon, and through whom no even transient desolation of these countries was effected. The whole argument is a simple begging of the question. "[k]The Egyptians cannot be meant; for the Cushites, who are threatened[l], themselves belong to the Egyptian army[m], and Psammetichus only besieged Ashdod which he also took, without emblazoning ought greater on his shield[n]. The Chaldæans come still less into account, because they did not found an independent kingdom until B. C. 625, nor threaten Judæa until after Josiah's death. On the other hand an unsuspicious and well-accredited account has been preserved to us, that somewhere about this time the Scyth-ians overflowed Palestine too with their hosts. Herodotus relates[o], that the Scyth-ians, after they had disturbed Cyaxares at the siege of Nineveh, turned toward Egypt; and when they had already arrived in Pales-tine, were persuaded by Psammetichus to re-turn, and in their return plundered a temple in Ascalon."

It is true that Herodotus says that " a large Scythian army did, under their king Madyes, burst into Asia in pursuit of the Cimmerians and entered Media,—keeping Mount Cauca-sus on the right," and that " the Medes op-posed and fought them and, being defeated, lost their rule[p]."

It is true also that Herodotus relates, that "[q]they went thence toward Egypt, and when they were in Palestine-Syria, Psammetichus king of Egypt, meeting them, turned them by gifts and entreaties from going further;

that when in their return they were in Asca-lon, a city of Syria, whereas most of the Scythians passed by without harming ought, some few of them, being left behind, plun-dered the temple of Venus Ourania." In this place also, it is true, Herodotus uses a vague expression, that "[r]for 28 years the Scythians ruled over Asia, and that all things were turned upside down by their violence and contempt. For beside the tributes, they ex-acted from each what they laid upon each, and beside the tribute, they drove together and took what each had. And most of them Cyaxares and the Medes entertaining as guests, intoxicated and slew. And then the Medes recovered their empire and *became masters of what they held before*."

But, apart from the inconsistency of the period here assigned to their power, with other history, it appears from the account itself, that by " all Asia " Herodotus means " all upper Asia," as he expresses himself more accurately, when relating the expe-dition of Darius against them. "[s]Darius wished to take revenge on the Scythians, because they first, making an inroad into Media and defeating in battle those who went against them, began the wrong. For the Scythians, as I have before said, *ruled upper Asia* for 28 years. For, pursuing the Cim-merians, they made an inroad into Asia, putting down the Medes from their rule; for these, before the Scythians came, ruled Asia." The Asia then, which Herodotus supposes the Scythians to have ruled, is co-extensive with the Asia which he supposes the Medes to have ruled previously. But this was all in the North ; for having said that "[t]Phra-ortes subdued Asia, going from one nation to another," he adds that, having brought Per-sia under his yoke, " he led an army against those Assyrians who had Nineveh, and there lost most of his army and his own life." Apart then from the fabulousness of this supposed empire, established by Phraortes[u], (Cyax-ares having been the real founder of the Median empire,) it is plain that, according to Herodotus himself, the Asia, in which the Scythians plundered and received tribute, were the lands North of Assyria. The expedi-tion against Egypt stands as an insulated pre-datory excursion, the object of which having been mere plunder, they were bought off by Psammetichus and returned (he tells us) do-ing no mischief[v] in their way, except that a few lingerers plundered a temple at Ascalon. It was to Media that they first came ; the Medes, whom they defeated ; the Median

---

selection of the Scythians as the object of the prophecy (which were a thing indifferent) but the grounds alleged for that selection.

[k] Hitzig.　　　　　　　　　　　　　[l] ii. 12.
[m] Jer. xlvi. 9.
[n] Herod. ii. 157.　　　　　　　　[o] Ib. i. 105.
[p] Ib. i. 103, 104.　　　　　　　　[q] Ib. 105.

[r] i. 106. He uses the same wide expression as to Cyrus, after the defeat of Crœsus. "Having sub-dued him, he thus ruled over all Asia," (i. 130); whereas he had not yet conquered Babylon.
[s] Ib. i. 106.　　　　　　　　　　　[t] iv. 4.
[u] i. 102. See above p. 119. and Rawlinson Herod. quoted ib.　　　　　　　　[v] ἀσινέων. Her. l. c.

empire to which they succeeded; Cyaxares and the Medes, who treacherously destroyed most of them; the Medes, whose empire was restored by the destruction of some, and the return of the rest to their own land. With this agrees the more detailed account of the Scythians by Strabo, who impeaches the accuracy of the accounts of Herodotus [w]. Having spoken of the migrations of leaders, and by name, of "[x] Madyes the Scythian " (under whom Herodotus states the irruption to have taken place), he says, "[y] the Sacæ made the like inroad as the Cimmerians and the Trerians, some longer, some nigh at hand; for they took possession of Bactriana, and acquired the best land of Armenia, which they also left, named after them Sacasene, and advanced as far as to the Cappadocians and especially those on the Euxine, whom they now call of Pontus (Pontians). But the generals of the Persians who were at the time there, attacking them by night, while they were making a feast upon the spoils, utterly extirpated them." The direction which he says they took, is the same as that of the Cimmerians, whom Herodotus says that they followed. "[z] The Cimmerians, whom they also call Trerians, or some tribe of them, often overrun the right side of the Pontus, sometimes making inroads on the Paphlagonians, at others, on the Phrygians. Often also the Cimmerians and Trerians made the like attacks, and they say that the Trerians and Cobus [their king] were, at last expelled by Madyes king of the [Scythians]." Strabo also explains, what is meant by the tributes, of which Herodotus speaks. He is speaking of the Nomadic tribes of the Scythians generally: "[a] Tribute was, to allow them at certain stated times, to overrun the country [for pasturage] and carry off booty. But when they roamed beyond the agreement, there arose war, and again reconciliations and renewed war. Such was the life of the nomads, always setting on their neighbors and then being reconciled again."

The Scythians then were no object of fear to the Jews, whom they passed wholly unnoticed and probably unconscious of their existence in their mountain country, while they once and once only swept unharming along the fertile tracks on the sea-shore, then occupied by the old 'enemies and masters of the Jews, the Philistines. But Herodotus must also have been misinformed as to the length of time, during which they settled in Media, or at least as to the period during which their presence had any sensible effects. For Cyaxares, whom he represents as having raised

the siege of Nineveh, in consequence of the inroad of the Scythians into Media, came to the throne, according to the numbers of Herodotus, B. C. 633. For the reign of Cyaxares having lasted according to him 40 years [b], that of Astyages 35 [c], and that of Cyrus 29 [d], these 104 years, counted back from the known date of the death of Cyrus, B. C. 529 or 530, bring us to B. C. 633 or 636 as the beginning of the reign of Cyaxares. But the invasion of the Scythians could not have taken place at the first accession of Cyaxares, since, according to Herodotus, he had already defeated the Assyrians, and was besieging Nineveh, when the Scythians burst into Media. According to Herodotus, moreover, Cyaxares "[e] first distributed Asiatics into troops, and first ordered that each should be apart, spearmen, and archers and cavalry; for before, all were mixed pele-mele together." Yet it would not be in a very short time, that those who had been wont to fight in a confused mass, could be formed into an orderly and disciplined army. We could not then, anyhow, date the Scythian inroad, earlier than the second or third year of Cyaxares. On the other hand the date of the capture of Nineveh is fixed by the commencement of the Babylonian Empire, Babylon falling to Nabopolassar. The duration of that empire is measured by the reigns of its kings [f], of whom, according to Ptolemy's Canon, Nabopolassar reigned 21 years; Nebuchadnezzar, (there called Nabocollasar) 43; Evil-Merodach (Iluaroadam) 2; Neriglissar (Niricassolassar) 4; Nabunahit (Nabonadius with whom his son Belshazzar was co-regent) 17; in all 87 years; and it ends in an event of known date, the capture of Babylon by Cyrus, B. C. 538. The addition of the 87 years of the duration of the empire to that date carries us back to the date assigned to the capture of Nineveh by Nabopolassar in conjunction with Cyaxares, B. C. 625. The capture then of Nineveh was removed by 8 or 9 years only from that, which Herodotus gives as the time of the accession of Cyaxares, and since the attack upon Nineveh can hardly have been in his first year, and the last siege probably occupied two, the 28 years of Scythian dominion would dwindle down into something too inconsiderable for history. Probably they represent some period from their first incursion into Media, to the final return of the survivors, during which they marauded in Media and Upper Asia. The mode, by which "the greater part" (Herodotus tells us) were destroyed, intoxication and subsequent murder at a banquet, implies that

---

[w] "More readily might we believe Homer and Hesiod in their tales of heroes, and the tragic poets, than Ctesias and Herodotus and Hellanicus and others of the same sort." xi. 6. 3.
[x] i. 3. 21.   [y] xi. 8. 4.
[a] Prol. i. 3. 21.   [a] xi. 8. 3.

[b] Herod. i. 106.   [c] Ib. 130.   [d] Ib. 214.   [e] Ib. 103.
[f] Berosus, in his Chaldæan history, agrees as to these dates, only adding 9 months for the son of Neriglissar, Laborosoarchod, in Jos. Ant. x. 11. combined with cont. Apion. i. 20, and Eus. Præp. Evang. ix. 40.

their numbers were no longer considerable.

History, with the exception of that one marauding expedition toward Egypt, is entirely silent as to any excursions of the Scythians, except in the North. No extant document hints at any approach of theirs to any country mentioned by Zephaniah. There was no reason to expect any inroad from them. With the exception of Bactriana, which lies some 18 degrees East of Media and itself extended over some 7 degrees of longitude, the countries mentioned by Strabo lie, to what the kings of Assyria mention as the far North, Armenia, and thence they stretched out to the West, yet keeping mostly to the neighborhood of the Euxine. Considering the occasion of the mention of the invasion of the Scythians, the relief which their invasion of Media gave to Nineveh, it is even remarkable that there is no mention of any ravages of theirs throughout Mesopotamia or Babylonia. Zephaniah speaks, not of marauding, but of permanent desolation of Assyria, Philistia, Moab, Ammon, and of destructive war also on Ethiopia. There is no reason to think that the Scythians approached any of these lands, except Philistia, which they passed through unharming. The sacred writers mention even smaller nations, by whom God chastised Judah in their times, *bands of the Syrians, of Moab, of the children of Ammon*, as well as Assyria and Babylon. Ezekiel [g], when he prophesies of the inroad of Northern nations, Meshech and Tubal, Gomer and Togarmah, speaks of it as far removed in the future, prophesies not their destroying but their own destruction.

It does not affect the argument from prophecy, whether Zephaniah did or did not know, through whom the events, which he predicted, should be brought to pass. But, setting aside the question whether he had from the prophecies of Habakkuk and Isaiah, a human knowledge of the Chaldees, or whether God instructed him, how what he foretold should be accomplished, or whether God spread out before his mind that which was to be, apart from time, in prophetic vision, Zephaniah *did* picture what came to pass. But it is an intense paradox, when men, 2500 years after his date, assert, not only that Zephaniah's prophecies had no relation to the Chaldees, in whom his words were fulfilled, and who are the objects of the prophecies of Habakkuk and Jeremiah, but

that *they* know, what *must* have been, and (as they assert) what *was* in the prophet's mind; and that he had in his mind, *not* those in whom his words were fulfilled, but others in whom they were *not* fulfilled, to whom he does not allude in one single trait, who left no trace behind them, and whose march along an enemy's tract on the sea-coast was of so little account, that no contemporary historian, nor Josephus, even alludes to it [h].

It has been already observed, that each prophet connects himself with one or more of those before them. They use the language of their predecessors in some one or more sentences, apparently with this precise object. They had overflowing fullness of words; yet they chose some saying of the former prophet, as a link to those before them. We have seen this in Amos [i], then in Obadiah [k], who uses the language of Balaam, David, Joel, Amos; of Jeremiah, in regard to Obadiah [l]; of Micah to his great predecessor, Micaiah, and Amos [m]; of Jeremiah, Habakkuk, Zephaniah, Ezekiel to Micah [n]; of Nahum to Jonah [o]; and of Isaiah (I think), to Nahum [p]; of Habakkuk, to Isaiah and Micah [q]. It is in conformity with this, that Zephaniah, even more than those before him, uses language of earlier prophets. It arises, not (as people have been pleased to say) from any declension in the originality of prophets at his date, but from his subject. It has been said, " If any one desire to see the utterances of the prophets in brief space, let him read through this brief Zephaniah." The office of Zephaniah was not to forewarn of any instrument of God's judgments. The destruction is prophesied, not the destroyer. His prophecy is, more than those of most other prophets, apart from time, to the end of time. He prophesies of *what* shall be, not *when* it shall be, nor *by whom*. He does not "expect" or "anticipate" or "forebode!" He absolutely declares the future condition of certain nations; but not the *how* of its coming to pass. If Nineveh, Edom and Ammon had not been desolated, his prophecy would have been falsified; each fulfillment became the earnest of a larger fulfillment; but all shall not be completed until *the earth and all that is therein shall be burned up.*

It belongs to this character of Zephaniah, that he gathers from other prophets before him, especially Isaiah, Joel, Amos, Habakkuk, expressions relating to, or bearing on,

---

[g] Ezek. xxxviii. xxxix.

[h] The name Σκυθόπολις, which Josephus says the Greeks gave to Bethshan, (Ant. 12. 8. 5) and which they alone can have given, is manifestly, as being Greek, too late to contain any tradition as to the presence of the Scythians in Palestine, three centuries before the Greeks, under Alexander, became acquainted with Palestine. S. Jerome regarded it as a corruption of *Succoth.* He says on Gen. xxxiii. 17, "In the Hebrew is read *Sucoth* (סכת). But

there is to this day a city beyond Jordan into which this name enters in part, Scythopolis." Quæstt. Hebr. ad Gen. [Opp. iii. 358. ed. Vall.] quoted by Reland, p. 992.

[i] See Introd. to Joel vol. i. p. 143.
[k] See Introd. to Obadiah vol. i. pp. 343-351.
[l] Ib. pp. 343-347.
[m] See Introd to Micah ab. p. 5.   [n] Ib.
[o] See Introd. to Nahum ab. p. 105.
[p] Ib. 125.   [q] Ib. 168.

judgment to come, or again to that his other great subject, God's love for the remnant of His people; yet mostly in fragments only and allusively. They were key-notes for those who knew the prophets. Thus, in calling on man to hushed submission before God, because a day of judgment was coming, he blends into one verse[r] Habakkuk's call, *hush before the Lord*, and the warning words of Isaiah, Joel, Obadiah, [t] *nigh is the day of the Lord;* the image of the *sacrifice*, which God had commanded, and the remarkable word, *consecrated*, of God's instruments. The allusion is contained in single words, *sacrifice*, *consecrated;* the context in which they are embodied is different. The idea only is the same, that Almighty God maketh, as it were, a sacrifice to Himself of those who incorrigibly rebel against Him. Else Isaiah draws out the image at much length; [u] *A sword of the Lord is full of bloods; it is smeared with fat, with the blood of lambs and of goats; with the fat of kidneys of rams: for the Lord hath a sacrifice in Bozrah, and a great slaughter in the land of Edom.* Jeremiah uses the image in equal fullness of the overthrow of Pharaoh-Necho at the Euphrates; [v] *This is a day of the Lord God of hosts, a day of vengeance, that He may avenge Him of His adversaries: and the sword shall devour, and it shall be satiate and made drunk with blood; for the Lord God hath a sacrifice in the North country by the river Euphrates.* Ezekiel expands it yet more boldly [w]. Zephaniah drops everything local, and condenses the image into the words, *The Lord hath prepared a sacrifice; He hath consecrated His guests*, adding the new bold image, that they whom God employed were, as it were, His invited guests[x], whom He consecrated[y] thereto.

In like way, as to the day of the Lord itself, he accumulates all words of terror from different prophets; from Joel the words, [z] *a day of darkness and of gloominess; a day of clouds and of thick darkness:* to these he adds [a] *of shouting and the sound of the trumpet*, used by Amos in relation to the destruction

of Moab; the two combinations, which precede, occur, the one in a different sense, the other with a slightly different grammatical inflection, in Job [b].

From Isaiah, Zephaniah adopts that characteristic picture of self-idolizing, which brings down God's judgments on its pride; (the city) [c] *that dwelleth securely, that said in her heart, I and no I beside.*

Even where Isaiah says, [d] *For a consumption and that decreed, the Lord God of hosts makes in the midst of all the earth* and, slightly varying it, [e] *For a consumption and that decreed, I have heard from the Lord God of hosts upon all the earth,* Zephaniah, retaining the two first words, which occur in both places, says more concisely, [f] *For a consumption, nought but terror, will He make all the inhabitants of the earth.* Yet simple as the words are, he pronounced, that God would not only *bring a desolation upon the earth*, or *in the midst of the earth*, but would make its inhabitants one consumption. Nahum had said of Nineveh, [g] *with an overflowing flood He will make the place thereof an utter consumption.* The most forceful words are the simplest.

He uses the exact words of Isaiah, [h] *From beyond the rivers of Cush*, than which none can be simpler, and employs the word of festive procession, though in a different form[i], and having thus connected his prophecy with Isaiah's, all the rest, upon which the prophecy turns, is varied.

In like way he adopts from Micah the three words[k], *her-that-halteth, and-will-gather her-that-is-driven-out.* The context in which he resets them is quite different.

It has been thought, that the words, [l] *I have heard the reproach of Moab*, may have been suggested by those of Isaiah, who begins his lament over Moab, *We have heard of the pride of Moab;* but the force and bearing of the words is altogether different, since it is God Who says, *I have heard*, and so He will punish.

The combination[m], *the exulters of pride*, is common to him with Isaiah: its meaning is

---

[r] i. 7.　[s] Hab. ii. 20.

[t] Is. xiii. 6. Jo. i. 15. iv. 15. Ob. 15. The words יום יי are used of a day of God's judgments, Is. xiii. 9, Jo. ii. 1, 11, Am. v. 18, 20. Ezek. xiii. 5. Mal. iii. 23, not with קרוב. In Is. ii. 12, it is יום ליי or in Jo. ii. 1. subordinately.

[u] Is. xxxiv. 6.　[v] Jer. xlvi. 10.

[w] Ezek. xxxix. 17.

[x] Zephaniah's word, קְרָאִים occurs beside only in 1 Sam. ix. 13.

[y] Isaiah's word (xiii. 3.) is מקדשׁי; Zephaniah's הקדישׁ.

[z] יום חשׁך ואפלה יום ענן וערפל Jo. ii. 2. Zeph. i. 15.

[a] שׁופר ותרועה Zeph. i. 16. Am. ii. 2.

[b] צד ומצוקה שׁואה ומשׁואה Job xxxviii. 27. xv. 24. Zeph. has ומצ. צרות stands parallel with מצוקות Ps. xxv. 17.

[c] היושׁבת לבטח האמרה בלבבה אני ואפסי עוד.

[d] Is. x. 23.　[e] Ib. xxviii. 22.

[f] כי כלה. He retains the simplest words, but substitutes אך נבהלה (a word formed by himself) for the ונחרצה of Isaiah.

[g] Nah. i. 8.

[h] מעבר לנהרי כושׁ Zeph. iii. 10. Is. xviii. 1.

[i] יובלון Zeph. iii. יבל Is. xviii. 7.

[k] והצלעה והנדחה אקבצה Mic. iv. 6. Zeph. iii. 19.

[l] שׁמעתי חרפת מואב Zeph. ii. 8. שׁמענו גאון מואב Is. xvi. 6.

[m] עליזי גאותך Is. xiii. 3. עליזי גאותי Zeph. iii. 11.

uncertain; but it is manifestly different in the two places, since the one relates to God, the other to man.

The words, [n] *They shall build houses and shall not dwell therein; they shall plant vineyards and not drink the wine thereof,* are from the original threat in Deuteronomy, from which also the two words, [o] *They-shall-walk as-the-blind,* may be a reminiscence, but with a conciseness of its own and without the characteristic expressions of Deuteronomy, adopted by other sacred writers: [p] *They shall grope at noonday, as the blind gropeth in darkness.*

Altogether these passages are evidence that Zephaniah is of later date than the prophecies in which the like language occurs; and the fact that he does employ so much language of his predecessors furnishes a strong presumption in any single case, that he in that case also adopted from the other sacred writer the language which they have in common.

It is chiefly on this ground, that a train of modern critics [q] have spoken disparagingly of the outward form and style of Zephaniah. It has however a remarkable combination of fullness with conciseness and force. Thus, he begins the enumeration of those upon whom the destruction should fall, with the words, [r] *consuming I will consume all:* to an enumeration co-extensive with the creation, he adds unexpectedly, [s] *and the stumblingblocks with the wicked,* anticipating our Lord's words of the Day of Judgment, [t] *they shall gather the stumblingblocks and them that do iniquity:* to the different idolatries he adds those of a divided faith, [u] *swearers to the Lord and swearers by Malcham;* to those who turned away from God he adds those who were unearnest in seeking Him [v].

Again, after the full announcement of the destruction in the Day of the Lord, the burst, in those five words, [w] *sift-yourselves and-sift (on) nation unlonged for,* is, in suddenness and condensation, like Hosea; and so again, in five words, after the picture of the future desolation of Nineveh. the abrupt turn to Jerusalem, [x] *Woe rebellious and-defiled (thou) oppressive city,* and then follow the several counts of her indictment, in brief disjointed sentences, first negatively, as a whole; each in three or four words [y], *she-listened not to-voice; she-received not correction; in-the-Lord she-trusted not; to-her-God she-approached not;*

then, in equally broken words, each class is characterized by its sins; [z] *her-princes in-her-midst* are *roaring lions; her-judges evening wolves; not gnawed-they-bones on-the-morrow; her-prophets empty-babblers, men of-deceits; her-priests profaned holiness, violated law.* Then in sudden contrast to all this contumacy, neglect, despite of God, He Himself is exhibited as *in the midst of her;* the witness and judge of all; there, where they sinned. [a] *The-Lord righteous in-her-midst; He-doth not iniquity; by-morning by-morning His-judgment He-giveth to-light; He-faileth not;* and then in contrast to the holiness and the judgments of God, follows in four words, the perseverance of man in his shamelessness, and—the fruit of all this presence and doings of the Holy and Righteous God and Judge is, and-*not knoweth the wrong-doer shame.* Zephaniah uses the same disjoining of the clauses in the description of God's future manifestation of His love toward them. Again it is the same thought [b], *The-Lord thy-God-(is) in-thy-midst;* but now in love; *mighty, shall-save; He-shall-rejoice over-thee with-joy; He-shall-keep-silence in-His-love; He-shall-rejoice over-thee with-jubilee.* The single expressions are alike condensed; [c] *she-hearkened not to-voice,* stands for what Jeremiah says at such much greater length, how God had sent all His servants [d] *the prophets, daily rising up early and sending them, but they hearkened not unto Me nor inclined their ear, but hardened their neck.* The words [e] *shall-be-silent in-His-love,* in their primary meaning, express the deepest human love, but without the wonted image of betrothal.

[f] *The whole people of Canaan* reminds one of Hosea; [g] *the-men-coagulated on-their-lees* is much expanded by Jeremiah [h], his word occurs before him in Job only and the song of Moses [i]. Single poetic expressions are, that Moab should become [k] *the possession of briars,* the word itself being framed by Zephaniah; in the description of the desolation of Nineveh, [l] *a voice singeth in the window; desolation is on the threshold,* the imagery is so bold, that modern criticism has thought that the word *voice* which occurs in the O. T. 328 times and with pronouns 157 times more, must signify "an owl," and *desolation* must stand for "a crow [m]." Very characteristic is the word, "He [n] *shall famish* all the gods of the earth," expressing with wonderful irony, the privation of their sacrifices, which was

with the LXX, into יַחְרִישׁ which does not occur elsewhere. But the LXX renders "shall renew thee;" Ewald, "(God) *becomes young* (sich verjüngt) in His love!"

[n] Zeph. i. 13. Deut. xxviii. 30, 39. The words are more exact than in Micah vi. 14. Am. v. 11.

[o] הֵלְכוּ כַעִוְרִים Zeph. i. 17. [p] Deut. xxviii. 29.

[q] Eichhorn, De Wette, Stähelin, and their followers. De Wette however does own, "In employing what is not his own, he is, at least, original in its expansion." Einl. 245. note b.

[r] i. 2.   [s] i. 3.   [t] S. Matt. xiii. 41.   [u] Zeph. i. 5.
[v] i. 6.   [w] ii. 1.   [x] ii. 1.   [y] iii. 2.   [z] Ib. 3, 4.
[a] Ib. 5,   [b] Ib. 17.   [c] iii. 2.   [d] Jer. vii. 24–28.
[e] iii. 17.   Some modern commentators take umbrage at the beautiful expression. Ewald alters,

[f] Zeph. i. 11. Comp. Hos. xii. 7.   [g] i. 12.
[h] Jer. xlviii. 11.   [i] Job x. 10. Ex. xv. 8.
[k] ii. 9.   [l] ii. 14.

[m] קוֹל must answer to the Ethiopian קָאַץ γλαὐξ and our *eule* (owl); and חֹרֶב seems equal יָרָב." Ewald Proph. ii. 25.
[n] See below on ii. 11.

the occasion of the first Heathen persecutions of the Christians.

When then a writer, at times so concise and poetic as Zephaniah is in these places, is, at others, so full in his descriptions, this is not prolixity, but rather vivid picturing; at one time going through all the orders of creation [o]; at another, different classes of the ungodly [p]; at yet another, the different parts of the scared woe-stricken city [q], to set before our eyes the universality of the desolation. Those who are familiar with our own great Northern poet of nature, will remember how the accumulation of names adds to the vividness of his descriptions. Yet here too there is great force in the individual descriptions, as when he pictures the petty plunderers for their master, and *fill their masters' houses*—not with wealth but—*with violence and fraud* [r], all which remains of wealth gained by fraud and extortion being the sins themselves, which dwell in the house of the fraudulent to his destruction.

In the strictly prophetic part of his office, Jerusalem having been marked out by Micah and Isaiah before him, as the place where God would make the new revelation of Himself, Zephaniah adds, what our Lord revealed to the Samaritan woman, [s]that Jerusalem should no longer be the abiding centre of worship. [t] *They shall worship Him, every man from his place, all the isles of the nations*, is a prophecy which, to this day, is receiving an increasing accomplishment. It is a prophecy, not of the spread of Monotheism, but of the worship of Him, to Whose worship at that time a handful of Jews could with difficulty be brought to adhere, the desertion or corruption or association of Whose worship with idolatry Zephaniah had to denounce and to foretell its punishment. The love which God should then shew to His own is expressed in words, unequaled for tenderness; and in conformity to that love is the increasing growth of holiness, and the stricter requirements of God's holy justice. Again, Zephaniah has a prelude to our Blessed Lord's words, [u] *to whom much is given, of him shall much be required*, or His Apostle's, of the great awe in working out our salvation [v]. Progress is a characteristic and condition of the Christian life; [w] *We beseech you, that as ye have received of us, how ye ought to walk and to please God, ye would abound more and more.* Even so Zephaniah bids [x] *all the meek of the earth, who have wrought His judgments or law to seek diligently* that *meekness*, which had already characterized them, and that, not in view of great things, but, if so be they might

be saved; *it may be that ye may be hid in the day of the Lord's anger*, as S. Peter saith, [y] *If the righteous scarcely be saved, where shall the ungodly and the sinner appear?* It is again remarkable, how he selects meekness, as the characteristic of the new state of things, which he promises. He anticipates the contrast in the Magnificat, in which the lowest lowliness was rewarded by the highest exaltation. As it is said there, [z] *He hath put down the mighty from their seat and hath exalted the humble and meek*, so the removal of the proud *from within thee*, and the "leaving of an afflicted and poor people *within thee* [a]," is the special promise by Zephaniah.

Little is said of the captivity. It is a future variously assumed [b]. Judah in the furthest lands, *beyond the rivers of Ethiopia*, is the daughter of *My dispersed* [c]; the whole earth is the scene of their shame [d]; their praises should be commensurate with their shame, *when I turn back your captivity before your eyes* [e]. But this turning away of their captivity is the only notice, that their punishment should be the going into captivity. The captivity itself is pre-supposed, as certain and as known. So neither are there any images from temporal exaltation. All pride should be removed, as utterly unbefitting God's holy presence: *thou shalt no more be haughty in My holy mountain* [f]. The words expressive of the abasement of those within her are proportionally strong, [g] *My afflicted and poor.* Some are wont, in these days, to talk of God's prophets as patriots. They were such truly, since they loved the land of the Lord with a Divine love. But what mere "patriot" would limit his promises to the presence of "a poor people in a low estate," with an unseen presence of God? The description belongs to *His* kingdom, which was *not of this world* [h]: the only king whom Zephaniah speaks of, *the king of Israel* [i], is Almighty God. The blessing which he promises, is the corresponding blessing of peace, [k] *Fear thou not; thou shalt not see evil any more, none shall make them afraid.* But the words [k] *Let not thy hands be slack*, imply that they shall be aggressive on the world; that they were not to relax from the work which God assigned to them, the conversion of the world.

An allusion to the prophet Joel [1] makes it uncertain whether words of Zephaniah relate to the first Coming of our Lord, or the times which should usher in the Second, or to both in one; and so, whether, in accordance with his general character of gathering into one all God's judgments to His end, he

---

[o] i. 3.   [p] Ib. 4–9.   [q] Ib. 10, 11.
[r] Ib. 9. Amos has the like idea (iii. 10) but no word is the same except חמס.
[s] S. John iv. 21.   [t] ii. 11.
[u] S. Luke xii. 48.   [v] Phil. ii. 12.
[w] 1 Thess. iv. 1.   [x] ii. 3.

[y] 1 S. Pet. iv. 18.   [z] S. Luke ii. 52.
[a] Zeph. iii. 12.   [b] Ib. 13.   [c] Ib. 10.
[d] Ib. 19.   [e] Ib. 20. add. ii. 7.   [f] Ib. 11.
[g] Ib. 12.   [h] S. John xviii. 36.
[i] Zeph. iii. 15.
[k] iii. 16.   [l] iii. 2. [iv. 2 Heb.]

is speaking of the first restoration of the one
purified language of faith and hope, when
[m] *the multitude of them that believed were of one
heart and of one soul,* or whether he had his
mind fixed rather on the end, *when* [n] *the fullness of the Gentiles shall come in.* The words
also (since they may be taken either way [o])
leave it uncertain whether the Gentiles are
spoken of as bringing in the people of God,
(as they shall at the end) or whether the

first conversion of the Jews, even in the most
distant countries, is his subject.

In any case, Zephaniah had a remarkable
office, to declare the mercy and judgment of
God, judgments both temporal and final,
mercies, not of this world, promised to a
temper not of this world, [p] *the wisdom which
is from above, pure, peaceable, gentle, easy to
be entreated, full of mercy and good fruits,
without partiality and without hypocrisy.*

[m] Acts iv. 32.   [n] Rom. xi. 25.   [o] See on Zeph. iii. 10.   [p] S. James iii. 7.

ZEPHANIAH.

CHAPTER I.

*God's severe judgment against
Judah for divers sins.*

THE word of the LORD
which came unto Zeph-
aniah the son of Cushi,
the son of Gedaliah, the

son of Amariah, the son
of Hizkiah, in the days of
Josiah the son of Amon,
king of Judah.

2 I † will utterly con-
sume all *things* from off
† the land, saith the LORD.

† Heb. *By taking
away I will
make an end.*
† Heb. *the face
of the land.*

CHAP. I., Ver. 1. *The word of the Lord
which came unto Zephaniah the son of Cushi, the
son of Gedaliah, the son of Amariah, the son of
Hezekiah.* It seems likely that more forefathers of the Prophet are named than is the
wont of Holy Scripture, because the last so
named was some one remarkable. Nor is
it impossible that Zephaniah should have
been the great grandson of the king Hezekiah ; for although Holy Scripture commonly
names the one son only who is in the sacred
line, and although there is one generation
more than to Josiah, yet if each had a son
early, Zephaniah might have been contemporary with Josiah. The names seem also
mentioned for the sake of their meaning ;
at least it is remarkable how the name of
God appears in most. Zephaniah, "whom
the Lord hid ;" Gedaliah, "whom the Lord
made great ;" Amariah, "whom the Lord
promised ;" Hezekiah, "whom the Lord
strengthened."

2. *I will utterly consume all things ;* better
all [1]. The word is not limited to "things"
"animate" or "inanimate" or "men ;" it is
used severally of each, according to the
context ; here, without limitation, of "all."
God and *all* stand over against one another ;
God and *all* which is not of God or in God.
God, he says, will *utterly consume all from off
the land* [*earth.*] The prophet sums up in

few words the subject of the whole chapter,
the judgments of God from his own times to
the day of Judgment itself. And this Day
Itself he brings the more strongly before the
mind, in that, with wonderful briefness, in
two words which he conforms, in sound also,
the one to the other, [2] he expresses the utter
final consumption of all things. He expresses
at once the intensity of action and blends
their separate meanings, *Taking away I will
make an end of all ;* and with this he unites
the words used of the flood, *from off the face of
the earth* [3]. Then he goes through the whole
creation as it was made, pairing *man and
beast,* which Moses speaks of as created on
the sixth day, and the creation of the fifth
day, *the fowls of the heaven and the fishes of the
sea ;* and before each he sets the solemn word
of God, *I will end,* as the act of God Himself.
The words can have no complete fulfillment,
until [4] *the earth and the works that are therein
shall be burned up,* as the Psalmist too, having
gone through the creation, sums up, [5] *Thou
takest away their breath, they die and return to
their dust ;* and then speaks of the re-creation,
[6] *Thou sendest forth Thy Spirit, they are created ;
and Thou renewest the face of the earth,* and,
[7] *Of old Thou hast laid the foundations of the
earth, and the heavens are the work of Thy
hands ; they shall perish, but Thou shalt endure,
yea, all of them shall wax old like a garment ;* as

---

[1] כל is used absolutely in a title of God, "Who
maketh all," יֹצֵר הַכֹּל, Is. xliv. 24; "Thou canst do
all," i. e. art Almighty, Job xlii. 2 ; "Thou hast put
all כֹּל שַׁתָּה, under his feet," Ps. viii. 7 ; and of
man, "mine eye hath seen all," Job xiii. 1 ; and
personally, gathering in one all which he had said
of God's doings, with לֹא תָחְסַר "want not any
thing," De. viii. 9. תֶחְסַר, חֹסֶר "want of every
thing," Jer. xliv. 18. De. xxviii. 48. 57 ; "all were
[lit. *was*] ashamed" (with sing. verb) כֹּל הֹבִאישׁ
Is. xxx. 5.

[2] So also Jeremiah viii. 13, in the same words,
אָסֹף אֲסִיפֵם. Rashi makes them one word, supposing אָסֹף to be for אַאֲסֹף. A. E. mentions those
who thought that א in אָסוּף was prefixed, as in
אֲרֹשׁ Is. xxviii. 28 ; but it is unnatural to assume
a rare and irregular form, when the word אָסוּף is
the regular form from the common word אָסַף.

[3] הָאֲדָמָה signifies "earth," almost always in the
phrase עַל פְּנֵי הָאֲדָמָה, always in the phrase
מֵעַל פְּנֵי הָאֲדָמָה, unless they be limited by some
addition, as "which the Lord sware that He would
give thee." עַל פְּנֵי הָאֲדָמָה is thus used Gen. vi.
1, vii. 23, Ex. xxxiii. 16, Nu. xii. 3, De. vii. 6, xiv. 2,
2 Sam. xiv. 7, Is. xxiii. 17, Jer. xxv. 26, Ezek.
xxxviii. 20. מֵעַל פְּנֵי הָאֲדָמָה "from the face of
the earth" occurs, unlimited by the context. Gen.
iv. 14, vi. 7, vii. 4, viii. 8, Ex. xxxii. 12, De. vi. 15. 1
Sam. xx. 15. 1 Kgs xiii. 34. Jer. xxviii. 16. Am. ix.
8. אֲדָמָה is used of cultivable land, and so
עַל פְּנֵי הָאֲדָמָה is used in connection with rain
falling on the ground, 1 Kgs xvii. 14 ; but מֵעַל פ.
הָא. suffers no exception, unless it be restrained
by an addition.

[4] 2 S. Pet. iii. 10   [5] Ps. civ. 29.
[6] Ps. civ. 30.   [7] Ib. cii. 25.

235

Before CHRIST cir. 630.

3 ^aI will consume man and beast; I will consume the fowls of the heaven, and the fishes of the sea, and ^bthe ‖stumbling blocks with the wicked; and I will cut off man

a Hos. 4. 3.

b Ezek. 7. 19.
& 14. 3, 4, 7.
Matt. 13. 41.
‖ Or, *idols.*

from off the land, saith the LORD.

4 I will also stretch out mine hand upon Judah, and upon all the inhabitants of Jerusalem; and ^cI will cut off the rem-

Before CHRIST cir. 630.

c Fulfilled, cir. 624.
2 Kin. 23. 4, 5.

---

a vesture shalt Thou change them, and they shall be changed. Local fulfillments there may, in their degree, be. S. Jerome speaks as if he knew this to have been. " [1] Even the brute animals feel the wrath of the Lord, and when cities have been wasted and men slain, there cometh a desolation and scarceness of beasts also and birds and fishes; witness Illyricum, witness Thrace, witness my native soil," [Stridon, a city on the confines of Dalmatia and Pannonia] "where, beside sky and earth and rampant brambles and deep thickets, all has perished." But although this fact, which he alleges, is borne out by natural history, it is distinct from the words of the prophet, who speaks of the fish, not of rivers (as S. Jerome) but of the sea, which can in no way be influenced by the absence of man, who is only their destroyer. The use of the language of the histories of the creation and of the deluge implies that the prophet has in mind a destruction commensurate with that creation. Then he foretells the final removal of offences, in the same words which our Lord uses of the general Judgment. [2] *The Son of Man shall send forth His Angels and they shall gather out of His kingdom all things that offend, and them that do iniquity.*

3. *The stumbling-blocks* [3] *with the wicked.* Not only shall the wicked be utterly brought to an end, or, in the other meaning of the word, *gathered into bundles to be taken away,* but all causes of stumbling too; everything, through which others can fall, which will not be until the end of all things. Then, he repeats, yet more emphatically, *I will cut off the whole race of man* [4] *from the face of the earth,* and then he closes the verse, like the

[1] S. Jer.   [2] S. Matt. xiii. 41.

[3] מַכְשֵׁלוֹת i. q. מִכְשֹׁלִים Jer. vi. 21, Ezek. xxi. 20. So Kim., Rashi, who limits it to idolatry (as Ges.) without reason. They are the wicked generally, not one class of them. In Is. iii. 6. (where alone the word occurs beside) it is used metaphorically of the state, "this ruin."

[4] אֶת־הָאָדָם, as in the history of the creation, Gen. i. 27, or the flood, Ib. vi. 7. vii. 21.

[5] Ex. vi. 6, De. iv. 34, v. 15, vii. 19. xi. 2, xxvi. 8, and thence Jer. xxxii. 21, Ps. cxxxvi. 12. Isaiah had, in the same phrase, prophesied God's judgments against Israel in the burden v. 25, ix. 11, 16, x. 4.

[6] Jer. ii. 10, 11.

[7] 1 S. Pet. iv. 17. Jer. xxv. 29.

[8] Is. xiv. 22.

foregoing, with the solemn words, *saith the Lord.* All this shall be fulfilled in the Day of Judgment, and all other fulfillments are earnests of the final Judgment. They are witnesses of the ever-living presence of the Judge of all, that God does take account of man's deeds. They speak to men's conscience, they attest the existence of a Divine law, and therewith of the future complete manifestation of that law, of which they are individual sentences. Not until the prophet has brought this circle of judgments to their close, does he pass on to the particular judgments on Judah and Jerusalem.

4. *I will also stretch out Mine Hand,* as before on Egypt [5]. Judah had gone in the ways of Egypt and learned her sins, and sinned worse than Egypt [6]. The *mighty Hand and stretched-out Arm,* with which she had been delivered, shall be again *stretched out,* yet not for her but *upon her, upon all the inhabitants of Jerusalem.* In this threatened destruction of all, Judah and Jerusalem are singled out, because *judgment* shall [7] *begin at the house of God.* They who have sinned against the greater grace shall be most signally punished. Yet the punishment of those whom God had so chosen and loved is an earnest of the general judgment. This too is not a partial but a general judgment "upon *all* the inhabitants of Jerusalem."

And I will cut off the remnant of Baal, i. e. to the very last vestige of it. Isaiah unites [8] *name and residue,* as equivalents, together with the proverbial, *posterity and descendant* [9]. Zephaniah distributes them in parallel clauses, "the *residue* [10] of Baal and the *name* of the Chemarim." Good and evil have each a root, which remains in the ground, when

[9] נִין וָנֶכֶד, which occur only together, Gen. xxi. 23, Job xviii. 19, Is. xiv. 22.

[10] שְׁאָר is not limited, like שְׁאֵרִית, to that which remains over when a former or larger part has ceased or is gone. It is mostly "the rest," after others who had been named, yet still it may be the larger number; as, "the rest of those chosen," 1 Chr. xvi. 41; "the rest of their brethren, the priests and the Levites," Ezr. iii. 9 (8. Eng.); "the rest of the chief of the fathers," Ib. iv. 3; "the rest of their companions," Ib. 7; "the rest of the people," Neh. x. 29, xi. 1., "the rest of Israel," Ib. 20; "the rest of the Jews," Esth. ix. 16. So in Isaiah, "the rest of Syria" beside Damascus. Is. xviii. 3, and "the rest of the Spirit" Mal. ii. 15. (See Ib.)

Before
C H R I S T
cir. 630.

⁴ Hos. 10. 5.

nant of B a a l from this place, *and* t h e name of ⁴the Chemarims with the priests;

Before
C H R I S T
cir. 630.

ᵉ 2 Kin. 23. 12.
ᶠ Jer. 19. 13.
ᶠ 1 Kin. 18. 21.
2 Kin. 17. 33, 41.

5 And them ᵉ that worship the host of heaven upon the housetops; ᶠand them that w o r s h i p *and*

---

the trunk has been hewn down. There is ¹ *a remnant according to the election of grace,* when *the rest* have been *blinded;* and this is a ² *holy seed* to carry on the line of God. Evil too has its remnant, which, unless diligently kept down, shoots up again, after the conversion of peoples or individuals. The ³ *mind of the flesh* remains in the regenerate also. The prophet foretells the complete excision of the whole *remnant of Baal,* which was fulfilled in it after the captivity, and shall be fulfilled as to all which it shadows forth, in the Day of Judgment. *From this place;* for in their phrensy, they dared to bring the worship of Baal into the very temple of the Lord⁴. "⁵ Who would ever believe that in Jerusalem, the holy city, and in the very temple idols should be consecrated? Whoso seeth the ways of our times will readily believe it. For among Christians and in the very temple of God, the abominations of the heathen are worshiped. Riches, pleasures, honors, are they not idols which Christians prefer to God Himself?"

And the name of the Chemarim with the priests. Of the *idolatrous priests*⁶ the very name shall be cut off, as God promises by Hosea, that He will ⁷ *take away the names of Baalim,* and by Zechariah, that He ⁸ *will cut off the names of the idols out of the land.* Yet this is more. Not the *name* only of *the Chemarim,* but themselves with their name, their posterity, shall be blotted out; still more, it is God Who cuts off all memory of them, blotting them out of the book of the living and out of His own. They had but *a name* before, ⁹ *that they were living, but were dead.* "¹⁰ The Lord shall take away names of vain glory, wrongly admired, out of the Church; yea, the very names of the priests with the priests who vainly flatter themselves with the name of Bishops and the dignity of Presbyters without their deeds. Whence he markedly says, not, *and the deeds of priests with the priests,* but the *names;* who only bear the false name of dignities, and with evil works destroy their own names." The

priests are *priests of the Lord,* who live not like priests, corrupt in life and doctrine and corrupters of God's people ¹¹. The judgment is pronounced alike on what was intrinsically evil, and on good which had corrupted itself into evil. The title of priest is no where given to the priest of a false God, without some mention in the context, implying that they were idolatrous priests; as the priests of Dagon ¹², of the high-places as ordained by Jeroboam ¹³, of Baal ¹⁴, of Bethel ¹⁵, of Ahab ¹⁶, of those who were not gods ¹⁷, or of On, where the sun was worshiped ¹⁸. *The priests* then were God's priests, who in the evil days of Manasseh had manifoldly corrupted their life or their faith, and who were still evil. The *priests* of Judah, with its kings its princes and the people of the land, were in Jeremiah's inaugural vision enumerated as those, who *shall,* God says, ¹⁹ *fight against thee, but shall not prevail against thee.* ²⁰ *The priests said not, Where is the Lord?* *and they that handle the law knew Me not.* In the general corruption, ²¹ *A wonderful and horrible thing is committed in the land, the prophets prophesy falsely, and the priests bear rule at their hands*²²; ²³ *the children of Israel and the children of Judah, their kings, their princes, their priests, and their prophets, and the men of Judah, and the inhabitants of Jerusalem, have turned unto Me the back, and not the face.* Jeremiah speaks specifically of heavy moral sins. ²⁴ *From the prophet even unto the priest every one dealeth falsely;* ²⁵ *both prophet and priest are profane;* ²⁶ *for the sins of her prophets, the iniquities of her priests, that have shed the blood of the just in the midst of her.* And Isaiah says of their sensuality; ²⁷ *the priests and the prophets have erred through strong drink; they are swallowed up of wine, they are out of the way through strong drink.*

5. *And them that worship the host of heaven upon the* [flat] *housetops.* This was fulfilled by Josiah who destroyed ²⁸ *the altars that were on the top of the upper chamber of Ahaz.* Jeremiah speaks as if this worship was almost universal, as though well-nigh every roof had been profaned by this idolatry. ²⁹ *The houses*

---

¹ Rom. xi. 5, 7.   ² Is. vi. 13.   ³ φρόνημα σαρκός.
⁴ 2 Kgs xxiii. 4.   ⁵ Rib.
⁶ The *chemarim* is the name of idolatrous priests generally, (it occurs also 2 Kgs xxiii. 5. Hos. x. 5). In 2 Kings, where is the account of the first fulfillment of this prophecy, they appear as priests of the idolatrous high-places, distinct from the priests of Baal and of the *host of heaven.* The name is probably the Syriac name of "priest," used in Holy Scripture of idolatrous priests, because the Syrians were idolaters. See Gesenius Gesch. d. Hebr. Sprache p. 58. In Chald. כומרא is limited to idolatrous priests. See Buxt. and Levy.

⁷ Hos. ii. 17.   ⁸ Zech. xiii. 2.   ⁹ Rev. iii. 1.
¹⁰ S. Jer.   ¹¹ See Jer. ii. 8. v. 31.   ¹² 1 Sam. v. 5.
¹³ 1 Kgs xiii. 2, 33, 2 Kgs xxiii. 20. 2 Chr. xi. 15.
¹⁴ 2 Kgs x. 19, xi. 18, 2 Chr. xxiii. 17.
¹⁵ Am. vii. 10.   ¹⁶ 2 Kgs x. 11.   ¹⁷ 2 Chr. xiii. 9.
¹⁸ Gen. xli. 45-50. &c. The name "Potipherah," probably belonging to "Phre," implies this.
¹⁹ Jer. i. 18, 19.   ²⁰ Ib. ii. 7, 8.   ²¹ Jer. v. 30, 31.
²² על ידיהם.   ²³ Jer. xxxii. 32, 33.
²⁴ Ib. vi. 13. viii. 10.   ²⁵ Jer. xxiii. 11.
²⁶ Lam. iv. 13.   ²⁷ Is. xxviii. 7.
²⁸ 2 Kgs xxiii. 12.   ²⁹ Jer. xix. 13.

of Jerusalem, and the houses of Judah, shall be defiled as the place of Tophet, because of all the houses upon whose roofs they have burned incense unto all the host of heaven, and have poured out drink-offerings unto other gods. [1] The Chaldæans that fight against this city, shall come and set fire on this city, and burn it with the houses, upon whose roofs they have offered incense unto Baal, and poured out drink-offerings to other gods, to provoke Me to anger. They worshiped on the house-tops, probably to have a clearer view of that magnificent expanse of sky, [2] the moon and stars which God had ordained; the queen of heaven, which they worshiped instead of Himself. There is something so mysterious in that calm face of the moon, as it [3] walketh in beauty; God seems to have invested it with such delegated influence over the seasons and the produce of the earth, that they stopped short in it, and worshiped the creature rather than the Creator. Much as men now talk of "Nature," admire "Nature," speak of its "laws," not as laws imposed upon it, but inherent in it, laws affecting us and our well-being; only not in their ever-varying vicissitudes, [4] doing whatsoever God commandeth them upon the face of the world in the earth, whether for correction, or for His land or for mercy! The idolaters [5] worshiped and served the creature more than the Creator, Who is blessed for ever; moderns equally make this world their object, only they idolize themselves and their discoveries, and worship their own intellect.

This worship on the house-tops individualized the public idolatry; it was a rebellion against God, family by family; a sort of family-prayer of idolatry. [6] Did we, say the mingled multitude to Jeremiah, make our cakes to worship her, and pour out our drink-offerings unto her, without our men? Its family character is described in Jeremiah. [7] The children gather wood, and the fathers kindle the fire, and the women knead the dough to make cakes to the queen of heaven, and to pour out drink-offerings unto other gods. The idolatry spread to other cities. [8] We will certainly do, they say, as we have done, we and our fathers, our kings and our princes, in the cities of Judah, and in the streets of Jerusalem. The incense went up continually as a memorial to God

from the Altar of incense in the temple: the roofs of the houses were so many altars, from which, street by street and house by house the incense went up to her, for whom they dethroned God, the queen of heaven. It was an idolatry, with which Judah was especially besotted, believing that they received all goods of this world from them and not from God. When punished for their sin, they repented of their partial repentance and maintained to Jeremiah that they were punished for [9] leaving off to burn incense to the queen of heaven.

And them that worship the Lord, but with a divided heart and service; that swear by [rather [10] to] the Lord, swear fealty and loyal allegiance to Him, while they do acts which deny it, in that they swear by Malcham, better [it is no appellative although allied to one] their king [11], most probably, I think, "Moloch."

This idolatry had been their enduring idolatry in the wilderness, after the calves had been annihilated; it is the worship, against which Israel is warned by name in the law [12]; then, throughout the history of the Judges, we hear of the kindred idolatry of Baal [13], the Lord (who was called also "[14] eternal king" and from whom individuals named themselves "son of [the] king," "servant of [the] king [15]"), or the manifold Baals [16] and Ashtaroth or Astarte. But after these had been removed on the preaching of Samuel [17], this idolatry does not reappear in Judah until the intermarriage of Jehoram with the house of Ahab [18]. The kindred and equally horrible worship of [19] Molech, the abomination of the children of Ammon, was brought in by Solomon in his decay, and endured until his high-place was defiled by Josiah [20]. It is probable then that this was their king [21], of whom Zephaniah speaks, whom Amos [22] and after him Jeremiah, called their king; but speaking of Ammon. Him, the king of Ammon, Judah adopted as their king. They owned God as their king in words; Molech they owned by their deeds; they worshiped and sware fealty to the Lord and they sware by their king; his name was familiarly in their mouths; to him they appealed as the Judge and witness of the truth

---

[1] Jer. xxxii. 29.   [2] Ps. viii. 3.
[3] Job xxxi. 26.   [4] Ib. xxxvii. 12, 13.
[5] Rom. i. 25.   [6] Jer. xliv. 19.   [7] Ib. vii. 18.
[8] Ib. xliv. 17.   [9] Ib. 2, 15, 18.
[10] As in the E. M., comp. 2 Chr. xv. 14. Is. xix. 18. xiv. 23. It can only mean this.
[11] מַלְכְּכֶם as מַלְכְּכֶם Am. v. 26. and מַלְכָּם Jer. xlix. 1, 3. where the E. V. too renders, their king. On his worship see vol. i. pp. 301–303.
[12] Lev. xviii. 21, xx. 2-4.
[13] Always used with the article expressed or understood, הַבְּעַל, לַבְּעַל, בַּבְּעַל, unless the specific name (Bael-berith, Bael-zebub, Bael-peor) is mentioned.
[14] Numid. 1, 2, 3 in Ges. Thes. p. 795.

[15] עַבְדִמְלֶךְ, בְּרֹמְלֶךְ ap. Ges. lc.
[16] הַבְּעָלִים in Judges, 1 Sam., 2 Kgs, 2 Chron., Jeremiah, Hosea.
[17] 1 Sam. vii. 6. xii. 10.
[18] 2 Kgs viii. 16–18. 26, 27. 2 Chr. xxi. 6, 12, 13. xxii 2-4.
[19] 1 Kgs xi. 7.   [20] 2 Kgs xxiii. 13, 14.
[21] Molech is always an appellative, except 1 Kgs xi. 7. Else (by a pronunciation belonging probably to Ammon) it is הַמֹּלֶךְ Lev. xx. 5, or לַמֹּלֶךְ Lev. xviii. 21, xx. 2, 4, 2 Kgs xxiii. 10, Jer. xxxii. 35. As a proper name, it is Milcom, 1 Kgs xi. 5, 33, 2 Kgs xxiii. 13.
[22] See on Amos i. 15. vol. i. p. 255.

Before
C H R I S T
cir. 630.

g Isai. 48. 1.
Hos. 4. 15.
‖ Or, *to the LORD.*

g that swear ‖ by the LORD, and that swear h by Malcham;

h Josh. 23. 7. 1 Kin. 11. 33.

6 And i them that are turned back from the LORD; and *those* that

Before
C H R I S T
cir. 630.

i Isai. 1. 4.
Jer. 2. 13, 17.
& 15. 6.

of their words, his displeasure they invoked on themselves, if they sware falsely. "¹ Those in error were wont to swear by heaven, and, as matter of reverence to call out, ' By the king and lord Sun.' Those who do so must of set purpose and wilfully depart from the love of God, since the law expressly says, ² *Thou shalt worship the Lord thy God, and serve Him alone, and swear by His Name.*"

The former class who *worshiped on the roofs* were mere idolaters. These *worshiped*, as they thought, *the Lord*, bound themselves solemnly by oath to Him, but with a reserve, joining a hateful idol to Him, in that they, by a religious act, owned it too as god. The act which they did was in direct words, or by implication, forbidden by God. The command to *swear by the Lord* implied that they were to swear by none else. It was followed by the prohibition to go after other gods³. Contrariwise to swear by other gods was forbidden as a part of their service. ⁴ *Be very courageous to keep and to do all that is written in the book of the Law of Moses, neither make mention of the name of their gods, nor cause to swear by them, neither serve them, but cleave unto the Lord your God.* ⁵ *How shall I pardon thee for this?* *Thy children have forsaken Me, and have sworn by those who are no gods.* ⁶ *They taught My people to swear by Baal.* They thought perhaps that in that they professed to serve God, did the greater homage to Him, professed and bound themselves to be His, (such is the meaning of *swear to the Lord*) they might, without renouncing His service, do certain things, *swear by their king*, although in effect they thereby owned him also as god. To such Elijah said, ⁷ *How long halt ye between two opinions?* *If the Lord be God, follow Him; but if Baal, then follow him;* and God by Jeremiah rejects with abhorrence such divided service. ⁸ *Ye trust in lying words, which will not profit. Will ye steal, murder, commit adultery, swear falsely, and burn incense unto Baal, and walk after other gods, and come and stand before Me in this house, which is called by My Name, saying, We are delivered to do all these abominations.* And Hosea, ⁹*Neither go ye to Beth-aven, and swear there, The Lord liveth.*

Such are Christians, " ¹⁰ who think that they can serve together the world and the Lord, and please two masters, God and Mammon ; who, *being soldiers of Jesus Christ* and having sworn fealty to Him, ¹¹ *entangle themselves with the affairs of this life* and offer the same image to God and to Cæsar." To such, God, Whom with their lips they own, is not their God ; their idol is, as the very name says, *their king*, whom alone they please, displeasing and dishonoring God. We must not only fear, love, honor God, but love, fear, honor all beside for Him Alone.

6. *And them that are turned back from* [lit. *have turned themselves back from following after* ¹²] *the Lord.* From this half-service, the prophet goes on to the avowed neglect of God, by such as wholly fall away from Him, not setting His Will or law before them, but *turning away from* Him. It is their misery that they were set in the right way once, but themselves *turned themselves back*, now no longer *following* God, but ¹³ *their own lusts*, *drawn away and enticed* by them. How much more Christians, before whose eyes Christ Jesus is set forth, not as a Redeemer only but as an Example that they should ¹⁴ *follow His steps!*

And those that have not sought the Lord, nor enquired for Him. This is marked to be a distinct class. *And those who.* These did not openly break with God, or turn away overtly from Him ; they kept (as men think) on good terms with Him, but, like *the slothful servant*, rendered Him a listless heartless service. Both words express diligent search ¹⁵. God is not found then in a careless way. They who *seek* Him not *diligently* ¹⁶, do not find Him. *Strive*, our Lord says, ¹⁷ *to enter in at the strait gate; for many, I say unto you, shall seek to enter in, and shall not be able.* She who had lost the one piece of silver, *sought diligently* ¹⁸, till she had found it.

Thus he has gone through the whole cycle. First, that most horrible and cruel worship of Baal, the *idolatrous priests* and those who had the name of *priests* only, mingled with them, yet not openly apostatizing ; then the milder form of idolatry, the star-worshipers ; then those who would unite the wor-

¹ S. Cyr.   ² Deut. vi. 13.
³ Ib. vi. 13, 14, x. 30. comp. Is. lxv. 16. Jer. iv. 2.
⁴ Josh. xxiii. 6–8. comp. Amos viii. 14.
⁵ Jer. v. 7.   ⁶ Ib. xii. 16.
⁷ 1 Kgs xviii. 21.   ⁸ Jer. vii. 8–10.
⁹ Hos. iv. 15. See vol. i., p. 53.   ¹⁰ S. Jer.
¹¹ 2 Tim. ii. 3, 4.
¹² Such is the uniform use of נָסוֹג. Its common

construction is with אָחוֹר; with מֵאַחַר, as here, Is. lix. 13 ; Kal, with מִן of pers., Ps. lxxx. 19 ; Nif. with מִן of thing, 2 Sam. i. 22.
¹³ S. Jas. i. 14.   ¹⁴ 1 S. Pet. ii. 21.
¹⁵ בָּקַק, intensive ; דָּרַשׁ of search below the surface.   ¹⁶ S. Matt. ii. 8.
¹⁷ S. Luke xiii. 24.   ¹⁸ Ib. xv. 8.

Before CHRIST
cir. 630.

k Hos. 7. 7.

l Hab. 2. 20.
Zech. 2. 13.

k have not sought the LORD, not enquired for him.

7 ¹Hold thy peace at the presence of the LORD

GOD: ᵐfor the day of the LORD is at hand: for ⁿthe LORD hath prepared a sacrifice, he hath † bid his guests.

Before CHRIST
cir. 630.

m Isai. 13. 6.
n Isai. 34. 6.
Jer. 46. 10.
Ezek. 39. 17.
Rev. 19. 17.
†.Heb. sanctified,
or prepared.

ship of God with idols, who held themselves to be worshipers of God, but whose real king was their idol; then those who openly abandoned God; and lastly those who held with Him, just to satisfy their conscience-qualms, but with no heart-service. And so, in words of Habakkuk and in reminiscence of his awful summons of the whole world before God, he sums up;

7. *Hold thy peace at the presence of the Lord God.* [lit. *Hush, in awe from the face of God.*] In the Presence of God, even the righteous say from their inmost heart, ¹ *I am vile, what shall I answer Thee? I will lay mine hand upon my mouth.* ² *Now mine eye seeth Thee, wherefore I abhor myself, and repent in dust and ashes.* ³ *Enter not into judgment with Thy servant, O Lord; for in Thy sight shall no man living be justified.* How much more must the ⁴ *man without the wedding garment* be *speechless*, and every false plea, with which he deceived himself, melt away before the Face of God! The voice of God's Judgment echoes in every heart, ⁵ *we indeed justly.*

For the Day of the Lord is at hand. Zephaniah, as is his wont, grounds this summons, which he had renewed from Habakkuk, to hushed silence before God, on Joel's prophetic warning⁶, to shew that it was not yet exhausted. *A* day of the Lord, of which Joel warned, had come and was gone; but it was only the herald of many such days; judgments in time, heralds and earnests, and, in their degree, pictures of the last which shall end time.

"⁷ All time is God's, since He Alone is the Lord of time; yet that is specially said to be His' time when He doth anything special. Whence He saith, ⁸ *My time is not yet come;* whereas all time is His." The Day of the Lord is, in the first instance, "⁹ the day of captivity and vengeance on the sinful people," as a forerunner of the Day of Judgment, or the day of death to each, for this too is near, since, compared to eternity, all the time of this world is brief.

For the Lord hath prepared a sacrifice. God had rejected sacrifices, offered amid unrepented sin; they were ¹⁰ *an abomination to Him.* When man will not repent and offer

himself as ¹¹ *a living sacrifice, holy and acceptable to God,* God, at last, rejects all other outward oblations, and the sinner himself is the sacrifice and victim of his own sins. The image was probably suggested by Isaiah's words, ¹² *The Lord hath a sacrifice in Bozrah, and a great slaughter in the Land of Idumea;* and Jeremiah subsequently uses it of the overthrow of Pharaoh at the Euphrates, ¹³ *This is the day of the Lord of Hosts; that He may avenge Him of His adversaries; for the Lord God hath a sacrifice in the north country by the river Euphrates.* ¹⁴ *The Lord hath made all things for Himself, yea even the wicked for the day of evil.* All must honor God, either fulfilling the will of God and the end of their own being and of His love for them, by obeying that loving Will with their own free-will, or, if they repudiate it to the end, by suffering It.

He hath bid [lit. *sanctified* ¹⁵] *His' guests.* God had before, by Isaiah, called the heathen whom He employed to punish Babylon, ¹⁶ *My sanctified ones.* Zephaniah, by giving the title to God's instruments against Judah, declares that themselves, having become in deeds like the heathen, were as heathen to Him. The instruments of His displeasure, not they, were so far His chosen, His called ¹⁷. Jeremiah repeats the saying, ¹⁸ *Thus saith the Lord against the house of the king of Judah;— I have sanctified against thee destroyers, a man and his weapons.* That is, so far, a holy war in the purpose of God, which fulfills His will; whence Nebuchadnezzar was ¹⁹ *His servant,* avenging His wrongs ²⁰. " ²¹ To be sanctified, here denotes not the laying aside of iniquity, nor the participation of the Holy Ghost, but, as it were, to be foreordained and chosen to the fulfillment of this end." That is in a manner hallowed, which is employed by God for a holy end, though the instrument, its purposes, its aims, its passions, be in themselves unholy. There is an awe about "the scourges of God." As with the lightning and the tornado, there is a certain presence of God with them, in that through them His Righteousness is seen; although they themselves have as little of God as the *wind and storm* which *fulfill His word.* Those who were

1 Job xl. 4.   2 Ib. xlii. 5, 6.   3 Ps. cxliii. 2.
4 S. Matt. xxii. 11, 12.   5 S. Luke xxiii. 41.
6 See on Joel i. 14. vol. i. p. 164, and ii. 1. p. 168.
7 Dion.   8 S. John vii. 6.   9 S. Jer
10 Is. i. 11-15.   11 Rom. xii. 1.
12 Is. xxxiv. 6.   13 Jer. xlvi. 10.

14 Prov. xvi. 4.   15 See E. M.
16 Is. xiii. 3.   17 קְרָאִיו.
18 Jer. xxii. 6, 7.   19 Ib. xxv. 9.
20 See on Joel iii. 9. vol. i. p. 137 and Micah iii. 5.
ab. p. 312.   21 S. Cyr.

8 And it shall come to pass in the day of the

LORD's sacrifice, that I will † punish ° the princes,

° Jer. 39. 6.   † Heb. *visit upon.*

---

once admitted to make offerings to God make themselves sacrifices to His wrath; these, still heathen and ungodly and in all besides reprobate, are His Priests, because in this, although without their will, they do His Will.

8. *I will punish* [lit. *visit upon*]. God seems oftentimes to be away from His own world. Men plot, design, say, in word or in deed, *who is Lord over us?* God is, as it were, a stranger in it, or as a man, who hath *taken a journey into a far country.* God uses our own language to us. *I will visit,* inspecting, (so to say), examining, sifting, reviewing, and when man's sins require it, allowing the weight of His displeasure to fall upon them.

The princes. The prophet again, in vivid detail (as his characteristic is), sets forth together sin and punishment. Amid the general chastisement of all, when all should become one *sacrifice,* they who sinned most should be punished most. The evil priests had received their doom. Here he begins anew with the mighty of the people and so goes down, first to special spots of the city, then to the whole, man by man. Josiah being a godly king, no mention is made of him. Thirteen years before his death [1], he, received the promise of God, *because thine heart was tender, and thou hast humbled thyself before the Lord—I will gather thee unto thy fathers, and thou shalt be gathered unto thy grave in peace, and thou shalt not see all the evil which I will bring upon this place.* In remarkable contrast to Jeremiah, who had to be, in detail and continual pleading with his people, a prophet of judgment to come, until these judgments broke upon them, and so was the reprover of the evil sovereigns who succeeded Josiah, Zephaniah has to pronounce God's judgments only on the *princes* and *the king's children.* Jeremiah, in his inaugural vision, was forewarned, that [2] *the kings of Judah, its princes, priests, and the people of the land* should war against him, because he should speak unto them all which God should command him. And thenceforth Jeremiah impleads or threatens kings and the princes together [3]. Zephaniah contrariwise, his office lying wholly within the reign of Josiah, describes the princes again as [4] *roaring lions,* but says nothing of the king, as neither does Micah [5], in the reign, it may be, of Jotham or Hezekiah. Isaiah speaks of

princes, as [6] *rebellious and companions of thieves.* Jeremiah speaks of them as idolaters [7]. They appear to have had considerable influence, which on one occasion they employed in defence of Jeremiah [8], but mostly for evil [9]. Zedekiah enquired of Jeremiah secretly for fear of them [10]. They brought destruction upon themselves by what men praise, their resistance to Nebuchadnezzar, but against the declared mind of God. Nebuchadnezzar unwittingly fulfilled the prophets's word, when he [11] *slew all the nobles of Judah, the eunuch who was over the war, and seven men of them that were near the king's person, and the principal scribe of the host.*

And the king's children. Holy Scripture mentions chief persons only by name. Isaiah had prophesied the isolated lonely loveless lot of descendants of Hezekiah who should be *eunuchs in the palace of the king of Babylon* [12], associated only with those intriguing pests of Eastern courts [13], a lot in itself worse than the sword (although to Daniel God overruled it to good) and Zedekiah's sons were slain before his eyes and his race extinct. Jehoiakim died a disgraced death, and Jehoiachin was imprisoned more than half the life of man.

And all such as are clothed with strange apparel. Israel was reminded by its dress, that it belonged to God. It was no great thing in itself; *a band of dark blue* [14] *upon the fringes at the four corners of their garments.* But *the band of dark blue* was upon the high-priest's mitre, with the plate engraved, [15] *Holiness to the Lord,* fastened upon it; *with a band of dark blue* also was the breastplate [16] bound to the ephod of the high-priest. So then, simple as it was, it seems to have designated the whole nation, as [17] *a kingdom of priests, an holy nation.* It was appointed to them, [18] *that ye may look upon it, and remember all the commandments of the Lord and do them, and that ye seek not after your own heart and your own eyes, after which ye use to go a whoring; that ye may remember and do all My commandments, and be holy unto your God.* They might say, "it is but *a band of blue;*" but the *band of blue* was the soldier's badge, which marked them as devoted to the service of their God; indifference to or shame of it involved indifference to or shame of the charge given them therewith, and to their calling as a peculiar people. The choice of the *strange apparel* involved the

---

[1] 2 Kgs xxii. 19. 20.   [2] Jer. i. 18.
[3] Ib. ii. 26, iv. 9, viii. 1, xxiv. 8, xxxii. 37, xxxiv. 21.
[4] Zeph. iii. 3.   [5] Mic. iii. 1, 9.
[6] Is. i. 23.   [7] Jer. xxxi. 32–34. xliv. 21.
[8] Ib. xxvi. 16.   [9] Ib. xxxvii. 15, xxxviii. 4, 16.
[10] Ib. xxxvii. 17. xxxviii. 14–27.

[11] Ib. xxxix. 6, lii. 25–27.
[12] Is. xxxix. 7. See Daniel the prophet p. 16.
[13] See Ib. p. 21, 22.
[14] Nu. xv. 38. De. xxii. 12.   [15] Ex. xxviii. 36.
[16] Ib. xxxix. 21.
[17] Ib. xix. 6.   [18] Nu. xv. 39, 40.

Before CHRIST cir. 630.	and the king's children, and all such as are clothed with strange apparel.

9 In the same day also will I punish all those that

Before CHRIST cir. 630.	leap on the threshold, which fill their masters' houses with violence and deceit.

10 And it shall come to

choice to be as the nations of the world; [1] *we will be as the heathen, as the families of the countries.*

All luxurious times copy foreign dress, and with it, foreign manners and luxuries; whence even the heathen Romans were zealous against its use. It is very probable that with the foreign dress foreign idolatry was imported [2]. The Babylonian dress was very gorgeous, such as was the admiration of the simpler Jews. [3]*Her captains and rulers clothed in perfection, girded with girdles upon their loins, with flowing dyed attire upon their heads.* Ezekiel had to frame words to express the Hebrew idea of their beauty. Jehoiakim is reproved among other things for his luxury [4]. Outward dress always betokens the inward mind, and in its turn acts upon it. An estranged dress betokened an estranged heart, whence it is used as an image of the whole spiritual mind [5]. "[6]The garment of the sons of the king and the apparel of princes which we receive in Baptism, is Christ, according to that, *Put ye on the Lord Jesus Christ,* and *Put ye on bowels of mercy, goodness, humility, patience,* and the rest. Wherein we are commanded to be clothed with the new man from heaven according to our Creator, and to [7] *lay aside* the clothing of *the old man with his deeds.* Whereas then we ought to be clothed in such raiment, for mercy we put on cruelty, for patience, impatience, for righteousness, iniquity; in a word, for virtues, vices; for Christ, Antichrist. Whence it is said of such an one, [8] *He is clothed with cursing as with a garment.* These the Lord will visit most manifestly at His Coming." "[9] Thinkest thou that hypocrisy is *strange apparel?* Of a truth. For what stranger apparel than sheeps' clothing to ravening wolves? What stranger than for him who [10]*within is full of iniquity,* to appear outwardly *righteous before men?*"

9. *I will punish all those that leap on the threshold.* Neither language nor history nor context allow this to be understood of the

idolatrous custom of Ashdod, not to tread on the threshold [11] of the temple of Dagon. It had indeed been a strange infatuation of idolatry, that God's people should adopt an act of superstitious reverence for an idol in the very instance in which its nothingness and the power of the true God had been shewn. Nothing is indeed too brutish for one who chooses an idol for the true God, preferring Satan to the good God. Yet this superstition belonged apparently to Ashdod alone; the worship of Dagon, although another form of untrue worship, does not appear, like that of Baal, to have fascinated the Jews; nor would Zephaniah, to express a rare superstition, have chosen an idiom, which might more readily express the contrary, that they "leapt *on* the threshold," not over it [12]. They are also the same persons, who *leap on the threshold,* and who *fill their masters' houses with violence and deceit.* Yet this relates, not to superstition, but to plunder and goods unjustly gotten. As then, before, he had declared God's judgments upon idolatry, so does he here upon sins against the second table, whether by open violence, or secret fraud, as do also Habakkuk [13], and Jeremiah [14]. All, whether open or hidden from man, every wrongful dealing, (for every sin as to a neighbor's goods falls under these two, violence or fraud) shall be avenged in that day. Here again all which remains is the sin. They enriched, as they thought, their masters, by art or by force; they schemed, plotted, robbed; they succeeded to their heart's wish; but, "ill-gotten, ill-spent!" They *filled their masters' houses* quite full; but wherewith? with violence and deceit, which witnessed against them, and brought down the judgments of God upon them.

10. *A cry from the fish-gate. The fish-gate* was probably in the North of the wall of *the second city.* For in Nehemiah's rebuilding, the restoration began at the sheep-gate [15], (so called doubtless, because the sheep for the

---

[1] Ezek. xx. 33.
[2] Jon. Rashi and S. Jer. connect it with idolatry.
[3] Ezek. xxiii. 12, 15.   [4] Jer. xxii. 14, 15.
[5] Rom. xiii. 14, Col. iii. 12, Eph. iv. 24.
[6] S. Jer.
[7] Eph. iv. 22.   [8] Ps. cix. 17.   [9] Rup.
[10] S. Matt. xxiii. 28.
[11] מִפְתָּן is used 1 Sam. v. 4, 5, Ezek. ix. 3, x. 4, 18, xlvi. 2, xlvii. 1; elsewhere סַף. There is a trace of this explanation in the Chald., "who walk in the laws of the Philistines," and in S. Jerome, doubt-

less from his Jewish teachers. Isaiah's reproof that they *have soothsayers like the Philistines,* ii. 6, is altogether different.

[12] דלג על is, in the only other place, Cant. ii. 8, "bounding *on* the mountains;" "bounding over" (like our "leapt a wall") happens to be expressed by an acc., 2 Sam. xviii. 30, Ps. xviii. 30; "passing over" had been expressed more clearly by פסח על, as in Ex. xii. 23, 27.
[13] Hab. i. 2, 3.   [14] Jer. v. 27.   [15] Neh. iii. 1.

Before
C H R I S T
cir. 630.

p 2 Chr. 33. 14.

pass in that day, saith the Lord, *that there shall be* the noise of a cry from p the

fish gate, and an howling from the second, and a great crashing from the hills.

Before
C H R I S T
cir. 630.

sacrifices were brought in by it) which, as being near the temple, was repaired by the priests ; then it ascended Northward, by two towers, *the towers of Meah* and *Hananeel ;* then two companies repaired some undescribed part of the wall[1], and then another company *built the fish-gate*[2]. Four companies are then mentioned, who repaired, in order, to the *old gate*, which was repaired by another company[3]. Three more companies repaired beyond these ; *and they left Jerusalem unto the broad wall*[4]. After three more sections repaired by individuals, two others repaired a *second measured portion, and the tower of the furnaces*[5]. This order is reversed in the account of the dedication of the walls. The people being divided [6] *into two great companies of them that give thanks*, some place near *the tower of the furnaces* was the central point, from which both parted to encompass the city in opposite directions. In this account, we have two additional gates mentioned, the *gate of Ephraim*[7], between *the broad wall* and the *old gate*, and *the prison-gate*, beyond *the sheep-gate*, from which the repairs had begun. The *gate of Ephraim* had obviously not been repaired, because, for some reason, it had not been destroyed. Else Nehemiah, who describes the rebuilding of the wall so minutely, must obviously have mentioned its rebuilding. It was obviously to the North, as leading to Ephraim. But the tower of Hananeel must have been a very marked tower. In Zechariah Jerusalem is measured from North to South, [8] *from the tower of Hananeel unto the king's winepresses*. It was then itself at the North-East corner of Jerusalem, where towers were of most importance to strengthen the wall, and to command the approach to

the wall either way. *The fish-gate* then, lying between it and *the gate of Ephraim*, must have been on the North side of the city, and so on the side where the Chaldæan invasions came ; yet it must have been much inside the present city, because the city itself was enlarged by Herod Agrippa on the North, as it was unaccountably contracted on the South[9]. The then limits of Jerusalem are defined. For Josephus thus describes *the second wall*. "[10] It took its beginning from that gate which they called *Gennath*, which belonged to the first wall ; it only encompassed the northern quarter of the city and reached as far as the tower of Antonia." The tower of Antonia was situated at the North-West angle of the corner of the temple. The other end of the wall, the Gennath or *garden* gate, must have opened on cultivated land ; and Josephus speaks of the gardens on the N. and N. W. of the city which were destroyed by Titus in levelling the ground[11]. But near the tower of Hippicus, the North-Western extremity of the first wall, no ancient remains have been discovered by excavation[12] ; but they *have* been traced North, from "an ancient Jewish semi-circular arch, resting on piers 18 feet high, now buried in rubbish." These old foundations have been traced at three places[13] in a line on the East of the Holy Sepulchre (which lay consequently outside the city) up to the judgment gate, but not North of it[14]. The line from West to East, i. e., to the tower of Antonia, is marked generally by "very large stones, evidently of Jewish work, in the walls of houses, especially in the lower parts[15]." They are chiefly in the line of the Via Dolorosa.

The fish-gate had its name probably from a

---

[1] Neh. iii. 2.   [2] Ib. 3.   [3] Ib. 4–6.   [4] Ib. 7, 8.
[5] Ib. 9–11.   [6] Ib. xii. 31–38.   [7] Ib. 39.
[8] Zech. xiv. 10.   [9] See ab. p. 50.   [10] B. J. v. 42.
[11] Ib. v. 32.
[12] Pierotti, "Jerusalem explored" p. 32, from whom this account is taken. Signor Pierotti's work is "the fruit of eight years of continual labor devoted to a study of the topography of Jerusalem upon the spot, in which I have been constantly occupied in excavating and removing the rubbish accumulated over the place during so many centuries, in retracing the walls, in examining the monuments and ancient remains, and in penetrating and traversing the conduits and vaults."—"I have," he says, "made excavations and watched those made by others, have formed intimacies with the inhabitants of the country, have sought for information on the spot, regardless of personal risk, have worked with my own hands underground, and so have obtained much knowledge of that which lies below the surface of the soil in Jerusalem." Jerusalem explored Pref. p. viii.
[13] 1) At the meat-bazaar near the convent of S. Mary the Great. "In digging down to the rock to lay the new foundations, 10 feet below the surface,

I came upon large stones, boldly rusticated and arranged in a manner that reminded me of the Phœnician work of the time of Solomon." 2) on the East of the Church of the Resurrection. 3) "close to the West of the present *judgment gate*." "In digging down for the rock, I found, 18 feet below the surface, a fragment of a wall, resembling, in all respects, that first described." Ib. p. 33.
[14] This appeared from excavations made in repairing the then Russian consulate, and from "enquiries of all who in former years had built in this neighborhood." Ib.
[15] "These were found when the Effendi Kadduti repaired and partly rebuilt the house in the Via Dolorosa at the *Station of Veronica*. A similar discovery was made by the Mufti in strengthening his house at the *Station of Simon of Cyrene*, and by the Effendi Soliman Giari, opposite to the Mufti's house on the North. The Armenian Catholic monks requested me to examine and level a piece of land, at the *Station of the first fall of Christ ;* which, as representative of his nation, he had just bought. In the lower part of the wall enclosing it on the north, very large stones and an ancient gate were found. In the foundations of the Austrian hospice,

11 ⁑Howl, ye inhabitants of Maktesh, for all the merchant people

are cut down; all they that bear silver are cut off.

fish-market (markets being in the open places near the gates¹) the fish being brought either from the lake of Tiberias or from Joppa. Near it, the wall ended, which Manasseh, after his restoration from Babylon², *built without the city of David, on the West side of Gihon, in the valley.* This, being unprotected by its situation, was the weakest part of the city. "³ The most ancient of the three walls could be considered as impregnable, as much on account of its extreme thickness, as of the height of the mountain on which it was built, and the depth of the valleys at its base, and David, Solomon and the other kings neglected nothing to place it in this state." Where they had made themselves strong, there God's judgment should find them.

And a howling from the second city, as it is supplied in Nehemiah, who mentions the prefect set over it⁴. It was here that Huldah the prophetess lived⁵, who prophesied the evils to come upon Jerusalem, after Josiah should be *gathered to* his *grave in peace.* It was probably the lower city, which was enclosed by the second wall. It was a second or new city, as compared to the original city of David, on Mount Moriah. On this the enemy who had penetrated by the fish-gate would first enter; then take the strongest part of the city itself. Gareb⁶ and Bezetha were outside of the then town; they would then be already occupied by the enemy before entering the city.

A great crashing from the hills. These are probably Zion, and Mount Moriah on which the temple stood, and so the capture is described as complete. Here should be not a cry or howling only, but an utter destruction⁷. Mount Moriah was the seat of the worship of God; on Mount Zion was the state, and the abode of the wealthy. In human sight they were impregnable. The Jebusites mocked at David's siege, as thinking their city impregnable⁸; but God was with David and he took it. He and his successors fortified it yet more, but its true defence was that *the Lord was round about His*

*people*⁹, and when He withdrew His protection, then this natural strength was but their destruction, tempting them to resist first the Chaldæans, then the Romans. Human strength is but a great *crash,* failing by its own weight and burying its owner. "This threefold cry¹⁰, from three parts of the city, had a fulfillment before the destruction by the Romans. In the lower part of the city Simon tyrannized, and in the middle John raged, and *there was a great crashing from the hills,* i. e., from the temple and citadel where was Eleazar, who stained the very altar of the temple with blood, and in the courts of the Lord made a pool of blood of divers corpses." "¹¹ In the assaults of an enemy the inhabitants are ever wont to flee to the tops of the hills, thinking that the difficulty of access will be a hindrance to him, and will cut off the assaults of the pursuers. But when God smiteth, and requireth of the despisers the penalties of their sin, not the most towered city nor impregnable circuits of walls, not height of hills, or rough rocks, or pathless difficulty of ground, will avail to the sufferers. Repentance alone saves, softening the Judge and allaying His wrath, and readily inviting the Creator in His inherent goodness to His appropriate gentleness. Better is it, with all our might to implore that we may not offend Him. But since human nature is prone to evil, and ¹² *in many things we all offend,* let us at least by repentance invite to His wonted clemency the Lord of all, Who is by nature kind."

11. *Howl, ye inhabitants of Maktesh,* lit. *Mortar*¹³, "in which," S. Jerome says, "corn is pounded; a hollow vessel, and fit for the use of medical men, in which properly ptisans are wont to be beaten (or made). Striking is it, that Scripture saith not, 'who dwell in the valley or in the alley,' but who *dwell in the mortar,* because as corn, when the pestle striketh, is bruised, so the army of the enemy shall rush down upon you¹⁴." The place intended is probably so much of the valley of the Tyropœon, which intersected Jerusalem from North to South, as was en-

---

laid in 1857, to the north of the Armenian property, large stones were discovered, and also further to the East, in the new convent of the Daughters of Sion." Pierotti pp. 33, 34.
¹ See 2 Kgs vii. 1. Neh. xiii. 16, 19.
² 2 Chr. xxxiii. 14.   ³ Jos. de B. J. v. 4. 2.
⁴ Neh. xi. 9, E. V. "was second over the city" on account of the absence of the article, עַל הָעִיר מִשְׁנֶה. I prefer taking it, as in a sort of apposition, as Ewald does, Lehrb. n. 287, l. p. 734. ed. 8.
⁵ 2 Kings xxii. 14. 2 Chr. xxxiv. 22. It is called by Josephus ἄλλη, "another" city, Ant. xv. 11, 5.

⁶ Jer. xxxi. 39.
⁷ Not, as some, "a cry of destruction" as in Is. xv. 5. Isaiah has indeed the words זַעֲקַת שֶׁבֶר "cry of destruction," but here שֶׁבֶר, יְלָלָה, צְעָקָה are plainly parallel to one another.
⁸ 2 Sam. v. 6.   ⁹ Ps. cxxv. 2.   ¹⁰ From Rup.
¹¹ S. Cyr.   ¹² S. James iii. 2.
¹³ Prov. xxvii. 22. It is also a proper name in Jud. xv. 19, since Lehi in which it was situate (אֲשֶׁר בַּלֶּחִי), was a proper name, Ib. and 9, and 14.
¹⁴ S. Jer.

Before
CHRIST
cir. 630.
12 And it shall come to pass at that time, *that* I will search Jerusalem with candles, and p u n i s h the men that are † ʳ settled on their l e e s : ˢ that say in Before
CHRIST
cir. 630.

ʳ Jer. 48. 11. Amos 6. 1. ˢ Ps. 94. 7.

† Heb. *curded*, or, *thickened*.

closed by the second wall, on the North, and the first wall on the South. The valley "¹ extended as far as the fountain of Siloam," and united with the valley of Jehoshaphat a little below Ophel. It was "² full of houses," and, from its name as well as from its situation, it was probably the scene of petty merchandise, where the occasions in which men could and did break the law and offend God, were the more continual, because they entered into their daily life, and were a part of it. The sound of the pestle was continually heard there ; another sound should thereafter be heard, when they should not bruise, but be themselves bruised. The name *Maktesh* was probably chosen to express how their false hopes, grounded on the presence of God's temple among them while by their sins they profaned it, should be turned into true fears. They had been and thought themselves *Mikdash*, " a holy place, sanctuary ;" they should be *Maktesh* ³, wherein all should be utterly bruised in pieces.

" ⁴ Whoso considereth the calamities of that siege, and how the city was pressed and hemmed in, will feel how aptly he calls them *the inhabitants of a mortar ;* for, as grains of corn are brought together into a mortar, to the end that, when the pestle descendeth, being unable to fly off, they may be bruised, so the people flowing together, out of all the countries of Judæa, was narrowed in by a sudden siege, and through the savage cruelty of the above leaders of the sedition, was unutterably tortured from within, more than by the enemy without."

For all the merchant people [lit. *the people of Canaan*] *are cut down ;* i. e., " ⁵ they who in deeds are like the people of Canaan," according to that, ⁶ *Thou art of Canaan and not of Judah,* and, ⁷ *Thy father is an Amorite and thy mother a Hittite.* So our Lord says to the reprobate Jews, ⁸ *Ye are of your father the devil.*

All they that bear [lit. ⁹ *all laden with*] *silver are cut off.* The silver, wherewith they lade themselves, being gotten amiss, is a load

upon them, weighing them down until they are destroyed.

12. *I will search* [lit. *diligently*]. The word is always used of a minute diligent search, whereby places, persons, things, are searched and sifted one by one in every corner, until it be found whether a thing be there or no ¹⁰. Hence also of the searching out of every thought of the heart, either by God ¹¹, or in repentance by the light of God ¹².

Jerusalem with candles : so that there should be no corner, no lurking-place so dark, but that the guilty should be brought to light. The same diligence, which Eternal Wisdom used, to *seek and to save that which was lost,* ¹³ *lighting a candle and searching diligently,* till It find each lost piece of silver, the same shall Almighty God use that no hardened sinner shall escape. " ¹⁴ What the enemy would do, using unmingled phrensy against the conquered, that God fitteth to His own Person, not as being Himself the Doer of things so foreign, but rather permitting that what comes from anger should proceed in judgment against the ungodly." It was an image of this, when, at the taking of Jerusalem by the Romans, they " ¹⁵ dragged out of common sewers and holes and caves and tombs, princes and great men and priests, who for fear of death had hid themselves." How much more in that Day when *the secrets of all hearts shall be revealed* by Him Who ¹⁶ *searcheth the hearts and reins, and to Whose Eyes* ¹⁷, *which are like flaming Fire, all things are naked and open!* The *candles* wherewith God searcheth the heart, are men's own consciences ¹⁸, His Own revealed word ¹⁹, the lives of true Christians ²⁰. These, through the Holy Ghost in each, may enlighten the heart of man, or, if he takes not heed, will rise in judgment against him, and shew the falsehood of all vain excuses. " ²¹ One way of escape only there is. If we judge ourselves, we shall not be judged. I will *search out my own ways* and my desires, that He Who *shall search out Jerusalem with candles,* may find nothing in me, unsought and unsifted.

¹ See Signor Pierotti's map.
² Jos. B. J. v. 4. 1.
³ The two words do so occur in an epistle of the Samaritans (Cellar. Epist. Sichemit. p. 25) Ges.
⁴ S. Jer.   ⁵ Ch.   ⁶ Hist. of Susannah 56.
⁷ Ezek. xvi. 3. See also on Hosea xii. 7, ab, p. 121.
⁸ S. John viii. 44.
⁹ A passive adj. (קָטִיל from קָטוּל). As an act. adj. (קָטִיל from קָטַל) it would rather imply that they cast it on others.
¹⁰ Nif. of Esau by enemies Ob. 6, Pih., for Laban's

idols, Gen. xxxi. 35 ; for Joseph's cup, Ib. xliv. 12 ; for David in hiding places, 1 Sam. xxiii. 23 ; Ahab's house, 1 Kgs xx. 6 ; for worshipers of God in Baal's temple, 2 Kgs x. 23 ; in Caves of Carmel, Am. ix. 3, (See vol. i. pp. 330–333) ; Divine wisdom Pr. ii. 4, God's ways, Ps. lxxvii. 7. The form is intensive here.   ¹¹ Pr. xx. 27.   ¹² Lam. iii. 40.
¹³ S. Luke xv. 8.   ¹⁴ S. Cyr.
¹⁵ S. Jer. See Jos. de B. J. vi. 94. vii. 2 fin.
¹⁶ Ps. vii. 9, xxvi. 2, Jer. xi. 20, xvii. 10, xx. 12, Rev. ii. 23.   ¹⁷ Ib. i. 14.   ¹⁸ Prov. xx. 27.
¹⁹ Ps. cxix. 104. Pr. vi. 23. 2 Pet. i. 19.
²⁰ Phil. ii. 15.   ²¹ S. Bern. Serm. 55 in Cant.

their heart, The LORD will not do good, neither will he do evil.

13 Therefore their

goods shall become a booty, and their houses a desolation: they shall also build houses, but [t]not in-

[t] Deut. 28. 30, 39.
Amos 5. 11.

For He will not twice judge the same thing. Would that I might so follow and track out all my offences, that in none I need fear His piercing Eyes, in none be ashamed at the light of His candles! Now I am seen, but I see not. At hand is that Eye, to Whom all things are open, although Itself is not open. Once [1] *I shall know, even as I am known.* Now *I know in part,* but I am not known in part, but wholly."

The men that are settled on their lees, stiffened and contracted[2]. The image is from wine which becomes harsh, if allowed to remain upon the lees, unremoved. It is drawn out by Jeremiah[3], *Moab hath been at ease [4]from his youth, and he hath settled on his lees, and hath not been emptied from vessel to vessel, neither hath he gone into captivity; therefore his taste remained in him, and his scent is not changed.* So they upon whom *no changes come, fear not God*[5]. The lees are the refuse of the wine, yet stored up (so the word [6] means) with it, and the wine rests, as it were, upon them. So do men of ease rest in things defiled and defiling, their riches or their pleasure, which they hoard up, on which they are bent, so that they "[7]lift not their mind to things above, but, darkened with foulest desires, are hardened and stiffened in sin."

That say in their heart, not openly scoffing, perhaps thinking that they believe; but people *do* believe as they love. Their most inward belief, the belief of their heart and affections, what they wish, and the hidden spring of their actions, is, *The Lord will not do good, neither will He do evil.* They act as believing so, and by acting inure themselves to believe it. They think of God as far away, [8] *Is not God in the height of heaven? And behold the height of the stars, how high they are! And thou sayest, How doth God know? Can He judge through the dark cloud? Thick clouds are a covering to Him, that He seeth not; and He walketh in the circuit of heaven.* [9] *The ungodly in the pride of his heart* (thinketh); *He will not enquire; all his devices* (speak), *There is no God. Strong are his ways at all*

times; *on high are Thy judgments out of his sight.* [10] *They slay the widow and the stranger, and murder the fatherless, and they say, The Lord shall not see, neither shall the God of Jacob regard it.* [11] *Such things they did imagine and were deceived; for their own wickedness blinded them. As for the mysteries of God, they knew them not.* [12] *Faith without works is dead.* Faith which acts not dies out, and there comes in its stead this other persuasion, that God will not repay. There are more Atheists than believe themselves to be such. These act as if there were no Judge of their deeds, and at last come, themselves to believe that God will not punish[13]. What else is the thought of all worldlings, of all who make idols to themselves of any pleasure or gain or ambition, but "God will not punish?" "God cannot punish the [wrongful, selfish,] indulgence of the nature which He has made." "God will not be so precise." "God will not punish with everlasting severance from Him, the sins of this short life." And they see not that they ascribe to God, what He attributes to idols i. e., not-gods. [14] *Do good or do evil, that we may be dismayed and behold it together.* [15] *Be not afraid of them; for they cannot do evil, neither also is it in them to do good.* These think not that God does good; for they ascribe their success to their own diligence, wisdom, strength, and thank not God for it. They think not that He sends them evil. For they defy Him and His laws, and think that they shall go unpunished. What remains but that He should be as dumb an idol as those of the heathen?

13. *Therefore their goods,* lit. *And their strength.* It is the simple sequel in God's Providence. It is a continued narrative. God will visit those who say, that God does not interfere in man's affairs, *and,* it shall be seen [16] *whose words shall stand,* God's or their's. All which God had threatened in the law shall be fulfilled. God, in the fulfillment of the punishment, which He had foretold in the law[17], would vindicate not only His present Providence, but His continual gov-

---

[1] 1 Cor. xiii. 12.
[2] קפא is used in two cases of the (as it were) congealing of the waves when they *stood on an heap* Ex. xv. 8; of the curdling into cheese Job x. 10. Jon. paraphrases "who are tranquil in their possessions." The Arabic authorities, Abulw. Tanch. David B. Abr. agree in the sense "congealed," and do not call in the Arab. פק which is primarily "dried," then is used of the wrinkling of a cloth in drying, or of the face of the old, not "contracted" as Ges. On Zech. xiv. 6, see ibid.

[3] Jer. xlviii. 11. [4] שקט. [5] See Ps. lv. 19.
[6] שמרים. [7] Dion.
[8] Job xxii. 12-14.
[9] Ps. x. 4, 5. [10] Ib. xciv. 5, 6.
[11] Wisd. ii. 21-22. [12] S. Jas. ii. 20.
[13] Is. v. 19, Mal. ii. 17.
[14] Is. xli. 23. Perhaps Zeph. meant to suggest this by using words which God by Isaiah had used of idols.
[15] Jer. x. 5. [16] Ib. xliv. 28.
[17] Lev. xxvi. 32, 33. Deut. xxviii.

habit *them;* and they shall
plant vineyards, but ^u not

^u Mic. 6. 15.   drink the wine thereof.

14 ^x The great d a y of
the LORD *is* near, *it is*
near, and hasteth greatly, ^x Joel 2. 1, 11.

---

ernment of His own world. All which is
strength to man, shall the rather fail, because it is strength, and they presume on it
and it deceives them. Its one end is to *become a prey* of devils. Riches, learning, rule,
influence, power, bodily strength, genius,
eloquence, popular favor, shall all fail a man,
and he, when stripped of them, shall be the
more bared because he gathered them around
him. "¹ Wealth is ever a runaway and has
no stability, but rather intoxicates and in-
clines to revolt and has unsteady feet. Exceeding folly is it to think much of it. For it
will not rescue those lying under the Divine
displeasure, nor will it free any from guilt,
when God decreeth punishment, and bringeth
the judgment befitting on the transgressors.
How utterly useless this eagerness after
wealth is to the ungodly, he teacheth, saying, that *their strength shall be a prey* to the
Chaldæan."
And their houses a desolation. "¹ For they
are, of whom it may be said very truly, ² *This
is the man that took not God for his strength, but
trusted unto the multitude of his riches, and
strengthened himself in his wickedness.* But if
indeed their houses are adorned costlily, they
shall not be theirs, for they shall be burned,
and themselves go into captivity, leaving all
in their house, and deprived of all which
would gladden. And this God said clearly
to the king of Judah by Jeremiah, ³ *Thou
hast builded thyself a large house and wide
chambers, ceiled with cedar, and painted with
vermilion. Shalt thou reign because thou closest
thyself with cedar?* " "⁴ As the house of the
body is the bodily dwelling, so to each mind
its house is that, wherein through desire it
is wont to dwell," and *desolate* shall they be,
being severed for ever from the things they
desired, and for ever deserted by God. *They
shall also build houses but not inhabit them,* as
the rich man said to his soul, ⁵ *Soul, thou hast
much goods laid up for many years.—Thou fool,
this night thy soul shall be required of thee;
then whose shall those things be, which thou hast
provided?* Before the siege by the Romans,
Jerusalem and the temple had been greatly
beautified, only to be destroyed. *And they
shall plant vineyards, but not drink the wine
thereof.* This is the woe, first pronounced in
the law ⁶, often repeated and ever found
true. Wickedness makes joy its end, yet
never finds it, seeking it where it is not, out
of God.
    14. *The great Day of the Lord is near.* The

Prophet again expands the words of Joel,
accumulating words expressive of the terrors
of that Day, shewing that though ⁷ *the great
and very terrible Day of the Lord, a day* (Joel
had said ⁸) *of darkness and gloominess, of
clouds and of thick darkness,* which was then
coming and *nigh at hand* ⁹, had come and was
gone, it was only a forerunner of others;
none of them final; but each, because it *was*
a judgment and an instance of the justice of
God, an earnest and forerunner of other
judgments to the end. Again, a *great Day
of the Lord* was *near.* This *Day* had itself, so
to speak, many hours and divisions of the
day. But each hour tolleth the same knell
of approaching doom. Each calamity in the
miserable reigns of the sons of Josiah was
one stroke in the passing-bell, until the destruction of Jerusalem by the Chaldæans, for
the time closed it. The judgment was complete. The completeness of that excision
made it the more an image of every other
like day until the final destruction of all
which, although around or near to Christ,
shall in the Great Day be found not to be
His, but to have rejected Him. "¹⁰ Truly
was vengeance required, ¹¹*from the blood of
righteous Abel to the blood of Zechariah, whom
they slew between the temple and the Altar,* and
at last when they said of the Son of God,
¹² *His blood be upon us and upon our children,*
they experienced a bitter day, because they
had provoked the Lord to bitterness; a Day,
appointed by the Lord, in which not the
weak only but the mighty shall be bowed
down, and wrath shall come upon them to
the end. For often before they endured the
wrath of the Lord, but that wrath was not to
the uttermost. What need now to describe
how great calamities they endured in both
captivities, and how they who rejected the
light of the Lord, walked in darkness and
thick darkness, and they who would not hear
the trumpet of the solemn feast-days, heard
the shout of the enemy. But of the *fenced
cities* and *lofty corner-towers* of Judæa, which
are till now destroyed even to the ground,
the eyes, I deem, can judge better than the
ears. We especially, now living in that
province, can see, can prove what is written.
We scarcely discern slight traces of ruins of
what once were great cities. At Shiloh,
where was the tabernacle and ark of the testament of the Lord, scarcely the foundations
of the altar are shewn. Rama and Bethoron
and the other noble cities built by Solomon,

¹ S. Cyr.   ² Ps. lii. 7.
³ Jer. xxii. 14, 15.   ⁴ S. Greg. Mor. viii. 14.
⁵ S. Luke xii. 19, 20.   ⁶ Deut. xxviii. 39.

⁷ Joel ii. 31.   ⁸ Ib. 2.   ⁹ Ib. 1.
¹⁰ S. Jer.   ¹¹ S. Matt. xxiii. 35.
          ¹² Ib. xxvii. 25.

Before
CHRIST
cir. 626. *even* the voice of the day of the LORD: the mighty man shall cry there bitterly.

15 ʸ That day *is* a day of wrath, a day of trouble and distress, a day of wasteness and desolation, Before
CHRIST
cir. 626.

ʸ Isai. 22. 5.
Jer. 30. 7.
Joel 2. 2, 11.
Amos 5. 18.
ver. 18.

are shewn to be little villages. Let us read Josephus and the prophecy of Zephaniah; we shall see his history before our eyes. And this must be said not only of the captivity, but even to the present day. The treacherous husbandmen, having slain the servants, and, at last, the Son of God, are prevented from entering Jerusalem, except to wail, and they purchase at a price leave to weep the ruin of their city, so that they who once bought the Blood of Christ, buy their tears ; not even their tears are costless. You may see on the day that Jerusalem was taken and destroyed by the Romans, a people in mourning come, decrepit old women and old men, in aged and ragged wretchedness, shewing in their bodies and in their guise the wrath of the Lord. The hapless crowd is gathered, and amid the gleaming of the Cross of Christ, and the radiant glory of His Resurrection, the standard also of the Cross shining from Mount Olivet, you may see the people, piteous but unpitied, bewail the ruins of their temple, tears still on their cheeks, their arms livid and their hair dishevelled, and the soldier asketh a guerdon, that they may be allowed to weep longer. And doth any, when he seeth this, doubt of the *day of trouble and distress, the day of darkness and gloominess, the day of clouds and thick darkness, the day of the trumpet and alarm?* For they have also trumpets in their sorrow, and, according to the prophecy, the voice of *the solemn feast-day is turned into mourning.* They wail over the ashes of the Sanctuary and the altar destroyed, and over cities once fenced, and over the high towers of the temple, from which they once cast headlong James the brother of the Lord."

But referring the Day of the Lord to the end of the world or the close of the life of each, it too is *near; near*, the prophet adds to impress the more its nearness ; for it is at hand to each ; and when eternity shall come, all time shall seem like a moment, [1] *A thousand years, when past, are like a watch in the night;* one fourth part of one night.

And hasteth greatly. For time whirls on more rapidly to each, year by year, and when God's judgments draw near, the tokens of them thicken, and troubles sweep one over the other, events jostle against each other. *The voice of the day of the Lord.* That Day, when it cometh, shall leave no one in doubt

what it meaneth ; it shall give no *uncertain sound*, but shall, trumpet-tongued, proclaim the holiness and justice of Almighty God ; its voice shall be the Voice of Christ, which [2] *all that are in the graves shall hear and come forth; they that have done good, unto the resurrection of life; and they that have done evil unto the resurrection of damnation.*

The mighty men shall cry there bitterly; for [3] *bitter is the remembrance of death to a man that liveth at rest in his possessions, unto the man that hath nothing to vex him, and that hath prosperity in all things;* and [4], *There is no mighty man that hath power over the spirit to retain the spirit; neither hath he power in the day of death; and there is no discharge in that war; neither shall wickedness deliver those that are given to it.* Rather, wrath shall come upon [5] *the kings of the earth, and the great men and the rich men and the mighty men, and* they shall will to hide themselves *from the Face of Him that sitteth on the Throne and from the wrath of the Lamb; for the great Day of His wrath is come: and who shall be able to stand?*

The mighty men shall cry there bitterly. The prophet has spoken of time, *the day of the Lord.* He points out the more vividly the unseen sight and place, *there;* so David says, [6] *There they feared a fear.* He sees the place ; he hears the bitter cry. So nigh is it in fact; so close the connection of cause and effect, of sin and punishment. There shall be a great and *bitter cry*, when there shall be no place for repentance. It shall be a [7] mighty cry, but mighty in the bitterness of its distress. [8] *Mighty men shall be mightily tormented*, i. e., those who have been mighty against God, weak against Satan, and shall have used their might in his service.

15. *A day of wrath*, in which all the wrath of Almighty God, which evil angels and evil men have treasured to them for that day, shall be poured out: *the* day of wrath, because then they shall be brought face to face before the Presence of God, but thenceforth they shall be cast out of it for ever.

A day of trouble and distress. Both words express, how anguish shall narrow and hem them in; so that there shall be no escape; above them, God displeased; below, the flames of Hell; around, devils to drag them away, and Angels casting them forth *in bundles to burn them;* without, *the books* which

---

[1] Ps. xc. 4.　　　　　[2] S. John v. 28, 29.
[3] Ecclus. xli. 1.　　　[4] Eccl. viii. 8.
[5] Rev. vi. 15–17.　　　[6] Ps. xiv. 5.

[7] The Arab. word, צָרַח, is used of "a loud shrill cry." It occurs only here and (Hif.) in Is. xlii. 12.
　　　　[8] Wisd. vi. 6.

a day of darkness and gloominess, a day of clouds and thick darkness,

16 A day of ᶻ the trumpet and alarm against the fenced cities, and against the high towers.

17 And I will bring

distress upon men, that they shall ᵃwalk like blind men, because they have sinned against the LORD: and ᵇtheir blood shall be poured out as dust, and their flesh ᶜas the dung.

Before
CHRIST
cir. 626.

ᵃ Deut. 28. 29.
Isai. 59. 10.

ᵇ Ps. 79. 3.

ᶜ Ps. 83. 10.
Jer. 9. 22.
& 16. 4.

---

shall be opened ; and within, conscience leaving them no escape.

A day of wasteness and desolation, in which all things shall return to their primeval void, before *the Spirit of God brooded upon the face of the waters,* His Presence being altogether withdrawn.

A day of darkness and gloominess ; for sun and moon shall lose their brightness, and no brightness from the Lamb shall shine upon the wicked, but they shall be driven into *outer darkness.*

A day of clouds and thick darkness, hiding from them the Face of the Sun of Righteousness, and covering Him, so that their *prayers* should *not pass through*[1].

16. *A day of the trumpet and alarm*[2], i. e., of the loud blast of the trumpet, which sounds alarm and causes it. The word[3] is especially the shrill loud noise of the trumpet (for sacred purposes in Israel itself, as ruling all the movements of the tabernacle and accompanying their feasts) ; then also of the " battle cry." They had not listened to the voice of the trumpet, as it called them to holy service ; now they shall hear [4] *the voice of the Archangel and the trump of God.*

Against the high towers, lit. *corners*[5], and so *corner-towers.* This peculiarity describes Jerusalem, whose walls " [6] were made artificially standing in a line curved inwards, so that the flanks of assailants might be exposed." By this same name[7] are called the mighty men and chiefs of the people, who, humanly speaking, hold it together and support it ; on these chiefs in rebellion against God, whether devils or evil men, shall punishment greatly fall.

17. *I will bring distress upon men.* I will

hem them in, in anguish on all sides. God Himself shall meet them with His terrors, wherever they turn. [8] *I will hem them in, that they may find it so.*

That they shall walk like blind men, utterly bereft of counsel, seeing no more than the blind which way to turn, grasping blindly and franticly at anything, and *going on* headlong to their own destruction. So God forewarned them in the law ; [9] *Thou shalt grope at noon day, as the blind gropeth in darkness ;* and Job, of the wicked generally, [10] *They meet with the darkness in the day-time, and grope in the noon-day as in the night ;* and, [11] *They grope in the dark without light, and He maketh them to stagger like a drunken man ;* and Isaiah foretelling of those times, [12] *We grope for the wall, as the blind ; and we grope, as if we had no eyes ; we stumble in the noon-day as in the night. Because they have sinned against the Lord,* and so He hath turned their wisdom into foolishness, and since they have despised Him, He hath made them objects of contempt[13]. *Their blood shall be poured out like dust,* as abundant and as valueless ; utterly disregarded by Him, as Asaph complains, [14] *their blood have they shed like water ;* contemptible and disgusting as what is vilest ; *their flesh* [15] *as the dung,* refuse, decayed, putrefied, offensive, enriching by its decay the land, which had been the scene of their luxuries and oppressions. Yet the most offensive disgusting physical corruption is but a faint image of the defilement of- sin. This punishment, in which the carrion-remains should be entombed only in the bowels of vultures and dogs, was especially threatened to Jehoiakim ; [16] *He shall be buried with the burial of an ass, dragged and cast forth beyond the gates of Jerusalem.*

---

[1] Lam. iii. 44.
[2] " Alarm " seems to be used in the sense of "sounding alarm," alarum.
[3] תְּרוּעָה.   [4] 1 Thess. iv. 16.   [5] See E. M. on iii. 6. It is the *corner* of a house, of a street, of a court, a city. Hence " the gate of the corner," 2 Kgs xiv. 13, 2 Chr. xxvi. 9, Jer. xxxi. 38. In 2 Chr. xxvi. 15, פִּנּוֹת cannot be " battlements " (as Ges. &c.) since the engines were erected upon them. Neither then here is there any ground to invent a new meaning for the word.
[6] Tac. Hist. v. 11. Jos. de B. J. v. 5. 3.
[7] Jud. xx. 2. 1 Sam. xiv. 38, Is. xix. 13. Zech. x. 4.
[8] Jer. x. 18. Moses had said this of His instru-

ments, *And He shall hem thee in, in all thy gates.* Deut. xxviii. 52.
[9] Ib. 29.   [10] Job v. 14.   [11] Ib. xii. 25.   [12] Is. lix. 10.
[13] 1 Sam. ii. 30.
[14] Ps. lxxix. 3. שָׁפַךְ is used of the pouring out both liquids and solids.
[15] Insulated the use is, לְחוּם must have had the meaning of the Arab. لَحْم "flesh." So LXX Ch. Vulg. Syr. David B. Abr. Abulw. Tanch., Anon-Arab. Tr., retain the word in Arabic ; Abulw. notices that " the Heb. is akin to the Arabic word." Tanch. cites Job vi. 7.   [16] Jer. xxii. 19.

Before
CHRIST
cir. 630.

d Prov. 11. 4.
Ezek. 7. 19.

18 ^d Neither their silver nor their gold shall be able to deliver them in the day of the LORD's wrath; but the whole land shall be

Before
CHRIST
cir. 630.

e ch. 3. 8.
f ver. 2, 3.

^e devoured by the fire of his jealousy: for ^f he shall make even a speedy riddance of all them that dwell in the land.

---

18. *Neither their silver nor their gold shall be able to deliver them in the day of the Lord's wrath.* Gain unjustly gotten was the cause of their destruction. For, as Ezekiel closes the like description; "¹ They shall cast their silver into the streets, and their gold shall be removed; their silver and their gold shall not be able to deliver them in the day of the wrath of the Lord; they shall not satisfy their souls nor fill their bowels: *because it is the stumbling block of their iniquity.*" Much less shall any possession, outward or inward, be of avail in the Great Day; since in death the rich man's ² *pomp shall not follow him,* and every gift which he has misused, whether of mind or spirit, even the knowledge of God without doing His Will, shall but increase damnation. "Sinners will then have nothing but their sins."

Here the prophet uses images belonging more to the immediate destruction; at the close the words again widen, and belong, in their fullest literal sense, to the Day of Judgment. *The whole land,* rather, as at the beginning, *the whole earth shall be devoured by the fire of His jealousy; for He shall make even a speedy riddance of all them that dwell in the land:* rather, *He shall make an utter, yea altogether* ³ *a terrific destruction* ⁴ *of all the dwellers of the earth.* What Nahum had foretold of Nineveh⁵, *He shall make the place thereof an utter consumption,* that Zephaniah foretells of all the inhabitants of the world. For what is this, *the whole earth shall be devoured by the fire of His jealousy,* but what S. Peter says, ⁶ *the earth also and the works that are therein shall be burned up?* And what is that he says, *He shall make all the dwellers of the earth an utter, yea altogether a hasty destruction,* but a general judgment of all, who belong to the world, whose home, citizenship, whose whole mind is in the world, not as true Christians, who are strangers and pilgrims here, and their ⁷ *citizenship is in Heaven?* These God shall make an utter, terrific, speedy destruction, a living death, so that they shall at once both be and not be; be, as continued in being; not be, as having no life of God, but only a continued death in misery. And this

shall be through the jealousy of Almighty God, that Divine quality in Him, whereby He loves and wills to be loved, and endures not those who give to others the love for which He gave so much and which is so wholly due to Himself Alone. " ⁸ Thou demandest my love, and if I give it not, art wroth with me, and threatenest me with grievous woes. Is it then a slight woe to love Thee not?" What will be that anger, which is Infinite Love, but which becomes, through man's sin, Hate?

II. Having set forth the terrors of the Judgment Day, the prophet adds an earnest call to repentance; and then declares how judgments, forerunners of that Day, shall fall, one by one, on those nations around, who know not God, and shall rest upon Nineveh, the great beautiful ancient city of the world. " ⁹ See the mercy of God. It had been enough to have set before the wise the vehemence of the coming evil. But because He willeth not to punish, but to alarm only, Himself calleth to repentance, that He may not do what He threatened." " ¹⁰ Having set forth clearly the savageness of the war and the greatness of the suffering to come, he suitably turns his discourse to the duty of calling to repentance, when it was easy to persuade them, being terrified. For sometimes when the mind has been numbed, and exceedingly bent to evil, we do not readily admit even the will to repent, but fear often drives us to it, even against our will. He calls us then to friendship with Himself. For as they revolted, became aliens, serving idols and giving up their mind to their passions, so they would, as it were, retrace their steps, and lay hold of the friendship of God, choosing to serve·Him, nay and Him Alone, and obey His commandments. Wherefore while we have time, while the Lord, in His forbearance as God, gives way, let us enact repentance, supplicate, say weeping, ¹¹ *remember not the sins and offences of my youth;* let us unite ourselves with Him by sanctification and sobriety. So shall we be sheltered in the day of wrath, and wash away the stain of our falls, before the Day of the Lord come

---

¹ Ezek. vii. 19. ² Ps. xlix. 17.

³ אַךְ "nothing but."

⁴ נְבְהָלָה unites here the senses of terror and destruction, as in Ps. civ. 29. *Thou hidest Thy face, they are troubled,* יִבָּהֵלוּן *and perish;* Is. lxv. 23, *they*

shall not bear לַבֶּהָלָה for destruction, ‖ לֹא יִגְעוּ לָרִיק.

⁵ See ab. on Nahum i. 8. p. 134.
⁶ 2 Pet. iii. 13.
⁷ Heb. xi. 13. Phil. iii. 20.
⁸ S. Aug. Conf. i. 5. p. 3. Oxf. Tr.
⁹ S. Jer. ¹⁰ S. Cyr. ¹¹ Ps. xxv. 7.

[a]GATHER yourselves together, yea, gather together, O nation ‖ not desired;

upon us. For the Judge will come, He will come from heaven at the due season, and will reward each according to his work."

1. *Gather yourselves together, yea gather together* [1], rather, *Sift yourselves, yea sift* [2]. The exact image is from gathering stubble or dry sticks, which are picked up one by one, with search and care. So must men deal with the dry and withered leaves of a past evil life. The English rendering however comes to the same meaning. We use, "collect one's self" for bringing one s self, all one's thoughts, together, and so, having full possession of one's self. Or *gathering ourselves* might stand in contrast with being "abroad," as it were, out of ourselves amid the manifoldness of things seen. "[3] Thou who, taken up with the business of the world, hurriest to and fro amid divers things, return to the Church of the saints, and join thyself to their life and assembly, whom thou seest to please God, and bring together the dislocated members of thy soul, which now are not knit together, into one frame of wisdom, and cleave to its embrace." *Gather yourselves* into one, wherein ye have been scattered; to the One God, from Whom they had wandered, seeking pleasure from His many creatures; to His one fold and Church, from which they had severed themselves outwardly by joining the worship of Baal, inwardly, by serving him and his abominable rites ; joining and joined to the assembly of the faithful, by oneness of faith and life.

In order to repent, a man must know himself thoroughly ; and this can only be done by taking act by act, word by word, thought by thought, as far as he can, not in a confused heap or mass, as they lie in any man's conscience, but one by one, each picked up apart, and examined, and added to the sear unfruitful heap, plucking them as it were, and gathering them out of himself, that so they may, by the Spirit of burning, the fire of God's Spirit kindling repentance, be burned up, and not the sinner himself be fuel for fire with them. The word too is intensive,

[1] The Eng. Vers. follows the LXX Ch. Syr., S. Jer., which render "Gather yourselves together," as if, from the first meaning, "gather dry sticks or stubble" it came to signify "gather" generally, and thence, in the reflective form, "gather yourselves together."
[2] The word is first used of gathering dry stubble together (Ex. v. 7, 12.) then of "dry sticks" one by one (Nu. xv. 32, 33, 1 Kgs xvii. 10, 12.). A heathen speaks of "gathering out thorns" (ἐξακανθίζειν) i. e., minutely examining and bringing out to light every fault. (Cic. ad Att. vi. 6. 2.) And another writes to his steward, "Shalt thou with stronger hand pull

" Gather together all which is in you, thoroughly, piece by piece " (for the sinner's whole self becomes chaff, dry and empty). To use another image, "Sift yourselves thoroughly, so that nothing escape, as far as your diligence can reach, and then—*And gather on,* i. e., "glean on ; " examine yourselves, "not lightly and after the manner of dissemblers before God," but repeatedly, gleaning again and again, to see if by any means anything have escaped : continuing on the search and ceasing not. The first earnest search into the soul must be the beginning, not the end. Our search must be continued, until there be no more to be discovered, i. e. when sin is no more, and we see ourselves in the full light of the Presence of our Judge. For a first search, however diligent, never thoroughly reaches the whole deep disease of the whole man; the most grievous sins hide other grievous sins, though lighter. Some sins flash on the conscience, at one time, some at another ; so that few, even upon a diligent search, come at once to the knowledge of all their heaviest sins. When the mist is less thick, we see more clearly what was before one dark dull mass of imperfection and misery. "[4] Spiritual sins are also with difficulty sifted, (as they are,) for one who is carnal. Whence it happens, that things in themselves heavier he perceives less or very little, and conscience is not grieved so much by the memory of pride or envy, as of impurities and crimes." So having said, "Sift yourselves through and through," he says, "sift on." A diligent sifting and search into himself must be the beginning of all true repentance and pardon. "[5] What remains, but that we give ourselves wholly to this work, so holy, and needful ? [6] *Let us search and try our ways and our doings,* and let each think that he has made progress, not if he find not what to blame, but if he blame what he finds. Thou hast not sifted thyself in vain, if thou hast discovered that thou needest a fresh sifting ; and so often has thy search not failed thee, as thou judgest that it must be renewed. But

out thorns from my field, or I from my mind ? "
Hor. Ep. i. 14. 4.　[3] S. Jer.　[4] S. Bern. de Cons. c. 5.
[5] Id. Serm. 58. in Cant. fin.
[6] Lam. iii. 40. The two words, *search* and *try,* חקר, חפר are both used of a deep search of a thing which lies deep and hidden. Both originally mean "dig." Both are used of a Divine knowledge of the inmost soul; the former of the mind as enlightened by God (Prov. xx. 27), the latter of God's searching it out Himself (Jer. xvii. 10. Ps. xliv. 22 (21) cxxxix. 1. Job xiii. 9, and of the Divine Wisdom, Job xxviii. 27.

Before
CHRIST
cir. 630.

2 Before the decree
bring forth, *before* the day
pass [b] as the chaff, before
[c] the fierce anger of t h e
LORD come u p o n y o u,
b e f o r e the day o f the
LORD's anger come upon
you.

[b] Job 21. 18.
Ps. 1. 4.
Isai. 17. 13.
Hos. 13. 3.
[c] 2 Kin. 23. 26.

3 [d] Seek ye the LORD,
[e] all ye meek of the earth,
which have wrought h i s
judgment ; seek righteousness, s e e k meekness : [f] it
may be ye shall be hid in
the day of the L o r d 's
anger,

Before
CHRIST
cir. 630.

[d] Ps. 105. 4.
Amos 5. 6.
[e] Ps. 76. 9.

[f] Joel 2. 14.
Amos 5. 15.
Jonah 3. 9.

---

if thou ever dost this, when there is need,
thou dost it ever. But ever remember that
thou needest help from above and the mercy
of Jesus Christ our Lord Who is over all,
God blessed for ever." The whole course of
self-examination then lies in two words of
Divine Scripture. And withal he warns
them, instead of gathering together riches
which shall *not be able to deliver them in the
day of trouble*, to gather themselves into themselves, and so *judge* themselves *thoroughly* [1],
that they be not judged of the Lord [2].

O nation not desired [3], i. e., having nothing
in itself to be desired or loved, but rather, for
its sin, hateful to God. God yearneth with
pity and compassion over His creatures ; He
[4] *hath a desire to the work of His Hands.* Here
Israel is spoken to, as what he had made himself, hateful to God by his sins, although still
an object of His tender care, in what yet remained to him of nature or grace which was
from Himself.

2. *Before the decree bring forth.* God's
word is full (as it were) of the event which
it foretelleth ; it contains its own fulfillment
in itself, and *travaileth* until it come to pass,
giving signs of its coming, yet delaying until
the full time. Time is said to bring forth
what is wrought in it. *Thou knowest not,
what a day shall bring forth.*

Before the day pass as the chaff, or, parenthetically, *like chaff the day passeth by.* God's
counsels lie wrapt up, as it were, in the womb
of time, wherein He hides them, until the
moment which He has appointed, and they
break forth suddenly to those who look not
for them. The mean season is given for repentance, i. e., the day of grace, the span of
repentance still allowed, which is continually whirling more swiftly by ; and woe, if it

be fruitless as chaff ! Those who profit not
by it shall also be as chaff, carried away pitilessly by the whirlwind to destruction. Time,
on which eternity hangs, is a slight, uncertain thing, as little to be counted upon, as the
light dry particles which are the sport of the
wind, driven uncertainly hither and thither.
But when it is *passed*, then *cometh*, not *to*
them, but *upon* them, from Heaven, overwhelming them, [5] *abiding upon* them, not to
pass away, *the heat of the anger of Almighty
God.* This warning he twice repeats, to impress the certainty and speed of its coming [6].
It is the warning of our Lord, [7] *Take heed,
lest that day come upon you unawares.*

3. *Seek ye the Lord.* He had exhorted sinners to penitence ; he now calls the righteous
to persevere and increase more and more.
He bids them *seek diligently* [8], and that with a
three-fold call, to seek Him from Whom they
received daily the three-fold blessing [9],
Father, Son, and Holy Ghost, as he had just
before threatened God's impending judgment with the same use of the mysterious
number, three. They, whom he calls, were
already, by the grace of God, *meek,* and *had
wrought His judgment.* " [10] Submitting themselves to the word of God, they had done and
were doing the judgment of God, *judging
themselves that they be not judged ;* the beginning of which judgment is, as sinners and
guilty of death, to give themselves to the
Cross of the Lord, i. e., to be [11] *baptized* in *His
Death and be buried with Him by Baptism into
death ;* but the perfection of that judgment or
righteousness is, to *walk in newness of life, as
He rose from the dead through the glory of the
Father."*

" [12] Since the meek already have God
through grace as the Possessor and Dweller

---

[1] διακρινατε, which answers to the intensive form
here, " judge yourselves through and through."
[2] 1 Cor. xi. 31, 32.
[3] The E. M. has " or not desirous," the word
ⁿⁿⁿⁿ signifying to long, Gen. xxxi. 30. Ps. lxxxiv.

3. But in both places the object of desire is mentioned, " thy father's house," in Gen., " the courts
of the Lord," in the Ps. Israel had strong but bad
longings. " Not desirous " would not by itself convey, " having no desire to return to God," or as Ch.,
" who willeth not to return to the law." The same
objection lies, over and above, to the rendering
" unashamed," coll. Chald. ⁿⁿⁿ " turned pale " from

shame, disgrace, horror. Buxt. For there is nothing to limit the " turning pale " to " shame." The
root ⁿⁿⁿ in Heb. only means " longed," Ps. xvii.
12, Job xiv. 15, of which ⁿⁿⁿⁿ is here the passive.
People turn pale from fear or horror, not from
shame.

[4] Job xiv. 15. The word is the same.
[5] S. John iii. 36.   [6] Gen. xli. 32.
[7] S. Luke xvi. 34.
[8] The Hebrew form is intensive.
[9] Nu. vi. 23-26.   [10] Rup.
[11] Rom. vi. 3, 4.   [12] Dion.

Before
C H R I S T
cir. 630.

g Jer. 47. 4, 5.
Ezek. 25. 15.
Amos 1. 6, 7, 8. Zech. 9. 5, 6.

4 ¶ For g Gaza shall be forsaken, and Ashkelon a desolation: they shall drive out Ashdod h at the noon day, and Ekron shall be rooted up.

in their heart, how shall they seek Him but that they may have Him more fully and more perfectly, knowing Him more clearly, loving Him more ardently, cleaving to Him more inseparably, that so they may be heard by Him, not for themselves only, but for others?" It is then the same Voice as at the close of the Revelation, [1] *the righteous, let him be still more righteous; the holy, let him be still more holy.* They are the *meek*, who are exhorted *diligently* to *seek meekness,* and they who had *wrought His judgment,* who are *diligently* to *seek Righteousness.* And since our Lord saith, [2] *Learn of Me, for I am meek and lowly of heart,* He bids " [3] those who imitated His meekness and did His judgment, to seek the Lord in their meekness." Meekness and Righteousness may be His Attributes, Who is All-gentleness and All-Righteousness, the Fountain of all, wheresoever it is, in gentleness receiving penitents, and as *the Righteous Judge, giving the crown of righteousness* to those who *love Him and keep His commandments,* yea He joineth righteousness with meekness, since without His mercy no man living could be justified in His Sight. " [4] God is sought by us, when, of our choice, laying aside all listlessness, we thirst after doing what pleases Him; and we shall do judgment too, when we fulfill His Divine law, working out what is good unshrinkingly; and we shall gain the prize of righteousness, when crowned with glory for well-doing and running the well-reported and blameless way of true piety to God and of love to the brethren; for [5] *love is the fulfilling of the law."*

It may be ye shall be hid in the day of the Lord's anger. " [6] Shall these too then scarcely be *hid in the day of the Lord's anger?* Doth not the Apostle Peter say the very same? [7] *If it first begin at us, what shall be the end of them that obey not the Gospel of God? And if the righteous scarcely be saved, where shall the ungodly and the sinner appear?* So then, although any be *meek,* although he *have wrought the judgment* of the Lord, let him ever suspect himself, nor think that he has *already attained,* since neither can any righteous be saved, if he be judged *without mercy."* " [8] He saith, *it may be;* not that there is any doubt that the meek and they who perseveringly seek God, shall then be saved, but, to convey how difficult it is to be saved, and how fear-

ful and rigorous is the judgment of God." To be hid is to be sheltered from wrath under the protection of God; as David says, [9] *In the time of trouble He shall hide me;* and, [10] *Thou shalt hide them [that trust in Thee] in the secret of Thy presence from the pride of man; Thou shalt keep them secretly in a pavilion from the strife of tongues.* And in Isaiah, [11] *A Man shall be as an hiding-place from the wind, and a covert from the tempest;* and, [12] *There shall be a tabernacle for a shadow in the daytime from the heat, and for a place of refuge, and for a covert from storm and from rain.*

4. *For.* As a ground for repentance and perseverance, he goes through Heathen nations, upon whom God's wrath should come. " [3] As Isaiah, Jeremiah, Ezekiel, after visions concerning Judah, turn to other nations round about, and according to the character of each, announce what shall come upon them, and dwell at length upon it, so doth this prophet, though more briefly." And thus under five nations, who lay West, East, South and North, he includes all mankind on all sides, and, again, according to their respective characters toward Israel, as they are alien from, or hostile to the Church; the Philistines [13], as a near, malicious, infesting enemy; Moab and Ammon [14], people akin to her (as heretics) yet ever rejoicing at her troubles and sufferings; Ethiopians [15], distant nations at peace with her, and which are, for the most part, spoken of as to be brought unto her; Assyria [16], as the great oppressive power of the world, and so upon it the full desolation rests. In the first fulfillment, because Moab and Ammon aiding Nebuchadnezzar, (and all, in divers ways, wronging God's people [17]), trampled on His sanctuary, overthrew His temple and blasphemed the Lord, the prophecy is turned against them. So then, before the captivity came, while Josiah was yet king, and Jerusalem and the temple were, as yet, not overthrown, the prophecy is directed against those who mocked at them. *Gaza shall be forsaken.* Out of the five cities of the Philistines, the Prophet pronounces woe upon the same four as Amos [18] before, Jeremiah [19] soon after, and Zechariah [20] later. Gath, then, the fifth, had probably remained with Judah since Uzziah [21] and Hezekiah [22]. In the sentence of the rest, regard is had (as is so frequent in the Old

1 Rev. xxii. 11.   2 S. Matth. xi. 29.
3 S. Jer.   4 S. Cyr.   5 Rom. xiii. 10.
6 Rup.   7 1 S. Pet. iv. 17, 18.   8 Dion.
9 Ps. xxvii. 5.   10 Ib. xxxi. 20.   11 Isai. xxxii. 2.
12 Ib. v. 6.   13 ii. 4–7.   14 Ib. 8–10.

15 v. 12.   16 13–15.
17 Is. xvi. 4, Am. i. 13–15. ii. 1–3. Jer. xlviii. 27–30,
42. xlix. 1. Ezek. xx. 3, 6, 8.
18 Am. i. 6–8.   19 Jer. xxv. 20.   20 Zech. ix. 5, 6.
21 2 Chr. xxvi. 6.   22 2 Kgs xviii. 8.

Testament) to the names of the places themselves, that, henceforth, the name of the place might suggest the thought of the doom pronounced upon it. The names expressed boastfulness, and so, in the Divine judgment, carried their own sentence with them, and this sentence is pronounced by a slight change in the word. Thus *'Azzah* (Gaza,) *strong* shall be *'Azoobah, desolated; Ekron, deep-rooting*[1], shall *Teaker, be uprooted;* the *Cherethites (cutters off)* shall become (*Cheroth*) *diggings; Chebel, the band* of the sea coast, shall be in another sense *Chebel,* an *inheritance*[2], divided by line to the remnant of Judah ; and *Ashdod (the waster*[3]) shall be taken in their might, not by craft, nor in the way of robbers, but *driven forth* violently and openly in the *noon-day.*
For Gaza shall be forsaken. Some vicissitudes of these towns have been noted already[4]. The fulfillment of the prophecy is not tied down to time; the one marked contrast is, that the old heathen enemies of Judah should be destroyed, the house of Judah should be restored, and should re-enter upon the possession of the land, promised to them of old. The Philistine towns had, it seems, nothing to fear from Babylon or Persia, to whom they remained faithful subjects. The Ashdodites (who probably, as the most important, stand for the whole[5]) combined with Sanballat, *the Ammonites and the Arabians*[6], to hinder the rebuilding of the walls of Jerusalem. Even an army was gathered, headed by Samaria[7]. They gave themselves out as loyal, Jerusalem as rebellious[8]. The old sin remaining, Zechariah renewed the sentence by Zephaniah against the four cities[9]; a prophecy, which an unbeliever also has recognized as picturing the march of Alexander[10]. "[11] All the other cities of Palestine having submitted," Gaza alone resisted the conqueror for two or five months. It had come into the hands of the Persians in the expedition of Cambyses against Egypt[12]. The Gazæans having all perished fighting at their posts, Alexander sold the women and children, and re-peopled the city from the neighborhood[13]. Palestine

lay between the two rival successors of Alexander, the Ptolemies and Seleucidæ, and felt their wars[14]. Gaza fell through mischance into the hands of Ptolemy[15], 11 years after the death of Alexander[16], and soon after, was destroyed by Antiochus[11] (B. C. 198), " preserving its faith to Ptolemy" as before to the Persians, in a way admired by a heathen historian. In the Maccabee wars, Judas Maccabæus chiefly destroyed the idols of Ashdod, but also [17] *spoiled their cities ;* Jonathan set it on fire, with its idol-temple, which was a sort of citadel to it[18]; Ascalon submitted to him[19]; Ekron with its borders were given to him by Alexander Balas[20]; he burnt the suburbs of Gaza[21]; Simon took it, expelled its inhabitants, filled it with believing Jews and fortified it more strongly than before[22] ; but, after a year's siege, it was betrayed to Alexander Jannæus, who slew its senate of 500 and razed the city to the ground[23]. Gabinius restored it and Ashdod[24]. After Herod's death, Ashdod was given to Salome[25] ; Gaza, as being a Greek city[26], was detached from the realm of Archelaus and annexed to Syria. It was destroyed by the Jews in their revolt when Florus was "procurator," A. D. 55[27]. Ascalon and Gaza must still have been strong, and were probably a distinct population in the early times of Antipater, father of Herod, when Alexander and Alexandra set him over all Idumæa, since " he is said " then "[28] to have made friendship with the Arabs, Gazites and Ascalonites, likeminded with himself, and to have attached them by many and large presents."
Yet though the inhabitants were changed, the hereditary hatred remained. Philo in his Embassy to Caius, A. D. 40, used the strong language, "[29] The Ascalonites have an implacable and irreconcilable enmity to the Jews, their neighbors, who inhabit the holy land." This continued toward Christians. Some horrible atrocities, of almost inconceivable savagery, by those of Gaza and Ascalon A. D. 361, are related by Theodoret[30] and Sozomen[31]. "[32] Who is ignorant of the madness of the Gazæans?" asks S. Gregory

---

[1] It seems to me most probable that the origin of the meanings is preserved in the Ch. עֲקָר, "root,"

(which itself is the source of other metaphoric meanings, as, "the root of a thing ;" "the root " i. e., the foundation "of faith," its fundamental doctrines; "the root," in Lexicography, see Buxtorf), and that the Chald. עֲקַר "pluck up, remove," and

עֲקַר, here and Eccl. iii. 2, is a denominative. The Proper Name is older probably than even Moses.
[2] ii. 5, 7.
[3] The root שָׁדַד has throughout the meaning of "wasting," not of "strength." שַׁדַּי "the Almighty," is probably from a kindred root, שָׂדָה.
[4] See on Amos i. 6-8, vol. i. p. 244-247.
[5] Their language alone is mentioned Neh. ix. 24, אַשְׁדּוֹדִית, in contrast with Jewish יְהוּדִית; but neither is it mentioned that the Jews married any

other Philistine women. If Gath was destroyed, Ashdod lay nearest to them.
[6] Neh. iv. 7.   [7] Ib. 2.   [8] Ib. ii. 19. vi. 6.
[9] Zech. ix.
[10] Eichhorn Einl. iv. 605. See Daniel the Proph. p. 280. sqq.
[11] Polyb. Reliq. xvi. 40.   [12] Mela i. 11.
[13] Arrian ii. 27.   [14] Polyb. v. 68.
[15] Diod. Sic. xix. 84.
[16] Hecat. in Jos. c. Ap. i. 22 Opp. ii. 455.
[17] 1 Macc. v. 68.   [18] Ib. x. 84.   [19] Ib. 86.   [20] Ib. 89.
[21] Ib. xi. 61.   [22] Ib. xiii. 43-48.
[23] Jos. Ant. xiii. 13. 3.   [24] Ib. xiv. 5. 3.
[25] Ib. xvii. 8. 1.   [26] B. J. ii. 6. 3.
[27] κατέσκαπτον, Jos. B. J. ii. 18. 1.
[28] Ant. xiv. 1. 3.
[29] Philo Leg. ad Caium T. ii. p. 576 Mang. The words are ἀσυμβατός τις καὶ ἀκατάλλακτος δυσμένεια.
[30] Theod. H. E. iii. 7.   [31] Soz. H. E. v. 10.
[32] Orat. 4. in Julian. c. 36.

of Nazianzus, of the times of Julian. This was previous to the conversion of the great Gazite temple of Marna into a Christian Church by Eudoxia[1]. On occasion of Constantine's exemption of the Maiumas Gazæ from their control, it is alleged, that they were "[2] extreme Heathen." In the time of the Crusades the Ascalonites are described by Christians as their "[3] most savage enemies." It may be, that a likeness of sin may have continued on a likeness of punishment. But the primary prediction was against the people, not against the walls. The sentence, *Gaza shall be forsaken*, would have been fulfilled by the removal or captivity of its inhabitants, even if they had not been replaced by others. A prediction against any ancient British town would have been fulfilled, if the Britons in it had been replaced or exterminated by Danes, and these by Saxons, and these subdued by the Normans, though their displacers became wealthy and powerful in their place. Even on the same site it would not be the same Gaza, when the Philistine Gaza became Edomite, and the Edomite Greek, and the Greek Arabian[4]. Ashdod (as well as Gaza) is spoken of as a city of the Greeks[5]; New Gaza is spoken of as a mixture of Turks, Arabians, Fellahs, Bedouins out of Egypt, Syria, Petræa[6]. Felix Faber says, "there is a wonderful commixture of divers nations in it, Ethiopians, Arabs, Egyptians, Syrians, Indians and eastern Christians; no Latins[7]." Its Jewish inhabitants fled from it in the time of Napoleon: now, with few exceptions it is inhabited by Arabs[8].

But these, Ghŭzzeh, Eskalon, Akir, Sedud, are at most successors of the Philistine cities, of which there is no trace above the surface of the earth. It is common to speak of "remnants of antiquity," as being or not being to be found in any of them; but this means, that, where these exist, there are remains of a Greek or Roman, not of a Philistine city.

Of the four cities, *Akkaron*, Ekron, ("the firm-rooting") has not left a vestage. It is mentioned by name only, after the times of the Bible, by some who passed by it[9]. There was "a large village of Jews" so called in the time of Eusebius and S. Jerome[10], "between Azotus and Jamnia." Now a village of "[11] about 50 mud houses without a single remnant of antiquity except 2 large finely built wells" bears the name of Akir. S. Jerome adds, "Some think that Accaron is the tower of Strato, afterward called Cæsarea." This was perhaps derived from misunderstanding his Jewish instructor[12]. But it shows how entirely all knowledge of Ekron was then lost.

Ashdod or Azotus which, at the time when Zephaniah prophesied, held out a twenty-nine years' siege against Psammetichus, is replaced by "[13] a moderate sized village of mud houses, situated on the Eastern declivity of a little flattish hill," "entirely modern, not containing a vestige of antiquity." "A beautiful sculptured sarcophagus with some fragments of small marble shafts," "near the Khan on the S. W." belong of course to later times. "The whole south side of the hill appears also, as if it had been once covered with buildings, the stones of which are now thrown together in the rude fences." Its Bishops are mentioned from the Council of Nice to A. D. 536[14], and so probably continued till the Mohammedan devastation. It is not mentioned in the Talmud[15]. Benjamin of Tudela calls it Palmis, and says, "it is desolate, and there are no Jews in it[16]." "[17] Neither Ibn Haukal [Yacut], Edrisi, Abulfeda, nor William of Tyre mention it."

Ascalon and Gaza had each a port, Maiuma Gazæ, Maiuma Ascalon; lit. "a place on the sea" (an Egyptian name[18]) belonging to Ascalon or Gaza. The name involves that Ascalon and Gaza themselves, the old Philistine towns, were not on the sea. They were, like Athens, built inland, perhaps (as

---

[1] "This too we see to be fulfilled *in our times.* The temple of Serapis at Alexandria, and of Marna at Gaza, rose to be temples of the Lord." S. Jerome on Is. xvii.
[2] ἐς ἄγαν Ἑλληνίζουσιν. Soz. v. 3.
[3] William of Tyre (pp. 917, 840, 865) calls them "hydra immanissima," "hostes immanissimi"— "like restless gnats persevering in the purpose of injuring." comp. pp. 781, 787, 797. "Ascalona was ever an adversary of Jerusalem." Robertus Monachus p. 77. in v. Raumer Palæst. p. 173, ed. 4. It was called "the spouse of Syria," as an impregnable fortress. [4] See on Amos i. 6. vol. i. p. 244.
[5] Ps. Epiphanius de vitis Proph. p. 246.
[6] Ritter xvi. 49.
[7] Fabri Evagatorium T. ii. p. 379.
[8] Schwartz, d. Heil. Land p. 91. 1853.
[9] "Passing through Azotus, between which and Jamnia, which is situate on the sea, [i. e. the maritime Jamnia] we left Accaron on one side." Fulcher. Carnot. A. D. 1100. Gesta Peregr. Franc. c. 23 p. 464 quoted Raumer's. verb.
[10] de locis Hebr. T. iii. p. 146. Vall.
[11] Porter Handb. p. 275.

[12] "The verse, *Ekron shall be uprooted,* the Talmud says, relates to Cæsarea, the daughter of Edom, which is situate among the sands. It does not mean that Ekron is Cæsarea, which would be absurd, but only shews its hatred against that city, and foretells its destruction, resting on a Biblical text, as is the habit of the talmudists." Neubauer Geogr. du Talmud p. 92. See also Ib. p. 12. Estori in his Kaftor uperach gives קסרי as another name of עקרן, but Zunz quotes the Succah f. 276. as distinguishing קיסרי from קיסריון Cæsarea (on the geogr. of Pal. App. to Benj. Tud. ii. 441.)
[13] Porter Handb. pp. 272, 273. [14] Reland p. 609.
[15] It does not appear in Neubauer, Geographie du Talmud.
[16] "Palmis, which is Ashdod of the Philistines." כמ. ed. Asher.
[17] Asher note Ib. T. ii. p. 99.
[18] "The name Maiuma seems to belong to the Egyptian language, and to offer the two words MA IOM "place by the sea." Quatremère, les sultans Mamlouks de Makrizi T. i. 2 App. p. 229.

has been conjectured) from fear of the raids of pirates, or of inroads from those who (like the Philistines themselves probably, or some tribe of them) might come from the sea. The port probably of both was built in much later times; the Egyptian name implies that they were built by Egyptians, after the time when its kings Necos and Apries, (Pharaoh-Necho and Pharaoh-Hophra, who took Gaza[1]) made Egypt a naval power[2]. This became a characteristic of these Philistine cities. They themselves lay more or less inland, and had a city connected with them of the same name, on the shore. Thus there was an "[3]Azotus by the sea," and an "Azotus Ispinus." There were "[4]two Iamniæ, one inland." But Ashdod lay further from the sea than Gaza; Yamnia, (the Yabneel of Joshua[5], in Uzziah's time, Yabneh[6]) further than Ashdod. The port of Yamnia was burnt by Judas[7].

The *name*, Maiumas, does not appear till Christian times, though "the port of Gaza" is mentioned by Strabo[8]: to it, Alexander brought from Tyre the machines, with which he took Gaza itself[9]. That port then must have been at some distance from Gaza. Each port became a town, large enough to have, in Christian times, a Bishop of its own. The Epistle of John of Jerusalem, inserted in the Acts of the Council of Constantinople, A. D. 536, written in the name of Palestine i., ii., and iii., is signed by a Bishop of Maiumen of Ascalon, as well as by a Bishop of Ascalon, as it is by a Bishop of Maiumas of Gaza as well as by a Bishop of Gaza[10]. Yabne, or Yamnia, was on a small eminence[11], 6½ hours from the sea[12]. The Maiumas Gazæ became the more known. To it, as being Christian, Constantine gave the right of citizenship, and called it Constantia from his son, making it a city independent of Gaza. Julian the Apostate gave to Gaza (which, though it had Bishops and Martyrs, had a heathen temple at the beginning of the 5th century) its former jurisdiction over it, and though about 20 furlongs off, it was called "the maritime portion of Gaza[13]." It had thenceforth the same municipal officers; but, "as regards the Church alone," Sozomen adds, "they still appear to be two cities; each has its own Bishop and clergy, and festivals and martyrs, and commemorations of those who had been their Bishops,

and *boundaries of the fields around*, whereby the altars which belong to each Episcopate are parted." The provincial Synod decided against the desire of a Bishop of Gaza, in Sozomen's time, who wished to bring the Clergy of the Maiumites under himself, ruling that "although deprived of their civil privileges by a heathen king, they should not be deprived of those of the Church."

In A. D. 400, then, the two cities were distinct, not joined or running into one another.

S. Jerome mentions it as "[14]Maiumas, the emporium of Gaza, 7 miles from the desert on the way to Egypt by the sea;" Sozomen speaks of "[15]Gaza by the sea, which they also call Maiumas;" Evagrius, "[16]that which they also call Maiumas, which is over against the city Gaza," "[17]a little city." Mark the deacon A. D. 421, says, "[18]We sailed to the maritime portion of Gaza, which they call Maiumas," and Antoninus Martyr, about the close of the vi[th] century, "[19]we came from Ascalon to Mazomates, and came thence, after a mile, to Gaza,—that magnificent and lovely city." This perhaps explains how an anonymous Geographer, enumerating the places from Egypt to Tyre, says so distinctly, "[20]after Rinocorura lies the new Gaza, being itself also a city; then the desert Gaza," (writing, we must suppose, after some of the destructions of Gaza); and S. Jerome could say equally positively; "[21]The site of the ancient city scarce yields the traces of foundations; but the city now seen was built in another place in lieu of that which fell."

Keith, who in 1844 explored the spot, found wide-spread traces of some extinct city.

"[22]At seven furlongs from the sea the manifold but minute remains of an ancient city are yet in many places to be found—Innumerable fragments of broken pottery, pieces of glass, (some beautifully stained) and of polished marble, lie thickly spread in every level and hollow, at a considerable elevation and various distances, on a space of several square miles. In fifty different places they profusely lie, in a level space far firmer than the surrounding sands," "from small patches to more open spaces of twelve or twenty thousand square yards." "The oblong sand-hill, greatly varied in its elevation and of an undulated surface, throughout

---

[1] Jer. xlvii. 1.
[2] See Herod. ii. 159, 161. and Rawlinson on ii. 182. Herod. T. ii. p. 277.
[3] Ἄζωτος πάραλος. Excerpta in Græca notitia Patriarch. in Reland p. 215. Schwarz (d. heil. Land p. 91.) places Ashdod at an hour from the "Mediterranean."
[4] Plin. N. H. v. 12.
[5] Josh. xv. 11.
[6] 2 Chr. xxvi. 6.
[7] 2 Macc. xii. 9.
[8] Strabo xvi. 2, 30. p. 759.
[9] "The engines, with which he took Tyre, being sent for by him, arrive from the sea." Arr. ii. 27.
[10] Conc. T. v. 1164. Col.

[11] Irby and Mangles p. 57.
[12] Michaud et Poujoulat Corresp. d'Orient v. p. 373, 374.
[13] Soz. v. 3.
[14] Vita S. Hilarion. n. 3. Opp. ii. 15. Vall.
[15] Soz. vii. 21.
[16] Ev. ii. 5.
[17] Ib. 8.
[18] Marcus Diac. A. D. 421, in vita S. Porphyrii, c. 8. ap. Bolland. Feb. 26.
[19] Itin. B. Antonini, pp. 24, 25.
[20] Hudson Geograph. Minores T. iv. p. 39.
[21] T. iii. p. 218.
[22] Keith on prophecy, from personal examination. pp. 378, 379.

which they recur, extends to the W. and W. S. W. from the sea nearly to the environs of the modern Gaza." "In attempts to cultivate the sand (in 1832) hewn stones were found, near the old port. Remains of an old wall reached to the sea.—Ten large fragments of wall were embedded in the sand. About 2 miles off are fragments of another wall. Four intermediate fountains still exist, nearly entire in a line along the coast, doubtless pertaining to the ancient port of Gaza. For a short distance inland, the débris is less frequent, as if marking the space between it and the ancient city, but it again becomes plentiful in every hollow. About half a mile from the sea we saw three pedestals of beautiful marble. Holes are still to be seen from which hewn stones had been taken."

On the other hand, since the old Ashkelon had, like Gaza, Jamnia, Ashdod, a sea-port town, belonging to it but distinct from itself, (the city itself lying distinct and inland), and since there is no space for two towns distinct from one another, within the circuit of the Ashkelon of the crusades, which is limited by the nature of the ground, there seems to be no choice but that the city of the crusades, and the present skeleton, should have been the Maiumas Ascalon, the sea-port. The change might the more readily take place, since the title "port" was often omitted. The new town obliterated the memory of the old, as Neapolis, Naples, on the shore, has taken place of the inland city (whatever its name was), or Utrecht, it is said, has displaced the old Roman town, the remains of which are three miles off at Vechten[1], or Sichem is called Neapolis, Nablous, which yet was 3 miles off[2]. Er-riha is, probably, at least the second representative of the ancient Jericho; the Jericho of the New Testament, built by Herod, not being the Jericho of the prophets. The Corcyra of Greek history gave its name to the island; it is replaced by a Corfu in a different but near locality, which equally gives its name to the island now. The name of Venetia migrated with the inhabitants of the province, who fled from Attila, some 23 miles, to a few of the islands on the coast, to become again the name of a great republic[3]. In our own country, "old Windsor" is said to have been the residence of the Saxon monarchs; the

present Windsor, was originally "new Windsor:" old Sarum was the Cathedral city, until the reign of Henry iii: but, as the old towns decayed, the new towns came to be called Windsor, Sarum, though not the towns which first had the name. What is now called Shoreham, not many years ago, was called "new Shoreham," in distinction from the neighboring village[4].

William of Tyre describes Ashkelon as "[5] situated on the sea-shore, in the form of a semi-circle, whose chord or diameter lies on the sea-shore; but its circumference or arc on the land, looking East. The whole city lies as in a trench, all declining toward the sea, surrounded on all sides by raised mounds, on which are walls with numerous towers of solid masonry, the cement being harder than the stone, with walls of due thickness and of height proportionate; it is surmounted also with outer walls of the same solidity." He then describes its four gates, E. N. S. toward Jerusalem, Gaza, Joppa, and the W., called the sea-gate, because "by it the inhabitants have an egress to the sea."

A modern traveler, whose description of the ruins exactly agrees with this, says, "[6] the walls are built on a ridge of rocks that winds round the town in a semicircular direction and terminates at each end in the sea; the ground falls within the walls in the same manner, that it does without, so that no part of it could be seen from the outside of the walls. There is no bay nor shelter for shipping, but a small harbor advancing a little way into the town toward its eastern extremity seems to have been formed for the accommodation of such small craft as were used in the better days of the city." The harbor, moreover, was larger during the crusades, and enabled Ascalon to receive supplies of corn from Egypt and thereby to protract its siege. Sultan Bibars filled up the port and cast stones into the sea, A. D. 1270, and destroyed the remains of the fortifications, for fear that the Franks, after their treaty with the king of Tunis, should bring back their forces against Islamism and establish themselves there[7]. Yet Abulfœda, who wrote a few years later, calls it "one of the Syrian ports of Islam[8]."

This city, so placed on the sea, and in which too the sea enters, cannot be the Ash-

---

[1] Reland who lived at Utrecht, says that Roman antiquities were daily dug up at Vechten, where were the remains of a Roman fort. Pal. p. 105.

[2] S. Jerome.

[3] Gibbon c. 35.

[4] In like way Alresford, Basford, Brentford, Goole, Isleworth, must have been at one time, New Alr. New Basford &c. but, as the more considerable, have appropriated the name which belonged to both the old and new places.

[5] Willermus Tyr. Hist. xvii. 22. in Gesta Dei per Francos p. 924. The solidity of the walls and of the cement are described in the same way, in the

latter part of the 17th. cent. by d'Arvieux and Padre Malone da Maleo Terra Santa p. 471.

[6] Dr. Richardson, Travels along the Mediterr. ii. p. 201.

[7] According to Ibn Férat in Reinaud Chroniques Arabes n. xcvi. Michaud, Biblioth. des. Croisades iv. 525.

[8] Ab. Tab. Syriæ p. 78. Köhler. תַעַר, a gap, opening, access, or an enemy's frontier, (Freytag) " is in ordinary Arabic, used for a port, as הַעַר בִּירוּת 'the port of Beyrout,' and תַעַר דמיטה 'the port of Damietta.'" Prof. Chenery.

17

kelon, which had a port, which was a town distinct from it. The Ascalon of the Philistines, which existed down into Christian times, must have been inland. Benjamin of Tudela in the 12th cent. who had been on the spot, and who is an accurate eyewitness [1], says, " From Ashdod are two parasangs to Ashkelonah [2]; this is new Ashkelon which Ezra the priest built on the seashore, and they at first called it Benibra [3], and it is distant from the old Ashkelon, which is desolate, four parasangs." When the old Ashkelon perished, is unknown. If, as seems probable from some of the antiquities dug up, the Ashkelon, at which Herod was born and which he beautified, was the seaport town, commerce probably attracted to it gradually the inhabitants of the neighboring town of Ascalon, as the population of the Piræus now exceeds that of Athens.

The present Ashkelon is a ghastly skeleton; all the frame-work of a city, but none there. " The soil is good," but the " peasants who cultivate it " prefer living outside in a small village of mud-huts, exposed to winds and sand-storms, because they think that God has abandoned it, and that evil spirits (the Jân and the Ghûl) dwell there [4].

Even the remains of antiquity, where they exist, belong to later times. A hundred men excavated in Ashkelon for 14 days in hopes of finding treasure there. They dug 18 feet below the surface, and found marble shafts, a Corinthian capital, a colossal statue with a Medusa's head on its chest, a marble pavement and white-marble pedestal [5]. The excavation reached no Philistine Ashkelon. " Broken pottery," " pieces of glass," " fragments of polished marble," " of ancient columns, cornices &c. [6]" were the relics of a Greek Gaza.

Though then it is a superfluity of fulfillment, and what can be found belongs to a later city, still what can be seen has an impressive correspondence with the words *Gaza is forsaken;* for there are miles of fragments of some city connected with Gaza. The present Gaza occupies the southern half of a hill built with stone for the Moslem conquer-

ors of Palestine. " [7] Even the traces of its former existence, its vestiges of antiquity, are very rare; occasional columns of marble or gray granite, scattered in the streets and gardens, or used as thresholds at the gates and doors of houses, or laid upon the front of watering-troughs. One fine Corinthian capital of white marble lies inverted in the middle of the street." These belong then to times later than Alexander, since whose days the very site of Gaza must have changed its aspect.

Ashkelon shall be a desolation. The site of the port of Ascalon was well chosen, strong, overhanging the sea, fenced from the land, stretching forth its arms toward the Mediterranean, as if to receive in its bosom the wealth of the sea, yet shunned by the poor hinds around it. It lies in such a living death, that it is " [8] one of the most mournful scenes of utter desolation " which a traveler " even in this land of ruins ever beheld." But this too cannot be the Philistine city. The sands which are pressing hard upon the solid walls of the city, held back by them for the time, yet threatening to overwhelm " the spouse of Syria," and which accumulated in the plain below, must have buried the old Ashkelon, since in this land, where the old names so cling to the spot, there is no trace of it.

Ekron shall be uprooted; and at Akîr and Esdûd " [9] celebrated at present, for its scorpions," the few stones, which remain, even of a later town, are but as gravestones to mark the burial place of departed greatness.

" [10] In like way, all who glory in bodily strength and worldly power and say, *By the strength of my hand I have done it,* shall be left desolate and brought to nothing in the day of the Lord's anger." And " the waster," they who by evil words and deeds injure or destroy others and are an offence unto them, these *shall be cast out* shamefully, *into outer darkness* " [11] when the saints shall receive the fullest brightness " in the *mid-day* of the Sun of Righteousness. The judgment shall not be in darkness, save to them, but in mid-day, so that the justice of God shall be clearly seen, and darkness itself shall be turned into

---

[1] ρ. מֵן. 2. ed. Asher. The enumeration of " about 200 Rabbanite Jews," with the names of the chief, " about 40 karaites, and about 300 Cuthæans " shews personal acquaintance. The former name of the " new Ascalon " and the supposed distance of the ruins of the old, he must have learned on the spot.
[2] Benj. Tud. pronounces the new city Ashkelona, as the Latins did. When speaking himself, he says Ashkelon.
[3] "Benibra" looks like a corruption of בֵּית מְרָה, " a place of pure water," like " Bebaten, Bedora, Beestera, Begabar " &c. in Reland. 617. sqq. The Gadite town of that name becomes in Eus. βηθναβρίς. S. Jerome has another Benamerium, N. of Zoar, now N'mairah. Tristram Land of Moab p. 57. A well in Ascalon is mentioned by Eusebius. " There are many wells (named) in Scripture and are yet shewn in the country of Gerar, and at Asca-

lon." v. φρέαρ. William of Tyre says: " It has no fountains, either within the compass of the walls, or near it; but it abounds in wells, both within and without, which supply palatable water, fit for drinking. For greater caution the inhabitants had built some cisterns within, to receive rain-water. Benj. of T. also says, " There in the midst of the city is a well which they call Beer Ibrahim-al-khalîl [the well of Abraham the friend (of God)] which he dug in the days of the Philistines." Keith mentions " 20 fountains of excellent water opened up anew by Ibrahim Pasha." p. 274.
[4] Mr. Cyril Graham in Keith p. 376.
[5] Travels of Lady H. Stanhope, iii. 159-169.
[6] Keith p. 378.   [7] Robinson Travels ii. 38.
[8] Smith Ib. p. 66 note.
[9] Volney Voyage en Syrie c. 31. p. 311. Keith p. 370.   [10] S. Jer.   [11] Rup.

Before
CHRIST
cir. 630.

i Ezek. 25. 16.

k Jos. 13. 3.

5 Woe unto the inhab-
itants of ¹ the sea coast, the
nation of the Cherethites!
the word of the LORD is
against you; O ᵏ Canaan,
the land of the Philistines, I
will even destroy thee, that

there shall be no inhabitant.

6 And the sea coast
shall be dwellings and cottages for shepherds, ¹ and
folds for flocks.

7 And the coast shall
be for ᵐ the remnant of

Before
CHRIST
cir. 630.

¹ See Is. 17. 2.
ver. 14.
ᵐ Isai. 11. 11.
Mic. 4. 7.
& 5. 7, 8.
Hag. 1. 12.
& 2. 2.
ver. 9.

light, as was said to David, ¹ *Thou didst this
thing secretly, but I will do it before all Israel
and before the sun;* and our Lord, ² *Whatsoever ye have spoken in darkness shall be heard in
the light; and that which ye have spoken in the
ear in closets shall be proclaimed upon the house-
tops;* and St. Paul, ³ *the Lord shall come, Who
both will bring to light the hidden things of darkness, and will make manifest the counsels of the
heart.* And "they who by seducing words in
life or in doctrine uprooted others, shall be
themselves rooted up ⁴."

5. The *woe* having been pronounced on the
five cities apart, now falls upon the whole
nation of the Cherethites or Philistines.
The Cherethites are only named as equivalent to the Philistines, probably as originally
a distinct immigration of the same people ⁵.
The name is used by the Egyptian slave of
the Amalekite ⁶ for those whom the author
of the first book of Samuel calls Philistines ⁷. Ezekiel uses the name parallel
with that of *Philistines*, with reference to the
destruction which God would bring upon
them ⁸.

The word of the Lord comes not to them, but
upon them, overwhelming them. To them
He speaketh not in good, but in evil; not in
grace, but in anger; not in mercy, but in
vengeance. Philistia was the first enemy
of the Church. It shewed its enmity
to Abraham and Isaac and would fain
that they should not sojourn among them ⁹.
They were the hindrance that Israel should
not go straight to the promised land ¹⁰.
When Israel passed the Red Sea, ¹¹ *sorrow*

took hold of them. They were close to salvation in body, but far in mind. They are
called *Canaan,* as being a chief nation of it ¹²,
and in that name lay the original source of
their destruction. They inherited the sins
of Canaan and with them his curse, preferring the restless beating of the barren, bitter
sea on which they dwelt, "the waves of this
troublesome world," to being a part of the
true Canaan. They would absorb the Church
into the world, and master it, subduing it to
the heathen Canaan, not subdue themselves
to it, and become part of the heavenly
Canaan.

6. *The sea-coast* ¹³ *shall be dwellings and cottages,* lit. cuttings or diggings ¹⁴. This is the
central meaning of the word; the place of
the Cherethites (the *cutters off*) shall be
cheroth of shepherds, places which they dug
up that their flocks might be enclosed therein.
The tracts once full of fighting men, the
scourge of Judah, should be so desolate of its
former people, as to become a sheep-walk.
Men of peace should take the place of its
warriors.

So the shepherds of the Gospel with their
flocks have entered into possession of warlike nations, turning them to the Gospel.
They are shepherds, the chief of whom is
that Good Shepherd, Who laid down His
Life for the sheep. And these are the sheep
of whom He speaks, ¹⁵ *Other sheep I have,
which are not of this fold; them also I must bring,
and they shall hear My Voice; and there shall
be one fold and One Shepherd.*

7. *And the coast shall be.* Or probably ¹⁶, *It*

---

¹ 2 Sam. xii. 12.   ² S. Luke xii. 3.   ³ 1 Cor. iv. 5.
⁴ S. Matth. xv. 13.   ⁵ See on Am. ix. 7. vol. i. p. 333.
⁶ 1 Sam. xxx. 14.   ⁷ Ib. 16.
⁸ הכרתי את כרתים Ezek. xxv. 16. It may be
that they were so called as coming from Crete as
the LXX supposed, rendering "Cretans" in Ezek.,
and here (as also the Syr.) "sojourners of the Cretans." Hence perhaps also Tacitus' statement
(Hist. v. 2.) that the Jews had been expelled from
Crete. The other versions render the word as an
appellative, "destroying" or "destroyed." Aq. and
ἐ, ἔθνος ὀλέθριον, Theod. ἔθνος ὀλεθρίας Symm. ἔθνος
ὀλεθρευόμενον. S. Jer. gives perditorem.
⁹ Gen. xxi. 34. xxvi. 14, 15, 28.   ¹⁰ Ex. xiii. 17.
¹¹ Ib. xv. 14.   ¹² Gen. xv. 21.
¹³ The words "band of the sea" are repeated with
emphasis, vers. 5, 6, and the first words v. 7.
¹⁴ So Kim. Ibn Denan has, "caves which shepherds
inhabit;" Arab. transl. "domiciles which shepherds dig." Abulw., and Tanchum derive it from
כרה 2 Kgs. vi. 23. "a feast." Abulw. thinks this not

improbable, as an irregular plural. Tanchum,
"stations of shepherds where they turn their flocks
to feed and sit down to eat, or places in which they
dig for watering the flocks." The climate of Judæa,
however, does not admit of underground habitations, like Nineveh, and in the country of the Philistines flocks would be supplied by wells with
trenches. No Arabic authority suggests a derivation from וכר "nest" (as Ewald). The allusion to
Cherethim would be lost by this invented root.
Rashi has "a place where the shepherds eat." A.
E. explains כרת, as if it were from כרת, "which
the shepherds כרת for themselves." The Moabite
stone has מכרתת l. 25. apparently, of "a ditch"
"or moat."
¹⁵ S. John x. 16.
¹⁶ Grammatically, חבל may be either the subject
or predicate. For even in prose (Josh xix. 29.) it is
used without the article, of the sea-coast, the mention of the sea having preceded, "the goings forth

Before
C H R I S T
cir. 630.
the house of Judah ; they shall feed thereupon ; i n the h o u s e s of Ashkelon shall they lie down in the

‖ Or, *when, &c.* evening : ‖ for the Lᴏʀᴅ

their God shall ⁿ visit them, and ° turn away their captivity.

8 ¶ ᵖ I. have heard the reproach of M o a b, and

Before
C H R I S T
cir. 630.
ⁿ Ex. 4. 31.
Luke 1. 68.
° Ps. 126. 1.
Jer. 29. 14.
ch. 3. 20.
ᵖ Jer. 48. 27.
Ezek. 25. 8.

---

shall be a portion for the remnant of the house of Judah. He uses the word, employed in the first assignment of the land to Israel[1]; and of the whole people as belonging to God, "[2] Jacob is the *lot* of His inheritance." The *tract of the sea*, which, with the rest, was assigned to Israel, which, for its unfaithfulness, was seldom, even in part, possessed, and at this time, was wholly forfeited, should be a portion for the mere *remnant* which should be brought back. David used the word in his psalm of thanksgiving, when he had brought the ark to the city of David, when God had "[3] confirmed the covenant to Israel, saying, Unto thee will I give the land of Canaan, the *lot* of your inheritance;" and Asaph,[4] *He cast out the heathen before them and divided to them an inheritance by line.* It is the reversal of the doom threatened by Micah, [5] *Thou shalt have none, that shall cast a cord by lot in the congregation of the Lord.* The word is revived by Ezekiel in his ideal division of the land to the restored people[6]. [7] *The gifts and calling of God are without repentance.* The promise, which had slumbered during Israel's faithlessness, should be renewed to its old extent. "[8] There is no prescription against the Church." The boat threatens to sink ; it is tossed, half-submerged, by the waves; but its Lord *rebukes the wind and the sea; wind and sea obey Him, and there is a great calm*[9].

For the remnant of the house of Juda Yet, who save He in Whose hand are human wills, could now foresee that Judah should, like the ten tribes, rebel, be carried captive, and yet, though like and worse than Israel in its sin[10], should, unlike Israel, be restored ? The re-building of Jerusalem was, their enemies pleaded, contrary to sound policy[11]: the plea was for the time accepted; for the rebellions of Jerusalem were recorded in the chronicles of Babylon[12]. Yet the falling short of the complete restoration depended on their own wills. God turned again their captivity ; but *they* only, *whose spirit God*

thereof were to the sea, מַחֲבֵל to Mizpeh." Yet there is no emphasis in the repetition of the word from the preceding verse. The LXX renders חבל as the subject, the Ch. Vulg. as the predicate.
[1] "The ten *portions* of Manasseh;" Josh. xvii. 5. "Why hast thou given me one lot and one *portion?*" Ib. 14. " out of the *portion* of the children of Judah was the inheritance of the children of Simeon." Ib. xix. 9.
[2] Deut. xxxii. 9.   [3] 1 Chr. xvi. 18. Ps. cv. 11.

stirred, willed to return. The temporal restoration was the picture of the spiritual. They who returned had to give up lands and possessions in Babylonia, and a remnant only chose the land of promise at such cost. Babylonia was as attractive as Egypt formerly.

In the houses of Ashkelon shall they lie down in the evening. One city is named for all. *They shall lie down,* he says, continuing the image from their flocks, as Isaiah, in a like passage[13], *The first-born of the poor shall feed, and the needy shall lie down in safety.*

The true Judah shall overspread the world ; but it too shall only be a *remnant;* these shall, in safety, [14]*go in and out and find pasture. In the evening* of the world they shall find their rest; for then also in the time of Anti-Christ, the Church shall be but a remnant still. *For the Lord their God shall visit them,* for He is the Good Shepherd, Who came to seek the one sheep which was lost and Who says of Himself, [15]*I will seek that which was lost, and bring again that which was driven away, and will bind up that which was broken, and will strengthen that which was sick;* and Who in the end will more completely *turn away their captivity,* bring His banished to their everlasting home, the Paradise from which they have been exiled, and separate for ever the sheep from the goats who now oppress and scatter them abroad[16].

8. *I,* "[17]God, Who know all things, *I heard* i. e., have known within Me, in My mind, not anew but from eternity, and now I shew in effect that I know it; wherefore I say that I hear, because I act after the manner of one who perceiveth something anew." *I, the just Judge, heard*[18]. He was present and *heard,* even when, because He avenged not, He seemed not to hear, but laid it up in store with Him to avenge in due time[19].

The reproach of Moab and the reviling of the children of Ammon, whereby they have reproached My people. Both words, *reproached, reviled,* mean, primarily, cutting speeches; both are

[4] Ps. lxxviii. 55. [5] Mic. ii. 5. [6] Ezek. xlvii. 13.
[7] Rom. xi. 29.
[8] "Nullum tempus ecclesiæ," though said of its property.
[9] S. Matt. viii. 26, 27.
[10] Jer. iii. 8–11. Ezek. xvi. 46–52. xxiii. 11.
[11] Ezra ix. 12–16. [12] Ib. 19–22. [13] Is. iv. 30.
[14] S. John x. 9. [15] Ezek. xxxiv. 16. [16] Ib. 17–19.
[17] Dion.
[18] See Is. xvi. 6. Jer. xlviii. 39. Ezek. xxxv. 12, 13.
[19] Deut xxxii. 34, 35.

q the revilings of the children of Ammon, whereby
q Ezek. 25. 3, 6. they have reproached my

people, and r magnified
themselves against their
border.
r Jer. 49. 1.

intensive, and are used of blaspheming God as unable to help His people, or reviling His people as forsaken by Him. If directed against man, they are directed against God through man. So David interpreted the taunt of Goliath, [1] reviled the armies of the living God, and the Philistine cursed David by his gods [2]. In a Psalm David complains, [3] the reproaches of them that reproached Thee are fallen upon me; and a Psalm which cannot be later than David, since it declares the national innocency from idolatry, connects with their defeats, the voice of him [4] that reproacheth and blasphemeth (joining the two words used here). The sons of Corah say, [5] with a sword in my bones, mine enemies reproach me, while they say daily unto me, where is thy God? So Asaph, [6] The enemy hath reproached, the foolish people hath blasphemed Thy Name; and, [7] we are become a reproach to our neighbors. Wherefore should the heathen say, where is their God? render unto our neighbors—the reproach wherewith they have reproached Thee, O Lord. And Ethan, [8] Remember, Lord, the reproach of Thy servants—wherewith Thine enemies have reproached, O Lord, wherewith they have reproached the footsteps of Thine Anointed.

In history the repeated blasphemies of Sennacherib and his messengers are expressed by the same words. In earlier times the remarkable concession of Jephthah, [9] Wilt not thou possess what Chemosh thy god giveth thee to possess? so whomsoever the Lord our God shall drive out before us, them will we possess, implies that the Ammonites claimed their land as the gift of their god Chemosh, and that that war was, as that later by Sennacherib, waged in the name of the false god against the True.

The relations of Israel to Moab and Ammon have been so habitually misrepresented, that a review of those relations throughout their whole history may correct some wrong impressions. The first relations of Israel toward them were even tender. God reminded His people of their common relationship and forbade him even to take the straight road to his own future possessions, across their land against their will. [10] Distress them not, nor contend with them, it is said of each, for I will not give thee of their land for a possession; for I have given it unto the children of Lot for a possession. Idolaters and hostile as they were, yet, for their father's

sake, their title to their land had the same sacred sanction, as Israel's to his. I, God says, have given it to them as a possession. Israel, to their own manifest inconvenience, [11] went along through the wilderness, and compassed the land of Edom, and the land of Moab, but came not within the border of Moab. By destroying Sihon king of the Amorites and Og king of Bashan, Israel removed formidable enemies, who had driven Moab and Ammon out of a portion of the land which they had conquered from the Zamzummim and Anakim [12], and who threatened the remainder. [13] Israel dwelt in all the cities of the Amorites.

Heshbon, Dibon, Jahaz, Medeba, Nophah were cities in the land of the Amorites, in which Israel dwelt. The exclusion of Moab and Ammon from the congregation of the Lord to the tenth generation [14] was not, of course, from any national antipathy, but intended to prevent a debasing intercourse; a necessary precaution against the sensuousness of their idolatries. Moab was the first [15] in adopting the satanic policy of Balaam, to seduce Israel by sensuality to their idolatries; but the punishment was appointed to the partners of their guilt, the Midianites [16], not to Moab. Yet Moab was the second nation, whose ambition God overruled to chasten His people's idolatries. Eglon, king of Moab, united with himself Ammon and Amalek against Israel. The object of the invasion was, not the recovery of the country which Moab had lost to the Amorites but, Palestine proper. The strength of Moab was apparently not sufficient to occupy the territory of Reuben. They took possession only of the city of palm trees [17]; either the ruins of Jericho or a spot close by it; with the view apparently of receiving reinforcements or of securing their own retreat by the ford. This garrison enabled them to carry their forays over Israel, and to hold it enslaved for 18 years. The oppressiveness of this slavery is implied by the cry and conversion of Israel to the Lord, which was always in great distress. The memory of Eglon, as one of the oppressors of Israel, lived in the minds of the people in the days of Samuel [18]. In the end, this precaution of Moab turned to its own destruction; for, after Eglon was slain, Ephraim, under Ehud, took the fords, and

1 1 Sam. xvii. 26, 36, 45. coll. 10. 25.
2 1 Sam. xvii. 43.   3 Ps. lxix. 10 (9).
4 Ib. xliv. 16 (17).   5 Ib. xlii. 10.
6 Ib. lxxiv. 10, 18.   7 Ib. lxxix. 4, 10, 12.
8 Ib. lxxxix. 50, 51.   9 Jud. xi. 24.
10 Deut. ii. 9, 19.   11 Jud. xi. 18.
12 Deut. ii. 10, 20, 21. 13 Nu. xxi. 25, 31.

14 Deut. xxiii. 3.
15 Nu. xxv. 1, 3. The rank of the Midianitish lady who gave herself as a partner of the sin of the Simeonite chief (Ib. 6, 14, 15, 18.) shews how much store the Midianites set on that seduction.
16 Ib. 17. and xxxi.
17 Jud. iii. 13.   18 1 Sam. xii. 9.

the whole garrison, 10,000 of Moab's warriors, [1] *every strong man and every man of
might,* were intercepted in their retreat and
perished. For a long time after this, we
hear of no fresh invasion by Moab. The
trans-Jordanic tribes remained in unquestioned possession of their land for 300
years [2], when Ammon, not Moab, raised the
claim, [3] *Israel took away my land,* although
claiming the land down to the Arnon, and
already being in possession of the Southern-
most portion of that land, Aroer, since Israel
smote him *from Aroer unto Minnith* [4]. The
land then, according to a law recognized by
nations, belonged by a twofold right to Israel;
1) that it had been won, not from Moab, but
from the conquerors of Moab, the right of
Moab having passed to its conquerors [5]; 2)
that undisputed and unbroken possession
"for time immemorial" as we say, 300 years,
ought not to be disputed [6]. The defeat by
Jephthah stilled them for near 50 years till
the beginning of Saul's reign, when they
refused the offer of the *men of Jabesh-Gilead*
to serve them, and, with a mixture of insolence and savagery, annexed as a condition
of accepting that entire submission, [7] *that I
may thrust out all your right eyes, to lay it as a
reproach to Israel.* The signal victory of
Saul [8] still did not prevent Ammon, as well
as Moab, from being among the enemies whom Saul *worsted* [9]. The term
enemies implies that *they* were the assailants.
The history of Naomi shews their prosperous
condition, that the famine, which desolated
Judah [10], did not reach them, and that they
were a prosperous land, at peace, at that
time, with Israel. If all the links of the
genealogy are preserved [11], Jesse, David's
father, was grandson of a Moabitess, Ruth,
and perhaps on this ground David entrusted
his parents to the care of the king of Moab [12].
Sacred history gives no hint, what was the
cause of his terrible execution upon Moab.
But a Psalm of David speaks to God of some

blow, under which Israel had reeled. [13] *O
God, Thou hast abhorred us, and broken us in
pieces; Thou hast been wroth: Thou hast made
the land to tremble and cloven it asunder; heal
its breaches, for it shaketh; Thou hast shewed
Thy people a hard thing, Thou hast made it
drink wine of reeling;* and thereon David expresses his confidence that God would humble Moab, Edom, Philistia. While David
then was engaged in the war with the Syrians
of Mesopotamia and Zobah [14], Moab must
have combined with Edom in an aggressive
war against Israel. *The valley of salt* [15], where
Joab returned and defeated them, was probably within Judah, since *the city of salt* [16] was
one of the six cities of the wilderness.
Since they had defeated Judah, they must
have been overtaken there on their return [17].
Yet this too was a religious war. "*Thou,*"
David says [18], "hast given a *banner to them
that fear Thee,* to be raised aloft because of
the truth."

There is no tradition, that the kindred
Psalm of the sons of Corah, Psalm xliv.
belongs to the same time. Yet the protestations to God of the entire absence of idolatry
could not have been made at any time later
than the early years of Solomon. Even
were there Maccabee Psalms, the Maccabees
were but a handful among apostates. They
could not have pleaded the national freedom
from unfaithfulness to God, nor, except in
two subordinate and self-willed expeditions [19],
were they defeated. Under the Persian rule,
there were no armies nor wars; no immunity
from idolatry in the later history of Judah.
Judah did not in Hezekiah's time go out
against Assyria; the one battle, in which
Josiah was slain, ended the resistance to
Egypt. Defeat was, at the date of this Psalm,
new and surprising, in contrast with God's
deliverances of old [20]; yet the inroad, by
which they had suffered, was one of spoiling [21], not of subdual. Yet this too was a
religious war, from their neighbors. They

---

[1] Jud. iii. 29.   [2] Ib. xi. 26.
[3] Ib. 13.   [4] Ib. 33.
[5] Grotius de jure belli et pacis, iii. c. vi. n. vii. and
notes.
[6] Id. Ib. ii. c. iv. n. ii. and ix. and notes.
[7] 1 Sam. xi. 1, 2.   [8] Ib. 11.
[9] הרשיע, not, "vexed." Ib. xiv. 47.
[10] Ruth i. 1.   [11] Ib. iv. 21, 22.
[12] 1 Sam. xxii. 3, 4.   [13] Ps. lx. 3-5.   [14] Ib. tit.
[15] It was probably the narrow valley some three
miles long between the Northern end of that remarkable salt mountain, the Jebel or Khasm Us-
dum and the dead sea. See the description in
Tristram's Land of Isr., p. 326 sqq. At its N. extremity at the mouth of Wady Zuweirah there are
considerable traces of (perhaps Roman) buildings.
A tower placed here would command the entrance
of the valley of salt, and this may well have been
the site of the *city of salt.*
[16] Jos. xv. 62.
[17] Seetzen guessed (Reisen ii. 356) and Robinson
considered it certain (ii. 109) that "the valley of
salt" was the lower part of the 'Arabah, close to the
Dead Sea, between Edom and Judæa. But i. This

is spoken of as a "great plain" (Seetzen p. 355) and
although the word אַיְג is twice used of as large valley; (1) the valley over against Baal Peor, where all
Israel was encamped Deut. iii. 29, iv. 46; 2) that of
Zephathah, where Asa, with an army of 580,000 men,
defeated Zerah the Ethiopian with 1,000,000 (2 Chr.
xiv. 10) this is the exception. In eleven other
places it is used of a narrow valley. ii. The depression, South of the Dead Sea down to the Red Sea,
had, in the time of Moses, the same title as now, the
"Arabah," Deut. i. 1. ii. 8. iii. The space, near the
Dead Sea, which is salt, "the Sebkha, or desolate
sand-swamp" (Tristram Moab, p. 41.) is impracti-
cable for men; much more for an army. "The
Sebkha or salt-flat is a large flat, of at least 6 by 10
miles from N. to S. Taught by the experience of
M. de Saulcy, we made no attempt to cross it to the
northwards, as the mud would have been far too
deep and treacherous for us to pass in safety" (Id.
Land of Israel, p. 336.). "The land South of the
Sebkha is not salt, but rich and fertile" (Id. p. 338).
See de Saulcy Voyage en Syrie &c. p. 248-256.
[18] Ps. lx. 4.   [19] 1 Macc. v. 56-60. 67.
[20] Ps. xliv. 1-3.   [21] Ib. 10, 12.

were slain for the sake of God [1], they were covered with shame on account of the reproaches and blasphemies [2] of those who triumphed over God, as powerless to help; they were a scorn and derision to the petty nations around them. It is a Psalm of unshaken faith amid great prostration: it describes in detail what the lxth Psalm sums up in single heavy words of imagery; but both alike complain to God of what His people had to suffer for His sake.

The insolence of Ammon in answer to David's message of kindness to their new king, like that to the men of Jabesh Gilead, seems like a deliberate purpose to create hostilities. The relations of the previous king of Ammon to David, had been kind [3], perhaps, because David being a fugitive from Israel, they supposed him to be Saul's enemy. The enmity originated, not with the new king, but with *the princes of the children of Ammon* [4]. David's treatment of these nations [5] is so unlike his treatment of any others whom he defeated, that it implies an internecine warfare, in which the safety of Israel could only be secured by the destruction of its assailants.

Mesha king of Moab records one war, and alludes to others, not mentioned in Holy Scripture. He says, that before his own time, " Omri, king of Israel, afflicted Moab many days;" that " his son [Ahab] succeeded him, and he too said, ' I will afflict Moab.' " This affliction he explains to be that " [6] Omri possessed himself of the land of Medeba" [expelling [7], it is implied, its former occupiers] " and that " (apparently, Israel [8]) " dwelt therein," " [in his days and in] the days of his son forty years." He was also in possession of Nebo, and " the king of Israel " (apparently Omri,) " buil[t] Jahaz and dwelt in it, when he made war with me.[9]" Jahaz was near Dibon. In the time of Eusebius, it was still " pointed out between Dibon and Medeba [10]." Mesha says, " And I took it to annex it to Dibon." It could not, according

to Mesha also, have been S. of the Arnon, since Aroer lay between Dibon and the Arnon, and Mesha would not have annexed to Dibon a town beyond the deep and difficult ravine of the Arnon, with Aroer lying between them. It was certainly N. of the Arnon, since Israel was not permitted to come within the border of Moab, but it was at Jahaz that Sihon met them and fought the battle in which Israel defeated him and gained possession of his land, *from the Arnon to the Jabbok* [11]. It is said also that [12] *Israel dwelt in the land of the Amorites from Aroer which is on the edge of the river Arnon* [13], *and the city which is in the river* [14] *unto Gilead.* [15] *Aroer on the edge of the river Arnon, and the city which is in the river* Arnon, again occur in describing the southern border of Reuben, among 'whose towns Jahaz is mentioned, with Beth-Baal-Meon and Kiriathaim, which have been identified.

The afflicting then of Moab by Omri, according to Mesha, consisted in this, that he recovered to Israel a portion of the allotment of Reuben, between 9 and 10 hours in length [16] from N. to S., of which, in the time of Israel's weakness through the civil wars which followed on Jeroboam's revolt, Moab must have dispossessed Reuben. Reuben had remained in undisturbed possession of it, from the first expulsion of the Amorites to the time at least of Rehoboam, about five hundred years [17]. " The men of Gad " still " dwelt in Ataroth," Mesha says, " from time immemorial."

The picture, which Mesha gives, is of a desolation of the southern portion of Reuben. For, " I rebuilt," he says, " Baal-Meon, Kiriathaim, Aroer, Beth-bamoth, Bezer, Beth-Diblathaim, Beth-baal-Meon." Of Beth-Bamoth, and probably of Bezer, Mesha says, that they had previously been destroyed [18]. But Reuben would not, of course, destroy his own cities. They must then have been destroyed either by Mesha's father, who reigned before him, when invad-

---

[1] Ps. xliv. 22. [2] Ib. 13, 14. [3] 2 Sam. x. 2. 3. [4] Ib. 3. [5] Ib. viii. 2. xii. 31.
[6] וירש עמרי את ארץ מה דבא.
[7] This lies in the word וירש.
[8] A gap in the broken stone probably contained the subject. I see that Schlottman also supplied, " Israel;" Dr. Ginsburg conjectured, less probably, " the enemy."
[9] In this place only Mesha speaks of the king of Israel's war with him in the past. Elsewhere he speaks of himself only as being on the offensive. " I fought against the city" [Ataroth]; " I fought against it" [Nebo]; " go down, fight against Horonaim." The king of Israel is apparently the same throughout, Omri.
[10] S. Jerome de situ loc. Hebr. Opp. iii. 230, v. Ἰεσσά, " Jassa, where Sihon king of the Amorites is defeated."
[11] Nu. xxi. 23–25. [12] Deut. ii. 36.
[13] " The ruins of Araayr (עי׳רעא׳ר) the Aroer of the Scriptures, standing on the edge of the precipice." Burckhardt, travels in Syria p. 372.

[14] " Near the confluence of the Ledjoum and the Mojeb" [Arnon] " about 1 mile E. of the bridge across the Mojeb, there seems to be a fine verdant pasture ground, in the midst of which stands a hill with some ruins upon it." Burckhardt Ib. 373, 4.
[15] Josh. xiii. 16, 18.
[16] The distance is taken from Porter's Hand-book pp. 299–301.
[17] The beginning of Rehoboam's reign is, in the received Chronology, 477. B. C.
[18] I built Beth-Bamoth, for it was destroyed; I built Bezer, for " [the rest is conjecture. There are only two letters, which may be עי or יע, perhaps עזב " forsaken "] בנה probably, in such simple Hebrew, signifies, in regard to *all* the towns, built. It is the one word used of the king of Israel and of Mesha, " he built;" " I built," although it is rarely used of building on to existing towns and fortifying them. (1 Kgs xv. 17. 2 Chr. xi. 7.) It is probably here used of re-building; since the cause of the building was the previous destruction.

ing Reuben, or by Omri, when driving back Moab into his own land, and expelling him from these cities. *Possibly* they were dismantled only, since Mesha speaks only of Omri's occupying Medeba, Ataroth, and Jahaz. He held these three cities only, leaving the rest dismantled, or dismantling them, unable to place defenders in them, and unwilling to leave them as places of aggression for Moab. But whether they ever were fortified towns at all, or how they were desolated, is mere conjecture. Only they were desolated in these wars.

But it appears from Mesha's own statement, that neither Omri nor Ahab invaded Moab proper. For in speaking of his successful war and its results, he mentions no town S. of the Arnon. He must have been a tributary king, but not a foot of his land was taken. The subsequent war was not a mere revolt, nor was it a mere refusal to pay tribute, of which Mesha makes no complaint. Nor could the tribute have been oppressive to him, since the spoils, left in the encampment of Moab and his allies shortly after his revolt, is evidence of such great wealth. The refusal to pay tribute would have involved nothing further, unless Ahaziah had attempted to enforce it, as Hezekiah refused the tribute to Assyria, but remained in his own borders. But Ahaziah, unlike his brother Jehoram who succeeded him, seems to have undertaken nothing, except the building of some ships for trade[1]. Mesha's war was a renewal of the aggression on Reuben.

Heshbon is not mentioned, and therefore must, even after the war, have remained with Reuben.

Mesha's own war was an exterminating war, as far as he records it. "I fought against the city," [Ataroth,] he says, "and took it, and killed all the mighty of the city for the well-pleasing of Chemosh and of Moab;" "I fought against it [Nebo] from break of day till noon and took it, and slew all of it, 7000 men; the ladies and maidens I devoted to Ashtar Chemosh;" to be desecrated to the degradations of that sensual idolatry. The words too "[2]Israel perished with an everlasting destruction" stand clear, whether they express Mesha's conviction of the past or his hope of the future.

The war also, on the part of Moab, was a war of his idol Chemosh against God. Chemosh, from first to last, is the agent. "Chemosh was angry with his land;"

"Chemosh [was pleased] with it in my days;" "I killed the mighty for the well-pleasing of Chemosh;" "I took captive thence all [   ] and dragged it along before Chemosh at Kiriath;" "Chemosh said to me, Go and take Nebo against Israel;" "I devoted the ladies and maidens to Ashtar-Chemosh;" "I took thence the vessels of IHVH and dragged[3] them before Chemosh;" "Chemosh drove him [the king of Israel] out before [my face];" "Chemosh said to me, Go down against Horonaim." "Chemosh [   ] it in my days."

Contemporary with this aggressive war against Israel must have been the invasion by [4] *the children of Moab and the children of Ammon, the great multitude from beyond the sea, from Syria,* in the reign of Jehoshaphat, which brought such terror upon Judah. It preceded the invasion of Moab by Jehoshaphat in union with Jehoram and the king of Edom. For the invasion of Judah by Moab and Ammon took place, while Ahab's son, Ahaziah, was still living. For it was *after this,* that Jehoshaphat joined with Ahaziah in making ships to go to Tarshish[5]. But the expedition against Moab was in union with Jehoram who succeeded Ahaziah. The abundance of wealth which the invaders of Judah brought with them, and the precious jewels with which they had adorned themselves, shew that this was no mere marauding expedition, to spoil; but that its object was, to take possession of the land or at least of some portion of it. They came by entire surprise on Jehoshaphat, who heard of them first when they were at Hazazon-Tamar or Engedi, some 36½ miles from Jerusalem[6]. He felt himself entirely unequal to meet them, and cast himself upon God. There was a day of public humiliation of Judah at Jerusalem. [7] *Out of all the cities of Judah they came to seek the Lord.* Jehoshaphat, in his public prayer, owned, [8]*we have no might against this great company which cometh against us; neither know we what to do; but our eyes are upon Thee.* He appeals to God, that He had forbidden Israel to invade Ammon, Moab, and Mount Seir, so that they turned away from them and destroyed them not; and now they rewarded them by "[9] coming to cast us out of Thy possession which Thou hast given us to inherit." One of the sons of Asaph foretold to the congregation, that they might go out fearlessly ; for they should not have occasion to fight. A Psalm, ascribed to Asaph, records a great invasion, the object of

[1] 2 Chr. xx. 35, 36.

[2] A break in the stone leaves the subject uncertain, "In my day said [   ], and I will look upon him and upon his house, and Israel perished with an everlasting destruction." Schlottman conjectures, probably, "Chemosh." Ganneau renders as if it were past, אבד, so Haug, Geiger, Neubauer, Wright; Schlottman, Nöldeke, and Ginsburg, as future, אבד, though Ginsburg alone renders,

"And Israel said, I shall destroy it for ever," which is impossible.

[3] The word in Hebrew is used of contumelious dragging along the ground.

[4] 2 Chr. xx. 1, 2.

[5] Ib. 35, 36. "And *after this* did Jehoshaphat king of Judah join himself with Ahaziah."

[6] 300 stadia. Jos. Ant. ix. 1. 2.

[7] 2 Chr. xx. 4.   [8] Ib. 13.   [9] Ib. 10.

which was the extermination of Israel. [1] *They have said ; Come and let us cut them off from being a nation,* that *the name of Israel may be no more in remembrance.* It had been a secret confederacy. [2] *They have taken crafty counsel against Thy people.* It was directed against God Himself, i. e. His worship and worshipers. [3] *For they have taken counsel in heart together ; against Thee do they make a covenant.* It was a combination of the surrounding petty nations ; Tyre on the N., the Philistines on the W.; on the South the Amalekites, Ishmaelites, Hagarenes ; Eastward, Edom, Gebal, Moab, Ammon. But its most characteristic feature was, that Assur (this corresponds with no period after Jehoshaphat) occupies a subordinate place to Edom and Moab, putting them forward and helping them. *Assur also,* Asaph says [4], *is joined with them; they have become an arm to the children of Lot.* This agrees with the description, *there is come against thee a great multitude from beyond the sea, from Syria.*

Scripture does not record, on what ground the invasion of Moab by Jehoram and Jehoshaphat, with the tributary king of Edom, was directed against Moab proper ; but it was the result doubtless of the double war of Moab against Reuben and against Judah. It was a war, in which the strength of Israel and Moab was put forth to the utmost. Jehoram had mustered all Israel [5]; Moab had gathered all who had reached the age of manhood and upward, [6] *every one who girded on a girdle and upward.* The three armies, which had made a seven days' circuit in the wilderness, were on the point of perishing by thirst and falling into the hands of Moab, when Elisha in God's name promised them the supply of their want, and complete victory over Moab. The eager cupidity of Moab, as of many other armies, became the occasion of his complete overthrow. The counsel with which Elisha accompanied his prediction, [7] *ye shall smite every fenced city and every choice city, and every good tree ye shall fell, and all springs of water ye shall stop up, and every good piece of land ye shall waste with stones,* was directed, apparently, to dislodge an enemy so inveterate. For water was essential to the fertility of their land and their dwelling there. We hear of no special infliction of death, like what Mesha records of himself. The war was ended by the king of Moab's sacrificing the heir-apparent of the king of Edom [8], which naturally created great displeasure against Israel, in whose cause

Edom thus suffered, so that they departed to their own land and finally revolted.

Their departure apparently broke up the siege of Ar and the expedition. Israel apparently was not strong enough to carry on the war without Edom, or feared to remain with their armies away from their own land, as in the time of David, of which Edom might take the advantage. We know only the result.

Moab probably even extended her border to the South by the conquest of Horonaim [9].

After this, Moab is mentioned only on occasion of the miracle of the dead man, to whom God gave life, when cast into Elisha's sepulchre, as he came in contact with his bones. Like the Bedaween now, or the Amalekites of old, [10] *the bands of Moab came into the land, as the year came.* Plunder, year by year, was the lot of Israel at the hands of Moab.

On the East of Jordan, Israel must have remained in part (as Mesha says of the Gadites of Aroer) in their old border. For after this, Hazael, in Jehu's reign, smote Israel [11] *from Aroer which is by the river Arnon ;* and at that time probably Ammon joined with him in the exterminating war in Gilead, destroying life before it had come into the world, *that they might enlarge their border* [12]. Jeroboam ii, B. C. 825, restored Israel *to the sea of the plain* [13], i. e., the dead sea, and, (as seems probable from the limitation of that term in Deuteronomy [14], *under Ashdoth-Pisgah Eastward*) to its Northern extremity, lower in latitude than Heshbon, yet above Nebo and Medeba, leaving accordingly to Moab all which it had gained by Mesha. Uzziah, a few years later, made the Ammonites tributaries [15] B. C. 810. But 40 years later B. C. 771, Pul, and, after yet another 30 years, 740, Tiglath-pileser having carried away the trans-jordanic tribes [16], Moab again possessed itself of the whole territory of Reuben. Probably before. For B. C. 726, when Isaiah foretold that [17] *the glory of Moab should be contemned with all that great multitude,* he hears the wailing of Moab throughout all his towns, and names all those which had once been Reuben's and of whose conquest or possession Moab had boasted [18], Nebo, Medeba, Dibon, Jahaz, Baiith ; as also those not conquered then, [19] Heshbon, Elealeh ; and those of Moab proper, Luhith, Horonaim, and its capitals, Ar-Moab and Kir-Moab. He hears their sorrow, sees their desolation and bewails with their weeping [20]. He had prophesied this before [21], and now, three

---

1 Ps. lxxxiii. 4. 2 Ib. 3. 3 Ib. 5. 4 Ib. 8.
5 2 Kgs. iii. 6. 6 Ib. 21. 7 Ib. 19.
8 See on Am. ii. 12. vol. i. p. 268.
9 This is marked on the Moabite stone, as a subsequent and distinct expedition.
10 2 Kgs xiii. 20. 11 Ib. x. 33.
12 See on Amos i. 13. vol. i. p. 252. 13 2 Kgs xvi. 25.

14 Deut. iii. 17. 15 2 Chr. xxvi. 8.
16 1 Chr. v. 26. 17 Is. xvi. 14.
18 Ib. xv. 1, 2, 4. 19 Ib. 4, 5. 1.
20 Ib. xvi. 9.
21 "That the prophecy must be from any other older prophet, is an inference from grounds of nought." Del.

years [1] before its fulfillment by Tiglath-Pileser, he renews it. This tender sorrow for Moab has more the character of an elegy than of a denunciation; so that he could scarcely lament more tenderly the ruin of his own people. He mentions also distinctly no sin there except pride. The pride of Moab seems something of common notoriety and speech. *We have heard* [2]. Isaiah accumulates words, to express the haughtiness of Moab; *the pride of Moab; exceeding proud; his pride and his haughtiness and his wrath* [3], pride overpassing bounds, upon others. His words seem to be formed so as to keep this one bared thought before us, as if we were to say "pride, prideful, proudness, pridefulness;" and withal the unsubstantialness of it all, *the unsubstantiality of his lies* [4]. Pride is the source of all ambition; so Moab is pictured as retiring within her old bounds, *the fords of Arnon*, and thence asking for aid; her petition is met by the counter-petition, that, if she would be protected in the day of trouble, the out-casts of Israel might lodge with her now: *be thou a covert to her from the face of the spoiler* [5]. The prophecy seems to mark itself out as belonging to a time, after the two and a half tribes had been desolated, as stragglers sought refuge in Moab, and when a severe infliction was to come on Moab: *the* [6] *remnant* shall be *small, small not great*.

Yet Moab recovered this too. It was a weakening of the nation, not its destruction. Some 126 years after the prophecy of Isaiah, 30 years after the prophecy of Zephaniah, Moab, in the time of Jeremiah, was in entire prosperity, as if no visitation had ever come upon her. What Zephaniah says of the luxuriousness of his people, Jeremiah says of Moab; [7] *Moab is one at ease from his youth; he is resting on his lees; and he hath not been emptied from vessel to vessel, neither hath he gone into captivity.* [8] They say, *We are mighty and strong men for the war.* Moab was [9] *a strong staff, a beautiful rod;* [10] *he magnified himself against the Lord;* [11] *Israel* was *a derision* to him; *he skipped for joy* at his distress. Jeremiah repeats and even strengthens Isaiah's description of his pride; [12] *his pride, proud,* he repeats, *exceedingly; his loftiness,* again *his pride, his arrogancy, and the haughtiness of his heart.* Its *strong holds* [13] were unharmed; all its cities, *far and near,* are counted one by one, in their prosperity [14]; its summer-fruits and vintage were plenteous; its vines, luxuriant; all was joy and shouting. Whence should this evil come? Yet so it was with

Sodom and Gomorrah just before its overthrow. It was, for beauty, [15] *a paradise of God; well-watered everywhere; as the garden of the Lord, like the land of Egypt.* In the morning [16] *the smoke of the country went up as the smoke of the furnace.* The destruction foretold by Jeremiah is far other than the affliction spoken of by Isaiah. Isaiah prophesies only a visitation, which should reduce her people: Jeremiah foretells, as did Zephaniah, captivity and the utter destruction of her cities. The destruction foretold is complete. Not of individual cities only, but of the whole he saith, [17] *Moab is destroyed.* [18] *The spoiler shall come upon every city, and no city shall escape, and the valley shall perish and the high places shall be destroyed, as the Lord hath spoken.* Moab himself was to leave his land. [19] *Flee, save your lives, and ye shall be like the heath in the wilderness. Chemosh shall go forth into captivity; his priests and his princes together. Give pinions unto Moab, that it may flee and get away, and her cities shall be a desolation; for there is none to dwell therein.* It was not only to go into captivity, but its home was to be destroyed. [20] *I will send to her those who shall upheave her, and they shall upheave her, and her vessels they shall empty, all her flagons* (all that aforetime contained her) *they shall break in pieces.* [21] *Moab is destroyed and her cities;* [22] *the spoiler of Moab is come upon her; he hath destroyed the strongholds.* The subsequent history of the Moabites is in the words, [23] *Leave the cities and dwell in the rock, dwellers of Moab, and be like a dove which nesteth in the sides of the mouth of the pit.* The purpose of Moab and Ammon against Israel which Asaph complains of, and which Mesha probably speaks of, is retorted upon her. [24] *In Heshbon they have devised evil against it; come and let us cut it off from being a nation. Moab shall be destroyed from being a people, because he hath magnified himself against the Lord.*

Whence should this evil come? They had, with the Ammonites, been faithful servants of Nebuchadnezzar against Judah [25]. Their concerted conspiracy with Edom, Tyre, Zidon, to which they invited Zedekiah [26], was dissolved. Nebuchadnezzar's march against Judæa did not touch them; for they [27] *skipped with joy* at Israel's distresses. The connection of Baalis, king of the Ammonites, with Ishmael [28] the assassin of Gedaliah, whom the king of Babylon made governor over the land [29] out of their own people, probably brought down the vengeance of Nebuchadnezzar. For Chaldæans too were included in

---

[1] Is. xvi. 13, 14.   [2] Ib. 6.
[3] גאון מואב גא מאד גאותו וגאונו ועברתו
לא כן בדיו [4].   [5] Is. xvi. 4, 5.
[6] Ib. 14.   [7] Jer. xlviii. 11.   [8] Ib. 14.
[9] Ib. 17.   [10] Ib. 26.   [11] Ib. 27.
[12] Ib. 29.   [13] Ib. 18.   [14] Ib. 1, 3, 5, 21–24.

[15] Gen. xiii. 10.   [16] Ib. xix. 28.
[17] Jer. xlviii. 4.   [18] Ib. 8.   [19] Ib. xvii. 6.
[20] Ib. xlviii. 12.   [21] Ib. 15.   [22] Ib. 18.
[23] Ib. 28.   [24] Ib. 2, 42.
[25] 2 Kgs xxiv. 2.   [26] Jer. xxvii. 2 sqq.
[27] Ib. xlviii. 27.   [28] Ib. xl. 14. xli. 10.
[29] 2 Kgs xxv. 22–26. Jer. xl. 6. xli. 1.

the slaughter[1]. The blow seems to have been aimed at the existence of the people; for the murder of Gedaliah followed upon the rallying of the Jews [2] *out of all the places whither they had been driven.* It returned on Ammon itself, and on Moab who probably on this, as on former occasions, was associated with it. The two nations, who had escaped at the destruction of Jerusalem, were warred upon and subdued by Nebuchadnezzar in the 23d year of his reign[3], the 5th after the destruction of Jerusalem.

And then probably followed that complete destruction and disgraced end, in which Isaiah, in a distinct prophecy, sees Moab trodden down by God as [4] *the heap of straw is trodden down in the waters[5] of the dunghill,* and he (Moab) *stretcheth forth his hands in the midst thereof, as the swimmer stretcheth forth his hands to swim, and He,* God, *shall bring down his pride with the treacheries of his hands.* It speaks much of the continued hostility of Moab, that, in prophesying the complete deliverance for which Israel waited, the one enemy whose destruction is foretold, is Moab and those pictured by Moab. [6] *We have waited for Him and He will save us—For in this mountain* (Zion) *shall the hand of the Lord rest, and Moab shall be trodden down under Him.* After this, Moab, as a nation, disappears from history. Israel, on its return from the captivity, was again enticed into idolatry by Moabite and Ammonite wives, as well as by those of Ashdod and others[7], Canaanites, Hittites, Perizzites, Jebusites, Egyptians, Amorites[8]. Sanballat also, who headed the opposition to the rebuilding of Jerusalem, was a Moabite[9]; Tobiah, an Ammonite[10]. Yet it went no further than intrigue and the threat of war. They were but individuals, who cherished the old hostility. In the time of the Maccabees, the Ammonites, not Moab, *with a mighty power and much people* were in possession of the Reubenite cities to Jazar[11]. It was again an exterminating war, in which the Jews were to be destroyed[12]. After repeated defeats by Judas Maccabæus[13] the Ammonites *hired the Arabians*[13] (not the

Moabites) *to help them,* and Judas, although victorious, was obliged to remove the whole *Israelite* population, [14] *all that were in the land of Gilead, from the least unto the greatest, even their wives, and their children, and their stuff, a very great host, to the end they might come into the land of Judæa.* The whole population was removed, obviously lest, on the withdrawal of Judas' army, they should be again imperilled. As it was a defensive war against Ammon, there is no mention of any city, south of the Arnon, in Moab's own territory. It was probably with the view to magnify descendants of Lot, that Josephus speaks of the Moabites as being "even yet a very great nation[15]." S. Justin's account, that there is "[16] even now a great multitude of Ammonites," does not seem to me to imply a national existence. A later writer says, "[17] Now not only the Edomites but the Ammonites and Moabites too are included in the one name of Arabians."

Some chief towns of Moab became Roman towns, connected by the Roman road from Damascus to Elath. Kir-Moab in Moab proper became Areopolis and Charac-Moab, and, as well as Medeba and Heshbon in the country which had been Reuben's, preserve traces of Roman occupancy. As such, they became Christian Sees. The towns, which were not thus revived as Roman, probably perished at once, since they bear no traces of any later building.

The present condition of Moab and Ammon is remarkable in two ways; 1) for the testimony which it gives of its former extensive population; 2) for the extent of its present desolation. "How fearfully," says an accurate and minute observer[18], "is this residence of old kings and their land wasted!" It gives a vivid idea of the desolation, that distances are marked, not by villages which he passes but by ruins[19]. "[20] From these ruined places, which lay on our way, one sees how thickly inhabited the district formerly was." Yet the ground remained fruitful. It was partly abandoned to wild plants, the wormwood and other shrubs[21];

[1] Jer. xli. 3.   [2] Ib. xl. 12.
[3] Jos. Ant. x. 9, 7.   [4] Is. xxv. 10–12.
[5] בְּמֵי Chethib.   [6] Is. xxv. 9. 10.
[7] Neh. xiii. 23–26.   [8] Ezr. ix. 1.
[9] Neh. ii. 10. iv. 1–8.   [10] Ib. iv. 2, 9.
[11] 1 Macc. v. 6, 8.   [12] Ib. 9, 10, 27.
[13] Ib. 39.   [14] Ib. 45.   [15] Ant. i. 11. 3.
[16] Dial. n. 119, p. 218. Oxf. Tr.
[17] Anon. in Job ap. Origen i. 852.
[18] Seetzen Reisen i. 412.
[19] e. g. "¾ of an hour further, we reached the ruins of el-Eale; 1½ hour further, we came to Hûsbân; beside some overthrown pillars, nothing important is found here. On the E., about 1½ hour, are the ruins of Shelûl: after an hour on this plain we came to 3 wasted places, close together; ½ an hour further, we reached the ruins of what formerly was Mádabá; ½ an hour further lay the ruined village of Tuême: above an hour to the W. the important ruins of Maéin." Ib. 407, 8.

[20] Ib. 411.
[21] "A little N. of el-Eale we came on good soil, which however lay wholly uncultivated and was mostly overgrown with the prickly little Bullân, which gave the country the look of moor-ground." Seetzen Travels, i. 406. "The soil here (Heshbon) is in this district excellent, but it lies wholly uncultivated and serves only for pasture to the little herds of sheep, goats, kine and camels of the Arabs." Ib. p. 407. "The Arabs cultivate a little ground near Madaba." p. 409. "The land (the other side the Mujeb [Arnon] and so in Moab proper) had little grass, but there was an extraordinary quantity of wormwood on it. Yet the soil seems excellent for wheat, although no spot was cultivated. Large spots had the look of our moors from the quantity of wormwood and other little shrubs." p. 410. "Here and there, there were tokens of cultivation, wheatfields; the wheat was good." p. 412.

partly, the artificial irrigation, essential to cultivation in this land, was destroyed[1]; here and there a patch was cultivated; the rest remained barren, because the crops might become the prey of the spoiler[2], or the thin population had had no heart to cultivate it. A list of 33 destroyed places, which still retained their names, was given to Seetzen[3], "of which many were cities in times of old, and beside these, a great number of other wasted villages. One sees from this, that, in the days of old, this land was extremely peopled and flourishing, and that destructive wars alone could produce the present desolation." And thereon he adds the names of 40 more ruined places. Others say: "[4] The whole of the fine plains in this quarter" [the S. of Moab] "are covered with sites of towns, on every eminence or spot convenient for the construction of one; and as all the land is capable of rich cultivation, there can be no doubt that this country, now so deserted, once presented a continued picture of plenty and fertility." "[5] Every knoll" [in the highlands of Moab] "is covered with shapeless ruins.—The ruins consist merely of heaps of squared and well-fitting stones, which apparently were erected without mortar." "[6] One description might serve for all these Moabite ruins. The town seems to have been a system of concentric circles, built round a central fort, and outside the buildings the rings continue as terrace-walks, the gardens of the old city. The terraces are continuous between the twin hillocks and intersect each other at the foot."

"[7] Ruined villages and towns, broken walls that once enclosed gardens and vineyards, remains of ancient roads; everything in Moab tells of the immense wealth and population, which that country must have once enjoyed." The like is observed of Ammon[8]. His was direct hatred of the true religion. It was not mere exultation at the desolation of an envied people. It was hatred of the worship of God. "[9] Thus saith the Lord God; *Because thou saidst, Aha, against My sanctuary, because it was profaned;* and against the land of Israel, because it was desolated; and against the house of Judah, because they went into captivity." The like temper is shewn in the boast, "[10] *Because that Moab and Seir do say ; Behold the house of Judah is like unto the heathen,*" i. e., on a level with them.

Forbearing and long-suffering as Almighty God is, in His infinite mercy, He does not, for that mercy's sake, bear the direct defiance of Himself. He allows His creatures to forget Him, not to despise or defy Him. And on this ground, perhaps, He gives to His prophecies a fulfillment beyond what the letter requires, that they may be a continued

---

[1] See Mr. Tristram's picture of "a ruin-covered ridge by an immense tank of solid masonry, 140 yards by 110 yards, at Ziza. From the surface of the water to the edge of the tank was 17 feet 6 inches. The masonry was simply magnificent. The whole system and artificial sluices were precisely similar to ancient works for irrigation in India and Ceylon.—Such works easily explain to us the enormous population, of which the ruined cities give evidence. Everywhere is some artificial means of retaining the occasional supplies of rain water. So long as these precious structures remained in order, cultivation was continuous and famines remained unknown.—The Islamite invasion left the miserable remnants of a dense and thriving nation entirely dependent on the neighboring countries for their supply of corn: a dependence which must continue till these border lands are secure from the inroad of the predatory bands of the East." Land of Moab pp. 183-186. At Kustul is "a massive wall in the plain, about 600 yards in length across the valley, and 18 feet thick, built to dam up the water in the gentle depression, the head of the wady." Ib. c. 12. p. 220. "Gôr el Mesráa, as far as the soil can be watered, evinces a luxuriant fertility. By far the greater part of it is a waste." Seetz. ii. 352. "Gôr el Záphia owes its fruitfulness entirely to the water of the Wady el Hôssa, which is guided to the fields in many canals. But only a very small portion of this exceedingly rich soil is cultivated, the rest is overgrown with bushes and shrubs, wherein very many wild boars, hyenas and other wild animals live." Ib. 355. "This water too [of the Nimméry] is said formerly to have been used for watering some fields, of which there is now no trace." Ib. 354.

[2] "True, the land is not our's, but our people are many, and who shall dare to prevent them from going where they please? You will find them everywhere, if the land is good for them." Answer of Beni Sakkr Sheikh, Tristram Moab. c. 15. p. 28.

[3] Ib. 416.

[4] Irby and Mangles (May 14) p. 113.

[5] Tristram, Land of Moab, pp. 100, 101.

[6] Ib. 99.

[7] Palmer, desert of the Exodus ii. 473, 474.

[8] "East of Assalt, including Ammon, are thirty ruined or deserted places of which names are given in Dr. Smith's Arabic lists." Keith Prophecy p. 274. "All this country, formerly so populous and flourishing, is now changed into a vast desert." Seetzen Brief account &c. p. 34. Ib. p. 263. "The far greater part of this country is uninhabited, being abandoned to the wandering Arabs, and the towns and villages are in a state of total ruin." Id. p. 37. Ib. "Two hours from Szalt we came upon some peasants, who were ploughing some little fields near what was a little fountain." Seetzen i. 405. "The soil was excellent; but only here and there we saw a little spot cultivated, and this by the Aduán Arabs." p. 406. "The country that lay in our route [near Daboah] though now bare of wood, presented a great extent of fertile soil, lying entirely waste, though equal to any of the very best portions of Galilee and Samaria, and capable of producing sustenance for a large population. Around us, in every direction, were remains of more than 50 towns or villages, once maintained by the productive soil, over which they were so thickly studded." Buckingham Travels among the Arab tribes p. 66. "At Mahanafish we had arrived at a very elevated part of the plain, which had continued fertile throughout the whole distance from Ammon." p. 81. "S. S. E. of Yedoody we pushed our way over a continuous tract of fertile soil, capable of the highest cultivation. Throughout the whole extent of the plain were seen ruined towns in every direction, before, behind, on each side, generally seated on small eminences, all at a short distance from each other, and all, as far as we had yet seen, bearing evident marks of former opulence. There was not a tree in sight; but my guide assured me, that the whole of the plain was covered with the finest soil, and capable of being made the most productive corn-land in the world." Ib. p. 85.

[9] Ezek. xxv. 3.

[10] Ib. 8.

witness to Him. The Ammonites, some 1600 years ago, ceased to " be remembered among the nations." But as Nineveh and Babylon, and the cities of Sodom and Gomorrah, by being what they are, are witnesses to His dealings, so the way in which Moab and Ammon are still kept desolate is a continued picture of that first desolation. Both remain rich, fertile; but the very abundance of their fertility is the cause of their desolation. God said to Ammon, as the retribution on his contumely: "[1] therefore, behold, I give thee to the children of the East for a possession, and they shall set their encampments in thee, and place their dwellings in thee; *they* shall eat thy fruit and *they* shall drink thy milk; and I will make Rabbah a dwelling-place of camels, and the children of Ammon a couching-place for flocks." Of Moab He says also, "[2] I will open the side of Moab from the cities, which are on his frontiers, the glory of the country, unto the men of the East with the Ammonites." And this is an exact description of the condition of the land at this day. All travelers describe the richness of the soil. We have seen this as to Moab. But the history is one and the same. One of the most fertile regions of the world, full of ruined towns, destitute of villages or fixed habitations, or security of property, its inhabitants ground down by those, who have succeeded the Midianites and the Amalekites, *the children of the East*. "Thou canst not find a country like the Belka," says the Arabic proverb [3], but "the inhabitants cultivate patches only of the best soil in that territory when they have a prospect of being able to secure the harvest against the invasion of enemies," said Lord Lindsay [4], "and the country has once been very populous, but, in 35 miles at least, we did not see a single village; the whole country is one vast pasturage, overspread by the flocks and herds of the Anezee and Beni Hassan Bedouins."
The site of Rabbath Amman was well chosen for strength. Lying "[5] in a long valley" through which a stream passed, "the city of waters" could not easily be taken, nor its inhabitants compelled to surrender from hunger or thirst. Its site, as the eastern bound of Peræa [6], "[7] the last place where water could be obtained and a frontier fortress against the wild tribes beyond," marked it for preservation. In Greek times, the disputes for its possession attest the sense of its

importance. In Roman, it was one of the chief cities of the Decapolis, though its population was said to be a mixture of Egyptians, Arabians, Phœnicians [8]. The coins of Roman Emperors to the end of the second century contain symbols of plenty, where now reigns utter desolation [9]. In the 4th century, it and two other now ruined places, Bostra and Gerasa, are named as "most carefully and strongly walled." It was on a line of rich commerce filled with strong places, in sites well selected for repelling the invasions of the neighboring nations [10]. Centuries advanced. It was greatly beautified by its Roman masters. The extent and wealth of the Roman city are attested both by the remains of noble edifices on both sides of the stream, and [11] by pieces of pottery, which are the traces of ancient civilized dwelling, strewed on the earth two miles from the city. "[12] At this place, Ammân, as well as Gerasa and Gamala, three colonial settlements within the compass of a day's journey from one another, there were five magnificent theatres and one ampitheatre, besides temples, baths, aqueducts, naumachia, triumphal arches." "[13] Its theatre was the largest in Syria; its colonnade had at least 50 columns." The difference of the architecture shews that its aggrandizement must have been the work of different centuries: its "castle walls are thick, and denote a remote antiquity; large blocks of stone are piled up without cement and still hold together as well as if recently placed." It is very probably the same which Joab called David to take, after the city of waters had been taken; within it are traces of a temple with Corinthian columns, the largest seen there, yet "not of the best Roman times."
Yet Amman, the growth of centuries, at the end of our 6th century was destroyed. For "[14] it was desolate before Islam, a great ruin." "[15] No where else had we seen the vestiges of public magnificence and wealth in such marked contrast with the relapse into savage desolation." But the site of the old city, so well adapted either for a secure refuge for its inhabitants or for a secure depository for their plunder, was, on that very ground, when desolated of its inhabitants, suited for what God, by Ezekiel, said it would become, a place, where the men of the East should stable their flocks and herds, secure from straying. What a change, that its temples, the centre of the worship of its successive idols, or its theatres, its places of

[1] Ezek. xxv. 4, 5.　　　　　　　[2] Ib. 8. 10.
[3] Burckhardt Syria p. 369. "On both sides of the road" (near Naour) "were the vestiges of ancient field-enclosures." Ib. 365.
[4] Travels p. 279.
[5] Irby and Mangles June 14. c. 8. p. 146.
[6] Jos. B. J. iii. 3. 3.
[7] Grote in Smith Bibl. Dict. v. Rabbah.

[8] Strabo xvi. 2. 33. p. 760. Cas.
[9] Ritter, West-Asien viii. 1157.
[10] Amm. Marc. xiv. 8. 13.
[11] Buckingham Arab Tribes p. 67, 73.　　[12] Ib. 77.
[13] See Burckhardt's description of its ruins. Travels in Syria pp. 357-360.
[14] Abulf. Tab. Syr. p. 91.
[15] Tristram Land of Israel p. 551.

Before
C H R I S T
cir. 630.

9 Therefore *as* I live,
saith the LORD of hosts,
the God of Israel, Surely
[s] Moab shall be as Sodom,
and [t] the children of Am-

[s] Isai. 15.
Jer. 48.
Ezek. 25. 9.
Amos 2. 1.
[t] Amos 1. 13.

mon as Gomorrah, [u] *even*
t h e breeding of nettles,
and saltpits, and a perpetual desolation : [x] the residue of my people s h a l l

Before
C H R I S T
cir. 630.
[u] Gen. 19. 25.
Deut. 29. 23.
Isai. 13. 19.
& 34. 13.
Jer. 49. 18.
& 50. 40.
[x] ver. 7.

luxury or of pomp, should be stables for that drudge of man, the camel, and the stream which gave it the proud title of "city of waters" their drinking trough! And yet of the cities whose destruction is prophesied, this is foretold of Rabbah alone, as in it alone is it fulfilled! "Ammon," says Lord Lindsay [1], "was situated on both sides of the stream; the dreariness of its present aspect is quite indescribable. It looks like the abode of death; the valley stinks with dead camels; one of them was rotting in the stream; and though we saw none among the ruins, they were absolutely *covered* in every direction with their dung." "Bones and skulls of camels were mouldering there [in the area of the ruined theatre] and in the vaulted galleries of this immense structure." "It is now quite deserted, except by the Bedouins, who water their flocks at its little river, descending to it by a *wady*, nearly opposite to a theatre (in which Dr. Mac Lennan saw great herds and flocks) and by the *akiba*. Re-ascending it, we met sheep and goats by thousands, and camels by hundreds." Another says [2], "The space intervening between the river and the western hills is entirely covered with the remains of buildings, now only used for shelter for camels and sheep." Buckingham mentions incidentally, that he was prevented from sleeping at night "[3] by the bleating of flocks and the neighing of horses, barking of dogs &c." Another speaks of "[4] a small stone building in the Acropolis now used as a shelter for flocks." While he was "[5] traversing the ruins of the city, the number of goats and sheep, which were driven in among them, was exceedingly annoying, however remarkable, as fulfilling the prophecies." "[6] Before six tents fed sheep and camels." "[7] Ezekiel points just to these, (xx. 5.) which passage Seetzen cites [8]. And

in fact the ruins are still used for such stalls."

The prophecy is the very opposite to that upon Babylon, though both alike are prophecies of desolation. Of Babylon Isaiah prophesies, "[9] It shall never be inhabited, neither shall it be dwelt in from generation to generation; neither shall the Arabian pitch tent there, neither shall the shepherds make fold there, but wild beasts of the desert shall lie there, and their houses shall be full of doleful creatures; and the ostriches shall dwell there, and the jackals shall cry in their desolate houses, and howling creatures in their pleasant palaces." And the ruins are full of wild beasts [10]. Of Rabbah Ezekiel prophesied that it should be "[11] a possession for the men of the East, and I," God says, "will make Rabbah a stable for camels, and the Ammonites a couching-place for flocks;" and man's lawlessness fulfills the will and word of God.

9. *Therefore as I live, saith the Lord of hosts.* Life specially belongs to God, since He Alone is Underived Life. [12] *He hath life in Himself.* He is entitled "the living God," as here, in tacit contrast with the dead idols of the Philistines [13], with idols generally [14]; or against the blasphemies of Sennacherib [15], the mockeries of scoffers [16], of the awe of His presence [17], His might for His people [18]; as the object of the soul's longings [19], the nearness in the Gospel, *children of the living God* [20]. Since He can swear by no greater, He sware by *Himself* [21]. Since mankind are ready mostly to believe that God means well with them, but are slow to think that He is in earnest in His threats, God employs this sanction of what He says, twice only in regard to His promises or His mercy [22]; everywhere else to give solemnity to His threats [23]. The appeal to the truth of His own being [24] in support of

[1] The Holy Land pp. 279. 281, 283.
[2] G. Robinson's travels in Palestine and Syria ii. 175.
[3] Travels among the Arab tribes, Ruins of Ammon, p. 73.
[4] Lord C. Hamilton in Keith p. 271.
[5] Id. Ib. p. 269.   [6] Seetzen Reisen i. 394.
[7] Prof. Kruse Anmerkung. Ib. T. iv. p. 216.
[8] l. 31.   [9] Is. xiii. 20.
[10] See Rich Mem. p. 27, 30. Buckingham ii. 307. Sir R. K. Porter Travels ii. 342. 387. Kenneir Memoirs p. 279. Keppel's Narr. i. 179, 180. Layard Nin. and Bab., quoted by Keith on Prophecy pp. 466, 467.   [11] Ezek. xxv. 4, 5.   [12] S. John v. 26.
[13] 1 Sam. xvii. 26, 36.   [14] Jer. x. 10.
[15] 2 Kgs xix. 4. 16.   [16] Jer. xxiii. 36.

[17] Deut. v. 25 (26 Heb.)   [18] Josh. iii. 10.
[19] Ps. of sons of Korah. xlii. 2. lxxxiv. 2.
[20] Hos. i. 10 [ii. 1. Heb.]   [21] Heb. vi. 13.
[22] Is. xlix. 18. Ezek. xxxiii. 10.
[23] Num. xiv. 21, [of the glory which God should have in all the world from his chastisement of Israel] 28. Deut. xxxii. 40, [adding לעולם] Jer. xxii. 24. Ez. v. 11. xiv. 16, 18, 20. xvi. 48. [as Judge] xvii. 16, 19. xviii. 3. [in rebuke] xx. 3, 31, 33. xxxiii. 27. xxxiv. 8. xxxv. 11. In the same sense, *I swear by Myself* Jer. xxii. 5. xlix. 13. *hath sworn by Himself* Am. vi. 8. by the excellency of Jacob, viii. 7.
[24] Ges. Maurer, &c. [with a strange conception of God] render "ita vivam." Ewald rightly, "as true as I live."

spoil them, and the remnant of my people shall possess them.

ʸ for their pride, because they have reproached and

the truth of His words is part of the grandeur of the prophet Ezekiel in whom it chiefly occurs. God says in the same meaning, *by Myself have I sworn,* of promises which required strong faith [1]. *Saith the Lord of Hosts.* Their blasphemies had denied the very being of God, as God, to Whom they preferred or likened their idols ; they had denied His power or that He could avenge, so He names His Name of power, *the Lord of the hosts* of heaven against their array against His border, I, *the Lord of hosts* Who can fulfill what I threaten, and *the God of Israel* Who Myself am wronged in My people, will make *Moab as Sodom, and the children of Ammon as Gomorrah.* Sodom and Gomorrah had once been flourishing cities, on the borders of that land, which Israel had won from the Amorite, and of which Moab and Ammon at different times possessed themselves, and to secure which Ammon carried on that exterminating war. For they were to the East of the plain *between Bethel and Ai,* where Lot made his choice, *in the plain or circle of Jordan* [2], the well known title of the tract, through which the Jordan flowed into the Dead Sea. Near this, lay Zoar, (Ziara [3]) beneath the caves whither Lot, at whose prayer it had been spared, escaped from its wickedness. Moab and Ammon had settled and in time spread from the spot, wherein their forefathers had received their birth. Sodom, at least, must have been in that part of the plain, which is to the East of the Jordan, since Lot was bidden to flee to the mountains, with his wife and daughters, and there is no mention of the river, which would have been a hindrance [4]. Then it lay probably in that " [5] broad belt of desolation " in the plain of Shittim, as Gomorrah and others of the Pentapolis may have lain in " the sulphur-sprinkled expanse " between El Riha [on the site of Jericho] and the dead sea, " covered with layers of salt and gypsum which overlie the loamy subsoil, literally fulfilling the descriptions of Holy Writ (says an eye witness), [6] *Brimstone and salt and burning, that it is not*

sown *nor beareth, nor any grass groweth therein :* [7] *a fruitful land turned into saltness.* [8] *No man shall abide there, neither shall a son of man dwell in it.*" An elaborate system of artificial irrigation was carried through that cis-Jordanic tract, which decayed when it was desolated of man, and that desolation prevents its restoration.

The doom of Moab and Ammon is rather of entire destruction beyond all recovery, than of universal barrenness. For the imagery, that it should be the *breeding* [lit. *possession*] *of nettles* would not be literally compatible, except in different localities, with that of *saltpits,* which exclude all vegetation. Yet both are united in Moab. The soil continues, as of old, of exuberant fertility ; yet in part, from the utter neglect and insecurity of agriculture it is abandoned to a rank and encumbering vegetation ; elsewhere, from the neglect of the former artificial system of irrigation, it is wholly barren. The plant named is one of rank growth, since outcasts could lie concealed under it [9]. The preponderating authority seems to be for *mollách* [10], the Bedawin name of the "mallow," Prof. E. H. Palmer says [11], "which," he adds, "I have seen growing in rank luxuriance in Moab, especially in the sides of deserted Arab camps."

The residue of My people shall spoil them, and the remnant of My people shall possess them. Again, a remnant only, but even these shall prevail against them, as was first fulfilled in Judas Maccabæus [12].

10. *This shall they ·have for their pride.* lit. *This to them instead of their pride.* Contempt and shame shall be the residue of the proud man ; the exaltation shall be gone, and all which they shall gain to themselves shall be *shame.* Moab and Ammon are the types of heretics [13]. As they were akin to the people of God, but hating it ; akin to Abraham through a lawless birth, but ever molesting the children of Abraham, so heretics profess to believe in Christ, to be children of Christ, and yet ever seek to overthrow the faith of Christians. As the Church says, [14]*My mother's children are*

[1] Gen. xxii. 16. (so often referred to) Is. xlv. 23, or by Thy Right Hand, i. e. the might which He would put forth.
[2] Gen. xiii. 1, 3, 11.
[3] See the description of Ziara "once a place of considerable importance " in Tristram, land of Moab pp. 328, 330. [4] Gen. xix. 17–23.
[5] Tristram, Land of Israel, p. 367.
[6] Deut. xxix. 23. [7] Ps. cvii. 34. [8] Jer. xlix. 18.
[9] Job xxx. 7.
[10] Jon. has חֲלוּחִין : the Peschito, מְלוּחָא, and, remarkably, does not use a name coincident with the

Heb. חָרוּל sc. חֲנֻגְלָא, a sort of vetch. Abulwalid prefers the מָלוּחַ, but mentions the חַרְשֻׁף "artichoke" (Höst Nachrichten von Maroko u. Fez. p. 538) as an "opinion;" R. Tanchum adopts it, but gives חַרְמָאן as an "opinion " and says that "altogether it belongs to the prickly plants;" Kimchi says, that "some count it a nettle; others, a thistle." On מָלוּחַ see Bochart Hieroz. ii. 223–228, ed. Leipz.
[11] Ms. letter. [12] 1 Macc. v. 6–8.
[13] S. Jer. and Rup. [14] Cant. i. 5.

magnified *themselves*
against the people of the
LORD of hosts.

11 The LORD *will be*

terrible unto them: for he
will † famish all the gods
of the earth; [z] and *men*
shall worship him, every

† Heb.
make lean.
[z] Mal. 1. 11.
John 4. 21.

---

angry with me. They seem to have escaped the overthrow of Sodom and Gomorrah (heathen sins), and to have found a place of refuge (Zoar); and yet they are in darkness and cannot see the light of faith; and in an unlawful manner they mingle, against all right, the falsehood of Satan with the truth of God; so that their doctrines become, in part, *doctrines of devils,* in part have some stamp of the original truth. To them, as to the Jews, our Lord says, *Ye are of your father the devil.* While they profess to be children of God, they claim by their names to have God for their Father (Moab) and to be of His people (Ammon), while in hatred to His true children they forfeit both. As Moab seduced Israel, so they the children of the Church. They too enlarge themselves against the borders of the Church, rending off its children and making themselves the Church. They too utter reproaches and revilings against it. "Take away their revilings," says an early father [1], "against the law of Moses, and the Prophets, and God the Creator, and they have not a word to utter." They too [2] *remove the old landmarks which the fathers* (the Prophets and Apostles) *have set.* And so, barrenness is their portion; as, after a time, heretics ever divide, and do not multiply; they are a desert, being out of the Church of God: and at last the remnant of Judah, the Church, possesses them, and absorbs them into herself.

11. *The Lord will be terrible unto* [*upon*] *them,* i. e. upon Moab and Ammon, and yet not in themselves only, but as instances of His just judgment. Whence it follows, *For He will famish all the gods of the earth.* "[3] Miserable indeed, to whom the Lord is terrible! Whence is this? Is not God by Nature sweet and pleasurable and serene, and an Object of longing? For the Angels ever desire to look into Him, and, in a wonderful and unspeakable way, ever look and ever long to look. For miserable they, whose conscience makes them shrink from the face of Love. Even in this life they feel this shrinking, and, as if it were some lessen-

ing of their grief, they deny it, as though this could destroy the truth, which they *hold down in unrighteousness* [4]."

For He will famish [5] *all the gods of the earth,* taking away [6] *the fat of their sacrifices,* and the *wine of their drink-offerings.* Within 80 years from the death of our Lord [7], the governor of Pontus and Bithynia wrote officially to the Roman Emperor, that "[8] the temples had been almost left desolate, the sacred rites had been for a long time intermitted, and that the victims had very seldom found a purchaser," before the persecution of the Christians, and consulted him as to the amount of its continuance. Toward the close of the century, it was one of the Heathen complaints, which the Christian Apologist had to answer, "[9] they are daily melting away the revenues of our temples." The Prophet began to speak of the subdual of Moab and Ammon; he is borne on to the triumphs of Christ over all the gods of the Heathen, when the worship of God should not be at Jerusalem only, but *they shall worship Him, every one from his place.*

Even all the isles of the heathen. For this is the very note of the Gospel, that "[10] each who through faith in Christ was brought to the knowledge of the truth, by Him, and with Him, *worshipeth from his place* God the Father; and God is no longer known in Judæa only, but the countries and cities of the Heathen, though they be separated by the intervening sea from Judæa, no less draw nigh to Christ, pray, glorify, thank Him unceasingly. For formerly [11] *His name was great in Israel,* but now He is well known to all everywhere; earth and sea are full of His glory, and so every one *worshipeth Him from his place;* and this is what is said, [12] *As I live, saith the Lord, 'all the earth shall be filled with the glory of the Lord."* The *isles* are any distant lands on the seashore [13], especially the very distant [14]; but also Asia Minor [15] and the whole coast of Europe, and even the Indian Archipelago [16], since the ivory and ebony came from its *many isles.* Zephaniah revives the term, by which Moses had spoken

[1] Tert. de Præscr. Hær. c. 42, p. 493. Oxf. Tr.
[2] Ib. c. 37. p. 488.　　　[3] Rup.
[4] Rom. i. 18.
[5] There is no reason to abate the irony by rendering "destroy." נרוה is contrasted with משמן Is. xvii. 4, as is רזון Is. x. 16; רזה, of the land, with שמנה Nu. xiii. 20; of the sheep, with בריה Ez. xxxiv. 20. In Ps. cvi. 15. רזון is used met. for a wasting, emaciating sickness: in Mic. vi. 10, of "an

ephah of emaciation" i. e. scant; in Is. xxiv. 6, רזי is sickness; (see Ew. Lehrb. 149. g.) [all.]
[6] Deut. xxxii. 38.
[7] Between A. D. 103–105.
[8] Pliny Epist. x. 32. p. 584. ed. Steph.
[9] Tert. Apol. c. 42. see p. 90. note o. Oxf. Tr.
[10] S. Cyr.
[11] Ps. lxxvi. 1.　　　[12] Nu. xiv. 21.
[13] Jer. xxv. 22. sqq. Ez. xxvi. 15. sqq. Ps. lxxii. 10.
[14] Is. lxvi. 19.　　　[15] Dan. xi. 1, 8.
[16] Ez. xxvii. 15. Ges. Thes. sub. v.

Before CHRIST cir. 630.

a Gen. 10. 5. one from his place, *even* all *a the isles of the hea- then.

12 ¶ *b Ye Ethiopians also, ye *shall be* slain by *c my sword.

Before CHRIST cir. 630.

b Isai. 18. 1. & 20. 4.
c Ps. 17. 13. Jer. 46. 9. Ezek. 30. 9.

of the dispersion of the sons of Japhet; "[1] By these were the *isles of the Gentiles* divided in their lands, every one after his tongue." He adds the word, *all ;* all, wherever they had been dispersed, every one from his place, shall worship God. One universal worship shall ascend to God from all everywhere. So Malachi prophesied afterward ; "[2] From the rising up of the sun even to the going down of the same My Name shall be great among the Gentiles, and *in every place* incense shall be offered unto God and a pure offering ; for My Name shall be great among the heathen, saith the Lord of hosts." Even a Jew [3] says here: "This, without doubt, refers to the time to come, when all the inhabitants of the world shall know that the Lord is God, and that His is the greatness and power and glory, and He shall be called the God of the whole earth." The *isles* or *coasts of the sea* are the more the emblem of the Church, in that, "[4] lying, as it were, in the sea of this world and encompassed by the evil events in it, as with bitter waters, and lashed by the most vehement waves of persecutions, the Churches are yet founded, so that they cannot fall, and rear themselves aloft, and are not overwhelmed by afflictions. For, for Christ's sake, the Churches cannot be shaken, and [5] *the gates of hell shall not prevail against them.*"

12. *Ye Ethiopians also, ye shall be slain by My sword.* lit. *Ye Ethiopians also, the slain of My sword are they.* Having summoned them to His throne, God speaks of them, not *to* them any more; perhaps in compassion, as elsewhere in indignation [6]. The Ethiopians were not in any direct antagonism to God and His people, but allied only to their old oppressor, Egypt. They may have been in Pharaoh Necho's army, in resisting which, as a subject of Assyria, Josiah was slain: they are mentioned [7] in that army which Nebuchadnezzar smote at Carchemish in the 4th year of Jehoiakim. The prophecy of Ezekiel implies rather, that Ethiopia should be involved in the calamities of Egypt, than that it should be itself invaded. "[8] Great

terror shall be in Ethiopia, *when the slain shall fall in Egypt.*" "[9] Ethiopia and Lybia and Lydia &c. and all the men of the land that is in league, shall fall *with these*, by the sword." "[10] They also *that uphold Egypt* shall fall." Syene [10], the frontier-fortress over against Ethiopia, is especially mentioned as the boundary also of the destruction. "Messengers," God says [11], "shall go forth from Me to make the careless Ethiopians afraid," while the storm was bursting in its full desolating force upon Egypt. All the other cities, whose destruction is foretold, are cities of lower or upper Egypt [12].

But such a blow as that foretold by Jeremiah and Ezekiel must have fallen heavily upon the allies of Egypt. We have no details; for the Egyptians would not, and did not tell of the calamities and disgraces of their country. No one does. Josephus, however, briefly but distinctly says [13], that after Nebuchadnezzar had in the 23d year of his reign, the 5th after the destruction of Jerusalem, "reduced into subjection Moab and Ammon, he invaded Egypt, with a view to subdue it," "killed its then king, and having set up another, captured for the second time the Jews in it and carried them to Babylon." The memory of the devastation by Nebuchadnezzar lived on apparently in Egypt, and is a recognized fact among the Mohammedan historians, who had no interest in the fulfillment of Jewish prophecy, of which it does not appear that they even knew. "Bokht-nasar [Nebuchadnezzar], they say, "[14] made war on the son of Nechas [Necho], slew him and ruined the city of Memphis and many other cities of Egypt: he carried the inhabitants captive, without leaving one, so that Egypt remained waste forty years without one inhabitant." Another says, "[15] The refuge which the king of Egypt granted to the Jews who fled from Nebuchadnezzar brought this war upon it: for he took them under his protection and would not give them up to their enemy. Nebuchadnezzar, in revenge, marched against the king of Egypt and destroyed the country." "One may be

[1] Gen. x. 5. The phrase, הגוים אי, occurs only in these two places.
[2] Mal. i. 11. [3] Abarbanel. [4] S. Cyr.
[5] S. Matt. xvi. 18.
[6] Is. xxii. 16, "What hast thou here, and whom hast thou here, that thou hast hewed thee here a sepulchre? Hewing him out on high his sepulchre, graving in the rock a dwelling for him." Mic. i. 2, "Hear, ye people, all of them." Deut. xxxii. 15, "Thou art waxen fat, art grown thick, art covered with fatness ; and he forsook God Who made him, and lightly esteemed the Rock of his salvation."

[7] Jer. xlvi. 9. [8] Ezek. xxx. 4.
[9] Ib. 5. [10] Ib. 6. [11] Ib. 9.
[12] Zoan, Aven, Pi-beseth, Tehaphnehes, Sin, on the Eastern boundary ; Noph [Memphis] the capital of Lower Egypt; Pathros, probably a district of Upper Egypt: No [Thebes] its capital ; Syene, its last town to the South.
[13] Ant. x. 9. 7. See further Sir G. Wilkinson, Manners and customs of the Ancient Egyptians, i. 173–179. Pusey's Daniel the Prophet pp. 275–277.
[14] Makrizi in De Sacy, Abdallatif Rélation de l'Egypte p. 247. [15] Abdallatif l. c. p. 184.

18

13 And he will stretch out his hand against the north, and [d]destroy As-

syria; and will make Nineveh a desolation, and dry like a wilderness.

certain," says a good authority [1], "that the conquest of Egypt by Nebuchadnezzar was a tradition generally spread in Egypt and questioned by no one." Ethiopia was then involved, as an ally, and as far as its contingent was concerned, in the war, in which Nebuchadnezzar desolated Egypt for those 40 years. But, although this fulfilled the prophecy of Ezekiel, Isaiah, some sixty years before Zephaniah, prophesied a direct conquest of Ethiopia. *I have given*, God says [2], *Egypt as thy ransom, Ethiopia and Seba for thee.* It lay in God's purpose, that Cyrus should restore His own people, and that his ambition should find its vent and compensation in the lands beyond. It may be that, contrary to all known human policy, Cyrus restored the Jews to their own land, willing to bind them to himself, and to make them a frontier territory toward Egypt, not subject only but loyal to himself. This is quite consistent with the reason which he assigns; [3] *The Lord God of heaven hath given me all the kingdoms of the earth; and He hath charged me to build Him an house at Jerusalem which is in Judah;* and with the statement of Josephus, that he was moved thereto by "[4] reading the prophecy which Isaiah left, 210 years before." It is, alas! nothing new to Christians to have mixed motives for their actions: the exception is to have a single motive, "for the glory of God." The advantage to himself would doubtless flash at once on the founder of a great empire, though it did not suggest the restoration of the Jews. Egypt and Assyria had always, on either side, wished to possess themselves of Palestine, which lay between them. Anyhow, one Persian monarch did restore the Jews; his

successor possessed himself of "Egypt, and part, at least, of Ethiopia." Cyrus wished, it is related [5], "to war in person against Babylon, the Bactrians, the Sacæ, and Egypt." He perished, as is known, before he had completed [6] the third of his purposed conquests. Cambyses, although after the conquest of Egypt he planned ill his two more distant expeditions, reduced "[7] the Ethiopians bordering upon Egypt" ["[8] lower Ethiopia and Nubia"], and these "brought gifts" permanently to the Persian Sovereign. Even in the time of Xerxes, the Ethiopians had to furnish their contingent of troops against the Greeks. Herodotus describes their dress and weapons, as they were reviewed at Doriscus [9]. Cambyses, then, did not lose his hold over Ethiopia and Egypt, when forced by the rebellion of Pseudo-Smerdis to quit Egypt.

13. Zephaniah began by singling out Judah amid the general destruction, [10] *I will also stretch out My Hand upon Judah;* he sums up the judgment of the world in the same way; *He will stretch out*, or, *Stretch He forth* [11], *His Hand against the North and destroy Asshur, and make Nineveh a desolation.* Judah had, in Zephaniah's time, nothing to fear from Assyria. Isaiah [12] and Micah [13] had already foretold, that the captivity would be to Babylon. Yet of Assyria alone the prophet, in his own person, expresses his own conformity with the mind of God. Of others he had said, *the word of the Lord is against you, O Canaan, and I will destroy thee; As I live, saith the Lord, Moab shall be as Sodom. Ye also, O Ethiopians, the slain of My sword are they.* Of Assyria alone, by a slight inflection of the word, he expresses that he goes along with this, which he announces.

---

[1] De Sacy l. c. who quotes Abulféda [see his hist. ante-Islam. p. 102. he could not find the names of Egyptian kings between Shishak and the Pharaoh who was the contemporary of Nebuch.] Masudi, Nosairi, also.
[2] Is. xliii. 3.   [3] Ezr. i. 2, 3.
[4] Ant. xi. 1. 2.   [5] Herod. i. 153.
[6] Ib. 214 and Rawl. notes p. 350.   [7] Herod. iii. 97.
[8] Sir G. Wilkinson in Rawl. Herod. ii. 487. n. 10.
[9] Her. vii. 69.   [10] i. 4.
[11] וַיֵּט. וַיָּשֶׂם. The ordinary force of the abridged form of the future with ו is consecutive, viz., that the action so joined on is the result of the preceding; "intercede with the Lord יַעְתַּר, that He may take away," lit. "and He may take away." Ex. x. 17. Gesenius' instances are all of this sort. In Hif. of the regular verb, Jud. xiv. 15, 1 Sam. vii. 3, Job xi. 6, xii. 7. Jer. xlii. 3. (Lehrg. p. 321.) verbs עו׳, Kal. Nu. xxv. 4, Jud. vi. 30, Is. l. 2, 1 Kgs xxi. 10, 2 Kgs. v. 10, 2 Chr. xxix. 10, xxx. 6, 8. (Ib. p. 403.)

Hif. Ex. viii. 4, x. 17, Nu. xxi. 7. (Ib. p. 405) verb לה, Ez. x. 12, Is. ii. 20, Is. xxxviii. 21, 1 Kgs xx. 20, Jer.

xxiii. 18. (Ib. p. 428). Such are also Hos. xiv. 6, 7, 9. Sometimes a prayer seems to be thus interwoven with prediction as, Nu. xxiv. 7, "her seed shall be in many waters, and exalted be (וְיָרֹם) his king above Amalek, and exalted shall be his kingdom" and Ib. 9, "And Israel doeth valiantly; and rule one (וְיֵרְדְּ) from Jacob." Is. xxxv. 1, 2, "Wilderness and dry-place shall be glad for them, and *let the desert rejoice* (וְתָגֵל) and it shall blossom as the Autumn-crocus. It shall blossom abundantly; *and joy it* (וְתָגֵל) yea with joy and jubilee: the glory of Lebanon is given to it; they shall see the glory of the Lord, the excellency of our God." The peculiarity here is, that it stands so apart and independent of the preceding, with which ו connects it. The shade of meaning is so fine, that the Verss. and Rabbins pass over it, rendering simply future as do modern commentators, except Keil, and Ewald who corrects וַיֹּאבֵד וַיֵּט arbitrarily and against history.   [12] Is. xxxix. 6.   [13] Mic. iv. 10.

Before
C H R I S T
cir. 630.

14 And ᵉ flocks shall lie down in the midst of her, all ᶠ the beasts of the nations: both the || ᵍ cormorant and the bittern shall lodge in the || upper lintels

ᵉ ver. 6
ᶠ Is. 13. 21, 22.
|| Or, *pelican*.
ᵍ Is. 34. 11, 14.
|| Or, *knops*, or, *chapters*.

of it; *their* voice shall sing in the windows; desolation *shall be* in the thresholds: || for he shall uncover the ʰ cedar work.

Before
C H R I S T
cir. 630.

|| Or, *when he hath uncovered*.

ʰ Jer. 22. 14.

He does not say as an imprecation, "May He stretch forth His hand;" but gently, as continuing his prophecies, *and*, joining on Asshur with the rest; only instead of saying "He will stretch forth," by a form almost insulated in Hebrew, he says, *And stretch He forth His Hand.* In a way not unlike, David having declared God's judgments, *The Lord trieth the righteous; and the wicked and the lover of violence doth His soul abhor,* subjoineth, *On the wicked rain He snares,* signifying that he (as all must be in the Day of judgment), is at one with the judgment of God. This is the last sentence upon Nineveh, enforcing that of Jonah and Nahum, yet without place of repentance now. He accumulates words expressive of desolateness. It should not only be a *desolation* [1], as he had said of Ashkelon, Moab and Ammon, but a dry, parched [2], unfruitful [3] land. As Isaiah, under the same words, prophesies that the dry and desolate land [4] should, by the Gospel, be glad, so the gladness of the world should become dryness and desolation. *Asshur* is named, as though one individual [5], implying the entireness of the destruction; all shall perish, as one man; or as gathered into one and dependent upon one, its evil King. *The North* is not only Assyria, in that its armies came upon Judah from the North, but it stands for the whole power of evil [6], as Nineveh for the whole beautiful, evil, world. The world with "the princes of this world" shall perish together.

14. *And flocks shall lie down in the midst of her.* No desolation is like that of decayed luxury. It preaches the nothingness of man, the fruitlessness of his toils, the fleetingness of his hopes and enjoyments, and their baffling when at their height. Grass in a court or on a once beaten road, much more, in a

town, speaks of the passing away of what has been, that man was wont to be there, and is not, or is there less than he was. It leaves the feeling of void and forsakenness. But in Nineveh not a few tufts of grass here and there shall betoken desolation, it shall be one wild rank pasture, where *flocks* shall not feed only, but *lie down* as in their fold and continual resting-place, not in the outskirts only or suburbs, but in the very centre of her life and throng and busy activity, *in the midst of her,* and none shall fray them away. So Isaiah had said of the cities of Aroer, [7] *they shall be for flocks, which shall lie down and none shall make them afraid,* and of Judah till its restoration by Christ, that it should be [8] *a joy of wild asses, a pasture of flocks.* And not only those which are wont to be found in some connection with man, but *all the beasts of a nation* [9], the troops of wild and savage and unclean beasts which shun the dwellings of man or are his enemies, these in troops have their lair there.

Both the pelican [10] *and the [hedgehog* [11]*] shall lodge in the upper lintels thereof.* The *chapiters* [E. M.] or capitals of the pillars of the temples and palaces shall lie broken and strewn upon the ground, and among those desolate fragments of her pride shall unclean animals haunt. The pelican has its Hebrew name from vomiting. It vomits up the shells which it had swallowed whole, after they had been opened by the heat of the stomach, and so picks out the animal contained in them [12], the very image of greediness and uncleanness. It dwells also not in deserts only but near marshes, so that Nineveh is doubly waste.

A voice shall sing in the windows. In the midst of the desolation, the muteness of the hedgehog and the pensive loneliness of the

[1] שְׁמָמָה Zeph. ii. 4. 9.

[2] צִיָּה of absence of water, Job xxx. 3. Ps. lxiii. 2. cv. 41. cvii. 35. Is. xli. 18. Jer. ii. 6. Ez. xix. 13. Hos. ii. 5.

[3] Is. liii. 2.

[4] מדבר ציה Is. xxxv. 1. Jer. joins מדבר ציה וְעֲרָכָה, l. 12.

[5] Asshur is used in this way of the people, considered in and with their king. Is. xxx. 31. xxxi. 8. [6] See Is. xiv. 13.   [7] Ib. xvii. 2.
[8] Ib. xxxii. 14. Comp. Jer. vi. 2.

[9] גּוֹי "nation," of gregarious creatures, locusts, Jo. i. 6, ii. 2; עַם, "ants," Pr. xxx. 25. "conies," Ib. 26. Comp. ἔθνεα χηνῶν &c. "apium populi," "equo-

rum gentes," Virg. Georg. iv. 430. Arab. אִמָּה Boch. Hieroz. ii. 468. Leipz.

[10] The most probable rendering, as explaining the etymology. The ὁ render "pelican" Ps. cii. 7. Lev. xi. 18; Aq. Symm. Th., Is. xxxiv. 11; Aq. here. The קִק of the Talmudists (קָק Jerus. Targ. ap. Levy Lex.) is probably the same. The pelican retires inland to consume its food. Tristram, Houghton, in Smith Bibl. Dict. v. Pelican. *note.*

[11] There seems a consent that the קִפֹּד is the hedgehog or porcupine (as in Aram. and Arab.) o, S. Jer. R. Nathan, Rashi, although the Arab. etym. "rolled himself round" seems uncertain.

[12] Aristot. Anim. ix. 10.

Before
CHRIST
cir. 630.

ⁱ Isai. 47. 8.
ᵏ Rev. 18. 7.

15 This *is* the rejoicing city ¹that dwelt carelessly, ᵏthat said in her heart, I *am*, and *there is* none beside me: how is she be-

come a desolation, a place for beasts to lie down in ! every one that passeth by her ¹shall hiss, *and* ᵐ wag his hand.

Before
CHRIST
cir. 630.

¹ Job 27. 23.
Lam. 2. 15.
Ezek. 27. 36.
ᵐ Nah. 3. 19.

solitary pelican, the musing spectator is even startled by the gladness of a bird, joyous in the existence which God has given it. Instead of the harmony of music¹ and men-singers and women-singers in their palaces shall be the sweet music of some lonely bird, unconscious that it is sitting *in the windows of* those, at whose name the world grew pale, portions of the outer walls being all which remain of her palaces. *Desolation* shall be *in the thresholds,* sitting, as it were, in them; everywhere to be seen in them; the more, because unseen. Desolation is something oppressive; we *feel* its presence. There, as the warder watch and ward at the empty portals, where once was the fullest throng, shall *desolation sit,* that no one enter. *For He shall uncover* [*hath uncovered* E. M.] *the cedar-work:* in the roofless palaces, the carved *cedar-work* shall be laid open to wind and rain. Any one must have noticed, how piteous and dreary the decay of any house in a town looks, with the torn paper hanging uselessly on its walls. A poet of our own said of the beautiful ruins of a wasted monastery :

"For the gay beams of lightsome day
Gild, but to flout the ruins gray."

But at Nineveh it is one of the mightiest cities of the world which thus lies waste, and the bared *cedar-work* had, in the days of its greatness, been carried off from the despoiled Lebanon² or Hermon³.

15. *This* utter desolation *is the rejoicing city* (so unlike is it, that there is need to point out that it is the same); this is she, who was full of joy, exulting exceedingly⁴, but in herself, not in God ; *that dwelt carelessly,*

¹ אֶרְזָה collective, like עֵצָה Jer. vi. 6.

² Is. xiv. 8. xxxvii. 24. Ezek. xxxi. 16. "In the fragment of another epigraph, we have mention of some objects also of wood, 'brought from Mt. Lebanon, (and taken up to the mound) from the Tigris.'" Layard, Nineveh and Babylon. p. 118. "At that time the countries that are upon Lebanon, I took possession of, to the great sea of the country of Akkari," (the Mediterranean,) from Inscription. Ib. p. 355, 356. "The conqueror from the upper passage of the Tigris to Lebanon and the Great Sea." Ib. p. 361. "Standing one day on a distant part of the mound, I smelt the sweet smell of burning cedar; the Arab workmen excavating in the small temple had dug out a beam, and the weather being cold, had at once made a fire to warm themselves. The wood was cedar, probably one of the very beams mentioned in the inscription, as brought from the forests of Lebanon, by the King who built the edifice. After a lapse of nearly 3000 years, it had retained its original fragrance." Ib. p. 357.

lit. *securely,* and so carelessly ; saying *Peace and safety*⁵, as though no evil would come upon her, and so perishing more certainly and miserably⁶. *That said in her heart,* this was her inmost feeling, the moving cause of all her deeds ; *I am and there is none beside me;* literally, ⁷ *and there is no I beside,* claiming the very attribute of God (as the world does) of self-existence, as if it alone were *I,* and others, in respect of her, were as nothing. Pantheism, which denies the being of God, as Author of the world, and claims the life in the material world to be God, and each living being to be a part of God, is only this self-idolatry, reflected upon and carried out in words. All the pride of the world, all self-indulgence which says, *Let us eat and drink, for to-morrow we die,* all covetousness which ends in this world, speaks this by its acts, *I and no I beside.*

How is she become a desolation, has passed wholly into it, exists only as a desolation, *a place for beasts to lie down in,* a mere den for *the wild beasts. Every one that passeth by her shall hiss* in derision, *and wag* [or *wave*] *his hand*] in detestation, as though putting the hand between them and it, so as not to look at it, or, as it were, motioning it away. The action is different from that of ⁸ *clapping the hands* in exultation.

"It is not difficult," S. Jerome says, "to explain this of the world, that when the Lord hath stretched forth His Hand over the North and destroyed the Assyrian, the Prince of this world, the world also perishes together with its Princes, and is brought to utter desolation, and is pitied by none, but all hiss and shake their hands at its ruin. But of the Church it

³ Rawl. 5. Emp. i. 385.

⁴ עָלַז, (verb, perhaps i. q. ἀλαλάζω,) is exulting joy, the exultation being good or bad, according to its object, in God or in self and the world ; in God, Ps. xxviii. 7, lxviii. 5, xcvi. 11, cxlix. 5, Hab. iii. 18 ; Zeph. iii. 14: in good, Pr. xxiii. 16 ; in God's gifts, Ps. lx. 8, cviii. 8 ; in evil, Ps. xciv. 3, Jer. xi. 15, xv. 17, l. 11, li. 39 ; over an enemy 2 Sam. i. 20. עָלִיז (intens.) Is. xxii. 2, xxiii. 7, xxiv. 8, xxxii. 13, is used, as here, of a city, full of its tumultuous, self-confident excitement, as is the verb Is. xxiii. 12. and עָלֵז of an individual, Jer. v. 14. [all.]

⁵ 1 Thess. v. 3.
⁶ See Jud. xviii. 27.
⁷ As we might say "no second I." This gives an adequate explanation of the ' in אֶפֶס, as no other rendering does.
⁸ Nah. iii. 19.

CHAPTER III.

1 *A sharp reproof of Jerusalem for divers sins.* 8 *An exhortation to wait for the restoration*

of Israel, 14 *and to rejoice for their salvation by God.*

WOE to || † her that is filthy and polluted, to the oppressing city !

|| Or, *gluttonous.*
† Heb. *craw.*

seems, at first sight, blasphemous to say that it shall be a pathless desert, and wild beasts shall dwell in her, and that afterward it shall be said insultingly over her ; ' This is the city given up to ill, which *dwelt carelessly and said in her heart, I and none beside.'* But whoso should consider that of the Apostle, wherein he says, [1] *in the last days perilous times shall come,* and what is written in the Gospel, that [2] *because iniquity shall abound, the love of many shall wax cold,* so that then shall that be fulfilled, *When the Son of Man cometh, shall He find the faith on the earth?* he will not marvel at the extreme desolation of the Church, that, in the reign of Antichrist, it shall be reduced to a desolation and given over to beasts, and shall suffer whatever the Prophet now describes. For if for unbelief *God spared not the natural branches, but brake them off,* and *turned rivers into a wilderness and the water-springs into a dry ground,* and a *fruitful land into barrenness, for the iniquity of them that dwelt therein,* why not as to those of whom He had said, [3] *He turneth the wilderness into a standing water, and dry ground into water-springs, and there He maketh the hungry to dwell;* and as to those whom *out of the wild olive He hath grafted into the good olive tree,* why, if forgetful of this benefit, they depart from their Maker and worship the Assyrian, should He not undo them and bring them to the same thirst wherein they were before ? Which, whereas it may be understood generally of the coming of Anti-christ or of the end of the world, yet it may, day by day, be understood of those who feign to be of the Church of God, and *in works deny it, are hearers of the word not doers,* who in vain boast in an outward show, whereas herds i. e. troops of vices dwell in them, and brute animals serving the body, and all the beasts of the field which devour their hearts [and pelicans, i. e. gluttons [4], whose *god is their belly*] and hedgehogs, a prickly animal full of spikes which pricketh whatever it toucheth. After which it is subjoined, that the Church shall therefore suffer this, or hath suffered it, because it lifted itself up proudly and raised

its head like a cedar, given up to evil works, and yet promising itself future blessedness, and despising others in its heart, nor thinking that there is any other beside itself, and saying, *I am, and there is no other beside me,* how is it become a solitude, a lair of beasts ! For where before, dwelt the Father, and the Son, and the Holy Ghost, and Angels presided over its ministries, there shall beasts dwell. And if we understand that, every one that passeth by shall hiss, we shall explain it thus ; when Angels shall pass through her, and not remain in her, as was their wont, they shall be amazed and marvel, and shall not support and bear her up with their hand, when falling, but shall lift up the hands and shall pass by. Or they shall make a sound as those who mourn. But if we understand this of the devil and his angels, who destroyed the vine also that was brought out of Egypt, we shall say, that through the soul, which before was the temple of God and hath ceased so to be, the serpent passeth, and hisseth and spitteth forth the venom of his malice in her, and not this only, but setteth in motion his works which figuratively are called *hands.*"

" [5] The earlier and partial fulfillment of prophecy does not destroy, it rather confirms, the entire fulfillment to come. For whoso heareth of the destruction of mighty cities, is constrained to believe the truth of the Gospel, that the fashion of this world passeth away, and that, after the likeness of Nineveh and Babylon, the Lord will in the end judge the whole world also."

C. III. I. The " woe," having gone round the heathen nations, again circles round where it began, the [6] *Jerusalem that killed the prophets and stoned those that were sent unto her.* Woe upon her, and joy to the holy Jerusalem, the *new Jerusalem* [7], *the Jerusalem which is from above, the mother of us all,* close this prophecy ; both in figure ; destruction of her and the whole earth, in time, the emblem of the eternal death ; and the love of God, the foretaste of endless joy in Him.

Wo [8] *rebellious and polluted* [9]; *thou oppressive*

---

[1] 2 Tim. iii. 1-5. [2] S. Matt. xxiv. 12. [3] Ps. cvii. 33-36.
[4] Rib. [5] Rup. [6] S. Matt. xxiii. 37.
[7] Rev. iii. 12. xxi. 10.
[8] הוֹי with the partic., as a vocative, as in Am. v. 18. Is. xlv. 9, 10. Mic. i. 1. Hab. ii. 6, 9, 12, 15, 19, &c.
[9] מוֹרָאָה from מרא = מרה. This seems more probable than E. V. (from a meaning given to יאר

Nah. iii. 6. and from מֹרְאָה crop of bird Lev. i. 16.) or LXX ἐπιφανὴς (as if מַרְאֶה, as a few Mss. de R.) or S. Jer. " embittering," provocatrix (as if הַמְרָה = מרא), or Abarb. " terrible " (as from ירא which is expressed by Nif. נוֹרָא) or Drus. " made a spectacle ; " παραδειγμα-τιζομένη, cf. מַרְאָה ; but this is not used elsewhere, though the verb is so common.

Before
CHRIST
cir. 630.

2 She ᵃobeyed not the voice; she ᵇreceived not || correction; s h e trusted not in the LORD; she drew not near to her God.

3 ᶜHer princes within

ᵃ Jer. 22. 21.
ᵇ Jer. 5. 3.
|| Or, instruction.

ᶜ Ezek. 22. 27.
Mic. 3. 9, 10, 11.

her *are* roaring lions; her judges *are* ᵈevening wolves; they gnaw not the bones till the morrow.

4 Her ᵉp r o p h e t s *are* light *and* treacherous per-

Before
CHRIST
cir. 630.

ᵈ Hab. 1. 8.

ᵉ Jer. 23. 11, 32.
Lam. 2. 14.
Hos. 9. 7.

---

city ¹ ! The address is the more abrupt, and bursts more upon her, since the prophet does not name her. He uses as her proper name, not her own name, "city of peace," but " rebellious," " polluted ; " then he sums up in one, *thou oppressive city.*

Jerusalem's sin is threefold, actively rebelling against God; then, inwardly defiled by sin; then cruel to man. So then, toward God, in herself, toward man, she is wholly turned to evil, not in passing acts, but in her abiding state, 1) rebellious, 2) defiled, 3) oppressive. She is known only by what she has become, and what has been done for her in vain. She is rebellious, and so had had the law; defiled, and so had been cleansed; and therefore her state is the more hopeless.

2. *She obeyed not the Voice,* of God, by the law or the prophets, teaching her His ways; and when, disobeying, He chastened her, *she received not correction,* and when He increased His chastisements, she, in the declining age of the state and deepening evil, turned not unto Him, as in the time of the judges, nor ceased to do evil.

In the Lord she trusted not, but in Assyria or Egypt or her idols. Our practical relation to God is summed up in the four words, " Mistrust self; trust God." Man reverses this, and when " self-trust " has of course failed him, then he " mistrusts God." " ² Such rarely ask of God, what they hope they may obtain from man. They strain every nerve of their soul to obtain what they want; canvass, flatter, fawn, bribe, court favor; and betake themselves to God when all human help fails. They would be indebted, not to God, but to their own diligence. For the more they receive of God, the less, they see, can they exalt their own diligence, the more they are bound to thank God, and obey Him the more strictly."

To her God she drew not nigh, even in trouble, when all draw nigh unto Him, who

are not wholly alien from Him; she drew not near by repentance, by faith, hope or love, or by works meet for repentance, but in heart remained far from Him. And yet He was *her* own *God,* as He had shewn Himself in times past, Who changes not, while we change; is faithful to us, while we fail Him; is still our God, while we forget Him; *waits, to have mercy upon us;* shines on us while we interpose our earth-born clouds between us and Him. " ³ Not in body nor in place, but spiritually and inwardly do we approach to the uncircumscribed God," owning Him as our Father, to Whom we daily say " Our Father."

3. The prophet having declared the wickedness of the whole city, rehearses how each in Church and state, the ministers of God in either, who should have corrected the evil, themselves aggravated it. Not enemies, without, destroy her, but

Her princes within her, in the very midst of the flock, whom they should in God's stead *feed with a true heart,* destroy her as they will, having no protection against them. *Her judges are evening wolves* ⁴; those who should in the Name of God redress all grievances and wrongs, are themselves like wild beasts, when most driven by famine. *They gnaw not the bones* ⁵ *till the morrow* or *on the morrow* [lit. *in the morning*]. They reserve nothing till the morning light, but do in darkness the works of darkness, shrinking from the light, and, in extreme rapacity, devouring at once the whole substance of the poor. As Isaiah says, ⁶ *Thy princes are rebellious and companions of thieves,* and ⁷ *The Lord will enter into judgment with the ancients of His people and the princes thereof : for ye have eaten up the vineyard : the spoil of the poor is in your houses.* And Ezekiel, ⁸ *Her princes in the midst thereof are like wolves, ravening the prey to shed blood, to destroy souls, to get dishonest gain.*

4. *Her prophets are light,* boiling and bubbling up, like water boiling over ⁹, empty

---

¹ הָעִיר as a separate vocative, as Nu. xv. 15. Cant. vi. 1. Is. lii. 18. Mi. ii. 7. &c., and in the N. T. ὁ βασιλεύς, S. Matt. xxvii. 29. ὁ υἱὸς, S. Mark x. 47. ὁ πατὴρ Ib. xiv. 36, &c.

² Rib. on Hos. vii. n. 39.   ³ Dion.

⁴ See Hab. i. 8.

⁵ The meaning of Piel, in Num. xxiv. 8, and met. Ez. xxiii. 34. as denom. from poetic גֶּרֶם. "bone." The Verss. gave the meaning, dropping the metaphor, the Lxx. and Vulg. rendering "left;" Ch. " deferring to," Syr. " waiting for." In Arab. צָרַם

signifies "cut off," spec. wool of sheep, fruit of palm-trees, and with ל p. " gaining for himself or his family." In Syr. it is 1) " cut off;" 2) "decreed;" not, "reserved." Abulw. Kim. Menach. render "break" as denom.

⁶ Is. i. 23.   ⁷ Ib. iii. 14.   ⁸ Ez. xxii. 27.

² פֹּחֲזוּת being used by Jeremiah (xxiii. 32.) of the false prophets who *prophesy false dreams and do tell them and cause My people to err by their lies and by their lightness,* it probably has the same meaning here; though פֹּהֵן is used of the boiling over of

Before C H R I S T cir. 630.	sons ; her priests have pol- luted the sanctuary, they
f Ezek. 22. 26.	have done f violence to the law.

5 g The just LORD h is in the midst thereof; he will not do iniquity : † every morning doth he bring his

g Deut. 32. 4.
h ver. 15, 17.
See Mic. 3. 11.
† Heb. morning
by morning.

boasters claiming the gift of prophecy, which they have not ; "boldly and rashly pouring out what they willed as they willed;" promising good things which shall not be. So they are *her* prophets, to whom they *prophesy smooth things*, "[1] the prophets of this people" not the prophets of God ; *treacherous persons* [lit. men of treacheries] wholly given to manifold treacheries against God in Whose Name they spake and to the people whom they deceived. "[2] They spake as if from the mouth of the Lord and uttered everything against the Lord." *The leaders of the people*, those who *profess* to lead it aright, Isaiah says[3], *are its misleaders. Thy prophets*, Jeremiah says[4], *have seen vain and foolish things for thee ; they have seen for thee false visions and causes of banishment.*

Her priests have polluted her sanctuary, lit. *holiness*, and so holy rites, persons[5], things, places (as the sanctuary), sacrifices. All these they polluted, being themselves polluted ; they polluted first themselves, then the holy things which they handled, handling them as they ought not ; carelessly and irreverently, not as ordained by God ; turning them to their own use and self-indulgence, instead of the glory of God ; then they polluted them in the eyes of the people, [6] *making them to abhor the offering of the Lord*, since, living scandalously, they themselves regarded the Ministry entrusted to them by God so lightly. Their office was to [7] *put difference between holy and unholy and between clean and unclean, and to teach the children all the statutes which the Lord hath spoken unto them by Moses ;* that they [8] *should sanctify themselves and be holy, for I the Lord your God am holy*. But they on the contrary, God says by Ezekiel, [9] *have done violence to My law and have profaned My holy things ; they have made no difference between holy and profane, and have taught none between clean and unclean. Holy* and *unholy* being the contradictory of each other, these changed what God had hallowed into its exact contrary. It was not a mere short-coming, but an annihilation (so to speak), of God's purposes.

" [10] The Priests of the Church then must

keep strict watch, not to profane holy things. There is not one mode only of profaning them, but many and divers. For Priests ought to be purified both in soul and body, and to cast aside every form of abominable pleasure. Rather should they be resplendent with zeal in well-doing, remembering what S. Paul saith, [11] *walk in the Spirit and ye shall not fulfill the lust of the flesh.*"

They have oppressed, done violence, to the law, openly violating it [12] ; or straining it, or secretly wresting and using its forms to wrong and violence, as in the case of Naboth and of Him, of Whom Naboth thus far bore the Image. " [13] *We have a law, and by our law He ought to die.* Law exists to restrain human violence ; these reversed God's ordinances ; violence and law changed places : first, they did violence to the majesty of the law, which was the very voice of God, and then, through profaning it, did violence to man. Forerunners herein of those, who, when Christ came, [14] *transgressed the commandment of God*, and *made it of none effect by their traditions ;* [15] *omitting also the weightier matters of the law, judgment and mercy and faith ; full of extortion and excess!*

5. But, beside these *evening wolves in the midst of her*, there standeth Another *in the midst of her*, Whom they knew not, and so, very near [16] to them although they would not draw near to Him. But He was near, to behold all the iniquities which they did in the very city and place called by His Name and in His very Presence ; He was in her to protect, foster her with a father's love, but she, presuming on His mercy, had cast it off. And so He was near to punish, not to deliver ; as a Judge, not as a Saviour. "[17] God is everywhere, Who says by Jeremiah, [18] *I fill heaven and earth.* But since, as Solomon attesteth, [19] *The Lord is far from the wicked*, how is He said here to be *in the midst* of these most wicked men ? Because the Lord is far from the wicked, as regards the presence of love and grace ; still in His Essence He is everywhere, and in this way He is equally present to all."

The Lord is in the midst thereof ; He will not

---

sensuality (Gen. xlix. 4.) and of *empty wanton men*, Jud. ix. 4. In Arabic, פּחז as well as רהק is used of vain-glory; in Syr. of " impurity."

1 See Mic. ii. 11.
3 Is. ix. 15. [16. Eng.]
5 Ezra viii. 28.
7 Lev. x. 10, 11.
9 Ezek. xxii. 26.
11 Gal. v. 16.
2 S. Jer.
4 Lam. ii. 14.
6 1 Sam. ii. 17.
8 Ib. xi. 44. xix. 2. &c.
10 S. Cyr.

12 The construction with the acc. of person occurs Ezek. xxii. 26, Prov. viii. 36, Jer. xxii. 3.
13 S. John xix. 7.   14 S. Matt. xv. 6.
15 Ib. xxiii. 23. 25.
16 The words in Hebrew correspond with each other, being from the same root, קרב "draw near;" בקרבה, " in the midst of her." ver. 2, 3, 5.
17 Dion.   18 Jer. xxiii. 24.
19 Pr. xv. 29.

Before
C H R I S T
cir. 630.

¹ Jer. 3. 3.
& 6. 15. & 8. 12.

judgment to light, he faileth not; but ¹the unjust
knoweth no shame.

6 I have cut off the na-

tions: their ‖ towers a r e
desolate; I m a d e their
streets waste, that n o n e
passeth by: t h e i r cities

Before
C H R I S T
cir. 630.

‖ Or, *corners.*

do iniquity. " ¹ Since He is the primal rule
and measure of all righteousness; therefore
from the very fact that He doeth anything,
it is just; for He cannot do amiss, being essentially holy. Therefore He will give to
every man what he deserves. Therefore we
chant, ² *The Lord is upright, and there is no
unrighteousness in Him.*" Justice and injustice, purity and impurity, cannot be together.
God's Presence then must destroy the sinners, if not the sin. He was *in the midst of
them,* to sanctify them, giving them His
judgments as a pattern of theirs; *He will not
do iniquity:* but if they heeded it not, the
judgment would fall upon themselves. It
were for God to become ³ *such an one as themselves,* and to connive at wickedness, were He
to spare at last the impenitent.

Every morning [lit. *in the morning, in the
morning*] one after the other, quickly, openly,
daily, continually, bringing all secret things,
all works of darkness, to light, as He said to
David, ⁴ *Thou didst it secretly, but I will do
this thing before all Israel, and before the sun.*
Doth He bring His judgments to light, so that
no sin should be hid in the brightness of His
Light, as He said by Hosea, *Thy judgments
are a light which goeth forth.* " ⁵ Morning by
morning, He will execute His judgments,
i. e., in bright day and visibly, not restrain-
ing His anger, but bringing it forth in the
midst, and making it conspicuous, and, as it
were, setting in open vision what He had
foreannounced." Day by day God gives some
warning of His judgments. By chastisements
which are felt to be His on this side or on
that or all around, He gives ensamples which
speak to the sinner's heart. *He faileth not.*
As God said by Habakkuk, that His promises, although they seem to *linger,* were not
behind ⁶ the real time, which lay in the
Divine mind, so, contrariwise, neither are
His judgments. His hand is never missing ⁷
at the appointed time. *But the unjust* ⁸, he,
whose very being and character, *iniquity,* is
the exact contrary to what he had said of the
perfection of God, ⁹ *Who doth not iniquity,* or,
as Moses had taught them in his song ¹⁰, *all
His ways are judgment, a God of truth and*

without iniquity ¹¹, *just and right is He.* Know-
eth no shame, as God saith by Jeremiah,
¹² *Thou refusedst to be ashamed.* ¹³ *They were not
at all ashamed, neither could they blush.* Even
thus they would not be ashamed of their
sins, ¹⁴ *that they might be converted and God
might heal them.*

6. *I have cut off* [the] *nations.* God appeals
to His judgments on heathen nations, not on
any particular nation, as far as we know;
but to past history, whether of those, of
whose destruction Israel itself had been the
instrument, or others. The judgments upon
the nations before them were set forth to
them, when they were about to enter on their
inheritance, as a warning to themselves ¹⁵.
*Defile not ye yourselves in any of these things;
for in all these have the nations defiled themselves,
which I cast out before you: and the land is
defiled; therefore I do visit the iniquity thereof
upon it, and the land vomiteth out her inhabitants. And ye, ye shall keep My statutes and
My judgments and shall not commit any of these
abominations—And the land shall not spue you
out when ye defile it, as it spued out the nations
which were before you.* The very possession
then of the land was a warning to them; the
ruins, which crowned so many of its hill-
tops ¹⁶, were silent preachers to them; they
lived among the memories of God's visitations; if neglected, they were an earnest of
future judgments on themselves. Yet God's
judgments are not at one time only. Sennacherib appealed to their own knowledge,
¹⁷ *Behold, thou hast heard what the kings of
Assyria have done to all lands by destroying
them utterly. Have the gods of the nations
delivered them which my fathers have destroyed?*
Hezekiah owned it as a fact which he knew:
¹⁸ *Of a truth, Lord, the kings of Assyria have
laid waste all the nations and their land.* And
God owns him as His instrument: ¹⁹ *Now I
have brought it to pass, that thou shouldest be to
lay waste defenced cities into ruinous heaps:* and,
²⁰ *I will send him against an ungodly nation, and
against the people of My wrath will I give him a
charge, to take the spoil and to take the prey, and
to tread them down as the mire of the streets,* and
says of him, *It is in his heart to destroy and to*

¹ Dion. ²Ps. xcii. 15. ³Ib. l. 21.
⁴2 Sam. xii. 12.
⁵ S. Cyr. ⁶ Hab. ii. 3.
⁷ נֶעְדָּר is used of one missing when a muster is
made (1 Sam. xxx. 19, 2 Sam. xvii. 22, met. Is. xxxiv.
16, xl. 26, lix. 15.); here only of God, that He does
not fail to visit at the time when He ought to be
looked for.
⁸ עַוָּל. ⁹ לֹא יִשְׂעֶה עוֹלָה. ¹⁰Deut. xxxii. 4.

¹¹ וְאֵין עַוֶל. ¹² Jer. iii. 3. ¹³ Ib. vi. 15, viii. 12.
¹⁴ Is. vi. 10.
¹⁵ Lev. xviii. 24, 25, 26, 28, add Ib. xx. 23.
¹⁶ This will be brought out by the "Ordnance survey" of Palestine, when completed. Isaiah alludes
to them, xvii. 9.
¹⁷ Is. xxxvii. 11, 13. ¹⁸ Ib. 18.
¹⁹ Ib. 26.
²⁰ Ib. x. 6, 7, and the graphic picture ib. 13, 14.

Before
CHRIST
cir. 630.
are destroyed, so that
there is no man, that there
is none inhabitant.

ᵏSo Jer. 8. 6.

7 ᵏ I said, Surely thou

wilt fear me, thou wilt receive instruction; so their
dwelling should not be cut
off, howsoever 1 punished

Before
CHRIST
cir. 630.

---

cut off nations not a few. The king of Babylon too he describes as ¹ *the man that made
the earth to tremble, that did shake kingdoms,
that made the world as a wilderness, and destroyed
the cities thereof.* Habakkuk recently described the wide wasting by the Babylonians,
and the helplessness of nations before him ².

Their towers, corner towers ³, the most carefully fortified parts of their fortified cities,
are desolate; I made their streets waste. The
desolation is complete, within as well as
without; ruin itself is hardly so desolate as
the empty habitations and forsaken streets,
once full of life, where

"The echoes and the empty tread
Would sound like voices from the dead."

7. *I said, surely thou wilt fear Me.* God
speaks of things here, as they are in their
own nature. *It could not but be,* that in the
very presence of the Hand of God, destroying others but as yet sparing them, they
must learn to fear Him; they must stand in
awe of Him for His judgments on others;
they must be in filial fear of Him for His
loving longsuffering toward themselves.
"Thou *wilt* receive instruction," corrected
and taught through God's correction of
others and the lighter judgments on themselves, as Solomon says, ⁴ *I looked, I set my
heart: I saw, I received instruction.* He saith,
receive, making it man's free act. God brings
it near, commends it to him, exhorts, entreats,
but leaves him the awful power to *receive* or
to refuse. God speaks with a wonderful tenderness. "Surely thou *wilt* stand in awe of
Me; thou *wilt* receive instruction; thou wilt
now do what hitherto thou hast refused to
do." There was (so to speak) nothing else
left for them ⁵, in sight of those judgments.
He pleads their own interests. The lightning was ready to fall. The prophet
had, in vision, seen the enemy within the

city. Yet even now God lingers, as it were,
⁶ *If thou hadst known in this thy day, the things
which are for thy peace.*
So their [*her*] *dwelling should not be cut off.*
His own holy land which He had given
them. A Jew paraphrases ⁷, "And He will
not cut off their dwellings from the land of
the house of My Shechinah" (God's visible
Presence in glory). Judah, who was before
addressed *thou,* is now spoken of in the third
person, *her;* and this also had wonderful
tenderness. It is as though God were musing over her and the blessed fruits of her
return to Him; "it shall not be needed to
correct her further." *Howsoever I punished
them:* lit. *all* (i. e., *all* the offences) *which I
visited upon her,* as God saith of Himself,
" ⁸ *visiting the sins* of the fathers *upon the
children,*" and this is mostly the meaning
of the words ⁹ *visit upon.* Amid and notwithstanding all the offences which God had
already chastised, He, in His love and compassion, still longeth, not utterly to remove
them from His Presence, if they would but
receive instruction *now;* but they would not.
How often, our Lord says ¹⁰, *would I have
gathered thy children together, even as a hen
gathereth her chickens under her wings, and ye
would not. But indeed,* probably, *Of a truth* ¹¹
(it is a word strongly affirming what follows)
they rose early, they corrupted all their doings;
God gave them His warnings, awaited the
result; they lost no time, they began with
morning light; they hasted to rise, burthened ¹²
themselves, made sure of having the whole
day before them, to—seek God as He had
sent His Prophets, ¹³ *rising early and sending
them?* No, nor even simply to do ill, but of
set purpose to do, not this or that corruptly,
but to *corrupt all their doings.* " ¹⁴ They with
diligence and eagerness rose early, that, with
the same haste wherewith they ought to
have returned to Me, they might shew forth

---

¹ Is. xiv. 16, 17. ² Hab. i. 14–16.
³ See on i. 16. Since also the subjects spoken of
in this verse are places, the metaph. meaning of
פִּנּוֹת "princes" i. e. corner-stones, is not probable
here, although נִשְׁמוּ is, in four places, used of
men.
⁴ Prov. xxiv. 32.
⁵ אַךְ, exclusively of all besides. All the meanings ascribed to אַךְ are but different ways of expressing in other languages the primary meaning,
"nothing but."
⁶ S. Luke xix. 42. ⁷ Jon.
⁸ Ex. xx. 5, xxxiv. 7. Nu. xiv. 18.
⁹ Ex. xxxii. 34, Is. xiii. 11, Jer. xxiii. 2, Hos. i. 4, ii.
13, iv. 9, Amos iii. 2, 14; beside the separate cases
of a) visiting upon, or b) visiting the sin. See
Ges.

¹⁰ S. Matt. xxiii. 37.
¹¹ אָכֵן probably (as Ges.)=הֲכִי Jos. iii. 17. iv. 5.
The adversative force, which Gesenius (Thes. p.
670) and Ewald (Lehrb. n. 105. d. p. 274. ed. 8.) think
to belong to a later style, lies (as so often in other
Heb. particles) in the tacit contrast of the sentences. Gesenius' instances of this "later usage"
are Ps. xxxi. 23. (David's) lxvi. 19. lxxxii. 7. Job
xxxii. 8. Is. xlix. 4. liii. 4. Jer. iii. 20, and this
place.
¹² The word means originally "placed on the
back;" then is used of a traveler, who taking his
baggage upon him, or setting it on his camels, sets
out in very early dawn, or before it, as is the practice in hot countries.
¹³ Jer. vii. 13, 25, xi. 7, xxvi. 5. xxix. 19.
¹⁴ S. Jer.

Before
CHRIST
cir. 630.

[1] Gen. 6. 12.
[m] Ps. 27. 14.
& 37. 34.
Prov. 20. 22.

them; but they rose early,
and [1]corrupted all their
doings.

8 ¶ Therefore [m] wait ye
upon me, saith the LORD,
until the day that I rise up

Before
CHRIST
cir. 630.

[n] Joel. 3. 2.

to the prey: for my determination *is* to [n] gather the
nations, that I may assemble the kingdoms, to pour
upon them mine indigna-
tion, *even* all my fierce an-

---

in deed what they had conceived amiss
in their mind." There are as many aggravations of their sin as there are
words. The four Hebrew words bespeak
eagerness, wilfulness, completeness enormity, in sin. They *rose early*, themselves
deliberately *corrupted*, of their own mind
made offensive, *all* their *doings*, not slight
acts, but *deeds*, great works done with a high
hand [1].

8. *Therefore wait ye upon* [*for*] *Me.* God
so willeth not to punish, but that all should
lay hold of His mercy, that He doth not here
even name punishment. Judah had slighted
His mercies; He was ready to forgive *all*
they had sinned, if they would *now* receive
instruction; they in return set themselves to
corrupt *all* their doings. They had wholly
forsaken Him. *Therefore*—we should have
expected, as elsewhere, "Therefore I will
visit all your iniquities upon you." But not
so. The chastisement is all veiled; the prophet points only to the mercy beyond. *Therefore wait ye for Me.* All the interval of
chastisement is summed up in these words;
i. e., since neither My mercies toward you,
nor My chastisement of others, lead you to
obey Me, *therefore* the time shall be, when
My Providence shall not seem to be over
you, nor My Presence among you [2]; but
then, *wait ye for Me* [3] earnestly, intensely,
perseveringly, *until the day, that I rise up to
the prey.* The *day* is probably in the first
instance, the deliverance from Babylon. But
the words seem to be purposely enlarged, that
they may embrace other judgments of God
also. For the words to *gather the nations,
assemble the kingdoms,* describe some array of
nations against God and His people; gathering themselves for their own end at that
time, but, in His purpose, gathering themselves for their own destruction, rather than
the mere tranquil reunion of those of
different nations in the city of Babylon, when

the Medes and Persians came against *them.*
Nor again are they altogether fulfilled in the
destruction of Jerusalem, or any other event
until now. For although then a vast number of the dispersed Jews were collected
together, and were at that time "[4]broken
off" and out of covenant with God, they
could hardly be called *nations,* (which are
here and before [5] spoken of in contrast with
Judah), much less *kingdoms.* In its fullest
sense the prophecy seems to belong to the
same events in the last struggle of Anti-Christ,
as at the close of Joel [6] and Zechariah [7].
With this agrees the largeness of the destruction; *to pour out upon them,* in full
measure, emptying out so as to overwhelm
them [8], *Mine indignation, even all My fierce
anger; for all the earth shall be devoured with
the fire of My jealousy.* The outpouring of *all*
God's wrath, the devouring of the *whole* earth,
in the fullest sense of the words, belongs to
the end of the world, when He shall say to the
wicked, "Depart from Me, ye cursed, into
everlasting fire." In lesser degrees, and less
fully, the substance of the prophecy has
again and again been fulfilled to the Jewish
Church before Christ, at Babylon and under
the Maccabees; and to the Christian, as when
the Mohammedans hemmed in Christendom
on all sides, and the waves of their conquests
on the East and West threatened to meet,
overwhelming Christendom. The Church,
having sinned, had to *wait* for a while *for God*
Who by His Providence withdrew Himself,
yet at last delivered it.

And since the whole history of the Church
lies wrapt up in the Person of the Redeemer,
the day that I rise up to the prey, is especially
the Day in which the foundation of His
Church was laid, or that in which it shall be
completed; the Day whereon He rose again,
as the first-fruits, or that Day in which He
shall [9] *stand again on the earth,* to judge it;
[10] *so coming even as He went up into Heaven.*

[1] עֲלִילוֹת are the "mighty works" of God, or
deeds of man's might, and, as such, mostly great
crimes in the sight of God. So even the heathen
have formed from "facio," "facinus," of deeds
which they too held to involve great guilt.
[2] See Hos. iii. 3–5.
[3] חכּה is mostly a longing persevering expectation for a thing or person which as yet comes not,
when the delay requires patience; for God, with לְ,
Ps. xxxiii. 20, Is. viii. 7, lxiv. 3; His promise, Hab.
ii. 3, and (part. Kal in sense of Pi.) Is. xxx. 18; with

negative Ps. cvi. 13; for death, Job iii. 20; of endurance, Dan. xii. 12. The only other cases are 'lying
in wait,' Hos. vi. 9. waiting for the end of Job's
words, Job xxxii. 4; for the issue of the message to
Jehu, 2 Kgs ix. 3; till dawn, Ib vii. 9; and of God,
waiting for us, till He can shew us mercy, Is. xxx.
18. [4] Rom. xi. 20. [5] v. 6. [6] Joel iii. 2, 9–16.
[7] Zech. xiv.
[8] See Ps. lxix. 24, lxxix. 6, Jer. vi. 11, x. 25, xiv.
16, Ezek. xxi. 31, Rev. xvi. 1.
[9] Job xix. 25. It is the same word.
[10] Acts i. 11.

ger; for all the earth ° shall be devoured with the fire of my jealousy.

9 For then will I turn to the people ᴾ a pure † language, that they may all

Then, *the prey*[1] must be, what God vouchsafes to account as His gain, *the prey* which is *taken from the mighty*[2], and *the lawful captivity, the prey of the terrible one,* which shall be delivered; even that spoil which the Father bestowed on Him *Who made His soul an offering for sin*[3], the goods of the strong man[4] *whom* He bound, and spoiled us, His lawful goods and captives, since we had *sold*[5] ourselves *under sin* to him. "[6] Christ lived again having spoiled hell, because [7] *it was not possible* [as it is written] *that He,* being by nature Life, *should be holden of death.*

Here, where spoken of with relation to the Church, *the jealousy* of Almighty God is that love for His people[8], which will not endure their ill-treatment by those who (as all Anti-Christian power doth) make themselves His rivals in the government of the world.

9. *For then,* in the order of God's mercies. The deliverance from Babylon was the forerunner of that of the Gospel, which was its object. The spread of the Gospel then is spoken of in the connection of God's Providence and plan, and time is overlooked. Its blessings are spoken of, as *then* given when the earnest was given, and the people, from whom according to the flesh Christ was to be born, were placed anew in the land where He was to be born. "[9] The prophet springs, as is his wont, to Christ and the time of the new law.' And in Christ, the End of the law, the prophet ends.

I will turn, contrary to what they had before, *to the people,* lit. *peoples,* the nations of the earth, *a pure language,* lit. *a purified lip.* It is a real conversion, as was said of Saul at

the beginning; [10] *God* [lit.] *turned to him another heart.* Before the dispersion of Babel the world was [11] *of one lip,* but that, impure, for it was in rebellion against God. Now it shall be again *of one lip,* but that, *purified.* The purity is of faith and of life, *that they may call upon the Name of the Lord,* not as heretofore on idols, but that every tongue should confess the one true God, Father Son and Holy Ghost, in Whose Name they are baptized. This is purity of faith. To [12] *call upon the Name of the Lord Jesus* is the very title of Christian worship; *all that called upon the Name* of Jesus, the very title of Christians[13]. *To serve Him with one consent,* lit. *with one shoulder,* evenly, steadfastly, not *unequally yoked,* but all with united strength, bearing Christ's *easy yoke* and *one another's burdens, fulfilling the law of Christ.* This is purity of life. The fruit of the lips is *the sacrifice of praise*[14]. God gave back one pure language, when, on the Day of Pentecost, the Holy Spirit, the Author of purity, came down in fiery tongues upon the Apostles, teaching them and guiding them *into the whole truth*[15], and to [16] *speak to every one in his own tongue, wherein he was born, the wonderful works of God.* Thenceforth there was to be a higher unity than that of outward language. For speech is not the outer sound, but the thoughts which it conveys and embodies. The inward thought is the soul of the words. The outward confusion of Babel was to hinder oneness in evil and a worse confusion. At Pentecost, the unity restored was oneness of soul and heart, wrought by One Spirit, Whose gift is the one Faith and the

---

[1] עַד commonly signifies "eternity," עַד or לְעַד; also Gen. xlix. 27, Is. xxxiii. 23. (as Ch עָדָא &c.) "prey;" nowhere, as Ew., "attack."
[2] Is. xlix. 24, 25. [3] Ib. liii. 10, 12.
[4] S. Matt. xii. 29.
[5] Rom. vii. 14. coll. Is. l. 1, lii. 3.
[6] S. Cyr. [7] Acts ii. 24.
[8] See on Nah. i. 2. [9] Lap.
[10] 1 Sam. x. 9. וַיַּהֲפָךְ יי לוֹ לֵב אַחֵר, as here
אהפך אל עמים שפה ברורה.
[11] Gen. xi. 1, 6, 7, 9. The Jews also saw that this was a reversal of the confusion of Babel. "God, blessed for ever, saith, 'in this world, on account of evil concupiscence (יֵצֶר הרע man's natural corruption) men were divided into 70 languages; but in the world to come, all shall agree with one mind to call upon My Name;'" alleging this place. Tanchuma f. 5. 1. ap. Schoettg. ad loc. "R. Chiia said, 'thou hearest from holy Scripture, that all hangeth from the word of the mouth;' for after the tongues were confounded, it is added, 'and God dispersed them thence' But in the time to come, what is written? 'Then will I turn &c.'" Sohar, Gen. f. 58. col. 217. (Schoettg. loc. gen n. 37). Again it is said, "when the days of the Messiah shall

come, boys shall know the hidden things of wisdom; for then shall all things be revealed, as is said, Then v ill I turn &c." Ib. f. 74. col. 291. Ib. ad loc. And of its fulfillment in the conversion of the world, "Who would have expected that God would raise up the tabernacle of David, which was fallen? and yet it is read, In that day I will raise &c. (Am. ix. 11). And who would have hoped that the whole world would be one band? as in, Then will I turn &c." Bereshith rabba n. 88 fin. Schoettg. loci gen. n. 18, and on Gen. xli. 44; "Why is, 'they shall praise Thee' repeated four times in Ps. lxvii. 4? He means, 'They shall praise Thee with their heart; they shall praise Thee with their mouth; they shall praise Thee with their good deeds, and they shall praise Thee with all these, as it is said, For then will I turn &c.' and the Name of the Lord is no other than the King Messiah, according to, 'and the Name of the Lord cometh from far.'" in Mart. Pug. Fid f. 327. It is also quoted with other places, as to be fulfilled in the time of the Messiah, *Tikkune Sohar* p. 60 (Schoettg. Loc. gen. n. 80), R. Moseh in Ibn Ezra, and Ibn Ezra himself, of the second temple. Kimchi "after the wars of Gog."
[12] Acts. xxii. 16. Rom. x. 13.
[13] Acts ix. 14, 21, 1 Cor. i. 2. [14] Heb. xiii. 15.
[15] S. John xvi. 13. [16] Acts ii. 8, 11.

Before CHRIST cir. 630.

call upon the name of the LORD, to serve him with one † consent.

10 ᵠ From beyond the rivers of Ethiopia my suppliants, *even* the daughter of my dispersed, shall bring mine offering.

† Heb. *shoulder*.
ᵠ Ps. 68. 31. Isai. 18. 1, 7. & 60. 4, &c. Mal. 1. 11. Acts 8. 27.

one Hope of our calling, in the One Lord, in Whom we are one, grafted into the one body, by our Baptism[1]. The Church, then created, is the One Holy Catholic Church diffused throughout all the world, everywhere with one rule of Faith, *the Faith once for all delivered unto the saints*, confessing one God, the Trinity in Unity, and serving Him in the one law of the Gospel with one consent. Christians, as Christians, speak the same language of Faith, and from all quarters of the world, one language of praise goes up to the One God and Father of all. "[2] God divided the tongues at Babel, lest, understanding one another, they should form a destructive unity. Through proud men tongues were divided; through humble Apostles tongues were gathered in one. The spirit of pride dispersed tongues; the Holy Spirit gathered tongues in one. For when the Holy Spirit came upon the disciples, they spake with the tongues of all, were understood by all; the dispersed tongues were gathered into one. So then, if they are yet angry and Gentiles, it is better for them to have their tongues divided. If they wish for one tongue, let them come to the Church; for in diversity of the tongues of the flesh, there is one tongue in the Faith of the heart." In whatever degree the oneness is impaired within the Church, while there is yet one Faith of the Creeds, He Alone can restore it and *turn to her a purified language*, Who first gave it to those who waited for Him. Both praise and service are perfected above, where the Blessed, with one loud voice, [3] *shall cry, Salvation to our God which sitteth upon the Throne and unto the Lamb; blessing and glory and wisdom and thanksgiving and honor and power and might be unto our God for ever and ever.* And they who *have come out of great tribulation and have washed their robes and made them white in the Blood of the Lamb*, shall be *before the Throne of God and serve Him day and night in His Temple*[4]."

10. *From beyond the rivers*[5] *of Ethiopia.* The furthest Southern people, with whom the Jews had intercourse, stand as the type of the whole world beyond. The utmost bound of the known inhabited land should not be the bound of the Gospel. The conversion of Abyssinia is one, but the narrowest fulfillment of the prophecy. The whole new world, though not in the mind of the prophet, was in the mind of Him Who spake by the prophet.

My suppliants. He names them as what they shall be when they shall come to Him. They shall come, as needy, to the Fountain of all good, asking for mercy of the unfailing Source of all mercy. He describes the very character of all who come to God through Christ. *The daughter of My dispersed*[6]. God is, in the way of Providence, the Father of all, although, by sin, alienated from Him; whence S. Paul says, *we are the offspring of God*[7]. They were *dispersed*, severed from the oneness in Him and from His house and family; yet still, looking on them as already belonging to Him, He calls them, *My dispersed*, as by Caiaphas, being high-priest, He prophesied that *Jesus should die for that nation; and not for that nation only, but that also He should gather together in one the children of God that were scattered abroad*[8].

Shall bring Mine offering[9]. The offering is the same as that which Malachi prophesies shall continue under the New Testament, which offering was to be offered to the Name of God, not in Jerusalem, but [10] *in every place from the rising of the sun unto the going down of the same.* The dark skin of the Ethiopian is the image of ingrained sin, which man could not efface or change [11]: their conversion then declares how those steeped in sin shall be cleansed from all their darkness of mind, and washed white from their sins in Baptism and beautified by the grace of God. "[12] The word of prophecy endeth in truth. For not only through the Roman empire is

[1] Eph. iv 3–6.
[2] S. Aug. in Ps. liv. 6.
[3] Rev vii. 10, 12
[4] Ib. vii. 14, 15.
[5] See Isaiah xviii. 1.
[6] Ewald conjectures בת פוט because Nahum speaks of Cush, Phut and Lubin among the allies of No-Ammon or Thebes, and renders עתרי "my incenses;" first rendering עתר (Ez. viii. 11) "*the smoke of the cloud of incense.*" But this sense is not itself proved (in both Syr and Arab. incense is עטר not עתר) nor is incense plural; nor is there any parallelism of Cush and Phut in Nahum, but Phut and Lubim are historically named as allies of No.

[7] Acts xvii. 28.
[8] S. John xi. 51, 52.
[9] It is possible also to render, "from beyond the rivers of Ethiopia, My suppliants the daughter of My dispersed shall they bring as Mine offering;" and this some have preferred on account of the like place in Isaiah lxvi. 20, "And they shall bring all your brethren for an offering unto the Lord out of all nations &c." But the word מנחה alone is common to the two passages, and the words מעבר לנהרי כוש which occur in Is. xviii. 1, and יובל שי לי' Ib. 7, make me think that this place rather was in the prophet's mind
[10] Mal. i. 11.
[11] Jer xiii. 23.
[12] S. Cyr.

Before
CHRIST
cir. 630.
11 In that day shalt thou not be ashamed for all thy doings, wherein thou hast transgressed against me : for then I will take away out of the midst of thee them that [r] rejoice in thy pride, and thou shalt no more be haughty † because of my holy mountain.

Before
CHRIST
cir. 630.

[r] Jer. 7. 4.
Mic. 3. 11.
Matt. 3. 9.
† Heb. *in my holy.*

---

the Gospel preached, but it circles round the barbarous nations. And there are Churches everywhere, shepherds and teachers, guides and instructors in mysteries, and sacred altars, and the Lamb is invisibly sacrificed by holy priests among Indians too and Ethiopians. And this was said plainly by another prophet also [1], *For I am a great King, saith the Lord, and My Name is great among the heathen, and in every place incense is offered to My Name and a pure sacrifice."*

11. *In that day shalt thou not be ashamed for all thy doings,* because God, forgiving them, will blot them out and no more remember them. This was first fulfilled in the Gospel. " [2] No one can doubt that when Christ came in the flesh, there was an amnesty and remission to all who believed. *For we are justified not by works of righteousness which we have done, but according to His great mercy.* But we have been released from shame. For *He* hath restored us to freedom of access to God, Who for our sakes arose from the dead, and for us ascended to heaven in the presence of the Father. *For Christ, our Forerunner, hath ascended for us now to appear in the presence of God.* So then He took away the guilt of all and freed believers from failures and shame." St. Peter, even in heaven, must remember his denial of our Lord, yet not so as to be *ashamed* or pained any more, since the exceeding love of God will remove all shame or pain. " [3] Mighty promise, mighty consolation. Now, before that Day comes, the Day of My Resurrection, thou wilt be ashamed and not without reason, since thou ownest by a true confession, [4] *all our righteousnesses are as filthy rags.* But at that Day it will not be so, especially when that shall be which I promise thee in the Prophets and the Psalms, [5] *There shall be a Fountain opened for sin and for uncleanness ;* whence David also, exulting in good hope of the Holy Spirit, saith, [6] *Thou shalt wash me and I shall be whiter than snow.* For though he elsewhere saith, [7] *they looked unto Him and were lightened, and*

their faces were not ashamed, yet in this mortal life, when the Day of My Resurrection doth not fully shine upon thee, thou art after some sort ashamed ; as it is written, [8] *What fruit had ye then in those things whereof ye are now ashamed?* but that shame will bring glory, and, when that glory cometh in its place, will wholly pass away. But when the fullness of that day shall come, the fullness of My Resurrection, when the members shall rise, as the Head hath risen, will the memory of past foulness bring any confusion ? Yea the very memory of the miseries will be the richest subject of singing, according to that, [9] *My song shall be alway of the loving-kindness of the Lord."* For how shall the redeemed forget the mercies of their redemption, or yet how feel a painful shame even of the very miseries, out of which they were redeemed by the fullness of the overstreaming Love of God ?

For then will I take away out of the midst of thee them that rejoice in thy pride. [those of thee who exult in pride [10].] All confusion shall cease, because all pride shall cease, the parent of sin and confusion. The very gift of God becomes to the carnal a source of pride. Pride was to the Jew also the great hindrance to the reception of the Gospel. He made his *boast of the law,* yea, in God Himself, that he *knew His will,* and was *a guide of others* [11], and so was the more indignant, that the heathen was made equal to him, and that he too was called to repentance and faith in Christ. So, *going about to establish his own rightcousness, he did not submit himself to the rightcousness of God,* but shut himself out from the faith and grace and salvation of Christ, and rejected Himself. So, [3] *thy pride* may be the pride in being the people of God, and having Abraham for their father. *And thou shalt no more be haughty* [12] *in My holy mountain,* " but thou shalt stand in the great and everlasting abiding-place of humility, knowing perfectly, that thou now 'knowest in part' only, and confessest truly that no one ever could or can

---

[1] Mal. i. 11.   [2] S. Cyr.   [3] Rup.
[4] Is. lxiv. 6.   [5] Zech. xiii. 1.
[6] Ps. li. 7.   [7] Ib. xxxiv. 5.
[8] Rom. vi. 21.   [9] Ps. lxxxix. 1.
[10] It cannot be "those that exult in thy highness;" for גאוה, as used of man, always has a bad sense, "self-exaltation."
[11] Rom. ii. 17, 18–20, 23.
[12] As in E. M., not, *because of.* גבה, as a mental quality, mostly occurs with לב and is used in a bad sense of high-mindedness=pride; Ps. cxxxi.

1, (David's), Pr. xviii. 12, Ez. xxviii. 2, 5, 17, 2 Chr. xxvi. 16, xxxii. 25; absol. in a bad sense, Is. iii. 16, Jer. xiii. 15, Ez. xvi. 50. It is used of eminence given by God, Job xxxvi. 7, and of the Messiah as exalted by Him, Is. lii. 13. Once only, 2 Chr. xvii. 6, נבה לבו is used in a good sense of Jehoshaphat, that, being exalted by God, "his heart was elevated in the ways of the law." The form לְגָבְהָה is like the inf. in Ex. xxix. 29, xxx. 18, xxxvi. 2, Lev. xv. 32, &c.

Before
CHRIST
cir. 630.

* Isai. 14. 32.
Zech. 11. 11.
Matt. 5. 3.
1 Cor. 1. 27, 28.
Jam. 2. 5.

12 I will also leave in the midst of thee * an afflicted a n d poor people, and they shall trust in the name of the LORD.

Before
CHRIST
cir. 630.

t Mic. 4. 7.
ch. 2. 7.
u Isai. 60. 21.
x Isai. 63. 8.
Rev. 14. 5.

13 ᵗ The remnant of Israel ᵘ shall not do iniquity, ˣ nor speak lies ; neither shall a deceitful tongue be found in their mouth : for

by his own works be justified in the sight of God. ¹ *For all have sinned and come short of the glory of God.*" Pride which is ever offensive to God, is yet more hideous in a holy place or a holy office, *in* Mount Sion where the temple was or in the Christian priesthood.

12. And *I will also leave* (over, as a remnant, it is still the same heavy prophecy, that *a remnant* only *shall be saved* ²) *an afflicted and poor people.* Priests, (except that *great company* who *were obedient to the faith* ³) scribes, lawyers, Pharisees, Sadducees were taken away ; and there remained " ⁴ the people of the land," the ⁵ *unlearned and ignorant,* ⁶ *the weak things of the world and the things despised* who bore the very title of their Master ⁷, *the poor and needy ; poor in Spirit* ⁸ ; poor also in outward things, since *they who had lands, sold them* and they *had all things common* ⁹. They were afflicted above measure outwardly in the ¹⁰persecutions, *reproaches, spoiling of their goods,* stripes, deaths, which they endured for Christ's sake. They knew too their own poverty; " ¹¹ knowing themselves to be sinners, and that they were justified only by faith in Jesus Christ." When the rest were cast out *of the midst of her,* these should be left *in the midst of her* (the words stand in contrast with one another) in the bosom of the Church. *And they shall trust in the name of the Lord.* " As they looked to be justified only in the Name of Christ," and " ¹² trusted in the grace and power of God alone, not in any power or wisdom or eloquence or riches of this world, they converted the world to a faith above nature." " ¹³ Conformed in this too to Christ, Who for our sakes became poor and almost neglected both His divine glory and the supereminence of His nature, to subject Himself to the condition of a servant. So then those instructed in His laws after His example, think humbly of them-

selves. They became most exceedingly loved of God, and chiefly the divine disciples, who were set as lights of the world."

13. *The remnant of Israel,* the same poor people, the *true Israel* of whom God said, *I leave over* (the word is the same) *a poor people,* few, compared with the rest who were blinded ; of whom the Lord said, *I know whom I have chosen* ¹⁴. These *shall not do iniquity nor speak lies.* " ¹³ This is a spiritual adorning, a most beautiful coronet of glorious virtues. For where meekness and humility are and the desire of righteousness, and the tongue unlearns vain words and sinful speech, and is the instrument of strict truth, there dawns a bright and most perfect virtue. And this beseems those who are in Christ. For the beauty of piety is not seen in the Law, but gleams forth in the power of Evangelic teaching."

Our Lord said of Nathanael, ¹⁵ *Behold an Israelite indeed, in whom is no guile,* and to the Apostles, ¹⁶ *I send you forth as sheep among wolves ; be ye therefore wise as serpents and harmless as doves ;* and of the first Christians it is said, ¹⁷ *they, continuing daily with one accord in the temple, and breaking bread from house to house did eat their meat with gladness and singleness of heart, praising God and having favor with all the people.* This is the character of Christians, as such, and it was at first fulfilled ; ¹⁸ *whosoever is born of God, doth not commit sin ;* ¹⁹ *whosoever is born of God sinneth not ; but he that is begotten of God keepeth himself, and that wicked one toucheth him not.* An Apologist, at the close of the second century, could appeal to the Roman Emperor ²⁰, that no Christian was found among their criminals, " unless it be only as a Christian, or, if he be anything else, he is forthwith no longer a Christian. We alone then are innocent ! What wonder if this be so, of necessity ? And truly of necessity it is so. Taught

---

¹ Rom. iii. 23.
² Ib. ix. 27. See ab. on Mic. ii. 12. p. 36.
³ Acts vi. 7.
⁴ הָאָרֶץ עַם the uneducated, *this people that knoweth not the law* (S. John vii. 49), " one in whom there are moral not intellectual excellences." Rambam in Buxt. Lex. Talm. col. 1626.
⁵ Acts iv. 13.   ⁶ 1 Cor. i. 27, 28.   ⁷ Ps. xli. 1.
⁸ עָנִי is not simply " poor," nor עָנָו simply " meek." עָנִי is one " afflicted," in whom affliction has produced its fruits; עָנָו. one " meek " but in whom patience has been tried and perfected; as the same class are meant by the πτωχοί, S. Luke vi. 20, and the πτωχοὶ τῷ πνεύματι, S. Matt. v. 3; and,

" no humility without humiliation," is become a Christian proverb.
⁹ Acts ii. 44, 45, iv. 32, 35.
¹⁰ Acts viii. 1, ix. 2, 13, 14. xii. 1, 2, xiii. 50, xiv. 5. 22. xxii. &c. Rom. viii. 17, 35, 36. xii. 14, 1 Cor. ix. 19, 2 Cor. i. 8, 9, xii. 10, 2 Thess. i. 4, 2 Tim. iii. 11, 12, Heb. x. 32–34, 8 James ii. 6, 7, 1 S. Pet. i. 6, 7. iv. 13, Rev. i. 9. vi. 9 &c.
¹¹ Rup.   ¹² Dion.   ¹³ S. Cyr.   ¹⁴ S. John xiii. 18.
¹⁵ Ib. i. 47.   ¹⁶ S. Mat. x. 16.   ¹⁷ Acts ii. 46, 47.
¹⁸ 1 S. John iii. 9.   ¹⁹ Ib. v. 18.
²⁰ Tert. Apol. c. 44, 45. See also Justin M. i. n. 34. S. Athenagoras, n. 2, Minutius Felix p. 333. Theodoret de cur. Græc. aff. Disp. xii. circ. med. p. 1021 sqq. ed Schultz; Lactant. v. 9. quoted Ib.

Before CHRIST cir. 630.
J Ezek. 34. 28.
Mic. 4. 4.
& 7. 14.
z Isai. 12. 6.
& 54. 1. Zech. 2. 10. & 9. 9.

ʸ they shall feed and lie down, and none shall make *them* afraid.

14 ¶ ᶻ Sing, O daughter

of Zion; shout, O Israel; be glad and rejoice with all the heart, O daughter of Jerusalem.

innocence by God, we both know it perfectly, as being revealed by a perfect Master; and we keep it faithfully, as being committed to us by an Observer, Who may not be despised." "¹ Being so vast a multitude of men, almost the greater portion of every state, we live silently and modestly, known perhaps more as individuals than as a body, and to be known by no other sign than the reformation of our former sins." Now in the Church, which "our earth dimm'd eyes behold," we can but say, as in regard to the cessation of war² under the Gospel, that God's promises are sure on His part, that still ³ *they that are Christ's have crucified the flesh with the affections and lusts,* that the Gospel is ⁴ *a power of God unto salvation,* that *the ⁵ preaching of the Cross is, unto us which are saved, the power of God;* ⁶ *unto them that are called, Christ is the power of God and the wisdom of God;* that those who will, ⁷ *are kept by God through faith unto salvation;* but that now too ⁸ *they are not all Israel, which are of Israel,* and that ⁹ *the faithlessness of man does not make the faith of God of none effect.* " ¹⁰ The Church of God is universally holy in respect of all, by institutions and administrations of sanctity; the same Church is really holy in this world, in relation to all godly persons contained in it, by a real infused sanctity; the same is farther yet at the same time perfectly holy in reference to the saints departed and admitted to the presence of God; and the same Church shall hereafter be most completely holy in the world to come, when all the members, actually belonging to it, shall be at once perfected in holiness and completed in happiness." Most fully shall this be fulfilled in the Resurrection. " ¹¹ O blessed day of the Resurrection, in whose fullness no one will sin in word or deed! O great and blessed reward to every soul, which, although it hath now *done iniquity* and *spoken falsehood,* yet willeth not to do it further! Great and blessed reward, that he shall now receive such immovableness, as no longer to be able to do iniquity or speak falsehood, since the blessed soul, through the Spirit of everlasting love inseparably united with God its Creator, shall now no more be capable of an evil will!"

For they shall feed; on the hidden manna,

" ¹² nourished most delicately by the Holy Spirit with inward delights, and spiritual food, the bread of life." In the things of the body too was ¹³ *distribution made unto every man according as he had need. And they shall lie down* in the green pastures where He foldeth them; *and none shall make them afraid,* " ⁷ for they were ready to suffer and to die for the Name of the Lord Jesus ¹⁴. ¹⁵ *They departed from the presence of the council rejoicing that they were counted worthy to suffer shame for His Name.* Before the Resurrection and the sending of the Holy Ghost, how great was the fearfulness, unsteadfastness, weakness of the disciples; how great, after the infusion of the Holy Spirit, was their constancy and imperturbableness, it is delightsome to estimate in their Acts," when they ¹⁶ *bare His Name before the Gentiles and kings, and the children of Israel,* and he who had been afraid of a little maid, said to the High Priest, ¹⁷ *We ought to obey God rather than men.* " ¹⁸ When Christ the Good Shepherd Who laid down His life for His sheep, shone upon us, we are fed in gardens and pastured among lilies, and lie down in folds; for we are folded in Churches and holy shrines, no one scaring or spoiling us, no wolf assailing nor lion trampling on us, no robber breaking through, no one invading us, to steal and kill and destroy; but we abide in safety and participation of every good, being in charge of Christ the Saviour of all."

14. *Sing, O daughter of Sion; shout, O Israel; be glad and rejoice with all the heart, O daughter of Jerusalem.* Very remarkable throughout all these verses is the use of the sacred number three, secretly conveying to the thoughtful soul the thought of Him, Father Son and Holy Ghost, the Holy and Undivided Trinity by Whose operation these things shall be. Threefold is the description of their being freed from sins; 1) they shall *not do iniquity,* 2) *nor speak lies,* 3) *neither shall a deceitful tongue be found in their mouth.* Threefold their blessedness; They shall 1) *feed,* 2) *lie down,* 3) *none make them afraid.* Threefold the exhortation to joy here; " ¹⁹ *Sing* to God the Father; *shout* to God the Son; *be glad and rejoice* in God the Holy Ghost, which Holy Trinity is One God, from Whom thou hast received it that

1 Id. ad Scap. n. 2, p, 145. Oxf. Tr.
2 See ab. on Mic. iv. 3 pp. 56, 57.
3 Gal. v. 24. See Dr. Pusey's Sermon, "The Gospel, the power of God." Lenten Sermons, pp. 300-321.
4 Rom. i. 16. 5 1 Cor. i. 18. 6 Ib. 24.

7 1 S. Pet. i. 5. 8 Rom. ix. 6. 9 Ib. iii. 3.
10 Bp. Pearson on the Creed, Art. ix.
11 Rup. 12 Dion.
13 Acts iv. 35. 14 Ib. xxi. 13. 15 Ib. v. 41.
16 Acts ix. 15. 17 Ib. v. 29. 18 S. Cyril. 19 Rup.

Before
C H R I S T
cir. 630.

15 The Lᴏʀᴅ hath taken away thy judgments, he hath cast out thine enemy: ᵃthe king of

ᵃ John 1. 49.

Israel, *even* the Lᴏʀᴅ, ᵇ *is* in the midst of thee: thou shalt not see evil any more.

Before
C H R I S T
cir. 630.

ᵇ ver. 5, 17.
Ezek. 48. 35.
Rev. 7. 15.
& 21. 3, 4.

thou art 1) *the daughter of Zion*, 2) *Israel*, 3) *the daughter of Jerusalem ; the daughter of Zion* by faith, *Israel* by hope, *Jerusalem* by charity." And this hidden teaching of that holy mystery is continued ; ¹ *The Lord*, God the Father, *hath taken away thy judgments ; He* God the Son, *hath cast out* (*cleared quite away*) *thine enemy ; the king of Israel, the Lord*, the Holy Ghost, *is in the midst of thee !* The promise is threefold, 1) *thou shalt not see evil any more ;* 2) *fear thou not ;* 3) *let not thine hands be slack.* The love of God is threefold. 1) *He will rejoice over thee with joy ;* 2) *He will rest in His love ;* 3) *He will joy over thee with singing.* Again the words in these four verses are so framed as to be *ful*-filled in the end. All in this life are but shadows of that fullness. First, whether the Church or the faithful soul, she is summoned by all her names, *daughter of Zion* (" the thirsty " athirst for God) *Israel* (" Prince with God ") *Jerusalem* (" City of Peace "). By all she is called to the fullest joy in God with every expression and every feeling. *Sing ;* it is the inarticulate, thrilling, trembling burst of joy ; *shout ;* again the inarticulate yet louder swell of joy, a trumpet-blast ; and then too, deep within, *be glad*, the calm even joy of the inward soul ; *exult*, the triumph of the soul which cannot contain itself for joy ; and this, *with the whole heart*, no corner of it not pervaded with joy. The ground of this is the complete removal of every evil, and the full Presence of God.

15. *The Lord hath taken away thy judgments ;* her own, because brought upon her by her sins. But when God takes away the chastisements in mercy, He removes and forgives the sin too. Else, to remove *the judgments* only, would be to abandon the sinner. *He hath cast out*, lit. *cleared quite away* ², as a man clears away all hindrances, all which stands in the way, so that there should be none whatever left—*thine enemy ;* the one enemy, from whom every hindrance to our salvation comes, as He saith, ³ *Now shall the prince of this world be cast out. The King of Israel, even the Lord*, Christ the Lord, *is in the midst of thee*, of Whom it is said, ⁴ *He that sitteth on the throne shall dwell among them*, and Who Himself saith, ⁵ *Lo I am with you always unto the end of the world.* ⁶ *Where two or three are gathered together in My Name, there am I*

in the midst of you. He Who had removed *from the midst of her* the proud, Who had left *in the midst of her* those with whom He dwelleth, shall Himself dwell *in the midst of her* in mercy, as He had before in judgment⁷. He cleanseth the soul for His indwelling, and so dwelleth in the mansion which He had prepared for Himself. *Thou shalt not see evil any more.* For even the remains of evil, while we are yet in the flesh, are overruled, and ⁸ *work together to good to those who love God.* They cannot separate between the soul and Christ. Rather, He is nearer to her in them. We are bidden to ⁹ *count it all joy when we fall into divers temptations*, for all sorrows are but medicine from a father's hand. " ¹⁰ And truly our way to eternal joy is to suffer here with Christ, and our door to enter into eternal life is gladly to die with Christ, that we may rise again from death and dwell with Him in everlasting life." So in the Revelation, it is first said that God should dwell with His people, and then that all pain shall cease. ¹¹ *Behold the tabernacle of God is with men, and He will dwell with them and be their God. And God shall wipe all tears from their eyes ; and there shall be no more death, neither sorrow nor crying, neither shall there be any more pain ; for the former things are passed away.* " ¹² In the inmost meaning of the words, he could not but bid her rejoice and be exceeding glad and rejoice with her whole heart, her sins being done away through Christ. For the holy and spiritual Zion, the Church, the multitude of believers, is justified in Christ Alone, and we are saved by Him and from Him, escaping the harms of our invisible enemies, and having in the midst of us the King and God of all, Who appeared in our likeness, the Word from God the Father, through Whom we see not evil, i. e. are freed from all who could do us evil. For He is the worker of our acceptableness, our peace, our wall, the bestower of incorruption, the dispenser of crowns, Who lighteneth the assaults of devils, Who giveth us to ¹³ *tread on serpents and scorpions and all the power of the enemy*—through Whom we are in good hope of immortality and life, adoption and glory, through Whom we shall not see evil any more."

¹ v. 15.
² Beside this place, the word is used of " the clearing of a house," Gen. xxiv. 31, Lev. xiv. 36 ; " a way," Is. xl. 3, lvii. 14, lxii. 10 ; Mal. iii. 1 ; " clearing ground," Ps. lxxx. 10.

³ S. John xii. 31.　　　⁴ Rev. vii. 15.
⁵ S. Matt. xxviii. 20.　　⁶ Ib. xviii. 20.
⁷ Verses 11, 12, 15, 5.　　⁸ Rom. viii. 28.
⁹ S. James i. 2.　¹⁰ Exhort. in Visit. of the sick.
¹¹ Rev. xxi. 3, 4.　¹² S. Cyril.　¹³ S. Luke x. 19.

Before
C H R I S T
cir. 630.

c Is. 35. 3, 4.
d Heb. 12. 12.
|| Or, faint.

16 In that day ᵉ it shall be said to Jerusalem, Fear t h o u not: *and to* Zion, ᵈ Let not thine hands be || slack.

17 The LORD thy God

ᵉ in the midst of thee *is* mighty; he will save, ᶠ he will rejoice over thee with joy; † he will rest in Ḥis love, he will joy over thee with singing.

Before
C H R I S T
cir. 630.

ᵉ ver. 15.
f Deut. 30. 9.
Isai. 62. 5.
& 65. 19.
Jer. 32. 41.
† Heb. *he will be
silent.*

---

16. *In that day it shall be said to Jerusalem, Fear thou not;* for ¹ *perfect love casteth out fear;* whence he saith, ² *Fear not, little flock; it is your Father's good pleasure to give you the kingdom.* Who then and what should the Church or the faithful soul fear, since *mightier is He that is in her, than he that is in the world?* And to Zion, Let not thine hands be *slack,* through faint-heartedness ³, but work with all thy might; be ready to do or bear anything; since Christ worketh with, in, by thee, and ⁴ *in due time we shall reap, if we faint not.*

17. *The Lord thy God in the midst of thee is mighty; He will save.* What *can* He then not do for thee, since He is Almighty? What *will* He not do for thee, since *He will save?* Whom then should we fear? ⁵ *If God be for us, who can be against us?* But then was He especially *in the midst of* us, when God ⁶ *the Word became flesh and dwelt among us; and we beheld His Glory, the Glory as of the Only-Begotten of the Father, full of grace and Truth.* Thenceforth He ever is in the midst of His own. He with the Father and the Holy Spirit ⁷ *come unto them and make Their abode with them,* so that they are *the temple of God. He will save,* as He saith, ⁸ *My Father is greater than all, and no man is able to pluck them out of My Father's hand. I and My Father are One.* Of the same time of the Christ, Isaiah saith almost in the same words; ⁹ *Strengthen ye the weak hands and confirm the feeble knees, Say to them that are of a feeble heart, Be strong, fear not, behold your God will come, He will come and save you;* and of the Holy Trinity, ¹⁰ *He will save us.*

He will rejoice over thee with joy. Love, joy, peace in man are shadows of that which is in God, by Whom they are created in man. Only in God they exist undivided, uncreated. Hence God speaks after the manner of men, of that which truly is in God. God joyeth "with an uncreated joy" over the works of His Hands or the objects of His Love, as man joyeth over the object of *his* love. So Isaiah saith ¹¹, *As the bridegroom rejoiceth over the bride, so shall thy God rejoice over thee.* As with uncreated love the Father resteth in good pleasure in His Well-beloved Son, so

¹² *God is well-pleased with the sacrifices of loving deeds,* and, ¹³ *the Lord delighteth in thee;* and, ¹⁴ *I will rejoice in Jerusalem and joy in My people;* and, ¹⁵ *the Lord will again rejoice over thee for good.* And so in a two-fold way God meeteth the longing of the heart of man. The soul, until it hath found God, is evermore seeking some love to fill it, and can find none, since the love of God Alone can content it. Then too it longeth to be loved, even as it loveth. God tells it, that every feeling and expression of human love may be found in Him, Whom if any love, he only ¹⁶ *loveth Him, because He first loved us.* Every inward and outward expression or token of love are heaped together, to express the love of Him Who broodeth and as it were yearneth *over* (it is twice repeated) His own whom He loveth. Then too He loveth thee as He biddeth thee to love Him; and since the love of man cannot be like the love of the Infinite God, He here pictures His own love in the words of man's love, to convey to his soul the oneness wherewith love unites her unto God. He here echoes in a manner the joy of the Church, to which He had called her ¹⁷, in words the self-same or meaning the same. We have *joy* here for *joy* there; *singing* or the uttered unutterable jubilee of the heart, which cannot utter in words its joy and love, and joys and loves the more in its inmost depths because it cannot utter it. A shadow of the unutterable, because Infinite Love of God, and this repeated thrice; as being the eternal love of the Ever-blessed Trinity. This love and joy the Prophet speaks of, as an exuberant joy, one which boundeth within the inmost self, and again is wholly *silent in His love,* as the deepest, tenderest, most yearning love broods over the object of its love, yet is held still in silence by the very depth of its love; and then, again, breaks forth in outward motion, and leaps for joy, and uttereth what it cannot form in words; for truly the love of God in its unspeakable love and joy is past belief, past utterance, past thought. " ¹⁸ Truly that joy wherewith *He will be silent in His love,* that exultation wherewith *He will joy over thee with singing,* ¹⁹ *Eye hath not seen nor*

---

¹ S. John iv. 18.
³ See Heb. xii. 12.
⁵ Rom. viii. 31.
⁷ Ib. xiv. 23.
⁹ Is. xxxv. 3, 4.

² S. Luke xii. 32.
⁴ Gal. vi. 9.
⁶ S. John i. 14.
⁸ Ib. x. 29, 30.
¹⁰ Ib. xxxiii. 22.

¹¹ Ib. lxii. 5.
¹³ Is. lxii. 4.
¹⁵ Deut. xxx. 9.
¹⁷ Verse 14.
¹⁸ Rup.

¹² Heb. xiii. 16.
¹⁴ Ib. lxv. 19.
¹⁶ 1 S. John iv. 19.

¹⁹ 1 Cor. ii. 9.

Before
CHRIST
cir. 630.

18 I will gather *them
that* ᵍ *are* sorrowful for the
solemn assembly, *who are*
of thee, *to whom* † the reproach of it *was* a burden.

19 Behold, at that time
I will undo all that afflict

ᵍ Lam. 2. 6.

† Heb. *the bur-
den upon it
was reproach.*

thee: and I will save her
that ʰ halteth, and gather
her that was driven out; ʰ Ezek. 34. 16.
and † I will get them praise
and fame in every land
† where they have b e e n
put to shame.

Before
CHRIST
cir. 630.

ʰ Ezek. 34. 16.

Mic. 4. 6, 7.
† Heb. *I will set
them for a
praise.*

† Heb. *of their
shame.*

---

ear heard, *neither hath it entered into the heart of
man.*" The Hebrew word¹ also contains the
meaning, "He in His love shall make no
mention of past sins², He shall not bring
them up against thee, shall not upbraid thee,
yea, shall not remember them." It also may
express the still, unvarying love of the Unchangeable God. And again how the very
silence of God, when He seemeth not to hear,
as He did not seem to hear S. Paul, is a very
fruit of His love. Yet that entire forgiveness
of sins, and that seeming absence are but
ways of shewing His love. Hence God
speaks of His very love itself, *He will be silent
in His love,* as, before and after, *He will rejoice,
He will joy over thee.*

18–21. In these verses still continuing the
number "three," the prophecy closes with
the final reversal of all which, in this imperfect state of things, seems turned upside
down, when those who now mourn shall be
comforted, they who now bear reproach and
shame shall have glory, and those who now
afflict the people of God shall be undone.

18. *I will gather them that are sorrowful³
for⁴ the solemn assembly,* in which they were
to *rejoice⁵* before God and which in their
captivity God made to cease⁶. *They were of
thee,* the true Israel who were⁷ *grieved for the
affliction of Joseph ; to whom the reproach of it
was a burden* [rather⁸, *on whom reproach was
laid*]: for this *reproach of Christ is greater
riches than the treasures of Egypt,* and such
shall inherit the blessing, ⁹*Blessed are ye,
when men shall hate you, and when they shall*

*separate you from their company, and shall re-
proach you and cast out your name as evil, for
the Son of Man's sake ; rejoice ye in that day,
and leap for joy ; for, behold your reward is
great in heaven.*

19. *Behold, at that time I will undo* [lit. *I
deal with*¹³]. While God punisheth not, He
seemeth to sit still¹¹, be silent¹², asleep¹³.
Then He shall act, He shall *deal* according
to their deserts with *all*, evil men or devils,
that afflict thee, His Church. The prophecy
looked for a larger fulfillment than the destruction of Jerusalem, since the Romans
who, in God's Hands, avenged the blood of
His Saints, themselves were among those
who *afflicted her. And will save her,* the flock
or sheep *that halteth*¹⁴, "¹⁵imperfect in virtue
and with trembling faith," *and gather,* like a
good and tender shepherd¹⁶, *her that was driven
out ;* scattered and dispersed through persecutions. All infirmities within shall be
healed ; all troubles without, removed.

And I will get them praise and fame [lit. *I
will make them a praise and a name*] *in every
land where they have been put to shame*¹⁷.
Throughout the whole world have they been
¹⁸*the offscouring of all things ;* throughout the
whole world should their praise be, as it is
said, ¹⁹*Thou shalt make them princes in all lands.*
One of themselves saith ²⁰, *Ye see your calling,
brethren, how that not many wise men after the
flesh, not many mighty, not many noble, are called.
But God hath chosen the foolish things of the world
to confound the wise ; and God hath chosen the weak
things of the world to confound the things which are*

---

¹ יָחֲרִישׁ.
² Jer. xxxi. 34, xxxiii. 8, Mic. vii. 18.
³ This is the common meaning of the root יָגָה,
though not so frequent in the verb as in nouns, and
5 out of the 8 cases are in Lam. i. 4 (where the same
form נוּגוֹת, Nif. occurs), 12. iii. 32, 33, the remaining being, this place, Job xix. 2, Is. li. 23. The
other sense "removed" (even if הֵנָה 2 Sam. xx. 13,
implies a פָּי in this sense) comes to the same general meaning, though with less force. The Arab
נ'ג, iv. is wrongly applied (e. g. Ges. Thes. p. 564) as
"procul a se removit." It is simply "abstained
from it," "refused one's self."
⁴ מִן is used of the ultimate cause. (See Ges.
Thes. s. v. 2) b. p. 802.
⁵ Lev. xxiii. 40. Deut. xii. 12, 18. xvi. 11, xxvii. 7.
⁶ Lam. i. 4. ii. 6.　　　　⁷ Amos vi. 6.
⁸ As in Ps. xv. 3, וְחֶרְפָּה לֹא נָשָׂא עַל קְרֹבוֹ, the
construction being like מִסְתָּר פָּנִים מִמֶּנּוּ, Is.
liii. 3.　　　　⁹ S. Luke vi. 22, 23.

¹⁰ as Ru. ii. 19. in a good sense ; Ez. vii. 27. xvii. 17,
xxiii. 25, in a bad; אוֹתוּ, אוֹתָם אוֹתְךָ, being probably for אַתָּם &c.　　　　¹¹ Is. xviii. 4.
¹² Hab. i. 13.　　　　¹³ Ps. xliv. 23.
¹⁴ See Micah iv. 6, 7.　　　¹⁵ Dion.
¹⁶ See Is. xl. 11.
¹⁷ The article is inserted in a way very unusual
and probably emphatic. Without it the words
would mean, as in the E. V. "in every land of their
shame." But it makes the meaning of the first
words, בְּכָל הָאָרֶץ, complete in itself; and they
mean, *in the whole earth.* בְּשֶׁתָּם then is probably
in apposition, *in the whole earth, their shame,* i. e. the
scene of *their shame ;* comp. the construction
הָאָרוֹן הַבְּרִית Jos. iii. 14. 17 and those Deut. viii.
15. 1 Kgs iv. 13 ; and "Daniel the Prophet" p. 476.
In the next verse, הָאָרֶץ is undoubtedly "the
earth."　　　¹⁸ 1 Cor. iv. 13.
¹⁹ Ps. xlv. 16.　　　²⁰ 1 Cor. i. 26–28.

| Before CHRIST cir. 630. | 20 At that time [1] will I bring you *again*, even in the time that I gather you: for I will make you a name | and a praise among all people of the earth, when I turn back your captivity before your eyes, saith the LORD. | Before CHRIST cir. 630. |

Isai. 11. 12.
& 27. 12.
& 56. 8.
Ezek. 28. 25.
& 34. 13. & 37. 21. Amos 9. 14.

mighty; and base things of this world, and things which are despised, hath God chosen, yea, and things which are not, to bring to nought things that are. "[1] These He maketh a praise and a name there, where they were without name and dispraised, confounding by them and bringing to nought those wise and strong and mighty, in whose sight they were contemptible."

20. *At that time will I bring you in* i. e. into the one fold, the one Church, the one *House-hold of God, even in the time that I gather you.* "That time" is the whole time of the Gospel; the one *day of salvation,* in which all who shall ever be gathered, shall be brought into the new Jerusalem. These words were fulfilled, when, at our Lord's first Coming, the remnant, the true Israel, those *ordained to eternal life* were brought in. It shall be fulfilled again, when "the fullness of the Gentiles shall be *come in,* and so all Israel shall be saved[2]." It shall most perfectly be fulfilled at the end, when there shall be no going out of those once *brought in,* and those who have gathered others into the Church, shall be a *name and a praise among all people of the earth,* those whom God hath [3] *redeemed out of every tribe and tongue and people and nation,* shining like stars for ever and ever.

When I turn back your captivity: "[1] that conversion, then begun, now perfected, when the dead shall rise and they shall be placed on the right hand, soon to receive the kingdom prepared for them from the foundation of the world. O mighty spectacle of the reversed captivity of those once captives; mighty wonder at their present blessedness, as they review the misery of their past captivity!" *Before your eyes,* so that we shall see what we now believe and hope for, the end of all our sufferings, chastisements, losses, achings of the heart, the fullness of our Redemption. That which our eyes have looked for, *our eyes shall behold and not another,* the everliving God as HE IS, face to Face; *saith the Lord,* Who is the Truth Itself, all Whose words will be fulfilled. [4] *Heaven and earth shall pass away, but My Words shall not pass away,* saith He Who is *God blessed for ever.* And so the Prophet closes in the thought of Him, Whose Name is I AM, the Unchangeable, the everlasting Rest and Centre of those who, having been once captives and halting and scattered among the vanities of the world, turn to Him, to Whom be glory and thanksgiving for ever and ever. Amen.

[1] Rup.   [2] Rom. xi. 25, 26.   [3] Rev. v. 9.   [4] S. Mark xiii. 31.

THE MOABITE STONE. See pp. 263, 264.

I MESHA, son of Chemosh-gad, king of Moab the Dibonite. My father reigned over Moab thirty years, and I reigned after my father; and I made this shrine to Chemosh in Kor-choh, a shr[ine of deli]verance, because he saved me from all [[1]] he let me look upon all who hate me, Om[r]i king of Israel; and he afflicted Moab many days, for Chemosh was wroth with his la[n]d; and his son succeeded him, and he too said, I will afflict Moab. In my days said [*Chemosh* [2]], and I will look upon him and upon his house, and Israel perisheth with an everlasting destruction. And Omri took possession of the land of Moh-deba and there dwelt in it [[2] Israel in *his days and in*] the days of his son, forty years; [*and looked*] on it Chemosh in my days, and I built Baal-Meon and I made in it the ditch [?] and I [built] Kiriathan. And the men of Gad dwelt in the land of [Atar]oth from time immemorial, and the kin[g of I]srael

built for him A[ta]roth and I warred against the city; and I took it and I slew all the mi[ghty men] of the city, for the well-pleas-ing of Chemosh and Moab; and I took captive thence the [   ] and [dr]agged it [or them] before Chemosh in Kiriath and I made to dwell in it the men of Siran, and the men of Macharath. And Chemosh said to me, Go take Nebo against Israel [and I] went by night and I fought against it from the break of the morning to midday and I took it, and I slew the whole of it, seven thous-and; [   ] the honorable women [and mai]dens, for to Ashtar Chemosh [I] dedicated [them] and I took thence [ves]sels of Yhvh and I dragged them before Chemosh. And the king of Israel bui[l]t Yahats, and dwelt in it when he warred with me; and Chemosh drove him from [my] [f]ace and] I took of Moab 200 men, all its chiefs and I took them against Yahats and took it to add to

[1] The stone has הַשְׁלְכֵן, whose meaning is conjectural. Nöldeke conjectures הַמְלָכֵ׃ "the kings."

[2] Schlottman's conjecture. Likely conjectures I have put in [ ]; mere guess-work I have omitted.

Dibon. I built Korchoh the wall of the forest, and the wall of Ophel[1] and I built the gates thereof, and I built the towers thereof, and I built the king's house, and I made prisons for the gui[lt]y in the mi[dst] of the city; and there was no cistern within the city, in Korchoh, and I said to all the people, make yourselves every man a cistern in his house, and I cut the cutting for Korchoh by m[en] of Israel. I built [A]roer and I made the high road[2] at the Arnon. I built

Beth-Bamoth, for it was destroyed. I built Bezer, for [it was] forsa[ken] me[n] of Dibon   fifty; for all Dibon was obedience, and I reig[ned] from Bikran which I added to the land and I buil[t]——and Beth Diblathan and Beth-Baal-Meon and I took there the — of the land and Horonan   dwelt in it — — — — [and] Che-mosh said to me, Go fight against Horonan and I   it—Chemosh in my days and on   [I] made

[1] חומת העפל occurs of Jerusalem, Neh. iii. 27.

[2] המסלת lit. " the way cast up " cannot possibly be a way over the river.

HAGGAI[a] is the eldest of the three-fold band, to whom, after the Captivity, the word of God came, and by whom He consecrated the beginnings of this new condition of the chosen people. He gave them these prophets, connecting their spiritual state after their return with that before the Captivity, not leaving them wholly desolate, nor Himself without witness. He withdrew them about 100 years after, but some 420 years before Christ came, leaving His people to long the more for Him, of Whom all the prophets spake. Haggai himself seems to have almost finished his earthly course, before he was called to be a prophet; and in four months his office was closed. He speaks as one who had seen the first house in its glory[b], and so was probably among the very aged men, who were the links between the first and the last, and who laid the foundation of the house in tears[c]. After the first two months[d] of his office, Zechariah, in early youth, was raised up to carry on his message; yet after one brief prophecy was again silent, until the aged prophet had ended the words which God gave him. Yet in this brief

space he first stirred up the people in one month to rebuild the temple[e], prophesied of its glory through the presence of Christ[f], yet taught that the presence of what was holy sanctified not the unholy[g], and closes in Him Who, when Heaven and earth shall be shaken, shall abide, and they whom God hath chosen in Him[h].

It has been the wont of critics, in whose eyes the Prophets were but poets[i], to speak of the style of Haggai as "tame, destitute of life and power," shewing "[j] a marked decline in" what they call "prophetic inspiration." The style of the sacred writers is, of course, conformed to their mission. Prophetic descriptions of the future are but incidental to the mission of Haggai. Preachers do not speak in poetry, but set before the people their faults or their duties in vivid earnest language. Haggai sets before the people vividly their negligence and its consequences; he arrests their attention by his concise questions; at one time retorting their excuses[k]; at another asking them abruptly, in God's name, to say why their troubles came[l]. Or he puts a matter of the law to

---

[a] His name is explained by S. Jerome "festive." But although there are Prop. Names with *ai* which are Adjectives, as שֵׁשַׁי בַּרְזִלַּי (Ezr. ix. 40. תַּלְמַי and שֵׁשַׁי are foreign names) יִשְׁשַׁי, the termination *ai* is more frequently an abbreviation of the Name of God, which enters so largely into Hebrew names, as indeed we have חֲנַנְיָה 1 Chr. vi 15. And this occurs not only, when the first part of the word is a verb, אָחִי יַעֲשִׂי יַעְנִי יַחְמִי יְהֻדִי אֲחַסְבַּי אַתְּרַי יְרִיבַי יִשְׁמְרַי, (as Köhler observes p. 2.) but when it is a noun, as שֻׁלַּמִי אֲמִתַּי הֻדַּי מַתְּנַי, צֶלְתַּי (coll. מַתָּנָיָה and שִׁמְשַׁי מַתַּנְיָהוּ Ezr. iv.

[a] פְּעֻלְתַי (1 Chr. xxvi. 5.) perhaps שַׁבְּתַי שִׁטְרַי or again אֵתַי.   [b] ii. 3.   [c] Ezr. iii. 12.

[d] The prophecies of Haggai and Zechariah are thus intertwined. Haggai prophesies in the 6th and 7th months of the 2d year of Darius Hystaspis, B. C. 520.) Hagg. i. 1. ii. 1) Zechariah first prophesies in the 8th month (Zech. i. 1.). Haggai resumes at the close of the 9th and there ends (ii. 10, 20). On the same day in the 11th month, the series of visions were given to Zechariah. (Zech. i. 7.)
[e] c. i.   [f] ii. 1–9.   [g] Ib. 12.   [h] Ib. 20–23.
[i] Eichhorn, De Wette, Bertholdt, Gesenius (Gesh. d. Hebr. Spr. p. 26.), Herzfeldt, (Gesch. d. Volkes Israel ii. 21) Stähelin.
[j] Dr. Davidson iii. 314.   [k] i. 4.   [l] i. 9.

the priests, that they may draw the inference, before he does it himself [m]. Or he asks them, what human hope had they [n], before he tells them of the Divine. Or he asks them (what was in their heart), "Is not this house poor [o]?" before he tells them of the glory in store for it. At one time he uses heaped and condensed antitheses [p], to set before them one thought; at another he enumerates, one by one, how the visitation of God fell upon all they had [q], so that there seemed to be no end to it. At another, he uses a conciseness, like S. John Baptist's cry, *Repent ye, for the kingdom of heaven is at hand,* in his repeated [r] *Set your heart to your ways;* and then, with the same idiom, *set your heart* [s] viz. to God's ways, what He had done on disobedience, what He would do on obedience. He bids them work for God, and then he expresses the acceptableness of that work to God, in the three words, [t] *And-I-will-take-pleasure in-it and-will-be-glorified.* When they set themselves to obey, he encouraged them in the four words, [u] *I with-you saith the-Lord.* This conciseness must have been still more impressive in his words, as delivered [v]. We use many words, because our words are weak. Many of us can remember how the House of Lords was hushed, so hear the few low, but sententious words of the aged general and statesman. But conceive the suggestive eloquence of those words, as a whole sermon, *Set your-heart on-your-ways.*

Of distant prophecies there are but two [w], so that the portion to be compared with the former prophets consists but of at most 7 verses. In these the language used is of the utmost simplicity. Haggai had but one message as to the future to convey, and he enforced it by the repeated use of the same word [x], that temporal things should be shaken, the eternal should remain, as S. Paul sums it up [y]. He, the long-longed for, the chosen of God, the signet on His Hand, should come; God would fill that house, so poor in their eyes, with glory, and there would He give peace. Haggai had an all-containing but very simple message to give from God. Any ornament of diction would but have impaired and obscured its meaning. The two or three slight idioms, noticed by one after another, are, though slight, forcible [z].

The office of Haggai was mainly to bring about one definite end, which God, Who raised him up and inspired him, accomplished by him. It is in the light of this great accomplishment of the work entrusted to him at the verge of man's earthly course, that his power and energy are to be estimated. The words which are preserved in his book are doubtless (as indeed was the case as to most of the prophets) the representatives and embodiment of many like words, by which, during his short office, he roused the people from their dejection indifference and irreligious apathy, to the restoration of the public worship of God in the essentials of the preparatory dispensation.

Great lukewarmness had been shewn in the return. The few looked mournfully to the religious centre of Israel, the ruined temple, the cessation of the daily sacrifice, and, like Daniel, [a] *confessed their sin and the sin of* their *people Israel, and presented* their *supplication before the Lord* their *God for the holy mountain of* their *God.* The most part appear, as now, to have been taken up with their material prosperity, and, at best, to have become inured to the cessation of their symbolical worship, connected, as it was, with the declaration of the forgiveness of their sins. Then too, God connected His declaration of pardon with certain outward acts: *they* became indifferent to the cessation of those acts. For few returned. The indifference was even remarkable among those, most connected with the altar. Of the 24 [b] orders of priests, ⅙ only, 4 orders [c] returned; of the Levites only 74 individuals [d]; while of those assigned to help them, the Nethinim and the children of Solomon's servants, there were 392 [e]. This coldness continued at the return of Ezra. The edict of Artaxerxes [f], as suggested by Ezra, was more pious than those appointed to the service of God. In the first instance no Levite answered to the invitation [g]; on the special urgency and message of Ezra, [h] *by the good hand of God upon us they brought us a man of understanding,* of the sons of Levi; some 3 or 4 chief Levites; their sons and brethren; in all, 38; but of the Nethinim, nearly six times as many, 220 [i]. Those who thought more of temporal prosperity than of their high spiritual nobility and destination, had flourished doubtless in that exile as they have in their present homelessness, as [j] *wanderers among the nations.* Haman calculated apparently on being able to *pay* out of their spoils *ten thousand talents of silver* [k], some £300,000,000, two-thirds of

[m] ii. 12. 13. [n] ii. 19. [o] Ib. 3. [p] i. 6. [q] i. 11.
[r] i. 5-7. [s] ii. 15-18. [t] i. 8. [u] i. 13.
[v] See on ii. 5, 9. [w] ii. 6-9, 21-23.
[x] מרעיש, ii. 6, 22, והרעשתי ii. 7.
[y] Heb. xii. 26.
[z] See on ii. 3, 5, 17. The junction of מעט אחת ii. 6, is a mistake of the critics.
[a] Dan. ix. 20. [b] 1 Chr. xxiv. 3-19.
[c] Ezr. ii. 36-39. [d] Ib. 40. [e] Ib. 58.
[f] Ib. vii. 13-14. [g] Ib. viii. 15. [h] Ib. 18, 19.
[i] Ib. 20. [j] See on Hos. ix. 17. vol. i. p. 97, 98.

[k] Esther iii. 9. Ahasuerus apparently, in acceding to Haman's proposal, made over to him the lives and property of the Jews. *The silver is given unto thee, the people also, to do with them as it seemeth good to thee.* (Ib. 11.) The Jews' property, was confiscated with their lives. On the contrary, it was noticed, that the Jews, when permitted to defend their lives, did *not lay their hands on the prey,* which, by the king's decree, was granted to them, with authority to take the lives of those who *should* assault them. Esth. viii. 11. ix. 10, 15, 16.

the annual revenue of the Persian Empire[1] *into the king's treasuries.*

The numbers who had returned with Zerubbabel had been (as had been foretold of all restorations) *a remnant* only. There were 42,360 free men, with 7337 male or female slaves[m]. The whole population which returned was not above 212,000, freemen and women and children. The proportion of slaves is about $\frac{1}{12}$, since in their case adults of both sexes were counted. The enumeration is minute, giving the number of their horses, mules, camels, asses[n]. The chief of the fathers however were not poor, since (though unspeakably short of the wealth, won by David and consecrated to the future temple) they [o] *offered freely for the house of God, to set it up in its place,* a sum about £117,100[p] of our money. They had, beside, a grant from Cyrus, which he intended to cover the expenses of the building, the height and breadth whereof were determined by royal edict[q].

The monarch, however, of an Eastern empire had, in proportion to its size, little power over his subordinates or the governors of the provinces, except by their recall or execution, when their oppressions or peculations notably exceeded bounds. The returned colony, from the first, were in fear of the nations, *the peoples of those countries*[r], their old enemies probably; and the first service, *the altar to offer burnt-offerings thereon,* was probably a service of fear rather than of love, as it is said, [r] *they set up the altar upon its bases; for it was in fear upon them from the peoples of the lands, and they offered burnt-offerings thereon unto the Lord.* They hoped apparently to win the favor of God, *that* He might, as of old, protect them against their enemies. However, the work was carried on [s] *according to the grant that they had of Cyrus king of Persia;* and the foundations of the temple were laid amidst mixed joy at the carrying on of the work thus far, and sorrow at its poverty, compared to the first temple[t]. The hostility of the Samaritans discouraged them. Mixed as the religion of the Samaritans was, —its better element being the corrupt religion of the ten tribes, its worse the idolatries of the various nations, brought thither in the reign of Esarhaddon,—the returned Jews could not accept their offer to join in their worship, without the certainty of admitting, with them, the idolatries, for which they had been punished so severely. For

the Samaritans pleaded the identity of the two religions. [u] *Let us build with you, for we serve your God, as ye do; and we do sacrifice unto Him since the days of Esarhaddon which brought us up hither.* But in fact this mixed worship, in which [v] *they feared the Lord and served their own gods,* came to this, that [w] *they feared not the Lord, neither did they after the law and commandment which the Lord commanded the children of Jacob.* For God claims the undivided allegiance of His creatures; these [x] *feared the Lord and served their graven images, both their children and their children's children: as did their fathers, so do they to this day.* But this worship included some of the most cruel abominations of heathendom, the sacrifice of their children to their gods[y].

The Samaritans, thus rejected, first themselves harassed the Jews in building, apparently by petty violence, as they did afterward in the rebuilding of the walls by Nehemiah. [z] *The people of the land weakened the hands of the people of Judah, and wore them out*[a] *in building.* This failing, they [b] *hired counsellors* (doubtless at the Persian court), *to frustrate their purpose, all the days of Cyrus king of Persia, until the reign of Darius king of Persia.* The object of the intrigues was probably to intercept the supplies, which Cyrus had engaged to bestow, which could readily be effected in an Eastern Court without any change of purpose or any cognizance of Cyrus.

In the next reign of Ahashverosh (i. e. Khshwershe, a title of honor of Cambyses) [c] they wrote accusations against the Jews, seemingly without any further effect, since none is mentioned. Perhaps Cambyses, in his expedition to Egypt, knew more of the Jews, than the Samaritans thought, or he may have shrunk from changing his father's decree, contrary to the fundamental principles of Persism, not to alter any decree, which the sovereign (acting, as he was assumed to do, under the influence of Ormuzd) had written[a]. Pseudo-Smerdis (who doubtless took the title of honor, Artachshatr) may, as an impostor, have well been ignorant of Cyrus' decree, to which no allusion is made[b]. From him the Samaritans, through Rehum the chancellor, obtained a decree prohibiting, until further notice, the rebuilding of *the city.* The accusers had overreached themselves; for the ground of their accusation was, the former rebellions of the city[c]; the prohibition accordingly extended only to the *city*[d], not to the temple. However, hav-

---

[1] 14,560 silver talents. Herod. iii. 95.

[m] Ezra ii. 64, 65, Neh. vii. 66, 67. In the time of Augustus, it was no uncommon thing for a person to have 200 slaves (Hor. Sat. i. 9. 11) it is said that very many Romans possessed 10000 or 20000 slaves. Athenæus vi. p. 272.

[n] 736 horses, 245 mules, 435 camels, 6720 asses. Ezra ii. 66, 67, Neh. vii. 68, 69.

[o] Ezr. ii. 68, 69.

[p] The golden daric being estimated at £1 2s., the

61,000 darics would be £67,100; the "maneh" being 100 shekels, and the shekel about 2s., the 5000 maneh of silver would be about £50,000.

[q] Ezr. iv. 3. [r] Ib. iii. 3. [s] Ezr. iii. 7. [t] Ib. 11–13.
[u] Ib. iv. 2.   [v] 2 Kgs xvii. 33.   [w] Ib. 34.

[x] Ib. 41.   [y] Ib. 31.   [z] בְּלָה Cheth.

[a] Ezr. iv. 4.   [b] Ib. 5.   [c] Ib. 6.
[a] See Daniel the prophet pp. 445–447.
[b] Ezr. iv. 7, sqq.   [c] Ib. 12, 13, 15, 16.   [d] Ib. 19. 21.

ing obtained the decree, they were not scru-
pulous about its application, and *made the
Jews to cease* [e] *by arm and power*, the governor
of the Jews being apparently unable, and the
governor of the cis-Euphratensian provinces
being unwilling, to help. As this, however,
was, in fact, a perversion of the decree, the
Jews were left free to build, and in the second
year of Darius Hystaspis, [f] *Haggai, and then
Zechariah, prophesied in the name of the God of
Israel* to Zerubbabel, the native Governor,
and Joshua the high-priest, and *the Jews in
Judah and Jerusalem; and they began to build
the house of God in Jerusalem.* Force was no
longer used. Those engaged in building appealed to the edict of Cyrus; the edict was
found at Ecbatana [g], and the supplies which
Cyrus had promised, were again ordered.
The difficulty was at the commencement.
The people had been cowed perhaps at first
by the violence of Rehum and his companions; but they had acquiesced readily in the
illegal prohibition, and had [h] *run each to his
own house*, some of them to their [i] *ceiled houses.*
All, employers or employed, were busy on
their husbandry. But nothing flourished.
The laborers' wages disappeared, as soon as
gained [j]. East and West wind alike brought
disease to their corn; both, as threatened
upon disobedience in the law [k]. The East
wind scorched and dried it up [l]; the warm
West wind turned the ears yellow [m] and barren; the hail smote the vines, so that when
the unfilled and mutilated clusters were
pressed out, two-fifths only of the hoped-
for produce was yielded; of the corn, only
one half [n].

In the midst of this, God raised up an
earnest preacher of repentance. Haggai was
taught, not to promise anything at the first,
but to set before them, what they had been
doing, what was its result. [o] He sets it before them in detail; tells them that God had
so ordered it for their neglect of His service,
and bids them amend. He bids them quit
their wonted ways; *go up into the mountain;
bring wood; build the house.* Conceive in
Christian England, after some potato-disease,
or foot-and-mouth-disease (in Scripture language "*a murrain among the cattle*"), a
preacher arising and bidding them, *consider
your ways*, and as the remedy, not to look to
any human means, but to do something,
which should please Almighty God; and not
preaching only but effecting what he

preached. Yet such was Haggai. He stood
among his people, his existence a witness of
the truth of what he said; himself one, who
had lived among the outward splendors of
the former temple; a contemporary of those,
who said [p] *the temple of the Lord, the temple of
the Lord, the temple of the Lord are these;* who
had held it to be impossible that Judah
should be carried captive; who had prophesied the restoration of the vessels of God [q],
which had been carried away, not, as God
foretold, after the captivity, but as an earnest
that the fuller captivity should not be [r]; yet
who had himself, according to the prophecies
of the prophets of those days, been carried
into captivity, and was now a part of that
restoration which God had promised. He
stood among them "in gray-haired might,"
bade them do, what he bade them, in the
name of God, to do; and they did it. When
they had set about the work, he assured
them of the presence of God with them [s]. A
month later, when they were seemingly discouraged at its poorness, he promised them
in God's name, that its glory should be
greater than that of Solomon's [t]. Three
days after, in contrast with the visitations
up to that time, while there was as yet
no token of any change, he promised them
in the name of God, [u] *From this day will I
bless you.*

He himself apparently saw only the commencement of the work; for his prophecies
lay within the second year of Darius and the
temple was not completed till the sixth [v].
Even the favorable rescript of Darius must
have arrived after his last prophecy, since
it was elicited by the enquiry of the governor, consequent upon the commenced rebuilding [w], three months only before his
office closed [x].

While this restoration of the public worship of God in its intregrity was his main
office, yet he also taught by parable [y] that
the presence of what was outwardly holy did
not, in itself, hallow those, among whom it
was; but was itself unhallowed by inward
unholiness.

Standing too amid the small handful of
returned exiles, not, altogether, more than
the inhabitants of Sheffield, he foretold, in
simple all-comprehending words, that central
gift of the Gospel, [z] *In this place will I give
peace, saith the Lord.* So had David, the sons
of Korah, Micah, Isaiah, Ezekiel prophe-

---

[e] Ezra iv. 23. [f] Ib. v. 1, 2.
[g] Ib. vi. 2. [h] Hagg. i. 9. [i] Ib. 4.
[j] Ib. 6. [k] Deut. xxviii. 22.
[l] שַׁדְפוֹן comp. שְׁדִיפוֹת קָדִים Gen. xli. 6, 23, 27.

[m] יֵרָק וֹן Forskäl (in Niebuhr, Beschreibung v.
Arabien, Pref. p. xlv.) took down from the mouth
of "Muri, a Jew of Mecca, that, in the month
Marchesvan, a warm wind sometimes blew, which
turned the ears yellow and they yielded no grain;

it was an unsteady wind, but spoils all it touches."
" M. Forskäl remarks that the fields, near the canal
of Alexandria. are sown in October and reaped in
Feb." Id. In Arabic the disease is called ירקאן

Ges. Thes.   [n] Hagg. ii. 16.
[o] Ib. 5-11.   [p] Jer. vii. 4.
[q] Ib. xxvii. 16, xxviii. 3. [r] Ib. xxviii. 2.
[s] Hagg. i. 13. [t] Ib. ii. 3-9. [u] ii. 19.
[v] Ezr. vi. 15. [w] Ib. v. 3. sqq.
[x] Hagg. i. 15. ii. 10, 20. [y] ii. 10-15. [z] ii. 9.

sied[a]; but the peace was to come, not then, but in the days of the Messiah. Other times had come, in which the false prophets had said[b], *Peace, peace, when there was no peace;* when God had taken away His peace from [c]*this people.* And now, when the chastisements were fulfilled, when the land lay desolate, when every house of Jerusalem lay burned with fire[d], and the "blackness of ashes" alone "marked where they stood;" when the walls were broken down so that, even when leave was given to rebuild them, it seemed to their enemies a vain labor to [e]*revive the stones out of the heaps of rubbish which were burned;* when [f]*the place of their fathers' sepulchres lay waste, and the gates thereof were consumed with fire;* when, for their sakes, Zion was [g]*ploughed as a field* and *Jerusalem was become heaps*—let any one picture to himself the silver-haired prophet standing, at first, alone, rebuking the people, first through their governor and the high-priest, then the collected multitude, in words, forceful from their simplicity, and obeyed! And then let them think whether anything of human or even Divine eloquence was lacking, when the words flew straight like arrows to the heart, and roused the people to do at once, amid every obstacle, amid every downheartedness or outward poverty, that for which God sent them. The outward ornament of words would have been misplaced, when the object was to bid a downhearted people, in the Name of God, to do a definite work. Haggai sets before his people cause and effect; that they denied to God what was

His, and that God denied to them what was His to give or to withhold. His sermon was, in His words Whom he foretold; *Seek ye first the kingdom of God and His righteousness, and all these things shall be added unto you.* He spake in the name of God, and was obeyed.

"[h] The Holy Ghost, Who spake by the mouth of the prophets, willed that he by a foreboding name should be called Haggai, i. e. 'festive,' according to the subject whereof He should speak by his mouth. Yet was there not another festiveness in the prophet's heart, than the joy which he had or could have with the people, from the rebuilding of that temple made with hands, again to be defiled and burned with fire irrecoverably? Be it that the rebuilding of that temple, which he saw before him, was a matter of great festive joy; yet not in or for itself, but for Him, the festive joy of saints and angels and men, Christ; because when the temple should be rebuilt, the walls also of the city should be rebuilt and the city again inhabited and the people be united in one, of whom Christ should be born, fulfilling the truth of the promise made to Abraham and David and confirmed by an oath. So then we, by aid of the Holy Spirit, so enter upon what Haggai here speaketh, as not doubting that he altogether aimeth at Christ. And so may we in some sort be called or be Haggais, i. e. 'festive,' by contemplating that same, which because he should contemplate, he was, by a Divine foreboding, called Haggai.".

[a] Ps. lxxii. 3–7, lxxxv. 8, 10. Mic. v. 5. Is. ix. 6, 7. xxvi. 12. xxxii. 17. lii. 7. liii. 5. liv. 10, 13. lvii. 19. lx. 17. lxvi. 12. Ezek. xxxiv. 25. xxxvii. 26.

[b] Jer. vi. 14. viii. 11. xiv. 13.
[c] Ib. xvi. 5.   [d] 2 Chr. xxxvi. 19.
[e] Neh. iv. 2,   [f] Ib. ii. 3.   [g] Mic. iii. 12.   [h] Rup.

HAGGAI.

CHAPTER I.

1 *Haggai reproveth the people for neglecting the building of the house.* 7 *He inciteth them to the building.* 12 *He promiseth God's assistance to them being forward.*

ᵃ Ezra 4. 24.
& 5. 1.
Zech. 1. 1.

IN ᵃ the second year of Darius the king, in the

sixth month, in the first day of the month, came the word of the LORD † by Haggai the prophet unto ᵇ Zerubbabel the son of Shealtiel, ‖ governor of Judah, and to ᶜ Joshua the son of ᵈ Josedech, the high priest, saying,

† Heb. *by the hand of Haggai.*
ᵇ 1 Chron. 3. 17, 19.
Ezra 3. 2.
Matt. 1. 12.
Luke 3. 27.
‖ Or, *captain.*
ᶜ Ezra. 3. 2.
& 5. 2.
ᵈ 1 Chr. 6. 15.

CHAP. I. 1. *In the second year of Darius,* i. e. Hystaspis. The very first word of prophecy after the Captivity betokens that they were restored, not yet as before, yet so, as to be hereafter, more than before. The earthly type, by God's appointment, was fading away, that the Heavenly truth might dawn. The earthly king was withdrawn, to make way for the Heavenly. God had said of Jeconiah, [1] *No man of his seed shall prosper, sitting upon the throne of David, and ruling any more in Israel:* and so now prophecy begins to be dated by the years of a foreign earthly ruler, as in the Baptism of the Lord Himself[2]. Yet God gives back in mercy more than He withdraws in chastisement. The earthly rule is suspended, that men might look out more longingly for the Heavenly.

In the sixth month. They counted by their own months, beginning with Nisan, the first of the ecclesiastical year, (which was still used for holy purposes and in sacred history) although, having no more any kings, they dated their years by those of the empire, to which they were subject[3]. In the sixth month, part of our July and August, their harvest was past, and the dearth, which they doubtless ascribed (as we do) to the seasons, and which Haggai pointed out to be a judgment from God, had set in for this year also. The months being lunar, *the first day of the month* was the festival of the new moon, a popular feast[4] which their forefathers had kept[5], while they neglected the weightier matters of the law, and which the religious in Israel had kept, even while separated from the worship at Jerusalem[6]. *In its very first day,* when the grief for the barren year was yet fresh, Haggai was stirred to exhort them to *consider their ways;* a pattern for Christian preachers, to bring home to peo-

ple's souls the meaning of God's judgments. God directs the very day to be noted, in which He called the people anew to build His temple, both to shew the readiness of their obedience, and a precedent to us to keep in memory days and seasons, in which He stirs our souls to build more diligently His spiritual temple in our souls[7].

By the hand of Haggai. God doth well-nigh all things which He doeth for a man through the hands of men. He committeth His words and works for men into the hands of men as His stewards, to dispense faithfully to His household[8]. Hence He speaks so often of the law, which He commanded [9] *by the hand of Moses;* but also as to other prophets, Nathan[10], Ahijah[11], Jehu[12], Jonah[13], Isaiah[14], Jeremiah[15], and the prophets generally[16]. The very Prophets of God, although gifted with a Divine Spirit, still were willing and conscious instruments in speaking His words.

Unto Zerubbabel (so called from being born in Babylon) *the son of Shealtiel.* By this genealogy Zerubbabel is known in the history of the return from the captivity in Ezra and Nehemiah[17]. God does not say by Jeremiah, that Jeconiah should have no children, but that he should in his life-time be childless, as it is said of those married to the uncle's or brother's widow, [18] *they shall die childless.* Jeremiah rather implies that he should have children, but that they should die untimely before him. For he calls Jeconiah, [19] *a man who shall not prosper in his days; for there shall not prosper a man of his seed, sitting on the throne of David, and ruling any more in Israel.* He should die (as the word means) *bared*[20] of all, alone and desolate. The own father of Shealtiel appears to have been Neri[21], of the line of Nathan son

---

[1] Jer. xxii. 30. [2] S. Luke iii. 1.
[3] See Zech. i. 7, vii. 1. [4] Pr. vii. 20.
[5] Is. i. 13, 14.
[6] 2 Kgs iv. 23. add Am. viii. 5. Hos. ii. 11.
[7] Castro. [8] S. Luke xii. 42.
[9] 12 times in the Pent.; 5 times in Joshua; in Judges once; in 1 Kgs viii.; 2 Chron. twice; Neh. ix. 14. Ps. lxxvii. 20. [10] 2 Sam. xii. 25.
[11] 1 Kgs xii. 15, xiv. 18. 2 Chr. x. 15.

[12] Ib. xvi. 7. [13] 2 Kgs xiv. 25.
[14] Is. xx. 2. [15] Jer. xxxvii. 2.
[16] Hos. vii. 20. 2 Chr. xxix. 25.
[17] Ezr. iii. 2, 8. v. 2. Neh. xii. 1.
[18] Lev. xx. 20, 21. [19] Jer. xxii. 30.
[20] עֲרִירִי from עָרַר, as the Samar. Vers. renders it in Lev. xx. 20, 21, "naked." Abraham uses it of his desolation in having no son. Gen. xv. 2. [all].
[21] S. Luke iii. 27.

299

2 Thus s p e a k e t h the
LORD of hosts, s a y i n g,
This people say, The time

is not come the time that
the LORD's house should
be built.

of David ; not, of the line of the kings of Judah. Neri married, one must suppose, a daughter of Assir, son of [1] Jeconiah whose grandson Shealtiel was; and Zerubbabel was the own son of Pedaiah, the brother of Shealtiel, as whose son he was in the legal genealogy inscribed, according to the law as to those who die childless [2]; or as having been adopted by Shealtiel being himself childless, as Moses was called the son of the daughter of Pharaoh [3]. So broken was the line of the unhappy Jehoiachin, two thirds of whose own life was passed in the prison [4], into which Nebuchadnezzar cast him.

Governor of Judah. The foreign name [5] betokens that the civil rule was now held from a foreign power, although Cyrus shewed the Jews the kindness of placing one of themselves, of royal extraction also, as his deputy over them. The lineage of David is still in authority, connecting the present with the past, but the earthly kingdom had faded away. Under the name *Sheshbazzar* Zerubbabel is spoken of both as *the prince* [6] and the *governor* [7] of Judah. With him is joined *Joshuah the son of Josedech, the high priest*, whose father went into captivity [8], when his grandfather Seraiah was slain by Nebuchadnezzar [9]. The priestly line also is preserved. Haggai addresses these two, the one of the royal, the other of the priestly, line, as jointly responsible for the negligence of the people; he addresses the people only through them. Together, they are types of Him, the true King and true Priest, Christ Jesus, Who by the Resurrection raised again the true temple, His Body, after it had been destroyed [10].

2. *Thus speaketh the Lord of hosts, saying, This people say.* Not Zerubbabel or Joshua, but *this people.* He says not, *My people,* but reproachfully *this people,* as, in acts, disowning Him, and so deserving to be disowned

by Him. *The time is not come,* lit. *It is not time to come, time for the house of the Lord to be built* [11]. They might yet sit still ; the time for them *to come* was not yet ; for not yet was the *time for the house of the Lord to be built.* Why it was not time, they did not say. The government did not help them ; the original grant by Cyrus [12] was exhausted ; the Samaritans hindered them, because they would not own them, (amid their mishmash of worship, *worshiping,* our Lord tells them, they [13] *know not what,*) as worshipers of the same God. It was a bold excuse, if they said, that the 70 years during which the temple was to lie waste, were not yet ended. The time had long since come, when, 16 years before, Cyrus had given command that the house of God should be built. The prohibition to build, under Artaxerxes or Pseudo-Smerdis, applied directly to the city and its walls, not to the temple, except so far as the temple itself, from its position, might be capable of being used as a fort, as it was in the last siege of Jerusalem. Yet in itself a building of the size of the temple, apart from outer buildings, could scarcely so be used. The prohibition did not hinder the building of stately private houses, as appears from Haggai's rebuke. The hindrances also, whatever they were, had not begun with that decree. Any how the death of Pseudo-Smerdis had now, for a year, set them free, had they had any zeal for the glory and service of God. Else Haggai had not blamed them. God, knowing that He should bend the heart of Darius, as He had that of Cyrus, requires the house to be built without the king's decree. It was built in faith, that God would bring through what He had enjoined, although outward things were as adverse now as before. And what He commanded He prospered [14].

There was indeed a second fulfillment of

---

[1] 1 Chr. iii. 17-19.   [2] Deut. xxiii. 5-10.
[3] Ex. ii. 10.   [4] Jer. lii. 31.
[5] See in Daniel the prophet pp. 570-572. Keil adduces a conjecture of Spiegel, "that *pechah* is from *pávan,* 'protector' (from *pá*) which in Sanskrit and old Persian occurs in compounds as *Khshatrapávan,* Satrap, but in the Avesta occurs in the abridged form *pávan.* Thence *might* be developed *paqvan,* as *dreqvat* from *drevat, huôgva* from *huóva.*" Max Müller kindly informs me ; "Phonetically pavâo could hardly become pagvâo, and even this would still be considerably different from Pechah. The insertion of a *g* before a *v* in Zend is totally anomalous. It rests entirely on the uncertain identification of *dreqvant,* "bad," with *drvant,* for in the second instance, *huova* is much more likely a corruption of *huogva,* than *vice versâ. Pavâo* in Zend would mean, protector, but like the Sanskrit *pávân,* it occurs only at the end of compounds. The one passage, quoted in support of its occurring as a

separate noun, seems to me to contain an etymological play, where *pavâo* is used as an independent noun in order to explain the two compounds, *pacca-pavâo* and *parâ-pavâo,* i. e., protecting behind and protecting in front, as if we were to say, 'he is a *tector,* both as a *pro-tector* and *sub-tector.'"
[6] Ezr. i. 8. In relation to Cyrus, he is called by his Persian name Sheshbazzar, by which name he is mentioned in Tatnai's letter to Darius, as having been commissioned by Cyrus to rebuild the temple and as having done so (Ezr. vi. 14-16) while, in the history of the restoration, he is related to have done it under his domestic name Zerubbabel. On these changes of names by their masters, see Daniel the Prophet p. 16.
[7] Ezr. v. 14.   [8] 1 Chr. vi. 15.
[9] 2 Kgs xxv. 18-21.   [10] S. Jer.
[11] The first sentence being left incomplete, for, "It is not time to come to build the Lord's house."
[12] Ezr. iii. 7.   [13] S. John iv. 22.   [14] Ezr. v. vi.

Before
CHRIST
cir. 520.

3 Then came the word of the LORD [e] by Haggai the prophet saying,

4 [f] *Is it* time for you, O ye, to dwell in your ceiled

[e] Ezra 5. 1.

[f] 2 Sam. 7. 2.
Ps. 132. 3, &c.

houses, and this house *lie* waste?

5 Now therefore t h u s † saith the LORD of hosts;
† [g] Consider your ways.

Before
CHRIST
cir. 520.

† Heb. *Set your heart on your ways.*
[g] Lam. 3. 40.
ver. 7.

seventy years, from the destruction of the temple by Nebuchadnezzar B. C. 586, to its consecration in the 6th year of Darius B. C. 516. But this was through the wilfulness of man, prolonging the desolation decreed by God, and Jeremiah's prophecy relates to the people not to the temple.

"[1] The prophet addresses his discourse to the chiefs [in Church and state] and yet accuses directly, not their listlessness but that of the people, in order both to honor them before the people and to teach that their sins are to be blamed privately not publicly, lest their authority should be injured, and the people incited to rebel against them; and also to shew that this fault was directly that of the people, whom he reproves before their princes, that, being openly convicted before them, it might be ashamed, repent, and obey God; but that indirectly this fault touched the chiefs themselves, whose office it was to urge the people to this work of God."
"[2] For seldom is the Prince free from the guilt of his subjects, as either assenting to, or winking at them, or not coercing them, though able."
Since also Christians are the temple of God, all this prophecy of Haggai is applicable to them. "[3] When thou seest one who has lapsed thinking and preparing to build through chastity the temple which he had before destroyed through passion, and yet delaying day by day, say to him, 'Truly thou also art of the people of the captivity, and sayest, *The time is not yet come for building the house of the Lord.*' Whoso has once settled to restore the temple of God, to him every time is suited for building, and the prince, Satan, cannot hinder, nor the enemies around. As soon as being thyself converted, thou callest upon the name of the Lord, He will say, *Behold Me.*" "[4] To him who willeth to do right, the time is always present; the good and right-minded have power to fulfill what is to the glory of God, in every time and place."

3. *And the word of the Lord came.* "[1] Before, he prophesied nothing, but only recited the saying of the people; now he refutes it in his prophecy, and repeats, again and again, that he says this not of himself, but from the mind and mouth of God." It is

characteristic of Haggai to inculcate thus frequently, that his words are not his own, but the words of God. Yet "[1] the prophets, both in their threats and prophecies, repeat again and again, *Thus saith the Lord,* teaching us, how we should prize the word of God, hang upon it, have it ever in our mouth, reverence, ruminate on, utter, praise it, make it our continual delight."

4. *Is it time for you,* [*you* [5],] being what you are, the creatures of God, *to dwell in your ceiled houses* [6], more emphatically, *in your houses,* and those *ceiled,* probably with costly woods, such as cedar [7]. But where then was the excuse of want of means? They imitated, in their alleged poverty, what is spoken of as magnificent in their old kings, Solomon and Shallum, but not having, as Solomon first did, [8] *covered the house* of God *with beams and rows of cedar.* "[3] Will ye dwell in houses artificially adorned, not so much for use as for delight, and shall My dwelling-place, wherein was the Holy of holies, and the Cherubim, and the table of shew-bread, be bestreamed with rains, desolated in solitude, scorched by the sun?"
"[9] With these words carnal Christians are reproved, who have no glow of zeal for God, but are full of self-love, and so make no effort to repair, build, or strengthen the material temples of Christ, and houses assigned to His worship, when aged, ruinous, decaying or destroyed, but build for themselves curious, voluptuous, superfluous dwellings. In these the love of Christ gloweth not; these Isaiah threateneth, [10] *Woe to you who join house to house and field to field, and regard not the work of the Lord!*"
To David and Solomon the building of God's temple was their heart's desire; to early Christian Emperors, to the ages of faith, the building of Churches; now mostly, owners of lands build houses for this world's profit, and leave it to the few to build in view of eternity, and for the glory of God.

5. And now, thus saith the Lord of hosts; *Consider,* [lit. *set your heart upon*] *your ways,* what they had been doing, what they were doing, and what those doings had led to, and would lead to. This is ever present to the mind of the prophets, as speaking God's words, that our acts are not only *ways* in

[1] Lap.   [2] à Castro from Alb.
[3] S. Jer.   [4] S. Cyr.
[5] לכם אתם, the pers. pron. repeated emphatically.
[6] The force of ספונים in appos. to בתיכם.

[7] ספון בארז 1 Kgs vii. 6, 7. Jer. xxii. 14.
[8] 1 Kgs vi. 9. ויספן.   [9] Dion.
[10] Is. v. 8, 12.

Before
CHRIST
cir. 520.

b Deut. 28. 38.
Hos. 4. 10.
Mic. 6. 14, 15.
ch. 2. 16.

6 Ye have ʰ sown much, and bring in little; ye eat, but ye have not enough; ye drink, but ye are not filled with drink; ye clothe

you, but there is none warm; and ¹he that earneth wages earneth wages *to put it* into a bag † with holes.

Before
CHRIST
cir. 520.

i Zech. 8. 10.

† Heb. *pierced through.*

which we go, each day of life being a continuance of the day before; but that they are *ways* which lead somewhither in God's Providence and His justice; to some end. of the *way*, good or bad. So God says by Jeremiah, ¹ *I set before you the way of life and the way of death;* and David, ² *Thou wilt shew me the path of life,* where it follows, *In Thy Presence is the fullness of joy and at Thy Right Hand there are pleasures for evermore;* and Solomon, ³ *Reproofs of instruction are the way of life;* and, he is in ⁴ *the way of life who keepeth instruction; and he who forsaketh rebuke, erreth;* and, ⁵ *The way of life is above to the wise, that he may depart from hell beneath;* and of the adulterous woman, ⁶ *Her house are the ways of hell, going down to the chambers of death;* and ⁷ *her feet go down unto death; her steps take hold on hell; lest thou shouldest ponder the path of life.* Again, ⁸ *There is a way that seemeth right unto a man, and the end thereof are the ways of death;* and contrariwise, ⁹ *The path of the righteous is a shining light, shining more and more until the midday.* ¹⁰ *The ways of darkness are the ways* which end in darkness; and when Isaiah says, ¹¹ *The way of peace hast thou not known,* he adds, *whosoever goeth therein shall not know peace.* They who choose not peace for their way, shall not find peace in and for their end.

On these your ways, Haggai says, *set your hearts,* not thinking of them lightly, nor giving a passing thought to them, but fixing your minds upon them; as God says to Satan, ¹² *Hast thou set thy heart on My servant Job?* and God is said to set His eye or His face upon man for good ¹³ or for evil ¹⁴. He speaks also, not of setting the mind, applying the understanding, giving the thoughts, but of *setting the heart,* as the seat of the affections. It is not a dry weighing of the temporal results of their ways, but a loving dwelling upon them; for repentance without love is but the gnawing of remorse.

" ¹⁵ *Set your heart on your ways;* i. e., your affections, thoughts, works, so as to be circumspect in all things; as the Apostle says, ¹⁶ *Do nothing without forethought,* i. e., without previous judgment of reason; and Solomon, ¹⁷ *Let thine eyes look right on, and let thine*

eyelids look straight before thee; and the son of Sirach, ¹⁸ *Son, do nothing without counsel and when thou hast done it thou wilt not repent.* For since, according to a probable proposition, nothing in human acts is indifferent, i. e., involving neither good nor ill deserts, they who do not thus *set* their *hearts upon* their *ways,* do they not daily incur well-nigh countless sins, in thought, word, desire, deed, yea and by omission of duties? Such are all fearless persons who heed not to fulfill what is written, ¹⁹ *Keep your heart with all watchfulness.*"

" ²⁰ He *sows much* to his own heart, but *brings in little,* who by reading and hearing knows much of the heavenly commands, but by negligence in deeds bears little fruit. *He eats and is not satisfied,* who, hearing the words of God, coveteth the gains or glory of the world. Well is he said *not* to be *satisfied,* who *eateth* one thing, hungereth after another. *He drinks and is not inebriated,* who inclineth his ear to the voice of preaching, but changeth not his mind. For through inebriation the mind of those who drink is changed. He then who is devoted to the knowledge of God's word, yet still desireth to gain the things of the world, *drinks and is not inebriated.* For were he inebriated, no doubt he would have changed his mind and no longer seek earthly things, or love the vain and passing things which he *had* loved. For the Psalmist says of the elect, ²¹ *they shall be inebriated with the richness of Thy house,* because they shall be filled with such love of Almighty God, that, their mind being changed, they seem to be strangers to themselves, fulfilling what is written, ²² *If any will come after Me, let him deny himself.*"

6. *Ye have sown much.* The prophet expresses the habitualness of these visitations by a vivid present. He marks no time and so expresses the more vividly that it was at all times. It is one continually present evil. *Ye have sown much and there is a bringing in little; there is eating and not to satisfy; there is drinking and not to exhilarate; there is clothing and not to be warm* ²³. It is not for the one or the other years, as, since the first year of Darius Hystaspis; it is one continued

¹ Jer. xxi. 8.   ² Ps. xvi. 11.   ³ Pr. vi. 23.
⁴ Ib. x. 17.   ⁵ Ib. xv. 24.   ⁶ Ib. vii. 27.
⁷ Ib. v. 5, 6.   ⁸ Ib. xiv. 12. xvi. 25.
⁹ Ib. iv. 18.   ¹⁰ Ib. ii. 13.   ¹¹ Is. lix. 8.
¹² Job i. 8.   ¹³ Jer. xxiv. 6.   ¹⁴ Ib. xxi. 10.
¹⁵ Dion.   ¹⁶ 1 Tim. v. 21.   ¹⁷ Pr. iv. 25.

¹⁸ Ecclus. xxxii. 19. Vulg.   ¹⁹ Pr. iv. 23.
²⁰ S. Greg. in Ezek. Hom. i. 10. n. 7. Opp. i. 1266.
²¹ Ps. xxxvi. 8.   ²² S. Matt. xvi. 24.
²³ לֶחֶם לוֹ. The לוֹ is not pleonastic, but from the impersonal לְ תַם 1 Kgs i. 1, 2. Eccl. iv. 11. (bis).

Before
CHRIST
cir. 520.

7 ¶ Thus saith the LORD of hosts; C o n s i d e r your ways.

8 Go up to the moun- tain, and bring wood, and build the house; and I will

Before
CHRIST
cir. 520.

visitation, coordinate with one continued negligence. As long as the sin lasted, so long the punishment. The visitation itself was twofold; impoverished harvests, so as to supply less sustenance; and various indisposition of the frame, so that what would, by God's appointment in nature, satisfy, gladden, warm, failed of its effect. *And he that laboreth for hire, gaineth himself hire into a bag full of holes* [lit. *perforated*]. The labor pictured is not only fruitless, but wearisome and vexing. There is a seeming result of all the labor, something to allure hopes; but forthwith it is gone. The heathen assigned a like baffling of hope as one of the punishments of hell. " [1] Better and wiser to seek to be blessed by God, Who bestoweth on us all things. And this will readily come to those who choose to be of the same mind with Him and prefer what is for His glory to their own. For so saith the Saviour Himself to us, [2] *Seek ye first the kingdom of God and His righteousness, and all these things shall be added unto you.*" " [3] *He* loses good deeds by evil acts, who takes account of his good works, which he has before his eyes, and forgets the faults which creep in between; or who, after what is good, returns to what is vain and evil." " [4] *Money* is seen in the pierced bag, when it is cast in, but when it is lost, it is not seen. They then who look how much they give, but do not weigh how much they gain wrongly, cast their rewards into a pierced bag. Looking to the Hope of their confidence they bring them together; not looking, they lose them." " [5] *They* lose the fruit of their labor, by not persevering to the end, or by seeking human praise, or by vain glory within, not keeping spiritual riches under the guardianship of humility. Such are vain and unprofitable men, of whom the Saviour saith, [6] *Verily I say unto you, they have their reward.*" 8. *Go up into the mountain.* Not Mount Lebanon, whence the cedars had been brought

for the first temple; whence also Zerubbabel and Joshua had procured some out of Cyrus' grant [7], at the first return from the captivity. They were not required to buy, expend, but simply to give their own labor. They were themselves to *go up to the mountain*, i. e. the mountainous country where the trees grew, *and bring* them. So, in order to keep the feast of tabernacles, Ezra made a proclamation [8] *in all their cities and in Jerusalem, go ye up to the mountain and bring leafy branches of vines, olives, myrtles, palms.* The palms, anyhow, were timber. God required not goodly stones, such as had been already used, and such as hereafter, in the temple which was built, were the admiration even of disciples of Jesus [9], but which were, for the wickedness of those who rejected their Saviour, *not to be left, one stone upon another.* He required not costly gifts, but the heart. The neglect to build the temple was neglect of Himself, Who ought to be worshiped there. His worship sanctified the offering; offerings were acceptable, only if made with a free heart. *And I will have pleasure in it.* God, Who has declared that He has no [10] *pleasure in thousands of rams, or ten thousands of rivers of oil,* had delight in [11] *them that feared Him,* that are *upright in their way* [12], that *deal truly* [13], in the *prayer of the upright* [14]; and so in the temple too, when it should be built to His glory. *And will be glorified* [15]. God is glorified in man, when man serves Him; in Himself, when He manifests aught of His greatness; in His great doings to His people [16], as also in the chastisement of those who disobey Him [17]. God allows that glory, which shines ineffably throughout His creation, to be obscured here through man's disobedience, to shine forth anew on his renewed obedience. The glory of God, as it is the end of the creation, so is it His creature's supreme bliss. When God is really glorified, then can He shew forth His glory, by His grace and acceptance. " [18] The glory of God is our glory.

[1] S. Cyr.   [2] S. Matt. vi. 33.   [3] Lap.
[4] S. Greg. Reg. Past. iii. 21. fin. Opp. ii. 68.
[5] Dion.   [6] S. Matt. vi. 2.
[7] Ezr. iii. 7.   [8] Neh. viii. 15.
[9] S. Matt. xxiv. 1. [10] Mic. vi. 7. [11] Ps. cxlvii. 11.
[12] Pr. xi. 20.   [13] Ib. xii. 22.   [14] Ib. xv. 8.
[15] There is no ground for the Kri וְאֶכָּבְדָה, *and so should I be glorified or honored.* It is a positive promise that God would shew forth His glory, as in וְאָרְצֶה immediately before. God says, "do this, and I will do that." Comp. Zech. i. 3. Of 65 instances which Böttcher (Lehrb. n. 965. c.) gives of ה ָ after the imperative, 61 relate to some wish of the human agent; 4 only relate to God. Deut. v.

31, "stand here by Me, וַאֲדַבְּרָה, that I may speak unto thee;" Is. xli. 22, 23. irony, including men, "that we may consider and know; that we may know;" Ps. l. 7. "hear Me and *I would speak,* and *testify;*" Mal. iii. 7. "Return to Me and I would return unto you;" the return of the creature being a condition that God could return to it. On the other hand the Ch. Lam. v. 21, "Turn Thou us unto Thee, נָשׁוּב, and we will return" expresses the absolute will to return; Ruth iv. 4, "tell me, וְאֵדְעָה, and I shall know," the certainty of the knowledge, upon which Boaz would act.
[16] Is. xxvi. 15, xliv. 23, lx. 21, lxi. 3.
[17] Ex. xiv. 4. Ezek. xxviii. 22.
[18] S. Aug. Serm. 380, n. 6.

take pleasure in it, and I will be glorified, saith the LORD.

9 [k] Ye looked for much, and, lo, *it came* to little; and when ye brought *it*

home, [1] I did ‖ blow upon it. Why? saith the LORD of hosts. Because of mine house that *is* waste, and ye run every man unto his own house.

The more sweetly God is glorified, the more it profits us : " yet not our profit, but the glory of God is itself our end ; so the prophet closes in that which is our end, *God will be glorified.*

" [1] Good then and well-pleasing to God is zeal in fulfilling whatever may appear necessary for the good condition of the Church and its building-up, collecting the most useful materials, the spiritual principles in inspired Scripture, whereby he may secure and ground the conception of God, and may shew that the way of the Incarnation was well-ordered, and may collect what appertains to accurate knowledge of spiritual erudition and moral goodness. Nay, each of us may be thought of, as the temple and house of God. For Christ *dwelleth in us* by the Spirit, and we are *temples of the living God,* according to the Scripture [2]. Let each then build up his own heart by right faith, having the Saviour as the *precious foundation.* And let him add thereto other materials, obedience, readiness for anything, courage, endurance, continence. So *being framed together by that which every joint supplieth,* shall we *become a holy temple, a habitation of God through the Spirit* [3]. But those who are slow to faith, or who believe but are sluggish in shaking off passions and sins and worldly pleasure, thereby cry out in a manner, *The time is not come to build the house of the Lord.*"

9. *Ye looked,* lit. *a looking ;* as though he said, it has all been one looking, *for much,* for increase, the result of all sowing, in the way of nature : *and behold it came to little,* i. e. less than was sown ; as Isaiah denounced to them of old by God's word, [4] *the seed of a homer shall yield an ephah,* i. e. one tenth of what was sown. *And ye brought it home, and I blew upon it,* so as to disperse it, as, not the wheat, but the chaff is blown before the wind. This, in whatever way it came to pass, was a further chastisement of God. The little seed which they brought in lessened through decay or waste. *Why? saith the Lord of hosts.* God asks by his prophet, what He asks in the awakened conscience. [5] *God with rebukes*

chastens man for sin. Conscience, when alive, confesses for *what* sin ; or it asks itself, if memory does not supply the special sin. Unawakened, it murmurs about the excess of rain, the drought, the blight, the mildew, and asks, not itself, why, in God's Providence, these inflictions came in these years ? They felt doubtless the sterility in contrast with the exceeding prolificalness of Babylonia [6], as they contrasted the *light bread* [7], the manna, with [8] the plenteousness of Egypt. They ascribed probably their meagre crops (as we mostly do) to mere natural causes, perhaps to the long neglect of the land during the captivity. God forces the question upon their consciences, in that Haggai asks it in His Name, in Whose hands all powers stand, *saith the Lord of hosts.* They have not to talk it over among themselves, but to answer Almighty God, *why?* That *why?* strikes into the inmost depths of conscience !

Because of My house which is waste, and ye run lit. *are running,* all the while, *each to his own house* [9]. They were absorbed in their material interests, and had no time for those of God. When the question was of God's house, they stir not from the spot ; when it is of their own concerns, they run. Our Lord says, [10] *Seek ye first the kingdom of God and His righteousness, and all these things shall be added unto you.* Man reverses this, seeks his own things first, and God withholds His blessing.

" [11] This comes true of those who prefer their own conveniences to God's honor, who do not thoroughly uproot self-love, whose penitence and devotion are shewn to be unstable ; for on a slight temptation they are overcome. Such are they who are bold, self-pleasing, wise and great in their own eyes, who do not ground their conversation on true and solid humility."

" [12] To those who are slow to fulfill what is for the glory of God, and the things whereby His house, the Church, is firmly stayed, neither the heavenly dew cometh, which enricheth hearts and minds, nor the fruitfulness of the earth ; i. e. right action ; not food nor wine nor use of oil. But they will be

---

1 S. Cyr.   2 2 Cor. vi. 16.   3 Eph. iv. 16, ii. 21, 22.
4 Is. v. 10.   5 Ps. xxxix. 11.
6 Herod. i. 193. Theophr. Hist. Plant. viii. 7. Berosus Fr. 1. Strabo xvi. 1. 14. Pliny Nat. Hist. xviii. 17. Amm. Marc. xxiv. 9.
7 Nu. xxi. 5.   8 Ib. xi. 5.

9 רוץ with ל is used of the direction whither a man goes ; if used of an action, hasting to do it ; as *runneth to evil* (Is. lix. 7, Pr. i. 16.) Here לביתו cannot be " on account of his house," but to it, viz. for his business there.
10 S. Matt. vi. 33.   11 Dion.   12 S. Cyr.

Before
C H R I S T
cir. 520.

10 Therefore ^mthe heaven over you is stayed from dew, and the earth is stayed *from* her fruit.

11 And I ⁿ called for a drought upon the l a n d, and upon the mountains, and upon the corn, and upon the new wine, and upon the oil, and upon *that* which the ground bringeth forth, and upon men, and

m Lev. 26. 19.
Deut. 28. 23.
1 Kin. 8. 35.
n 1 Kin. 17. 1.
2 Kin. 8. 1.

upon cattle, and °upon all the labor of the hands.

12 ¶ ^p Then Zerubbabel the son of Shealtiel, and Joshua the son o f Josedech, the high priest, with all the remnant of the people, obeyed the voice of the LORD their God, and the words of Haggai the prophet, as the LORD their God had sent him, and the

Before
C H R I S T
cir. 520.

° ch. 2. 17.
p Ezra 5. 2.

ever strengthless and joyless, unenriched by spiritual oil, and remain without taste or participation of the blessing through Christ."

10. *Therefore, for you,* on your account [1]; for your sins [2], He points out the moral cause of the drought, whereas men think of this or that cause of the variations of the seasons, and we, e. g. take into our mouths Scripture-words, as *murrain of cattle,* and the like, and think of nothing less than why it was sent, or Who sent it. Haggai directs the mind to the higher Cause, that as they withheld their service from God, so, on their account and by His will, His creatures withheld [3] their service from them.

11. *And I called for a drought upon the land.* God called to the people and they would not hear. It is His ever-repeated complaint to them. *I called unto you, and ye would not hear.* He called to His inanimate creatures to punish them, and *they* obeyed. So Elisha tells the woman, whose son he had restored to life, [4] *The Lord hath called to the famine, and it shall also come to the land seven years.*

And upon men, in that the drought was oppressive to man. The Prophet may also allude to the other meaning of the word, "waste," "desolation." They had left the house of the Lord [5] waste, therefore God called for waste, desolation, upon them.

12. *Then Zerubbabel, and all the remnant of the people,* not, "the rest of people" but "the

[1] As in Ps. xliv. 43.   [2] Jon.

[3] כלא being everywhere transitive, and in this V. also, is probably transitive here.

[4] 2 Kgs viii. 1.

[5] חֲרֵב, Hagg. i. 4, 9; חֹרֶב, i. 11.

[6] This is the almost uniform usage of שְׁאֵרִית, "remnant which remains over," mostly after the rest have been destroyed or carried captive. See vol. i. on Am. i. 8; add, *the remnant of Judah,* Jer. xl. 11, xlii. 19, xliii. 5, xliv. 12, 14, *of Israel,* Zeph. iii. 13. Ez. xi. 13; *whole remnant of the people,* Jer. xli. 10, 16; *of Ashdod,* Jer. xxv. 20; *of the coast of Caphtor,* Ib. xlvii. 4; *of their valley,* Ib. 5; *of the coast of the sea,* Ez. xxv. 16; *of the nations,* Ib. xxxvi. 3, 4, 5; *of the land,* אֲרָמָה, Is. xv. 9; *of My people,* Zeph. ii. 9;

remnant [6]," those who remained over from the captivity, the fragment of the two tribes, which returned to their own land, *hearkened unto the voice of the Lord.* This was the beginning of a conversion. In this one thing they began to do, what, all along, in their history, and most in their decay before the captivity they refused to do—obey God's word. So God sums up their history, by Jeremiah, [7] *I spake unto thee in thy prosperity, thou saidst, I will not hear. This is thy way from thy youth, that thou hearkenedst not unto My voice.* Zephaniah still more briefly, [8] *she hearkened not unto* [any] *voice.* Now in reference, it seems, to that account of their disobedience, Haggai says, using the self-same formula, [9] *they hearkened unto the voice of the Lord,* [10] *according to the words of Haggai.* They obeyed, not vaguely, or partly, but exactly, *according to the words* which the messenger of God spake.

And they feared the Lord. "[11] Certainly the presence of the Divine Majesty is to be feared with great reverence." "[12] The fear of punishment at times transports the mind to what is better, and the infliction of sorrows harmonizes the mind to the fear of God; and that of the Proverbs comes true, [13] *He that feareth the Lord shall be recompensed,* and [14] *the fear of the Lord tendeth to life;* and Wisdom, [15] *The fear of the Lord is honor and glory,* and [16] *the fear of the Lord shall rejoice*

of His heritage, Mi. vii. 18; *thy remnant,* Is. xiv. 30, Ez. v. 10; *its remnant,* Is. xliv. 17; *their remnant,* Jer. xv. 9; and of those who had actually returned, Zech. viii. 6, 11, 12. In two places in which it signifies "the rest" (Jer. xxxix. 3, 1 Chr. xii. 38.) it is at least the rest of a whole, already mentioned. A third only, Neh. vii. 72. is uncertain. The word is used almost exclusively by the prophets.

[7] Jer. xxii. 21.

[8] לֹא שָׁמְעָה בְקוֹל. See Introd. to Zeph. p. 225.

[9] וַיִּשְׁמַע בְקוֹל יְיָ.

[10] This is the only place in which שְׁמַע עַל דְּבָרֵי is used.

[11] Dion.   [12] S. Cyr.   [13] Pr. xiii. 13.

[14] Ib. xix. 23.   [15] Ecclus. i. 11.   [16] Ib. 12.

Before
CHRIST
cir. 520.

people did fear before the LORD,

13 Then spake Haggai the Lord's messenger in the LORD's message unto the people, saying, [q] I *am* with you, saith the Lord.

14 And [r] the Lord

[q] Matt. 28. 20.
Rom. 8. 31.
[r] 2 Chr. 36. 22.
Ezra 1. 1.

Before
CHRIST
cir. 520.

stirred up the spirit of Zerubbabel the son of Shealtiel, [s] governor of Judah, and the spirit of Joshua the son of Josedech, the high priest, and the spirit of all the remnant of the people; [t] and they came

[s] ch. 2. 21.

[t] Ezra 5. 2, 8.

---

the heart, and giveth joy and gladness and a long life. See how gently and beseemingly God smites us."

" [1] See how the lovingkindness of God forthwith goes along with all changes for the better. For Almighty God changes along with those who will to repent, and promises that He will be with them; which what can equal? For when God is with us, all harm will depart from us, all good come in to us."

13. *And Haggai, the Lord's messenger.* Malachi, whose own name was framed to express that he was *the Lord's messenger,* and Haggai alone use the title, as the title of a prophet; perhaps as forerunners of the great prophet whom Malachi announced. Malachi also speaks of the priest, as [2] *the messenger of the Lord of hosts,* and prophesies of John Baptist as [3] *the messenger* of the Lord, who should *go before His face.* Haggai, as he throughout repeats that his words were God's words, frames a new word [4], to express, in the language of the New Testament [5]; that he had an embassy from God; *in the Lord's message.*

I am with you. All the needs and longings of the creature are summed up in those two words, *I with-you.* "Who art Thou and who am I? Thou, He Who Is; I, he who am not;" nothing, yea worse than nothing. Yet *if* [6] *God be for us,* S. Paul asks, *who can be against us?* Our Blessed Lord's parting promise to the Apostles, and in them to the Church, was, [7] *Lo I am with you alway, even to the end of the world.* The all-containing assurance goes beyond any particular promise of aid, as, " [8] I will help you, and will protect you, so that your building shall have its completion." This is one fruit of it; " [9] since I am in the midst of you, no one shall be able to hinder your building." But, more widely, the words bespeak *His* presence in love, Who knows all our needs, and is Almighty to support and save us in all. So David says, [10] *when I walk through the valley of the shadow of death, I will fear no evil; for*

Thou art with me: and God says by another, [11] *I* will be *with him in trouble,* and by Isaiah, [12] *When thou passest through the waters, I* will be *with thee.*

14. *And the Lord stirred up the spirit.* The words are used of any strong impulse from God to fulfill His will, whether in those who execute His will unknowingly as Pul [13], to carry off the trans-Jordanic tribes, or the Philistines and Arabians against Jehoram [14], or the Medes against Babylon [15]; or knowingly, as of Cyrus to restore God's people and rebuild the temple [16], or of the people themselves to return [17]. " [9] The spirit of Zerubbabel and the spirit of Joshua were stirred, that the government and priesthood may build the temple of God: the spirit of the people too, which before was asleep in them; not the body, not the soul, but the spirit, which knoweth best how to build the temple of God." " [18] The Holy Spirit is stirred up in us, that we should enter the house of the Lord, and do the works of the Lord."

" [19] Again, observe that they did not set themselves to choose to do what should please God, before He was with them and stirred up their spirit. We shall know hence also, that although one choose zealously to do good and be in earnest therein, yet he will accomplish nothing, unless God be with him, raising him up to dare, and sharpening him to endure, and removing all torpor. For so the wondrous Paul says of those entrusted with the divine preaching, [20] *I labored more abundantly than they all,* yet added very wisely, *yet not I, but the grace of God which was with me,* and the Saviour Himself saith to the holy Apostles, [21] *Without Me ye can do nothing.* For He is our desire, He, our courage to any good work; He our strength, and, if He is with us, we shall do well, [22] *building ourselves to a holy temple, a habitation of God in the Spirit;* if He depart and withdraws, how should any doubt, that we should fail, overcome by sluggishness and want of courage?"

[1] S. Cyr.   [2] Mal. ii. 7.   [3] Ib. iii. 1.
[4] מלאכות.   [5] 2 Cor. v. 20.
[6] Rom. viii. 31.   [7] S. Matt. xxviii. 20.
[8] Dion.   [9] S. Jer.   [10] Ps. xxiii. 4.

[11] Ib. xci. 15.   [12] Is. xliii. 2.   [13] 1 Chr. v. 26.
[14] 2 Chr. xxi. 16.   [15] Jer. li. 11.
[16] Ezr. i. 1.   [17] Ib. 5.   [18] ap. Lap.
[19] S. Cyr.   [20] 1 Cor. xv. 11.
[21] S. John xv. 5.   [22] Eph. ii. 21, 22.

and did work in the house of the LORD of hosts, their God.

15 In the four and twentieth day of the sixth month, in the second year of Darius the king.

CHAPTER II.

1 He encourageth the people to the work, by promise of greater glory to the second temple than was in the first. 10 In the type of holy things and unclean he sheweth their sins hindered the work. 20 God's promise to Zerubbabel.

IN the seventh *month*, in the one and twentieth

day of the month, came the word of the LORD † by the prophet Haggai, saying,

2 Speak now to Zerubbabel the son of Shealtiel, governor of Judah, and to Joshua the son of Josedech, the high priest, and to the residue of the people, saying,

3 ª Who *is* left among you that saw this house in her first glory? and how do ye see it now? ᵇ *is it* not in your eyes in comparison of it as nothing?

† Heb. *by the hand of.*

ª Ezra 3. 12.

ᵇ Zech. 4. 10.

---

15. *In the four and twentieth day of the month.* The interval of twenty-three days must have been spent in preparation, since the message came on the first of the month, and the obedience was immediate.

II. 1. *In the seventh month, in the one and twentieth day of the month.* This was the seventh day of the feast of tabernacles[1], and its close. The eighth day was to be a sabbath, with its [2]*holy convocation,* but the commemorative feast, the dwelling in booths, in memory of God's bringing them out of Egypt, was to last seven days. The close then of this feast could not but revive their sadness at the glories of their first deliverance by God's *mighty hand and outstretched arm,* and their present fewness and poverty. This depression could not but bring with it heavy thoughts about the work, in which they were, in obedience to God, engaged; and that, all the more, since Isaiah and Ezekiel had prophesied of the glories of the Christian Church under the symbol of the temple. This despondency Haggai is sent to relieve, owning plainly the reality of its present grounds, but renewing, on God's part, the pledge of the glories of this second temple, which should be thereafter.

3. *Who is left among you?* The question implies that there were those among them, who had seen the first house in its glory, yet but few. When the foundations of the first temple were laid, there were many. [3] *Many of the priests and Levites and chief of the fa-*

thers, *ancient men, that had seen the first house, when the foundations of this house were laid before their eyes, wept with a loud voice.* Fifty-nine years had elapsed from the destruction of the temple in the eleventh year of Zedekiah to the first of Cyrus; so that old men of seventy years had seen the first temple, when themselves eleven years old. In this second of Darius seventy years had passed, so that those of 78 or 80 years might still well remember it. Ezra's father, Seraiah, was slain in the eleventh year of Zedekiah; so he must have been born at latest a few months later; yet he lived to the second of Artaxerxes.

Is not such as it is[4]*, as nothing?* Beside the richness of the sculptures in the former temple, everything, which admitted of it, was overlaid with gold ; [5] *Solomon overlaid the whole house with gold, until he had finished all the house, the whole altar by the oracle, the two cherubim, the floor of the house, the doors of the holy of holies* and the ornaments of it, *the cherubims* thereon and *the palm trees he covered with gold fitted upon the carved work ;* [6] *the altar of gold and the table of gold, whereupon the shewbread was, the ten candlesticks of pure gold, with the flowers and the lamps and the tongs of gold, the bowls, the snuffers and the basons and the spoons and the censers of pure gold, and hinges of pure gold for all the doors of the temple.* [7] *The porch that was in the front of the house, twenty cubits broad and 120 cubits high, was overlaid within with pure gold ;* the house

---

[1] Lev. xxiii. 34, 36, 40–42.
[2] Ib. 39.   [3] Ezr. iii. 12.
[4] Such is probably the force of כְּמוֹהוּ. Comp. כְּמוֹךְ כְּפַרְעֹה [Gen. xliv. 18] "one such as thou is like Pharaoh," and perhaps כָּמֹהוּ, Ex. ix. 18, and

אֲשֶׁר כָּמֹנִי, 2 Sam. ix. 8. הוּא כְאַיִן (which Ewald says older writers would have used) would have been weaker.
[5] 1 Kgs vi. 22. 28, 30, 32, 35.   [6] Ib. vii. 48–50.
[7] 2 Chr. iii. 4–9.

4 Yet now [c] be strong,
O Zerubbabel, saith the
LORD; and be strong, O
Joshua, son of Josedech,
the high priest; and be
strong, all ye people of the

[c] Zech. 8. 9.

land, saith the LORD, and
work: for I *am* with you,
saith the LORD of hosts:

5 [d] *According to* the
word that I covenanted
with you when ye came

[d] Ex. 29. 45, 46.

---

glistened with precious stones; and the gold
(it is added) was *gold of Parvaim*, a land distant of course and unknown to us. *Six
hundred talents of gold* (about £4,320,000 [1],)
were employed in overlaying the Holy of
holies. *The upper chambers were also of gold ;
the weight of the nails was fifty shekels of gold.*
4. *Yet now be strong—and work.* They are
the words with which David exhorted Solomon his son to be earnest and to persevere in
the building of the first temple. [2] *Take heed
now, for the Lord hath chosen thee to build an
house for the sanctuary : be strong and do.* [3] *Be
strong and of good courage, and do.* This combination of words occurs once only elsewhere [4],
in Jehoshaphat's exhortation to *the* [5] *Levites
and priests and chiefs of the fathers of Israel,*
whom he had set as judges in Jerusalem.
Haggai seems then to have adopted the
words, with the purpose of suggesting to the
down-hearted people, that there was need of
the like exhortation, in view of the building
of the former temple, whose relative glory
so depressed them. The word *be strong*
(elsewhere rendered, *be of good courage*) occurs commonly in exhortations to persevere
and hold fast, amid whatever obstacles [6].
5. *The words which I covenanted.* The words
stand more forcibly, because abruptly [7]. It
is an exclamation which cannot be forced

into any grammatical relation with the preceding. The more exact idiom would have
been "Remember," "take to heart." But
the Prophet points to it the more energetically, because he casts it, as it were, into the
midst, not bound up with any one verb.
This would be the rather done in speaking
to the people, as David to his followers [8],
*That which the Lord hath given us and hath
preserved us and given the company against us
into our hands !* i. e. "Would you deal thus
with it ?" The abrupt form rejects it as
shocking. So here, *The word which I covenanted with you,* i. e. this, *I will be with you,*
was the central all-containing promise, to
which God pledged Himself when He
brought them out of Egypt. He speaks to
them as being one with those who came up
out of Egypt, as if they were the very persons. The Church, ever varying in the individuals of whom it is composed, is, throughout all ages, in God's sight, one; His promises to the fathers are made to the children
in them. So the Psalmist says, *There* (at the
dividing of the Red Sea and the Jordan) *do we
rejoice in Him,* as if present there; and our
Lord promises to the Apostles, [9] *I am with
you always even to the end of the world,* by an
ever-present Presence with them and His
Church founded by them in Him.

---

[1] Reckoning the silver shekel at 2s., the talent of
silver,=3000 shekels, would be £300 ; reckoning the
gold talent, as, in weight, double the silver talent,
and the relation of gold to silver as 12 to 1, (H. W.
Poole in Smith Bibl. Dict. p. 1734, 1735.) the gold
talent would be £300 x 24,= £7,200 ; and 600 gold
talents £4,320,000. This would not be so much as
Solomon imported yearly, 666 talents = £4,795,200.
[2] 1 Chr. xxviii. 10.   [3] Ib. 20.
[4] 2 Chr. xix. 11.   [5] Ib. 8.
[6] Gesenius (v. חָזַק) refers to the following; 2
Sam. x. 12, (Joab to Abishai in the war with the
Syrians); 2 Chr. xxv. 8. (the prophet to Amaziah);
2 Sam. xiii. 28 (Absalom to his servants about the
murder of Amnon); Ps. xxvii. 14, xxxi. 25, (with
the corresponding promise that God would *establish
their hearts*); Is. xli. 6, (in mockery of the laborious
process of making an idol). It occurs also, supported by וַאֲמִיץ Jos. i. 6, 7, 9, 18 (God's words to
Joshua); Deut. xxxi. 7, (Moses to Joshua); Ib. 6,
(to Israel); Josh. x. 25 (Joshua to the people); 2
Chr. xxxii. 7 (Hezekiah to the people); חָזַק itself
is repeated Dan. x. 19. חֲזַק וַחֲזָק.
[7] Less probable seems to me, 1) To make אֵת
הַדָּבָר depend on עֲשׂוּ in v. 4, as Kim. A. E. a) on
account of the idiom in 1 Chr., in which, as here,
עֲשׂוּ stands absolutely, "do work;" b) Haggai is

exhorting them to this one work of rebuilding the
temple, not to obedience to the law generally ; c)
he speaks of what God had promised them, not of
their duties to God. 2) To supply זְכֹר "remember," or any like word, is arbitrary, unless it means
that *we* should fill up the meaning by some such
word. 3) To construe, "Remember the word which
I covenanted with you, fear not" (Ew.); a) gives
undue prominence to the absence of fear, which
was one consequence of God's covenant that He
would be their God, they His people, not the covenant itself; b) *Fear not,* is elsewhere the counterpart and supplement of the exhortation, "be
strong," 2 Chr. xxv. 8, Is. xxxv. 41. c) In Ex. xx. 20,
(referred to by Ew.) "fear not" is only Moses'
exhortation on occasion of the terrors of the manifestation of God on Mt. Sinai. 4) It is doubly
improbable, that it, as well as רוּחַ, should be the
subject of the sing. עֲבֹדַת. The אֵת הַדָּבָר and
the רוּחִי seem to be different constructions, in
order to prevent this. Böttcher terms it, "an acc.
abs. of the object," and cites Deut. xi. 2, Ezek.
xliii. 7, xlvii. 17-19, ("unless one correct אֵת for
זֹאת ") Zech. viii. 17. (Lehrb. n. 516. *e.*)
[8] 1 Sam. xxx. 23, which Ewald compares, Lehrb.
n. 329. *a.* p. 811, ed. 8. and in his Die Proph. iii. 183.
Only he, not very intelligibly, makes it a sort of
oath, *By the word, By that which the Lord hath given
us.* But he suggests the like broken sentence
Zech. vii. 7.   [9] S. Matt. xxviii. 20.

Before CHRIST cir. 520.	
e Neh. 9. 20. Isai. 63. 11.	

out of Egypt, so ^e my spirit remaineth among you: fear ye not.

6 For thus saith the Lord of hosts; ^f Yet once; it *is* a little while, and ^g I

Before CHRIST cir. 520.	
f ver. 21. Heb. 12. 26. g Joel 3. 16.	

My Spirit abideth among you, as the Psalmist says, [1] *they* [the heavens] *perish and Thou abidest;* [2] *The counsel of the Lord standeth forever;* [3] *His righteousness endureth forever.* The Spirit of God is God the Holy Ghost, with His manifold gifts. Where He is, is all good. As the soul is in the body, so God the Holy Ghost is in the Church, Himself its life, and bestowing on all and each every good gift, as each and all have need. As S. Paul says of the Church of Christ; [4] *There are diversities of gifts, but the same Spirit; and there are diversities of operations, but it is the same God, Who worketh all in all. All these worketh one and the self-same Spirit, dividing to every man severally as He will.* But above and beyond all gifts He is present as the Spirit of holiness and love, making the Church and those in whom He individually dwells, acceptable to God. Special applications, such as *the Spirit of wisdom and might;* a spirit such as He gave to Moses to judge His people [5]; the spirit of prophecy [6]; or the spirit given to Bezaleel and Aholiab for the work of the sanctuary [7]—these recognize in detail the one great truth, that all good, all wisdom, from least to greatest, comes from God the Holy Ghost; though one by one they would exclude more truth than they each contain.

6. *Yet once, it is a little while.* This, the rendering of S. Paul to the Hebrews, is alone grammatical [8]. *Yet once.* By the word *yet* he looks back to the first great shaking of the moral world, when God's revelation by Moses and to His people broke upon the darkness of the pagan world, to be a monument against heathen error till Christ should come; *once* looks on, and conveys that God would again shake the world, but *once* only, under the one dispensation of the Gospel, which should endure to the end.

It is a little while. "[9] The 517 years, which were to elapse to the birth of Christ, are called *a little time,* because to the prophets, ascending in heart to God and the eternity of God, all times, like all things of this world, seem, as they are, only a little thing, yea a mere point;" which has neither length nor breadth. So S. John calls the time of the

new law, *the last hour;* [10] *Little children, it is the last hour.* It was *little* also in respect to the time, which had elapsed from the fall of Adam, upon which God promised the Saviour Christ [11]; little also in respect to the Christian law, which has now lasted above 1800 years, and the time of the end does not seem yet nigh.

I will shake the heavens and the earth, and the sea and the dry land. It is one universal shaking of all this our world and the heavens over it, of which the Prophet speaks. He does not speak only of [12] *signs in the sun and in the moon and in the stars,* which might be, and yet the frame of the world itself might remain. It is a shaking, such as would involve the dissolution of this our system, as St. Paul draws out its meaning; [13] *This word, once more, signifieth the removing of the things that are shaken, that those things which cannot be shaken may remain.* Prophecy, in its long perspective, uses a continual foreshortening, speaking of things in relation to their eternal meaning and significance, as to that which shall survive, when heaven and earth and even time shall have passed away. It blends together the beginning and the earthly end; the preparation and the result; the commencement of redemption and its completion; our Lord's coming in humility and in His Majesty. Scarce any prophet but exhibits things in their intrinsic relation, of which time is but an accident. It is the rule, not the exception. The Seed of the woman, Who should bruise the serpent's head, was promised on the fall; to Abraham, the blessing through his seed; by Moses, the prophet like unto him; to David, an everlasting covenant [14]. Joel unites the out-pouring of the Spirit of God on the Day of Pentecost, and the hatred of the world till the Day of Judgment [15]; Isaiah, God's judgments on the land and the Day of final judgment [16]; the deliverance from Babylon, and the first coming of Christ [17]; the glories of the Church, the new heavens and the new earth which shall remain forever, and the unquenched fire and undying worm of the lost [18]; Daniel, the persecutions of Antiochus Epiphanes, of Anti-

---

[1] Ps. cii. 27.   [2] Ib. xxxiii. 11.
[3] Ib. cxi. 3.   [4] 1 Cor. xii. 4, 6, 11.
[5] Alb. quoting Num. xi. 25.
[6] Jon. "My prophets shall teach you, fear not."
[7] Included by Lap.
[8] אחת 2 Kgs vi. 10, Ps. lxii. 12, Job. xl. 5: אחד, as an adj., follows the noun. In the only exception alleged by Ges., Dan. viii. 13, it is used of one certain angel, as contrasted with another. מעט is

used of time, Job x. 20, xxiv. 24. ו אחת עוד is the like construction as ו מעט עוד Ex. xvii. 4, Ps. xxxvii. 10, Hos. i. 4.   [9] Lap.
[10] 1 S. John ii. 18.   [11] Gen. iii. 15.
[12] S. Luke xxi. 25.   [13] Heb. xii. 27.
[14] 2 Sam. xxiii. 5.   [15] Joel ii. 28-32, iii.
[16] Is. xxiv.
[17] Ib. xl.-lxvi.   [18] Ib. lxvi. 22-24.

will shake the heavens, and the earth, and the sea, and the dry *land;*

7 And I will shake all nations, [h] and the desire of all nations shall come: and

[h] Gen. 49. 10.
Mal. 3. 1.

Christ, and the Resurrection [1]; Obadiah, the punishment of Edom and the everlasting kingdom of God [2]; Zephaniah, the punishment of Judah and the final judgment of the earth [3]; Malachi, our Lord's first and second Coming [4].

Nay, our Lord Himself so blends together the destruction of Jerusalem and the days of Anti-Christ and the end of the world, that it is difficult to separate them, so as to say what belongs exclusively to either [5]. The prophecy is an answer to two distinct questions of the Apostles, 1) *When shall these things* (viz. the destruction of the temple) *be?* 2) *and what shall be the sign of Thy coming and of the end of the world?* Our Lord answers the two questions in one. Some things seem to belong to the first Coming, as [6] *the abomination of desolation spoken of by Daniel,* and the flight from [7] *Judæa into the mountains.* But the exceeding deceivableness is authoritatively interpreted by St. Paul [8] of a distant time; and our Lord Himself, having said that *all these things,* of which the Apostles had enquired, should take place in that generation [9], speaks of His absence as of a man taking a far journey [10], and says that *not the angels in heaven knew that hour, neither the Son* [11]; which precludes the idea, that He had just before declared that the whole would take place in that generation. For this would be to make out, that He declared that the Son knew not the hour of His Coming, which He had just (on this supposition) declared to be in that generation.

So then, here. There was a general shaking upon earth before our Lord came. Empires rose and fell. The Persian fell before Alexander's; Alexander's world-empire · was ended by his sudden death in youth; of his four successors, two only continued, and they too fell before the Romans; then were the Roman civil wars, until, under Augustus, the temple of Janus was shut. " [12] For it greatly beseemed a work ordered by God, that many kingdoms should be confederated in one empire, and that the universal preaching might find the peoples easily accessible who were held under the rule of one state." In the Heavens was the

star, which led the wise men, the manifestation of Angels to the shepherds; the preternatural darkness at the Passion; the Ascension into the highest Heaven, and the descent of the Holy Ghost with [13] *a sound from heaven as* [*of*] *a rushing mighty wind.* " [14] God had moved them [heaven and earth] before, when He delivered the people from Egypt, when there was in heaven a column of fire, dry ground amid the waves, a wall in the sea, a path in the waters, in the wilderness there was multiplied a daily harvest of heavenly food [the manna], the rock gushed into fountains of waters. But He moved it afterward also in the Passion of the Lord Jesus, when the heaven was darkened, the sun shrank back, the rocks were rent, the graves opened, the dead were raised, the dragon, conquered in his waters, saw the fishers of men, not only sailing in the sea, but also walking without peril. The dry ground also was moved, when the unfruitful people of the nations began to ripen to a harvest of devotion and faith,—so that *more were the children of the forsaken, than of her which had a husband,* and [15] *the desert flourished like a lily.*" " [16] He moved earth in that great miracle of the birth from the Virgin: He moved the sea and dry land, when in the islands and in the whole world Christ is preached. So we see all nations moved to the faith."

And yet, whatever preludes of fulfillment there were at our Lord's first Coming, they were as nothing to the fulfillment which we look for in the Second, *when* [17] *the earth shall be utterly broken down; the earth, clean dissolved; the earth, moved exceedingly; the earth shall reel to and fro like a drunkard, and shall be removed like a hanging-cot in a vineyard* [18], *and the transgression thereof is heavy upon it; and it shall fall and not rise again;* whereon follows an announcement of the final judgment of men and angels, and the everlasting kingdom of the blessed in the presence of God.

Of that *day of the Lord,* St. Peter uses our Lord's image, [19] that it *shall* [20] *come as a thief in the night, in which the heavens shall melt with fervent heat, the earth also and the works therein shall be burned up.*

7. *And the desire of all nations shall come.*

---

[1] Dan. xi. xii.
[2] Ob. 18–21.
[3] See on Zeph. i. 2, 3. p. 235, 236.
[4] Mal. iii. 1–5. 17, 18. lv.
[5] The second question about the end of the world occurs only in S. Matthew (xxiv. 3); the first, *When shall these things be?* occurs in S. Mark also (xiii. 3) and S. Luke (xxi. 6). The words in S. Mark, *This generation shall not pass till all these things be done* (xiii. 30) seem to me to be cast in the form of their question, *When shall these things be?* viz. the things about which they had asked.

[6] S. Matt. xxiv. 15, 16.
[7] Ib. 24.
[8] 2 Thess. v. 2–10.
[9] S. Mark xiii. 30.
[10] Ib. 34.
[11] Ib. 32.
[12] S. Leo Hom. 82 in Nat. Ap. Petri et Pauli. c. 2. col. 322. Ball.
[13] Acts ii. 2.
[14] S. Ambr. Ep. 30 ad Iren. n. 11, 12. Opp. ii. 913 Ben.
[15] Is. xxxv. 1.
[16] S. Aug. de Civ. Dei. xviii. 25.
[17] Is. xxiv. 19, 20.
[18] מְלוּנָה. See a picture of one in Niebuhr.
[19] S. Matt. xxiv. 43.
[20] 2 S. Pet. iii. 10.

The words can only mean this, *the* central longing of all nations[1]; He whom they longed for, either through the knowledge of Him spread by the Jews in their dispersion, or mutely by the aching craving of the human heart, longing for the restoration from its decay. *The earnest expectation of the creature* did not begin with the Coming of Christ, nor was it limited to those, who actually came to Him. [2] *The whole creation,* Saint Paul saith, *groaneth and travaileth in pain together until now.* It was enslaved, and the better self longed to be free; every motion of grace in the multitudinous heart of man was a longing for its Deliverer; every weariness of what it was, every fleeting vision of what was better, every sigh from out of its manifold ills, were notes of the one varied cry, "Come and help us." Man's heart, formed in the image of God, could not but ache to be re-formed by and for Him, though *an unknown God,* Who should reform it.

This longing increased as the time drew nigh, when Christ should come. The Roman biographer attests the existence of this expectation, not among the Jews only, but in the East[3]; this was quickened doubtless among the heathen by the Jewish Sibylline book, in that, amid the expectations of one sent from heaven, who should found a kingdom of righteousness, which the writer drew from the Hebrew prophets, he inserted denunciations of temporal vengeance upon the Romans, which Easterns would share. Still, although written 170 years before our Lord came[4], it had not apparently much effect until the time, when, from the prophecies of Daniel it was clear, that He must shortly come[5]. Yet the attempt of the Jewish[6] and heathen[7] historian to wrest it to Vespasian, shews how great must have been the influence of the expectation, which they attempted to turn aside. The Jews, who rejected our Lord Whom Haggai predicted, still were convinced that the prediction must be fulfilled before the destruction of the second temple. The impulse did not cease even after its destruction. R. Akiba, whom they accounted "[8] the first oracle of his time, the first and greatest guardian of the tradition

---

[1] חמד is "coveted." It is the passion forbidden in the tenth commandment, Ex. xx. 14, (bis) Deut. v. 18, vii. 25, Ex. xxxiv. 24, Jos. vii. 21, Pr. vi. 25, Mi. ii. 2. In Pr. xii. 12, it is a passionate desire which ends in choice. It is united with "loved" and "hated," Ib. i. 22; of the passionate idolatry, Is. i. 29. It is used of God's passionless good-pleasure in that which He chooses, yet speaking after the manner of men, Ps. lxviii. 17, and of man's not longing for Jesus, Is. liii. 2. The Piel is used once of intense longing. Cant. ii. 3. Men covet things for some real or seeming good; and so the passive form of the verb, נֶחְמָד or חָמוּד, are things which are the object of coveting, and so things desirable; נֶחְמָד Job xx. 20, Ps. xxxix. 12, s. xliv. 9; מַחְמָד Gen. ii. 9, iii. 6, Ps. xix. 11. Pr. xxi. 20. מַחְמָד with the gen. is "the desire of the eye," what it covets or desires, 1 Kgs xx. 6, Ex. xxiv. 16, 21, 25, Lam. ii. 4; or desirable things, belonging to one, Jo. iv. 5, Is. lxiv. 10, Lam. i. 10, 2 Chron. xxxvi. 19, or from it, מַחֲמַדֵּי בִטְנָם Hos. ix. 16. "the desires of the womb," "the desired children that their womb had borne," or with לְ, "the desired things consisting in their silver," מַחְמַד לְכַסְפָּם, Ib. ix. 6. or abs. Cant. v. 16. מַחְמָד occurs in the same sense, Lam. i. 7, 11; חֲמֻדוֹת or אִישׁ ח. of Daniel, as the object of the love of God, Dan. ix. 23, x. 11, 19; and of desirable things, Gen. xxvii. 15, 2 Chr. xx. 25, Dan. x. 3, xi. 38, 43, Ezr. viii. 27.

As to חֶמְדָה itself, two idioms have been confused; 1) that in which it is accessory to another word, as כְּלִי חֶמְדָה "vessels of desire," Hos. xiii. 15, Jer. xxv. 34, 2 Chr. xxxii. 27, Dan. xi. 8, Nah. ii. 10; אֶרֶץ חֶמְדָּה, "land of desire," Ps. cvi. 24, Jer. iii. 19, Zech. vii. 14; בָּתֵּי חֶמְדָּתְךָ "houses of thy desire," or "thy houses of desire," Ez. xxvi. 12; חֶלְקַת חֶמְדָּתִי "my portion of desire," Jer. xii. 10. These we might paraphrase "pleasant vessels," "pleasant land," as we might say "desirables." Not that the word חֶמְדָּה means, in itself, "pleasant things," any more than the word "coveted" signifies *pleasant,* though those things only are "coveted," which are thought to be pleasant. The original sense of the root, to "desire," is obviously

brought out the more, when the idea is not subsidiary, but the chief. There are four cases, in which *Chemdah* is so used. (1) "Jehoram died בְּלֹא חֶמְדָּה, unregretted," we should say; "no one longing for him," 2 Chr. xxi. 20; (2) "To whom is כָּל חֶמְדַת יִשְׂרָאֵל, the whole longing of Israel?" 1 Sam. ix. 20; (3) The well-known words חֶמְדַת נָשִׁים *Chemdath Nashim,* "the desire of women," Dan. xi. 37. If (as this is now generally understood) this means "the object of the longing of women," so much the more must חֶמְדַּת כָּל הַגּוֹיִם mean, "the object of the longing of all nations." They cannot mean, "the most desirable of all nations," "die liebsten aller Völker," Ew. formerly; "die edelsten aller Völker," Hitzig; "die auserlesensten derselben;" Umbreit. This must have been expressed by aid of the passive participle in any of the forms, by which a superlative is expressed. Nor can it mean "the costly things of all people;" ("die höhen Schätzen aller der völker," Ewald, "die Köstbarkeiten aller Nationen," Scholz). This, if expressed by the word at all, would have been, מַחְמַדֵּי כָּל הַגּוֹיִם. Rashi, A. E., Kimchi, explain as if בְּ were omitted. R. Isaac (Chizzuk Emunah, in Wagens. Tela ignea p. 288) quotes 2 Kgs xii. 13, where בֵּית יי stands as the acc. of place; R. Tanchum omits the verse, Abulwalid the instance. It is not noticed by R. Parchon, Kimchi, Menahem ben Saruk, David b. Abraham, in their dictionaries. Aberbanel retains the meaning, "the desire of all nations," interpreting it of the holy land. He paraphrases וִיבֹאוּ ח. כָּל הַג. "that they shall come to the holy land and there shall He be avenged of them, and then at that time 'I will fill this house with glory.' v. p. עֵץ, 4. The Anon. Arab. (Hunt. 206) renders "the most precious things of all nations shall come." [2] Rom. viii. 19–22. [3] Suet. Vesp. c. 4. [4] See Pusey's "Daniel the Prophet," pp. 364–368. [5] Ib. pp. 230–233. [6] Jos. B. J. vi. 5. 4. [7] Tac. Hist. v. 13. [8] "He was President of the academies of Lidda and Jafna, disciple and successor of Rabban Gamaliel, and a man of such learning and repute, that he was accounted among the Hebrews the first oracle &c." De Rossi Diz. stor. d. Autori Ebr. sub v.

and old law," of whom they said, that "[1] God revealed to him things unknown to Moses," was induced by this prophecy to acknowledge the impostor Bar-cochab, to the destruction of himself and of the most eminent of his time; fulfilling our Lord's words, [2] *I am come in My Father's name, and ye receive Me not; if another shall come in his own name, him ye will receive.* Akiba, following the traditional meaning of the great prophecy which rivetted his own eyes, paraphrased the words, "[3] Yet a little, a little of the kingdom, will I give to Israel upon the destruction of the first house, and after the kingdom, lo! I will shake heaven, and after that will come the Messiah."

Since the words can only mean "the Desire of all nations," he or that which all nations long for, the construction of the words does not affect the meaning. Herod doubtless thought to advance his own claims on the Jewish people by his material adorning of the temple; yet, although mankind do covet gold and silver, few could seriously think that, while a heathen immoral but observant poet could speak of "gold undiscovered and so better placed [4]," or our own of the "pale and common drudge 'Tween man and man," a Hebrew prophet could recognize gold and silver as *the desire of all nations.* R. Akiba and S. Jerome's Jewish teachers, after our Lord came, felt no difficulty in understanding it of a person. We cannot in English express the delicacy of the phrase, whereby manifoldness is combined in unity, the Object of desire containing in itself many objects of desire. To render "the desire of all nations" or "the desires of all nations" alike fail to do this. A great heathen master of language said to his wife, "fare you well, my longings [5]," i. e., I suppose, if he had analyzed his feelings, he meant that she manifoldly met the longings of his heart; she had in herself manifold gifts to content them. So St. Paul sums up all the truths and gifts of the Gospel, all which God shadowed out in the law and had given us in Christ, under the name of "[6] the good things to come." A pious modern writer [7] speaks of "the unseen *desirables* of the spiritual world." A psalmist expresses at once the collective, "God's Word" and the "words" contained in it, by

an idiom like Haggai's, joining the feminine singular as a collective with the plural verb; [8] *How sweet are Thy word unto my taste* lit. *palate.* It is God's word, at once collectively and individually, which was to the Psalmist so *sweet.* What was true of the whole, was true, one by one, of each part; what was true of each part, was true of the whole. So here, the object of this longing was manifold, but met in one, was concentrated in One, [9] *in Christ Jesus, Who of God is made unto us wisdom and righteousness and sanctification and redemption.* That which the whole world sighed and mourned for, knowingly or unknowingly, light to disperse its darkness, liberty from its spiritual slavery, restoration from its degradation, could not come to us without some one, who should impart it to us.

But if Jesus was *the longed-for of the nations* before He came, by that mute longing of need for that which it wants (as the parched ground thirsteth for the rain [10]) how much more afterward! So Micah and Isaiah describe many peoples inviting one another, [11] *Come ye, and let us go up to the mountain of the Lord, to the house of the God of Jacob; and He will teach us of His ways, and we will walk in His paths.* And in truth He became the *desire of the nations,* much more than of the Jews; as, St. Paul says [12], God foretold of old; *Moses saith, I will provoke you to jealousy by them that are not a people: by a foolish nation I will anger you. But Esaias is very bold and saith, I was found of them that sought Me not.*

So till now and in eternity, "[13] Christ is the longing of all holy souls, who long for nothing else, than to please Him, daily to love Him more, to worship Him better. So S. John longed for Him; *Come, Lord Jesus* [14]. So Isaiah; [15] *The desire of our soul is to Thy Name and to the remembrance of Thee: with my soul have I desired Thee in the night; yea, with my spirit within me, will I seek Thee early.* So S. Ignatius, "[16] Let fire, cross, troops of wild beasts, dissections, rendings, scattering of bones, mincing of limbs, grindings of the whole body, ill tortures of the devil come upon me, only may I gain Jesus Christ.—I seek Him Who for us died; I long for Him Who for us rose."

"[13] Hungerest thou and desirest food? Long for Jesus! He is the bread and refreshment of Angels. He is manna, *containing in Him*

---

[1] R. Bechai. See ab. p. 48. note 12.
[2] S. John v. 43.
[3] Sanhedrin. dist. *chelek* in Mart. Pug. fid. p. 305. R. Gedaliah B. Yechaiah quotes R. Akiba, rejecting his interpretation. "And not as Rabbi Akibah, who was interpreting this section; ' *Yet once, it is a little and I shake the heaven and the earth.*' He interprets, that when Israel went to the captivity of Babylon, Haggai the prophet spake this section, and its meaning is, that in this house there will be little glory, and after this I will bring the desire of the heathen to Jerusalem." Shalsheleth Hakkabbala extracted in the Carm. R. Lipmanni confut. p. 619. in Wagenseil Tela ignea satanæ.

[4] "Aurum irrepertum et sic melius situm." Hor. Od. iii. 3. 49.
[5] "Valete, mea desideria, valete." Cic. Ep. ad Famil. xiv. 2. fin.
[6] Heb. x. 1. τῶν μελλόντων ἀγαθῶν.
[7] Dr. Watts Vol. i. Serm. 4.
[8] Ps. cxix. 103. מה נמלצו לחכי אמרתך.
[9] 1 Cor. i. 30.
[10] Euripides so uses ἐρᾶν, of the ground longing for the rain.
[11] Mi. iv. 2. Is. ii. 3.
[12] Rom. x. 19, 20; quoting Deut. xxxii. 21. Is. lxv. 2.
[13] Lap.   [14] Rev. xxii. 20.   [15] Is. xxvi. 8, 9.
[16] Ep. ad Rom. in Ruinart Acta Mart. p. 703.

| Before
C H R I S T
cir. 520. | I will fill this house with glory, saith the LORD of hosts. | 8 The silver *is* mine and the gold *is* mine, saith the LORD of hosts. | Before
C H R I S T
cir. 520. |

all sweetness and pleasurable delight. Thirstest thou? Long for Jesus! He is the well of *living water*, refreshing, so that thou shouldest thirst no more. Art thou sick? Go to Jesus. He is the Saviour, the physician, nay, salvation itself. Art thou dying? Sigh for Jesus! He is *the resurrection and the life.* Art thou perplexed? Come to Jesus! He is *the Angel of great counsel.* Art thou ignorant and erring? Ask Jesus; He is *the way, the truth and the life.* Art thou a sinner? Call on Jesus! For *He shall save His people from their sins.* To this end He came into the world: *This is all His fruit, to take away sin.* Art thou tempted by pride, gluttony, lust, sloth? Call on Jesus! He is humility, soberness, chastity, love, fervor: *He bare our infirmities, and carried,* yea still beareth and carrieth, *our griefs.* Seekest thou beauty? He is *fairer than the children of men.* Seekest thou wealth? In Him are *all treasures,* yea in Him *the fullness of the Godhead dwelleth.* Art thou ambitious of honors? *Glory and riches are in His house. He is the King of glory.* Seekest thou a friend? He hath the greatest love for thee, Who for love of thee came down from heaven, toiled, endured the Sweat of Blood, the Cross and Death; He prayed for thee by name in the garden, and poured forth tears of Blood! Seekest thou wisdom? He is the Eternal and Uncreated Wisdom of the Father! Wishest thou for consolation and joy? He is the sweetness of souls, the joy and jubilee of Angels. Wishest thou for righteousness and holiness? He is *the Holy of holies;* He is *everlasting Righteousness,* justifying and sanctifying all who believe and hope in Him. Wishest thou for a blissful life? He is *life eternal,* the bliss of the saints. Long then for Him, love Him, sigh for Him! In Him thou wilt find all good; out of Him, all evil, all misery. Say then with S. Francis, ' My Jesus, my love and my all!' O Good Jesus, burst the cataract of Thy love, that its streams, yea seas, may flow down upon us, yea, inebriate and overwhelm us."

And I will fill this house with glory. The glory then was not to be anything, which came from man, but directly from God. It was the received expression of God's manifestation of Himself in the tabernacle [1], in Solomon's temple [2], and of the ideal temple [3] which Ezekiel saw, after the likeness of that of Solomon, that *the glory of the Lord*

filled the house. When then of this second temple God uses the self-same words, that He will *fill it with glory,* with what other glory should He fill it than His own? In the history it is said, *the glory of the Lord filled the temple;* for there man relates what God did. Here it is God Himself Who speaks; so He says not, *the glory of the Lord,* but, *I will fill the house with glory,* glory which was His to give, which came from Himself. To interpret that *glory* of anything material, is to do violence to language, to force on words of Scripture an unworthy sense, which they refuse to bear.

The gold upon the walls, even had this second temple been adorned like the first, did not fill the temple of Solomon. However richly any building might be overlaid with gold, no one could say that it is filled with it. A building is filled with what it contains; a mint or treasure-house may be filled with gold: the temple of God was *filled,* we are told, *with the glory of the Lord.* His creatures bring Him such things as they can offer; they bring [4] *gold and incense;* they [5] *bring presents* and *offer gifts;* they do it, moved by His Spirit, as acceptable to Him. God is nowhere said, Himself to give these offerings to Himself.

8. *The silver is Mine, and the gold is Mine.* These words, which have occasioned some to think, that God, in speaking of the glory with which He should fill the house, meant our material riches, suggest the contrary. For silver was no ornament of the temple of Solomon. Everything was overlaid with gold. In the tabernacle there were bowls of silver [6], in Solomon's temple they and all were of gold [7]. Silver, we are expressly told, *was nothing accounted of* [8] *in the days of Solomon: he* [9] *made silver to be in Jerusalem as stones—for abundance.* Rather, as God says by the Psalmist, [10] *Every beast of the forest is Mine, so are the cattle upon a thousand hills: I know all the fowls of the mountains, and the wild beasts of the field are Mine. If I were hungry, I would not tell thee: for the world is Mine and the fullness thereof:* so here He tells them, that for the glory of His house He needed not gold or silver: for all the wealth of the world is His. They had no ground " [11] to grieve then, that they could not equal the magnificence of Solomon who had abundance of gold and silver." All was God's. He

---

[1] Ex. xl. 34, 35.
[2] 1 Kgs viii. 11. 2 Chr. v. 14. vii. 1–12.
[3] Ezek. xliii. 5. xliv. 4.
[4] Is. lx. 6.   [5] Ps. lxxii. 10.
[6] Nu. vii. 19, 25, 31. &c. The "charger" (קְעָרָה)

which in the tabernacle was of silver (Nu. vii. 13. &c.) does not appear in the temple of Solomon.
[7] 1 Kgs vii. 50. 2 Chr. iv. 8.
[8] 1 Kgs x. 21.
[9] Ib. 27.   [10] Ps. l. 10–12.   [11] Lap.

9 [1] The glory of this latter house shall be greater

than of the former, saith
the LORD of hosts : and in

would fill it with divine glory. The Desire
of all nations, Christ, should come, and be a
glory, to which all created glory is nothing.

"[1] God says really and truly, that the silver and gold is His, which in utmost bounty
He created, and in His most just government
administers, so that, without His will and
dominion, neither can the bad have gold and
silver for the punishment of avarice, nor the
good for the use of mercy. Its abundance
does not inflate the good, nor its want crush
them : but the bad, when bestowed, it blinds:
when taken away, it tortures."

"[2] It is as if He would say, Think not the
temple inglorious, because, may be, it will
have no portion of gold or silver, and their
splendor. I need not such things. How
should I? For Mine is the silver and Mine
the gold, saith the Lord Almighty. I seek
rather true worshipers : with their brightness will I guild this temple. Let him come
who hath right faith, is adorned by graces,
gleams with love for Me, is pure in heart,
poor in spirit, compassionate and good."
"These make the temple, i. e. the Church,
glorious and renowned, being glorified by
Christ. For they have learned to pray [3], The
glory of the Lord our God be upon us."

9. The glory of this latter house shall be greater
than of the former, or, perhaps, more probably,
the later glory of this house shall be greater than
the former; for he had already spoken of the
present temple, as identical with that before
the captivity; "[4] Who is left among you
that saw this house in her first glory, and how
do you see it now?" He had spoken of its
first glory. Now he says, in contrast, its later
glory should be greater than that of its most
glorious times [5]. In this case the question,
whether the temple of Herod was a different
material building from that of Zerubbabel,
falls away. In either case, the contrast is
between two things, either the temple in

that its former estate, and this its latter
estate after the captivity, or the two
temples of Solomon and Zerubbabel. There
is no room for a third temple. God holds
out no vain hopes. To comfort those distressed by the poverty of the house of God
which they were building, God promises a
glory to this house greater than before. A
temple, erected, after this had lain waste
above 1800 years, even if Anti-Christ were
to come now and to erect a temple at Jerusalem, could be no fulfillment of this
prophecy.

In material magnificence the temple of
Solomon, built and adorned with all the
treasures accumulated by David and enlarged
by Solomon, far surpassed all which Herod,
amid his attempts to give a material meaning to the prophecy, could do. His attempt
shews how the eyes of the Jews were fixed
on this prophecy, then when it was about to
be fulfilled. While taking pains, through
the gradualness of his rebuilding, to preserve
the identity of the fabric, he lavished his
wealth, to draw off their thoughts from the
king, whom the Jews looked for, to himself.
The friendship of the Romans who were
lords of all, was to replace the all nations, of
whom Haggai spoke; he pointed also to the
length of peace, the possession of wealth, the
greatness of revenues, the surpassing ex-
penditure beyond those before [6]. A small
section of Erastians admitted these claims of
the murderer of his sons. The Jews generally were not diverted from looking on to
Him Who should come. Those five things,
the absence whereof they felt, were connected
with their atoning worship or God's Presence among them; "[7] the ark with the
mercy-seat and the Cherubim, the Urim and
Tummim, the fire from heaven, the Shechinah, the Holy Ghost." Material magnificence could not replace spiritual glory. The

---

[1] S. Aug. Serm. 50. (de Ag. 2.) n. 4, 5.   [2] S. Cyr.
[3] Ps. xc. 17.
[4] ii. 3. So the LXX. " Wherefore great will be
the last glory of this house above the first [glory]."
In the other case, the order would have probably
been, הזה האחרון הבית כבוד as in Ex. iii. 3,
De. ii. 7, iv. 6, 1 Sam. xii. 16, 1 Kgs iii. 9, xx. 13, 28,
Jon. i. 12; but, as Köhler observes, this is not quite
uniform, as in 2 Chr. i. 10.
[6] This interpretation involves a change in the
wording of the argument from this prophecy, as to
the time of our Lord's first coming. For thus interpreted, it does not speak of a second house, and so
does not, in terms, speak of the material building
which was destroyed. R. Isaac made use of this :
"a difficulty need not be raised, that he said, 'this
house' of the house which is to be built, since of
the first house, which in their time was of old
waste, he said 'this house' in the words, 'who is

left among you, who hath seen this house in its
first glory?' and as 'this house' is spoken of the
house of the sanctuary which was then desolate,
which was passed away, so he saith, 'this house,'
of the house which shall be." Chizzuch Emunah,
c. 34. Wagens. p. 292.
[6] In his oration to the Jews, " Our forefathers
built this temple to the supreme God after the
return from Babylon, yet in size it lacks 60 cubits
in height; for so much did the first, which Solomon
built, exceed.—But since, by the counsel of God, I
now rule, and we have a long peace, and ample
funds and large revenues; and chief of all, the
Romans, who, so to speak, are lords of all, are our
friends and kindly disposed," (Joseph. Ant. xv. 11.
1.) and a little later (n. 3) "exceeding the expendi-
ture of those aforetime, in a way in which no other
appears to have adorned the temple." See Hengst.
Christ. iii. 257, 258. ed. 2.
[7] Yoma 21. b.

Before
C H R I S T
cir. 520.

k Ps. 85. 8, 9.
Luke 2. 14.
Eph. 2. 14.

this place will I give [k] peace, saith the LORD of hosts.

10 ¶ In the four and twentieth *day* of the ninth *month*, in the second year

Before
C H R I S T
cir. 520.

explanations of the great Jewish authorities [1], that the second temple was superior to the first in structure (which was untrue) or in duration, were laid aside by Jews who had any other solution wherewith to satisfy themselves. "The Shechinah and the five precious things," says one [2], "which, according to our wise of blessed memory, were in it, and not in the second house, raised and exalted it beyond compare." Another [3] says, "When Haggai saith, 'greater shall be the glory of this later house than the first,' how is it, that the house which Zerubbabel built through the income which the king of Persia gave them was more glorious than the house which Solomon built? And though it is said that the building which Herod made, was exceeding beautiful and rich, we should not think that it was in its beauty like to the house which Solomon built. For what the wise of blessed memory have said of the beauty of the house of Herod is in relation to the house which Zerubbabel built. How much more, since Scripture saith not, 'Great shall be the *beauty* or the *wealth* of this latter house above the first,' but the *glory:* and the glory is not the wealth or the beauty, or the largeness of the dimensions of the building, as they said in their interpretations; for the 'glory' is in truth spoken of the glory of God, which filled the tabernacle, after it was set up, and of the glory of God which filled

the house of God, which Solomon built, when he brought the ark into the holy of holies, which is the Divine cloud and the Light supreme, which came down thither in the eyes of all the people, and it is said, 'And it was when the priests came out of the holy place, the cloud filled the house of God, and the priests could not stand to minister because of the cloud, for the glory of God filled the house of God.' And this glory was not in the second house. And how shall it be said, if so, 'great shall be the glory of this later house above the first'?" The poor unconverted Jew did not know the answer to his question: "Through the Presence of God, in the substance of our flesh; through *the Son given to us*, Whose *name* should be *Mighty God.*" The glory of this temple was in Him Who [4] *was made Flesh and dwelt among us, and we beheld His glory, the glory as of the Only Begotten of the Father, full of grace and truth.* "[5] There Christ, the Son of God, was, as a Child, offered to God: there He sat in the midst of the Doctors; there He taught and revealed things, hidden from the foundation of the world. The glory of the temple of Solomon was, that in it the majesty of God appeared, veiling itself in a cloud: in this, that same Majesty shewed itself, in very deed united with the Flesh, visible to sight: so that Jesus Himself said, [6] *He that hath seen Me hath seen the Father.* This it was which

[1] "Rab and Samuel disputed hereon, or, as others, R. Jochánan and R. Eliezer. The former said, 'it shall be more glorious in structure;' the latter, 'in years.'" Baba bathra c. 1. f. 30. R. Asariah quotes also from the Shir hashshirim Rabba on Cant. ii. 12 and viii. 1, and adds, "We have found that the best interpreters explained this prophecy literally as to the second house." This is followed by Kimchi, Rashi, A. E., Lipmann (Nizz. n. 260), Manasseh ben Israel (de ternf. vitæ) iii. 4. (Hilpert de gloria Templi post., Thes. Theol.-Phil. p. 1086 sqq.) Tanchum. Of the magnificence of the building they allege only that the building was in *size* equal to that of Solomon, while even in material magnificence it was beyond measure inferior. The relative duration they underrate; "the first, 410 years; the second 420;" for from the xi[th] of Solomon's reign, B. C. 1005, to the burning of the temple in the xi[th] of Zedekiah, were 417 years; but from the vi[th] of Darius when the 2d temple was finished, B. C. 515, to the burning of the temple under Titus A.D. 70, were 585 years. But mere duration is not glory. R. Isaac says as Abarbanel; "But it is a difficulty in what they say, that Scripture says not, 'great shall be the building of the house,' or, 'the time of the house,' only 'great shall be the glory of the house;' for what that the 2d house stood ten years more than the 1st, this was not such great glory, that for this the prophet should say what he said: and again though the days during which the 2d house stood were 100 years more than the duration of the first house, and though in its building it were twofold greater than the first house, how saith Scripture of it on this account, that its glory

[2] R. Asariah de Rossi *Imre Binah*, c. 51, in Hilpert l. c. n. 8. His own solution is that the glory was not in the temple itself, but in that kings brought presents to it. Ib. 10.

[3] Abarbanel Quæst. iv. in Hagg. f. עיר. He says that "the interpreters, all of them explained it of the second house." p. ער 2. Abarb subjoins a criticism, which R. Asaria, *Imre-Binah* c. 54, saw to be mistaken, that ראשון and אחרון could not be said of two things of which אחר and שני are, he says, used) against which R. Asariah quotes Jer. l. 17. Gen. xxxiii. 2. Add Ex. iv. 8. Deut. xxiv. 3, 4. Ru. iii. 10, Is. viii. 23. [ix. 1. Eng.]

[4] S. John i. 14.   [5] Lap.   [6] S. John xiv. 9.

was greater than the first, since the glory which dwelt in the first house did not dwell in it?" Chizz. Em. l. c. pp. 287, 288. "Wherefore it is rather the true glory which is the abiding of the glory of the Shechinah in this house for ever; which did not abide continually in the first house; but in the second house the glory did not dwell at all; for they had not the ark and the mercy seat and the cherubim, or the Urim and Tummim, nor the Holy Spirit, nor the heavenly fire, nor the anointing oil, as it was in the 1st house." Ib. p. 293. Others made the glory to consist in the absence of idolatry, quoted Ib. p. 286. R. Lipmann Nizz. p. 42, makes in it to consist in the uninterruptedness of the worship of God there, whereas the temple was shut by Ahaz and Manasseh [as was the second at least desecrated by Antiochus Epiphanes for 3 years. 1 Macc. i. 54, iv. 59.]

Before CHRIST cir. 520.	of Darius, câme the word of the LORD by Haggai the prophet saying,
[1] Lev. 10. 10, 11. Deut. 33. 10. Mal. 2. 7.	11 Thus saith the LORD of hosts; [1] Ask now t h e

priests *concerning* the law saying,	Before CHRIST cir. 520.

12 If one bear holy flesh in the skirt of his garment, and with his

Malachi sang with joy: [1] *The Lord Whom ye seek shall suddenly come to His temple, even the Messenger of the covenant, whom ye delight in." And in this place I will give peace.* Temporal peace they had now, nor was there any prospect of its being disturbed. They were quiet subjects of the Persiam empire, which included also all their former enemies, greater or less. Alexander subdued all the bordering countries which did not yield, but spared themselves. Temporal peace then was nothing to be then given them; for they had it. In later times they had it not. The temple itself was profaned by Antiochus Epiphanes. "[2] Her sanctuary was laid waste like a wilderness. As had been her glory, so was her dishonor increased." Again by Pompey[3], by Crassus[4], the Parthians[5], before it was destroyed by Titus and the Romans. Jews saw this and, knowing nothing of the peace in Jesus, argued from the absence of outward peace, that the prophecy was not fulfilled under the second temple. "[6] What Scripture says, 'and in this place I will give peace,' is opposed to their interpretation. For all the days of the duration of the 2d house were *in strait of times* and not in peace, as was written in Daniel, *and threescore and two weeks: the street shall be built again and the fosse, and in strait of time,* and, as I said, in the time of Herod there was no peace whatever, for the sword did not depart from his house to the day of his death; and after his death the hatred among the Jews increased, and the Gentiles straitened them, until they were destroyed from the face of the earth."

But spiritual peace is, throughout prophecy, part of the promise of the Gospel. Christ Himself was to be [7] *the Prince of peace : of the increase of His government and of His peace there was to be no end;* in His days [8] *the mountains were to bring peace to the people; there should be abundance of peace, so long as the moon endureth; the work of righteousness* was to be *peace* [9]; *the chastisement of our peace* [that which obtained it] *was upon*

Him [10]; *great* should be *the peace of her children* [11]; in the Gospel God would give *peace,* true *peace,* to the *far off and the near* [12]; He would extend [13] *peace to her like a river :* the good things of the Gospel was *the publishing of peace* [14]. The Gospel is described as [15] *a covenant of peace:* the promised king [16] *shall speak peace to the Heathen;* He Himself should be *our peace* [17]. And when He was born, the angels proclaimed [18] *on earth peace, goodwill toward men :* [19] *The Dayspring from on high visited us, to guide our feet into the way of peace.* He Himself says, [20] *My peace I leave with you.* He spake, that [21] *in Me ye might have peace.* S. Peter sums up *the word which God sent unto the children of Israel,* as [22] *preaching peace by Jesus Christ :* [23] *the kingdom of God is joy and peace;* [24] Christ *is our peace; made peace; preaches peace. God calleth us to peace* [25], in the Gospel: [26] *being justified by faith, we have peace with God through Jesus Christ our Lord;* [27] *the fruit of the Spirit is love joy peace.* Spiritual peace being thus prominent in the Gospel and in prophecy, as the gift of God, it were unnatural to explain *the peace* which God promised here to give, as other than He promised elsewhere; peace in Him Who is *our peace, Jesus Christ.*

"[28] Peace and tranquillity of mind is above all glory of the house; because peace passeth all understanding. This is peace above peace, which shall be given after the third shaking of heaven sea earth, dry land, when He shall destroy all powers and principalities [in the day of judgment].—And so shall there be peace throughout, that, no bodily passions or hindrances of unbelieving mind resisting, Christ shall be all in all, exhibiting the hearts of all subdued to the Father."

11–14. *Ask now the priests concerning the law.* The priests answer rightly, that, by the law, insulated unholiness spread further than insulated holiness. The flesh of the sacrifice hallowed whatever it should touch [29], but not further; but the human being, who was defiled by touching a dead body, defiled all he might touch [30]. Haggai does not

[1] Mal. iii. 1. [2] 1 Macc. i. 39, 40.
[3] Jos. Ant. xiv. 4. 4. B. J. i. 7.
[4] Ant. xiv. 7. 1. B. J. i. 9. 8.
[5] Ant. xiv. 13. 3. 4.
[6] "Abraham B. Dior in his book of the Cabbala, p. 43" in R. Isaac Chizz. Em. l. c. p. 287. R. Isaac makes as if he had answered the explanation as to Jesus by quoting S. Matt. x. 34. l. c. p. 292, 293.
[7] Is. ix. 6, 7. [8] Ps. lxxii. 3. 7.
[9] Is. xxxii. 17. [10] Ib. liii. 5.

[11] Ib. liv. 13. [12] Ib. lvii. 19.
[13] Ib. lxvi. 12. [14] Ib. lii. 7.
[15] Ez. xxxiv. 25. [16] Zech. ix. 10.
[17] Mi. v. 5. [18] S. Luke ii. 14. [19] Ib. i. 79.
[20] S. John xiv. 27. [21] Ib. xvi. 33.
[22] Acts x. 36. [23] Rom. xiv. 17.
[24] Eph. ii. 14, 15, 17. [25] 1 Cor. vii. 15.
[26] Rom. v. 1. [27] Gal. v. 22.
[28] S. Ambr. l. c. n. 14. Opp. ii. 913.
[29] Lev. vi. 19 (27 Eng.) [30] Nu. xix. 22.

skirt do touch bread, or pottage, or wine, or oil, or any meat, shall it be holy? And the priest answered and said, No.

13 Then said Haggai, m Num. 19. 11. If *one that is* m unclean by a dead body touch any of these, shall it be unclean? And the priests answered and said, It shall be unclean.

14 Then answered Haggai, and said, n So *is* this n Tit. 1. 15. people, and so *is* this nation before me, saith the LORD; a n d s o *is* every work of their hands; and

that which they offer there *is* unclean.

15 A n d n o w, I pray y o u, °consider from this °ch. 1. 5. day and upward, from before a stone was laid upon a stone in the temple of the LORD:

16 S i n c e t h o s e *days* were, P when *one* came to P ch. 1. 6, 9. Zech. 8. 10. an heap of twenty *measures*, there were *but* ten: when *one* c a m e to t h e pressfat for to draw out fifty *vessels* o u t o f t h e press, t h e r e w e r e *but* q Deut. 28. 22. twenty. 1 Kin. 8. 37. ch. 1. 9.

17 q I smote y o u with Amos 4. 9.

---

apply the first part; viz. that the worship on the altar which they reared, while they neglected the building of the temple, did not hallow. The possession of a holy thing does not counterbalance disobedience. Contrariwise, one defilement defiled the whole man and all which he touched, according to that, [1] *whosoever shall keep the whole law and yet offend in one point, he is guilty of all.*

In the application, the two melt into one; for the holy thing, viz. the altar which they raised out of fear on their return, so far from hallowing the land or people by the sacrifices offered thereon, was itself defiled. *This people* and *this nation* (not " My people ") since they in act disowned Him. *Whatever they offer there*, i. e. on that altar, instead of the temple which God commanded, is unclean, offending Him Who gave all.

15. *And now, I pray you.* Observe his tenderness, in drawing their attention to it [2]. *Consider from this day and upward.* He bids them look backward, *from before a stone was laid upon a stone*, i. e. from the last moment of their neglect in building the house of God; *from since those* days *were*, or *from* the time backward *when those things were*, (resuming, in the word, *from-their-being* [3], the date which

[1] S. James ii. 10.
[2] As expressed by נָא, here and 18.
[3] מֵהְיוֹתָם.
[4] Ruth iii. 7. Neh. xiii. 15. 2 Chr. xxxi. 6–9.
[5] Vulg.   [6] LXX.
[7] פּוּרָה only occurs beside, Is. lxiii. 3; where it is the winefat itself. The LXX render it μετρηταὶ ; Jon. נַרְבִּין (which they use for נֵבֶל 1 Sam. x. 3, xxv. 18, Jer. xiii. 12) Vulg. *lagenas.*
[8] Deut. xxviii. 27.   [9] Am. iv. 9.

he had just given, viz. the beginning of their resuming the building backward, during all those years of neglect) *one came to a heap of twenty* measures. The precise measure is not mentioned [4]: the force of the appeal lay in the proportion : *the heap* of corn which, usually, would yield *twenty*, (whether bushels [5] or *seahs* [6] or any other measure, for the heap itself being of no defined size, neither could the quantity expected from it be defined) *there were ten* only ; *one came to the pressvat to draw out fifty* vessels out of the *press*, or perhaps *fifty poorah*, i. e. the ordinary quantity drawn out at one time from the press [7], *there were*, or *it had become*, *twenty*, two-fifths only of what they looked for and ordinarily obtained. The dried grapes yielded so little.

17. *I smote you with blasting and mildew*, two diseases of corn, which Moses had foretold [8] as chastisements on disobedience and God's infliction, of which Amos had spoken in these self-same words [9]. Haggai adds the *hail*, as destructive of the vines [10]. *Yet [And]* ye turned *you not to Me* lit. *there were none— you*, (accusative [11]) i. e. who turned you unto Me. The words are elliptical, but express the entire absence of conversion, of any who turned to God.

[10] Ps. lxxviii. 47.
[11] אֶתְכֶם marking the acc., אֵין אֶתְכֶם is not for אֵינְכֶם, which itself, according to the common Hebrew construction, would require a participle, to express action on their part. See instances in Fürst Conc. p. 45. v. אֵין, Ex. v. 19, De. i. 42, Is. i. 15, Jer. xiv. 12 (bis), xxxvii. 14; אֵינֶךְ Gen. xx. 7, xliii. 5, Ex. viii. 17, Jud. xii. 3, 1 Sam. xix. 11, 2 Sam. xix. 8, 1 Kgs xxi. 5, Neh. ii. 2, Eccl. xi. 5, 6. Jer. vii. 17; אֵינָם, De. i. 32, iv. 12, 2 Kgs xii. 8, Ez. xx. 39,

Before
CHRIST
cir. 520.

ʳ ch. 1. 11.
ˢ Jer. 5. 3.
Amos 4. 6, 8, 9,
10, 11.

blasting and mildew and with hail ʳ in all the labors of your hands; ˢ yet ye *turned* not to me, saith the LORD.

18 Consider now from this day and upward, from the four and twentieth day of the ninth *month, even* from ᵗ the day that the foundation of the LORD's

ᵗ Zech. 8. 9.

temple was laid, consider it.

Before
CHRIST
cir. 520.

19 ᵘ Is the seed yet in the barn? yea, as yet the vine, and the fig tree, and the pomegranate, and the olive tree, hath not brought forth: from this day will I bless you.

ᵘ Zech. 8. 12.

20 ¶ And again the word of the LORD came

---

18. *From the day that the foundation of the Lord's house.* Zechariah, in a passage corresponding to this, uses the same words ¹, *the day that the foundation of the house of the Lord of hosts was laid, that the temple might be built,* not of the first foundation, but of the work as resumed in obedience to the words by *the mouth of the prophets,* Haggai and himself, which, Ezra also says, was ² *in the second year of Darius.* But that work was resumed, not now at the time of this prophecy, but three months before, on the 24th of the sixth month. Since then the word translated here, *from* ³, is in no case used of the present time, Haggai gives two dates, the resumption of the work, as marked in these words, and the actual present. He would then say, that even in these last months, since they had begun the work, there were as yet no signs for the better. There was yet no *seed in the barn,* the harvest having been blighted and the fruit-trees stripped by the hail before the close of the sixth month, when they resumed the work. Yet though there were as yet no signs of change, no earnest that the promise should be fulfilled, God pledges His word, *from this day I will bless you.*

Thenceforth, from their obedience, God would give them those fruits of the earth, which in His Providence had been, during their negligence, withheld. *God,* said St.

Mal. ii. 2, 9; אֵינְנּוּ, De. xxi. 18, 20, Jud. iii. 25, 1 Sam. xi. 7, 2 Chr. xvii. 7, Esth. v. 13, Eccl. v. 11, viii. 7, 13, 16, ix. 2, Jer. xxxviii. 4, xliv. 16; אַיִן, 2 Kgs xvii. 26, 34 bis, Eccl. iv. 17, ix. 5, Neh. xiii. 24, Jer. xxxii. 33, Ezek. iii. 7. אֲלֵיכֶם וְאֵינְכֶם would have signified, "and ye were not [well disposed] toward Me," as in Hos. iii. 3, Jer. xv. 1, 2 Kgs vi. 11 (Ewald's instances Lehrb. n. 217 c), Gen. xxxi. 5; not (as required here) "ye turned you not unto Me," as in Am. iv. 6, 8, 9, 10, 11. Böttcher (Lehrbuch n. 516. d.) compares bene te (which implies a verb), en illum (where en is as a verb.) These however are exclamations, not parts of sentences. He thinks that אֵין is joined, 1) with a nom., and then an acc. after יֵשׁ, 1 Sam. xxvi. 16; that יֵשׁ has an acc. Gen. xxiii. 8, 2 Kgs x. 15, and אֵין /הֵן Zech. vii. 7.
¹ Zech. viii. 9.
² Ezr. iv. 24, v. 1.
³ Such use of לְמִן would be inconsistent with any

Paul and Barnabas, ⁴ *left not Himself without witness, in that He did good, and gave us rain from heaven and fruitful seasons, filling our hearts with food and gladness.*

All the Old and New Testament, the Law, the Prophets and the Psalms, the Apostles and our Lord Himself, bear witness to the Providence of God Who makes His natural laws serve to the moral discipline of His creature, man. The physical theory, which presupposes that God so fixed the laws of His creation, as to leave no room for Himself to vary them, would, if ever so true, only come to this, that Almighty God knowing absolutely (as He must know) the actions of His creatures (in what way soever this is reconcilable with our free-agency, of which we are conscious), framed the laws of His physical creation, so that plenty or famine, healthiness of our cattle or of the fruits of the earth or their sickness, should coincide with the good or evil conduct of man, with his prayers or his neglect of prayer. The reward or chastisement alike come to man, whether they be the result of God's Will, acting apart from any system which He has created, or in it and through it. It is alike His Providential agency, whether He have established any such system with all its minute variations, or whether those variations are the immediate result of His sovereign

force of לְ. It is used of a *terminus à quo,* distant from the present, and is equivalent to "up to and from." So Jud. xix. 30, "No such deed was seen or done from the day that the children of Israel came up," i. e. looking back to that time and from it. So 2 Sam. vii. 6, "Since the time that I brought up the children of Israel out of Egypt," lit. "up to from the day." Add Ex. ix. 18, Deut. iv. 32, ix. 7, 2 Sam. vii. 11, xix. 25, Is. vii. 17, Jer. vii. 7, 25, xxv. 5, xxxii. 31, 1 Chr. xvii. 10, Mal. iii. 7. But there is no ground for thinking that Haggai used the word in any sense, in which it had not been used before him. The only construction consistent with the use of לְמִן elsewhere is, that the *terminus ad quem,* elsewhere expressed by וְעַד, having been expressed by the present מִיּוֹם, the distant *terminus à quo* is, as elsewhere, expressed by לְמִן.
⁴ Acts xiv. 17.

Before
C H R I S T
cir. 520.

unto Haggai in the four and twentieth *day* of the month, saying,

21 Speak to Zerubbabel, *governor of Judah, saying, *I will s h a k e t h e heavens and the earth;

22 And *I w i l l overthrow the throne of king-

x ch. 1. 14.
y ver. 6. 7.
Heb. 12. 26.

z Dan. 2. 44.
Matt. 24. 7.

doms, and I will destroy the strength of the kingdoms of the heathen; *I will overthrow the chariots, and those that ride in them; and the horses and their r i d e r s shall come down, every one by the sword of his brother.

Before
C H R I S T
cir. 520.

a Mic. 5. 10.
Zech. 4. 6.
& 9. 10.

Will. If He has instituted any physical system, so that the rain, hail, and its proportions, size, destructiveness, should come in a regulated irregularity, as fixed in all eternity as the revolutions of the heavenly bodies or the courses of the comets, then we come only to a more intricate perfection of His creation, that in all eternity He framed those laws in an exact conformity to the perfectly foreseen actions of men good and evil, and to their prayers also: that He, knowing certainly whether the creature, which He has framed to have its bliss in depending on Him, would or would not cry unto Him, framed those physical laws in conformity therewith; so that the supply of what is necessary for our wants or its withholding shall be in all time inworked into the system of our probation. Only, not to keep God out of His own world, we must remember that other truth, that, whether God act in any such system or no, He [1] *upholdeth all things by the word of His power* by an ever-present working; so that it is He Who at each moment doth what is done, doth and maintains in existence all which He has created, in the exact order and variations of their being. [2] *Fire and hail, snow and vapor, stormy wind fulfilling His word*, are as immediate results of His Divine Agency, in whatever way it pleaseth Him to act, and are the expression of His Will.

21. *I will shake.* Haggai closes by resuming the words of a former prophecy to Zerubbabel and Joshua, which ended in the coming of Christ. Even thus it is plain, that the prophecy does not belong personally to Zerubbabel, but to him and his descendants, chiefly to Christ. There was in Zerubbabel's time no shaking of the heaven or of nations. Darius had indeed to put down an unusual number of rebellions in the first few years after his accession; but, although he magnified himself on occasion of their suppression, they were only so many distinct and unconcerted revolts, each under its own head. All were far away in the distant East, in Baby-

lonia, Susiana, Media, Armenia, Assyria, Hyrcania, Parthia, Sagartia, Margiana, Arachosia [3]. The Persian *empire*, spread " [4] probably over 2,000,000 square miles, or more than half of modern Europe," was not threatened; no foreign enemy assailed it; one impostor only claimed the throne of Darius. This would, if successful, have been, like his own accession, a change of dynasty, affecting nothing externally. But neither were lasting, some were very trifling. Two decisive battles subdued Babylonia: of Media the brief summary is given; " [5] the Medes revolted from Darius, and having revolted were brought back into subjection, defeated in battle." The Susianians slew their own pretender, on the approach of the troops of Darius. We have indeed mostly the account only of the victor. But these are only self-glorying records of victories, accomplished in succession, within a few years. Sometimes the satrap of the province put the revolt down at once. At most two battles ended in the crucifixion of the rebel. The Jews, if they heard of them, knew them to be of no account. For the destroyer of the Persian empire was to come from the West [6]; the fourth sovereign was to stir up all against the realm of Grecia [7], and Darius was but the third. In the same second year of Darius, in which Haggai gave this prophecy, the whole earth was exhibited to Zechariah as [8] *sitting still and at rest.*

The overthrow prophesied is also universal. It is not one throne only, as of Persia, but *the throne*, i. e. the sovereigns, *of kingdoms;* not a change of dynasty, but a destruction of their *strength;* not of a few powers only, but *the kingdoms of the heathen;* and that, in detail; that, in which their chief strength lay, the chariots and horsemen and their riders, and this, man by man, *every one by the sword of his brother.* This mutual destruction is a feature of the judgments at the end of the world against Gog and Magog [9]; and of the yet unfulfilled prophecies of Zechariah [10]. Its stretching out so far does not hinder its par-

[1] Heb. i. 3. [2] Ps. cxlviii. 8.
[3] Rawlinson v. Empires iv. pp. 407–415. chiefly from Behistun Inscription.

[4] Id. Ib. p. 2. [5] Herod i. 130.
[6] Dan. viii. 5. [7] Ib. xi. 2. [8] Zech. i. 11.
[9] Ezek. xxxviii. 21. [10] Zech. xiv. 17.

23 In that d a y, saith the LORD of hosts, will I

take thee, O Zerubbabel, my servant, the son of She-

tial fulfillment in earlier times. Zerubbabel stood, at the return from the captivity, as the representative of the house of David and heir of the promises to him, though in an inferior temporal condition; thereby the rather shewing that the main import of the prophecy was not temporal. As then Ezekiel prophesied, [1] *I will set up One Shepherd over them, and He shall feed them, My servant David;* [2] *And David My servant* shall be *king over them; and My servant David shall be their prince forever;* and Jeremiah, [3] *They shall serve the Lord their God and David their king, whom I will raise up unto them;* and Hosea, that [4] *after many days shall the children of Israel return and seek the Lord their God, and David their king,* meaning by David, the great descendant of David, in whom the promises centered, so in his degree, the promise to Zerubbabel reaches on through his descendants to Christ; that, amid all the overthrow of empires, God would protect his sons' sons until Christ should come, the King of kings and Lord of lords, Whose [5] *kingdom shall never be destroyed, but it shall break in pieces and consume all those kingdoms, and shall stand fast for ever.*

23. *I will make thee as a signet.* God reverses to Zerubbabel the sentence on Jeconiah for his impiety. To Jeconiah He had said, [6] *though he were the signet upon My right hand, yet would I pluck thee thence; and I will give thee into the hand of them that seek thy life.* The signet was very precious to its owner, never parted with, or only to those to whom authority was delegated (as by Pharaoh to Joseph [7], or by Ahasuerus to Haman [8] and then to Mordecai [9]); through it his will was expressed. Hence the spouse in the Canticles says, [10] *Set me, as a seal upon thy heart, as a seal upon thy arm.* The signet also was an ornament to him who wore it. *God is glorified in His saints* [11]; by Zerubbabel in the building of His house. He gave him estimation with Cyrus, who entrusted him with the return of his people, and made him (who would have been the successor to the throne of Judah, had the throne been re-established) his governor over the restored people. God promises to him and his descendants protection amid all shaking of empires. " [12] He was a type of Christ in bringing back the people from Babylon, as Christ delivered us from sin death and hell: he built the temple, as Christ built the Church; he protected his people against the Samaritans who would

hinder the building, as Christ protects His Church: he was dear and joined to God, as Christ was united to Him, and hypostatically united and joined His Humanity to the Word. The true Zerubbabel then, i. e. Christ, the son and antitype of Zerubbabel, is the signet in the hand of the Father, both passively and actively, whereby God impresses His own Majesty and His own Image on men angels and all creatures." " [13] The Son is the Image of God the Father, having His entire and exact likeness, and in His own beauty beaming forth the nature of the Father. In Him too God seals us also to His own likeness, since, being conformed to Christ, we gain the image of God." " [12] Christ, as the Apostle says, is [14] *the Image of the invisible God, the brightness of His Glory and the express Image of His Person,* Who, as the Word and Seal and express Image, seals it on others. Christ is here called a *signet,* as Man not as God. For it was His Manhood which He took of the flesh and race of Zerubbabel. He is then, in His Manhood, the signet of God; 1) as being hypostatically united with the Son of God; 2) because the Word impressed on His Humanity the likeness of Himself, His knowledge, virtue, holiness, thoughts, words, acts and conversation; 3) because the Man Christ was the seal, i. e. the most evident sign and witness of the attributes of God, His power, justice, wisdom, and especially His exceeding love for man. For, that God might shew this, He willed that His Son should be Incarnate. Christ thus Incarnate is as a seal, in which we see expressed and depicted the love power justice wisdom &c. of God; 4) because Christ as a seal, attested and certified to us the will of God, His doctrine law commands, i. e. those which He promulgated and taught in the Gospel. *No one,* St. John saith, [15] *hath seen God at any time: the Only-Begotten Son Who is the Image of the Father, He hath declared Him.* Hence God gave to Christ the power of working miracles, that He might confirm His words as by a seal, and demonstrate that they were revealed and enjoined to Him by God, as it is in S. John, [16] *Him hath God the Father sealed."* " [12] Christ is also the seal of God, because by His impress, i. e. the faith grace virtue and conversation from Him and by the impress in Baptism and the other Sacraments, He *willed to conform us to the Image of His Son* [17], that, [18] *as we have borne the image of*

[1] Ezek. xxxiv. 23. [2] Ib. xxxvii. 24, 25.
[3] Jer. xxx. 9. [4] Hos. iii. 5.
[5] Dan. ii. 44. [6] Jer. xxii. 24.
[7] Gen. xli. 42. [8] Esther iii. 10.

[9] Ib. viii. 2. [10] Cant. viii. 6.
[11] 2 Thess. i. 10. [12] Lap. [13] S. Cyr.
[14] Heb. i. 3. [15] S. John i. 18.
[16] S. John vi. 27. [17] Rom. viii. 29. [18] 1 Cor. xv. 49.

Before
C H R I S T
cir. 520. altiel, saith the LORD, [b]and will make thee as a signet :

[b] Cant. 8. 6. Jer. 22. 24.

for [c]I have chosen thee, Before
C H R I S T
cir. 520. saith the LORD of hosts.

[c] Isai. 42. 1. & 43. 10

the earthly Adam, *we may also bear the image of the Heavenly.* Then, Christ, like a seal, seals and guards His faithful against all temptations and enemies. The seal of Christ is the Cross, according to that of Ezekiel, [1] *Seal a mark upon the foreheads of the men who sigh,* and in the Revelation, [2] *I saw another Angel having the seal of the living God.* For the Cross guardeth us against the temptations of the flesh, the world and the devil, and makes us followers, soldiers, and martyrs of Christ crucified. Whence the Apostle says, [3] *I bear in my body the marks of the Lord Jesus."*

" This is said without doubt of the Messiah, the expected ; " says even a Jewish controversialist [4], " who shall be of the seed of Zerubbabel ; and therefore this promise was not fulfilled at all in himself : for at the time of this prophecy he had aforetime been governor of Judah, and afterward he did not rise to any higher dignity than what he was up to that day : and in like way we find that God said to Abraham our father in the covenant between the pieces, [5] *I am the Lord who brought thee out of Ur of the Chaldees to give thee this land to inherit it,* and beyond doubt this covenant was confirmed of God to the seed of Abraham, as He Himself explained it there afterward, when He said, *In that day God made a covenant with Abraham, saying, To thy seed have I given this land &c.,* and many like these.

Abarbanel had laid down the right principles, though of necessity misapplied. "[6]Zerubbabel did not reign in Jerusalem and did not rule in it, neither he nor any man of his seed ; but forthwith after the building of the house, he returned to Babylon and died there in his captivity, and how saith he, 'In that day I will take thee?' For after the fall of the kingdom of Persia Zerubbabel is not known for any greatness, and his name is not mentioned in the world. Where then will be the meaning of 'And I will place thee as a signet, for thee have I chosen?' For the signet is as the seal-ring which a man putteth on his hand, it departeth not from it, night or day. And when was this fulfilled in Zerubbabel? But the true meaning, in my opinion, is, that God shewed Zerubbabel that this very second house would not abide; for

after him should come another captivity, and of this he says, 'I shake the heaven &c.,' and afterward, after a long time, will God take His vengeance of these nations 'which have devoured Jacob and laid waste his dwelling place;' and so he says 'I will overthrow the thrones &c.,' and He sheweth him further that the king who shall rule over Israel at the time of the redemption is the Messiah of the seed of Zerubbabel and of the house of David ; and God saw good to shew him all this to comfort him and to speak to his heart ; and it is as if he said to him, 'It is true that thou shalt not reign in the time of the second temple, nor any of thy seed, but in that day when God shall overthrow the throne of the kingdoms of the nations, when He gathereth His people Israel and redeemeth them, then shalt thou reign over My people ; for of thy seed shall he be who ruleth from Israel at that time forever, and therefore he saith, 'I will take thee, O Zerubbabel &c.,' for because the Messiah was to be of his seed he saith, that he will take him ; and this is as he says, '[7]And David My servant shall be a prince to them for ever ;' for the very Messiah, he shall be David, he shall be Zerubbabel, because he shall be a scion going forth out of their hewn trunk [8]."

For I have chosen thee. God's forecoming love is the ground of all the acceptableness of His creatures. [9] *We love Him, because He first loved us.* Zerubbabel was a devoted servant of God. God acknowledges his faithfulness. Only, the beginning of all was with God. God speaks of the nearness to Himself which He had given him. But in two words [10] He cuts off all possible boastfulness of His creature. Zerubbabel was all this, not of himself, but *because God had chosen* him. Even the Sacred Manhood of our Lord (it is acknowledged as a theological Truth) was not chosen for any foreseen merits, but for the great love, with which God the Father chose It, and God the Son willed to be in such wise incarnate, and God the Holy Ghost willed that that Holy Thing should be conceived of Him. So God says of Him, [11] *Behold My Servant whom I uphold, Mine elect in whom My soul delighteth ;* and God bare witness to Him, [12] *This is My Beloved Son in Whom I am well pleased.*

[1] חן Ezek. ix. 4.   [2] Rev. vii. 2.   [3] Gal. vi. 17.
[4] R. Isaac Chiz. Em. l. c. pp. 289, 290.
[5] Gen. xv. 7, 18.   [6] p. רעט.

[7] Ezek. xxxvii. 24.   [8] Is. xi. 1.
[9] 1 S. John iv. 19.   [10] כי בחרתיך.
[11] Is. xlii. 1.   [12] S. Matt. iii. 17. xvii. 5.

INTRODUCTION

TO

THE PROPHET

ZECHARIAH.

ZECHARIAH entered on his prophetic office, two months after Haggai's first prophecy. He was still a youth, when God called him [a], and so, since in the second year of Darius Hystaspis 18 years had elapsed from the first of Cyrus, he must have been brought in infancy from Babylon. His father Berechiah probably died young, since, in Ezra, the prophet is called after his grandfather, *Zechariah the son of Iddo* [b]. He succeeded his grandfather in the office of *the priests, the chief of the fathers,* (of which there were twelve) in the days of Joiakim the son of Joshua, the High priest [c]. Since then, while he prophesied together with Haggai, Joshua was still high-priest, and it is Joshua whom he sees in his vision in that same year [d], he must have entered on his prophetic office before he succeeded to that other dignity. Yet neither is there any reason to think that he ever laid it aside, since we hear not of any prophet, called by God, who did abandon it. Rather, like Jeremiah, he exercised both; called to the priesthood by the birth given to him by God, called to the prophetic office by Divine inspiration.

Like Jeremiah, Zechariah was called in early youth to the prophetic office. The same designation, by which Jeremiah at first excused himself as unfit for the office, is given to Zechariah, *youth* [e]. The term does not indeed mark any definite age; for Joseph, when he was so designated [f] by the chief but-

ler, was 28 [g]; Benjamin and Absalom had sons of their own [h]. They were probably so called as terms of affection, the one by his brother Judah [i], the other by David his father [k]. But his grandfather Iddo was still in the discharge of his office. The length of his ministry is equally unknown. Two years after his first entrance upon it [l], when Haggai's office was closed, he was bidden to answer from God those who enquired whether, now that they were freed from the captivity, they should keep the national fasts which they had instituted on occasion of some of the mournful events which had ushered it in. His remaining prophecies bear no date. The belief, that he lived and prophesied to old age, may have a true foundation, though to us unknown. We only know that he survived the high priest, Joshua, since his own accession to his office of head of the priests, in his division, was in the days of Joiakim, the son of Joshua.

His book opens with a very simple touching call to those returned from the captivity, linking himself on to the former prophets, but contrasting the transitoriness of all human things, those who prophesied and those to whom they prophesied, with the abidingness of the word of God. It consists of four parts, differing in outward character, yet with a remarkable unity of purpose and end. All begin with a foreground subsequent to the captivity; all reach on to a further end;

---

[a] Zech. ii. 4.
[b] Ezr. v. 1. vi. 14.
[c] Neh. xii. 10, 12, 16.   [d] Zech. iii. 1.
[e] נַעַר. Jer. i. 6, Zech. ii. 4.
[f] Gen. xli. 12.
[g] Joseph was 30, when he stood before Pharaoh (Ib. 46), but the interpretation of the dreams of Pharaoh's servants was given two years before. (Ib. 1.)
[h] Benjamin had 10 sons when Jacob went down into Egypt (Gen. xlvi. 21); Absalom's 3 sons (2 Sam. xiv. 27.) were dead (Ib. xviii. 18). Absalom was David's third son. (2 Sam. iii. 3.) [i] Gen. xliii. 8. xliv. 22, 30, 33. [k] 2 Sam. xviii. 5, 12, 29, 32. [l] vii. 1.

the two first to the coming of our Lord ; the third from the deliverance of the house then built, during the invasion of Alexander, and from the victories of the Maccabees, to the rejection of the true Shepherd and the curse upon the false ; the last, which is connected with the third by its title, reaches from a future repentance for the death of Christ to the final conversion of the Jews and Gentiles.

The outward difference, that the first prophecy is in visions ; the second, a response to an enquiry made of him ; the two last in free delivery, obviously did not depend upon the prophet. The occasion also of the two first bodies of prophecy involved that they were written in prose. For the imagery was borne on the prophet's mind in visions. The office of the prophet was only to record them and the explanations given to him of parts of them, which could only be done in prose. He was so far like the Apostles, who enquired of our Lord, when in the flesh, the meaning of His parables. There is, as in the later chapters, abundance of imagery ; and it may have pleased God to adapt the form of His revelation to the imaginative mind of the young prophet who was to receive it. But the visions are, as the name implies, pictures which the prophet *sees*, and which he describes. Even a rationalist writer saw this. " [m] Every vision must form a picture, and the description of a vision must have the appearance of being read from a picture. It follows from the nature of the description of a vision, that for the most part it cannot be composed in any elevated language. The simplest prose is the best vehicle for a relation (and such is the description of a vision), and elaborate ornament of language were foreign to it. The beauty, greatness, elevation of a vision, as described, must lie in the conception, or in the symmetry, or wondrous boldness in the grouping of the images. Is the whole group, piece by piece, in all its parts, to the most minute shading, faithful and described with the character of truth, the exhibition of the vision in words is perfect."

The four portions were probably of different dates, as they stand in order in the prophet's book, as indeed the second is dated two years later than the first [n]. For in the first part God's people are exhorted to come from Babylon [o], which command, many in the time of Ezra, obeyed, and doubtless individuals subsequently, when a prosperous polity was restored ; in the latter part, Babylon is mentioned no more ; only in one place, in the imagery of earlier prophets, the future gathering of God's people is symbolized under the previous deliverance from West and East, Egypt and Assyria [p].

But they agree in this, that the foreground is no longer, as in the former prophets, deliverance from Babylon. In the first part, the reference to the vision of the four empires in Daniel removes the promise of the Deliverer to the fourth Empire. For the series of visions having closed with the vision of the four chariots, there follows at once the symbolic act of placing the crown or crowns on the head of the high priest and the promise of the Messiah, Who should be king and priest [q]. In the later part the enemies spoken of are in one place the Greeks [r], subsequent to the protection of the temple under Alexander [s] ; in another the final gathering of all nations against Jerusalem [t], which Joel also places at the end of all things [u], after the outpouring of the Spirit, as it was outpoured on the day of Pentecost.

In both parts alike, there is no mention of any king or of any earthly ruler ; in both, the ruler to come is the Messias. In both, the division of the two kingdoms is gone. The house of Israel and house of Judah are united, not divided [v] ; they had been distinct wholes, now they are in interests as one. Zechariah promises a future to both collectively, as did Jeremiah [w] long after the captivity of Israel, and Ezekiel promised that they should both again be one in the hand of God [x]. The *brotherhood between Judah and Israel* still existed, after they had weighed the thirty pieces of silver for the Good Shepherd. The captivity, in God's Providence, ended at once the kingdom of Israel and the religious schism, the object of which was to maintain the kingdom. Even before the captivity, [y] *divers of Asher and Manasseh and Zebulun humbled themselves, and came to Jerusalem*, to the passover of Hezekiah ; nay, [z] *a great multitude of the people from Ephraim and Manasseh, Issachar and Zebulun*, who had neglected or despised the first invitation [a], came subsequently. In the great passover of Josiah, we hear [b] of *all Judah and Israel that were*

---

[m] Eichhorn Einl. n. 603. iv. pp. 435, 436. "The style in these visions borders closely on prose : for they relate what the Seer saw ; and prose is the natural vehicle of relation." Ib. n. 605. p. 442. Eichhorn also draws attention to what he calls "the hymns, songs of victory or consolation, with which the visions are sometimes closed, and which are a more elevated finale." Ib.

[n] "In the 2d year of Darius." i. 1. "In the 4th year of Darius." vii. 1.   [o] ii. 7.
[p] Zech. x. 10. Comp. Is. xi. 11, 16, Hos. xi. 11.
[q] vi. 10–13.   [r] ix. 13.

[s] Ib. 8. See Pusey's "Daniel the Prophet." pp. 279–282.   [t] xii. 2, 3, 9. xiv. 2, 3, 14, 16.
[u] Joel iii. 2.
[v] "As ye were a curse among the heathen, O house of Judah and house of Israel" viii. 13 ; "these are the horns which scattered Judah, Israel, Jerusalem," i. 19. (ii. 2. Heb.) So in x. 6. "I will strengthen the house of Judah, and I will save the house of Joseph, and I will bring them again to place them."   [w] Jer. xxiii. 6. l. 20.
[x] Ez. xxxvii. 16–19.   [y] 2 Chr. xxx. 11.
[z] Ib. 18.   [a] Ib. 10.   [b] Ib. xxxv. 18.

present. The edict of Cyrus related to the *° people of the Lord God of heaven, and was published throughout all his kingdom,* which included *d the cities of the Medes,* whither Israel had been removed. The sacred history is confined to Jerusalem, whence the Gospel was to go forth ; yet even *e the sons of Bethel,* the centre of the rival, idolatrous worship, which was *among the mountains of Ephraim,* were among those of the people of Israel who returned with Zerubbabel. It is inconceivable that, as the material prosperity of Palestine returned, even many of the ten tribes should not have returned to their country. But place was no condition of the unity of the Church. Those who returned recognized the religious oneness of all the twelve tribes, wherever dispersed. At the dedication of the house of God, they *f offered a sin-offering for all Israel, twelve he-goats, according to the number of the tribes of Israel.* At that passover were present, not only *the children of Israel which had come again out of the captivity,* but, *g all such as had separated themselves unto them from the defilements of the people of the land, to seek the Lord God of Israel,* i. e., Israelites, who had been defiled by the heathen idolatries. The *house of David* h is mentioned ; for of his seed according to the flesh Messiah was to be born, but it is his *house,* not any earthly ruler in it.

In both parts alike, Zechariah connects his prophecies with the former prophets, the fulfillment of whose warnings he impressed upon his people in his opening exhortation to them i, and in his answer to the question about keeping the fasts k which related to the destruction of the city and temple. In the first part, the title "l the Branch" is used as a proper name, recalling the title of the Messiah in Isaiah and Jeremiah, *the Branch of the Lord* m, *a righteous Branch* n, *a Branch of righteousness* o, whom God would raise up to David. The prophecy of the mutual exhortation of peoples and cities to worship at Jerusalem p is an echo of those of Isaiah and Micah, prolonging them. The prophecy of the four chariots q, the symbol of those world-empires, would be unintelligible without the visions in Daniel which it presupposes. The union of the offices of priest and king in the Messiah is a renewal of the promise through David r. In the last chapters, the continuousness of the prophet's diction admits still

more of this interweaving of the former prophecies, and these alike from the earlier and later prophets. The censure of Tyre for its boast of its wisdom is a renewal of that of Ezekiel s ; the prophecy against the Philistine cities, of that of Zephaniah t ; the remarkable prediction that, when the king should come to Zion, chariots and horses, not of the enemy but of Judah should be cut off, is renewed from Micah u ; the extent of his peaceful kingdom is from a psalm of Solomon v ; the loosing of the exile from the pit, and God's rendering double unto them, are in Isaiah w. The description of the sifting, in which, two parts having been cut off, even the remaining third should be anew tried and cleansed, is condensed from Ezekiel, so that, *shall be cut off, shall expire,* correspond to the natural and violent deaths, by famine and by the sword, spoken of in Ezekiel x. The words, *y I have said, it is My people, and it will say, the Lord my God,* are almost verbally from Hosea, *I say to not-my-people, thou art My people, and it will say, my God ;* only omitting the allusion to the significant name of the prophet's son. *" z The first part of xiv. 10, the whole land shall be turned as a plain from Gebah to Rimmon, and Jerusalem shall be exalted,* reminds of Isaiah and Ezekiel, the latter part, *it shall be inhabited in her place from the tower of Hananeel to the king's wine-presses, and men shall dwell in it and there shall be no more utter desolation, but Jerusalem shall dwell securely,* reminds of Jeremiah, *a The city shall be built to the Lord from the tower of Hananeel unto the gate of the corner ; it shall not be plucked up nor thrown down any more.* The words, *b and every one that is left of all the nations shall go up to worship the king, the Lord of hosts, and to keep the feast of tabernacles,* reminds of Isaiah, *c From new-moon to his new-moon, and from sabbath to his sabbath shall all flesh come to worship before Me, saith the Lord.* v. 17–19 are an expansion of Isaiah lx. 12 ; v. 20 expresses the thought of Ez. xliii. 13 : the prophecy, *d there shall be no more the Canaanite in the house of the Lord for ever,* refers back to Ezekiel e." The symbolizing of the Gospel by the life-giving waters which should flow forth from Jerusalem, originally in Joel iii. 18, is a miniature of the full picture in Ezekiel f. The promise, "g I will cut off the names of the idols from the land and they shall be no more remembered," in part verbally

---

c Ezr. i. 1, 2.　　　d 2 Kgs xvii. 6.
e Ezr. ii. 2, 28.　　f Ib. vi. 17.　　g Ib. 21.
h Zech. xii. 7. The *king's wine-presses* (Zech. xiv. 10.) is but the name of a locality in Jerusalem, which retained its former name. Wine-presses were often hewn out in the rock. Bleek, who alleged this, afterward (Einl. p. 563. note) laid no stress on it.　　　　　　　i i. 4–6.
k vii. 7-14.　　　　　l iii. 8. vi. 12.
m Is. iv. 2.　　　　　n Jer. xxiii. 5.
o Ib. xxxiii. 15.
p Zech. viii. 20-22. comp. Mic. iv. 1, 2. Is. ii. 3.

q Zech. vi. coll. Dan. ii. vii. See below on c. vi. and "Daniel the Prophet" pp. 359–361.
r Zech. vi. 13. coll. Ps. cx.
s ix. 2. and Ezek. xxviii. 3.
t ix. 5. Zeph. ii. 4.　　　　　u ix. 10. Mic. v. 10.
v Ib. Ps. lxxii. 8.　　　　w Ib. 12. Is. li. 14. lxi. 7.
x xiii. 8, 9. Ezek. v. 12. Hengst.
y Hengst. Zech. xiii. 9, Hos. ii. 25.
z Hengst.　　a Jer. xxxi. 38. 40.　　b Zech. xiv. 16.
c Is. lxvi. 23.　　d Zech. xiv. 21.　　e Ezek. xliv. 9.
f Zech. xiv. 8, Ezek. xlvii. 1–13.
g Zech. xiii. 2. Hos. ii. 17.

agrees with that of Hosea, "And I will remove *the names of the* Baalim *from* her mouth, *and they shall be no more remembered* by their names;" only, since the Baal-worship was destroyed by the captivity, the more general name of *idols* is substituted.

Equally, in descriptions not prophetic, the symbolizing of the wicked by the title of the goats, *I punished the goats*[h], is renewed from Ezekiel; *I judge between flock and flock, between the rams and the he-goats.* The description of the shepherds who destroyed their flocks retains from Jeremiah the characteristic expression, [i] *and hold themselves not guilty.* The minuteness of the enumeration of their neglects and cruelties is the same (amid differences of the words whereby it is expressed): " [k] the perishing shall he not visit, those astray shall he not seek, and the broken shall he not heal; the sound shall he not nurture, and the flesh of the fat shall he eat and their claws he shall split. In Ezekiel, " [l] Ye eat the fat and clothe you with the wool; the fat ye slay; the flock ye feed not; the diseased have ye not healed; and the broken have ye not bound, and the wandering have ye not sought." The imagery of Obadiah, that Israel should be a flame amidst corn to consume it, is retained; the name of Edom is dropped, for the prophecy relates to a larger gathering of enemies. Zechariah has, " [m] In that day I will make the governors of Judah like a hearth of fire among wood and like a lamp of fire in a sheaf of corn, and they shall eat on the right hand and on the left all nations round about:" Obadiah; "The house of Jacob shall be *fire* and the house of Jacob a *flame,* and the house of Esau stubble, and it shall kindle on them and shall eat them." Even so slight an expression as *the pride of Jordan* [n], as designating the cane-brake around it, is peculiar to Jeremiah [o].

Zechariah is eminently an Evangelic prophet, as much as Isaiah, and equally in both portions.

[h] Zech. x. 3. Ezek. xxxiv. 17.
[i] ולא יאשמו Zech. xi. 5. לא נאשם Jer. i. 7.
[k] Zech. xi. 16.   [l] Ezek. xxxiv. 3, 4.   [m] Zech. xii. 6. Obad. 18.   [n] Zech. xi. 3.   [o] Jer. xii. 5. xlix. 19. l. 44.
[p] Prof. Stanley Leathes, "The witness of the Old Testament to Christ. Note on the Authorship of Isaiah," (pp. 282, 283.) gives the following summary as to the occurrence of words in poems of Milton and Tennyson; "L'Allegro is a poem of 152 lines: it contains about 450 words; Il Penseroso is a poem of 176 lines, and contains about 578 words; Lycidas is a poem of 193 lines, which are longer than those of either of the other two, most of them being heroics: its words are about 725. It is plain, therefore, that Milton must have used for Il Penseroso 128 words not in L'Allegro, and for Lycidas 275 not in L'Allegro, and 147 not in Il Penseroso.
"But what is much more remarkable, is the fact that there are only about 125 words common to L'Allegro and Il Penseroso; only about 140 common to Lycidas and Il Penseroso; only about 61 common to all three. That is; Milton must have used for Il Penseroso 450 words not in L'Allegro, and for Lycidas 590 not in L'Allegro. He must have used for

The use of different words in unlike subjects is a necessary consequence of that unlikeness. In contrast with that pseudo-criticism, which counts up the unlike words in different chapters of a prophet, the different words used by the same modern poet have been counted [p]. A finer perception will see the correspondence of a style, when the rhythm, subject, words, are different. No one familiar with English poetry could doubt that "the Bard," and "the Elegy in a country Churchyard," however different in subject and style and words, were by the same hand, judging alone from the labored selection of the epithets, however different. Yet there is not one characteristic word or idiom which occurs in both. But the recurrence of the same or like words or idioms, if unusual elsewhere, is a subordinate indication of sameness of authorship.

They are thus enumerated by the writers who have answered the attacks on the authorship of Zechariah.

"Common to both parts are the idioms, *from him who goeth and from him who returneth,* which do not occur elsewhere [q]; the whole Jewish people are throughout designated as " [r] the house of Israel and the house of Judah," or " [s] the house of Judah and the house of Joseph," or " [t] Judah Israel and Jerusalem," or " [u] Ephraim and Jerusalem," or " [v] Judah and Ephraim," or " [w] Judah and Israel." There is in both parts the appeal to future knowledge of God's doings to be obtained by experience [x]; in both, internal discord is directly attributed to God, Whose Providence permits it [y]; in both the prophet promises God's gifts of the produce of the earth [z]; in both he bids Jerusalem burst out for joy; in the first, " [a] *for lo,* God says, *I come and will dwell in the midst of thee;* in the second, [b] *behold thy King cometh unto thee.*

The purity of language is alike in both parts of the book. No one Syriasm occurs in Lycidas some 585 words not in Il Penseroso, and more than 660 not occurring in both together. Also, there must be in L'Allegro some 325 words not in Il Penseroso, and 315 not in Lycidas; and there must be in Il Penseroso nearly 440 words not in Lycidas.
"Again, Tennyson's Lotos-Eaters contains about 590 words; Œnone has about 720. Thus the latter must contain 130 words not in the former: but a comparison shows that there are only about 230 words common to the two poems. That is, there must be 490 words in Œnone which are not in the Lotos-Eaters, and there must be in the Lotos-Eaters about 360 words not occurring in Œnone; that is,— the shorter poem has 360 words which the longer one does not contain."

[q] מעבר ומשב vii. 14, ix. 8. In Ez. xxxii. 27, the expression עברו ושוב, "pass through and return," is not proverbial; in Ezek. xxxv. 7, it is "I will cut off from it" עבר ושב:

[r] viii. 13.   [s] x. 6.   [t] i. 19, [ii. 2. Heb.]   [u] ix. 10.
[v] ix. 13.   [w] xi. 14.   [x] ii. 13, 15. [v] xi. 11.
[y] viii. 10. xi. 6.   [z] viii. 12. x. 1.
[a] ii. 14. [10. Eng.]   [b] ix. 9.

the earlier chapters[c]. The prophet, who returned as a child to Judæa, formed his language upon that of the older prophets.

In both there is a certain fullness of language, produced by dwelling on the same thought or word [d]: in both, the whole and its parts are, for emphasis, mentioned together[e]. In both parts, as a consequence of this fullness, there occurs the division of the verse into five sections, contrary to the usual rule of Hebrew parallelism.

This rhythm will appear more vividly in instances [f];

" [g] And *he* shall build the temple of the Lord ;
And *he* shall bear majesty ;
And he shall sit and rule on his throne ;
And he shall be a priest on his throne ;
And a counsel of peace shall be between them both.

[h] Ashkelon shall see, and shall fear ;
Gaza, and shall tremble exceedingly ;
And Ekron, and ashamed is her expectation ;
And perished hath a king from Gaza,
And Ashkelon shall not be inhabited.

[i] And I will take away his blood from his mouth,
And his abominations from between his teeth :
And he too shall be left to our God,
And he shall be as a governor in Judah,
And Ekron as a Jebusite.

" [k] In that day, saith the Lord,
I will smite every horse with astonishment,
And his rider with madness ;
And upon the house of Judah I will open my eyes,
And every horse of the nations I will smite with blindness."

With one considerable exception[l], those

who would sever the six last chapters from Zechariah, are now at one in placing them before the captivity. Yet Zechariah here too speaks of the captivity as past. Adopting the imagery of Isaiah, who foretells the delivery from the captivity as an opening of a prison, he says, in the name of God, " [m] By the blood of thy covenant *I have sent forth thy* prisoners out of the pit wherein is no water." Again, " [n] The Lord of hosts hath visited His flock, the house of Judah. I will have mercy upon them [Judah and Joseph] and they shall be *as though I had not cast them off*." The mention of the mourning of all the *families that remain* [o] implies a previous carrying away. Yet more ; Zechariah took his imagery of the future restoration of Jerusalem, from its condition in his own time. " [p] It shall be lifted up and inhabited in its place from Benjamin's gate unto *the place* of the first gate, unto the corner-gate, and from the tower of Hananeel unto the king's winepresses." " The gate of Benjamin " is doubtless " the gate of Ephraim," since the road to Ephraim lay through Benjamin ; but the gate of Ephraim existed in Nehemiah's time [q], yet was not then repaired, as neither was the tower of Hananeel [r], having been left, doubtless, at the destruction of Jerusalem, being useless for defence, when the wall was broken down. So [s] at the second invasion the Romans left the three impregnable towers, of Hippicus, Phasaelus, and Mariamne, as monuments of the greatness of the city which they had destroyed. Benjamin's gate, the corner gate, the tower of Hananeel, were still standing ; " the king's winepresses" were naturally uninjured, since there was no use in injuring them ; but *the first gate* was destroyed, since not itself, but *the place* of it is mentioned.

The prophecy of the victory over the Greeks fits in with times when Assyria or Chaldæa were no longer the instruments of God in the chastisement of His people. The notion that the prophet incited the few Hebrew slaves, sold into Greece, to rebel against

[c] וְאֶסְעָרֵם vii. 14 is no Syriasm (as so often alleged) but has Hebrew analogies as גֵּוָה Job xxii. 29. xxiii. 7, from נֵּאָוָה for נַּאֲוָה (Ew. Lehrb. n. 62. b); but which of these critics would argue from the points except in favor of what he wished to maintain? Böttcher (Lehrbuch n. 437. g. 498. 3. p. 304.) regards the as emphatic. 2) "That מְהֹלְכִים (iii. 7.) comes from a מַהֲלָךְ is self-evident." Ew. ad. loc. 3) עֹזֵר לְ (i. 16.) is not "joined with acc. of object," but is simply our, "helped to evil."

[d] As in the repetition of שְׁכַנְתִּי בְתוֹכֵךְ ii. 14, 15; of וּבָנָה אֶת הֵיכַל יי וְהוּא יִבְנֶה, in vi. 10; וּבָנָה אֶת הֵיכַל יי vi. 12, 13; בְּרֶחְבָּתִיהָ,וּרְחֹבוֹת,בִּרְחֹבוֹת, 3 times in viii. 4. 5; וְאֶרְעֶה Ib. 23; יְחַזְּקוּ-וְהַחֲזִיקִי אֶת הַצֹּאן at the beginning and end of xi. 7;

ישבה ירושלם לבטח and ישבה תחתיה at the end, xiv. 10, 11. וְנָלְחַם כְּיוֹם הִלָּחֲמוֹ בְּיוֹם קְרָב &c.,

xiv. 3. In xiv. 4. the sentence וּמָשׁ explains the same event in different words: וְנַסְתֶּם-וְנַסְתֶּם כַּאֲשֶׁר נַסְתֶּם xiv. 5.

[e] v. 4. "the house, and its stones, and its timbers," x. 4. "out of him the corner; out of him the nail; out of him the battle bow; out of him every oppressor together." x. 11. "the land shall mourn, every family apart," and then follows the enumeration of the families. 12, 13.

[f] This was observed by Köster, Meletemata crit. et exeg. in Zech. part. post. c. ix.-xiv. pp. 54-56.

[g] vi. 13.   [h] ix. 5.   [i] Ib. 7.

[k] xii. 4. Köster further refers to i. 4, 17. iii. 5, 9. and on the other hand to ix. 9, 10, 13, 15. x. 11. xi. 2, 7, 9, 17. xii. 10. xiv. 4, 8.

[l] Böttcher.   [m] ix. 11.   [n] x. 3-5.   [o] xii. 14.

[p] xiv. 10.   [q] Neh. viii. 16. xii. 39.   [r] Ib. iii. 1.

[s] Jos. B. J. vii. 1.

their masters, is so absurd, that one wonders that any one could have ventured to forge it and put it upon a Hebrew prophet [t].

Since, moreover, all now, who sever the six last chapters from the preceding, also divide these six into two halves, the evidence that the six chapters are from one author is a separate ground against their theory. Yet not only are they connected by the imagery of the people as the flock of God [u], whom God committed to the hand of the Good Shepherd [v], and on their rejecting Him, gave them over to an evil shepherd [w]; but the Good Shepherd is One with God [x]. The poor of the flock, who would hold to the Shepherd, are designated by a corresponding word [y].

A writer has been at pains to shew that two different conditions of things are foretold in the two prophecies. Granted. The first, we believe, has its foreground in the deliverance during the conquests of Alexander, and under the Maccabees, and leads on to the rejection of the true Shepherd and God's visitation on the false. The later relates to a later repentance and later visitation of God, in part yet future. By what law is a prophet bound down to speak of one future only?

For those who criticize the prophets, resolve all prophecy into mere "anticipation" of what *might*, or might *not* be, denying to them all certain knowledge of any future, it is but speaking plainly, when they imagine the author of the three last chapters to have "anticipated" that God would interpose miraculously to deliver Jerusalem, then, when it was destroyed. It would have been in direct contradiction to Jeremiah, who for 39 years in one unbroken dirge predicted the evil which should come upon Jerusalem. The prophecy, had it preceded the destruction of Jerusalem, could not have been earlier than the reign of the wretched Jehoiakim, since the mourning for the death of Josiah is spoken of as a proverbial sorrow of the past. This invented prophet then would have been one of the false prophets, good, who contradicted Jeremiah, prophesying good, while Jeremiah prophesied evil; who encouraged Zedekiah in his perjury, the punishment whereof Ezekiel solemnly denounced [z], prophesying his captivity in Babylon as its penalty; he would have been one of those, of whom Jeremiah said, that they spake lies [a] in the name of the Lord. It was not "anticipation" on either side. It was the statement of those who spoke more certainly than we could say, "the sun will rise to-morrow." They were

the direct contradictories of one another. The false prophets said, "[b] the Lord hath said, Ye shall have peace;" the true, "[c] they have said, Peace, peace, when there is no peace:" the false said, "[d] sword and famine shall not be in the land;" the true, "[d] By sword and famine shall their prophets be consumed;" the false said, "[e] ye shall not serve the king of Babylon; thus saith the Lord, even so will I break the yoke of Nebuchadnezzar, king of Babylon, from the neck of all nations within the space of two full years;" the true, "[f] Thus saith the Lord of hosts, Now have I given all these lands into the hand of Nebuchadnezzar the king of Babylon, My servant, and all nations shall serve him, and his son and his son's son." The false said, "[g] I will bring again to this place Jeconiah, with all the captives of Judah, that went into Babylon, for I will break the yoke of the king of Babylon;" the true, "[h] I will cast thee out and the mother that bare thee, into another country, where ye were not born, and there ye shall die. But to the land, whereunto they desire to return, thither they shall not return." The false said; "[i] The vessels of the Lord's house shall now shortly be brought again from Babylon;" the true, "[k] the residue of the vessels that remain in this city,—they shall be carried to Babylon."

If the writer of the three last chapters had lived just before the destruction of Jerusalem in those last reigns, he would have been a political fanatic, one of those who, by encouraging rebellion against Nebuchadnezzar, brought on the destruction of the city, and, in the name of God, told lies against God. "That which is most peculiar in this prophet," says one [l], "is the uncommon high and pious hope of the deliverance of Jerusalem and Judah, notwithstanding all visible greatest dangers and threatenings. At a time when Jeremiah, in the walls of the capital, already despairs of any possibility of a successful resistance to the Chaldees and exhorts to tranquillity, this prophet still looks all these dangers straight in the face with swelling spirit and divine confidence, holds, with unbowed spirit, firm to the like promises of older prophets, as Is. c. 29, and anticipates that, from that very moment when the blind fury of the destroyers would discharge itself on the sanctuary, a wondrous might would crush them in pieces, and that this must be the beginning of the Messianic weal within and without."

---

[t] Hitzig. Ewald avoids this; but would have it, that the prophet in Joel's time was stirring up the Jews to war with the Greeks. Other evasions see in Pusey's "Daniel the Prophet" pp. 281, 282. note.   [u] ix. 16. x. 3.   [v] xi. 4–14.   [w] Ib. 15–17.   [x] xi. 7–12. xiii. 7.   [y] הַצֹּאן עֲנִיֵּי, xi. 7, 11. הַצְּעָרִים, xiii. 7, the same as the הַצְּעִירֵי צְּעִירֵי Jer. xlix. 20, l. 45.

[z] Ezek. xiii. 10–19.   [a] Jer. xiv. 14, xxiii. 22, xxvii. 15, xxviii. 15, xxix. 8, 9.   [b] Jer. viii. 11. xxiii. 17.   [c] Ezek. xiii. 2–10.   [d] Jer. xiv. 15.   [e] Ib. xxvii. 9–14, xxviii. 11.   [f] Ib. xxvii. 4, 6, 7.   [g] Ib. xxviii. 4.   [h] Ib. xxii. 26, 27.   [i] Ib. xxvii. 16.   [k] Ib. 19–22.   [l] Ewald Proph. ii. 52, 53. ed. 1868.

Chapter 14 is to this writer a modification of those anticipations. In other words there was a greater human probability, that Jeremiah's prophecies, not his, would be fulfilled : yet he cannot give up his sanguineness, though his hopes had now become fanatic. This writer says on chap. 14, " [m] This piece cannot have been written till somewhat later, when facts made it more and more improbable, that Jerusalem would not any how be conquered, and treated as a conquered city by coarse foes. Yet then too this prophet could not yet part with the anticipations of older prophets and those which he had himself at an earlier time expressed : so boldly, amid the most visible danger, he holds firm to the old anticipation, after that the great deliverance of Jerusalem in Sennacherib's time (Is. c. 37.) appeared to justify the most fanatic hopes for the future. (comp. Ps. 59). And so now the prospect moulds itself to him thus, as if Jerusalem must indeed actually endure the horrors of the conquest, but that then, when the work of the conquerors was half-completed, the great deliverance, already suggested in that former piece, would come, and so the Sanctuary would, notwithstanding, be wonderfully preserved, the better Messianic time would notwithstanding still so come."

It must be a marvelous fascination, which the old prophets exercise over the human mind, that one who can so write should trouble himself about them. It is such an intense paradox, that the writing of one convicted by the event of uttering falsehood in the name of God, incorrigible even by the thickening tokens of God's displeasure, should have been inserted among the Hebrew prophets, in times not far removed from those whose events convicted him, that one wonders that any one should have invented it, still more that any should have believed in it. Great indeed is "the credulity of the incredulous."

And yet this paradox is essential to the theories of the modern school which would place these chapters before the captivity. English writers, who thought themselves compelled to ascribe these chapters to Jeremiah, had an escape, because they did not bind down prophecy to immediate events. Newcome's criticism was the conjectural criticism of his day; i. e. bad, cutting knots instead of loosing them. But his faith, that God's word is true, was entire. Since the prophecy, placed at the time where he placed

it, had no immediate fulfillment, he supposed it, in common with those who believe it to have been written by Zechariah, to relate to a later period. That German school, with whom it is an axiom, "that all definite prophecy relates to an immediate future," had no choice but to place it just before the destruction of the temple by the Chaldees, or its profanation by Antiochus Epiphanes ; and those who placed it before the Captivity, had no choice, except to believe, that it related to events, by which it was falsified.

Nearly half a century has passed, since a leading writer of this school said, " [n] One must own, that the division of opinions as to the real author of this section and his time, as also the attempts to appropriate single oracles of this portion to different periods, leave the result of criticism simply *negative ;* whereas on the other hand, the view itself, since it is not yet carried through exegetically, lacks the completion of its proof. It is not till criticism becomes *positive,* and evidences its truth in the explanation of details, that it attains its completion ; which is not, in truth, always possible." Hitzig did what he could, " to help to promote the attainment of this end according to his ability." But although the more popular theory has of late been that these chapters are to be placed before the captivity, the one portion somewhere in the reigns of Uzziah, Jotham, Ahaz, or Hezekiah ; the other, as marked in the chapters themselves, after the death of Josiah. there have not been wanting critics of equal repute, who place them in the time of Antiochus Epiphanes. Yet criticism which reels to and fro in a period of near 500 years, from the earliest of the prophets to a period, a century after Malachi, and this on historical and philological grounds, certainly has come to no definite basis, either as to history or philology. Rather, it has enslaved both to preconceived opinions ; and at last, as late a result as any has been, after this weary round, to go back to where it started from, and to suppose these chapters to have been written by the prophet whose name they bear [o].

It is obvious that there must be some mistake either in the tests applied, or in their application, which admits of a variation of at least 450 years from somewhere in the reign of Uzziah (say B. C. 770) to "later than B. C. 330."

Philological and historical criticism, bearing on events (as it is assumed) of the day,

[m] Ewald Proph. p. 59.

[n] Hitzig. über d. abfassungszeit der Orakel Zach. ix-xiv, in the Theol. Studien u. Kritiken 1830. 1. p. 25.

[o] De Wette ed. 4 (after maintaining the contrary ed. 1–3) and Stähelin, Einl. 1862. " De Wette often assured me orally, that since he felt himself compelled to admit, that this portion evinces acquaintance with the latest prophets, he could not deny it to be Zechariah's." Stähelin p. 323. De

Wette, Stähelin, Köster, Bürger, were of a different school from Hengstenberg, Havernick, Keil, or again from Jahn and Herbst. Stähelin says, " in the investigation I kept myself free from any influence from without, and first found the facts, which attest the post-exile origin of this section, given by Hengstenberg and de Wette, when I subsequently compared the labors of others, especially those two scholars." Messian. Weissag. p. 174. 1847.

which should, in its variations, oscillate between the reign of John or of Charles I, or (to bring it nearer to ourselves) the first half of the xiv[th] century or the latter part of the xviii[th], would not gain much attention. Indeed, it is instructive, that after the philological argument has figured so much in all questions about the date of books of Holy Scripture, it is virtually admitted to be absolutely worthless, except negatively. For, in regard to Zechariah, the argument is not used, except in proof that the same writer cannot have written prose and poetry, which would establish that Hosea did not write either his three first chapters or his nine last; or Ezekiel his inaugural vision, the visions of the ninth and tenth chapters, and the simple exhortations to repentance in his eighteenth and thirty-third. Only I know not on the same evidence, how, of modern writers, Scott and Southey could be supposed to have written their prose and their poetry. How easy it would be to prove that the author of Thalaba did not write the life of Wesley or the history of the peninsular war, nor Shakespeare Macbeth and any comedy which criticism may yet leave to him; still more that he cannot have written the deep tragic scenes of Hamlet and that of the grave-diggers.

Yet such negations have been practically considered as the domain of the philological neo-criticism. Style is to be evidence that the same prophet did not write certain prophecies; but, this being demonstrated, it is to yield no evidence, whether he wrote, when Hebrew was a dead language or in the time of its richest beauty. Individuals indeed have their opinions; but philological criticism, as a whole, or as relates to any acknowledged result, is altogether at fault. Having done its office of establishing, that, in the mind of the critic and his disciples, certain chapters are *not* Zechariah's, the witness is forthwith dismissed, as incompetent even to assist in proving anything beside. The rest is to be established by historical allusions, which are by some adapted to events in the reign of Uzziah, by others to those of the Maccabees: or rather, it being assumed that there is no prophecy, this latter class assumes that the book is to belong to the times of the Maccabees, because one part of it predicts their victories. Those who tell us [p] of the unity of the results of this modern criticism, must have been thinking of the agreement of its negations. As to the positive results, a table will best shew their har-

mony. Yet the fault is not in the want of an ill-exercised acumen of the critics; their principle, that nothing in the prophets can relate to any distant future, even though that future exactly realized the words, is the mainspring of their confusions. Since the words of Zechariah do relate to, and find their fulfillment in, events widely separated from each other, and the theory of the critics requires that they should belong to some proximate event, either in the present or some near future, they have to wrest those words from the events to which they relate, some in this way, some in that; and the most natural interpretations are those which are least admitted. Certainly since the descriptions in c. ix. suit with the wars of Alexander and the Maccabees, no one, but for some strong antecedent exigency, would assume that they related to some expected expedition of an Assyrian monarch, "[q]which may be conjectured as very probable, but which, for want of historical data, cannot be indicated more circumstantially," or to "[r]a plan of the Assyrians which was not then carried out," or "[s]Uzziah's war with the Philistines[t], and some imagined "[u]attitude of Jeroboam II against Damascus and Hamath," or "[u]a concealed denunciation against Persia," against which Zechariah did not wish to prophesy openly, or to have had no special meaning at all[v].

It is marvelous, on what slight data this modern school has satisfied itself that these chapters were written before the captivity. To take the statement of an epitomator[w] of German pseudo-criticism: " *Damascus, Tyre, and Sidon, Philistia, Javan (ix. 1, 6–12) Assyria and Egypt (x. 10.) are the enemies of Judah.*" " *The historical stand-point is different from that of Zech. i-viii.*" Of all these, Javan, the Greeks, alone are spoken of as enemies of Judah, who before the captivity were known only as purchasers of Hebrew captives; the only known wars are those of the Maccabees.

" *The two kingdoms of Judah and Israel still exist. Surely the language,* 'that I might break the brotherhood between Judah and Israel,' *implies that both kingdoms existed as part of the covenant nation.*"

Zechariah speaks of Judah and Israel, but not as *kingdoms.* Before the captivity, except during the effects of the inter-marriage with Athaliah, there was not *brotherhood* but enmity. In the reigns of Amaziah and Ahaz there was war.

" *The house of David is spoken of xiii.* 1."

---

[p] Essays and Reviews, p. 340. "Among German commentators there is, for the first time in the history of the world, an approach to agreement and certainty. For example the diversity among German writers on prophecy is far less than among English ones."

[q] Bertholdt p. 1715.   [r] Knobel ii. 170.

[s] Hitzig Vorbemerk. z. ii. and iii. Zech. Kl. Pr. p. 354.

[t] 2 Chr. xxvi. 6.   [u] De Wette Einl. p. 337.

[v] "The uncertain hopes of the future, here expressed by the prophet, are not to be referred to certain events." Rosenmüller on Zech. ix. 13. ed. 1.

[w] Dr. S. Davidson iii. 321, 322.

The *house*, not the kingdom. The house existed after the captivity. Zerubbabel, whom the Persians made governor, was its representative.

" *Idols and false prophets (x. 2. xiii. 2 &c.) harmonize only with a time prior to the exile.*"

Idolatry certainly was not the prevailing national sin, after God had taught the people through the captivity. It is commonly taken for granted, that there was none. But where is the proof? Malachi would hardly have laid the stress on [x] *marrying the daughters of a strange god*, had there been no danger that the marriage would lead to idolatry. [y] Nehemiah speaks of the sin, into which Solomon was seduced by "outlandish women," as likely to recur through the heathen marriages; but idolatry was that sin. Half of the children could only speak the language of their mothers[z]. It were strange, if they had not imbibed their mothers' idolatry too. In a battle in the Maccabee war, it is related " [a] under the coats of every one that was slain they found things consecrated to the idols of the Jamnites, which is forbidden the Jews by their law."

The *Teraphim* were, moreover, an unlawful and forbidden means of attempting to know the future, not any coarse form of idolatry [b]; much as people now, who more or less earnestly have their fortunes told, would be surprised at being called idolaters. But Zechariah was probably speaking of sins which had brought on the captivity, not of his own day. The prediction repeated from an older prophet, that in the true Judah, the Church, God would *cut off* even *the names* and the memory *of idols*, does not imply that they existed [c].

False prophets continued after the captivity. Shemaiah, who *uttered a prophecy against* Nehemiah, *the prophetess Noadiah*, and *the rest of the prophets*, are known to us from Nehemiah's relation[d]. Such there were before our Lord came, of whom He said, that they [e] *were thieves and robbers: He* warned against them, [f] *as coming in sheep's clothing*, but *inwardly they are ravening wolves; He* foretold that [g] *many false prophets shall arise and deceive many;* the Acts tell us of the *false prophet* [h], *a Jew, Bar-jesus;* and *Theudas*, and *Judas* of Galilee[i]. S. John says, [k] *many false prophets have gone out into the world.* False

prophets aggravated the resistance to the Romans and the final destruction of Jerusalem[1].

" *The mention of a king or kingdom, in xi. 6, xiii. 7, does not suit the age of Zechariah.*"

Zechariah had already implied that they had no king then, for he had bidden Zion to rejoice that her king *would come* to her ; accordingly she had none. In xi. 6, God says, "I will no more pity the land; I will deliver man, every one into the hand of his king." It is an event, not of the prophet's time, but of the future; in xiii. 7, there is no mention of any king at all.

Such being the entire absence of proof that these chapters were written before the captivity [m], the proof that c. xi. relates to the time of Menahem is even absurd. The process with those who maintained this, has been, assuming as proved, that it was written before the captivity, and that it contained no prophecy of the future, to ask, to what period before the captivity does it relate? One verse [n] relates to civil confusion, such as is foretold also, with the same metaphor, by Isaiah and Jeremiah. The choice was large, since the kingdom of Israel had the curse of discord and irreligion entailed upon it, and no king ventured to cut off the entail by cutting off the central sin, the worship of the calves, which were to consolidate it by a worship, the rival of that at Jerusalem. Of the 18 kings between Jeroboam and Hosea, 9, including Tibni, died violent deaths. The choice was directed to Menahem, because of the words in Zechariah, *three shepherds also I cut off in one month*, and Shallum murdered Zachariah the son of Jeroboam ; and he himself, after he had *reigned a full month in Samaria*, was murdered by Menahem. Here then were two kings cut off. But the third? Imagination is to supply it. One [o] conjectures Menahem ; but *he* reigned 10 years, and so, he invents a meaning for the word, that the prophet does not mean *cut off*, but *denied* them, leaving it open whether he meant "removed" or merely "did not acknowledge them, as Menahem at first certainly found no recognition with the prophetic order (2 Kgs xv. 16, 19);" another [p] imagined "some third rival of Zachariah and Shallum, of whom there is no mention in the historical books;" but there is no room for a third king, since Shallum murdered Zachariah;

---

[x] Mal. ii. 11.   [y] Neh. xiii. 26.
[z] Ib. 23, 24.   [a] 2 Macc. xii. 40.
[b] See below on x. 2.
[c] See ab. p. 325, and bel. on xiii. 2.
[d] Neh. vi. 12. 14.   [e] S. John x. 8.
[f] S. Matt. vii. 15.
[g] Ib. xxiv. 11, 24. S. Mark xiii. 22.   [h] Acts xiii. 6.
[i] Acts v. 36, 37.   [k] 1 S. John iv. 1.
[l] "The cause of this destruction [of those who took refuge in the temple] was a false prophet, who at that day preached to those in the city, that God bade them go up to the temple, to receive the signs of salvation. But there were many at that time suborned by the tyrants to the people, bidding them wait the help from God, that they might not desert, and that hope might master to their ill, those who were beyond fear or watching.—The deceivers, telling lies against God, then misdeceived the wretched people." Jos. B. J. vi. 5. 2 and 3.
[m] The questions 1) whether the six last chapters were Zechariah's, and 2) whether they were written before the captivity, are entirely apart.
[n] xi. 6. Comp. Is. ix. 20. xlix. 26. Jer. xix. 9.[l]
[o] Hitzig ad loc. p. 373. ed. 3.
[p] Maurer, followed by Bunsen Bibelwerk on Zech., Dr. Davidson Intr. ii. 330.

and Menahem, Shallum; another [q] found in Hebrew words [r] which had crept into the LXX, an usurper Kobal-am, of whom he says truly, "we hear nothing;" another [s] conceived of some usurper after the murder of Zachariah or of Shallum (this is left free), who about this time *may* have set himself at the head of the kingdom, but scarcely maintained himself some weeks; another [t] says, "This refers probably to the Interregnum 784–773, in which many *may* have set themselves as kings, but none have maintained themselves." Another [u] "An anti-king *may* at this time have set himself up in other parts of the kingdom, whom Menahem overthrew as he did that murderer." Others [v] say of the whole, "The symbolical representation, verss. 3 sqq., admits of no detailed explanation, but can be understood only as a whole. It describes the evil condition of Judah under Ahaz." Another [w], equally certain that it relates to Ahaz, says, "the three shepherds, who perished in one and the same month, were probably men who, in the long anarchy before Hosea ascended the throne, contended for the sceptre."

Yet another is so confident in this interpretation as to the three kings, Shallum, Zechariah and Menahem, that, whereas the book of Kings says expressly that Shallum reigned "[x] a full month" lit. "a month of days," the commentator says, "The month cannot have been full [y]; Zechariah xi. 8 evidently refers to the three Kings, Sachariah, Sallum and Menahem," while others [z] will have it that Zechariah by *one month* means some indefinite space more than a month. This is indeed required (although not stated) by all these theories, since Shallum alone reigned "a full month," and, consequently, the other two kings (if intended at all by the term "shepherds") must have been cut off at some period, outside of that "one month."

Truly, theory is a very exacting taskmaster,

though strangely fascinating. It is to be one of the triumphs of the neo-criticism to distinguish between the authorship of Zech. ix–xi and xii–xiv. The point alleged to prove that c. xi. belongs to the time of Menahem is one at variance with history. It is not that the whole is like, while in one point the likeness is imperfect. It is *the* point, alleged as the keystone of the whole, which fails. The words of God by the prophet are, "*Three shepherds* have I cut off in *one month.*" It lies on the surface of the history, that Zachariah, son of Jeroboam, was murdered by Shallum, after reigning 6 months; and that Shallum, after reigning one full month, was himself murdered by Menahem [a]. The succession of murders was not so rapid as when Zimri had murdered Elah, Baasha's son, and after reigning 7 days, committed suicide, lest he should fall into the hands of Omri [b]. Elah and Zimri were cut off in one month; Zachariah and Shallum, in two. But in neither case was there any visible result, except a partial retribution of God's justice. The last executioner of God's justice *slept with his fathers;* his retribution was after death. He was *not* cut off. And this is the proof, which is to supplant the testimony to Jesus. The Apostle's words come true, as so often beside: [c] *They shall turn away their ears from the truth and shall be turned unto fables.*

[d] *Thou art wearied in the greatness of thy way, yet saidst thou not, there is no hope.* One should have thought that some must have, at times, thought of the old days, when the prophecy was interpreted of the Good Shepherd and of the 30 pieces of silver which were the price of His Blood, and which *were* cast into the house of the Lord [e]. But this would have been fatal to "historical criticism," whose province was to find out events of the prophet's own day to fill up the words of prophecy.

The human authorship of any books of

---

[q] Ewald (Gesch. d. V. Israel iii. 644.), followed as elsewhere by Dr. Stanley, Jewish Church ii. 364.
[r] The original text of the LXX seems to have corresponded with the Hebrew. The meaning of the two Hebrew words, קבל עם, is very simple, "before people" i. e. publicly; קבל העם would (as Böttcher observed, Jen. Lit. Zeit. 1847. p. 1144) have signified "before the people publicly assembled together." The Syro-Hexaplar version by Paul of Tela translates the words, and introduces "Kebdaam" with Origen's asterisk, and so, as not belonging to the LXX. The Alexandrian and two other MSS. (one of Constantinople cent. x.) also retain the rendering. The singular "conspired," which excludes "Keblaam" from the place which it commonly occupies, occurs in 3 MSS., the Syro-Hex. Georg. Slav-Ostrog. Verss. and the Complut.; "and smote him" is also sing. in 3 MSS. and Compl. The word "Keblaam" was doubtless only the Hebrew words, written by one, who did not know how to translate them, and is variously written and placed as if the scribes did not know what to do with it. Four MSS. make it the name of a place, "in Ieblaam." They are retained in the place of

the Hebrew words in the Vat. MS., but more commonly are added to "Shallum son of Jabis:" in some MSS. and a note in the Syr. Hex., they are followed by "and Selem or Selêm his father." They are written, "Kebdaam, Kebdiam, Kebdam, Kaddaam, Kaibdaam, Keblaam, Keddaam, Kebdaan, Ieblaam, Iebaan, Iebdaam, Bdaam, Beldaam." See LXX ed. Parsons.
[s] Bleek Einl. p. 559.   [t] Knobel, Proph. ii. 171.
[u] Bunsen Gott in d. Gesch. i. 450.
[v] Bertholdt Einl. iv. 1716, and so seemingly Rosenmüller. "Single traits are not to be pressed here; that of v. 8, that Jehovah had slain 3 bad shepherds in one month, belongs merely to poetic individualising." Gramberg ii. 523.
[w] Herzfeld, Gesch. d. Volkes Isr. Excurs. ii. §3. p. 283.   [x] 2 Kgs. xv. 13.
[y] Thenius on 2 Kgs l. c. p. 351.
[z] "Three kings were dethroned by sedition in nearly one month." G. L. Bauer, Addit. Schulzii. Scholia viii. "Three kings followed in a short time on each other." E. Meier Gesch. d. poet. nation. lit. d. Hebr. p. 307.
[a] 2 Kgs xv. 8–14.   [b] 1 Kgs xvi. 15–18.
[c] 2 Tim. iv. 4.   [d] Is. lvii. 10.
[e] S. Matt. xxvi. 14–16, xxvii. 3–10.

Holy Scripture, and so of these chapters of Zechariah is, in itself, a matter which does not concern the soul. It is an untrue imputation, that the date of books of the Bible is converted into matter of faith. In this case Jesus has not set His seal upon it; God the Holy Ghost has not declared it. But, as in other cases, what lay as the foundation of the theory was the unbelief that God, in a way above nature, when it seemed good to Him, revealed a certain future to His creature man. It is the postulate, (or axiom, as appears to these critics), that there is no super-human prophecy, which gives rise to their eagerness, to place these and other prophetic books or portions of books where they can say to themselves that they do not involve such prophecy. To believers it has obviously no religious interest, at what time it pleased Almighty God to send any of His servants the prophets. Not the dates assigned by any of these self-devouring theories, but the grounds alleged in support of those dates, as implying unbelief in God's revelation of Himself, make the question one of religious interest, viz. to shew that these theories are as unsubstantial, as their assumed base is baseless.

It is an infelicity of the modern German mind, that it is acute in observing detailed differences, rather than comprehensive in grasping deeper resemblances. It has been more busied in discovering what is new, than in observing the grounds of what is true. It does not, somehow, acquire the power of balancing evidence, which is habitual to the practical minds of our own countrymen. To take an instance of criticism, apart from Theology, the genuineness of a work of Plato.

"The genuineness of the Laws," says their recent translator[f], "is sufficiently proved by more than 20 citations of them in the writings of Aristotle [whom Plato designated "[g] the intellect of the school," and who must

have been intimate with him for some 17 years[h]] who was residing at Athens during the last years of the life of Plato, and who returned to Athens at the time when he was himself writing his Politics and Constitutions; 2) by the allusion of Isocrates, writing B. C. 346, a year after the death of Plato, and not more than 2 or 3 years after the composition of the Laws—3) by the reference of the comic poet Alexis, a younger contemporary of Plato (B. C. 356.); [*] 4) by the unanimous voice of later antiquity, and the absence of any suspicion among ancient writers worth noticing."

Yet German acuteness has found out reasons, why the treatise should not be Plato's. Those reasons are plausible, as most untrue things are. As put together carefully by one who yet attaches no weight to them, they look like a parody of the arguments, produced by Germans to take to pieces books of Holy Scripture. Mutatis mutandis, they have such an absurdly ludicrous resemblance, that it provokes a smile. Some 50 years ago, there was a tradition at Göttingen, where Heyne had lived, that he attributed the non-reception of the theories as to Homer in England to the English Bishops, who "apprehended that the same principle would be applied to Holy Scripture." Now, for half a century more, both sets of critics have had full scope. The classical sceptics seem to me to have the advantage. Any one, who knew but a little of the uncritical criticism, applied to the sacred books, could imagine, what a jubilee of triumph it would have occasioned, could such differences as those pointed out between "the Laws" and other treatises of Plato, have been pointed out to detach any book of Holy Scripture from its traditional writer. Yet it is held inadequate by one, of whom an admirer said, that "[i] his peculiar mode of criticism cut the very sinews of belief." I insert the criticisms[k], (omitting the details of

[f] Prof. Jowett, Translation of Plato's Dialogues. T. iv. p. 1.

[g] Philopon. de Ætern. mundi vi. 27. in Smith Gr. & Rom. Biogr. i. 317.

[h] From B. C. 364. to Plato's death B. C. 347.

[i] Pall Mall Gaz. March 28, 1868.

[k] "The style of the Laws differs in several important respects from the other dialogues of Plato: 1) in the want of character, power and lively illustration; 2) in the frequency of mannerisms; 3) in the form and rhythm of the sentences; 4) in the use of words. On the other hand, there are many passages 5) which are characterized by a sort of ethical grandeur; and 6) in which perhaps, a greater insight into human nature, and a greater reach of practical wisdom is shewn than in any other of Plato's writings.

"The Laws fall very short of the other Platonic dialogues in the refinements of courtesy. Partly the subject did not properly take the form of dialogue and partly the dramatic vigor of Plato had passed away.—Plato has given the Laws that form which was most suited to his own powers of writing in the decline of life.

"The fictions of the Laws have no longer that

verisimilitude, which we find in the Phædrus, and the Timæus or even in the Politicus—Nor is there any where in the Laws that lively ἐνάργεια, that vivid mise en scène, which is as characteristic of Plato, as of some modern novelists.

"We no longer breathe the atmosphere of humor which pervades the earlier writings of Plato, and which makes the broadest Aristophanic joke as well as the subtlest refinement of wit possible; and hence the impression made upon us is bald and feeble—The irony of the earlier dialogues, of which some traces occur in the 10th book, is replaced by a sort of severity which hardly condescends to regard human things.

"The figures of speech and illustrations are poor in themselves and are not assisted by the surrounding phraseology. In the Republic and in the earlier dialogues—notes are struck which are repeated from time to time, as in a strain of music. There is none of this subtle art in the Laws.—The citations from the poets have lost that fanciful character, which gave them their charm in the earlier dialogues.

2. "The clumsiness of the dialogue leads to frequent mannerisms—This finish of style [in the

illustration) because their failure may open
the eyes of some to the utter valuelessness
of this sort of criticism. The accuracy of the
criticisms is not questioned ; the statements
are not said to be exaggerated; yet they are
held invalid. The question then comes with
great force to the conscience ; "Why, rejecting arguments so forcible as to a treatise of
Plato, do I accept arguments very inferior,
as to such or such a book of the Old or New
Testament,—certain chapters of Isaiah, or
Ecclesiastes, or these chapters of Zechariah,
or the Epistle to the Hebrews, or the Revelation of S. John the Divine,—except on
grounds of theology, not of criticism, and
how am I true to myself in rejecting such
arguments as to human books, and accepting
them as to Divine books ?"

dialogue] is no longer discernible in the Laws.
Again and again the speaker is charged or charges
himself with obscurity; he repeats again and
again that he will explain his views more clearly.
—A tendency to a paradoxical form of statement is
also observable.—More than in other writings of
Plato the tone is hortatory ; the Laws are sermons
as well as laws; they are supposed to have a religious sanction, and to rest upon a religious sentiment in the mind of the citizens—Resumptions of
subjects which have been half disposed of in a
previous passage, constantly occur : the arrangement has neither the clearness of art, nor the freedom of nature. Irrelevant remarks are made here
and there, or illustrations used which are not properly filled in. The dialogue is generally weak and
labored ; and is in the later books fairly given up;
apparently, because unsuited to the subject of the
work.
3. "From this [perfection of style in the Sympos-
ium and Phædrus] there are many fallings off in
the Laws, first, in the structure of the sentences,
which are rhythmical and monotonous :—second,
they are often of enormous length, and the latter
end frequently appears to forget the beginning of
them : they seem never to have received the
second thoughts of the author : either the emphasis is wrongly placed, or there is a want of point in
the clause, or an absolute case occurs, which is not
properly separated from the rest of the sentence ;
or words are aggregated in a manner, which fails
to shew their relation to one another ; or the connecting particles are omitted at the beginning of
sentences ; the use of the relative and the antecedent is more indistinct, the changes of number
and person more frequent; examples of pleonasm,
tautology and periphrasis, unmeaning antitheses
of positive and negative, and other affectations, are
more numerous than in the other writings of
Plato; there is also a more common and sometimes
unmeaning use of qualifying formulæ—and of
double expressions—; again there is an over-curious adjustment of verb and participle, noun and
epithet : many forms of affected variety: thirdly,
the absence of metaphorical language is remarkable ; the style is not devoid of ornament but the
ornament is of a debased rhetorical kind, patched
on it instead of growing out of the subject; there
is a great command of words, and a labored use of
them ; forced attempts at metaphor occur in several passages—(compare also the unmeaning ex-
travagance of language in other passages); poor
and insipid illustrations are also common : fourthly,
we may observe an unmeaning use of climax and
hyperbole—
4. "The peculiarities in the use of words, which
occur in the Laws, have been collected by Zeller
and Stallbaum; first, in the use of nouns, such as"
[8 are given]; "secondly, in the use of adjectives,
such as" [5 instances] "and of adverbs, such as"
[3 instances] "thirdly in the use of verbs such as"
[5 instances]——
"Zeller and Stallbaum have also collected forms
of words in the Laws differing from the forms of
the same words, which occur in other places [7 instances, "and the Ionic word——"]. Zeller has
noticed a fondness for substantives ending in μα
and σις, such as [9 instances "and others "]; also a
use of substantives in the plural, which are commonly found only in the singular [five instances.]
Also a peculiar use of prepositions in composition
as in [five instances " and others "] also a frequent
use of the Ionic datives plural in αισι and οισι.
"To these peculiarities he has added a list of
peculiar expressions and constructions [9 are
given]. He remarks also on the frequent use of
the abstract for the concrete [11 instances]. He
further notes some curious instances of the geni-
tive case—and of the dative—and also some rather
uncommon periphrases; also the pleonastic use of
the enclitics τις and of γε, of τανῦν, of ὡς, and the
periphrastic use of the preposition περί. Lastly he
observes the tendency to hyperbata or transposi-
tion of words ; and to rhythmical uniformity as
well as grammatical irregularity in the structure
of the sentences.
"For nearly all the expressions, which are adduced by Zeller against the genuineness of the
Laws, Stallbaum finds some sort of authority.
There is no reason for suspecting their genuineness, because several words occur in them, which
are not found in the other writings of Plato. An
imitator will often preserve the usual phraseology
of a writer, better than he would himself." From
Prof. Jowett's Introduction to the Laws of Plato,
T. iv. pp. 11-16.

TABLE OF DATES, WHICH IN THIS CENTURY HAVE BEEN ASSIGNED TO ZECHARIAH IX—XIV[a].

AFTER THE DATE OF ZECHARIAH.

c. ix–xiv.	"At the earliest, in the first half and middle of the fifth century."	Vatke[1].
	"The younger poet, whose visions were added to those of Zechariah."	Geiger[2].
	Last years of Darius Hystaspis, or first of Xerxes[3].	Gramberg[4].
	After the battle of Issus B. C. 333.	Eichhorn[5].
	After 330.	Böttcher[6].

[a] J. D. Michaelis, 1786, was uncertain. The opinions or doubts in the last century were altogether vague. "I have as yet no certainty, but am seeking: am also not opposed, if any deny these chapters to be Zechariah's." Neue Orient. u. Exeg. Biblioth. i. 128.

Augusti stated attack and defence, but gave no opinion, Einl. 1806. G. L. Bauer (1793) said generally, "c. ix.–xiv. seem not to be Zechariah's," but professed himself in utter uncertainty as to the dates. Scholia T. viii. On ix.–xiv. he says, "which seems not to be Zechariah's," but whether Flügge was right who thought c. ix. belonged to the time of Jeroboam ii., or Eichhorn, who doubted whether it was not later than Zechariah, he says, "I decide nothing, leaving the whole question uncertain." p. 74. On xi. he says, "we find no indication when the desolation was inflicted," though he would rather understand the Assyrians, than Ant. Epiph. or the Romans. pp. 96, 97. Of xii.–xiv. he leaves subject and time uncertain. pp. 109. 119. 121. Döderlein also seems uncertain, Auserl. theol. Biblioth. iv. 2. p. 81. (1787.)

[1] Biblische Theologie wissenschaftlich dargestellt. i. 553. "It seems to have been occasioned by the Persian-Egyptian wars, and by the feuds of the Jews with the neighboring people. Nehemiah found Jerusalem half destroyed [rather not rebuilt]. The want of historical accounts makes it impossible to explain to what details refer."

[2] (Rabbiner d. Synag. Gem. Breslau) Urschrift u. Uebersetz. d. Bibl. p. 55, 57. 1857.

[3] "When the fame of the Greeks, even in Palestine, must have been great enough to suggest to the poet the thought, that so mighty and warlike a people could only be conquered by Jehovah and his Israelites; then would mere peace and prosperity prevail.

[4] Religions-Ideen d. A. T. (with preface by Gesenius) ii. 520.

[5] Einl. ins. A. T. n. 605. iv. 445, 449. 450. 1824. "If it is true, that all prophecies start from the present, and prophets threaten with no people, and promise nothing of any, till the people itself is come on the scene and into relation with their people, the poet cannot have spoken of the relation of Alexander to the Jews, till after the battle of Issus." "Altogether, no explanation of the whole section (ix. 1.–x. 17.) is possible, if it be not gained from the history of Alexander the Great. History relates expressly, how after the battle of Issus he took possession of all Syria and Zidon without great difficulties; how, with an employment of military contrivance unheard of elsewhere, he conquered and destroyed island-Tyre; how, of the maritime cities of Philistia, with indomitable perseverance he is specified to have besieged and taken Gaza, punished with death the opposition of its commander and its in-

habitants, can any require more to justify this explanation?" "The portions xi. xii.–xiii. 6. have no matter, from which their age could be determined; yet neither do they contain any thing to remove them to an early time; rather has the language much which is late; if then the contents of xiii. 7–end, set it late, they too may be accounted late. This last must either have been to comfort the people on the first tidings of the death of Judas Maccabi in the battle with Bacchides, or have no definite subject.—In that case it would belong to B. C. 161, yet one must own that there is not the same evidence for this, as that ix. 1.–x. 17, belongs to the time of Alexander.—These must be the proofs, that the 2d half of Zechariah cannot have the same author as the first, or one must allow what tradition gives out, and since there are great doubts against it, one must regret that one can come to no clear result as to Zechariah. For the other proofs which could be brought are not decisive." pp. 450, 451.

Corrodi had on the same grounds assigned c. ix. to the time of Alexander; c. xiv. to that of Antiochus Epiphanes. Versuch e. Beleuchtung d. Gesch. d. Jüd. u. Christl. Bibel-Canons i. 107.

[6] Ausf. Lehrbuch d. Hebr. Sprache. n. 45. p. 23. 1868. "The way in which Greece is named as a chief enemy of Zion (quite different from that of Joel iv. 6. Is. lxvi. 19.), chiefly shews that the sections Zech. ix. sqq. which resist every assured collocation in the præ-exile or ante-Macedonian period, could only have been written after Alexander's march through Palestine. With this agree the later coloring, the Levitical spirit, the style full of compilation and of imitation, as also the phantastic messianic hopes. These last must have been revived among the Jews after the overthrow through Alexander. In comparison with the lifeless language of these chapters, as to which we cannot at all understand how any can have removed them into so early præ-exile times, the Psalms attributed to the times of the Maccabees are amazingly fresh. On this, as well as other grounds, we can admit of no Psalms of the Maccabee times." Neue Aehrenlese ii. 215–127. One ground, which has by others of this school been alleged for not ascribing them to Zechariah, had been that they were so much more poetic &c. "In regard to language also, the style in the second Part is wholly different. c. 9. and 10, are energetic, vivid, &c." Hitzig, Vorbemerkk. z. d. ii. u. iii. Zech. n. 2. "Rosenmüller says truly:—How much the poetic, weighty, concise, fervid style of the six last chapters differs from the prosaic, languid, humble style of the eight first." Maurer on Zech. ix.–xiv. p. 667. "These prophecies [Zech. ix.–xiv.] cannot be from Zechariah, not on account of the un-symbolic style (comp. xi. 4–17.) but on account of the more forceful style" &c. De Wette Einl § 250 ed. 2.

TABLE OF DATES.

c. xiv.	Antiochus Epiphanes.	"many interpreters[1]."
c. ix.	On Hyrcanus i, as the Messiah.	Paulus[2].

ZECHARIAH HIMSELF.

[Beckhaus[3] 1792] Jahn[4], Koster[5], Henstenberg[6], Burger[7], De Wette (edd. 4–6). A. Theiner[8], Herbst[9], Umbreit[8], Hävernick[9], Keil[9], Stähelin[9], von Hoffmann[10], Ebrard, Schegg, Baumgarten[8], Neumann[8], Kliefoth[8], Köhler[8], Sandrock[11].

DATES BEFORE THE CAPTIVITY.

ix–xiv.	Uzziah B.C. 772.	Hitzig[12], Rosenmüller[13].
ix–xi.	Under Ahaz, during war with Pekah.	Bertholdt[11].
ix–xi.	Beginning of Ahaz.	Credner[15], Herzfeld[16].
ix–xi.	Later time of Hezekiah.	Baur[17].
ix–xi.	Between B.C. 771–740, i. e. between the invasion of Pul, (2 Kgs xv. 19.) and the capture of Damascus by Tiglath-Pileser (2 Kgs xvi. 9.) i. e. between the 40th of Uzziah and the 3d of Ahaz.	Knobel[18].
ix–xi. and xiii. 7–9.	In the first 10 years of Pekah before the war with Ahaz [i. e. between B.C. 759–749].	Ewald[19].
ix–xi. xiii. 7–9.	"Very probably Uzziah's favorite prophet in his prosperous days."	Stanley[20].
ix–xi.	Contemporary with Isaiah under Ahaz toward B.C. 736.	Bunsen[21].
ix. x.	Perhaps contemporary with Zephaniah [in the time of Josiah].	De Wette[22].
xi.	Might be put in the time of Ahaz.	Id.
ix.	Perhaps out of the time of Zephaniah.	Gesenius[23].

[1] in Bertholdt Einl. iv. 1715.
[2] Comm. z. N.T. iii.130–139. Else he follows Eichhorn 1832.
[3] ub. d. Integrität d. Proph. Schriften d. A. B. p. 337. sqq.
[4] Einl. ii. 675. sqq.
[5] Meletemata crit. et exeg. in Zach. proph. part. post. 1818.
[6] Beiträge zur Einl. ins. A. T. i. 361. sqq.
[7] Etudes exégét. et critiques sur le proph. Zacharie. Strasburg 1841.
[9] In their commentaries on Zechariah.
[9] In their Introductions to the O. T.
[10] Schriftbeweis ii. 2. p.550.
[11] Prioris et posterioris Zach. partis vaticin. ab uno eodemque auct. profecta. 1857.
[12] Theol. Studien u. Kritiken 1830. 1. p. 25. sqq. followed by v. Lengerke, d. Buch Daniel, Einl. p. lxxvii.
[13] Scholia in V. T. vii. 4. p. 254. sqq. ed. 2. In ed. 1. he had followed Jahn.

[14] Einl. ins A. T. iv. n. 431. pp. 1712–1716. In p. 1722 he conjectures the prophet to have been Zechariah son of Jeberechiah (Is. viii. 2); a conjecture recommended by Gesenius, Jesaia i. 527 as "an acute combination." Ewald calls the theory of one or more Zechariahs, "an over-ingenious device (erklügelte) idle conjecture, a plea of those who will not look straight at the truth." Proph. i. 249.
[15] Joel. vol. i. p. 105.
[16] Gesch. d. Volkes Isr., Excurs. ii. n. 3. pp. 280–282.
[17] d. Proph. Amos, voi. i.
[18] Prophetismus d. Hebräer ii. 168–170.
[19] Kl. Proph. i. 248–251, followed mostly by E. Meier Gesch. d. poet. national. lit. d. Hebraer p. 308.
[20] Jewish Church ii. 444, add 364, 366.
[21] Gott. in d. Geschichte i. 453. In p. 247, he placed ch. ix. at "a generation after Ahaz."
[22] Einl. ins. A. T. n. 250. p. 338. edd. 1–3.
[23] On Is. xxiii. p. 713.

TABLE OF DATES.

ix.	Uzziah.	Bleek [1], Forberg [2].
x.	Ahaz, soon after war with Pekah and Rezin.	Bleek.
xi. 1–3.	Invasion of some Assyrian king.	
xii. 4–17.	Menahem, and end of Uzziah.	
ix.	Between the carrying away of 2½ tribes and the fall of Damascus.	Maurer [3].
x.	Between 739–731, the 7 years' anarchy between Hosea's murder of Pekah and his own accession.	
xi.	In reign of Hosea.	
ix.	Under Uzziah and Jeroboam.	
x.	The Anarchy after death of Jeroboam ii. [B.C. 784–772.]	v. Ortenberg [4].
xi. 1–3.	B.C. 716.	
xi. 4–17. xiii. 7–9.	Shortly after the war of Pekah and Rezin.	
ix–x.	Not before Jeroboam, nor before Uzziah's accession, but before the death of Zechariah son of Jeroboam.	Hitzig [5].
xi.	Beginning of reign of Menahem.	Hitzig [5].
xi.	Possibly contemporary with Hosea.	Bauer [6].
ix.	After capture of Damascus by Tiglath-Pileser.	Movers [7].
xii–xiv.	Manasseh, in view of a siege by Esarhaddon.	Hitzig [8].
	Between B.C. 607–604 (though falsified.)	Knobel [9].
	Soon after Josiah's death, by Uriah, Jeremiah's contemporary, B.C. 607 or 606.	Bunsen [10].
	Most probably, while the Chaldees were already before Jerusalem, shortly before Jerusalem was first conquered (599).	Schrader [11].
xii. 1–xiii. 6.	Under Joiakim or Jeconiah or Zedekiah in Nebuchadnezzar's last expedition (no objection that it was falsified).	Bertholdt [12].
xiii. 7.–end.	Soon after Josiah's death.	Bertholdt [13].
xii. 1–xiii. 6.	The last years of Jehoiakim, or under Jehoiachin or Zedekiah.	Bleek [14].
xiii.–7. end.	" Exceeding probably under Josiah or Jehoiakim."	Bleek [15].
xii. 1–xiii. 6.	Fourth year of Jehoiakim.	Maurer [16].
xiii. 7.–end.	Fifth.	
xii. 1–xiii. 6.	The latter half of 600 B.C.	v. Ortenberg [17].
xiv.	Later than xii. 1.–xiii. 6.	

[1] Einl. ins. A. T. p. 555–560.
[2] Comm. crit. et exeg. in part. post. Zach. P. i.
[3] Maurer Comm. p. 669.
[4] Die Bestandtheile d. Buchs Sacharia pp. 68. 72. 75, 79, followed by Kahnis Lutherische Dogm. i. 354–357.
[5] D. Kl. Proph. ii. und iii. Zacharia, Vorbemerk. n. 4. p. 351. ed. 2., followed by *Schrader* in his re-writing of De Wette's Einl. n. 308, only placing c. ix. definitely in the time of Jeroboam ii.

[6] "What I think, or rather, conjecture." Schulzii Scholia continuata viii. 100.
[7] Phœnicien ii. 1. p. 383, 384.
[8] Kl. Proph. ii. und iii. Sach. n. 5. 6. ed. 2, 3.
[9] Prophetismus ii. 289.
[10] Gott in d. Geschichte i. 451, 452.
[11] De Wette's Einleitung, re-written from his Ed. vi. n. 308. a new § p. 382.   [12] Einl. iv. 1717.
[13] Ib. 1719.   [14] Einl. p. 560.   [15] Ib. 563.
[16] Proph. Min. p. 670.   [17] Bestandtheile &c. p. 87.

TABLE OF DATES.

xii–xiii. 6.	12 years after Habakkuk [about B.C. 607, Ewald] shortly before the destruction of Jerusalem.	Ewald [1].
xiii. 7–9.	Same date as ix. xi. (see above).	
xiv.	A little later than xii–xiii.	
	or, In the first rebellion against Nebuchadnezzar "[3] by Chananiah, or one of the many prophets who contradicted Jeremiah."	Ewald [2].
xii–xiii. 6. xiv.	Zedekiah, "Beginning of revolt."	Stanley [4]
xii. 1–xiii. 6.	"Prophecies of fanatic contents, which deny all	De Wette ed. 2 [5].
xiii. 7. end.	historical explanation, but xiii. 7. must rather be conceived as future than 'past,' as Bertholdt."	
xii. 1–xiii. 6. xiv.	After death of Josiah, yet relating to the repentance for the putting the Messias to death, and so independent of the times in which it is placed.	Kahnis [6].

[1] Kl. Proph. ii. 52.
[2] Ib. ii. 59. "At a time when the earnest and more threatening condition of the world softened the proud certainty of victory, and occasioned the anticipation of the fulfillment of a judgment on the holy city." xiv. 1–2.
[3] Geschichte d. Volkes Isr. iii. 803. Ewald says that he often balanced between them, but always ended by coming back to the first, since xiv. 2, probably referred to the capture under Jehoiachin.

[4] Jewish Church. Sect. xi. "special authorities." p. 513. Passing him over in the history, he escapes the consequence which Ewald drew out, that he would have been a false prophet, although he says, that "in Hananiah," whose death Jeremiah prophesied for "telling lies in the name of the Lord," "passed away the last echo of the ancient invincible strain of the age of Isaiah." p. 545.
[5] Einl. n. 250. p. 338 ed. 1822.
[6] Lutherische Dogm. i. 359–361.

ZECHARIAH.

CHAPTER I.

1 *Zechariah exhorteth to repent-*
ance. 7 *The vision of the*
horses. 12 *At the prayer of*
the angel comfortable promises
are made to Jerusalem. 18
The vision of the horns, and
the four carpenters.

ᵃ Ezra 4. 24.
Hag. 1. 1.

ᵇ Ezra 5. 1.
Matt. 23. 35.

IN the eighth month, ᵃ in
the second year of Da-
rius, came the word of the
LORD ᵇ unto Zechariah, the

son of Berechiah, the son
of Iddo the prophet, saying,

2 The LORD hath been
† sore displeased with your
fathers.

† Heb. *with*
displeasure.

3 Therefore say thou
unto them, Thus saith the
LORD of hosts ; Turn ᶜ ye
unto me, saith the LORD
of hosts, and I will turn
unto you, saith the LORD
of hosts.

ᶜ Jer. 25. 5.
& 35. 15.
Mic. 7. 19.
Mal. 3. 7.
Luke 15. 20.
James 4. 8.

CHAP. I. 1. *In the eighth month* [1]. The
date joins on Zechariah's prophecy to those
of Haggai. Two months before, *in the sixth*
month [2], had Haggai, conjointly with Zechariah [3], exhorted Zerubbabel and the people to resume the intermitted building of the
temple. These had used such diligence,
notwithstanding the partial discouragement
of the Persian Government [4], that God gave
them *in the seventh month*, the magnificent
promise of the later glory of the temple
through the Coming of Christ [5]. Still as
Haggai too warned them, the conversion was
not complete. So Zechariah in the eighth,
as Haggai in the ninth [6] month, urges upon
them the necessity of thorough and inward
repentance, as the condition of partaking of
those promises.

" [7] Thrice in the course of one saying, he
mentions the most holy name of God ; partly
to instruct in the knowledge of Three Persons in one Nature, partly to confirm their
minds more strongly in the hope of the salvation to come."

2. lit. *Wroth was the Lord against your*
fathers with wrath [8], i. e., a wrath which was
indeed such, whose greatness he does not
further express, but leaves to their memories
to supply. " [9] Seest thou how he scares
them, and, setting before the young what
befell those before them, drives them to
amend, threatening them with the like or
more grievous ills, unless they would wisely
reject their fathers' ways, esteeming the
pleasing of God worthy of all thought and
care. He speaks of *great wrath*. For it indicates no slight displeasure that He allowed

the Babylonians to waste all Judah and
Samaria, burn the holy places and destroy
Jerusalem, remove the elect Israel to a piteous slavery in a foreign land, severed from
sacrifices, entering no more the holy court
nor offering the thank-offering, or tithes, or
first-fruits of the law, but precluded by
necessity and fear even from the duty of
celebrating his prescribed and dearest festivals. The like we might address to the
Jewish people, if we would apply it to the
mystery of Christ. For after they had *killed*
the prophets and had *crucified the Lord of glory*
Himself, they were captured and destroyed ;
their famed temple was levelled, and Hosea's
words were fulfilled in them ; [10] *The children*
of Israel shall abide many days without a kin⸗
and without a prince, without a sacrifice and
without an image, without an ephod and without
teraphim."

3. *Therefore say thou.* lit. *And thou sayest*, i. e.,
this having been so, it follows that thou
sayest or must say [11], *Turn ye unto Me.* In
some degree they had turned to God, for
Whose sake they had returned to their land ;
and again when, after some negligence [12],
they renewed the building of the temple, and
God had said, [13] *I am with you.* But there
needed yet a more inward completer turning,
whereon God promises a yet nearer presence,
as Malachi repeats the words [14], and S. James
exhorts [15], *Draw nigh to God and He will draw*
nigh to you. Those who have turned to God
need ever to turn more into the centre of the
narrow way. As the soul opens itself more
to God, God, Whose communication of Himself is ever hindered only by our closing the

---

[1] Not as Kim. in the 8th new-moon ; for though
חֹדֶשׁ is used of the new-moon, Num. xxviii. 14, 1
Sam. xx. 5, 18, 24 ; Am. viii. 5. (not Ex. xix. 1. or
Hos. v. 7.) it is not so used in dates, in which it
would be ambiguous.
[2] Hagg. i. 1.   [3] Ezr. v. 1, 2.   [4] Ib. 3–5.
[5] Hagg. ii. 1–9.   [6] Ib. 10–14.   [7] Osor.
[8] As we might express by the indefinite article

"a blow" for "such a blow." The LXX fill up
ὀργὴν μεγάλην. Ewald (Lehrb. n. 281. p. 702.) quotes
χαρᾷ χαίρει, S. John iii. 29.
[9] S. Cyr.   [10] Hos. iii. 4. See vol. i. p. 44.
[11] The force of וְאָמַרְתָּ. The duty is implied in
v. 2.   [12] Hagg. i. 2–11.   [13] Ib. 13.
[14] Mal. iii. 7.   [15] S. James iv. 8.

Before
CHRIST
cir. 520.
d 2 Chron. 36.
15, 16.
e Isai. 31. 6.
Jer. 3. 12.
& 18. 11.
Ezek. 18. 30.
Hos. 14. 1.

4 Be ye not as your fa-thers, ^d unto w h o m t h e former prophets have cried, s a y i n g, Thus saith the LORD of hosts; ^e Turn ye

now from your evil ways, and *from* your evil doings : but they did not hear, nor hearken unto me, saith the LORD.

Before
CHRIST
cir. 520.

door of our hearts against Him, enters more into it. ¹ *If a man love Me, he will keep My words, and My Father will love him, and We will come unto him, and make Our abode with him.*

" ² Men are said to be converted, when leaving behind them deceitful goods, they give their whole mind to God, bestowing no less pains and zeal on Divine things than before on the nothings of life."

" ³ When it is said in Holy Scripture, *Turn unto Me and I will turn unto you,* we are admonished as to our own freedom ; when we answer, *Turn us, Lord, unto Thee, and we shall be turned,* we confess that we are fore-come by the grace of God."

4. *Be ye not like your fathers.* Strangely infectious is the precedent of ill. Tradition of good, of truth, of faith, is decried ; only tradition of ill and error are adhered to. The sin of Jeroboam was held sacred by every king of Israel : ⁴ *The statutes of Omri were diligently kept, and all the works of the house of Ahab. They turned back and were treacherous like their forefathers ; they turned themselves like a deceitful bow* ⁵, is God's summary of the history of Israel. " ⁶ Absurd are they who follow the ignorances of their fathers, and ever plead inherited custom as an irrefrag-able defence, though blamed for extremest ills. So idolaters especially, being called to the knowledge of the truth, ever bear in mind the error of their fathers and, embrac-ing their ignorance as an hereditary lot, remain blind."

The former prophets. The prophets spake God's words, as well in their pastoral office as in predicting things to come, in enforcing God's law and in exhorting to repentance, as in announcing the judgments on disobedience. The predictive as well as the pastoral office were united in Nathan ⁷, Gad ⁸, Shemaiah ⁹, Azariah ¹⁰, Hanani ¹¹, Elijah ¹², Elisha ¹³, Micaiah the son of Imla, whose habitual pre-dictions against Ahab induced Ahab to say ¹⁴, *I hate him, for he doth not prophesy good con-cerning me, but evil.* The specific calls to con-

version here named and their fruitlessness, are summed up by Jeremiah as words of all the prophets. For ten years he says, ¹⁵ *The word of the Lord hath come unto me, and I have spoken unto you, rising early and speaking, and ye have not hearkened. And the Lord hath sent unto you all His servants the prophets, rising early and sending ; but ye have not hearkened nor inclined your ear to hear. They said, Turn ye again now every one from his evil ways and from the evil of your doings, and dwell in the land that the Lord hath given unto you and to your fathers for ever and ever ; and go not after other gods to serve and worship them, and provoke Me not to anger with the works of your hands, and I will do you no hurt. But ye have not hearkened unto Me, saith the Lord ; that ye might provoke Me to anger with the works of your hands to your own hurt. Therefore, thus saith the Lord of hosts, Because ye have not heard My words &c.* The prophetic author of the book of Kings sums up in like way, of *all the pro-phets and all the seers.* ¹⁶ *The Lord testified against Israel and against Judah by the hand of all the prophets and all the seers, saying, Turn ye from your evil ways and keep My command-ments, My statutes, according to all the law which I commanded your fathers, and which I sent to you by My servants the prophets, and they did not hear, and hardened their neck, like the neck of their fathers.*

The characteristic word ¹⁷, *turn from your evil ways and the evil of your doings* occurring in Jeremiah, it is probable, that this sum-mary was chiefly in the mind of Zechariah, and that he refers not to Isaiah, Joel, Amos &c., (as all the prophets were preachers of repentance), but to the whole body of teachers, whom God raised up, analogous to the Chris-tian ministry, to recall men to Himself.

The title, *the former prophets,* contrasts the office of Haggai and Zechariah, not with definite prophets before the captivity, but with the whole company of those, whom God sent as He says, so unremittingly.

And they hearkened not unto Me. " ¹⁸ They heard not the Lord warning through the pro-

¹ S. John xiv. 23.	² Osor.
³ Conc. Trid. Sess. vi. c. 5.	⁴ Mic. vi. 16.
⁵ Ps. lxxviii. 57.	⁶ S. Cyr.
⁷ 2 Sam. vii. 4-16, xii. 1-14.	⁸ 1 Sam. xxii. 5, xxiv. 11.
⁹ 2 Chr. xi. 2-4, xii. 5-8.	¹⁰ Ib. xv.	¹¹ Ib. xvi. 7-9.
¹² 1 Kgs xvii. 1, 14, xviii. 1, 41, xxi. 19, 21, 23, 29, 2
Kgs i. 4, 16.
¹³ 2 Kgs iii. 17, 18. iv. 16, v. 27, vii. 1, 2, viii. 10-13, xiii. 14-19.
¹⁴ 1 Kgs xxii. 8.	¹⁵ Jer. xxv. 3-8.	¹⁶ 2 Kgs xvii. 13.

¹⁷ Zech. שׁוּבוּ נָא מִדַּרְכֵיכֶם הָרָעִים וּמַעֲלִילֵיכֶם
Jer. xxv. 5. שָׁבוּ נָע אִישׁ מִדַּרְכּוֹ הָרָעָה הָרָעִים
וּמֵרֹעַ מַעֲלִילֵיכֶם. In Jer. xviii. 11. the second clause is, וַהֲשִׁיבוּ כִבוּד כִיכֶם וּמַעֲלִילֵיכֶם ; in Jer. xxxv. 15, it is, וְהֵיטִיבוּ מַעֲלִילֵיכֶם. In Zech., the Kri מַעֲלֵיכֶם substitutes Jeremiah's word for the ἀπ. λεγ. מַעֲלִילִים.
¹⁸ S. Jer.

Before
C H R I S T
cir. 520.

5 Your fathers, where *are* t h e y ? and the prophets, do t h e y l i v e for ever?

f Isai. 55. 1.

6 But *'my words and my statutes, which I commanded my servants the p r o p h e t s, did they not

‖ Or, *overtake.*

‖ take h o l d of your fathers? and they returned

g Lam. 1. 18.
& 2. 17.

and said, *g L i k e* as the LORD of hosts thought to do unto us, according to our ways, a n d according

to our doings, so hath he dealt with us.

7 ¶ Upon the four and t w e n t i e t h day of the eleventh month, which *is* the month Sebat, in the s e c o n d year of Darius, c a m e t h e word of the LORD unto Zechariah, the son of Berechiah, the son of Iddo the prophet, saying,

8 I saw by night, and behold *h* a man riding upon

Before
C H R I S T
cir. 520.

cir. 519.

h Josh. 5. 13.
Rev. 6. 4.

phets, attended not—not to the Prophets who spake to them but—not to Me, saith the Lord. For I was in them who spake and was despised. Whence also the Lord in the Gospel saith, [1] *He that receiveth you, receiveth Me.*"

5. *Your fathers, where are they* [2] ? The abrupt solemnity of the question seems to imply an unexpected close of life which cut short their hopes, plans, promises to self. [3] *When they* said, *Peace and safety, then sudden destruction cometh upon them.* Yet not they only but the prophets too, who ministered God's word to them, these also being men, passed away, some of them before their time as men, by the martyr's death. Many of them saw not their own words fulfilled. But God's word which they spake, being from God, passed not away.

6. *Only My words and My decrees* [4], which God spake by them, *did not they overtake them ?* Heathen reminiscence of God's justice acknowledged, " [5] Rarely hath punishment with limping tread parted with the forerunning miscreant." *All these curses,* Moses foretells [6], *shall come upon thee and overtake thee* [7], *until thou art destroyed.*

And they returned to God and said. The history of the Jews in Babylon is omitted in Holy Scripture, except as to His special dealings with Daniel and his three companions. Yet Jeremiah confesses in words, what Zechariah had apparently in his mind; [8] *The Lord hath done that which He purposed; He hath fulfilled His word, which He commanded in the days of old.* The Lamentations are one

long confession of deserved punishment, such as Daniel too made in the name of his people with himself [9].

It was one long waiting for God and for the restoration of His visible worship. Yet repentance was a condition of their restoration.

7. *On the twenty-fourth day,* exactly five months after the building of the temple was resumed [10], and two months after Haggai's last prophecy [11]. The series of visions, leading onward, from the first deliverance from the enemies who oppressed them, to the Coming of Christ, is given as a reward to their first whole-hearted endeavor to restore their worship of Him. The visions are called *the word of the Lord,* because they were prophecy, made visible to the eye, conveying the revelation to the soul, and in part explained by Him.

8. *I saw in the night,* i. e. that following on *the twenty-fourth* day. The darkness of the night perhaps was chosen, as agreeing with the dimness of the restored condition. Night too is, " [12] through the silence of the senses and of the fancy, more suited for receiving Divine revelations."

A man riding upon a red horse. The man is an angel of God, appearing in form of man, as Daniel says, " [13] *The man* Gabriel, whom I had seen in the vision at the beginning, touched me." He is doubtless the same who appeared to Joshua in form of man, preparing thereby for the revelation of *God manifest in the flesh*— He, before whom Joshua fell on his face and in him worshiped God, through whom also

[1] S. Matt. x. 40.
[2] It is probably for emphasis, that (here alone) the full אַיֵּה הֵם stands for the contracted אַיָּם; our, "where are *they ?*"
[3] 1 Thess. v. 3. [4] As Ps. ii. 7. Zeph. ii. 2.
[5] Hor. Od. iii. 9. fin.
[6] Deut. xxviii. 45.
[7] The same word הִשִּׂיג (as here) occurs also Ib.

15; of the Divine wrath, Ps. lxix. 25; of iniquities, Ps. xl. 13.
[8] Lam. ii. 17. זָמַם is used of God, in connection with עָשָׂה in both places and in Jer. li. 12. זָמַם is used of God beside only in Jer. iv. 28. The verb is used only 13 times in all.
[9] Dan. ix. 4–16. [10] Hagg. ii. 15. [11] Ib. ii. 20.
[12] Dion. [13] Dan. ix. 21.

Before
CHRIST
cir. 519.
a red horse, and he stood
among the myrtle trees
that *were* in the bottom;
and behind him *were there*
[i] ch. 6. 2,–7.
|| Or, *bay.*
[i] red horses, ||speckled, and
white.

9 Then said I, O my
lord, what *are* these? And
the angel that talked with

me said unto me, I will
shew thee what these *be.*
Before
CHRIST
cir. 519.

10 And the man that
stood among the myrtle
trees answered and said,
[k] These *are they* whom the [k] Heb. 1. 14.
LORD hath sent to walk
to and fro through the
earth.

God required the same tokens of reverence
as He had from Moses [1]. *Joshua lifted up his
eyes, and looked, and behold there stood a man
over against him with a sword drawn in his hand,
who said, as Captain of the Lord's host am I
come.* He rides here, as Leader of the host
who follow Him ; to Him the others report,
and He instructs the Angel who instructs the
prophet. Red, being the color of blood,
symbolizes doubtless "[2] the vengeance of
God to be inflicted on the enemies of the
Jews for their sins committed against the
Jews," exceeding the measure of chastisement allowed by God. It probably was S.
Michael [3], who is entitled in Daniel, *your
prince* [4], *the great prince which standeth up for
the children of thy people* [5].
And he was standing, almost as we say, stationary, abiding in that one place. The description is repeated [6], apparently as identifying this angel, and so he and *the angel of the* [7]
Lord are probably one.
The myrtle trees [8], from their fragrance and
lowness, probably symbolize the Church, as
at once yielding a sweet odor, and in a low
estate, or lowly. The natural habits of the
myrtle make it the fitter symbol [9].
And behind him. The relation of the

Angel as their chief is represented by their
following him. This is consistent with their
appearing subsequently as giving report to
him. The red and white horses are well-
known symbols of war and glory, whence He
Who sits on *the white horse* [10] in the Revelations, *went forth conquering and to conquer.*
The remaining color is somewhat uncertain.
If it be *ashen gray,* it would correspond to *the
pale horse* [11] of the Revelations, and the union
of the two colors, black and white, is calculated to be a symbol of a chequered state of
things, whereas a mingled color like " chestnut " is not suggestive of any symbol.
9. *What are these ?* He asks, not *who,* but
what [12] they import.
The angel that talked with me. lit. "spake *in*
me." The very rare expression [13] seems
meant to convey the thought of an inward
speaking, whereby the words should be borne
directly into the soul, without the intervention of the ordinary outward organs. God
says to Moses, [14] *If there is a prophet among you,
I, the Lord, will make Myself known unto him in
a vision, I will speak* [lit.] *in him in a dream.
My servant Moses is not so—In him will I
speak mouth to mouth ;* and Habakkuk says of
the like inward teaching, [15] *I will watch to see,*

---

[1] Josh. v. 13–15. See on "the Angel of the Lord"
in "Daniel the Prophet," pp. 519–525.
[2] Dion.   [3] Dan. x. 13.   [4] Ib. 21.
[5] Ib. xii. 1. S. Jerome observes, "The Jews suppose
the man on the red horse to be the Angel Michael,
who was to avenge the iniquities and sins against
Israel."   [6] ver. 10.   [7] ver. 11.
[8] The name of the plant, הֲדַס, occurs in the
Arabic of Yemen (Kam. p. 812 and Abulwalid) and
is probably the basis of Esther's original name,
הֲדַסָּה, perhaps i. q. 'Ατοσσα. Ges.
[9] מְצֻלָה, ἅπ. in form is doubtless the same as צָלַל
מְצוּלָה, being used of sinking in the water, Ex.
xv. 10. "In profundo," S. Jer. (Virg. Georg. ii. 112,
litora myrtetis gratissima, and Ib. iv. 124, amantes
litora myrti.) The LXX κατασκίων would rather
have been מְצִלָּה, and the myrtles make shade, but
do not grow in a shady place. Hitz. Ew. Maur.
correct מְצִלָּה, "the tent," (as Arab. מַטֲלָה) i. e.
"of God," they say. But the tabernacle, while it
existed, was not so called ; nor did myrtles grow
before it. Bottcher n. 641. γ.) מְצָלָה, "schatten-
dach."   [10] Rev. vi. 2.

[11] Rev. vi. 8, ψαροὶ, ό; varū, S. Jer., ξανθοί Aq. The
קוּחִין of the Targum is itself uncertain. It is a
conjecture only of Levy, that it may be i. q.
κυανοχαίτης, "dark-maned." Rashi and Kim. own
that they do not know. The Peshito פִּיסְבְּיָא corresponds to the Heb. טְלוּא in Gen. xxx. 32. (bis)
33, 35 (bis) 39. but its meaning, in itself, is equally
unknown. The Hebrew root occurs beside, only
of a choice vine, pl. Is. xvi. 8, שֹׂרֵק Is. v. 2. Jer. ii.
21, שְׂרֵקָה Gen. xlix. 11 ; in Arab. سريق, Abulw.
But although this vine, growing only in Syria, has
small blue-black grapes (Kim.), it is mere guess
that it is so called from its color, or that שׂרק
signifies red or dark. It is equally a guess that
שרק is transposed from Arab. أَشْقَر "chestnut,"
(as distinct from "bay" כֻּמַיְת). שֻׁקְרָא is used of
the color of fire.
[12] מַה, not מִי.   [13] דִבֶּר בִּי.   [14] Nu. xii. 6–9.
[15] Hab. ii. 1. These are the only additional instances
of the construction, unless Jer. xxxi. 20, be used of
tender speaking, "in (elsewhere in the heart of)
Ephraim."

Before
CHRIST
cir. 519.
11 ¹ And they answered the angel of the LORD

¹ Ps. 103. 20, 21.
that stood among the myrtle trees, and said, We have walked to and fro through the earth, and, behold, all the earth sitteth still, and is at rest.

12 ¶ Then the angel of the LORD answered and said, ᵐ O LORD of hosts, how long wilt thou not

Before
CHRIST
cir. 519.

ᵐ Ps. 102. 13.
Rev. 6. 10.

what He will speak in me. It is the characteristic title of one attendant-angel, who was God's expositor of the visions to Zechariah [1]. "² By his ministry God shewed me things to come, in that that angel formed in the spirit and imaginative power of Zechariah phantasms or images of things which were foreshewn him, and gave him to understand what those images signified."

11. *And the man answered* to the question addressed to the attendant-angel. He himself took the word.

These are they whom the Lord sent to walk up and down. Satan says of himself that he came ³ *from going to and fro in the earth and from walking up and down in it.* As he for evil, so these for good. Their office was not a specific or passing duty, as when God sent His angels with some special commission, such as those recorded in Holy Scripture. It was a continuous conversation with the affairs of men, a minute course of visiting, inspecting our human deeds and ways, a part of the "⁴ wonder.'ul order," in which God has "ordained and constituted the services of Angels and men." Nor is it said that the Angels were limited, each to his own peculiar province, as we learn through Daniel, that certain great Angels, *Princes* among them, had the charge of empires or nations, even of the heathen [5]. These Angels had apparently only the office of inspecting and reporting to Angels of a higher order, themselves a subordinate order in the heavenly Hierarchy. Nor are they spoken of, as executing any judgments of God, or as pacifying the earth; they may have been so employed ; but they are only said to have reported the state in which they found it.

These *answered* the unexpressed inquiry of *the angel of the Lord,* as he had answered the unuttered question of the angel, attendant on Zechariah.

Sitteth still and is at rest, at rest, as the word

¹ i. 13, 14, 19 (ii. 2 Heb.) ii. 3. [7] iv. 1, 4, 5. v. 5. 10. vi. 4.　　　　² Dion.
³ Job ii. 2.　　　⁴ Collect for S. Michael's day.
⁵ See "Daniel the Prophet" pp. 525, 526.
⁶ קשׁט is the word used in the book of Judges
of the rest given to the land under judges until its fresh departure from God, Jud. iii. 11, 30, v. 31, viii. 28. ; of the undisturbed life of the people of Laish, Jud. xviii. 7, 27; "from war," מִפְּלְחָמָה, is added, Jos. xi. 23, xiv. 15. of the rest after the war whereby Israel was put in possession of Canaan.

seems to express ⁶, from its wonted state of tumult and war. Wars, although soon to break out again, were in the second year of Darius for the time suspended. The rest, in which the world was, suggests the contrast of the yet continuing unrest allotted to the people of God. Such rest had been promised to Israel, on its return from the captivity [7], but had not yet been fulfilled. Through the hostility of the Samaritans the building of the temple had been hindered and was just recommenced ; the wall of Jerusalem was yet broken down [8]; its fire-burned gates not restored ; itself was a waste [9]; its houses unbuilt [10]. This gives occasion to the intercession of *the Angel of the Lord.*

12. *And the Angel of the Lord answered* the implied longing, by intercession with God. As the angel-interpreter in Job had " [11] the office of no mere created angel, but one, anticipative of *His,* Who came at once to redeem and justify," so *the* Angel of the Lord, in whom God was, exercised at once a mediatorial office with God, typical of our Lord's High Priest's prayer [12], and acted as God.

These seventy years. The seventy years of the captivity, prophesied by Jeremiah [13], were on the eve of their conclusion at the time of Daniel's great prayer of intercession [14] ; they ended with the capture of Babylon, and the edict of Cyrus, permitting the Jews to return [15]. Yet there seems to have been a secondary fulfillment, from the destruction of the temple and city, in Zedekiah's eleventh year [16], 588 B. C. to the second year of Darius, 519 B. C. Such double fulfillments of prophecy are not like alternative fulfillments. They are a more intricate and fuller, not an easier fulfillment of it. Yet *these* 70 *years* do not necessitate such a double fulfillment. It might express only a reverent wonder, that the 70 years being accomplished, the complete restoration was not yet brought to pass. " [17] God having fixed the time of the cap-

It is used of the rest in Asa's days, 2 Chr. xiii. 23, Heb. given him by God, xiv. 4, 5. of the rest of the city after the death of Athaliah, 2 Kgs xi. 20, 2 Chr. xxiii. 21 ; of the earth, after the destruction of Babylon, Is. xiv. 7.
⁷ with the same word קשׁט Jer. xxx. 10, xlvi. 27.
⁸ Neh. i. 3.　　⁹ Ib. ii. 3.　　¹⁰ Ib. vii. 4.
¹¹ See " Daniel the Prophet" p. 523.
¹² S. John xvii.
¹³ Jer. xxv. 11, 12. xxix. 10.
¹⁴ Dan. ix. 2.　　¹⁵ 2 Chr. xxxvi. 22, 23. Ezr. i. 1.
¹⁶ 2 Kgs xxv. 2, 8, 9.　　¹⁷ S. Cyr.

·[n] Jer. 25. 11, 12.
Dan. 9. 2.
ch. 7. 5.

[o] Jer. 29. 10.

have mercy on Jerusalem and on the cities of Judah, against which thou hast had indignation [n] these three-score and ten years?

13 And the LORD answered the angel that talked with me *with* [o] good

words *and* comfortable words.

14 So the angel that communed with me said unto me, Cry thou, saying, Thus saith the LORD of hosts; I am [p]jealous for Jerusalem and for Zion with a great jealousy.

[p] Joel 2. 18.
ch. 8. 2.

---

tivity to the 70th year, it was necessary to be silent, so long as the time was not yet come to an end, that he might not seem to oppose the Lord's will. But, when the time was now come to a close and the fear of offending was removed, he, knowing that the Lord cannot lie, entreats and ventures to enquire whether His anger has come to an end, as had those who sinned; or whether, fresh sins having accrued, there shall be a further delay, and their forlorn estate shall be yet further extended. They then who worship God have a good and not uncertain hope, that, if they should offend from infirmity, yet have they those who should entreat for them, not men only, but the holy angels themselves, who render God gracious and propitious, soothing His anger by their purity, and in a manner winning the grieved judge. *Then* the Angel entreated for the synagogue to the Jews; but we, who believe and have been sanctified in the Spirit, [1] *have an Advocate with the Father Jesus Christ the righteous, and He is the propitiation for our sins*, and as the Divine Paul writes, [2] *God hath set Him forth as a propitiation through faith*, freeing from sin those who come to Him."

13. *And the Lord answered the angel that talked with me.* Either directly, at the intercession of *the angel of the Lord*, or mediately through an answer first given to him, and by him communicated to the subordinate angel. Neither is expressed.

Good words, as God had promised[3], *after seventy years shall be accomplished at Babylon, I will visit you and perform My good word unto you, causing you to return to this place;* and Joshua says, [4] *There failed not ought of any good word which the Lord spake unto the house of Israel.*

Comfortable words, lit. *consolations* [5]. Perhaps the Angel who received the message had, from their tender compassion for us, whereby they [6] *joy over one sinner that re-*

penteth, a part in these *consolations* which he conveyed.

14. *Cry thou.* The vision was not for the prophet alone. What he saw and heard, *that* he was to proclaim to others. The vision, which he now saw alone, was to be the basis and substance of his subsequent preaching[7], whereby he was to encourage his people to persevere.

I am jealous for Jerusalem, lit. *I have been*, not now only but in time past even when I did not shew it, *and am jealous*[8], with the tender love which allows not what it loves to be injured [9]. The love of God, until finally shut out, is unchangeable, He pursues the sinner with chastisements and scourges in His love, that he may yet be converted and live [10]. But for God's love to him and the solicitations of His grace, while yet impenitent and displeasing Him, he could not turn and please Him.

And for Zion, which especially He had chosen to put His Name there, and there to receive the worship of His people; [11] *the hill which God desired to dwell in,* [12] *which He loved.* " [13] With great and special love have I loved the people of the Jews and what pertained to them, and out of that love have I so diligently and severely corrected her excesses, that she may be more careful for the time to come, as a husband corrects most sharply a wife most dear to him, if she be unfaithful. Whence in the book of Maccabees it is written, " [14] It is a token of His great goodness, when wicked doers are not suffered any long time, but are forthwith punished. For not as with other nations, whom the Lord patiently forbeareth to punish, till they become to the fullness of their sins, so dealeth He with us; lest, being come to the height of sin, afterward He should take vengeance of us. And therefore He never withdraweth His mercy from us, and though He punisheth

---

[1] 1 S. John ii. 1, 2.   [2] Rom. iii. 25.
[3] Jer. xxix. 10.
[4] Josh. xxi. 43 (45 Eng.) add xxiii. 14, 15.
[5] as Is. lvii. 18.   [6] S. Luke xv. 10.
[7] קָרָא, ab. 4. Jon. i. 2. Is. xl. 2, 6.
[8] Ewald compares יָדַעְתִּי, οἶδα, novi; זָכַרְתִּי,

memini, Nu. xi. 5, הוֹחִיל, חסית, Ps. xxxviii. 16.
&c. Lehrb. n. 135. *b.* p. 129. ed. 8.
[9] See on Nah. i. 1, p. 129.   [10] S. Aug. Conf. iii. 1.
[11] Ps. lxviii. 16.
[12] Ib. lxxviii. 68, add Ps. cxxxii. 13, 14.
[13] Dion.   [14] 2 Macc. vi. 13–16.

Before CHRIST cir. 519.	15 And I am very sore displeased with the heathen *that are* at ease: for ᑫ I was but a little displeased, and they helped forward the affliction. 16 Therefore thus saith	the LORD; ʳ I am returned to Jerusalem with mercies: my house shall be built in it, saith the LORD of hosts, and ˢ a line shall be stretched forth upon Jerusalem.	Before CHRIST cir. 519.
ᑫ Isai. 47. 6.			ʳ Isai. 12. 1. & 54. 8. ch. 2. 10. & 8. 3. ˢ ch. 2. 1, 2.

with adversity, yet doth He never forsake His people."

15. *I am sore displeased*, lit. *with great anger am I angered against the nations which are at ease.* The form of the words [1] shews that the greatness of the displeasure of God against those who oppress His people, is proportionate to the great and tender love toward themselves. God had been angered indeed [2] with His people; with their enemies He was *angered with a great anger;* and that the more, because they were *at ease* [3], in unfeeling self-enjoyment amid the miseries of others.

I was a little displeased [4]; little, in comparison with our deserts; little in comparison with the anger of the human instruments of His displeasure; little in comparison with their's who, in their anger, sought their own ends.

They helped forward the affliction [5]. " [6] He is wroth with the nations at ease, because He delivered His people to be corrected, but they used cruelty toward those delivered; He wills them to be amended as a son by a schoolmaster; they set themselves to slay and punish them, as an enemy. Like that in Isaiah, ᵗ *I gave them into thy hands; thou didst shew them no mercy; upon the ancients hast thou very heavily laid thy yoke.*"

Or it may be, *helped for evil,* in order to bring about evil, as in Jeremiah [8], *Behold I set My face against you for evil* [9], *and to destroy all Judah* i. e., as we should say, they were the instruments of God, " [10] coöperated in the execution of My justice toward you, but cruelly and with perverse intention. For although the Assyrians and Chaldæans

wasted the Jewish people, God so ordaining in as far as He willed through them to punish in the present the sins of His people, yet they did it, not in view of God and out of zeal for righteousness, but out of pride covetousness and with the worst ends. Hence God says by Isaiah [11], *Wo to Asshur, the rod of Mine anger, and the staff in his hand is Mine indignation. Howbeit he thinketh not so, but his heart is to destroy and cut off nations not a few.*

16. *Therefore.* This being so, since God was so jealous for His people, so displeased with their persecutors, *thus saith the Lord,* " [10] *I* Who [12] *in wrath remember mercy, am returned* [13], not by change of place, Who am uncircumscribed, not existing in place, to the people of Judah and Jerusalem in mercies, manifoldly benefiting them by various effects of My love." The single benefits, the rebuilding of His House, and so the restoration of His public worship, and the rebuilding of Jerusalem, are but instances of that all-containing mercy, His restored presence in tender mercies [14]. *I am returned,* God says, although the effects of His return were yet to come.

A line shall be stretched forth over Jerusalem, before, when it stood, this had been done to destroy [15]; now, when destroyed, to rebuild [16].

" [17] The temple was built then, when the foundations of the walls were not yet laid. In man's sight it would have seemed more provident that the walls should be first builded, that then the temple might be builded more securely. To God, in Whom

---

[1] קצף גדול אני קצף על ver. 15, as contrasted with קנאתי ל. קנאה גדולה ver. 14.

[2] קצף קצפתי i. 2.

[3] שַׁאֲנָן, as applied to persons, is always used in a bad sense; the noun, 2 Kgs xix. 28, Is. xxxvii. 29; the adj. Is. xxxii. 9, 11, Job xii. 5, Am. vi. 1, Ps. cxxiii. 4, and here.

[4] קצפתי מעט is obviously contrasted with קצף גדול: others "for a little while." But beside this contrast, מעט is seldom, comparatively, used of time, and that, as indicated by the context. Gen. xlvii. 9, "my days have been few;" Lev. xxv. 52, "if a little remains of the years;" Ru. ii. 7, "she sat a little in the house;" Job x. 20, "are not my days few?" xxiv. 24, "they are exalted a little, and are not." Add Ps. xxxvii. 10, Jer. li. 33, Hos. i. 4,

"yet a little, and." Hagg. ii. 6; "yet once, it is a little, and;" [all, except the doubtful Ps. viii. 6.]

[5] As 2 Chr. xx. 23, עָזְרוּ לְמַשְׁחִית "aided the destruction."

[6] S. Jer.   [7] Is. xlvii. 6.   [8] Jer. xliv. 11.

[9] לְרָעָה וּלְהַכְרִית.   [10] Dion.   [11] Is. x. 5, 7.

[12] Hab. iii. 2.   [13] שׁבתּי, although ינשה, יבנה, נְתַה.

[14] רחמים occurs 27 times of the tender love of God; 12 times only, of the compassion of man, and in 6 of these, of compassion of man as given by God, נתן פ. לרחמים; 2ce with the word נכמרו.

[15] 2 Kgs xxi. 13, Is. xxxiv. 11.

[16] It is used of the creation of the earth, Job xxxviii. 5. The Chethib, probably קָוֶה, occurs 1 Kgs vii. 23, Jer. xxxi. 19, and here.   [17] Osor.

Before
C H R I S T
cir. 519.

17 Cry yet, saying, Thus saith the LORD of hosts; My cities through † prosperity shall yet be spread abroad; ᵗand the LORD shall yet comfort Zion, and ᵘshall yet choose Jerusalem.

† Heb. *good.*

ᵗ Isai. 51. 3.

ᵘ Isai. 14. 1.
ch. 2. 12.
& 3. 2.

18 ¶ Then lifted I up mine eyes, and saw, and behold four horns.

19 And I said unto the angel that talked with me, What *be* these? And he answered me, ˣThese *are* the horns which have scat-

Before
C H R I S T
cir. 519.

ˣ Ezra 4. 1, 4, 7.
& 5. 3.

Alone is the most firm stay of our life and salvation, it seemed otherwise. For it cannot be that he, to whom nothing is dearer than zeal for the most l oly religion, should be forsaken of His help."

17. *Cry yet*, a further promise; not only should Jerusalem be rebuilt, but should as we say, *overflow with good*[1]; and God, Who had seemed to cast off His people, should yet comfort her, and should shew in act that He had chosen her[2]. Zechariah thrice[3] repeats the promise, given through Isaiah[4] to Jerusalem, before her wasting by the Chaldæans, reminding the people thereby, that the restoration, in the dawn whereof they lived, had been promised two centuries before. *Yet*, against all appearances. *My* cities shall overflow with good, as being God's; *yet* would the Lord comfort Zion; *yet* would He choose Jerusalem.

"⁵ What is the highest of all goods? what the sweetest solace in life? what the subject of joys? what the oblivion of past sorrow? That which the Son of God brought upon earth, when He illumined Jerusalem with the brightness of His light and heavenly discipline. For to that end was the city restored, that in it, by the ordinance of Christ, for calamity should abound bliss; for desolation, fullness; for sorrow, joy; for want, affluence of heavenly goods."

This first vision having predicted the entire restoration, the details of that restoration are given in subsequent visions.

18. ⁶*And I lifted up mine eyes.* "⁷ Not those of the body (for such visions are invisible to the eyes of the flesh), but rather the inner eyes of the heart and mind." It seems as though, at the close of each vision, Zechariah sank in meditation on what had been shewn him; from which he was again roused by the exhibition of another vision.

I saw four horns. The mention of the horns naturally suggests the thought of the creatures which wielded them; as in the first vision that of the *horses* following the chiefs, implies the presence of the riders upon them. And this the more, since the word "fray them away" implies living creatures, liable to fear. "⁸ The horn, in inspired Scripture, is always taken as an image of strength, and mostly of pride also, as David said to some, ⁹ *I said unto the fools, Deal not so foolishly, and to the ungodly, Lift not up the horns. Lift not up your horns on high and speak not with a stiff neck.* The prophet then sees *four horns*, i. e. four hard and warlike nations, who could easily uproot cities and countries."

These are the horns which have scattered. "¹⁰ The four horns which scattered Judah, Israel and Jerusalem, are four nations, Babylonians, Medes and Persians, Macedonians and Romans; as the Lord, on the prophet's enquiry, explains here, and Daniel unfolds most fully ¹¹; who in the vision of the image with golden head, silver breast, belly and thighs of brass, feet of iron and clay, explained it of these four nations, and again in another vision of four beasts ¹², lion, bear, leopard and another unnamed dreadful beast, he pointed out the same nations under another figure. But that the Medes and Persians, after the victory of Cyrus, were one kingdom, no one will doubt, who reads secular and sacred literature.—When this vision was beheld, the kingdom of the Babylonians had now passed away, that of the Medes and Persians was instant; that of Greeks and Macedonians and of the Romans was yet to come. What the Babylonians, what the Medes and Persians, what the Greeks i. e. the Macedonians, did to Judah, Israel and Jerusalem, a learned man acknowledgeth, especially under Antiochus, surnamed Epiphanes,

1 "affluent bonis," S. Jer.; "effluent bonis," Vulg. more exactly. The word פרץ is used of the "gushing forth of a fountain," Pr. v. 16; also of the dispersion of people; not of the spreading abroad of a people for good.
2 בחר is always "choose," not (as Ges. and others) "love." In all the cases, which Ges. cites as meaning "love," (Gen. vi. 2, 1 Sam. xx. 30, 2 Sam. xv. 15, Pr. i. 29, iii. 31, Is. i. 29) the sense would be injured by rendering, "loved."

3 here, ii. 12, iii. 2.
4 Is. xiv. 1. בחר עוד בישראל. Isaiah has the same cadence as Zechariah, though Zechariah only retains the characteristic words בחר עוד.
5 Osor.
6 The Eng. Vers. follows the LXX and S. Jer. in adding the 2d vision to the first chapter.
7 S. Cyril on ii. 1.   8 S. Cyr.   9 Ps. lxxv. 4.
10 S. Jer. Kimchi and Abarbanel agree with him in the general line.   11 Dan. ii.   12 Ib. vii.

tered Judah, Israel, and Jerusalem.

20 And the L O R D shewed me four carpenters.

21 Then said I, What come these to do? And he spake, saying, These *are* the horns which have scattered Judah, so that no man did lift up his head: but these are come to fray them, to cast out the horns of the Gentiles, which ʸ lifted up *their* horn over the land of Judah to scatter it.

ʸ Ps. 75. 4, 5.

CHAPTER II.

1 *God, in the care of Jerusalem, sendeth to measure it.* 6 *The redemption of Zion.* 10 *The promise of God's presence.*

I LIFTED up mine eyes again, and looked, and behold ᵃ a man with a measuring line in his hand.

2 Then said I, Whither goest thou? And he said unto me, ᵇ To measure Jerusalem, to see what *is* the breadth thereof, and what *is* the length thereof.

ᵃ Ezek. 40. 3.

ᵇ Rev. 11. 1. & 21. 15, 16.

---

to which the history of the Maccabees belongs. After the Coming of our Lord and Saviour, when Jerusalem was encompassed, Josephus, a native writer, tells most fully, what the Israelites endured, and the Gospel fore-announced. These horns dispersed Judah almost individually, so that, bowed down by the heavy weight of evils, no one of them raised his head." Though these were successive in time, they are exhibited to Zechariah as one. One whole are the efforts against God's Church; one whole are the instruments of God, whether angelic or human, in doing or suffering, to repel them. Zechariah then exhibits these hostile powers as past and gone[1], as each would be at the end, having put forth his passing might, and perishing. They scattered, each in its day, and disappeared; for the next displaced it.

The long schism being ended, Judah and Israel are again one; and Jerusalem, the place of God's worship, belongs to Israel as well as to Judah[2].

The explanation of the number *four*, as symbolizing contemporaneous attacks from the four quarters of the heavens, fails in matter of fact, that, in these later times, the Jews suffered always from one power at a time. There was no such fourfold attack. In Zechariah's time all around was Persian.

" [3] Those horns, broken by the angels' ministry, portended that no guilt against the Church of Christ should be unpunished. Never will there be wanting fierce enemies from E. W. N. or S., whom God will strengthen, in order by them to teach His own. But when He

ᵃ וירן.

[2] This is expressed by the use or omission of the את. Its use coördinates Judah and Israel; its omission subordinates Jerusalem.

shall see His work finished, i. e. when He shall have cleansed the stains of His own and brought back His Church to her former purity, He will punish those who so fiercely afflicted her."

Spiritually, " [4] those who destroy vices, build up virtues, and all the saints who, possessing these remedies, ever build up the Church, may be called 'builders.' Whence the Apostle says, [5] *I, as a wise builder, laid the foundation;* and the Lord, when wroth, said that He would [6] *take away* from Jerusalem *artificer and wise man.* And the Lord Himself, Son of the Almighty God and of the Creator of all, is called [7] *the son of the carpenter."*

II. 1. *A man with a measuring line in his hand.* Probably the Angel of the Lord, of whom Ezekiel has a like vision. " [4] He who before, when he lift up his eyes, had seen in the *four horns* things mournful, now again lifts up his eyes to see a man, of whom it is written, [8] *Behold a man whose name is the Branch;* of whom we read above, [9] *Behold a man riding upon a red horse, and he stood among the myrtle trees, which were in the bottom.* Of whom too the Father saith; He builded My city,[10] *whose builder and maker is God.* He too is seen by Ezekiel in a description like this, [11] *a man whose appearance was like the appearance of brass,* i. e. burnished [12] and shining as fire, *with a line of flax in his hand and a measuring reed."* The office also seems to be one of authority, not to measure the actual length and breadth of Jerusalem, but to lay down what it should be, " [13] to mark it out broad and very long."

[3] Osor.   [4] S. Jer.   [5] 1 Cor. iii. 10.   [6] Is. iii. 3.
[7] S. Matt. xiii. 55.   [8] Zech. vi. 12.   [9] Ib. i. 8.
[10] Heb. xi. 10.   [11] Ezek. xl. 3.
[12] Ib. i. 7.   [13] S. Cyr.

Before
CHRIST
cir. 519.

3 And, behold, the angel that talked with me went forth, and another angel went out to meet him,

4 And said unto him,

Run, speak to this young man, saying, ° Jerusalem shall be inhabited *as* towns without walls for the multitude of men and cattle therein:

Before
CHRIST
cir. 519.

° Jer. 31. 27.
Ezek. 36. 10, 11.

3. *The angel that talked with me went forth,* probably to receive the explanation which was given to him for Zechariah; *and another angel,* a higher angel, since he gives him a commission, *went forth to meet him,* being (it seems probable) instructed by the Angel of the Lord, who laid down the future dimensions of the city. The indefiniteness of the description, *another angel,* implies that he was neither the Angel of the Lord, nor (were they different) Michael, or *the man with the measuring line,* but an angel of intermediate rank, instructed by one higher, instructing the lower, who immediately instructed Zechariah.

And said unto him, Run, speak unto this young man, the prophet himself, who was to report to his people what he heard. Jeremiah says, [1] *I am a youth;* and [2] *the young man, the young prophet,* carried the prophetic message from Elisha to Jehu. "Youth," common as our English term in regard to man, is inapplicable and unapplied to angels, who have not our human variations of age, but exist, as they were created.

Jerusalem shall be inhabited as towns without walls, or as villages[3], viz. an unconfined, uncramped population, spreading itself freely, without restraint of walls, and (it follows) without need of them. Clearly then it is no earthly city. To be inhabited as villages would be weakness, not strength; a peril, not a blessing. The earthly Jerusalem, so long as she remained unwalled, was in continual fear and weakness. God put it into the heart of His servant to desire to restore her; her wall was built, and then she prospered. He Himself had promised to Daniel, that [4] *Her street shall be rebuilt, and her wall, even in strait of times.* Nehemiah mourned 73 years after this, B. C. 443, when it was told him, [5] *The remnant that are left of the captivity there in the province* are *in great affliction and reproach: the wall of Jerusalem also is broken down, and the gates thereof are burned with fire.* He said to Artaxerxes, [6] *Why should not my countenance be sad, when the city, the place of my fathers' sepulchres, lieth waste, and the gates thereof are consumed with fire?* When permitted by Artaxerxes to return, he addressed the rulers of the Jews, [7] *Ye see the*

distress *that we are in, how Jerusalem lieth waste, and the gates thereof are burned with fire; come, and let us build up the wall of Jerusalem, that we be no more a reproach; and they said, let us rise and build. So they strengthened their hands for this good work.* When [8] *the wall was finished and our enemies heard,* and *the heathen about us saw it, they were much cast down in their own eyes; for they perceived that this work was wrought of our God.*

This prophecy then looks on directly to the time of Christ. Wonderfully does it picture the gradual expansion of the kingdom of Christ, without bound or limit, whose protection and glory God is, and the character of its defences. It should *dwell as villages,* peacefully and gently expanding itself to the right and the left, through its own inherent power of multiplying itself, as a city, to which no bounds were assigned, but which was to fill the earth. "[9] *For us God hath raised a Church,* that truly holy and far-famed city, which Christ fortifieth, consuming opponents by invisible powers, and filling it with His own glory, and as it were, standing in the midst of those who dwell in it. For He promised; *Lo, I am with you always even unto the end of the world.* This holy city Isaiah mentioned: [10] *thine eyes shall see Jerusalem, a quiet habitation; a tabernacle that shall not be taken down; not one of the stakes thereof shall ever be removed, neither shall any of the cords thereof be broken;* and to her he saith, [11] *enlarge the place of thy tent, and let them stretch forth the curtains of thine habitation; spare not; lengthen thy cords and strengthen thy stakes. For thou shalt break forth on the right hand and on the left.* For the Church of Christ is widened and extended boundlessly, ever receiving countless souls who worship Him." "[12] What king or emperor could make walls so ample as to include the whole world? Yet, without this, it could not encircle that Jerusalem, the Church which is diffused through the whole world. This Jerusalem, the pilgrim part of the heavenly Jerusalem, is, in this present world, inhabited without walls, not being contained in one place or one nation. But in that world, whither it is daily being removed hence, much more can there not, nor ought to be,

[1] נַעַר Jer. i. 6.
[2] הַנַּעַר הַנַּעַר הַנַּבִיא 2 Kgs ix. 4.
[3] See on Hab. iii. 14. p. 218.   [4] Dan. ix. 25.

[5] Neh. i. 3.   [6] Ib. ii. 3.   [7] Ib. 17, 18.
[8] Ib. vi. 15, 16.   [9] S. Cyr.   [10] Is. xxxiii. 20.
[11] Ib. liv. 2, 3.   [12] Rup.

Before
CHRIST
cir. 519.

d Isai. 26. 1.
ch. 9. 8.
e Isai. 60. 19.
Rev. 21. 23.
f Isai. 48. 20.
& 52. 11.
Jer. 1. 14.
& 50. 8.
& 51. 6, 45.

5 For I, saith the LORD, will be unto her [d] a wall of fire round about, [e] and will be the glory in the midst of her.

6 ¶ Ho, ho, *come forth,* and flee [f] from the land of the north, saith the LORD: for I have [g] spread you abroad as the four winds of the heaven, saith the LORD.

7 [h] Deliver thyself, O Zion, that dwellest *with* the daughter of Babylon.

Before
CHRIST
cir. 519.

g Deut. 28. 64.
Ezek. 17. 21.

h Rev. 18. 4.

nor is, any wall around, save the Lord, Who is also the glory in the midst of it."

5. *And I, Myself[1] in My own Being, will be to her a wall of fire,* not protection only, an inner circle around her, however near an enemy might press in upon her, but destructive to her enemies. Isaiah says, [2] *No weapon that is formed against thee shall prosper, and every tongue that shall rise in judgment against thee thou shalt condemn.* Its defence, Isaiah says, shall be immaterial. [3] *We have a strong city ; salvation shall God appoint for walls and bulwarks ;* [4] *thou shalt call thy walls salvation and thy gates praise.* By a different figure it is said, [5] *I will encamp about mine house because of the army.*

And glory will I be in the midst of her, as Isaiah says, [6] *The Lord shall be unto thee an everlasting light, and thy God thy glory ;* and of Christ, [7] *In that day shall the Branch of the Lord be Beauty and Glory—to the escaped of Israel.*

6. *Ho! ho! and flee.* Such being the safety and glory in store for God's people in Jerusalem, He Who had so provided it, the Angel of the Lord, bids His people everywhere to come to it, saving themselves also from the peril which was to come on Babylon. So Isaiah bade them, [8] *Go ye forth of Babylon; flee ye from the Chaldæans with a voice of singing ; declare ye, tell this, utter it to the end of the earth ; say ye, The Lord hath redeemed His servant Jacob.* [9] *Depart ye, depart ye, go ye out from thence ; touch no unclean thing : go ye out of the midst of her ; be ye clean, that bear the vessels of the Lord ;* and Jeremiah, [10] *Flee ye out of the midst of Babylon, and deliver every man his soul ; be not cut off in her iniquity, for this is the time of the Lord's vengeance ; He will render unto her a recompense ;* [11] *My people, go ye out of the midst of her, and deliver ye, every man his soul from the fierce anger of the Lord.*

The words, *flee, deliver thyself,* imply an imminent peril on Babylon, such as came upon her, two years after this prophecy, in the fourth year of Darius. But the earnestness of the command, its repetition by three prophets, the context in Isaiah and Jeremiah, imply something more than temporal peril, the peril of the infection of the manners of Babylon, which may have detained there many who did not return. Whence in the New Testament, the words are cited, as to the great evil city of the world ; [12] *Wherefore come out from among them and be ye separate, and touch not the unclean thing, and I will receive you ;* and under the name of Babylon ; [13] *I heard another voice from heaven, saying, Come out of her, My people, that ye be not partakers of her sins, and that ye receive not of her plagues.*

For I have spread you abroad as the four winds of heaven. The north country, although its capital and centre was Babylon, was the whole Babylonian empire, called "the North[14]" because its invasions always came upon Israel from the North. But the book of Esther shews that, sixty years after this, the Jews were dispersed over the 127 provinces of the Persian empire, *from India* (the Punjaub) *to Ethiopia*[15], whether they were purposely placed by the policy of the conquerors in detached groups, as the ten tribes were *in the cities of the Medes*[16], or whether, when more trusted, they migrated of their own accord. God, in calling them to return, reminds them of the greatness of their dispersion. He had dispersed them abroad as the four winds of heaven[17]: He, the Same, recalled them.

7. *Dwellest* with *the daughter of Babylon.* The unusual idiom[18] is perhaps chosen as expressive of God's tenderness, even to the people who were to be destroyed, from which Israel was to escape.

1 אני emph.   2 Is. liv. 17.
3 Ib. xxvi. 1.   4 Ib. lx. 18.   5 Zech. ix. 8.
6 Is. lx. 19.   7 Ib. iv. 2.
8 Is. xlviii. 20.   9 Ib. lii. 11.   10 Jer. li. 6. add. l. 8.
11 Ib. li. 45.   12 2 Cor. vi. 17.   13 Rev. xviii. 4.
14 Jer. i. 13, 14, iii. 18, iv. 6, vi. 1. 22. xxiii. 8.
15 Esther i. 1, iii. 8, 12–14. viii. 5, 9.
16 2 Kgs xvii. 6.
17 "As the four winds of heaven are distant one from the other." Sal. b. Mel. Kim. AE. The LXX alone paraphrase, "For from the winds of heaven I will gather you." Others take the word of an intended diffusion of them, through the favor of God,

the future being spoken of, as if past. But although פרש is used of dispersion, beside, in Ps. lxviii. 15, Nif. Ez. xvii. 21, it is no where used of diffusion, only of the spreading out of what remained coherent, as hands, wings, a garment, tent, veil, cloud, letter, light. See instances Ges. Thes. p. 1132.

18 יושבת בת בבל *dweller of the daughter of Babylon,* as Jer. xlvi. 19. יושבת בת מצרים, Ib. xlviii. 18, ישבת בת דיבון. In Jeremiah however, it is the same people, Egypt or Dibon; here, Israel as settled in Babylon.

Before
CHRIST
cir. 519.

8 For thus saith the
LORD of hosts; After the
glory hath he sent me unto
the nations which spoiled
you: for he that [1]toucheth
you toucheth the apple of
his eye.

[1] Deut. 32. 10.
Ps. 17. 8.
2 Thess. 1. 6.

9 For, behold, I will
[k]shake mine hand upon
them, and they shall be a
spoil to their servants: and
[l]ye shall know that the
LORD of hosts hath sent
me.

Before
CHRIST
cir. 519.

[k] Isai. 11. 15.
& 19. 16.

[l] ch. 4. 9.

---

8. *After the glory*[1], "[2]which it is promised
to bring upon you." This being the usual
construction, the words involve a great course
of God's dealing, of first shewing favor to
those who *will* receive favor, then abandoning
or punishing the rest; as, when the eight
souls had been received into the ark, the
flood came; when Lot and his had escaped
out of Sodom, the fire came down from
heaven; when Israel had passed the Red
Sea, Pharaoh's hosts were drowned; the election obtained what Israel sought for, the rest
were blinded[3]. *The glory* then would be the
glory, of which God says, *I will be the glory in
the midst of you.*
But further He Who speaketh is Almighty
God, *Thus saith the Lord of Hosts, He hath
sent*[4] *me; For lo I wave My hand against
them—and ye shall know that the Lord of hosts
hath sent me; Lo I come and dwell in the midst
of thee, saith the Lord, and many nations shall
cleave unto the Lord in that day, and they shall
be to Me a people and I will dwell in the midst
of thee, and thou shalt know, that the Lord of
hosts hath sent me unto you.* In all which
series of promises, the *I,* of whom Israel were
to know that the Lord of hosts had sent Him,
is the *I,* Who affirms of Himself what belongs to Almighty God only, inflicting punishment on the enemies of Judah, indwelling
the Church and people, receiving the Heathen
as His own; and it is precisely by all these
acts of power and love, that Israel shall know
that the Lord of hosts had sent Him.

"[5] In what follows, *Thus saith the Lord of
hosts, After glory, He hath sent Me &c.,* the
Saviour is introduced speaking, Who, being
Almighty God, saith that He was sent by the
Father Almighty, not according to that
whereby He was Almighty, but according to
that, that, *after glory,* He was sent, [6] *Who
being in the Form of God, thought it not robbery
to be equal with God; but emptied Himself, taking the form of a servant, and was made obedient
unto the Father even unto death; and that, the
death of the Cross.* Nor is it marvel that
Christ is called Almighty, in Whose Person
we read in the Apocalypse of John, [7] *These
things saith the faithful Witness—I am Alpha
and Omega, the beginning and the ending, saith
the Lord, which was and which is and which is
to come, the Almighty,* [8] *to Whom all power is
given in heaven and in earth;* and Who saith,
[9] *All things of the Father's are Mine.* But if
all things, i. e. God from God, Lord from
Lord, Light from Light, therefore also Almighty from Almighty; for it cannot be,
that diverse should be the glory of those
whose Nature is One."
For he who toucheth, so as to injure [10] *you,*
toucheth the apple of His eye, i. e. of Him Who
sent Him, Almighty God [11], as in the song of
Moses, [12] *He led him about, He instructed him,
He kept him as the apple of His eye;* and David
prays, [13] *Keep me as the apple of the eye.*
9. *For behold I will shake My hand against
them,* as God promised of old against the
enemies of His people [14], and they shall

[1] שָׁלַח is used with acc. pers., and אַחֲרֵי also of
persons, 2 Sam. iii. 26, 2 Kgs viii. 14, or with אַחֲרֵי
of pers. alone, 2 Kgs xiv. 9. שָׁלַח אַחַר is not elsewhere used like our "sent after a thing." So generally אַחַר is used with verbs of motion, הָלַךְ אַחַר,
Gen. xxxvii. 17, 2 Kgs xxiii. 3; בָּא אַחַר, Nu. xxv.
8; הָיָה אַחַר, 1 Sam. xii. 14; רָדַף אַחַר, 2 Kgs xxv.
5; יָצָא אַחַר, 1 Sam. xi. 7: or, spiritually, הַהֹלְכִים
אַחַר כְּחַשְׁבוֹתֵיהֶם Is. lxv. 2; אַחַר רוּחַם, Ez. xiii.
3; אַחַר עֵינִי הָלַךְ לִבִּי, Job xxxi. 7; but אַחַר is
not used in our sense of *seeking,* "going after a
thing," except in the one phrase וְאַחַר כָּל יָרוֹק
יִדְרוֹשׁ Job xxxix. 8, "searcheth after every green
thing." It is the less probable here, because, apart
from this, (beside the 5 duplicate passages in
Isaiah and 2 Kings, 2 Sam. and 1 Chronicles) the
construction of שָׁלַח with acc. of the person sent
and אֶל of the person to whom he is sent, occurs in

71 passages, (Ges. cites 23 of them) and in no one
case is the object for which they were sent, added
by any preposition. Four are in Zechariah himself ii. 12, 15, iv. 9, vi. 15. To "send for" is expressed
by שָׁלַח לְ Jer. xiv. 3, 1 Kgs xx. 7.
[2] Jon.   [3] Rom. xi. 7.   [4] ver. 8-10.   [5] S. Jer.
[6] Phil. ii. 6.   [7] Rev. i. 5, 8.   [8] S. Matt. xxviii. 18.
[9] S. John xvi. 15.
[10] נָגַע בְּ, as in Gen. xxvi. 11, Jos. ix. 19, 2 Sam.
xiv. 10, Jer. xii. 14, Ezek. xvii. 10, Ps. cv. 15; with
acc. Gen. xxvi. 29, Ru. ii. 9; of God, 1 Sam. vi. 9, Job
i. 11. xix. 21.
[11] So S. Jer. Theod. Others, as S. Cyr., of his own
eye, turning to evil to himself; but the analogy of
the other passages is against it. בָּבַת עַיִן [ἄπ.]
is doubtless the same as בַּת עַיִן with the same reduplication as in Arab. Syr. Ch. The reduplication
is plain in the Arab. بؤبؤ from بأبأ "papavit,"
not from a separate root, as Ges. Thes. p. 841.
[12] Deut. xxxii. 10.   [13] Ps. xvii. 8.
[14] The same idiom, Is. xi. 15. xix. 16.

Before CHRIST cir. 519.	10 ¶ ^m Sing and rejoice, O daughter of Zion: for, lo, I come, and I ⁿ will dwell in the midst of thee, saith the LORD.

10 ¶ [m] Sing and rejoice, O daughter of Zion: for, lo, I come, and I [n] will dwell in the midst of thee, saith the LORD.

11 [o] And many nations shall be joined to the LORD [p] in that day, and shall be [q] my people: and I will dwell in the midst of thee,

be a spoil to those who served them habitually [1].

And ye shall know that the Lord of hosts hath sent Me. "[2] He was sent, not as God, but as Man. For as God He is equal to the Father. For He saith, [3] *I am in the Father and the Father in Me,* and, *The Father Who dwelleth in Me He doeth the works,* and, [4] *I and My Father are one,* and [5] *He who hath seen Me hath seen the Father.* But He is sent, as Man, fulfilling the dispensation for us, not lessening the Divine Nature. The Prophet then intimated not the duality only, but the equality of the Persons."

10. *Sing and rejoice, O daughter of Zion.* It is a great jubilee of joy, to which Zion is invited. Thrice beside is she invited with this same word, and all for the restored or renewed Presence of God. [6] *Cry aloud for joy, thou barren which bare not,* as here, on the coming in of the Gentiles, [7] *Cry aloud for joy, O daughter of Zion; jubilate, O Israel; rejoice and exult with all the heart, O daughter of Jerusalem; the Lord, the King of Israel, is in the midst of thee.* [8] *Shout and cry aloud for joy, O inhabitant of Zion; for great in the midst of thee is the Holy One of Israel.* The source of joy is a fresh coming of God, *a coming,* whereby He should *dwell* abidingly among them : truly what is this, but the Incarnation ? As S. John saith, [9] *The Word was made Flesh and dwelt among us ;* and, [10] *Behold the tabernacle of God is with men, and He will dwell with them, and they shall be His people, and God Himself shall be with them and shall be their God.* "[11] Hence too you may learn how great a subject of contentment above is the Presence of the Saviour upon earth. He could not then but bid the spiritual Zion, [12] *which is the Church of the Living God,* the most sacred multitude of those saved by faith, to cry aloud for joy and rejoice. But it was announced that He should come and be in the midst of her. For S. John saith to us, *The Word* [13] *was in the world,* and, being God, was not severed from His creatures, but He was

Himself the Source of life to all living, and holding all things together to well-being and life ; but [13] *the world knew Him not :* for it worshiped the creature. But He came among us, when, taking our likeness, He was conceived by the holy Virgin, and [14] *was seen upon earth and conversed with men,* and the divine David witnesseth saying, [15] *Our God shall come manifestly, and shall not keep silence.* Then also was there a haven for the Gentiles. For now no longer was the race of Israel alone taught, but the whole earth was engoldened with the evangelical preachings, and in every nation and country *great is His Name.*"

"[16] This too is to be understood of the Person of the Lord, that He exhorts His people, being restored from the captivity to their former abode, to be *glad and rejoice,* because *the Lord* Himself *cometh* and *dwelleth in the midst of her,* and *many nations* shall believe in Him, of Whom it is said, [17] *Ask of Me and I will give Thee nations for Thine inheritance, and the ends of the earth for Thy possession,* and He shall *dwell in the midst of them,* as He saith to His disciples, [18] *Lo, I am with you always, even unto the end of the world.*"

11. *And many nations shall join themselves,* cleaving to Him by a close union. Isaiah had so spoken of single proselytes [19] ; Jeremiah had used the word of Israel's self-exhortation after the return from Babylon ; [20] *going and weeping, they shall go and seek the Lord their God,* saying, *Come and let us join ourselves unto the Lord, in a perpetual covenant that shall not be forgotten.* This Zechariah now predicts of *many nations.* The Jews were scarcely half-restored themselves, a mere handful. They had wrought no conversions among the heathen, yet prophecy continues its unbroken voice, *many nations shall join themselves unto the Lord.*

And shall be My people, lit. *be to Me a people.* This is exactly the history of the Christian Church, unity amid diversity ; many nations still retaining their national

---

[1] The force of the part. יֹעֲבָדֶיהֶם, instead of עֲבָדֵיהֶם. So עֲבָד אֲדָמָה, Zech. xiii. 5. Is. xxx. 24; עֹבֵר אֲדָמָתוֹ Pr. xii. 11; עֹבֵר אֱלֹהִים Mal. iii. 18: הָעֹבֵד הַבַּעַל Ib. 17. עֹבְדֵי הַבַּעַל 2 Kgs x. 19, 21, 22, 23, פֶּסֶל ע. Ps. xcvii. 7. עֹבְדֵי הָעִיר Ez. xlviii. 18, הָעֹבֵד הָעִיר, Ib. 19. So כֹּל הָעֹבֵד בְּאֹהֶל מוֹעֵד Nu. iv. 37, 41. עֲבַדְתֶּם אֲשֶׁר הֶם עֹבְדִים Ib. xviii.

21. הָעֹבֵד the laborer, Eccl. v. 11. In Gen. iv. 2, xlix. 15, Jos. xvi. 10, 1 Kgs v. 1, 2 Kgs xvii. 33, 41, it has this force from the preceding הָיָה.
[2] Theod.　[3] S. John xiv. 10.　[4] Ib. x. 30.
[5] Ib. xiv. 9.　[6] Is. liv. 1.　[7] Zeph. iii. 14, 15.
[8] Is. xii. 6.　[9] S. John i. 14.　[10] Rev. xxi. 3.
[11] S. Cyr.　[12] 1 Tim. iii. 15.　[13] S. John i. 10.
[14] Baruch iii. 37.　[15] Ps. l. 3.　[16] S. Jer.
[17] Ps. ii. 8.　[18] S. Matt. xxviii. 20.
[19] Is. lvi. 3-6.　[20] Jer l. 4, 5.

Before
C H R I S T
cir. 519.

r Ezek. 33. 33.
ver. 9.

and ^rthou shalt know that the LORD of hosts hath sent me unto thee.

12 And the LORD shall

Before
C H R I S T
cir. 519.

s Deut. 32. 9.
t ch. 1. 17.

^sinherit Judah his portion in the holy land, and ^tshall choose Jerusalem again.

---

existence, yet owned by God as one people and His own. The words are those in which God adopted Israel in Egypt; [1] *I will take you to Me for a people, and I will be your God.* This was the covenant with them, [2] *that thou shouldest enter into covenant with the Lord thy God,—that He may establish thee to-day for a people unto Himself, and that He may be unto thee a God.* The contrary was the title of the heathen, [3] *not a people; with whom God said, I will move Israel to jealousy.* The closeness of union Jeremiah expresses; [4]*As the girdle cleaveth to the loins of a man, so have I caused to cleave to Me the whole house of Israel and the whole house of Judah, saith the Lord, that they might be unto Me for a people and for a name and for a praise and for a glory.* This was the object of the existence of Israel; to this it was to be restored [5] by conversion [6]; to this special privilege of Israel *many nations* were to be admitted; yet not so as to be separate from Israel, for He adds, *and I will dwell in* the midst of thee, Judah. God would dwell in His Church, formed of Israel and the Gentiles, yet so that the Gentiles should be grafted into Israel, becoming one with them.

12. *And the Lord shall inherit Judah His portion.* The *inheritance of the Lord* is the title which God commonly gave to Israel [7]. God is said to be the *portion* of Israel [8]; of the pious [9]; once only beside, is Israel said to be the portion of God [10]; once only is God said to inherit Israel, [11] *Pardon our iniquity*

and our sin, and take us for thine inheritance. Zechariah unites the two rare idioms.

In the holy land. The land is again made holy by God, and sanctified by His Presence. So He calls the place where He revealed Himself to Moses, *holy ground* [12]. So it is said, [13] *the holy place,* [14] *the holy house,* [15] *the holy ark,* [16] *the holy city,* [17] *the holy mountain,* [18] *the holy people,* [19] *the holy chambers,* or, with reference to their relation to God Who consecrates them, [20] *My holy mountain,* [21] *Thy holy habitation,* [22] *Thy holy dwelling-place,* [23] *Thy holy temple,* [24] *Thy holy mountain,* [25]*Thy holy oracle,* [26] *Thy holy city,* [27] *cities,* [28] *His holy place,* [29] *His holy border.* It is not one technical expression, as people now by a sort of effort speak of "the holy land." ⁋Everything which has reference to God is holy. The land is holy, not for any merits of theirs, but because God was worshiped there, was specially present there. It was an anticipation and type of "Thy holy Church throughout all the world doth acknowledge Thee." This land their fathers had [30] *polluted with blood;* God says, [31] *they defiled My land;* Ezekiel called her eminently, [32] *the land that is not cleansed.* Now God said, [33] *I will remove the iniquity of the land,* and she was again a *holy land,* as hallowed by Him.

It is not a mere conversion of the heathen, but, as Isaiah [34] and Micah [35] foretold; a conversion, of which Jerusalem should be the centre, as our Lord explained to the Apostles after His Resurrection, [36] *that repentance and*

---

[1] Exod. vi. 7.
[2] Deut. xxix. 12, 13, add Lev. xxvi. 12, Deut. xxvii. 9. 1 Sam. xii. 22, 2 Sam. vii. 23, 24, 2 Kgs xi. 17, 1 Chr. xvii. 22, 2 Chr. xxiii. 16, Jer. vii. 23, xi. 4.
[3] Deut. xxxii. 21.
[4] Jer. xiii. 11.
[5] Ib. xxiv. 7, xxx. 22, xxxi. 1, xxxii. 38.
[6] Ez. xi. 20, xiv. 11, xxxvi. 28, xxxvii. 23, 27, Zech. viii. 8.
[7] Deut. iv. 20, ix. 26, 29, 1 Sam. xxvi. 19, 2 Sam. xiv. 16, xx. 19, xxi. 3, 1 Kgs viii. 51, Ps. xxviii. 9, xxxiii. 12, lxviii. 10, lxxviii. 62, 71, lxxix. 1, cvi. 40, Joel ii. 17, iii. 2, [Heb.] Is. xix. 25, xlvii. 6, Jer. xii. 7-9, l. 11.
[8] Jer. x. 16. li. 19.

[9] Ps. xvi. 5, lxxiii. 26, cxix. 57, cxli. 6, Lam. iii. 24.
[10] Deut. xxxii. 9.   [11] Ex. xxxiv. 9.
[12] אַדְמַת קֹדֶשׁ, Ex. iii. 5.
[13] מְקוֹם הַקֹּדֶשׁ, Lev. x. 17, xiv. 13.
[14] בֵּית הֻק׳, 1 Chr. xxix. 3.
[15] אֲרוֹן הֻק׳, 2 Chr. xxxv. 3.
[16] עִיר הֻק׳, Neh. xi. 1, 18, Is. xlviii. 2, lii. 1.
[17] הַר הֻק׳, Is. xxvii. 13, Jer. xxxi. 23, Zech. viii. 3.
[18] עַם הֻק׳, Is. lxii. 12.

[19] לִשְׁכוֹת הֻק׳. Ez. xlii. 13. [all.]
[20] הַר קָדְשִׁי Ps. ii. 6. Is. xi. 9. lvi. 7, lvii. 13, lxv. 11, 25, lxvi. 20, Ez. xx. 40. Jo. ii. 1, iv. 17, Ob. 16. Zeph. iii. 11.
[21] נְוֵה קָדְשֶׁךָ Ex. xv. 13.
[22] מְעוֹן ק׳ Deut. xxvi. 15. *His holy hab.* Ps. lxviii. 6, Jer. xxv. 30, Zech. ii. 17.
[23] הֵיכַל ק׳ Ps. v. 8, lxxix. 1, cxxxviii. 2, Jon. ii. 5, 8, *His holy temple,* Mi. i. 2. Hab. ii. 20.
[24] הַר ק׳ Ps. xv. 1, xliii. 3, Dan. ix. 16. *His holy hill,* Ps. iii. 5, xlviii. 2, xcix. 9.
[25] דְּבִיר ק׳ Ps. xxviii. 2.   [26] עִיר ק׳ Dan. ix. 24.
[27] עָרֵי ק׳ Is. lxiv. 9.
[28] מְקוֹם ק׳ Ps. xxiv. 3.
[29] גְּבוּל ק׳ Ps. lxxviii. 54.   [30] Ps. cvi. 38.
[31] Jer. ii. 7, iii. 9, xvi. 18.   [32] Ezek. xxii. 24.
[33] Zech. iii. 9.   [34] Is. ii. 3.
[35] Micah iv. 2.   [36] S. Luke xxiv. 47.

13 [u] Be silent, O all flesh, before the LORD: for he is raised up [x] out of † his holy habitation.

[u] Hab. 2. 20.
Zeph. 1. 7.
[x] Ps. 68. 5.
Isai. 57. 15.
† Heb. *the habitation of his holiness.*
Deut. 26. 15.
Isai. 63. 15.

CHAPTER III.

1 Under the type of Joshua, the restoration of the church, 8 Christ the Branch is promised.

AND he shewed me [a] Joshua the high priest standing before the angel of the LORD, and [b] ‖ Satan standing at his right hand † to resist him. 2 And the LORD said unto Satan, [c] The LORD rebuke thee, O Satan ; even

[a] Hag. 1. 1.

[b] Ps. 109. 6.
Rev. 12. 10.
‖ That is, *an adversary.*
† Heb. *to be his adversary.*
[c] Jude 9.

---

remission of sins should be preached in His name among all nations, beginning at Jerusalem.

13. *Be silent,* lit. *hush*[1], *all flesh, before the Lord;* man in his weakness[2], *flesh and blood* in the language of the New Testament[3], before God his Maker. *All flesh,* the whole human race[4], is to·be hushed before God, because His judgments, as His mercies, are over all.

For God ariseth. God seemeth to be quiescent, as it were, when He bears with us; to arise, when He puts forth His power, either for us, when we pray, [5] *Lord, awake to help me;* or in displeasure. His *holy habitation* is alike the tabernacle[6], temple[7], heaven[8], since His presence is in all.

III. 1. *And He,* God, (for the office of the attendant angel was to explain, not to shew the visions) *shewed me Joshua the High Priest, standing before the Angel of the Lord;* probably to be judged by him[9]; as in the New Testament, *to stand before the Son of Man;* for although *standing before,* whether in relation to man[10] or God[11], expresses attendance upon, yet here it appears only as a condition, contemporaneous[12] with that of Satan's, to accuse him. Although, moreover, the Angel speaks with authority, yet God's Presence in him is not spoken of so distinctly, that the High Priest would be exhibited as standing before him, as in his office before God.

And Satan, etymologically, *the enemy,* as, in the New Testament, [13] *your adversary the devil,* etymologically, *the accuser.* It is a proper name of the Evil one, yet its original meaning, *the enemy*[14], was not lost. Here, as in Job, his malice is shewn in accusation; [15] *the accuser of our brethren, who accused them before our God, day and night.* In Job[16], the accusations were calumnious; here, doubtless, true. For he accused Job of what would have been plain apostacy[17]; Joshua and Zerubbabel had shared, or given way to, the remissness of the people, as to the rebuilding of the temple and the full restoration of the worship of God[18]. For this, Haggai had reproved the people, through them[19]. Satan had then a real charge, on which to implead them. Since also the whole series of visions relates to the restoration from the captivity, the guilt, for which Satan impleads him with Jerusalem and Jerusalem in him, includes the whole guilt, which had rested upon them, so that for a time God had seemed to have *cast away His people*[20]. Satan *stands at his right hand,* the place of a protector[21], to shew that he had none to save him, and that himself was victorious.

2. *And the Lord said unto Satan, The Lord rebuke thee.* "[22] This they so explain, that the Father and the Son is Lord, as we read in the 110th Psalm, *The Lord said unto my*

---

[1] See on Hab. ii. 20. p. 207.
[2] Gen. vi. 3, 2 Chr. xxxii. 8, Job x. 4, Ps. lvi. 4, lxxviii. 39, Is. xxxi. 3, Jer. xvii. 5.
[3] S. Matt. xvi. 17, 1 Cor. xv. 50, Gal. i. 16.
[4] Gen. vi. 12, Ps. lxv. 3, cxlv. 21, Is. xl. 5, 6, xlix. 26, lxvi. 23, Jo. iii. 1, Ez. xxi. 4, 9, 10.
[5] Ps. lix. 4. add Ps. vii. 7, xliv. 24.   [6] 1 Sam. ii. 29, 32, Ps. xxvi. 9, lxviii. 6.   [7] 2 Chr. xxxvi. 15.
[8] Deut. xxvi. 15, Jer. xxv. 30, 2 Chr. xxx. 27.
[9] "Stand before" is used judicially, Nu. xxxv. 12, Deut. xix. 17. Jos. xx. 6, and of plaintiffs, Nu. xxvii. 2, 1 Kgs iii. 16; *stand before God,* Rev. xx. 12; *before the judgment-seat of Christ,* Rom. xiv. 10; and be acquitted, S. Luke xxi. 36.
[10] Joseph before Pharaoh, Gen. xli. 46; Joshua before Moses, Deut. i. 38; David before Saul, 1 Sam. xvi. 21; the young virgin before David. 1 Kgs i. 2; Solomon's servants, Ib. x. 8; his councillors, 2 Chr. x. 6; Gedaliah, of serving the Chaldæans, Jer. xl. 10; Nebuzaradan, Jer. lii. 12; Daniel and his companions, of office *before the king* of Babylon, Dan. i. 5. But it is also used of presence with a commission to the person: Moses before Pharaoh, Ex. viii. 20, ix. 13; of an office toward others, to minister

unto them, as the Levites before the congregation, Nu. xvi. 9; degraded priests, "to serve them." Ezek. xliv. 11.
[11] The tribe of Levi, Deut. x. 8, 2 Chr. xix. 11; the High Priest, Jud. xx. 28, Ezek. xliv. 15; Elijah, 1 Kgs xvii. 1, xviii. 15; Elisha, 2 Kgs iii. 14, v. 16; Jonadab's descendants, Jer. xxxv. 19. It is used of standing to intercede with God, of Abraham, Gen. xviii. 22; Moses and Samuel, Jer. xv. 1; Jeremiah, Ib. 19. Also of worship, Jer. vii. 10.
[12] The two עֹמֵד express a correlative condition.
[13] 1 S. Pet. v. 8.
[14] As in other appellatives, יָרֵדֶן (יָרֵדֶן) twice only), הַבַּעַל, but in its contracted form, when the etymology was lost, בֵּל, &c. שָׂטָן as a Prop. Name, without the article, occurs 1 Chr. xxi. 1, Ps. cix. 6; with the article, eleven times here, and fourteen times in the first narrative chapters of Job.
[15] Rev. xii. 10.   [16] Job i. 8-11, ii. 3-5.
[17] Ib. i. 11. ii. 5.
[18] Ezr. iii. iv.   [19] Hagg. i. 1-11.   [20] Rom. xi. 1.
[21] Ps. xvi. 8. cix. 31, cxxi. 5, cxli. 4.   [22] S. Jer.

23

Before C H R I S T cir. 519.
d ch. 1. 17. Rom. 8. 33. e Amos 4. 11. Rom. 11. 5. Jude 23.

the LORD that ^d hath cho-sen Jerusalem rebuke thee: ^e *is* not this a brand plucked out of the fire?

3 Now Joshua was

clothed with ^f filthy gar-ments, and stood before the angel.

4 And he answered and spake unto those that stood

Before C H R I S T cir. 519.
f Isai. 64. 6.

Lord, Sit Thou on My right hand. The Lord speaketh of another Lord; not that He, the Lord Who speaketh, cannot rebuke, but that, from the unity of nature, when the Other rebuketh, He Himself Who speaketh rebuk-eth. For ¹ *he who seeth the Son, seeth the Father also.*" It may be that God, by such sayings ², also accustomed men, before Christ came, to believe in the Plurality of Persons in the One Godhead.

The rebuke of God must be with power. ³ *Thou hast rebuked the nations, Thou hast de-stroyed the ungodly.* ⁴ *Thou hast rebuked the proud, accursed.* ⁵ *They perish at the rebuke of Thy Countenance.* ⁶ *At Thy rebuke, O God of Jacob, both the chariot and horse are cast into a deep sleep.* ⁷ *God shall rebuke him, and he fleeth far off, and shall be chased as the chaff of the mountains before the wind.* ⁸ *He rebuked the Red Sea and it dried up.* ⁹ *The founda-tions of the world were discovered at Thy rebuke, O Lord.* He ¹⁰ *rebuked the seed,* and it per-ished; *the devourer* ¹¹, and it no longer de-voured. The rebuke then of the blasted spirit involved a withering rejection of him-self and his accusations, as when Jesus re-buked the unclean spirit and he departed out of his victim ¹².

The Lord hath chosen Jerusalem. Joshua then is acquitted, not because the accusation of Satan was false, but out of the free love of God for His people and for Joshua in it and as its representative. ¹³ *Who shall lay any-thing to the charge of God's elect? It is God that justifieth. Who is he that condemneth?* The *high priest,* being ¹⁴ *himself also compassed with infirmity,* needed daily to offer up sacrifices first *for his own sins, and then for the people's.* As Isaiah said, on the sight of God, ¹⁵ *I am undone, because I am a man of unclean lips, and I dwell in the midst of a people of unclean lips,* and, until cleansed by the typical coal, dared not offer himself for the prophetic

office, so here Satan, in Joshua, aimed at the whole priestly office, and, in it, at Israel's re-lation to God.

Is not this a brand plucked out of the fire? " ¹⁶ As if he should say, Israel confessedly has sinned, and is liable to these charges. Yet it has suffered no slight punishment; it has endured sufferings, and has scarce been snatched out of them, as a half-burned *brand out of the fire.* For not yet had it shaken off the dust of the harms from the captivity; only just now and scarely had it escaped the flame of that most intolerable calamity. Cease then imputing sin to them, on whom God has had mercy."

3. *Now Joshua was clothed with filthy gar-ments;* such, it is expressed, was his habitual condition ¹⁷ ; he was one so clothed. The *filthy garment,* as defilement generally, is, in Scrip-ture, the symbol of sin. ¹⁸ *We are all as the unclean, and all our righteousnesses are as filthy rags.* ¹⁹ *He that is left in Zion and he that re-maineth in Jerusalem shall be called holy—when the Lord shall have washed away the filth of the daughters of Zion.* ²⁰ *There is a generation, pure in its own eyes, and it is not washed from its filthiness.* The same is expressed by different words, signifying pollution, defilement by sin ; ²¹ *Wo unto her that is filthy and polluted ;* ²² *The land was defiled with blood ;* ²³ *they were defiled with their own works.* It is symbolized also by the ²⁴ *divers washings* of the law, rep-resenting restored purity; and the use of the word by Psalmists and Prophets; ²⁵ *Wash me thoroughly from mine iniquity ;* ²⁶ *wash you, make you clean ; put away the evil of your doings from before Mine eyes ;* ²⁷ *O Jerusalem, wash thy heart from wickedness.* In later times at least, the accused were clothed in black ²⁸, not in defiled ²⁹ garments.

4. *And He spake to those who stood before Him,* the ministering Angels who had waited on the Angel of the Lord to do His bidding.

---

¹ S. John xiv. 9.
² As in those, " *the Lord rained upon Sodom and upon Gomorrah brimstone and fire from the Lord out of heaven,"* Gen. xix. 24, and others in which God speaks of Himself in the third person, the Lord. Gen. xviii. 14, 19.
³ Ps. ix. 5.　　⁴ Ib. cxix. 21.　　⁵ Ib. lxxx. 16.
⁶ Ib. lxxvi. 6.　　⁷ Is. xvii. 13.　　⁸ Ps. cvi. 9.
⁹ Jacob, xviii. 15. add. Nah. i. 4.　¹⁰ Mal. ii. 3.
¹¹ Ib. iii. 11. נֵעַר is used 11 times of God, only 3 times of man; Gen. xxxvii. 10, Ruth ii. 16, Jer. xxix. 27. גְּעָרָה 8 times of God; 3 times in Prov. and Eccl. vii. 5, of rebuke of man, and Is. xxx. 17.
¹² S. Mark i. 25, 26, ix. 25, S. Luke iv. 35, ix. 42.
¹³ Rom. viii. 33, 34.　¹⁴ Heb. v. 2, 3.　¹⁵ Is. vi. 5.

¹⁶ S. Cyr.　¹⁷ The force of the participle with הָיָה.
¹⁸ Is. lxiv. 6.　　　　¹⁹ Ib. iv. 3, 4.
²⁰ Pr. xxx. 12. Filth, *filthiness,* in Is. iv. 4 also, is צוֹאָה, the abstract of the ἅπ. λεγ. in Zech., צוֹא.
²¹ Zeph. iii. 1, מֹרָאָה וְנִגְאָלָה. See ib.
²² Ps. cvi. 38. חָנֵף i. q. טָנַף Cant. v. 3.
²³ Ps. cvi. 39. טָמֵא opp. to טָהוֹר.　²⁴ Heb. ix. 10.
²⁵ Ps. li. 4, כַּבְּסֵנִי [2 Eng.]　²⁶ Is. i. 16. רַחֲצוּ.
²⁷ Jer. iv. 14, כַּבְּסִי.
²⁸ Jos. Ant. xiv. 10. 4. " Whosoever is brought before the tribunal to be judged, is set, as lowly, before it, and is clothed with black raiment."
²⁹ As in Latin, "sordidati." Liv. ii. 54, vi. 20.

Before
C H R I S T
cir. 519.

ᵍ Isai. 61. 10.
Luke 15. 22.
Rev. 19. 8.

ʰ Ex. 29. 6.
ch. 6. 11.

before him, saying, Take away the filthy garments from him. And unto him he said, Behold, I have caused thine iniquity to pass from thee, ᵍand I will clothe thee with change of raiment.

5 And I said, Let them set a fair ʰ mitre upon his head. So they set a fair

mitre upon his head, and clothed him with garments. And the angel of the LORD stood by.

6 And the angel of the LORD protested unto Joshua, saying,

7 Thus saith the LORD of hosts; If thou wilt walk in my ways, and if thou wilt ⁱkeep my ‖ charge,

Before
C H R I S T
cir. 519.

ⁱ Lev. 8. 35.
1 Kin. 2. 3.
Ezek. 44. 16.
‖ Or, *ordinance.*

See, I have caused thine iniquity to pass from thee; the pardoning words of the Lord to David by Nathan, ¹ *The Lord too hath put away thy sin. And clothe thee*² *with change of raiment*³, i. e. such as were taken off and reserved for great occasions. As the *filthy garments* were not necessarily other than the High Priest's vesture, symbolically defiled through the sins of the people, so neither need these be other than the priestly garments in their purity and freshness. The words imply the condition, not the nature of the vestment. "⁴ The high-priest having been thus taken to represent the whole people, the filthy garments would be no unclear symbol of the wickedness of the people. For clad, as it were, with their sins, with the ill-effaceable spot of ungodliness, they abode in captivity, subject to retribution, paying the penalty of their unholy deeds. But when God had pity on them, He bade them be freed from their defilements, and in a manner re-clad with justifying grace. He indicates to them the end of their toils. For where remission of sin is, there follows of necessity freedom from the evils brought through sin."—He adds that *a clean mitre should be put upon his head,* "⁵ that so we might understand that the glory of the priesthood ever, in a sort, concurs with the condition of the people. For the boast of the priesthood is the purity of those in their charge.—As then when the people was in sin, the raiment of the priest also was in a manner defiled, so if it were again well-approved, pure and bright is the fashion of the priesthood, and free its access to God. So the divine Paul having ministered to the Gentiles the Gospel óf Christ,

seeing them advancing in graces, writes, ⁶ *By your boast, brethren, which I have in Christ Jesus,* and, ⁷ *my joy and crown."*

5. *And I said, let them set a fair mitre*⁸ *on his head.* This seems to have been purposely omitted, in order to leave something, and that, the completion of all, to be done at the intercession of the prophet. The glory and complement of the High Priest's sacrificial attire was the *mitre* with the *holy crown upon it* and *the plate of pure gold, on which was graven, Holiness to the Lord*⁹; which was to *be upon* the High-priest's *forehead, that* he *may bear the iniquity of the holy things which the children of Israel shall hallow in all their holy gifts;* which was *always* to be *upon his forehead, that they may be accepted before the Lord.* The renewed gift of this was reserved for the intercession of man co-working with God.

And the angel of the Lord standing by, seeing that all was done aright, and, now that the acquittal was complete, *standing* to give the charge.

6. *And the angel of the Lord protested* solemnly (etymologically, *called* God *to witness*) as in, ¹⁰ *Did I not make thee swear by the Lord and protested unto thee,* laying it as an obligation upon him ¹¹. The charge is given to Joshua, and in him to all successive high-priests, while Israel should continue to be God's people, as the condition of their acceptance.

7. *If thou wilt walk in My ways and if thou wilt keep My charge.* Both of these are expressions, dating from the Pentateuch, for holding on in the way of life, well-pleasing to God and keeping the charge given by God ¹². It was the injunction of the dying David to Solomon, ¹³ *Keep the charge of the*

---

¹ 2 Sam. xii. 13, חטאתך העביר יי גם. The idiom occurs Ib. xxiv. 10. add. Job vii. 21.
² The inf. expresses the more, the contemporaneousness of the acts. See below vii. 5, xii. 10, and others in Ewald Lehrb. § 351. *c.* p. 853. ed. 8.
³ מחלצות recurs Is. iii. 22. ⁴ S. Cyr.
⁵ S. Cyr. ⁶ 1 Cor. xv. 31. ⁷ Phil. iv. 1.
⁸ צָנִיף is used of the turban of women, Is. iii. 23; or of nobles, Job xxix. 14: i. q. צָנוּף of royalty, Is.

lxii. 3. Here it is put for מִצְנֶפֶת, the Pentateuch name for the high-priest's mitre, as distinct from the מִגְבָּעָה of ordinary priests.
⁹ Ex. xxviii. 36–38, xxix. 6. ¹⁰ 1 Kgs ii. 42.
¹¹ העֵד with בְ Gen. xliii. 3, Deut. viii. 19, xxxii. 46, Ps. l. 7, &c.
¹² שָׁמַר מִשְׁמֶרֶת first used of Abraham, Gen. xxvi. 5, then Lev. xviii. 30, xxii. 9, Deut. xi. 1, Jos. xxii. 3.
¹³ 1 Kgs ii. 3.

Before
C H R I S T
cir. 519.

k Deut. 17. 9.
Mal. 2. 7.
† Heb. *walks.*

l ch. 4. 14.
& 6. 5.

then thou shalt also ᵏjudge my house, and shalt also keep my courts, and I will give thee † places to walk among these that ˡstand by.

8 Hear now, O Joshua

Before
C H R I S T
cir. 519.

m Ps. 71. 7.
Isai. 8. 18.
& 20. 3.
† Heb. *men of wonder,* or, *sign,* as Ezek. 12. 11. & 24. 24.

n Isai. 42. 1. & 49. 3, 5. & 52. 13. & 53. 11. Ezek. 34. 23, 24.

o Isai. 4. 2. & 11. 1. Jer. 23. 5. & 33. 15. ch. 6. 12. Luke 1. 78.

the high priest, thou and thy fellows that sit before thee: for they *are* ᵐ† men wondered at : for, behold, I will bring forth ⁿ my servant the ᵒBRANCH.

Lord thy God, to walk in His ways, to keep His statutes &c.

Then shalt thou also judge My house. Judgment, in the place of God, was part of the High-priest's office ¹. Yet these judgments also were given in the house of God. The cause was directed to be brought to God, and He through His priests judged it. Both then may be comprehended in the world, the oversight of the people itself and the judgment of all causes brought to it. "²Thou shalt judge those who minister in the house of My sanctuary."

*And I will give thee place to walk among those who stand by*³, i. e. among the ministering spirits, who were ⁴*standing before the Angel of the Lord.* This can be fully only after death, when the saints shall be received among the several choirs of angels. "²In the resurrection of the dead I will revive thee and give thee feet walking among these Seraphim." Even in this life, since ⁵*our conversation is in heaven,* and the life of priests should be an angel-life, it may mean, that he should have free access to God, his soul in heaven, while his body was on this earth.

8. *Thou and thy companions which sit before thee; yea* ⁶ *men of marvelous signs are they*⁷. It seems probable that the words addressed to Joshua begin here; else *the men of signs* would be the companions of Joshua, to the exclusion of Himself. His companions are probably ordinary priests, who *sit* as sharing his dignity as priest, but *before him,* as inferiors. So Ezekiel says, ⁸*I was sitting in my house, and the elders of Israel were sitting before me.* They are ⁹*images of the things to come.*

Isaiah's two sons, with their prophetic names, *Haste-spoil speed-prey,* and *a-remnant shall-return,* were with his own name, *salvation-of-the-Lord,* ¹⁰*signs and portents* of the future Israel. Isaiah, walking naked and barefoot, was ¹¹*a sign and portent* against Egypt. God tells Ezekiel, that in the *removal of his stuff, as stuff for the captivity,* ¹²*I have set thee for a portent unto the house of Israel. I,* he explains his act ¹³, *am your portent; like as I have done, so shall it be done unto you.* When forbidden to mourn on the death of his wife; ¹⁴*Ezekiel is unto you for a portent; according to all that he hath done, shall ye do; and when this cometh, ye shall know that I am the Lord God.* Wherein then were Joshua and the other priests portents of what should be? One fact alone had stood out, the forgiveness of sins. Accusation and full forgiveness, out of God's free mercy, were the substance of the whole previous vision. It was the full reinstatement of the priesthood. The priesthood so restored was the portent of what was to come. To ¹⁵*offer the offering of the people, and make an atonement for them;* ¹⁶*to make an atonement for the children of Israel for all their sins once a year,* was the object of the existence of the priesthood. Typical only it could be, because they had but *the blood of bulls and goats to offer, which could,* in themselves, ¹⁷*never take away sins.* But in this their act they were portents of what was to come. He adds here, *For, behold, I will bring My Servant the Branch.*

The Branch had now become, or Zechariah made it, a proper name. Isaiah had prophesied, ¹⁸*In that day shall the Branch of the Lord be beautiful and glorious for the escaped of*

---

¹ Deut. xvii. 9–13, xix. 17, Mal. ii. 7. דין is used of judging a cause (with דין, Jer. v. 28, xxx. 13; with משפט, Ib. xxi. 12) or persons; with the personal pronoun, Gen. xxx. 6; or people, peoples, the ends of the earth, the poor and needy, 17 times: ביתי is used metaphorically of the people of God, only in Nu. xii. 7, *he is faithful in all My house,* or at most Jer. xii. 7, *I have left My house.* Here the parallel word *My courts,* shews that the house is the literal temple.

² Jon.

³ Against the rendering, " those who shall make thee to go," i. e., guide thee, (מהליכים for מהלכים) there were valid objections; 1) that the Hif. is always הוליך, except הילך Ex. ii. 9. The Partic.

מוליך occurs 9 times, once in Zech. v. 10. 2) It would have been probably "out of these" or at least "from among these." מהלכים is then probably from a sing. מהלך like מהפך, מעבר, מחצב for מהלך Jon. iii. 3, 4, Ez. xlii. 4.

⁴ verse 4. ⁵ Phil. iii. 20.

⁶ כי is inserted in the like way in Gen. xviii. 20, Ps. cxviii. 10–12, cxxviii. 2.

⁷ The subject addressed in the nominative is resumed by the pronoun of the 3d person, as in Zeph. ii. 12.

⁸ Ezek. viii. 1.   ⁹ Heb. x. 1.   ¹⁰ Is. viii. 18.
¹¹ Ib. xx. 3.   ¹² Ezek. xii. 6.   ¹³ Ib. 11.
¹⁴ Ib. xxiv. 24.   ¹⁵ Lev. ix. 7.
¹⁶ Lev. xvi. 34.   ¹⁷ Heb. x. 4.   ¹⁸ Is. iv. 2.

Before CHRIST cir. 519.

9 For behold the stone that I have laid before Joshua; [p] upon one stone *shall be* [q] seven eyes: be-

[p] Ps. 118. 22. Isai. 28. 16.
[q] ch. 4. 10. Rev. 5. 6.

Israel; and, in reference to the low estate of him who should come, [1] *There shall come forth a rod out of the stump of Jesse, and a Branch shall grow out of his roots;* and Jeremiah, [2] *Behold the days come, saith the Lord, that I will raise unto David a righteous Branch, and a king shall reign and prosper, and shall execute judgment and justice in the earth, and this is the name whereby He shall be called, The Lord our Righteousness;* and, [3] *In those days and at that time, will I cause the Branch of righteousness to grow up unto David, and he shall execute judgment and righteousness in the land.* Of him Zechariah afterward spoke as, [4] *a man whose name is the Branch.* Here Zechariah names him simply, as a proper name, *My servant* [the] *Branch*, as Ezekiel prophesied of [5] *My servant David.* The title *My servant*, which is Isaiah's chiefest title of the Messiah, occurs in connection with the same image of His youth's lowly estate, and of His atoning Death. [6] *He shall grow up before Him as a sucker, and as a root from a dry ground;* [7] *a scion shall grow out of his roots.* "[8] He alone was above all marked by this name, who never in anything withdrew from the Will of God." "[9] God had before promised to Joshua, i. e. to the priesthood of the law, that they should judge His house and fulfill the types of the legal worship. Yet not long after, the things of the law were to be translated into the true worship, and the unloveliness of the types to be recast into the lovely spiritual polity. [10] *A righteous king was to reign and princes to rule with judgment,* as the Prophet spake. Another priest was to arise, after the order, [11] *not of Aaron but of Melchisedec,* [12] *a minister of the sanctuary and of the true tabernacle which God pitched and not man.* For our Lord Jesus Christ entered the holy of holies, [13] *not by the blood of bulls and goats, but by His own Blood, having obtained eternal redemption,* and [14] *having by One Oblation perfected for ever them that are sanctified.* Lest then God should seem to have spoken untruly, in promising to the legal priesthood that it should ever have the oversight over His house, there was need to fore-announce the mystery of Christ, that the things of the law should cease and He Himself should judge His own house through the Scion from Himself, His Son."

"[8] Look ye to the Branch of the Lord; set Him as the example of life; in Him, as a most strong tower, place with most becoming faith all your hope of salvation and immortality. For He is not only a Branch, who shall fill you with the richness of Divine fruit, but a stone also, to break all the essays of the enemy."

9. *For behold the stone, that I have laid before Joshua.* This must be an expansion of what he had said, or the ground of it, being introduced by, *for.* It must be something future, to be done by God Himself, since God says, *I will grave the graving thereof;* something connected with the remission of sins, which follows upon that graving. The stone, then, cannot be the stone of foundation of the material temple [15]. For this had long before been laid. The head-corner-stone, the completion of the building [16], had nothing remarkable, why God should be said to grave it. The plumbline [17] was not a part even of the material temple. *The stone* is *one stone.* But to interpret it by other prophecy, one stone there is, of which God says, [18] *Behold I lay in Zion for a foundation, a stone, a tried stone, a precious corner-stone, a sure foundation, he that believeth shall not make haste;* that stone, of which our Lord reminded the Jews, [19] *the stone which the builders refused is become the head-stone of the corner;* [20] *Jesus Christ Himself, the chief corner-stone, in whom all the building, fitly framed together, groweth into an holy temple in the Lord, in whom ye also are builded together for an habitation of God through the Spirit.*

On this stone had Joshua, with all those typical priests, to look, in Whom Alone they and all have forgiveness, Whose Sacrifice their sacrifices pictured and pleaded. "It," says an old mystical Jewish book [21], "is the stone of foundation, on which the earth is founded, which God Himself laid, that the world might receive blessing from it." "[22] The Shechinah is called the stone, through which the world subsisteth; of which

[1] Is. xi. 1. [2] Jer. xxiii. 5, 6. [3] Ib. xxxiii. 15.
[4] Zech. vi. 12.
[5] עַבְדִּי דָוִד Ezek. xxxiv. 23, 24, xxxvii. 24, as here עבדי צמח.
[6] Is. liii. 2. [7] Ib. xi. 1. [8] Osor. [9] S. Cyr.
[10] Is. xxxii. 1. [11] Heb. vii. 11. [12] Ib. viii. 2.
[13] Ib. ix. 12. [14] Ib. x. 14. [15] Rashi.
[16] Kim. Nor, of course, were either foundation-stone or head-stone engraven.
[17] Also in Kim. [18] Is. xxviii. 16.
[19] Ps. cxviii. 22. S. Matt. xxi. 42. add Acts iv. 11. The passages of the Psalm and of Isaiah are united 1 S. Pet. ii. 4–7. [20] Eph. ii. 20, 21.
[21] Zohar Gen. fol. 124. col. 492.
[22] Ib. Num. f. 100. col. 397. quoted by Schoettg. de Mess. p. 218. "Both passages," he subjoins, "are again adduced as parallel, Zohar Deut. f. 118. col. 472." Jonathan seems to identify the Branch, the Messiah, and the Stone; "Lo I am bringing My Servant Messiah, and He shall be revealed. Lo, the stone which I have set before Joshua, upon one stone seven eyes, beholding it; lo, I revealed the vision thereof, saith the Lord of hosts, and will re-

hold, I will engrave the graving thereof, saith the Lord of hosts, and

ʳ I will remove the iniquity of that land in one day.

it is said, *A stone of seven eyes,* and, *the stone which the builders refused.*" This *stone,* God says, *I have laid* or *set before Joshua,* i. e. for him to consider ; as He speaks to Solomon and his children, of *My commandments which I have set before you*[1]. "[2] That the stone is the Lord Jesus Christ, *the head corner-stone, elect, laid as a foundation;* and that the *seven eyes on the one stone* are the sevenfold Spirit of God which rested upon Him, is or ought to be unknown to no one. For to Him [3] *God giveth not the Spirit by measure,* and [4] *in Him dwelleth all the fullness of the Godhead bodily.* This stone was rejected by men, but chosen and honored by God." "[5] This stone then, on which the house of God and our whole salvation resteth, is placed by God before that high priest. That is, the most holy Name of Jesus, the virtue piety and largeness of Jesus is, by the Divine Spirit, shewed to the priest, that he might understand the End of the law and holiness, to Whom all the actions of life and the offices of the priesthood were to be referred. In which stone was foreshewn to the divine man, not the invisible strength only, but also the manifold light of the Divine intelligence. For it follows ;"

Upon this *one stone* are *seven eyes,* whether they are *the eyes* of God, resting in loving care upon it, or whether, as the *wheels* in Ezekiel's vision were [6] *full of eyes round about,* the eyes are pictured as on the stone itself, marking that it symbolized a being with manifold intelligence. Zechariah speaks of the eyes of [7] *the Lord which run to and fro on the earth,* and S. John, of the [8] *Lamb, as it had been slain, having seven horns and seven eyes, which are the seven spirits of God, sent forth into all the earth.* Either symbol harmonizes with the context, and is admissible in language[9]. The care of God for this stone is expressed before and afterward, *I have laid it, I will engrave the graving thereof;* and so it corresponds

to the [10] *It shall grow up before Him as a tender plant.* But the contrast, that on *one* stone there are *seven* eyes, perhaps rather suggests that the eyes are on the stone itself, and He, the *Living Stone,* is pictured with an universality of sight, whereby, with a Divine knowledge, He surveys and provides for the well-being of His whole Church. It has some analogy too to the sevenfold Spirit which was to rest upon Him. "[11] For this stone to have seven eyes is to retain in operation the whole virtue of the Spirit of sevenfold grace. For according to the distribution of the Holy Spirit, ones receives prophecy ; another, knowledge ; another, miracles ; another, kinds of tongues ; another, interpretation of words ; but no one attaineth to have all the gifts of that same Spirit. But our Creator taking on Him our infirmities, because, through the power of His Divinity, He shewed that He had at once in Him all the virtues of the Holy Spirit, united beyond doubt the bright gleams of the sevenfold constellation." "None among men had together all the operations of the Holy Spirit, save the Mediator of God and man Alone, Whose is that same Spirit, Who proceeds from the Father before all worlds." "[12] The stone is one. For as we have in God One Spirit, one faith, one sacrament of that most pure laver, so we worship One Christ, the one only Deliverer of the human race, and Author of our righteousness and everlasting salvation ; and strengthened by His guardianship, we hope for immortality and eternal glory. Who, though He be One, governs all things with ineffable wisdom. For His wisdom is aptly described by the seven eyes. For the number seven generally describes an universality of good."

Behold I will engrave the graving [13] *thereof,* as of a costly stone. What the graving is, is not explained ; but manifestly it is every-

---

move the guilt of that land in one day." The Zohar chadash (f. 76. 1.) joins the mention of the stone in Dan. ii. 35, Ps. cxviii. 22, Gen. xlix. 24. and this place, in Schoettg. l. c. p. 140. n. cv.
[1] 1 Kgs ix. 6. The idiom is the same, נָתַתִּי לִפְנֵיכֶם.
See also Deut. iv. 8, xi. 32, Jer. ix. 12, xxvi. 4, xliv. 10 ; of two things, between which to choose, Deut. xi. 26, xxx. 15. In Ezek. xxiii. 24, נָתַתִּי לִפְנֵיהֶם מִשְׁפָּט, "I have placed before them judgment," which they are to consider and to execute.
[2] Rup.   [3] S. John iii. 34.   [4] Col. ii. 9.   [5] Osor.
[6] Ezek. i. 18, x. 12.   [7] iv. 10.   [8] Rev. v. 6.
[9] In Ps. xxxii. 8. it is אִיעֲצָה עָלֶיךָ עֵינִי *I will counsel, My Eye upon thee;* in Ps. xxxiii. 18, עֵין יי ; in Ps. xxxiv. 16. עֵינֵי יי אֶל צַדִּיקִים ; but אֶל רָאיו ; "directed toward, or resting *upon,*" are only shades

of the same meaning. In Gen. xliv. 21. is וְאָשִׂימָה עֵינִי עָלָיו ; Jer. xxiv. 6, וְשַׂמְתִּי עֵינִי עֲלֵיהֶם and xl. 4, for good, אָשִׂים אֶת עֵינִי עָלֶיךָ.
[10] Is. liii. 2.
[11] S. Greg. on Job L. xxix. c. 31. n. 74. Opp. i. 951.
[12] Osor.
[13] פִּתּוּחַ only occurs besides of the carved wood of the house of God, 1 Kgs vi. 29, Ps. lxxiv. 6, or of the carving of a precious stone, Ex. xxviii. 11, 21, 36, xxxix. 6, 14, 30. פָּתַח is used of engraving things on wood, 1 Kgs vii. 36, 2 Chr. iii. 7 ; on precious stones, Ex. xxxviii. 9. The whole idiom, "skilled to *grave gravings,*" to *grave all graving,* recurs 2 Chr. ii. 6, 13 ; *thou shalt grave on it* with the *engravings of a signet, holiness to the Lord;* Ex. xxviii. 36.

Before
CHRIST
cir. 519.

ᵃch. 2. 11.

ᵗ1 Kin. 4. 25.
Isai. 36. 16.
Mic. 4. 4.

10 ᵃIn that day, saith the LORD of hosts, shall ye call every man his neighbor ᵗunder the vine and under the fig tree.

CHAPTER IV.

1 *By the golden candlestick is foreshewed the good success of*

Zerubbabel's foundation. 11 *By the two olive trees the two anointed ones.*

AND ᵃthe angel that talked with me came again and waked me, ᵇas a man that is wakened out of his sleep,

---

thing which concurs to its beauty. "[1] This stone is of earth, and of the power and workmanship of God." "[2] It signifies Him Who had His birth in virgin-earth, but framed skillfully by the power of the Holy Spirit." That Precious stone was further graven, through the Providence and Will of God, when "[3] He caused it to be wounded by the nails of the Cross and the soldier's lance, and in His Passion took away the *iniquity of the earth in one day,* of which it is written, [4] *This is the day which the Lord hath made, we will rejoice and be glad in it.*" Beautiful were the gifts and graces which Christ received, as Man; but beautiful beyond all beauty must be those glorious scars, with which He allowed His whole Body to be riven, that "[5] throughout the whole frame His love might be engraven." "[6] What even in the Body of the Lord can be lovelier or more lightful than those five Wounds, which He willed to retain in His immortal Being, lest the blessed should be deprived of that splendor, surpassing far the light of sun and stars?"

And I will remove the iniquity of the land in one day. On one day in the year was the typical atonement; in *one day* absolutely, God Himself would *make the iniquity of that land to depart.* One *day* is always emphatic [7], that things are crowded into it, which seemed too much for *one day.* Year by year came the *day of atonement:* its yearly repetition shewed that nothing lasting was effected. On *one day* that removal should be, which needed no renewal [8]. A Jewish writer confessed the mystery, while he said [9], "*One day;* I know not what that day is." Ask any Christian child, "On what day was iniquity removed, not from the land only, but from all lands?" he would say, "On the day when Jesus Died."

10. *Under the vine and under the fig tree.* Micah had already made the description of

the peaceful days of Solomon [10], a symbol [11] of the universal fearless peace of the time of Christ. "[12] Christ by His Passion shall not only take away iniquity, but also bring peace, delight, free communication of all things, so that all things among Christians should be common. For the law of Christ enjoineth charity, forgiveness of injuries, patience, love of enemies &c., all which bring temporal peace."

IV. 1. *The angel came again.* The angel (as before [13]) had gone forth to receive some fresh instruction from a higher angel or from God.

And awakened me, as a man is awakened out of sleep. Zechariah, overwhelmed by the greatness of the visions, must have sunk down in a sort of stupor, as after the vision of the ram and he-goat, *as Gabriel was speaking with him,* Daniel says, [14] *I was in a deep sleep on my face toward the ground, and he touched me and set me upright;* and again at the voice of the angel, who, after his three weeks' fast [15], came to declare to him [16] *the scripture of truth;* and at the Transfiguration, [17] *Peter and they that were with him were heavy with sleep, and when they were awake, they saw His glory.* "[18] Wondrous and stupendous mysteries were they which were shewn to the divine man. He saw the Branch of the Lord; he saw His invincible might; he saw His brightness of Divine intelligence and Providence; he saw the amplitude of beauty and dignity. Nailed then and struck still with amazement, while he revolved these things in his mind, sunk in a sort of sleep, he is borne out of himself and, mantled around with darkness, understands that the secret things of Divine wisdom cannot be perfectly comprehended by the mind of any. This then he attained that, his senses being overpowered, he should see nothing, save that wherein is the sum of wisdom, that this

---

[1] S. Iren. Hær. iii. 21. 7.   [2] Lap. as from S. Iren.
[3] S. Jer.   [4] Ps. cxviii. 24.
[5] "Cernis, ut in toto corpore sculptus amor." in Lap.   [6] Rib.
[7] Gen. xxvii. 45, "why should I be deprived of you both *in one day?*" 1 Sam. ii. 34, "*in one day* they shall die both of them;" 1 Kgs xx. 29, "Israel slew of the Syrians 100,000 footmen *in one day;*" 2 Chr. xxviii. 6, "Pekah slew in Judah 120,000 *in one day;*" Is. ix. 14, "shall cut off branch and rush *in one day;*"

x. 17, "devour his thorns and briers *in one day:*" Is. xlvii. 9, "two things shall come to thee *in one day;*" Ib. lxvi. 8, "shall the earth be made to bring forth *in one day?*"
[8] It includes then the ἐφάπαξ of Heb. vii. 27, ix. 12, x. 10, though the idiom is different.
[9] Rashi.   [10] 1 Kgs iv. 25.
[11] Mi. iv. 4. See ab. p. 59.   [12] Lap.
[13] ii. 3.   [14] Dan. viii. 18.   [15] Ib. x. 9.   [16] Ib. 21.
[17] S. Luke ix. 32.   [18] Osor.

Before
CHRIST
cir. 519.

2 And said unto me, What seest thou? And I said, I have looked, and behold [e] a candlestick all of gold, [†] with a bowl upon the top of it, [d] and his seven lamps thereon, and [||] seven pipes to the seven lamps, which *are* upon the top thereof:

3 [e] And two olive trees by it, one upon the right *side* of the bowl, and the

[e] Ex. 25. 31.
Rev. 1. 12.
[†] Heb. *with her bowl.*
[d] Ex. 25. 37.
Rev. 4. 5.

[|] Or, *seven several pipes to the lamps, &c.*

[e] ver. 11. 12.
Rev. 11. 4.

other upon the left *side* thereof.

4 So I answered and spake to the angel that talked with me, saying, What *are* these, my lord?

5 Then the angel that talked with me answered and said unto me, Knowest thou not what these be? And I said, No, my lord.

6 Then he answered and spake unto me, saying,

Before
CHRIST
cir. 519.

---

immensity of the Divine excellence cannot be searched out. By this sleep he was seized, when he was roused by the angel to see further mysteries.' "[1]Such is the condition of our mind, so far inferior to that in the holy angels, that their state may be called wakefulness, our's a sleep."

2. *And I said[2], I have looked and behold a candlestick all of gold.* The candlestick is the seven-branched candlestick of the tabernacle[3], but with variations purposely introduced to symbolize the fuller and more constant supply of the oil, itself the symbol of God's Holy Spirit, Who

" Enables with perpetual light
The dullness of our blinded sight."

The first variation is *her bowl[4] on the top of the candlestick,* containing the oil; then (as dependent on this) the pipes to derive the oil into each lamp, *seven several[5] pipes to the seven lamps,* i. e., seven to each; and the *two olive* trees on either side of the bowl, whose extreme and fine branches poured through two golden pipes the golden oil into the bowl which supplied the lamps. The multiplied conduits imply the large and perfect supply of oil unceasingly supplied, the seven being symbolic of perfection or of the reconciling of God (symbolized by 3) unto the world (svm-

[1] S. Cyr.
[2] The Kri וָאֹמַר must be right, "וַיֹּאמֶר‎, a manifest blunder, which the Kri corrects; countless Mss. correct in the text also, the Bibl. Brix., an old folio without date, and the Soncin. Prophets, 1486." De Rossi ad loc. All the Verss. agree with the Kri. The text would suppose that, in the silence of the prophet, the angel-interpreter related the vision which he also saw. But this is unlike all the other cases. Kim. supposes that the prophet speaks of himself in the third person. There is the same variation in 2 Sam. i. 8, Neh. v. 9, vii. 3.
[3] Ex. xxv. 31.
[4] נֵזֶר ἅπ. λεγ. for גֻּלָּה, like other rare masculines, as תְּבוּנֹם, Hos. xiii. 2; צִירָם, Ps. xlix. 15; בְּעֶרְכְּמָם

bolized by 4, *its four quarters*); the spontaneous flow of the golden oil from the olive trees symbolizes the free gift of God.

4. "[6]Awakened from his state of sleep, even thus the prophet seemed slowly to understand what was shewn him. He asks then of the instructing angel. The angel, almost amazed, asks if he knows it not, and when he plainly declares his ignorance, makes clear the enigma of the vision."

6. *This is the word of the Lord unto Zerubbabel.* "[6]As if he were to say, the meaning of the vision and scope of what has been exhibited is, 'God's doings have almost cried aloud to Zerubbabel that all these visions shall come to an end in their time, not effected by human might nor in fleshly strength, but in power of the Holy Ghost and through Divine Will.' For the Only Begotten became Man as we: but He warred not after the flesh, to set up the Church as a candlestick to the world, nor did He, through sensible weapons and armed phalanxes, make those two people His own, or place the spiritual lights on the candlestick; but in the might of His own Spirit He appointed in the Church [7]first Apostles, then prophets and evangelists, and all the rest of the saintly band, filling them with Divine gifts and enriching them abundantly by the influx of His Spirit."

Job v. 13; פָּנָה Pr. vii. 8, as פָּנִים Zech. xiv. 10; בִּמְגוּרָם Ps. lv. 16; סֻכּוֹ Ps. lxxvi. 3; שִׁיבוּ, 1 Kgs xiv. 4; מַטָּהֵרוּ, Ps. lxxxix. 45.

[5] lit. *seven and seven,* i. e., seven to each, as in Gen. vii. 2, without the לַגֻּלְגֹּלֶת ,וֹ חֲמֵשֶׁת חֲמֵשֶׁת שְׁקָלִים "five shekels apiece by the poll," Nu. iii. 47; "the fingers of his hands, and the fingers of his feet were שֵׁשׁ וָשֵׁשׁ, six and six, four and twenty in number," 2 Sam. xxi. 20; "his fingers (including as in 2 Sam. those of his feet) were six and six, twenty-four." 1 Chron. xx. 6.
[6] Osor.
[7] 1 Cor. xii. 28.

Before
CHRIST
cir. 519.

f Hos. 1. 7.
‖ Or, *army.*

g Jer. 51. 25.
Matt. 21. 21.

This *is* the word of the
LORD unto Zerubbabel,
saying, f Not by ‖ might,
nor by power, but by my
spirit, saith the LORD of
hosts.

7 Who *art* thou, g O
great mountain? before
Zerubbabel *thou shalt be-*
come a plain : and he shall
bring forth h the headstone
thereof i *with* s h o u t i n g s,
crying, Grace, grace unto
it.

Before
CHRIST
cir. 519.

h Ps. 118. 22.

i Ezra 3. 11, 13.

" [1] *Not* then *in* great *power nor in* fleshly
might were the things of Christ, but in power
of the Spirit was Satan spoiled, and the ranks
of the adverse powers fell with him ; and
Israel and those who aforetime served the
creature rather than the Creator, were called
to the knowledge of God through faith. But
that He saved all under heaven, not by
human arm, but by His own power as God
Emmanuel, Hosea too protested [2], *I will have
mercy upon the house of Judah and will save
them by the Lord their God, and will not save
them by bow nor by sword nor by battle nor by
chariots nor by horses nor by horsemen.* But
exceeding fittingly was this said to Zerubbabel, who was of the tribe of Judah and at,
that time administered the royal seat at
Jerusalem. For that he might not think
that, since such glorious successes were fore-
announced to him, wars would in their season
have to be organized, he lifts him up from
these unsound and human thoughts, and bids
him be thus minded, that the force was divine,
the might of Christ, Who should bring such
things to pass, and not human."
    Having given this key of the whole vision,
without explaining its details, God enlarges
what He had said to Zerubbabel, as He had
in the preceding chapter to Joshua [3].
    7. *Who art thou, O great mountain* [4] ? *Before
Zerubbabel thou shalt be a plain.* The words
have the character of a sacred proverb ;
b *Every one that exalteth himself shall be abased.*
Isaiah prophesies the victories of the Gospel
in the same imagery, [6] *Every valley shall be
exalted and every mountain and hill shall be
made low ; and the crooked shall be made straight
and the rough places plain.* And in the New
Testament S. Paul says, [7] *The weapons of our
warfare are not carnal, but mighty through God
to the pulling down of strongholds, casting down
imaginations and every high thing that exalteth
itself against God, and bringing into captivity
every thought to the obedience of Christ.* As it is
the character of Anti-Christ, that he [8] *opposeth*

and *exalteth himself above everything that is called*
God, so of Satan himself it had been said in
the former vision, that he stood at the right
hand of Joshua [9] *to resist him.* So then the
mountain symbolizes every resisting power ;
Satan and all his instruments, who, each in
his turn, shall oppose himself and be brought
low. In the first instance, it was Sanballat
and his companions, who opposed the rebuilding of the temple, on account of the
" exclusiveness " of Zerubbabel and Joshua [10],
because they would not make the temple the
abode of a mixed worship of him whom they
call *your* God and of their own idolatries.
In all and each of his instruments, the persecuting Emperors or the heretics, it was the
one adversary. " [11] The words seem all but
to rebuke *the great mountain,* i. e. Satan, who
riseth up and leadeth against Christ the
power of his own stubbornness, who was
figuratively spoken of before [9].—For that as far
as it was allowed and in him lay, he warred
fiercely against the Saviour, no one would
doubt, who considered how he approached
Him when fasting in the wilderness, and seeing Him saving all below, willed to make Him
his own worshiper, shewing Him [12] *all the
kingdoms of the world,* saying that all should
be His, if He *would fall down and worship* him.
Then out of the very choir of the holy
Apostles he snatched the traitor disciple,
persuading him to become the instrument of
the Jewish perverseness. He asks him, *Who
art thou ?* disparaging him and making him of
no account, *great* as the *mountain* was and
hard to withstand, and in the way of every
one who would bring about such things for
Christ, of Whom, as we said, Zerubbabel was
a type."
    And he shall bring forth the headstone [13].
The foundation of the temple had long
been laid. Humanly it still hung in the
balance whether they would be permitted to
complete it [14] : Zechariah foretells absolutely
that they would. Two images appear to be

[1] S. Cyr.   [2] Hos. 1. 7.   [3] Zech. iii. 8–10.
[4] הַר הַגָּדוֹל ; the construction as שַׁעַר הָרִאשׁוֹן
xiv. 10; עֵד בּוֹר הַגָּדוֹל 2 Sam. xii. 4; לְאִישׁ הָעָשִׁיר
1 Sam. xix. 22; הַזֶּה 1 Sam. xvii. 12;
אִישׁ אֶפְרָתִי Jer. xxxviii. 14; דָּבָר הַזֶּה Ib. xl.
3; סֵפֶר הַגָּלוּי הַזֶּה Ib. xxxii. 14. also 1 Kgs vii. 8,
12. Ges. Lehrg. n. 168. p. 659.

[5] S. Luke xiv. 11, xviii. 14.
[6] Is. xl. 4. The same word לְמִישׁוֹר, there with
וְהָיָה.
[7] 2 Cor. x. 4, 5.   [8] 2 Thess. ii. 4.   [9] iii. 1.
[10] See ab. Introd. to Haggai. p. 293.   [11] S. Cyr.
[12] S. Matt. iv. 8, 9.

[13] רֹאשָׁה is a form, perhaps framed by Zechariah,
here in apposition to הָאֶבֶן.
[14] Ezr. v.

8 Moreover the word of
the LORD came unto me,
saying,

9 The hands of Zerub-
babel [k] have laid the foundation of this house; his
hands [l] shall also finish it;
and [m] thou shalt know that

the [n] LORD of hosts hath
sent me unto you.

10 For who h a t h de-
spised the day of [o] small
things? || for they shall re-
joice, and s h a l l see the
† plummet in the hand of
Zerubbabel *with* those

[k] Ezra 3. 10.

[l] Ezra 6. 15.
[m] ch. 2. 9, 11.
& 6. 15.

[n] Isai. 48. 16.
ch. 2. 8.
[o] Hag. 2. 3.
|| Or, *since the
seven eyes of the
Lord shall re-
joice.*
† *Heb. stone of
tin.*

used in Holy Scripture, both of which
meet in Christ: the one, in which the stone
spoken of is the foundation-stone; the other,
in which it is the head corner-stone binding
the two walls together, which it connects.
Both were corner stones; the one at the base,
the other at the summit. In Isaiah the
whole emphasis is on the foundation; [1] *Behold Me Who have laid in Zion a stone, a tried
stone, a precious corner-stone, well-founded.* In
the Psalm, the building had been commenced; those who were building had disregarded and despised the stone, but *it became
the head of the corner,* crowning and binding
the work in one [2]. Both images together
express, how Christ is the Beginning and
the End, the First and the Last; the Foundation of the spiritual building, the Church,
and its summit and completion; the unseen
Foundation which was laid deep in Calvary,
and the Summit to which it grows and which
holds it firm together. Whence S. Peter
unites the two prophecies, and blends with
them that other of Isaiah, that Christ would
[3] *be a stone of stumbling, and a rock of offence.
To Whom coming, as unto a living stone, disal-
lowed indeed of men but chosen of God and precious, ye also are built up a spiritual house—
Whence also it is contained in the Scripture,
Behold, I lay in Zion a chief corner-stone, elect,
precious:—unto you which believe He is precious,
but · unto them which be disobedient, the same
stone which the builders refused is made the head
of the corner, and a stone of stumbling and a rock
of offence, to them which stumble at the word being
disobedient.*
A Jew paraphrases this of the Messiah;
" [4] And He shall reveal His Messiah, whose

name was spoken from the beginning, and
he shall rule over all nations."
With shoutings [5], *grace, grace unto it,* i. e. all
favor from God unto it, redoubled favors,
grace upon grace. The completion of the
building was but the commencement of the
dispensation under it. It was the beginning
not the end. They pray then for the continued and manifold grace of God, that He
would carry on the work, which He had
begun. Perseverance, by the grace of God,
crowns the life of the Christian; our Lord's
abiding presence in grace with His Church
unto the end of the world, is the witness
that He Who founded her upholds her in
being.
8. *And the word of the Lord.* "[6] This word
of the Lord is not addressed through 'the
interpreting angel,' but direct from the Lord,
and that through the 'Angel of the Lord.'
[7] For though in the first instance the words,
the hands of Zerubbabel &c., relate to the
building of the material temple, and announce
its completion through Zerubbabel, yet the
inference, *and thou shalt know that the 'Lord of
hosts hath sent me unto you,* shews that the
meaning is not exhausted thereby, but that
here too this building is mentioned only as a
type of the building of the spiritual temple [8];
and the completion of the typical temple is
but a pledge of the completion of the true
temple. For not through the completion of
the material temple, but only through the
building of the kingdom of God, shadowed
forth by it, can Judah know, that the Angel
of the Lord was sent to him."
10. The simplest rendering is marked by
the accents. *For who hath despised* [9] *the day*

[1] Is. xxviii. 16.
[2] Ps. cxviii. 22. This is implied in the Midrash,
quoted by De Lira. " They explain it of a certain
stone of this building, which was frequently offered
by the stone-masons for the building of the wall,
but was always found too long or too short, and so
was often rejected by them as unfit, but in the completion of the wall, in the coupling of the two walls,
it is found most fit, which was then accounted a
marvelous thing." in Ps. cxvii. (118) 22. רֹאשׁ
" head," is a natural metaphor for the summit; the
tops of mountains, Gen. viii. 5 &c.; of a hill over
valleys, Is. xxviii. 1, 4; of a tower, Gen. xi. 4; of
columns, 1 Kgs vii. 19: the rounded top of a throne,
Ib. x. 19; of a bed, Gen. xlvii. 31 [Heb.]; ear of
corn, Job xxiv. 24; the starry heavens above us,

Job xxii. 12; of the head of a people, tribes, nations,
a family, in many places. Although used of the
chief among things, it cannot, any more than
κεφαλή, be used of " the base," as Gesenius would
have it. Thes. p. 1251. v. רֹאשָׁה.
[3] 1 S. Pet. ii. 4–7.   [4] Jon.
[5] תְּשֻׁאוֹת always plur.; of the cries of a city, Is.
xxii. 2; of the exactor, Job xxxix. 7; crash of
thunder, Ib. xxxvi. 29. [all]
[6] Keil.
[7] " comp. v. 9 [b] with ii. 13 [b] and 15 [b]."
[8] " as in vi. 12. sq."
[9] בָּזָ i.q. בָּזָה (and with its const. with לְ) as מַט for
מַט, Is. xliv. 18.

Before
CHRIST
cir. 519.

P 2 Chr. 16. 9.
Prov. 15. 3.
ch. 3. 9.

q ver. 3.

seven; P they *are* the eyes of the Lord, which run to and fro through the whole earth.

11 ¶ Then answered I, and said unto him, What *are* these q two olive trees upon the right *side* of the candlestick and upon the left *side* thereof?

12 And I answered again, and said unto him, What *be these* two olive branches which † through the two golden pipes ‖empty † the golden *oil* out of themselves?

13 And he answered me and said, Knowest thou

Before
CHRIST
cir. 519.

† Heb. *by the hand.*

‖ Or, *empty out of themselves* oil into *the gold.*

† Heb. *the gold.*

---

of small things [1]? *and* [i. e. *seeing that* [2],] *there have rejoiced and seen the plummet in the hand of Zerubbabel, these seven, the Eyes of the Lord, they are running to and fro in all the earth,* i. e. since God hath with joy and good-pleasure beheld the progress of the work of Zerubbabel, *who can despise the day of small things?* The day of small things was not only that of the foundation of the temple, but of its continued building also. The *old men* indeed, *that had seen the first house, wept with a loud voice, when the foundation of this house was laid before their eyes* [3]. But while in progress too, Haggai asks, [4] *Who is left among you that saw this house in its first glory? And how do ye see it now? is not in your eyes such as it, as nothing?* But that temple was to see the day of great things, when [5] *the later glory of this house shall be greater than the former, and in this place will I give peace, saith the Lord of hosts.*

They are the eyes of the Lord which run to and fro. He uses almost the words of the prophet Hanani to Asa [6], *the eyes of the Lord run to and fro throughout the whole earth, to shew Himself strong in behalf of those whose heart is perfect toward Him.* Yet this assurance that God's watchful Providence is over *the whole earth,* betokens more than the restoration of the material temple, whose only hindrance could be the will of one man, Darius.

The day of small things is especially God's day, Whose *strength is made perfect in weakness;*

[1] נְעִמוֹת ,נִפְלָאוֹת ,רֵעוּת as קְטֻנוֹת Ps. xvi. 11. sing. קְטַנָה אוֹ גְדוֹלָה Num. xxii. 18.

[2] This is not a mere relation of a contemporaneous fact, in which the noun is placed first. (Ew. Lehrb. § 341 p. 835). It is a contrast; in which case the word, in which the contrast lies, is placed first, whether noun or verb. Here the contrast being between "despising" and "rejoicing," וְשָׂמְחוּ is placed first. So in Ps. v. 12, וְיִשְׂמְחוּ; Ib. xxv. 3, *all that trust in Thee shall not be ashamed; ashamed be they who &c.;* Ps. xxxviii. 17. *The arms of the ungodly shall be broken, and upholdeth the Lord the righteous,* יְי וְסוֹמֵךְ צַדִּיקִים.

[3] Ezr. iv. 12. [4] Hagg. ii. 3. [5] Ib. 9.

[6] 2 Chr. xvi. 9. עֵינָיִם is masc. in Zech. both here and iii. 9, which is rare, but also Ps. xxxviii. 11. עַיִן m. Cant. iv. 9. Ch. Ps. lxxiii. 7.

[7] Rib. vita S. Ther. ap. Lap.

Who raised Joseph from the prison, David from the sheepfold, Daniel from slavery, and converted the world by the fishermen and the tentmaker, having Himself first become the Carpenter. "Wouldest thou be great? Become little." "Whenever," said S. Theresa [7], "I am to receive some singular grace, I first annihilate myself, sink into my own nothingness, so as to seem to myself to be nothing, be capable of nothing."

11. *And I answered and said.* The vision, as a whole, had been explained to him. The prophet asks as to subordinate parts, which seemed perhaps inconsistent with the whole. If the whole imports that everything should be done by the Spirit of God, not by human power, what means it that there are these *two olive-trees?* And when the Angel returned no answer, to invite perhaps closer attention and a more definite question, he asks again;

12. *What are the two spikes* [8] *of the olive?* comparing the extreme branches of the olivetree, laden with their fruit, to the ears of corn, which *were by* or *in the hand of* [9] the golden pipes[10], *which empty forth the golden oil from themselves.* Zechariah's expression, *in the hand of* or, if so be, *by the hand of* the two pipes, shews that these two were symbols of living agents, for it is nowhere used except of a living agent, or of that which it personified as such [11].

[8] שִׁבֲּלֵי, ἅπ. after the analogy of שִׁבֹּלֶת, of ears of corn.

[9] Kim., by his explanation "in the midst" and that the olive trees were pressed in the midst of the golden pipes, seems to mean that the branches with their olives fell into those pipes as hands, and yielded in them their oil; Rashi renders "near it" like אֶל יְדֵי 2 Sam. xiv. 30, as בְּיַד Job xv. 23.

[10] צַנְתָּרוֹת is doubtless the same as Ch. צִנְתָּרִין Esth. (ii.) i. 2, "tubes" צִנּוּרֵי תְהוֹכְמָא Eccl. i. 7, Targ. in Buxt., yet larger than the מוֹצֵק, both from its etymology, and since the oil was derived through two tubes to the bowl, but by 7 x 7 = 49 to the lamps.

[11] Of the 276 cases beside this, in which בְּיַד occurs, in three only is it used of any other than a personal agent, and in these the agent is personified; Job viii. 4, *and he cast them away in the hand of their transgression;* Prov. xviii. 21, *death and life are*

Before
C H R I S T
cir. 519.

▪ Rev. 11. 4.

not what these *be?* And I
said, No, my lord.

14 Then said he, ʳ These

are the two † anointed
ones, ˢ that stand by ᵗ the
Lord of the whole earth.

Before
C H R I S T
cir. 519.

† Heb. *sons of oil.*
ˢ ch. 3. 7. Luke 1. 19.   ᵗ See Josh. 3. 11, 13.   ch. 6. 5.

14. *These are the two sons of oil,* probably not as themselves anointed, (for another word is used for this [1], and the whole vision has turned on the use of oil as an instrument of light, not of anointing) but as themselves abundantly ministering the stream which is the source of light [2].

Which stand by the Lord of the whole earth, as His servants and ministers.

The candlestick is almost authoritatively interpreted for us, by the adoption of the symbol in the Revelation, where our Lord is exhibited [3] *as walking in the midst of the seven golden candlesticks,* and, it is said, [4] *the seven candlesticks are the seven Churches;* and our Lord says to the Apostles, on whom He founded the Church; [5] *Ye are the light of the world: men light a candle, and put it on a candlestick, and it giveth light to them that are in the house.*

" [6] The golden candlestick is the Church, as being honored in the world, most bright in virtues, raised on high exceedingly by the doctrines of the true knowledge of God. But there are seven lamps, having light, not of their own, but brought to them from without, and nourished by the supplies through the olive tree. These signify the holy Apostles, Evangelists, and those who, each in their season, were teachers of the Churches, receiving, like lamps, into their mind and heart the illumination from Christ, which is nourished by the supplies of the Spirit, casting forth light to those who are in the house." " [7] The pipes of the lamps, which pour in the oil, signify the unstinted prodigality of the loving-kindness of God to man."

The most difficult of explanation (as is plain from the variety of interpretations) is this last symbol of the spikes of the olive-tree, through whom flows the oil of the Holy Spirit to the candlesticks, and which yet represent created beings, ministers, and servants of God. Perhaps it represents that, in the Church, grace is ministered through men, as S. Paul says, [8] *Unto every one of us is given grace according to the measure of the gift of Christ. Wherefore he saith, when He as-*

cended up on high, He led captivity captive and gave gifts unto men. And He gave some, apostles; and some, prophets; and some, evangelists; and some, pastors and teachers, for the perfecting of the saints, for the work of the ministry, for the edifying of the body of Christ—that we—may grow up into Him in all things which is the Head, even Christ, from Whom the whole body, fitly joined together and compacted by that which every joint supplieth, according to the effectual working in the measure of every part, maketh increase of the body unto the edifying of itself in love. What S. Paul expresses by [9] all the body, having nourishment ministered and being knit together by joints and bands, from the Head, and so increasing with the increase of God, (as he elsewhere speaks of [10] the ministration of the Spirit; [11] he that ministereth to you the Spirit) that* Zechariah may express by the oil being poured, through the living [12] tubes, the bowl, the sevenfold pipes, into the lamps, which shone with the God-given light. So S. Paul speaks again, of [13] *having this treasure in earthen vessels.* Joshua and Zerubbabel, as representatives of the priestly and royal offices, shadowed forth what was united in Christ, and so, in their several offices, they might be included in the symbol of the olive-tree, they could not exhaust it; for men who, having served God in their generation, were to pass away, could not be alone intended in a vision, which describes the abiding being of the Church.

" [14] Christ is both All-holy Priest and supreme Eternal King. In both ways He supplies to us the light which He brought. For from Him piety and righteousness flow unceasingly to the Church, that it never lack the heavenly light. The oil is expressed into tubes; thence passed through pipes into the vessel which contains the lamps; to designate the various suppliers of light, which, the nearer they are to the effluence of the oil, the more they resemble Him by Whom they are appointed to so Divine an office. The seven lamps are the manifold Churches, distinct in place but most closely bound together by the consent of one faith and by the

in the power, lit. *the hand, of the tongue;* Is. lxiv. 6, *thou hast made us to melt away by the hand of our iniquities.* With regard to ʙᴇʏᴀᴅᴋ, ʙᴇʏᴀᴅᴋ, this could not be otherwise; but also in the 92 cases in which ʙᴇʏᴀᴅᴏ; 6, in which ʙᴇʏᴀᴅᴀʜ; and 34, in which ʙᴇʏᴀᴅᴀᴍ, occurs, the pronoun relates to a personal agent.

[1] רָה_, in the other 20 places where it occurs, is always united with other natural products: both תִּירוֹשׁ (not יַיִן), the fresh wine, and דָּגָן "wheat." שֶׁמֶן is used of the oil as derived from the olive

(שֶׁמֶן זַיִת, Ex. xxvii. 20, Lev. xxiv. 2.) for the candlestick, Ex. xxvii. 20, as well as for the anointing oil, but not יִצְהָר.

[2] So בֶּן שֶׁמֶן Is. v. 1, and the other idioms of qualities, בֶּן עֹלָה, בֶּן בְּלִיַּעַל, בֶּן חַיִל &c.

[3] Rev. i. 13. ii. 1.		[4] Ib. i. 20.
[5] S. Matt. v. 14, 15. cf. Phil. ii. 15.	[6] S. Cyr.
[7] Theod.		[8] Eph. iv. 7, 8, 11, 12, 14–16.
[9] Col. ii. 19.	[10] 2 Cor. iii. 8.	[11] Gal. iii. 5.
[12] See ab. on ver. 12.	[13] 2 Cor. iv. 7.	[14] Osor.

Before
CHRIST
cir. 519.

CHAPTER V.

1 *By the flying roll is shewed the curse of thieves and swearers.* 5 *By a woman pressed in an ephah, the final damnation of Babylon.*

THEN I turned, and lifted up mine eyes, and looked, and behold a flying [a] roll.

[a] Ezek. 2. 9.

2 And he said unto me, What seest thou? And I answered, I see a flying roll; the length thereof is t w e n t y cubits, and the breadth thereof ten cubits. 3 Then said he unto me, This is the [b] curse that goeth forth over the face of

Before
CHRIST
cir. 519.

[b] Mal. 4. 6.

---

bond of charity. For although the Church is one, yet it is distinct according to the manifold variety of nations. They are said to be seven, both on account of the seven gifts of the Spirit, mentioned by Isaiah, and because in the numbers 3 and 4, is contained an emblem of piety and righteousness. There are 7 pipes to each lamp, to signify that each has need of many instruments, that the light may be maintained longer. For as there are diversities of gifts, so must there needs be the functions of many ministers, to complete one work. But the lamps are set in a circle, that the oil of one may flow more readily into others, and it, in turn, may receive from others their superabundance, to set forth the communion of love and the indissoluble community of faith."

V. 1. Hitherto all had been bright, full of the largeness of the gifts of God; of God's favor to His people[1]; the removal of their enemies[2]; the restoration and expansion and security of God's people and Church under His protection[3]; the acceptance of the present typical priesthood and the promise of Him, through Whom there should be entire forgiveness[4]: the abiding illumining of the Church by the Spirit of God[5]. Yet there is a reverse side to all this, God's judgments on those who reject all His mercies. "[6] Prophecies partly appertain to those in whose times the sacred writers prophesied, partly to the mysteries of Christ. And therefore it is the wont of the prophets, at one time to chastise vices and set forth punishments, at another to predict the mysteries of Christ and the Church."

And I turned and, or, *Again* [7] *I lifted up my eyes,* having again sunk down in meditation on what he had seen, *and behold a roll flying ;* as, to Ezekiel was shewn *a hand with a roll of*

a *book therein, and he spread it before me.* Ezekiel's roll also was [8] *written within and without, and there was written therein lamentation and mourning and woe.* It was a wide unfolded roll, as is involved in its *flying ;* but its "[9] flight signified the very swift coming of punishment ; its flying from heaven that the sentence came from the judgment-seat above."

2. *And he* (the interpreting angel) *said unto me.* It cannot be without meaning, that the dimensions of the roll should be those of the tabernacle [10], as the last vision was that of the candlestick, after the likeness of the candlestick therein. The explanations of this correspondence do not exclude each other. It may be that [11] *judgment shall begin at the house of God ;* that the punishment on sin is proportioned to the nearness of God and the knowledge of Him; that the presence of God, which was for life, might also be to death, as S. Paul says ; [12] *God maketh manifest the savor of this knowledge by us in every place ; for we are unto God a sweet savor of Christ in them that are saved and in them that perish ; to the one we are the savor of death unto death, and to the other the savor of life unto life ;* and Simeon said, [13] *This child is set for the fall and rising again of many in Israel.*

Over the face of the whole earth, primarily *land,* since the perjured persons, upon whom the curse was to fall [14], were those who swore falsely by the name of God : and this was in Judah only. The reference to the two tables of the law also confines it primarily to those who were under the law. Yet, since the moral law abides under the Gospel, ultimately these visions related to the Christian Church, which was to be spread *over the whole earth.* The roll apparently was shewn, as

---

[1] Vision 1. i. 7-17.   [2] Vision 2. Ib. 18-21.
[3] Vis. 3. c. ii.   [4] Vis. 4. c. iii.   [5] Vis. 5. c. iv.
[6] S. Aug. de Civ. Dei. xvii. 3. Rib.
[7] Gen. xxvi. 18, 2 Kgs i. 11, 13. Jer. xviii. 14.
[8] Ez. ii. 9, 10.   [9] Rib.
[10] The length of the tabernacle is fixed by the 5 curtains which were to be on each side, *the breadth of each curtain four cubits.* Exod. xxvi. 1, 2. The whole, including the holy of holies, is determined by the *twenty boards* on each side, *a cubit and a half, the breadth of each board ;* Ib. 16, 18. The breadth

is fixed by the *six boards,* i. e. nine cubits, with the *two boards for the corners of the tabernacle in the two sides.* Ib. 22, 23. Josephus gives the whole thirty cubits long, (the holy of holies being ten cubits square) ten broad (Ant. 3. 6. 3.). Kimchi strangely neglects this, and refers to the porch of Solomon's temple, in which the dimensions of the tabernacle were repeated (1 Kgs vi. 3.), but which was itself only an ornament to the temple.
[11] 1 Pet. iv. 17.   [12] 2 Cor. ii. 14-16.
[13] S. Luke ii. 34.   [14] ver. 4.

Before
CHRIST
cir. 519.

the whole earth: for ‖every one that stealeth

‖ Or, *every one of this people that stealeth holdeth* him-self *guiltless as it doth.*

shall be cut off *as* on this side according to it; and every one t h a t sweareth shall be cut off *as* on that side according to it.

4 I will bring it forth, saith the LORD of hosts,

and it shall enter into the house of the thief, and into the h o u s e of °him that sweareth f a l s e l y by my name: and it shall remain in the midst of his house, and ᵈ shall consume it with the timber thereof and the stones thereof.

Before
CHRIST
cir. 519.

° Lev. 19. 12.
ch. 8. 17.
Mal. 3. 5.

ᵈ See Lev. 14. 45.

---

written on both sides; the, commandments of the first table, in which perjury is for-bidden, on the one side; those relating to the love of our neighbor, in which stealing is for-bidden, on the other [1]. "[2] He calleth *curse* that vengeance, which goeth through the whole world, and is brought upon the workers of iniquity. But hereby both prophets and people were taught, that the God of all is the judge of all men, and will exact meet pun-ishment of all, bringing utter destruction not on those only who live ungodly toward Him-self, but on those also who are unjust to their neighbors. For let no one think that this threat was only against thieves and false-swearers; for He gave sentence against all iniquity. For since all the law and the prophets hang on this word, *Thou shalt love the Lord thy God with all thy heart and thy neigh-bor as thyself,* He comprised every sort of sin under false swearing and theft. The viola-tion of oaths is the head of all ungodliness. One who so doeth is devoid of the love of God. But theft indicates injustice to one's neighbor; for no one who loves his neigh-bor will endure to be unjust to him. These heads then comprehend all the other laws."

Shall be cut off, lit. *cleansed away* [3], as some-thing defiled and defiling, which has to be cleared away as offensive: as God says, [4] *I will take away the remnant of the house of Jero-boam, as a man taketh away dung, till it be all gone,* and so often in Deuteronomy, *thou shalt put the evil away from the midst of thee* [5], or of

Israel [6], and in Ezekiel, [7] *I will disperse thee in the countries and will consume thy filthiness out of thee.* [8] *Set it empty upon the coals thereof, that the brass of it may be hot and may burn, and the filthiness of it may be molten, that the scum of it may be consumed.*

4. *I will bring it forth* out of the treasure-house, as it were; as he says, [9] *He bringeth forth the wind out of His treasures;* and, [10] *Is not this laid up in store with Me, sealed up among My treasures? To Me belongeth vengeance and recompense."*

And it shall remain, lit. "lodge for the night [11]," until it was accomplished that for which it was sent, its utter destruction. "[12] So we have seen and see at this day powerful families, which attained to splendor by rapine or ill-gotten goods, destroyed by the just judgment of God, that those who see it are amazed, how such wealth perceptibly yet in-sensibly disappeared." "[13] Why doth it overthrow the stones and the wood of the swearer's house? In order that the ruin may be a correction to all. For since the earth must hide the swearer, when dead, his house, overturned and become a heap, will by the very sight be an admonition to all who pass by and see it, not to venture on the like, lest they suffer the like, and it will be a lasting witness against the sin of the departed." Heathenism was impressed [14] with the doom of him who consulted the oracle, whether he should foreswear himself for gain [15]. "Swear," was the answer, "since death awaits too the man, who keeps

---

[1] מִזֶּה מִזֶּה, in two corresponding sentences, can only be partitive, as in Ex. xvii. 12, xxv. 19, xxvi. 13, xxxii. 15, of the two tables of the law, written on both sides; xxxvii. 8, xxxviii. 15, Nu. xxii. 24; Jos. viii. 22, and ten other places. So also מִזֶּה מִזֶּה וּמִזֶּה לָאָרוֹן Jos. viii. 33. מִזֶּה וּמִזֶּה Ez. xlvii. 7, 12, as in other partitives מִפֹּה, מִפֹּה, or מִפֹּו Ez. xl. 10, 12, 21, 26, xli. 2. מִזֶּה also, when used of place, always means "from here," i. e. a definite place where people are, Gen. xxxvi. 17, xlii. 15, Exod. xi. 1 (Maurer's instances). [2] Theod.
[3] So is καθαρίζω used Mark vii. 19, (See reff. notes 10-14.) For נקה is not simply "clear," but "cleanse out," as καθαίρω Soph. Tr. 1012, 1061, Plutarch Thes. n. 7, Maʳ. n. 6. "of monsters and robbers." (Gese-nius in comparing Arab. אשתנק, "emptied clean

out" (Vita Tim. i. 576.), יָן אשתחלי, "appropriated it exclusively to himself" (Lane), אשתצפי "took away the whole" (Freyt.), "cleared it all off," misses the moral meaning of the Heb. word.
[4] 1 Kgs xiv. 10, add xxi. 21. [5] Deut. xiii. 5 (6 Heb.), xvii. 7, xix. 19, xxi. 21, xxii. 21, 24, xxiv. 7.
[6] Ib. xvii. 12, xxiii. 22 [7] Ezek. xxii. 15.
[8] Ib. xxiv. 11. [9] Jer. x. 13, li. 16.
[10] Deut. xxxii. 34, 35.
[11] לָנָה for לָנָה in verb *āπ.*; in part. pass. זָרֶה Is. lix. 5. [12] Lap.
[13] S. Chrys. on the statues 15. n. 13. p. 259. Oxf. Tr.
[14] "The story of Glaucus is alluded to by Plutarch (ii. p. 556 D) Pausanias (11. xviii. n. 2.) Juvenal (xiii. 199-208) Clemens (Strom. vi. p. 749) Dio Chrysostom (Or. lxiv. p. 640) and others." Rawl. Herod. iii. 477.
[15] Herod. vi. 85.

Before
C H R I S T
cir. 519.

5 ¶ Then the angel that talked with me went forth, and said unto me, Lift up now thine eyes, a n d see what *is* this t h a t goeth forth.

6 And I said, What *is*

it? And he said, This *is* an ephah that goeth forth.

Before
C H R I S T
cir. 519.

He said moreover, This *is* their resemblance through all the earth.

7 And, behold there was lifted up a ‖ talent of lead :

‖ Or, *weighty piece.*

---

the oath; yet Oath hath a son, nameless, handless, footless; but swift he pursueth, until he grasp together and destroy the the whole race and house." "[1] In the third generation, there was nought descended from him," who had consulted about this perjury, "nor hearthstone reputed to be his. It had been uprooted and effaced." A Heathen orator[2] relates, as well known, that " the perjurer escapes not the vengeance of the gods, and if not himself, yet the sons and whole race of the foresworn fall into great misfortunes." God left not Himself without witness.

"[3] The prophet speaks of the curse inflicted on the thieves and false swearers of his own day; but à fortiori he includes that which came upon them for slaying Christ. For this was the greatest of all, which utterly overthrew and consumed Jerusalem, the temple and polity, so that that ancient and glorious Jerusalem exists no longer, as Christ threatened. [4] *They shall lay thee even with the ground, and they shall not leave in thee one stone upon another.* This resteth upon them these" 1800 " years."

5. *Then the angel went forth* from the choirs of angels, among whom, in the interval, he had retired, as before[5] he had gone forth to meet another angel.

6. *This is the ephah that goeth forth.* "[6] We too are taught by this, that the Lord of all administers all things *in weight and measure.* So, foretelling to Abraham that his seed should be a sojourner and the cause thereof, He says, [7] *for the iniquity of the Amorites is not yet full,* i. e., they have not yet committed sins enough to merit entire destruction, wherefore I cannot yet endure to give them over to the slaughter, but will wait for the measure of their iniquity." The relation then of this vision to the seventh is, that the seventh

tells of God's punishment on individual sinners; this, on the whole people, when the iniquity of the whole is full.

This is their *resemblance,* as we say, *their look* [8], i. e. the *look,* appearance, of the inhabitants [9] *in all the land.* This then being the condition of the people of the land, at the time to which the vision relates, the symbolical carrying away of the full measure of sin cannot be its forgiveness, since there was no repentance, but the taking away of the sin with the sinner. "[10] The Lord of all is good and loving to mankind; for He is patient toward sinners and endures transgressors, waiting for the repentance of each; but if one perseveres long in iniquity, and come to the term of the endurance allowed, it remains that he should be subjected to punishment, and there is no account of this long forebearance, nor can he be exempt from judgment proportioned to what he has done. So then Christ says to the Jewish people, rushing with unbridled phrensy to all strange excess, [11] *Fill ye up the measure of your fathers.* The measure then, which was seen, pointed to the filling up of the measure of the transgression of the people against Himself." "[12] The angel bids him behold the sins of the people Israel, heaped together in a perfect measure, and the transgression of all fulfilled—that the sins, which escaped notice, one by one, might, when collected together, be laid open to the eyes of all, and Israel might go forth from its place, and it might be shewn to all what she was in her own land." "[13] I think the Lord alluded to the words of the prophet, as though He would say, *Fill up the measure of sins* which your fathers began of old, as it is in Zechariah, i. e. ye will soon fill it; for ye so haste to do evil, that ye will soon fill it to the utmost."

7. *And behold there was lifted up a talent of*

---

[1] Herod. vi. 85, 86.
[2] Lycurgus Or. in Leocr. p. 157 fin.   [3] Lap.
[4] S. Luke xix. 44.   [5] ii. 3 (7 Heb.)   [6] Theod.
[7] Gen. xv. 16.
[8] עַיִן our *look,* as in Lev. xiii. 55. *and the leprosy hath not changed* עֵינוֹ *its look;* Nu. xi. 7, of the manna, *its look* (עֵינוֹ) *was like the look* (כְּעֵין) *of bdellium;* Ezek. x. 9. *the appearance of the wheels was like the look* (כְּעֵין) *of stone of Tarshish.* Add Ez. i. 4, 7, 16, 27, and Dan. x. 6. *like the look* (כְּעֵין) *of polished brass.*

[9] The ם relates to the persons, implied though not expressed in the כָּל הָאָרֶץ, as in Ps. lxv. 10, *thou preparest* דְּגָנָם *their corn;* xxxix. 7, *he heapeth up and knoweth not,* אֹסְפָם, *who gathereth them,* Eccl. v. 17, (18 Eng.) *to see good* (בְּכָל עֲמָלוֹ) *in all his labor;* Ib. vii. 1, *better is the day of death than the day* הִוָּלְדֹו *of his birth;* Hagg. i. 6, lit. *to clothe, yet not for warmth* לוֹ, *to him.* Ew. Lehrb. n. 294. l. p. 754. ed. 8.   [10] S. Cyr.
[11] S. Matt. xxiii. 32.   [12] S. Jer.   [13] Rib.

Before
CHRIST
cir. 519.

and this *is* a woman that sitteth in the midst of the ephah.

8 And he said, This *is* wickedness. And he cast it into the midst of the ephah; and he cast the weight of lead upon the mouth thereof.

9 Then lifted I up mine eyes, and looked, and, behold, there came out two women, and the wind *was* in their wings; for they

had wings like the wings of a stork: and they lifted up the ephah between the earth and the heaven.

10 Then said I to the angel that talked with me, Whither do these bear the ephah?

11 And he said unto me, To ᵉ build it an house in ᶠ the land of Shinar: and it shall be established, and set there upon h e r own base.

Before
CHRIST
cir. 519.

• Jer. 29. 5, 28.

ᶠ Gen. 10. 10.

---

lead, the heaviest Hebrew weight, elsewhere of gold or silver; the golden talent weighing, 1,300,000 grains; the silver, 660,000; here, being lead, it is obviously an undefined mass, though circular [1], corresponding to the Ephah. The Ephah too was the largest Hebrew measure, whose compass cannot now, with certainty, be ascertained [2]. Both probably were, in the vision, ideal. " [3] Holy Scripture calleth the punishment of sin, *lead*, as being by nature heavy. This the divine David teacheth us, [4] *mine iniquities are gone over my head: as an heavy burden, they are too heavy for me.* The divine Zechariah seeth sin under the image of a woman; for most evils are engendered by luxury. But he seeth the punishment, like most heavy lead, lying upon the mouth of iniquity, according to a Psalm, [5] *all iniquity shall stop her mouth.*" " [6] Iniquity, as with a talent of lead, weighs down the conscience."

This is a woman, lit. *one woman*, all sin being concentrated and personified in one, as he goes on to speak of her as *the*, personified, *wickedness* [7]. The *sitting* may represent her abiding tranquil condition in her sins, according to the climax in the first Psalm, [8] *and hath not sat in the seat of the scornful;* and, [9] *thou sittest and speakest against thy brother;* " [10] not standing as by the way, but sitting, as if of set purpose, of wont and habit." " [11] Whoso hath peace in sins is not far from lying down in them, so that, oppressed by a spirit of slumber, he neither sees light, nor feels any blow, but is kept down by the leaden talent of his obduracy."

8. *And cast her into the midst of the Ephah.* As yet then the measure was not full. " [12] She had the lower part within the Ephah, but the upper, especially the head, without. Though the Jews had slain the prophets and done many grievous things, the greatest sin of all remained to be done. But when they had crucified Christ and persecuted the Apostles and the Gospel, the measure was full; she was wholly within the Ephah, no part remained without, so that the measure was filled."

And he cast the weight of lead upon the mouth thereof, i. e. doubtless of the Ephah; as in Genesis [13], *a great stone was on the mouth of the well*, so that there should be no access to it.

9. *There came out two women.* It may be that there may be no symbol herein, but that he names women because it was a woman who was so carried; yet their wings were the wings of an unclean bird, strong, powerful, borne by a force not their own; with their will, since they flew; beyond their will, since the wind was in their wings; rapidly, inexorably, irresistibly, they flew and bore the Ephah between heaven and earth. No earthly power could reach or rescue it. God would not. It may be that evil spirits are symbolized, as being like to this personified human wickedness, such as snatch away the souls of the damned, who, by serving them, have become as they.

11. *To build it an house in the land of Shinar.* The name of Shinar, though strictly Babylonia, carries back to an older power than the world-empire of Babylon; which now too

---

[1] According to its etymology.
[2] It is thought that Josephus (Ant. 15. 9. 2.) put the μεδιμνος by mistake for the μετρητης, which is ³⁄₄ of the μεδιμνος; the μετρητης holding nine of our gallons, the μεδιμνος twelve. The Ephah was probably an Egyptian measure, since the LXX substitute οιφι &c. corresponding to the Egyptian word for "measure," and Ephah has no Semitic etymology.

[3] Theod.   [4] Ps. xxxviii. 4.   [5] Ib. cvii. 42.
[6] S. Ambr. in Ps. 35. n. 9. Opp. i. 769.
[7] הרשעה, ἅπ. with art. as הצדקה absolutely, only in Dan. ix. 7. Thine, O Lord, is הצדקה, העולה does not occur at all.
[8] Ps. i. 1.   [9] Ib. l. 20.   [10] Lap.
[11] Sanct.   [12] Rib.   [13] Gen. xxix. 2.

Before
C H R I S T
cir. 519.

CHAPTER VI.

1 *The vision of the four chariots.*
9 *By the crowns of Joshua is
shewed the temple and kingdom
of Christ the Branch.*

AND I turned, and lifted
up m i n e   e y e s, and
looked, and behold, there
came four c h a r i o t s out
from between two moun-
tains; and the mountains
were mountains of brass.

2 In the first c h a r i o t
were [a] red horses; and in
the second chariot [b] black
horses;

3 And in the third char-
iot [c] white horses; and in
the fourth chariot grisled
and || bay horses.

4 Then I answered [d] and
said unto the angel that
talked with me, What *are*
these, my lord?

Before
C H R I S T
cir. 519.

a ch. 1. 8.
Rev. 6. 4.
b Rev. 6. 5.

c Rev. 6. 2.

|| Or, *strong.*

d ch. 5. 10.

---

was destroyed. *In the land of Shinar* [1] was
that first attempt to array a world-empire
against God, ere mankind was yet dispersed.
And so it is the apter symbol of the antithe-
ist or Anti-Christian world, which by violence, art, falsehood, sophistry, wars against
the truth. To this great world-empire it
was to be removed; yet to live there, no
longer cramped and confined as within an
Ephah, but in pomp and splendor. A house
or temple was to be built for it, for its honor
and glory; as Dagon [2] or Ashtaroth [3], or
Baal [4] had their houses or temples, a great
idol temple, in which the god of this world
should be worshiped.

And it—" the house," *shall be established*
firmly on its base, like the house of God, *and
it,* (wickedness [5]) shall be tranquilly rested on
its base, as an idol in its temple, until the
end come. In the end, the belief of those
of old was, that the Jews would have great
share in the antagonism to Christ and His
empire. At the first, they were the great
enemies of the faith, and sent forth, S. Justin
says [6], those everywhere who should circu-
late the calumnies against Christians, which
were made a ground of early persecutions.
In the end, it was believed, that Anti-Christ
should be from them, that they would receive
him as their Christ, the last fulfillment of
our Lord's words, [7] *I am come in My Father's
name and ye receive Me not; another shall come
in his own name, him ye will receive.*

VI. 1. *Behold, four chariots going forth*
" [8] by the secret disposal of God into the
theatre of the world," *from between two mountains of brass.* Both Jews [9] and Christians
have seen that the four chariots relate to the
same four empires, as the visions in Daniel.

" *The* two mountains." It may be that the
imagery is from the two mountains on either
side of the valley of Jehoshaphat, which Joel
had spoken of as the place of God's judgment [10], and Zechariah afterward [11]. It may
then picture that the judgments go forth
from God. Anyhow the powers, symbolized
by the four chariots, are pictured as closed in
on either side by these mountains, strong as
brass, unsurmountable, undecaying, " [12] that
they should not go forth to other lands to
conquer, until the time should come, fixed by
the counsels of God, when the gates should
be opened for their going forth." The
mountains of brass may signify the height of
the Divine wisdom ordering this, and the
sublimity of the power which putteth them
in operation; as the Psalmist says, [13] *Thy
righteousnesses are like the mountains of God.*

2. 3. The symbol is different from that in
the first vision. There [14], they were horses
only, with their riders, to go to and fro to enquire; here they are war-chariots with their
horses, to execute God's judgments, each in
their turn. In the first vision also, there is
not the characteristic fourfold division, which
reminds of the four world-empires of Daniel [15]; after which, in both prophets, is the
mention of the kingdom of Christ. Even if
the *grisled* horses be the same as the *speckled*
of the first vision, *the black horses* are wanting
there, as well as the succession, in which they
go forth. The only resemblance is, that
there are horses of divers colors, two of
which, red and white, are the same. The
symbol of the fourth empire, *grizzled, strong* [16],
remarkably corresponds with the strength
and mingled character of the fourth empire
in Daniel.

---

[1] Gen. xi. 2.   [2] 1 Sam. v. 2–5.
[3] Ib. xxxi. 10.   [4] 2 Kgs x. 23.
[5] The subjects are marked by the genders; בי״ה
being masc., רשׁעה fem.
[6] S. Just. Dial. n. 17 (n. 91. Oxf. Tr.) and n. 108. p.
205. Eusebius quotes the first passage, H. E. iv. 18,
and repeats the statement on Is. xviii.

[7] S. John v. 43.   [8] Alb.
[9] Saadiah in Kim., Kim., Rashi, the Jews in the
time of S. Jerome. Jon. paraphrases vi. 5, "four
kingdoms."   [10] Jo. iii. 2.   [11] Zech. xiv. 4.
[12] Rib.   [13] Ps. xxxvi. 6.   [14] i. 8.   [15] Dan. ii.
[16] The guess of Abulwalid and Kimchi that אמץ
might be i. q., חמוּץ *bright red,* Is. lxiii. 1, is at

Before
CHRIST
cir. 519.

• Ps. 104. 4.
Heb. 1. 7, 14.
‖ Or, *winds*.

f 1 Kin. 22. 19.
Dan. 7. 10.
ch. 4. 14.
Luke 1. 19.

5 And the angel answered and said unto me, **e** These *are* the four ‖ spirits of the heavens, which go forth from **f** standing before the Lord of all the earth.

6 The black horses which *are* therein go forth into **g** the north country; and **g** the white go forth after them; and the grisled go forth toward the south country.

Before
CHRIST
cir. 519.

g Jer. 1. 14.

---

5. *These are the four spirits of the heavens.* They cannot be literal winds: for spirits, not winds, *stand before God*, as His servants, as in Job, [1] *the sons of God came to present themselves before the Lord.* This they did, "[2] for these four kingdoms did nothing without the will of God." Zechariah sums up in one, what former prophets had said separately of the Assyrian, the Babylonian, Egyptian, Persian. [3] *O Assyria, the rod of Mine anger—I will send him against an ungodly nation, and against the people of My wrath I will give him a charge.* [4] *I will send and take all the families of the north, and Nebuchadrezzar, the king of Babylon, My servant, and will bring them against this land.* [5] *The Lord shall hiss for the fly, that is in the uttermost part of Egypt, and for the bee that is in the land of Assyria, and they shall come, and shall rest, all of them, in the desolate valleys.* [6] *I will call all the families of the kingdoms of the north, saith the Lord; and they shall come, and shall set every one his throne at the entering of the gates of Jerusalem.* Whatever the human impulse or the human means, all *stand before the Lord of the whole earth*, ministering to *His* will Whose are all things, the Judge of all, Who withholdeth the chastisement till the iniquity is full, and then, through man's injustice, executes His own just judgment. "[7] He says that they went forth from where they had stood before the Lord of the whole earth, to shew that their power had been obtained by the counsel of God, that they might serve His will. For no empire was ever set up on earth without the mind, counsel and power of God. He exalts the humble and obscure, He prostrates the lofty, who trust overmuch in them-

variance with the whole use of the Hebrew root, which occurs 40 times in the verb, אָמַץ; 7 times in the adj. אַמִּיץ; and once each in מַאֲמָץ, אֲמָצָה, אַמִּיץ, beside the Proper Names אָמֹץ, Isaiah's father; אֲמִצַי, of two persons, אֲמַצְיָה, of four persons. The Arab. וְמָצַ, which Eichhorn and Henderson compare, is no name of a color, but is used apparently of the "slight summer lightning." The ground with some was, that the word is united with names of colors; with Ewald, to replace the red horses, on which the prophet is silent. See "Daniel the prophet" p. 360. The single case too, in which ח and א are supposed to be interchanged in Heb., is that a Proper Name תַּחְרֵעַ 1 Chr. ix. 41, is written תַּאְרֵעַ Ib. viii. 35, but the pronunciation

selves, arms one against the other, so that no fraud or pride shall be without punishment."

6. *The black horses which are therein go forth.* lit. *That chariot wherein the black horses are, these go forth.* "[2] Most suitably is the first chariot, wherein the red horses were, passed over, and what the second, third, fourth did is described. For when the prophet related this, the Babylonian empire had passed, and the power of the Medes possessed all Asia." Red, as the color of blood, represented Babylon as sanguinary; as it is said in the Revelation, [8] *There went out another horse, red, and power was given to him that sat thereon, to take peace from the earth, and that they should kill one another, and there was given him a sharp sword. The black* were to go forth to the North country, the ancient title of Babylon. For Babylon, though taken, was far from being broken. They had probably been betrayed through the weakness of their kings. Their resistance, in the first carefully prepared [9] revolt against Darius, was more courageous than that against Cyrus: and more desperate [10]. Since probably more Jews remained in it, than returned to their own country, what was to befall it had a special interest for them. They had already been warned in the third vision [11] to escape from it. The color *black* doubtless symbolizes the heavy lot, inflicted by the Medo-Persians; as in the Revelation it is said, [12] *the sun became black as sackcloth of hair;* and to the beast in Daniel's vision which corresponded with it, [13] it was *said, Arise, devour much flesh;* and in the Revelation [14], *he that sat on the black horse* was the angel charged

of Proper Names varies in all languages. See "Daniel the prophet" p. 405. Fürst's instances (Handwört. p. 368) are conjectures of his own. Within Arabic, אַתָּ, i. q., חַתִּי; אֲרֹם i. q., חֹרֹם; אַרֹם i. q., חָרַת; (Eichh. in Ges. Thes. p. 2.) are without authority; אֲבָס is not owned by Lane; else, if it means "imprisoned," it would be a softer pronunciation of חֲבָס in this one sense; אָצָר and נָצַר are perhaps from the same biliteral root.

[1] Job i. 6, ii. 1.   The same idiom הִתְיַצֵּב עַל.
[2] S. Jer.   [3] Is. x. 5.   [4] Jer. xxv. 9.
[5] Is. vii. 18, 19.   [6] Jer. i. 15.   [7] Osor.   [8] Rev. vi. 4.
[9] Herod. iii. 150.
[10] See "Daniel the Prophet," pp. 129, 130. ed. 2.
[11] ii. 7.   [12] Rev. vi. 12.
[13] Dan. vii. 5.   [14] Rev. vi. 5, 6.

Before
CHRIST
cir. 519.

h Gen. 13. 17.
ch. 1. 10.

7 And the bay went forth, and sought to go that they might [h] walk to and fro through the earth: and he said, Get you hence, walk to and fro through the earth. So they walked to and fro through the earth.

8 Then cried he upon me, and spake unto me, saying, Behold, these that

Before
CHRIST
cir. 519.

---

with the infliction of famine. Of the Medes, Isaiah had said[1], *I will stir up the Medes against them* [Babylon], *which shall not regard silver; and gold, they shall not delight in it. Their bows also shall dash the young men to pieces; and they shall have no pity on the fruit of the womb; their eye shall not spare children.*

The white went forth after them: for the Greek empire occupied the same portion of the earth as the Persian. White is a symbol of joy, gladness[2], victory[3], perhaps also, from its relation to light, of acute intelligence. It may relate too to the benevolence of Alexander to the Jewish nation. "[4] Alexander used such clemency to the conquered, that it seemed as though he might be called rather the founder than the destroyer of the nations whom he subdued."

And the grizzled, the Romans in their mingled character, so prominent in the fourth empire of Daniel[5], *go forth* to the south country, i. e. Egypt; as Daniel speaks of [6] *the ships of Chittim* and the intervention of the Romans first in regard to the expulsion of Antiochus Epiphanes from Egypt; in Egypt also, the last enduring kingdom of any successor of Alexander, that of the Ptolemies, expired. "30 years afterward, the Son of God was to bring light to the earth. The prophet so interweaves the prediction, that from the series of the four kingdoms it is brought to the Birth of the Eternal King[7]."

7. *And the strong went forth and sought to go, that they might walk to and fro through the earth.* The mention of their strength corresponds to the extent of the power and commission, for which they asked, to *go to and fro,* up and down, at their will, unhindered, through the whole earth. The Babylonian empire held Egypt only out of Asia; the Persian was conquered in its efforts against Europe, in Greece; Alexander's was like a meteor, gleaming but breaking into the four:

the Roman combined East and West and within large limits tranquilly.

And he said go, walk to and fro in the earth. He commanded, and they, which were before withheld, went, *and they walked to and fro* [8] *on the earth,* ordering all things at their will, under the Providence of God, whereby He gave free access to the Gospel in all their wide empire. The Greek empire being extinguished, the Romans no longer went into any given country, but superintended and governed all human things in (it is the language of the New Testament) *all the world.* "[9] These same, the dappled and ashen grey horses were commanded to traverse the earth, and they did traverse it; for they mastered all under heaven, and ruled the whole earth, God consenting and arraying those who swayed the Roman might with this brilliant glory. For, as God, He knew beforehand the greatness of their future piety."

8. *Then* God, or *the Angel of the Lord,* who speaks of what belonged to God alone, *called me* (probably "loudly [10]"), so as to command his attention to this which most immediately concerned his people.

These have quieted My spirit in the North country, or rather, *have made My anger to rest* [11] *on,* i. e. have carried it thither and deposited it there, made it to rest upon them, as its abode, as S. John saith of the unbelieving, [12] *The wrath of God abideth on him.* Babylon had been the final antagonist and subduer of the people of God. It had at the outset destroyed the temple of God, and carried off its vessels to adorn idol-temples. Its empire closed on that night when it triumphed over God [13], using the vessels dedicated to Him, to the glorifying of their idols. *In that night was Belshazzar the king of the Chaldæans slain.* This final execution of God's anger upon that their destroyer was the earnest of the rest to *them;* and in this the visions pause.

[1] Is. xiii. 17, 18.   [2] Eccl. ix. 8.   [3] Rev. vi. 2.
[4] See note 16, p. 369. [5] Dan. ii. 41–43. [6] Ib. xi. 30.
[7] Osor. See "Daniel the Prophet," pp. 142–150.

[8] The fem. תַהְלַכְנָה may have been occasioned by the symbol מֶרְכָּבוֹת v. 1, or the explanation רוּחוֹת, v. 5; but since their going was consequent on the permission to go, which they asked and obtained, it must relate to the empire symbolized by the 4th chariot, not (as some) to all.   [9] S. Cyr.
[10] הֹזְעִיק, with acc. p. is used elsewhere of calling together people. Jud. iv. 10, 13, 2 Sam. xx. 4, 5.

[11] הֲנִיחוֹתִי הַנִיחַ אֶת רוּחִי, with בְ, as Ez. v. 13. הֵנִיחוֹתִי
בְּכַלּוֹתִי חֲמָתִי בָם, followed by חֲמָתִי בָם Ib. xxiv. 13: *thou shalt not be cleansed any more, until I have made my anger to rest upon thee.* The idiom, "to cause to rest upon" a person, involves that that person is the object, on whom it abides; not that anger or spirit was quieted in him whose it was, (as Kim.). רוּחַ is "anger," Jud. viii. 3, Eccl. x. 4.
[12] S. John iii. 36.
[13] Dan. v. See in Daniel the Prophet pp. 450–453.

Before
CHRIST
cir. 519.

Judg. 8. 3.
Eccles. 10. 4.

go toward the north coun-
try have quieted my [i]spirit
in the north country.

9 ¶ And the word of
the LORD came unto me,
saying,

10 Take of *them of* the

captivity, *even* of Heldai,
of Tobijah, and of Jeda-
iah, which are come from
Babylon, and come thou
the same day, and go into
the house of Josiah the
son of Zephaniah ;

Before
CHRIST
cir. 519.

---

9. *And the word of the Lord came to me.* The
visions being closed, Zechariah marks the
change by adopting the usual formula, with
which the prophets authenticated, that they
spake not of themselves, but by the Spirit of
God. The act enjoined is a symbolic act,
pointing and summing up and interpreting
the visions, as some of the visions had been
already expanded by fresh revelations following immediately upon them.

10. *Take of the captivity*, of that which they
had brought with them [1]. *The captivity* was,
in Jeremiah [2], and Ezekiel [3], the title of those
who had been actually carried captive and
were at that moment in captivity. Ezra continues it of those who had been in captivity,
though now returned from exile. Yet not
without a reference to the circumstances or
causes of that captivity. It is *the captivity* [4]
which Sheshbazzar brings from Babylon, or
Ezra subsequently [5]; the *children of the captivity*, who set themselves to build the temple
of God [6]; who dedicated it and kept the
passover [7]. The title is used apparently as
an aggravation of sin, like that which had
been chastened by that captivity [8]. Here,
the term seems to imply some blame, that
they remained of their own accord in this
state of severance from the altar, where alone
special worship of God and sacrifice could be
offered. They had been removed against
their will; yet, as Christians often do, acquiesced in the loss, rather than forego their
temporal advantages. Still they wished to

take part in the work of restoring the public
worship, and so sent these men, with their
contribution of gold and silver, to their brethren, who had returned ; as, in the first times
of the Gospel, the Christians everywhere
made collections for the poor saints, who
dwelt in Jerusalem. And this their imperfect zeal was instantly accepted.

And go thyself, to make the act more impressive, *on that same day*, as matter of urgency,
*and thou shalt come to the house of Josiah son of
Zephaniah, whither they have come from Babylon* [9]. The exiles who had brought presents
for the building of the temple, lodged, it
seems, in the house of Josiah, whether they
doubted or no that their presents would be
accepted, since they chose Babylon, not Jerusalem for their abode. This acceptance of
their gifts symbolized the incoming of those
from afar. It is remarkable that all five
names express a relation to God. *Tobiah*,
" [10] The Lord is my good ;" *Yedaiah*, " God
knoweth " or " careth for ;" *Josiah*, " The
Lord supporteth [11] ;" *Zephaniah*, " The Lord
hideth," and perhaps *Cheldai*, " The Lord's
world [12]." They had taken religious instead
of worldly names. Probably Zechariah was
first to accept the offerings from the three
exiles, and then to take the actual gold from
the house of Josiah whither they had brought
it. The pilgrims from Babylon and their
host are included in one common blessing.

And make crowns ; or *a crown* [13], as in Job,
[14] *I would bind it as a crown unto me*, and our

---

[1] לָקַח מֵאֵת, as Ex. xxv. 2, xxx. 16, xxxv. 5, Lev.
vii. 34.

[2] Jer. xxviii. 6, xxix. 1, 4, 20, 31. (גָּלוּת) Ib. xxiv. 5,
xxviii. 4, xxix. 22, xl. 1.)

[3] Ezek. i. 2, iii. 11, 15, xi. 24, 25. [4] Ezr. i. 11.

[5] Ib. viii. 35.   [6] Ib. iv. 1.

[7] *the children of the captivity* Ib. vi. 16. Ch. 19, 20.

[8] הַגּוֹלָה Ib. ix. 4, x. 6, בְּנֵי הַגּוֹלָה Ib. x. 7. 16,
קְהַל הַגּוֹלָה Ib. 8.

[9] As in 1 Kgs xii. 2, אֲשֶׁר בָּרַח *whither he had
fled* ; add Gen. xlv. 25, for the like accus. of place.
Kim. renders, " who have come from Babylon"
expressly including Josiah. Yet this too is an
impossible construction.

[10] טוֹבִיָּהוּ. Tobias happens only to occur after
the exile, in Ezr. ii. 60, Neh. vii. 62; 2) in Neh. ii.
10, vi. 1 ; 3) the Tobiah here and 14; 4) Tobit and
Tobias in his book.

[11] Josiah only occurs beside, as the name of the
well-known king.

[12] חֶלְדִּי. The name is preserved, though obelised,
in the LXX. Ἐλδαΐ, Ελδαΐ ; not from Aq. who has
Ὀλδὰ. Jon. retains the name ; the Syr. and S. Jer.
Holdai (the Syr. in v. 14. also.) The LXX only
παρὰ τῶν ἀρχόντων.

[13] " great crown," Jon.; " a crown," Syr.

[14] עֲטָרוֹת Job xxxi. 36. The plural form is used
only in these two places, and as, or in, the Proper
Name of four towns ; 1) עֲטָרוֹת a town of the
Gadites, Nu. xxxii. 3, 34; 2) of Ephraim, Josh. xvi.
27, also עֲטָרוֹת אַדָּר " crown of Addar," Ib. xvi. 5,
xviii. 13 ; 3) of Judah בֵּית יוֹאָב עֲטָרוֹת (" crown
of the house of Joab ") 1 Chr. ii. 54; and 4) and of
Gad, שׁוֹפָן עֲטָרוֹת, (mentioned with Ataroth) Nu.
xxxii. 35. In all these it must needs be singular.

Before
CHRIST
cir. 519.

k Ex. 28. 36.
& 29. 6.
Lev. 8. 9. ch. 3. 5.

11 Then take silver and gold, and make [k] crowns, and set *them* upon the head of Joshua the son of Josedech the high priest;

Before
CHRIST
cir. 519.

Lord is seen in the Revelation, [1] *on His Head were many crowns.* The singular is used of [2] *a royal crown,* apparently of a festive crown [3]; and figuratively [4]; even of Almighty God Himself as a crown [5]; but no where of the mitre of the high-priest.

The characteristic of the act is, that *the crown* or crowns (it is not in the context said, which) were placed on the head of the one high priest, Joshua; *and thou shall place [it or them,* it is not said which] *upon the head of Joshua son of Josedech the high-priest, and shalt say unto him.* If crowns were made of each material, there were two crowns. But this is not said, and the silver might have formed a circlet in the crown of gold, as, in modern times, the iron crown of Lombardy, is called iron, because it had " [6] a plate of iron in its summit, being else of gold and most precious." In any case the symbolical act was completed by the placing of a royal crown upon the head of the high-priest. This, in itself, represented that He, Whom he and all other priests represented, would be also our King. It is all one then, whether the word designate one single crown, so entitled for its greatness, or one united royal crown, i. e., one crown uniting many crowns, symbolizing the many kingdoms of the earth, over which our High Priest and King should rule. Either symbol, of separate crowns [7], or an united crown [8], has been used in the same meaning, to symbolize as many empires, as there were crowns.

On Zerubbabel no crown was placed. It would have been confusing; a seeming restoration of the kingdom, when it was not to be restored; an encouragement of the temporal hopes, which were the bane of Israel. God had foretold, that none of the race of Jehoiakim should prosper, *sitting on the throne of David, or ruling any more in Israel.* Nehemiah rejects the imputation of Sanballat [9], *Thou hast also appointed prophets to preach of thee at Jerusalem,* There is *a king in Judah.* He answers, *There are no such things done as thou sayest; and thou feignest them out of thine own heart.* But Isaiah had foretold much of the king who should reign : Zechariah, by placing the royal crown on the head of Joshua, foreshewed that the kingdom was not to be of this world. The royal crown had been taken away in the time of Zedekiah, [10] *Thus saith the Lord God, Remove the diadem and take away the crown; this shall not be this; exalt the low and abase the high; an overthrow, overthrow, overthrow will I make it; this too is not; until he come whose the right is, and I will give it.*

But the Messiah, it was foretold, was to be both priest and king; [11] *a priest after the order of Melchizedec,* and *a king, set* by the Lord [12] *upon His holy hill of Zion.* The act of placing the crown on the head of Joshua the high-priest, pictured not only the union of the offices of priest and king in the person of Christ, but that He should be King, being first our High Priest. Joshua was already High Priest; being such, the kingly crown was added to him. It says in act, what S. Paul says, that [13] *Christ Jesus, being found in fashion as a man, humbled Himself and became*

---

[1] Rev. xix. 12.   In Rev. xii. 3, the 7 crowns are for the 7 heads of the dragon. קְשָׁרִים is used of the one girdle, Jer. ii. 32.

[2] עֲטֶרֶת מַלְכֻם 2 Sam. xii. 30, 1 Chr. xx. 2; also of a king, Ps. xxi. 4, Cant. iii. 11, Jer. xiii. 18; perhaps Esther viii. 15, (coll. vi. 8.) possibly Ezek. xvi. 12, (coll. 13); fig., parallel with מְלוּכָה צְנוּף Is. lxii. 3; comp. also צוּר מְעַטִּירָה *Tyre the crowning* i. e., the kingmaker, in her colonies, Is. xxiii. 8.

[3] Is. xxviii. 1, 3, Lam. v. 16; of festive array, Ez. xxiii. 42

[4] Job xix. 9. [plur. Ib. xxxi. 36] Pr. iv. 9, xii. 4, xiv. 24, xvi. 31. xvii. 6.

[5] Is. xxviii. 5. is contrasted with "the crown of pride" Ib. 1, 3. [all]

[6] Ceremoniale Rom. L. 1. sect. 5. in Du Cange Glossar. v. Corona Ferrea.

[7] Ptolemy Philadelphus "set two crowns upon his head," the crown of Asia and of Egypt (1 Macc. xi. 13); Artabanus, "in whom the kingdom of Parthia ended," used two diadems (Herodian Hist. vi. 2. p. 119 Bekk.); "the Emperor of Germany received three crowns: first, silver (at Aix) for Germany; one of iron at Monza in the Milanese or Milan (for Lombardy); that of gold in divers places," (Alber. Index

v. *Corona* in Du Cange v. Corona Imperialis) "the golden at Rome." Du Cang. Otto of Frisingen said that Frederic received 5 crowns; the first at Aix for the kingdom of the Franks; a second at Ratisbon for that of Germany; a third at Pavia for the kingdom of Lombardy; the fourth at Rome for the Roman empire from Adrian iv; the fifth of Monza for the kingdom of Italy." In our own memory, Napoleon I. having been crowned in France, was crowned with the iron crown at Monza.

[8] "The headdress of the king, on state occasions, was the crown of the upper or of the lower country, or the *pshent,* the union of the two. Every king, after the sovereignty of the Thebaid and lower Egypt had become once more vested in the same person, put on this double crown at his coronation, and we find in the grand representation given of this ceremony at Medeenet Haboo that the principal feature of the proclamation, on his ascension to the throne, was the announcement that Remeses had put on the crown of the upper and lower country.—When crowned, the king invariably put on the two crowns at the same time, though on other occasions he was permitted to wear each separately, whether in the temple, the city, or the field of battle." Wilkinson's Ancient Egypt, iii. 351-353.

[9] Neh. vi. 6-8.   [10] Ezek. xxi. 31, 32 [26, 27, Eng.]
[11] Ps. cx. 4.   [12] Ib. ii. 6.   [13] Phil. ii. 8, 9.

Before CHRIST cir. 519.	

12 And speak unto him, saying, Thus speaketh the LORD of hosts, saying, Behold [1]the man whose name *is* The [m]BRANCH; and

Before CHRIST cir. 519.

[1]See Luke 1. 73.
John 1. 45.
[m] ch. 3. 8.

he shall ||grow up out of his place, [n]and he shall build the temple of the LORD:

13 Even he shall build

Before CHRIST cir. 519.
|| Or, *branch up from under him.*
[n] ch. 4. 9. Matt. 16. 18. Eph. 2. 20, 21, 22. Heb. 3. 3.

---

obedient unto death, even the death of the Cross. Wherefore God also hath highly exalted Him.

12. The Prophet is taught to explain his own symbolic act. *Behold the Man whose name is the Branch* [1]. "Not for himself, but for Christ, Whose name Joshua bare, and Whose Priesthood and Princedom he represented," was the crown given him. The Prophet had already foretold the Messiah, under the name of the Branch. Here he adds,

And he shall grow up out of His place [2], lowly and of no seeming account, as God foretold by Jeremiah, [3]*I will cause the Branch of righteousness to grow up unto David;* and Jesus Himself said, [4]*Except a grain of wheat fall into the earth and die, it abideth alone; but if it die, it bringeth forth much fruit.* Alone He grew up before God, as a tender plant [5], unknown of man, known to God. It is that still, Divine life at Nazareth, of which we see only that one bright flash in the temple, the deep saying, ununderstood even by Joseph and Mary, and then, [6]*He went down with them and came to Nazareth and was subject unto them.*

And he shall build the temple of the Lord. The material temple was soon to be finished, and that by Zerubbabel, to whom this

had been promised [7], not by Joshua. It was then a new temple, to be built from the foundation, of which He Himself was to be *the foundation* [8], as He said, [9]*On this rock I will build My Church;* and *in* Him [10] *all the building, fitly framed together, groweth unto an holy temple to the Lord.* "[11]He it is, Who built the house; for neither Solomon nor Zerubbabel nor Joshua son of Josedech could build a house worthy of the majesty of God. For [12]*the most High,* S. Stephen says, *dwelleth not in temples made with hands, as saith the prophet; Heaven is My throne and earth is My footstool; what house will ye build Me, saith the Lord?* For if they could have built a house for God, He would not have allowed His house to be burned and overthrown. What then is the house of God which Christ built? The Church, founded on faith in Him, dedicated by His Blood, stablished by the stayedness of Divine virtue, adorned with Divine and eternal riches, wherein the Lord ever dwelleth."

13. *Even He,* lit. *He Himself* [13]. The repetition shews that it is a great thing, which he affirms; *and He,* again emphatic, *He,* the same who shall build the temple of the Lord, *He shall bear the glory.* Great must be the

---

[1] The consent of the ancient Jews in interpreting "the Branch" of the Messiah is very remarkable. "R. Berachiah (about A. D. 200, Wolf. Bibl. Hebr. ii. 870) said, that 'God, blessed for ever, saith to Israel, Ye say before Me, we are become orphans and have no father; the Redeemer too, Whom I am about to make to stand before you, He shall have no father, as is said, Behold the Man Whose name is the Branch, and he shall shoot [lit. from below him] from his place; and so saith Isaiah, And He grew up like a sucker before him.'" (Bereshith Rabba on Gen. xxxvi. 22. in Martini Pug. Fid. f. 594 quoted also by a Jewish convert, Joshua Hallorki, known among us as Hieron. de S. Fide, c. Jud. i. 5. Bibl. Max. Patr. xxvi. 536. His quotation is independent of Martini, since he adds the quotation from Ps. ii. "and elsewhere, 'The Lord said unto me, Thou art my Son,'") Jon. paraphrases, "Behold a Man, Whose name is Messiah, Who shall be revealed, and shall be multiplied," (ויתרב, by which צמח is rendered Ps. lxxxv. 12.) "and *he* shall build the temple of the Lord, and *he* shall bear glory, and he shall sit and shall rule on his throne, and he shall be a great priest on his throne, and counsel of peace there shall be between them both." Rashi says, "He hints at the Messiah, and so paraphrases Jonathan, Behold a Man Whose name is Messiah, &c." (in Mart. p. 376. The printed edit. substitute "And some interpret it of king Messiah.") R. Nachman observes on the force of the word man, "Man (in Nu. i. 4.) is not said here but of the Messiah the Son of David, as is said, 'Behold the Man, Whose name is the Branch,' Jonathan paraphrases The Man Messiah, and so it is said, 'a man of sorrows and acquainted with grief.'" (Mart. p. 664). The Echa Rabati, f.

59, 2. and Jerus. Bereshith f. 5, 1. quote R. Joshua B. Levi (end of 2d cent., Wolf. B. H. ii. 842, coll. pp. 834, 841) as alleging this place in proof that "Branch is a name of the Messiah." Schöttgen [ad loc.]. Schöttgen quotes also the Pirke Elieser c. 38, "God will free Israel at the end of the 4th kingdom, saying, I have put forth a germ unto you, Behold my servant the Branch." Bammidbar R. sect. 18 f. 236, 1, Tanchuma f. 68, 3. "Behold the Man, whose name is the Branch. This is the Messiah, of Whom it is said (Jer. xxiii. 5.) And I will raise up unto David a righteous Branch." Midrash Mishle xix. 21 f. 57, 1. quotes, "R. Huna (3d cent.) said, The name of Messiah is Branch, as in, 'Behold a man.'" Ib. After all this Kimchi says, "*Some* interpret it of king Messiah."

[2]צמחתי as Ex. x. 23, "neither rose any from his place," מתחתיו.

[3] Jer. xxxiii. 15. This is the natural construction, 1) צמח being the common word for the shooting of plants, (Gen. ii. 5, xli. 6, 23, Is. xliv. 4, Ez. xvii. 6,) the name of "the branch," having preceded, is the idiomatic subject to צמח; 2) the impers. would have been plural, since the meaning would have been plural, *they* i. e. many, *shall grow up,* 3) it is unnatural to assume an impersonal, since a subject has been mentioned in the preceding clause to which it is united by 1; and 4) it is followed by a personal verb, with that same subject for its subject.

[4] S. John xii. 24.
[5] Is. liii. 2.
[6] See S. Luke ii. 49–51.
[7] iv. 10.
[8] Is. xxviii. 16, 1 Cor. iii. 11, Eph. ii. 20, 21.
[9] S. Matt. xvi. 18.
[10] Eph. ii. 21.
[11] Osor.
[12] Acts vii. 48, 49.
[13] הוא emph.

Before
C H R I S T
cir. 519.

o Isai. 22. 24.

the temple of the LORD;
and he °shall bear the
glory, and shall sit and
rule upon his throne; and

P he shall be a priest upon
his throne: and the coun-
sel of peace shall be-
tween them both.

Before
C H R I S T
cir. 519.

p Ps. 110. 4.
Heb. 3. 1.

glory, since it is affirmed of Him as of none
beside, "*He* shall bear glory," "*He* should
build the temple of the Lord," as none
beside ever built it; *He* should *bear glory,* as
none beside ever bare it, [1] *the glory as of the
Only Begotten of the Father, full of grace and
truth.* This word *glory* is almost always used
of the special glory of God [2], and then,
although seldom, of the Majesty of those, on
whom God confers majesty as His representatives, as Moses, or Joshua [3], or *the glory of
the kingdom* given to Solomon [4]. It is used
also of Him, a likeness of Whom these vice-
gerents of God bare, in a Psalm whose language belongs (as Jews too have seen,) to
One more than man [5], although also of glory
given by God, either of grace or nature [6].
So in our Lord's great High Priest's prayer
He says, [7] *Father, glorify Thou Me with Thine
ownself with the glory which I had with Thee
before the world was;* and prays, [8] *that they
also whom Thou hast given Me, be with Me,
where I am; that they may behold My glory
which Thou hast given Me.* So S. Paul, applying the words of the eighth Psalm, says of
our Lord, [9] *We see Jesus, Who was made a
little lower than the angels, crowned with glory
and honor;* and the angels and saints round
the Throne say, [10] *Worthy is the Lamb which
was slain to receive power and wisdom and
strength and honor and glory and blessing,* and
those on earth answer, *Blessing and honor and
glory and power be unto Him that sitteth upon
the Throne and unto the Lamb for ever and ever.*
That glory Isaiah saw [11]; in His miracles He
manifested forth His glory [12], which resided in
Him; in His Transfiguration, the three
Apostles *saw His glory* [13], shining out from
within Him; *into* this *His glory* [14], He told
the disciples at Emmaus, the *prophets* said,
that He was *to enter,* having first suffered
what He suffered; *in* this *His glory* He is to
sit, when He judges [15]. *And He shall sit and
rule on His Throne.* His rule shall be, not
passing but abiding, not by human might,
but in peaceful majesty, as God says, [16] *Yet
have I set My king upon My holy hill of Zion,*
and again, [17] *Sit Thou on My Right Hand,
until I make Thine enemies Thy footstool;* and

the angel said to Mary, [18] *The Lord God shall
give unto Him the throne of His father David,
and He shall reign over the house of Jacob for
ever, and of His kingdom there shall be no
end.*
And He shall be a priest upon His Throne.
He shall be at once king and priest, as it is
said, *Thou art a priest for ever after the order of
Melchizedec.* When the Christ should reign,
He should not cease to be our Priest. He,
having *all power given to Him in heaven and
earth,* reigneth over His Church and His
elect by His grace, and over the world by
His power, yet *ever liveth to make intercession
for us.* "[19] Not dwelling now on what is
chiefest, that [20] *by Him were all things created,
that are in heaven and that are in earth, visible
and invisible, whether they be thrones or dominions or principalities or powers; all things were
created by Him and for Him, and He is before
all things, and by Him all things consist,* how
many crowns of glory belong to Him, One
and the Same, God and man, Christ Jesus!
He then *will bear glory and will sit upon His
throne and shall be a priest on His throne.* How
just this is, it is easier to think than to express, that *He should sit and rule all things,* by
Whom all things were made, and He should be
a *Priest for ever,* by Whose Blood all things
are reconciled. *He shall rule* then *upon His
throne,* and *He shall be a priest upon His
throne,* which cannot be said of any of the
saints, because it is the right of none of them,
to call the throne of his rule or of his priesthood his own, but of this Only Lord and
Priest, Whose majesty and throne are one
and the same with the Majesty of God, as He
saith, [21] *When the Son of Man shall come in His
Majesty* [Glory], *then shall He sit upon the
throne of His Majesty* [Glory]. And what
meaneth that re-duplication, *and He shall
rule on His Throne,* but that One and the
Same, of Whom all this is said, should be
and is King and Priest. He Who is King
shall rule on His Throne, because kingdom
and priesthood shall meet in One Person,
and One shall occupy the double throne of
kingdom and priesthood." He Alone should
be our King; He Alone our Saviour: He

---

1 S. John i. 14.
2 הוד והדר Ps. xcvi. 6, (1 Chr. xvi. 27.) civ. 1, cxi.
3, Job xl. 10. of Christ, Ps. xlv. 4; הדר כבוד הדרך
Ps. cxlv. 5; הוד alone, Job xxxvii. 22, Is. xxx. 30, 1
Chr. xxix. 11, Ps. viii. 2, cxlviii. 13, Hab. iii. 3.
3 Nu. xxvii. 20.   4 1 Chr. xxix. 25.
5 Ps. xxi. 6. See in Schöttgen de Messia ad loc.
6 It is used of the inward glory given to regenerate Israel, Hos. xiv. 7. (6 Eng.); or as glorified by

God, Zech. x. 3; of kingly glory, Jer. xxii. 18, Dan.
xi. 21; of the inward glory of man, as such, Dan. x.
8, Pr. v. 9, or even of the horse, as the creation of
God, Job xxxix. 20 [all].   7 S. John xvii. 5.
8 Ib. 24.   9 Heb. ii. 9.   10 Rev. v. 12, 13.
11 S. John xii. 41.   12 Ib. ii. 11.   13 S. Luke ix. 32.
14 Ib. xxiv. 26; add 1 S. Pet. i. 11, 12.
15 S. Matt. xix. 28, S. Luke ix. 26.   16 Ps. ii. 6.
17 Ib. cx. 1.   18 S. Luke i. 32, 33.   19 Rup.
20 Col. i. 16, 17.   21 S. Matt. xxv. 31.

Before CHRIST cir. 519.

14 And the crowns shall be to Helem, and to Tobijah, and to Jedaiah, and

to Hen the son of Zephaniah, q for a memorial in the temple of the LORD.

Before CHRIST cir. 519.

q Ex. 12. 14.
Mark 14. 9.

Alone the Object of our love, obedience and adoration.

And the counsel of peace shall be between them both. The *counsel of peace* is not merely *peace,* as S. Jerome seems to interpret : " He is both king and priest, and shall sit both on the royal and sacerdotal throne, and there shall be peaceful counsel between both, so that neither should the royal eminence depress the dignity of the priesthood, nor the dignity of the priesthood, the royal eminency, but both should be consistent in the glory of the One Lord Jesus." For had this been all, the simple idiom, *there shall be peace between them,* would have been used here, as elsewhere [1]. But *counsel of peace,* must, according to the like idioms[2], signify "a *counsel* devising or procuring *peace*" for some other than those who counsel thereon. We have the idiom itself, *counsellors of peace*[3].

They twain might be said of things[4] : but things are naturally not said to *counsel,* so that the meaning should be, that the thrones of the priests and of the Branch should counsel. For the throne is in each case merely subordinate. It is not as we might say, "the See of Rome," or "of Constantinople," or "of Canterbury," meaning the successive Bishops. It is simply the material throne, on which He sits. Nor is anything said of any throne of a priest, nor had a priest any throne. His office was *to stand before the Lord*[5], his intercessorial office to [6] *offer gifts and sacrifices for sin.* To [7] *offer up sacrifice, first for his own sins and then for the people's,* was his special office and honor. There are then not two thrones. One sits on His Throne, as King and Priest. It seems only to remain, that the *counsel of peace* should be between Jesus and the Father; as S. Jerome says, "I read in the book of some, that this, *there shall be a peaceful counsel be-*

tween the two, is referred to the Father and the Son, because He [8] *came to do not His own will, but the Will of the Father,* and [9] *the Father is in the Son, and the Son in the Father.*" In Christ all is perfect harmony. There is a counsel of peace between Him and the Father Whose temple He builds. The Will of the Father and the Son is one. Both had one Will of love toward us, the salvation of the world, bringing forth peace through our redemption. God the Father [10] *so loved the world, that He gave His Only-Begotten Son, that whosoever believeth in Him should not perish but have everlasting life ;* and God the Son [11] *is our peace, Who hath made both one, that He might reconcile both unto God in one body by the Cross, and came and preached peace to them which were afar off and to them that were nigh.* Others seem to me less naturally to interpret it of Christ in His two offices. " [12] There shall be the counsel of peace between them, the ruler and the priest, not that Christ is divided, but that those two princedoms, which were hitherto divided, (the priest and the king being different persons) should be united in the One Christ. *Between these two* princedoms, being inseparably joined in one, shall be the *counsel of peace,* because through that union we have peace ; and through Him [13] *it pleased the* Father to *reconcile all things unto Himself, and that all things should be brought to* peace *through the Blood of His cross, whether things in earth or things in heaven.*"

14. *And the crowns shall be to Helem.* There is no ground apparent to us, why the name *Helem* appears instead of *Holdai*[14], or *Hen* for *Josiah:* yet the same person must have been called both Hen *and* Josiah, since the father's name is the same in both places. They cannot both be intended as explanations of the former names, since *Helem* stands insulated in Hebrew, its meaning conjectural[15].

---

[1] Jud. iv. 17, 1 Sam. vii. 14, 1 Kgs v. 16 (12 Eng.).
[2] The verbal noun retaining the active force of the verb, as היוֹעֲצִים עֲצַת רָע Ez. xi. 2. as in the verb הוּא זִמּוֹת יָעָץ Is. יָעַץ בֹּשֶׁת לְבֵיתֶךָ Hab. ii. 10; xxxii. 7 ; נְדִיב נְדִיבוֹת יָעָץ, Ib. 8.
[3] Pr. xii. 20.
[4] שְׁנֵיהֶם is used of things, throughout Nu. vii. of the offerings of the princes of the 12 tribes; also Ex. xxvi. 24, xxxvi. 29, De. xxiii. 19, Pr. xx. 10, xxvii. 3, Eccl. xi. 6: but not with any verb implying action.
[5] See ab p. 353, note 12.   [6] Heb. v. 1, ix. 9.
[7] Ib. vii. 27.   [8] S. John v. 30, vi. 38.
[9] Ib. xiv. 10.   [10] Ib. iii. 16.   [11] Eph. ii. 14, 16, 17.
[12] Rup.   [13] Col. i. 19, 20.
[14] All MSS. and the Versions (except the Syr. which repeats here the names of v. 10) have or imply the names *Helem* and *Hen.* Aq. and Jon. have the names *Helem* here; Symm. translated it as

Holem, τῷ ὁρῶντι ἐνύπνια. The LXX render the names common to both verses by the same words, (τῶν χρησίμων αὐτῆς, τῶν ἐπεγνωκότων αὐτήν) but use different words for *Holdai* and *Helem;* for *Holdai* (v. 10) ἀρχόντων ; for *Helem,* τοῖς ὑπομένουσι, as if יחילים. (The Prop. Name יְחַלְאֵל is, in Gen. xlvi. 14, the third son of Zabulon, the patronymic יַחְלְאֵלִי, Nu. xxvi. 26, and the adj. יָחִיל Lam. iii. 26). The Jews in S. Jerome's time identified the three with Ananias Azarias and Misael, and *Hen,* "grace" with Daniel.

[15] In Syr. the central meaning of חלד seems to be "crept," hence used of a "cancer" or a "mole." Neither חלדי nor חלם signify "strong." חלד is rather used of "the world" as "fleeting." חלד Arab. is perhaps originally "lingered," hence was "slow in becoming grey," "lingered," abode in a place ever, "everlastingly," in heaven or hell. It is

Before
CHRIST
cir. 519.

r Isai. 57. 19.
& 60. 10.
Eph. 2. 13, 19.
s ch. 2. 9.
& 4. 9.

15 And *they *that are* far off shall come and build in the temple of the LORD, and *ye shall know that the LORD of hosts

hath sent me unto you. And *this* shall come to pass, if ye will diligently obey the voice of the LORD your God.

Before
CHRIST
cir. 519.

Perhaps then they were the own names of the individuals, and the names compounded with the name of *God*, honorable names which they had taken.

For a memorial in the temple of the Lord. They brought a passing gift, but it should be for a lasting memorial in their behalf. It is a renewal of the well-known term of the law[1]. The *two stones*, engraven with the names of the children of Israel, *upon the shoulders of the Ephod*, were to the end, that *Aaron should bear their names before the Lord upon his two shoulders for a memorial*[2]; *continually*, it is added of the *breastplate with its twelve precious stones*[3]; *the atonement money of the children of Israel* was to be *appointed for the service of the tabernacle of the congregation, that it may be a memorial for the children of Israel before the Lord, to make atonement for their souls*[4]; *to make an atonement for their souls before the Lord.* They were to *blow with the trumpets over their burnt-offerings, and over the sacrifice of their peace-offerings, that they may be to you for a memorial before your God*[5]. When Midian had been smitten before Israel, and not one of Israel had been slain, they brought all the gold which had accrued to them, and *Moses and Eleazar took the gold, and brought it into the tabernacle, a memorial for the children of Israel before the Lord*[6]. So the angel said to Cornelius, [7] *thy prayers and thy alms are come up for a memorial before God.* "[8] This is what we look for, that to all the saints and friends of God, whom these signify, those crowns which they made of their gold and silver for the Lord Jesus, shall be an everlasting memorial in that heavenly temple of the Lord." The tradition of the Jews, that this was literally observed[9], can hardly be without foundation. "[10] These their offerings shall be for grace to those who dedicated them and an occasion of doxology. For the piety of princes becomes to the rest a path to the love of God. But when Christ is crowned by us, then shall also the multitude of the Gentiles haste to the knowledge of Him."

And they who are far off shall come. They who came from Babylon with offerings to God, became types of the Gentiles, of whom the Apostle says, [11] *Now in Christ Jesus ye who sometimes were far off have become nigh through the blood of Christ;* and, [12] *He came and preached peace to you which were far off and to them that were nigh;* and [13] *the promise is to you and to your children, and to all that are far off, as many as the Lord our God shall call.*

And build in, or *upon, the temple of the Lord*[14], not "build in" for it was to be built by the *Branch*, but *build on*, labor on, it. It was a building, which should continually be enlarged; of which S. Paul says, [15] *I, as a wise master-builder, according to the grace given unto me, laid the foundation, and another buildeth thereon; let every man take heed how he buildeth thereupon.* "[16] What shall they build? Themselves, compacting themselves with the saints, and joining together in faith to oneness with those of Israel, Jesus Christ Himself being the head corner-stone and uniting together in harmony through Himself, what was of old divided. For He united [17] *the two peoples into one new man, making peace, and reconciling in His own Body all things unto the Father*, which being accomplished, we shall own the truth of the holy prophets, and know clearly that it was God Who spake in them and declared to us beforehand the mystery of Christ."

15. *And this shall be ;* not as though the coming of Christ depended upon their faithfulness, but their share in it. *Ye shall know* (he had said) *that the Lord of hosts hath sent me unto you ;* but whether this knowledge should reach to individuals, depends upon their obedience and their willingness to know ; *it shall be,* [18] *if ye will diligently obey the voice of the Lord your God.* For *none of the wicked,* Daniel says [19], *shall understand ;* and Hosea, [20] *Who is wise, and he shall understand these things? prudent, and he shall know them? For the ways of the Lord are right, and the just shall walk in them and the transgressors shall*

not used of strength. חלם is used of "good condition" of an animal, Job xxxix. 4; (as in Arab.); in Hif. is "restored one to health" (Is. xxxviii. 16), as Syr. in Ethp. In Syr. חלים is used of *recovered* health, S. Mark v. 34, S. John v. 11, Acts iv. 10; as opposed to sickness, S. Mark ii. 17; or sound *healthy* words, S. John vi. 3, 2 Tim. i. 11. In Arab. חלם conj. i. is "dreamt" ii. "was kind, forbearing," v. "became fat" (of animals). Other senses are derived from dreaming.
[1] זכרון.   [2] Ex. xxviii. 12, 22, xxxix. 7.

[3] Ib. xxviii. 29.   [4] Ib. xxx. 16.   [5] Nu. x. 10.
[6] Ib. xxxi. 50, 54.   [7] Acts x. 4, 31.   [8] Rup.
[9] "The crowns were hung in windows in the height of the temple," as we learn from the tract Middot. a. f. 36. Rashi ad loc.
[10] S. Cyr.
[11] Eph. ii. 13.   [12] Ib. 17.   [13] Acts ii. 39.
[14] בנה ב.   Neh. iv. 4, 11 [10, 17 Eng.]
[15] 1 Cor. iii. 10.   [16] S. Cyr.
[17] Eph. ii. 15, 16.
[18] So Marck.   [19] Dan. xii. 10.
[20] Hosea xiv. 9. [10 Heb.] see vol. i. p. 141.

Before
C H R I S T
cir. 518.

CHAPTER VII.

1 *The captives enquire of fasting.*
4 *Zechariah reproveth their
fasting.* 8 *Sin the cause of
their captivity.*

518.

AND it came to pass in
the fourth year of king
Darius, *that* the word of

the LORD came unto Zech-
ariah in the fourth *day* of
the ninth month, *even* in
Chisleu ;

2 When they had sent
unto the h o u s e of God
Sherezer a n d Regem-me-
lech, and their men, † to
pray before the LORD,

Before
C H R I S T
cir. 518.

† Heb. *to
intreat the
face of the
LORD;*
1 Sam. 13. 12.
ch. 8. 21.

---

stumble at them ; and the wise man, [1] *he that
keepeth the law of the Lord getteth the understanding thereof.* So our Lord said, [2] *If any
man will do His will, he shall know of the doctrine,
whether it be of God or whether I speak of Myself ;* [3] *He that is of God heareth God's words :
ye therefore hear them not because ye are not of
God :* [4] *Every one that is of the truth heareth
My voice.* "[5] Because he had said, *And ye
shall know that the Lord hath sent me unto you,*
he warns them, that the fruit of that coming will reach to those only, who should hear
God and with ardent mind join themselves to
His name. *For as many as believed in Him
were made sons of God ;* but the rest *were cast
into outer darkness.* But *they* receive Christ,
who hear His voice and do not refuse His
rule. For He *was made the cause of eternal
salvation to all who obey Him.*"

VII. 1. *In the fourth year of Darius.* Two
years after the series of visions, shewn to
him, and two years before the completion of
the temple. Chisleu being December, it was
the end of B. C. 518.

2. *When they had sent unto the house of God.*
Rather, *And Bethel sent ;* i. e. the inhabitants
of Bethel sent. *The house of God is nowhere
in Holy Scripture called Bethel.* Bethel is
always the name of the place [6]. The *house
of God* is designated by historians, Psalmists,

prophets, by the name, *Beth-elohim,* more
commonly *Beth-Ha-elohim, the God ;* or *of the
Lord,* YHVH [7]. Zechariah and Haggai use
these names. It is not likely that the name,
Beth-el, should have first been given to the
house of God, when it had been desecrated
by the idolatries of Jeroboam. Bethel also
is, in the Hebrew order of the words, naturally the subject [8]. Nor is there any reason
why they should have sent to Bethel, since
they sought an answer from God. For it
would be forced to say that they sent to
Bethel, in order that those at Bethel should
send to Jerusalem ; which is not said. It
were unnatural also that the name of the
sender should not have been mentioned,
when the names of persons inferior, because
sent, are recorded [9]. Bethel, in Nehemiah's
time [10], was one of the chief places of Benjamin. *Two hundred twenty and three of the
men of Bethel and Ai* [11] had returned with
Zerubbabel. The answer being to *the people
of the land,* such were doubtless the enquirers,
not those still in Babylon. The answer shews
that the question was not religious, though
put as matter of religion. It is remarkable that, whereas in the case of those who
brought presents from Babylon, the names
express some relation to God, these names
are singularly, the one of a parricide son of

---

[1] Ecclus. xxi. 11.   [2] S. John vii. 17.
[3] Ib. viii. 47.   [4] Ib. xviii. 37.
[5] Osor.
[6] The LXX, Jon., Syr. render in the accusative,
to Bethel. The Vulg. alone has "ad domum Dei."

[7] Although בֵּית is used alike of the "tent" and
the "house," it is used but little of the "house of
God" before Solomon's temple ; יְ בֵּית Ex. xxiii.
19, xxxiv. 26, Deut. xxiii. 18, Jos. vi. 24, Jud. xix. 18,
1 Sam. i. 7, 24, iii. 15, 2 Sam. xii. 20; בֵּית הָאֱלֹהִים
Jud. xviii. 31. Subsequently יְ בֵּית occurs in the
books of Kings, 73 times ; in the Chronicles, 92 ; in
the Psalms, 7; in Isaiah, 6; in Jeremiah, 32; in
Lam., 1; Ezek. 6; Hosea, 2; Joel, 3; Micah, 1;
Haggai, 2; Zechariah, 5; Ezra, 7; in all 246; בֵּית
אֱלֹהִים occurs Gen. xxviii. 17, 22 ; in two of David's
Psalms (Ps. lii. 10, lv. 15,); once in the Chronicles, 2
Chron. xxxiv. 9; in all 5; and בֵּית הָאֱלֹהִים in
Eccl. iv. 17; in Chronicles, 33 times (intermingled
'th יְ בֵּית); Daniel i. 2; Ezra, 7 times; Nehemiah,
imes ; in all 50.
‡ So Ibn Ezra, although regarding Bethel as the

name of a man, who sent the others. Rashi and S.
Jerome's Hebrew instructors made Shareser and
Regemmelech the senders. Rashi says that they
sent to their kinsmen in Bethel, that these should
come to *entreat the face of God* at Jerusalem. S. Jerome's teachers said more naturally, that "Shareser
and Regemmelech sent to the house of God ;" only
"Bethel" is not so used, and the theory that they
were "Persian officers of Darius fearing God," is
inconsistent with the question as to a Jewish political fast of long standing. The interposition of the
place whither they were sent, between the verb and
the subject, would be unnatural. The E. V. follows
Kimchi, taking וַיִּשְׁלַח as impersonal. But here it
is a formal message from some definite person or
persons. In Gen. xlviii. 1, וַיֹּאמֶר לְיַעֲקֹב is altogether like our "one told Jacob." In Esth. ix. 30,
the subject is probably Mordecai, mentioned v. 29.

[9] Abarbanel notices this difficulty.
[10] Neh. xi. 31.   [11] Ezr. ii. 28.

Before CHRIST cir. 518.	

3 *And* to ᵃ speak unto the priests which *were* in the house of the LORD of hosts, and to the prophets, saying, Should I weep in ᵇ the fifth month, separating myself, as I have done these so many years?

ᵃ Deut. 17. 9, 10, 11. & 33. 10. Mal. 2. 7.

ᵇ Jer. 52. 12. ch. 8. 19.

4 ¶ Then came the word of the LORD of hosts unto me, saying,

5 Speak unto all the people of the land, and to the priests, saying, When ye ᶜ fasted and mourned in the fifth ᵈ and s e v e n t h

Before CHRIST cir. 518.

ᶜ Isai. 58. 5. ᵈ Jer. 41. 1. ch. 8. 19.

Sennacherib [1], and of one, chief among the King of Babylon's princes [2]; the other probably a secular name, "the king's friend [3]."

" [4] I do not see why under the name of Bethel, the city so called is not understood. For since Jerusalem was not yet fortified, the Jews chose them sites in various places, where they should be less harassed. All hatred was concentrated on that city, which the neighbors wished not to be restored to its former greatness. Other cities they did not so molest. Bethel then, i. e. the assembly of the city, sent messengers to Jerusalem to offer sacrifices to God and consult the wise there."

To entreat the face of the Lord. They wished, it seems, (so to speak) to ingratiate themselves with God with an account of their past self-humiliation, on the day when the house of God was burned by Nebuchadnezzar. In regard to God, the word is always used of entreating Him by earnest prayer [5].

3. *Should I weep in the fifth month, separating myself?* In the fifth month, from the seventh to the tenth day, Jerusalem was in flames, fired by Nebuchadnezzar. [6] *He burnt the house of the Lord, and the king's house, and all the houses of Jerusalem and every great man's house he burnt with fire.*

" [7] Now since it is said that the temple is builded and we see that no cause of sorrow remaineth, answer, we pray, are we to do this or to change our sorrow into joy ? "

Separating myself. This seems to be added,

[1] Is. xxxvii. 38, 2 Kgs xix. 37.
[2] Nergal-Shar-ezer, "Nergal preserve the prince," Jer. xxxix. 3, 13. νεριγλισσάρ. The omission of the name of the idol left it less openly idolatrous, but retained the prayer originally idolatrous.
[3] רֵעַ occurs as a proper name, 1 Chr. ii. 47. The Kamoos and Fasee say that the Arab. רֶגֶם is "friend," [see Lane] and, though this meaning is wholly insulated from the rest of the root, their authority is, of course, decisive.
[4] Osor.
[5] The explanation of the idiom, *stroked the face of,* in regard to which critics have so descanted about anthropomorphisms, is altogether imaginary. The phrase occurs, in all, 13 times in regard to God; three of these are in Zechariah, here, and viii. 21, 22; and beside Ex. xxxii. 11, 1 Sam. xiii. 12, 1 Kgs xiii. 6, (bis) 2 Kgs xiii. 4, Jer. xxvi. 19, Dan. ix. 13, Ps. cxix. 58, 2 Chr. xxxiii. 12, Mal. i. 9, and all the simplest prose. Of man it occurs only 3 times Ps. xlv. 13, Pr. xix. 6, Job xi. 19. In no dialect is there any

to intensify the fast which they had kept. The Nazarite was bound to [8] *separate himself from wine and strong drink,* and so, they severed themselves to the Lord, and consecrated themselves to Him [9]. These had severed themselves from food, from things pleasant, from pleasure, from sin, it may be, for the day, but not abidingly : they had not given themselves to God.

As I have done these so many years, lit. *how many* [10]. As if, although they knew that they were seventy years, they could not count them.

5. *Speak unto all the people of the land.* They of Bethel had spoken as one man, as Edom said to Israel, [11] *Thou shalt not pass by me ;* and [12] *the men of Israel said to the Hivite ; Perhaps thou dwellest in the midst of me, and how shall I make a league with thee ?* God gives the answer not to them only, but to all likeminded with them, *all the people of the land,* the whole population (in our language) ; as Jeremiah says, [13] *ye and your fathers, your kings and your princes and all the people of the land,* and, [14] *the scribe who mustered the people of the land.*

When ye fasted and that, mourning. It was no mere abstinence from food (severe as the Jewish fasts were, one unbroken abstinence from evening to evening) but with real mourning, the word being used only of mourning for the dead [15], or, in a few instances [16], for a very great public calamity ; probably with beating on the breast.

trace of the meaning *lœvis* or *palpo.* The Arab חלא is, any how, used of hard friction, as to bruising collyrium, rubbing off hair from skin [tanning], striking with sword, &c. חלא (ult. י) is, "sweet;" חלי is "adorned with jewels."

[6] 2 Kgs xxv. 9, Jer. lii. 13. Jeremiah mentions *the tenth day ;* the book of Kings, *the seventh.*
[7] S. Jer. [8] Nu. vi. 3.
[9] Ib. 5. See on Am. ii. 11. vol. i. p. 265.
[10] כמה is used in exclamation, not interrogatively, here, Ps. lxxviii. 40, Job xxi. 17.
[11] Nu. xx. 18. [12] Josh. ix. 7. [13] Jer. xliv. 21.
[14] Ib. lii. 25.
[15] Gen. xxiii. 2, l. 10, 1 Sam. xxv. 1, xxviii. 3, 2 Sam. i. 12, iii. 31, xi. 26, 1 Kgs. xiii. 29, 30, xiv. 13, 18, Eccl. xii. 5, Jer. xvi. 4, 5, 6, xxii. 18, [bis], xxv. 33, xxxiv. 5, Ezek. xxiv. 16, 23, Zech. xii. 10, 12.
[16] Is. xxxii. 12, Jo. i. 13, Mic. i. 8, Jer. iv. 8, xlix. 3. In Eccl. iii. 4, it is "mourning" as opposed to רקד,

Before
C H R I S T
cir. 518.

e ch. 1. 12.
f See Rom. 14. 6.

‖ Or, be
not ye they
that &c.

‖ Or, Are
not these
the words.

month e even those seventy years, did ye at all fast f unto me, *even* to me?

6 And when ye did eat, and when ye did drink, ‖ did not ye eat *for your-selves*, and drink *for your-selves?*

7 ‖ *Should ye* not *hear* the words which the LORD

hath cried † by the former prophets, when Jerusalem was inhabited and in pros-perity, and the cities there-of round about her, when *men* inhabited g the south and the plain?

8 ¶ And the w o r d of the LORD came unto Zech-ariah, saying,

Before
C H R I S T
cir. 518.

† Heb. *by the
hand of, &c.*

g Jer. 17. 26.

In the seventh month. The murder of Geda-liah, *whom the king of Babylon made governor of the land,* completed the calamities of Jeru-salem, in the voluntary, but prohibited exile to Egypt, for fear lest the murder should be avenged on them [1].

Did ye at all fast unto Me, Me [2]? God em-phatically rejects such fasting as their's had been, as something, unutterably alien from Him, *to Me, Me* [3]! Yet the fasting and mourning had been real, but irreligious, like remorse for ill-deeds, which has self only for its ground. He prepares the way for His answer by correcting the error of the ques-tion. "[4] Ye fasted to yourselves, not to Me. For ye mourned your sorrows, not your mis-deeds ; and your public fast was undertaken, not for My glory, but out of feeling for your own grief. But nothing can be pleasing to God, which is not referred to His glory. But those things alone can be referred to His glory, which are done with righteousness and devotion."

6. *And when ye eat and when ye drink, is it not ye who eat and ye who drink?* Conversely now that, after your return, ye feast for joy, this is no religious act ; ye have all the good of it, there is no thanksgiving to God. Con-trary to the Apostle's saying, [5] *Whether ye eat or drink, or whatever ye do, do all to the glory of God.* "[6] He eateth and drinketh to himself, who receiveth the nourishments of the body, which are the common gifts of the

Creator, without the needy. And any one fasts to himself, if he doth not give to the poor what for the time he withdraweth from himself, but keepeth it to be thereafter of-fered to his appetite. Hence it is said by Joel, *sanctify a fast.* For to ' sanctify a fast ' is to shew an abstinence worthy of God through other good deeds. Let anger cease, quarrels be hushed. For in vain is the flesh worn, if the mind is not refrained from evil pleasures, since the Lord says by the Pro-phet, [7] *Behold, in the day of your fast ye find pleasure. Behold, ye fast for strife and debate &c.*

7. Should ye *not* hear *the words,* or, Know ye *not the words?* The verb is presupposed in the emphatic question, as in, [8] *Shall I, the blood of these men?* David omits the word "drink" for abhorrence.

By the former prophets Isaiah and Jere-miah [9], *when Jerusalem was dwelling abidingly* [10], *at ease,* as the whole world then was, except herself, *and the south and the low-country,* both belonging to Judah, *were inhabited.* The re-storation then was still very incomplete, since he contrasts their *then* condition with the present, as inhabited or no. *The mountain, the south, and the low country,* known still by its name of Sephêla to Greeks [11], made up the territory of Judah [12].

8. Instead of quoting the former prophets, Zechariah gives the substance of their exhor-tations, as renewed to himself.

"bounding" for joy [all]. The noun מִסְפֵּד is in like way used of "mourning" for the dead, Gen. l. 10, Jer. vi. 26, Nu. v. 16, Zech. xii. 10, 11, 12 ; for the destruction of a people or place, Jer. xlviii. 38, Ez. xxvii. 34, Mi. i. 8, 11 ; for imminent destruction, Am. v. 17, Esth. iv. 3 ; or great public calamity, Jo. ii. 12, Is. xvii. 12. In Ps. xxx. 12, it stands contrasted with a great outward expression of joy, dancing, מָחוֹל. [all.]

[1] Jer. xli.–xliii.

[2] צַמְתֻּנִי. The affix is almost a dative, as in Is. xliv. 21, lxv. 5, Job xxxi. 18 ; and Ch. Dan. v. 6.

שְׁנֵי עָלֵיהוּ, for which, שְׁנֵיהוּ, occurs ver. 9.

[3] The pronoun repeated after the affix, as in בִּי אָנִי 1 Sam. xxv. 24 ; פְּגַרֵיכֶם אַתֶּם Nu. xiv. 32, and with בָּם, גַּם אָנִי, בֵּרְכַנִי גַם אָנִי Gen. xxvii. 38 ; 2 Sam. xvii. 5, 1 Kgs xxi. 19, Pr. xxiii. 15, Jer. xxv. 14, xxvii. 7.

[4] Osor.   [5] 1 Cor. x. 31.

[6] S. Greg. in Evang. Hom. 16, n. 6. Opp. 1495.

[7] Is. lvii. 3, 4.

[8] 2 Sam. xxiii. 17.

[9] Is. lviii. 4, Jer. xiv. 12. Since Isaiah's is the chief passage and Jeremiah's scarcely more than allusive, Zechariah, just after the captivity, knew that the prophecy Is. lviii. was Isaiah's, not by a prophet after the captivity.

[10] יָשַׁב וּשְׁקֵט–יָשֶׁבֶת וּשְׁלֵוָה as ab. i. 11, שֶׁבֶת וּשְׁקֵטַת ; "the state of ease is conveyed by the הָיָה with the act. partic.

[11] 1 Macc. xii. 38. "It is still called Sephêla." Eus. Onom.

[12] Josh. x. 40, Jud. i. 9, Jer. xvii. 26, xxxii. 44, xxxiii. 13.

| Before CHRIST cir. 518. | 9 Thus speaketh the LORD of hosts, saying, [h] † Execute true judgment, and shew mercy and compassions every man to his brother: 10 And ! oppress not the widow, nor the fatherless, the stranger, nor the poor; [k] and let none of you imagine evil against his brother in your heart. | 11 But they refused to hearken, and [1]† pulled away the shoulder, and † [m] stopped their ears, that they should not hear. 12 Yea they made their [n] hearts as an adamant stone, [o] lest they should hear the law, and the words which the LORD of hosts hath sent in his spirit † by the former prophets: | Before CHRIST cir. 518. |

Left margin references:
[h] Is. 58. 6, 7. Jer. 7. 23. Mic. 6. 8. ch. 8. 16. Matt. 23. 23.
† Heb. Judge judgment of truth.
[1] Ex. 22. 21, 22. Deut. 24. 17. Isai. 1. 17. Jer. 5. 28.
[k] Ps. 36. 4. Mic. 2. 1. ch. 8. 17.

Right margin references:
[1] Neh. 9. 29. Jer. 7. 24.
† [m] Hos. 4. 16.
† Heb. they gave a backsliding shoulder.
† Heb. made heavy.
[m] Acts 7. 57.
[n] Ezek. 11. 19.
& 36. 26.
[o] Neh. 9. 29, 30.
† Heb. by the hand of.

9. *Thus spake the Lord,* i. e. through the former prophets, for he goes on to speak of their rejection in the past. *Execute true judgment.* He retains the words of Ezekiel [1]. The injunction itself runs throughout the prophets [2]. *Shew mercy,* i. e. tender love, to all; *compassion,* to the unhappy. Omit no act of love, God so loves the loving. " [3] Like S. Paul to the Romans [4], he names only the duties to the neighbor, but understands what relates to God. For the love of our neighbor presupposes the love of God, from which it springs." " [5] After strictness of justice, let mercy to all follow, and specially to brethren, of the same blood and of one faith. Brother and neighbor we ought to account the whole human race, since we are all born of one parent, or those who are of the household of faith, according to the parable of the Gospel [6], which willeth us to understand by neighbor, nor our kin, but all men."

10. *And oppress not.* He had commanded positive acts of love; he now forbids every sort of unlove. *He that oppresseth the poor,* Solomon had said [7], *reproacheth his Maker. The widow, the orphan, the stranger, the afflicted,* are, throughout the law, the special objects of God's care. This was the condition which God made by Jeremiah [8]; *If ye thoroughly amend your ways and your doings, if ye thoroughly execute judgment between a man and his neighbor; if ye oppress not the stranger the fatherless and the widow, and shed not innocent blood in this place, neither walk after other gods to your hurt, then will I cause you to dwell in this place.* It was on the breach of the covenant to set their brethren free in the year of release,

[1] מִשְׁפַּט אֱמֶת occurs beside in Ezek. xviii. 8, only. In Deut. xvi. 18, occurs מִשְׁפַּט צֶדֶק.
[2] As Is. i. 17, 23, lviii. 6, 7, Jer. vii. 5, Ezek. xviii. 8. Hos. xii. 6 &c.
[3] Lap.   [4] Rom. xiii. 9.   [5] S. Jer.
[6] S. Luke x. 30 sqq.   [7] Prov. xxiv. 31.
[8] Jer. vii. 5-7.   [9] Ib. xxxiv. 17.   [10] הֵשֵׁב.
[11] Mic. ii. 1, 3.   [12] Hos. iv. 16.   [13] Neh. ix. 29.

that God said; [9] *I proclaim a liberty for you to the sword, to the pestilence and to the famine, and I will make you to be removed into all the kingdoms of the earth.*

And let none of you imagine, i. e. devise [10], as, by Micah, God retorted the evil upon them. They [11] *devised evil on their beds; therefore, behold, against this family do I devise an evil, from which ye shall not remove your necks.*

11. *But they gave a backsliding shoulder,* like a restive animal, which would not endure the yoke, dull and stupid as the beasts: as Hosea says, [12] *Israel slideth back like a backsliding heifer.* Nehemiah confesses the same; [13] *they gave a backsliding shoulder and hardened their neck and would not hear.*

And made heavy their ears, fulfilling in themselves what God foretold to Isaiah would be the result of his preaching, *make their ears heavy* [14]. The heart, which will not hearken, becomes duller by the outward hearing, as S. Paul says, [15] *The earth which drinketh in the rain that cometh oft upon it, and bringeth forth herbs meet for them by whom it is dressed, receiveth blessing from God; but that which beareth thorns and briars is rejected.*

12. *Harder than adamant.* The stone, whatever it be, was hard enough to cut ineffaceable characters [16]: it was harder than flint [17]. It would cut rocks; it could not be graven itself, or receive the characters of God.

This is the last sin, obduracy, persevering impenitence, which [18] *resisted the Holy Ghost,* and [19] *did despite to the Spirit of grace.* Not through infirmity, but of set purpose, they hardened themselves, lest [20] *they should convert and be healed.* They feared to trust them-

[14] The same words; וְאָזְנָיו הַכְבֵּד Is. vi. 5, הַכְבִּידוּ Zech.
[15] Heb. vi. 7, 8.
[16] Jer. xvii. 1. "The sin of Judah is written with a pen of iron, with the point of a (שָׁמִיר) diamond." E. V.
[17] Ezek. iii. 9, "As an adamant harder than flint."
[18] Acts vii. 51.   [19] Heb. x. 29.   [20] Is. vi. 10.

Before
CHRIST
cir. 518.

P2 Chr. 36. 16.
Dan. 9. 11.

q Prov. 1.
24—28.
Isa. l. 15.
Jer. 11. 11.
& 14. 12.
Mic. 3. 4.

P therefore c a m e a great wrath from the LORD of hosts.

13 Therefore it is come to pass, *that* as he cried, and they would not hear; so q they cried, and I would not hear, saith the LORD of hosts:

14 But r I scattered them with a whirlwind among all the nations s whom they knew not. Thus t the land was desolate after them, that no man passed through nor returned: for they laid u the † pleasant land desolate.

Before
CHRIST
cir. 518.

r Deut. 4. 27.
& 28. 64.
Ezek. 36. 19.
ch. 2. 6.
s Deut. 28. 33.
t Lev. 26. 22.

u Dan. 8. 9.
† Heb. *land of
desire.*

selves to God's word, lest He should convert them by it.

Lest they should hear the law and the words which the Lord God sent by His Spirit by the hand of the former prophets. The Holy Ghost was the chief agent; *by His Spirit;* the inspired prophets were His instruments; *by the hand of.* Nehemiah confesses the same to God: [1] *Thou didst protest to them by Thy Spirit by the hand of Thy prophets.* Moses was one of the greatest prophets. The law then may be included, either as delivered by Moses, or as being continually enforced by all the prophets. Observe the gradations. 1) The words of God are not heard. 2) The restive shoulder is shewn; men turn away, when God, by the inner motions of His Spirit or by lesser chastisements, would bring them to the yoke of obedience. "[2] They would not bear the burden of the law, whereas they willingly bore that most heavy weight of their sins." 3) Obduracy. "[2] Their adamantine heart could be softened neither by promises nor threats." Therefore nothing remained but the *great wrath,* which they had *treasured to themselves against the day of wrath.* And so Zechariah returns to that, wherewith his message and visions of future mercy began, the *great wrath* which fell upon their fathers [3].

"[2] I sought not,' He says, ' for your tears; I enjoined not bitterness of sorrow; but what, had they been done, the calamity, for which those tears were meet, had never befallen you. What was it which I admonished you formerly by the former prophets to recall you from sin? What I bid you by Zechariah now. This I preach, admonish, testify, inculcate upon you.'"

13. *And it came to pass,* i. e. this which God had said, *As He cried and they heard not, so shall they cry and I will not hear, saith the Lord of hosts.* God had often said this. "It

shall be too late to cry for mercy, when it is the time of justice." So Wisdom had said by Solomon; [4] *then,* i. e. *when distress and anguish cometh upon them, they shall call upon Me, but I will not answer; they shall seek Me early, and they shall not find Me.* So by Isaiah, [5] *When ye spread forth your hands, I will hide Mine eyes from you; yea, when ye make many prayers, I will not hear; your hands are full of bloods.* So by Hosea [6], by Micah [7], by Jeremiah [8]. It was one message which was verified in every day of chastisement, "there will be a 'too late;'" not a final "too late," until the end of ends comes, but a "too late" for them, a "too late" to avert that particular judgment of God, whereby the sinner's earthly trial and future were changed permanently [9].

14. *But I scattered them,* rather, *And I will scatter them* [10]. The saying continues what God had said that He had said, and which had come to pass. *Among all nations whom they knew not.* So God had repeatedly said by Jeremiah, [11] *I will cast you out of this land into a land that ye know not, ye nor your fathers; where I will not shew you favor.* This was the aggravation of the original woe in the law: [12] *The Lord shall bring a nation against thee from far, from the end of the earth, a nation whose tongue thou shalt not understand, a nation of fierce countenance.* There was no mitigation of suffering, when the common bond between man and man, mutual speech, was wanting.

That no man passed through nor returned, lit. *from passer through and from returner;* as in the prophecy of Alexander's march and return, [13] *because of him that passeth by and of him that returneth;* and of Seir God saith, [14] *I will cut off from him, passer-through and returner* [15]. As we say, there shall be no traffic more through her.

[1] Neh. ix. 30.   [2] Osor.
[3] i. 7. קָף; here קָצֶף גָדוֹל.   [4] Prov. i. 27, 28.
[5] Is. i. 15.   [6] Hos. v. 6. see vol. i. pp. 58, 59.
[7] iii. 4. see ab. pp. 40, 41.   [8] Jer. xi. 14, xiv. 12.
[9] See Pusey's Parochial Sermons, Vol. I. Serm. 12.
" Irreversible chastisements."
[10] The form וָאֵסָעֲרֵם for -אֵ, is remarkable chiefly, if the punctuation comes, (as is assumed)

from Zechariah's time, for the care with which the vowel pronunciation has been preserved. It has no exact parallel. The conjugation recurs with the שׁ, Job xxvii. 21. See Introd. to Zech. p. 327. n. c.
[11] Jer. xvi. 13; add xv. 14, xvii. 4.
[12] Deut. xxviii. 49, 50.   [13] ix. 8.
[14] Ezek. xxxv. 7.
[15] The form implies that the same did, or did not, pass and return, whence he came. Ezek. xxxii. 27.

Before
C H R I S T
cir. 518.

CHAPTER VIII.

1 *The restoration of Jerusalem.*
9 *They are encouraged to the building by God's favor to them.* 16 *Good works are required of them.* 18 *Joy and enlargement are promised.*

AGAIN the word of the LORD of hosts came *to me,* saying,

2 Thus saith the LORD of hosts ; [a] I was jealous for Zion with great jealousy, and I was jealous for her with great fury.

3 Thus saith the LORD ; [b] I am returned unto Zion, and [c] will dwell in the

Before
C H R I S T
cir. 518.

[a] Nah. 1. 21. ch. 1. 14.

[b] ch. 1. 16.

[c] ch. 2. 10.

And they made the pleasant land [1] *desolate.* They were the doers of what they by their sins caused, by bringing down the judgments of God. Heretofore the land which God had given them, had been in our language "the envy" of all who knew it now they had made it into a desolation, one wide waste [2].

"[3] What is said in the beginning of the chapter against Jews who abstained indiscreetly, applies mystically to all, not inward, but rude Christians, who not being diligent enough but rather negligent about acts of piety and inward prayer and reformation of the powers of the soul, account highly of bodily exercises and outward observances, and use no slight scrupulosity as to things of less moment, and do not attend to the chief things, charity, humility, patience meekness. On these it must be inculcated, that if they wish their fasts and other outward exercises to please God, they must judge true judgment, and be compassionate, kind, liberal to their neighbors, keep their mind ever steadfast in God, cast away wholly all hardness of heart, and be soft and open to receive within them the word of God. Otherwise *their land will be desolate,* i. e. deprived of the indwelling of the Holy Spirit, and they scattered amid various vices." "[4] That which was formerly *a pleasant land,* and the hospice of the Trinity, is turned into a desert and dwelling-place of dragons."

VIII. "[3] After the Lord had, in the preceding chapter, manifoldly rebuked the Jewish people, He now comforts it with renewed promises, as a good physician, who after a bitter draught employs sweet and soothing remedies ; as that most loving Samaritan poured in wine and oil." The chapter falls into two portions, each marked by the words, *The Word of the Lord of hosts came* [5], or *came unto me,* the first [6] declaring the reversal of the former judgments, and the complete,

though conditional, restoration of God's favor ; the 2d [7] containing the answer to the original question as to those fasts, in the declaration of the joy and the spread of the Gospel. The first portion has, again, a sevenfold, the second, a threefold subordinate division ; marked by the beginning, *Thus saith the Lord of hosts.*

2. *Thus saith the Lord of hosts.* "[8] At each word and sentence, in which good things, for their greatness, almost incredible are promised, the prophet premises, *Thus saith the Lord of hosts,* as if he would say, Think not that what I pledge you are my own, and refuse me not credence as man. What I unfold are the promises of God."

I was jealous, lit. *I have been and am jealous for* [9]. He repeats in words slightly varied, but in the same rhythm, the declaration cf His tender love wherewith He opened the series of visions, thereby assuring beforehand that this was, like that, an answer of peace. The form of words shews, that this was a jealousy *for,* not *with* her ; yet it was one and the same strong, yea infinite love, whereby God, as He says, [10] *clave unto their fathers to love them and chose their seed after them out of all nations.* His jealousy of their sins was part of that love, whereby, "[3] without disturbance of passion or of tranquillity, He inflicted rigorous punishment, as a man fearfully reproves a wife who sins." They are two different forms of love according to two needs. "[11] The jealousy [12] of God is good, to love men and hate the sins of men. Contrariwise the jealousy of the devil is evil, to hate men and love the sins of men." "[13] Since God's anger had its origin in the vehemence of His love (for this sort of jealousy arises from the greatness of love), there was hope that the anger might readily be appeased toward her."

3. *I am returned.* "[3] Without change in

---

[1] ארץ חמדה occurs Ps. cvi. 24, Jer. iii. 19. On חמדה see ab. on Hagg. ii. 7. pp. 310, 311.

[2] This idiom שׁית לשׁמה or שׁית רֹשׁ. or שֹׁום שׁ. had been used by Jo. i. 7, Is. xiii. 9, Jer ii. 15, iv. 7, xviii. 16, xix. 8, xxv. 9, l. 3, li. 29.

[3] Dion.

[4] S. Jer.

[5] אל, ver. 1, which is added in 22 Kenn. MSS., 13 De R. ; 7 at first, 3 corrected ; 2 early edd. ; Jon. Syr.,

is only an explanatory addition. It is noted to be "wanting in correct MSS." De R.

[6] 1—17.

[7] 18—23.

[8] S. Jer.

[9] It is the inverted Hebrew parallelism 1, 2 ; 4, 3. *I am jealous for Zion with a great jealousy, and with great wrath am I jealous for her,* only substituting קנאתי גדול for חמה גדולה, in it.

[10] חָשַׁק בּ De. x. 15. [11] Rup. [12] Zelus. [13] Osor.

Before
CHRIST
cir. 518. midst of Jerusalem : and
Jerusalem [d] shall be called

[d] Is. 1. 21, 26.
[e] Is. 2. 2, 3. a city of truth ; and [e] the
mountain of the LORD of

[f] Jer. 31. 23. hosts [f] the holy mountain.

4 Thus saith the LORD

of hosts ; [g] There shall yet Before
CHRIST
cir. 518.
old men and old women
dwell in the streets of Je- [g] See 1 Sam. 2
31. Is. 65, 20, 22.
rusalem, and every man Lam. 2. 20, &c.
& 5. 11,—14.
with his staff in his hand [†] Heb. for
multitude
of days.
[†] for very age.

Myself, I am turned to that people from the
effect of justice to the sweetness of mercy,
and I will dwell in the midst of Jerusalem, in
the temple and the people, indwelling the
hearts of the good by charity and grace.
Christ also, Very God and Very Man, visibly conversed and was seen in Zion."
"[1] When He says, 'I am turned,' He shews
that she was turned too. He had said, *Turn
unto Me and I will turn unto you ;* otherwise
she would not have been received into favor
by Him. As the fruit of this conversion, He
promises her His presence, the ornaments of
truth, the hope of security, and adorns her
with glorious titles."

God had symbolized to Ezekiel the departure of His special presence, in that the *glory
of the God of Israel* which was over the temple, at the very place where they placed *the
image of jealousy* [2], [3] *went up from the Cherub,
whereupon it was, to the threshold of the house;*
then [4] *stood over the Cherubim ;* and then
[5] *went up from the midst of the city and stood
upon the mountain, which is on the east side of
the city,* so removing from them. He had
prophesied its return in the vision of the
symbolic temple, how [6] *the glory of the Lord
came into the house by the way of the gate looking
toward the East, and the Spirit took me up and
brought me into the inner court, and behold, the
glory of the Lord filled the house.* This renewed
dwelling in the midst of them, Zechariah too
prophesies, in the same terms as in his third
vision [7], *I will dwell in the midst of Jerusalem.*

And Jerusalem shall be called the city of truth,
being what she is called, since God would not
call her untruly ; so Isaiah says, [8] *afterward
thou shalt be called the city of righteousness, the
faithful city,* and [9] *they shall call thee the city of
the Lord, the Zion of the Holy One of Israel.* So
Zephaniah prophesied, [10] *The remnant of
Israel shall not do iniquity, nor speak lies.* Truth
embraces everything opposite to untruth ;
faithfulness, as opposed to faithlessness ; sincerity, as opposed to simulation ; veracity, as
opposed to falsehood ; honesty, as opposed to

untruth in act ; truth of religion or faith, as
opposed to untrue doctrine.   "[11] *It shall be
called the city of truth,* i. e. of the True God or
of truth of life, doctrine, and justice.   It is
chiefly verified by the Coming of Christ,
Who often preached in Jerusalem, in Whom
the city afterward believed."

And the mountain of the Lord of hosts, Mount
Zion, on which the temple shall be built, shall
be called and be *the mountain of holiness.*
This had been the favorite title of the
Psalmists [12], and Isaiah [13] ; and Obadiah had
foretold, [14] *upon Mount Zion there shall be holiness;* and Jeremiah, [15] *As yet they shall use
this speech in the land of Judah and in the cities
thereof, when I shall bring again their captivity ;
The Lord shall bless thee, O habitation of justice, and mountain of holiness.*   It should be
called and be ; it should fulfill the destination
of its titles ; as, in the Apostles' Creed we profess our belief of "the holy Catholic Church,"
and holiness is one of its characteristics.

4. *There shall yet dwell old men and old
women.*   "[11] Men and women shall not be
slain now, as before in the time of the Baby-
lonish destruction, but shall fulfill their
natural course."   It shall not be, as when
[16] *He gave His people over unto the sword ; the
fire consumed their young men and their maidens
were not given to marriage ; the priests were slain
by the sword and their widows made no lamentation ;* apart from the horrible atrocities of
heathen war, when the unborn children were
destroyed in their mothers' womb [17], with
their mothers.   Yet [18], once more as in the
days of old, and as conditionally promised in
the law [19].   As death is the punishment of
sin, so prolongation of life to the time which
God has now made its natural term, seems
the more a token of His goodness.   This
promise Isaiah had renewed [20], *There shall no
more be an infant of days, nor an old man that
hath not filled his days.*   In those fierce wars
neither young nor very old were spared.   It
implied then a long peace, that men should
live to that utmost verge of human life.

[1] Osor.   [2] Ezek. viii. 4, 5.   [3] Ib. ix. 3.
[4] Ib. x. 4, 18.   [5] Ib. xi. 23.   [6] Ib. xliii. 4.
[7] ושכנתי בתוכך ii. 14. Heb. [10 Eng.]
[8] Is. i. 26.
[9] Ib. lx. 14.   So Jer. iii. 17, *At that time they shall call
Jerusalem the throne of the Lord.*
[10] Zeph. iii. 13.   [11] Dion.
[12] David, Ps. ii. 6, iii. 4, xv. 1, sons of Korah, xliii.
3, xlviii. 1, lxxxvii. 1, and anon., Ps. xcix. 9.

[13] Is. xi. 9, lvi. 7, lvii. 13, lxv. 11, 25, lxvi. 20, also in
Jo. ii. 1, iii. 17, Ob. 16, Zeph. iii. 11, Dan. ix. 16, 20.
[14] Ob. 17.
[15] Jer. xxxi. 23.   [16] Ps. lxxviii. 63, 64.
[17] 2 Kgs xv. 16, Hos. xiii. 16, Am. i. 13.
[18] As in Zech. i. 17.
[19] De. iv. 10, v. 16, 33, vi. 2, xi. 9, xvii. 20, xxii. 7,
xxxii. 47, Ezek. xx. 17.
[20] Is. lxv. 20.

5 And the streets of the city shall be full of boys and girls playing in the streets thereof.

6 Thus saith the LORD of hosts; If it be || marvelous in the eyes of the remnant of this people in these

|| Or, *hard,* or, *difficult.*

The man, whose staff is in his hand for the multitude of days. The two opposite pictures, the old men, "[1] so aged that they support with a staff their failing and trembling limbs," and the young in the glad buoyancy of recent life, fresh from their Creator's hands, attest alike the goodness of the Creator, Who protecteth both, the children in their yet undeveloped strength, the very old whom He hath brought through "all the changes and chances of this mortal life," in their yet sustained weakness. The tottering limbs of the very old, and the elastic perpetual motion of childhood are like far distant chords of the diapason of the Creator's love. It must have been one of the most piteous sights in that first imminent destruction of Jerusalem[2], how [3] *the children and the sucklings swooned in the streets of the city;* how *the young children fainted for hunger in the top of every street.* We have but to picture to ourselves any city in which one lives, the ground strewed with these little all-but corpses, alive only to suffer. We know not, how great the relief of the yet innocent, almost indomitable joyousness of children is, until we miss them. In the dreadful Irish famine of 1847 the absence of the children from the streets of Galway was told me by Religious as one of its dreariest features[4]. In the dreary back-streets and alleys of London, the irrepressible joyousness of children is one of the bright sun-beams of that great Babylon, amid the oppressiveness of the anxious, hard, luxurious, thoughtless, careworn, eager, sensual, worldly, frivolous, vain, stolid, sottish, cunning, faces, which traverse it. God sanctions by His word here our joy in the joyousness of children, that He too taketh pleasure in it, He the Father of all. It is precisely their laughing[5], the fullness of her streets of these merry creations of His hands, that He speaks of with complacency.

6. *If it should be marvelous in the eyes of the remnant of this people in those* [6] [*not these*] *days, shall it be marvelous in Mine eyes also? saith the Lord of hosts.* Man's anticipations, by reason

of his imperfections and the chequered character of earthly things, are always disappointing. God's doings, by reason of His infinite greatness and goodness, are always beyond our anticipations, past all belief. It is their very greatness which staggers us. It is not then merely that the temporal promises seemed "too good to be true" (in our words) "[7] in the eyes of the people who had come from the captivity, seeing that the city almost desolate, the ruins of the city-walls, the charred houses shewed the doings of the Babylonians." It is in the day of the fulfillment, not of the anticipation, that they would seem marvelous in their eyes, as the Psalmist says, [8] *This is the Lord's doing: and it is marvelous in our eyes.* The temporal blessings which God would give were not so incredible. They were but the ordinary gifts of His Providence: they involved no change in their outward relations. His people were still to remain under their Persian masters, until their time too should come. It was matter of gladness and of God's Providence, that the walls of Jerusalem should be rebuilt: but not so marvelous, when it came to pass. The mysteries of the Gospel are a marvel even to the blessed Angels. That fulfillment being yet future, so the people, in whose eyes that fulfillment should be marvelous, were future also. And this was to be *a remnant* still. It does not say, *this people which is a remnant,* nor *this remnant of the people,* i. e., those who remained over out of the people who went into captivity, or *this remnant,* but "the remnant of *this* people," i. e. those who should remain over of it, i.e., of the people who were returned. It is the *remnant* of the larger whole, *this people*[9]. It is still *the remnant according to the election of grace; that election* which *obtained* what all Israel sought, but, seeking wrongly, were *blinded*[10].

Shall it be marvelous in Mine eyes also? It is an indirect question in the way of exclamation[11]. *It be marvelous in Mine eyes also,* rejecting the thought, as alien from the na-

---

[1] Dion.   [2] Jer. vi. 11, ix. 21.   [3] Lam. ii. 11. 19.
[4] See other pictures of that time in Pusey's "Chastisements neglected forerunners of greater," in "Occasional Sermons."   [5] מִשְׂחֲקִים.
[6] בַּיָּמִים הָהֵם as in Gen. vi. 4, Ex. ii. 11, De. xvii. 9, בַּיָּמִים הָהֵמָּה are the times of the Gospel, Jo. iii. 2, iv. 1; bel. 25.   [7] S. Jer.
[8] Ps. cxviii. 23. The phrase occurs beside only 2 Sam. xiii. 2.
[9] See on Am. i. 8, vol. i. p. 247, n. 28, and on Hagg. i. 12, p. 305.   [10] Rom. xi. 5-7.

[11] As in 2 Sam. xvi. 17, *This thy kindness!* for, *Is this thy kindness?* Gen. xxvii. 24, *Thou, this my son Esau!* for, *Art thou my very son Esau?* 1 Sam. xxii. 7, *Yea, to you all the son of Jesse shall give!* for, *shall he give?* Job ii. 9, *Thou still holding fast thine integrity!* for, *art thou?* Jud. xiv. 16, *I have not told my father and my mother,* וְלָךְ אַגִּיד *and to thee I shall tell!* i. e., shall I tell thee? Jer. xxv. 29, *For lo, on the city which is called by My Name, I begin to bring evil, and ye shall be utterly unpunished!* as we should say, "and ye be utterly unpunished." Ew. Lehrb. n. 324. p. 802. ed. 8.

Before
C H R I S T
cir. 518.
ᵇGen. 18. 14.
Luke 1. 37.
& 18. 27.
Rom. 4. 21.
ⁱ Is. 11. 11, 12. &
43. 5, 6.
Ezek. 37. 21.
Amos 9. 14, 15.

days, ʰshould it also be marvelous in mine eyes? saith the LORD of hosts.

7 Thus saith the LORD of hosts; Behold, ⁱI will save my people from the

east c o u n t r y, and from †the west country;

8 And I will bring them, and they shall dwell in the midst of Jerusalem: ᵏ and they shall be my people,

Before
C H R I S T
cir. 518.

† Heb. the coun-
try of the going
down of the
sun:
See Ps. 50. 1.
& 113. 3.
Mal. i. 11.
ᵏ Jer. 30. 22.
& 31. 1, 33. ch. 13. 9.

ture of God, to Whom ¹ *all things are possible,* yea, what *with men is impossible.* As God says to Jeremiah, ² *Behold, I am the Lord, the God of all flesh. Is there anything too hard for Me?* ³ *For with God nothing shall be impossible.* ⁴ *The things which are impossible with men are possible with God.* ⁵ *For with God all things are possible.* "⁶ For He is the Lord of all powers, fulfilling by His will what exceedingly surpasseth nature, and effecting at once what seemeth Him good. The mystery of the Incarnation passeth all marvel and discourse, and no less the benefits redounding to us. For how is it not next to incredible, that the Word, Begotten of God, should be united with the flesh and be in the form of a servant, and endure the Cross and the insults and outrages of the Jews? Or how should one not admire above measure the issue of the dispensation, whereby sin was destroyed, death abolished, corruption expelled, and man, once a recreant slave, became resplendent with the grace of an adopted son?"

7. *I will save My people from the East country and from the West country,* "⁷ i. e. the whole world; for Israel has been scattered in every part of the world." God had said to Israel, ⁸ *I will bring thy seed from the east and gather thee from the west; I will say to the north, Give up, and to the south, Keep not back.* The two tribes had been carried to Babylon and had been dispersed, or had been allowed to migrate to the various provinces of the Babylonian or Persian empire. But these were in the East, though commonly called the North, because they invaded Israel from the North. Those who had migrated to Egypt were in the South. As yet none were in the West. The dispersion, as well as the gathering, was still future. When our Lord came, they had migrated Westward. Greece, Italy, Asia minor, were full of them; and from all they were gathered. All S. Paul's Epistles written to named Churches, were written to Churches formed from converts in the West. In all these countries God would gather His one people, His Church, not of ⁹ *the Jews only, but also of the Gentiles,* grafted into them, as our Lord said, ¹⁰ *I say unto you, that many shall come from the East and from the West, and shall*

sit down with Abraham, and Isaac, and Jacob, in the kingdom of heaven ; but the children of the kingdom (the unbelieving Jews, who were not the remnant) shall be cast out into outer darkness.

8. *They shall dwell in the midst of Jerusalem,* not the literal Jerusalem ; for this would not contain the Jews from all quarters of the world, whom, as they multiplied, the whole land could not contain ; but the promised Jerusalem, the Jerusalem, which *should be inhabited as towns without walls,* to which the Lord should be *a wall of fire round about.*

And they shall be My people. He promises this as to those who were already His people; *I will save My people—and will bring them, and they shall dwell—and they shall be My people.* And this they were to be in a new way, by conversion of heart, as Jeremiah says, ¹¹ *I will give them an heart to know Me, that I am the Lord, and they shall be My people, and I will be their God: for they shall return unto Me with their whole heart,* and, ¹² *This shall be the covenant that I will make with the house of Israel ; After those days, saith the Lord, I will put My law in their inward parts, and will write it in their hearts; and will be their God, and they shall be My people.*

" ¹³ The circuit of one city will not contain so great a multitude. But one confession of faith, one conspiration of sanctity, one communion of religion and righteousness, can easily enfold all born of the holy fathers, united to them in faith and piety. And God is specially called the God of all these. For He specially consults for these, loads them with benefits, fences them in with most strong protection, illumines them with His light, crowns them, when confirmed in the Image of His beauty, with glory immortal and Divine."

In truth and in righteousness. This too is on account of their former relation to God. Isaiah had upbraided them for a worship of God, ¹⁴ *not in truth and righteousness.* Jeremiah had said, ¹⁵ *Thou shalt swear, the Lord liveth, in truth, in judgment, and in righteousness.* God should be their God *in truth and righteousness ;* " ¹⁶ truth in fulfilling His promises; righteousness in rewarding every man according to his works."

¹ S. Matt. xix. 26.   ² Jer. xxxii. 27.
³ S. Luke i. 37.   ⁴ Ib. xviii. 27.   ⁵ S. Mark x. 27.
⁶ S. Cyr.   ⁷ Dion.   ⁸ Is. xliii. 5, 6.

⁹ Rom. ix. 24.   ¹³ S. Matt. viii. 11, 12.
¹¹ Jer. xxiv. 7, add xxx. 22.   ¹² Ib. xxxi. 33.
¹³ Osor.   ¹⁴ Is. xlviii. 1.   ¹⁵ Jer. iv. 2.   ¹⁶ Rib.

Before
C H R I S T
cir. 518.

and I will be their God, [1] in truth and in righteousness.

9 ¶ Thus saith the LORD of hosts; [m] Let your hands be strong, ye that hear in these days these words by the mouth of [n] the prophets, which *were* in [o] the day *that* the foundation of the house of the LORD of hosts was laid,

Marginal references (left column):

[1] Jer. 4. 2.

[m] Hag. 2. 4. ver. 18.

[n] Ezra 5. 1, 2.

[o] Hag. 2. 18.

that the temple might be built.

10 For before these days [‖] Or, *the hire of man became nothing, &c.* [‖] there was no [p] hire for man, nor any hire for [p] Hag. 1. 6, 9, 10. & 2. 16. beast; [q] neither *was there* [q] 2 Chr. 15. 5. *any* peace to him that went out or came in because of the affliction: for I set all men every one against his neighbor.

Before
C H R I S T
cir. 518.

---

9 *Let your hands be strong.* The fulfillment of God's former promises are the earnest of the future; His former providences, of those to come. Having then those great promises for the time to come, they were to be earnest in whatever meantime God gave them to do. He speaks to them, as *hearing in these days*, i. e. that *fourth* year of Darius in which they apparently were, *these words from the mouth of the prophets, which* were *in the day* when *the foundation of the house of the Lord was laid, the temple, that it might be built.* Haggai was now gone to his rest. His voice had been silent for two years. But his words lived on. The fulfillment of what the prophets had then spoken in God's Name, was a ground, why their hands should be strong, now and thereafter, for every work which God gave or should give them to do. "[1] Some things are said to Jerusalem, i. e. to the Jews, which belong to them only; some relate to what is common to them and the other members of the Church, i. e. those who are called from the Gentiles. Now he speaks to the Jews, but not so as to seem to forget what he had said before. He would say, Ye who hear the words, which in those days when the temple was founded, Haggai and Zechariah spake, be strong and proceed to the work which ye began of fulfilling the will of the Lord in the building of the temple, and in keeping from the sins, in which ye were before entangled. For as, before ye began to build the temple, ye were afflicted with many calamities, but after ye had begun, all things went well with you, as Hag-

gai said [2], so, if you cultivate piety and do not depart from God, ye shall enjoy great abundance of spiritual good." "[3] The memory of past calamity made the then tranquillity much sweeter, and stirred the mind to greater thanksgiving. He set forth then the grief of those times when he says; "

10. *There was no hire for man,* lit. *hire for man came not to pass* [4]. It was longed for, waited for, and came not. So little was the produce, that neither laborer nor beast of burden were employed to gather it in.

Neither was there peace to him who went out or came in because of the affliction, better, *of the adversary.* In such an empire as the Persian, there was large scope for actual hostility among the petty nations subject to it, so that they did not threaten revolt against itself, or interfere with the payment of tribute, as in the Turkish Empire now, or in the weak government of Greece. At the rebuilding of the walls, after this time, the Samaritans, *Arabians, Ammonites, Ashdodites conspired to fight against Jerusalem,* and to *slay them* [5]. They are summed up here in the general title used here, *our adversaries* [6].

For I set; lit. *and I set.* Domestic confusions and strife were added to hostility from without. Nehemiah's reformation was, in part, to stop the grinding usury in time of dearth or to pay the king's taxes, through which men sold lands, vineyards, even their children [7].

God (lit.) *let them loose, each against his neighbor,* in that He left them to their own ways and withheld them not.

---

[1] Rib.   [2] Hagg. ii. 15–19.   [3] Osor.

[4] נָהְיָה לֹא נִהְיָה occurs only in 19 other places: "it came to pass," with מֵאֵת, "it was from," i. e. his doing, 1 Kings i. 27, xii. 24, 2 Chr. xi. 4; of a thing which had not its like, with כְּ or כְּמוֹ Ex. xi. 6, Deut. iv. 32, Jo. ii. 2, Jud. xix. 30, Dan. xii. 1, or abs., Jud. xx. 3, 12, Jer. v. 30, xlviii. 19, Ezek. xxi. 12, xxxix. 8. There remain five insulated cases; "was made God's people," Deut. xxvii. 9; "a desire accomplished," Pr. xiii. 19; "hath not been done," (rejecting an imputation) Neh. vi. ⁸; "was departed," Dan. ii. 1; as if he had ceased to be, Ib. viii. 27.

[5] Neh. iv. 7–11.

[6] צָרֵינוּ Neh. iv. 5 Heb. (11 Eng.), צַר, as calamity, is very rare, except in the idiom בְּצַר לְ. It is used twice in the construct, as a sort of adj., לֶחֶם צַר, *bread of affliction* Is. xxx. 20; עֵת צַר *time of affliction*, Job xxxviii. 23; and as united with the synonyme וּמְצוּקָה, Job xv. 24, וּמְצוּק, Ps. cxix. 143; absolutely, once only, Is. v. 30. The fem. צָרָה occurs, in all, 72 times.

[7] Neh. v. 1–12.

Before
C H R I S T
cir. 518.

11 But now I *will* not
be unto the residue of this
people as in the former days,
saith the LORD of hosts.

ʳ Hos. 2. 21, 22.
Joel 2. 22.
Hag. 2. 19.
† Heb. *of peace.*

ˢ Ps. 67. 6.

ᵗ See Hag. 1. 10.

12 ʳ For the seed *shall
be* † prosperous ; the vine
shall give her fruit, and
ˢ the ground shall give her
increase, and ᵗ the heavens

shall give their dew ; and
I will cause the remnant
of this people to possess all
these *things.*

13 And it shall come to
pass, *that* as ye were ᵘ a ᵘ Jer. 42. 18.
curse among the heathen,
O house of Judah, and
house of Israel ; so will I

Before
C H R I S T
cir. 518.

---

11. *And now.* The words imply a contrast
of God's dealings, rather than a contrast of
time. *I am not to the remnant of this people.*
He had said, *I will be to them God ;* so now
He does not say that He will not *do* to them,
as in former days, but *I am not to the remnant*
of this people as heretofore. He would be,
as He was in Jesus, in a new relation to
them.
12. *For the seed* shall be *peace*[1]. " [2] Your
seed shall be peace and a blessing, so that
they will call it 'a seed of peace.' " The
unusual construction is perhaps adopted, in
order to suggest a further meaning. It is a
reversal of the condition, just spoken of,
when there was *no peace to him that went, or to
him that returned.*
*The vine shall give her fruit and the ground
shall give her increase.* The old promise in
the law on obedience[3], as the exact contrary
was threatened on disobedience[4]. It had
been revived in the midst of promise of
spiritual blessing and of the coming of Christ,
in Ezekiel[5]. " [6] By the metaphor of sensible
things he explains (as the prophets often do)
the abundance of spiritual good in the time
of the new law, as did Hosea[7], Joel[8],
Amos[9], and many others." *And I will cause
the remnant of the people to inherit.* " [6] As if
he said, I promised these things not to you
who live now, but to the future remnant of
your people, i. e. those who shall believe in
Christ and shall be saved, while the rest
perish. These shall possess these spiritual
goods, which I promise now, under the image
of temporal." As our Lord said [10], *He that
overcometh shall inherit all things, and I will be
his God, and he shall be My son.*

[1] It cannot be, *the seed shall be safe,* (Jon.), for
םוֹלָשַׁה is never used except of *peace ;* nor is even
םוֹלָשׁ used as a predicate, except of human beings,
either directly or as implied, as in Job v. 24, *thy
tent,* םוֹלָשׁ לֶהֹאַ ; Job xxi. 9, *their houses are peace
from fear,* דַחָפִּמ םוֹלָשׁ םֶהיֵתָּב. The sense in-
columitas, integritas, is wrongly assumed in Röd.
Ges. Thes. Deut. xxix. 18, 1 Kgs ii. 33, Ps. xxxvii.
11, 37, lxxii. 3, 7, Is. lii. 7, lvii. 19, 21, Jer. iv. 10, vi.
14, except as far as this may be involved in " peace."
Nor can םוֹלָשַׁה עַרֶז be a noun. abs. before ןֶבֶג,

13. *As ye were a curse among the nations, O
house of Judah and house of Israel, so I will
save you.* The ten tribes bore the name of
Israel, in contrast with the two tribes with
the name of Judah, not only in the history
but in the prophets ; as Hosea says [11], *I will
no more have mercy upon the house of Israel,* and
on the house of Judah I will have mercy. Here
he unites both ; both, in the time of their
captivity, were *a curse,* were held to be a
thing accursed, as it is said, [12] *He that is hanged
is the curse of God,* i. e. a thing accursed by
Him ; and God foretold of Judah, that they
should be [13] *a desolation and a curse,* and by
Jeremiah, [14] *I will deliver them to be removed
into all the kingdoms of the earth for hurt, a reproach and a proverb, a taunt and a curse in all
places whither I shall drive them ;* and in deed,
when it was so, [15] *therefore is your land a desolation and an astonishment and a curse without
an inhabitant, as at this day.* Now the sentence was to be reversed as to both. *As ye
were a curse, among the nations,* naming each,
so I will save you. There would have been no
proportion between the curse and the blessing, unless both had been included under the
blessing, as they were under the curse. But
Israel had no share in the temporal blessing,
not returning from captivity, as Zechariah
knew they were not returned hitherto.
Therefore the blessings promised must be
spiritual. Even a Jewish commentator saw
this. " [16] It is possible, that this may have
been spoken of the second temple, on condition that they should keep the commandments of the Lord ; or, it is still future,
referring to the days of the Messiah : and
this is proved by the following verse which

" a seed of peace, the vine shall yield her fruit ;"
for " seed " has no relation to the " vine."
[2] Kim.　　[3] Lev. xxvi. 4.　　[4] Ib. 20.
[5] Ezek. xxxiv. 27.　[6] Rib.　[7] Hos. ii. 21, 22.
[8] Jo. ii. 23–25, iii. 18.　　　[9] Am. ix 13.
[10] Rev. xxi. 7.　[11] Hos. i. 6, 7.　[12] De. xxi. 23.
[13] 2 Kgs xxii. 19.
[14] Jer. xxiv. 9, add Ib. xxv. 18, *to make thee a desolation, an astonishment, a hissing and a curse ;* and of
those who went in rebellion to Egypt, *ye shall be an
execration* [הָלָאְ] *and an astonishment and a curse and
a reproach* (Ib. xlii. 18), *and that ye might be a curse
and a reproach among all the nations of the earth* (Ib.
xliv. 8.)　　[15] Ib. xliv. 22.　　[16] Kim. on ver. 12.

Before
C H R I S T
cir. 518.

save you, and ˣye shall be a blessing: fear not, *but*

ʸlet your hands be strong.

14 For thus s a i t h the L O R D of hosts; ᶻAs I t h o u g h t to punish you, when your f a t h e r s provoked me to wrath, saith

ˣGen. 12. 2.
Ruth 4. 11, 12.
Is. 19. 24, 25.
Zeph. 3. 20.
Hag. 2. 19.
ʸver. 9.
ᶻJer. 31. 28.

the LORD of hosts, ᵃand I repented not:

15 So a g a i n h a v e I thought in these days to do well unto Jerusalem and to the house of Judah: fear ye not.

16 ¶ These *are* the

Before
C H R I S T
cir. 518.

ᵃ2 Chr. 36. 16.
ch. 1. 6.

says, *O house of Judah and house of Israel.* During the second temple the house of Israel did not return."

And ye shall be a blessing. This is a revival and an application of the original promise to Abraham, [1]*thou shalt be a blessing;* which was continued to Jacob, [2] *God give thee the blessing of Abraham, to thee and to thy seed with thee.* And of the future king, of whom it is said, [3] *Thou gavest him length of days for ever and ever,* David says, *Thou hast made him blessings for ever,* and again, [4] *They shall be blessed in Him.* So Isaiah had said of the days of Christ, [5] *In that day shall Israel be the third with Egypt and with Assyria, a blessing in the midst of the land;* and symbolically of the cluster of grapes, [6] *Destroy it not: for a blessing is in it;* and Ezekiel, [7] *I will make them and the places round about My hill a blessing.* They were this; for of them, [8] *according to the flesh, Christ came, Who is over all, God blessed for ever;* of them were the Apostles and Evangelists, of them every writer of God's word, of them those who carried the Gospel throughout the world. " [9] Was this fulfilled, when the Jews were under the Persians? or when they paid tribute to the Greeks? or when they trembled, hour by hour, at the mention of the Roman name? Do not all count those who rule much happier than those oppressed by the rule of others? The prediction then was fulfilled, not then, but when Christ, the Sun of Righteousness, shone on the earth, and He chose from the Hebrews lights, through whom to dissipate darkness and illumine the minds of men who were in that darkness. The Jews, when restored from the captivity, seemed born to slavery." They were reputed to be of slaves the most despised. "But when they had through Christ been put in possession of that most sure liberty, they overthrew, through their empire, the power and tyranny of the evil spirits."

14. *As I thought to punish you* (lit. *to do evil to you*) *and repented not.* In like way God says in Jeremiah [10], *I have purposed and will not repent.*

15. *So have I turned and purposed* [11] *in these days to do well unto Jerusalem.* " [12] God, to be better understood, speaketh with the feelings and after the manner of men, although, in the passionless and unchangeable God, there is no provocation to anger, nor turning, implying change in Himself." So He says by Jeremiah, [13] *I know the thoughts that I think toward you, saith the Lord, thoughts of peace and not of evil.* And, with the same contrast as here, [14] *As I have watched over them to pluck up and to break down and to throw down, and to destroy and to afflict, so will I watch over them, to build and to plant, saith the Lord.* His having done what He purposed before was an earnest the more, that He would do what He purposed now. His chastisements were the earnests of His mercies; for they too were an austere form of His love. " [9] When the Lord stretches out His hand to strike those who are contumacious in guilt, none can hold His hand that He exact not the due punishment. Therefore He says, that He *repented not;* so, when He receives to grace those who repent of their sins, no one can any way delay the course of His benevolence. [15] *For the gifts and calling of God are without repentance."*

And to the house of Judah. [16] He speaks to the two tribes, not to, or of, the ten, because Christ was to come to the two tribes, and Zechariah was prophesying to them, and they were to be admonished to prepare themselves in good works, lest the coming of Christ should not profit them, on account of their depraved ways. But the ten tribes were far off in the cities of the Medes, nor was Christ to come to them; but they were to hear the Gospel through the Apostles, and so he prophesies of the conversion of all to the glory of Christ, yet he could not admonish all, but those only to whom he was sent.

16. *These are the things that ye shall do.* He exhorts them to the same duties, to which the former prophets had exhorted their fathers [17], and, as before, first positively to *truth* and *peace;* then to avoid everything

[1] Gen xii. 2.
[3] Ps. xxi. 4, 6.
[5] Is. xix. 24.
[7] Ezek. xxxiv. 26.
[2] Ib. xxviii. 4.
[4] Ib lxxii. 17.
[6] Ib lxv. 8.
[8] Rom. ix. 5.

[9] Osor.
[11] On ϽϽϽ see above on i. 6, p. 341, note 8.
[12] Dion.   [13] Jer. xxix. 11.
[15] Rom. xi. 29.   [16] Rib.
[10] Jer. iv. 28.

[14] Ib. xxxi. 28.
[17] vii. 9, 10.

Before
C H R I S T
cir. 518.

things that ye shall do ; ^bSpeak ye every man the truth to his neighbor ; †execute the j u d g m e n t of truth and peace in your gates :

17 ^cAnd let none of you imagine evil in your hearts against his neighbor ; and ^dlove no false oath : for all these *are things* that I hate, saith the LORD.

18 ¶ And the word of the LORD of hosts came unto me, saying,

b ch. 7. 9.
ver. 19.
Ephes. 4. 25.
† Heb. *judge
truth, and the
judgment of
peace.*

c Prov. 3. 29.
ch. 7. 10.

d ch. 5. 3, 4.

19 Thus saith the LORD of hosts ; ^eThe fast of the fourth *month,* ^fand the fast of the fifth, ^gand the fast of the seventh, ^hand the fast of the tenth, shall be to the house of Judah ⁱjoy and gladness, and cheerful ‖feasts ; ^kt h e r e f o r e love the truth and peace.

20 Thus saith the LORD of hosts ; *It shall* yet *come to pass,* that there s h a l l come people, and the inhabitants of many cities :

Before
C H R I S T
cir. 518.

e Jer. 52. 6, 7.
f Jer. 52. 12, 13.
ch. 7. 3, 5.
g 2 Kin. 25. 25.
Jer. 41. 1, 2.
h Jer. 52. 4.

i Esth. 8. 17.
Isai. 35. 10.

‖ Or, *solemn*, or,
set times.
k ver. 16.

---

contrary to it. *Judgment of peace* must be judgment which issues in peace, as all righteous judgment righteously received, in which case each party acquiesces, must. "¹ If ye judge righteousness, there will be peace between the litigants, according to that proverb, '²He that hath his coat taken from him by the tribunal, let him sing and go his way' [" because," says a gloss ³, " they have judged the judgment of truth, and have taken away that which would have been stolen property, if he retained it," being in fact not his]. And they have quoted that, ⁴*And all this people shall go to their place in peace.*" "⁵*All this people,* even he that is condemned in judgment. It is also interpreted of arbitration. What sort of judgment is that, in which there is peace ? It is that of arbitration."

17. *For all these things do I hate.* lit. emphatic, ⁶ *For they are all these things which I hate.* This is the sum of what I hate ; for they comprise in brief the breaches of the two tables, the love of God and of man.

19. *The fast of the fourth month.* On the ninth day *of the fourth month* ⁷ of Zedekiah's eleventh year, Jerusalem, in the extremity of famine, opened to Nebuchadnezzar, and his princes sat in her gate ; in the *tenth month* ⁸ of his ninth year Nebuchadnezzar began the siege. Ezekiel was bidden ⁹ *on its*

¹ Kim.
² Sanhedr. f. 7. a. quoted by Mc. Caul, p. 78.
³ Rashi, quoted Ib.   ⁴ Exod. xviii. 23.
⁵ Judah b. Korcha in Sanhr. f. 6 b. Ib.
⁶ את כל אלה is a sort of noun abs., as Hagg.
ii. 5.   ⁷ Jer. xxxix. 2, 3 ; lii. 6, 7.
⁸ 2 Kgs xxv. 1, Jer. xxxix. 1, lii. 4.
⁹ Ezek. xxiv. 1, 2.
¹⁰ Ib. 6–14. The Jews in S. Jerome's time added, that in the fourth month Moses brake the tables of the law ; in the fifth month was the rebellion on the return of the spies, and the sentence of the

tenth day ; *write thee the name of the day, of this same day,* as the beginning of God's uttermost judgments against *the bloody city* ¹⁰. The days of national sorrow were to be turned into exuberant joy, *joy and gladness and cheerful feasts* ¹¹, for the sorrows, which they commemorated, were but the harbingers of joy, when the chastisements were ended ; only He adds, *love the truth and peace ;* for such love whereby they would be Israelites indeed, in whose spirits is no guile, were the conditions of their participating the blessings of the Gospel, of which he goes on to speak ;

20. It shall *yet* be *that.* The promises are those which God had already made by Isaiah ¹² and Micah ¹³. Yet where was the shew of their fulfillment ? The Jews themselves, a handful : the temple unfinished ; its completion depending, in human sight, upon the will of their heathen masters, the rival worship at Samaria standing and inviting to coalition. Appearances and experience were against it. God says virtually, that it was, in human sight, contrary to all expectations. But "weakness is aye Heaven's might." Despite of all, of the fewness of those who were returned, their downheartedness, broken condition, hopelessness, though all had hitherto failed, though, or rather because, all human energy and strength were gone, as

forty years' wandering. This is true. For since Moses went up into the mount in the third month (Ex. xix. 1, 16, xxiv. 12, 16.), the end of the forty days (Ib. 18), after which he came down and brake the tables (Ex. xxxii. 15, 19) would fall in the fourth month. Ribera calculates the fourth month thus : setting off from Sinai, 20th day of 2d month, Nu. x. 11 ; 3 days' journey, Ib. 33 ; halt of one month, Ib. xi. 20, 21 ; of 7 days, Ib. xii. 15 ; 40 days' search of spies, Ib. xiii. 25.
¹¹ טוב as יום טוב, Esth. viii. 17. ix. 19, 22, Eccl. vii. 14.   ¹² Is. ii. 2, sqq.   ¹³ Mic. iv. 1. sqq.

Before
C H R I S T
cir. 518.
i Isai. 2. 3.
Mic. 4. 1, 2.
‖ Or, *continually.*
† Heb. *going.*
† Heb. *to intreat the face of the* LORD, ch. 7. 2.

21 And the inhabitants of one *city* shall go to another, saying, [1] Let us go ‖ † speedily † to pray before the LORD, and to seek the

LORD of hosts: I will go also.

22 Yea, [m] many people and strong nations shall come to seek the LORD of

Before
C H R I S T
cir. 518.

m Isai. 60. 3, &c. & 66. 23.

God had said before, *The Lord shall yet*[1] *choose Jerusalem,* so now, It shall yet[2] be *that. Nations and many cities shall come.* He describes vividly the eagerness and mutual impulse, with which not only many but mighty nations should throng to the Gospel, and every fresh conversion should win others also, till the great tide should sweep through the world.

21. *The inhabitants of one* city *shall go to another.* It is one unresting extension of the faith, the restlessness of faith and love. "[3] They shall not be satisfied with their own salvation, careless about the salvation of others; they shall employ all labor and industry, with wondrous love, to provide for the salvation of others as if it were their own." It is a marvelous stirring of minds. Missionary efforts, so familiar with us as to be a household word, were unknown then. The time was not yet come. *Before the faith* in Christ *came,* the Jewish people were not to be the converters of mankind. They were to await for Him, the Redeemer of the world, through Whom and to Whom they were to be first converted, and then the world through those who were of them. This mutual conversion was absolutely unknown. The prophet[4] predicts certainly that it would be, and in God's time it was. *From you,* S. Paul writes to a small colony in Greece[5], *sounded out the word of the Lord, not only in Macedonia and Achaia, but also in every place your faith to God-ward is spread abroad.* [6] *Your faith,* he writes to the heathen capital of the world, *is spoken of throughout the whole world.* Within eighty years after our Lord's Ascension, the Roman governor of Bithynia reported, on occasion of the then persecution, that it spread as a contagion. "[7] The contagion of that superstition traversed not cities only but villages and scattered houses too." Before the persecution, the temples had been desolated, the solemn rites long intermitted, the sacrificed animals had very rarely found a purchaser. An impostor of the same date says, "[8] Pontus is full of atheists and Christians." "[9] There is no one race of men," it was said before the middle of the second

century[10], "whether Barbarians or Greeks or by whatsoever name called, whether of those wandering houseless tribes who live in wagons or those pastoral people who dwell in tents, in which there are not prayers and Eucharists to the Father and Creator of all things, through the name of the crucified Jesus." "The word of our teacher," said another[11], "abode not in Judæa alone, as philosophy in Greece; but was poured out throughout the whole world, persuading Greeks and barbarians in their several nations and villages and every city, whole houses and each hearer individually, and having brought over to the truth no few even of the very philosophers. And if any ordinary magistrate forbid the Greek philosophy, forthwith it vanishes; but our teaching, forthwith at its first announcement, kings and emperors and subordinate rulers and governors with all their mercenaries and countless multitudes forbid, and war against us and try to extirpate; but it the rather flourishes." The second century had not closed, before another said, "[12] We are a people of yesterday, and yet we have filled every place belonging to you, cities, islands, castles, towns, assemblies, your very camp, your tribes, companies, palace, senate, forum! We leave you your temples only. We can count your armies; our numbers in a single province will be greater." "[13] Men cry out that the state is beset; that the Christians are in their fields, in their forts, in their islands. They mourn, as for a loss, that every sex, age, condition, and now even rank is going over to this sect." "[14] On whom besides have all nations believed, except on Christ Who hath already come?" Then having enumerated the nations mentioned in the Acts[15], he adds, "And now the varieties of the Getulians, and the many tracts of the Moors, all the bounds of the Spains, and the divers nations of the Gauls, and places of the Britons, unreached by the Romans but subdued to Christ; of Sarmatians, Dacians, Germans, and Scythians, and of many remote nations, and many provinces and islands, unknown to us, and which we can

1 i. 17, ii. 16 [12 Eng.]
2 עוד is premised emphatically.   3 Osor.
4 See below on ix. 12.   5 1 Thess. i. 8.
6 Rom. i. 8.   7 Plin. ad. Traj. Ep. x. 97.
8 Alexander in Lucian. Alexander.
9 S. Justin M. Dial. n. 117, on Mal. i. 10. p. 216.
Oxf. Tr.

10 Trypho says, "I escaped from the late war."
(A. D. 132–135) Dial. init. p. 70.
11 Clem. Alex. Strom. vi. fin.
12 Tert. Apol. n. 37, p. 78. Oxf. Tr.
13 Ib. n. 1. pp. 2. 3.
14 Tert. adv. Jud. c. 7 p. 113 Rig.
15 Acts ii. 9–11.

Before
C H R I S T
cir. 518.
hosts in Jerusalem, and to pray before the LORD.

23 Thus saith the LORD

of hosts; In those days *it shall come to pass*, that ten men shall [n] take hold out
Before
C H R I S T
cir. 518.
[n] Isai. 3. 6.
& 4. 1.

scarce enumerate. In all which places the name of Christ, Who hath already come, reigneth, seeing that before Him the gates of all cities are opened and none are shut against Him, before Whom [1] *the bars of iron are broken in pieces and the gates of brass are opened.* In all these places dwelleth a people called by the name of Christ. For who could reign over all, save Christ the Son of God, Who was foretold as about to reign over all nations forever?" Then having contrasted the limited rule of Solomon, Darius, the Pharaohs, Nebuchadnezzar, Alexander, "the Romans who protect their own empire by the strength of their legions and are unable to extend the might of their kingdom beyond these nations [Germans, Britons, Moors, Getulians], he sums up, "but the kingdom and the Name of Christ is extended everywhere, is believed in everywhere, is worshiped by all the nations above enumerated. Everywhere He reigns, everywhere is adored, is given everywhere equally to all. With Him no king hath greater favor; no Barbarian inferior joy; no dignities or birth enhance the merit of any; to all He is equal; to all, King; to all Judge; to all, God and Lord." A little later, a heathen owns, while calumniating, "[2] Those most foul rites of that impious coalition are growing throughout the whole world, as bad things come up most luxuriantly, evil ways creeping on daily." The Christian answers, "[3] That our number increases daily, this is no imputation of error, but a testimony to praise. For in a good mode of life, its own persevere, aliens accrue to it."

Let us go on and on, [4] perseveringly, until we attain *to entreat the face of the* Lord. It is not a Theism or Monotheism, but the God, Who had revealed Himself to Israel, Who, when our Lord came, was worshiped in Jerusalem, to which those invited say, *I too would go with thee.* Yet not so, but the words seem to speak of that which is a special gift of the Gospel, continued progress, "[5] *forgetting those things which are behind, and reaching forth unto those things which are before,* to *press toward the mark of the prize of the high calling of God in*

Christ Jesus. Let us go on and on ; whence it is a Christian proverb, "[6] not to go on is to go back." "[7] The whole life of a good Christian is a holy longing to make progress." "[8] The one perfection of man is, to have found that he is not perfect." "[9] If thou sayest, It sufficeth, thou art lost." "[10] To be unwilling to increase, is to decrease."

23. *Ten men of all languages of the nations.* Ten [11] is the symbol of a whole, all the numbers before it meeting in it and starting again from it. The day of Pentecost was to be the reversal of the confusion of Babel; all were to have one voice, as God had said, [12] *It* (the time) *shall come to gather all nations and tongues, and they shall come and see My glory.*

They shall lay hold of the skirt of one man who is a Jew, "[13] that is, of the Lord and Saviour, of Whom it is said, [14] *A prince shall not depart from Judah, nor a lawgiver from between his feet, until He shall come, for Whom it is laid up, and for Him shall the Gentiles wait ;* for [15] *there shall be a rod of Jesse, and He who shall arise to rule over the Gentiles, to Him shall the Gentiles seek.* And when they shall lay hold of Him, they shall desire to tread in His steps, since God is with Him. Or else, whosoever shall believe out of all nations, *shall lay hold of a man who is a Jew,* the Apostles who are from the Jews, and shall say, Let us go with you ; for we have known through the prophets and from the voice of all the Scriptures, that the Son of God, Christ, God and Lord, is with you. Where there is a most manifest prophecy, and the coming of Christ and His Apostles and the faith of all nations is preached, let us seek for nothing more."

"[16] Christ turning our sorrow into joy and a feast and good days and gladness, and transferring lamentation into cheerfulness, the accession to the faith and union to God by sanctification in those called to salvation shall not henceforth be individually ; but the cities shall exhort each other thereto, and all nations shall come in multitudes, the later ever calling out to those before them, *I too will go.* For it is written, [17] *iron sharpeneth iron, so doth a man the countenance of another.*

[1] Is. xlv. 2.
[2] Cæcil. in Minut. Fel. p. 80. Ouz.
[3] Minut. Fel. Ib. p. 312. Other like sayings are in Origen, (de Princ. iv. 1. c. Cels. i. 7, 67, ii. 13, iii. 24,) Lactantius, (v. 13) Arnobius (i. p. 33, ii. 50, Lugd.), who argues thence to the divinity of the Gospel, Jul. Firmicus, (c. 21 B. P. iv. 172.)
[4] נלכה הלוך.   [5] Phil. iii. 13, 14.
[6] "non progredi est regredi."
[7] S. Aug. in 1 Ep. S. Joann. Hom. iv. n. 6. p. 1144. Oxf. Tr.

[8] Id. Serm. 120, [170. Ben.] c. 8. p. 877. Oxf. Tr.
[9] Id. Serm. 119, [169.] fin. ib. p. 871. Oxf. Tr.
[10] Nolle proficere deficere est. S. Bern. Ep. 254 ad Guarin. n. 4.
[11] As in Gen. xxxi. 7, *he hath changed my wages these ten times ;* Lev. xxvi. 26, *when I have broken your staff of bread, ten women shall bake your bread in one oven ;* Nu. xiv. 22, *those men which have seen My glory, have tempted Me now these ten times, and have not hearkened to My voice.*
[12] Is. lxvi. 18.   [13] S. Jer.   [14] Gen. xlix. 8–10.
[15] Is. xi. 10.   [16] S. Cyr.   [17] Pr. xxvii. 17.

of all languages of the nations, even shall take hold
of the skirt of him that is
a Jew, saying, We will go
with you: for we have
heard °*that* God *is* with
you.

°1 Cor. 14. 25.

1 *God defendeth his church.* 9
*Zion is exhorted to rejoice for
the coming of Christ, and his
peaceable kingdom.* 12 *God's
promises of victory and defence.*

THE ªburden of theªJer. 23. 33.
word of the LORD in

For the zeal of some is ever found to call
forth others to fulfill what is good. But what
is the aim proposed to the cities, that is, the
Gentiles ? *To entreat and to seek the face of the
Lord,* i. e. Christ, Who is the exact image of
God the Father, and, as is written, ¹*the
brightness of His glory, and the express image of
His Person,* of Whom also the divine David
saith, ²*Shew Thy countenance to Thy servant.*
For the Image and Countenance of God the
Father hath shone upon us. Having Him
propitious and kind, we lay aside the injury
from sin, being justified through faith, ³*not
by works of righteousness, which we have done,
but according to His great mercy.*—But how
they shall come, he explains. By the *ten men*
you are to understand the perfect number of
those who come. For the number *ten* is the
symbol of perfection. But that those of the
Gentiles, who cleave to the holy Apostles,
took in hand to go the same way with them,
being justified by the faith in Christ, he sets
evidently before us. For little children, if
they would follow their fathers, lay hold of
the hem of their dress, and, aided by the
touch and hanging from their dress, walk
steadily and safely. In like way, they too
who ⁴*worshiped the creature rather than the
Creator,* choosing as their true fathers the
bringers-in of the Gospel-doctrines, and joining themselves by like-mindedness to them,
follow them, being still of childlike minds,
and go the same way, ever shewing themselves zealous followers of their life, and by
continued progress advancing ⁵*to a perfect
man, to the measure of the stature of the fullness of
Christ.* But why do they follow them?
Being persuaded that God is with them, i. e.
Emmanuel, *God with us.* But that this
calling belongs not only to those of the blood
of Israel but to all nations throughout the
world, he indicated by saying, that those who
laid hold of that hem should be *of all languages.* But when were the nations called to
the knowledge of the truth, and when did
they desire to seek the face of the Lord and
to entreat it, and to go the same way, as it
were, as the holy Apostles, except when the

Only-Begotten came to us, Who is ⁶the
expectations of the nations ; to Whom also the
divine David singeth, ⁷*All the nations, whom
Thou hast made, shall come and worship before
Thee, O Lord ?* For the multitude of the
nations also is saved through Him."
The startling condescension of this passage
is, that our Lord is spoken of as "a man, a
Jew." Yet of His Human Nature it is not
only the simple truth, but essential to the
truth. Pilate said to Him in scorn, *Am I a
Jew* ⁸*?* *Thine own nation and the Chief Priests
have delivered Thee unto me.* But it was essential to the fulfillment of God's promises.
The Christ was to be ⁹*the Son of David.*
¹⁰*Hath not the Scripture said, That Christ cometh
of the seed of David, and out of the town of
Bethlehem, where David was ?* David, ¹¹*being a
prophet and knowing that God had sworn with an
oath to him, that of the fruit of his loins according to the flesh, He would raise up Christ to sit
on his throne ;* ¹²*Of this man's seed hath God,
according to promise, raised unto Israel a Saviour, Jesus.* Whence S. Paul begins his
great doctrinal Epistle with this contrast,
¹³*the Gospel of God concerning His Son Jesus
Christ, which was made of the seed of David according to the flesh, and declared to be the Son of
God with power.* He was that ¹⁴*one Man
among a thousand,* whom Solomon says, *I
found ;* but *a woman among all those have I not
found ;* the one in the whole human race. It
was fulfilled in the very letter when ¹⁵*they
brought to Him all that were diseased, and besought Him that they might only touch the hem of
His garment : and as many as touched were made
perfectly whole.* ¹⁶*The whole multitude sought to
touch Him, for there went virtue out of Him
and healed all.*
Even the Jews saw the reference to the
Messiah. "¹⁷All nations shall come, falling
on their faces before the Messiah and the
Israelites, saying, Grant, that we may be
Thy servants and of Israel. For as relates to the doctrine and the knowledge of the
law, the Gentiles shall be their servants, according to that, *In those days ten men &c.*"
IX. 1. *The burden* ¹⁸ *of the word of the Lord*

---

¹ Heb. i. 3.	² Ps. cxix. 135.	³ Tit. iii. 5.
⁴ Rom. i. 25.	⁵ Eph. iv. 13.	⁶ Gen. xlix. 10.
⁷ Ps. lxxxvi. 9.
⁸ S. John xviii. 35.	⁹ S. Matt. i. 1. xxii. 42.
¹⁰ S. John vii. 42.	¹¹ Acts ii. 30.	¹² Ib. xiii. 23.
¹³ Rom. i. 1-4.	¹⁴ Eccl. vii. 28.

¹⁵ S. Matt. xiv. 35, 36.
¹⁶ S. Luke vi. 19. add Ib. viii. 46, S. Mark v. 30.
¹⁷ Pesikta Rabbathi, in Yalkut Shim 'oni ii. 56. 4.
in Schöttgen ad loc.
¹⁸ On the word "Burden" see above on Nah. i. 1.
p. 129.

the land of Hadrach, and ᵇ Damascus *shall be* the rest

thereof: when ᶜ the eyes of man, as of all the tribes of

in [or. *upon* [1]] *the land of Hadrach.* The foreground of this prophecy is the course of the victories of Alexander, which circled round the holy land without hurting it, and ended in the overthrow of the Persian empire. The surrender of Damascus followed first, immediately on his great victory at the Issus; then Sidon yielded itself and received its ruler from the conqueror, Tyre he utterly destroyed; Gaza, we know, perished; he passed harmless by Jerusalem. Samaria, on his return from Egypt, he chastised.

It is now certain that there was a city called Hadrach in the neighborhood of Damascus and Hamath, although its exact site is not known. "It was first found upon the geographical tablets [2] among the Assyrian inscriptions." "[3] In the catalogue of Syrian cities, tributary to Nineveh, (of which we have several copies in a more or less perfect state, and varying from each other, both in arrangement and extent) there are three names, which are uniformly grouped together and which we read Manatsuah, Magida [Megiddo] and Du'ar [Dor]. As these names are associated with those of Samaria, Damascus, Arpad, Hamath, Carchemish, *Hadrach,* Zobah, there can be no doubt of the position of the cities [4]." In the Assyrian Canon, Hadrach is the object of three Assyrian expeditions, [5] 9183 (B. C. 818), 9190 (811) and 9200 (801). The first of these follows upon one against Damascus, 9182 (817). In the wars of Tiglath-pileser ii. (the Tiglath-pileser of Holy Scripture,) it has been twice deciphered; 1) in the war B. C. 738, 737, after the mention of "the

cities to Saua the mountain which is in Lebanon were divided, the land of Bahalzephon to Ammana" (Ammon), there follows Hadrach [6]; and subsequently there are mentioned as joined to the league, "19 districts of Hamath, and the cities which were round them, which are beside the sea of the setting sun." 2) In his "war in Palestine and Arabia," "[7] the city of Hadrach to the land of Saua," and six other cities are enumerated, as "the cities beside the upper sea," which, he says, "I possessed, and six of my generals as governors over them I appointed." No other authority nearly approaches these times. The nearest authority is of the second century after our Lord, A.D. 116. "[8] R. Josè, born of a Damascene mother, said," answering R. Yehudah ben Elai [9], "I call heaven and earth to witness upon me, that I am of Damascus, and that there is a place called Hadrach." S. Cyril of Alexandria says [10] that "the land of Hadrach must be somewhere in the Eastern parts, and near to Emath (now Epiphania of Antioch) a little further than Damascus, the metropolis of the Phœnicians and Palestine." A writer of the 10th century [11] says that there was "a very beautiful mosque there, called the Mesjed-el-Khadra, and that the town was named from it." The conjecture that Hadrach might be the name of a king [12], or an idol [13], will now probably be abandoned, nor can the idea, (which before seemed the most probable and which was very old), that it was a symbolic name, hold any longer. For the Prophets *do* use symbolic names [14]; but then they are

---

[1] As Is. ix. 8, "The Lord sent a word *upon* Jacob (בְּיַעֲקֹב) and it lighted on Israel" (בְּיִשְׂרָאֵל).

[2] Published in the British Museum Series vol. ii. Pl. 53, Prof. Rawlinson.

[3] Sir H. Rawlinson, Athenæum, No. 1869, Aug. 22, 1863, p. 246, where he "published his reading, some time after he identified it." "It has since been identified by others."

[4] Sir H. Rawlinson adds in a note; "From the position on the lists, I should be inclined to identify it with Homs or Edessa which was certainly a very ancient capital, (being the Kedesh of the Egyptian records) and which would not otherwise be represented in the Assyrian inscriptions." Note 26. Ib.

[5] Oppert in the Révue Archéologique 1868. T. 2. p. 323.

[6] G. Smith's Assyrian discoveries p. 276.

[7] Ib. p. 284.

[8] in Siphre sect. Debarim (ed. Friedm. p. 65.)

[9] In the time of Hadrian. Wolf Bibl. Hebr. i. 411.

[10] Here.

[11] David ben Abraham, MS. Opp. Add. f. 25, quoted by Neubauer, Geogr. du Talmud p. 298. The account of one Joseph Abassi that "it was once a large city, but now small; that the Arabs told much of its kings and princes; that it was said to have had giants and was about 10 miles from Damascus," no doubt relates to Edrei. See Hengstenberg Christol. ii. 92 sqq. A. v. Kremer, Beiträge zur Geographie des nördlichen Syriens (in d. Denkschriften d. Kais.

Akad. d. Wissensch. [Wien] philos. hist. Classe, A. 1852. I. Abth. p. 21 sqq.) and Topographie v. Damascus (Ib. 1854. 2 Abth. p. 1 sqq. ; 1855 2 Abth. p. 1 sqq.) and Wetzstein d. Markt v. Damascus (ZDMG. 1857. p. 476 sqq.) Reisebericht üb. Hauran u. d. Trachonen (1860), carry out the evidence that no trace of such a place can now be found. Köhler ad loc. T. ii. p. 7.

[12] The idiom, *the land of,* is used of a people, Cannan, Benjamin, Israel, Judah, Assyria, the Philistines; or of the actual king, speaking of his territory, (as Neh. ix. 22, *they possessed the land of Sihon, and the land of the king of Heshbon and the land of Og, king of Bashan,* (Sihon and Og and the king of Heshbon being, at the time spoken of, in actual possession of that land; but it is nowhere used of any past king or of an idol; much less would it be used in reference to an unknown king or idol. Scotland might, in oratory, be called "land of the Bruce," or England perhaps, "thou land of Mammon." But it would not be called, without emphasis, "land of Stephen" or "Edgar" or any obscure Saxon king.

[13] The people, not the land, is called "the people of Chemosh" (i. e. the people who worshiped it) Nu. xxi. 29. Jer. xlviii. 46. Nor is there any like name of an idol. "Derketo" (v. Alphen) would be תַּרְעָתָא. Hitzig gave up the combination, by which he made the name of an idol. (Kl. Proph. Ed. 3.)

[14] As "Ariel," Is. xxix. 1, 2, 7; "The burden of the

names which they themselves frame. Micah again selects several names of towns, now almost unknown and probably unimportant, in order to impress upon his people some meaning connected with them [1], but then he does himself so connect it. He does not name it (so to say), leaving it to explain itself. The name Hadrach [2] would be a real name, used symbolically, without anything in the context to shew that it is a symbol.

The cities, upon which the burden or heavy prophecy tell, possessed no interest for Israel. Damascus was no longer a hostile power; Hamath had ever been peaceable, and was far away ; Tyre and Sidon did not now carry on a trade in Jewish captives. But the Jews knew from Daniel, that the empire, to which they were in subjection, would be overthrown by Greece [3]. When that rapid attack should come, it would be a great consolation to them to know, how they themselves would fare. It was a turning point in *their* history and the history of the then known world. The prophet describes [4] the circuit, which the conqueror would take around the land which God defended ; how the thunder-cloud circled round Judæa, broke irresistibly upon cities more powerful than Jerusalem, but was turned aside from the holy city *in going and returning*, because God encamped around it.

" [5] The selection of the places and of the whole line of country corresponds very exactly to the march of Alexander after the battle of Issus, when Damascus, which Darius had chosen as the strong depository of his wealth, of Persian women of rank, confidential officers and envoys [6]," was betrayed, but so opened its gates to his general, Parmenio. Zidon, a city renowned for its antiquity and its founders, surrendered freely ; Tyre, here specially marked out, was taken after a 7 months' siege ; Gaza too resisted for 5 months, was taken, and, as it was said, "plucked up [7]."

And Damascus shall be *the rest thereof.* God's judgment fell first upon Damascus. But the word "resting-place" is commonly used of quiet peaceful resting, especially as given by God to Israel ; of the ark, the token of the Presence of God, after its manifold removals, and of the glorious dwelling-place of the Christ among men [8]. The prophet seems then purposely to have chosen a word of large meaning, which should at once express (as he had before [9]), that the word of God should fall heavily on Damascus and yet be its resting-place. Hence, about the time of our Lord, the Jews interpreted this of the coming of the Messiah, that " [10] Jerusalem should reach to the gates of Damascus. Since Damascus shall be the place of His rest, but the place of His rest is only the house of the sanctuary, as it is said, *This is My rest for ever ; here will I dwell.*" Another added [11], " All the prophets and all prophesied but of the years of redemption and the days of the Messiah." Damascus, on the conversion of S. Paul, became the first resting-place of the word of God, the first-fruits of the Gentiles

---

desert of the sea," Ib. xxi. 1; "the sea," Jer. xlix. 23; "Sheshac," of Babylon, (whatever the explanation is, perhaps from sinking down, coll. שכך Gen. viii. 1) Jer. xxv. 26, li. 41; "the land Merathaim," ("double rebellion"), and "the inhabitants of Pekod " ("visitation") of Babylon (Jer. l. 21); not Dumah, which is probably a real proper name, Is. xxi. 11; nor לב קמי, (Jer. li. 1.) for כשדים ; for כשדים could not be mentally substituted for it, since ישבי כשים would be an impossible combination. For inhabitants are of a land, city &c; but כשדים are the people themselves.

[1] See ab. on Micah i. 10, p. 221.

[2] The word, divided into two halves, would signify, "sharp-soft." חד is used of sharpness (see on Hab. i. 8. comp. Ps. lvii. 5, Is. xlix. 2.); רך of delicacy, Deut. xxxiii. 54–56; of weakness, Ib. xx. 8, 2 Chr. xiii. 7. And so it would signify, what was in one respect or at one time "sharp," and in or at another, "soft." A Jewish tradition, extant in times soon after our Lord, so explained it: "Severe to the Gentiles, and tender to Israel." (R. Judah ben Elai, a disciple of R. Akibah. Wolf. Bibl. Hebr. ii. 690.) S. Jerome has the same from his Jewish teacher, "The burden of the word of the Lord is on the land of Hadrach ; on which the Lord exercised both His austerity and clemency; austerity on those who would not believe, clemency on those who, with the Apostles, returned to Him." The name would have singularly suited Persia, whose empire Alexander was engaged in destroying, when this prophecy was fulfilled, and which was aimed at in them. It would describe them as they were, fierce and cruel, as conquerors, but infamous, even among the Heathen, for their incests. Sins of the

flesh, destroying pure love, brutalizing the soul, disorganizing the frame, are parents of ferocity, from which voluptuousness seems at first sight most alien.

[3] Dan. viii. 20, 21.   [4] See below on ver. 8.

[5] Pusey's "Daniel the Prophet," pp. 279, 280.

[6] Grote's Greece xii. 173, 4.

[7] κατεσπασμένη. Strabo xvi. 2. 30.

[8] מנוחה is used of rest or a place of rest, given by God, Deut. xii. 9, Ps. xxiii. 2, xcv. 11, Mi. ii. 10, Is. xxviii. 12, xxxii. 18 ; dwelling of God, Ps. cxxxii. 8, 14, Is. lxvi. 1; for the ark, 1 Chr. xxviii. 2; of the Messiah, Is. xi. 10. It is probably a proper name, Jud. xx. 43.

[9] הניח Zech. vi. 8.

[10] R. Johanan in Midrash Shir Hasshirim on Cant. vii. 4 in Raym. Pug. Fid. 643. This Midrash gives a second mystical interpretation of Hadrach. "Hadrach (הדריך) is the King Messiah, Who is to guide (להדריך) all who come into the world by repentance before God, Blessed be for ever." Ib. "R. Johanan was a disciple of the elder Hillel and Shammai, according to the Pirkè Aboth c. 2 ; prince of Israel for 40 years, 5 of them after the destruction of the temple. Rashi on cod. Rosh Hasshana, end." Wolf Bibl. Hebr. ii. 844.

[11] Mar (quoted by Rashi) i. e. Rabbi ben Nachman "Rector of the Academy of Pombedita in 300." De Rossi Dict. St. v. Rabboth. Ibn Ezra has; "the rest of the prophecy shall be on Damascus; for this prophecy shall be fulfilled, connected with the second temple ; For the eyes of man are to the Lord; for many from the men of Damascus shall return to worship the Lord and to turn to the obedience of Israel in Jerusalem." And so Kimchi, "Damascus shall be His resting-place, i. e. the Shechinah of His glory and prophecy."

Israel, *shall be* toward the LORD.

2 And [d] H a m a t h also

shall border thereby; [e] Ty-rus, and [f] Zidon, though it be very [g] wise.

Before
CHRIST
cir. 487.

[e] Isai. 23.
Ezek. 26, & 27,
& 28. Amos 1. 9. [f] 1 Kin. 17. 9. Ezek. 28. 21. Obad. 20.
[g] Ezek. 28. 3, &c.

whom the Apostle of the Gentiles gathered from East to West throughout the world.

When [or *For*] *the eyes of man, as* [lit. *and* i. e. especially beyond others] *of all the tribes of Israel,* shall be *toward the Lord.* This also implies a conversion of Gentiles, as well as Jews. For *man,* as contrasted with Israel, must be the heathen world, mankind [1]. "[2] The eyes of all must needs look in adoration to God, expecting all good from Him, because the Creator of all provided for the well-being of all, as the Apostle says, [3] *Is He the God of the Jews only? Is He not also of the Gentiles? Yea, of the Gentiles also.* God's time of delivering His people is, when they pray to Him. So Jehoshaphat prayed, [4] *O our God, wilt Thou not judge them? For we have no strength against this great company, which is come against us, and we know not what we shall do; but our eyes are on Thee* [5]; and the Psalmist says, [6] *The eyes of all wait toward Thee;* and, [7] *as the eyes of servants are unto the hand of their masters, and as the eyes of a maiden are unto the hand of her mistress, so our eyes are unto the Lord our God, until He have mercy upon us.* "For in those days," says a Jew, who represents the traditional interpretation [8], "man shall look to his Creator, and his eyes shall look to the Blessed One, as it was said above, *we will go with you,* and they shall join themselves, they and their cities, to the cities of Israel." And another [9]; "In those days the eyes of all mankind shall be to the Lord, not to idols or images; therefore the land of Hadrach and Damascus, and the other places near the land of Israel—shall be included among the cities of Judah, and shall be in the faith of Israel."

2. *And Hamáth also shall border thereby* [10].

Near to it in place and character, it shall share its subdual. After the betrayal of Damascus, Parmenio was set over all Syria. "[11] The Syrians, not as yet tamed by the losses of war, despised the new empire, but, swiftly subdued, they were commanded."

And Zidon. Zidon, although probably older than Tyre [12], is here spoken of parenthetically, as subordinate. Perhaps, owing to its situation, it was a wealthy [13], rather than a strong place. Its name is "Fishing-town;" in Joshua, it is called "the great [14]," perhaps the metropolis; while Tyre is named from its strength [15]. It infected Israel with its idolatry [16], and is mentioned among the nations who oppressed them and from whom God delivered them on their prayers [17], probably under Jabin. In the time of the Judges, it, not Tyre, was looked to for protection [18]. In the times of Ezekiel it had become subordinate, furnishing "rowers [19]" to Tyre; but Esarhaddon, about 80 years before, boasts that he had taken it, destroyed its inhabitants, and repeopled it with men from the East, building a new city which he called by his own name [20]. Tyre too had been taken by Nebuchadnezzar [21]. At the restoration from the captivity, Sidon had the first place [22], which it retained in the time of Xerxes [23]. But Artaxerxes Ochus gained possession of it by treachery, when all Phœnicia revolted from Persia, and, besides those crucified, 40,000 of its inhabitants perished by their own hands [24], twenty years before the invasion of Alexander, to whom it submitted willingly [25].

The prophet having named Tyre and Zidon together, yet continues as to Tyre

[1] So Israel and *man* (הָאָדָם) are contrasted in Jer. xxxii. 20.
[2] Rib.   [3] Rom. iii. 29.   [4] 2 Chron. xx. 12.
[5] כִּי עָלֶיךָ עֵינֵינוּ.
[6] אֵלֶיךָ יְשַׂבֵּרוּ Ps. cxlv. 15; without עֵינֵי Ps. civ. 27; and in the same sense, with לְ, שָׂבַּרְתִּי לִישׁוּעָתְךָ Ps. cxix. 166.
[7] Ps. cxxiii. 2. God's eye is said to be אֶל יְרֵאָיו, *toward them that fear Him.* Ps. xxxiii. 18, or in Ezra's Chaldee, *The eye of their God was upon the elders* (עַל שָׂבֵי) *of the Jews* (Ezr. v. 5.), or, *the eyes of the Lord thy God are upon it* (the land) בָּהּ, De xi. 12; but there is no construction like עֵין לְיֵי אָדָם "the Lord hath an eye on (obj.) man" (as lxx. Jon. Syr.) The passages, *Whose eyes are opened* (פְּקָחוֹת) *upon all the ways of the sons of men, to give &c.* (Jer. xxxii.

[19] "His eyes behold the nations" (בְּגוֹיִם תִּצְפֶּינָה Ps. lxvi. 7), are altogether different. "The eye of" must be construed as "his own eye."
[8] Rashi.   [9] Kimchi.
[10] It might be also, *and Hamath too, which bordereth thereby,* viz. shall be *the place of its rest,* as well as Damascus, but it seems not so forcible.
[11] Q. Curtius iv. 1.
[12] "The Tyrians are often called Sidonians; the Sidonians are never called Tyrians."
[13] Its manufactures of silver bowls and of female robes of great beauty, are mentioned by Homer (Il. vi. 289, xxiii. 743, 744; Od. iv. 614–618.); Homer does not name Tyre.
[14] Jos. xi. 8, xix. 28.   [15] Ib. xix. 29.   [16] Jud. x. 6.
[17] Ib. 12.   [18] Ib. xviii. 7, 28.   [19] Ezek. xxvii. 8.
[20] Inscription of Esarhaddon (Annals of the past iii. 112). Such names, in the East, last only with the conquerors.
[21] See vol. i. pp. 249, 250, and, more fully, "Daniel the Prophet," pp. 289, 290.
[22] Ezr. iii. 7.   [23] Herod. viii. 67, see also vii. 9. 6.
[24] Diod. xvi. 41 sqq. Mela i. 12.   [25] Curt. iv. 3.

Before
C H R I S T
cir. 487.

ʰ Job 27. 16.
Ezek. 28. 4, 5.

3 And Tyrus did build herself a strong hold, and ʰ heaped up silver as the dust, and fine gold as the mire of the streets.

4 Behold, ¹the LORD will cast her out, and he will smite ᵏ her power in the sea; and she shall be devoured with fire.

Before
C H R I S T
cir. 487.

ⁱ Isai. 23. 1.
ᵏ Ezek. 26. 17.

---

alone, as being alone of account in the days of which he is speaking, those of Alexander. *Although*, rather, *because she is very wise*. Man's own wisdom is his foolishness and destruction, as *the foolishness of God is his wisdom and salvation*. God ¹ *taketh the wise in their own craftiness.* ² *For after that, in the wisdom of God, the world by wisdom knew not God, it pleased God by the foolishness of preaching to save them that believe.* Of the Hagarenes it is said, they ³ *seek wisdom upon earth; none of these know the way of wisdom, or remember her paths.* The wisdom of Tyre was the source of her pride, and so of her destruction also. ⁴ *Because thy heart is lifted up, and thou hast said, I am a god, I sit in the seat of God, in the midst of the seas; yet thou art a man and not God, though thou hast set thine heart as the heart of God; behold thou art wiser than Daniel, there is no secret that they can hide from thee. Therefore I will bring strangers upon thee—they shall bring thee down to the pit.* So of Edom Obadiah says, ⁵ *The pride of thy heart hath deceived thee, thou that dwellest in the clefts of the rock. Shall I not destroy the wise men out of Edom, and understanding out of the mount of Esau?*

3. *And Tyre did build herself a stronghold.* She built it for herself, not for God, and trusted to it, not to God, and so its strength brought her the greater fall. The words in Hebrew express yet more. "Tyre" (*Zor*) lit. " *the rock*," built herself *mazor, tower,* a rock-like fort, as it were, a rock upon a rock for exceeding strength, binding her together. " ⁶ The walls, 150 feet high and of breadth proportionate, compacted of large stones, embedded in gypsum," seemed to defy an enemy who could only approach her by sea. " ⁷ In order to make the wall twice as strong they built a second wall ten cubits broad, leaving a space between of five cubits, which they filled with stones and earth." Yet high walls do not fence in only; they also hem in. *Mazor* is both " a stronghold " and " a siege." Wealth and strength, without God, do but invite and embitter the spoiler and the conqueror."

And she heaped up silver as the dust, and fine

gold *as the mire of the streets.* Though *he heap up silver as the dust,* Job says. ⁸ *The King,* Solomon, *made silver in Jerusalem as stones*⁹. Through her manifold commerce she gathered to herself wealth, as abundant as the mire and the dust, and as valueless. " Gold and silver," said a heathen, " are but red and white earth." Its strength was its destruction. Tyre determined to resist Alexander, " ¹⁰ trusting in the strength of the island, and the stores which they had laid up," the strength within and without, of which the Prophet speaks.

4. *Behold.* Such were the preparations of Tyre. Over against them, as it were, the prophet sets before our eyes the counsels of God. " ¹¹ Since they had severed themselves from the providence of God, they were now to experience His power." *The Lord will cast her out* ¹², lit. deprive her of her possessions, give her an heir of what she had amassed, viz: the enemy ; *and he will smite her power or wealth* ¹³, of which Ezekiel says, ¹⁴ *With thy wisdom and with thine understanding thou hast gotten thee riches, and hast gotten gold and silver into thy treasures: by the greatness of thy wisdom and by thy traffic thou hast increased thy riches, and thine heart is lifted up because of thy riches* ¹⁵. All wherein she relied, and so too the stronghold itself, God would *smite in the sea.* The sea was her confidence and boast. She said ¹⁶ *I am a God; I sit in the seat of God, in the midst of the seas.*

The scene of her pride was to be that of her overthrow; the waves, which girt her round, should bury her ruins and wash over her site. Even *in the sea* the hand of God should find her, and *smite her in it,* and *into it,* and so that she should abide in it. " ¹⁷ They mocked at the king, as though he thought to prevail against Neptune [the sea]." " ¹⁸ Ye despise this land-army, through confidence in the place, that ye dwell in an island," was the message of Alexander, " but soon will I shew you that ye dwell on a continent."

Every device had been put in force in its defence : the versatility by which the inhabitants of an island, some 2½ miles in circumference, held at bay the conqueror of the

---

¹ Job v. 13.   ² 1 Cor. i. 21.   ³ Baruch iii. 23.
⁴ Ezek. xxviii. 2, 8.   ⁵ Ob. 3, 8.   ⁶ Arrian ii. 21.
⁷ Diod. Sic. xvii. 43.   ⁸ Job xxvii. 16.
⁹ 2 Chron. ix. 27.   ¹⁰ Diod. Sic. xvii. 40.   ¹¹ Theod.
* ¹² וֵּרַשׁ, of God, is chiefly used of the driving out the Canaanitish nations before Israel, Ex. xxxiv. 24, Nu. xxxii. 21, Ps. xliv. 3, 1 Kgs xiv. 24, xxi. 26, 2 Kgs xvi. 3, xvii. 8. xxi. 2.

¹³ חֵיל cannot be here the outer wall (on which see Nah. iii. 8, ab. p. 156, n. 2.) which was useless in island Tyre, whose walls rising from the sea needed no outer wall and admitted of no fosse or pomœrium.
¹⁴ Ezek. xxviii. 4, 5.   ¹⁵ יחל.
¹⁶ Ezek. xxviii. 2.
¹⁷ Diod. Sic. xvii. 41.   ¹⁸ Q. Curt. iv. 7.

Before
C H R I S T
cir. 487.

1 Jer. 47. 1, 5.
Zeph. 2. 4.

5 [1] Ashkelon shall see *it*, and fear; Gaza also *shall see it*, and be very sorrow-ful, and Ekron; for her expectation shall be ashamed; and the king

Before
C H R I S T
cir. 487.

battle of Issus with unlimited resources, " [1] engineers from Cyprus and all Phœnicia," and " [2] a fleet of 180 ships from Cyprus," attests the wisdom in which the prophet says, she would trust. " [3] She had already a profusion of catapults and other machines useful in a siege, and easily prepared manifold others by the makers of war-engines and all sorts of artificers whom she had, and these invented new engines of all sorts; so that the whole circuit of the city was filled with engines." Divers who should loosen the mole; grappling hooks and nets to entangle near-assailants; melted metal or heated sand to penetrate between the joints of their armor; bags of sea-weed to deaden the blows of the battering machines; a fireship navigated so as to destroy the works of the enemy, while its sailors escaped; fiery arrows; wheels set in continual motion, to turn aside the missiles against them [4], bear witness to an unwearied inventiveness of defence. The temporary failures might have shaken any mind but Alexander's (who is even said to have hesitated [5]) but that he dared not, by abandoning the enterprise, lose the prestige of victory. Yet all ended in the massacre of 6, 7, or 8000 of her men, the crucifixion of 2000, the sale of the rest, whether 13,000 or 30,000, into slavery [6]. None escaped save those whom the Sidonians secreted in the vessels [7], with which they had been compelled to serve against her. *And she herself* [8], when her strength is overthrown, *shall be devoured with fire.* " [7] Alexander, having slain all, save those who fled to the temples, ordered the houses to be set on fire."

5. *Ashkelon shall see and fear.* The words express that to *see* and *fear* shall be as one [9]. The mightiest and wealthiest, Tyre, having fallen, the neighbor cities of Philistia who had hoped that her might should be their stay, shall stand in fear and shame. Tyre, being a merchant-city, the mother-city of the cities of the African coast and in Spain, its desolation caused the more terror [10].

And the [a] *king shall perish from Gaza*, i. e. it shall have no more kings. It had been the policy of the world-empires to have tributary kings in the petty kingdoms which they conquered, thus providing for their continued tranquil submission to themselves [11]. The internal government remained as before: the people felt no difference, except as to the payment of the tribute. The policy is expressed by the title "king of kings," which they successively bore. Sennacherib speaks of the kings of Ascalon, Ekron and Gaza [12]. A contemporary of Alexander [13] mentions, that the king of Gaza was brought alive to Alexander on its capture. Alexander's policy was essentially different from that of the world-monarchs before him. *They* desired only to hold an empire as wide as possible, leaving the native kings, if they could; and only, if these were intractable, placing their own lieutenants. Alexander's policy was to blend East and West into one [14]. These petty sovereignties, so many insulated centres of mutual repulsion, were essentially at variance with this plan, and so this remnant of sovereignty of 1500 years was taken away by him, when, after a siege in which he himself was twice wounded, he took it. Alexander wholly depopulated it, and repeopled the city with strangers.

And Ashkelon shall not be inhabited. Ashkelon yielded at once to Jonathan, when he " camped against it [15]," after he had taken and " burned Ashdod and the cities round about it." In another expedition of Jonathan its inhabitants " [16] met him honorably," while " they of Gaza shut him out" at first. " [17] Simon—passed through the country unto Ascalon, and the holds there adjoining," without resistance, whereas " he turned aside to Joppe, and won it." He placed Jews in Gaza, but of Ascalon nothing is said. The ruins of a Christian city, built on its site, " khirbet-Ascalon," have been lately discovered in the hills near Tell Zakariyeh [18], and so, a little South of Timnath, a Philistine city in the days of Samson, whence

---

[1] Arr. ii. 21. [2] Q. Curt. iv. 13. [3] Diod. Sic. xvii. 41. [4] Q. Curt. iv. 11–16. Arrian ii. 18–22. [5] Diod. Sic. xvii. 42–46. [6] Diod. xvii. 46. Q. Curt. iv. 19, Arr. ii. 24. [7] Q. Curt. l. c. [8] וְהִיא emph. [9] תֵּרֶא־וְתִירָא. [10] Is. xxiii. 5–11. [11] Herodotus states it to have been the wont of the Persian monarchs to put the sons even of revolted kings on their fathers' thrones (iii. 15), and in the review of the Persian troops under Xerxes mentions different tributary kings, among whom the king of Sidon had first rank; then the king of Tyre; then the rest (viii. 67). Josephus speaks of " the kings of Syria." (Ant. xi. 8. 5.)

[12] in Layard Nin. and Bab. p. 144. [13] Hegesias in Dionys. Hal. de comp. verb. c. 18. T. V. p. 125, Reiske. There is much obscurity about the individual. Dion. Hal. has, "its king Baistis or Baistios;" Arrian (ii. 25) mentions Batis, an Eunuch and so a Persian officer, as "having supreme authority over Gaza;" κρατῶν τ. Γαζαίων πόλεως. Q. Curtius says, "Betis was over the city" (iv. 26). "Josephus (Ant. xi. 84.) says that "the name of the commandant of the garrison was Babemēsēs." [14] See "Daniel the Prophet," pp. 142–145. [15] 1 Macc. x. 86. [16] Ib. xi. 60, 61. [17] Ib. xii. 33. [18] "The name was given twice to Lieut. Conder and 3 times to Corporal Brophy by different wit-

| Before CHRIST cir. 487. | shall perish **f r o m** Gaza, and Ashkelon shall not be inhabited. |
| m Amos 1. 8. | 6 And a bastard shall dwell in **m** Ashdod, and I will cut off the pride of the Philistines. |

| 7 And I will take away his †blood out of his mouth, and his abominations from between his teeth: but he that remaineth, even he, *shall be* for our God, and he shall be as a governor | Before CHRIST cir. 487. † Heb. *bloods.* |

Samson went to it, to gain the 30 changes of raiment[1]. Commentators have assigned reasons, why Samson might have gone so far as the maritime Ascalon, whereas, in fact, he went to a city close by. That city, in 536 A.D., had its Bishop[2]. " [3] The site shews the remains of an early Christian Church or convent: " as a great lintel of stone[4], resembling somewhat the Maltese Cross, lies on the ground." It was probably destroyed by the inundation of Mohammedan conquest. In 1163 A. D. it was a ruin. The distance of the ruins from the Ascalon Maiumas corresponds to that assigned by Benjamin of Tudela, being twice the distance of that city from Ashdod[5]; but since he was at Beth Jibrin[6], he must have been not far from the spot where it has been lately discovered[7]. The Ashkelon, which was Herod's birth-place and which he beautified, must have been the well-known city by the sea; since the distance from Jerusalem assigned by Josephus[8] is too great for the old Ashkelon, and he speaks of it as on the sea[9].

6. *And a bastard shall dwell at Ashdod*[10].

The " mamzer " was one born unlawfully, whether out of marriage, or in forbidden marriage, or in adultery[11]. Here it is, probably, like our " spurious brood[12]; " whether it was so itself or in the eyes of the Ashdodites; whence he adds, *I will cut off the pride of the Philistines.* Pride would survive the ruin of their country, the capture of their cities, the loss of independence. It would not survive the loss of their nationality; for they themselves would not be the same people, who were proud of their long descent and their victories over Israel. The breaking down of nationalities, which was the policy of Alexander, was an instrument in God's hands in cutting off their pride.

7. *And I will take away his bloods out of his mouth.* The *abominations* being idol-sacrifices[13], the *bloods* will also be, the blood mingled with the wine of sacrifices, of which David says, [14] *Their drink-offerings of blood will I not offer;* and Ezekiel unites the offences, " [15] *Ye eat with the blood, and lift up your eyes toward your idols, and shed blood.*"

But *he that remaineth,* better, *And he too*

---

nesses," " so that there is no doubt (Lieut. Conder subjoins) that it is a well-known site." Lieut. Conder's Report N. xxxiv. p. 153.   [1] Jud. xiv. 19.
[2] See ab. p. 244.   [3] Lieut. Conder, Ib.   [4] "Such lintels are to be found in all that class of ruins, which date from about the 5th to the 7th century."Ib.
[5] He says that the new Ashkelon, that on the sea, is 2 parasangs from Ashdod, 4 from the old Ashkelon.   [6] Travels, p. בכ.
[7] Jeremiah, xlvii. 7, *How can it* (the sword of the Lord) *be quiet, seeing that the Lord has given it a charge against Ashkelon, and against the sea-shore?* has often been wrongly quoted in proof that Ashkelon was on the sea-shore." On the contrary, Jeremiah speaks of them as distinct; "against Ashkelon and against the sea-shore." The חוף הים, in the 3 other places, in which it occurs, is only a title for Philistia itself, as lying between the Shephelah and the sea. Thus in Deut. i. 7, Palestine is divided into the hill country, the 'Arabah, the Shephelah, the Nejeb, and the חוף הים. In Joshua, ix. 1, the division is, "the hill country, the Shephelah, and the whole coast of the great sea, כל חוף הים הגדול." Ezekiel (xxv. 16.) uses חוף הים, as equivalent to the Cherethim and Philistim, whom he had named in v. 5. Jeremiah names together the whole tract and a whole city of it, as the prophets so often speak of "Judah and Jerusalem."
[8] 520 stadia. B. J. iii. 2. 1.   [9] Ib. iv. 11. 5.
[10] On the omission of Gath see on Am. i. 6.
[11] ἐκ πορνῆς, ό in Deut. xxiii. 3; "de scorto," Vulg. and so Saad.; " son of adultery," Syr. With this

agrees the opinion of R. Joshua A. D. 73, "every one, for whom they are guilty of death in the house of judgment." R. Joshua b. Azai says, 'I have found a roll of genealogies in Jerusalem, and there was written in it, ' M., a mamzer from a man's wife;' to confirm the words of R. Joshua." in Yebamoth c. 4, § 13. R. Akiba's opinion was, that "it was any near of kin, with whom marriage was forbidden;" Simon the Temanite said, "any liable to excision at the hands of God." Ib. in Ges. Thes. p. 781 sub. v. Of the etymologies, Kimchi's is perhaps the most probable, that it is from זור, the two מ's being added, as in מַמְגֻרוֹת, Joel i. 17.
[12] The Lxx. Jon. Syr. agree in the rendering, "strangers," Jon. and the Syr. using the same word; נוכרַיֵא Pesh.; "and the children of Israel shall dwell in Ashdod, who were in it, as strangers " (כנוכראיֵן). Jon. Aq. Symm. Theod. retain the Hebrew word, as do Onk. and Sam. in Deut.
[13] שקוץ always retains its appellative sense. It is not merely " idols," but idols, in that they were " abominations." It is generally in constr., " the abomination of " such a nation, 1 Kgs xi. 5, 7 [bis], 2 Kgs xxiii. 13 [bis], " the abomination of his, their, eyes," Ezek. xx. 7, 8; or with the personal pronoun as here, Deut. xxix. 16, Is. lxvi. 3, Jer. [5 times] Ezek. [6 times]. In a few places it stands absolutely, in its original appellative sense, Nah. iii. 6; allusively to the idol abominations, Hos. ix. 10; with art. the [idol] abominations (2 Kgs xxiii. 24, 2 Chr. xv. 8); and the abomination of desolation. Dan. ix. 27, xi. 31. xii. 11. [all].
[14] Ps. xvi. 4.   [15] Ezek. xxxiii. 25.

Before
CHRIST
cir. 487.

n Ps. 34. 3.
ch. 2. 5.

in Judah, and Ekron as a Jebusite.

8 And n I will encamp about mine house because

of the army, because of
him that passeth by, and
because of him that re-
turneth: and o no oppressor

Before
CHRIST
cir. 487.

o Isai. 60. 18.
Ezek. 28. 24.

shall remain over to our God. Of the Philistines too, as of Israel, *a remnant shall be saved.* After this visitation their idolatry should cease ; God speaks of the Philistine nation as one man; He would wring his idol-sacrifices and idol-enjoyments from him; he should exist as a nation, but as God's. *And he shall be as a governor in Judah,* lit. " a captain of a thousand," merged in Judah as in a larger whole, as each tribe was divided into its " thousands," yet intimately blended, in no inferior position, with the people of God, as each converted nation became an integral yet unseparated whole in the people of God. *And Ekron as a Jebusite.* Ekron was apparently the least important of the few remaining Philistine cities[1]; yet he shall be, as those of the Canaanite nations who were not destroyed, nor fled, but in the very capital and centre of Israel's worship, [2] *dwelt with the children of Benjamin and Judah,* and were, as a type of the future conversion and absorption of the heathen, incorporated into Judah.

8. *And I will encamp about my house (for*[3] *my house's sake) because of the army*[4] ; *because,* it is added in explanation, *of him that passeth by and of him that returneth;* Alexander, who *passed by* with his army, on his way to Egypt, and *returned,* having founded Alexandria.

It was a most eventful march ; one of the most eventful in the history of mankind. The destruction of the Persian empire, for which it prepared, was in itself of little moment ; Alexander's own empire was very brief. As Daniel had foretold[5], he came, *cast down* Persia *to the ground, waxed very great,* and *when he was strong, the great horn was broken.* But with the marvelous perception which characterized him, he saw and impressed upon his successors the dependibleness of the Jewish people. When he came into Judæa, he sent to the high priest for aid against Tyre and for the like tribute as he used to pay to Darius, promising that

he would not repent of choosing the friendship of the Macedonians[6]. The high priest refused on the ground of the oath, by which his people were bound in fealty to the earthly king of kings, whom Alexander came to subdue. Alexander threatened to teach all, through its fate, to *whom* fealty was due. This, after the conquest of Gaza, he prepared to fulfill. He came, he saw, he was conquered. [7] Jaddua and his people prayed to God. Taught by God in a dream not to fear, he went to meet the conqueror. The gates of the city were thrown open. There marched out, not an army such as encountered the Romans, but as he had been taught, a multitude in white garments, and the priests going before in their raiment of fine linen. The high priest, in his apparel of purple and gold, having on his head the mitre, and on it the golden plate[8], whereon was written the name of God, advanced alone, and the Conqueror, who was expected to give the city to be plundered, and the high priest to be insulted and slain, kissed the name of God, recognizing in the priest one whom he had seen in the like dress in a dream, who had bidden him, when hesitating, cross to Asia ; for that he would go before his army and deliver the Persian empire to him.

The result is related to have been, that Alexander promised to allow the Jews in Judæa to live according to their own laws, remitted the tribute of every seventh year, acceded beforehand to the terms to be proposed by those in Babylonia and Media, and that many Jews joined his army, under condition that they might live under their own laws.

Rationalism, while it remains such, cannot admit of Daniel's prophecies which the high priest shewed him, declaring that a Greek should destroy the Persian empire, which Alexander rightly interpreted of himself. But the facts remain ; that the conqueror, who, above most, gave way to his anger, bestowed privileges almost incredible

[1] See on Jo. i. 8, vol. i.
[2] Josh. xv. 63. Jud. i. 21.   [3] לִבְיָתִי.
[4] צָבָה, for צָבָא, according to the Masorites as in the verb also, Is. xxix. 7. So Symm. κωλύων στρατείας. The context also favors the reading; for unless the *passers by* and *returners* had been a powerful army, there had been no occasion for that defence of which God speaks. The correction מַצָבָה would come to the same, "a military post;" only, in actual use, this is a " fort," " fortress," 1 Sam. xiv. 12, i. q. מַצָב Ib. xiii. 23, xiv. 1, 4, 6, 11, 15,

[2] Sam. xxiii. 14. מָצָב Is. xxix. 3, is a work on the offensive, not defensive. Ewald comes to the same sense, that God would protect her against any one coming against her.
[5] Dan. viii. 7, 8.   [6] Jos. Ant. xi. 8, 3.   [7] Ib. n. 5.
[8] Justin says, "then he, Alexander, goes to Syria, where many kings of the East with fillets met him. Of these, according to their deserts, he received some into alliance; others he deprived of their kingdom, putting other kings in their place." xi. 10.

shall pass through them any more: for now p have I seen with mine eyes.

9 ¶ q Rejoice greatly, O daughter of Zion; shout, O daughter of Jerusalem:

Before
CHRIST
cir. 487.

q Isai. 62. 11.
ch. 2. 10.
Matt. 21. 5. John 12. 15.

on a nation, which under the Medes and Persians had been "[1] the most despised part of the enslaved;" made them equal in privileges to his own Macedonians[2], who could hardly brook the absorption of the Persians, although in inferior condition, among themselves[3]. The most despised of the enslaved became the most trusted of the trusted. They became a large portion of the second and third then known cities of the world. They became Alexandrians, Antiochenes, Ephesians[4], without ceasing to be Jews. The law commanded faithfulness to oaths, and they who despised their religion respected its fruits.

The immediate successors of Alexander, Ptolemy Lagi[5] and Antiochus Nicator, followed his policy; Ptolemy especially on the ground of the fealty shewn to Darius; Nicator, as having observed their faithfulness as soldiers, who had served with him[6]; but they were so enrolled on this visit to Jerusalem. The Heathen kings multiplied, in their own purpose, faithful subjects to themselves; in God's design, they prepared in Asia and Egypt a seed-plot for the Gospel. The settlement of the Jews at Alexandria formed the language of the Gospel; that wonderful

blending of the depth of the Hebrew with the clearness and precision of the Greek. Everywhere the seed of the preparatory dispensation was sown, to be fostered, grow and ripen with the harvest of the Gospel.

For now have I seen with Mine eyes. This is the counterpart of what the Psalmists and pious men so often pray, [7] *Awake to help me and behold;* [8] *Look down from heaven, behold and visit this vine;* [9] *Look upon my trouble from them that hate me;* [10] *Look upon my affliction and my trouble; look upon my enemies, for they are many;* [11] *Look upon my adversity and deliver me;* [12] *O Lord, behold my affliction;* [13] *Behold, O Lord, for I am in distress;* [14] *Look and behold my reproach;* [15] *Open Thine eyes, O Lord, and see;* [16] *Look down from heaven, and behold from the habitation of Thy holiness and glory.* With God, compassion is so intrinsic an attribute, that He is pictured as looking away, when He does not put it forth. With God, to behold is to help.

9. From the protection, which God promised to His people and to His House, the Prophet passes on to Him Who was ever in his thoughts, and for Whose sake that people and temple were preserved. He had described the great conqueror of this world,

---

[1] Tacitus limits the description to the time, "when the East belonged to the Assyrians, Medes and Persians." Hist. v. 8.

[2] "Alexander gave them (the Jews) a place to dwell in, and they obtained equal rank with the Macedonians. I know not what Apion would have said, had they been settled near the Necropolis and not near the palace, and were not their race now too called 'Macedonians.' If then he (Apion) has read the Epistles of Alexander the King, and has met with the rescripts of Ptolemy Lagi and the kings after him, and has lighted on the column which stands in Alexandria and contains the rights given by the great Cæsar to the Jews; if, I say, he knows these things, and, knowing them, has dared to write the contrary, he is unprincipled; if he knew nothing of them, he is ill-instructed." "Alexander collected some of our people there, not for want of such as should colonize the city which he founded with great earnestness. But carefully proving all as to good faith and probity, he gave this distinction to our people. For he honored our nation, as Hecatæus too says of us, that, for the probity and good faith which the Jews evinced toward him, he gave them in addition the territory of Samaria to hold, free from tribute. And Ptolemy Lagi too was like-minded with Alexander as to those who dwelt in Alexandria." Jos. lb. This early equalizing of the Jews with Alexandrians is recognized in the edict of Claudius; "Having learnt that the Jews in Alexandria were from the first called Alexandrians, having been settled there together with the Alexandrians straightway at the earliest period, and having received from the kings equal citizenship, as appeared plain both from their letters and from the ordinances," &c. [in Jos. Ant. xix. 5, 2.] in Pusey's "Daniel the Prophet," p. 146, n. 3. [3] Arr. vii. 6.

[4] "His (Apion's) marveling, how, being Jews, they were called Alexandrians, betrays the same ignorance. For all who are invited into a given colony, much as they differ in race, take their name from its founders. Those of us, who dwell at Antioch, are called Antiochenes. For Seleucus, the founder, gave them citizenship. And so too in Ephesus, and the rest of Ionia, they bear the same name with the natives, the Successors (of Alexander) having given it to them." Jos. c. Ap. ii. 4. See Pusey's "Daniel the Prophet," p. 146. n. 2.

[5] Ptolemy Lagi, "understanding that, those from Jerusalem were most reliable as to their oaths and fealty, (from the answer which they gave to the embassy of Alexander after he had conquered Darius,) having located many of them in the garrisons and given them equal rights of citizenship with the Macedonians in Alexandria, took an oath of them that they would keep fealty to the descendants of him who gave them this charge. And no few of the other Jews came of their own accord into Egypt, invited by the goodness of the soil and the liberality of Ptolemy." Jos. Ant. xii. 1. lb. p. 145. n. 8.

[6] "They (the Jews) obtained the honor from the kings of Asia also, having served in the army with them. For Seleucus Nicator, in the cities which he founded in Asia and lower Syria, and in the metropolis itself, Antioch, conferred on them citizenship, and made them rank with the Macedonians and Greeks who were settled therein, so that this citizenship remains even now also." Ant. xii. 3. lb. p. 146. n. 1.

[7] Ps. lix. 4. [8] lb. lxxx. 14. [9] lb. ix. 13.
[10] lb. xxv. 18, 19. [11] lb. cxix. 153.
[12] Lam. i. 9. add 11, ii. 20. [13] lb. i. 20.
[14] lb. v. 1.
[15] Is. xxxvii. 17. Dan. ix. 18. [16] Is. lxiii. 15.

behold, ͬ thy King cometh

ͬ Jer. 23. 5. & 30. 9. Luke 19. 38.
John 1. 49.

unto thee: he *is* just, and

sweeping along in his course of victory. In contrast with such as he, he now exhibits to his people the character and procession of their king. *Rejoice greatly.* Not with this world's joy. God never exhorts man to *rejoice greatly* in this world's fleeting joys. He allows us to be glad, as children, before Him; He permits such buoyancy of heart, if innocent; but He does not command it. *Now* He commands His people to burst out into a jubilee of rejoicing : they were to dance and shout for gladness of spirit; "despising the poor exultation of this world and exulting with that exceeding" yet chaste joy, which befits the true bliss to be brought by their King and Saviour. "[1] This word, *greatly*, means that there should be no measure whatever in their exultation; for the exultation of the children of the bridegroom is far unlike to the exultation of the children of this world." "[2] He biddeth the spiritual Zion rejoice, inasmuch as dejection was removed. For what cause of sorrow is there, when sin has been removed, death trampled under foot, and human nature called to the dignity of freedom, and crowned with the grace of adoption and illumined with the heavenly gift?"

Behold, thy king cometh unto thee. He does not say "*a* king," but "*thy* king;" thy king, thine own, the long-promised, the long-expected; He Who, when they had kings of their own, given them by God, had been promised as the king[3]; [4] *the righteous Ruler among men*, of the seed of David; He Who, above all other kings, was *their* King and Saviour; Whose kingdom was to absorb in itself all kingdoms of the earth; *the King of kings, and Lord of lords.* Her king was to come *to her.* He was in a manner then "of her," and "not of her;" "of her," since He was to be *her king*, "not of her," since He was to "*come to* her." As Man, He was born of her : as God, the Word made flesh, He *came* to her. "[5] *To thee*, to be manifest unto thee[6]; to be thine by communion of nature[7]; as He is thine, by the earnest of the Eternal Spirit and the gift of the Father, to procure thy good. [8] *Unto us a Child is born, unto us a Son is given.*" Of this, His entry into Jerusalem was an image. But how should He come? "He shall come to

thee," says an old Jewish writing[9], "to atone thee; He shall come to thee, to upraise thee; He shall come to thee, to raise thee up to His temple, and to espouse thee with an everlasting espousal."

He is just and having salvation. Just or righteous, and the Fountain of justice or righteousness. For what He is, *that* He diffuseth. Righteousness which God *Is*, and righteousness which God, made Man, imparts, are often blended in Holy Scripture[10]. This is also the source of the exceeding joy. For the coming of their king in righteousness would be, to sinful man, a cause, not of joy but of fear. This was the source of the Angel's message of joy; "[11] *I bring you good tidings of great joy, which shall be to all people ; for unto you is born this day, in the city of David, a Saviour.*

He is just, "[12] because in the Divine Nature, He is the Fountain of all holiness and justice." "[13] As Thou art righteous Thyself, Thou orderest all things righteously. For Thy power is the beginning of righteousness." According to the nature which He took, He was also most just; for He ever sought the glory of the Father, and [14] *He did no sin, neither was guile found in His Mouth.* In the way also of justice He satisfied for men, delivering Himself for their faults to the pain of the most bitter death, to satisfy the honor of the Divine Majesty, so that sin should not remain unpunished. Hence He saith of Himself; [15] *He that seeketh His glory that sent Him, the same is true, and no unrighteousness is in Him.* Of Whom also Stephen said to the Jews, [16] *Your fathers slew them which shewed before of the coming of the Just One, of Whom ye have been now the betrayers and murderers.* Righteousness is an awful attribute of God. It is a glory and perfection of His Being, for the perfect to gaze on and adore. Mercy, issuing in our salvation, is the attribute which draws us sinners. And this lies in the promise that He should *come to them*, however the one word *nosha'* be rendered[17]. The meaning of such a prophecy as this is secure, independent of single words. The whole context implies, that He should come as a ruler and deliverer, whether the word *nosha'* signify

[1] Rup.   [2] S. Cyr.
[3] e. g. Ps. ii. lxxii. Is. xxxii. 1. Jer. xxiii. 5.
[4] 2 Sam. xxiii. 3.   [5] Cocc.   [6] 1 Tim. iii. 16.
[7] Heb. ii. 14.   [8] Is. ix. 6.
[9] Zohar Levit. f. 3. col. 9 in Schöttg. on Hos. ii. 21.
[10] Is. xlv. 21. liii. 11, Jer. xxiii. 5, 6, xxxiii. 15, 16, Mal. iv. 2.
[11] S. Luke ii. 10, 11.   [12] Dion.   [13] Wisd. xii. 15, 16.
[14] 1 S. Pet. ii. 22. [15] S. John vii. 18. [16] Acts vii. 52.
[17] The Jewish Versions as well as the Christian render, actively, "Saviour," LXX, σώζων ; Jon. ‫פריק‬,

as well as the Christian, the Syr. and S. Jerome. The participle ‫נושׁע‬ might, according to analogy, be a reflective, but it only occurs elsewhere as a passive; with ‫ב‬ p., Deut. xxxiii. 29, Is. xlv. 17; with ‫ב‬ r., Ps. xxxiii. 16. Imperat. "look unto Me and be ye saved," ‫וְהִוָּשְׁעוּ‬ Is. xlv. 22; being "saved by God" implied Nu. x. 9. Ps. xviii. 4. [2 Sam. xxii. 4.] lxxx. 4, 8, 20, cxix. 117, Pr. xxviii. 18, Is. xxx. 15, lxiv. 4, Jer. iv. 14, viii. 20, xvii. 14, xxiii. 6, xxx. 7, xxxiii. 16. [all]

|| having salvation; lowly, and riding u p o n an ass,

| Or, *saving himself.*

and upon a colt the foal of an ass.

"endued with salvation," (whereas the old versions rendered it, "Saviour") or whether it be, "saved." For as He came, not for Himself but for us, so, in as far as He could be said to be saved, He was "saved," not for Himself but for us. Of our Lord, as Man, it is, in like way, said, [1] *Thou shalt not leave His soul in Hell,* or, [2] *Whom God raised up, having loosed the pains of death, because it was not possible that He should be holden of it.* As Man, He was raised from the dead; as God, He raised Himself from the dead, for our sakes, for whom He died. For us, He was born a Saviour; for us, He was endued with salvation; for us, He was saved from being held of death; in like way as, of His Human Nature, the Apostle says, [3] *He was heard, in that He feared.* To us, as sinners, it is happiest to hear of the Saviour; but the most literal meaning "saved" has its own proper comfort: for it implies the Sufferings, by which that salvation was procured, and so it contains a hint of the teaching by Isaiah, *He was taken from oppression and from judgment;* upon which that same wide reign follows, of which David, in his picture of the Passion [4], and Isaiah [5] prophesy. "[6] This 'saved' does not imply, that He obtained salvation for His own otherwise than from Himself. *Mine own arm,* He saith in Isaiah, [7] *brought salvation unto Me.* But as Man, He obtained salvation from the indwelling Godhead. For when He destroyed the might of death, when, rising from the dead, He ascended into heaven, when He took on Him the everlasting kingdom of heaven and earth, He obtained salvation from the glory of the Father, i. e. from His own Divinity, to impart it to all His. The Hebrew word then in no way diminishes the amplitude of His dignity. For we confess, that the Human Nature of Christ had that everlasting glory added to It from His Divine Nature, so that He should not only be Himself adorned with those everlasting gifts, but should become the cause of everlasting salvation to all who obey Him."

Lowly. Outward lowliness of condition, is, through the grace of God, the best fosterer of the inward. The word *lowly* wonderfully expresses the union of both; lowness of outward state with lowliness of soul. The Hebrew word expresses the condition of one, who is bowed down, brought low

through oppression, affliction, desolation, poverty, persecution, bereavement; but only if, at the same time, he had in him the fruit of all these, in lowliness of mind, submission to God, piety. Thus our Lord pronounces the blessedness of "the poor" and "the poor in spirit," i. e. poor in estate, who are poor in soul also. But in no case does it express lowliness of mind without lowness of condition. One lowly, who was not afflicted, would never be so called. The Prophet then declares that their king should come to them in a poor condition, *stricken, smitten, and afflicted* [8], and with the special grace of that condition, meekness, gentleness and lowliness of soul; and our Lord bids us, [9] *Learn of Me, for I am meek and lowly of heart.* "[10] He saith of Himself in the Gospel, [11] *The foxes have holes and the birds of the air have nests, but the Son of Man hath not where to lay His Head.* [12] *For though He was rich, He for our sakes became poor, that we through His poverty might be rich.*

Lowly and riding upon an ass. Kings of the earth ride in state. The days were long since by, when the sons of the judges rode on asses [13]. Even then the more distinguished rode on *white* (i. e. roan [14]) asses. The mule, as a taller animal, was used by David [15] and his sons [16], while asses were used for his household [17], and by Ziba, Shimei, Mephibosheth, Ahitophel [18], and, later, by the old prophet of Bethel [19]. David had reserved horses for 100 chariots [20], after the defeat of the Syrians, but he himself did not use them. Absalom employed *chariots and horses* [21] as part of his pomp, when preparing to displace his father; and Solomon multiplied them [22]. He speaks of it as an indignity or reverse; [23] *I have seen servants upon horses, and princes walking, as servants, upon the earth.* The burial of an ass became a proverb for a disgraced end [24]. There is no instance in which a king rode on an ass, save He Whose kingdom was not of this world. The prophecy, then, was framed to prepare the Jews to expect a prophet-king, not a king of this world. Their eyes were fixed on this passage. In the Talmud, in their traditional interpretations, and in their mystical books, they dwelt on these words. The mention of the ass, elsewhere, seemed to them typical of this ass, on which their Messiah should ride. "If a man in a dream seeth an ass," says

[1] Ps. xvi. 10.   [2] Acts ii. 24.   [3] Heb. v. 7.
[4] Ps. xxii. 27, 28.   [5] Is. liii. 10–12.   [6] Osor.
[7] Is. lxiii. 5.   [8] Is. liii. 4.   [9] S. Matt. xi. 29.
[10] Dion.   [11] S. Matt. viii. 20.   [12] 2 Cor. viii. 9.
[13] Jud. x. 4, xii. 14.   [14] Ib. v. 10.
[15] 1 Kgs i. 33, 38, 44.   [16] 2 Sam. xiii. 29, xviii. 9.

[17] Ib. xvi. 2.
[18] Ib. xvi. 1, xvii. 23, xix. 26, 1 Kgs ii. 40.
[19] 1 Kgs xiii. 13, 23, 27.   [20] 2 Sam. viii. 4.
[21] Ib. xv. 1.
[22] 1 Kgs iv. 26, x. 26, 2 Chr. i. 14, ix. 25.
[23] Eccl. x. 7.   [24] Jer. xxii. 19.

the Talmud [1], " he shall see salvation." It is an instance of a prophecy which, humanly speaking, a false Messiah could have fulfilled, but which, from its nature, none would

fulfill, save the True. For *their* minds were set on earthly glory and worldly greatness: it would have been inconsistent with the claims of one, whose kingdom was of this

[1] Berachoth f. 56. 2 (in Schöttgen ad loc.). There was a general consent among the Jews, that this prophecy related to the Messiah. *R. Joseph* (probably " the pious," the disciple of Jochanan, the disciple of Hillel, Wolf, Bibl. Hebr. ii. 848, 844) used it as an argument against R. Hillel, who disbelieved in any Messiah. "R. Hillel, ' Israel has no Messiah, for they enjoyed him in the days of Hezekiah.' R. Joseph said, ' Lord, forgive R. Hillel!' When did Hezekiah live? In [the time of] the first temple. But Zechariah prophesied in [the time of] the second temple; ' Rejoice greatly, daughter of Zion, behold, thy king cometh unto thee, righteous and *nosha*'." He said also, "O that he may come, and that I may be worthy to sit in the shadow of the dung of his ass." Sanhedrin, f. 99. 1. " *R. Alexandri* said, that *R. Joshua ben Levi* set against each other the Scriptures, ' Lo there came with the clouds of heaven one like unto the Son of Man,' and that, ' lowly and riding on an ass.' Deserve he [Israel], ' with the clouds of heaven;' deserve he not, ' lowly and riding on an ass.' " Ib. f. 98. " All these goods, which I will do to them through the merits of the Messiah, shall be extended in all those years." *R. Jannai* (about A. D. 130) said from *Raf*, " whoever looketh for salvation, God will give him rest in the garden of Eden, according to that, ' I will feed my flock and cause them to lie down ' (Ezk. xxxiv. 15.) 'Just and nosha.' This is the Messiah, who justifieth his judgment against Israel because they mocked him, because he sat in prison, so he is called ' just.' But why נושע, but that he justifieth the judgment upon them. He says to them, ' ye are my sons; are ye not all to be saved only by the mercy of the Holy One, blessed be He?' ' Afflicted and riding on an ass.' This is the Messiah. But why is his name called 'עני, ' afflicted ?' Because he was afflicted all those years in prison, and the transgressors of Israel mocked him, because he rideth upon an ass on account of the wicked who have no desert." (a dislocated passage, Schöttg. says, of the *Pesikta Rabbathi* f. 61. 1. 2. in Schöttg. de' Messia, loci gen. n. xcvii. p. 136. The Hebrew of the latter part is given by Wünsche d. Leiden des Messias p. 66.) And in a remarkable passage on Cant. i. 4, " Let us exult and rejoice in thee." " The Matrona is like a royal bride, whose husband the king, her sons and sons-in-law, were gone beyond sea. When they brought her word that her sons were returned, she said, ' What cause of joy have I? Let my daughters-in-law rejoice !' Another messenger came, that her sons-in-law were returned, she answered, ' What cause of joy have I? Let my daughters rejoice !' But when they told her that the king, her husband, was returned, she said, ' This is perfect joy, a joy above all joys!' So also in the time to come, the time of the Messiah, the prophets shall come to Jerusalem and say, (Is. lx. 4) ' thy sons shall come from far;' she will answer, ' What cause of joy have I ?' The prophets will add, ' Thy daughters shall be nurtured by thy side; ' she will answer in like way. But when they shall say to her, ' Behold, thy king cometh unto thee, just and a Saviour,' then she shall say, ' This is perfect joy;' as in, ' Exult greatly, daughter of Zion,' and elsewhere, ' Sing and rejoice, O daughter of Zion.' Then she shall say, ' I will greatly rejoice in the Lord, my soul shall be joyful in my God (Is. lxi. 10.) ' " *Shir hasshirim Rabba* fol. 7. 3 (in Schöttg. loc. gen. n. v., Martini f. 512). They quote the prophecy also as to the union of the royal and priestly offices of the Messiah. The *Bereshith Rabba* had on Gen. xiv. 18, " ' And Melchizedec, king of Salem.' This is the name of Shem, the son of Noah. What would that teach, ' he brought forth bread and wine ?' *R. Samuel Bar Nachman* said, He delivered to him the ways of the priesthood, and he offered bread and wine to God, as it is said, ' He was priest of the

most High God, king of Salem.'—Otherwise; Melchizedec; this is what Scripture saith, ' The Lord sware and will not repent, Thou art a Priest for ever after the order of Melchizedec.' And who is he? This is the king, righteous and נושע, the king Messiah, according to, ' Behold thy king cometh unto thee, righteous and נושע.' And what would that teach, ' He brought forth bread and wine?' It is as is said, ' Be there a handful of corn upon the earth.' (Ps. lxxii. 16.) This is what is written, ' And he was a priest of the most High God.' " (in Mart. f. 654 end.) Or they argue from נושע, as to the free mercy of God, " God says to Israel, If your merit is not of such account, I do it for my own sake; for day by day, when you are in trouble, I am with you, as in, ' I am with him in trouble,' (Ps. xci. 15); and so I deliver myself, ' And he saw that there was no one, and wondered ' (Is. lix. 16.); and elsewhere, ' Exult greatly, daughter of Zion—behold thy king cometh unto thee, just and נושע.' It is not written ומושיע [" and saving "] but ונושע [" and saved "]; whereby it is hinted that, though your merits are not of such account, God will act for His own sake, according to, ' For my salvation is near to come.' " (*Shemoth Rabba* sect. 30.¦fol. 129. 1. Schöttg. loc. gen. n. ix.) Martini quotes a like saying from the *Bereshith Rabba* on Gen. xlix. 8. " R. Berachiah the priest, son of Rabbi, said, See what is written, ' Rejoice greatly &c.' It is not written, ' Just and מושיע, a Saviour,' but ' Just and נושע saved,' and thus he says, (Is. lxii. 11.) ' Say ye to the daughter of Sion—it is not written, ' thy Saviour (מושיע) cometh,' but, ' Behold thy salvation (ישע) cometh.' As if one might so speak, ' Israel was redeemed, and it is as if God were redeemed,' and this is one of the hard Scriptures, that the salvation of Israel is the salvation of God." fol. 518. Martini quotes also from a comment on Isaiah lvii. 1. " The righteous perisheth." " This is Messiah, of Whom it is said, ' Just and saved.' " f. 334.

In other places, the riding upon the ass is dwelt upon. *Midrash Coheleth* on Eccl. i. 9. f. 73. 3. " *R. Berachiah* said from *R. Isaac*, As was the first redeemer, so also shall be the last redeemer. What did the first redeemer? (Ex. iv. 20.) ' And Moses took his wife and his sons and placed them on an ass;' the second, as is written, ' lowly and riding on an ass.' " (Martini f. 380, and 690, Schöttg. Hor. Hebr. on S. Matt. xxi. 5.) In the *Midrash Shemuel* f. 66. 1. the saying is ascribed to *R. Levi* (Schöttg. on this place). And the *Pirke R. Eliezer* c. 31, of Abraham's ass, " This is the ass, on which the son of David shall ride, according to, ' Rejoice greatly, daughter of Zion.' " (Ib.) The *Zohar* owns that the prophecy relates to the Messiah, but apologizes for it. " It is not the custom that the king and his Matrona should ride on an ass, but rather on horses, as in (Hab. iii. 7.) ' For thou shalt ride on thy horses, and thy chariots are salvation.' For they do not esteem a matrona so slightly, that she should ride on an ass, as the king wonteth not to ride on an ass, like one of the people. And therefore it is said of the Messiah, ' Poor and riding upon an ass.' And he is not there called king, until he ride upon his horses, which are the people of Israel." (on Levit. f. 38. col. 151. in Schöttg. de Mess. vi. 213. p. 543.) Or they say great things of the ass. " This ass is son of the she-ass, which was created within the six days in the twilight. This is the ass, which Abraham saddled, when he purposed to sacrifice Isaac. This is the ass, on which Moses was carried when he went to Egypt. This is the ass, on which the son of David shall ride hereafter." *Yalkut Reubeni* (f. 79, 3, 4 on Exod. iv.

world. It belonged to the character of Him, Who was buffeted, mocked, scourged, spit upon, crucified, died for us, and rose again. It was Divine humiliation, which, in the

purpose of God, was to be compensated by Divine power. In itself it would, if insulated, have been unmeaning. The Holy Ghost prophesied it, Jesus fulfilled it, to shew the

---

20 in Schöttg. on S. Matt. xxi. 5.) They connect it with Balaam's ass. "This is the ass destined for the Messiah, as it is written, 'Poor and riding on an ass.'" (*Zohar Num.* f. 83. col. 332.) Or they speak of his reigning thereon. 'This is the ass, on which the Messiah shall reign,' as it is written, 'Poor and riding on an ass.'" *Zohar Num.* f. 83, col. 332 (on Deut. xxii. 10.) in Schöttg. de Messia vi. 2. 12. p. 543. The mention of an 'ass' in Holy Scripture suggests the thought of this prophecy, as relating to the Son of David. "'And I have oxen and asses.' Messiah son of David is hinted at here, of whom it is written, 'Meek and riding upon an ass'" *Tanchuma* on Gen. xxxii. 6. f. 12. 2. (in Schöttg. on S. Matt. xxi. 5). And the *Bereshith Rabba* on Gen. xlix. 14, had, "By the foot of the ox (Is. xxxii. 20.) is understood Messias son of Joseph, according to Deut. xxxiii. 17. 'His glory is of the firstling of a bullock.' But by the foot of the ass, Messiah son of David, as in Zach., 'Meek and riding on an ass.'" (in Mart. f. 330. See also Schöttg. loc. gen. n.'liii. and lxxiv.) "When he shall come, of Whom it is written, ''ני and riding upon an ass,' he will wash his garments in wine, i. e. make clear to them the words of the law, and his clothes in the blood of grapes, i. e. cleanse them from their errors." Ib. f. 95. col. 4. And in the *Bereshith ketanna* on Gen. xlix. 11. "binding his foal unto the vine and his ass's colt unto the choice vine." "This is he of whom it is written, ''ני and riding &c.' and he it is who planteth Israel as a choice vine (Jer. ii. 21): and how will he do it? As it is written, I will sprinkle clean water &c. Ezek. xxxvi. 21." *Zohar* Deut. f. 118. col. 471. in Schöttg. Horæ H. on Hab. ii. 3. p. 215. "After that depth (of the fulfillment of the vision, Hab. ii. 3.) was opened, whoever fell into it, never came up. The Messiah Ben David fell into it, with the Messiah ben Joseph, of whom one is 'poor and riding upon an ass,' the other, 'the firstling of his bullock' (Deut. xxxiii. 17.), viz. the Messiah ben Joseph. And this is alluded to in (Ex. xxi. 23.) 'If any one dig a pit and cover it not, and an ox or an ass fall therein.' And therefore the Messiah is called 'Bar naphli' 'son of the fallen.'" The *Bereshith Rabba* quoted the prophecy also in proof of His meekness. "When the king Messias shall come to Jerusalem to save Israel, he shall bind his ass and ride upon it and come to Jerusalem, that he may conduct himself in lowliness, as it is said, 'lowly and riding upon an ass.' And his ass's foal unto the choice vine, when he shall come to gather the congregation of Israel, ["which is called a vine in that, Thou hast brought a vine out of Egypt," added in Schöttg. loc. gen. n. lix.] as in Zech. x. 8. 'I will kiss to them and will gather them,' then he shall ride on the foal of his ass, as in Zech. ix. 9. 'Rejoice greatly &c.' And is it not of old said of the Messiah, 'And in the clouds of heaven cometh one like the Son of man?' (Dan. vii. 13.) If Israel deserveth, 'He cometh with the clouds of heaven,' and if he deserveth not, 'lowly and riding on an ass.' on Gen. xlix. 11 in Martini f. 656 (or latter part as in Sanhedrin above). In times not far from our Lord, the Messiah seems to be mentioned, as under a well-known name, "he who is borne upon an ass." The *Zohar* quotes a revelation to *R. Eliezer and R. Abba,* "Did I not say to you that the precept of the king lasts, until he shall come who is borne on an ass?" (*Zohar* Gen. in Schöttg. loc. gen. n. xxxi. 7 p. 79.) And ''ני "afflicted" becomes an indication that the passage relates to the Messiah. Thus 'the steps of the needy,' 'ני, (Is. xxvi. 6.) is explained 'This is the Messiah, 'ני and riding on an ass.' (Bereshith R. on Gen. xlix. 10. Mart. f. 656.) The *Midrash Tehillim* explains Ps. xc. 15, "'according to the days of the Messiah.' The word, ויתנו 'ני 'hast afflicted

us' corresponds to the other, ''ני afflicted and riding on an ass,' as if he would say 'according to the days of our afflicted.'" (in Schöttg. ad loc. p. 242.) and the Zohar Chadash on Eccl. ix. 14. sqq. "A little city is Zion; 'and a few men in it:' these are the six days of the creation; and there came a great king against it,' this is a certain one; 'and there was found in it a poor wise man.' This is Messiah Ben David, as it is said, ''ני and riding upon an ass' and 'the righteous perisheth' (Is. lvii. 1.) so long as the overflowing cometh not upon him, it is said, 'the river shall be wasted and dried up.' (Is. xix. 5.) 'The ass,' that is Samael, and the wise man, that is Messiah Ben David, and of him it is said, 'and he delivered the city by his wisdom.' And he shall be the deliverer of Messiah ben Ephraim. And this is a redemption from above." (f. 63. 2. in Schöttg. loc. gen. n. 103. filled up from Wünsche Leiden d. Mess. p. 105.) Schöttgen ad loc. quotes also from the Zohar Deut. 117. col. 465. The name חמור is understood as indicating the Messiah. "By the word חמור, 'ass' is indicated the king Messiah, according to that, 'poor and riding on an ass.'" Bereshith Rabba sect. 75, f. 74. 2. in Schöttg. ad loc.

In later times, *R. Saadiah Gaon* said on Daniel vii. 13; "'And behold with the clouds of heaven one came like a Son of man.' This is the Messiah our righteousness, and is it not written of the Messiah, ''ני and riding upon an ass?' i. e. he shall come with meekness, for he shall not come on horses with pride; and 'the clouds of heaven' they are the Angels of the heavenly host. This is the exceeding greatness, which the Creator shall give to the Messiah." And *Rashi* says, "This cannot be explained, except of king Messiah; for it is said of him, 'and his dominion shall be from sea to sea;' but we do not find that such an one ruled over Israel in the time of the second house;" and (on Exod. iv. 20) "On an ass the Messiah will reveal himself, according to 'Meek and riding on an ass.'" (in Schöttg. ad loc.) The first who referred it to any other was *R. Moseh Haccohen* (A. D. 1148), whom *Ibn Ezra* quotes, as explaining it of "Nehemiah, the Tirshatha, because of him it was said, 'There is a king in Judah;' and that there was no mention of a horse, because he was poor;" which, Ibn Ezra says, was contrary to the fact in Nehemiah, and also the mention of the Greeks did not suit his times. *Ibn Ezra* says that, as far as he knows, "it was the king Judas the Hasmonæan, whose might suited that, 'I have made thee like the sword of a mighty man,' and his hand was mighty against the Greeks, and at first he had not wealth or horses." These were private opinions, for *Ibn Ezra* says, "The expositors are divided about it; some say, this king is Messiah ben David, and some say, Messiah ben Joseph." Both then agreed that he was a Messiah. *Abarbanel* says of Ibn Ezra; "I wonder that his ill intent blinded his understanding; for lo, Judas the Hasmonæan was never called king, all his days, much less of Zion; that had he prophesied of the Hasmonæan, what had he to do with Ephraim, since the kingdom of Ephraim was not in the second temple; also he did not speak peace to all nations, and did not rule from sea to sea." (On his own exposition see below.) Even *R. Isaac* (Chizz. Emunah c. 35 p. 293 Wagenseil), denying it as to our Lord, insists upon it as relating to their Messiah whom they looked for. *R. Bechai* says that "Jacob (Gen. xlix. 11) used the words עירה 'his ass' and ובני אתונו 'the foal of his ass,' because it is written of him (the king Messiah) 'and upon a colt, the foal of an ass' (the same words being used, עיר בן אתונות. Binat-hatthorah ad loc. f. 58 col. 3. Amst.) *R. Tanchum* admits the difficulty of supposing it to relate to a future Messiah,

Jews, of what nature His kingdom was. Hence the challenge; " ¹ Let us look at the prophecy, that in words, and that in act. What is the prophecy? *Lo, thy king cometh unto thee, meek, and sitting upon an ass, and upon a colt;* not driving chariots as other kings, not in pomp nor attended by guards, but shewing herein also all gentleness. Ask the Jew then, What king, riding on an ass, came to Jerusalem? He could name none, save this One alone." An ancient writer says, " ² The Greeks too " (not the Jews only) " will laugh at us, saying, that ' The God of the Christians, Who is called Christ, sat upon an ass.' " The same mockery was probably intended by Sapor³ king of Persia, which the Jews met with equal pride. The taunt continues till now. " ⁴ It is not hid from you, O congregation of Christians, that ' rider upon an ass' indicates Christ." The Mohammedans appropriate the title "rider upon a camel" to Mohammad, as the grander animal ⁵. The taunt of worshiping " Him Who sat upon an ass" was of the same class as those of the

worship of the Crucified; " ⁶ one dead and crucified, who could not save himself;" " a crucified Man," " that great Man," or (if it suited them so to speak) " that great sophist who was crucified," but Who now, for above 1800 years, reigns, " to all, the King; to all, the Judge; to all, Lord and God." " ⁷ Christ did not only fulfill prophecies or plant the doctrines of truth, but did thereby also order our life for us, everywhere laying down for us rules of necessary use and, by all, correcting our life." Even Jews, having rejected our Lord, say this. " Not from poverty," says one ⁸, " for behold the whole world shall be in his power—but from humility he will ride upon an ass; and further to shew that Israel [viz. the establishment of His kingdom or Church] shall not want horse nor chariot: therefore it is added, *And I will cut off the chariot from Ephraim and the horse from Jerusalem.*" And another ⁹ ; " He, i. e. thy true king David, shall come to thee; and he mentions of his qualities that he shall be *righteous and nosha'* ¹⁰ in his wars; but his salvation

or, since as a Jew, he could not interpret it of Jesus, of interpreting it of any one in the time of the second temple. " Some of the interpreters make this consolation an announcement of the Expected (may he soon be revealed!) and this is found in most of the Midrashoth of the ancient wise (blessed be their memory!) and the obvious meaning of his words, ' and his dominion is from sea to sea and from the river unto the ends of ths earth ' supports this; and some of them think, that from the context it relates to the circumstances of the second house, and this is supported by his words in the passage, 'And I will raise thy sons, O Zion, against thy sons, O Greece,' which was in the second house, through the Hasmonæans, and now the empire of Greece is dispersed and gone. How then should he promise help against it in the future? And altogether the word of the prophecies admits of the interpretation. And many vary therein from one meaning to the other. And therefore we will mention how the language can be explained according to each opinion. And God, most high, knows what is hidden ! The meaning then of '`יני` and riding upon an ass' is, in my opinion, in the first way, beautiful; as `יני` means one who humbles himself, like (Is. lxvi. 2) ' And to this man will I look, to the humble (`יני`) and contrite of spirit,' not weak in condition; on account then of his lowliness he will ride upon an ass." (He compares the reduplication to that in Gen. xlix. 11.) " Or," he says, " the whole of this may be a metaphor for self-abjection, not an actual history; and what is known, is that this is his condition at first for his weakness and lowness; afterward he will attain his later condition in strength and felicity. And so for the second way, this points to the return of the kingdom to Israel through the Hasmonæans, and his saying ' meek and riding upon an ass ' indicates their first king, Judas the Hasmonæan, and he, at the outset, was weak, because he followed upon the oppression of Greece, according to what has been transmitted of that history; and that, ' his dominion shall be from sea to sea &c.' this is the kingdom to which he attained at last, and the extension of his house; and he means by this, ' from the red sea to the sea of the Philistines and from the river to the end of the habitable land; ' and this is, ' And from the river &c.' and thus words, ' I will raise up thy sons, O Zion, against thy sons, O Greece,' will fit. And in the first way : · from sea to sea ' will be the encircling sea [the Ocean] and from the river which is the bound of the land of Israel to the fur-

thest habitable earth." He answers the reference to Nehemiah, but ends by leaving the other two open. *Moses ben Nâchman* quotes it in illustration of the contempt of the Messiah spoken of in Isaiah lii. 13. liii. 3. 7. " Theirs [the kings'] astonishment was shewn by mocking him, when he first arrived, and by asking, how one ' despised, meek and riding upon an ass,' could conquer all the kings of the world who had laid hold on Israel?—He was ' despised,' for he had no army and no people, but was ' meek and riding on an ass,' like the first redeemer Moses our master, when he entered in Egypt with his wife and children riding upon an ass. (Ex. iv. 20.) ' He was oppressed and he was afflicted,' for when he first comes ' meek and riding upon an ass,' the oppressors and officers of every city will come to him, and afflict him with revilings and insult, reproaching both him and the God in whose name he appears, like Moses our master, who, when Pharaoh said, I know not the Lord, answered him not." In Jewish Commentaries on Is. liii. p. 80, 81.

The modern school, which rids itself of definite prophecy, would have this relate to "the ideal Messiah." One does not see, how a literal prophecy, fulfilled to the letter, can relate to an ideal king; unless on the implied assumption, "There can be no prophecy of a definite event." ¹ S. Chrys. in S. Matt. Hom. 66. p. 656 marg. Ed. Oxon.

² Author of the Hom. in S. Matt. xxi. 2. in the Dubia of S. Athan. n. 6. Opp. ii. 77.

³ " King Sapor said to R. Samuel, 'Ye say that the Messiah comes upon an ass, I will send him a horse [epithet uncertain] which I have, He answered, ' Hast thou one with 100 colors' (so Rashi) or, 'with 1000 qualities.' (Aruch and Reland Diss. ix. T. i. 288, 298.) Sanhedr. f. 98. 1. " In the deep humility of the Messiah," subjoins Lightfoot, "they dream of pride even in his ass." Hor. Hebr. on S. Matt. xxi. 5.

⁴ Epist. Mohammedan. Anon. inserted by Hackspan Nizzach. pp. 397–401.

⁵ The titles " rider on an ass," " rider on a camel," are derived from Is. xxi. 14.

⁶ See Lucian de morte Peregrini c. 11, 13. Trypho in S. Justin Dial. n. 14. p. 83. Oxf. Tr. Celsus in Origen c. Cels. viii. 12. 14. 15. and others in Pusey's Lenten Sermons pp. 454, 455. Liddon's Bampton Lectures pp. 4. c. 4 pp. 31–36.

⁷ S. Chrys. l. c. p. 655.   ⁸ Kimchi.

⁹ Abarbanel in his Mashm'a Yeshu'ah p. 73.

¹⁰ I leave the word *nosha'* untranslated, in order not to give any possible color to his words, though

Before
CHRIST
cir. 487.
* Hos. 1. 7.
& 2. 18.
Mic. 5. 10.
Hag. 2. 22.

10 And I * will cut off the chariot from Ephraim, and the horse from Jerusalem, and the battle bow shall be cut off: and he shall speak ᵗ peace unto the heathen: and his dominion ᵗ Eph. 2. 14, 17. shall be ᵘ from sea *even* to ᵘ Ps. 72. 8.

Before
CHRIST
cir. 487.

shall not be from strength of his wars, for he shall come *lowly* and *riding upon an ass* [1].

And *riding on an ass*, this is not on account of his want, but to shew that peace and truth shall be in his days; and therefore he says forthwith, *And I will cut off the chariot from Ephraim and the horse from Jerusalem;* viz. that such shall be the peace and stillness in the world, that in Ephraim (i. e. the tribes) and in Jerusalem (i. e. the kingdom of Judah) they shall *trust* no more in horse and in rider, but *in the name of God.* And because it is the way of princes and chiefs to take example from the life of their kings, and to do as they, therefore he saith, that when the king Messiah rideth upon an ass, and *has no pleasure in the strength of a horse*, there will be no other in Jerusalem or the lands of the tribes, who will have pleasure in riding on a horse. And therefore he says, *And I will cut off the chariot from Ephraim and the horse from Jerusalem;* and he assigns the reason for this, when he says, *And the battle-bow shall be cut off, and he shall speak peace among the nations*, i. e. there shall be no more war in the world, because he shall *speak peace unto the world, and by the word of his lips* [2] *he shall dispose peace unto them.*"

And upon a colt, the foal of an ass. The word rendered *colt*, as with us, signifies the young, as yet unbroken animal. In the fulfillment, our Lord directed His disciples to find [3] *an ass tied, and a colt with her, whereon never man sat.* The prophet foretold that He would ride on both animals; our Lord, by commanding both to be brought, shewed that the prophet had a special meaning in naming both. S. Matthew relates that both were employed. "They brought the ass and the colt, and put on *them* their clothes, and they set Him thereon." The untrained colt, an appendage to its mother, was a yet humbler animal. But as the whole action was a picture of our Lord's humility and of the unearthliness of His kingdom, so, doubtless, His riding upon the two animals was a part of that picture. There was no need of two animals to bear our Lord for that short distance. S. John notices especially, [4] *These things understood not His disciples at the first.* The ass, an unclean stupid debased ignoble drudge, was in itself a picture of unregenerate man, a slave to his passions and to devils,

toiling under the load of ever-increasing sin. But, of man, the Jew had been under the yoke and was broken; the Gentiles were the wild unbroken colt. Both were to be brought under obedience to Christ.

10. *And I will cut off the chariot.* The horse is the symbol of worldly power, as the ass is of meekness. *Some*, says the Psalmist, [5] *put their trust in chariots, and some in horses; but we will remember the name of the Lord our God.* [6] *A horse is but a vain thing to save a man.* [7] *He delighteth not in the strength of a horse.* In scarcely any place in Holy Scripture is the horse spoken of in relation to man, except as the instrument of war. It represents human might, which is either to be consecrated to the Lord, or destroyed by Him [8]. As the [9] *stone, cut out without hands*, broke in pieces and absorbed into itself all the kingdoms of the world, so here He, Whose Kingdom should not be of this world, should supersede human might. His kingdom was to begin by doing away, among His followers, all, whereby human kingdoms are established. He first cuts off the chariot and the horse, not from His enemies, but from His own people; His people, not as a civil polity, but as the people of God. For the prophet speaks of them as Ephraim and Judah, but Ephraim had no longer a distinct existence.

And He shall speak peace unto the heathen, as the Apostle says, [10] *He came and preached peace to you which were afar off, and to them that were nigh.* He shall speak it to them, as He Who hath power to give it to them, peace with God, peace in themselves, the reconciliation of God and man, and the remission of their sins.

"[11] At His birth the heavenly host announced peace to men; all His doctrine has peace for its end; when His death was at hand, He especially commended peace to His disciples, that peace which the world knoweth not, which is contained in tranquillity of mind, burning zeal for charity. Divine grace. This same peace He brought to all who gathered themselves to His empire and guidance, that, emerging from intestine wars and foul darkness, they might behold the light of liberty, and, in all wisdom keep the grace of God."

And His dominion shall be from sea to sea.

he seems from the context to take it actively "Saviour." [1] He says here that יְנִי is like יָנִי.
[2] Is. xxvi. 12.
[3] S. Matt. xxi. 2, S. Mark xi. 2, S. Luke xix. 30.
[4] S. John xii. 16.
[5] Ps. xx. 7.
[6] Ib. xxxiii. 17.
[7] Ib. cxlvii. 10.
[8] See Mi. v. 10.
[9] Dan. ii. 34.
[10] Eph. ii. 17.
[11] Osor.

Before
CHRIST
cir. 487.
sea, and f r o m the river *even* to the ends of the earth.

|| Or, *whose cove-
nant is by
blood.*
Ex. 24. 8.
Heb. 10. 29.
& 13. 20.
11 As for thee also, || by the blood of thy covenant

I have sent forth thy ˣ pris- oners out of the pit where- in *is* no water.

12 ¶ Turn you to the strong hold, ʸ ye prisoners

Before
CHRIST
cir. 487.

ˣ Isai. 42. 7.
& 51. 14.
& 61. 1.
ʸ Isai. 49. 9.

The bounds of the promised land, in its utmost range, on the West, were the Mediterranean sea ; on the East, *the great river,* the Euphrates. The prophet pictures its extension, so as to embrace the whole world, taking away, first the one bound, then the other. *From sea to sea* is from the Mediterranean to the extremest East, where the Ocean encircles the continent of Asia ; *from the river to the ends of the earth,* is from the Euphrates to the extremest West, embracing the whole of Europe ; and whatever may lie beyond, to the ends of the earth, where earth ceaseth to be[1]. It is this same lowly and afflicted king, Whose entry into Jerusalem is on a despised animal, Who shall, by His mere will, make war to cease, Who shall, by His mere word, give peace ｔ the heathen.

11. *As for thee also.* The Prophet turns from the deliverance of the whole world to the former people, the sorrows which they should have in the way, and the protection which God would bestow upon them for the sake of Him, Who, according to the flesh, was to be born of them. *Thou too;* he had spoken of the glories of the Church, such as her king, when He should come, should extend it, embracing earth's remotest bounds : he turns tò her, Israel after the flesh, and assures her of the continued protection of God, even in her lowest estate. The deliverᴸ ance under the Maccabees was, as those under the judges had been, an image of the salvation of Christ and a preparation for it. They were martyrs for the One God and for the faith in the Resurrection, and, whether by doing or by suffering, preserved the sacred line, until Christ should come.

By the blood of thy covenant. " [2] Not by the blood of those victims of old, but *by the blood of thy covenant,* wilt thou be united to the empire of Christ, and so obtain salvation. As the Lord Himself says, *This is the blood of covenant, which is shed for you.*" [3] *The gifts and calling of God are without repentance.*

That symbolic blood, by which, fore-signifying the new Covenant, He made them His own people, [4] *Behold the blood of the covenant, which the Lord hath made with you concerning all these words,* endured still, amid all their unfaithfulness and breaches of it. By virtue of it God would send forth her imprisoned ones *out of the deep, dry pit, the dungeon* wherein they could be kept securely, because life was not threatened [5]. Out of any depth of hopeless misery, in which they seemed to be shut up, God would deliver them ; as David says, [6] *He brought me up also out of a horrible pit, out of the miry clay, and set my feet upon a rock and established my goings;* and Jeremiah, [7] *They have cut off my life in the dungeon, and cast a stone upon me. I called upon Thy Name, O Lord ; out of the low dungeon Thou hast heard my voice.* "[8] The dry and barren depth of human misery, where are no streams of righteousness, but the mire of iniquity."

12. *Turn ye to the stronghold* [9], i. e. Almighty God ; as the Psalmists so often say [10], *The Lord is the defence of my life;* and Joel [11], *The Lord shall be a stronghold of the children of Israel ;* and Nahum [12], *The Lord is a stronghold in the day of trouble;* And, David said, [13] *Thou hast been a shelter for me, a strong tower against the enemy* [14]; *the Name of the Lord is a strong tower, the righteous runneth into it and is safe;* and again, [15] *Be Thou to me a rock of strength, a house of defence to save me—Bring me forth out of the net that they have laid privily for me ; for Thou art my stronghold.* The *stronghold,* " cut off" from all approach from an enemy, stands in contrast with the deep dungeon of calamity. The *return* must be a willing return, one in their own power ; *return to the stronghold,* which is Almighty God, must be by conversion of heart and will. Even a Jewish commentator [16] paraphrases, "Turn ye to God ; for He is a stronghold and tower of strength."

Ye prisoners of [*the*] *hope* [17] not, accordingly, any hope, or generally, *hope,* but *the* special

[1] See " Daniel the Prophet." p. 483.   [2] Osor.
[3] Rom. xi. 29.   Exod. xxiv. 8.
[5] As in Gen. xxxvii. 24.   [6] Ps. xl. 2.
[7] Lam. iii. 53, 55, 56.   [8] S. Aug. de Civ. Dei. xviii. 35. 3.   [9] בצדון is ἄπ. λεγ.
[10] Ps. xxvii. 1. add xxxi. 5, xxxvii. 39, xliii. 2, lii. 9.
[11] Joel iv. 16. [iii. 16 Eng.]   [12] Nah. i. 7.
[13] עז כנדל Ps. lxi. 3.   [14] Pr. xviii. 10.
[15] Ps. xxxi. 3, 5. [2, 4, Eng.]   [16] Kim.
[17] התקוה. The only place, where it has the art.

It is used 12 times with different pronouns ; 6 times with the gen., of him whose expectation is spoken of ; it is used absolutely 13 times, viz. 5 times of a hope which will not fail, in the idiom יש תקוה
Ruth i. 12. Jer. xxxi. 17. כי יש ת. Job xi. 18, xiv. 7, Pr. xix. 18, modified by אולי Lam. iii. 29, with ל, a solid expectation which a person has, Job v. 16, Pr. xxvi. 12, xxix. 20 : given by God, Hos. ii. 17, Jer. xxix. 11 ; twice with the neg., the absence of *all* hope, Job vii. 6, Pr. xi. 7. [all.]

of hope: even to day do I declare *that* ᶻ I will render double unto thee;

13 When I have bent Judah for me, filled the

bow with Ephraim, and raised up thy sons, O Zion, against thy sons, O Greece, and made thee as the sword of a mighty man.

---

hope of Israel, *the hope* which sustained them in all those years of patient expectations, as S. Paul speaks of [1] *the hope of Israel, for* which he says, *I am bound with this chain.* [2] *I stand to be judged for the hope of the promise made by God unto our fathers, unto which* promise *our twelve tribes, serving God instantly day and night, hope to come; for which hope's sake, King Agrippa, I am accused of the Jews.* And in his Epistles, [3] *the hope laid up for you in heaven;* [4] *the hope of the Gospel;* and, [5] *looking for the blessed hope and the glorious appearing of the great God and our Saviour Jesus Christ.* He writes also of " [6] keeping the rejoicing of *the* hope firm unto the end;" of " [7] the full assurance of *the* hope unto the end;" of " [8] fleeing to lay hold on *the* hope set before us; which hope we have as an anchor of the soul, both sure and steadfast." He does not speak of hope as a grace or theological virtue, but, objectively, as the thing hoped for. So Zechariah calls to them as bound, held fast by *the hope*, bound, as it were, to it and by it, so as not to let it go, amid the persecution of the world, or weariness of expectation; as S. Paul also says, [9] *before faith came, we were guarded*, kept in ward, *under the law, shut up unto the faith* [10] *which was about to be revealed.*

Even to-day, amid all contrary appearances, *do I declare, that I will render double unto thee;* as He had said by Isaiah [11], *For your shame ye shall have double.*

13. *When,* or *For I have bent* [12] *Judah for me,* as a mighty bow which is only drawn at full human strength, the foot being placed to

steady it. It becomes a strong instrument, but only at God's Will. God Himself bends it. It cannot bend itself. *And filled the bow with Ephraim* [13]. The bow is filled, when the arrow is laid upon it. God would employ both in their different offices, as one. *And raised up* [14] *thy sons, O Zion, against thy sons, O Greece.* Let men place this prophecy where they will, nothing in the history of the world was more contradictory to what was in human sight possible. " [15] Greece was, until Alexander, a colonizing, not a conquering, nation. The Hebrews had no human knowledge of the site or circumstances of Greece. There was not a little cloud, like a man's hand, when Zechariah thus absolutely foretold the conflict and its issue. Yet here we haveᵃ a definite prophecy later than Daniel, fitting in with his temporal prophecy, expanding part of it, reaching on beyond the time of Antiochus, and fore-announcing the help of God in two definite ways of protection; 1) *without war*, against the army of Alexander [16]; 2) *in the war* of the Maccabees; and these, two of the most critical periods in their history after the captivity [17]. Yet, being expansions of part of the prophecy of Daniel, the period, to which they belong, becomes clearer in the event by aid of the more comprehensive prophecies. They were two points in Daniel's larger prediction of the 3d empire."

And I will make thee as the sword of a mighty man. The strength is still not their own. In the whole history of Israel, they had only once met in battle an army of one of the

---

[1] Acts xxviii. 20.   [2] Ib. xxvi. 6, 7.
[3] Col. i. 5.   [4] Ib. 23.   [5] Tit. ii. 13.
[6] Heb. iii. 6.   [7] Ib. vi. 11.
[8] Ib. 18, 19.   [9] Gal. iii. 23.
[10] ἐφρουρούμεθα, συγκεκλεισμένοι εἰς.
[11] Is. lxi. 7. The same word, מִשְׁנֶה.
[12] קֶשֶׁת דְּרַךְ, in different inflections is too common an idiom to leave any ambiguity, though the word קֶשֶׁת occurs in the following clause only. The idiom occurs Ps. vii. 13, xxxvii. 14, Is. v. 28, xxi. 15. Jer. xlvi. 9, l. 14, 29, li. 3, Lam. ii. 4, iii. 12, 1 Chr. v. 18, viii. 40, 2 Chr. xiv. 7. דְּרַךְ is used twice in the same sense, when the arrow is made the object, Ps. lviii. 8, lxiv. 4.   [13] It is the common construction of מִלֵּא with a double acc., "fill a thing with;" which, in different idioms, occurs 38 times beside. [Gen. xxi. 19. xxvi. 15, xli. 25, Ex. xxviii. 3, xxxi. 3, xxxv. 31, 35, 1 Sam. xvi. 1, 1 Kgs xviii. 35, 2 Kgs xxiii. 14, xxiv. 4, 2 Chr. xvi. 14, Job iii. 15, viii. 21, xv. 2, xxii. 18. xxiii. 4, Ps. xvii. 14, lxxxiii. 17, cvii. 9, cxxix. 7. Pr. i. 13, Is. xxxiii. 5,

Jer. xiii. 13, xv. 17, xxxiii. 5, xli. 9, li. 14, 34, Ezek. iii. 3, ix. 7, x. 2, xi. 7, xxxii. 5, xxxv. 8. Nah. ii. 13, Zeph. i. 9, Hagg. ii. 7.] It is therefore entirely unidiomatic to render with Ges. &c., "pulled with full strength a bow, Ephraim." The Arab. פִּי אֶמְלָא does not bear this out, being for אֶמְלָא אֶלְקוֹם. The Syr. קֶשְׁתָּא מְלוֹ Ps. xi. 2. אֶלְגֹּנְעַ פִּי אֶלְקוֹם. קֶשְׁתָּא דְמְלִיא Is. xxi. 15, probably mean, "filled the bow" "the bow filled" viz. with the arrow
[14] Since עוֹרֵר occurs of rousing a person, Cant. ii. 7, iii. 5, viii. 4, 5, Is. xiv. 9, or living thing, Job iii. 8, or His might, (of God) Ps. lxxx. 3, it would be unidiomatic to interpret it here, "lift up as a spear," on the ground of the idioms חֲנִיתוֹ עוֹרֵר אֶת 2 Sam. xxiii. 18, 1 Chr. xi. 11, 20, שׁוֹט עוֹרֵר Is. x. 26, since here no instrument is mentioned, but a person, and עוֹרֵר is not used of any one instrument, nor, by itself, signifies "wave."
[15] Pusey's "Daniel the Prophet" pp. 282, 283.
[16] Zech. ix. 1–8.   [17] Ib. 9–16.

Before
CHRIST
cir. 487.

* Ps. 18. 14.
& 77. 17.
& 144. 6.

ᵇ Isai. 21. 1.

14 And the LORD shall be seen over them, and ᵃ his arrow shall go forth as the lightning: and the Lord GOD shall blow the trumpet, and shall go ᵇ with whirlwinds of the south.

15 The LORD of hosts

shall defend t h e m ; and they shall d e v o u r, and || subdue with sling stones ; and they shall drink, and make a noise as through wine ; and they || shall be filled like bowls, and as ᶜ the corners of the altar.

Before
CHRIST
cir. 487.

|| Or, *subdue the stones of the sling.*

|| Or, *shall fill both the bowls, &c.*
ᶜ Lev. 4. 18, 25.
Deut. 12. 27.

world-Empires and defeated it, at a time, when Asa's whole population which could bear arms were 580,000 [1], and he met Zerah the Ethiopian with his million of combatants, besides his 500 chariots, and defeated him. And this, in reliance on the [2] *Lord his God,* to Whom he cried, *Lord, it is nothing to Thee to help, whether with many, or with them that have no power ; help us, O Lord our God; for we rest on Thee, and in Thy Name we go against this multitude.* Asa's words found an echo in Judas Maccabæus [3], when the "small company with him asked him, How shall we be able, being so few, to fight against so great a multitude and so strong ? " "It is no hard matter," Judas answered, "for many to be shut up in the hands of a few, and with Heaven it is all one to deliver with a great multitude or a small company. For the victory of battle standeth not in the multitude of an host; but strength cometh from Heaven." But his armies were but a handful; 3000, on three occasions [4], on one of which they are reduced by fear to 800 [5]; 10,000 on two occasions [6] ; on another, two armies of 8000 and 3000, with a garrison, not trusted to fight in the open field [7] ; on one, 20,000 [8] ; once only 40,000, which Tryphon treacherously persuaded Jonathan to disperse [9] ; these were the numbers with which, always against "great hosts," God gave the victory to the lion-hearted Judas and his brothers. But Who save He, in Whose hands are the hearts of men, could foresee that He, at that critical moment, would raise up that devoted family, or inspire that faith, through which they [10] *out of weakness were made strong, waxed valiant in fight, turned to flight the armies of the aliens ?*

14. *And the Lord shall be seen over them* [11], " [12] He will reveal Himself," protecting them. " [13] He says plainly, that the Lord God will

be with them and will fight in serried array with them and will with them subdue those who resist them." It is as if he would say, "When they go forth and preach everywhere, [14] *the Lord* shall *work with* them *and confirm the word with signs following." And His arrow shall go forth as the lightning.* Habakkuk directly calls the lightnings the arrows of God [15]: *at the light of Thine arrows they went.* Here it is probably of an invisible agency, and so compared to that awful symbol of His presence, the lightning.

And the Lord God shall blow with the trumpet, as their Commander, ordering their goings. The blowing of the trumpet by the priests in war was commanded, as a reminiscence of themselves before God, [16] *If ye go to war in your land against the enemy that oppresseth you, then ye shall blow an alarm with the trumpets, and ye shall be remembered before the Lord your God, and ye shall be saved from your enemies.* Abijah said, [17] *God Himself is with us for our captain, and His priests with sounding trumpets to cry alarm against you.*

And shall go with whirlwinds of the south, as being the most vehement and destructive. So Isaiah, [18] *As whirlwinds in the south sweep by, He cometh from a desert, from a terrible land.* Such smote the four corners of the house where Job's children were [19], and they perished.

15. *The Lord of hosts shall defend them.* As God says [20], *I will defend this city to save it, for Mine own sake and for My servant David's sake.* The word is used by Isaiah only before Zechariah, and of the protection of Almighty God. The image of the complete protection on all sides stands first in God's words to Abraham [21], *I am thy shield ;* David thence says to God, [22] *Thou, O Lord, art a shield around me.*

And they shall devour, and subdue, or more

[1] Chr. xiv. 8–10 sqq. [2] Ib. 11. [3] 1 Macc. iii. 16–19.
[4] 1 Macc. iv. 6, vii. 40. ix. 5. [5] Ib. ix. 6.
[6] Ib. iv. 29, x. 74. [7] Ib. v. 17–20. [8] Ib. xvi. 4.
[9] Ib. xii. 41–47. See more in detail in "Daniel the Prophet" p. 371. note 5. [10] Heb. xi. 34.
[11] עַל as with the word גנן, בסה סכך, עטה.
[12] Jon. [13] S. Cyr. [14] S. Mark xvi. 20.
[15] Hab. iii. 11. The arrows of God, and the lightnings, stand in parallel or connected clauses, Ps. xviii. 14, lxxvii. 17, 18. cxliv. 6.

[16] Nu. x. 9. [17] 2 Chr. xiii. 12.
[18] Is. xxi. 1.
[19] Job i. 19. In Job xxxvii. 9, E. V. has followed Kim. who explains מִן הַחֶדֶר by חַדְרֵי תֵימָן Job ix. 9 ; but in this case the chief characteristic word would be omitted.
[20] Is. xxxvii. 35, 2 Kgs xix. 34. Is. xxxviii. 6, 2 Kgs xx. 6. It occurs again Zech. xii. 8.
[21] Gen. xv. 1, מָגֵן from the same root.
[22] Ps. iii. 4. (3 Eng.)

Before
CHRIST
cir. 487.

16 And the LORD their
God shall s a v e them in
that day as the flock of his
people: for [d] they shall be

[d] Isai. 62. 3.
Mal. 3. 17.

as the stones of a crown,
[e] lifted up as an ensign
upon his land.

17 For [f] how great is his

Before
CHRIST
cir. 487.

[e] Isai. 11. 12.

[f] Ps. 31. 19.

probably [1], *shall tread on, the stones of the sling,*
as in the image of leviathan in Job, [2] *The
son of the bow will not make him flee ; sling-
stones are to him turned into stubble ; clubs are
counted as stubble ; he laugheth at the shaking of
a spear.* Their enemies shall fall under them,
as harmless and as of little account as the sling-
stones which have missed their aim, and lie
as the road to be passed over. It is not expressed what they shall devour, and so the
image is not carried out, but left indefinite,
as destruction or absorption only ; as in that,
[3] *thou shalt consume* [lit. *eat*] *all the people
which the Lord thy God shall deliver thee ;* and,
[4] *they are our bread ;* and in that, [5] *they shall
devour* [lit. *eat*] *all the people round about,*
where the image is of fire, not of eating.
The one thought seems to be, that their
enemies should cease to be, so as to molest
them any more, whether by ceasing to be
their enemies or by ceasing to be. There is no
comparison here, (as in Balaam) with the
lion ; or of eating flesh or drinking blood,
which, apart from the image of the wild
beast, would be intolerable to Israel, to whom
the use of blood, even of animals, was so
strictly forbidden. They should disappear,
as completely as fuel before the fire, or food
before the hungry. The fire was invigorated,
not extinguished, by the multitude of the
fuel : the multitude of the enemies but
nerved and braced those, whom they sought
to destroy.
*And they shall be filled like bowls, like the
corners of the altar.* They shall be consecrated
instruments of God ; they shall not prevail
for themselves, but for Him ; they shall be
hallowed like the bowls of the temple, from
which the sacrificial blood is sprinkled on
His altar, or as *the corners of the altar* which
receive it.

16. *And the Lord their God shall save them in
that day.* Still all should be God's doing ; they
themselves were but as a flock, as sheep
among wolves, ready for the slaughter ; but
they were *the flock, His people*[6], as He says,
[7] *I will increase them like the flock, men, as the
flock of holy things, as the flock of Jerusalem*

*in her solemn feasts ; so shall the waste cities be
filled with flocks, men.* "[8] As a man saves his
flock with all his strength, so He will save
His people ; for they are His flock." As in,
[9] *Thou leddest Thy people like sheep by the hand
of Moses and Aaron.*
They shall be as the stones of a crown. While
God's enemies shall be trampled under foot,
as a common thing which has failed its end,
these shall be precious stones ; a consecrated
[10] diadem of king or priest, *raised aloft*[11], so
that all can see. *On His land.* It was laid
down, as the title-deed to its whole tenure,
[12] *the land is Mine,* and much more our Christian land, bought and purified by the blood
of Christ.
17. *For how great is His goodness.* For it is
unutterable ! As the Psalmist said, [13] *O Lord,
our Lord, how excellent is Thy Name in all the
earth !* and Jacob, [14] *How awful is this place !*
and the Psalmist, *How awful are Thy doings !*
The goodness and the beauty are the goodness and beauty of God, Whose great doings
had been his theme throughout before. Of
the goodness the sacred writers often speak [15],
since of this we have extremest need. And
this He shewed to Moses, [16] *I will cause all My
goodness to pass before thy face.* Of this we
know somewhat personally in this life ; for
beside the surpassing amazingness of it in the
work of our redemption, we are surrounded
by it, immersed in it, as in a fathomless,
shoreless ocean of infinite love, which finds
entrance into our souls, whenever we bar it
not out.
Goodness is that attribute of God, whereby He loveth to communicate to all, who can
or will receive it, all good ; yea, Himself,
"[17] Who is the fullness and universality of
good, Creator of all good, not in one way, not
in one kind of goodness only, but absolutely,
without beginning, without limit, without measurement He possesseth and embraceth
all excellence, all perfection, all blessedness,
all good." This Good His Goodness bestoweth on all and each, according to the
capacity of each to receive it, nor is there

[1] As in margin.
[2] Job xli. 20, 21 (28, 29 Eng.)   [3] Deut. vii. 16.
[4] Nu. xiv. 9.   [5] Zech. xii. 6.
[6] כְּצֹאן עָמוֹ in apposition, as in Ezek. כְּצֹאן אָדָם.
[7] Ezek. xxxvi. 37, 38.   [8] Kim.   [9] Ps. lxxvii. 20.
[10] The etymology implies this, properly "conse-
cration," then the diadem of one consecrated, as
the נֵזֶר הַקֹּדֶשׁ Ex. xxix. 6, xxxix. 30, Lev. viii. 9.
or the נֵזֶר of the king.

[11] Comp. Ar. צָע "lifted on high," נָצַע "throne
exalted."
[12] Lev. xxv. 23.   [13] Ps. viii. 1.   [14] Gen. xxviii. 17.
[15] טוּב "the goodness" of the Lord, Ps. xxv. 7,
xxvii. 13, xxxi. 20, cxlv. 7, Is. lxiii. 7, Jer. xxxi. 12,
14. Hos. iii. 5.
[16] אַעֲבִיר כָּל טוּבִי עַל פָּנֶיךָ Ex. xxxiii. 19.
[17] Blaise Palma in "Paradise of the Christian
soul," P. 1. c. vi. n. 4. pp. 90, 91.

goodness, and how great *is* his beauty! г corn shall make

the young men || cheerful, and new wine the maids.

any limit to His giving, save His creature's capacity of receiving, which also is a good gift from Him. "From Him all things sweet derive their sweetness; all things fair, their beauty; all things bright, their splendor; all things that live, their life; all things sentient, their sense; all that move, their vigor; all intelligences, their knowledge; all things perfect, their perfection; all things in any wise good, their goodness."

The beauty of God belongs rather to the beatific vision. Yet David speaks of the Beauty of Christ [1], *Thou art exceeding fairer than the children of men;* and Isaiah says, [2] *Thine eyes shall behold the King in His beauty.* But the Beauty of God "eye hath not seen nor ear heard nor can heart of man conceive." Here, on earth, created beauty can, at least when suddenly seen, hold the frame motionless, pierce the soul, glue the heart to it, entrance the affections. Light from heaven kindles into beauty our dullest material substances; the soul in grace diffuses beauty over the dullest human countenance; the soul, ere it has passed from the body, has been known to catch, through the half-opened portals, such brilliancy of light, that the eye even for some time after death has retained a brightness, beyond anything of earth [3]. "[4] The earth's form of beauty is a sort of voice of the dumb earth. Doth not, on considering the beauty of this universe, its very form answer thee with one voice, ' Not I made myself, but God ' ? " Poets have said,

" [5] Old friends . . . . shall lovelier be,
    As more of heaven in each we see,"
or,
            " [6] When he saw,
"—God within him light his face."

and Holy Scripture tells us that when S. Stephen, *full of faith and of the Holy Ghost,* was about to speak of Jesus to the council which arraigned him, [7] *all that sat in the council, looking steadfastly at him, saw his face as it had been the face of an Angel.* It has been said, that if we could see a soul in grace, its beauty would so pierce us, that we should die. But the natural beauty of the soul transcends all corporeal beauty which so attracts us; the natural beauty of the last Angel surpasseth all natural beauty of soul. If we could ascend from the most beautiful form, which the soul could here

imagine, to the least glorious body of the beatified, on and on through the countless thousands of glorious bodies, compared wherewith heaven would be dark and the sun lose its shining; and yet more from the most beautiful deified soul, as visible here, to the beauty of the disembodied soul, whose image would scarce be recognized, because " [8] the bodily eyes gleamed with angelic radiancy ; " yea, let the God-enlightened soul go on and on, through all those choirs of the heavenly hierarchies, clad with the raiment of Divinity, from choir to choir, from hierarchy to hierarchy, admiring the order and beauty and harmony of the house of God ; yea, let it, aided by divine grace and light, ascend even higher, and reach the bound and term of all created beauty, yet it must know that the Divine power and wisdom could create other creatures, far more perfect and beautiful than all which He hath hitherto created. Nay, let the highest of all the Seraphs sum in one all the beauty by nature and grace and glory of all creatures, yet could it not be satisfied with that beauty, but must, because it was not satisfied with it, conceive some higher beauty. Were God forthwith, at every moment to create that higher beauty at its wish, it could still conceive something beyond; for, not being God, its beauty could not satisfy its conception. So let him still, and in hundred thousand, hundred thousand, thousand years with swiftest flight of understanding multiply continually those degrees of beauty, so that each fresh degree should ever double that preceding, and the Divine power should, with like swiftness, concur in creating that beauty, as in the beginning He said, *let there be light and there was light ;* after all those millions of years, he would be again at the beginning, and there would be no comparison between it and the Divine Beauty of Jesus Christ, God and Man. For it is the bliss of the finite not to reach the Infinite [9]. That city of the blest which is lightened by the glory of God, and the Lamb is the light thereof, sees It, enabled by God, as created eye can see It, and is held fast to God in one jubilant exstacy of everlasting love.

" [10] The Prophet, borne out of himself by consideration of the Divine goodness, stands amazed, while he contemplates the beauty and Deity of Christ: he bursts out with unwonted admiration ! How great is His goodness, Who, to guard His flock, shall come

---

[1] Ps. xlv. 2.   [2] Is. xxxiii. 17.   [3] This I saw once.
[4] S. Aug. in Ps. cxliv. n. 13.
[5] Christian Year. Morning Hymn.
[6] Tennyson, In memoriam.   T. has " *The* God."
[7] Acts vi. 5, 15.

[8] S. Flavian, of Successus a martyr, whom he saw after death. Passio SS. Montani, Lucii &c. cxxxi. in Ruinart, Acta martyr. sincera p. 241.
[9] abridged from Joannes a Jesu Maria, ars amandi Deum c. 3. Opp. ii. 301–304.   [10] Osorius.

CHAPTER X.

1 *God is to be sought unto, and not idols.* 5 *As he visited his flock for sin, so he will save and restore them.*

A SK ye [a]of the LORD [b]rain [c]in the time of the latter rain; *so* the LORD shall make || bright clouds, and give them

[a] Jer 14. 22.
[b] Deut. 11. 14.
[c] Job 29. 23.
Joel 2. 23.
|| Or, *lightnings.* Jer. 10. 13.

down on earth to lay down His life for the salvation of His sheep! How great His beauty, Who is the *brightness of the glory and the Image of the Father,* and comprises in His Godhead the measure of all order and beauty! With what firm might does He strengthen, with what joy does He overwhelm the souls which gaze most frequently on His beauty, and gives largely and bountifully that corn, by whose strength the youths are made strong. He supplieth abundantly the wine, whereby the virgins, on fire with His love, are exhilarated and beautified. But both are necessary, that the strength of the strong should be upheld by the *bread from heaven,* and that sound and uncorrupt minds, melted with the sweetness of love, should be re-created with wine, i. e. the sweetness of the Holy Spirit, and be borne aloft with great joy, in the midst of extreme toils. For all who keep holily the faith of Christ, may be called *youths,* for their unconquered strength, and virgins for their purity and integrity of soul. For all these that heavenly bread is prepared, that their strength be not weakened, and the wine is inpoured, that they be not only refreshed, but may live in utmost sweetness."

X. 1. *Ask ye of the Lord rain. Ask and ye shall receive,* our Lord says. Zechariah had promised in God's name blessings temporal and spiritual: all was ready on God's part; only, he adds, ask them of the Lord, the Unchangeable, the Self-same, not of Teraphim or of diviner, as Israel had done aforetime [1]. He had promised, [2] *If ye shall hearken diligently unto My commandments, to love the Lord your God, I will give you the rain of your land in his due season, the first rain and the latter rain, and I will send grass in thy field for thy cattle.* God bids them ask Him to fulfill His promise. The *latter rain* [3] alone is mentioned, as completing what God had begun by the former rain, filling the ears before the har-

vest. Both [4] had been used as symbols of God's spiritual gifts, and so the words fit in with the close of the last chapter, both as to things temporal and eternal. " [5] He exhorts all frequently to ask for the dew of the divine grace, that what had sprung up in the heart from the seed of the word of God, might attain to full ripeness."

The Lord maketh bright clouds, [rather] *lightnings* [6], *into rain,* as Jeremiah says, [7] *He causeth the vapors to ascend from the ends of the earth; He maketh lightnings into rain;* and the Psalmist, [8]*He maketh lightnings into rain,* disappearing as it were into the rain which follows on them. *And giveth them.* While man is asking, God is answering. *Showers of rain* [9], "rain in torrents," as we should say, or "in floods," or, inverted, "floods of rain." *To every one grass,* rather, *the green herb, in the field,* as the Psalmist says, [10] *He causeth the grass to grow for the cattle, and green herb for the service of men.* This He did with individual care, as each had need, or as should be best for each, as contrariwise He says in Amos, [11] *I caused it to rain upon one city, and caused it not to rain upon another city; one piece was rained upon, and the piece, whereon it rained not, withered.* The Rabbins observed these exceptions to God's general law, whereby He [12] *sendeth rain on the just and on the unjust,* though expressing it in their way hyperbolically; " [13] In the time when Israel doeth the will of God, He doeth their will; so that if one man alone, and not the others, wants rain, He will give rain to that one man; and if a man wants one herb alone in his field or garden, and not another, He will give rain to that one herb; as one of the saints used to say, This plot of ground wants rain, and that plot of ground wants not rain [14]." Spiritually the rain is divine doctrine bedewing the mind and making it fruitful, as the rain doth the earth. So Moses saith, [15] *My doctrine shall drop as the rain, my speech shall distill as the dew,* as the

[1] Hos. ii. 5-12, Jer. xliv. 15-28. [2] Deut. xi. 13-15.
[3] It is mentioned alone in Pr. xvi. 15.
[4] See vol. i. on Hos. vi. 3, p. 64; Jo. ii. 23. pp. 190, 191. [5] Osorius.
[6] חזיז, Its etymology is unknown, its meaning is determined by the idiom חזיז קולות Job xxviii. 26, xxxviii. 25. The Arab. חז only signifies " made incisions, notches, cut the heart," (of misgivings of conscience.)
[7] Jer. x. 13, li. 16. [8] Ps. cxxxv. 7.
[9] As the words are transposed in Job xxxvii. 6, גֶּשֶׁם ונשם מטר occurs, de-

fined by גדול 1 Kgs xviii. 45; by שוטף Ezek. xiii. 11, 13, xxxviii. 22; by נדבות Ps. lxviii. 10, המון הגשם 1 Kgs xviii. 41. " The clouds are full of גשם." Eccl. xi. 3. The waters of the flood are called הגשב Gen. vii. 12, viii. 2. Kim. compares the two synonymes, אדמת עפר (Dan. xii. 2) טיט היון Ps. xl. 3.
[10] Ps. civ. 14. See also Gen. i. 30, iii. 18.
[11] Am. iv. 7. See note vol. i. p. 284.
[12] S. Matt. v. 49.
[13] Taanith f. ix. 2 in Kim. Mc. Caul pp. 111, 112.
[14] S. Cyril. [15] Deut. xxxii. 2.

Before CHRIST cir. 487.	

showers of rain, to every one grass in the field.

2 For the [d] † idols have spoken v a n i t y, and the diviners have seen a lie, and have told false dreams; they [e] comfort in v a i n : therefore they went their way as a flock, they || were

[d] Jer. 10. 8. Hab. 2. 18.
† Heb. *tera-phims.* Judg. 17. 5.

[e] Job 13. 4.

| Or, *answered that, &c.*

troubled, [f] because *t h e r e* *was* no shepherd.

3 Mine anger was kin-dled against the shepherds, [g] and I † p u n i s h e d the goats : for the L O R D of hosts [h] hath v i s i t e d his flock the house of Judah, and [i] hath made them as

[f] Ezek. 34. 5.

[g] Ezek. 34. 17.
† Heb. *visited upon.*

[h] Luke 1. 68.

[i] Cant. 1. 9.

---

small rain upon the tender herb and as the showers upon the grass. " [1] The law of Moses and the prophets were the former rain."

2. *For the teraphim have spoken vanity,* rather, *spake vanity.* He appeals to their former experience. Their fathers had sought of idols, not of God ; therefore they went into captivity. The *teraphim* were used as instruments of divination. They are united with the *ephod,* as forbidden, over against the allowed, means of enquiry as to the future, in Hosea, [2] *without an ephod and without teraphim ;* they were united in the mingled worship of Micah [3] ; Josiah *put them away* together with [4] *the workers with familiar spirits and the wizards,* to which are added, *the idols.* It was probably, a superstition of Eastern origin. Rachel brought them with her from her father's house, and Nebuchadnezzar used them for divination [5]. Samuel speaks of them, apparently, as things which Saul himself condemned. [6] *Rebellion is as the sin of divination, and stubbornness as iniquity or idolatry, and teraphim.* For it was probably in those his better days, that [7] *Saul had put away those that had familiar spirits and wizards out of the land.* Samuel then seems to tell him, that the sins to which he clave were as evil as those which he had, in an outward zeal, like Jehu, condemned. Anyhow, the *teraphim* stand united with the *divination* which was expressly condemned by the law [8]. The use of the teraphim by Rachel [9] and Michal [10] (for whatever purpose) implies that it was some less offensive form of false worship, though they were probably the *strange gods* [11] which Jacob bade his household to put away, or, anyhow, among them, since Laban calls them, [12] *my gods.*

Zechariah uses anew the words of Jeremiah and Ezekiel, [13] *Hearken ye not to your prophets, nor to your diviners, nor to your dreamers, nor to your enchanters, nor to your sorcerers ;* and, [14] *let not your prophets and your diviners, that be in the midst of you, deceive you, neither hearken to your dreams, which ye cause to be dreamed ;* and Ezekiel, [15] *While they see vanity unto thee, while they divine a lie unto thee.* The words not only joined on the Prophet's warning with the past, but reminded them of the sentence which followed on their neglect. The echo of the words of the former prophets came to them, floating, as it were, over the ruins of the former temple.

Therefore they went their way as a flock, which, having no shepherd, or only such as would mislead them, removed [16], but into captivity. *They were troubled* [17]. The trouble lasted on, though the captivity ended at the appointed time. Nehemiah speaks of the exactions of former governors, [18] *The former governors which were before me, laid heavy weights upon the people* [19], *and took from them in bread and wine, after forty shekels of silver ; also their servants used dominion over* [20] *the people ; and I did not so, because of the fear of God.*

Because there was no shepherd. As Ezekiel said of those times, [21] *They were scattered, because there is no shepherd ; and they became meat to all the beasts of the field, when they were scattered : My flock was scattered upon all the face of the earth ; and none did search or seek after them.*

3. *Mine anger was kindled against the shepherds.* As Ezekiel continued, [22] *Thus saith the Lord God ; Behold I am against the shepherds, and I will require My flock at their hand. I punished the he-goats.* The evil powerful

[1] S. Cyril.
[2] Hos. iii. 4. Every fresh attempt to find an etymology for תְרָפִים attests the unsatisfactoriness of those before it, without finding anything better.
[3] Jud. xvii. 5, xviii. 14, 17, 18, 20.
[4] 2 Kgs xxiii. 24.   [5] Ezek. xxi. 21.
[6] 1 Sam. xv. 23.   [7] Ib. xxviii. 3.
[8] De. xviii. 13, 14.   [9] Gen. xxxi. 19, 34, 35.
[10] 1 Sam. xix. 13, 16.   [11] Gen. xxxv. 2, 4.
[12] Ib. xxxi. 3 1, 32.   [13] Jer. xxvii. 9.   [14] Ib. xxix. 8.
[15] Ezek. xxi. 29 ; add xxii. 28.
[16] The etym. meaning of נָסַע, " plucked up " pegs of tent, in order to removal, must have been lost in

the idiom. The captivity is spoken of as past, and the idolatry as before the captivity, which was its punishment.
[17] עָנָה occurs in this sense Ps. cxvi. 10, cxix. 67, of man ; with בְ of wearisome labor Eccl. i. 13, iii. 10 ; of the lion, Is. xxxi. 4 ; of the song of the terrible, Ib. xxv. 5 [4 Eng.] all.   [18] Neh. v. 15.
[19] הַכְבִּידוּ with עַל p., like " made our, your, yoke heavy," 1 Kgs xii. 10, 14, 2 Chr. x. 10, 14. "thy yoke,"Is. xlvii. 6. " my chain " Lam. iii. 7. or עָבְטִים Hab. ii. 6.
[20] שָׁלְטוּ עַל   [21] Ezek. xxxiv. 5, 6.   [22] Ib. 10.

Before
C H R I S T
cir. 487.
his goodly h o r s e in the battle.

4 Out of him came forth

k Num. 24. 17.
1 Sam. 14. 38.
Isa⸴. 19. 13.
l Isai. 22. 23.
ᵏ the corner, out of him ¹ the nail, out of him the battle bow, out of him every oppressor together.

5 ¶ And they shall be as

mighty *men*, which ᵐ tread down *their enemies* in the mire of the streets in the battle: and they shall fight, because the LORD *is* with them, and ‖ the riders on horses shall be confounded.

6 And I will strengthen

Before
C H R I S T
cir. 487.

ᵐ Ps. 18. 42.

‖ Or, *they shall make the riders on horses ashamed.*

---

are called the *he-goats of the earth* ¹ ; and in Ezekiel God says, ²*I will judge between cattle and cattle, between rams and he-goats ;* and our Lord speaks of the reprobate as goats, the saved as sheep ³. God *visited upon* ⁴ these in His displeasure, *because* He *visited His flock, the people of Judah,* to see to their needs and to relieve them.

And hath made them as the goodly horse, as, before, He said, ⁵ *I made thee as the sword of a mighty man.* Judah's might was not in himself; but, in God's hands, he had might like and above the might of this world; he was fearless, resistless; as S. Paul says, ⁶ *the weapons of our warfare are not carnal, but mighty through God to the pulling down of strongholds.*

4. *Out of him* ⁷ *came forth,* or rather, *From him is the corner,* as Jeremiah ⁸, *Their nobles shall be from themselves,* and *their governor shall go forth from the midst of them.* Her strength, though given by God, was to be inherent in her, though from her too was to come He Who was to be the *head-corner-stone,* the sure Foundation and Crowner of the whole building.

From thee the nail, an emblem of fixedness in itself, (as Isaiah says, ⁹ *I will fasten him a nail to a sure place*) and of security given to others dependent on Him, as Isaiah says further, ¹⁰ *And they shall hang upon him all the glory of his father's house, the offspring and the issue, from the vessels of cups to the vessels of flagons ;* all, of much or little account, the least and the greatest. "¹¹ Christ is the corner-stone; Christ is the nail fixed in the wall, whereby all vessels are supported. The word of Christ is the bow, whence the arrows rend the king's enemies."

¹ Is. xiv. 9. ² Ezek. xxxiv. 17.
³ S. Matt. xxv. 32.
⁴ פָּקַד עַל, as commonly, of chastisement; פָּקַד,
like ἐπεσκέψατο, of visiting to shew favor.
⁵ ix. 13. ⁶ 2 Cor. x. 4.
⁷ The word יָצָא does not suit פִּנָּה or יָתֵד unless (which is not probable as to יָתֵד) the metaphor was lost. ⁸ Jer. xxx. 21. ⁹ Is xxii. 23.
¹⁰ Ib. 24. ¹¹ Osor. ¹² Zech. ix. 8.

¹³ Is. xiv. 2. נָגַשׂ is no where used of a ruler or king, as in Æthiopic. The idea of "oppressors" remains in Is. iii. 12, (comp. נָגַשׂ Ib. iii. 5) xiv. 2. add Is. lx. 17, where the contrast is of change of the inferior for the better; *for brass I will bring*

From it every exactor shall go forth together. God had promised ¹² that no *oppressor,* or *exactor* ¹³, *shall pass through them any more.* He seems to repeat it here. *From thee shall go forth every oppressor together ; go forth,* not to return : as Isaiah had said, ¹⁴ *Thy children shall make haste* to return ; *thy destroyers and they that made thee waste shall go forth of thee.* "From it, its corner-stone ; from it, the sure nail ; from it, the battle bow ; *from it,"*—he no longer unites closely with it, that which should be from it, or of it, but—*from it shall go forth every oppressor together ;* one and all, as we say ; a confused pêle-mêle body, as Isaiah, ¹⁵ *all that are found of thee are bound together ;* ¹⁶ *together shall they all perish ;* or, in separate clauses ¹⁷, *they are all of them put to shame ; together they shall go into confusion.*

5. *And they* [the house of Judah ¹⁸, of whom he had said, *He hath made them as the goodly horse in the battle*] *shall be as mighty men, trampling on the mire of the streets.* Micah had said, ¹⁹ *she shall be a trampling, as the mire of the streets,* and David, ²⁰ *I did stamp them as the mire of the street.* Zechariah, by a yet bolder image, pictures those trampled upon, as what they had become, *the mire of the streets,* as worthless, as foul ; as he had said, ²¹ *they shall trample on the sling-stones. And they shall fight, because the Lord is with them,* not in their own strength, he still reminds them ; they shall have power, because God empowers them ; strength, because God instrengthens them ²² ; in presence of which, the goodly war-horse of God, human strength, *the riders on horses, shall be ashamed.*

6. *I will bring them again to place them.* Zechariah seems to have condensed into one

gold &c. It is summed up and it ends in, *I will make their exactors righteousness.* [all alleged.]
¹⁴ Is. xlix. 17. יָצָאוּ. as here יָצָא מִמְּךָ ‏מִמֶּנּוּ יֵצֵא
¹⁵ With the same idiom, כָּל נִמְצָאַיִךְ אֻסְּרוּ יַחְדָּו
‏כֻּל יַחְדָּו; Is. xxii. 3.
¹⁶ Is. xxxi. 3, יְכַלָּיוּן יַחְדָּו כֻּלָּם יֵהֹדוּ.
¹⁷ Ib. xlv. 16, ‏וְגַם נִכְלְמוּ כֻלָּם יַחְדָּו הָלְכוּ בַכְּלִמָּה
¹⁸ They are the main subject in v. 3. The words in v. 4. could not be the subject: for neither corner-stone, nor nail, nor bow, can be said to be like mighty men &c.
¹⁹ Mic. vii. 10. ²⁰ 2 Sam. xxii. 43. ²¹ ix. 15.
²² ἐν τῷ ἐνδυναμοῦντί με χριστῷ. Phil. iv. 13.

Before CHRIST cir. 487.	the house of Judah, and I will save the house of Joseph, and ⁿ I will bring them again to place them; for I ^ohave mercy upon them: and they shall be as though I had not cast them off: for I *am* the LORD their God, and ^pwill hear them.
ⁿ Jer. 3. 18. Ezek. 37. 21.	
^o Hos. 1. 7.	
^pch. 13. 9.	

7 And *they of* Ephraim shall be like a mighty *man*, and their ^qheart shall rejoice as through wine: yea, their children shall see *it*, and be glad; their heart shall rejoice in the LORD.

8 I will ^rhiss for them, and gather them; for I have redeemed them: ^sand

Before CHRIST cir. 487.
^qPs. 104. 15. ch. 9. 15.
^rIsai. 5. 26.
^sIsai. 49. 19. Ezek. 36. 37.

word two[1] of Jeremiah, [2] *I will bring them again* unto this place, and *I will cause them to dwell* safely. " [3] The two ideas are here both implied, he will cause them to return to their land, and will cause them to dwell there in peace and security."

For I will have mercy upon them. " [4] For the goodness and lovingkindness of God, not any merits of our's, is the first and principal cause of our whole salvation and grace. Therefore the Psalmist says, [5] *neither did their own arm save them; but Thy right hand and Thine arm, and the light of Thy countenance, because Thou hadst a favor unto them.*

And they shall be, as though I had not cast them off. (etymologically, "loathed," "cast off as a thing abhorrent [6]".) God is ever "the God of the present." He does not half-forgive. [7] *Their sins and their iniquities I will remember no more.* God casts off the sinner, as being what he is, a thing abhorrent, as penitence confesses of itself that it is " [8] a dead dog, a loathsome worm, a putrid corpse." God will not clothe with a righteousness, which He does not impart. He restores to the penitent all his lost graces, as though he had never forfeited them, and cumulates them with the fresh grace whereby He converts him [9]. It is an entire re-creation. *They shall be, as though I had not cast them off.* [10] *I will settle you as in your old estates, and will do good, more than at your beginnings, and ye shall know that I am the Lord.*

For I am the Lord their God, and will hear them, as He says by Malachi [11], *I am the Lord; I change not.* His unchangeableness belongs to His Being; *I Am; therefore ye sons of Jacob are not consumed;* and by Hosea, [12] *The Lord of hosts, The Lord is His memorial, therefore turn thou to thy God.* Because God was *their God,* and as surely as He was *their*

God, He would hear them. His Being was the pledge of His hearing. [13] *I, the Lord, will hear them; I, the God of Israel, will not forsake them.*

7. *And Ephraim, they shall be like a mighty man.* Prophecy, through the rest of the chapter, turns to Ephraim, which had not yet been restored. With regard to them, human victory retires out of sight, though doubtless, when their wide prison was broken at the destruction of the Persian empire, many were free to return to their native country, as others spread over the West in Asia Minor, Greece, Rome, and so some may have taken part in the victories of the Maccabees. Yet not victory, but strength, gladness beyond natural gladness, as through wine, whereby the mind is exhilarated above itself; and that, lasting, transmitted to their children, large increase, holy life in God, are the outlines of the promise.

Their heart shall rejoice in the Lord, " [5] as the principal object, the first, highest, most worthy Giver of all good, to Whom is to be referred all gladness, which is conceived from created goods, that [14] *whoso glorieth may glory in the Lord,* in Whom Alone the rational creature ought to take delight."

8. *I will hiss for them.* Formerly God had so spoken of His summoning the enemies of His people to chastise them. [15] *It shall be in that day, that the Lord shall hiss for the fly, that is in the uttermost part of the rivers of Egypt, and for the bee that is in the land of Assyria, and they shall come, and shall rest all of them in the desolate valleys, and in the holes of the rocks, and upon all thorns and upon all bushes.* [16] *He will hiss unto them from the ends of the earth, and behold they shall come with speed swiftly; none shall be weary or stumble among them.* He would gather them, like the countless num-

---

[1] הוֹשִׁבוֹתִים from הִשְׁבַּתִּים, and הֲשִׁיבֹתִים.
[2] Jer. xxxii. 37.
[3] Kim. It is not a confusion of forms, but the blending of two words into one. So also Ibn E.
[4] Dion. [5] Ps. xliv. 3.
[6] זָנַח. Arab used of "rancid" oil. Observe הָאֹזְנִיתוֹ Is. xix. 6.

[7] Heb. viii. 12.
[8] Bp. Andrewes' devotions. Morn. Pr.
[9] See vol. i. on Joel ii. 25 pp. 192, 193.
[10] Ezek. xxxvi. 11. [11] Mal. iii. 6.
[12] Hos. xii. 5, 6. [6, 7 Heb.] See vol. i. pp. 119, 120.
[13] Is. xli. 17. [14] 2 Cor. x. 17. [15] Is. vii. 18, 19.
[16] Ib. v. 26, 27. The word is only used in this same sense in these three places.

they shall increase as they have increased.

Before CHRIST cir. 487.

t Hos. 2. 23.

u Deut. 30. 1.

9 And [t] I will sow them among the people: and they shall [u] remember me in far countries; and they shall live with their children, and turn again.

10 [x] I will bring them again also out of the land of Egypt, and gather them out of Assyria; and I will

Before CHRIST cir. 487.

x Is. 11. 11. 16. Hos. 11. 11.

---

bers of the insect creation, which, if united, would irresistibly desolate life. He would summon them, as the bee-owner, by his shrill call, summons and unites his own swarm. Now, contrariwise God would summon with the same His own people. The fulfillment of the chastisement was the earnest of the ease of the fulfillment of the mercy.

For I have redeemed them. Then they are His, being redeemed at so dear a price. " [1] For Christ, as far as in Him lay, redeemed all." God had done this in purpose, as S. John speaks of [2] *the Lamb slain from the foundation of the world.*

And they shall increase as they increased. " [3] As they increased in Egypt, so shall they increase at that time." The marvels of God's favor in Egypt shall be repeated. The increase there had been promised beforehand. [4] *Fear not to go down into Egypt; for I will there make of thee a great nation.* The fulfillment is recorded, [5] *the children of Israel were fruitful, and increased abundantly, and multiplied, and waxed exceeding mighty; and the land was filled with them.* God appointed that this should be part of their confession at their yearly prosperity, the offering of the basket of first-fruits; [6] *A Syrian ready to perish was my father, and he went into Egypt and sojourned there with a few, and became there a nation, great, mighty, and populous.* The Psalmist dwelt upon it. [7] *He increased His people greatly, and made them stronger than their enemies.* It became then one of the resemblances between the first deliverance and the last. " [1] For the Apostles and others converted from Judaism, had more spiritual children, all those whom they begat in Christ, than the synagogue ever had after the flesh."

9. *And I will sow them among the nations.* Such had been the prophecy of Hosea; [8] *I will sow her unto Me in the earth,* as the prelude of spiritual mercies, *and I will have mercy on her that had not obtained mercy, and I will say to not-my-people, Thou art My people, and they shall say, my God.* Hosea's saying, *I will sow her in the earth* i. e. the whole earth, and that *to Me,* corresponds to, and explains Zechariah's brief saying, *I will sow them among*

the nations. The sowing, which was future to Hosea, had begun; but the purpose of the sowing, the harvest, was wholly to come; when it should be seen, that they were indeed sown by God, that *great* should *be the day of Jezreel* [9]. And Jeremiah said, [10] *Behold the days come, saith the Lord, that I will sow the house of Israel and the house of Judah, with the seed of man and with the seed of beast.* The word is used of sowing to multiply, never of mere scattering [11].

And they shall remember Me in far countries. So Ezekiel had said, [12] *And they that escape of you shall remember Me among the nations, whither they shall be carried captive—and they shall loath themselves for the evils which they have committed in all their abominations, and they shall know that I am the Lord.*

And shall live. As Ezekiel again says, [13] *Ye shall know that I am the Lord, when I open your graves, and bring you up out of your graves, O My people, and shall put My Spirit in you, and ye shall live.* *With their children.* A continuous gift, as Ezekiel, [14] *they and their children, and their children's children for ever: and My servant David shall be their prince for ever.*

And shall turn again to God, being converted, as Jeremiah had been bidden to exhort them ; [15] *Go and proclaim these words toward the North,* the cities of the Medes whither they were carried captive, *and say, Return, thou backsliding Israel, and I will not cause Mine anger to fall upon you ;* [16] *Turn, O backsliding children—and I will take you, one of a city, and two of a family, and will bring you to Zion, and I will give you pastors according to Mine heart.* [17] *Return, ye backsliding children ; I will heal your backslidings.* And they answer, *Behold, we come unto Thee ; for Thou art the Lord our God.* So Isaiah had said, [18] *A remnant shall return, the remnant of Jacob, unto the mighty God.* " [1] They shall return by recollection of mind and adunation and simplification of the affections toward God so as ultimately to intend that one thing, which alone is necessary."

10. *I will bring them again also out of the land of Egypt.* Individuals had fled to Egypt [19]; but here probably Egypt and Assyria stand,

---

[1] Dion. [2] Rev. xiii. 8. [3] Kim. [4] Gen. xlvi. 3.
[5] Ex. i. 7. [6] De. xxvi. 5. [7] Ps. cv. 24.
[8] Hos. ii. ult. See vol. i. pp. 27, 28, etc.
[9] Ib. i. 11. See vol. i. p. 25. [10] Jer. xxxi. 27.
[11] זרע (Kal and Pi.), "dispersed," is contrariwise never to "sow."

[12] Ezek. vi. 9. [13] Ib. xxxvii. 13, 14. [14] Ib. 25.
[15] Jer. iii. 12. [16] Ib. 14, 15. [17] Ib. 22.
[18] Is. x. 21. comp. שָׁבְיךָ, "her converts," Is. 1. 27, and וְשָׁבוּ in Solomon's prayer, 2 Chr. vi. 24.
[19] See Hos. viii. 13, vol. i., p. 86, ix. 3, p. 88.

bring them into the land of Gilead and Lebanon ; and *place* shall not be found for them.

y Isai. 49. 20.

11 ᶻ And he shall pass through the sea with afflic-tion, and shall smite the

ᶻ Isai. 11. 15. 16.

waves in the sea, and all the deeps of the river shall dry up : and ᵃ the pride of Assyria shall be brought down, and ᵇ the sceptre of Egypt shall depart away.

ᵃ Isai. 14. 25.

ᵇ Ezek. 30. 13.

---

as of old, for the two great conflicting em-pires, between which Israel lay, at whose hands she had suffered, and who represent the countries which lay beyond them. Hosea unites, [1] *the West, Assyria, Egypt,* the three then known divisions of the world, Europe, Asia, Africa [2]. Asshur, after Nineveh perished, stands clearly for the world-empire of the East at Babylon [3], and then in Persia [4]. Balaam includes under Asshur, first Babylon, then the third world-empire [5]. Babylon, which was first subject to Nineveh, then subjected it, was at a later period known to Greek writers (who proba-bly had their information from Persian sources) as part of Assyria [6].

And I will bring them into the land of Gilead and Lebanon, their old dwellings, East and West of Jordan. *And place shall not be found for them* [7], as Isaiah says, [8] *The children of thy bereaved estate shall yet say in thine ears, The place is too strait for me: give place, that I may dwell.*

11. *And He,* i. e. Almighty God, *shall pass through the sea, affliction* [9], as He says, [10] *When thou walkest through the waters, I* will be *with thee ; and through the rivers, they shall not overflow thee. And shall smite the waves in the sea,* as in Isaiah, [11] *The Lord shall utterly de-stroy the tongue of the Egyptian sea.* The image is from the deliverance of Egypt : yet it is said, that it should not be any exact repetition of the miracles of Egypt ; it would

be as the Red Sea [12], which would as effectu-ally shut them in, and in presence of which they might again think themselves lost, through which God would again bring them. But it would not be the Red sea itself; for *the sea* through which they should be brought, would be *affliction ;* as our own poet speaks of "taking arms against a sea of troubles." " [13] The promise of succor to those who believe in Christ is under the likeness of the things given to those of old; for as Israel was conveyed across the Red sea, braving the waves in it ; [14] *for the waters stood upright as an heap,* God bringing this to pass marvellously ; and as [15] they passed the Jordan on foot, so he says, those who are called through Moses to the knowledge of Christ, and have been saved by the ministries of the holy Apostles, they shall pass the waves of this present life, like an angrily foaming sea, and, being removed from the tumult of this life, shall, undisturbed, worship the true God. And they shall pass through temptations, like sweeping rivers, saying with great joy, in like way, [16] *Unless the Lord had been for us, may Israel now say, the waters had drowned us, the stream had gone over our souls." He shall smite the waves in the sea.* There, where the strength of the powers of this world is put forth against His people, there He will bring it down. *All the deeps of the river,* i. e. of the Nile [17], *shall be dried up.* The Nile as a mighty river is substituted for the

---

[1] Hos. xi. 10, 11, Is. xi. 15, 16; add Ib. xix. 23-25, xxvii. 13, lii. 4, Mic. vii. 12. See ab. p. 96.
[2] See on Hos. xi. 11. vol. i., p. 115.
[3] 2 Kgs xxiii. 29, Lam. v. 6; and, unless it refers to earlier history, Jer. ii. 18; also Judith i. 5, ii. 1, v. 1 &c.
[4] Ezra vi. 22.   [5] Nu. xxiv. 22-24. coll. Dan. xi. 30.
[6] Thus Herodotus, in the familiar passages, speaks of "Assyria, all but the Babylonian por-tion." i. 106. " Those Assyrians, to whom Nineveh belongs." Ib. 102. " Assyria possesses a vast num-ber of cities, whereof the strongest at this time was Babylon, whither after the fall of Nineveh the seat of government was removed." Ib. 178. " many sovereigns have ruled over this city of Babylon, and lent their aid to the building of its walls and the adornment of its temples: of whom I shall make mention in my Assyrian history." Ib. 184. " Babylon supplies food during four, the other regions of Asia during eight months [to the great king] by which it appears that Assyria in respect of resources is ¼ of the whole of Asia." Ib. 192. " Little rain falls in Assyria. The whole of Baby-lonia is, like Egypt, intersected with canals. The largest is carried from the Euphrates into another

stream called the Tigris, upon which the city Nine-veh formerly stood." Ib. 193. so Strabo xiv. init., Arrian Exp. Al. vii. 2. 6. Ammian xxiii. 20.
[7] לֹא מָצְאוּ לָהֶם Jud. xxi. 14, is, "they found not (enough) for themselves ;" thence here, Nif. "there was not found for them."
[8] Is. xlix. 20.
[9] צָרָה is in appos. to בַיָּם. Against the render-ing of the LXX ἐν θαλάσσῃ στενῇ, 1) יָם, as the sea, no where occurs as fem.: in 2 Kgs xvi. 17. it is "the brazen sea" which is spoken of; 2) the narrowness of the sea, if physical, would facilitate the crossing, not aggravate it; 3) omitting the art., בַיָּם צָרָה would be "in a sea of affliction," but would drop the reference to the sea, or "the red sea," "sea" becoming a mere metaphor.
[10] Is. xliii. 2.   [11] Ib. xi. 15.   [12] Ex. xiv. 10, 12.
[13] S. Cyr.   [14] Ex. xv. 8.   [15] Josh. iii. 17.
[16] Ps. cxxiv. 1-5.
[17] יְאֹר, always the Nile, except Dan. xii. 5, where it is part of his revival of words of the Pentateuch. So Gesenius also. It has been conjectured that a canal now connecting the Tigris and Euphrates,

12 And I will strengthen
them in the LORD; and
c they shall walk up and
down in his name, saith
the LORD.

CHAPTER XI.

1 The destruction of Jerusalem.
The elect being cared for, the

rest are rejected. 10 The staves
of Beauty and Bands broken
by the rejection of Christ. 15
The type and curse of a foolish
shepherd.

OPEN a thy doors, O
Lebanon, that the fire
may devour thy cedars.

a ch. 10. 10.

Jordan, symbolizing the greater putting
forth of God's power in the times to come.
*And the pride of Asshur shall be brought
down.* " 1 When the good receive their reward, then their enemies shall have no power
over them, but shall be punished by Me,
because they injured My elect.—By the Assyrians and Egyptians he understands all their
enemies."

12. *I will strengthen them in the Lord,* as our
Lord said to S. Paul, *My strength is made perfect in weakness,* and S. Paul said in turn,
*When I am weak, then am I strong. And in
His Name shall they walk up and down,* have
their whole conversation " 2 in Him according to His will, and diligent in all things to
speak and act in His grace and Divine hope."
" 3 Christians walk in the Name of Christ,
and there is written on the new white stone
given to them *a new name* 4, and under the
dignity of a name so great, they walk with
God, as 5 Enoch walked and pleased God and
was translated."

Saith the Lord. " 2 Again the Lord God
speaks of the Lord God, as of Another, hinting the plurality of Persons in the Godhead."
XI. " 6 *All the ways of the Lord are mercy
and truth,* saith the Psalmist 7, and, 8 *I will
sing to Thee of mercy and judgment.* So is this
prophecy divided. Above 9, almost all were
promises of mercy, which are now fulfilled in
deed; and from this, 10 *Open, O Lebanon, thy
doors,* all are terrible edicts of truth and
tokens of just judgment. How much sweetness and softness and pleasantness is therein,
*Rejoice greatly, daughter of Zion: shout, O
daughter of Jerusalem;* what bitterness and
acerbity and calamity to those, to whom
he says, *Open, O Lebanon, thy doors, that the fire
may devour thy cedars; howl, O fir tree; howl, O ye
oaks of Basan.* As then, before, we beheld His
mercy in those who believed and believe; so
now let us contemplate His just judgment on

those who believed not." Gilead and Lebanon 11 had been named as the restored home
of Ephraim; but there remained a dark side
of the picture, which the prophet suddenly
presents, with the names of those self-same
lands, 1* *Open thy doors, O Lebanon; howl, O
ye oaks of Basan."*

1. *Open thy doors, O Lebanon.* Lebanon,
whose cedars had stood, its glory, for centuries,
yet could offer no resistance to him who felled
them and were carried off to adorn the palaces of its conquerors 13, was in Isaiah 14 and
Jeremiah 15 the emblem of the glory of the
Jewish state; and in Ezekiel, of Jerusalem,
as the prophet himself explains it 16; glorious, beauteous, inaccessible, so long as it was
defended by God; a ready prey, when abandoned by Him. The centre and source of
her strength was the worship of God; and
so Lebanon has of old been understood to be
the temple, which was built with cedars of
Lebanon, towering aloft upon a strong summit; the spiritual glory and the eminence
of Jerusalem, as Lebanon was of the whole
country, and " 17 to strangers who came to it,
it appeared from afar like a mountain full of
snow; for, where it was not gilded, it was exceeding white, being built of marble." But
at the time of destruction, it was 18 *a den of
thieves,* as Lebanon, amidst its beauty, was of
wild beasts.

" 6 I suppose Lebanon itself, i. e. *the temple,*
felt the command of the prophet's words,
since, as its destruction approached, its doors
opened without the hand of man. Josephus
relates how " 19 at the passover, the Eastern
gate of the inner temple, being of brass and
very firm, and with difficulty shut at eventide
by twenty men; moreover with bars strengthened with iron, and having very deep bolts,
which went down into the threshold, itself
of one stone, was seen at six o'clock at night
to open of its own accord. The guards of the

---

called *Bahr-el-Nil,* may have had that name in the
time of Daniel and been the river in his vision
(Stanley Jewish Church iii. 12). 1) The *Bahr-el-Nil* is
only the *modern* Arabic name for the Nile. 2) Had
the canal been so called in Daniel's time and had
he meant it (which is unlikely) he would naturally
have called it by its name, not have translated it
into the old Egyptian and Hebrew name.
1 Rib.   2 Dion.   3 S. Jer.   4 Rev. ii. 17.

5 Gen. v. 24.   6 Rup.
7 Ps. xxv. 11.   8 Ib. ci. 1.
9 " viii. 19–x. end."   10 " all c. xi."
11 x. 10.   12 xi. 1, 2.
13 See ab. on Zeph. ii. 14. and note 2. p. 276.
14 Is. xiv. 8, xxxvii. 24.   15 Jer. xxii. 6, 7.
16 Ezek. xvii. 3, 12.   17 Joseph. de Bello J. 5. 5, 6.
18 S. Matt. xxi. 13.
19 de Bell. J. 6. 5. 3 quoted by Rup.

Before
CHRIST
cir. 487.

‖ Or, *gallants.*

[b] Isai. 32. 19.
‖ Or, *the defenced
forest.*

2 Howl, fir tree; for
the c e d a r is fallen; because the ‖ m i g h t y are
spoiled : howl, O ye oaks
of B a s h a n; [b]for ‖the
f o r e s t of the vintage is
come down.

3 ¶ *There is* a voice of

the howling of the shep-
herds; for their glory is
spoiled : a voice of the roaring of young lions; for the
pride of Jordan is spoiled.

4 Thus saith the LORD
my God; [c] Feed the flock [c] ver. 7.
of the slaughter;

Before
CHRIST
cir. 487.

temple running told it to the officer, and he,
going up, with difficulty closed it. This the
uninstructed thought a very favorable sign,
that God opened to them the gate of all
goods. But those taught in the Divine
words, understood that the safety of the
temple was removed of itself, and that the
gate opened." A saying of this sort is still
exstant. "[1] Our fathers have handed down,
forty years before the destruction of the
house, the lot of the Lord did not come up
on the right hand, and the tongue of splendor
did not become white, nor did the light from
the evening burn, and the doors of the temple opened of their own accord, until Rabban
Johanan ben Zaccai rebuked them, and said,
'O temple, why dost thou affright thyself?, I
know of thee that thy end is to be destroyed,
and of this Zechariah prophesied, *Open thy
doors, O Lebanon, and let the fire devour thy
cedars.*'" The "forty years" mentioned in
this tradition carry back the event exactly to
the Death of Christ, the temple having been
burned A. D. 73[2]. Josephus adds that they
opened at the passover, the season of His Crucifixion. On the other hand, the shutting of
the gates of the temple, when they had [3] *seized
Paul and dragged him out of the temple,* seems
miraculous and significant, that, having thus
violently refused the preaching of the Gospel,
and cast Paul out, they themselves were also
shut out, denoting that an entrance was
afterward to be refused them.

And let a fire devour thy cedars. Jerusalem,
or the temple, were, after those times, burned
by the Romans only. The destruction of
pride, opposed to Christ, was prophesied by
Isaiah in connection with His Coming [4].

2. *Howl, O cypress, for the cedar is fallen.*
Jerusalem or the temple having been likened
to Lebanon and its cedars, the prophet carries on the image, speaking of the priests

princes and people, under the title of firs,
cypresses and oaks, trees inferior, but magnificent. He shews that it is imagery, by ascribing to them the feelings of men. The
more glorious and stately, *the cedars,* were
destroyed. Woe then to the rest, *the
cypress;* as our Lord says, [5] *If they do these
things in the green tree, what shall be done,
in the dry?* and S. Peter, [6] *If the righteous
scarcely be saved, where shall the ungodly and
the sinner appear?*

For the *defenced* [7] *forest is come down;* that
which was closed and inaccessible to the
enemy. All which was high and lifted up
was brought low, *came down,* even to the
ground [8].

3. *A voice of the howling of the shepherds,
for their glory is spoiled.* It echoes on from
Jeremiah before the captivity, [9] *Howl, ye
shepherds—A voice of the cry of the shepherds,
and an howling of the principal of the flock; for
the Lord hath spoiled their pasture.* There is
one chorus of desolation, the mighty and the
lowly; the shepherds and the young lions;
what is at other times opposed is joined in
one wailing. *The pride of Jordan* is the
stately oaks on its banks, which shroud it
from sight, until you reach its edges, and
which, after the captivity of the ten tribes,
became the haunt of lions and their chief
abode in Palestine, "on account of the burning heat, and the nearness of the desert, and
the breadth of the vast solitude and jun-
gles [10]."

4. *Thus saith the Lord my God, Feed the
flock of the slaughter.* The fulfillment of the
whole prophecy shews, that the person addressed is the prophet, not in, or for himself,
but (as belongs to symbolic prophecy) as representing Another, our Lord. It is addressed,
in the first instance, to Zechariah. For
Zechariah is bidden, [11] *take unto thee yet the*

[1] Yoma f. 39 b. quoted by Mart. Pug. fid. f. 297.
Eusebius (Dem. Evang. vii. 4) says, "He calls the
temple Lebanon, as is his wont, since in other
prophecies it has been shewn that the temple itself
is called Lebanon. This the Jews themselves still
confess."
[2] Euseb. Chron.   [3] Acts xxi. 30.
[4] Is. x. 34, xi. 1.   [5] S. Luke xxiii. 31.
[6] 1 S. Pet. iv. 18.
[7] As in E. M. The E. V. has followed the Kri,
correcting הבציר יער for יער הבצור, probably

in order to substitute the common nom. and gen.
for the less usual construction of the subj. and adj.
being defined by the art. of the adj. as in Zech.
himself, iv. 7, xiv. 10.
[8] As in Is. xxxii. 19, ii. 12, sqq. [9] Jer. xxv. 34, 36.
[10] S. Jer. See Jerem. xlix. 19, l. 44, 2 Kgs xvii. 25.
The lion lingered there even to the close of the
XIIth cent. Phocas in Reland Palæst. i. 274. S.
Cyril says in the present, "there are very many
lions there, roaring horribly and striking fear into
the inhabitants."   [11] v 15.

Before
C H R I S T
cir. 487. 5 Whose possessors slay
them, and ^dhold themselves

^d Jer. 2. 3. & 50. 7.

not guilty: and they that Before
C H R I S T
cir. 487.
sell them ^esay, Blessed be ____

^e Deut. 29. 19. Hos. 12. 8.

instruments of a foolish shepherd, in words addressed to himself, personally ; *And the Lord said unto me.* But he who was to represent the foolish shepherd, had represented the True Shepherd, since it is said to him, " Take unto thee *yet*." But He, the Shepherd addressed, who does the acts commanded, speaks with the authority of God. He says, ¹ *I cut off three shepherds in one month ;* ² *I broke My covenant which I had made with all the peoples ;* ³ *the poor of the flock waited upon Me ;* ⁴ *I cut asunder Mine other staff, Bands, that I might break the brotherhood between Judah and Israel.* But in Zechariah's time, no three shepherds were cut off, the covenant made by God was not broken on His part, there was no such visible distinction between those who waited on God, and those who, outwardly too, rejected Him.

Feed the flock of the slaughter ⁵, those who were, even before the end, slain by their evil shepherds whom they followed, and who in the end would be given to the slaughter, as the Psalmist says, ⁶ *we are counted as sheep for the slaughter,* because they would not hear the voice of the True Shepherd, and were not His sheep. They were already, by God's judgment, a prey to evil shepherds ; and would be so yet more hereafter. As a whole then, they were *sheep of the slaughter.* It is a last charge given to feed them. As our Lord says, ⁷ *Last of all, He sent unto them His Son, saying, They will reverence My Son.* This failing, nothing remained but that the flock would be given up, as they themselves say, ⁸ *He will miserably destroy those wicked men, and will let out His vineyard unto other husbandmen, which shall render Him the fruits in their seasons,* i. e. our Lord explains it, ⁹ *The kingdom of heaven shall be taken from them, and given to a nation bringing forth the fruits thereof.* Yet a *remnant should be saved,* for whose sake the larger flock was still to be fed : and, as our Lord, as Man, wept over Jerusalem, whose sentence He pronounced, so He still feeds those who would not turn to Him that they might be saved, and who would in the end be *a flock of slaughter,* ¹⁰ *Death their shepherd,* since they chose death rather than Life.

5. *Whose possessors* [*buyers* ¹¹] *slay them and hold themselves not guilty,* rather, *are not guilty,*

either in their own eyes, or in the sight of God, since He gave them up and would no more avenge them. They contract no guilt. Aforetime God said ; ¹² *Israel was holiness to the Lord, the first-fruits of His increase ; all that devour him shall be guilty* ¹³ : *evil shall come upon them, saith the Lord.* Now God reversed this, as He said by the same prophet, ¹⁴ *My people hath been lost sheep ; their shepherds have caused them to go astray ; they have turned them away on the mountains ;—all that found them have devoured them ; and their adversaries say, We are not guilty* ¹⁵ ; *because they have sinned against the Lord, the habitation of justice, yea, the hope of their fathers, the Lord.* The offence of injuring Israel was that they were God's people : when He cast them forth, they who chastened them were His servants ¹⁶, His instruments, and offended only when through pride they knew not in Whose hands they themselves were ¹⁷, or through cruelty exceeded their office ¹⁸, and so they became guilty.

And they that sell them say, Blessed be the Lord, for I am rich. Even Sennacherib felt himself in part, or thought best to own himself, to be an instrument in God's hand ¹⁹. But Titus when he " ²⁰ entered Jerusalem, marveled at the strength of the city and its towers, which 'the tyrants' in phrensy abandoned. When then he had beheld their solid strength and the greatness of each rock, and how accurately they were fitted in, and how great their length and breadth, he said 'By the help of God we have warred : and God it was Who brought down the Jews from those bulwarks : for what avail the hands of man or his engines against such towers?' Much of this sort he said to his friends." The Jews also were *sold* in this war, as they had not been in former captures ; and that, not by chance, but because the Roman policy was different from all, known by "experience" in the time of Zechariah. Into Babylon they had been carried captive, as a whole, because it was the will of God, after the *seventy years* to restore them. In this war, it was His will to destroy or disperse them ; and so those above 17 were sent to Egypt to the works ; those below 17 were sold. " ²¹ The whole number taken

¹ v. 8.   ² v. 10.   ³ v. 11.   ⁴ v. 14.
⁵ צֹאן הַהֲרֵגָה, as גֵּיא הֵהִנֹּם. Jer. vii. 32, xix. 6.
יֹום ה Ib. xii. 3.
⁶ Ps. xliv. 22. צֹאן טִבְחָה. ⁷ S. Matt. xxi. 37.
⁸ Ib. 41.   ⁹ Ib. 43.   ¹⁰ Ps. xlix. 14.
¹¹ קֹנֵיהֶן stands opposed to מֹכְרֵיהֶן, as in Is.
xxiv. 2, כַּקֹּונֶה כַּמֹּוכֵר.

¹² Jer. ii. 3.   ¹³ יֶאְשָׁמוּ כָּל אֹכְלָיו.   ¹⁴ Jer. l. 6, 7.
¹⁵ לֹא נֶאְשָׁם. The same word.
¹⁶ Jer. xxv. 9, xxvii. 6, xliii. 10.
¹⁷ Is. x. 7. וְאָשֵׁם Hab. i. 11.
¹⁸ Is. xlvii. 6, Zech. i. 18.   ¹⁹ Is. xxxvi. 10.
²⁰ Jos. de B. J. 6. 9. 1.
²¹ Jos. ib. § 2. 3.

Before
CHRIST
cir. 487.

† Heb. *make to
be found.*

the LORD; for I am rich:
and their own shepherds
pity them not.

6 For I will no more
pity the inhabitants of the
land, saith the LORD: but,
lo, I will † deliver the men

Before
CHRIST
cir. 487.

every one into his neigh-
bor's hand, and into the
hand of his king: and
they shall s m i t e the
land, and out of their
hand I will not deliver
them.

---

prisoners during the wars were 1,100,000,"
beside those who perished elsewhere.
"[1] Read we the ancient histories and the
traditions of the mourning Jews, that at the
Tabernaculum Abrahæ (where now is a very
thronged mart every year) after the last destruction, which they endured from Adrian,
many thousands were sold, and what could
not be sold were removed into Egypt, and
destroyed by shipwreck or famine and slaughter by the people. No displeasure came upon
the Romans for the utter destruction, as
there had upon the Assyrians and Chaldæans."

And their own shepherds (in contrast to those
who *bought* and *sold* them, who accordingly
were not their own, temporal or spiritual)
they to whom God had assigned them, who
should have fed them with the word of God,
[2]strengthened the diseased, healed the sick,
bound up the broken, and sought the lost,
pity them not. He says what they should
have done, in blaming them for what they
did not do. They owed them a tender compassionate love [3]; they laid aside all mercy,
and became wolves, as S. Paul says; [4] *After
my departure shall grievous wolves enter in
among you, not sparing the flock. Also of your
own selves shall men arise, speaking perverse
things, to draw away disciples after them.* They
who owed them all love, shall have none.
"[1] No marvel then, he says, if enemies shall
use the right of conquest, when their very
shepherds and teachers spared them not,
and, through their fault, the flock was given
over to the wolves." All were corrupted,
High Priest, priests, scribes, lawyers, Pharisees, Sadducees. No one[5] had pity on
them.

6. *For I will no more pity.* Therefore were
they a *flock of the slaughter,* because God

would *have no pity* on those who went after
shepherds who *had no pity* upon them, but
corrupted them; who [6]*entered not in themselves, and those who were entering in, they hindered.*

The inhabitants of the land, "that land, of
which he had been speaking," Judæa. *And
lo.* God, by this word, *lo,* always commands
heed to His great doings with man; *I, I,*
Myself [7], visibly interposing, *will deliver man,*
the whole race of inhabitants, *every one into
his neighbor's hand,* by confusion and strife
and hatred within, *and into the hand of his
king,* him whom they chose and took as their
own king, when they rejected Christ as their
King, repudiating the title which Pilate
gave Him, to move them pity. Whereas
He, their Lord and God, was their King,
they formally [8] *denied Him in the presence of
Pilate, when he was determined to let Him go;*
they *denied the Holy One and the Just,* and
said, [9] *We have no king but Cæsar.*

And they, the king without and the wild
savages within, *shall smite,* bruise, crush in
pieces, like a broken vessel [10], *the land, and
out of their hand I will not deliver* them.
Their captivity shall be without remedy or
end. Holy Scripture often says, *there is no
deliverer* [11], or [12]*none can deliver out of My
hand,* or, since God delighteth in doing
good, I [13], He [14], will deliver, or delivered [15]
from the hands of the enemy, or their
slavery, or their own fears, or afflictions, or
the like. God nowhere else says absolutely
as here, *I will not deliver* [16]. "Hear, O Jew,"
says S. Jerome, "who holdest out to thyself
hopes most vain, and hearest not the Lord
strongly asserting, *I will not deliver* them *out
of their hands,* that thy captivity among the
Romans shall have no end." In the threatened captivity before they were carried to

---

[1] S. Jer. [2] Ezek. xxxiv. 4.
[3] יַחְמְלוּ. [4] Acts xx. 29, 30.
[5] This is expressed by the Hebrew idiom, "their
shepherds [plur.] one by one, pity [sing.] them
not." [6] S. Luke xi. 52. [7] אָנֹכִי emphatic.
[8] Acts iii. 13, 14. [9] S. John xix. 15.
[10] Of which כָּתַת is used, Is. xxx. 14; of the
golden calf, De. ix. 21. So כָּתַת, of the brazen
serpent, 2 Kgs xviii. 4; the idols, 2 Chr. xxxiv. 7.
[11] אֵין מַצִּיל Jud. xviii. 28, 2 Sam. xiv. 6, Job v. 4,
Ps. vii. 3, l. 22, lxxi. 11, Is. v. 29, xlii. 22, Hos. v. 14,
Mic. v. 7, 8.

[12] De. xxxii. 39, Job x. 7, Ps. l. 22, lxxi. 11. Is. xliii.
13. Dan. viii. 4, 7.
[13] Ex. vi. 6, 2 Kgs xx. 6, Jer. xv. 21, xxxix. 17,
Ezek. xxxiv. 27.
[14] 1 Sam. vii. 3, Ps. xviii. 15, lxxii. 12, 2 Kgs xvii.
39, Is. xix. 20, xxxi. 5, Job v. 19.
[15] Ex. xviii. 10, Josh. xxiv. 10, Jud. vi. 9, 1 Sam. x.
18, xiv. 10, 2 Sam. xxii. 1, Ps. xxxiv. 5, 18, liv. 9, Ezr.
viii. 31, Jer. xx. 13.
[16] Once only on one of the brief repentances in
the Judges, God answers their prayer, *I will not save
you; go and cry to the gods which ye have chosen; let
them save you:* but only to save them on their
renewed repentance and prayer. Jud. x. 13-16.

Before CHRIST cir. 487.	7 And I will ᶠfeed the flock of slaughter, ‖ *even* you, ᵍO poor of the flock. And I took unto me two
ᶠver. 4. ‖ Or, *verily the poor.* ᵍZeph. 3. 12. Matt. 11. 5.	

staves; the one I called Beauty, and the other I called ‖ Bands; and I fed ‖ the flock.

Before CHRIST cir. 487.

‖ Or, *binders.*

Babylon, the prophet foretold the restoration: here only it is said of Judah, as Hosea had said of Israel, that there should be no deliverer out of the hand of the king whom they had chosen.

7. The prophetic narrative which follows, differs in its form, in some respects, from the symbolical actions of the prophets and from Zechariah's own visions. The symbolical actions of the prophets are actions of their own: *this* involves acts, which it would be impossible to represent, except as a sort of drama. Such are the very central points, the feeding of the flock, which yet are intelligent men who understand God's doings: the cutting off of the three shepherds; the asking for the price; the unworthy price offered; the casting it aside. It differs from Zechariah's own visions, in that *they* are for the most part exhibited to the eye, and Zechariah's own part is simply to enquire their meaning and to learn it, and to receive further revelation. In one case only, he himself interposes in the action of the vision[1]; but this too, as asking that it might be done, not, as himself doing it. Here, he is himself the actor, yet as representing Another, Who alone could cut off shepherds, abandon the people to mutual destruction, annulling the covenant which He had made. Maimonides, then, seems to say rightly; "[2] This, *I fed the flock of the slaughter*, to the end of the narrative, where he is said to have asked for his hire, to have received it, and to have cast it into the temple, to the treasurer, all this Zechariah saw in prophetic vision. For the command which he received, and the act which he is said to have done, took place in prophetic vision or dream." "This," he adds, "is beyond controversy, as all know, who are able to distinguish the possible from the impossible."

"[3] The actions, presented to the prophets are not always to be understood as actions but as predictions. As when God commands Isaiah, to make the heart of the people dull[4] i. e. to denounce to the people their future blindness, through which they would,

with obstinate mind, reject the mercies of Christ. Or when He says, that He appointed Jeremiah [5] to destroy and to build; to root out and to plant. Or when He commanded the same prophet to cause the nations to drink the cup, whereby they should be bereft of their senses[6], Jeremiah did nothing of all this, but asserted that it would be. So here."

And I will feed the flock of the slaughter, rather *And* [our, *so*] *I fed* [7]. The prophet declares, in the name of our Lord, that He did what the Father commanded Him. He fed the flock, committed to His care by the Father, who, through their own obstinacy, became *the flock of slaughter*. What could be done, He did for them; so that all might see that they perished by their own fault. The symbol of our Lord, as the Good Shepherd, had been made prominent by Isaiah, Jeremiah and Ezekiel, [8] *Behold the Lord will come, as a Mighty One—He shall feed His flock like a shepherd: He shall gather the lambs with His arm and carry them in His bosom: He shall gently lead those that are with young.* And Jeremiah, having declared God's judgments on the then shepherds [9], [10] *I will gather the remnant of My flock out of all countries whither I have driven them, and will bring them again to their fold; and they shall be fruitful and increase. And I will set up shepherds over them which shall feed them. Behold the days come, saith the Lord, that I will raise unto David a righteous Branch, and a king shall reign and prosper—and this is the name whereby He shall be called, the Lord our Righteousness.* And Ezekiel with the like context[11]; [12] *Therefore will I save My flock and they shall be no more a prey; and I will judge between cattle and cattle. And I will set One Shepherd over them, and He shall feed them: My servant David, He shall feed them; and He shall be their Shepherd;* and, uniting both offices, [13] *David, My servant, shall be king over them, and they shall all have One Shepherd.* It was apparent then beforehand, Who this Shepherd was to be, to Whom God gave the feeding of the flock.

"Even *you*, or *for you, ye poor of the flock;* or, *therefore*, being thus commanded, [*fed I*]

[1] iii. 15.
[2] More Neboch. ii. 46, p. 123, 6. Buxt. Tr. p. 326. Abarbanel (ad loc.) regards the act as real, but symbolic. "God commanded him to do an act, in deed and awake, which was a declaration and a sign of what should be in God's guidance of Israel. See at length in McCaul's transl. of Kimchi on Zech. pp. 198–208.

[3] Osor. [4] Is. vi. 10. [5] Jer. i. 10. [6] Id. xxv. 15 sqq.
[7] ה retained in וָאֶרְעֶה as in verbs לה in 1 Sam. i. 7, 2 Sam. xxiii. 15, 1 Kgs xiv. 9, 2 Kgs ii. 8, 14 [bis] Jer. xx. 2.
[8] Is. xl. 10, 11. [9] Jer. xxiii. 2. [10] Ib. 3–6.
[11] Ezek. xxxiv. 1–21. [12] Ib. 22, 23.
[13] Ib. xxxvii. 24.

8 Three shepherds also I cut off [h] in one month ; and

my soul † loathed them, and their soul also abhorred me.

† Heb. *was straitened for them.*

the poor of the flock [1]. The whole flock was committed to Him to feed. He had to seek out all [2] *the lost sheep of the house of Israel.* "[3] *He fed,* for the time, the Jews destined to death, until their time should come;" the fruit of His labor was in the [4] *little flock,* "the faithful Jews who believed in Him, out of the people of the flock aforesaid, or the synagogue, Who in the primitive Church despised all earthly things, leading a most pure life." So He says, [5] *I will feed My flock and I will cause them to lie down, saith the Lord God : I will seek that which was lost, and bring again that which was driven away, and will bind that which was broken, and will strengthen that which was sick: but I will destroy the fat and the strong, I will feed them with judgment.*

The elect are the end of all God's dispensations. He fed all; yet the fruit of His feeding, His toils, His death, the travail of His soul, was in those only who are saved. So S. Paul says, [6] *Therefore I endure all things for the elect's sakes, that they may also obtain the salvation which is in Christ Jesus, with eternal glory.* He fed all ; but the *poor of the flock* alone, those who were despised of men, because they would not follow the pride of the High Priests and Scribes and Pharisees, believed on Him, as they themselves say, [7] *Have any of the rulers or the Pharisees believed on Him?* and S. Paul says, [8] *Not many wise men after the flesh, not many mighty, not many noble are called ; but God hath chosen the foolish things of the world to confound the wise ; and God hath chosen the weak things of the world to confound the things that are mighty ; and base things of the world, and things despised, hath God chosen, yea, and things which are not, to bring to nought things that are.*

And I took unto Me two [shepherd's] *staves,* as David says, [9] *Thy rod and Thy staff they comfort me.* The one *I called Beauty* or *Loveliness* [10], as the Psalmist longs to *behold the beauty* or *loveliness* of God in His temple [11], and says; let [12] *the beauty of the Lord our God be upon us.*

And the other I called Bands, lit. *Binders* [13]. The one staff represents the full favor and loving-kindness of God; when this was

broken, there yet remained the other, by which they were held together as a people in covenant with God. *And I fed the flock.* This was the use of his staves ; He tended them with both, ever putting in exercise toward them the loving beauty and grace of God, and binding them together and with Himself.

8. *And I cut off three shepherds in one month.* "[14] I have read in some one's commentary, that the shepherds, cut off in the indignation of the Lord, are to be understood of priests and false prophets and kings of the Jews, who, after the Passion of Christ, were all cut off in one time, of whom Jeremiah speaketh, [15] *The priests said not, Where is the Lord? and they that handle the law knew Me not ; the pastors also transgressed against Me, and the prophets prophesied by Baal, and walked after things which do not profit,*" and again, "[16] *As the thief is ashamed when he is found, so is the house of Israel ashamed ; they, their kings, their princes, and their priests and their prophets ;* and [17] *they said, Come, let us devise devices against Jeremiah ; for the law shall not perish from the priest, nor counsel from the wise, nor the word from the prophet.* "[18] He speaks of the kings of the Jews, and prophets and priests ; for by the three orders they were shepherded." "[19] The true and good Shepherd having been already pointed out, it was right and necessary that the hirelings and false shepherds should be removed, the guides of the Jews in the law. The three shepherds were, I deem, those who exercised the legal priesthood, and those appointed judges of the people, and the interpreters of Scripture, i. e. the lawyers. For these too fed Israel. Those who had the glory of the priesthood were of the tribe of Levi only ; and of them Malachi says, [20] *The priest's lips shall keep knowledge, and they shall seek the law at his mouth.* But those who received authority to judge were also selected, yet were appointed out of every tribe. In like way the lawyers, who were ever assessors to the judges, and adduced the words of the law in proof of every matter.— But we shall find that our Lord Jesus Christ

---

[1] The masora parva says that "the לְכֵן is a feminine," i. e. so punctuated for לָכֵן, as in the 3d pers. כָּהֶם 2 Sam. xxiv. 3, Eccl. ix. 12 ; בָּהֶן Gen. xix. 29, xxx. 26. Yet לָכֵן being, so often, some 60 times, illative, *therefore,* it would be arbitrary to take it otherwise here, since even כֵּן itself nowhere occurs as a pronoun.

[2] S. Matt. x. 6, xv. 24.   [3] Dion.
[4] S. Luke xii. 32.   [5] Ezek. xxxiv. 15, 16.
[6] 2 Tim. ii. 10.   [7] S. John xii. 48.

[8] 1 Cor. i. 26–28.   [9] Ps. xxiii. 4.
[10] κάλλος, ὁ; εὐπρέπεια, Aq. Sym. (Theodot. also, see Field Hexapl. on v. 10.) "decus." S. Jer.
[11] נֹעַם Ps. xxvii. 4.   [12] Ps. xc. 17.
[13] From the common חָבַל "rope;" in Arab. verb, "bound fast as with rope," "made covenant;" noun, "band of marriage, friendship, covenant of God or man, personal security," Lane. σχοίνισμα, ὁ Aq. Sym.; funiculos, S. Jer.
[14] S. Jer.   [15] Jer. ii. 8.   [16] Ib. 26.   [17] Ib. xviii. 18.
[18] Theodoret.   [19] S. Cyr.   [20] Mal. ii. 7.

Before
CHRIST
cir. 487.

j Jer. 15. 2.
& 43. 11.

9 Then said I, I will not feed you : [1]that that dieth, let it die ; and that that is to be cut off, let it be cut off ;

and let the rest eat every one the flesh † of another.

Before
CHRIST
cir. 487.

10 ¶ And I took my staff, *even* Beauty, and cut

† Heb. *of his fellow*, or, *neighbor*.

Himself expressly pronounced woe on the Pharisees and scribes and lawyers. For He said, [1] *Woe unto you scribes and Pharisees.* And when one of the lawyers hereupon answered Him saying, [2] *Master, so saying Thou reproachest us also,* He said, *Woe unto you also, ye lawyers! for ye lade men with burdens grievous to be borne, and ye yourselves touch not the burdens with one of your fingers.* These *three Shepherds* then, priests and judges and lawyers [3], who remained in their own orders and places, until the coming of Christ, were very justly taken away *in one month.* For since [4] *they killed the Prince of life,* thereby also are they mown down, and that in the month of the first fruits, in which Emmanuel endured to be slain for us. They remained indeed administering Israel, even after the Saviour's Cross, through the long-suffering and compassion of Almighty God calling them to repentance ; but, in the sentence passed by God, they were taken away, at that time, when they delivered to the Cross the Saviour and Redeemer of all. They were taken away then *in one month ;* " Nisan. A. D. 33. The three offices, King, Divine Teacher, Priest, were to be united in Christ : they might have been held under Him : those who rejected them in Him, forfeited them themselves. These then He made to disappear, effaced them from the earth [5].
And My soul was straightened for them [6]. It is used of the Divine grief at the misery of His people [7]. *And their soul abhorred Me, nauseated Me* [8]. " [9] When it is said, *Their soul also abhorreth Me,* the meaning is, 'My soul did not loathe them first, but their soul first despised Me, therefore My Soul abhorred

them.' " The soul which drives away God's good Spirit, comes at last to loathe Him and the thought and mention of Him.
9. And I said, I will not feed you. God, at last, leaves the rebellious soul or people to itself, as He says by Moses, [10] *Then My anger shall be kindled against them in that day, and I will forsake them, and will hide My Face from them, and they shall be devoured, and many evils and troubles shall find them :* and our Lord tells the captious Jews ; [11] *I go My way, and ye shall seek Me and shall die in your sins.*
That which dieth, let it die. Zechariah seems to condense, but to repeat the abandonment in Jeremiah ; [12] *Cast them out of My sight, and let them go forth. And it shall be, if they shall say unto thee, Whither shall we go forth ?* then *thou shalt tell them, Thus saith the Lord, Such as are for death, to death ; and such as are for the sword, to the sword ; and such as are for the captivity, to the captivity.* First, God gives over to death without violence, by famine or pestilence, those whose lot it should be ; another portion to violent death by the sword ; *that which is cut off shall be cut off ; and the rest,* the flock of slaughter, would be turned into wolves ; and, as in the awful and horrible siege of Jerusalem, those who had escaped these deaths, *the left-over, shall eat every one of the flesh of his neighbor,* every law of humanity and of nature broken. " [13] So should they understand at last, how evil and bitter a thing it is for all who lived by My help to be despoiled of that help."
10. *And I took my staff Beauty, and cut it asunder.* Not, as aforetime, did He chasten His people, retaining His relation to them : for such chastening is an austere form of love.

---

[1] S. Luke xi. 44.   [2] Ib. 45, 46.
[3] No other explanation of the 'three shepherds' seems to me at all to recommend itself. The Jews made them Moses Aaron and Miriam (Taanith f. 9a.) and from them, S. Jerome ; J. Kim. and (as one solution) Ibn Ezra, suggested Haggai, Zechariah, Malachi ; " ' After whom,' the rabbis say, ' prophecy departed from Israel ' " (" on account of the cutting off of prophecy at their death," opinion in Tanchum.) Abraham Lev. " the principality of the sons of David, and the monarchy of the Hasmonæans, and that of their servants." D. Kim., " the three sons of Josiah, Jehoahaz, Jehoiakim and Zedekiah : " Abarbanel, " the Maccabees, Judas Jonathan and Simon : " Rashi, " the house of Ahab and the house of Ahaziah, and his brethren and all the posterity of the kingdom of David (except Joash) slain by Ahab and Athaliah : " Tanchum, " Joshua the high-priest and the second priest and the anointed for war : " (Buxtorf refers for his office to Maimonides, Hilchos melachin umilchama c. 7. and massecheth Sota c. 8. Lex. Chald. col. 1267). " And it is said, Joshua, Zerubbabel and Nehemiah," Tanchum. Theodorus of Mops. interpreted it of " the priests " generally, not of any

three classes of persons. Three classes, Priests, Pharisees and Sadducees, were adopted by some older ; Pharisees Sadducees and Essenes by Lightfoot (Horæ Hebr. on S. John x.). On the abortive guesses of a German school, see ab. Introd. to Zechariah p. 509.   [4] Acts iii. 15.
[5] הכחוד lit. " hid," Job xx. 12, as כחד uniformly (15 times), thence ἀφανίζω. It is used of numbers ; the 7 nations, Ex. xxiii. 23 ; of Israel, in the intention of their enemies, from being a nation, מגּוי, Ps. lxxxiii. 5 ; of the house of Jeroboam from the face of the earth, 1 Kgs xiii. 34 ; of Sennacherib's army, 2 Chr. xxxii. 21.
[6] As in E. M.
[7] Jud. x. 16 also with בּ p. Gesenius' comparison of Arab. נבן is wrong. Its primary meaning is " cut off from," See Lane p. 419.
[8] Such is the traditional meaning of בחל. " loathed My worship," Ch. ; " loathed," Abulw. Tanch. coll. Syr. בחילא. " one so nauseating as to vomit his food."
[9] Kim.   [10] De. xxxi. 17.   [11] S. John viii. 21.
[12] Jer. xv. 1, 2, and similarly xliii. 11.   [13] Osor.

Before
CHRIST
cir. 487.

it asunder, that I might
break my covenant which
I had made with all the
people.

11 And it was broken
in that day: and ‖ so [k] the
poor of the flock that
waited upon me knew that

‖ Or, *the poor of
the flock, &c.*
*certainly
knew.*
[k] Zeph. 3. 12.
ver. 7.

it *was* the word of the
LORD.

12 And I said unto
them, † If ye think good,
give *me* my price; and if
not, forbear. So they
[1] weighed for my price
thirty *pieces* of silver.

Before
CHRIST
cir. 487.

† Heb. *If it be
good in your
eyes.*

[1] Matt. 26. 15.
See Ex. 21. 32.

By breaking the staff of His tender love, He
signified that this relation was at an end.

*That I might dissolve My covenant which I had
made with all the people,* rather, *with all the
peoples,* i. e. with all nations. Often as it is
said of Israel, that they brake the covenant
of God [1], it is spoken of God, only to deny
that He would break it [2], or in prayer that
He would not [3]. Here it is not absolutely
the covenant with His whole people, which
He brake; it is rather, so to speak, a covenant with the nations in favor of Israel, allowing thus much and forbidding more, with regard to His people. So God had said of the
times of Christ [4]; *In that day I will make a covenant for them with the beasts of the field and with
the fowls of the heaven, and with the creeping things
of the ground;* and, [5] *I will make with them a
covenant of peace, and will cause the evil beasts to
cease out of the land;* and in Job [6] *thou shalt
be in league with the stones of the field, and the
beasts of the field shall be at peace with thee.*
This covenant He willed to annihilate. He
would no more interpose, as He had before
said, [7] *I will not deliver from their hand.* Whoever would might do, what they would, as the
Romans first, and well nigh all nations since,
have inflicted on the Jews, what they willed;
and Mohammedans too have requited to
them their contumely to Jesus.

11. *And so the poor of the flock that waited
upon Me* [8] *knew.* The rest were blinded;
those who listened to God's word, observed
His Prophet, waited on Him and observed His
words, knew from the fulfillment of the
beginning, that the whole was God's word.
Every darkening cloud around the devoted
city was an earnest, that the storm, which
should destroy it, was gathering upon it. So
our Lord warned, [9] *When ye shall see Jerusalem compassed with armies, then know that the
desolation thereof is nigh. Then let them which
are in Judæa flee to the mountains; and let
them which are in the midst of it depart.* The

little flock which waited upon the Good Shepherd, obeyed the warning, and, fleeing
to Pella, escaped the horrible judgment which fell on those who remained.
" [10] They remembered that it had been predicted many centuries before, and that the
Lord, by Whose Spirit the prophet spake,
foretold that in that city [11] *one stone should not
be left upon another.*"

12. *And I said unto them, If ye think good,
give Me My price.* God asks of us a return,
not having any proportion to His gifts of
nature or of grace, but such as we can render.
He took the Jews out of the whole human
race, made them His own, *a peculiar people,*
freed them from *the bondage and the iron furnace of Egypt,* gave them *the land flowing with
milk and honey,* fed and guarded them by His
Providence, taught them by His Prophets.
He, the Lord and Creator of all, was willing
to have them alone for His inheritance, and,
in return, asked them to love Him with their
whole heart, and to do what He commanded
them. [12] *He sent His servants to the husbandmen, that they might receive the fruits of the vineyard; and the husbandmen took His servants,
and beat one, and killed another, and stoned
another.* Last of all, *He sent unto them His Son,*
to ask for those fruits, the return for all His
bounteous care and His unwearied acts of
power and love. " [13] Give Me," He would
say, "some fruits of piety, and tokens of
faith."

" [10] What? Does He speak of a price? Did
the Lord of all let out His toil? Did He
bargain with those, for whom he expended it
for a certain price? He did. He condes-
cended to serve day and night for our
salvation and dignity; and as one hired,
in view of the reward which He set
before Him, to give all His care to
adorn and sustain our condition. So He
complains by Isaiah, that He had undergone
great toil to do away our sins. But what

[1] Lev. xxvi. 15, De. xxxi. 16, 20, Is. xxiv. 5, Jer.
xi. 10, xxxi. 32, Ezek. xvi. 59, xliv. 7.
[2] Lev. xxvi. 44, Jud. ii. 1. and, strongly, Jer.
xxxiii. 20, 21.
[3] Jer. xiv. 21.   [4] Hos. ii. 18, [20, Heb.]
[5] Ezek. xxxiv. 25.   [6] Job v. 23.
[7] v. 6.
[8] שמר השמרים את׳. שמר occurs more commonly w.

acc. of thg., commandments &c. but w. acc. pers., in
good sense, שמר דני׃· "he that observeth his
master," Pr. xxvii. 18; also of God, Hos. iv. 10; of
idols, Ps. xxxi. 7; and of observing for evil, 1 Sam.
xix. 11, Job x. 14.
[9] S. Luke xxi. 20, 21.   [10] Osor.
[11] S. Matt. xxiv. 2.   [12] S. Matt. xxi. 34–37.
[13] Eus. Dem. Ev. x. 4. So Theod.

Before CHRIST cir. 487. 13 And the LORD said unto me, Cast it unto the

ᵐpotter: a goodly price that I was prized at of Before CHRIST cir. 487.
ᵐ Matt. 27. 9, 10.

reward did He require? Faith and the will of a faithful heart, that thereby we might attain the gift of righteousness, and might in holy works pant after everlasting glory. For He needeth not our goods; but He so bestoweth on us all things, as to esteem His labor amply paid, if He see us enjoy His gifts. But He so asketh for this as a reward, as to leave us free, either by faith and the love due, to embrace His benefits, or faithlessly to reject it. This is His meaning, when He saith,"
And if not, forbear. God does not force our free-will, or constrain our service. He places life and death before us, and bids us choose life. By His grace alone we can choose Him; but we can refuse His grace and Himself. [1] *Thou shalt say unto them,* He says to Ezekiel, *Thus saith the Lord God, He that heareth, let him hear, and he that forbeareth, let him forbear.* This was said to them, as a people, the last offer of grace. It gathered into one all the past. As Elijah had said, [2] *If the Lord be God, follow Him; but if Baal, then follow him;* so He bids them, at last to choose openly, whose they would be, to whom they would give their service; and if they would refuse in heart, to refuse in act also. *Forbear,* cease, leave off, abandon; and that for ever.
So they weighed for My price thirty pieces of silver; the price of a slave, gored to death by an ox[3]. Whence one of themselves says, "[4] you will find that a freeman is valued, more or less, at 60 shekels, but a slave at thirty." He then, Whom the prophet represented, was to be valued at *thirty pieces of silver.* It was but an increase of the contumely, that this contemptuous price was given, not to Him, but for Him, the Price of His Blood. It was matter of bargain. [5] *Judas said, What will ye give me, and I will deliver Him unto you?* The High Priest, knowingly or unknowingly, fixed on the price, named by Zechariah. As they took into their mouths willingly the blasphemy mentioned in the Psalm; [6] *they shoot out the lip, they shake the head,* saying, *He trusted in the Lord, that He would deliver Him; let Him deliver Him, seeing that He delighted in Him;* so perhaps they fixed on the *thirty pieces of silver,*

because Zechariah had named them as a sum offered in contumely to him, who offered to be a shepherd and asked for his reward.
13. *And the Lord said unto me, Cast it,* as a thing vile and rejected, as torn flesh was to be cast to dogs[7], or a corpse was cast unburied[8], or the dead body of Absalom was cast into the pit[9], or the dust of the idol-altars into the brook Kedron by Josiah[10], or the idols to the moles and the bats[11]; or Judah and Israel from the face of God[12] into a strange land[13]; Coniah and his seed, a vessel in which is no pleasure[14], into a land which they knew not; or the rebels against God, said, [15] *let us cast away their cords from us;* or wickedness was cast into the Ephah[16]; once it is added[17], *for loathing.*
Unto the potter. The words exactly correspond with the event, that the *thirty pieces of silver* were *cast* or flung away[18]; that their ultimate destination was the potter, whose field was bought with them; but that they were not cast directly to him, (which were a contemptuous act, such as would not be used whether for a gift or a purchase), but were cast to him *in the house of the Lord.* They were *flung away* by the remorse of Judas, and, in God's Providence, came to the potter. Whether any portion of this was a direct symbolic action of the prophet, or whether it was a prophetic vision, in which Zechariah himself was an actor, and saw himself in the character which he described, doing what he relates, cannot now be said certainly, since God has not told us. It seems to me more probable, that these actions belonged to the vision, because in other symbolic actions of the prophets, no other actors take part; and it is to the last degree unlikely, that Zechariah, at whose preaching Zerubbabel and Joshua and all the people set themselves earnestly to rebuild the temple, should have had so worthless a price offered to him; and the casting a price, which God condemned, into the house of God, at the command of God, and so implying His acceptance of it, were inconsistent. It was fulfilled, in act consistently, in Judas' remorse; in that he *flung*[19] *away the pieces of silver,* which had stained his soul with innocent blood, *in the*

[1] Ezek. iii. 27; add ii. 5, 7, iii. 11.
[2] 1 Kgs xviii. 21. [3] Ex. xxi. 32.
[4] Maimonides More Neboch. c. 40. P. 3.
[5] S. Matt. xxvi. 15. [6] Ps. xxii. 7, 8.
[7] Ex. xxii. 31.
[8] Is. xiv. 19, xxxiv. 3, Jer. xxiv. 16, xii. 19, xxvi. 23, xxxvi. 30.
[9] 2 Sam. xviii. 17. [10] 2 Kgs xxiii. 12.
[11] Is. ii. 20, add Ezek. xx. 8.
[12] 2 Kgs xiii. 23, xvii. 20, xxiv. 21, Jer. lii. 3.
[13] De. xxix. 27 [28 Eng.] [14] Jer. xxii. 28.

[15] Ps. ii. 3. [16] Zech. v. 18. [17] Ezek. xvi. 5.
[18] ῥίψας τὰ ἀργύρια ἐν τῷ ναῷ S. Matt. xxvii. 5.
[19] This is in itself (as Keil observed) decisive against the substitution of צָר, for אוֹצָר, as Jon. and the Syr. have, if it be interpreted of any act of Zechariah. If it were taken only of the result of the ordering of God's Providence, the man substance of the prophecy would equally remain, that the Good Shepherd was valued at this contemptuous price; and that the money itself was flung

them. And I took the
thirty *pieces* of silver, and

cast them to the potter in
the house of the LORD.

---

temple, perhaps remembering the words of
Zechariah ; perhaps wishing to give to pious
uses, too late, money which was the price of
his soul ; whereas God, even through the
Chief Priests, rejected it, and so it came to
the potter, its ultimate destination in the

into the treasury; only in this case the second
clause " to the treasury in the house of the Lord "
would add nothing to the first, whereas, if יוֹצֵר be
rendered in its natural sense " potter," this accounts for the use of the word "fling," and contains what was brought about by the joint agency
of Judas and the Pharisees. But 2) no two words,
in any language, are more distinct than אוֹצָר and
יוֹצֵר, both of them also being, in their several
senses, common words. אוֹצָר, " treasure," or at
times, " treasury," occurs 79 times in the O. T. ;
יוֹצֵר, lit. " former," occurs 41 times beside these
verses. There is not the slightest approximation of the meaning of the two roots ; אָצַר is
" treasured up;" יָצַר, " made." Since then, apart
from inspiration, every writer wishes to be understood, it is, in the nature of things, absurd to suppose, that, had Zechariah meant to say, " cast into
the treasury," he should not have used the word,
which everywhere else, 79 times, is used to express
it, but should have used a word, which is always,
viz. 41 times, used of something else. The particular form moreover, with the art. occurs 11 times in
the O. T. as " the potter;" once in Isaiah (xxix.
16), seven times in 2 chapters of Jeremiah, xviii. 2,
3, 4 (bis) 6 (bis) xix. 11, of " the potter," once only
of Almighty God (Ps. xxxiii. 15) and that, in a different idiom. Of God, it is never used as a substantive, " the Creator." It remains a part., " Maker
of," it being added, of what He is the Maker. ' He
that maketh the eye,' Ps. xciv. 9, the hearts, Ib.
xxxiii. 15, light, Is. xlv. 7; the earth, Ib. 18; the
universe, הַכֹּל Jer. x. 15, li. 19; mountains, Amos
iv. 13; grasshoppers, Ib. vii. 1; the spirit of man,
Zech. xii. 1; or with pronouns, my Maker Is. xlix.
5; thy Maker Is. xliii. 1; our Maker xliv. 2, 24, his
Maker Is. xxvii. 11, xxix. 16, xlv. 9, 11. The rendering then of the Jews in S. Jerome's time, D.
Kim., Abraham of Toledo apparently, Abarb., Alsheikh, " the Creator," is unidiomatic, as well as
that of Rashi, J. Kim. Tanch., Isaac (xvii. cent.)
Chizzuk Emunah (Wagnseil Tel. ign. Sat. p. 146.),
" treasury," which the modern Anti-Messianic interpreters follow. Aquila has τὸν πλάστην; the LXX
and Symm. χωνευτήριον, " foundry ;" in that יָצַר is
used with regard to metals, Is. xliv. 12, liv. 17, Hab.
ii. 18, as well as, more commonly, of clay. יוֹצֵר is
used of the " potter " 2 Sam. xvii. 28, 1 Chr. iv. 23,
Ps. ii. 9, Is. xxx. 14, xli. 25, lxiv. 7, Jer. xix. 1, Lam.
iv. 2 (beside the use of הַיּוֹצֵר above); also " the
former thereof " contrasted with the clay, Is. xlv.
9. The Hebrew-Arabic translation, which Pococke
so much valued (12th cent.) has twice אַלצַאֱגﱠ,
(used chiefly of a gold-smith). Abulwalid does not
notice it in either lexicon, nor Saadyah Ibn Danân
nor Parchon. They must therefore have had nothing to remark on it, interpreting it as elsewhere,
' potter.'
    It is not then necessary even to say, that the
dicta as to the interchange of א and ' in Hebrew
are much too vague, the instances heterogeneous.
All the words, in which א and ' occur as the first
letter, are allied words of the same meaning, not
interchanged. Such are אָחֵר and יָחֵר, and אֲשֶׁר and
יֵשׁ, (whence the Proper Names אֲשָׂרְאֵלָה 1 Chr.
xxv. 2. and יִשְׂרָאֵלָה Ib. 14.). אָחֵר and יָחֵר ἁπ. λεγ.

Providence of God. " [1] He saith, *cast it unto
the potter,* that they might understand
that they would be broken as a potter's
vessel."
    A goodly price, that I was prized at of them,
lit. *the magnificence of the value* [2], *at which I was*

(2 Sam. xx. 5) are again allied, the Maltese also
having a root *wacchar* (Vassali Lex. melit. pp. 82,
651, in Ges. v. חֵר). אָמֵן " was stable " was, probably, the basis of יָמִין. The use of the ἁπ. λεγ.
הֵאָמִינוּ for תֵּימִינוּ " turn to the right " Is. xxx. 21,
would have been anyhow a substitution of the gut-
tural for the ', not the ' for the א, and any ambiguity is precluded by the contrast of תַּשְׂמְאִילוּ
" turn to the left." The Kri מִיוֹנִים (Jer. v. 8) is
only a bad correction for the Ch. מוּזָנִים, and so not
Biblical Hebrew. These are all the instances collected by Böttcher (Lehrb. n. 430.) In like way in the
middle radical הָאֵה (Lev. x. 14) and הָיֵה Deut. xiv.
13. Böttch, 1103, 4. adds תַּתְמִירוּ, which Saad. and
Rashi, more probably, derive from מֵר, Jer. ii. 11.
In Ezek. vi. 6, שֵׁי and אֵשַׁם both occur, as variations, not of each other, but of שֵׁמֵם, vi. 4.
    Other cases are simple omissions of the א, not an
interchange at all ; as קִיק from קִיק (med. i. Arab.
Æth.) Jer. xxv. 27, בְּרִיה for בְּרִיאָה Ez. xxxiv. 20.
בְּיר Jer. vi. 7 is a mere correction for בּוּר. and so,
again, not Biblical Hebrew. דּוּג (1 Sam. xxii. 18,
22 Ch.) is a mere corruption of דָּאן, as, in all languages proper names are the most easily corrupted. (See Daniel the prophet p. 405 ed. 2). אֵשׁ (2
Sam. xx. 5. Mic. vi. 19) and the common שׁ, each
lose one letter of the original form, which has
both. (See on Daniel the prophet p. 50 note. ed. 2)
There is not then the slightest countenance for
assuming that הַיּוֹצֵר is *not,* what according to its
form it is, " the potter." [1] Osor.

[2] אֶרֶךְ occurs in this sense, here only. In Mi. ii.
8, it is used of a wide garment i. q. אַדֶּרֶת. יָקָר, " of
value " only occurs else in כְּלִי יָקָר " a vessel of
value " Pr. xx. 15; כְּלִי־יְקָר " every precious thing "
Job. xxviii. 10; כָּל יְקָרָה " all its magnificence,"
Jer. xx. 5; " costliness," Ez. xxii. 25; not directly a
" price."
    " Jewish writers who could satisfy themselves
that the ' thirty pieces of silver ' were anything but
what they are, some thirty precepts given to the
sons of Noah (mystical interpretation in the גֵיד
הַנָּשֶׁה ap. Abarb. ad loc. p. 219. v.), or thirty dignities of royalty (" the wise of blessed memory," in
Abarb. Ib. p. 292. v.) or the thirty righteous in each
generation, promised (as they say) by God to Abraham (Midrash Aggadah in Rashi), or the thirty in
that generation (Kim.), or who went up with Nehemiah, or were priests in his time [Tanchum has
    It is said, that perhaps it is an image of the thirty
righteous or priests, who were the noblest of the
followers of Zerubbabel or Nehemiah."] Ibn E., or
thirty days of imperfect repentance (Kim.), or
thirty years of the reigns of the kings of the pious
Hasmonæans (Abrah. Toled. in McCaul on Zech. ad
loc.), or who scrupled not to own that they could
not explain them at all (Rashi) ;—Jewish writers,
who could, in any of these ways, escape from thinking of those thirty pieces of silver, at which their
forefathers priced the Blood of Jesus, doubt not
that the Good Shepherd Who fed them, Whom

Before CHRIST cir. 487.

‖ Or, *Binders.*

14 Then I cut asunder mine other staff, *even* ‖ Bands, that I might break the brotherhood between Judah and Israel.

Before CHRIST cir. 487.

valued of them! The strong irony is carried on by the, *at which I was valued of them*, as in the idiom, *thou wert precious in my sight* [1]. Precious the thought of God to David [2]; precious the redemption of the soul of man [3]; and precious was the Shepherd Who came to them; precious was the value, whereat He was valued by them [4]. And yet He, Who was so valued, was Almighty God. For so it stands: *Thus saith the Lord God, Cast it unto the potter, the goodly price that I was prized at of them.* The name, *the potter*, connects the prophecy with that former prophecy of Jeremiah [5], denouncing the judgment of God for the shedding of innocent blood, whereby they had defiled *the valley of the son of Hinnom, which was at the entry of the gate of the pottery* [6], and which, through the vengeance of God there, should be called *the valley of slaughter* [7]. The price of this innocent Blood, by the shedding of which the iniquities of their fathers were filled up, should rest on that same place, for whose sake God said, [8] *I will break this people and this city, as one breaketh a potter's vessel, that cannot be made whole again.* So then S. Matthew may have quoted this prophecy as Jeremiah's, to signify how the woes, denounced on the sins committed in this same place, should be brought upon it through this last crowning sin, and *all the righteous blood which had been shed, should come upon that generation* [9].

14. *And I cut asunder mine other staff, Bands,*

they rejected, Who gave them up, Who speaks of Himself, "the goodly price that *I* was prized at of them' (however they may have distorted these words too) was Almighty God." Pusey's University Sermons pp. 151, 152.

[1] יָקָר בְּעֵינַי פ 1 Sam. xxvi. 21, Ps. lxxii. 14, 2 Kgs i. 13, 14, Is. xliii. 4. [2] Ps. cxxxix. 17. [3] Ib. xlix. 9. [4] יָקָר מֵעֲלֵיהֶם. See Ewald Lehrb. n. 219a. p. 573. ed. 8. [5] Jer. xix. [6] שַׁעַר הַחַרְסוּת Ib. 2. See Ges. Thes. sub v. p. 522. [7] Jer. xix. 6. [8] Ib. 11.

[9] S. Augustine suggests that S. Matthew wished to lead the reader to connect the prophecy of Zechariah with Jerem. xxxii. 9. " All copies," he says, "have not 'Jeremiah' but only 'by the prophet;' but more Mss. have the name of Jeremiah; and those who have considered the Gospel carefully in the Greek copies, say that they have found it in the older Greek copies; and there is no reason why the name should be added, so as to occasion a fault; but there was a reason *why* it should be removed from some copies, this being done by a bold unskillfulness [imperitia] being distracted by the question, that this testimony was not found in Jeremiah." "S. Matthew," he says further, "would have corrected it in his life-time at least, when admonished by others who could read this, while he was yet in the flesh, unless ... thought that one name of a prophet instead of another did, not without reason, occur to his memory, which was ruled by the Holy Spirit, but that the Lord appointed that

to dissolve the brotherhood between Judah and Israel. Hitherto prophecy had spoken of the healing of the great breach between Israel and Judah, in Christ. *The Lord,* Isaiah said, [10] *shall assemble the outcasts of Israel, and gather together the dispersed of Judah from the four corners of the earth. The envy of Ephraim shall depart, and the adversaries of Judah shall be cut off : Ephraim shall not envy Judah, and Judah shall not vex Ephraim ;* and Hosea, [11] *Then shall the children of Judah and the children of Israel be gathered together and shall appoint themselves one Head ;* and Jeremiah, [12] *In those days the house of Judah shall walk with the house of Israel.* And Ezekiel, in the midst of the captivity, in a symbolic action the counterpart of this, is bidden, [13] *Take thee one stick, and write upon it, For Judah, and for the children of Israel his companions ; then take another stick, and write upon it, For Joseph, the stick of Ephraim and all the house of Israel his companions, and join them one to another into one stick, and they shall become one in thy hand ;* and, when asked the meaning of this act, he was to say, *Thus saith the Lord God,* [14] *I will take the stick of Joseph, which is in the hand of Ephraim, and the tribes of Israel his fellows, and will put them with him, even with the stick of Judah, and will make them one stick, and they shall be one in Mine hand.* And dropping the symbol ; [15] *Thus saith the Lord God, Behold, I will take the children of Israel from among the heathen, whither they be gone—and I will make*

it should be so written," 1) to shew that all the prophets, speaking by the Spirit, agreed together by a marvelous consent, which is much more than if all the things of the prophets were spoken by the mouth of one man, and so that, whatever the Holy Spirit said by them, should be received undoubtingly, and each belonged to all and all to each &c. 2) to combine it with the selling the field of Hananeel, of which the evidence was put in an earthen vessel. de Cons. Evang. L. iii. n. 30, 31. T. iii. 2. p. 114–116.

None of the other cases of mixed quotation come up to this. S. Mark quotes two prophecies, of Malachi and of Isaiah as Isaiah's (S. Mark i. 2. 3). S. Matthew blends in one, words of Isaiah (lxii. 1) and Zechariah (ix. 9) as "the prophet" (S. Matt. xxi 4, 5). Our Lord unites Is. lvi. 7, and Jer. vii. 11, with the words, " It is written."

Of earlier fathers *Tertullian* simply quotes the prophecy as Jeremiah's (adv. Marc. iv. 40). *Origen* says, "Jeremiah is not said to have prophesied this anywhere in his books, either what are read in the Churches, or reported (referuntur) among the Jews. I suspect that it is an error of writing, or that it is some secret writing of Jeremiah wherein it is written." (in S. Matt. p. 916.) *Eusebius* says, "Consider since this, is not in the Prophet Jeremiah, whether we must think that it was removed from it by some wickedness, or whether it was a clerical error of those who made the copies of the Gospels carelessly." Dem. Ev. x. p. 481.

[10] Is. xi. 12, 13. [11] Hos. i. 11. [12] Jer. iii. 18. [13] Ezek. xxxvii. 16, 17. [14] Ib. 19. [15] Ib. 21, 22, 23, 24.

Before
C H R I S T
cir. 487.

n Ezek. 34. 2, 3, 4.

15 ¶ And the Lord said unto me, n Take unto thee yet the instruments of a foolish shepherd.

16 For, lo, I will raise up a shepherd in the land, *which* shall not visit those

that be ‖ cut off, neither shall seek the young one, nor heal that that is broken, nor ‖ feed that that stand- eth still : but he shall eat the flesh of the fat, and tear their claws in pieces.

Before
C H R I S T
cir. 487.

‖ Or, *hidden.*

‖ Or, *bear.*

them one nation in the land upon the mountains of Israel : and one king shall be king to them all : and they shall be no more two nations, neither shall they be divided into two kingdoms any more at all—I will cleanse them, and they shall be My people and I will be their God, and David My servant shall be king over them, and they all shall have one Shepherd. Such should be the unity of those who would be gathered under the One Shepherd. And so it was. [1] *The multitude of them that believed were of one heart and of one soul;* and long afterward it was a proverb among the Heathen [2], "See how these Christians love one another." Zechariah is here speaking of those who had rejected the Good Shepherd, the Israel and Judah after the flesh, who shut themselves out from the promises of God. This had its first fulfillment in the terrible dissolution of every band of *brotherhood* [3] and of our common nature, which made the siege of Jerusalem a proverb for horror, and precipitated its destruction. " [4] Having thus separated the believing from the unbelieving, He bared the rest of His care. And what we now see bears witness to the prophecy. For the Jews, being deprived of prophets and priests and kings and temple and ark and altar and mercy-seat and candlestick and table and the rest, through which the legal worship was performed, have come to be deprived also of the guardianship from above; and, scattered, exiled, removed, serve against their will those who preach Christ : denying Him as Lord, they yield service to His servants. The prophet having foretold these things of Christ, our God and Saviour, and reproved the obstinacy of the Jews, naturally turns his prophecy straight to the God-opposed christ whom they expect, as they say. So said the Lord in the holy Gospels to them, [5] *I am come in My Father's name, and ye receive Me not ; another will come in his own name, and him ye will receive.* This the blessed Paul also prophesied of them, [6] *Because they*

received not the love of the truth, that they might be saved, God shall send them strong delusion that they should believe a lie, that all might be damned, who believe not the truth, but have pleasure in unrighteousness. The like does the blessed Zechariah prophesy, having received the power of the Holy Spirit."

15. *Take to thee yet the instrument* [7] *of a foolish* [8] *shepherd.* " [9] Yet. He had enacted one tragedy, in which he clearly set forth the future guilt of Judas; now another is set forth, the accumulated scoffing through Anti-Christ. For as Paul said, because they receive not the Spirit of truth, the All-righteous Judge shall send them a spirit of *delusion, that they should believe a lie* [10]. He calls him a foolish shepherd, for since the extremest folly consists in the extremest wickedness, he will be the most foolish, who reached the highest impiety, and this he will do by arrogating to himself divinity and claiming divine honors [11].

This is the only action, which the prophet had to enact or to relate. If it was a visible act, the instrument might be a staff which should bruise, an instrument which should bear a semblance to that of the good shepherd, but which should be pernicious. " [12] Good shepherds, who understood their business, had slight staves, that, if there should be occasion to strike, the stricken sheep might not be bruised; but one who understandeth not, beats them with thicker clubs." Or it may mean also, whatever he would use for the hurtful treatment of the sheep, such as he proceeds to speak of. He is spoken of as, in fact, foolishly sinful [8]: for sin is the only real folly, and all real folly has sin mingled in it. The short-lived wisdom of the foolish shepherd for his own ends should also be his destruction.

16. *I will raise up.* God supplies the strength or wisdom which men abuse to sin. He, in His Providence, disposeth the circumstances, of which the ambitious avail themselves

[1] Acts iv. 32.
[2] Tert. Apol. n. 39. p. 82. and notes, Oxf. Tr.
[3] אַחְוָה The word occurs only here, but is in Arab. Syr. Ch. Zab.
[4] Theod.
[5] S. John v. 43.
[6] 2 Thess. ii. 10–12.
[7] Ezekiel has the idiom, "his instrument of destruction," כְּלִי מַשְׁחֵתוֹ ix. 1; "his instrument of

slaughter," מַכַּתוֹ כ. Ib. 2; Isaiah, "for his work," כְּלִי לְמַעֲשֵׂהוּ liv. 16.

[8] אֱוִילִי ἅπ., אֱוִיל being often a subst., אֱוִיל is a sinful fool, Job. v. 2, 3, and throughout the Proverbs, though more marked in some places, Pr. vii. 22, xiv. 3, xv. 5, xx. 3, xxiv. 7, xxvii. 22; and in the plural, Ps. cvii. 17, Pr. i. 7. x. 21, xiv. 9.
[9] Osor. [10] 2 Thess. ii. 10, 11. [11] Ib. 4. [12] S. Cyr.

17 °Woe to the idol shepherd that leaveth the flock! the sword *shall be* upon his arm, and upon

his right eye: his arm shall be clean dried up, and his right eye shall be utterly darkened.

---

selves. Anti-Christ, whom the Jews look for, will be as much an instrument of God for the perfecting the elect, as the Chaldees [1] or the Assyrians [2] whom God raised up, for the chastisement of His former people, or the Medes against Babylon [3].

Which shall not visit them that be cut off. Zechariah uses the imagery, yet not the exact words of Jeremiah [4] and Ezekiel [5]. Neglect of every duty of a shepherd to his flock, to the sick, the broken, the sound; direct injury of them, preying upon them, make up the picture.

Which shall not visit, or tend, *that which is cut off:* fulfilling God's judgment [6], *that which is to be cut off, let it be cut off.*

Neither shall seek the young one, better, *the scattered* [7], *dispersed,* as the Good Shepherd [8] *came to seek and to save that which was lost. Nor heal that which is broken; bound not,* Ezekiel says [9]. " [10] The broken legs of sheep are healed no otherwise than those of men; rolled in wool impregnated with oil and wine, and then bound up with splinters placed round about it."

Nor feed that which standeth still, better, *the whole* [11], as the word always means, "in its good estate," like our prayer, "that Thou wouldest strengthen those who do stand."

17. *Wo to the idol shepherd,* (a *shepherd of nothingness,* one who hath no quality of a shepherd [12];) *who leaveth the flock.* The condemnation of the evil shepherd is complete in the abandonment of the sheep; as our Lord says, [13] *He that is an hireling and not the Shepherd, whose own the sheep are not, seeth the wolf coming and leaveth the sheep and fleeth: and the wolf catcheth them and scattereth the sheep. The hireling fleeth, because he is an hireling and careth not for the sheep.*

Or it may equally be, *Shepherd,* [14] *thou idol,* including the original meaning of nothingness, such as Anti-Christ will be, " [15] while he calleth himself God, and willeth to be

worshiped." " [15] This shepherd shall therefore arise in Israel, because the true Shepherd had said, *I will not feed you.* He is prophesied of by another name in Daniel the Prophet [16], and in the Gospel [17], and in the Epistle of Paul to the Thessalonians [18], as *the abomination of desolation,* who shall sit in the temple of the Lord, and make himself as God. He cometh, not to heal but to destroy the flock of Israel. This shepherd the Jews shall receive, whom the *Lord Jesus shall slay with the breath of His mouth, and destroy with the brightness of His coming.*"

The sword shall be upon [*against*] *his arm and right eye.* His boast shall be of intelligence, and might. The punishment and destruction shall be directed against the instrument of each, the eye and the arm. " [15] The eye, whereby he shall boast to behold acutely the mysteries of God, and to see more than all prophets heretofore, so that he shall call himself son of God. But the word of the Lord shall be upon his arm and upon his right eye, so that his strength and all his boast of might shall be dried up, and the knowledge which he promised himself falsely, shall be obscured in everlasting darkness." " [19] Above and against the power of Anti-Christ, shall be the virtue and vengeance and sentence of Christ, Who shall *slay* him *with the breath of His mouth.*" The right arm, the symbol of might, and the right eye which was to direct its aim, should fail together, through the judgment of God against him. He, lately boastful and persecuting, shall become blind and powerless, bereft alike of wisdom and strength.

The "right" in Holy Scripture being so often a symbol of what is good, the left of what is evil, it may be also imagined, that " [20] the left eye, i. e. the acumen and cunning to devise deadly frauds, will remain uninjured: while the *right eye,* i. e. counsel to guard against evil, will be sunk in thick

---

[1] הִנְנִי מֵקִים Hab. i. 6.   [2] Am. vi. 14.

[3] חנני מֵעִיר. Is. xiii. 17.   [4] Jer. xxiii. 1, 2.

[5] Ezek. xxxiv. 3, 4.   [6] ab. v. 9.

[7] τὸ ἐσκορπισμένον, ό; dispersum, S. Jer. "who have wandered or gone astray," Syr. "He who hireth a flock is forbidden לנער. What is this! To lead it from place to place." Talm. Hieros. Tr. Sheviith c. 3, in Burt. Lex. p. 1363. Arab. מִן אֵין נערת אלינא "Whence camest thou to us?" c. פ, "traversed country" (Kam.). נער is not used of young of animals.

[8] S. Luke xix. 10, S. Matt. xviii. 11.
[9] Ezek. xxxiv. 4.   [10] Colum. de re rust. viii. 5.

[11] "Which was set firm, or set himself firm." Nif. as in Ps. xxxix. 6, "Every man in his firm estate (נִצָּב) is all vanity." τὸ ὁλόκληρον, ό. "id quod stat," S. Jer. So Syr. The Arab. "נָצַב was weary" (quoted C. B. Mich. Ges.) has only this force as intrans.; נצב c. acc. r., and אנתצב agree with Heb. Yet Jon. renders as Eng.

[12] רְעִי הָאֱלִיל, as אֱלָל רֹפְאֵי, "physicians of no value," Job xiii. 4.   [13] S. John x. 12, 13.

[14] רֹעִי, as a form for רֹעֶה, occurs in Is. xxxviii. 12. אֹהֶל רֹעִי.

[15] S. Jer.   [16] Dan. ix.   [17] S. Mark xiii.
[18] 2 Thess. ii.   [19] Dion.   [20] Osor.

CHAPTER XII.

1 *Jerusalem a cup of trembling
to herself,* 3 *and a burdensome
stone to her adversaries.* 6
*The victorious restoring of Ju-
dah.* 9 *The repentance of Jerusalem.*

THE burden of the word
of the LORD for Israel,
saith the LORD, [a] which
stretcheth forth the heavens, and layeth the foun-
dation of the earth, and

[a] Isai. 42. 5.
& 44. 24.
& 45. 12, 18.
& 48. 13.

---

darkness. And so, the more he employs his
ability to evil, the more frantically will he
bring to bear destruction upon himself."
XII. "[1] From 'I will make Jerusalem'
to 'Awake, O sword,' there is a threefold exposition. For some of the Jews say that
these things have already been fulfilled in
part from Zorobabel to Cn. Pompey who,
first of the Romans, took Judæa and the
temple, as Josephus relates. Others think
that it is to be fulfilled at the end of the
world, when Jerusalem shall be restored,
which the miserable Jewish race promiseth
itself with its anointed, of whom we read
above as the foolish shepherd. But others,
i. e. we who are called by the name of
Christ, say that these things are daily fulfilled, and will be fulfilled in the Church to
the end of the world."
1. *The burden of the word of the Lord for,*
rather, *upon*[2] *Israel.* If this prophecy is a
continuation of the last, notwithstanding its
fresh title, then *Israel* must be the Christian
Church, formed of the true Israel which believed, and the Gentiles who were grafted
into them. So S. Cyril; "Having spoken
sufficiently of the Good Shepherd Christ,
and of the foolish, most cruel shepherd who
butchered the sheep, i. e. Anti-Christ, he
seasonably makes mention of the persecutions which would from time to time arise
against Israel; not the Israel according to
the flesh, but the spiritual, that Jerusalem
which is indeed holy, [3] *the Church of the
Living God.* For as we say, that *he* is spiritually a Jew, who hath the [4] *circumcision in
the heart,* that through the Spirit, *and not* in
the flesh *through the letter;* so also may *Israel*
be conceived, not that of the blood of Israel,
but rather that, which has a mind beholding
God. But such are all who are called to
sanctification through the faith in Christ,
and who, in Him and by Him, know of God
the Father. For this is the one true elected
way of beholding God."

Since the Good Shepherd was rejected by
all, except the *poor of the flock,* the *little flock*
which believed in Him, and thereupon the
band of brotherhood was dissolved between
Israel and Judah, *Israel* in those times could
not be Israel after the flesh, which then too
was the deadly antagonist of the true Israel,
and thus early also chose Anti-Christ, such
as was Bar-Cochba, with whom so many
hundreds of thousands perished. There was
no war then against Jerusalem, since it had
ceased to be [5].
But Zechariah does not say that this prophecy, to which he has annexed a separate
title, follows, in time, upon the last; rather,
since he has so separated it by its title, he
has marked it as a distinct prophecy from
the preceding. It may be, that he began
again from the time of the Maccabees and
took God's deliverances of the people Israel
then, as the foreground of the deliverances
to the end [6]. Yet in the times of Antiochus,
it was one people only which was against
the Jews, and Zechariah himself speaks
only of the Greeks [7]; here he repeatedly
emphasizes that they were *all nations* [8]. It
may then rather be, that the future, the
successive efforts of the world to crush the
people of God, and its victory amid suffering,
and its conversions of the world through the
penitent looking to Jesus, are exhibited in
one great perspective, according to the manner of prophecy, which mostly exhibits the
prominent events, not their order or sequence. "[9] The penitential act of contrite
sinners, especially of Jews, looking at Him
Whom they pierced, dates from the Day of
Pentecost, and continues to the latter days,
when it will be greatly intensified and will
produce blessed results, and is here concentrated into one focus. The rising up of
God's enemies against Christ's Church,
which commenced at the same time, and has
been continued in successive persecutions
from Jews, Gentiles, and other unbelievers

[1] S. Jer.
[2] See on Nah. i. 1, p. 129. The עַל of the title is
repeated in the עַל־יְהוּדָה עַל־יְרוּשָׁלַם ver. 2.
[3] 1 Tim. iii. 15.   [4] Rom. ii. 29.
[5] See at length, ab. on Mic. iii. 12, pp. 46–50.
[6] So Lap. "That Zechariah speaks literally of the
times of the Maccabees which were shortly to
follow, appears both from the sequence of the
times, and the connection and congruency of these
oracles with the deeds of the Maccabees, as also

because v. 10. ends in the Passion of Christ. For
this followed the times of the Maccabees. As then
Isaiah, Jeremiah, Hosea, Daniel, Ezekiel &c. foretold what was shortly to befall the Jews from Sal-
manassar, Nebuchadnezzar, Cyrus, Darius, so Zechariah foretells what should presently befall them
from Antiochus under the Maccabees." Synops.
c. xii.   [7] Zech. ix. 13.   [8] כָּל הָעַמִּים xii. 2, 3, 6, 9.
[9] Bp. C. Wordsworth here, and the like in Keil on
xiv. 20. p. 661.

Before
CHRIST
cir. 487.

b Num. 16. 22.
Eccles. 12. 7.
Isai. 57. 16. Heb. 12. 9.

b formeth the spirit of man within him.

2 Behold, I will make

Before
CHRIST
cir. 487.

c Isai. 51. 17, 22, 23.

Jerusalem °a cup of || trembling unto all the people round about, || when

|| Or, *slumber*, or, *poison*. || Or, *and also against Judah shall he be which shall be in siege against Jerusalem*.

---

in every age, and which will reach its climax in the great Anti-Christian outbreak of the last times, and be confounded by the Coming of Christ to judgment, is here summed up in one panoramic picture, exhibited at once to the eye."
Which stretcheth forth the heavens. God's creative power is an ever-present working, as our Lord says, [1] *My Father worketh hitherto and I work.* His preservation of the things which He has created is a continual re-creation. All "forces" are supported by Him, Who Alone hath life in Himself. He doth not the less *uphold all things by the word of His power*, because, until the successive generations, with or without their will, with or against His Will for them, shall have completed His Sovereign Will, He upholds them uniformly in being by His Unchanging Will. Man is ever forgetting this, and because, [2] *since the fathers fell asleep, all things continue as from the beginning of the creation,* they relegate the Creator and His creating as far as they can to some time, as far back as they can imagine, enough to fill their imaginations, and forget Him Who made them, in Whose hands is their eternity, Who will be their Judge. So the prophets remind them and us of His continual working, which men forget in the sight of His works; [3] *Thus saith the Lord; He that createth the heavens, and stretcheth them out; He that spreadeth forth the earth and its produce, Who giveth breath to the people upon it, and spirit to them that walk therein;* and, [4] *I am the Lord Who maketh all things, Who stretcheth out the heavens alone, Who spreadeth abroad the earth by Myself;* speaking at once of that, past in its beginning yet present to us in its continuance, but to Him ever-present present; and of things actually present to us, [5] *that frustrateth the tokens of the liars;* and of things to those of that day still future, [6] *that confirmeth the word of His servant, and performeth the counsel of His messengers:* the beginning of which was not to be till the taking of Babylon. And the Psalmist unites past and present in one, [7] *Donning light as a garment, stretching out the heavens as a curtain; Who layeth the beams of His chambers on the waters, Who maketh the clouds His chariot; Who walketh on the wings of the wind; Who maketh His angels*

spirits, *His ministers a flame of fire; He founded the earth upon its base.* And Amos, [8] *He that formeth the mountains and createth the winds, and declareth unto man his thoughts;*— adding whatever lieth nearest to each of us.

And formeth the spirit of man within him, both by the unceasing creation of souls, at every moment in some spot in our globe, or by the re-creation, for which David prays, [9] *Create in me a clean heart, O God, and renew a right spirit within me.* He Who formed the hearts of men can overrule them as He wills. "[10] But the spirit of man is formed by God in him, not by being called to the beginnings of being, although it was made by Him, but, as it were, transformed from weakness to strength, from unmanliness to endurance, altogether being transelemented from things shameful to better things."

"[10] It is the wont of the holy Prophets, when about to declare beforehand things of no slight moment, to endeavor to shew beforehand the Almightiness of God, that their word may obtain credence, though they should declare what was beyond all hope, and (to speak of our conceptions) above all reason and credibility."

2. *I will make Jerusalem a cup of trembling*[11]. For encouragement, He promises the victory, and at first mentions the attack incidentally. Jerusalem is as a cup or basin, which its enemies take into their hands; a stone, which they put forth their strength to lift; but they themselves reel with the draught of God's judgments which they would give to others, they are torn by the stone which they would lift to fling. The image of the *cup* is mostly of God's displeasure, which is given to His own people, and then, His judgment of chastisement being exceeded, given in turn to those who had been the instruments of giving it[12]. Thus Isaiah speaks of *the cup of trembling.* [13] Thou, *Jerusalem, hast drunk the dregs of the cup of trembling, hast wrung them out. Therefore hear thou this, thou afflicted and drunken but not with wine. Thus saith thy Lord, the Lord, and thy God that pleadeth the cause of His people, Behold, I have taken out of thine hand the cup of trembling, the dregs of the cup of My fury; thou shalt no more drink it again: but I will put it into the hand of them that afflict thee.* Jere-

[1] S. John v. 17.   [2] S. Pet. iii. 4.   [3] Is. xlii. 5.
[4] Ib. xliv. 24.   [5] Ib. 25.   [6] Ib. 26.
[7] Ps. civ. 2-5.   [8] Am. iv. 13. add v. 8.
[9] Ps. li. 10.   [10] S. Cyr.

[11] רעל aπ. in the sense. The form תרעלה

occurs in the like idioms, כוס תרעלה, Is. li. 17, 22; יין תרעלה Ps. lx. 5.
[12] See on Obad. 16, vol. i. pp. 362-365.
[13] Is. li. 17, 21-23.

Before
CHRIST
cir. 487.
ᵈ ver. 4, 6, 8, 9.
11. & ch. 13. 1.
& 14. 4, 6, 8, 9.
13.

they shall be in the siege b o t h against Judah *and* against Jerusalem.

3 ¶ ᵈ And in that day will

I make Jerusalem ᵉ a burdensome stone for all people; all that burden themselves with it shall be cut in

Before
CHRIST
cir. 487.

ᵉ Matt. 21. 44.

miah speaks of *the cup of God's anger*, as given by God first to Jerusalem, then to all whom Nebuchadnezzar should subdue, then to Babylon itself[1]; and as *passing through* to Edom also[2]; Ezekiel, of *Aholibah*[3] (Jerusalem) *drinking the cup of Samaria.* In Jeremiah alone, Babylon is herself the cup. [4] *Babylon is a golden cup in the Lord's hand, that made all the nations drunken; the nations have drunken of the wine; therefore the nations are mad.* Now Jerusalem is to be, not an ordinary cup, but a large basin[5] or vessel, from which all nations may drink what will make them reel.

And also upon Judah will it be in the siege against Jerusalem, i. e. *the burden of the word*[6] *of the Lord which was on Israel* should be upon Judah, i. e. upon all, great and small.

3. *I will make Jerusalem a burdensome stone to all nations.* What is *a stone to all nations?* It is not a rock or anything in its own nature immovable, but *a stone*, a thing rolled up and down, moved, lifted, displaced, piled on others, in every way at the service and command of men, to do with it what they willed. So they thought of that [7] *stone cut out without hands;* that [8] *tried stone and sure foundation, laid in Zion;* that *stone* which, God said in Zechariah[9], *I have laid;* of which our Lord says, [10] *the stone, which the builders rejected, is become the head of the corner;* [11] *whosoever shall fall on this stone shall be broken, but on whomsoever it shall fall, it will grind him to powder.* The Church, built on the stone,

seems a thing easily annihilated; ten persecutions in succession strove to efface it; Diocletian erected a monument, commemorating that the Christian name was blotted out[12]. It survived; he perished. The image may have been suggested by the custom, so widely prevailing in Judæa, of trying the relative strength of young men, by lifting round stones selected for that end[13]. "[14] The meaning then is, I will place Jerusalem to all nations like a very heavy stone[15] to be lifted up. They will lift it up, and according to their varied strength, will waste it; but it must needs be, that, while it is lifted, in the very strain of lifting the weight, that most heavy stone should leave some scission or rasure on the bodies of those who lift it. Of the Church it may be interpreted thus; that all persecutors, who fought against the house of the Lord, are inebriated with that cup, which Jeremiah gives to all nations, to drink and be inebriated and fall and vomit and be mad. Whosoever would uplift the stone shall lift it, and in the anger of the Lord, whereby He chastens sinners, will hold it in his hands; but he himself will not go unpunished, the sword of the Lord fighting against him."

All that burden themselves with it will be cut to pieces[16], more exactly, *scarified, lacerated;* shall bear the scars. *Though* (rather, *and*) *all the people* [*peoples, nations*] *of the earth shall be gathered together against it.* The prophet marshals them all against Jerusalem, only to

[1] Jer. xxv. 15–26.   [2] Lam. iv. 21. Jer. xlix. 12.   [3] Ezek. xxiii. 31–33.   [4] Jer. li. 7.

[5] קֻב is the basin, which received the blood of the Paschal lamb, Ex. xii 22; סִפִּים, with beds and earthen vessels, were brought to David by Barzillai and the others, 2 Sam. xvii. 28. Else they are only mentioned as instruments of the temple-services. 1 Kgs vii. 50, 2 Kgs xii. 14, Jer. lii. 19.

[6] מֵי אֵן is the only natural subject, as in ix. 1, *the burden of the Lord is on the land of Hadrach,* but it is subjoined, *Damascus is the resting place thereof, &c.* The E. V. does not seem grammatical. The E. M. is too elliptical, as also that other, "it will be laid upon Jerusalem *to be* in the siege against Jerusalem." Had "the cup of trembling" been the subject, it had probably been לִיהוּדָה, as לְכָל הָעַמִּים. Nor can מָצוֹר be the subject; for countries, as Judah, are not the objects of siege.

[7] Dan. ii. 45.   [8] Is. xxviii. 16.   [9] Zech. iii. 9.
[10] S. Luke xx. 17.
[11] S. Matt. xxi. 44. S. Luke xx. 18.
[12] Baronius speaks of two inscriptions as still existing at Clunia (Corunna dal Conde) in Spain. The one had, "amplificato per Orientem et Occid. Impe. Rom. et nomine Christianor. deleto qui remp. evertebant;" the other, "superstitione Christi ubiq. deleta. Cultu Deorum propagato." A. 304. n. I.

[13] " It is the custom in the cities of Palestine, and that old usage is kept up to this day throughout Judæa, that in villages towns and forts, round stones are placed, of very great weight, on which young men are wont to practise themselves, and according to their varying strength, lift them, some to the knees, others to the navel, others to the shoulders and head; others lift the weight above the head, with their two hands raised straight up, shewing the greatness of their strength. In the Acropolis at Athens, I saw a brass globe, of very great weight, which I, with my little weak body, could scarcely move. When I asked its object, I was told by the inhabitants, that the strength of wrestlers was proved by that mass, and that no one went to a match, until it was ascertained by the lifting of that weight, who ought to be set against whom." S. Jer.
[14] S. Jer.
[15] lit. "a stone of lading," which whoso lifteth would be laden or burthened. It is the only noun formed from עָמַס; and the root itself existed only in Hebrew.

[16] שׂרט is a root, revived by Zechariah from the Pentateuch. It occurs only Lev. xix. 28, xxi. 5, of the forbidden incisions for the dead. Arab. שׂרט and Syr. סָרַט, "scarified" Syr. אתסרט "was branded."

Before
CHRIST
cir. 487.

pieces, though all the people of the earth be gathered together against it.

4 In that day, saith the LORD, [f] I will smite every horse with astonishment, and his rider with madness: and I will open mine eyes upon the house of Judah, and will smite every

[f] Ps. 76. 6. Ezek. 38. 4.

horse of the people with blindness.

Before
CHRIST
cir. 487.

5 And the governors of Judah shall say in their heart, || The inhabitants of Jerusalem *shall be* my strength in the LORD of hosts their God.

|| Or, There is strength to me and to the inhabitants, &c. Joel 3. 16.

6 ¶ In that day will I make the governors of Ju-

---

say how they should perish before it. So in Joel God says, [1] *I will also gather all nations, and will bring them down to the valley of Jehoshaphat,* speaking of that last closing strife of Anti-Christ against God. Wars against Israel had either been petty, though Antitheistic, wars of neighboring petty nations, pitting their false gods against the True, or one, though world-empire wielded by a single will. The more God made Himself known, the fiercer the opposition. The Gospel claiming [2] *obedience to the faith among all nations,* provoked universal rebellion. Herod and Pontius Pilate became friends through rejection of Christ; the Roman Cæsar and the Persian Sapor, Goths and Vandals, at war with one another, were one in persecuting Christ and the Church. Yet in vain;

4. *In that day, saith the Lord, I will smite every horse with astonishment, stupefying.* Zechariah revives the words concentrated by Moses, to express the stupefaction at their ills, which God would accumulate upon His people, if they perseveringly rebelled against Him. Each expresses the intensity of the visitation [3]. *The horse and his rider* had, through Moses' song at the Red Sea, become the emblem of worldly power, overthrown. That song opens; [4] *I will sing unto the Lord; for He hath triumphed gloriously : the horse and his rider hath He cast into the sea.* The scared cavalry throws into confusion the ranks, of which it was the boast and strength.

And on the house of Judah I will open My eyes, in pity and love and guidance, as the Psalmist says, [5] *I will counsel, with Mine eye*

[1] Jo. iii. 2. See vol. i. pp. 200, 201, and p. 207 on Jo. iii. 9.   [2] Rom. i. 5.
[3] Deut. xxvii. 28, תִּמָּהוֹן (the only noun derived from תִּמָּה (and with the same word, כֵּה) עֵנָּרוֹן occurs only there beside; שִׁנָּע, beside, only in 2 Kgs ix. 20. Only לֵבָב is omitted after תִמָּהוֹן since it stands in connection with the horse in the parallelism.   [4] Ex. xv. 1.   [5] Ps. xxxii. 8.
[6] אֶמְצָה *ἅπ*.; as is the form אֹמֶץ, Job xvii. 19, כְּאָמֵץ Ib. xxxvi. 19.   [7] Zech. i. 17, ii. 12. iii. 2.
[8] כִּיּוֹר, in 1 Sam. ii. 14, is 'a vessel, in which the

---

upon thee, in contrast with *the blindness* with which God would smite the powers arrayed against them.

5. *And the princes of Judah.* He pictures the onemindedness of the Church. No one shall assume anything to himself; each shall exalt the strength which the other was to him; but all, *in the Lord. The princes of Judah* shall say *in their heart,* not outwardly or politically, but in inward conviction, *strength to me* [6] (all speak as one) *are the inhabitants of Jerusalem in the Lord of hosts their God.* The highest in human estimation acknowledge that their strength is in those who are of no account in this world; as, in fact, the hearts of the poor are evermore the strength of the Church ; but that, *in the Lord of hosts;* in Him, in Whose hands are the powers of heaven and earth, over against the petty turmoil on earth. God had chosen Jerusalem [7]; therefore she was invincible. "That most glorious prince of Judah, Paul, said, '*I can do all things in Christ Who instrengtheneth me.*'"

6. *I will make the governors of Judah like a hearth* or *cauldron* [8] of fire, large, broad, deep, and full of fire, *among the wood* which is prepared for burning [9], *and like a torch of fire in a sheaf.* The fire could not kindle the wood or the sheaf, of itself, unless applied to it. All is of the agency of God : *I will make.*

"[10] He foretells the increase of the Church, which by such persecutions shall not be diminished, but shall be marvelously increased. The preachers of the Church shall raise up all the peoples round about, shall destroy all unbelief, and shall kindle the

food is cooked;' in 2 Chr. vi. 13 'a pulpit;' so that the vessel, to which it is likened, must have been large ; as must have been the brazen laver of the tabernacle (Ex. Lev.) or temple (2 Kgs), of which the word is elsewhere used. Each laver of Solomon's temple *contained forty baths,* or about 300 gallons, and was four cubits (1 Kgs vii. 38) square apparently (coll. 27.).
[9] עֵצִים (pl.) is used of wood cut up, 1) for burning, especially on an altar, or 2) for building, unless it is plain from the context, that they are living trees, as in Jos. x. 26, Jud. ix. 48, in Jotham's fable Ib. 9-15, or Ps. xcvi. 12, civ. 16, Cant. iv. 14, Is. vii. 2. &c.   [10] Rib.

Before
C H R I S T
cir. 487.

‖Obad. 18.

dah ⁶ like an hearth of fire among the wood, and like a torch of fire in a sheaf; and they shall devour all the people round about, on the right hand and on the left: and Jerusalem shall be inhabited again in her own place, *even* in Jerusalem.

7 The LORD also shall

save the tents of Judah first, that the glory of the house of David a n d the glory of the inhabitants of Jerusalem do not magnify *themselves* against Judah.

8 In that day shall the LORD defend the inhabitants of Jerusalem; and ʰ he that is ‖ † feeble among them at that day shall be

Before
C H R I S T
cir. 487.

ʰ Joel 3. 10.
‖ Or, *abject.*
† Heb. *fallen.*

hearts of hearers with the fire of the Divine word." *On the right hand and on the left.* "¹ He indicates the strength and success of the preachers, whom no one can resist nor hinder," as our Lord says, ² *I will give you a mouth and wisdom, which all your adversaries shall not be able to gainsay nor resist.*

And Jerusalem shall again, rather, *yet, be inhabited.* "Yet" is a sort of burden in Zechariah's prophecies³. "⁴They at once burned up by the flame all the defilement of vices, and kindled the minds of men with the torch of Divine love; at once consumed the enemy and cast a heavenly fire into the human heart: *yet;* in despite of all appearances, of all which is against her. *She shall yet dwell in her own place in Jerusalem;* for, however the waves of this world chafe and lash themselves into foam against her, they break themselves, not her; as soon as they have reached their utmost height, they fall back; if they toss themselves, and, for a moment, hide her light, they fall down at all sides, and the ray shines out, steady as before; for she is *founded on a rock,* against which ⁵ *the gates of hell should not prevail.*

7. *The Lord also shall save the tents of Judah first.* Still it is, *the Lord shall save.* We have, on the one side, *the siege,* the gathering of all the peoples of the earth *against Jerusalem, the horse and his rider.* On the other, no human strength; not, as before, in the prophecy of the Maccabees, the bow, the arrow, and the sword, though in the hand of God⁶. It is thrice, *I will make* ⁷; *I will smite* ⁸; and now, *The Lord shall save.* By the *tents,* he probably indicates their defencelessness. God would save them first; that *the glory* ⁹ *of the house*

of David—*be not great against* or *over Judah,* may not overshadow it; but all may be as one; for all is the free gift of God, the mere grace of God, that ¹⁰ *he that glorieth may glory in the Lord,* and both "¹¹ may own that, in both, the victory is the Lord's."

"¹²*In Christ Jesus is neither Jew nor Greek; neither bond nor free* ¹³, neither rich nor poor; *but all are one,* viz. a new creation; yea in Christendom the poor are the highest, both because Christ ¹⁴ *preached to the poor,* and pronounced the ¹⁵ *poor blessed,* and He made the Apostles, being poor, nobles in His kingdom, through whom He converted kings and princes, as is written, ¹⁶ *ye see your calling, brethren, that not many wise men after the flesh, not many mighty, not many noble* are called, *but God hath chosen the foolish things of the world to confound the wise, and the weak things of the world to confound the things which are mighty &c.;* and, ¹⁷ *Hath not God called the poor in this world, rich in faith, and heirs of the kingdom, which God has promised to them that love Him?* The rich and noble have greater hindrances to humility and Christian virtues, than the poor. For honors puff up, wealth and delights weaken the mind; wherefore they need greater grace of Christ to burst their bonds than the poor. Wherefore, for the greater grace shewn them, they are bound to give greater thanks unto Christ."

8. *In that day the Lord shall defend the inhabitants of Jerusalem; and he that is feeble,* rather, *he that stumbleth among them, shall be as David.* The result of the care and the defence of God is here wholly spiritual, "the strengthening of such as do stand, and the raising up of such as fall." It is not simply one feeble, but one *stumbling* ¹⁸ and ready to

¹ Rib.   ² S. Luke xxi. 15.
³ See reff. note 2.   ⁴ Osor.
⁵ S. Matt. xvi. 18.   ⁶ Zech. ix. 13.
⁷ ver. 2, 3, 6.   ⁸ ver. 4 bis.
⁹ הָפְאָרֶת is nowhere "gloriatio," as Ges., but
simply "glory," "beauty," though, rarely, it is implied in the context, that he who has it, is proud of
it, as Is. iii. 18. x. 12, xiii. 9.
¹⁰ Jer. ix. 24, 1 Cor. i. 31, 2 Cor. x 17.

¹¹ S. Jer.   ¹² Lap.   ¹³ Gal. iii. 28.
¹⁴ S. Luke iv. 18.   ¹⁵ Ib. vi. 20.   ¹⁶ 1 Cor. i. 26.
¹⁷ S. James ii. 5.
¹⁸ 1 Sam. ii. 4, is the only case alleged by Ges., in
which נִכְשָׁל is to signify "weak." Yet here too
"stumble," as in the E. V., is the natural rendering.
In the other 19 cases it is confessedly stumbling,
though in some it is stumbling, so as to fall.

Before CHRIST cir. 487. as David; and the house of David *shall be* as God, as the angel of the LORD before them.

9 ¶ And it shall come to pass in that day, *that I*

will seek to [1] destroy all the nations that come against Jerusalem.

10 [k] And I will p o u r upon the house of David, and upon the inhabitants

Before CHRIST cir. 487.

[1] Hag. 2. 22. ver. 3.
[k] Jer. 31. 9. & 50. 4.
Ezek. 39. 29.
Joel 2. 28.

---

fall, who becomes as David, the great instance of one who fell, yet was raised. Daniel says of a like trial-time, [1] *And some of those of understanding shall stumble, to try them and to purge and to make them white, to the time of the end.* "[2] Such care will God have of protecting the sons of the Church, when it shall be infested with persecutions, that he who shall have fallen through human infirmity, either deceived by heretics or overcome by fear of tortures, shall arise the more fervent and cautious, and with many tears shall make amends for his sins to God, as did David. *He who stumbled shall be as David*, because the sinner returneth to repentance. This is not said of all times, nor of all (for many have stumbled, who never rose) but chiefly of the first times of the Church and of men of great sanctity, such as were many then."

And the house of David shall be as God. They who stumbled became really like David; but he, though mighty and a great saint of God, though he once fell, was man. How then could the house of David be really like God? Only fully in Him, Who, [3] *being in the form of God, thought it not robbery to be equal with God;* Who said, [4] *He who hath seen Me, hath seen My Father also;* [5] *I and the Father are one.* And this the prophet brings out by adding, *as the Angel of the Lord before them*, i. e. that one Angel of the Lord, in whom His very Presence and His Name was; Who went before them, to guide them [6]. Else, having said, *like God*, it had been to lessen what he had just said, to add, *like the Angel of the Lord.* Our Lord prayed for those who are truly His, [7] *As Thou, Father, art in Me and I in Thee, that they may be one in Us; that they may be one as We are one, I in them, and Thou in Me, that they may be perfect in one;* and S. Paul saith, [8] *Christ is formed in us;* [9] *Christ dwelleth*

in our hearts by faith; [10] *Christ liveth in me;* [11] *Christ is in you;* [12] *Christ is our life;* [13] *Christ is all and in all;* [14] *we grow into Him which is the Head, even Christ;* [15] *we are in Christ;* and S. Peter, we are [16] *partakers of the Divine nature;* and S. John, [17] *As He is, so are we in this world.* Then in a degree the glory of Christ passeth over to those who dwell in Him, and in whom He dwells by the Spirit, as S. Paul says; [18] *Ye received me, as an angel of God, as Christ Jesus.*

9. *In that day, I will seek to destroy.* Woe indeed to those, whom Almighty God shall "*seek* to destroy!" Man may seek earnestly to do, what at last he cannot do. Still it is an earnest seeking. And whether it is used of human seeking which fails [19], or which succeeds [20], inchoate [21] or permitted [22], it is always used of seeking to do, what it is a person's set purpose to do if he can [19]. Here it is spoken of Almighty God [23]. "[2] He saith not, ' I will destroy' but *I will seek to destroy*, i. e. it shall ever be My care to destroy all the enemies of the Church, that they may in no way prevail against it: this I will do alway to the end of the world."

10. *And I will pour,* as He promised by Joel [24], *I will pour out My Spirit upon all flesh,* largely, abundantly, *upon the house of David and the inhabitants of Jerusalem,* all, highest and lowest, from first to last, the *Spirit of grace and supplication,* i. e. the *Holy Spirit* which conveyeth *grace,* as [25] *the Spirit of wisdom and understanding* is the *Spirit* infusing *wisdom and understanding,* and *the Spirit of counsel and might* is that same Spirit, imparting the *gift of counsel* to see what is to be done and *of might* to do it, and the Spirit *of the knowledge and of the fear of the Lord* is that same *Spirit,* infusing loving acquaintance with God, with awe at His infinite Majesty. So *the Spirit of grace and supplication,* is that same Spirit,

---

[1] Dan. xi. 35.   [2] Rib.   [3] Phil. ii. 6.
[4] S. John xiv. 9.   [5] Ib. x. 30.
[6] See "Daniel the prophet" pp. 519–523.
[7] S. John xvii. 21, 22, 23.   [8] Gal. iv. 19.
[9] Eph. iii. 17.   [10] Gal. ii. 20.
[11] Rom. viii. 10.
[12] Col. iii. 4.   [13] Ib. 11.   [14] Eph. iv. 15.
[15] Rom. xvi. 7, 2 Cor. v. 17, Gal. i. 22.
[16] 2 Pet. i. 4.   [17] 1 S. John iv. 17.   [18] Gal. iv. 14.
[19] בקשׁ with לְ and inf. "Pharaoh sought to slay Moses," Ex. ii. 15; "Saul, my father, seeketh to slay thee," 1 Sam. xi. 2; "Saul sought to smite

David," Ib. 20; Solomon, to kill Jeroboam, 1 Kgs xi. 40; "Sought to lay hand on the king," Esth. vi. 2; Haman sought to destroy the Jews. Ib. iii. 6.
The inf. without לְ, occurs Jer. xxvi. 21.
[20] 1 Sam. xiv. 4, xxiii. 10, Eccl. xii. 10.
[21] "sought to turn away," De. xiii. 11. "seekest to destroy a city," 2 Sam. xx. 19.
[22] 1 Kgs xi. 22, Zech. vi. 7.
[23] In Ex. iv. 24 only, it is said, "God sought to slay Moses," i. e. shewed that He would, unless his son had been circumcised.
[24] Jo. ii. 28. See vol. i. pp. 193, 194.   [25] Is. xi. 2.

of Jerusalem, the spirit of grace and of supplications: and they shall [1]look upon

me whom they have pierced, and they shall mourn for him, [m]as one

infusing grace and bringing into a state of favor with God, and a *Spirit of supplication*[1] is that Spirit, calling out of the inmost soul the cry for a yet larger measure of the grace already given. S. Paul speaks of [2]*the love of God poured out in our hearts by the Holy Spirit which is given unto us ;* and of [3] *insulting*

the *Spirit of grace,* rudely repulsing the Spirit, Who giveth grace. "[4]When God Himself says, '*I* will pour out,' He sets forth the greatness of His bountifulness whereby He bestoweth all things."

And they shall look, with trustful hope and longing, on *Me*[5], Almighty God, *Whom they*

---

[1] תחנונים is chosen in allusion to חן "grace." תחנונים is, almost everywhere, the cry to God for His grace and favor. It occurs mostly in the Psalms united with קול. "the voice of my supplications," Ps. xxviii. 2, 6, xxxi. 23, xxxvi. 6, cxvi. 1, cxxx. 2, cxi. 7; also of the cry to God, without קול, Ps. cxliii. 1, Dan. ix. 3, 17, 18, 33, Jer. iii. 21. xxxi. 9. It is used of man to man, only Prov. xviii. 23, and else, in irony, of what leviathan would not do to man, Job xl. 27, 6. [xli. 3. Eng.]
[2] Rom. v. 5.
[3] Heb. x. 29, τὸ πνεῦμα τῆς χάριτος ἐνυβρίσας.
[4] Osor.
[5] There is no critical doubt about the reading, אלי, *to Me.* It is the reading of all the old Verss., Jewish or Christian; LXX. Aq. Sym. Theod. Chald. Syr. Vulg. In the ixth cent., the Jews had begun to make a marginal correction into אליו, but did not venture to change the text. "Where we, according to the faith of Holy Scripture, read, in the Person of God, 'and they shall look to Me Whom they pierced,' though, in the text itself of the book, they were deterred by God's Providence from making a change, yet without, in the margin, they have it noted, 'they shall look to *him* whom they pierced.' And so they hand down to their disciples, that they should transcribe, as it is contained in the text, and read, as they have noted, outside; so that they may hold, according to their phrensy, that the Jews look to him, whom Gog and Magog pierced." Rabanus Maurus c. Jud. n. 12. In the 13th. cent. Martini says, that "*all* the old MSS. of the Jews have אלי ;" and that the "perfidy of *some modern* Jews, unable to deprave so evident a testimony to the divinity of the Messiah, say, that it is not אלי but אליו." f. 666. In f. 328, he again says, "*some* Jews falsify the text ;" and (f. 329) that "*now* (jam) in many MSS. they have corrupted their text, but that they are refuted by the Targum, the Talmud, *and by many ancient* MSS., in which this text is *not yet* corrupted, and by the exposition of Rashi." R. Isaac, at the end of the 16th. cent. A. D. 1593, quoted the reading אלי without doubt, though he was expressly controverting the Christian argument. "They say, that hereafter the sons of Israel shall mourn, because they pierced and slew the Messiah sent to them, Jesus who is compounded of Godhead and Manhood, and they say, that this is (the meaning of) 'they shall look *to me* whom they pierced.'" (Chizzuk Emunah in Wagenseil Tela ign. Sat. pp. 303, 304.) He explains it of the wars of Gog and Magog. 'If they shall see that they [their enemies] shall pierce through even one of them, they shall be amazed and shall look *to me,* eth asher dakaroo, i. e. on account of him, whom they pierced—So that the Nazarenes have no help from the words והביטו אלי את אשר דקרו ;' (Ib. pp. 307, 308;) and he subjoins, that if he who was wounded had been the same as he to whom they should look, it ought to have gone on in the first

person, ספדו עלי, and והמר עלי, like והביטו. אלי. Ib. 309. R. Lipmann (A. D. 1399) uses the same argument, "He should have said, *and they shall mourn for me,* as he began, *they shall look to me.*" p. 144 ed. Hacksp. *Ibn Ezra* agrees with this, for he explains it in the first person, "Then shall all nations look to me (אלי) to see what I shall do to those who have slain Messiah b. Joseph." *Alsheikh's* commentary requires the same, "And I will yet do a third thing. And this that they shall look אלי, is that they shall hung their eyes on Me in perfect repentance when they see &c." and *R. Obadiah Siporno,* (Bibl. Rabb.) "and they shall look to Me in their prayer." Rashi also gives the Targ. "and they shall seek *of Me* " מן קדמי as the interpretation of והביטו אלי "they shall look to me." *R. Tanchum* of Jerusalem, "a learned son of a learned father," in the latter part of the 13th cent. (Grätz vii. 144, 145) knew in the East of no other reading. He explains it; "They shall flee to Me, when they see the slaying of those whom the enemy had slain of them" (Poc. 344). His contemporary, *Parchon,* in his lexicon *Mechabberoth,* cites the passage with אלי, and explains the word "piercing of a sword in the body," v. דקר. The Heb. Arab. version, so often quoted by Pococke (Hunt. 206) renders, "And they turned to me, whom they rent (בענו) the word, used by Abulwalid, only Abulwalid further explains this by שע.) Abulwalid does not notice the *reading* in either of his lexica, nor Menahem b. Sarug, nor David b. Abraham. With regard to MSS., even in later times Peter Niger [Schwarz] (a learned Benedictine of the 17th cent.) wrote, "some false and lying Jews say that it is not written, 'And they shall look on me whom they have pierced,' but 'they shall seek to him whom they have pierced'—I answer, that on my conscience and on the Christian truth I say, I have seen many Jewish Bibles [Spanish, doubtless, since he studied Hebrew in Spain] and I never, in any Bible, found it written other than *vehibbitu elai* 'and they shall look to me,' and not *vehibbitu elav,* 'and they shall look to him,' as I will shew any one who desires to see." Stella Messiæ Tract. ii. c. 2. A. D. 1477 in Wolf Bibl. Hebr. iv. p. 543. Norzi, a Jewish critic, says that אליו is not found in the Scriptures, only in *Rashi and the Gemara.* The codex Babyl. Petropol. (I am told, of the ixth cent.) has אלי. In the collated MSS. there is the variation, common where there is a real or virtual kri, 33 Kenn. MSS. and 6 de R. have אליו ; 3 have אלי marked on the marg., one as a kri; 7 K. and 5 de R. had אלי corrected into אליו ; 4 K., 5 de R. had אליו corrected into אלי: 11 K., 5 de R. had a kri in marg. אליו. "The most and best MSS. have אלי." De R. . Ewald's ground for rejecting the reading אלי illustrates the Jewish. "דקר is, from the context which speaks of mourning for the dead, and the

mourneth for *his* only *son,* and shall be in bitterness | for him, as one that is in bitterness for *his* firstborn.

have pierced [1]; the Head with the thorns, the Hands and Feet with the nails, the Side with the soldier's lance. The prophecy began to be fulfilled as soon as the deed was completed, and Jesus had yielded up His Spirit: when [2] *all the people that came together to that sight, beholding the things which were done, smote their breasts and returned.* " [3] When they had nailed the Divine Shrine to the Wood, they who had crucified Him, stood around, impiously mocking.—But when He had laid down His life for us, [4] *the centurion and they that were with him, watching Jesus, seeing the earthquake and those things which were done, feared greatly, saying, Truly this was the Son of God.*" As it ever is with sin, compunction did not come till the sin was over: till then, it was over-laid; else the sin could not be done. At the first conversion, the three thousand *were pricked* [5] *in the heart,* when told that He [6] *Whom they had taken and with wicked hands had crucified and slain, is Lord and Christ.* This awoke the first penitence of him who became S. Paul. *Saul, Saul, why persecutest thou Me?* This has been the centre of Christian devotion ever since, the security against passion, the impulse to self-denial, the parent of zeal for souls, the incentive to love; this has struck the rock, that it gushed forth in tears of penitence: this is the strength and vigor of hatred of sin, to look to Him Whom our sins pierced, *Who* S. Paul says, *loved me and gave Himself for me.* " [7] We all lifted Him up upon the Cross; we trans-fixed with the nails His Hands and Feet; we pierced His Side with the spear. For if man had not sinned, the Son of God would have endured no torment."

And they shall mourn for Him, as one mourneth for an only son, and shall be in bitterness for Him, as one that is in bitterness for a first-born. We feel most sensibly the sorrows of this life,

language of the prophet (xiii. 3) clear; but for אֵלַי, we must, with many MSS., read אֵלָיו. The first person were wholly unsuited here. It is at variance with the following וְסָפְדוּ עָלָיו, and introduces into the Old Testament the senselessness, that one is to weep over Jahve, (for Jahve [Almighty God] must be the subject,) as over one dead, (who should never come back again !)." De Rossi suggests that the אֵלָיו came in accidentally, the scribe having in his mind Ps. xxxiv. 6, הִבִּיטוּ אֵלָיו.

[1] There can equally be no question about the meaning of דְקֹר (as even Ew. and Hitz. admit) or about the construction. דָקַר (which occurs 11 times, is everywhere "thrust through." In one place only, Lam. iv. 9. מְדֻקָּרִים. "thrust through," occurs as a synonym of חַלְלֵי רָעָב "those wounded by hunger" and that, in contrast with

passing as they are; and of these, the loss of an only son is a proverbial sorrow. [8] *O daughter of My people, gird thee with sackcloth and wallow thyself in ashes,* God says; *make thee the mourning of an only son, most bitter lamentation.* [9] *I will make it as the mourning of an only son.* The dead man carried out, *the only son of his mother and she was a widow,* is recorded as having touched the heart of Jesus. " [10] And our Lord, to the letter, was the Only-Begotten of His Father and His mother." He was [11] *the first-begotten of every creature,* and [12] *we saw His glory, the glory as of the Only-Begotten of the Father, full of grace and truth.* This mourning for Him Whom our sins pierced and nailed to the tree, is continued, week by week, by the pious, on the day of the week, when He suffered for us, or in the perpetual memorial of His Precious Death in the Holy Eucharist, and especially in Passion-Tide. God sends forth anew *the Spirit of grace and supplication,* and the faith-ful mourn, because of their share in His Death. The prophecy had a rich and copious fulfillment in that first conversion in the first Pentecost; a larger fulfillment awaits it in the end, when, after the destruction of Anti-Christ, [13] *all Israel shall* be converted and *be saved.* There is yet a more awful fulfillment; when [14] *He cometh with clouds, and every eye shall see Him, and they which pierced Him, and all kindreds of the earth shall wail because of Him.* But meanwhile it is fulfilled in every solid conversion of Jew Heathen or careless Christian, as well as in the devotion of the pious. Zechariah has concentrated in few words the tenderest devotion of the Gospel, *They shall look on Me Whom they pierced.* " [15] Zechariah teaches that among the various feelings which we can elicit from the meditation on the Pas-sion of Christ, as admiration, love, gratitude,

חַלְלֵי חֶרֶב "wounded by the sword." So also the noun, מַדְקְרוֹת חֶרֶב, "the piercings of the sword," Ps. xii. 18. In regard to the construction, אֵת אֲשֶׁר occurs in 97 places in the Bible, and in every place in the meaning "he who," "that which," "this that." In one place only Zech. xxix. 13, 14, אֵת having been previously used as a preposition, "and not with you only, (אֶתְכֶם) do I make this cove-nant," the אֵת is again used as a preposition, carry-ing on the construction, "but with him who, אֵת אֲשֶׁר. Frischmuth (de Messia confixo) mentions 14 ways, by which "because" might without ambi-guity have been expressed (see Pusey's Univ. Sermons p. 142). There is then no excuse for the renderings ἀνθ᾽ ὧν, LXX. or Aq. σὺν ᾧ. Theod. has πρὸς μὲ εἰς ὃν ἐξεκέντησαν.

[2] S. Luke xxiii. 48. [3] S. Cyr. [4] S. Matt. xxvii. 54. [5] κατενύγησαν Acts ii. 37. [6] Ib. 23, 36. [7] Osor. [8] Jer. vi. 26. [9] Amos viii. 10. [10] Alb. [11] Col. i. 15. [12] S. John i. 14. [13] Rom. xi. 26. [14] Rev. i. 7. [15] Lap.

Before
CHRIST
cir. 487.

11 In that day shall there be a great ⁿ mourning in Jerusalem, ° as the mourning of Hadadrimmon in the valley of Megiddon

12 ᴾ And the land shall mourn, † every family apart; the family of the house of David apart, and their wives apart; the fam-

ᵃ Acts 2. 37.
° 2 Kin. 23. 29.
Chr. 35. 24.

ᴾ Matt. 24. 30.
Rev. 1. 7.
† Heb. *families,*
families.

ily of the house of ᑫ Nathan apart, and their wives apart;

13 The family of the house of Levi apart, and their wives apart; the family ‖ of Shimei apart, and their wives apart;

14 All the families that remain, every family apart, and their wives apart.

Before
CHRIST
cir. 487.

ᑫ 2 Sam. 5. 14.
Luke 3. 31.

‖ Or, *of Simeon*
as LXX.

compunction, fear, penitence, imitation, patience, joy, hope, the feeling of compassion stands eminent, and that it is this, which we peculiarly owe to Christ suffering for us. For who would not in his inmost self grieve with Christ, innocent and holy, yea the Only-Begotten Son of God, when he sees Him nailed to the Cross and enduring so lovingly for him sufferings so manifold and so great? Who would not groan out commiseration, and melt into tears? Truly says S. Bonaventure in his 'goad of Divine love:' 'What can be more fruitful, what sweeter than, with the whole heart, to suffer with that most bitter suffering of our Lord Jesus Christ?'"

11. *As the mourning of Hadadrimmon in the valley of Megiddo.* This was the greatest sorrow, which had fallen on Judah. Josiah was the last hope of its declining kingdom. His sons probably shewed already their unlikeness to their father, whereby they precipitated their country's fall. In Josiah's death the last gleam of the sunset of Judah faded into night. Of him it is recorded, that *his pious acts, according to what was written in the law of the Lord,* were written in his country's history[1]; for him the prophet *Jeremiah wrote a dirge*[2]; *all* the minstrels of his country *spake of him in their dirges*[2]. The dirges were *made an ordinance* which survived the captivity; *to this day*[2], it is said at the close of the Chronicles. Among the gathering sorrows of Israel, this lament over Josiah was written in the national collection of *dirges*[2]. *Hadadrimmon,* as being compounded of the name of two Syrian idols, is, in its name, a witness how Syrian idolatry penetrated into the kingdom, when it was detached from the worship of God. It was "[3] a city near Jezreel, now called Maximinianopolis in the plain of Megiddon, in which the

righteous king Josiah was wounded by Pharaoh Necho." This "[4] was 17 miles from Cæsarea, 10 from Esdraelon." Its name still survives in a small village, south of Megiddon[5], and so, on the way back to Jerusalem.

12-14. This sorrow should be universal but also individual, the whole land, and that, family by family; the royal family in the direct line of its kings, and in a branch from Nathan, a son of David and whole brother of Solomon[6], which was continued on in private life, yet was still to be an ancestral line of Jesus[7]: in like way the main priestly family from Levi, and a subordinate line from a grandson of Levi, *the family of Shimei*[8]; and all the remaining families, each with their separate sorrow, each according to Joel's call, [9] *let the bridegroom go forth of his chamber and the bride out of her closet,* each denying himself the tenderest solaces of life.

"[10] The ungrateful and ungodly, daily, as far as in them lies, crucify Christ, as S. Paul says, [11] *crucifying to themselves the Son of God afresh and putting Him to an open shame.* And on these Christ, out of His boundless pity, poureth forth a spirit of grace and supplication, so that, touched with compunction, with grieving and tearful feeling, they look on Christ, suffering with His suffering, and bewailing their own impurities."

"[12] The likeness is in the sorrow, not in its degree. Josiah had restored religion, removed a dire superstition, bound up relaxed morals by healthful discipline, recalled to its former condition the sinking state. In their extremest needs light shone on them, when there came his unlooked-for death, Therewith the whole state seemed lost. So in the Death of Christ, they who loved Him, saw His Divine works, placed their whole hope

[1] 2 Chr. xxxv. 26, 7.   [2] Ib. 25.   [3] S. Jer.
[4] Itin. Hieros. in Reland p. 891.
[5] "About ¾ of an hour to the S. of Megiddo lies a small village called Rumûni." Van de Velde Travels i. 355.
[6] 1 Chr. iii. 5.   [7] S. Luke iii. 31.

[8] Nu. iii. 21. Had the allusion been to the tribe of Simeon, as supplying, the teachers of Israel, as S. Jerome thought, it had been, not שִׁמְעִי, but שִׁמְעֹנִי as in Nu. xxv. 14, Jos. xxi. 4. 1 Chr. xxvii. 15.
[9] Jo. ii. 16.   [10] Dion.   [11] Heb. vi. 6   [12] Osor.

Before
C H R I S T
cir. 487.

CHAPTER XIII.

1 *The fountain of purgation for Jerusalem, 2 from idolatry, and false prophecy. 7 The death of Christ, and the trial of a third part.*

ᵃch. 12. 3.
ᵇ Heb. 9. 14.
1 Pet. 1. 19.
Rev. i. 5.

IN ᵃ that day there shall be ᵇ a fountain opened to the house of David and to the inhabitants of Jerusalem for sin and for † uncleanness.

2 ¶ And it shall come to pass in that day, saith the LORD of hosts, *that I* will ᶜ cut off the names of the idols out of the land, and they shall no more be

Before
C H R I S T
cir. 487.

† Heb. *separation for uncleanness.*

ᶜ Ex. 23. 13.
Josh. 23. 7.
Ps. 16. 4.
Ezek. 30. 13.
Hos. 2. 17.
Mic. 5. 12, 13.

of salvation in His goodness, suddenly saw the stay of their life extinct, themselves deprived of that most sweet intercourse, all hope for the future cut off. But the grief in the death of Christ was the more bitter, as He awoke a greater longing for Himself, and had brought a firmer hope of salvation."

XIII. 1. *In that day there shall be a fountain opened.* Zechariah often repeats, *in that day*[1], resuming his subject again and again, as a time not proximate, but fixed and known of God, of which he declared somewhat. It is *that day* which [2] *Abraham desired to see, and saw it,* whether by direct revelation, or in the typical sacrifice of Isaac, *and was glad:* it was [3] *that day* which *many prophets and kings and righteous men desired to see,* and in patience waited for it: *the* one *day of salvation* of the Gospel. He had spoken of repentance, in contemplation of Christ crucified; he now speaks of forgiveness and cleansing, of sanctification and consequent obedience. The *fountain shall be* not simply *opened,* but shall remain open[4]. Isaiah had already prophesied of the refreshment of the Gospel. [5] *When the poor and needy seek water and there is none,* and *their tongue faileth for thirst, I, the Lord, will hear them, I, the God of Israel, will not forsake them. I will open rivers in high places and fountains in the midst of the valleys;* here it is added, *for sin and for uncleanness.* There were *divers*[6] symbolical *washings* under the law; the Levites were [7] *sprinkled with the water of purifying,* lit. *the water of taking away of sin: living waters*[8], put to the ashes of an

heifer, were appointed as a [9] *water for* (removing) *defilements; a cleansing of sin*[10]. Now, there should be one ever-open fountain for all *the house of David.* "[11] Who that fountain is, the Lord Himself teacheth through Jeremiah, [12] *they have forsaken Me, the fountain of living waters;* and in the Gospel He says, [13] *If any man thirst, let him come unto Me and drink;* and [14] *The water which I shall give him, is a fountain of living water, gushing up to everlasting life.* This was *open to the house of David;* for of that kindred He took human nature. It was opened also *for the dwellers of Jerusalem,* for the sprinkling of holy Baptism, through which we have received remission of sins." "[15] That, receiving Divine and holy Baptism, we are sprinkled with the Blood of Christ to the remission of sins, who can doubt?" "[16] Of this fountain much was foretold by Ezekiel[17], that a fountain should issue forth from the temple of the Lord, and *go down into the desert,* and *every soul, to whom it shall come, shall live;* and Joel, [18] *A fountain shall come forth of the house of the Lord, and water the valley of Shittim.* Of this fountain Peter said to the Jews, when pricked in the heart and seeking forgiveness, [19] *Let every one of you be baptized in the Name of Jesus Christ for the remission of sins.*"

2. *I will cut off the names of the idols.* This had been a fence against idolatry. To name evil is a temptation to evil. Wrong words are the parents of wrong acts. To speak of evil awakens curiosity or passion; curiosity is one of the strongest incentives to act. All

[1] xii. 3, 4, 6, 8, 9, 11, xiii. 1, 2, 4, xiv. 6, 8, 13, 20.
[2] S. John viii. 56.
[3] S. Matt. xiii. 17, S. Luke x. 24.
[4] The force of יִהְיֶה נִפְתָּח.   [5] Is. xli. 17, 18.
[6] Heb. ix. 10.   [7] מֵי הַטָּאת Num. viii. 7.
[8] Ib. xix. 17.
[9] מֵי נִדָּה Ib. xix. 9, 13, 20, 21 bis xxxi. 23.
[10] הַטָּאת Ib. xix. 9.   [11] Theod.
[12] Jer. ii. 13. The word is the same, מָקוֹר, and
Ib. xvii. 13. מָקוֹר is, etymologically, a place "dug;"
but a "mere well" could not be "a fountain of living water." They dug to obtain anyhow a larger supply of water. Is. xxxvii. 25; Isaac's servants by digging obtained "a well of living" i.e. flowing "water" Gen. xxvi. 19. It is parallel with מַעְיָן Hos. xiii. 15., where cistern or reservoir would

be unmeaning. Metaphorically, *fountain of living waters* Jer. xxii. 13. *fountain of life* Ps. xxxvi. 10. Pr. x. 11. xiii. 14. xiv. 27. xvi. 22. *of wisdom* Ib. xviii. 4. *of tears* Jer. viii. 23. *of blood* Lev. xii. 7. xx. 18. *of Israel* Ps. lxviii. 17, are like one fountain which supplies a stream, rather than a reservoir, and מַיִם חַיִּים is of running water, Gen. l. c. Lev. xiv. 5, 6, 50-52. xv. 13. Num. xix. 17. Cant. ix. 15. Zech. xiv. 8. מְקוֹר מָשְׁחָת Pr. xxv. 28. is rather "a fountain corrupted," spoiled from without, than stagnant water in a reservoir, where the spoiling is from itself. In Jer. li. 36. מָקוֹר (sing.) stands collectively for the whole supply of water. Tanchum has מנבע מא.   [13] S. John vii. 37.   [14] Ib. iv. 14.
[15] S. Cyr.   [16] Dion.   [17] Ezek. xlvii. 1, 8, 9.
[18] Jo. iii. 18. See vol. 1. pp. 212, 213.
[19] Acts ii. 37, 38.

Before CHRIST cir. 487.

remembered: and a l s o I will cause [d] the prophets and the unclean spirit to pass out of the land.

[4] 2 Pet. 2. 1.

3 And it shall come to pass, *that* when any shall yet prophesy, then his father and his mother that

begat him shall say unto him, Thou shalt not live; for thou speakest lies in the name of the LORD: and his father and his mother that begat him [e] shall thrust him through when he prophesieth.

Before CHRIST cir. 487.

[e] Deut. 13. 6.
8. & 18. 20.

---

public mention of terrible crimes (it has been observed) produces imitation of the specific form of crime. Hence it was commanded, [1] *make no mention of the name of other gods, neither let it be heard out of thy mouth.* And Joshua names it in his dying charge to Israel, [2] *Be ye therefore very strong to keep and to do all that is written in the book of the law of Moses—neither make mention of the name of their gods, nor cause to swear* by them. Hence they changed the names of cities [3], which bare idol names. David speaks of it, as part of fealty to God. [4] *I will not take their names upon my lips.* Hosea prophesies of the times of the new covenant; [5] *I will take away the names of Baalim out of her mouth, and they shall be no more remembered by their name.* Isaiah, [6] *The idols he shall utterly abolish.* Zechariah foretells their abolition with a turn of words, formed apparently on those of Hosea [7]; but slightly varied, because the worship of Baal, such a plague-spot in the time of Hosea, one, which continued until the year before the captivity [8], was gone. He implies nothing as to his own times, whether idolatry still existed. He predicts its entire abolition in the whole compass of the enlarged Judah, i. e. of Christendom.

And also I will cause the prophets and the unclean spirit to pass out of the land. False prophecy sets itself to meet a craving of human nature to know something of its future. False prophets there were, even in the time of Nehemiah [9], and those in some number, hired to prophesy against the word of God. Our Lord warns against them. [10] *Beware of false prophets, which come to you in sheep's clothing, but inwardly they are ravening wolves.* [11] *Many false prophets shall arise and shall deceive many. Many false prophets,* S. John says, [12] *are gone out into the world.* False prophets at-

tended the decline of Judaism. Such was the author of the Jewish Sibylline book, prophesying the destruction of the Romans [13], and fixing the mind of his people on temporal aggrandizement [14]: false prophets were suborned by the Jewish "tyrants" and encouraged the Jews in the resistance which ruined the devoted city [15]: false prophets have arisen in Christianity; but, like the Phrygian women who led Tertullian astray, they "went out," were cast out "from it, as not being of it." "[16] After that the Only-Begotten Word of God appeared to us, the dull and childish toys of idolatry perished and were utterly destroyed, and with it were taken away the strange and impious devices of the false prophets, who were full of the evil, unclean spirit, and could be readily detected as laboring under a kindred disease to the idolaters. For both had one president of impiety, Satan." Not 50 years after the Crucifixion, a heathen [17] wrote his work, "on the failure of oracles." The outpouring of the Holy [18] *Spirit of grace and supplication,* should sweep away [19] *the unclean spirit,* (Zechariah alone anticipates the language of the New Testament [19]) which became [20] *a lying spirit in the mouth of the prophets* of those who sought to them.

3. *His father and mother that begat him* [21] *shall say unto him, Thou shalt not live.* The prophet describes the zeal against false prophecy, with reference to the law against those who seduced to apostasy from God. [22] The nearest relations were themselves to denounce any who had secretly tried to seduce them, and themselves, as the accusers, to cast the first stone at them. "[16] Such shall in those times be the reverence to God-wards, so careful shall they be of perfect probity and laudable life, that parents themselves shall be stimu-

---

[1] Ex. xxiii. 13.　　　[2] Jos. xxiii. 6, 7.
[3] Nebo and Baalmeon, Num. xxxii. 38.
[4] Ps. xvi. 4.　　[5] Hos. ii. 17.　　[6] Is. ii. 18.
[7] Hos. ii. 19. Heb. "*I will* remove the *names* of Baalim *out of* his mouth; *and they shall be no more remembered,* עוֹד יִזָּכְרוּ וְלֹא, by their names " Zech. *I will* cut off *the names* of the idols *from* the land, *and they shall be no more remembered,* עוֹד יִזָּכְרוּ וְלֹא.
[8] Jer. xxxii. 19. The prophecy was in the tenth year of Zedekiah, ver. 1. So far then from its implying a date before the captivity (Speaker's Comm.

p. 735.), there could have been no ground for the change *then.*
[9] See Introd. p. 330.　　[10] S. Matt. vii. 15.
[11] Ib. xxiv. 11.　　[12] 1 S. John iv. 1.
[13] See Pusey's "Daniel the Prophet" p. 162.
[14] Ib. pp. 364–368　　[15] Jos. B. J. vi. 5. 2.
[16] S. Cyr.　[17] Plutarch A. D. 80.　[18] Zech. xii. 10.
[19] הַטֻּמְאָה רוּחַ here only in the O. T.; πνεῦμα ἀκάθαρτον, in our Lord's words, S. Matt. xii. 43. S. Mark v. 8. S. Luke viii. 29, xi. 24. add Rev. xviii. 2, xvi. 13.
[20] 1 Kgs xxii. 21–23.　[21] לֵידְין.　[22] De xiii. 6–10.

Before
C H R I S T
cir. 487.

*Mic. 3. 6, 7.

§2 Kin. 1. 8.
Isai. 20. 2.
Matt. 3. 4.
† Heb. *a garment* § of hair.
† Heb. *to lie.*

4 And it shall come to pass in that day, *that* ᶠ the prophets shall be ashamed every one of his vision, when he hath prophesied; neither shall they w e a r § † a rough garment † to deceive:

5 ʰ But he shall say, I am no prophet, I *am* an husbandman; f o r m a n ʰ taught me to keep cattle from my youth.

6 And *one* shall say unto him, What *are* t h e s e wounds in thine h a n d s?

Before
C H R I S T
cir. 487.

ʰ Amos 7. 14.

lated against their children, if they should speak falsely anything from their own heart, as though God spake by them—How true that word is, and how accredited the prophecy! This indicates clearly a great advance toward godliness, God transforming things for the better. What aforetime was held in great esteem, is now hated and accursed and held intolerable."

4. *The prophets shall be ashamed, every one of them.* They who before their conversion, gave themselves to such deceits, shall be ashamed of their deeds; as, after the defeat of the seven sons of the chief priest Sceva, ¹ *fear fell on them all, and the name of the Lord Jesus was magnified, and many that believed came and confessed and shewed their deeds: many of them also which used curious arts brought their books together and burned them before all, and they counted the price of them, and found it fifty thousand pieces of silver.* So mightily, S. Luke subjoins, *grew the word of God and prevailed.*

Neither shall wear a rough garment to deceive, feigning themselves ascetics and mourners for their people, as the true prophets were in truth. The sackcloth, which the prophets wore ², was a rough garment of hair ³, worn next to the skin ⁴, whence Elijah was known to Ahaziah, when described as ⁵ *a hairy man,*

and girt with a girdle of leather about his loins. It was a wide garment, enveloping the whole frame ⁶, and so, afflictive to the whole body. " ⁷ This was the habit of the prophets, that when they called the people to penitence, they were clothed with sackcloth."

5. *And he shall say,* repudiating his former claims, *I am a husbandman* ⁸: for *a man hath taught* ⁹ *me from my youth.* There was no room then for his having been a false prophet, since he had had from his youth one simple unlettered occupation, as Amos said truly of himself; ¹⁰ *I was no prophet, neither was I a prophet's son: but I was an herdsman and a gatherer of sycamore fruit.* The prophet does not approve the lie, any more than our Lord did the injustice of *the unjust steward.* Our Lord contrasted the wisdom *in their generation* of a bad man for his ends, with the unwisdom of *the children of light,* who took no pains to secure their God. Zechariah pictures vividly, how men would anyhow rid themselves of all suspicion of false-prophesying.

6. *And one shall say unto him, What* are *those wounds in thy hands?* The words are simple; the meaning different ¹¹, according as they are united with what immediately precedes, or the main subject, Him Whom

¹ Acts xix. 13-20.   ² Is. xx. 2.
³ Ib. xxii. 12, Jer. iv. 8, vi. 26.
⁴ 1 Kgs xxi. 27, 2 Kgs vi. 30, Job xvi. 15.
⁵ 2 Kgs i. 8.
⁶ אַדֶּרֶת שֵׂעָר occurs Gen. xxv. 25, as describing the whole appearance of the new-born Esau; אַדֶּרֶת alone, of Elijah's mantle, 1 Kgs xix. 13, 19, 2 Kgs ii. 8, 13, 14; of the robes of the king of Nineveh Jon. iii. 6. אַדֶּרֶת שִׁנְעָר is the large Babylonian garment which incited Achan's covetousness. Jos. vii. 21-24. [all]   ⁷ S. Jer.

⁸ The phrase עֹבֵד אֲדָמָה is from Gen. iv. 2.

⁹ הִקְנַנִי, occurring in this place only, is uncertain. Against the modern rendering " sold " (which would be the obvious causative of קנה), or

" bought " (taking *Hifil* as *Kal*) it seems decisive, that this would be contrary to the Levitical law. For since, if bought or sold as a slave, he would have been set free in the 7th year, he would not have been sold or bought from his youth. הקנה might equally be, " made me to possess," as " made another to possess me." In either case it governs a double accusative, of which one only is expressed.

Kim. " made me a shepherd and husbandman: Rashi, quoting Menahem, " set me to keep his flocks," Ibn Ezra, " made me to possess ground i. e. made me a husbandman." Tanchum " tilled his land, which his father put him in possession of by inheritance." Hunt. 206. translates הִקְנַנִי by אֶשְׁתִּרְאָנֵי " bought me."
¹⁰ Am. vii. 14.
¹¹ A prevalent modern explanation has been of the self-inflicted wounds of the prophets of Baal. But 1) the idolatrous incisions have a technical name, יִתְגֹּרָר " cut himself;" De. xiv. 1, 1 Kgs xviii. 28, Jer. xvi. 16, xli. 5, xlvii. 5. גְּדֻדִים Jer. xlviii. 37. 2) מַכָּה, מַכּוֹת, מַכִּים, are used of fresh unhealed wounds themselves, not of the scars. Pr. xx. 30, 1 Kgs xxii. 35, 2 Kgs viii. 29, ix. 15, Is. i. 6, xxx. 26, Mi. i. 9, Nah iii. 19, Jer. vi. 7, x. 19, xv. 18, xxx. 12, 17. 3) Self-infliction was characteristic of the idolatrous cuttings. They were probably to appease the displeased god or goddess. The only support of it, that מַאֲהֲבִים is used of idolatrous, and so adulterous, objects of love, is neutralized by the fact that the metaphor of male and female is never dropped. Of 14 times in which it occurs, 11 times, in Hosea, Jeremiah, Ezekiel, it is united with the fem. pronoun, מְאַהֲבֶיהָ, מְאַהֲבַיִךְ; 3 times in the first pers. of the city personified.

Before CHRIST cir. 487.	Then he shall answer, *Those* with which I was wounded *in* the house of my friends. 7 ¶ Awake, O sword,	against [l] my shepherd, and against the man [k] *that is* my fellow, saith the LORD of hosts : [l] smite the shepherd,	Before CHRIST cir. 487. [i] Isai. 40. 11. Ezek. 34. 23. [k] John 10. 30. & 14. 10, 11.

[l] Matt. 26. 31. Mark 14. 27.　　Phil. 2. 6.

they pierced, for Whom they were to mourn, and, on their mourning, to be cleansed, and of Whom it is said in the next verse, *Awake, O sword, against My Shepherd.* S. Jerome and others [l] explain it of the punishment inflicted by parents. "These wounds and bruises I received, condemned by the judgment of my parents, and of those who did not hate but loved me. And so will truth prevail dissipating falsehood, that he too, who was punished for his own fault, will own that he suffered rightly." But wounds of chastisement are not inflicted on the hands, and the punishment of false prophecy was not such wounds [2], but death. Wounds in the hands were no punishment, which parents would inflict. They were the special punishment of the cross [3], after sustaining which, One only lived. The most literal interpretation, then, of the wounds in the hands harmonizes with the piercing before, and the smiting of the Good Shepherd which follows, of Whom David too prophesie l, [4] *They pierced My Hands and My Feet.* "[5] What are those wounds of Thy hands? How long, think you, and how and by whom will this be said to Him? For ever and ever, unceasingly, and with unspeakable admiration it will be said, both by God the Father, [6] *to Whom He was obedient unto death, the death of the Cross:* it will be said also both by the holy [l] *angels* who *desire to look into* Him, and by men whom He has redeemed. O great miracle, wonderful spectacle, especially in the Lord of all, to bear wounds in the midst of His Hands! And He shall say ; *With these I was wounded in the house of those who loved Me.* O great sacrilege, sacrilegious homicide, that such wounds were inflicted in the house of those who loved. He will not say, '.with these I was wounded by those who loved Me,' but ' in the house of those who loved Me.' For they who inflicted them, loved Him not. But they were the house of Abraham and Isaac and Jacob and David, and the rest like them, who loved Me, and expected Me,

Who was promised to them. Yet so to speak is not to answer the question, *what are these wounds?* For it is one thing to ask, what are these wounds, another to say, where they were inflicted. Having said, that they were inflicted in the house of those who loved Me, He says, what they are, *the Cup which My Father hath given Me to drink.* For what He subjoins, is the Voice of the Father giving the Cup. *Sword, awake &c.* is as though he said, Ask ye, What are these wounds? I say, ' the tokens of obedience, the signs of the Father's will and command. The Lord of hosts, God the Father *hath not spared* Me, *His own Son, but hath given* Me *for* you *all.* And He said, *Awake, o sword, against My Shepherd, and against the Man cohering to Me,* which is as much as, 'O Death, have thou power over My Son, My good Shepherd, the Man Who cohereth to Me, i. e. Who is joined in unity of Person with the Word Who is consubstantial with Me!' And then, as though the sword asked, how or how far shall I arise against this Thy Shepherd, he subjoins, *Smite the shepherd, and the sheep shall be scattered.* Hence the Shepherd Himself, when about to be smitten, spake, [8] *All ye shall be offended because of Me this night. For it is written, I will smite the Shepherd and the sheep shall be scattered.* So then to those who say, *what are those wounds in the midst of Thy hands ?* is appositely subjoined the Voice of the Father, saying, *Awake, O sword, against My Shepherd &c.* in the meaning, 'They are monuments of the Father's love, the tokens of My Obedience, because He *spared not His own Son,* and I *became obedient* to Him for you all, *even unto death, and that, the death of the Cross.'* "

7. *Awake, O sword.* So Jeremiah apostrophises the sword, [9] *O thou sword of the Lord, when wilt thou be quiet ?* The prophets express what *will be,* by a command that it should be ; [10] *Make the heart of this people heavy.* But by this command he signifies that human malice, acting freely, could do

---

[l] So S. Cyr. also; but S. Cyril was misled by the rendering of the LXX, συμποδιοῦσιν, whereas Aq. Symm. Theod. have ἐκκεντήσουσιν.

[2] Hence Kim. explains it of the binding him hand and foot to keep him at home; Rashi of scourging the back, which would be the very opposite of בין ידים, and would not be visible. Ibn Ezra makes it refer to ומקרוה ver. 3. Tanchum explains " when one asks as to the marks of beating which are on his body," and, paraphrasing

בין ידיך, explains "in front of thee." The Arab. version [Hunt. 206] has simply בין ידאך.

[3] S. Jerome makes the question answered in the words, "They are the wounds &c." inconsistently, " Why hangest thou on the Cross ? why are thy hands transfixed by nails? What hast thou done, to be subjected to this punishment and torture ? "
[4] Ps. xxii. 16.　[5] Rup.　[6] Phil. ii. 8.
[7] 1 S. Pet. i. 12.
[8] S. Matt. xxvi. 31.　[9] Jer. xlvii. 6.　[10] Is. vi. 10.

Before CHRIST cir. 487.	and the sheep shall be scattered: and I will turn	mine hand upon [m] the little ones.	Before CHRIST cir. 487.

[m] Matt. 18. 10, 14. Luke 12. 32.

no more than [1] His *Hand and* His *counsel determined before to be done.* The envy and hatred of Satan, the blind fury of the Chief priests, the contempt of Herod, the guilty cowardice of Pilate, freely accomplished that Death, which God had before decreed for the salvation of the world. The meaning then is, " [2] the *sword shall be aroused against* My Shepherd, i. e. I will allow Him to be smitten by the Jews. But by *the sword* he designates death, persecution, wounding &c. as above, the [3] *sword upon his right arm,* and, where the Passion of Christ is spoken of, [4] *Deliver my soul from the sword.* So also, [5] *All the sinners of the people shall die by the sword,*" [6] which cannot be taken literally; for many sinners perish by shipwreck, poison, drowning, fire." Amos then " [5] so spake, because many died by war, yet not all by the sword, but others by pestilence and famine, all which he includes under *the sword.* This smiting began, when the Lord was taken, and His sheep began to be scattered; but the prophecy which, before, was being gradually fulfilled, was fully fulfilled in His Death, and the Apostles were dispersed till the day of the Resurrection at eventide."

Against the Man, My Fellow [7], i. e. One united by community of nature. A little before, God had spoken of Himself as priced at *the thirty pieces of silver,* yet as breaking the covenant which He had made with all nations for His people; as *pierced through,* yet as *pouring the spirit of grace and supplication* on those who pierced Him, that they should mourn their deed, and, thereon, ever cleansing them from sin. As Man, God was sold, was pierced. " [8] God, in flesh, not working with aught intervening as in the prophets, but having taken to Him a Manhood connatural [9] with Himself and made one, and through His flesh akin to us, drawing up to Him all humanity. What was the manner of the Godhead in flesh ? As fire in iron, not transitively but by communication. For the fire does not dart into the iron, but remains there and communi-

cates to it of its own virtue, not impaired by the communication, yet filling wholly its recipient." The bold language of the Fathers only expressed the actuality of the Incarnation. Since the Manhood was taken into God, and in Him dwelt all the fullness of the Godhead bodily, and God and Man were one Christ, then was it all true language. His Body was " [10] the Body of God;" His flesh " [11] the flesh of the Word ;" and it was lawful to speak of " [12] the flesh of the Deity," of " [13] the Passion of the Word," " [14] the Passion of Christ, my God," " [15] the Passion of God," " [16] God dead and buried," " [17] God suffered," " [18] murderers of God," " [19] the Godhead dwelt in the flesh bodily, which is all one with saying that, being God, He had a proper body, and using this as an instrument, He became Man for our sakes, and, because of this, things proper to the flesh are said to be His, since He was in it, as hunger, thirst, suffering, fatigue and the like, of which the flesh is capable, while the works proper to the Word Himself, as raising the dead and restoring the blind, He did through His own Body," is but a continuance of the language of Zechariah, since He Who was sold, was priced, was Almighty God. Jesus being God and Man, the sufferings of His Humanity were the sufferings of God, although, as God, He could not suffer. Now, conversely, God speaks of the Shepherd Who was slain, as *My Fellow,* united in Nature with Himself, although not the Manhood of Jesus which suffered, but the Godhead, united with It in one Person, was Consubstantial with Himself. The name might perhaps be most nearly represented by " connatural." " [20] When then the title is employed of the relation of an individual to God, it is clear that that individual can be no mere man, but must be one, united with God by unity of Being. The Akin of the Lord is no other than He Who said in the Gospel [21] *I and My Father are One,* and Who is designated as [22] *the Only-Begotten Son, Who is in the Bosom of the Father.* The word,

---

[1] Acts iv. 28. [2] Rib. [3] ch. xi. 17.
[4] Ps. xxii. 20. [5] Am. ix. 10. [6] S. Jer.
[7] The word עֲמִית, in form, abstract, is always personal. It stands alone in the dialects, having probably been framed by Moses, to express more than "neighbor," "our common nature," as we speak. It occurs 11 times in Leviticus (v. 21 bis, [vi. 2 Eng.] xviii. 20, xix. 11, 15, 17, xxiv. 19, xxv. 14 (bis) 15, 17.) always with the pronominal affix, "thy" or "his;" and always in enjoining things or forbidding things by virtue of our common humanity. Though feminine in form, it is always masc. in fact, as in, "the wife of" עֲמִיתֶךָ Lev. xviii. 20, and עֲלִיו, Ib. xix. 17. The word, being revived out of

the Pentateuch by Zechariah, received no modification in the Hebrew of the intermediate period.
[8] Hom. in Sanct. Christi gener. App. S. Basil. Opp. ii. 596 quoted in Newman on S. Ath. ag. Arian. p. 444. note k. Oxf. Tr.
[9] " συμφυῆ ἡ i. e. joined on to His Nature." Ib.
[10] S. Ath. ag. Arians iii. 9. p. 444. Oxf. Tr.
[11] Ib. n. 34 p. 449. [12] S. Leo, Serm. 65. fin.
[13] Tert. de carn. Christi, 5. [14] S. Ignat. Rom. 6.
[15] Tert. l. c. Ib. [16] Vigil. c. Eut. ii. p. 502.
[17] S. Melito in Anast. Hodeg. 12.
[18] Tert. l. c. all quoted on S. Ath. l. c. note i.
[19] S. Ath. ag. Ar. iii. n. 31 p. 443 O. T. See more ibid. [20] Hengst. Christ. iii. 530 ed. 2.
[21] S. John x. 30. [22] Ib. i. 18.

Before
C H R I S T
cir. 487.

8 And it shall come to pass *that* in all the land, saith the LORD, two parts

therein shall be cut off *and* die ; [n] but the third shall be left therein.

Before
C H R I S T
cir. 487.

[n] Rom. 11. 5.

it seems, was especially chosen, as being used in the Pentateuch, only in the laws against injuring a fellow-man. The prophet thereby gives prominence to the seeming contradiction between the command of the Lord, *Awake, O sword, against My Shepherd,* and those of His own law, whereby no one is to injure his fellow. He thus points out the greatness of that end, for the sake of which the Lord regards not that relation, Whose image among men He commanded to be kept holy. He speaks after the manner of men. He calls attention to the greatness of that sacrifice, whereby He [1] *spared not His own Son, but freely gave Him up for us all.* The word ' *Man* ' forms a sort of contrast with *My Fellow.* He Whom the sword is to reach must unite the Human Nature with the Divine." Jews too have seen that the words, *My Fellow,* imply an equality with God ; only since they own not Him, Who was God and Man, they must interpret it of a false claim on the part of man[2], overlooking that it is given Him by God.

And I will turn My hand [3] *upon the little ones,* doing to them as He had done to the Shepherd. So our Lord forewarned them : [4] *If they have persecuted Me they will also persecute you:* [5] *If the world hate you, ye know that it hated Me, before it hated you:* [6] *Ye shall be hated of all men for My name's sake:* [7] *they will deliver you up to the councils and scourge you in the synagogues; and ye shall be brought before governors and kings for My name's sake:* [8] *they shall deliver you up to be afflicted, and shall kill*

you: and ye shall be hated of all men for My name's sake; and to the Scribes and Pharisees, [9] *I send unto you prophets and wise men and scribes, and some of them ye shall kill and crucify, and some of them shall ye scourge in your synagogues and persecute them from city to city, that upon you may come all the righteous blood shed upon the earth.*

The little ones [10], as Jeremiah speaks of [11] *the least of the flock,* and the Lord said, [12] *fear not, little flock,* little and weak in itself, but mighty in Him and in His grace. Three centuries of persecution, alike in the Roman empire and beyond it in Persia, fulfilled the prophet's words and deepened the foundation of the Church and cemented its fabric.

8. *In all the land, two parts therein shall be cut off and die.* " In all the land of Israel," says a Jewish interpreter [13] ;—the land, in which the Good Shepherd had been slain and the sheep scattered, *that upon you,* our Lord had said, *may come all the righteous blood.* As David punished Moab, [14] *with two lines measured he to put to death, and with one full line to keep alive ;* and Ezekiel prophesied, [15] *A third part of thee shall die with the pestilence, and with famine shall they be consumed in the midst of thee : and a third part shall fall by the sword round about thee ;* so now, the greater part should be destroyed, but a remnant should be saved. *But the third part shall be left therein.* Even so then at this present time also, S. Paul says[16], *there is a remnant according to the election of grace.* " [17] The third part only shall be saved from the common de-

---

[1] Rom. viii. 32.

[2] Ibn Ezra interprets it in this sense, " He prophesieth again many wars, which shall be in all the earth, at the death of Messiah ben Joseph, and the meaning of My Shepherd, is every king of the nations, whom God made to rule over the earth; and he estimates of himself that he is as God ; therefore (he saith) and against the man my fellow." Kimchi adopting the interpretation, adds " i. e. who thinks himself my fellow." R. Isaac (Chizzuk Emunah, Wagenseil Tela Ignea Satanæ p. 310) interprets the whole of the king of Ishmael, called also the king of Turkey, and ruling over Asia and Africa, under whose hand the majority of the people of Israel are in captivity. God calls him my shepherd, because He has given His people into his hand to feed them in their captivity. He calls him 'the man my fellow and companion,' because in the pride and greatness of his heart he accounteth himself like God, like that, Behold man is become like one of us (Gen. iii.)." Abarbanel gives, as the one of three interpretations which he prefers, a modification of R. Isaac's, explaining the words " my shepherd " of Mohammed, and directing his interpretation of " the man, my fellow " against our Lord. " The words, ' the man my fellow' are spoken of Jesus the Nazarene, for according to the sentiment of the children of Edom and their faith, he was the Son of God, and of the same substance, and therefore he is called according to

their words, ' The man, my fellow." Rashi alone has " My shepherd, whom I set over the sheep of my captivity, and the man my fellow whom I associated with myself, to keep my sheep, even as I did;" but " I smite the shepherd," he explains " the wicked king of Moab," or " king of the border of wickedness " [i. e. Edom] or in one MS. " the wicked Roman king, who shepherdeth my flock." *R. Tanchum* has, " that they think in themselves on account of my setting them over the creation that they are my administrators in the kingdom and government." The Heb. Ar. [Hunt. 206] " against the man, my companion " (עלי אלרגל כאחבי).

[3] Such is the force of השיב על Am. i. 9, turning the hand against Ekron or against the other cities of Philistia; in Is. i. 25, upon Judah, and thoroughly cleansing her by affliction ; Ezek. xxxviii. 12, of Gog against the restored Israel; Ps. lxxxi. 15 of God's turning upon its adversaries, His Hand which was now upon her [all]. It were in itself improbable that men alone should be in a good sense, as Ges.   [4] S. John xv. 20.   [5] Ib. 18.

[6] S. Matt. x. 22, S. Luke xxi. 17.
[7] S. Matt. x. 17, 18; add S. Luke xxi. 12.
[8] S. Matt. xxiv. 9.   [9] Ib. xxiii. 34, 35.

[10] הצערים äπ.   [11] Jer. xlix. 20 הצאן צעירי

[12] S. Luke xii. 32.   [13] Kim.   [14] 2 Sam. viii. 2.

[15] Ezek. v. 12.   [16] Rom. xi. 5.   [17] Osor.

Before CHRIST cir. 487.

9 And I will bring the third part [o] through the fire, and will [p] refine them as silver is refined, and will try them as gold is tried: [q] they shall call on my name, and I will hear them: [r] I will say, It *is* my people: and they shall say, The LORD *is* my God.

[o] Isai. 48. 10.
[p] 1 Pet. i. 6, 7.
[q] Ps. 50. 15. & 91. 15. ch. 10. 6.
[r] Ps. 144. 15. Jer. 30. 22. Ezek. 11. 20. Hos. 2. 23. ch. 8. 8.

CHAPTER XIV.

1 *The destroyers of Jerusalem destroyed.* 4 *The coming of Christ, and the graces of his kingdom.* 12 *The plague of Jerusalem's enemies.* 16 *The remnant shall turn to the Lord,* 20 *and their spoils shall be holy.*

Before CHRIST cir. 487.

BEHOLD, [a] the day of the LORD cometh, and thy spoil shall be divided in the midst of thee.

[a] Isai. 13. 9. Joel 2. 31. Acts 2. 20.

struction; yet not so, that they should suppose that glory was to be obtained amid ease."

9. *I will bring the third part through the fire.* Such is always God's ways. [1] *Thou hast proved us, O God; Thou hast tried us, like as silver is tried. Thou broughtest us into the snare, Thou laidest trouble upon our loins: we went through fire and water, and Thou broughtest us out into a wealthy place.* [2] *I have refined thee, but not with silver, I have chosen thee in the furnace of affliction;* and, [3] *Through much tribulation we must enter into the kingdom of God.*

"[4] In adversity virtue is most tried, and it is shewn what advance a person has made; for *patience* hath *a perfect work* [5]; and it is called the touchstone of all other virtues, as is written; '[6] God tried His elect as gold in the furnace and received them as a burnt offering;' and, '[7] All the faithful who have pleased the Lord have passed through many tribulations.' And the angel Raphael saith to Tobias, '[8] Because thou wert accepted of God, need was that temptation should prove thee.'" "Adversities are granted to the elect of God, and therefore to be rejoiced in with the whole heart." "[9] Fire, crosses, racks were prepared; swords executioners torturers were put in action; new forms of suffering were invented, and yet Christian virtue remained moveless, unconquered: the fiercer the onslaught, the more glorious was the triumph." "[10] The more suffered, the more believed in Christ." "[9] Whose virtue they admired, these they imitated, and shared the suffering, that they might be partakers of the glory. This was that fire, whereby God willed that His own should be tried and purified, that, with Christ Whom they gave themselves to imitate, they might enjoy everlasting glory."

I will bless him and will say, It is My people, "[4] not only by creation as the rest, but by devotion and worship, by predestination and infusion of grace, by singular Providence, by mutual love; *and it shall say, The Lord is my God,* Whom Alone above all things, I long for, love, worship."

This promise is oftentimes renewed through the prophets, oftentimes fulfilled in Christ, whenever the Church is recalled from listlessness by fiery trials, and through them her children are restored to deeper devotedness and closer union with God.

XIV. "The Jews," S. Jerome says, "say that these things are to be fulfilled under Gog; others that they were accomplished in part, in the times of the Macedonians, Egyptians, and other nations. We, leaving the truth of the time to the judgment of the Lord, would explain what is written." Eusebius [11] points out that it cannot be said to have been fulfilled under Antiochus Epiphanes; "If any think that these things are, then let him consider again and again, whether he can refer the rest of the prophecy also to the times of Antiochus; as, that [12] *the feet of the Lord* stood *on the mount of Olives,* that [13] *the Lord in that day,* became *king over the whole earth;* and so, as to the rest of the prophecy." And although more was fulfilled in the last siege by the Romans, still those who would explain it solely of this, are obliged to mingle explanations partly literal, as that Jerusalem should be the earthly Jerusalem, which was destroyed, partly metaphorical, as to the mount of Olives, its division into two parts &c. It seems then probable that, like the kindred prophecy of Joel [14], it relates chiefly to the time of the end, and that as our Lord unites the destruction of Jerusalem with His Coming in the Day of Judgment, so here are united that first destruction with the last rebellion of man, in the times of Anti-Christ. Since then much or most may be yet future, it seems safer, as S. Jerome suggests, to explain the Prophet's symbolic language, leaving the times of the fulfillment to Him, in Whose hands they are.

1. *Behold the Day of the Lord cometh,* lit. *a day cometh, the Lord's,* in which He Himself

[1] Ps. lxvi. 9–11. [2] Is. xlviii. 10. [3] Acts xiv. 22. [4] Dion. [5] S. James i. 4. [6] Wisd. iii. 6. [7] Judith viii. 23. Vulg. [8] Tobit. xii. 13 Vulg. [9] Osor.

[10] S. Aug. in Ps. xc. Serm. i. n. 8. See more in Tert. Apol. c. ult. p. 105. note a. Oxf. Tr. [11] Dem. Evang. vi. 18. [12] ver. 4. [13] ver. 9. [14] Jo. ii. 30, iii. 18. See vol. 1. pp. 196–212.

› Joel 3. 2.

c Isai. 13. 16.

2 For **b** I will gather all
nations against Jerusalem
to battle ; and the city shall
be taken, and **c** the houses
rifled, and the women rav-
ished ; and half of the city
shall go forth into captiv-

ity, and the residue of the
people shall not be cut off
from the city.

3 Then shall the LORD
go forth, and fight against
those nations, as when he
fought in the day of battle.

---

shall be Judge, and no longer leave man to
fulfill his own will, and despise God's ; in
which His glory and holiness and the righteousness of all His ways shall be revealed.

And thy spoil shall be in the midst of thee.
"[1] How great will the strait be, that the
spoils should be divided in the midst of her.
It often happens that what, by a sudden
assault, is plundered in the city, is divided
in the field or in solitude, lest the enemy
should come upon them. But now there
will be such a heavy weight of ills, such will
be the security of conquest, that the spoils
shall be divided in the midst of the city."

2. *I will gather all nations against Jerusalem
to battle.* This is a feature which belongs to
the end. It had been dwelt upon by Joel[2] ;
Ezekiel spoke of the [3] *many nations* which
should come under Gog. S. John foretells
of an universal strife at the end, when [4] *The
spirits of devils, working miracles, go forth unto
the kings of the earth and of the whole world, to
gather them to the battle of that great day of God
Almighty ;* and [5] *Satan shall be loosed out of his
prison and shall go out to deceive the nations
which are in the four quarters of the earth, Gog
and Magog, to gather them together to battle, the
number of whom is as the sand of the sea. And
they went up on the breadth of the earth, and
compassed the camp of the saints round about,
and the beloved city.* Since no creature can do
aught but what God wills, and, in his
phrensy against God's people, is but His
instrument, [6] *to try them and to purge and to
make white to the time of the end ;* and the
strength of body or intellect, which is abused
against His law, He continuously in the
order of nature supplies, God may be said to
do what Satan does against Him. Satan, in
his blind fury, crowns martyrs, fills the
thrones of heaven, works, against his will,
the All-wise Will of God.

And the houses rifled, and the women &c.
The horrors of heathen war repeat themselves through men's ever-recurring passions.
What was foretold as to Babylon is repeated
in the same words as to the Church of God.
Seemingly *all things come alike to all :* [7] *there
is one event to the righteous and to the wicked ;*

*to the good and to the clean and to the unclean : to
him that sacrificeth and to him that sacrificeth
not : as is the good, so is the sinner.* The outward event is the same, the hidden part is
known to God Alone. *And the residue of the
people shall not be cut off from the city,* unlike
the lot of the earthly Jerusalem, in the destruction both by Nebuchadnezzar (which
was past) and the Romans[8]. At the first,
[9] *Nebuzaradan, the captain of the guard, carried
away the rest of the people left in the city, and
the fugitives that fell away to the king of Babylon, with the remnant of the multitude,* so that
Jeremiah mourned over it, [10] *Because of the
mountain of Zion which is desolate, foxes walk
[habitually] upon it.* The Romans "[11] effaced
the city." Now *a remnant is not cut off,*
because [12] *for the elect's sake those days shall be
shortened ;* for our Lord had said[13], that *the
gates of hell should not prevail against His
Church.*

3. *The Lord shall go forth and shall fight,*
"[14] is to be taken like that in Habakkuk,
[15] *Thou wentest forth for the salvation of Thy
people, for salvation with Thine Anointed,* and
in Micah, [16] *For behold, the Lord cometh forth
out of His place, and will come down and will
tread upon the high places of the earth, and the
mountains shall be molten under Him, and the
valleys shall be cleft ;* and Isaiah also, [17] *The
Lord shall go forth as a mighty man ; He shall
stir up jealousy like a man of war ; He shall
cry ; He shall prevail over His enemies.* "God
is said to *go forth,* when by some wondrous
deed He declares His Presence—His Deity
is, as it were, laid up, so long as He holds
Himself in, and does not by any token shew
His power. But He *goes forth,* and bursts
forth, when He exercises some judgment, and
worketh some new work, which striketh
terror." God then will *go forth out of His
place,* when He is constrained to break
through His quietness and gentleness and
clemency, for the amendment of sinners. He
Who elsewhere speaketh through the prophet, [18] *I, the Lord, change not,* and to Whom
it is said, [19] *Thou art the same,* and in the
Epistle of James, [20] *With Whom is no change,*
now *goeth forth* and fighteth *as in the day of*

[1] S. Jer.   [2] iii. 2–9, 11.   [3] Ezek. xxxviii. 6, 15, 22.
[4] Rev. xvi. 14.   [5] Ib. xx. 7, 8, 9.
[6] Dan. xi. 35. xii. 10.   [7] Eccl. ix. 2.
[8] See on Mic. iii. 12. pp. 46–50.   [9] 2 Kgs xxv. 11.

[10] Lam. v. 18.   [11] See on pp. 46, 47.
[12] S. Matt. xxiv. 32.   [13] Ib. xvi. 18.   [14] S. Jer.
[15] Hab. iii. 13.   [16] Mic. i. 3, 4.   [17] Is. xlii. 13.
[18] Mal. iii. 6.   [19] Ps. cii. 28.   [20] S. James i. 17.

4 ¶ And his feet shall stand in that day [d] upon the mount of Olives, which *is* before Jerusalem on the east, and the mount of Olives shall cleave in the midst thereof toward the

east and toward the west, [e] *and there shall be* a very great valley; and half of the mountain shall remove toward the north, and half of it toward the south.

battle, when He overwhelmed Pharaoh in the Red sea; and *fought for Israel."* The *Lord shall fight for you,* became the watchword of Moses[1] and the warrior Joshua in his old age[2], after his life's experience[3], and Nehemiah[4]. *Be not afraid by reason of this great multitude,* said Jahaziel, son of Zachariah[5], when *the Spirit of the Lord came upon* him; *for the battle is not your's, but God's.*

As He fought in the day of battle. " [6] All wars are so disposed by the power of God, that every victory is to be referred to His counsel and will. But this is not seen so clearly, when men, elate and confident, try to transfer to themselves all or the greater part of the glory of war. Then may the war be eminently said to be the Lord's, when no one drew sword, as it is written, [7] *The Lord shall fight for you, and ye shall hold your peace.* Of all God's wars, in which human insolence could claim no part of the glory, none was more wondrous than that, in which Pharaoh and his army were sunk in the deep. *The Lord,* said Moses[b], *is a man of war: the Lord is His Name. That day of battle* was the image of one much greater. In that, Pharaoh's army was sunk in the deep; in this, the power of evil, in Hell: in that, what could in some measure be conquered by human strength, was subdued; in this, a tyranny unconquerable; in that, a short-lived liberty was set up; the liberty brought by Christ through subdual of the enemy, is eternal. As then the image yields to the truth, earthly goods to heavenly, things perishable to eternal, so the glory of that ancient victory sinks to nothing under the greatness of the latter."

4 *And His feet shall stand in that day upon the mount of Olives,* "over against Jerusalem to the East, wherein riseth the Sun of Righteousness." The Mount of Olives is the central eminence of a line of hills, or rather more than a mile in length, overhanging the city, from which it is separated only by the narrow bed of the valley of the brook Cedron. It rises 187 feet above Mount Zion, 295 feet above Mount Moriah, 443 feet above Gethsemane, and lies between the city and the

wilderness toward the dead sea: around its Northern side, wound the road to Bethany and the Jordan[9]. There, probably, David worshiped[10]; his son, in his decay, profaned it[11]; Josiah desecrated his descrations[12]; there[13] *upon the mountain, which is on the East side of the city, the glory of the Lord stood,* when it had *gone up from the midst of the city;* it united the greatest glory of the Lord on earth, His Ascension, with its deepest sorrow, in Gethsemane. Since the Angel said, [14] *This same Jesus, which is taken up from you into heaven, shall so come in like manner as ye have seen Him go into heaven,* the old traditional opinion is not improbable, that our Lord shall come again to judge the earth, where He left the earth, near the place of His Agony and Crucifixion for us. So shall *the Feet* of God literally *stand upon the Mount of Olives.* Else it may be that "[15] the *Feet* of the uncircumscribed and simple God are to be understood not materially, but that the loving and fixed assistance of His power is expressed by that name."

Which is true, or whether, according to an old opinion, the last act of Anti-Christ shall be an attempt to imitate the Ascension of Christ (as the first Anti-Christ Simon Magus was said to have met his death in some attempt to fly[16]) and be destroyed by His Coming there, the event must shew.

And the Mount of Olives shall cleave [*be cleft*] *in* [*from*] *the midst thereof toward the East and toward the West,* i. e. the cleft shall be East and West, so as to form *a very great valley* through it—from Jerusalem toward the Jordan Eastward; and this shall be, in that *half of the mountain shall remove Northward, and half thereof Southward.* If this be literal, it is to form an actual way of escape from Jerusalem; if figurative, it symbolizes how that which would be the greatest hindrance to escape, the mountain which was higher than the city, blocking, as it were, the way, should itself afford the way of escape; as Zechariah speaks, [17] *O great mountain, before Zerubbabel thou shalt become a plain;* and Isaiah,[18] *Every valley shall be ex-*

[1] Exod. xiv. 14. Deut. i. 30, xiii. 22, xx. 4.
[2] Josh. xxiii. 10; comp. x. 14, 42, xxiii. 3.
[3] Ib. x. 14, 42, xxiii. 3. [4] Neh. iv. 20.
[b] 2 Chr. xx. 15. [6] Osor. [7] Ex. xiv. 14.
[8] Ib. xv. 3. [9] Van de Velde, Memoir 179.

[13] 2 Sam. xv. 32. [11] 1 Kgs xi.7. [12] 2 Kgs xxiii. 13.
[13] Ezek. xi. 23. [14] Acts i. 11. [15] Dion.
[16] The evidence would be late, except as seemingly confirmed by a like history in Suetonius vi. 12. [17] Zech. iv. 7. [18] Is. xl. 4.

Before CHRIST cir. 487.

5 And ye shall flee *to the valley of* || the mountains ; || for the valley of the mountains shall reach unto Azal: yea, ye shall flee, like as ye fled from

| Or, *my mountains.*
| Or, *when he shall touch the valley of the mountains to the place he separated.* cir. 787.

before the ᶠ earthquake in the days of Uzziah king of Judah : ᵍand the LORDᶠ my God shall come, *and* ʰ all the saints with thee.

6 And it shall come to

Before CHRIST cir. 487.

ᶠ Amos 1. 1.
ᵍ Matt. 16. 27.
& 24. 30, 31.
& 25. 31.
Jude 14.
ʰ Joel 3. 11.

---

alted and every mountain and hill shall be brought low, and the crooked shall be made straight, and the rough places plain ; i. e. every obstacle should be removed.

5. *And ye shall flee to the valley of the mountains,* rather, *along* ¹ *the valley of My mountains* ² viz. of those mountains, which God had just formed by dividing the mount of Olives. *For the valley of the mountains shall reach unto Azal,* i. e. *Azel,* the same word which enters into Beth-Azel of Micah, where the allusion probably is to its firm-rootedness. It is more probable that the name of a place should have been chosen with an allusive meaning, as in Micah, than that an unusual appellative should have been chosen to express a very common meaning. S. Cyril had heard of it as the name of a village at the extremity of the mountain ³. Else it might very probably have been destroyed in the destructive Roman wars. The Roman camp in the last siege must have been very near it ⁴. The destruction of villages, after the frantic revolt under Bar-Chocab, was enormous ⁵.

Yea, ye shall flee like as ye fled from before the earthquake. An earthquake in the time of Uzziah, whose memory survived the captivity to the time of Zechariah, nearly two centuries, must have been very terrible, but no historical account remains of it, Josephus having apparently described the past earthquake in the language which Zechariah uses of the future ⁶. Such an earthquake is the more remarkable a visitation in Jerusalem, because it was out of the line of earthquakes. These were to the North and East of Palestine : within it, they were almost unknown ⁷. Interpositions of God even in man's favor,

are full of awe and terror. They are tokens of the presence of the All-Holy among the unholy. Fear was an accompaniment of special miracles in the Gospel, not only among the poor Gadarenes ⁸, or the people ⁹, but even the Apostles ¹⁰ ; apart from the effect of the sight of Angels on us who are in the flesh ¹¹. It is then quite compatible, that the valley so formed should be the means of deliverance, and yet an occasion of terror to those delivered through it. The escape of the Christians in Jerusalem to Pella, during the break of the siege, after the withdrawal of Cestius Gallus was a slight image of this deliverance.

And the Lord thy God shall come, and all the saints with Thee, O God. The prophet, having spoken of God as *my God,* turns suddenly to speak to Him, as present. " ¹² This is manifestly said of the second Coming of the Saviour, of which John too in his Apocalypse says, ¹³ *Behold He shall come with the clouds, and every eye shall see Him, and they also which pierced Him.* And the Lord Himself in the Gospel declareth, that ¹⁴ *the Son of Man shall come in the clouds of heaven with power and great glory.* He shall *come with the clouds,* i. e. with the Angels, who are *ministering spirits* and are sent for different offices, and with the Prophets and Apostles." " ¹⁵ Whenever Scripture says that the saints and angels come with Christ, it is always speaking of His second Coming, as in that, ¹⁶ *When the Son of Man shall come in His glory and all His holy Angels with Him,* and in the Epistle of Jude ¹⁷, *Behold the Lord cometh with ten thousand of His saints, to execute judgment.*"

6. *The light shall not be clear nor dark,* or, more probably, according to the original

---

¹ According to the principle of words of motion, בּוֹא עָבַר יָצָא הלך. See Ew. Lehrb. n. 282a, 1. pp. 706, 707, ed. 8.
² E. vers has followed Kim.; yet there is no need to assume that הֲרֵי is an old plur. form.
³ אָצֵל for אַצֵל, in pause, as in the man's name both forms occur 1 Chr. viii. 38, ix. 44. The LXX had 'Ασαήλ in S. Jerome's time; Aq. 'Ασέλ; Theod. 'Ασήλ; Symm. alone translates it, πρὸς τὸ παρακείμενον. Jon. retains אָצֵל. So Kim., I. E., Abarb. The Syr. and Sym. (whom S. Jerome follows,) paraphrases. So Menahem and Rashi, giving an impossible explanation, "height." S. Cyril says, "it is a village, it is said, at the extremity of the mountain."
⁴ Jos. B. J. v. 1. 8.

⁵ "985 very well known villages." Dio Cass. lxix. 14. See ab. p. 48. ⁶ See Introd. to Amos vol. i. pp. 224, 225. ⁷ See Am. iv. 11, vol. i. p. 286.
⁸ S. Mark v. 15, S. Luke viii. 25.
⁹ On the restoration of Zacharias' speech, S. Luke i. 65; of the son of the widow of Nain Ib. vii. 16.
¹⁰ At the walking on the sea, S. Matt. xiv. 26, S. John vi. 19; the rebuking of the wind, S. Mark vi. 48, S. Luke viii. 25; the Transfiguration, S. Matt. xvii. 6, S. Mark ix. 6; the draught of fishes, S. Luke v. 3–10.
¹¹ To Zacharias, S. Luke i. 12; the B. Virgin, Ib. 29, 30; the shepherds, Ib. ii. 9; to the women after the Resurrection, S. Mark xvi. 8; the Apostles "supposing they had seen a spirit." S. Luke xxiv. 37. ¹² S. Jer. on vv. 6, 7. ¹³ Rev. i. 7.
¹⁴ S. Matt. xxiv. 30. ¹⁵ Rib. ¹⁶ S. Matt. xxv. 31.
¹⁷ S. Jude 14, 15.

Before
C H R I S T
cir. 487.

pass in that day, || *that* the light shall not be † clear,

|| *i. e.* it shall not be clear in some places, and dark in other places of the world.
† Heb. *precious.*
† Heb. *thickness.*
|| Or, *the day shall be one.*　¹ Rev. 22. 5.　ᵏ Matt. 24. 36.

nor † dark :

7 But || it shall be ¹one day ᵏ which shall be known to the LORD, not day, nor night : but it shall come to

pass, *that* at ¹ evening time it shall be light.

Before
C H R I S T
cir. 487.

8 And it shall be in that day, *that* living ᵐ w a t e r s shall go out from Jerusalem ; half of them toward the || former sea, and half

¹ Isai. 30. 26. & 60. 19, 20.
Rev. 21. 23.
ᵐ Ezek. 47. 1.
Joel 3. 18.
Rev. 22. 1.
|| Or, *eastern.*
Joel 2. 20.

---

reading ¹, *In that day there will be no light ; the bright ones* ² *will contract themselves,* as it is said, ³ *The stars shall withdraw their shining.*

This is evermore the description of the Day of Judgment, that, in the presence of God Who is Light, all earthly light shall grow pale. So Joel had said, ⁴ *The sun and moon shall be darkened, and the stars shall withdraw their shining.* And Isaiah,⁵ *The moon shall be confounded and the sun ashamed, when the Lord of hosts shall reign in Mount Zion and in Jerusalem and before His ancients gloriously;* and, ⁶ *Behold the day of the Lord cometh,—The stars of heaven and the constellations thereof shall not give their light : the sun shall be darkened in his going forth, and the moon shall not cause her light to shine.* All know well our Lord's words ⁷. S. John, like Zechariah, unites the failure of the heavenly light ⁸ *with a great earthquake, and the sun became as sackcloth of hair : and the moon became as blood ; and the stars of heaven fell upon the earth.*

7. *And it shall be one day : it shall be known unto the Lord : not day, and not night; and at the eventide it shall be light.* One special *day ; one,* unlike all beside ; known unto God, and to Him Alone. For God Alone knows the day of the consummation of all things, as He saith, ⁹ *Of that day and that hour knoweth no one, neither the angels in Heaven, nor the Son,* (so as to reveal it) *but the Father only.* Neither wholly *day,* because overclouded

with darkness; nor wholly *night,* for the streaks of light burst through the darkness chequered of both ; but in *eventide,* when all seems ready to sink into the thickest night, *there shall be light.* Divine light always breaks in, when all seems darkness ; but then the chequered condition of our mortality comes to an end, then comes the morning, which has no evening ; the light which has no setting ; "perpetual light, brightness infinite ;" when ¹⁰ *the light of the moon shall be as the light of the sun, and the light of the sun shall be sevenfold ;* and ¹¹ *the glory of God doth lighten* the eternal city, *and the Lamb is the light* thereof ; and ¹² *in Thy light we shall see light.* " ¹³ Christ shall be to us eternal light, a long perpetual day."

And it shall be, that living waters. " ¹⁴ This is what is said in the prophecy of Joel, ¹⁵ *A fountain shall come forth from the house of the Lord ;* and in that of Ezekiel, ¹⁶ *And behold there ran out waters."* Zechariah leaves to the mind to supply what the former prophets had said of the fertilizing life-giving character of those waters. He adds that they should pervade the whole land, West as well as East ; *to the former,* rather *the Eastern sea* ¹⁷, into which they would by nature flow, and toward *the hinder,* i. e. the Western sea, the Mediterranean, which natural waters could not *reach.* This their flow, he adds, should be perpetual. " ¹⁸ These streams shall not

---

¹ The E. V. follows Kim. "The light shall be neither קָרוֹת 'preciousnesses' nor קִפָּאוֹן 'thickness.'"

² יְקָפְאוּן קָרוֹת.

³ קָרוֹת as Job xxxi. 26. "the moon, יָקָר הֹלֵךְ, walking in beauty." יִקָפְּאוּן "shall contract themselves," as it is said in Ex. xv. 8, קָפְאוּ תְהֹמֹת "the depths (lit.) coagulated in the heart of the sea." According to the Kri, וְיָקָרוֹן, the meaning of יְקָרוֹת is mere conjecture. Kimchi (Lex.) Ibn Ezra Rashi suppose it to be used of "clear light," as contrasted with cloudy, expressed by קִפָּאוֹן, so that the meaning of the whole should be the same as that of v. 7. Our version follows this. Abulwalid and Parchon explain it of heavy thick clouds, and make the words synonymous. Tanchum mentions both. The LXX seem further to have read וְקָרוֹת, καὶ ψύχη; but it is not supported by any MS. or any other version : for the "but" in Symm.

Chald. Syr. may only express the contrast of the sentences ; "there shall not be light ;—and—," as Asyndeton. The LXX. however, "There shall not be light and cold and ice," could only mean to deny the presence of any of them, not (as Ewald) "there shall be no alternation of light with cold and ice." Proph. ii. 62. Light too and cold are not alternatives. The Kri וְקִפָּאוֹן, as always, occurs in some MSS., 8 Spanish of De Rossi, 2 at first, 15 old editions. The Jewish authorities (as far as I know) including Abulwalid Tanchum Parchon &c., take no notice of the Kethibh.

⁴ Joel iii. 15.　⁵ Is. xxiv. 23.　⁶ Ib. xiii. 9, 10.
⁷ S. Matt. xxiv. 29.　⁸ Rev. vi. 12, 13.
⁹ S. Mark xiii. 32.　¹⁰ Is. xxx. 26.
¹¹ Rev. xxi. 23.　¹² Ps. xxxvi. 9.　¹³ S. Cyr.
¹⁴ Kim.　¹⁵ Joel iii. 18.　¹⁶ Ezek. xlvii. 2.
¹⁷ Joel ii. 20, where the preternaturalness of the deliverance is pictured by the driving the *locust,* the symbol of the enemy, into two opposite seas. The Eastern sea, i. e. the dead sea, is spoken of there and Ezek. xlvii. 18 ; the hinder sea, i. e. the Mediterranean, Joel ii. 20, Deut. xi. 24, xxxiv. 2.
¹⁸ See Joel vol. i. pp. 212-215.

Before C H R I S T cir. 487	of them toward the hinder sea : in summer and in winter shall it be.

9 And the LORD shall

■ Dan. 2. 44.
Rev. 11. 15. be ⁿ king over all the earth: in that day shall there be

● Eph. 4. 5, 6. °one LORD, and his name one.

10 All the land shall be || turned ^p as a plain from Geba to Rimmon south of Jerusalem: and it shall be lifted up, and ^q || inhabited in her place, from Benjamin's gate unto the place of the first gate, unto the

Before
C H R I S T
cir. 487.

‖ Or, compassed.
P Isai. 40. 4.

q ch. 12. 6.
‖ Or, shall abide.

---

dry up and their waters shall not fail [1]; " therefore drought shall not lessen them, nor winter-cold bind them. " [1] From Jerusalem as from a fountain shall stream forth living waters of wisdom and grace to all nations."

" [2] Again he tells us, under a figure, that exceeding great and large shall be that outpouring of the Holy Spirit upon the saints, especially when they shall be removed to that holy eternal life in the world to come. For now through faith in Christ we are enriched, as with an earnest, with the first-fruits of the Holy Spirit. But after the Resurrection, sin being wholly taken away, the Holy Spirit will be in us, not as an earnest or in a measure; but richly bounteously and perfectly shall we enjoy the grace through Christ. He calleth, then, *living water*, the Spirit which, he says, will come forth from the Jerusalem which is from above.—But that the holy Scripture is wont to liken the Divine Spirit to *water*, the Giver thereof, the Son, accredits, saying [3], *he that believeth on Me, as the Scripture hath said, Out of his belly shall flow rivers of living water.* This the Evangelist explains, [4] *This spake He of the Spirit, which they who believe in Him should receive.* Since then the Spirit is life-giving, rightly does he liken it to that, which is life-giving to the frame."

9. *And the Lord shall be king over all the earth.* Such should be the influence of the living water, i. e. of the Spirit of God. God Who has ever reigned and will reign, [5] *a great King over all the earth,* shall be owned by His creatures, as what He is.

There shall be one Lord, more exactly, *The Lord shall be One, and His Name One.* He had before prophesied, [6] *I will cut off the names of the idols out of the land.* The Church being thus cleansed, no other lord or object of wor-

ship should be named but *Himself.* This is one of those prophecies, of continued expansion and development, ever bursting out and enlarging, yet never, until the end, reaching its full fulfillment. " [7] Since in this life we contemplate God in His effects, in which His whole perfection shineth not forth, now we know Him obscurely and imperfectly, His perfections being in divers diversely represented. In our home we shall see Him as He is, face to Face, through His Essence. Therefore then He will be represented by one name, as He shall be beheld by one gaze."

10. *All the land shall be turned as a plain from Rimmon to Gebah.* " [8] All the land, which is round about Jerusalem, which is now mountains, is as is said, [9] *The mountains are round about Jerusalem,* shall be level as a plain, but Jerusalem itself shall be exalted [10], and high above all the earth." The dignity of the Church, as [11] *a city set upon a hill, which cannot be hid,* is symbolized here by the sinking of all around and its own uprising; as in Micah and Isaiah, [12] *The mountain of the Lord's house shall be established on the top of the mountains, and shall be exalted above the hills. Gebah,* lit. *hill,* now, *Jeva,* was a frontier-garrison, held once by the Philistines [13], and fortified by Asa [14], in the northern boundary of Benjamin [15], together with Michmash [16] (now Mûkhmas), commanding an important pass, by which Jerusalem was approached [17]. *Rimmon, south of Jerusalem* is mentioned in Joshua among the southern towns of Judah [18], given to Simeon [19]. Both survived the Captivity [20]. They mark then the N. and S. of the kingdom of Judah, a long mountain chain, which is pictured as sinking down into a plain, that Jerusalem alone might be exalted.

---

[1] Kim. קוץ וחרף make up the whole year. Gen. viii. 22, Ps. lxxiv. 17. חרף is winter Pr. xx. 4, Am. iii. 15, Jer. xxxvi. 22.

[2] S. Cyr.   [3] S. John vii. 38.   [4] Ib. 39.
[5] Ps. xlvii. 3, 8.   [6] Zech. xiii. 2.   [7] Dion.   [8] Kim.
[9] Ps. cxxv. 2.
[10] ר, ראבה, as קאם, ר, Hos. x. 14. א is substituted in the name of the animal ראם, ראמים; the appell., ראמות Pr. xxiv. 7; the precious substance,

Ezek. xxvii. 16, Job xxviii. 18; the town, Deut. iv. 43, Jos. xx. 8, 1 Chr. vi. 65.
[11] S. Matt. v. 14.   [12] Is. ii. 2. Mic. iv. 1.
[13] 1 Sam. xiv. 5.   [14] 1 Kgs xv. 22.
[15] From Gebah to Beer-sheba," 2 Kgs xxiii. 8, as here, "from Gebah to Rimmon." It is named among the northern towns of Benjamin, Jos. xviii. 24.
[16] 1 Sam. l. c.   [17] Is. x. 28, 29.
[18] Jos. xv. 32.   [19] Ib. xix. 7, 1 Chron. iv. 32.
[20] Gebah, mentioned with Michmash, Neh. xi. 31, Rimmon, Ib. 29.

Before
CHRIST
cir. 487.

r Neh. 3. 1.
& 12. 39.
Jer. 31. 38.

s Jer. 31. 40.

t Jer. 23. 6.
‖ Or, *shall abide.*

corner gate, [r] and *from* the tower of Hananeel unto the king's winepresses.

11 And *men* shall dwell in it, and there shall be [s] no more utter destruction ; [t] but Jerusalem ‖ shall be safely inhabited.

12 ¶ And this shall be the plague wherewith the LORD will smite all the people that have fought

against Jerusalem ; Their flesh shall consume away while they stand upon their feet, and their eyes shall consume away in their holes, and their tongue shall consume away in their mouth.

13 And it shall come to pass in that day, *that* [u] a great tumult from the LORD shall be among

Before
CHRIST
cir. 487.

u 1 Sam. 14. 15, 20.

From Benjamin's gate unto the place of the first gate. Benjamin's gate[1] must obviously be a gate to the North, and doubtless the same as *the gate of Ephraim*[2], the way to Ephraim lying through Benjamin. This too has probably reference to the prophecy of Jeremiah, that [3] *the city shall be built to the Lord from the tower of Hananeel unto the gate of the corner.* [4] *Jehoash, king of Israel, brake down the wall of Jerusalem to the corner-gate, four hundred cubits,* after the war with Amaziah. Zechariah seems to speak of Jerusalem, as it existed in his time. For the tower of Hananeel[5] still existed ; the *first gate* was probably destroyed, since he speaks not of it, but of its *place ;* the gate of Benjamin and the corner-gate probably still existed, since Nehemiah[6] mentions the building of the sheep-gate, the fish-gate, the old gate, or gate of the old city, the valley-gate, the dung-gate, the gate of the fountain ; but not these.

11. *And they shall dwell in it,* in peace, going forth from it, neither into *captivity,* nor in flight[7] ; for God should exempt from curse the city which He had chosen, against which the gates of hell shall not prevail, and He says of the heavenly Jerusalem, [8] *there shall be no more curse.*

12. Again, upon the restoration of His people follows the destruction of His enemies. It shall, first and chiefly, be God's doing, not man's. *This shall be the plague.* The word is used of direct infliction by pestilence,

wherewith the Lord shall smite[9] all the people [peoples] that fought against Jerusalem. The awful description is of living corpses. "[10] The enemies of Jerusalem shall waste, not with fever or disease, but by a plague from God, so that, being sound, standing, living, in well-being, they should waste and consume away," as Isaiah speaks of the [11] *carcases of the men, that have transgressed against Me ; for their worm shall not die—and they shall be an abhorring unto all flesh.*

Their flesh shall consume away, rather, *wasting away the flesh of each one.* It is the act of God, in His individual justice to each one of all those multitudes gathered against Him. One by one, *their eyes,* of which they said, [12] *let our eye look on Zion,* i. e. with joy at its desolation, *shall consume away in their holes, and their tongue,* wherewith[13] they blasphemed God[13], *shall consume away in their mouths.* Appalling, horrible, picture! *standing on their feet,* yet their flesh mouldering away as in a grave-yard, their sightless balls decaying in their holes, the tongue putrefying in their mouth, a disgust to themselves and to others ! Yet what, compared to the horrible inward decay of sin, whereby men [14] *have a name that they live and are dead!* "[15] Let us read Ecclesiastical histories, what Valerian, Decius, Diocletian, Maximian, what the savagest of all, Maximin, and lately Julian suffered, and then we shall prove by deeds, that the truth of prophecy was fulfilled in the letter also."

13. *A great tumult,* and panic fear, such as

1 Mentioned beside, Jer. xx. 2. xxxvii. 12, 17. Jeremiah goes through it, "to go into the land of Benjamin." Jer. xxxvii. 12, 13.
2 Mentioned 2 Chr. xxv. 23, Neh. viii. 16, xii. 39.
3 Jer. xxxi 38.   4 2 Kgs xiv. 13. 2 Chr. xxv. 23.
5 Neh. iii. 1.   6 Neh. iii. 1, 3, 6, 13, 14, 15.
7 v. 2, 5.   8 Rev. xxii. 3.
9 נגף occurs 20 times of God's striking ; 2ce of a foot stumbling ; once (like נגח) of an ox goring another, once of a man's accidental blow, both in Ex. . . מגפה, in like way, occurs 17 times of death inflicted by God (once only of an individual, Eze-

kiel's wife, Ez. xxiv. 16), and 3 times only, of slaughter in battle by men, 1 Sam. iv. 17, 2 Sam. xvii. 9, xviii. 7. The form Hif., הכם; is ἀπ. Nif. is used of a putrefying wound, Ps. xxxviii. 6, and מק subst. Is. iii. 24. Nif. is also used of man's wasting away through (ב) his sins Lev. xxvi. 39 (bis) Ez. xxiv. 33, xxxiii. 10 [not 'under the weight of' as Ges.] and of the dissolution of the host of heaven, Is. xxxiv. 4.
10 Lap.   11 Is. lxvi. 24.   12 Mi. iv. 11.
13 comp. Ps. xxii. 3. Is. xxxvi. 15, 18. xxxviii. 3, 4. 17, 23, 29.   14 Rev. iii. 1.   15 S. Jer.

Before
CHRIST
cir. 487.

x Judg. 7. 22.
2 Chr. 20. 23.
Ezek. 38. 21.

them; and they shall lay hold every one on the hand of his neigh-bor and x his hand shall rise up against the

God said He would send upon the Canaanites before Israel[1], or on Israel itself, if disobe-dient[2]; or which fell on the Philistines after Jonathan's capture of the garrison at Mich-mash, when every man's *sword was against his fellow.* There is no real unity, except in God; elsewhere, since each seeks his own, all must be impregnated with mutual suspi-cion, ready at any moment to be fanned into a flame; as when, at the blowing of Gideon's trumpets, *[4] the Lord set every man's sword against his fellow;* or when, at Jehoshaphat's prayer[5], *the children of Ammon and Moab stood up against the inhabitants of Mount Seir, utterly to slay and destroy; and when they had made an end of the inhabitants of Seir, every one helped to destroy another.*

And they shall lay hold, every one on the hand of his neighbor.· Every one shall be every one's foe. Each shall, in this tumultuous throng, grasp the other's hand, mastering him powerfully[6]. *And his hand shall rise up [7] against the hand of his neighbor,* as was prophesied of Ishmael, [8] *his hand will be against every man, and every man's hand against him.*

14. *And Judah also shall fight at Jerusalem.* This seems more probable than the alter-native rendering of the E. M., "against." For Judah is united with Jerusalem as one, in the same context[9]; and, if it had shared with the heathen, it must also have shared their lot. It is Judah itself, not "a remnant of Judah," as it is [10] *every one that is left of all the nations,* which is thus united to Jerusalem:

1 De vii. 23. 2 Ib. xxviii. 20. 3 1 Sam. xiv. 20. The same word is used. 4 Jud. vii. 22. 5 2 Chr. xx. 32.
6 הֶחֱזִיק, with acc., is used adversely though figuratively. Anguish (Jer. vi. 24, 1. 43) amazement (Ib. viii. 21) pangs (Mic. iv. 9) are said to seize on—; and David "I seized (הֶחֱזַקְתִּי) by the beard the lion and the bear," 1 Sam. xvii. 35. It is used of a man grasping with violence (with בְּ) De. xxii. 25, 2 Sam. xiii. 11; forcibly detaining prisoners, Ex. ix. 2, Jer. l. 33; the head of an opponent, "they seized each his fellow by the head, and his sword in his fellow's side," 2 Sam. ii. 16; "the ears of a dog," Pr. xxvi. 17. Here the context precludes ambig-uity; the use of the acc. is poetic.
7 עָלָה "rise" = "be raised up," as even of in-animate things, Am. iii. 5, Pr. xxvi. 9, Job. v. 26; of a people carried away, Ib. xxxvi. 20. Gesenius' in-stances, Thes. p. 1023 n. 2.
8 Gen. xvi. 12. 9 v. 21. 10 v. 16.
11 "Yea, and those of the house of Judah the na-tions will bring, constrained, to carry war against Jerusalem." Jon. 12 v. 2, 3.
13 On the one hand, נִלְחַם בָּעִיר "fought against the city," Jud. ix. 45; בְּרַבָּה "against Rabbah" 2

hand of his neighbor.

Before
CHRIST
cir. 487.

‖ Or. thou also,
O Judah, shalt.
‖ Or, against.
y Ezek. 39. 10,
17, &c.

14 And ‖ Judah also shall fight ‖ at Jerusalem ; y and the wealth of all the heathen round about shall

it is that same Judah, as a whole, of which it is said, *it shall fight.* Nor is anything spoken of "conversion," which is said of those left from the heathen nations, who had fought against her. Yet for Judah to have joined an exterminating Heathen war against Jeru-salem, even though constrained, had, like the constrained sacrifices to Heathen gods, been apostasy. But there is not even a hint that, as Jonathan apologetically paraphrases[11], they were "constrained." The war is to be Judah's free act: *Judah also shall fight.* Again, those gathered against Jerusalem, and their warfare against it, had been described at the outset, as [12] *all nations:* here the subject is not the gathering or fighting, but the over-throw. Nor is there any decisive contrary idiom; for, although when used of people, it always means "fight against," yet, of place, it as often, means "fight in [13]." Probably then the Prophet means, that not only should God fight for His people, but that *Judah also* should do its part, as S. Paul says, [14] *We, then, as workers together with Him;* and, [15] *we are laborers together with God;* and, [16] *I labored more abundantly than they all; yet not I, but the grace of God which was with me;* or, [17] *work out your own salvation with fear and trembling; for it is God which worketh in you both to will and to do of His good pleasure.* God so doth all things in the Church, for the conversion of the heathen, and for single souls, as to wait for the cöoperation of His creature. "[18] God made thee without thee; He doth not justify thee without thee."

Sam. xii. 27; בִּקְעִילָה "against Keilah," 1 Sam. xxiii. 1: on the other, בְּתַעֲנָךְ "fought at Taanach," Jud. v. 19; בִּרְפִידִים, "at Rephidim," Ex. xvii. 8; בְּבִקְעַת מְגִדּוֹ "in the valley of Megiddo," 2 Chr. xxxv. 22, and so probably in the immediate context, (Ib. 20) בְּכַרְכְּמִישׁ, "at Carchemish," since it is hardly probable, that Carchemish should be men-tioned as *the* object of such an expedition, and the decisive battle between Egypt and Chaldæa was "*at,*" not "*in* Carchemish," בְּכַרְכְּמִשׁ, where Ne-buchadnezzar smote his army. Jer. xlvi. 2. For such a large army as Pharaoh's would not have been shut up in a town, which was of importance only as a key to the passage of the Euphrates. Also in Isaiah xxx. 32, the Chethib בָּהּ must be "in her," Zion, which the Kri has corrected into the more common idiom, בָּהּ, "against them." The LXX. renders thus, παραταξεται ἐν Ἱερουσαλήμ.
14 2 Cor. vi. 1. 15 1 Cor. iii. 9. 16 Ib. xv. 10.
17 Phil. ii. 12. 18 S. Aug. Serm. 169. n. 13. Opp. v. 815. (on N. T. p. 866 O. T.)

be gathered together, gold, and silver, and apparel, in great abundance.

* ver. 12.

15 And [z] so shall be the plague of the horse, of the mule, of the camel, and of the ass, and of all t h e beasts that shall be in these tents, as this plague.

16 ¶ And it shall come to pass, *that* every one that is left of all the nations which came against Jerusalem shall even [a] go up from year to year to worship the King, the LORD of hosts, and to keep [b] the feast of tabernacles.

[a] Is. 60. 6, 7, 9.
& 66. 23.

[b] Lev. 23. 34, 43.
Neh. 8. 14.
Hos. 12. 9.
John 7. 2.

And the wealth of all the heathen round about shall be gathered. Whatever the world had taken in their war against the Church shall be abundantly repaid. *All the heathen* had combined to plunder Jerusalem [1]; *the wealth of all the heathen* shall be gathered to requite them. " [2] As Isaiah says, The nations, converted to Christ, brought all their wealth to the Church, whence he congratulates the Church, saying, " [3] *Thou shalt also suck the milk of the Gentiles, and shalt suck the breasts of kings—For brass I will bring gold, and for iron I will bring silver;* under which he typically understands, " [4] wisdom, philosophy, eloquence, learning, and all the other arts and sciences, liberal and mechanical, wherewith the heathen shall be adorned, who are converted to the faith. So shall the gifts of nature be perfected by the gifts of grace, and *they* shall defend the Church who erstwhile attacked it."

15. *And so shall be the plague of the Lord &c.* " [4] So, when God sendeth the plague, all the irrational animals of Anti-Christ and his satellites shall perish, as the aforesaid men, who used them, perished. For, for the sins of men, God, to their greater confusion, sometimes slays their beasts, sometimes also for their loving correction." " [5] The imagery is from the Mosaic law of the ban. If a whole city became guilty of idolatry, not the inhabitants only, but the beasts were to be destroyed[6], so that here, in miniature, should be repeated the relation of the irrational to the rational part of the creation, according to which, for the sins of men, *the creature is*, against its will, *made subject to vanity.* Analogous is it also, that on the offence of Achan [7], beside him and his children, his oxen, asses and sheep were [stoned and] burned with him."

16. *Every one that is left of the nations.* God so gives the repentance, even through His visitations, that, in proportion to the largeness of the rebellion and the visitation upon it, shall be the largeness of the conversion. [8] *Jerusalem shall be trodden down of the*

Gentiles, *until the times of the Gentiles shall be fulfilled.* And S. Paul, [9] *Blindness in part is happened to Israel, until the fullness of the Gentiles shall be come in; and so all Israel shall be saved.* Hitherto prophets had spoken of a [10] *remnant* of Jacob, who should *return to the mighty God*, and should be saved; now, upon this universal rebellion of the heathen. He foretells the conversion of a remnant of the heathen also.

Shall even go up from year to year to worship the King, the Lord of hosts. There is a harmony between the rebellion and the repentance. The converted shall go to worship God there, where they had striven to exterminate His worshipers. The prophet could only speak of the Gospel under the image of the law. *The Feast of Tabernacles* has its counterpart, not, like the Pascha or the Pentecost, in any single feast, but in the whole life of the Gospel. It was a thanksgiving for past deliverance; it was a picture of their pilgrim-life from the passage of the Red sea, until the parting of the Jordan opened to them the entrance to their temporary rest in Canaan [11]. " [12] In that vast, wide, terrible wilderness, where was no village, house, town, cave, it made itself tents, wherein to sojourn with wives and children, avoiding by day the burning sun, by night damp and cold and hurt from dew; and it was [13] *a statute forever in their generations; ye shall dwell in booths seven days; all, that are Israelites born, shall dwell in booths, that your generations may know, that I made the children of Israel to dwell in booths, when I brought them out of the land of Egypt.*" " [2] Much more truly do Christians keep the feast of tabernacles, not once in the year only, but continually, unceasingly. This is, what S. Peter admonisheth, [14] *Dearly beloved, I beseech you, as strangers and pilgrims, abstain from fleshly lusts.* And S. Paul often teacheth that we, like Abraham, are strangers on earth, but [15] *citizens of heaven with the saints, and of the household of God.* Faith, he says, [16] *is the substance of things hoped for, the evidence of things not seen. By*

---

[1] ver. 2.   [2] Lap.   [3] Is. lx. 16, 17.   [4] Dion.
[5] Hengst.   [6] Deut. xiii. 15.   [7] Josh. vii. 24, 25.
[8] S. Luke xxi. 24.   [9] Rom. xi. 25, 26.   [10] Is. x. 21.

[11] See at greater length Hos. xii. 9. vol. i. p. 122.
[12] S. Jer.   [13] Lev. xxiii. 41–43.   [14] 1 S. Pet. ii. 11.
[15] Eph. ii. 19.   [16] Heb. xi. 1, 9, 10.

Before CHRIST cir. 487.

• Is. 60. 12.

17 º And it shall be, *that* whoso will not come up of *all* the families of the earth unto Jerusalem to worship

the King, the LORD of hosts, even upon them shall be no rain.

Before CHRIST cir. 487.

18 And if the family of

---

faith *Abraham sojourned in the land of pro-mise as in a strange country, dwelling in ta-bernacles with Isaac and Jacob, the heirs with him of the same promise; for he looked for a city which hath foundations, whose builder and maker is God."* "[1] As long as we are in progress, in the course and militant, we dwell in tabernacles, striving with all our mind to pass from the tabernacles to the firm and lasting dwelling-place of the house of God. Whence also holy David said, [2] *I am a stranger with Thee and a sojourner, as all my fathers were.* So speaketh he, who is still in Egypt and yet placed in the world. But he who goeth forth out of Egypt, and entereth a desert from vices, holdeth his way and says in the Psalm, [3] *I will pass through to the place of the tabernacle of the Wonderful unto the house of God.* Whence also he says else-where, [4] *How amiable are Thy dwellings. Thou Lord of hosts; my soul longeth, yea, even fainteth for the courts of the Lord;* and a little after, [5] *Blessed are they who dwell in thy house, they shall be alway praising Thee.* [6] *The voice of rejoicing and salvation is in the taber-nacles of the righteous.* [7] *One thing have I de-sired of the Lord, that will I seek after; that I may dwell in the house of the Lord all the days of my life, to behold the beauty of the Lord and to enquire in His temple.* Whoso dwelleth in such tabernacles, and hastes to go from the tabernacles to the court, and from the court to the house, and from the house to the temple of the Lord, ought to celebrate the feast of Tabernacles &c." It symbolizes how, "[8] in the New Testament, Christians, being delivered through Christ from the slavery to sin and satan, and sojourning in this vale of misery, by making progress in virtues go up to the home of the heavenly paradise, the door of glory being open by the merit of the Lord's Passion, and so the faithful of Christ celebrate the feast of tabernacles; and, after the destruction of Anti-Christ, they will celebrate it the more devoutly, as there will then be among them a fuller fervor of faith."

17. *Whoso will not go up.* "[9] To those who go not up, he threatens the same punishment as persecutors would endure. For enemies, and they who will not love, shall have the same lot. This is, I think, what Christ

Himself said, [10] *Whoso is not with Me is against Me, and whoso gathereth not with Me scattereth.*"

Upon them there shall be no rain. Rain was the most essential of God's temporal gifts for the temporal well-being of His people. Moses marked out this, as his people were entering on the promised land, with recent memory of Egypt's independence of rain in Egypt itself, and that this gift depended on obedience. [11] *The land, whither thou goest in to possess it,* is *not as the land of Egypt, whence ye came out, where thou sowedst thy seed and water-edst it with thy foot, as a garden of herbs:* but *a land of hills and valleys,—it drinketh water of the rain of heaven; a land which the Lord thy God careth for; the eyes of the Lord are always upon it, from the beginning of the year even unto the end of the year. And it shall be, if ye shall hearken diligently unto My commandments—I will give you the rain of your land in its season, the first rain and the latter rain, that thou mayest gather in thy corn and thy wine and thine oil. And I will send grass in thy fields for thy cattle, that thou mayest eat and be full.* But the threat on disobedience corresponded therewith. [12] *Take heed to yourselves,* Moses continues, *that your heart be not deceived, and ye turn aside and serve other gods—and the Lord's wrath be kindled against you, and He shut up the heaven, that there be no rain, and that the land yield not her fruit, and ye perish quickly from off the good land, which the Lord giveth you;* and, [13] *Thy heaven, that is over thee, shall be brass, and the earth, that is under thee, shall be iron; the Lord shall make the rain of thy land powder and dust.* Amos speaks of the withdrawal of rain as one of God's chastise-ments [14]: the distress in the time of Ahab is pictured in the history of the woman of Sarepta [15], and Ahab's directions to Obadiah [16]. But it is also the symbol of spiritual bles-sings; both are united by Hosea [17] and Joel [18], as Joel and Amos also speak of spiritual blessings exclusively under the figure of temporal abundance [19]. In Isaiah it is simply a symbol, [20] *Drop down, ye heavens, from above, and let the skies pour down right-eousness; let the earth open, and let them bring forth salvation, and let righteousness spring up together.*

18. *And if the family of Egypt go not up,*

---

[1] S. Jer.   [2] Ps. xxxix. 12.   [3] Ib. xli. 5. Vulg.
[4] Ib. lxxxiv. 1.   [5] Ib. 4.   [6] Ib. cxviii. 15.
[7] Ib. xxvii. 4.   [8] Dion.   [9] S. Cyr.
[10] S. Luke xi. 23.   [11] De. xi. 10–15   [12] Ib. 16, 17.
[13] Ib. xxviii. 23, 24.   [14] Am. iv. 7. See vol. i. p. 281.
[15] 1 Kgs xvii. 9–16.   [16] Ib. xviii. 5.

[17] Hosea vi. 3. See vol. i. p. 64.
[18] Jo. ii. 23. See vol. i. pp. 190, 191.
[19] Jo. iii. 18. See vol. i. pp. 212–215. Am. ix. 13. See vol. i. p. 333.
[20] Is. xlv. 8. See also Ib. v. 6, both together Ib. xxx. 23.

Before CHRIST cir. 487.

Egypt got n o t up, and come not, † ᵈ that *have* no

† Heb. *upon whom there is not.*
ᵈ Deut. 11. 10.

rain; there shall be the plague, wherewith t h e LORD will smite the heath-

en that come not up to keep the feast of tabernacles.

19 This shall be t h e || punishment of E g y p t,

Before CHRIST cir. 487.

|| Or, *sin.*

and the punishment of all

---

and come not, that have *no* rain ; rather, *and there shall not be* [1]. It may be that the prophet chose this elliptical form, as well knowing that the symbol did not hold as to Egypt, which, however it ultimately depended on the equatorial rains which overfilled the lakes which supply the Nile, did not need that fine arrangement of the rains of Autumn and Spring which were essential to the fruitfulness of Palestine. The omission leaves room for the somewhat prosaic supply of Jonathan, "The Nile shall not ascend to them." More probably the words are left undefined with a purposed abruptness, *there shall not be upon them,* viz. whatever they need: the omission of the symbol in these two verses might the more suggest, that it is a symbol only. Egypt, the ancient oppressor of Israel, is united with Judah as one, in the same worship of God, as Isaiah had said, [2] *In that day shall Israel be the third with Egypt and with Assyria;* and since it is united in the duty, so also in the punishment for despising it.

"[3] Let not Egypt be proud, that it is watered by the Nile, as if it needed no rain : i. e. let no one be secure in this life. For though we stand by faith, yet may we fall. For although bedewed by the efflux of Divine grace, and filled with its richness, yet if we give not thanks continually for such great gifts, God will count us as the rest, to whom such copious goodness never came. The safety of all then lies in this, that while we are in these tabernacles, we cherish the Divine benefits, and unceasingly praise the Lord, Who hath heaped such benefits upon us."

"[4] Under the one nation of the Egyptians, he understands those who are greatly deceived, and chose idolatry most unreasonably, to whom it will be a grave inevitable judgment, the pledge of destruction, that

they despise the acceptable grace of salvation through Christ. For they are murderers of their own souls, if, when they could lay hold of eternal life and the Divine gentleness, open to all who will choose it and put off the burden of sin, they die in their errors ; the stain and pollution from transgression and error uncleansed, although the Divine light illumined all around and called those in darkness to receive sight. Of each of these I would say, [5] *Better is an untimely birth than he ; for he cometh in with vanity, and departeth in darkness, and his name shall be covered with darkness.* [6] *Good had it been for them, if* they *had never been born,* is the Saviour's word. That this is not said of the Egyptians only, but shall come true of all nations, who shall altogether be punished, if they are reckless of the salvation through Christ and honor not His festival, he will establish in these words ;

19. *This shall be the sin of Egypt and the sin of all nations that come not up to keep the feast of tabernacles.* For before the coming of the Saviour, good perhaps had been in part the excuse of the heathen, that they had been called by none. For no one had preached unto them. Wherefore the Saviour also, pointing out this in the Gospel parables, said, [7] *the laborers,* called *at the eleventh hour, said, No man hath hired us.* But when Christ cast His light upon us, [8] *bound the strong man,* removed from his perverseness those subject to him, justified by faith those who came to Him, laid down His life for the life of all, they will find no sufficient excuse who admit not so reverend a grace. It will be true of the heathen too, if Christ said of them, [9] *If I had not come and spoken unto them, they had not had sin : but now they have no cloke for their sin.*"

The prophet says *sin,* not punishment [10], for sin includes *the punishment,* which is its

---

[1] The E. V., following Kim., takes וְלֹא עֲלֵיהֶם as a subordinate clause, "and there is not upon them," viz. rain at any time; but it is unnatural that, in two consecutive verses, the words should be taken in such divergent senses. The omission of וְלֹא by the LXX., followed so far (as so often) by the Pesh., is supported only by 4 Kenn. MSS., against those in S. Jerome's time, and Symm. Theod. Jon., and is evidently a makeshift, followed by Ewald.
[2] Is. xix. 24.   [3] Osor.   [4] S. Cyr.
[5] Eccl. vi. 3, 4.   [6] S. Matt. xxvi. 24.   [7] Ib. xx. 7.
[8] Ib. xii. 29.   [9] S. John xv. 22.
[10] The E. V. follows Kim. in rendering "punish-

ment." Ges. combines the two in his rendering of אָשָׁם, n. 2 "culpam sustinuit," not in his "culpæ pœnas dedit." The rendering "shall be guilty" unites sin and punishment in his instances, Ps. xxxiv. 22, 23, Is. xxiv. 6, Jer. ii. 3, Hos. x. 2, [E. V., in the same sense, "shall be found faulty"] xiv. 1 [xiii. 16 Eng.] Pr. xxx. 10, ["be found guilty," E. V.] So also in אָ ם ן Lam. iii. 39, חַטָּאת Ib. iv. 6. When the Lord said, *It shall be more tolerable in the day of judgment for Sodom and Gomorrah than for that city,* He meant, that both guilt and punishment would be greater. In Is. v. 18, חַטָּאָה, and, Ib. xl. 2, חַטָּאת is "sin." So also עָוֹן Is. v. 18, Ps. xxxi. 11.

Before
C H R I S T
cir. 487.
nations that come not up to
keep the feast of tabernacles.

20 ¶ In that day shall

I Or, *bridles.*
there be upon the || bells of

• Isai. 23. 18.
the horses, ᶜ HOLINESS
UNTO THE LORD; and

the pots in the L O R D ' S
house shall be like t h e
bowls before the altar.

Before
C H R I S T
cir. 487.

21 Yea, every pot in
Jerusalem and in Judah
shall be holiness unto the

---

due, and which it entails: it does not express the punishment, apart from the sin. It was *the sin* which comprised and involved all other sin, the refusal to worship God as He had revealed Himself, and to turn to Him. It was to say, [1] *We will not have Him to reign over us.*

20. *In that day there shall be upon the bells* [2] *of the horses, Holiness unto the Lord.* He does not say only, that they should be consecrated to God, as Isaiah says of Tyre, [3] *Her merchandise and her hire shall be holiness to the Lord;* he says that, *the bells of the horses,* things simply secular, should bear the same inscription as the plate on the high priest's forehead. Perhaps the comparison was suggested by the bells on the high priest's dress [4]; not the lamina only on his forehead, but bells (not as his, which were part of his sacred dress), bells, altogether secular, should be inscribed with the self-same title, whereby he himself was dedicated to God.

Holiness to the Lord. He does not bring down what is sacred to a level with common things, but he uplifts ordinary things, that they too should be sacred, as S. Paul says, ᵇ *whether ye eat or drink or whatsoever ye do, do all to the glory of God.*

And the pots of the Lord's house shall be like bowls before the altar. The pots are mentioned, together with other vessels of the Lord's house [6], but not in regard to any sacred use. They were used, with other vessels, for dressing the victims [7] for the partakers of the sacrifices. These were to be sacred, like those made for the most sacred use of all, *the bowls for sprinkling* [8], whence that sacrificial blood was taken, which was to make the typical atonement.

21. *And every pot in Jerusalem and in Judah shall be holiness to the Lord.* Everything is to be advanced in holiness. All the common utensils everywhere in the people of God shall not only be holy, but *holiness,* and capa-

ble of the same use as the vessels of the temple.

And there shall be no more the Canaanite in the house of the Lord of hosts. The actual Canaanite had long since ceased to be; the Gibeonites, the last remnant of them, had been absorbed among the people of God. But *all Israel* were not *of Israel.* Isaiah had called its princes and people, [9] *rulers of Sodom, people of Gomorrah.* Ezekiel had said, [10] *Thus saith the Lord God unto Jerusalem; Thy birth and thy nativity is of the land of Canaan; thy father was an Amorite, and thy mother a Hittite.* Hosea used at least the term of two-fold meaning, [11] *Canaan, in whose hands are the balances of deceit;* and Zephaniah, [12] *All the people of Canaan are destroyed.* After the time of the Canon, Daniel is introduced saying, " [13] O thou seed of Canaan and not of Judah." Ezekiel had spoken of ungodly priests, not only as uncircumcised in heart (according to the language of Deuteronomy [14]), but uncircumcised in flesh also, altogether alien from the people of God [15]. The prophet then speaks, as Isaiah, [16] *It shall be called the way of holiness; the unclean shall not pass over it,* and Joel, [17] *then shall Jerusalem be holy, and there shall no strangers pass through her any more.* This shall have its full fulfillment in the time of the end. [18] *There shall in no wise enter into it anything that defileth, neither whatsoever worketh abomination or a lie;* and, *without are dogs and sorcerers and whoremongers and murderers and idolaters, and whatsoever loveth and maketh a lie.*

" [19] Although born of the blood of Israel, those of old eagerly imitated the alien Canaanites. But after that the Only-Begotten Word of God came among us, and, having justified by faith, sealed with the Holy Spirit, those who came to His grace, our mind hath been steadfast, unshaken, fixed in piety. Nor will any one persuade those who are sanctified, to honor any other god

---

[1] S. Luke xix. 14.

[2] מִצְלָה, ἀπ. Yet the rendering "bells" has the analogy of מְצִלְתַּיִם 1 Chr. xiii. xv. xvi. xxv. 2 Chr. v. xxix. Ezr. iii. 10, Neh. xii. 27. The other guesses, "bridles" (lxx. Syr.), "trappings of horses" [Jon.] or "warlike ornaments" (S. Jerome's Jewish teacher) have none; the βυθὸν of Aq. and περίπατον οὐσκιον of Symm. (as from מְצֻלָה) give no meaning.

[3] Is. xxiii. 18.

[4] פַּעֲמוֹן Ex. xxviii. 34, xxxix. 25, 26, used of it only, and there only.   [5] 1 Cor. x. 31.
[6] Ez. xxxviii. 3, 1 Kgs vii. 45, 2 Kgs xxv. 14, 2 Chr. iv. 11, 16, Jer. lii. 18, 19.
[7] 2 Chr. xxxv. 13.   [8] מִזְרָקִים.   [9] Is. i. 10.
[10] Ezek. xvi. 3.   [11] Hosea xii. 7.   See vol. i. p. 121.
[12] Zeph. i. 11.   See ab. p. 244.
[13] Hist. of Sus. ver. 56.   [14] Deut. x. 16, xxx. 6.
[15] Ezek. xliv. 7.   [16] Is. xxxv. 8.
[17] Joel iii. 17.   See vol. i. p. 211.
[18] Rev. xxi. 27, xxii. 15.   [19] S. Cyr.

Before CHRIST cir. 487. LORD of hosts: and all they that sacrifice s h a l l come and take of them, and seethe therein: and in

that day there shall be no more t h e [f] Canaanite i n [g] the house of the LORD of hosts.

Before CHRIST cir. 487.

[f] Isai. 35. 8.
Joel 3. 17.
Rev. 21. 27.
& 22. 15.
[g] Eph. 2. 19, 20, 21, 22.

---

save Him Who is, by nature and in truth, God, Whom we have known in Christ. For in Himself He hath shewn us the Father, saying, [1] *He that hath seen Me hath seen the Father.* Wherefore *in that day,* i. e. at that time, he says, *there shall be no Canaanite,* i. e. alien and idolater, *in the house of the Lord Almighty."* " [2] But may the Almighty God

bring the saying true at this time also, that no Canaanite should be seen among us, but that all should live according to the Gospel-laws, and await that blessed hope and the appearance of our great God and Saviour Jesus Christ, with Whom be glory to the Father with the Holy Ghost, now and ever and to endless ages. Amen."

[1] S. John xiv. 9.

[2] Theod.

INTRODUCTION

TO

THE PROPHET

MALACHI.

THE last prophet of the Old Testament, like the Forerunner of our Lord, whom he foreannounced under his own name, "ᵃ the messenger of the Lord," willed to be but "the voice of one crying in the wilderness;" as his great successor, who took up his message, when asked, *Who art thou? What sayest thou of thyself?* said, ᵇ *I am the voice of one crying in the wilderness, Make straight the way of the Lord.* He mentions neither his parentage, nor birthplace, nor date; nor did he add the name of his office ᶜ, and has left it to be guessed, whether the name under which he is known, was the name which he bore among men; so wholly did he will to be hidden. No one before him is recorded to have borne his name. It may be that he framed it for himself, and willed to be known only as what it designated, "the messenger of the Lord." This was a favorite title with him, since, in this brief prophecy, he uses it, as describing the priest's office, and that of the forerunner ᵈ; whereas, before him, except once by Haggai and once by Isaiah ᵉ, it had been used only of the blessed Angels.

There is, however, no ground to think that it was not his name. Even the Seventy, who paraphrase it, "His messenger," prefix to the book the name Malachi; and the title,

"my messenger," would not have described that he was "the messenger of God," since the name of God had not preceded. "If names are to be interpreted," S. Jerome says, "ᶠ and history is to be framed from them, not a spiritual meaning to be derived, then Hosea who is called Saviour, and Joel whose name means, 'Lord God,' and the other prophets will not be men, but rather angels or the Lord and Saviour, according to the meaning of their name." No special stress was laid upon the name, even by the Origenists, who supposed Haggai, Malachi and S. John Baptist to have been angels ᵍ. Origen himself supposed S. John Baptist to have been an angel in human form ʰ, and Melchisedek ⁱ, as well as Malachi. More widely, that "ʲ they became the words in the prophets."

At the time of our Lord, some accounted him to have been Ezra, perhaps for his zeal for the law. His date must, however, have been later, since there is no mention of the building of the temple, whose service was in its regular order. In the New Testament, like others of the twelve, he is cited without his name ᵏ, or the substance of his prophecy, is spoken of or alluded to, without any reference to any human author ˡ; so entirely was his wish to remain hidden fulfilled.

ᵃ מַלְאָכִי, the extremest abridgement of the fuller form, יֶשַׁעְיָהוּ, יְשַׁעְיָה, as אוּרִי, Bezaleel's father (and two others) for אוּרִיָה, 'Uriah' or אוּרִיָּהוּ, Urijah the prophet Jer. xxvi. 20. sq. The same person אַבִי 2 Kgs xviii. 2 is אֲבִיָּה in 2 Chr. xix. 1; זַכְרִי (the name of 11 persons) is doubtless abridged from זְכַרְיָה זְכַרְיָהוּ.

ᵇ S. John i. 23.

ᶜ Habakkuk and Haggai add the title of their office, "the prophet." Hab. i. 1. Hagg. i. 1.
ᵈ Mal. ii. 7, iii. 1.   ᵉ Hagg. i. 13, Is. xlii. 19.
ᶠ Præf. ad Mal. T. i. p. 939 Vall.
ᵍ Id. on Hagg. i. 13 p. 751 Vall.
ʰ Orig. Comm. in S. Joan. T. ii. n. 25. Opp. iv. 85 de la Rue.   ⁱ S. Jer. Ep. 73 ad Evang. n. 2.
ʲ In Matt. Tom. ii. n. 30. Opp. iii. 549.
ᵏ "It is written." S. Matt. xi. 10. S. Luke vii. 27, or, with Isaiah, "in the prophets," S. Mark i. 2.
ˡ S. Luke i. 17, 76. S. Matt. xvii. 10, S. John i. 21.

Yet he probably bore a great part in the reformation, in which Nehemiah coöperated outwardly, and to effect which, after he had, on the expiring of his 12 years of office [m], returned to Persia, he obtained leave to visit his own land again [n], apparently for a short time. For he mentions his obtaining that leave, in connection with abuses at Jerusalem, which had taken place in his absence, and which he began reforming, forthwith on his arrival. But three chief abuses, the neglect of God's service, the defilement of the priesthood and of their covenant, and the cruelty to their own Jewish wives, divorcing them to make way for idolatresses, are subjects of Malachi's reproofs. Nehemiah found these practices apparently rampant. It is not then probable that they had been, before, the subjects of Malachi's denunciation, nor were his own energetic measures probably fruitless, so that there should be occasion for these denunciations afterward. It remains, then, as the most probable, that Malachi, as the prophet, coöperated with Nehemiah, as the civil authority, as Haggai and Zechariah had with Zerubbabel. "°So Isaiah coöperated with Hezekiah; Jeremiah with Josiah. Of a mere external reformation there is no instance" in Jewish history.

It does not appear, whether Nehemiah, on his return, was invested by the king of Persia with extraordinary authority for these reforms, or whether he was appointed as their governor. The brief account affords no scope for the mention of it. It is not then any objection to the contemporaneousness of Malachi and Nehemiah, that, whereas Nehemiah, while governor, *required not the bread of the governor,* i. e. the allowance granted him by the Persian government, as an impost upon the people, Malachi upbraids the people that they would not offer to their governor the poor things which they offered to Almighty God, or that the governor would not accept it, in that it would be an insult rather than an act of respect. For 1) the question in Malachi is of a free-offering, not of an impost; 2) Nehemiah says that he did not *require it,* not that he would not accept it; 3) there is no evidence that he was now governor, nor 4) any reason why he should not accept in their improved condition, what he did not *require,* [p] *because the bondage was heavy upon this people.* Presents were, as they are still, a common act of courtesy in the East.

Like S. John Baptist, though afar off, he prepared the way of the Lord by the preaching of repentance. More than other prophets, he unveils priests and people to themselves, interprets their thoughts to them, and puts those thoughts in abrupt naked language, picturing them as demurring to every charge which he brought against them. They were not, doubtless, conscious hypocrites. For conscious hypocrisy is the sin of individuals, aping the graces which others possess and which they have not, yet wish to be held in estimation for having. Here, it is the mass which is corrupt. The true Israel are the exception; [q] *those who feared the Lord, the jewels of* Almighty God. It is the hypocrisy of self-deceit, contented with poor, limited, outward service, and pluming itself upon it. Malachi unfolds to them the meaning of their acts. His thesis is themselves, whom he unfolds to them. He interprets himself, putting into their mouths words, betokening a simple unconsciousness either of God's goodness or their own evil. [r] *Yet ye say, Wherein hast Thou loved us?* This was their inward thought, as it is the thought of all, ungrateful to God. But his characteristic is, that he puts these thoughts into abrupt, bold bad words, which might startle them for their hideousness, as if he would say, "This is what your acts mean." He exhibits the worm and the decay, which lay under the whited exterior. [s] *Ye say, Wherein have we despised Thy Name?* Perhaps, they were already learning, not to pronounce the proper Name of God, while they caused it to be despised. Or they pronounced it with reverent pause, while they shewed that they held cheap God and His service. [t] *Ye say, The table of the Lord is contemptible.* [u] *Ye say, the table of the Lord is polluted; and the fruit thereof, his meat, is contemptible.* Their acts said it. What a reading of thoughts! [v] *Ye said also, Behold, what a weariness!* It is the language of the heart in all indevotion. [w] *Ye say, Wherefore?* as if innocently unconscious of the ground of God's judgment. [x] *Wherein have we robbed Thee?* The language of those who count the earth as their own. [y] *Ye say, Wherein have we wearied Him? When ye say, Every one that doeth evil is good in the sight of the Lord, and in them doth He delight, or, Where is the God of judgment?* The heart's speech in all envy at the prosperity of the wicked!

Yet the object of all this unfolding them to themselves, is their repentance. We have already the self-righteousness of the Pharisees, and the Sadducees' denial of God's Providence. And we have already the voice of S. John Baptist, *of the wrath to come.* They professed to [z] *delight* in the coming of *the messenger of the covenant;* yet their deeds were such as would be burned up with the fire of His Coming, not, rewarded.

Pharisees and Sadduces are but two offshoots of the same ungodliness; Pharisees,

---

[m] Neh. v. 14.   [n] Ib. xiii. 6.   [o] Hengst. Christ. iii. 583.
[p] Neh. v. 18.   [q] Mal. iii. 16.   [r] i. 2.   [s] i. 6.

[t] Ib. 7.   [u] Ib. and 12.   [v] Ib. 13.   [w] ii. 14.
[x] iii. 8.   [y] ii. 17.   [z] iii. 1. iv. 1.

while they hoped by outward acts to be in favor with God, they become, at least, secret Sadducees, when the hope fails. First, they justify themselves. God had said to them, [a] *Ye are departed out of the way: I have made you base, as ye have not kept My ways.* They say [b], *It is vain to serve God; and what profit, that we have kept His ordinance?* (affirming that they had done, what God called them to repentance for not doing). God said [c], *Ye have covered the altar of the Lord with tears,* the tears of their wronged wives; they insist on their own austerities, [b] *we have walked mournfully before the Lord our God.* Then comes the Sadducee portion. God had called them to obedience and said, [d] *Prove Me now herewith: they say,* [e] *the workers of wickedness have proved God, and are saved.* God promised, [f] *All nations shall call you blessed;* they answer, [g] *and now we call the proud blessed. What have we spoken against Thee?* is the last self-justifying question, which Malachi records of them; and this, while reproaching God for the uselessness of serving Him, and choosing the lot of those who rejected Him.

Thereon Malachi abandons this class to their own blindness. There was hope amid any sin, however it rebelled against God. This was a final denial of God's Providence and rejection of Himself. So Malachi closes with the same prophecy, with which S. John Baptist prepared our Lord's coming, *His* [h] *fan is in His hand, and He will thoroughly purge His floor, and will gather the wheat into His garner, but the chaff He shall burn with fire unquenchable.* The unspeakable tenderness of God toward *those who fear His name,* and the severity to those who finally rebel, are perhaps nowhere more vividly declared, than in these closing words of the Old Testament. Yet the love of God, as ever, predominates; and the last prophet closes with the word "Remember," and with one more effort to avert the curse which they were bringing upon themselves. Yet no prophet declares more expressly the rejection of the people, to whom he came to minister, the calling of the Gentiles, the universal worship, in all the earth, of Him Who was hitherto worshiped by the Jews only; and that, not at Jerusalem, but each offering, in his own place, the sacrifice which hitherto (as they had recently experienced, in their captivity at Babylon) could be offered up in Jerusalem only. To him alone it was reserved to prophesy of the unbloody Sacrifice, which should be offered unto God *in every place* throughout

the world *from the rising of the sun unto the going down thereof.* It has been said, "[i] Malachi is like a late evening, which closes a long day, but he is at the same time the morning twilight which bears in its bosom a glorious day."

"[k] When Prophecy was to be withdrawn from the ancient Church of God, its last light was mingled with the rising beams of *the Sun of Righteousness.* In one view it combined a retrospect of the Law with the clearest specific signs of the Gospel advent. [l] *Remember ye the law of Moses My servant, which I commanded him in Horeb, for all Israel,* with *the statutes and the judgments. Behold I will send you Elijah the prophet, before the great and dreadful day of the Lord.* Prophecy had been the oracle of Judaism and of Christianity, to uphold the authority of the one, and reveal the promise of the other. And now its latest admonitions were like those of a faithful departing minister, embracing and summing up his duties. Resigning its charge to the *personal* Precursor of Christ, it expired with the Gospel upon its lips."

A school, which regards the "prophets" chiefly as "poets," says that "the language is prosaic, and manifests the decaying spirit of prophecy." The office of the prophets was, to convey in forceful words, which God gave them, His message to His people. The poetic form was but an accident. God, Who knows the hearts of His creatures whom He has made, knows better than we, why He chose such an instrument. Zechariah, full of imagination, He chose some years before. But He preserved in history the account of the words which Zechariah spoke, not the words wherewith he urged the rebuilding of the temple, in his own book. Had Malachi spoken in imaginative language, like that of Ezekiel, to whom God says, [m] *thou art unto them like a very lovely song of one that hath a pleasant voice and can play well on an instrument, and they hear thy words and they do them not,* it may be that they would have acted then, as they did in the time of Ezekiel. It may be, that times like those of Malachi, apathetic, self-justifying, murmuring, self-complacent, needed a sterner, abrupter, more startling voice to awaken them. *Wisdom was justified of her children.* God wrought by him a reformation for the time being: He gave through him a warning to the generation, when our Lord should come, that He should come, as their Judge as well as their Saviour, and, how they should stand in the day of His

---

[a] ii. 8, 9.   [b] iii. 14.
[c] ii. 13.   [d] iii. 10 וּבְחָנוּנִי   [e] iii. 15. בָּחֲנוּ

וַאֲשֵׁרוּ אַתְכֶם iii. 12.

[g] אָנַחְנוּ כְּאַשֵּׁרִים iii. 15. These last contrasts are Hengstenberg's Christ. iii. 597. ed. 2.
[h] S. Luke iii. 17.
[i] Nägelsbach in Herzog Real-Encycl.

[k] Davison on prophecy pp. 456, 457. "Malachi, the last of the prophets, as in order, so in time; and even for that reason, by me chosen to fix my thoughts on, before others, because nearest, therefore, in conjunction with the Gospel; to which it leads us by the hand, and delivers us over; for that begins, where he ends." Pococke, Dedication.
[l] iv. 4.   [m] Ezek. xxxiii. 32.

Coming. He gave it as a book to His whole Church, whereby to distinguish seeming from real service. Parting words are always solemn, as closing the past, and opening out a future of expectation before us. The position of Malachi, as the last of the prophets, bids us the more solemnly prepare for that dread Day, our Lord's Second Coming, which he foretold, in one with the First, warning us that we deceive not ourselves, in unconsciousness of our own evil and remembrance of our seeming good, until He profess unto us, [n] *I never knew you; depart from Me, ye that work iniquity.*

[n] S. Matt. vii. 23.

MALACHI.

CHAPTER I.

1 *Malachi complaineth of Israel's unkindness,* 6 *Of their irreligiousness,* 12 *and profaneness.*

THE burden of the word of the LORD to Israel †by Malachi.

2 ᵃI have loved y o u,

† Heb. *by the hand of Malachi.*
ᵃ Deut. 7. 8. & 10. 15.

saith the LORD. Yet ye say, Wherein hast t h o u loved us? *Was* not Esau Jacob's brother? saith the L O R D: yet ᵇI loved Jacob.

3 And I hated E s a u, and ᶜlaid his mountains

ᵇ Rom. 9. 13.

ᶜ Jer. 49. 18. Ezek. 35. 3, 4, 7, 9, 14, 15. Obad. 10, &c.

CHAP. I. 1. *The burden of the word of the Lord to Israel.* "¹The word of the Lord is heavy, because it is called a *burden,* yet it hath something of consolation, because it is not 'against,' but *to Israel.* For it is one thing when we write *to* this or that person; another, when we write 'against' this or that person; the one being the part of friendship, the other, the open admission of enmity." *By the hand of Malachi;* through him, as the instrument of God, deposited with him; as S. Paul speaks of ²*the dispensation of the Gospel,* ³*the word of reconciliation,* ⁴*the Gospel of the uncircumcision,* being committed to him.

2. *I have loved you, saith the Lord.* What a volume of God's relations to us in two simple words, *I-have-loved you*⁵. So would not God speak, unless He still loved. "I have loved and do love you," is the force of the words. When? and since when? In all eternity God loved; in all our past, God loved. Tokens of His love, past or present, in good or seeming ill, are but an effluence of that everlasting love. He, the Unchangeable, ever loved, as the Apostle of love says; ⁶*we love Him, because He first loved us.* The deliverance from the bondage of Egypt, the making them His ⁷*peculiar people, the adoption, the covenant, the giving of the law, the service of God and His promises,* all the several mercies involved in these, the feeding with manna, the deliverance from their enemies whenever they returned to Him, their recent restoration, the gift of the prophets, were so many single pulses of God's everlasting love, uniform in itself, manifold in its manifestations. But it is more than a declaration of His everlasting love. "I have loved *you;*" God would say; with "⁸a special love, a more than ordinary love, with greater tokens of

love, than to others." So God brings to the penitent soul the thought of its ingratitude: I have loved *you:* I, you. *And ye have said, Wherein hast Thou loved us?* It is a characteristic of Malachi to exhibit in all its nakedness man's ingratitude. This is the one voice of all men's murmurings, ignoring all God's past and present mercies, in view of the one thing which He withholds; though they dare not put it into words: *Wherein hast Thou loved us?* ⁹*Within a while they forgat His works, and the wonders that He had shewed them:* ¹⁰ *they made haste, they forgat His works.* *Was* not *Esau Jacob's brother? saith the Lord: and I loved Jacob, and Esau have I hated.* "¹¹ While they were yet in their mother's womb, before any good or evil deserts of either, God said to their mother, ¹²*The elder shall serve the younger.* The hatred was not a proper and formed hatred, (for God could not hate Esau before he sinned) but only a lesser love," which, in comparison to the great love for Jacob, seemed as if it were not love. "¹¹ So he says, ¹³ *The Lord saw that Leah was hated;* where Jacob's neglect of Leah, and lesser love than for Rachel, is called 'hatred;' yet Jacob did not literally hate Leah, whom he loved and cared for as his wife." This greater love was shewn in preferring the Jews to the Edomites, giving to the Jews His law, Church, temple, prophets, and subjecting Edom to them; and especially in the recent deliverance, "¹¹ He does not speak directly of predestination, but of præelection, to temporal goods." God gave both nations alike over to the Chaldees for the punishment of their sins; but the Jews He brought back, Edom He left unrestored.

3. *And I made his mountains a waste, and his heritage for the jackals* ¹⁴ *of the wilderness.*

---

¹ S. Jer. ²¹ Cor. ix. 17, Tit. i. 3. ³ 2 Cor. v. 19.
⁴ Gal. ii. 7. · 1 Tim. 18. ⁵ אֲהַבְתִּי אֶתְכֶם.
⁶ 1 S. John iv. 19. ⁷ Rom. ix. 4. ⁸ Poc.
⁹ Ps. lxxviii. 11. ¹⁰ Ib. cvi. 13. ¹¹ Lap.
¹² Gen. xxv. 23. ¹³ Ib. xxix. 31.
¹⁴ תַּנּוֹת, in this fem. form, is but a variation from the form elsewhere, תַּנִּים, as we have אַיָּל and אַיֶּלֶת, Ewald. Lehrb. n. 147b. p. 458. ed. 8. Ges.'s rendering "dwellings" (after the LXX. δώματα ἐρήμου, and Syr.) fails in many ways. The Arab تَنَاءَة

which he, after Pococke, compares, is a nomen actionis, "a remaining, staying, dwelling, abiding [in a country, town, place], not "the dwelling" itself. 2) he supposes תַּנּוֹת to be = תַּנָּאוֹת (with dag. forte euphon.) as מִקְשָׁה for מִקְשָׁאָה, כְּבָלָה for מְכַלְאָה," (see Röd. in Ges. Thes.) But this would be to derive it from תָּנָא, with the characteristics of תנן and none of תָּנָא. 3) "dwellings of the

---

and his heritage waste for the dragons of the wilderness.

4 Whereas Edom saith, We are impoverished, but we will return and build the desolate places; thus saith the LORD of hosts, They shall build, b u t I will throw down ; and they shall call them, The border of wickedness, and, T h e people against whom the LORD hath indignation for ever.

5 And your eyes shall see, and ye s h a l l say, [d] The LORD will be magnified || † from the border of Israel.

[d] Ps. 35. 27.
|| Or, *upon.*
† Heb. *from upon.*

Malachi attests the first stage of fulfillment of Joel's prophecy, [1] *Edom shall be a desolate wilderness.* In temporal things, Esau's blessing was identical with Jacob's; *the fatness of the earth and of the dew of heaven from above;* and the rich soil on the terraces of its mountain-sides, though yielding nothing now except a wild beautiful vegetation, and its deep glens, attest what they once must have been, when artificially watered and cultivated. The first desolation must have been through Nebuchadnezzar [2] in his expedition against Egypt, when he subdued Moab and Ammon; and Edom lay in his way, as Jeremiah had foretold [3].

4. *Whereas Edom saith* [4], *We are impoverished* [5], or, more probably, *we were crushed.* Either gives an adequate sense. Human self-confidence will admit anything, as to the past ; nay, will even exaggerate past evil to itself, "Crush us how they may, we will arise and repair our losses." So Ephraim said of old, "[6] *in the pride and stoutness of heart, The bricks are fallen down, but we will build with hewn-stones : the sycamores are cut down, but we will change* them into *cedars.* It is the one language of what calls itself, "indomitable ;" in other words, "untameable," conquerors or every other gambler; "we will repair our losses." All is again staked and lost.

They shall call them the border of wickedness. Formerly it had its own proper name, *the border of Edom,* as other countries, [7] *all the border of Egypt,* [8] *the border of Moab,* [9] *the whole border of Israel,* [10] *the border of Israel,* [11] *the whole wilderness,*" is the contradictory of what is meant, complete desolation. [1] Joel iii. 19. vol. i. pp. 214, 215.

[2] Jos. Ant. x. 11. See vol. i. on Obad. 16. p. 362.

[3] Jer. xxv. 9, 21.

[4] אָמַר, Edom, for Idumæa, and so fem.

[5] So Jon. and Syr. here κατέστραπται, LXX: destructi sumus, Vulg. R. Tanchum gives both, here and on Jer. v. 17, and Sal. b. Mel. here out of Kim. on Jer. v. 17," Poc. On Jerem., Tanchum says the meaning "cut off" suits best the mention of the sword. Perhaps רשׁשׁ may be = רצץ, and תרשׁשׁ, "Tarshish," may be so called, as a boast, "she crushes." Syr., in Jerem. also has "impoverished ;" Jon. "destroy ;" S. Jer. "conteret." The αλοησουσι of the LXX. probably implies a misreading, ישׁשׁ.

border of the Amorite. Henceforth it should be known no more by its own name; but as *the border of wickedness,* where wickedness formerly dwelt, and hence the judgment of God and desolation from Him came upon it, "an accursed land." Somewhat in like way Jeremiah says of Jerusalem, [12] *Many nations shall pass by this city, and they shall say, every man to his neighbor, Wherefore hath the Lord done this unto this great city?* Then they shall answer, *Because they have forsaken the covenant of the Lord their God, and worshiped other gods and served them.* Only Israel would retain its name, as it has; Edom should be blotted out wholly and for ever.

5. *And your eyes shall see.* Malicious pleasure in looking on at the misery of Judæa and Jerusalem, had been a special sin of Edom: now God would shew Judah the fruit of its reversal, and His goodness toward themselves. "[13] Ye have assurance of His love toward you and providence over you, when ye see that ye are returned to your own land, and can inhabit it, but they cannot do this : but *they build and I throw down,* and ye therefore praise and magnify My name for this, and ye shall say, *The Lord shall be magnified on the border of Israel,* i. e. His greatness shall be always manifest upon you ;" high above and exalted over the border of Israel [14], which shall retain its name, while Edom shall have ceased to be. Wickedness gives its name to Edom's border, as in Zechariah's vision it was removed and settled in Babylon [15].

[6] Is. ix. 9, 10.　[7] Ex. x. 14, 19.　[8] De. ii. 18.

[9] 1 Sam. xi. 3, 7, xxvii. 1, 1 Chr. xxi. 12.

[10] 2 Chr. xi. 13.　[11] Jud. xi. 22.

[12] Jer. xxii. 8, 9. Comp. Deut. xxix. 23–28.

[13] Tanchum in Poc. here. Tanchum gives, as constructions of others, "the Lord, Who protecteth the border of Israel," or "ye from the border of Israel," or, "it had been fitting that ye should do this and abide in it; but ye have done the contrary," as he explains afterward.

[14] מֵעַל, as in Eccl. v. 7, גָּבֹהַ מֵעַל גָּבֹהַ "One high from above the high ;" Ezek. i. 25. "a voice from the firmament (מֵעַל) from above their heads," Gen. i. 7, "the waters above the firmament."

[15] Zech. v. 8, 11.

Before
C H R I S T
cir. 397.

6 ¶ A son ᵉ honoreth *his* father, and a servant his master: ᶠ if then I *be* a father, where *is* mine honor?

e Ex. 20. 12.
f Luke 6. 46.

and if I *be* a master, where *is* my fear? saith the LORD of hosts unto you, O priests, that despise my

Before
C H R I S T
cir. 397.

---

6. *A son honoreth his father, and a slave his lord.* Having spoken of the love of God, he turns to the thanklessness of man. God appeals to the first feelings of the human heart, the relation of parent and child, or, failing this, to the natural self-interest of those dependent on their fellow-men. *A son* by the instinct of nature, by the unwritten law written in the heart, *honoreth his father.* If he fail to do so, he is counted to have broken the law of nature, to be an unnatural son. If he is, what by nature he ought to be, he does really honor him. He does not even speak of love, as to which they might deceive themselves. He speaks of *honor,* outward reverence only; which whoso sheweth not, would openly condemn himself as an unnatural son, a bad slave. "Of course," the Jews would say, "children honor parents, and slaves their masters, but what is that to us?" God turns to them their own mental admission.

If I am a Father. "[1] Although, before ye were born, I began to love you in Jacob as sons, yet choose by what title ye will name Me: I am either your Father or your Lord. If a Father, render me the honor due to a father, and offer the piety worthy of a parent. If a Lord, wl y despise ye Me? why fear ye not your Lord?" God was their Father by creation, as He is Father of all, as Creator of all. He had come to be their Father in a nearer way, by temporal redemption and adoption as His peculiar people, creating them to be a nation to His glory. This they were taught to confess in their psalmody, [2] *He hath made us, and not we ourselves; we are His people and the sheep of His pasture.* This title God had given them in sight of the Egyptians, [3] *Israel is My son, My firstborn:* of this Hosea reminded them; [4] *When Israel was a child, then I loved him, and called My son out of Egypt;* and Jeremiah reassured them, [5] *I am a Father to Israel and Ephraim is My first-born :* this, Isaiah had pleaded to God; [6] *Doubtless Thou art our Father, though Abraham be ignorant of us, and Israel acknowledge us not. Thou, O Lord, art our Father, our Redeemer, Thy name is from everlasting.* [7] *And now, O Lord, Thou art our Father ; we the clay, and Thou our potter ; and we all, the work of Thy hands.* God had impressed this His relation of Father, in Moses' prophetic warn-

ing; [8] *Do ye thus requite the Lord, O foolish people and unwise? Is not He thy Father that hath bought thee? hath He not made thee and established thee?* "[9] God is the *Father* of the faithful; 1) by creation; 2) by preservation and governance; 3) by alimony; 4) by fatherly care and providence; 5) by faith and grace, whereby He justifies and adopts us as sons and heirs of His kingdom."

If I am a Father. He does not throw doubt, that He is our Father; but, by disobedience, we in deeds deny it. Our life denies what in words we profess. *Where is My honor?* "[10] Why obey ye not My precepts, nor honor Me with acts of adoration; praying, praising, giving thanks, sacrificing, and reverently fulfilling every work of God? For [11] *cursed is he that doeth the work of the Lord deceitfully.*"

And if I am your Lord, "as I certainly am, and specially by singular providence." "[12] He is our Lord by the same titles, that He is our Father, and by others, as that He has redeemed us, and purchased us to Himself by the Blood of His Son ; that He is the Supreme Majesty, Whom all creation is bound to serve; that, setting before us the reward of eternal glory, He has hired us as servants and laborers into His vineyard." God Alone is Lord through universal sovereignty, underived authority, and original source of laws, precepts, rights; and all other lords are but as ministers and instruments, compared to Him, the Lord and original Doer of all. Hence He says, [13] *I am the Lord ; that is My Name, and My glory will I not give to another.*

Where is My fear? which ought to be shewn Me. "[14] If thou art a servant, render to the Lord the service of fear; if a son, shew to thy Father the feeling of piety. But thou renderest not thanks, neither lovest nor fearest God. Thou art then either a contumacious servant or a proud son." "[12] Fear includes reverence, adoration, sacrifice, the whole worship of God." "[15] Whoso feareth is not over-curious, but adores; is not inquisitive, but praises, and glorifies."

"[10] Fear is twofold; servile, whereby punishment, not fault, is dreaded; filial, by which fault is feared. In like way service is twofold. A servant with a service of fear, purely servile, does not deserve to be called

---

[1] S. Jer.   [2] Ps. c. 3
[3] Ex. iv. 22.   [4] Hos. xi. 1. See vol. i. p. 109.
[5] Jer. xxxi. 9.   [6] Is. lxiii. 16.   [7] Ib. lxiv. 8.
[8] Deut. xxxii. 6.   [9] Lap.

[10] Dion.   [11] Jer. xlviii. 10.   [12] Lap.   [13] Is. xlii. 8.
[14] Lap. as from S. Ambr.
[15] S. Chrys. de Incompr. Dei. Hom. ii. T. i. p. 459.
Ben.

Before
CHRIST
cir. 397.
ᵍ ch. 2. 14, 17.
& 3. 7, 8, 13.

name. ᵍ And ye say,
Wherein have we despised
thy name?

7 ‖ Ye offer ʰ polluted
bread upon mine altar;
and ye say, Wherein have

Before
CHRIST
cir. 397.
‖ Or, Bring
unto, &c.
ʰ Deut. 15. 21.

a son of God, nor is in a state of salvation, not having love. Whence Christ, distinguishing such a servant from a son of God by adoption, saith, ¹ *The servant abideth not in the house forever, but the son abideth ever:* and again, ² *The servant knoweth not what his Lord doeth.* But a servant, whose service is of pure and filial love, is also a son, of whom the Saviour saith, ³ *Well done, good and faithful servant, enter thou into the joy of thy Lord.* But since a distinction is made here between the son and the servant, he seems to be speaking of servile fear, which, although it doth not good well and meritoriously, i. e. witĥ a right intention and from love, yet withdraws from ill, and is the beginning of wisdom, because it disposeth to grace. Whence it is written, '⁴ The fear of the Lord driveth away sins,' and again Scripture saith, ⁵ *By the fear of the Lord men depart from evil.*"

"⁶ God requireth to be feared as a Lord, honored as a Father, loved as a Husband. Which is chiefest of these? Love. Without this, fear has torment, honor has no grace. Fear, when not enfreed by love, is servile. Honor, which cometh not from love, is not honor, but adulation. Honor and glory belong to God Alone; but neither of them will God accept, unless seasoned with the honey of love."

Saith the Lord unto you, O priests, who despise My Name, lit. *despisers of My Name,* habitually beyond others. The contempt of God came specially from those bound most to honor him. Priests, as consecrated to God, belonged especially to God. "⁷ Malachi begins his prophecy and correction by the correction of the priests; because the reformation of the state and of the laity hangs upon the reformation of the clergy and the priest; for ⁸ *as is the priest, such also is the people.*" He turns, with a suddenness which must have been startling to them, to them as the centre of the offending.

And ye say, Wherein have we despised Thy Name? Before, it was ignorance of God's

love: now it is ignorance of self and of sin. They affect to themselves innocence and are unconscious of any sin. They said to themselves doubtless, (as many do now) "we cannot help it; we do the best we can, under the circumstances." Without some knowledge of God's love, there can be no sense of sin; without some sense of sin, no knowledge of His love. They take the defensive, they are simply surprised, like Cain, ⁹ *Am I my brother's keeper?* or many of the lost in the Day of judgment, ¹⁰ *Many will say to Me in that day, Lord, Lord, have we not prophesied in Thy Name? and in Thy Name have cast out devils? and in Thy Name done many wonderful works?* and yet were all the while *workers of iniquity,* to whom He will say, *I never knew you:* and, ¹¹ *Lord, when saw we Thee an hungered, or athirst, or a stranger, or naked, or sick, or in prison, and did not minister unto Thee?* And yet they *shall go away into everlasting punishment.*

7. *Offering polluted bread upon Mine altar.* This, continuing on the words, *despisers of My Name* ¹², is the answer to their question, *Wherein have we despised Thy Name? Bread* might stand, in itself, either for the shewbread, or for the "minchah," meal-offering, which was the necessary accompaniment of sacrifices and sometimes the whole. But here the *polluted bread* cannot be the shewbread, since this was not put upon the altar, but upon its own table; and although the altar is, as here, also called "a table ¹³" in regard to the sacrifice hereon consumed, "the table" of the shewbread is nowhere called "altar." The prophet then means by *bread,* either the meal-offering, as representing the sacrifice, or the offerings by fire altogether, as in Ezekiel, ¹⁴ *When ye offer My bread, the fat and the blood;* and in Leviticus, ¹⁵ *the offerings of the Lord, made by fire, the bread of their God, do they offer;* and of the *peace-offering* ¹⁶, the *priest shall burn it upon the altar; the bread of the offering made by fire unto the Lord:* and specifically, of animals with blemish, as these, it is forbidden, ¹⁷ *Neither from a*

¹ S. John viii. 35.   ² Ib. xv. 15.
³ S. Matt. xxv. 21, 23. ⁴ Ecclus. i. 21. ⁵ Pr. xvi. 6.
⁶ S. Bern. Serm. 83 in Cant. n. 4. Opp. i. 1560 Ben. Lap.   ⁷ Lap.   ⁸ Hos. iv. 9.   ⁹ Gen. iv. 9.
¹⁰ S. Matt. vii. 22, 23.   ¹¹ Ib. xxv. 44, 46.
¹² The collocation of מְנִישִׁים is probably subordinate to the verb, expressed in the question, *ye despise, offering;* as the participle often is to the expressed finite verb. Nu. xxvi. 27. Jud. viii. 4. Ps. vii. 3. lxxviii. 4, Job xiv. 20, xxiv. 5, Ezr. x. 1, Jer. xliii. 2 (instances out of those in Ewald Lehrb. § 341. b 3. p. 836. ed. 3.) This case is however more developed than the rest, as not being contemporaneous only, but in explanation of that expressed

by the finite verb. הִגִּישׁ is used with לְ, of offerings to God, Am. v 25, Mal. ii. 12; with עַל, here only.
¹³ In Ezek. xli. 22, the "altar" is called *the table that is before the Lord,* and in regard to the offering of the sacrifice, it is said, *they shall come near to my table,* Ezek. xli. 15, 16.   ¹⁴ Ezek. xliv. 7.
¹⁵ Lev. xxi. 6: more briefly, *the bread of thy God,* ib. 8, *of his God,* ib. 17 and (parallel with *to offer the offerings of the Lord made by fire,*) 21; *to eat the bread of his God* (in contrast with offering it) ib. 22, and in Nu. xxxiii. 2, "*thy offering, thy bread for thy sacrifices made by fire, shall ye observe to offer to Me.*"
¹⁶ Lev. iii. 11.   ¹⁷ Ib. xxii. 25.

Before CHRIST cir. 397.

we polluted thee? In that ye say, [1] The table of the LORD is contemptible.

8 And [k] if ye offer the blind † for sacrifice, is it not evil? and if ye offer

the lame and sick, is it not evil? offer it now unto thy governor; will he be pleased with thee, or [1] accept thy person? saith the LORD of hosts.

[1] Ezek. 41. 22. ver. 12.
[k] Lev. 22. 22. Deut. 15. 21. ver. 14.
† Heb. to sacrifice.

Before CHRIST cir. 397.

[1] Job 42. 8.

---

stranger's hand shall ye offer the bread of your God of any of these, because their corruption is in them, blemishes in them: they shall not be accepted for you. It was, as it were, a feast of God with man, and what was withdrawn from the use of man by fire, was, as it were, consumed by God, to Whom it was offered.

It was polluted, in that it was contrary to the law of God which forbade to sacrifice any animal, lame or blind or with any ill blemish, as being inconsistent with the typical perfection of the sacrifice. Even the Gentiles were careful about the perfection of their sacrifices. "[1] Blind is the sacrifice of the soul, which is not illumined by the light of Christ. Lame is his sacrifice of prayer, who comes with a double mind to entreat the Lord." "[2] He offereth one weak, whose heart is not established in the grace of God, nor by the anchor of hope fixed in Christ. These words are also uttered against those who, being rich, offer to the Creator the cheaper and least things, and give small alms."

And we say, Wherewith have we polluted Thee [3]? It is a bold expression. Yet a word, to which we are but too ill-accustomed, which expresses what most have done, "dishonor God," comes to the same. Though less bold in expression, they are yet like in meaning. [4] Will ye pollute Me any more among My people? or, [5] that My Name should not be polluted before the heathen. [6] My holy Name shall Israel no more defile; [7] I will not let them pollute My Name any more. "[8] Much more in the new law, in which the Sacrifice is Christ Himself our God, whence the Apostle says expressly, [9] Whoso eateth this bread and drinketh this Cup of the Lord unworthily, shall be guilty of the Body and Blood of the Lord. "[1] For when the Sacraments are violated, Himself, Whose Sacraments they are, is violated." God speaks of our acts with an unveiled plainness, which we should not dare to use. "[2] As we are said to sanctify God, when we minister to Him in holiness and righteousness, and so, as far as in us lies,

shew that He is holy; so we are said to pollute Him, when we conduct ourselves irreverently and viciously before Him, especially in His worship, and, thereby, as far as in us lies, shew that He is not holy and is to be dishonored."

In that ye say, the table of the Lord is contemptible, lit. contemptible is it [10], and so any contemptible thing might be offered on it. They said this probably, not in words, but in deeds. Or, if in words, in plausible words. "[11] God doth not require the ornamenting of the altar, but the devotion of the offerers." "[1] What good is it, if we offer the best? Be what we offer, what it may, it is all to be consumed by fire." "[8] The pretext at once of avarice and gluttony!" And so they kept the best for themselves. They were poor, on their return from the captivity. Anyhow, the sacrifices were offered. What could it matter to God? And so they dispensed with God's law.

"[12] So at this day we see some priests and prelates, splendid in their tables and feasts, sordid in the altar and temple; on the table are costly napkins and wine; on the Altar torn linen and wine-mace [13] rather than wine." "[1] We pollute the bread, that is, the Body of Christ, when we approach the Altar unworthily, and, being defiled, drink that pure Blood, and say, The table of the Lord is contemptible; not that any one dareth to say this, but the deeds of sinners pour contempt on the Table of God."

8. And if ye offer the blind for sacrifice, is it not evil? Others, it is not evil, as we should say, "there is no harm in it." Both imply, alike, an utter unconsciousness on the part of the offerer, that it was evil: the one, in irony, that this was always their answer, "there is nothing amiss;" the other is an indignant question, "is there indeed nought amiss?" And this seems the most natural.

The sacrifice of the blind and lame was expressly forbidden in the law [14], and the sick in manifold varieties of animal disease. Whatever hath a blemish ye shall not offer,

---

[1] S. Jer.   [2] Dion.
[3] The conj. גָּאַל occurs only here: the pass. גֹּאָל, here and 12, Ezr. ii. 62, Neh. vii. 64, in one idiom.
[4] Ezek. xiii. 19.   [5] Ib. xx. 9, 14, 22.
[6] Ib. xliii. 7.   [7] Ib. xxxix. 7.   [8] Lap.
[9] 1 Cor. xi. 27.
[10] נִבְזֶה הוּא; the noun being prefixed absolutely,

as in Gen. xxxiv. 21, "these men, peaceful are they," Ib. xlii. 11; "all of us, sons of one man are we." Ewald n. 297. b. pp. 761, 762.
[11] Remig.
[12] Lap. referring to Card. Bellarmine de gemitu columbæ.
[13] "villum ("the refuse of kernels and skins,"), potius quam vinum."   [14] Deut. xv. 21.

Before
CHRIST
cir. 397.

9 And now, I pray you, beseech † God that he will be gracious unto us : ^m this hath been † by your means : will he regard your persons? saith the LORD of hosts.

10 Who *is there* e v e n

† Heb. *the face of God.*
^m Hos. 13. 9.
† Heb. *from your hand.*

among you that would shut the doors *for n o u g h t ?* ⁿ neither do ye kindle *fire* on mine altar for nought. I have no pleasure in you, saith the LORD of hosts, ^o neither will I accept an offering at your hand.

Before
CHRIST
cir. 397.

ⁿ 1 Cor. 9. 13

^o Isai. 1. 11.
Jer. 6. 20.
Amos 5. 21.

[1] *blind* or with limb *broken, or wounded or mangy or scabby or scurfy.* Perfectness was an essential principle of sacrifice ; whether, as in the daily sacrifice, or the sin or trespass-offering, typical of the all-perfect Sacrifice, or in the whole-burnt-offering, of the entire self-oblation. But these knew better than God, what was fit for Him and them. His law was to be modified by circumstances. He would not be so particular, (as men now say so often.)

Is it then fit to offer to God what under the very same circumstances man would not offer to man ? Against these idle, ungrateful, covetous thoughts God saith,

Offer it now unto thy governor. He appeals to our own instinctive thought of propriety to our fellow creature, which may so often be a test to us. No one would think of acting to a fellow-creature, as they do to Almighty God. Who would make diligent preparation to receive any great one of the earth, and turn his back upon him, when come ? Yet what else is the behavior of most Christians after Holy Communion ? If thou wouldest not do this to a mortal man, who is but dust and ashes, how much less to God Almighty, the King of kings and Lord of lords ! "[2] The words are a reproof to those most negligent persons, who go through their prayers to God without fear, attention, reverence or feeling ; but if they have to speak to some great man, prelate or prince, approach him with great reverence, speak carefully and distinctly and are in awe of him. Do not thou prefer the creature to the Creator, man to God, the servant to the Lord, and that Lord, so exalted and so Infinite."

9. *And now entreat, I pray you, God* [3], *that He will be gracious unto you.* This is not a call to repentance, for he assumes that God would not accept them. It is rather irony ; " go now, seek the favor of God, as ye would not that of your governor." *From your hand,* not from your fathers, not from aliens, *hath this been : will He accept persons from you?* The unusual construction seems to imply a

difference of meaning ; as if he would say, that it consisted not with the justice of God, that He should be an *accepter of persons,* (which He declares that He is not) which yet He would be, were He to accept them, while acting thus.

10. *Who* is there *even among you ?* This stinginess in God's service was not confined to those offices which cost something, as the sacrifices. Not even services absolutely cost-less, which required only a little trouble, as that of closing the folding-doors of the temple or the outer court, or bringing the fire to consume the sacrifices, would they do without some special hire. All was mercenary and hireling service. Others have rendered it as a wish, *who is there among you !* i. e. would that there were one among you, who would close the doors altogether ; or shall ye not kindle fire on Mine altar for nought, i. e. fruitlessly ! But apart from the difficulty of the construction, it is not God's way to *quench the smouldering flax.* He Who bids, *Gather up the fragments that remain, that nothing be lost,* accepts any imperfect service rather than none. He does not break off the last link, which binds man to Himself. Then, if or when God willed His service to surcease, He would do it Himself, as He did by the destruction of the temple before the Captivity, or finally by the Romans. It would have been an ungodly act, (such as was only done by Ahaz, perhaps the most ungodly king of Israel [4]), and one which especially called down His wrath [5], to close the doors, and therewith to break off all sacrifice. Manasseh carried the worship of false gods into the temple itself ; Ahaz, as far as in him lay, abolished the service of God. A prophet of God could not express a wish, that pious Israelites (for it is presupposed that they would do this out of zeal for God's honor) should bring the service of God to an end.

He sums up with an entire rejection of them, present and future. *I have no pleasure in you ;* it is a term of repudiation [6], sometimes of disgust [7], *neither will I accept an offer-*

[1] Lev. xxii. 22.   [2] Dion.

[3] אל seems to be used purposely in contrast with man, as in Is. xxxi. 3, *The Egyptians are men and not God.*

[4] 2 Chron. xxviii. 24.   [5] Ib. xxix. 8.
[6] חפץ אין 1 Sam. xviii. 25. Eccl. v. 3. [4 Eng.]
[7] כלי אין חפץ בו Jer. xxii. 28, xlviii. 38, Hos. viii. 8.

Before CHRIST cir. 397.	11 For [p] from the rising of the sun even unto the going down of the same my name *shall be* great	[q] among the Gentiles ; [r] and in every p l a c e [s] incense *shall be* offered unto my name, and a pure offering :	Before CHRIST cir. 397.

[p] Ps. 113. 3.
Isai. 59. 19.

[q] Isai. 60. 3, 5.
[r] John 4. 21, 23.
1 Tim. 2. 8.
[s] Rev. 8. 3.

ing at your hands. He says not simply, [1] *your burnt-offerings are not acceptable, nor your sacrifices sweet unto Me,* but, *I will not accept* it. Such as they were, such they would be hereafter. God would not accept their sacrifices, but would replace them.

11. *For.* The form of words does not express whether this declaration relates to the present or the future. It is a vivid present, such as is often used to describe the future. But the things spoken of it to be future. The Jewish sacrifices had defects, partly incidental, partly inherent. Incidental were those, with which the Prophet had upbraided them; inherent, (apart from their mere typical character)that they never could be the religion of the world, since they were locally fixed at Jerusalem. Malachi tells them of a new sacrifice, which should be offered throughout the then heathen world, grounded on His new revelation of Himself to them. *For great* shall be *My Name among the heathen.* The prophet anticipates an objection[2], which the Jews might make to him. [3] *What then will God do unto His great Name?* Those by which He would replace them, would be more worthy of God in two ways, 1) in themselves, 2) in their universality. *Then,* whatsoever the heathen worshiped, even if some worshiped an *unknown God,* His *Name* was not known to .them, nor *great among* them. Those who knew of Him, knew of Him, not as the Lord of heaven and earth, but as the God of the Jews only; their *offerings* were not *pure,* but manifoldly defiled. A Hebrew prophet could not be an apologist for heathen idolatry amidst its abominations, or set it on a level with the worship which God had, for the time, appointed ; much less could he set it forth as *the* true acceptable service of God[4]. Malachi himself speaks of it, as an aggrava-

tion of cruelty in their divorcing of their wives, that they [5] *married the daughter of a strange god.* The worship of those Jews, who remained, out of secular interests, in foreign countries, could not be represented as *the* " pure offering ; " for they made no offerings : then as now, these being forbidden out of Jerusalem ; nor would the worship of such Jews, as were scattered in the large empire of Persia, be contrasted with that at Jerusalem, as *the* pure worship ; else why should the Jews have returned ? It would have been an abolition of the law before its time. Malachi prophesies then, as had Micah, Isaiah, Zephaniah [6], of a new revelation of God, when, and in which, men should *worship Him, every one from his place, even all the isles of the heathen.*

Our Lord Himself explains and expands it in His words to the Samaritan woman ; [7] *Woman, believe Me, the hour cometh, when ye shall neither in this mountain, nor yet at Jerusalem, worship the Father.—The hour cometh, and now is, when the true worshipers shall worship the Father in spirit and in truth ; for the Father seeketh such to worship Him. God is a Spirit : and they that worship Him must worship Him in spirit and in truth,* and declared the rejection of the Jews, sealing their own sentence against themselves, [8] *I say unto you, The kingdom of God shall be taken from you, and given to a nation bringing forth the fruits thereof ;* and before, [9] *Many shall come from the East and West, and shall sit down with Abraham and Isaac and Jacob in the kingdom of heaven, and the children of the kingdom shall be cast out into outer darkness.*

Incense shall be *offered unto My name,* lit. I think, *there* shall be *incense, oblation made unto My name* [this is a mere question of construction [10]], *and a pure oblation.*

מְקֻטָּר מֻגָּשׁ are, I think most probably, two independent impersonal passive participles, taken as future, " will be incensed, offered [wird geräuchert, dargebrachtas Ewald ג (Lehrb. 295 a) הוּחַל, " there is begun," שֻׁדַּד, " there is wasted," מְדֻבָּר " there is spoken " (Ps. lxxxvii. 3), and this place. Tanchum praises Abulwalid for taking מקטר as a noun = קְטוֹרָה (Lib. Rad. col. 634). He adds, " The rest (יְיֹרֵה) take them as adjectives with an unexpressed substantive." This, I think right : for, although מקטר might be ' what is incensed,' and so a subst. הִגַּשׁ is used elsewhere of offering a sacrifice, not of offering incense, and so מקטר could not be the subject to it.

[1] Jer. vi. 20.   [2] Poc.   [3] Jos. vii. 9.
[4] So in Rashi ; Our rabbis say, that " they [the heathen] called Him [the Lord] God of gods ; he too who hath an idol, knoweth, that He [the Lord] is God, that He is above all those things, and that in every place the Gentiles also, of their own accord, offer unto my name. But our rabbis have expounded, that they [those spoken of] are the disciples of the wise, who in every place are occupied in the rules of the Divine worship ; so also all the prayers of Israel, which they make in every place, these are like a pure oblation (Minchah), and so Jonathan interprets, ' at whatever time ye shall do My will, I receive your prayers, and My great name is sanctified by you, and your prayer is like a pure oblation before Me.'" See Ibn Ezra, D. Kim., Tanchum, Abarb., in Poc.
[5] Mal. ii. 11.   [6] Zeph. ii. 11.
[7] S. John iv. 21, 23, 24.   [8] S. Matt. xxi. 41, 43.
[9] Id. viii. 11, 12.

This sacrifice, which should be offered, is designated by the special name of *meal-offering*[1]. God would not accept it from the Jews; He would, from the Heathen. It was a special sacrifice, offered by itself as an unbloody sacrifice, or together with the bloody sacrifice. [2] *It is most holy, as the sin-offering and as the trespass-offering.* In the daily sacrifice it was offered morning and evening, with the lamb. As this was typical of the precious blood-shedding of the *Lamb without spot* upon the Cross, so was the meal-offering which accompanied it, of the Holy Eucharist.

The early Christians saw the force of the prediction, that sacrifice was contrasted with sacrifice, the bloody sacrifices which were ended by the "One full perfect and sufficient Sacrifice Oblation and Satisfaction" made by our Lord "on the Altar of the Cross for the sins of the whole world," and those sacrifices which He commanded to be made on our Altars, as a memorial of Him. So S. Justin, who was converted probably A.D. 133, within 30 years from the death of S. John, says, "[3] God has therefore beforehand declared, that all who through this name offer those sacrifices, which Jesus, Who is the Christ, commanded to be offered, that is to say, in the Eucharist of the Bread and of the Cup, which are offered in every part of the world by us Christians, are well-pleasing to Him. But those sacrifices, which are offered by you and through those priests of yours, He wholly rejects, saying, *And I will not accept your offerings at your hands. For from the rising of the sun even to the going down of the same, My Name is glorified among the Gentiles; but ye profane it.*"

He points out further the failure of the Jewish explanation as to *their* sacrifices, in that the Church was everywhere, not so the Jews. "[3] You and your teachers deceive yourselves, when you interpret this passage of Scripture of those of your nation who were in the dispersion[4], and say that it speaks of their prayers and sacrifices made in every place, as pure and well-pleasing, and know that you speak falsely, and endeavor in every way to impose upon yourselves; first, because your people are not found, even now, from the rising to the setting of the sun, but there are nations, in which none of your race have ever dwelt: whilst there is not one nation of men, whether Barbarians, or Greeks, or by whatsoever name distinguished, whether of those (nomads) who live in wagons, or of those who have no houses, or those pastoral people that dwell in tents, among whom prayers and thanksgivings are not offered to the Father and

Creator of all things, through the name of the crucified Jesus. And you know that at the time when the prophet Malachi said this, the dispersion of you through the whole world, in which you now are, had not yet taken place; as is also shewn by Scripture."

S. Irenæus in the same century, "[5] He took that which is part of the creation, viz. bread, and gave thanks, saying, *This is My Body.* And the Cup likewise, which is of the creation which appertains unto us, He professed to be His own Blood, and taught men the new oblation of the New Testament; which the Church receiving from the Apostles offers unto God in the world :—unto Him Who giveth us nourishment, the first-fruits of His own gifts, in the New Testament; of which in the twelve prophets Malachi gave beforehand this intimation [quoting Mal. i. 10, 11]; most evidently intimating hereby, that while the former people should cease to make offerings to God, in every place sacrifice should be offered unto Him, and that in pureness; His Name also is glorified among the Gentiles. Now what other name is there, which is glorified among the Gentiles, than that which belongs to our Lord, by Whom the Father is glorified, and man is glorified? And because man belongs to His Own Son, and is made by Him, He calls him His Own. And as if some King were himself to paint an image of his own son, he justly calls it his own image, on both accounts, first that it is his son's, next, that he himself made it: so also the Name of Jesus Christ, which is glorified in the Church throughout the whole world, the Father professes to be His own, both because it is His Son's, and because He Himself wrote and gave it for the salvation of men. Because therefore the Name of the Son properly belongs to the Father, and in God Almighty through Jesus Christ the Church makes her offering, well saith He on both accounts, *And in every place incense is offered unto My Name, and a pure sacrifice.* And *incense,* John in the Apocalypse declares to be *the prayers of the Saints.* Therefore the offering of the Church, which the Lord hath taught to be offered in the whole world, is accounted with God as a pure sacrifice, and accepted of Him."

Tertullian contrasts the "[6] sacerdotal law through Moses, in Leviticus, prescribing to the people of Israel, that sacrifices should in no other place be offered to God than in the land of promise, which the Lord God was about to give to the people Israel and to their brethren, in order that on Israel's introduction thither, there should be there

---

[1] Lev. ii. 7 (14 Eng.) sqq.
[2] Ib. vi. 17. [10. Heb.]
[3] Dial. c. Tryph. § 117 pp. 215, 216 Oxf. Tr. also § 28, 29 pp. 104, 105. Ib.
[4] The Jews then must have interpreted it of

themselves in the present, and so of the times of Malachi after the return of others from Babylon.
[5] iv. 17. 5. pp. 356, 357. Oxf. Tr. See also his Fragment xxxvi. p. 554, 555. Oxf. Tr. [6] c. Jud. i. 5. p. 214 Edinb. Tr. Add c. Marcion. iii. 22.

celebrated sacrifices and holocausts, as well for sins as for souls, and nowhere else but in the holy land [1]," and this subsequent prediction of "the Spirit through the prophets, that in every place and in every land there should be offered sacrifices to God. As He says through the angel Malachi, one of the twelve prophets, (citing the place)."

S. Hippolytus, a disciple of S. Irenæus, A. D. 220. martyr, in a commentary on Daniel, says that "[2] when Anti-Christ cometh, the sacrifice and libation will be taken away, which is now in every place offered by the Gentiles to God." The terms "Sacrifice offered in every place" are terms of Malachi.

So S. Cyprian, in his Testimonies against the Jews, sums up the teaching of the passage under this head, "[3] That the old sacrifice was to be made void, and a new sacrifice instituted."

In the "[4] Apostolic Constitutions," the prophecy is quoted as "said by God of His œcumenical Church."

Eusebius says, "[5] The truth bears witness to the prophetic word, whereby God, rejecting the Mosaic sacrifices, foretells that which shall be among us. *For from the rising of the sun &c.* We sacrifice then to the supreme God the sacrifice of praise; we sacrifice the Divine, reverend and holy oblation: we sacrifice, in a new way according to the New Testament, the pure sacrifice. The broken heart is also called a sacrifice to God—We sacrifice also the Memory of that great Sacrifice, performing it according to the mysteries which have been transmitted by Him."

S. Cyril of Jerusalem [6] speaks of it only as prophesying the rejection of the Jews and the adoption of the Gentiles.

In the liturgy of S. Mark [7], it is naturally quoted, only, as fulfilled "in the reasonable and unbloody sacrifice, which all nations offer to Thee, O Lord, from the rising of the sun to the setting thereof," not in reference to the cessation of Jewish sacrifices.

S. Chrysostom dwells on its peculiar force, coming from so late a prophet [8]. "Hear Malachi, who came after the other prophets. For I adduce, for the time, no testimony either of Isaiah or Jeremiah or any other before the Captivity, lest thou shouldest say that the terrible things which he foretold were exhausted in the Captivity. But I adduce a prophet, after the return from

Babylon and the restoration of your city, prophesying clearly about you. For when they had returned, and recovered their city, and rebuilt the temple and performed the sacrifices, foretelling this present desolation then future, and the taking away of the sacrifice, Malachi thus speaks in the Person of God [ver. 10 fin.—12 beg.]. When, oh Jew, happened all this? When was incense offered to God in every place? when a pure sacrifice? Thou couldest not name any other time, than this, after the Coming of Christ. If the prophet foretelleth not this time and our sacrifice, but the Jewish, the prophecy will be against the law. For if, when Moses commandeth that sacrifice should be offered in no other place than the Lord God should choose, and shutteth up those sacrifices in one place, the prophet says that incense should be offered in every place and a pure sacrifice, he opposeth and contradicteth Moses. But there is no strife nor contention. For Moses speaketh of one sacrifice, and Malachi of another. Where doth this appear? [From the place, not Judæa only; from the mode, that it should be pure; from the offerers, not Israel, but the nations,] from East to West, shewing that whatever of earth the sun surveys, the preaching will embrace.—He calls the former sacrifice impure, not in its own nature but in the mind of the offerers; if one compares the sacrifice itself, there is such a boundless distance, that this [that offered by Christians] might in comparison be called 'pure.'"

Even the cold, but clear, Theodoret has, "[9] Foretelling to the Jews the cessation of the legal priesthood, he announces the pure and unbloody sacrifice of the Gentiles. And first he says to the Jews, *I have no pleasure in you, saith the Lord of hosts, and I will not accept a sacrifice at your hands.* Then he foreshews the piety of the Gentiles, *For from the rising of the sun &c,* (Mal. i. 11.) You then I will wholly reject; for I detest altogether what you do. Wherefore also I reject the sacrifice offered by you; but instead of you, I have the whole world to worship Me. For the dwellers in the whole earth, which the rising and setting sun illumines, will everywhere both offer to Me incense, and will sacrifice to Me the pure sacrifice, which I love. For they shall know My name and My will, and shall offer to Me reverence due. So the Lord said

---

[1] Lev. xvii. 1–6, Deut. xii. 5–14, 26, 27.

[2] Interpret. in Dan. n. xxii. p. 110, published from the Chisian codex of cent. x. in Daniel sec. LXX. Romæ 1772. The passage is quoted loosely by S. Jerome in Dan. c. 9. Opp. v. 689. Vall.

[3] Testim. ad Quirin. i. 16. pp. 23 and 31. Oxf. Tr.

[4] vii. 30 [on their age, especially of that of their substance, see Pusey, The Real Presence the doctrine of the early Church pp. 605–609.]

[5] Dem. Ev. i. 10. fin. He also quotes the passage in proof of the abolition of the Jewish sacrifices,

although without allusion to the Eucharistic sacrifice, Ib. i. 6. p. 19; and in ii. 29. pp. 55, 56, of the rejection of the Jewish nation and their bodily worship according to the law of Moses, and the spiritual worship given to all nations through Christ."

[6] Cat. xviii. 25. [7] Assem. Cod. Lit. vii. 19, 20.

[8] Ad. Jud. v. 12. Opp. i. 647, 648 Montf. See also his Expos. in Ps. 112. n. 2. Opp. v. 288, 289, and Quod Christus sit Deus Opp. i. 582, "Seest thou, how plainly he both cast out Judaism and exhibited Christianity effulgent and extended over the whole world?" [9] ad. loc.

Before
CHRIST
cir. 397.

t for my name *shall be* great among the heathen, saith the LORD of hosts.

t Isai. 66. 19, 20.

12 ¶ But ye have profaned it, in that ye s a y, u The table of the LORD *is* polluted: and the fruit

u ver. 7.

thereof, *even* his meat *is* contemptible.

13 Ye said also, Behold, w h a t a weariness *is it !* || and ye have snuffed at it, saith t h e L O R D of hosts: and ye b r o u g h t

|| Or, *whereas ye might have blown it away.*

Before
CHRIST
cir. 397.

---

to the Samaritan woman, *Woman, believe Me, that the hour cometh and now is, when neither in this mountain, nor in Jerusalem shall ye worship the Father.*—The blessed Paul, being instructed in this, says, [1] *I will that men pray everywhere &c*, and the Divine Malachi clearly taught us in this place the worship now used ; for the circumscribed worship of the priests is brought to an end, and every place is accounted fit for the worship of God, and the sacrifice of irrational victims is ended, and He, our spotless Lamb, Who taketh away the sin of the world, is sacrificed."

Lastly, S. Augustine, " [2] Malachi, prophesying of the Church which we see propagated through Christ, says most plainly to the Jews in the person of God, *I have no pleasure in you, and will not receive an offering at your hands. For from the rising of the sun &c.* Since we see this sacrifice through the priesthood of Christ after the order of Melchisedek, now offered to God in every place from the rising of the sun to its setting ; but the sacrifice of the Jews, of which it is said, *I have no pleasure in you, neither will I accept an offering from your hands,* they cannot deny to have ceased; why do they yet expect another Christ, since what they read as prophesied and see fulfilled, could not be fulfilled, except through Him ? "

12. *And ye have profaned* [[3] *are habitually profaning it*], *in that ye say.* It was the daily result of their daily lives and acts. " [4] It is probable that the priests did not use such words, but that by their very deeds, they proclaimed this aloud: as in the, *The fool hath said in his heart, There is no God.* For in that he is seen to be a despiser, though he say it not in words, yet, by their very deeds and by the crookedness of their lives, they all-but cry out, There is no God. For they who live as though God beheld not, and do all things recklessly and unholily, by their own deeds and works deny God. So they who are not

earnest to preserve to the holy Altar the reverence becoming to it, by the very things which they do, say,

The table of the Lord is despised. Not *the table of shewbread,* since it is so called in reference to the sacrifice offered thereon. Ezekiel had probably so called the altar, which he saw in his vision of the new temple [5]. It is what was before called *the altar ;* an *altar,* in regard to the sacrifices offered to God ; a *table,* in regard to the food of the sacrifice therefrom received. Both names, "altar [6]" and "table [7]" being received in the New Testament, both were received in the early Church. For each represented one side of the great Eucharistic action, as it is a Sacrifice and a Sacrament. But the title "altar" was the earliest [8].

It may be here a different profaneness of the priests. They connived at the sin of the people in sacrificing the maimed animals which they brought, and yet, since they had their food from the sacrifices, and such animals are likely to have been neglected and ill-conditioned, they may very probably have complained of the poverty of their lot, and despised the whole service. For the words used, *its produce, the eating thereof is contemptible* belong to their portion, not to what was consumed by fire. With this agrees their cry,

13. *What a weariness !* What an onerous service it is ! The service of God is its own reward. If not, it becomes a greater toil, with less reward from this earth, than the things of this earth. Our only choice is between love and weariness.

And ye have snuffed [*puffed*] *at it* [9], i. e. at the altar; as a thing contemptible. *Ye have brought* that which was *taken by violence* [10]. In despising any positive law of God, they despised the lawgiver ; and so, from contempt of the ceremonial law, they went on to break the moral law. It were in-

[1] 1 Tim. ii. 8.   [2] de Civ. Dei. xviii. 35. 3.
[3] אתם מחללים אתו
[4] S. Cyr.   [5] Ezek. xliv. 16.
[6] S. Matt. v. 23, Heb. xiii. 10.   [7] 1 Cor x. 21.
[8] S Ignat. ad Philad. n. 4. p. 32. Cotel.
[9] This too is one of the Tikkunē Sopherim, as if, had it not been profane, the prophet would have said, *at Me.* On the character of these hypothetic corrections, see on Hab. i. 12. p. 186. n. 17.
[10] This is the one sense of גזל, which occurs in 34

separate passages (beside two met. Job. xxiv. 19, Pr. iv. 16.) It is used specially of the robbery of the poor, whether by wrong judgment (Eccl. v. 7, [Heb.] Is. x. 2) or open violence. The meaning "torn" was gained, as if the animal had been carried off by beasts (θηριάλωτον), the *eating* of which was forbidden, Ex. xxii. 30, Lev. vii. 24, xxii. 8. Ezek. iv. 14, xliv. 31. But this had its own name, טרֵפָה, and could not be used in sacrifices, since it was dead already.

Before
C H R I S T
cir. 397.
that which was torn, and the lame, and the sick: thus ye brought an offer-

x Lev. 22. 20, &c. ing: ˣshould I accept this of your hand? saith the LORD.

y ver. 8.
‖ Or, *in whose flock is.*

14 But cursed *be* ʸthe deceiver, ‖ which hath in

his flock a male, and voweth, and sacrificeth unto the Lord a corrupt thing: for ᶻI *am* a great King,

Before
C H R I S T
cir. 397.

z Ps. 47. 2.
1 Tim. 6. 15.

saith the LORD of hosts, and my name *is* dreadful among the heathen.

---

deed a mockery of God, to break a law whereby He bound man to man, and therefrom to seek to appease Himself. Yet in rough times, people, even in Christianity, have made their account with their souls, by giving to the poor a portion of what they had taken from the rich. " God," it was said to such an one, " rejects the gifts obtained by violence and robbery. He loves mercy, justice and humanity, and by the lovers of these only will He be worshiped." " ¹ He that sacrificeth of a thing wrongfully gotten, his offering is ridiculous, and the gifts of unjust men are not accepted. The Most High is not pleased with the offerings of the wicked, neither is He pacified for sin by the multitude of sacrifices. Whoso bringeth an offering of the goods of the poor doeth as one that killeth the son before the father's eyes."

14. *Cursed is the deceiver.* " ² The fraudulent, hypocritical, false or deceitful dealer, who makes a show of one thing, and doth or intends another, nor doth to his power what he would make a show of doing ; as if he could deceive God in doing in His service otherwise than He required, and yet be accepted by Him." The whole habit of these men was not to break with God, but to keep well with Him on as easy terms as they could. They even went beyond what the law required in making vows, probably for some temporal end, and then substituted for that which had typical perfection, the less valuable animal, the ewe ³, and that, diseased. It was probably, to prevent self-deceit, that the law commanded that the oblation for a vow should be ⁴*a male without blemish, perfect ;* lest (which may be a temptation in impulsive vows) repenting of their vow, they should persuade themselves, that they had vowed less than they had. Ordinarily, then, it would not have been allowed to one, who had not the best to offer, to vow at all. But, in their alleged poverty, the prophet supposes that God would so far dispense with His own law, and accept the best which any

one had, although it did not come up to that law. Hence the clause, *which hath in his flock a male.* " ⁵ If thou hast not a male, that curse in no wise injureth thee. But saying this, he sheweth, that they have what is best, and offer what is bad."

They sinned, not against religion only, but against justice also. " ⁶ For as a merchant, who offers his goods at a certain price, if he supply them afterward adulterated and corrupted, is guilty of fraud and is unjust, so he who promised to God a sacrifice worthy of God, and, according to the law, perfect and sound, is fraudulent and sins against justice, if he afterward gives one, defective, mutilated, vitiated, and is guilty of theft in a sacred thing, and so of sacrilege."

Clergy or " all who have vowed, should learn hence, that what they have vowed should be given to God, entire, manly, perfect, the best.—For, reverence for the supreme and Divine Majesty to Whom they consecrate themselves demandeth this, that they should offer Him the highest, best and most perfect, making themselves a whole-burnt-offering to God."

" ⁷ They who abandon all things of the world, and kindle their whole mind with the fire of Divine love, these become a sacrifice and a whole-burnt-offering to Almighty God." " ⁸ Man himself, consecrated and devoted in the name of God, is a sacrifice." He then offers a corrupt thing who, like Ananias, keeps back *part of the price,* and is the more guilty, because, while it was his own, it was in his own power.

I am a great King. " ⁹ As God is Alone Lord through His universal Providence and His intrinsic authority, so He Alone is King, and a King so great, that of His greatness or dignity and perfection there is no end."

My Name is dreadful among the heathen. Absence of any awe of God was a central defect of these Jews. They treated Him, as they would not a fellow-creature, for whom they had any respect or awe or fear. Some remaining instinct kept them from parting

¹ Ecclus. xxxiv. 18–20.   ² Poc.

³ מָשְׁחַת fem. for מָשְׁחָת, as מְשָׁרֵת for מְשָׁרֶתֶת, Kgs i. 15. and מַחֲנַת Lev. ii. 5, Ewald Lehrb. n. 188. p. 495 ed. 8. Keil would read מָשְׁחָת (masc.) and make it a separate case, " the deceiver, whereas in

his flock is a male ; and he who voweth &c. : " but then nothing would be said, wherein the deceit consisted.

⁴ Levit. xxii. 19, 21.   ⁵ S. Jer.   ⁶ Lap.
⁷ S. Greg. in Ezek. L. i. Hom. xii. 30. Opp. i. 305 Ben. L.
⁸ S. Aug. de Civ. Dei. x. 6. L.   ⁹ Dion.

Before
CHRIST
cir. 397.

CHAPTER II.

1 *He sharply reproveth the priests for neglecting their covenant,* 11 *and the people for idolatry,* 14 *for adultery,* 17 *and for infidelity.*

A ND now, O ye priests, this commandment is [a] for you.

2 [a] If ye will not hear,

[a] Lev. 26. 14, &c.
Deut. 28, 15,
&c.

and if ye will not lay *it* to heart, to give glory unto my name, saith the LORD of hosts, I will even send a curse upon you, and I will curse your blessings : yea, I have cursed them already, because ye do not lay *it* to heart.

Before
CHRIST
cir. 397.

with Him ; but they yielded a cold, wearisome, heartless service. Malachi points to the root of the evil, the ignorance, how awful God is. This is the root of so much irreverence in people's theories, thoughts, conversations, systems, acts, of the present day also. They know neither God or themselves. The relation is summed up in those words to a saint [1], "Knowest thou well, Who I am, and who thou art ? I am He Who Is, and thou art she who is not." So Job says in the presence of God, [2]*I have heard of Thee by the hearing of the ear, but now mine eye seeth Thee: wherefore I abhor myself and repent in dust and ashes.* To correct this, God, from the beginning, insists on the title which He gives Himself. [3] *Circumcise the foreskin of your hearts and be no more stiff-necked: for the Lord your God is God of gods and Lord of lords, the great God, the mighty and the terrible;* and in warning, [4] *If thou wilt not observe to do all the words of this law that are written in this book, that thou mayest fear this glorious and fearful name, The Lord thy God, then the Lord thy God will make thy plagues wonderful &c.*

II. 1. *And now this is My commandment unto you,* not a commandment, which He gave them, but a commandment in regard to them. As God said of old, upon obedience, [5] *I will command My blessing unto you,* so now He would command what should reach them, but a curse. "[6] He returns from the people to the priests, as the fountain of the evil, whose carelessness about things sacred he had rebuked before. Let the priests of the new law hear this rebuke of God, and conceive it dictated to them by the Holy Spirit to hear, from whom God rightly requires greater holiness, and so will punish them more grievously, if careless or scandalous in their office." All Christians are, in some sense, [7] *a royal, holy priesthood,* over and above the special "Christian priesthood;" as the

Jews, over and above the special priesthood of Aaron, were *a* [8] *kingdom of priests.* What follows then belongs, in their degree, to them and their duties.

2. *If ye will not lay to heart,* viz. the rebukes addressed to them, *to give glory to God.* For the glory of God is the end and aim of the priesthood. This should be the principle and rule of their whole life, "[9] to the greater glory of God." *I will send the curse upon you,* viz. that which He had threatened in the law upon disobedience; and will *curse your blessings,* will turn your blessings into a curse. He does not say, I will send you curses instead of blessings, but, I will make the blessings themselves a curse. [10] *The things which should have been to their wealth became to them an occasion of falling;* to the proud, the things which lift them up; to the gluttonous, their abundance; to the avaricious, their wealth; which, if used to the glory of God, become blessings, do, when self not God is their end, by God's dispensation and Providence, become a curse to them. "[11] The goods of nature, the goods of fortune, the goods of the Church allowed to you, I will turn to your greater damnation, permitting you to abuse them to pride; and your damnation shall be the more penal, the more good things ye have received from Me. Whence Christ declares in the Gospel, [12] *Unto whomsoever much is given, of him shall be much required.*"

Yea, I have cursed them [lit. *it*], i. e. each one of the blessings, *already.* God's judgments as well as His mercies are individual with a minute care, shewing that it is His doing. The curse had already gone forth, and had begun to seize upon them from the time that they began to despise His Name. His judgments do not break in at once, but little by little, with warnings of their approach, that so we may turn to Him, and *escape the wrath to come.*

[1] S. Catherine of Sienna.   [2] Job xlii. 5, 6.
[3] Deut. x. 16, 17, vii. 21. Nehemiah uses it in his prayers (i. 5, ix. 32) and Daniel (ix 4.) It occurs also Neh. iv. 8 (14 Eng.) Ps. xlvii. 3, lxviii. 36, lxxxix. 8, xcvi. 4, xcix. 3, cxi. 9, Zeph. ii. 11.
[4] Deut. xxviii. 58, 59.

[5] Lev. xxv. 21, וצויתי את ברכתי לכם.
[6] Lap.   [7] 1 S. Pet. ii. 9.   [8] Ex. xix. 6.
[9] "Ad majorem Dei. gloriam," the motto of S. Ignatius Loyola.
[10] Ps. lxix. 23.
[11] Dion.   [12] S. Luke xii. 48.

Before
C H R I S T
cir. 397.

3 Behold, I will ‖ cor-
rupt y o u r s e e d, and
† spread dung upon your
faces, *even* the dung of
your solemn feasts ; and
‖ one shall ᵇtake you away
with it.

4 And ye shall know

| Or, *reprove.*
† Heb. *scatter.*

| Or, *it shall
take you away
to it.*
ᵇ 1 Kin. 14. 10.

that I have sent this commandment unto you, that
my covenant m i g h t be
with Levi, saith the LORD
of hosts.

5 ᶜMy c o v e n a n t was
w i t h h i m o f l i f e and
peace ; and I gave them

Before
C H R I S T
cir. 397.

ᶜ Num. 25. 12.
Ezek. 34. 25.
& 37. 26.

---

3. *Lo, I will rebuke the seed*¹ *for your sake,*
i. e. that it should not grow. He Who worketh by His sustaining will all the operations of nature, would at His will withhold
them. Neither priests nor Levites cultivated
the soil ; yet, since the tithes were assigned to
them, the diminution of the harvest affected
them. The meal-offering too was a requisite
part of the sacrifice².

*And spread dung upon your faces, the dung*³
of your solemn feasts, or, *of your sacrifices*⁴. It
was by the law carried without the camp
and burned with the animal itself. They
had brought before the face of God maimed,
unfitting sacrifices ; they should have them
cast back, with their refuse, upon them ;
"⁵ as a lord that rejecteth a gift, brought to
him by his servant, casts it back in his face."
"⁶ Of your sacrifices,* not of Mine ; for I am
not worshiped in them : ye seek to please,
not Me, but yourselves." So God said of
Eli, ⁷ *them that honor Me I will honor, and they
that despise Me shall be lightly esteemed.*

And one shall take you away with it, lit. *to it.*
They should be swept away, as if they were
an appendage to it, as God said, ⁸ *I will take
away the remnant of the house of Jeroboam, as a
man taketh away dung, till all be gone.* As are
the offerings, so shall it be with the offerers.

4. *And ye shall know that I have sent this
commandment unto you :* this, which He had
just uttered. They who believe not God
when threatening, know that He is in earnest and not to be trifled with, through His
punishing. *That My covenant might be with
Levi*⁹. God willed to punish those who at
that time rebelled against Him, that He

might spare those who should come after
them. He chastened the fathers, who shewed
their contempt toward Him, that their sons,
taking warning thereby, might not be cut off.
He continues to say, what the covenant was,
which He willed still to be, if they would
repent.

5. *My covenant was with him life and peace ;*
lit. *the life and the peace ;* that, which alone
is true *life and peace.* The covenant was not
with Levi himself, but with Aaron, his representative, with whom the covenant was
made in the desert, as is indeed here expressed ; and, in him, with all his race¹⁰
after him, who succeeded him in his office ;
as, when it is said, that ¹¹*Aaron and his sons
offered upon the altar of burnt offering,* it must
needs be understood, not of Aaron in person
alone and his sons then living, but of any of
his race that succeeded in his and their
room. So our Lord promised to be with
His Apostles, ¹²*always to the end of the world,*
i. e. with them and those whom they should
appoint in their stead, and these others,
until He should Himself come. God
promised, if they would keep the law, that
they should live in peace on the earth ; yea,
that they should have peace of mind and a
life of grace. *Life* is an indefectible being,
which man does not forfeit by sin, to which
death is no interruption, changing only the
place of the soul's life.

And I gave them to him, in, or as, *fear,*
"¹³ *Fear,* not servile but filial and pure, as S.
Paul bids Christians, ¹⁴*work out your own salvation with fear and trembling.*" God gave
them an awful gift, to be held with fear

---

¹ Keil objects to this rendering of the text and
adopts the punctuation יְהוֹרֵעַ from lxx. Aq. Vulg.
"the arm," i. e. render it useless and incapable of
discharging its office. But when זְרֹעַ is used of
other than men themselves, it is a whole, as to
which the metaphor is used," either being animate,
as "the devourer," Mal. iii. 11, or pictured as animate, as "the sea," Ps. cvi. 9. Nah. i. 4.
² See also Joel i. 13. ii. 14.
³ פֶּרֶשׁ is only used of the dung, as it lies in the
animal killed for sacrifice, Ex. xxix. 4, Lev. iv. 11,
viii. 7, xxi. 27, Nu. xix. 5, and here.
⁴ חַג is certainly the animal sacrificed at the
feast, Ex. xxiii. 18, Ps. cxviii. 27, and so probably
here. So Kim.

⁵ Abarb. Poc.   ⁶ Rib.   ⁷ 1 Sam. ii. 30.
⁸ 1 Kgs xiv. 10.
⁹ Keil says that הָיָה means indeed to "exist,"
but not to "continue existence." But the continuance is involved in the existence in the future,
for the being in the future involves the continued
being. His own rendering, "that this should be
My covenant with Levi ;" requires a more definite
subject ; and it should rather be, "that My covenant with Levi should come to this." In ver. 5, 6,
he speaks of the past emphatically, " My covenant
was with him," "the law of truth *was* in his
mouth." So it shall be with you, if you become
like him.
¹⁰ By the art. in הַלֵּוִי v. 8. See Num. xxv. 12, 13.
¹¹ 1 Chr. vi. 49.   ¹² S. Matt. xxviii. 20.   ¹³ Dion.
¹⁴ Phil. ii. 12.

Before
C H R I S T
cir. 397.

to him ᵈ*for* the fear wherewith he feared me, a n d
ᵈ Deut. 33. 8, 9.   was afraid before my name.

6 ᵉ The law of truth
was in his mouth, and in-
iquity was not found in ᵉ Deut. 33. 10.

Before
C H R I S T
cir. 397.

and awe, for its very preciousness, as one
would hold anxiously what is very precious,
yet very fragile and easily marred.

*And he feared Me, and was afraid before My
Name.* Malachi unites two words, the second
expressive of strong fear, by which a man is,
as it were, crushed or broken. They are
often united in Hebrew, but as expressing
terror, which men are bidden not to feel
before men. Toward man it is ever said,
[1] *fear not, neither be ye dismayed ;* toward God
Alone, it is a matter of praise. Man's highest fear is too little ; for he knows not, Who
God is. So Isaiah says, [2] *Fear ye not their
fear* [*the fear of this people*], *nor be afraid.
Sanctify the Lord of hosts Himself, and let Him
be your fear and let Him be your dread.*
" [3] What can be more precious (than this
fear) ? For it is written, [4] *He who feareth the
Lord will be rewarded.* ' [5] The fear of the
Lord is honor and glory and gladness and a
crown of rejoicing.' He saith, *the fear, wherewith he feareth Me and was afraid,* i. e. he received the fear of God in his whole heart
and soul. For these reduplications and em-
phases suggest to the hearer how rooted in
virtue are those thus praised."

6. *The law of truth was in his mouth.* Apart
from those cases, which were brought to the
priests at the tabernacle [6], in which their
voice was the voice of God through them, to
teach the law was part of the office both of
the priest and Levite. Of the priest God
says ; [7] *that ye may teach the children of Israel
all the statutes, which the Lord hath spoken unto
them by the hand of Moses :* of the tribe of
Levi generally Moses says, [8] *They shall teach
Jacob Thy judgments and Israel Thy law.*
After the schism of the ten tribes, a prophet
says to Asa, that *Israel* had [9] *for a long time
been without the true God and without a teaching priest and without law.* They are evil
times, of which Ezekiel says, [10] *the law shall
perish from the priest ;* and God says of corrupt priests, [11] *The priest said not, where is the
Lord ? and they that handle the law knew Me
not.* [12] *They did violence to My law.* On
their return from the captivity Ezra was
known to Artaxerxes as [13] *a scribe of the law
of the God of heaven,* and he looked upon him
apparently, as one who should keep the peo-

ple in good order by teaching it. [14] *Thou,
Ezra, after the wisdom of thy God which is in
thy hand, set magistrates and judges, which may
judge all the people which are beyond the river,
all such as know the laws of thy God, and teach
ye them that know them not : and whosoever will
not do the law of thy God or the law of the king,
let judgment be executed speedily upon him.*
Ezra says of himself, that he [15] *had prepared
his heart to seek the law of the Lord and to do it
and to teach in Israel statutes and judgments.*

" [16] God's [17] *law is the truth :* the true doctrine of this law did he teach the people,
and instruct them in the true meaning and
intent thereof, that, according to the right
rule, they might frame all their actions ;
nothing of it did he conceal from them, nor
teach any thing contrary to it or false. This
was in his mouth ; nothing contrary to it
was found in his lips."

And iniquity was not found in his lips. He
expresses the perfectness of that teaching,
first positively, then negatively. The true
priest taught truth without any admixture
of wrong. " [11] Not he only is a betrayer of
the truth, who, transgressing the truth,
openly teaches a lie for the truth ; but he
too, who does not freely utter the truth,
which he ought to utter freely, or who does
not freely defend the truth which he ought
to defend freely, is a betrayer of the truth.
[19] *For with the heart man believeth unto righteousness, and with the mouth confession is made
unto salvation.*" " Nothing," says S. Ambrose [20] to the Emperor Theodosius, " is so
perilous to the priest with God, so disgrace-
ful with men, as not to utter freely what he
thinks. For it is written, [21] *I spake of Thy
testimonies before kings, and was not ashamed.*
And therefore a priest's silence ought to displease your Clemency ; his freedom, to please
you. For you are involved in the peril of
my silence, art aided by the good of my free
speech."

He walked with Me. To awe of God,
truthfulness of teaching, he adds a devout
continual intercourse with God. Like the
patriarchs of old, Enoch and Noah, he
[22] *walked with God.* He not only lived in the
Presence, but walked up and down with
Him, through his whole life, as a Friend ;

[1] Deut. i. 21, xxxi. 8, Josh. i. 9, x. 25, 1 Chr. xxii.
13, xxviii. 20, 2 Chr. xx. 15, 17, xxxii. 7, Is. li. 7, Jer.
xxiii. 4, xxx. 10, xlvi. 27, Ez. ii. 6, iii. 9.
[2] Is. viii. 12, 13.   [3] S. Cyr.   [4] Pr. xiii. 13.
[5] Ecclus. i. 11.
[6] Deut. xvii. 9, 10, 11, xix. 17 ; (add Deut. xxi. 5,
Ezek. xliv. 23, 24.) hence the use of אֱלֹהִים Ex.
xxi. 6, xxii. 7, 8.

[7] Lev. x. 11.   [8] Deut. xxxiii. 10.   [9] 2 Chr. xv. 3.
[10] Ezek. vii. 26.   [11] Jer. ii. 8.
[12] Ezek. xxii. 26, Zeph. iii. 4.   [13] Ezr. vii. 12, 21.
[14] Ib. 25, 26.   [15] Ib. 10.   [16] Poc.   [17] Ps. cxix. 142.
[18] Opus imp. in S. Matt. ap. S. Chrys. Hom. 25. T.
vi. App. p. cix. Ben.
[19] Rom. x. 10.
[20] S. Ambr. Ep. xi. ad Theod. n. 2. 3. Ben. L.
[21] Ps. cxix. 46.   [22] Gen. v. 24, vi. 9.

Before
C H R I S T
cir. 397.
f Jer. 23. 22.
Jam. 5. 20.
g Lev. 10. 11.
Deut. 17. 9, 10.
& 24. 8.
Ezra 7. 10.
Jer. 18. 18. Hag. 2. 11, 12.

his lips : he walked with
me in peace and equity,
and did ʳturn many away
from iniquity.

7 ᵍFor the priest's lips

should keep knowledge, Before C H R I S T cir. 397.
and they should seek the
law at his mouth : ʰ for ʰGal. 4. 14.
he *is* the messenger of the
Lᴏʀᴅ of hosts.

" having respect in all things to Him and His glory."

In peace and equity. The inward peace with God overflowing in peace to men. The brief words comprise the duties of both tables ; as that, ¹ *Follow peace with all men, and holiness, without which no man shall see God ;* ² *Live in peace, and the God of love and peace shall be with you ;* ³ *blessed are the peacemakers, for they shall be called the children of God.* "⁴ God's covenant with him was of peace⁵ ; so he observed it on his part." Even *equity,* or real considerate justice, would alienate those, whom it found wrong, so he joins with it *peace,* that even equity was not administered but with love. "⁶To have peace with God, what is it but to will to be mended and to do what He willeth, and in nothing to offend Him ? "

And turned away many from iniquity. They, the true priests of the Old Testament then, were not satisfied with their own sanctification, but were zealous for the salvation of souls. What a history of zeal for the glory of God and the conversion of sinners in those, of whom the world knows nothing ; of whose working, but for the three words ⁷ in the closing book of the Old Testament, we should have known nothing ! The Prophets upbraid the sins of the many ; the Psalms are the prayers given to and used by the pious ; such incidental sayings as these, record some of the fruits. " Be of the disciples of Aaron," said Hillel⁸, "who loved peace and followed peace, and who loved men and brought them near to the law." Yet even under the Gospel S. Gregory complains, " ⁹The world is full of priests ; yet in the harvest of God the laborers are few. For we undertake the priestly office, but do not fulfill its work. We receive the fruit of holy Church in daily stipend, but labor not for the everlasting Church in preaching." " ¹⁰There are many priests," says a writer in the IVth cent., "and few priests ; many in name, few in deed. See then, how ye sit on your thrones ; for the throne maketh not the priest, but the priest the throne ; the place sanctifieth not the man, but the man

the place. Whoso sitteth well on the throne, receiveth honor from the throne ; whoso ill, doth injustice to the throne. Thou sittest in judgment. If thou livest well and teachest well, thou wilt be a judge of all ; if thou teachest well and livest ill, thine own only. For by teaching well and living well thou instructest the people, how it ought to live ; by teaching well and living ill, thou teachest God, how He should condemn thee." " ¹¹We who are called priests, above the ills which we have of our own, add also the deaths of others. For we slay as many as we, in tepidity and silence, see daily go to death.—He who is placed under thee dies without thee, when in that which causes his death, thou hast withstood him. For to that death, which thou hast not withstood, thou wilt be added. "

7. *For the priest's lips should keep knowledge.* " ¹²He assigns the reason for what he had just said, *the law of truth was in his mouth ;* they had done what it was their duty to do ; as in Ecclesiasticus it is said of Aaron ; ‘ ¹³God gave unto him His commandments, and authority in the statutes of judgments, that he should teach Jacob the testimonies, and inform Israel in His laws.' So S. Paul requires of Titus to ordain such Bishops, as shall be able to ¹⁴ *exhort by sound doctrine and to convince gainsayers.* Wherefore S. Ambrose ¹⁵ calls the Bible, which contains the law of God, ‘the book of priests,' as specially belonging to them, to be specially studied by them. S. Jerome notes that he says *keep,* not ‘give forth,' that they should speak seasonably, and give their fellow-servants meat in due season."

For he is the messenger [or *angel*] *of the Lord of hosts.* Malachi gives to the priest the title which belongs to the lowest order of the heavenly spirits, as having an office akin to theirs ; as Haggai does to the prophet ¹⁶, as an extraordinary *messenger* of God ; and S. Paul tells the Galatians, ¹⁷ *ye received me as an angel of God, as Christ Jesus ;* and Christ, by S. John, speaks to the Bishops of the seven Churches, good or bad, or of mixed good and bad, as *the angels* ¹⁸ *of those Churches.*

¹ Heb. xii. 14. Rom. xii. 18.　² 2 Cor. xiii. 11.
³ S. Matt. v. 9.　⁴ Poc.　⁵ ver. 5.　⁶ S. Cyr.
⁷ ורבים השיב מעון.
⁸ Pirke Aboth c. i. § 13 Poc.
⁹ S. Greg. Hom. xvii. in Evang. n. 3 and 8. Opp. i. 1496, 1499. Ben. L.

¹⁰ Op. Imperf. in S. Matt. cxxiii. Hom. xliii. App. p. clxxxiii. Ben. L.
¹¹ S. Greg. Hom. in Ezek. L. i. Hom. xi. nn. 9. and 11. Opp. i. 1285. L.
¹² Lap.　¹³ Ecclus. xlv. 17.　¹⁴ Tit. i. 9.
¹⁵ de fide iii. c. 15. n. 128. Opp. i 519. Ben.
¹⁶ Hagg. ii. 11.　¹⁷ Gal. iv. 14.　¹⁸ Rev. i. 20.

Before
C H R I S T
cir. 397.

i 1 Sam. 2. 17.
Jer. 18. 15.
‖ Or, *fall in the
law.*
k Neh. 13. 29.

8 But ye are departed out of the way; ye [1]have caused many to ‖ stumble at the law; [k] ye have corrupted t h e covenant of Levi, saith the LORD of hosts.

9 Therefore [1]have I also made you contemptible and base before all the people, according as ye have not kept my ways, but ‖ †have been partial in the law.

Before
C H R I S T
cir. 397.

i 1 Sam. 2. 30.

‖ Or, *lifted up
the face
against.*
† Heb. *accepted
faces.*

" [1]Since in the heavenly hierarchy the order of Angels is the lowest, and in the Eucharistical hierarchy the order of the priesthood is the highest," " [2] most truly is the priest of God called angel, i. e. messenger, because he intervenes between God and man, and announces the things of God to the people; and therefore were the Urim and Thummim placed on the priest's *breastplate of* judgment, that we might learn, that the priest ought to be learned, a herald of Divine truth." Much more in the New Testament. " [3] Who, as it were in a day, can form one of earth, to be the defender of truth, to stand with angels, to give glory with Archangels, to transmit the sacrifices to the altar above, to be partaker of the priesthood [4] of Christ, to reform the thing formed, and present the image, to re-create for the world above, to be a god [5] and make men *partakers of the Divine Nature* [6] ?" " [7] The priesthood is enacted on earth, but is ranked with the heavenly ranks. Very rightly. For not man, not angel, not archangel, not any other created power, but the Paraclete Himself hath ordained this office, and persuaded them, while yet abiding in the flesh, to conceive the ministry of the Angels. Wherefore, he who is consecrated as priest, ought to be pure, as if he stood among the heavenly powers." " [8] The throne of the priesthood is placed in the heavens, and he is entrusted with ministering things of heaven. Who saith this? The King of heaven Himself. For He saith, *Whatsoever ye shall bind on earth, shall be bound in heaven, and whatsoever ye shall loose on earth, shall be loosed in heaven.*—So the priest standeth in the middle between God and human nature, bringing down to us Divine benefits, and transmitting thither our supplications."

8. *But ye* [9] *are departed out of the way* " [10] of knowledge, truth, equity, fear of God, which I appointed to Aaron and the Levites." *Ye have caused many to stumble at the law.* He does not simply say, *in the law,* but *at* it. The law was what they stumbled at. They

did not only misunderstand the law, through the false teaching of the priests, as though it allowed things which in truth were sins (although this too) ; itself was their source of stumbling. As Jesus Himself was *a rock of offence* whereon they stumbled, because through His Divine holiness He was not what they expected Him to be, so contrariwise the law became an offence to them through the unholiness and inconsistency of the lives and ways of those who taught it; much as we now hear Christianity spoken against, because of the inconsistency of Christians. So S. Paul saith to the Jews, [11] *The name of God is blasphemed among the Gentiles through you, as it is written;* and, for the sins of Eli's sons [12], *men abhorred the offering of the Lord.*

And have corrupted the covenant of Levi; as it is said in Nehemiah, [13] *They have defiled the priesthood, and the covenant of the priesthood and of Levi,* that *covenant* which was *life and peace* [14], and therefore forfeited them.

9. *Therefore have I made you contemptible.* They had said in their hearts, [15] *The table of the Lord is contemptible.* So God would require them " [16] measure for measure." Yet not only so, but in their office as judges, against the repeated protestations in the law, [17] *Thou shalt not respect the person of the poor, nor honor the person of the mighty, in righteousness shalt thou judge thy neighbor;* [18] *ye shall not respect persons in judgment;* [19] *thou shall not wrest judgment,* he says,

Ye have accepted persons in the law. You have interpreted the law differently for rich and poor, or have put it in force against the poor, not against the rich. It would include actual bribery; but there are many more direct offences against equal justice. How differently is the like offence against the eighth commandment visited upon the poor who have real temptation to it, and the rich who have none, but the lust of the eyes!

" Crows he condones, vexes the simple dove."

That contempt which they cast upon God and His law, by wresting it out of respect to

[1] Dion.   [2] S. Jer.
[3] S. Greg. Naz. Orat. ii. n. 73. p. 48 Ben.
[4] συνιερευσοντα.
[5] Θεον εσομενον και θεοποιησοντα.   [6] 2 S. Pet. i. 4.
[7] S. Chrys. de Sacerdotio iii. 4. Opp. i. 382 Ben.

[8] Id. in Is. vi. 1. Hom. v. 1. Opp. vi. 132.
[9] בֶּם, emphatic.   [10] Lap.
[11] Rom. ii. 24.   [12] 1 Sam. ii. 17. Poc.   [13] Neh. xiii. 29.
[14] ii. 5.   [15] i. 7.   [16] Kim.   [17] Lev. xix. 15.
[18] Deut. i. 17.   [19] Ib. xvi. 19.

Before
C H R I S T
cir. 397.

■ 1 Cor. 8. 6.
Eph. 4. 6.
■ Job 31. 15.

10 ᵐHave we not all one father? ⁿhath not one God created us? why do we deal treacherously every man against his brother, by profaning the covenant of our fathers?

11 ¶ Judah hath dealt

treacherously, and an abomination is committed in Israel and in Jerusalem; for Judah hath profaned the holiness of the LORD which he || loved, and hath married the daughter of a strange god.

Before
C H R I S T
cir. 397.

‖ Or, *ought to love.*
º Ezra 9. 1.
& 10. 2.
Neh. 13. 23.

persons, that so they might gain favor and respect from them, so honoring them more than Him, and seeking to please them more than Him, will He cast back on them making them contemptible even in the eyes of those, from whom they thought by that means to find respect.

10. *Have we not all one Father*[1]*? Hath not one God created us?* Malachi turns abruptly to another offence, in which also the priests set an evil example, the capricious dismissal of their Hebrew wives and taking other women in their stead. Here, as before, he lays down, at the outset, a general moral principle, which he applies. The *one Father*, (it appears from the parallel), is manifestly Almighty God, as the Jews said to our Lord, [2] *We have one Father, even God.* He created them, not only as He did all mankind, but by the spiritual relationship with Himself, into which He brought them. So Isaiah speaks, [3] *Thus saith the Lord that created thee, O Jacob, and He that formed thee, O Israel. Every one that is called by My Name; I have created Him for My glory; I have formed him; yea I have made him. This people have I formed for Myself; they shall shew forth My praise.* And from the first in Moses' song, [4] *Is not He thy Father that created*[5] *thee? Hath He not made thee and established thee?* This creation of them by God, as His people, gave them a new existence, a new relation to each other; so that every offence against each other was a violation of their relation to God, Who had given them this unity, and was, in a nearer sense than of any other, the common Father of all. *Why then,* the prophet adds, *do we deal treacherously, a man against his brother, to profane the covenant of our fathers?* He does not yet say, wherein this treacherous dealing consisted; but awakens them to the thought, that sin against a

brother is sin against God, Who made him a brother; as, and much more under the Gospel, in which we are all members of one mystical body; [6] *when ye sin so against the brethren, and wound their weak conscience, ye sin against Christ.* He speaks of the sin, as affecting those who did not commit it. Why do *we* deal treacherously? So Isaiah, before his lips were cleansed by the mystical coal, said, [7] *I am a man of unclean lips, and I dwell in the midst of a people of unclean lips,* and the high-priest Joshua was shewn in the vision, clothed with defiled garments[8]; and the sin of Achan became the *sin of the children of Israel*[9], and David's sinful pride in numbering the people was visited upon all [10]. He teaches beforehand, that, [11] *whether one member suffer, all the members suffer with it, or one member be honored, all the members rejoice with it.* They *profaned* also *the covenant of their fathers,* by marrying those whom God forbade, and who would seduce, as heathen wives had Solomon, from His worship. S. Paul in sanctioning the remarriage of widows, adds, *only* [12] *in the Lord,* i. e. Christian husbands. "[13]He who treated as null the difference between the Israelites and a heathen woman, shewed that the difference between the God of Israel and the God of the heathen had before become null to him, whence it follows;

11. *Treacherously has Judah dealt; an abomination is committed in Israel.* The prophet, by the order of the words, emphasizes the *treachery* and the *abomination.* This have they done; the very contrary to what was required of them as the people of God. He calls the remnant of Judah by the sacred name of the whole people, of whom they were the surviving representatives. The word "abomination[14]" is a word belonging to the Hebrew, and is used especially of

[1] Jews (Ibn E., Tanchum, Kim. Abarb. ap. Poc.) have understood the *one father* to be Jacob; S. Cyril, to be Abraham. The parallelism is, I think, decisive against both. Although Abraham is specially spoken of as their father, yet the appeal to that relation would not hold against the marriage, condemned here, since he was the father of the descendants of Ishmael as of Isaac, of the bitterest foes of Israel, the heathenish Edomites. Ammon and Moab, inveterate persecutors of Israel, were his near kindred. Ammonitesses and Moabitesses were as

much forbidden by Ezra (ix. 2) as women of the different nations of Canaan, Ashdod or Egypt.
[2] S. John viii. 41.
[3] Is. xliii. 1. 7. 21. add xliv. 2, 21, 24.
[4] Deut. xxxii. 6.   [5] אָבִיךָ קָנֶךָ.
[6] 1 Cor. viii. 12.   [7] Is. vi. 5.
[8] Zech. iii. 3, 4. See ab. pp. 354, 355.
[9] Josh. vii. 1, 11.   [10] 2 Sam. xxiv.
[11] 1 Cor. xii. 26.   [12] Ib. vii. 39.
[13] Hengst. Christ. iii. 595.   [14] תּוֹעֵבָה.

31

Before
C H R I S T
cir. 397.
12 The LORD will cut off the man t h a t doeth this, ‖ the master and the scholar, out of the taber-nacles of Jacob, [p] and him that offereth a n offering unto the LORD of hosts.

13 A n d this have ye

‖ Or, *him that waketh, and him that an-swereth.*
[p] Neh. 13. 28, 29.

done again, covering the altar of the LORD with tears, with weeping, and with crying out, insomuch that he regardeth not the offering any more, or re-ceiveth *it* with good will at your hand.

Before
C H R I S T
cir. 397.

---

things offensive to, or separating from, Almighty God; idolatry, as the central dereliction of God, and involving offences against the laws of nature, but also all other sins, as adultery, which violate His most sacred laws and alienate from Him.

Hath profaned the holiness of the Lord which He loved, in themselves, who had been sepa-rated and set apart by God to Himself as a [1] *holy nation.* [2] *Israel* was *holiness to the Lord.* "[3] The Lord is holy, perfect holiness ; His name, holy ; all things relating to Him, holy ; His law, covenant and all His ordinances and institutions holy ; Israel, His peculiar people, an holy people ; the temple and all things therein consecrated to Him, holy ; Jerusalem, the city of the great God, holy ; yea, the whole land of His inheritance, holy ; so that whosoever doth not observe those due respects which to any of these belong, may be said to have *profaned the holiness which He loved.*"

Unlawful marriages and unlawful lusts were in themselves a special profanation of that holiness. The high priest was to [4] *take a virgin of his own people to wife,* and *not to profane his seed among the people.* The priests who *married strange wives, defiled the priesthood and the covenant of the priesthood* [5]. The marriage with idolatresses brought, as one consequence, the profanation by their idolatries. The prohibition is an anticipa-tion of the fuller revelation in the Gospel, that [6] the body is the temple of the Holy Ghost, and so, that *sins against the body* are profanations of the temple of God. "[3] As those who acknowledge, worship and serve the true God are called His [7] *sons and daugh-ters,* so they that worshiped any strange god are, by like reason, here called the daughters of that god. Hence the Jews say, '[8] He that marrieth a heathen woman is, as if he made himself son-in-law to an idol.' "

Hath married the daughter of a strange god.

And so he came into closest relation with idols and with devils.

12. *The Lord will cut off the man that doeth this, the master and the scholar,* lit. *The Lord cut off from the man that doeth this, watcher* [9] *and answerer.* A proverbial saying apparently, in which the two corresponding classes com-prise the whole [10]. Yet so, probably, that the one is the active agent ; the other, the pas-sive. The one as a *watcher* goes his rounds, to see that nothing stirreth against that which he is to guard ; the other *answereth,* when roused. Together, they express the two opposite classes, active and passive sin ; those who originate the sin, and those who adopt or retain it at the instigation of the inventor or active propagator of it. It will not exempt from punishment, that he was led into the sin.

From the tabernacles of Jacob. Perhaps "he chose the word, to remind them of their unsettled condition," out of which God had brought them.

And him that offereth an offering unto the Lord of hosts ; i. e. him, who, doing these things, offereth an offering to God, to bribe Him, as it were, to connivance at his sin. In the same meaning, Isaiah says, that God hateth [11] *iniquity and the solemn meeting,* and, [12] *I hate robbery with burnt-offering ;* or Sol-omon, [13] *The sacrifice of the wicked is an abom-ination to the Lord ;* [14] *he that turneth away his ear from hearing the law, his prayer shall be an abomination.* And God by Amos says, [15] *I hate, I despise, your feast-days, and will not accept your solemn assemblies.* In one sense the sacrifice was an aggravation, in that the worship of God made the offence either a sin against light, or implied that God might be bribed into connivance in the breaking of His laws. The ancient discipline of remov-ing from Communion those guilty of grievous sin was founded on this principle.

13. *And this ye have done again,* adding the second sin of cruelty to their wives to the

---

[1] Ex. xix. 6.   [2] Jer. ii. 3.   [3] Poc.
[4] Lev. xxi. 14, 15.   [5] Neh. xiii. 29.
[6] 1 Cor. vi. 15-20.
[7] Deut. xxxii. 19, 2 Cor. vi. 18.
[8] Maim. in Issure biah, c. 12. § 1. Poc.
[9] Not "the awakener," as if עֵר were active: for עוּר is always intransitive, except in the correction

of the text, Job xli. 2. In Chald. עִיר is "a watcher." Dan. iv. 10, 14.
[10] Dietrich, Abhandll. zur Hebr. Gram. p. 201 sqq., has instances from the Arabic, but not so energetic as those in the O. T., except when they are the same.
[11] Is. i. 13.   [12] Ib. lxi. 8.   [13] Prov. xv. 8.
[14] Ib. xxviii. 9.   [15] See vol. i. p. 299 on Am. v. 21.

Before CHRIST cir. 397.	
q Prov. 5. 18.	
r Prov. 2. 17.	

14 ¶ Yet ye say, Wherefore? Because the LORD hath been witness between thee and q the wife of thy youth, against whom thou hast dealt treacherously: r yet is she thy companion, and the wife of thy covenant.

15 And s did not he make one? Yet had he the || residue of the spirit. And wherefore one? That he might seed † t a godly

Before CHRIST cir. 397.	
s Matt. 19. 4, 5.	
|| Or, excellency. † Heb. a seed of God. t Ezra 9. 2.	
1 Cor. 7. 14.	

taking foreign women; *they covered the altar of God with tears*, in that they by ill-treatment occasioned their wives to weep there to God; and God regarded this, as though they had stained the altar with their tears.

Insomuch that He regardeth not the offering any more. God regarded the tears of the oppressed, not the sacrifices of the oppressors. He would not accept what was thus offered Him as a thing well-pleasing [1] to Him, acceptable to win His good pleasure.

14. *And ye say, Wherefore?* They again act the innocent, or half-ignorant. What had they to do with their wives' womanly tears? He Who knows the hearts of all was Himself the witness between them and the wife of youth of each; her to whom, in the first freshness of life and their young hearts, each had plighted his troth, having been entrusted by her with her earthly all. [2] *The Lord*, said even Laban, when parting from his daughters, *watch between me and thee, when we are absent, the one from the other; if thou shalt afflict my daughters, or if thou shalt take wives beside my daughters, no man is with us; see, God is witness between me and thee.*

And he dealt treacherously against her, violating his own faith and her trusting love, which she had given once for all, and could not now retract. *And she is thy companion;* she has been another self, the companion of thy life, sharing thy sorrows, joys, hopes, fears, interests; different in strength, yet in all, good and ill, sickness and health, thy associate and companion; the help meet for the husband and provided for him by God in Paradise; and above all, the *wife of thy covenant*, to whom thou didst pledge thyself before God. These are so many aggravations of their sin. She was the wife of their youth, of their covenant, their companion; and God was the witness and Sanctifier of their union. Marriage was instituted and consecrated by God in Paradise. Man was to leave father and mother (if so be), but to cleave to his wife indissolubly. For they were to be [3] *no more twain, but one flesh*. Hence, as a remnant of Paradise, even the heathen knew of marriage, as a religious act, guarded by religious sanctions. Among God's people, marriage was a [4] *covenant of their God*. To that original institution of marriage he seems to refer in the following;

15. *And did not He*, God, of Whom he had spoken as the witness between man and his wife, *make one*, viz. Adam first, to mark the oneness of marriage and make it a law of nature, appointing "that out of man (created in His own image and similitude,) woman should take her beginning, and, knitting them together, did teach that it should never be lawful to put asunder those, whom He by matrimony had made one [5]?" "[6] Between those two, and consequently between all other married, to be born from them, He willed that there should be one indivisible union; for Adam could be married to no other save Eve, since no other had been created by God, nor could Eve turn to any other man than Adam, since there was no other in the world. 'Infringe not then this sanction of God, and unity of marriage, and degenerate not from your first parents, Adam and Eve.'" "[7] If divorce had been good, Jesus says, God would not have made one man and one woman, but, having made one Adam, would have made two women, had He meant that he should cast out the one, bring in the other; but now by the mode of creation, He brought in this law, that each should have, throughout, the wife which he had from the beginning. This law is older than that about divorce, as much as Adam is older than Moses."

Yet had he the residue of the spirit; [8] *the breath of life, which He breathed into Adam, and man became a living soul.* All the souls, which God would ever create, are His, and He could have called them into being at once. Yet in order to designate the unity of marriage, He willed to create but one. So our Lord argues against divorce, [9] *Have ye not read, that He which made them at the beginning, made them male and female?* They both together are called *one man* [10], and therefore should be of one mind and spirit also, the unity of which they ought faithfully to preserve.

---

[1] יצר.
[2] Gen. xxxi. 49, 50.
[3] S. Matt. xix. 6.
[4] Prov. ii. 17.
[5] Marriage Service.
[6] Lap.

[7] S. Chrys. de libello repud. n 2. Opp. iii. 28. Ben. Rib.
[8] Gen. ii. 7.   [9] S. Matt. xix. 4–6.   [10] Gen. i. 27.

Before
CHRIST
cir. 397.

seed. Therefore take heed to your spirit, and let none deal ‖ t r e a c h e r o u s l y against the w i f e of his youth.

16 For ᵘ the LORD, the God of Israel, saith ‖ that he hateth † putting away: for *one* covereth violence with his garment, s a i t h the LORD of hosts : therefore take heed to y o u r

‖ Or, *unfaith-
fully.*

ᵘ Deut. 24. 1.
Matt. 5. 32.
& 19. 8.
‖ Or, *if he hate
her, put* her
away.
¶ Heb. *to put
away.*

spirit, that ye d e a l not treacherously.

17 ¶ ˣ Ye have wearied the LORD with your words. Yet ye say, Wherein have we wearied *him?* When ye say, Every one that doeth evil *is* good in the sight of the LORD, and he delighteth in t h e m; or, Where *is* the God of judgment?

Before
CHRIST
cir. 397.

ˣ Isai 43. 24.
Amos 2. 13.
ch 3. 13, 14, 15.

And wherefore one? Seeking a seed of God, i. e. worthy of God ; for from religious marriage, religious offspring may most be hoped from God; and by violating that law, those before the flood brought in a spurious, unsanctified generation, so that God in His displeasure destroyed them all. *And take heed to your spirit*[1], which ye too had from God, which was His, and which He willed in time to create. He closes, as he began, with an appeal to man's natural feeling, *let none deal treacherously against the wife of his youth.*

16. *He hateth putting away*[2]. He had allowed it *for the hardness of their hearts*, yet only in the one case of some extreme bodily foulness[3], discovered upon marriage, and which the woman, knowing the law, concealed at her own peril. Not subsequent illness or any consequences of it, however loathsome (as leprosy), were a ground of divorce, but only this concealed foulness, which the husband *found* upon marriage. The capricious tyrannical divorce, God saith, *He hateth:* a word[4] naturally used only

[1] The רוחכם, "your spirit," manifestly refers back to " the residue of the spirit," שאר רוח which, he says, was God's.
[2] The E. M. "*If he hate* her, *put* her *away,*" (which follows Jon.) seems to enjoin what Malachi reproves these for, their cruelty to their wives, as also it gives an unbounded license of divorce.
[3] ערות דבר Deut. xxiv. 1, used of disgusting foulness in the chapter before, xxiii. 15.
[4] Things spoken of as objects of God's hatred, are, "a proud look, a lying tongue, hands that shed innocent blood, a heart that deviseth wicked imaginations, feet that be swift in running to mischief, a false witness that speaketh lies, and he that soweth discord among brethren," Prov. vi. 16–19; " pride, arrogancy, the evil way, and the froward mouth," Ib. viii. 13; idolatry, De. xvi. 22, Jer. xliv. 4, " robbery with burnt-offering," Is. lxi. 8; heathen abominations, Deut. xii. 31; worship with sin, Am. v. 21, Is. i. 14.
[5] No Jewish-Arabic writer notices the meaning, which Pococke suggested, and Gesenius, Fürst, Ewald follow ; as if לבש signified " wife," because in the Koran לבאם is used, not directly for ' husband ' or " wife," but in its original sense, " cover-

as to sin, and so stamping such divorce as sin.

One *covereth violence with his garment*[5] or, *and violence covereth his garment*[6], or, it might be, in the same sense, *he covereth his garment with violence*[7], so that it cannot be hid, nor washed away, nor removed, but envelopes him and his garment; and that, to his shame and punishment. It was, as it were, an outer garment of violence, as Asaph says, [8]*violence covereth them as a garment;* or David, [9] *he clothed himself with cursing as with a garment.* It was like a garment with *fretting leprosy*, unclean and making unclean, to be burned with fire[10]. Contrariwise, the redeemed saints had [11] *washed their robes and made them white in the Blood of the Lamb.* Having declared God's hatred of this their doing, he sums up in the same words, but more briefly; *and* this being so, *ye shall take heed to your spirit, and not deal treacherously.*

17. *Ye have wearied the Lord with your words.* " [12] By your blasphemous words, full of unbelief and mistrust, you have in a manner," of each reciprocally, הן הג לבאס לכם ואנתם (לבאס להן " they (your wives) are a garment to you, and you are a garment to them." So Abimelech said to Sarah, "*he* [Abraham] is *to thee a covering* (כסות) *of the eyes, unto all which are with thee,* (Gen. xx. 16). But לבאס does not signify, either husband or wife. In Arabic, חלה and אואר loose dresses, (See Lane Arab. Lex. p. 53, 621) are used metaph. of a wife: (ראאז also of a person's self or family as well). But there is no trace of this in Heb.

[6] According to the constr., Nu. xvi. 33, Lev. iv. 8, Job xxi. 26, where the thing covering is the nominative and על is put before the thing covered. So Vulg. and LXX. originally, as shewn by the Arabic transl., though now the LXX. has ἐνθύματα for ἐνδύματα. (De Dieu.)
[7] In Ez. xxiv. 7, Job xxxvi. 32, the thing covering is in the acc., with על of thing covered.
[8] Ps. lxxiii. 6.   [9] Ib. cix. 18.   [10] Lev. xiii. 47–58.   [11] Rev. vii. 14.   [12] Dion.

CHAPTER III.

1 *Of the messenger, majesty and grace of Christ.* 7 *Of the rebellion,* 8 *sacrilege,* 13 *and infidelity of the people.* 16 *The promise of blessing to them that fear God.*

BEHOLD, [a] I will send my messenger, and he shall [b] prepare the way before me: and the Lord, whom ye seek, shall suddenly come to his temple,

a Matt. 11. 10.
Mark 1. 2.
Luke 1. 76.
& 7. 27.
b Isai. 40. 3.

---

ner wearied God. He speaks of God, after the manner of men, as a man afflicted by the ills of others. Whence also the Lord says in Isaiah, [1] *I am weary to bear them,* and [2] *thou hast made Me to serve with thy sins ; thou hast wearied Me with thine iniquities.* In like way the Apostle says, [3] *Grieve not the Holy Spirit of God.*"

With the same contumacy as before, and unconsciousness of sin, they ask, *Wherein?* It is the old temptation at the prosperity of the wicked. " Does God love the wicked? if not, why does He not punish them?"

"[4] The people, when returned from Babylon, seeing all the nations around, and the Babylonians themselves, serving idols but abounding in wealth, strong in body, possessing all which is accounted good in this world, and themselves, who had the knowledge of God, overwhelmed with want, hunger, servitude, is scandalized and says, ' There is no providence in human things ; all things are borne along by blind chance, and not governed by the judgment of God ; nay rather, things evil please Him, things good displease Him ; or if God does discriminate all things, where is His equitable and just judgment?' Questions of this sort minds, which believe not in the world to come, daily raise to God, when they see the wicked in power, the saints in low estate; such as Lazarus, whom we read of in the Gospel, who, before the gate of the rich man in his purple, desires to support his hungry soul with the crumbs which are thrown away from the remnants of the table, while the rich man is of such savagery and cruelty, that he had no pity on his fellowman, to whom the tongues of the dogs shewed pity ; not understanding the time of judgment, nor that those are the true goods, which are for ever, say, He is pleased with the evil, and, Where is the God of judgment?"

Where is the God of the judgment? "[5] i. e. of that judgment, the great, most certain, most exact, clearsighted, omniscient, most just, most free, wherein He regards neither powerful nor rich nor gifts, nor aught but justice? For He is the *God of the judgment,* to Whom it belongs by nature to judge all men and things by an exact judgment: for His

nature is equity itself, justice itself, providence itself, and that, most just, most wise.— To Him it belongs to be the Judge of all, and to exercise strict judgment upon all ; and He will exercise it fully on that decisive and last day of the world, which shall be the horizon between this life and the next, parting off time from eternity, heaven from hell, the blessed from the damned forever, through Christ, Whom He constituted Judge of all, quick and dead."

III. 1. God answers their complaints of the absence of His judgments, that they would come, but would include those also who clamored for them. For no one who knew his own sinfulness would call for the judgment of God, as being himself, *chief of sinners.* S. Augustine pictures one saying to God, "Take away the ungodly man," and that God answers, " Which?"

Behold, I send My messenger before My face, and he shall prepare My way before Me. They, then, were not prepared for *His* Coming, for Whom they clamored. The messenger is the same whom Isaiah had foretold, whose words Malachi uses [6] ; [7] *The voice of one crying in the wilderness, Prepare ye the way of the Lord, make straight in the desert a high-way for our God.* [8] *Thou, child,* was the prophecy on S. John Baptist's birth, *shalt be called the prophet of the Highest ; for thou shalt go before the face of the Lord to prepare His way, to give knowledge of salvation unto His people, for the remission of their sins.* Repentance was to be the preparation for the kingdom of Christ, the Messiah, for Whom they looked so impatiently.

He Who speaks, is He Who should come, God the Son. For it was before Him Who came and dwelt among us, that the way was to be prepared. He speaks here in His Divine Nature, as the Lord Who should send, and Who should Himself come in our flesh. In the Gospel, when He *was* come in the flesh, He speaks not of His own Person but of the Father, since "[9] indivisible are the operations of the Trinity, and what the One doth, the other Two do, since the Three are of one nature, power and operation." Whence Christ, in order to give no excuse to the Jews to speak against Him before the time, refers

---

[1] Is. i. 14. [2] Ib. xliii. 24. [3] Eph. iv. 30.
[4] S. Jer. [5] Lap.
[6] פִּנָּה דֶרֶךְ had been used only by Isaiah, xl. 3,

lvii. 14, lxii. 10, although פִּנָּה לְפָנַי, abs., had been used Ps. lxxx. 10.
[7] Is. xl. 3. [8] S. Luke i. 76. [9] Lap.

Before
C H R I S T
cir. 397.

e Isai. 63. 9.

e even the messenger of the covenant, whom ye delight

in: behold, d he shall come, saith the LORD of hosts.

Before
C H R I S T
cir. 397.

d Hag. 2. 7.

it, as He does His life[1], His doctrine[2], words[3] and works[4] to the Father.

" [5] Those works, which do not relate to that which belongs peculiarly to each Person, being common, are ascribed now to One Person, now to Another, in order to set forth the One Substance in the Trinity of Persons." Thus, S. John says[6], Isaiah spoke of the unbelief of the Jews, when he *saw the glory* of God the Son *and spake of Him*, and S. Paul says[7] that the *Holy Ghost spake* then *by* him.

And he shall prepare the way before Me. " [8] The same is God's way here, and Christ's there, an evident proof that Christ is one God with the Father, and that, in Christ, God came and was manifest in the flesh." The prophets and all who turned men to righteousness, or who retained the knowledge of the truth or of righteousness or of God in the world, did, in their degree, prepare the way for Christ. But John was His immediate forerunner *before His Face*, the herald of His immediate approach; whence he is called " [9] the end of the law, and the beginning of the Gospel," " [10] the lamp before the Light, the voice before the Word, the mediator between the Old and the New Testament;" " [11] the link of the law and of grace; a new morning star; a ray, before the true Sun should burst forth," the end of night, the beginning of day.

And the Lord, Whom ye seek, shall suddenly come to His temple. He, Whose Coming they sought for, was Almighty God, *the God of Judgment* [12]. He Who should come, was *the*

Lord, again Almighty God, since, in usage too, none else is called " *the* Lord [13]," as none else can be. The temple also, to which He was to come, the temple of God, is His own. *The messenger*, or *the Angel of the covenant*, plainly, even from the parallelism, is the same as *the Lord*. It was *one*, for whom they looked; one, of whose absence they complained; [14] *where is the God of judgment?* one, who should come to His temple [15]; one, whose coming they sought and prepared to *have pleasure in* [16]; one, of whom it is repeated, *lo, He cometh* [17]; one, in the day of whose coming, at whose appearing, it was asked, *who shall stand?* " [18] All Christian interpreters are agreed that this Lord is Christ, [19] *Whom God hath made both Lord and Christ*, and [20] *Who is Lord over all*; by Whom all things were made, are sustained and governed; Who is (as the root of the word [21] imports) the basis and foundation, not of any private family, tribe or kingdom, but of all; [22] *by Whom are all things and we by Him:* and Whose we are also by right of redemption; and so He is [23] *Lord of lords and King of kings*, deservedly called *the* Lord." As then the special presence of God was often indicated in connection with *the Angel of the Lord*, so, here, He Who was to come was entitled the Angel or messenger of the covenant, as God also calls Him the covenant itself, [24] *I will give Thee for a covenant of the people, a light of the Gentiles.* He it was, [25] *the Angel of His Presence*, Who saved His former people, *in* Whom His *Name was*, and Who,

[1] S. John vi. 57.　　　　[2] Ib. vii. 16.
[3] Ib. iii. 11, v. 43, viii. 38, 40, 47, 55, xii. 49, xiv. 10, 24.
[4] Ib. iv. 19, 20, 26, 30, 36, vi. 38, viii. 28, ix. 4, x. 25, 32, 37, 38, xiv. 10, 11.
[5] Rib.　　　[6] S. John xii. 41.　　　[7] Acts xxviii. 25.
[8] S. Thom. 3 p. q. 38. art. 1. ad 2. See Tert. in Marc. iv. 33. pp. 317, 318. Edinb. Tr.
[10] S. Greg. Naz. Orat. 21. n. 3 p. 387 Ben.
[11] S. Chrysol. Serm. 21. Bibl. Patr. vii. 917.
[12] Rashi, "The God of judgment." Ibn Ezra says, " This is the glory; this is *the messenger of the covenant*; for the sense is doubled." Abarbanel, " Haadon is the Name which is glorified, who will then come to His temple, the house of His sanctuary, and His glorious name and His Shechinah shall dwell there; and this is what they sought in their murmurings." In the "Mashmia' yeshu'ah," "he says, " Haadon may be explained of the king Messiah." Kimchi also gives it as his first explanation; " Haadon, he is the king Messiah, and he is the angel of the covenant;" but he gives an alternative explanation, "or he calls Elijah the messenger of the covenant." Saadiah Gaon admits the ' *Me*,' before whom the messenger is sent, to be the Messiah b. David. "The forerunner of the Messiah b. David will be like his embassador, and as one who prepareth the people, and cleareth the way, as in what is said, Behold I send &c." Sepher Haemunoth Tr. 8 de redemptione, (quoted by Voisin on the P. F. f. 127.)

The author of the older Nizzachon (whether seriously or to have something to say) said, "He is sent and is not God." Wagenseil p. 126. Tanchum says, "they are promised a time, in which transgressors will be requited with a swift retribution by the just king whom God will raise up to the rule, and he is the king Messiah."
The Jews are agreed also that the messenger is no ordinary person. Ibn Ezra supposes him to be the Messiah b. Joseph, holding accordingly that he, before whose face he should come, was the Messiah ben David: Kimchi, that it was an angel from heaven (as in Ex. xxiii. 20.) to guard them in the way. But to guard *in* the way is not to prepare the way *before* him; Rashi and the author of the Abkath rochel, "the angel of death who should clear away the wicked;" Abarbanel, that it was Malachi himself; but he who is promised through Malachi, was yet to come.

[13] הָאָרוֹן Ex. xxiii. 17, xxxiv. 23, Is. i. 24, iii. 1, x. 16, 33, xxix. 4. [all, beside this place.]
[14] ii. 17.　　　[15] יָבוֹא אֶל הֵיכָלוֹ, iii. 1.
[16] רְפָצִים, מְבַקְשִׁים Ib.　　[17] חִנֵּה בָא Ib.　　[18] Poc.
[19] Acts ii. 36.　　　　　　　　[20] Ib. x. 36.
[21] Poc., (as Abulwalid, Menahem, Parchon, Kimchi) derives אָרוֹן from אָרַן.
[22] 1 Cor. viii. 6.　　　　[23] Rev. xvii. 14, xix. 16.
[24] Is. xlii. 6.　　　　　　[25] Ib. lxiii. 9.

Before C H R I S T cir. 397.	2 But who may abide ^e the day of his coming? and ^f who shall stand when

he appeareth? for ^g he *is* like a refiner's fire, and like fullers' soap:

by the prerogative of God, would [1] *not pardon* their *transgressions*. He should be [2] *the Mediator of the new and better covenant* which is promised; [3] *not according to the covenant, that I made with their fathers, in the day when I took them by the hand to lead them out of the land of Egypt,* which *My covenant they brake, although I was a husband unto them, saith the Lord ; but this shall be the covenant, that I will make with the house of Israel after those days, saith the Lord, I will put My law in their inward parts, and write it in their hearts, and will be their God and they shall be My people.*

Whom ye seek, are seeking, Whom ye delight in, i. e. profess so to do; *He will come,* but will be very different from Him whom ye look for, an Avenger on your enemies. Judgment will come, but it will begin with yourselves.

Shall suddenly come, " [4] unawares, when men should not think of them; whence perhaps it is that the Jews reckon the Messiah among what shall come *unawares* [5]. As, it is here said of His first Coming, so it is said of His second Coming (which may be comprehended under this here spoken of) that except they diligently watch for it, [6] *it shall come upon them unawares,* [7] *suddenly,* [8] *in such an hour as they think not.* " [9] The Lord of glory always comes, like a thief in the night, to those who sleep in their sins."

Lo, He will come : he insists again and calls their minds to that Coming, certain, swift, new, wonderful, on which all eyes should be set, but His Coming would be a sifting-time.

2. *And who may abide the day of His coming ? And who shall stand when He appeareth ?* The implied answer is, "No one ; " as in the Psalm, [10] *If Thou, Lord, wilt mark iniquities, O Lord, who shall stand ?* Joel had asked the same, [11] *The day of the Lord is great and very terrible ; and who can abide it ?* " [12] How can the weakness of man endure such might ; his blindness, such light; his frailty, such power; his uncleanness, such holiness ; the chaff, such a fire ? *For He is like a refiner's fire.* Who would not fail through stupefaction, fear, horror, shrinking reverence, from such majesty ? "

Malachi seems to blend, as Joel, the first and second coming of our Lord. The first Coming too was a time of sifting and severance, according as those, to whom He came, did or did not receive Him. The severance was not final, because there was yet space for repentance ; but it was real, an earnest of the final judgment. [13] *For judgment,* our Lord says, *I am come into this world, that they which see not may see, and they which see might be made blind ;* and again, [14] *Now is the judgment of this world ;* and, [15] *He that believeth not is condemned already, because he hath not believed on the name of the Only-Begotten Son of God ;* [16] *He that believeth not the Son, shall not see life, but the wrath of God abideth on him.* As, on the other hand, He saith, [17] *whoso eateth My Flesh and drinketh My Blood hath eternal life ;* and [18] *he that believeth on the Son hath everlasting life ;* "hath," He saith ; not, "shall have ; " *hath* it, in present reality and earnest, though he may forfeit it : so the other class *is condemned already,* although the one may repent and be saved, the other may [19] *turn from his righteousness and commit iniquity ;* and if he persevere in it, *shall die therein.* It is then one ever-present judgment. Every soul of man is in a state of grace or out of it ; in God's favor or under His wrath ; and the judgment of the Great Day, in which the secrets of men's hearts shall be revealed, will be but an outward manifestation of that now hidden judgment. But the words, in their fullest sense, imply a passing of that judgment, in which men do or do not stand, as in those of our Lord, [20] *As a snare shall that day come on all those that dwell on the face of the whole earth. Watch ye, therefore, and pray always, that ye may be accounted worthy to escape all these things which shall come to pass, and to stand before the Son of Man ;* and S. Paul, [21] *Take unto you the whole armor of God, that ye may be able to withstand in the evil day, and, having done all, to stand ;* and in the Revelation, [22] *They said to the mountains and rocks ; Fall on us, and hide us from the wrath of Him that sitteth upon the throne, and from the wrath of the Lamb. For the great day of His wrath is come, and who shall*

---

[1] Ex. xxiii. 21.   [2] Heb. xii. 24, viii. 6.
[3] Jer. xxxi. 32, 33, Heb. viii. 9.   [4] Poc.
[5] "Buxt. Lex. Ch. et Talm. v. נסם" Poc.
[6] S. Luke xxi. 35.
[7] S. Mark xiii. 36.
[8] S. Matt. xxiv. 44.   [9] Schmieder.
[10] Ps. cxxx. 3.
[11] Jo. ii. 11, כילנו ומי; Jer. x. 10, " *The nations shall not abide* (יכל) *His indignation."* Vulg. has,

cogitare, i. e. who shall comprehend ? But כלכל, in this sense, is used of actual containing, (the *heaven of heavens cannot contain* the Infinite God, (1 Kgs viii. 27, 2 Chr. ii. 5, [6 Eng.] vi. 18.) not of intellectually comprehending.
[12] Lap.   [13] S. John ix. 39.   [14] Ib. xii. 31.
[15] Ib. iii. 18.   [16] Ib. 36.
[17] Ib. vi. 54.   [18] Ib. 47.
[19] Ezek. xxxiii. 18.   [20] S. Luke xxi. 35, 36.
[21] Eph. vi. 13.   [22] Rev. vi. 16, 17.

Before
CHRIST
cir. 397.

h Isai. 1. 25.
Zech. 13. 9.

3 And ^h he shall sit *as*
a refiner and purifier of
silver: and he shall purify
the sons of Levi, and

purge them as gold and
silver, that they may ⁱ offer unto the LORD an of-
fering in righteousness.

Before
CHRIST
cir. 397.

i 1 Pet. 2. 5.

be able to stand? Asaph says of a temporal,
yet, for this life, final destruction; [1] *At Thy
rebuke, O God of Jacob, both the chariot and
horse are cast into a deep sleep. Thou art to be
feared, and who may stand in Thy sight, when
Thou art angry?*

*For He is like a refiner's fire, and like fuller's
soap.* Two sorts of materials for cleansing
are mentioned, the one severe, where the
baser materials are inworked with the rich
ore; the other mild, where the defilement is
easily separable. "[2] He shall come like a
refining fire; [3] *a fire shall burn before Him,
and it shall be very tempestuous round about
Him.* Then He shall call the heaven from above,
and the earth, that He may judge His people; *
streams of fire shall sweep before, bearing
away all sinners. For the Lord is called a
fire, and a [4] *consuming fire,* so as to burn our
[5] *wood, hay, stubble.* And not fire only, but
fuller's soap [6]. To those who sin heavily, He
is a refining and *consuming fire,* but to those
who commit light sins, *fuller's soap,* to restore
cleanness to it, when washed." Yet, though
light in comparison, this too had its severity;
for clothes which were washed (of which the
word is used) were trampled [7] on by the feet.
"[8] The nitrum and the fuller's soap is penitence." Yet the whiteness and purity so
restored, is, at the last, perfected. Inspiration could find no more adequate comparison
for us, for the brightness of our Lord's
raiment from the glory of the Transfiguration, than, [9] *exceeding white as snow; so as no
fuller on earth can white them.*

Our Lord is, in many ways, as a fire. He
says of Himself; [10] *I am come to send a fire
upon earth, and what will I, if it be already
kindled?* S. John Baptist said of Him, [11] *He
shall baptize you with the Holy Ghost and
with fire.* He kindles in the heart "a fire of
love," which softens what is hard, will

"[12] Wash whate'er of stain is here,
   Sprinkle what is dry or sere,
     Heal and bind the wounded sprite;
   Bend whate'er is stubborn still,
   Kindle what is cold and chill,
     What hath wandered guide aright."

But as God is *a consuming fire,* Who must
burn out the dross, unless we be [13] *reprobate
silver* which *the founder melteth in vain,* either
He must, by His grace, consume the sin
within us, or must consume us with it, in
hell.

3. *And He shall sit* [14], as a King and Judge
on His throne, with authority, yet also to
try accurately the cause of each, separating
seeming virtues from real graces; hypocrites,
more or less consciously, from His true servants.

He shall purify [15] *the sons of Levi.* These
had been first the leaders in degeneracy, the
corrupters of the people by their example
and connivance. Actually [16] *a great company
of the priests were obedient to the faith.* Barnabas also was a Levite [17]. But more largely,
as Zion and Jerusalem are the titles for the
Christian Church, and Israel who believed
was the true Israel, so *the sons of Levi* are the
true Levites, the Apostles and their successors in the Christian priesthood.

It was through three centuries of persecutions that the Church was purified by fire.

That they may offer, lit. *and they shall be
unto the Lord offerers of a meal-offering in
righteousness,* i. e. they shall be such, and
that, habitually, abidingly. Again, here and
in the next words, *and the meal-offering of
Judah shall be pleasant unto the Lord,* it is remarkable, that the *meal-offering,* to which the
Holy Eucharist corresponds, is alone mentioned. Of bloody offerings Malachi is silent;
for they were to cease.

[1] Ps. lxxvi. 6, 7.   [2] S. Jer.   [3] Ps. l. 3, 4.
[4] Deut. iv. 24.   [5] 1 Cor. iii. 12.

[6] בְּרִית is a generic name for materials for cleansing; but various plants, possessing alkaline qualities, grew and grow in Palestine, and "kali" is
still an article of trade. Being united with נתר
Jer. ii. 22, it has been supposed the "borith" is a
vegetable, as contrasted with נתר, a mineral.
"For the herb *Borith,* the LXX. have translated
πόαν, to signify the herb of fullers, which according to the wont of Palestine grows in luxuriant moist
places, and has the same virtue for cleansing defilements as nitrum." S. Jer. on Jerem. ii. 21.

[7] כבס, (only used in Piel, except in the part. of
the obsolete Kal. Comp., with Ges., כבש and בוס.
[8] S. Jer. ib.   [9] S. Mark ix. 3.   [10] S. Luke xii. 49.
[11] Ib. iii. 16.
[12] Transl. of Whitsun-hymn, Veni Sancte Spiritus,

in Hymns for the Week and the Seasons p. 105.
1848.
[13] Jer. vi. 29, 30.
[14] The usual word for sitting on a throne, Ex. xii.
29, Deut. xvii. 18, 1 Kgs i. 13, 17, 46, 48, ii. 12, 24, iii.
6, viii. 20, 25, xvi. 11, xxii. 10, 2 Kgs x. 30, xi. 19, xiii.
13, xv. 12, Ps. cxxxii. 12, Pr. xx. 8, Is. xvi. 5, Jer.
xiii. 13, xvii. 25, xxii. 4, 30, xxxiii. 17, xxxvi. 30,
Zech. vi. 13; or for judgment, Ex. xviii. 13. Jud. v.
10, Ps. cxxii. 5, Is. xxviii. 6, Jer. xxix. 16, Dan. vii.
9, 26, Jo. iii. 12. Of God, Ps. ii. 4, ix. 5, 8, xxix. 10,
xlvii. 8, lv. 20, 1 Kgs xxii. 19, Is. vi. 1. and others.

[15] זקק, probably originally "strained," used of
wine, Is. xxvi. 6, but thence perhaps, the first
meaning being lost, of precious metals; gold, Job
xxviii. 1, 1 Chr. xxviii. 18, silver, Ps. xii. 7, 1 Chr.
xxix. 4.
[16] Acts vi. 7.   [17] Ib. iv. 36.

Before
CHRIST
cir. 397.

k ch. 1. 11.

‖ Or, *ancient.*

4 Then ᵏ shall the offering of Judah and Jerusalem be pleasant unto the LORD, as in the days of old, and as ‖in former years.

Before
CHRIST
cir. 397.

¹ Zech. 5. 4.
Jam. 5. 4, 12.

5 And I will come near to you to judgment; and I will be a swift witness against the sorcerers, and against the adulterers, ¹ and against false swearers, and

---

In righteousness, as Zacharias prophesied, *that we might serve Him in holiness and righteousness before Him all the days of our life.*

4. *Then* [*And*] *shall the offering of Judah and Jerusalem.* The *law,* the new revelation of God, was to ¹ *go forth from Zion and the word of the Lord from Jerusalem.* Judah and Jerusalem then are here the Christian Church. They *shall be pleasant* [lit. *sweet*] *unto the Lord.* It is a reversal [using the self-same word] of what God had said of them in the time of their religious decay, ² *they shall not offer wine-offerings to the Lord, neither shall they be sweet unto Him;* ³ *your burnt-offerings are not acceptable, nor your sacrifices sweet unto Me.*

As in the days of old, before the days of degeneracy; as it stands in the ancient Liturgies, "⁴ Vouchsafe to look upon them [the consecrated oblations] with a propitious and serene Countenance, and to accept them, as Thou vouchsafedst to accept the gifts of Thy righteous Abel and the sacrifice of our Patriarch Abraham, and the holy sacrifice, the immaculate offering, which Thy high priest Melchisedec offered unto Thee." "⁵ The oblation of the sacrament of the Eucharist, made by the Jews who should believe in Christ, which is known to have been first instituted by Christ in the city of Jerusalem, and afterward to have been continued by His disciples ⁶, shall be pleasing unto the Lord, as the sacrifices of the Patriarchs, Melchisedec, Abraham, and the holy priests in the law, as Aaron; yea, the truth takes precedence of the figure and shadow; the sacrifice of the new law is more excellent

and acceptable to God, than all the sacrifices of the law or before the law. With this agrees what the Lord saith to the synagogue, ⁷ *I will turn My hand upon thee, and purely purge away thy dross, and take away all thy tin; and I will restore thy judges as at the first, and thy counsellors, as at the beginning: and the destruction of the transgressors, and of the sinners, shall be together, and they that forsake the Lord shall be consumed.*" So now it follows;

5. *And I will come near to you to judgment.* They had clamored for the coming of the *God of judgment;* God assures them that He will come to judgment, which they had desired, but far other than they look for. The few would be purified; the great mass of them (so that He calls them *you*), the main body of those who had so clamored, would find that He came as a Judge, not for them but against them.

And I will be a swift witness. "⁵ In judging I will bear witness, and witnessing, I, the Same, will bring forth judgment, saith the Lord; therefore the judgment shall be terrible, since the judge is an infallible witness, whom the conscience of no one will be able to contradict."

God would be a *swift witness,* as He had said before, *He shall come suddenly.* Our Lord calls Himself ⁸ *the Faithful and True witness,* when He stands in the midst of the Church, as their Judge. God's judgments are always unexpected by those, on whom they fall. The sins are those specially condemned by the law; the use of magical arts as drawing men away from God, the rest as sins of special malignity. Magical arts were rife at the time of the Coming of our Lord ⁹; and

---

¹ Is. ii. 3. ² Hos. ix. 4. ³ Jer. vi. 20.
⁴ Canon Missæ. So in S. James' Liturgy, in the prayer of the incense, "O God, Who didst receive the gift of Abel, and the sacrifice of Noah and Abraham, the incense of Aaron and Zachariah." Ass. Cod. Lit. T. v. p. 5. "Receive from the hand of us sinners this incense, as Thou didst receive the oblation of Abel and Noah and Aaron and all Thy saints." Ib. p. 6. "Grant us, Lord, with fear and a pure conscience to present to Thee this spiritual and unbloody Sacrifice, which, when Thou hast received on Thy holy supercelestial and spiritual altar, as a sweet savor, do Thou send back to us the grace of Thine All-holy Spirit, and look upon us, O God, and regard this our reasonable service, and accept it, as Thou didst accept the gifts of Abel, the sacrifice of Noah, the priesthoods of Moses and Aaron, the peace-offerings of Samuel, the repentance of David, the incense of Zachary. As Thou didst receive this true worship from the

hand of Thine Apostle, so, in Thy goodness, receive also from us sinners the gifts which lie before Thee, and grant that our oblation may be acceptable, hallowed in the Holy Spirit, &c." Ib. p. 29, 30.
⁵ Dion. ⁶ S. Matt. xxvi. [29] Acts ii. 42, 46.
⁷ Is. i. 25, 26, 28.
⁸ Rev. iii. 14, i. 5, "I, and not other witnesses, having seen with My own eyes." Theod. S. Jer.
⁹ See Introduction to Zechariah pp. 330, 331, and on Zech. xiii. 2. p. 442. Lightfoot, on S. Matt. xxiv. 24., quotes Maimonides, alleging that one "elected in the Sanhedrin ought to be learned in the arts of astrologers, diviners, soothsayers &c. that he might be able to judge those guilty thereof." Sanhedrin c. 2. He mentions the belief that many had perished thereby (Hieros. Sanhedr. f. 18, 3), 80 women hung in one day for it at Ascalon, (Ib. f. 23, 3, Babyl. Sanh. f. 44, 2;) for that "the Jewish women had greatly broken out into such practices." Gloss Ib.

against those that || oppress the hireling in *his* wages, the widow, and the fatherless, and that turn aside the stranger *from his right*, and fear not me, saith the LORD of hosts.

6 For I *am* the LORD,

---

adultery, as shewn in the history of the woman taken in adultery, when her accusers were convicted in their own consciences[1].

Oppress the hireling, lit. *oppress the hire*,[2] i. e. deal oppressively in it. *Behold*, says S. James[3], *the hire of the laborers who have reaped down your fields, which is by you kept back by fraud, crieth; and the cries of them which have reaped are entered into the ears of the Lord of Sabaoth.* The mere delay in the payment of the wages of the laborer brought sin unto him, against whom he cried to God[4]. It is no light sin, since it is united with the heaviest, and is spoken of as reaching the ears of God. The widow and the fatherless stand in a relation of special nearness to God.

And fear not Me. He closes with the central defect, which was the mainspring of all their sins, the absence of the fear of God. The commission of any of these sins, rife as they unhappily are, proves that those who did them had no fear of God. "[5] Nothing hinders that this should be referred to the first Coming of Christ. For Christ, in preaching to the Jews, exercised upon them a judgment of just rebuke, especially of the priests, Scribes and Pharisees, as the Gospels shew."

6. *I am the Lord, I change not*, better, more concisely, *I, the Lord*[6], *change not.* The proper name of God, *He Who Is*, involves His Unchangeableness. For change implies imperfection; it changes to that which is either more perfect or less perfect: to somewhat which that being, who changes, is not or has not. But God has everything in Himself perfectly. "[7] Thou Alone, O Lord, Art what Thou Art, and Thou Art Who Art. For what is one thing in the whole and another in parts, and wherein is anything subject to change, is not altogether what Is. And what beginneth from not being, and can be conceived, as not being, and only subsisteth through another thing, returns to not-being; and what hath a 'has been,' which now is not, and a 'to be,' which as yet is not, that *is* not, properly and absolutely. But Thou Art what Thou Art. For whatever Thou Art in any time or way, *that* Thou Art wholly and always; and Thou Art, Who Art properly and simply, because Thou hast neither 'to have been' or 'to be about to be; ' but only to be present; and canst not be conceived, ever not to have been." "[8] There is only one simple Good, and therefore One Alone Unchangeable, which is God."

Our life is a "becoming" rather than a simple "being; " it is a continual losing of what we had, and gaining what we had not; for "[9] in as far as any one is not what he was, and is what he was not, so far forth he dieth and ariseth; " dieth to what he was, ariseth to be something otherwise.

"[10] Increase evidences a beginning; decrease, death and destruction. And therefore Malachi says, *I am God, and I change not*, ever retaining His own state of being; because what has no origin cannot be changed."

So the Psalmist says, [11] *As a vesture, Thou shalt change them and they shall be changed, but Thou art the Same, and Thy years shall not fail;* and Balaam, controlled by God, [12] *God is not a man, that He should lie, or the son of man, that He should repent;* and, [13] *with Whom is no variableness, neither shadow of turning.*

Of this unchangeableness of God, His holy ones partake, as far as they fix themselves on God. "[14] The soul of man hangs upon Him, by Whom it was made. And because it was made, to desire God Alone, but everything which it desires below is less than He, rightly doth not *that* suffice it, which is not God. Hence is it, that the soul is scattered hither and thither, and is repelled from everything, toward which it is borne, through satiety of them. But holy men guard themselves by

---

[1] S. John viii. 9, *adulterous generation.* S. Matt. xii. 39. Lightfoot on S. John viii. 3 quotes Sotah f. 47. 1. " From the time that homicides were multiplied, the beheading of the heifer ceased: from the time that adulterers were multiplied, the bitter waters ceased: " and Maimonides on Sotah, c. 3, "When the adulterers multiplied under the 2d Temple, the Sanhedrin abolished the ordeal of the adulteresses by the bitter water; relying on its being written, 'I will not visit your daughters when they commit whoredom, nor your spouses when they commit adultery.'" Lightfoot subjoins, "The Gemarists teach that Johanan b. Zacchai was the author of that advice, who was still alive, in the Sanhedrin, and perhaps among those who brought the adulteress before Christ. For some things make it probable, that the *Scribes and Pharisees*, mentioned here, were elders of the Synagogue."

S. Justin reproaches them with having fresh wives, wherever they went throughout the world. Dial. fin. p. 243. Oxf. Tr.

[2] עָשְׁקֵי שְׂכַר שָׂכִיר, as in Mi. ii. 2, עָשְׁקוּ גֶבֶר וּבֵיתוֹ *oppress a man and his house.*
[3] S. Jas. v. 4.　　[4] Deut. xxiv. 14, 15.　　[5] Dion.
[6] *The Lord* is in apposition to *I*, as, in the following clause, *the sons of Jacob* to ye. The two clauses correspond in form,
　　I, (אֲנִי) the Lord, change not;
　　Ye, (וְאַתֶּם) sons of Jacob, are not consumed.
[7] S. Anselm Prosl. c. 22. p. 34 Ben.
[8] S. Aug. de Civ. Dei xi. 10.
[9] S. Aug. Conf. xi. 7. p. 291. Oxf. Tr.
[10] Novatian de Trin. c. 4.　　[11] Ps. cii. 27.
[12] Nu. xxiii. 19.　　[13] S. Jas. i. 17.
[14] S. Greg. Mor. xxvi. 44. n. 79. Ben.

Before
C H R I S T
cir. 397.

ᵐ Num. 23. 19.
Rom. 11. 29.
Jam. 1. 17.
ⁿ Lam. 3. 22.
ᵒ Acts 7. 51.

ᵖ Zech. 1. 3.

ᵐ I change not; ⁿ therefore ye sons of Jacob are not consumed.

7 ¶ Even from the days of ᵒ your fathers ye a r e gone away from mine ordinances, and h a v e not kept *them*. ᵖ Return unto me, and I will return unto you, saith the LORD of hosts. �q But ye said, Wherein shall we return?

8 ¶ Will a man rob God? Yet ye have robbed me. But ye say, Wherein have we robbed thee? ʳ In tithes and offerings.

9 Ye *are* cursed with a curse: for ye have robbed me, *even* this whole nation.

Before
C H R I S T
cir. 397.

q ch. 1. 6.

ʳ Neh. 13. 10, 12.

---

cautious observation, lest they should be relaxed from their intentness by change, and because they desire to be the same, wisely bind themselves to the thought, whereby they love God. For in the contemplation of the Creator, they will receive this, that they should ever enjoy one stability of mind. No changeableness then dissipates them, because their thought ever perseveres, free from unlikeness to itself. This therefore they now imitate, striving with effort, which hereafter they shall with joy receive as a gift. To which unchangeableness the prophet had bound himself by the power of love, when he said, [1] *One thing I required of the Lord, which I will require, that I may dwell in the house of the Lord.* To this unity Paul clave intently, when he said, [2] *One thing I do, forgetting those things which are behind and stretching forth to those things which are before, I press forward toward the mark for the prize of the high calling of God in Christ Jesus.*"

And ye sons of Jacob are not consumed. Man would often have become weary of man's wickedness and waywardness. We are impatient at one another, readily despair of one another. God might justly have cast off them and us; but *He* changes not. He abides by the covenant which He made with their fathers; He consumed them not; but with His own unchangeable love awaited their repentance. Our hope is not in ourselves, but in God.

7. *Even from the days of your fathers.* Back to those days and from them [3], *ye are gone away from My ordinances.* "[4] I am not changed from good; ye are not changed from evil. I am unchangeable in holiness; ye are unchangeable in perversity."

Return unto Me. The beginning of our return is from the preventing grace of God. [5] *Turn Thou me, and I shall be turned; for Thou art the Lord my God,* is the voice of the soul to God, preparing for His grace; [6] *turn*

us, O God of our salvation. For, not in its own strength, but by His grace can the soul turn to God. *Turn thou to Me and I will return unto you,* is the Voice of God, acknowledging our free-will, and promising His favor, if we accept His grace in return.

And ye say, Wherein shall we return? Strange ignorance of the blinded soul, unconscious that God has aught against it! It is the Pharisaic spirit in the Gospel. It would own itself doubtless in general terms a sinner, but when called on, wholly to turn to God, as being wholly turned from Him, it asks, "In what? What would God have of me?" as if ready to do it.

8. *Shall a man rob* or *cheat,* defraud God? God answers question by question, but thereby drives it home to the sinner's soul, and appeals to his conscience. The conscience is steeled, and answers again, *In what?* God specifies two things only, obvious, patent, which, as being material things, they could not deny. *In tithes and offerings.* The offerings included several classes of dues to God, a) the first fruits [7]; b) the annual half-shekel [8]; c) the offerings made for the tabernacle [9], and the second temple [10] at its first erection; it is used ·of ordinary offerings [11]; d) of the tithes of their own tithes, which the Levites paid to the priests [12]; e) of the portions of the sacrifice which accrued to the priests [13].

9. *Ye have been cursed with the curse* (not "with *a* curse"). The curse threatened had come upon them: but, as fore-supposed in Leviticus by the repeated burthen, *If ye still walk contrary to Me,* they had persevered in evil. God had already shewn His displeasure. But they, so far from being amended by it, were the more hardened in their sin. Perhaps as men do, they pleaded their punishment, as a reason why they should not amend. They *defrauded* God, under false pretences. They were impoverished by His curse, and

[1] Ps. xxvii. 4.   [2] Phil. iii. 13, 14.   [3] למימי.
[4] Rup.
[5] Jer. xxxi. 18. Lam. v. 21.
[6] Ps. lxxxv. 4.   [7] תרומה Num. xv. 19, 20.
[8] Ex. xxx. 13–15.

[9] Ib. xxv. 2, 3, xxxv. 5, 21, 24, xxxvi. 3, 6.
[10] Ezr. viii. 25.
[11] 2 Chr. xxxi. 10. 12 (where המעשר and התרומה are joined, as here, but in inverse order.)
[12] Nu. xviii. 26, 28, 29.   [13] Lev. vii. 14.

10 *Bring ye all the tithes into ᵗ the storehouse, that there may be meat in mine house, and prove me

now herewith, saith t h e LORD of hosts, if I will not open you the ᵘ windows of heaven, and †ˣpour

so they could not afford to pay the tithes; as men say, "the times are bad; so we cannot help the poor" of Christ. *And Me ye still are defrauding*[1]; *Me*, ye; man, God. And that not one or other, but *this whole people.* It was a requital as to that, in which they had offended. "² Because ye have not rendered tithes and first-fruits, therefore ye are cursed in famine and penury." "² Because the people did not render tithes and first-fruits to the Levites, the Lord saith, that He Himself suffered fraud, Whose ministers, constrained by hunger and penury, deserted the temple. For, if He is visited by others in prison, and sick, is received and cared for, and, hungry and athirst, receives food and drink, why should He not receive tithes in His ministers, and, if they are not given, be Himself deprived of His portion?"

10. *Bring the whole tithes*, not a part only, keeping back more or less, and, as he had said, *defrauding* God, offering, like Ananias, a part, as if it had been the whole; *into the treasury*, where they were collected in the time of Hezekiah[3], and again, at this time, by the direction of Nehemiah, *so that there shall be food*[4], not superfluity, *in My house*, "⁵ for those who minister in the house of My sanctuary." ⁶ *The Levites and singers had*, before the reformation, *fled every one to his field*, because *the portion of the Levites had not been given them.* On Nehemiah's remonstrance, aided by Malachi, *the tithe of corn and the wine and the new oil were brought into the treasuries.*

Bring the whole tithes. "⁷ Thou knowest that all things which come to thee are God's, and dost not thou give of His own to the Creator of all? The Lord God needeth not: He asketh not a reward, but reverence: He asketh not anything of thine, to restore to Him. He asketh of thee *first-fruits* and tithes. Niggard, what wouldest thou do, if He took nine parts to Himself, and left thee the tenth?—What if He said to thee; 'Man,

thou art Mine, Who made thee; Mine is the land which thou tillest; Mine are the seeds, which thou sowest; Mine are the animals, which thou weariest; Mine are the showers, Mine the winds, Mine the sun's heat; and since Mine are all the elements, whereby thou livest, thou who givest only the labor of thine hands, deservest only the tithes.' But since Almighty God lovingly feeds us, He gives most ample reward to us who labor little: claiming to Himself the tithes only, He has condoned us all the rest."

And prove Me now herewith, in or *by this thing.* God pledges Himself to His creatures, in a way in which they themselves can verify. "If you will obey, I will supply all your needs; if not, I will continue your dearth." By whatever laws God orders the material creation, He gave them a test, of the completion of which they themselves could judge, of which they themselves must have judged. They had been afflicted with years of want. God promises them years of plenty, on a condition which He names. What would men think now, if any one had, in God's name, promised that such or such a disease, which injured our crops or our cattle, should come at once to an end, if any one of God's laws should be kept? We should have been held as fanatics, and rightly; for we had no commission of God. God authenticates those by whom He speaks; *He* promises, Who alone can perform.

"⁸ There be three keys which God hath reserved in His own hands, and hath not delivered to any to minister or substitute, the keys of life, of rain, and of the resurrection. In the ordering of the rain they look on His great power, no less than in giving life at first, or afterward raising the dead to it; as S. Paul saith, ⁹ *God left not Himself without witness, in that He did good and gave rain from heaven and fruitful seasons.*"

If I will not open the windows of heaven[10]. In the time of the flood, they were, as it were,

---

¹ קְבֵעים. According to its probable etym. ("withdrew and so hid," Arab.), it might be defrauding rather than open robbery. But it has not this metaph. meaning in Arabic. Abulw. Tanchum, Hunt. 206., render it of open violence צָבַע. קְבַע occurs, beside, in Hebrew only in Pr. xxii. 23, *The Lord will plead their cause and will spoil those who spoil them*, i. e. He will requite them as they have done; in the same bold language, as in Ps. xviii. 17.
² S. Jer.
³ 2 Chr. xxxi. 11. sqq. Neh. x. 38, 32, xii. 44. xiii. 12.   ⁴ טֶרֶף, food, as Pr. xxxi. 15, Ps. cxi. 5.

⁵ Jon.   ⁶ Neh. xiii. 10–23.
⁷ App. Serm. S. Aug. 277. Opp. v. App. p. 461. "Not S. Augustine's; more like Cæsarius than S. Aug." Ben.
⁸ Poc. quoting Sanhedr. c. Chelek, and Taanith c. 1.   ⁹ Acts xiv. 17.
¹⁰ The exact expression occurs only in the history of the flood, Gen. vii. 11, viii. 2; in the scoffing courtier's speech, ironically, of God "making windows in heaven" (בַּשָּׁמַיִם), 2 Kgs ii. 2. and, perhaps in reference to the flood, Isaiah says, "*windows* from on high *are opened*, and the foundations of the earth do shake." Is. xxiv. 18.

Before CHRIST cir. 397. you out a blessing, that *there shall* not *be room* enough *to receive it.*

11 And I will rebuke

ʸ Amos 4. 9. ʸ the devourer for y o u r sakes, and he shall n o t

† Heb. *corrupt.* † destroy the fruits of your ground ; neither shall your vine cast her fruit before

the time in the field, saith the LORD of hosts.

Before CHRIST cir. 397.

12 And all nations shall call you blessed : for ye shall be ᶻ a delightsome ⁿ Dan. 8. 9. land, saith the LORD of hosts.

13 ¶ ᵃ Your words have ᵃ ch. 2. 17. been s t o u t against me,

---

opened, to man's destruction : now, God would rain abundantly *for you*, for their sakes. *And pour you out*, lit. *empty out to you*, give to them fully, holding back nothing. So in the Gospel it is said, that the love of God is *shed abroad*¹, poured out and forth *in our hearts by the Holy Ghost which is given to us.*

That *there be not* room *enough* to receive it; lit. *until there be no sufficiency*². The text does not express what should not suffice, whether it be on God's part or on man's. Yet it were too great irony, if understood of God. His superabundance, *above all which we can ask or think*, is a first principle in the conception of God, as the Infinite Source of all being. But to say of God, that He would pour out His blessing, until man could not contain it, is one bliss of eternity, that God's gifts will overflow the capacity of His creatures to receive them. The *pot of oil* poured forth the oil, until, on the prophet's saying, ³ *Bring me yet a vessel*, the widow's son said, There is *not a vessel more. And the oil stayed.* God's gifts are limited only by our capacity to receive them.

11. *And I will rebuke the devourer*, the locust, caterpillar, or any like scourge of God. It might be, that when the rain watered the fields, the locust or caterpillar &c. might destroy the corn, so that the labors of man should perish ; wherefore he adds, *I will rebuke the devourer.* Neither shall *your vine cast her fruit⁴ before the time*, holding out a fair promise, but cut off by the frost-wind or the hail ; the blossoms or the unripe fruit strewing the earth, as a token of God's displeasure.

12. *All nations shall call you blessed.* The promise goes beyond the temporal prosperity of their immediate obedience. Few could

know or think much of the restored prolificalness of Judæa ; none could know of its antecedents. A people, as well as individuals, may starve, and none know of it. Had the whole population of Judah died out, their Persian masters would not have cared for it, but would have sent fresh colonists to replace them and pay the tribute to the great king. The only interest, which *all nations* could have in them, was as being the people of God, from whom He should come, *the Desire of all nations, in* Whom *all the families of the earth* would *be blessed.* Of this, God's outward favor was the earnest ; they should have again the blessings which He had promised to His people.

And ye shall be called a delightsome land, lit. *a land of good pleasure.* It was not so much the land as the people ; *ye shall be called.* The land stands for the people upon it, in whom its characteristics lay. The river Jordan was not so bright as Abana and Pharpar : "the aspect of the shore" is the same, when the inhabitants are spiritually or morally dead ; only the more beautiful, in contrast with the lifeless "spirit of man." So Isaiah says, ⁵ *The nations shall see thy righteousness, and all kings thy glory ; and thou shalt be called by a name, which the mouth of the Lord shall name— Thou shalt no more be called Forsaken, nor shall thy land be called Desolate, but thou shalt be called My-delight-is-in-her, and thy land Married : for the Lord delighteth in thee and thy land shall be married.* God and man should delight in her.

13. *Your words have been stout against Me*, probably *oppressive to* ⁶ *Me*, as it is said, *the famine was strong upon the land. And ye have said, What have we spoken among ourselves⁷ against Thee ?* Again, the entire unconscious-

---

¹ ἐκκέχυται Rom. v. 5.

² In Ps. lxxii. 3 (quoted by Ges. Ros. &c.) *"there shall be abundance of peace* עַד בְּלִי יָרֵחַ, lit *"until there be no moon,"* has a literal meaning, that the peace should last until the end of our creation, without saying anything of what lies beyond.

³ 2 Kgs iv. 6.

⁴ שִׁכֵּל, used elsewhere as to the animal world, is used of a land, 2 Kgs ii. 19, whence מְשַׁכֶּלֶת Ib. 21.

of "immaturity." Pliny speaks of "arborum abortus." H. N. xii. 2, 6. Ges. ⁵ Is. lxii. 2–4.

⁶ הֵזַק, with בְּ on the land, Gen. xli. 56, 57 ; the city, 2 Kgs xxv. 3, Jer. lii. 6 ; with עַל, of persons, Gen. xlvii. 20 ; hand of God was strong upon the prophet, Ez. iii. 14 ; they were urgent, pressed upon. Ez. xii. 33

⁷ The force of Nif. as in iii. 16. Ps. cix. 23, Ezek. xxxiii. 30. The constr. with עַל as Pih. in Ps. cix. 20, Hos. vii. 13, Jer. xxix. 32.

Before
CHRIST
cir. 397. saith the LORD. Yet ye say, What have we spoken *so much* against thee?

[b] Job 21. 14, 15, & 22. 17.
Ps. 73. 13.
Zeph. 1. 12.

14 [b] Ye have said, It *is* vain to serve God: and what profit *is it* that we have kept † his ordinance, and that we have walked

† Heb. *his observation.*

† mournfully before the LORD of hosts?

Before
CHRIST
cir. 397.

15 And now [n] we call the proud happy; yea, they that work wickedness † are set up; yea, *they that* [d] tempt God are even de- livered.

† Heb. *in black.*
[c] Ps. 73. 12, ch. 2. 17.

† Heb. *are built.*

[d] Ps. 95. 9.

---

ness of self-ignorance and self-conceit! They had criticised God, and knew it not. " [1] Before, he had said, [2] *Ye have wearied the Lord with your words, and ye said, Wherein have we wearied Him? When ye said, Every one that doeth evil is good in the sight of the Lord &c.* Now he repeats this more fully. For the people who returned from Babylon seemed to have a knowledge of God, and to observe the law, and to understand their sin, and to offer sacrifices for sin; to pay tithes, to observe the sabbath, and the rest, commanded in the law of God, and seeing all the nations around them abounding in all things, and that they themselves were in penury, hunger and misery, was scandalized and said, ' What does it benefit me, that I worship the One True God, abominate idols, and, pricked with the consciousness of sin, walk mournfully before God?' A topic, which is pursued more largely in the 73d Psalm." Only the Psalmist relates his temptations to God, and God's deliverance of him from them; these adopted them and spake them against God. They claim, for their partial and meagre service, to have fulfilled God's law, taking to themselves God's words of Abraham, *he kept My charge* [3].

14. *Ye have said, It is vain to serve the Lord:* " [4] as receiving no gain or reward for their service. This is the judgment of the world, whereby worldlings think pious, just, sincere, strict men, vain, i. e. especially when they see them impoverished, despised, oppressed, afflicted, because they know not the true goods of virtue and eternal glory, but measure all things by sight, sense and taste.—Truly, if the righteous had not hope of another and better life, in vain would they afflict themselves, and bear the afflictions of others. For, as the Apostle says, [5] *If in this life only we have hope in Christ, we are of all men most miserable.* But now, hoping for another blessed

and eternal life for the slight tribulations of this, we are the happiest of all men."
And we have walked mournfully [6]. Again they take in their mouths the words of Psalmists, that they took the garb of mourners, going about mourning before God for their country's afflictions.

15. *And now we call the proud happy* [*blessed*]. This being so, they sum up the case against God. God had declared that all nations should *call* them *blessed* [7], if they would obey. They answer, using His words; *And now we,* (they lay stress on the word, [8] *we,*) *pronounce blessed,* in fact, those whom God had pronounced cursed: [9] *Thou hast rebuked the proud, who are cursed.* Their characteristic, among other bad men, is of insolence [10], arrogance, *boiling* over with self-conceit, and presumptuous toward God. The ground of Babylon's sentence was, [11] *she hath been proud toward the Lord, the Holy One of Israel;* Jethro says of the Egyptians, as a ground of his belief in God, [12] *for, in the thing that they dealt proudly, He was above them.* It describes the character of the act of Israel, when God bade them *not go up, neither fight,* and they *would not hear, and went up presumptuously into the battle* [13]; the contumacious act of those, who, appealing to the judgment of God, afterward refused it [14]; of Johanan's associates, who accuse Jeremiah of speaking falsely in the name of God [15]; they are persons who rise up [16], forge lies against [17], dig pits for [18], deal perversely with [19], hold in derision [20], oppress [21], the pious. Whether or no, they mean specifically the heathen, those, whom these pronounced *blessed,* were those who were contemptuous toward God.

Yea, the workers of wickedness, those who habitually work it, whose employment it is, *are built up; yea, they have tried God and have escaped.* God had promised that, if [22] they

---

[1] S. Jer.
[2] ii. 17.
[3] וישמר משמרתי Gen. xxvi. 5; add Lev. xviii. 30, xxii. 9, Deut. xi. 1, Jos. xxii. 3. 2 Kgs in. 3, 2 Chr. xiii. 11, xxiii. 6, Zech. iii. 7.
[4] Lap.
[5] 1 Cor. xv. 19.
[6] הלכנו קדרנית. The form ק is one found only here; the phrase in the Ps. is קדר הלך Ps. xxxv. 14, xxxviii. 7, xlii. 10, xliii. 2.
[7] verse 12.
[8] אנחנו emph.

[9] Ps. cxix. 21.
[10] Pr. xxi 24.
[11] זדה אל Jer. l. 29. It is used in regard to Babylon together with עריצים (as in Ps. lxxxvi. 14.) Is. xiii. 11.
[12] Ex. xviii. 11. It is used of Egypt toward Israel. Neh. ix. 16.
[13] Deut. i. 41, 43.
[14] Ib. xvii. 12, 13.
[15] Jer. xliii. 2.
[16] Ps. lxxxvi. 14.
[17] Ib. cxix. 69.
[18] Ib. 85.
[19] Ib. 78.
[20] Ib. 51.
[21] Ib. 122.
[22] Jer. xii. 16.

Before CHRIST cir. 397.	16 ¶ Then they [e]that feared the LORD [f]spake often one to another: and the LORD hearkened, and heard *it*, and [g]a book of remembrance was written	before him for them that feared the LORD, and that thought upon his name.	Before CHRIST cir. 397.
[e] Ps. 66. 16. ch. 4. 2. [f] Heb. 3. 13. [g] Ps. 56. 8. Isai. 65. 6. Rev. 20. 12.		17 And [h]they shall be mine, saith the LORD of hosts, in that day when I	[h] Ex. 19. 5. Deut. 7. 6. Ps. 135. 4. Tit. 2. 14. 1 Pet. 2. 9.

will diligently learn the ways of My people, they shall be built up in the midst of My people; these say, the workers of wickedness *had been built up:* God had bidden themselves, [1]*make trial of Me in this;* these answer, the wicked *had* made trial of Him, and had been unpunished.

16. *Then they that feared the Lord spake often among themselves.* The proud-speaking of the ungodly called out the piety of the Godfearing. "[2]The more the ungodly spake against God, the more these *spake among themselves* for God." Both went on till the great Day of severance. True, as those said, the distinction between righteous and wicked was not made yet, but it was stored up out of sight. They *spake among themselves,* strengthening each other against the ungodly sayings of the ungodly.

And the Lord hearkened and heard it. God, Whom these thought an idle looker-on, or regardless, all the while (to speak after the manner of men) was *bending the ear*[3] from heaven *and heard.* Not one pious loyal word for Him and His glory, escaped Him.

And a book of remembrance was written before Him. Kings had their chronicles written[4], wherein men's good or ill deeds toward them were recorded. But the image is one of the oldest in Scripture, and in the self-same words, [5]*the Lord said to Moses, Write this, a memorial in a book.* God can only speak to us in our own language. One expression is not more human than another, since all are so. Since with God all things are present, and memory relates to the past, to speak of God as "remembering" is as imperfect an expression in regard to God, as to speak of "a book." "[6]Forgetfulness hath no place with God, because He is in no way changed; nor remembrance, because He forgetteth not." Both expressions are used, only to picture vividly to our minds, that our deeds are present with God, for good or

for evil; and in the Day of Judgment He will make them manifest to men and angels, as though read out of a book, and will requite them. So Daniel had said, [7]*the judgment was set, and the books were opened.* And S. John says, [8]*The books were opened, and another book was opened, which is the book of life; and the dead were judged out of those things which were written in the books, according to their works.* So Moses says to God, [9]*If not, blot me out of Thy book which Thou hast written;* and David, prophesying, prays, [10]*Let them be blotted out of the book of the living, and not be written among the righteous;* and our Lord bids His disciples, [11]*Rejoice in this, that your names are written in heaven.*

And that thought upon His name, rather, esteemed, prized, it, in contrast with those who [12]*despised;* as, of Christ, when He should come, it is said, [13]*He was despised, and we esteemed Him not.* "[14]The thinking on His Name imports, not a bare thinking of, but a due esteem and awful regard of, so as with all care to avoid all things which may tend to the dishonor of it, as always in His presence and with respect to Him and fear of Him." "[15]Those are meant who always meditate on the ways of the Lord and the knowledge of His Godhead; for His name is Himself, and He is His Name;" "[16]the wise in heart who know the mystery of the awful glorious Name."

17. *And they shall be Mine, saith the Lord of hosts, in that day when I make up My jewels*[17], or perhaps better, *And they shall be to Me, saith the Lord of hosts, in that day which I make* (or, *in which I do* this) *a peculiar treasure*[18]. "[19]In the day of judgment, those who fear Me and believe and maintain My providence shall be to Me a peculiar treasure, i. e. a people peculiarly belonging and precious to Me, blessed in the vision and fruition of Me. For as in the old law, Israel was a peculiar treasure[20], a special people[21] and inher-

---

[1] ch. iii. 10.　　　　　　　　　[2] à Castro.
[3] ויקשב.　　　[4] ספר הזכרונות Esth. vi. 1.
[5] כתב זאת זכרון בספר Ex. xvii. 14.
[6] S. Aug. in Ps. xxxvii. n. 5.　　[7] Dan. vii. 10.
[8] Rev. xx. 12.　　　　　[9] Ex. xxxii. 32.
[10] Ps. lxix. 28.
[11] S. Luke x. 20.　　[12] Mal. i. 6.　　[13] Is. liii. 3.
[14] Poc.　　[15] Kim. ib.　　[16] Ibn Ezr. ib.
[17] The grounds for this rendering are 1) the recurrence of the words, יום אשר אני עשה, ver. 21.

Heb. [iv. 3. Eng.], and the והייתם לי סגלה Ex. xix. 5; so that we have both phrases elsewhere. In Deut. vii. 6, there is the equivalent להיות לו לעם סגלה, and the like, Deut. xiv. 2, Ps. cxxxv. 4.
[18] Beside the places in which Israel is spoken of such, it occurs only of David's treasures, laid up for building the temple 1 Chr. xxix. 3. and of the public treasures of kings and provinces. Eccl. ii. 8.
[19] Lap.　　[20] סגלה Ex. xxix. 5, Ps. cxxxv. 4.
[21] עם סגלה Deut. vii. 6.

Before
CHRIST
cir. 397.
make up my ‖ [1] jewels;
and [k] I will spare them, as
a man spareth his own son
that serveth him.

18 [1] Then shall ye re-
turn, and discern between
the righteous and the
wicked, between him that
serveth God and him that
serveth him not.

‖ Or, *special
treasure.*
[i] Isai. 62. 3.
[k] Ps. 103. 13.
[l] Ps. 58. 11.

CHAPTER IV.

Before
CHRIST
cir. 397.

1 *God's judgment on the wicked,*
2 *and his blessing on the good.*
He exhorteth to the study of
the law, 5 *and telleth of Eli-*
jah's coming and office.

FOR, behold, [a] the day
cometh, that shall burn
as an oven; and all [b] the
proud, yea, and all that do

[a] Joel 2. 31.
ch. 3. 2.
2 Pet. 3. 7.
[b] ch. 3. 18.

---

itance of God, chosen out of all nations, so in the new law Christians, and those who are righteous through grace, are the special treasure of God, and in heaven shall be His special treasure in glory, possessed by God and possessing God.' The *peculiar treasure,* is something, much prized, made great store of, and guarded. Such are Christians, bought at a great price, even by the precious Blood of Christ; but much more evidently such shall they be, Malachi says, in all eternity, which that Day of final retribution shall decide, "[1] joying in the participation of their Creator, by Whose eternity they are fixed, by Whose truth they are assured, by Whose gift they are holy."

And I will spare them. It is a remarkable word, as used of those who should be to Him a *peculiar treasure,* teaching that, not of their own merits, they shall be such, but by His great mercy. It stands in contrast with the doom of the wicked, whom that day shall sentence to everlasting loss of God. Still, the saved also shall have needed the *tender mercy* [2] of God, whereby He pardoned their misdeeds and had compassion upon them. [3] *If Thou, Lord, shalt lay up iniquities, O Lord, who shall stand?* Among those whom God will spare on that day, will be countless, whom the self-righteous despised as sinners. "[4] I will spare them, although formerly sinners; I will spare them, repenting, and serving Me with the service of a pious confession, as a man spareth his own son which served him." For our Lord saith of the son, who refused to go work in his Father's vineyard, and afterward repented and went, that he [5] *did the will of his Father.*

18. *Then shall ye return,* or *turn,* not, "return" in the sense of *returning* to God, for in that day will be the time of judgment, not of repentance; nor yet, "then shall ye again see;" for this is what they denied; and, if they had ceased to deny it, they would have been converted, not in that day, but before,

when God gave them grace to see it. They shall turn, so as to have other convictions than before; but, as Judas. The Day of judgment will make a great change in earthly judgment. Last shall be first, and first last; this world's sorrow shall end in joy, and worldly joy in sorrow; afflictions shall be seen to be God's love: [6] *Thou in very faithfulness hast afflicted me;* and the unclouded prosperity of the ungodly to be God's abandonment of them. The picture of the surprise of the wicked in the Day of judgment, in the Wisdom of Solomon, is a comment on the Prophet. "[7] Then shall the righteous man stand in great boldness before the face of such as have afflicted him, and made no account of his labors; when they see it, they shall be troubled with terrible fear, and shall be amazed with the strangeness of his salvation, so far beyond all they looked for: and they, repenting and groaning for anguish of spirit, shall say within themselves, This was he whom we had sometimes in derision and a proverb of reproach: we fools counted his life madness and his end to be without honor: how is he numbered among the children of God, and his lot is among the saints!"

IV. 1. *For, behold, the day cometh, which shall burn as an oven.* He had declared the great severance of the God-fearing and the God-blaspheming, those who served and those who did not serve God; the righteous and the wicked; now he declares the way and time of the severance, the Day of Judgment. Daniel had described the fire of that day, [8] *The throne [of the Ancient of days] was a fiery flame; his wheels a burning fire: a fiery stream issued and came forth from Him: the judgment was set and the books were opened.* Fire is ever spoken of, as accompanying the judgment. [9] *Our God shall come, and shall not keep silence, a fire shall devour before Him;* [10] *Behold the Lord will come with fire: for by fire and by the sword will the Lord plead with all*

---

[1] S. Aug. in Civ. Dei x. 7.

[2] חמל has originally the meaning of tender compassion.

[3] Ps. cxxx. 3.　　[4] Rup.　　[5] S. Matt. xxi. 31.
[6] Ps. cxix. 75.　　　　　　　　[7] Wisd. v. 1-5.
[8] Dan. vii. 9, 10.　　[9] Ps. l. 3.　　[10] Is. lxvi. 15, 16.

wickedly, shall be ᶜstubble:
and the day that cometh
shall burn them up, saith
the Lord of hosts, that it

ᶜObad. 18.

shall ᵈleave them neither
root nor branch.

2 ¶ But unto you that ᵈAmos 2. 9.
ᵉfear my name shall the ᵉch. 3. 16.

---

flesh: [1] *every man's work shall be made manifest, for the Day shall declare it, because it shall be revealed by fire: and the fire shall try every man's work, of what sort it is.* S. Peter tells us that fire will be of this burning world; [2] *the heavens and the earth which are now, by the same word are kept in store, reserved unto fire against the day of judgment and perdition of ungodly men; —in the which the heavens shall pass away with a great noise, and the elements shall melt with fervent heat, the earth also and the works that are therein shall be burned up.*

The *oven*, or furnace, pictures the intensity of the heat, which is white from its intensity, and darts forth, fiercely, shooting up like a living creature, and destroying life, as the flame of the fire of Nebuchadnezzar's [3] *burning fiery furnace slew those men that took up Shadrach Meshach and Abednego.* The whole world would be one burning furnace.

And all the proud and all that do wickedly. All those, whom those murmurers pronounced *blessed* [4], yea and *all* who should thereafter be like them (he insists on the universality of the judgment), *every doer of wickedness*, up to that day and those who should then be, *shall be stubble.* " [5] The proud and mighty, who in this life were strong as iron and brass, so that no one dared resist them, but they dared to fight with God, these, in the Day of Judgment, shall be most powerless, as stubble cannot resist the fire, in an everlasting death."

That shall leave them neither root nor branch " i. e. [6] they shall have no hope of shooting up again to life; that life, I mean, which is worthy of love, and in glory with God, in holiness and bliss. For when the root has not been wholly cut away, nor the shoot torn up as from the depth, some hope is retained, that it may again shoot up. For, as it is written, [7] *There is hope of a tree, if it be cut down, that it will sprout again, and that the tender branch thereof will not cease.* But if it be wholly torn up from below and from its very roots, and its shoots be fiercely cut away, all hope, that it can again shoot up to life, will perish also. So, he saith, will all hope of the lovers of sin perish. For so the Divine Isaiah clearly announces, [8] *their worm shall not die and their fire shall not be quenched, and they shall be an abhorring to all flesh.*"

2. *But* (And) *unto you, who fear My Name,*

shall the Sun of Righteousness arise. It is said of God, [9] *The Lord God is a sun and a shield,* and, [10] *The Lord shall be to thee an everlasting light, and thy God thy glory; thy sun shall no more go down; for the Lord shall be thine everlasting light;* and Zacharias, speaking of the office of S. John Baptist in the words of Malachi, *thou shalt go before the face of the Lord to prepare His way,* speaks of [11] *the tender mercy of our God, whereby the Dayspring from on high hath visited us, to give light to them that sit in darkness.* " [12] He Who is often called Lord and God, and Angel and Captain of the Lord's host, and Christ and Priest and Word and Wisdom of God and Image, is now called *the Sun of Righteousness.* He, the Father promises, will arise, not to all, but to those only who fear His Name, giving them the light of the Sun of Righteousness, as the reward of their fear toward Him. This is God the Word Who saith, *I am the Light of the world,* Who was *the Light of every one who cometh into the world.*" Primarily, Malachi speaks of our Lord's second Coming, when [13] *to them that look for Him shall He appear, a second time unto salvation.* For as, in so many places [14], the Old Testament exhibits the opposite lots of the righteous and the wicked, so here the prophet speaks of the Day of Judgment, in reference to the two opposite classes, of which he had before spoken, the proud and evil doers, and the fearers of God. The title, *the Sun of Righteousness,* belongs to both Comings; " [5] in the first, He diffused rays of righteousness, whereby He justified and daily justifies any sinners whatever, who will look to Him, i. e. believe in Him and obey Him, as the sun imparts light, joy and life to all who turn toward it." In the second, the righteousness which He gave, He will own and exhibit, cleared from all the misjudgment of the world, before men and Angels. Yet more, healing is, throughout Holy Scripture, used of the removal of sickness or curing of wounds, in the individual or state or Church, and, as to the individual, bodily or spiritual. So David thanks God, first for the forgiveness, [15] *Who forgiveth all thine iniquities;* then for healing of his soul, *Who healeth all thy diseases;* then for salvation, *Who redeemeth thy life from destruction;* then for the crown laid up for him, *Who crowneth thee with*

¹ 1 Cor. iii. 13. ² 2 S. Pet. iii. 7-10. ³ Dan. iii. 22.
⁴ ch. iii. 15. ⁵ Lap. ⁶ S. Cyr. ⁷ Job xiv. 7.
⁸ Is. lxvi. ult. ⁹ Ps. lxxxiv. 11. ¹⁰ Is. lx. 19, 20.
¹¹ S. Luke i. 76, 78, 79.
¹² Eus. Dem. Ev. iv. 29. ¹³ Heb. ix. 28.
¹⁴ As. Ps. i. 6, ii. 12, iii. 7, 8, v. 10-12, vi. 8-10, vii. 16,

17, ix. 17-20, x. 16-18, xi. 6, 7, xvii. 13-15, xx. 8, xxvi. 9-12, xxxi. 23, xxxii. 10, 11, xxxiv. 21, 22, xxxv. 26-28, xxxvi. 10-12, xxxvii. 38-40, xl. 15-17, l. 22, 23, lii. 5-9, lv. 22, 23, lviii. 10, 11, lxiii. 10, 11, lxiv. 9, 10, lxxiii. 27, 28, civ. 33-35, cxii. 9, 10, cxxvi. 5, cxlix. 9.
¹⁵ Ps. ciii. 3-5.

32

Before
CHRIST
cir. 397.

f Luke 1. 78.
Eph. 5. 14.
2 Pet. 1. 19.
Rev. 2. 28.
g 2 Sam. 22. 43.
Mic. 7. 10.
Zech. 10. 5.

f Sun of righteousness arise with healing in his wings; and ye shall go forth, and grow up as calves of the stall.

3 g And ye shall tread down the wicked; for they shall be ashes under the soles of your feet in the day that I shall do *this*, saith the LORD of hosts.

4 ¶ Remember ye the

Before
CHRIST
cir. 397.

loving-kindness and tender mercies; then, with the abiding sustenance and satisfying joy, *Who satisfieth thy mouth with good things.* Healing then primarily belongs to this life, in which we are still encompassed with infirmities, and even His elect and His Saints have still, whereof to be healed. The full then and complete healing of the soul, the integrity of all its powers will be in the life to come. There, will be " [1] understanding without error, memory without forgetfulness, thought without distraction, love without simulation, sensation without offence, satisfying without satiety, universal health without sickness." " [2] For through Adam's sin the soul was wounded in understanding, through obscurity and ignorance; in will, through the leaning to perishing goods; as concupiscent, through infirmity and manifold concupiscence. In heaven Christ will heal all these, giving to the understanding light and knowledge; to the will, constancy in good; to the desire, that it should desire nothing but what is right and good. Then too the healing of the soul will be the light of glory, the vision and fruition of God, and the glorious endowments consequent thereon, overstreaming all the powers of the soul and therefrom to the body." " [3] God has made the soul of a nature so mighty, that from its most full beatitude, which at the end of time is promised to the saints, there shall overflow to the inferior nature, the body, not bliss, which belongs to the soul as intelligent and capable of fruition, but the fullness of health that is, the vigorousness of incorruption."

And ye shall go forth, as from a prison-house, from the miseries of this lifeless life, *and grow up,* or perhaps more probably, *bound* [4], as the animal, which has been confined, exults in its regained freedom, itself full of life and exuberance of delight. So the Psalmist, [5] *The saints shall exult in glory.* And our Lord uses the like word [6], as to the way, with which they should greet persecution to the utmost, for His Name's sake. Swiftness of

motion is one of the endowments of the spiritual body, after the resurrection; as the angels, to whom the righteous shall be like [7], [8] *ran and returned as the appearance of a flash of lightning.*

3. *And ye shall tread down the wicked; for they shall be ashes under the soles of your feet.* It shall be a great reversal. *He that exalteth himself shall be abased, and he that humbleth himself shall be exalted.* Here the wicked often have the pre-eminence. This was the complaint of the murmurers among the Jews; *in the morning of the Resurrection* [9] *the upright shall have dominion over them.* The wicked, he had said, shall be *as stubble,* and that day [10] *shall burn them up;* here, then, they are as the ashes, the only remnant of the stubble, as the dust under the feet. " [11] The elect shall rejoice, that they have, in mercy, escaped such misery. Therefore they shall be kindled inconceivably with the Divine love, and shall from their inmost heart give thanks unto God." And being thus of one mind with God, and seeing all things as He seeth, they will rejoice in His judgments, because they are His. For they cannot have one slightest velleity, other than the all-perfect Will of God. So Isaiah closes his prophecy, [12] *And they shall go forth, and look upon the carcases of the men, that have transgressed against Me; for their worm shall not die, neither shall their fire be quenched, and they shall be an abhorring to all flesh.* So [13] *The righteous shall rejoice, when he seeth the vengeance;* and another Psalmist, [14] *The righteous shall see and rejoice; and all wickedness shall stop her mouth;* and Job, [15] *The righteous see and are glad, and the innocent laugh them to scorn.*

4. *Remember ye the law of Moses, My servant.* [16] *The law was our schoolmaster to bring us unto Christ.* They then who were most faithful to the law, would be most prepared for Christ. But for those of his own day, too, who were negligent both of the ceremonial and moral law, he says, " [11] Since the judgment of God will be so fearful, remem-

[1] Pomerius de vit. contempl. i. 4.　　[2] Lap.
[3] S. Aug. Ep. 118 ad Diosc. n. 14 Opp. ii. 334. L.
[4] So LXX. Vulg. Syr. (and on Jer. l. 11) Jon. (here "go" only); of modern Jews, Tanchum here and on Jer. l. 11. Pococke says more cautiously than moderns generally, " *not far from* this signification is the Arab. פאש, which signifies to 'vaunt' or 'boast' or 'go strutting' or 'proudly.'" For "arro-

gance," not "exuberance of joy," seems the meaning of the Arabic word. The E. V., "grow," "enlarge," follows the interpretation given by most Heb. Comm. or lexicographers.
[5] Ps. cxlix. 5.　　[6] σκιρτήσατε S. Luke vi. 23.
[7] S. Luke xx. 36.　[8] Ezek. i. 14.　[9] Ps. xlix. 14.
[10] iv. 1.　　　　[11] Dion.　　[12] Is. lxvi. 24.
[13] Ps. lviii. 10.　　　　　[14] Ib. cvii. 42.
[15] Job xxii. 19.　　　　　[16] Gal. iii. 24.

Before
CHRIST
cir. 397.

h Ex. 20. 3. &c.
i Deut. 4. 10.
k Ps. 147. 19.

[h] law of Moses my servant, which I commanded unto him [i] in Horeb for all Israel, with [k] the statutes and judgments.

5 ¶ Behold, I will send you [l] Elijah the prophet [m] before the coming of the great and dreadful day of the LORD:

Before
CHRIST
cir. 397.

l Matt. 11. 14.
& 17. 11.
Mark 9. 11.
Luke 1. 17.
m Joel 2. 31.

ber now unceasingly and observe the law of God given by Moses."

Which I commanded[1] *unto him for* [lit. *upon*, incumbent *upon*] *all Israel*. Not Moses commanded them, but God by His servant Moses ; therefore He " [2] would in the day of judgment take strict account of each, whether they had or had not kept them. He would glorify those who obeyed, He would condemn those who disobeyed them." They had asked, *Where is the God of judgment? What profit, that we have kept the ordinance?* He tells them of the judgment to come, and bids them take heed, that they did indeed keep them ; for there was a day of account to be held for all.

With *the statutes and judgments*, better, *statutes and judgments*, i. e. consisting in them ; it seems added as an explanation of the word, *law*, individualizing them. Duty is fulfilled, not in a general acknowledgment of law, or an arbitrary selection of some favorite commandments, which cost the human will less ; as, in our Lord's time, they minutely observed the law of tithes, but [3] *omitted weightier matters of the law, judgment, mercy, and faith*. It is in obedience to the commandments, one by one, one and all. Moses exhorted to the keeping of the law, under these same words : [4] *Now, therefore hearken, O Israel, unto the statutes and judgments which I teach you, to do them, that ye may live.— Ye shall not add unto the word that I command you, neither shall ye diminish it.—Behold, I have taught you statutes and judgments, even as the Lord my God commanded me.— What nation so great, that hath statutes and judgments, righteous as all this law, which I set before you this day? The Lord commanded me at that time, to teach you statutes and judgments, that ye might do them in the land, whither ye go to possess it.*

5. *Behold I will send* [*I send*, as a future, proximate in the prophet's mind] *you Elijah the prophet.* The Archangel Gabriel interprets this for us, to include the sending of S. John Baptist. For he not only says [5] that he·shall *go before* the Lord *in the spirit and power of Elias*, but describes his mission in the characteristic words of Malachi, *to turn the hearts of the fathers to the children:* and

those other words also, *and the disobedient to the wisdom of the just*, perhaps represent the sequel in Malachi, *and the hearts of the children to the fathers;* for their hearts could only be so turned by conversion to God, Whom the fathers, patriarchs and prophets, knew, loved and served ; and Whom *they* served in name only. S. John Baptist, in denying that he was Elias[6], denied only, that he was that great prophet himself. Our Lord, in saying, [7] *This is Elias, which was for to come,* [8] *that Elias is come already and they knew him not, but have done unto him whatsoever they listed,* met the error of the Scribes, that He could not be the Christ, because Elias was not yet come [9]. When He says, [10] *Elias truly shall first come and restore all things,* He implies a coming of Elias, other than that of S. John Baptist, since *he* was already martyred, and *all things* were not yet *restored*. This must also be the fullest fulfillment. For *the great and terrible Day of the Lord* is the Day of judgment, of which all earthly judgments, however desolating, (as the destruction of Jerusalem) are but shadows and earnests. Before our Lord's coming all things looked on to His first Coming, and, since that Coming, all looks on to the Second, which is the completion of the first and of all things in time.

Our Lord's words, *Elias truly shall first come and restore all things,* seem to me to leave no question, that, as S. John Baptist came, in the spirit and power of Elias, before His First Coming, so, before the Second Coming, Elias should come in person, as Jews and Christians have alike expected. This has been the Christian expectation from the first. S. Justin Martyr asked his opponent [11], " Shall we not conceive that the Word of God has proclaimed Elias to be the forerunner of the great and terrible day of His second Coming? " " Certainly," was Trypho's reply. S. Justin continues, " Our Lord Himself taught us in His own teaching that this very thing shall be, when He said that *Elias also shall come;* and we know that this shall be fulfilled, when He is about to come from Heaven in glory." *Tertullian* says [12], " Elias is to come again, not after a departure from life, but after a translation ; not to be re-

1 צוה with double accus.   2 Lap.
3 S. Matt. xxiii. 23.   4 Deut. iv. 1, 2, 5, 8, 14.
5 S. Luke i. 17.   6 S. John i. 21.
7 S. Matt. xi. 14.   8 Ib. xvii. 12.
9 The error of the Jews consisted, not in their rooted belief, as founded on these words, that

Elijah should come before the great and terrible Day of the Lord, but in their denial that He should have any forerunner of His Coming in His great humility. They erred, not in what they believed, but in what they disbelieved.
10 S. Matt. xvii. 11.   11 Dial. c. 49. p. 131. Oxf. Tr.
12 De anima c. 35. p. 539. Rig.

stored to the body, from which he was never taken; but to be restored to the world, from which he was translated; not by way of restoration to life, but for the completion of prophecy; one and the same in name and in person." "[1] Enoch and Elias were translated, and their death is not recorded, as being deferred; but they are reserved as to die, that they may vanquish Antichrist by their blood." And, in proof that the end was not yet, "[2] No one has yet received Elias; no one has yet fled from Antichrist." And the ancient *author of the verses against Marcion*; "[3] Elias who has not yet tasted the debt of death, because he is again to come into the world." *Origen* says simply in one place[4], that the Saviour answered the question as to the objection of the Scribes, "not annulling what had been handed down concerning Elias, but affirming that there was another coming of Elias before Christ, unknown to the scribes, according to which, not knowing him, and, being in a manner, accomplices in his being cast into prison by Herod and slain by him, they had done to him what they listed." *S. Hippolytus* has; "[5] As two Comings of our Lord and Saviour were indicated by the Scriptures, the first in the flesh, in dishonor, that He might be set at naught—the second in glory, when He shall come from Heaven with the heavenly host and the glory of the Father—so two forerunners were pointed out, the first, John, the son of Zacharias, and again—since He is manifested as Judge at the end of the world, His forerunners must first appear, as He says through Malachi, *I will send to you Elias the Tishbite before the great and terrible day of the Lord shall come.*" *S. Hilary*; "[6] The Apostles enquire in anxiety about the times of Elias. To whom He answereth, that *Elias will come and restore all things,* that is, will recall to the knowledge of God, what he shall find of Israel; but he signifies that John came in *the spirit and power of Elias,* to whom they had shewn all severe and harsh dealings, that, foreannouncing the Coming of the Lord, he might be a forerunner of the Passion also by an example of wrong and harass." "[7] We understand that those same prophets [Moses and Elias] will come before His Coming, who, the Apocalypse of John says, will be slain by Antichrist, although there are various opinions of very many, as to Enoch or Jeremiah, that one of them is to die, as Elias."

Hilary the Deacon, A.D. 355, has on the words,

I suppose God hath set forth us the Apostles last; "[8] He therefore applies these to his own person, because he was always in distress, suffering, beyond the rest, persecutions and distresses, as Enoch and Elias will suffer, who will be Apostles at the last time. For they have to be sent before Christ, to make ready the people of God, and fortify all the Churches to resist Antichrist, of whom the Apocalypse attests, that they will suffer persecutions and be slain." "[9] When the faithless shall be secure of the kingdom of the devil, the saints, i. e. Enoch and Elias being slain, rejoicing in the victory, and *sending gifts, one to another,* as the Apocalypse says[10], sudden destruction shall come upon them. For Christ at His Coming, shall destroy them all." *S. Gregory of Nyssa* quotes the prophecy under the heading, that "[11] before the second Coming of our Lord, Elias should come."

S. Ambrose; "[12] Because the Lord was to come down from heaven, and to ascend to heaven, He raised Elias to heaven, to bring him back to the earth at the time He should please." "[13] The beast, Antichrist, ascends from the abyss to fight against Elias and Enoch and John, who are restored to the earth for the testimony to the Lord Jesus, as we read in the Apocalypse of John."

S. Jerome gives here the mystical meaning; "God will send, in Elias, (which is interpreted 'My God' and who is of the town Thisbe, which signifies 'conversion' or 'penitence')the whole choir of the Prophets, to *convert the heart of the fathers to the sons,* viz. Abraham and Isaac and Jacob and all the patriarchs, that their posterity may believe in the Lord the Saviour, in whom themselves believed: for *Abraham saw the day of the Lord and was glad.*" Here, he speaks of the "coming of Elias before *their* anointed," as a supposition of Jews and Judaizing heretics. But in commenting on our Lord's words in S. Matthew, he adheres twice to the literal meaning. "[14] Some think that John is therefore called Elias, because, as, according to Malachi, at the second Coming of the Saviour[15], Elias will precede and announce the Judge to come, so did John at His first Coming, and each is a messenger of the first or second Coming of the Lord:" and again concisely, "[15] He who is to come in the second Coming of the Saviour in the actual body, now comes through John in spirit and power;" and he speaks of Enoch and Elias as "[16] the *two witnesses* in the Revelation,

---

[1] Id. ib. c. 50, p. 549.
[2] de res. carnis c. 22. p. 385. Rig.
[3] Carm. incert. Auct. adv. Marcion. L. iii. p. 802. col. 1 Rig.
[4] in S. Matt. xvii. 10. Opp. iii. 567.
[5] de Antichristo c. 44-46 pp. 21, 22.
[6] in Matt. c. xvii. n. 4. Opp. p. 694, 695.
[7] Id. Ib. c. xx. n. 10. p. 710. Ben.

[8] App. S. Ambros. ii. 125. in 1 Cor. iv. 9.
[9] Ib. p. 282. in 1 Thess. v. 1.   [10] Rev. xi. 10.
[11] adv. Jud. Opp. ii. p. 266.   [12] de poenit. i. 8.
[13] in Psalm 45, n. 10. Opp. i. 930. "Only one MS. has, 'and John.'" Ben. note.
[14] On S. Matt. xi. 14, 15.
[15] On S. Matt. xvii. 11, 12.
[16] Ep 59 [al. 148] ad Marcell. Opp. i. 326. Vall.

since, according to the Apocalypse of John, Enoch and Elias are spoken of, as having to die."

S. Chrysostom, "[1] When He saith that Elias *cometh and shall restore all things,* He means Elias himself, and the conversion of the Jews, which shall then be; but when He saith, *which was to come,* He calls John, Elias, according to the manner of his ministry."

In *S. Augustine's* time it was the universal belief. "[2] When he [Malachi] had admonished them to remember the law of Moses, because he foresaw, that they would for a long time not receive it spiritually, as it ought, he added forthwith ; *And I will send you Elias the Thisbite &c.* That when, through this Elias, the great and wonderful prophet, at the last time before the judgment, the law shall have been expounded to them, the Jews shall believe in the true Christ, i. e. in our Christ, is everywhere in the mouths and hearts of the faithful. For not without reason is it hoped, that he shall come before the Coming of the Saviour, as Judge, because not without reason is it believed that he still lives. For he was carried in a chariot of fire from things below ; which Scripture most evidently attests. When he shall come then, by expounding the law spiritually, which the Jews now understand carnally, he shall turn the heart of the fathers to the children."

S. Cyril of Alexandria, his antagonist *Theodoret,* and *Theodore* of Mopsuestia, who was loose from all tradition, had the same clear belief. *S. Cyril ;* " It is demonstrative of the gentleness and long-suffering of God, that Elias also the Tishbite shall shine upon us, to foreannounce when the Judge shall come to those in the whole world. For the Son shall come down, as Judge, in the glory of the Father, attended by the angels, and shall *sit on the throne of His glory,* judging *the world in righteousness,* and *shall reward every man according to his works.* But since we are in many sins, well is it for us, that the Divine Prophet goes before Him, bringing all those on earth to one mind ; that all, being brought to the unity through the faith, and ceasing from evil intents, may fulfill that which is good, and so be saved when the Judge cometh down. The blessed Baptist John came before Him *in the spirit and power of Elias.* But, as he preached saying, *Prepare ye the way of the Lord, make His paths straight,* so also the divine Elias proclaims His then being near and all-but-present, that He may *judge the world in righteousness.*"

Theodoret ; "[3] Malachi teaches us how, when Antichrist shall presume on these things, the great Elias shall appear, preaching to the Jews the Coming of Christ: and he shall convert many, for this is the meaning of, *he*

shall turn the heart of the fathers to the children, i. e. the Jews (for these he calls fathers, as being older in knowledge) to those who believed from the Gentiles. They who shall believe through the preaching of the great Elias, and shall join themselves to the Gentiles who seized the salvation sent to them, shall become one Church. He hints, how when these things are done by Antichrist, S. Michael the Archangel will set all in motion, that Elias should come and foreannounce the Coming of the Lord, that the then Jews may obtain salvation." And on this place, " Knowing well, that they would neither obey the law, nor receive Him when He came, but would deliver Him to be crucified, He promises them, in His unspeakable love for man, that He will again send Elias as a herald of salvation, *Lo, I will send you Elias the Tishbite.* And signifying the time, He added, *Before the great and terrible Day of the Lord shall come :* He named the Day of His Second Coming. But He teaches us, what the great Elias shall do, when he comes, *Who shall bring back the heart of the father to the son* &c. And pointing out the end, for which Elias should first come, *Lest I come and smite the earth utterly.* For lest, finding you all in unbelief, I send you all to that endless punishment, Elias will first come, and will persuade you, O Jews, to unite you indissolubly with those, who from the Gentiles believe in Me, and to be united to My one Church."

Theodore of Mopsuestia paraphrases: "In addition to all which I have said, I give you this last commandment, to remember My law, which I gave to all Israel through Moses, plainly declaring what they ought to do in each thing, and as the first token of obedience, to receive the Lord Christ when He cometh, appearing for the salvation of all men : Who will end the law, but shew His own perfection. It had been well, had you immediately believed Him when He came, and known Him, as He Whom Moses and all the prophets signified, Who should put an end to the law, and reveal the common salvation of all men, so that it should be manifest to all, that this is the sum and chief good of the whole dispensation of the law, to bring all men to the Lord Christ, Who, for those great goods, should be manifested in His own time. But since, when He manifested Himself, ye manifested your own ungainliness, the blessed Elias shall be sent to you before the second Coming of Christ, when He will come from Heaven, to unite those who, for religion, are separated from each other, and, through the knowledge of religion, to bring the fathers to one-mindedness with the children, and in a word, to bring all men to one and the same harmony, when those, then

[1] In S. Matt. Hom. 57. Opp. vii. 577. [2] de Civ. Dei, xx. 29. Opp. vii. 613. [3] On Daniel, c. xii. init.

6 And he shall turn the heart of the fathers to the children, and the heart of the children to their fathers, lest I come and ⁿ smite the earth with ° a curse.

found in ungodliness, shall receive from him the knowledge of the truth in the communion with the godly thence ensuing."

The African author of the work on the promises and predictions of God. (between A. D. 450–455.)

" [1] Against Antichrist shall be sent two witnesses, the prophets Enoch and Elijah, against whom shall arise three false prophets of Antichrist."

Isidore of Seville A. D. 595.;

" [2] Elias, borne in a chariot of fire, ascended to heaven, to come according to the prophet Malachi at the end of the world, and to precede Christ, to announce His last Coming, with great deeds and wondrous signs, so that, on earth too, Antichrist will war against him, be against him, or him who is to come with him, and will slay them; their bodies also will lie unburied in the streets. Then, raised by the Lord, they will smite the kingdom of Antichrist with a great blow. After this, the Lord will come, and will slay Antichrist with the word of His mouth, and those who worshiped him."

" [3] This will be in the last times, when, on the preaching of Elias, Judah will be converted to Christ."

To add one more, for his great gifts, S. *Gregory the Great.* " [4] It is promised, that when Elias shall come, he shall bring back the hearts of the sons to their fathers, that the doctrine of the old, which is now taken from the hearts of the Jews, may, in the mercy of God, return, when the sons shall begin to understand of the Lord God, what the fathers taught." " [5] Although Elias is related to have been carried to heaven, he deferred, he did not escape, death. For it is said of him by the mouth of the Truth Himself, *Elias shall come and restore all things.* He shall come to *restore all things;* for to this end is he restored to this world, that he may both fulfill the office of preaching, and pay the debt of the flesh." " [6] The holy Church, although it now loses many through the shock of temptation, yet, at the end of the world, it receives its own double, when, having received the Gentiles to the full, all Judæa too, which shall then be, agrees to

hasten to its faith. For hence it is written, *Until the fullness of the Gentiles shall come, and so all Israel shall be saved.* Hence in the Gospel the Truth says, *Elias shall come and shall restore all things.* For now the Church has lost the Israelites, whom it could not convert by preaching; but then, at the preaching of Elias, while it collects all which it shall find, it receives in a manner more fully what it has lost." " [7] John is spoken of as to come in the spirit and power of Elias, because, as Elias shall precede the second Coming of the Lord, so John preceded His first. For as Elias will come, as precursor of the Judge, so John was made the precursor of the Redeemer. John then was Elias in spirit; he was not Elias in person. What then the Lord owned as to spirit, that John denies as to the person."

Whether Elias is one of the *two witnesses* [8], spoken of in the Apocalypse, is obviously a distinct question. Of commentators on the Apocalypse, Arethas [9] remarks that as to Elias, there is clear testimony from Holy Scripture, this of Malachi; but that, with regard to Enoch, we have only the fact of his being freed from death by translation, and the tradition of the Church. S. John Damascene fixed the belief, in the Eastern Church [10]. In the West, Bede e. g. who speaks of the belief that the two witnesses were Elijah and Enoch, as what was said by " [11] some doctors," takes our Lord's declaration, that Elias shall return, in its simple meaning [12]. Yet it was no matter of faith [13]. When the belief as to a personal Antichrist was changed by Luther and Calvin, the belief of a personal forerunner of Christ gave way also.

6. *And he shall turn the hearts of the fathers unto the children.* Now they were unlike, and severed by that unlikeness from each other. Yet not on earth; for on earth parents and children were alike alienated from God, and united between themselves in wickedness or worldliness. The common love of the world or of worldly pursuits, or gain or self-exaltation, or making a fortune or securing it, is, so far, a common bond of interest to those of one family, through a common selfishness,

[1] Dimid. Temp. c. 13. App. to S. Prosper. Enoch and Elias are spoken of, as the two witnesses, by Ammonius in the Comm. variorr. on Daniel. Mai Scriptt. Vett. Nov. Coll. T. 1. P. iii. p. 52.
[2] de ort. et ob. Patr. c. 35. Opp. v. 167, 168.
[3] c. Jud. ii. 5. 9. Opp. vi. 79.
[4] Moral. xi. 15. n. 24. Ben.
[5] Ib. xx. 34. n. 66. Ben.
[6] Ib. xxxv. 14. n. 24. See also on Ezek. L. i. Hom. 12. n. 8, 9, where he speaks of the coming of Enoch also.

[7] in Evang. Hom. vii. n. 1. [8] See vol. i. p. 45.
[9] Comm. on Apocalypse printed with Œcumenius p. 942. ed. 1530.
[10] De fide iv. 26. [11] on Rev. c. xi.
[12] on S. Matt. xvii. 11. S. Mark ix.
[13] Rupertus says here; " Of the coming of Elias I dare not define anything, because some doctors, with whom almost all agree, believe that he will come in the letter, and will restore all things, and will pay the debt of death; but others not, with whom the illustrious S. Jerome seems to agree.

though that selfishness is the parent of general discord, of fraud, violence, and other misdeeds. Nay, conversion of children or parents becomes rather a source of discord, embittering the unconverted. Whence our Lord says, *Think not, that I* [1] *am come to send peace on the earth. I came not to send peace on earth, but a sword. For I am come to set a man at variance against his father, and the daughter against her mother, and the daughter-in-law against her mother-in-law: and a man's foes shall be they of his own household;* a prophecy fulfilled continually in the early persecutions, even to the extent of those other words of our Lord, [2] *the brother shall deliver up the brother to death, and the father the ·child; and the children shall rise up against their parents, and cause them to be put to death.* It is fulfilled also in the intense hatred of the Jews at this day, to any who are converted to Christ; a hatred which seems to have no parallel in the world. Nor do the words seem to mean that fathers and children should be united in one common conversion to God, as one says, "[3] All shall be one heart to return to the Lord, both fathers and children;" for he speaks primarily of their mutual conversion to one another, not to God.

The form of the expression seems to imply that the effect of the preaching of Elias shall be, to bring back the children, the Jews then in being, to the faith and love which their

fathers, the Patriarchs, had; that "[4] as these believed, hoped for, longed exceedingly for, and loved Christ to come, so their sons should believe, hope in, long exceedingly for and love Christ, Who was come, yea is present; and so the heart of fathers, which before was turned from their unbelieving children, he should turn to them, now believing, and cause the Patriarchs to own and love the Jews believing in Christ, as indeed their children; for [5] your father Abraham rejoiced to see My day; he saw it and was glad,' Christ saith."

Lest I come and smite the earth with a curse, i. e. with an utter destruction, from which there should be no redemption. [6] In the end, God will so smite the earth, and all, not converted to Him. The prayer and zeal of Elijah will gain a reprieve, in which God will spare the world for the gathering of His own elect, the full conversion of the Jews, which shall fulfil the Apostle's words, [6] *So shall all Israel be saved.*

After the glad tidings, Malachi, and the Old Testament in him, ends with words of awe, telling us of the consequence of the final hardening of the heart; the eternal severance, when the unending end of the everlasting Gospel itself shall be accomplished, and its last grain shall be gathered into the garner of the Lord. The Jews, who would be wiser than the prophet, repeat the previous verse [7], because Malachi closes so aw-

---

[1] S. Matt. x. 34–36.   [2] Ib. 21.
[3] Ibn Ezra. The Jews, although mixed up, that Elijah will come, are disagreed as to the end of his coming. By some he is spoken of as a Redeemer. *Tanchuma,* (f. 31. 1.) "God said to Israel, In this world I sent an angel to cast out the nations before you, but in the future [or, in the world to come, Yalkut Shim'oni f. 98–29] myself will lead you and will 'send you Elijah the prophet.'" Pesikta rabbathi (in Yalkut Shim'oni ii. f. 32. 4) "Both redeemed Israel: Moses in Egypt, and Elias in that which is to come." (Id. ib. f. 53. 2.) "I send you a redeemer." Midrash Shocher tof Ib. f. 884, "Israel said, 'It is written of the first redemption, *He sent Moses His servant, Aaron whom He had chosen;* send me two like them.' God answered; 'I will send you Elijah the prophet: this is one, the other is he, of whom Isaiah spoke (xlii. 1.) *Behold, my servant whom I have chosen.*'" "Shemoth Rabba [Sect. 3. col. 108. 2. ad loc.] 'In the second redemption, ye shall be healed and redeemed by the word *I,* i. e. *I will send.*" Or, as a comforter, "I will send you Elias, he shall come and comfort you." Debarim rabba sect. 3. fin. Or to pronounce some things clean, others unclean. Shir hashirim rabba f. 27. 3. [all the above in Schöttgen ad loc.] Others, in different ways, to settle, to which tribe each belongs. Kimchi on Ezek. xlvii. and this with different explanations as to strictness. (See Edaioth fin. Mishnah T. iv. p. 362. Surenhus.) "Rabbi Simeon says, 'To remove controversies.' And the wise and doctors say, To make peace in the world, as is said, "Behold I send." R. Abraham B. David explains the peace to be "from the nations," and adds, "to announce to them the coming of the redeemer, and this in one day before the coming of the Messiah;" and to "turn the hearts &c." he explains "the hearts of the fathers and children (on whom softness had fallen from fear, and they fled, some here, some there, from their distresses) on

that day they shall return to their might and to one another and shall comfort each other." Abarbanel says, that Elijah shall be the instrument of the resurrection, and that, through those who rise, the race of man shall be directed in the recognition of God and the true faith." Ibn. Ezra, "that he shall come at the collection of the captives, as Moses at the redemption of Egypt, not for the resurrection." [These are collected by Frischmuth de Eliæ adventu. Thes. Theol. Phil. V. T. T. i. p. 1070. sqq.] R. Tanchum, from Maimonides, says, "This is without doubt a promise of the appearance of a prophet in Israel, a little before the coming of the Messiah; and some of the wise think that it is Elias the Tishbite himself, and this is found in most of the *Midrashoth,* and some think that it is a prophet like him in rank, occupying his place in the knowledge of God and the manifesting His Name and that so he is called Elijah. And so explained the great Gaon, Rab Mosheh ben Maimon, at the end of his great book on jurisprudence, called 'Mishneh Torah.' And, perhaps he [the person sent] may be Messiah ben Joseph, as he says again—And the exactness of the matter in these promises will only be known, when they appear: and no one has therein any accredited account, but each of them says what he says, according to what appears to him, and what preponderates in his mind of the explanation of the truth." "The turning of the heart of the father to the children," he explains to be, "the restoration of religion,' until all should be of one heart in the obedience to God." [5] Lap.

[4] S. John viii. 56.
[6] Rom. xi. 26.
[7] The Masora at the end of Malachi notices, that in the reading of קקך, i. e. Isaiah, the Twelve [as one book, ending with Malachi], the Lamentations Ecclesiastes, the last verse but one is repeated.

fully. The Maker of the heart of man knew better the hearts which He had made, and taught their authors to end the books of Isaiah and Ecclesiastes with words of awe, from which man's heart so struggles to escape. To turn to God here, or everlasting destruction from His presence there, is the only choice open to thee. "[1] Think of this, when lust goads thee, or ambition solicits thee, or anger convulses thee, or the flesh blandishes thee, or the world allures thee, or the devil displays his deceitful pomp and enticement. In thy hand and thy choice are life and death, heaven and hell, salvation

The three do end heavily; but Ecclesiastes only ends with the declaration of a day of judgment,

and damnation, bliss or misery everlasting. Choose which thou willest. Think, 'A moment which delighteth, eternity which tortureth;' on the other hand, 'a moment which tortureth, eternity which delighteth.'"

"I see that all things come to an end: Thy commandment is exceeding broad."
Ps. cxix. 96.

"As the hart panteth after the water brooks, So panteth my soul after Thee, O God."
Ps. xlii. 1.

which, it must be supposed, they did not like to dwell upon.   [1] Lap.